THE BEST OF

YANK

THE ARMY WEEKLY

1942-1945

With Notes from

DWIGHT D. EISENHOWER AND HARRY S TRUMAN

Selected by Ira Topping

A Note to the Reader

This volume was reproduced from original copies of *Yank*, which were published during World War II. Those original issues have, of course, deteriorated with the passage of time. The publisher has taken advantage of all available means to insure the best possible reproduction under those circumstances.

Library of Congress Cataloging in Publication Data

Main entry under title:

The Best of Yank, the Army weekly.

    1.   World War,   1939-1945—United States—Addresses, essays, lectures. 2. United States—History—1933-1953—Addresses, essays, lectures.
I. Yank.
D769.2.B47   940.53'73   80-15806
ISBN 0-405-13289-1

Special contents of this edition
copyright © 1980 by Arno Press Inc.

Manufactured in the United States of America

CONTENTS

HARRY S TRUMAN

INDEPENDENCE, MISSOURI

April 11, 1967

The Army Weekly, known to all as YANK was as much a
part of those who were in the uniform of their country
as were their uniforms.

The servicemen were informed of events, and about
people from all of the countries, and in all of the
campaigns of Africa, Europe, and the Far East, in
World War II.

By it the servicemen were also kept informed of events
at home. The publication spoke in the soldier's language
and helped them to understand why they were called
upon to serve their country.

The preservation of the past volumes on the 25th Anniversary of the YANK will keep and preserve the good
things that were then published for the new generation.

Harry S Truman

DDE

GETTYSBURG
PENNSYLVANIA 17325

August 4, 1967

I was delighted to hear that Yank, the Army Weekly, is to be republished for few more important records of World War II can be found anywhere.

Yank was unique. The Weekly performed a truly indispensable function as a medium of communication. Its highly professional staff represented the soldiers' point of view and produced a running history of the war in the soldiers' own words.

The fascination of browsing through the written and pictorial record in Yank is never-ending. Veterans can relive those momentous years, and their children -- and grandchildren -- can share in some of the world's most dramatic history as it was being made and reported at first hand.

Dwight D Eisenhower

INTRODUCTION

What was life like for the GI in World War II? Let *Yank* tell you...and show you. *Yank* was there.

Everywhere in the world, every phase of the war was covered by and for the enlisted man, from battles with the enemy to battles with the Brass. Every reporter, artist, photographer and editor, as well as the entire production and circulation staff, was strictly GI, on active duty.

The pages of *Yank* provide a remarkable record of hardships and humor, front lines and chow lines, pin-ups and flare-ups. Whatever interested the enlisted man, from hard news of the fighting to sensitive glimpses of the home front, was included, to make *Yank* the special medium it became.

Coverage of sports enabled soldiers everywhere to follow the fortunes of their favorite teams. Pin-ups were sedate by today's standards, but the GI's saved and admired the poses of Betty Grable, Lena Horne, Jane Russell, Rita Hayworth and whatever other current beauty appeared in each issue.

There were many superb talents on the staff: writers like Walter Bernstein, Marion Hargrove and Merle Miller; cartoonists like Ralph Stein, Dave Breger and George Baker, whose Sad Sack still amuses soldiers and civilians alike; artists like Howard Brodie, whose battle sketches made under fire were amazingly realistic and vivid. And some of the most popular contributions came from writers to the editor in "Mail Call" and "What's Your Problem?," the only places, incidentally, where officers could occasionally get a word in.

Soldiers frequently looked forward to the arrival of *Yank* as the highlight of the week. Over 2 million copies of each issue were read avidly, distributed from 17 different printing locations, even in an airmail edition for troops inaccessible through normal channels.

Many interesting stories can be told about *Yank's* difficulties in getting started, with $25,000 borrowed from the Army Post Exchange, or in improvising production facilities, often under seemingly impossible circumstances.

But the reason for *Yank's* unique place in publishing lore—and the reason why it is so fascinating today—is the single-minded point of view it consistently maintained, despite the frequently strong opposition it faced from officers like General George Patton. *Yank* was the enlisted man's magazine, from first to last. It portrayed the war through the eyes of the average GI. It helps you live with him, laugh with him, be frustrated with him, suffer with him and eventually triumph with him. It's a view of history and war you won't find in history books.

Included in this volume are 18 complete issues, faithfully reproduced exactly as they appeared in the 1940s. Only an American army could have allowed its soldiers to publish a magazine of their own.

It's unique. It's *Yank*!

YANK
THE ARMY NEWSPAPER

5¢ *By the men for the men in the service*
JUNE 17, 1942
VOL. 1, NO. 1

F.D.R.: WHY WE FIGHT

See page 2

SPOILING FOR ACTION *U.S. gun battery in Australia ready for foe. "Let 'em come," they say, "we'll murder 'em."*

TO THE ARMED FORCES OF THE UNITED STATES

President Roosevelt Greets Fighting Men On All Fronts Through First YANK Issue, Calls Them 'Delegates of Freedom.'

THE WHITE HOUSE
WASHINGTON

May 28, 1942

To you fighting men of our armed forces overseas your Commander in Chief sends greetings in this, the first issue of your own newspaper.

In YANK you have established a publication which cannot be understood by your enemies. It is inconceivable to them that a soldier should be allowed to express his own thoughts, his ideas and his opinions. It is inconceivable to them that any soldiers -- or any citizens, for that matter -- should have any thoughts other than those dictated by their leaders.

But here is the evidence that you have your own ideas, and the intelligence and the humor and the freedom to express them. Every one of you has an individual mission in this war -- this greatest and most decisive of all wars. You are not only fighting for your country and your people -- you are, in the larger sense, delegates of freedom.

Upon you, and upon your comrades in arms of all the United Nations, depend the lives and liberties of all the human race. You bear with you the hopes of all the millions who have suffered under the oppression of the war lords of Germany and Japan. You bear with you the highest aspirations of mankind for a life of peace and decency under God.

All of you well know your own personal stakes in this war: your homes, your families, your free schools, your free churches, the thousand and one simple, homely little virtues which Americans fought to establish, and which Americans have fought to protect, and which Americans today are fighting to extend and perpetuate throughout this earth.

I hope that for you men of our armed forces this paper will be a link with your families and your friends. As your Commander in Chief, I look forward myself to reading YANK -- every issue of it -- from cover to cover.

Franklin D Roosevelt

More Money Now En Route

PROSPERITY AT LAST

WASHINGTON — The enlisted men of the Army are practically on higher pay right now. It's $50 a month for privates instead of $21, and substantial increases for grades and ratings, unless the President exercises his power of veto. The new pay, effective June 1, may reach you men at the June 30 pay call.

There are a few snarls to be ironed out yet by a Congressional committee but the big problems are solved, including the date the pay hike is effective.

Apprentice Navy seamen will receive the same $50 monthly base pay as Army's buck privates.

The Figures

Here is what a soldier, sailor, marine or coast guardsman will draw this month as compared with previous earnings:

	Present Pay	New Pay
Master sergeant, chief petty officer	$126	$138
First or technical sergeant, petty officer first class	84	114
Staff sergeant, petty officer 2nd class	72	96
Sergeant, petty officer 3rd class	60	78
Corporal, seaman 1st class	54	66
Private 1st class, seaman 2nd class	36	54
Private, apprentice seaman	30	50
Private, less than four months' service	21	50

With his $50 a month, the American buck private will rank second only to the Australian as the highest paid G.I. in the world. The Australian private draws $62.50; the Canadian, $30.00; German, $21.60; Mexican, $12.40; British, $12.20; Argentine, $4.76; Russian, $4.00; Brazilian, $2.80; Italian, $1.51; Turkish, 40 cents; Japanese, 30 cents; Chinese, 20 cents.

The new bill raises the pay of Army shavetails and Navy ensigns from $1,500 to $1,800 and nurses from $70-130 to $90-150. It increases the rental and subsistence allowances of officers in the higher grades.

Under the new bill, rental allowances for officers without dependents range from $45 monthly for second lieutenants and ensigns to $105 for colonels and naval captains. Correspondingly, the range for these same officers with dependents is $60 to $120.

Subsistence allowance ranges from 70 cents to $2.10 per day.

Under existing minimum pay scales in the Army, second lieutenants either with or without dependents receive $40 per month rental allowance and $18 per month subsistence. Colonels without dependents receive a minimum of $80 rental, $120 with dependents. Subsistence allowances are $18 minimum for colonels without dependents, $54 with dependents.

Delayed Three Months

A difference of opinion between House and Senate on how liberally to pay the fighting forces delayed final action on the bill for more than three months. It was first introduced March 4 in the Senate by Senator Johnson, Democrat, of Colorado, and called for a 100 per cent increase in privates' pay to $42 a month. In the House, however, Rep. Rankin of Mississippi offered an amendment to $50, which the Senate refused to accept in a joint conference committee. A compromise of $46 a month was reached after a long fight by Rep. Rankin to hold the pay at $50.

When the compromise was returned to the Senate for final approval last week, Senator Robert M. LaFollette of Wisconsin proposed that the Senate meet the House at $50 a month and this was approved June 9.

Meanwhile the House brought almost to final approval a bill which helps dependents of enlisted men. Now passed by both House and Senate and awaiting only adjustment of minor differences, the measure gives a soldier's dependent wife $50 a month, of which $22 is mandatorily deducted from the soldier's pay. The government kicks in the other $28. Each dependent child would receive $12 a month additional.

The same bill makes war risk insurance compulsory for U. S. fighting men. A $10,000 policy would cost you $3.50 a month from your pay, with Uncle Sam adding $3 from his own pocket to make up the $6.50 monthly premium.

Even in a South Seas island, it's the same old story—pay day means fresh paper, hard cash, and an old G.I. blanket. Must be too hot down there for this buck to stand at attention.

A SCREWBALL?

The 1942 Inventors' Exposition includes a round tank invented by E. P. Aghnides, who thinks it's an answer to a tankman's prayer. Built like a bowling ball with treads, it rights itself immediately after turning over. The occupants will spin around a little but, what the hell, tankmen are tough already, aren't they?

Flag Day

It happened one night at a port somewhere west of Suez.

British sailor tipsy. Goes in saloon. Meets three U. S. sailors. Limey slams U. S. Navy. Yankees buy him a drink. Limey slams U. S. Navy again. Yankees buy him another drink. Limey slams U. S. Navy third time. Yankees buy him third drink. . . . buy him tenth drink.

Limey passes out. Yankees sympathetic. Take him back to ship. Stop en route at tattoo shop. Limey still out.

Limey comes to. U. S. battleship on chest. Also red, white, and blue inscription, "God Bless America."

A Flaming Nightmare

Time was running out on Corregidor. Everyone knew the siege was nearly over. They had started to kill the horses; the meat was tough, but it was better than nothing. A man could fight on its nourishment, and fight well.

Out of the fortress' vaults the finance officers brought $100,000,000 in currency—useless paper. It couldn't be taken off the island, and it couldn't be left for the Japs. The only thing to do was to burn it.

Ten thousand dollar bills burn well. Around the fire stood silent soldiers, watching a fortune go up in smoke. A dirty-faced private stepped forward, picked up a $100 bill, turned it over and over in his hands. He put a cigarette in his mouth, bent and let the $100 touch the flames, then lit his cigarette from the blazing currency. "Always wanted to do that," he said.

Other soldiers followed him silently, doing the same thing. For once, money didn't matter much. Time was running out on Corregidor.

CABLE HOME AT 60¢ PER

Sixty-cent cables and microfilm mail are now available to American expeditionary forces.

A list of 103 fixed-test phrases, covering practically every situation in the life of a G.I., have been written. The sender may incoporate up to three of these texts in a cable or radiogram. Cost of the entire message will be 60 cents plus Federal tax, including address and signature. The ordinary cable rate is 20 to 40 cents a word.

Soldiers send the new Expeditionary Force Messages to the U.S. from Britain, Alaska, Newfoundland, Puerto Rico, Panama, Hawaii and the Caribbean. Plans may extend the service to Australia, New Caledonia, Egypt, India, China and Iceland.

Relatives and friends may send outbound E.F.M. cables and radiograms to you under the same conditions. Service overseas will be handled through central stations, with local deliveries and collections made by the Army Postal Service. The location of foreign posts to and from which messages are sent will not be indicated.

Very Expressive

The guy who prepared the 103 available texts didn't miss any tricks. If you get cleaned in a blackjack game, you need only go jawbone for sixty cents to wire home for seconds. If you need it quick for a Saturday night date with a blonde in Melbourne, you may group your phrases this way: "Urgent. Please send me ten dollars. Best wishes for a speedy return."

Or if you suspect that "Somebody Else Is Taking My Place," you can make a comeback with "No news of you for some time. Are you all right. Loves and kisses."

Light for Postmen

A new mail service, known as V-Mail, is now in operation between Army units in England and Northern Ireland and the United States. Mail is dispatched to a central station, censored and photographed on small rolls of microfilm. The British have used this system for some time.

The microfilm rolls are dispatched to America, where they are developed and photostatic copies made on special forms, which are sent through regular mail to the addressees.

V-Mail so far is handled only on a one-way basis between England, Northern Ireland and the United States, but it may soon be extended to U.S. armed forces in other parts of the world.

I CCC Foot in Grave, Other Soon Follows

WASHINGTON—The Civilian Conservation Corps, known to two and a half million old grads as the C's, may soon come to an end.

An appropriation of $75,000,000 to operate 350 CCC camps, most of them on military reservations, has been turned down by the House of Representatives.

Unless the Senate restores these funds to the appropriation bill, the CCC is doomed next month.

YES, Y'GOTTA FILE A RETURN

WASHINGTON—Like it or not, there's always the income tax.

The Treasury Department, queried this week by your YANK correspondent, gave out with answers to some pertinent questions about filing of returns by soldiers.

Each case which might cause serious worry to the taxpayer has a slightly different angle, but on the whole the idea is:

1. A soldier in the continental United States, meaning the 48 and D.C., has to file a return. That's final.

2. If outside continental U.S., filing is deferred until the fifteenth day of the third month of his return.

3. Any person in the military service may obtain deferment of income tax, due either now or in the future, until six months after the termination of his military service—if he has a valid cause. No interest can be charged on the amount due.

There's the Rub

Therein lies the clincher. The "valid cause" has to be proven. You've got to sell it to the Collector of Internal Revenue in your home state. The Treasury Department says, to write the C. of I.R. back home, explaining the reason why deferment of payment is asked. It's up to him to rule on your case. If your reason is valid he'll grant deferment and you don't have to worry until six months after you are mustered out.

The law (Soldiers' and Sailors' Relief Act of 1940) reads very simply:

"Sec. 513. The collection from any person in the military service of any tax on the income of such person, whether falling due prior to or during his period of military service, shall be deferred for a period extending not more than six months after the termination of his period of military service if such person's ability to pay such tax is materially impaired by reason of such service. No interest on any amount of tax, collection of which is deferred for any period under this section, and no penalty for nonpayment of such amount during such period, shall accrue for such period of deferment by reason of such nonpayment."

Joe and His Dough

Joe Louis (now Cpl. Barrow) may be one guy who'll bless this little paragraph. Joe owes the government $117,000 in taxes on his ring earnings, and there's talk that he may not be allowed to fight for his own benefit anymore.

Now if he hasn't got $117,000 and isn't allowed to pick up some more coin, he's still out of danger. It seems safe to say that his "ability to pay such tax is materially impaired by reason of such service."

Less publicized but more important is the guy who earned a moderate salary in private life. He knew his folks weren't starving, but he knew too that a five or a ten slipped into a letter home would do a lot of good.

He couldn't legally claim anyone as a dependent, so he paid income tax on his full salary, minus legal deductions. Then he went into the Army still owing Uncle Sam part of the tax.

To him, this deferment means a breathing spell until he gets back in the civilian groove.

Seeing Double

The parlor "peep show" of the Gay Nineties has been resurrected to get vital information about enemy military objectives.

A contour-finder, similar in principle to the old-fashioned stereoscope which was the forerunner of modern motion pictures, now is used by U. S. military intelligence officers to locate enemy information from aerial photographs taken on reconnaissance flights.

Stereoscopic lenses of the contour-finder are focused until two tiny red dots engraved in each lens merge into a single floating dot. Apparently flat photographs are then shown in three-dimensional or model relief which produces an image of the terrain. By maneuvering the floating dot over objects such as hills, buildings and gun emplacements, measurements of their height and other dimensions can be obtained with the aid of a computing table.

Small enough to be carried in a soldier's kit, the contour-finder is expected to aid field operations by recording in aerial photographs data that would take G-2 officers many weeks to explore.

It's a Sour Apple Tree

We got a letter the other day from a smart little blonde in Canarsie who does occasional espionage work for us on the side, usually along the Gowanus Canal. She's pretty upset, and with good reason. Seems that all of the new popular music about the war is being slanted for civilians, especially for The Girl He Left Behind. The soldier doesn't fit into the deal, which is O.K. with us, but our Canarsie friend is beginning to wilt under the strain.

This doll (her name is Irma), who had a perfectly good male chum until his outfit went to Ireland, has always been a radio fan. During a recent blackout, as a matter of fact, she carried a portable radio into the bathroom and sat there, knitting in the dark, happy as a clam, while some Jersey station cooled her coccyx with a Back-From-The-Grave mellerdrammer. Now, however, she's really boined, as they say in Canarsie.

"I'm going to turn that damned radio off for the duration," she wrote. "All it plays is 'Don't Sit Under The Apple Tree With Anyone Else But Me.' I can't take it no longer. Every time it comes over the ether I see myself sitting with my head against the antimacassar, being true to a bum who's probably out drinking beer right now with some Killarney *schlemiel*. 'Begob,' she'll be saying, 'do yez love anybody but me, Joe?' 'Begob, I do not,'

he'll be saying right back at her, and him slipping into the soft talk as though he'd never touched borscht in his life. The hell with the apple tree. Male men are so scarce around here there's nobody to sit under one with, anyway. And in the first place, there's only three apple trees in Canarsie, and they're just little small ones. It's time I tooken to drink."

Touched, and not a little upset, we checked up on the popular song business by the simple method of walking up to a naked jukebox with three nickels in our hand. The first nickel went into a number called "Three Little Sisters." These three tomatoes loved (a) a soldier, (b) a sailor, and (c) a Marine. Their boy friends went away, so they all sat around the gas works and read *True Story*. The second number was called "I Threw A Kiss In The Ocean," and it was about some poor nut on a convoy who looked down and saw his girl's face smiling at him from the waves. "I threw a kiss in the ocean," this ape said, "and it threw it right back to me." Salty kisses never appealed to us, so we went to the men's room when the number was about half played. When we came back we laid our last nickel on the nose of a tune called "The Jersey Bounce." It was a nice number, simple and loud. We're beginning to understand how things are in Canarsie.

Goddard, Chaplin Call It Quits

EL PASO, Tex.—The team of Charles Chaplin and Paulette Goddard, which for some years appeared in a successful skit entitled "Are We Married?" has reached the end of the circuit.

A civil court at Juarez, Mexico, granted Paulette a full-fledged divorce. The charges were incompatibility and separation of more than a year.

Chaplin and Paulette met in 1933 when she was a chorus cutie in Eddie Cantor's "Kid From Spain." The truth or falseness of their secret marriage kept the hearts of fainting fans palpitating for five years. Chaplin first called Paulette "my wife" at the premiere of "The Great Dictator" in 1940.

Did that cause confusion? It most certainly did cause confusion. Chaplin wouldn't give details. Movie reporters went crazy trying to find the details. But nobody found the details — not till last week.

During the divorce suit it became known that the two were married in 1936 in Canton, China. Of all places.

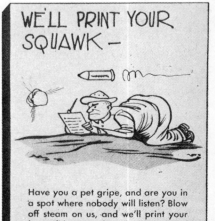

WE'LL PRINT YOUR SQUAWK—

Have you a pet gripe, and are you in a spot where nobody will listen? Blow off steam on us, and we'll print your letter if the squawk is a legitimate one. Send it to YANK, 205 East 42nd St., New York City.

Army May Drop Credit, Including PX and Barber

WASHINGTON—The Army has decided to find out whether charge accounts can be abolished for enlisted men.

Under a plan which will receive a test in the field soon, no more credit will be issued at Army Exchanges, barber shops, shoeshops and pool rooms. Object is two-fold: relieve the Army of a lot of paper work, and teach the soldier to budget his pay.

At present an enlisted man can get credit at Army Exchanges up to one-third of his pay, such debt being entered on the company collection sheet. Credit available for other facilities can be extended for another third of the soldier's pay.

R. G. HERBERT
Sergeant, Commandos

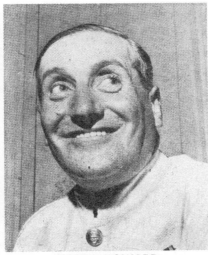

HARRY HOWARD
Artificer, Royal Navy

M. A. D. RIDDELL
F/Sgt., R.A.F.

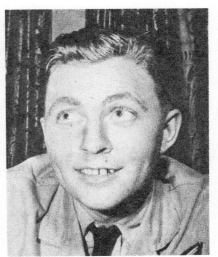

D. N. HUNTLEY
F/Sgt., R.A.F.

Four Who Came Back

Non-Coms Tell How They Won Those Medals; Two Were With Commandos at St. Nazaire

The ballroom of the big hotel was crowded. Reporters and cameramen crowded around. Fifteen heroes, men of war who had earned a respite from battle and who were getting a king's welcome.

Ten of the heroes were British, five were American. The Americans were Ensign Donald F. Mason, who "Sighted sub, sank same"; Lt. Comdr. Harold Smith, who was master of the destroyer Stewart in the Bandoeing Strait, off Java; Lt. Eliot Vandevanter Jr., who raided the Japs on Luzon; Lt. William Carrithers, cited for special skill as a bomber navigator during attacks on Jap installations and troops; and 2d Lt. George Welch, who shot down four Jap planes at Pearl Harbor.

In a corner of the ballroom stood four British non-commissioned officers. Two were flight sergeants in the R.A.F., one was a petty officer in His Majesty's fleet, and one was a sergeant of Commandos. They were tired. There had been a parade that morning, and many ceremonies. They had just finished an elaborate luncheon and now they wanted to go somewhere and lie down. It was hard being a hero.

Flight Sergeant D. N. Huntley thought it was hard. Huntley is young and blond, from Salisbury, South Africa. Once he worked for an oil company, now he is the front gunner on a bomber. On his left breast he wears the ribbon of the Distinguished Conduct Medal. He got it for a little trip to Augsburg on a sunny morning. "It wasn't so much," he said. "I do that sort of thing quite often. Just happened that they liked the way I did it this time, I guess."

Huntley strafed a strip of Germany all the way from England to Augsburg. He had a wonderful time. "I get the most men when we fly low," he said, "and this time we flew 50 feet off the ground all the way. I really don't know how many I killed. It must have been plenty. Especially officers. I hate those Jerry officers."

Flight Sergeant Maxwell Alexander Dick Riddell gets 20 shillings a day, and is pretty pleased about it. He's from Hamilton, Lanarkshire, Scotland. Riddell has been on 81 separate operations, and has been wounded twice. A German pilot put two bullets in his arm over the Channel one day. "I didn't know it for about five minutes," he said.

Riddell, a radio operator, has been in almost every important bombing. He was over Rostock and over Lubeck, and the Channel ports seem like home to him.

"A radio operator has a rum time of it," he said. "There he is, not knowing what's really going on, never sure but a bullet's going to nip him off through the fuselage. He has to sit tight and take it. Gets on a bloke's nerves sometimes."

A Commando has to be tough, and Sgt. R. G. Herbert is a tough baby. He looked very tough and out of place in the plush surroundings of the hotel. He's a thirsty guy, too, and while the reporters milled around him he lulled himself with a scotch and soda. Herbert is an old British Army man.

"I joined up in 1931," he said, "and stayed in till 1938. Then I got out and worked on the docks for awhile. A man likes a change now and again."

When the war began, Herbert got back into khaki. In January, 1941, he went to France, and he was with the Royal North Hampshires when they blew the Albert Canal to blazes in the fatal May of that year. "I was at Dunkirk, too," he said, "had two boats shot out from under me.

Pvt. Jaro Fabry

When they started the Commandos I was one of the first to volunteer. A man likes a bit of action now and again."

Herbert has been on all the important Commando raids, but it was during a raid on Vaagso that he picked up the Distinguished Conduct Medal he wears. He got it for taking 17 prisoners single-handed. The way he tells it, though, it sounds easy.

"What happened," he said, "was that I chased this one Jerry into an air raid shelter, and when I went down after him I found he wasn't alone. There were 17 of them down there, and one officer with them. I started to say me prayers, meanwhile aiming me tommy gun where it would do the most good. Then the Jerries surrendered." He smiled, a trifle grimly. "You know, there are only 10 men left of the original 65 in my troop."

Sergeant Herbert looked pensively at his glass. "A man likes a bit of scotch now and again," he said.

John Bull might be personified in the square, smiling face of Chief Engine Room Artificer Harry Howard. He's not so young any more, but he's still game for a "good go," as he calls it. He was in on a good go last Spring at St. Nazaire, and he has the Distinguished Service Medal to show for it. Howard was on the destroyer that rammed the locks at St. Nazaire.

"It was on one of those jolly old tubs you gave us," he said. "The Buchanan. Saintly old ship, she was. We sent her down right where we wanted her, and she went down just right—quick and easy."

There were 84 men on the Buchanan when she left England, but only 24 returned from St. Nazaire. There were no officers among them.

"When we hit the shore," Howard said, "I was the only petty officer left, so I was in command. Those of us who could still walk fought our way along the shore until we struck one of our motor boats and hopped aboard. We had to fight our way with pistols and tommy guns, and the Jerries were thick as flies. There weren't so many of them left when we'd gone, though."

Before the St. Nazaire raid Howard was on a ship ferrying supplies to Tobruk in Libya when the Australians were under siege there. "That was a good go, too," he said.

Around and about America

Remember Pearl Harbor

Where once stood the New York's World Fair, residents of Flushing Meadows Park and members of the Flushing Ridge Civic Association requested removal of the old Japanese Pavilion. Take it away or we'll tear it down piece by piece, they said. Park Commissioner Moses complied.

Yeah, Just Wait!

Antoinette Heim, who looked like a genteel little black-clad governess and said she was a cousin of Franz von Papen, almost ripped the roof off New York's General Sessions Court, where she was convicted of swindling German domestics of their life savings. Reviling officials and denouncing Jews, Fräulein Heim screamed, "Wait till Hitler comes over here! He'll take care of you!" Judge Owen W. Bowan replied that for the next three years the penitentiary would take care of her.

So Did Goliath

At Camp Shelby, Miss., a Maine infantry major was giving his men effective instruction in learning to duck from enemy observers. During such drills he toured the field in a jeep and popped away at exposed heads with a sling-shot.

Associate Justice Hugo Lafayette Black of the U. S. Supreme Court drove the wrong direction on a one-way thoroughfare. Fine: five dollars.

Patriotism was working on the night shift in Philadelphia this week. Miss Eileen Whitney, 24, was discharged from a hospital after being treated for submersion and alcoholism. Overcome by patriotic fervor, she had jumped into the Delaware River singing REMEMBER PEARL HARBOR.

Latrine Duty

In Los Angeles, a farmer named Sam Phillips appealed to the War Production Board for permission to buy a bathroom set. After working in a dirty chicken yard all day in the desert heat he felt entitled to a bath. Besides, he said, he wanted to get married and the lady had said he must have a bathroom.

Seven honor students at Pratt Institute in Brooklyn were given photographs of the bronze medals they would have received if there hadn't been a metal shortage. They were told that they will get the real awards eventually.

Not All in a Name

In Detroit, Adolph Hitler of Moscow, Mich., who first broke into print last February when he registered for the draft, made the headlines again. He was arrested by state police, who charged they found him spying on the Army Ferry Command at Wayne County Airport.

Learn to Fight Dirty

CHAMPAIGN, Ill.—Students at the University of Illinois may take a course called PEM 58 which is designed to teach prospective soldiers "how to fight dirty."

Use of the clenched fist is frowned on by the course's two mild-mannered instructors. "Hitting a clenched fist against a bony structure is a good way to break your knuckles," they teach. "Strike with the sharp, flat hand against the side of the neck or face. You can stun a man by hitting that way.

"Then, say you're sneaking up on a sentry. You jump on his back, reach both arms around his neck and shove a foot against the back of his knee. The impact is guaranteed to double him up like a jackknife and if you twist at the same time you'll sever his spinal cord."

The neatest and best trick of all, according to PEM 58, is to "go for his eyes if you get a chance. Gouge a man in the eye, that's the way."

The ten essentials of defense in dirty fighting are:

1. Get in the best possible physical condition and stay in condition.
2. In civil life, never initiate an attack regardless of provocation.
3. When facing an opponent intent on injuring you, allow him to show his hand first.
4. The counter-attack has greater possibility of success. Let him swing and then duck and strike under his guard.
5. When conditions are such that it is the only way out, take your opponent by surprise.
6. Fighting should be indulged in only for protection of self, family or nation.
7. The man who observes the rules of a gentleman when defending himself against an attack is using poor judgment.
8. If required to make a frontal attack, approach in such a way as to make your opponent lash out first—but it's better to get behind a foe if you can.
9. Remember your weak spots and your opponent's are the groin, solar plexis, neck, throat and chin.
10. If you can, gouge his eyes.

News From Home

RALEIGH, N. C.—Josephus Daniels, Secretary of the Navy in World War I, wants all West Point cadets and Annapolis midshipmen in future to be chosen from the ranks, instead of being nominated by Congressmen, the President and by competitions.

LOS ANGELES — George D. Hauptmann, lumber company executive, ground his teeth in rage after an automobile collision and sued for $16,250 damages: loss of one tooth.

LOGANSPORT, Ind.—The combined civic clubs called off a big rally in honor of two Canadian Air Force heroes who told of shooting down 126 planes. They were in the county jail as impostors.

BROOKLYN — Andrew Derby, attorney for the Brooklyn Dodgers, promised to soften the sound of the organ which plays during games at Ebbets Field. A neighbor three blocks away complained about the noise.

NEW YORK —"Brenda Diana Duff Frazier, former glamour girl and wife of John S. (Shipwreck) Kelly, attained to woman's estate. The estate: $1,400.00 in cash and a life interest in $2,500,000.

NASHVILLE, Tenn.—Don Calfee, 32, business manager of the Johnson City Press and Chronicle, who has traveled all over the U. S. and Canada, took his first train ride. Destination a state press convention in Nashville. Cost: price of the ticket and forfeiture of a $25 bet that he wouldn't ride a train before he was 35. Tire rationing and priorities on air travel left the train the only available conveyance.

CANTON, N. Y.—Malcolm MacDonald, United Kingdom High Commissioner to Canada, had automobile trouble on his way to Canton, where he was to receive an honorary degree at Lawrence University. The High Commissioner hitch-hiked the 15 miles from Ogdensburg.

WAYNE, Neb. — Mr. and Mrs. Fred Lutt returned to their farm to find their house burned. They had gone to town to buy matches.

COLUMBUS, Ohio—Gov. Bricker has appointed a commission to collect and preserve for future historians the records of Ohio's part in the present war.

NEW YORK—Myrna Loy went to the altar with John Hertz, Jr., advertising. Her second trip; first was with film producer Arthur Hornblow.

WASHINGTON — War Department announced perfection of a field unit to supply 4,000 men with daily bread ration. Sets up in an hour and a half.

DETROIT—Dick Reading, son of former Detroit mayor, was convicted of participation in a $30,-000,000-a-year gambling racket.

BELCHERSTOWN, Mass.—Constance Carpenter of Springfield, a 16-year-old who had been missing for five days, was found alive in a swamp.

TRENTON, N. J. — Supreme Court ruled to allow Norman Lichtman the right to keep pigs on his farm. There are 85,000 pigs in the vicinity, records show.

PHILADELPHIA, Pa.—A strike of musicians failed to stall the Ringling Circus. The management carried on with a caliope.

TRENTON, N. J.—Two thousand strawberry pickers are needed for the New Jersey strawberry harvest.

LEWISTON, Me.—Erskine Caldwell, Jr., son of the author of "Tobacco Road," was inducted into the Marine Corps.

ST. LOUIS, Mo.—A new plastic has been developed for tooth-filling which looks just as good as porcelain and feels like a real tooth.

INDIANAPOLIS—State officials were informed that naval officers assigned to the new battleship Indiana would appreciate a juke box instead of the silver table service usually given by the state for which a ship is named.

WEST DENNIS, Mass.—The airplane spotter who first sights an enemy plane over the Cape Cod area will receive $50 from Albert Gifford, a local resident.

NEW YORK — On eight hours' notice, the 321 square miles of New York City were completely blacked out in the first city-wide drill of the war. The result, said Mayor Fiorello H. LaGuardia, was "really beyond expectation."

ROCHESTER, N. Y.—Some 300 business and professional men are working midnight shifts in war plants here after their regular day's work. The idea sprang spontaneously from men who wanted to do "more than I'm already doing to help win this war." Their night "wages" are turned over to war relief funds.

NEW YORK—Mme. Liliana Teruzzi, estranged Jewish wife of General Attilio Teruzzi, who organized Mussolini's Black Shirt Militia, has found a practical patriotic use for her seven languages. She works as a volunteer censor in the U. S. Post Office.

LEWISBURG, Pa. — M. L. Annenberg, Philadelphia publisher, was released on parole from the penitentiary because of illness. He had served 23 months of a three-year sentence in the largest individual income-tax case on record.

WASHINGTON—A new three-cent postage stamp, with the inscription "Win the War," will be issued July 4. Central motive: An American eagle with wings outstretched to form a large V.

CHATTANOOGA, Tenn.—George W. Christians, leader of the Crusader White Shirts, was found guilty of sedition and faced a possible total of 80 years in prison and $40,000 fine. He was found guilty on two counts of attempting to foment rebellion and mutiny in the armed forces and two counts of attempting to discourage enlistments in the armed services.

LAGRANGE, Ga.—Lloyd Bradfeld, formerly of LaGrange and now in the Army, volunteered and reported to Ft. McPherson 25 years to the day that he reported for duty in the First World War at the same camp.

BATON ROUGE, La. — A bill passed unanimously by the Louisiana Senate would make it a crime to kill, wound or hold in possession living or dead racing pigeons which are used in wartime to carry messages.

CHICAGO—General forecasts of the wheat crop of 1942 indicate high yields to the acre for both Spring and Winter variety.

"Oh, some slip-up somewhere. I imagine we'll be back on regular rations in a day or two."

"Sorry, sir, but Harkins refuses to submerge."

"They're from the Morale Office. They say nobody ever plans anything to cheer *them* up!"

"I'm his lawyer."

"Corporal of the guard! Post number Seven!"

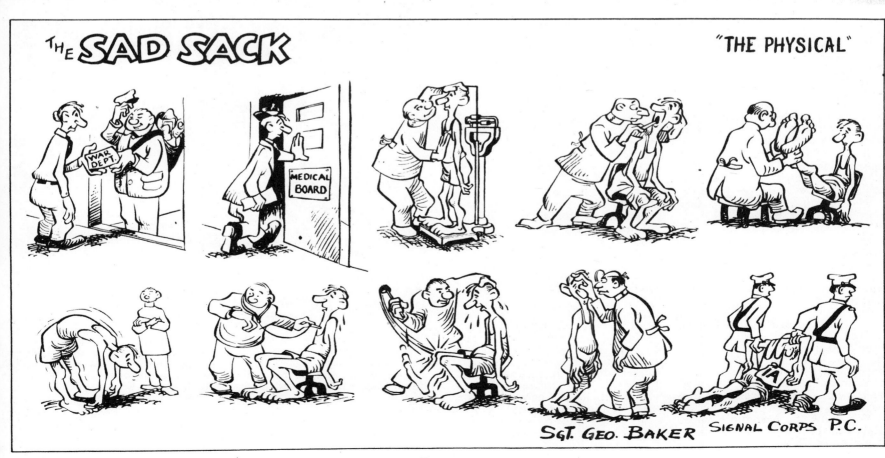

THE **SAD SACK**   "THE PHYSICAL"

SGT. GEO. BAKER   SIGNAL CORPS P.C.

THE BITTER BAYONET OF COLONEL BIDDLE

By Pvt. Lloyd Shearer

A pot-bellied fellow with eagles on his shoulders and store teeth upstairs pointed his bayonetted Springfield toward a hard-boiled infantry regiment at Ft. Bragg.

"All right, now," he shouted, "kill me."

Nobody moved.

The chicken-claws pointed to the ranks.

"You, come and get me." But the kid he singled out was scared.

"Dammit, I want you to cut my throat."

The Private made a half-hearted bayonet thrust.

Don't Be Yellow

"You're yellow," the Colonel yelled, prancing up and down in his black sneakers. "I want a man who's not afraid to kill. Step out, you there," he commanded a tough-looking 30-year-old sergeant. The buck stepped from the ranks.

"Now come running at me with your bayonet," he ordered, "and go for my throat."

The sergeant wet his lips. He clenched his gun and lunged full speed at the Colonel's neck.

Col. Anthony J. Drexel Biddle, who knows more about bayonets, knives and jiujitsu than any other man, parried the thrust with his own bayonet. Before the sergeant could mumble, "Holy smoke," Biddle had his own bayonet alongside the sergeant's throat, and the big buck was sweating.

"That's how it's done," the Colonel said. "Now let's all try it."

A Leatherneck

Ever since World War I in which he saw actual service on a half dozen fronts, Marine Corps Colonel Biddle, now 67, has been risking his Adam's Apple on behalf of recruit training. Loaned to the Army by the Marines, the former world's amateur heavyweight boxing champion has taught the fundamentals of in-fighting to parachutists at Lakehurst, raider battalions at Quantico, and thousands of camp trainees along the Eastern seaboard.

Of the scores of ambitious recruits who've tried to beat the old boy, either in jiujitsu, wrestling, boxing, or bayoneting, only one succeeded. A marine at Quantico supposedly got him in the groin with a knife. Thus far no one has been able to locate a witness to the event or find out the marine's name. Marine Headquarters says, "So far as we can determine, it never happened."

Biddle Is McCoy

The present crop of Army men he's trained swear by the Colonel. "Biddle is the real McCoy," they say. "In one hour this old guy teaches us more about bayonets and self-defense than we've learned in a whole year. He really knows how to kill. Some of us who've been in the artillery shooting shells five miles away never realized that death could be dished out to us six inches away."

And the colonel yelled: "Dammit, I want you to cut my throat." The colonel wasn't kidding either, because it'll be a long day from now when anybody can grab off the colonel with a bayonet. Why? The answer is on this page.

Private Joe Hill of Ft. Bragg, N. C., said: "I tried to get him myself today. You know what the old geezer did? He knocked the damn gun outa my hand. I think this Biddle is nuts."

"Nuts?" another yardbird asked.

"Yeah," Hill answered. "Look at him. He's a Philadelphia Biddle. He's got more money than you could shake a stick at. He's old enough to be our grandfather. And still he wantsa risk his neck. I tell you he's nuts. Only trouble with Army is that we ain't got more nuts just like him."

A Sentimental Cuss

At the other end of the pole, Biddle, despite his outward leatherneck hard-heartedness, is sentimental about his charges. "All the men in this new Army," he says, "are a great bunch of fellows, fine boys to teach."

"Do you find many of them gun-shy," we asked, "or reluctant to use a bayonet?"

Biddle reflected for a moment, closing his right eye. "Not many of them. They're not like Mussolini's soldiers. When I come across a man who looks as if he might hesitate to use the knife on the enemy, I tell him, 'Son, when you meet a Jap in battle, say to him real fast, "How is your dear old mother?" Then cut his throat.'"

"Does that help any?"

"Don't know exactly," replied the Colonel. "But it's good for their conscience...specially on Mother's Day."

Cold Steel!

Sixteen inches of steel at the end of a rifle can be a lease on life when "Assault Fire" comes and men fight hand-to-hand, no holds barred.

The bayonet is the last souvenir of days when men slugged it out with sword and battle-axe. Artillery and automatic weapons kill at a distance, chemicals sometimes inflict casualties days after first released.

There is nothing delicate or deceiving about a bayonet. Grooved for blood letting and cast for bitter service, it is a fearful weapon in the hands of a trained fighter.

It is the weapon of the individual soldier. It is vicious. And it is still important in warfare of tanks and mechanized equipment. Today we fight not in masses but in combat teams in which every man is a unit within himself.

The supposedly-expert Jap felt American steel burn on Bataan. Those same Japs have been accused by Chiang Kai-Shek's guerillas of refusing the challenge of man-to-man fight. But if the Jap's courage to face steel is questioned, his training in the weapon is not. He is drilled incessantly in its use.

British Commandos have developed the bayonet and a dozen variations of it. Their use of steel is as great as the German's aversion to it.

The long, thin blade of the Russian soldier has helped withstand Hitler on the Eastern Front.

The bayonet cannot and does not pretend to be more effective than fire power. But as long as there are armies there will be bayonets, because where there are armies men will come together in personal combat.

In that kind of fight steel wins. From time immemorial, it has been the same. Caesar had his battle pikes, and what were they but bayonets when you come to think of it. In the Middle Ages, they had their swords, and swords slash like bayonets.

You know the part the bayonet played in the World War. The part it played in China.

Men and Machines Put Hell on High

By Pvt. Leonard Rubin

Over London the anti-aircraft barrage was, and still is, a curtain of flame in the sky. In Australia, Panama, Iceland, Hawaii, and on both American coasts the snouts of the ack-acks poke into the sky. Most of them are virgin barrels, but they're ready for instant action.

Ack-acks may look simple, but they're touchy babies to shoot. Their crews need teamwork, courage, and strength.

Trained spotters pick out enemy ships trying to pull a sneak. They pick up a phone and bark an identification. "Enemy aircraft spotted. Height—10,000—12 ships—heading southeast." Other reports come in. The information center figures where the planes are from, where they're going, how fast they're flying. All this dope is relayed to anti-aircraft crews and fighter commands. If the raid is at night the searchlights get it, too.

Experts race to the guns. The mechanical "brains" start "thinking." The altitude crew sets its machine scanning the sky. What this instrument "sees" is flashed by electricity to the director, which aims the gun.

Eight hundred million candles probe the night. This baby can pick 'em out—and hold 'em.

From finder data the director picks up the plane and trains the gun for correct range. As the flying target moves the finder keeps the gun moving along with it.

All the brainwork is done for the gun crew. They ram 90 mm. shells into the breach and blaze away as soon as the plane is in range. Ack-ack fire is effective even at long distances. Exploding shells rock by impact — or flying shrapnel stings them.

Many shells scream out of the guns per minute — as long as the enemy is within range—and once the raider is out of "sight" the process starts again on any ships that may be following him.

When the "Jerries" or the "Little Yellow Bellies" hit low — under 5,000—rapid firing 50's and 37's get set. These smaller guns pester the low-flyers so they can't think enough about bombing or strafing to do their job. Arch enemies of these guns are the vaunted Stukas and Jap Zeros, both of which have licked wounds from American batteries.

Spears of Light

At night searchlight spears pierce the blackness. These 800,-000,000 candlepower needles have their own directors. With help from the gleamers the guns can spot the raiders with daytime ease. Fancy airobatics are easy for the searchlighters to follow. Sharp eyes and good coordiantion make our AA light beams feared by the enemy.

Before they know, enemy planes are in the middle of a barrage. Formations are dispersed, calculations for bombing thrown off. A burst several yards from a plane takes its toll. It may stun the pilot, or jar a delicate mechanism.

The batteries maintain constant touch with the secret information center for hint of approaching ships. The "hot loop" is always open with information steadily coming through. The battery commander makes his HQ in a command post where he keeps in telephonic touch with each gun. In the battery room is a plotting chart which is used to keep continuous track of a target as it approaches.

Seconds after the command post sounds the alert, men are at battle posts. They rip off gun covers—kick aside camouflage — raise barrels. Signals come through. The gun swivels into position. On target — Fire.

It's an old Army custom, and a wise one, never to under-estimate an enemy. The battery commander knows that once his gun is on a target and shells are sent screaming up, the target itself will locate the gun and take any kind of action to evade a hit.

"Hot loop" phone circuit is kept constantly open for alert from spotters.

Precision instruments are so set as to lead a plane flying at a certain altitude and a certain speed. If that speed or altitude should be altered, the target will be too far away for any burst to be effective. For example, it takes about 15 seconds for a shell to get up 10,000 feet, and everything is set up accordingly.

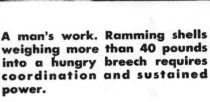

A man's work. Ramming shells weighing more than 40 pounds into a hungry breech requires coordination and sustained power.

Should the pilot of a raider see the gun flash on the ground, or if the first few shots were to be off target enough to lack effect, he would become a hard man to touch from there on out. Nobody is going to be a willing clay pigeon if he can do anything about it. And he can.

So the speed and timing — the only human element of a mechanical operation — come into their own. Here split seconds count, because the speed of modern aircraft is such that tardy information, faltering team-work, any mistake or miscalculation throws the whole thing into a cocked hat. Here nothing, down to the finest detail, can go wrong.

Gun crews of American anti-air batteries are among the finest trained teams in the world. Schooled since childhood by fast-breaking basketball or football plays, these men have since learned the value of coordination—and here they put it to its greatest use.

Director. A sensitive precision instrument for use in directing gun to its target.

Men on altitude finder get rough data from CP and search skies for raiders. Computed altitude is relayed to "brains" of system, the director.

Fifty calibre crew skeet shoots for keeps. This AA weapon is hell on strafing aircraft.

Wind, Sand and Mars

By Cpl. Harry Brown

The desert was there in the beginning and it will be there in the end. The Italians tried to beat it and it beat them. They put up neat white houses, and their officers wore scented uniforms, and they rode in their tanks as though they were parading. The British built nothing. They left the desert alone. They lived in their tanks and their armored cars, and they caught the Italians and they broke them. The parading tanks became twisted metal, and the scented officers were led away . . .

The worst enemy in Libya is the desert. It plays no favorites, and it has two irresistible weapons—sun and sand. The sun makes metal too hot to touch. Tank men fight, stripped to the waist, in temperatures of 130° and 140°. A Libyan sandstorm, called a khamseen, is a nightmare. The khamseen picks up surface dust as fine as talcum powder and blows it a thousand miles across North Africa. It gets in men's eyes and noses and mouths and ears. Khamseens can last for days; during their course soldiers, driven to desperation, live in gas masks. Some vomit continually.

Somehow, nevertheless, men live and fight and manage to be happy. During the siege of Tobruk, perhaps the worst phase of the six Libyan campaigns, the Australians even managed to achieve some form of contentment. They published a newspaper, "Dinkum Oil" ("Straight Dope"), on a captured Italian printing press. They had no beer or cigarettes, but cigars captured from Italians and beer brewed right on the desert took their place. They had outdoor concerts, and games of cricket and soccer, played at dawn, before the burning sun made exercise impossible.

Distance—An Empty Phrase

Sun and sand condition the style of warfare. The various Libyan campaigns have been tank warfare in its purest form. Tanks maneuver like battleships. Conquered territory means nothing; ultimate success depends on the destruction of the enemy. Patrols venture 500 or 600 miles into enemy territory, but distance is an empty phrase. To win in the desert, one must destroy—not the foe's towns and cities, but his tanks, his armored cars, his gasoline supplies, his oil dumps. Failing that, one fails all.

Desert soldiers are not military fashion plates. Tanned, unshaven, oil-smeared, they get little chance to keep clean. Their eyes grow narrow in the glare of the sun and fine little wrinkles appear in the corners. They are always in their tanks or under them. They live on tinned foods; the desert produces nothing. Water is more important to them than bombs. One great danger is boredom. As far as the eye can see, there is nothing. Desert, sand, plateaus, escarpments—nothing else. Brown, yellow and gray are the colors of the desert, and the camouflaged tanks are equally drab.

The Cannoneers

There are all kinds of weapons in the desert. Tanks are most important, after them the planes. The artillery and the infantry come next.

Italian artillery saved the face of the Italian army. It was made up of old guns, some of them holdovers from 1918. Many of its shells were duds, and its precision instruments were of poor grade. Yet it was good artillery, especially on fixed targets. When the Italians fell back it was the artillery that stayed behind, fighting a rear guard action at long range.

There is no trench warfare. The only trenches in Libya are slit trenches, used as protection against air attack. Slit trenches are simply narrow graves dug four feet deep in the sand. When a tank or an armored car or a Bren gun carrier stops for the night, the first duty of its crew is to dig a slit trench. For defense, there are land mines. Great fields of them lie hidden along miles of desert and in the passes between the plateaus and escarpments. It was mine fields that trapped General Rommel in his most recent offensive. A master of the flank attack, Rommel slipped around the end of the British line, only to be caught between British armored columns and mine fields.

Yank Tanks

American tanks had much to do with Rommel's plight, too. For some months the British had been receiving numbers of American M-3 and M-4 medium tanks, mounting 75-mm. cannon. Rommel didn't know it. He found his columns being blasted into the air from a distance of 1500 yards, 500 yards further than his 37-mm. tank guns could carry.

When night falls on Libya the desert is full of fantastic terrors. Darkness brings no cessation of battle.

On all sides signal lights flare, but in the desert distances are deceptive. The flare might be 500 feet away or five miles; there is no sure system of knowing.

The escarpments are dotted with dead tanks, smouldering steel skeletons, German and British alike. Distant gunfire sounds, and comes closer and closer as the battle veers toward the observer.

Death Above, Below

Overhead race the planes, invisible against the sky. Underfoot are the mine fields. Tanks must move slowly and uncertainly, feeling their way across terrain covered with mines. Should the track of a tank touch off their delicate mechanisms, destruction and oblivion follow.

On every side the tanks and armored cars fire their guns. The night is filled with flashes of fire. Patrols stumble into ambushes, and their vehicles are left flaming on

"Slammin' 'er 'ome!" British gun crew fires at point-blank range during desperate fighting in current Libyan battle.

Sixty-pounders let go at German positions during night bombardment in the desert. Note camouflage against air attack.

Desert battle wagons. British infantry tanks, pennants waving, plough in formation on movement "outside the perimeter of Tobruk." Libyan sun heats heavy plates to kitchen-stove degree.

e sand, lighting up the gully or
ne escarpment where they were
aught. At last, toward dawn, the
desert moon comes up. The firing
es down. Attackers and attacked
ait restlessly to join the battle
gain under the glare of a merciless
n.

The Germans are giving the Brit-
h a fight, but for once they are not
ufficiently equipped. Supplies from
e United States have given the
ritish a preponderance of equip-
ent. Moreover, the British have a
rge army in Libya, too, and a
olyglot army in the bargain. Free
oles, Free French and Free Czechs
re fighting in the desert, as are
dians, South Africans, New Zea-
nders and Australians. On the
xis side, German troops have
urped the Italian command, and
ehrmacht men outnumber the
ascisti.

ch is Desert War

When the Germans came to Libya
ey came suddenly. The story is
ill told in Cairo of the first meet-
g between British and German
rces. Three British armored cars
ere roaring down the coast road
etween Benghazi and Tripoli
hen three German armored cars
me from the opposite direction.
he two patrols actually shot past
ch other.

"My God," the British command-
said, "did you see who they
ere? Germans."

*The Germans, like the British, are not fighting the desert, and British
nd Germans have a common respect for each other. In the desert a man
as to be tough and he knows that another man in the desert, enemy or
ot, is a tough man too. The Germans built no houses. They live in their
anks. They remember that the Italians tried to beat the desert and were
eaten themselves. They know—as the British know—that the desert was
ere in the beginning and it will be there in the end.*

God, it's hot! British gunner, tanned,
tough, alert for attack. It's a Bren gun
under the cover. Maybe it looks like
Malibu Beach, but, brother, it ain't.
It's part of General Sherman's hell.

"Fust Class Fightin' Man." New Zea-
lander with Tommy gun lights a butt.
Note rough surface of desert, also the
rough surface of the Anzac's mugg.
This is a man who marched on Tobruk
once, singing with thousands of others
"The Wonderful Wizard of Oz." That
was their song. And it was their own
wizardry which held that isolated citadel for month after torturous month.
Men like this made Tobruk a name for
history and a synonym for bravery.

Bivouac. Helmeted British troopers in
Egypt move out on practice march. This
is a reinforcement unit.

ike tins of less-precious gasoline, these containers of water are being unloaded
t a desert base. Special convoys search out water holes, often travel hundreds
f miles to supply troops.

READY ON THE RIGHT . . . READY ON THE LEFT

. . . READY ON THE
FIRING LINE

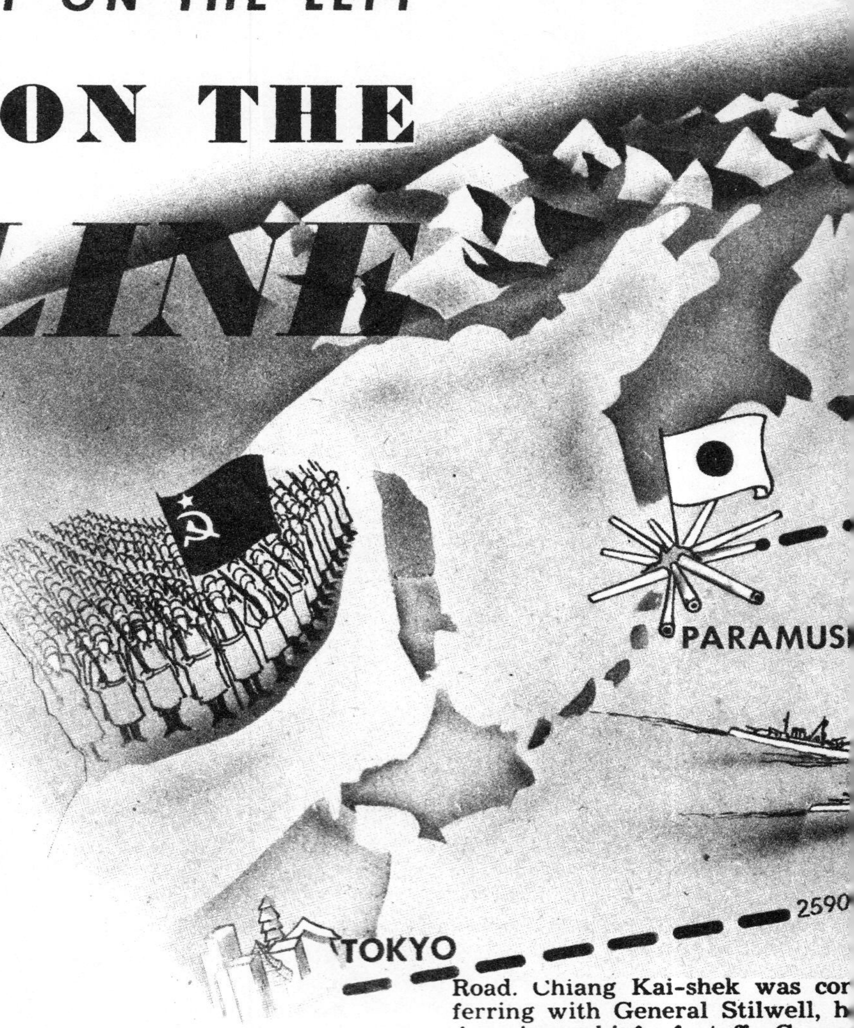

Six months to the day after Pearl Harbor, the honorable ancestors of Japan's Emperor Hirohito stirred uneasily in their graves.

A mighty Jap fleet, attempting what might have been intended as a prelude to invasion of Hawaii, stabbed at Midway, 1,300 miles to the west and was promptly hurled back with staggering losses by the U. S. Army, Navy and Marine Corps forces. Two or three enemy aircraft carriers were sunk, one or two severely damaged and the planes from three or more lost. Three battleships, six cruisers and three transports took terrific punishment. Some would never reach port.

Upon us the Japs inflicted only slight damage. A U. S. aircraft carrier was hit and a destroyer sunk. Casualties were few.

Two Battles

The battle, biggest so far in the Pacific, was one of two simultaneous engagements which U. S. naval authorities said might well decide the course of the war in that ocean. The other was being fought in the vicinity of the Aleutian Islands, which string from Alaska toward Japan and form a constant threat to raid-jittery Tokio. What was happening there, however, was obscure. The weather was bad and the opposing naval units had tangled intermittently for several days without decisive action.

It was the first time since Dec. 7 that the Japanese had returned in force to the north Pacific.

On June 3, at Dutch Harbor, in the Aleutians, the soldiers who had been performing such duties as K. P. with no more excitement than their comrades in the States, or at other quiet outposts, got their first taste of war. The fog that enfolds the islands most of the year parted. Out of the sky came planes with the Rising Sun insignia. They dropped bombs and flashed away, leaving a few warehouses burning beneath them.

Next day they struck at Midway. There were no planes lined up on the ground ready for destruction, as once there were at Pearl Harbor.

This time the planes were in the air, not only to defend the island against the raiding force but to take heavy toll of the warships battling American vessels in the surrounding seas. Two days later, as the Jap fleet finally ducked its American pursuers under cover of darkness, the conservative commander of the U. S. Pacific Fleet gave his report on the respective losses.

"This," he declared, "is the balance sheet that Army, Navy and Marine Corps forces in this area offer their country this morning."

Soldiers hearing the news over barrack-room radios got the significance: Pearl Harbor had, in part, been avenged.

Whether the Japanese could bring up sufficient reinforcements immediately for a second attack was unknown, but the defenders were more than ready—they were eager.

Strategy Uncertain

Exactly what the Japs hoped to accomplish in their blows at Dutch Harbor and Midway was uncertain. Generally, however, it was believed that their plan was to divert American naval forces toward Alaska, then strike south and seize Midway as a preliminary to invasion of Hawaii. Supporting this belief were two reports: First, that the three transports sunk were laden with troops; second, that 14 such vessels had recently been observed en route northward from Jap-controlled Marshall Islands.

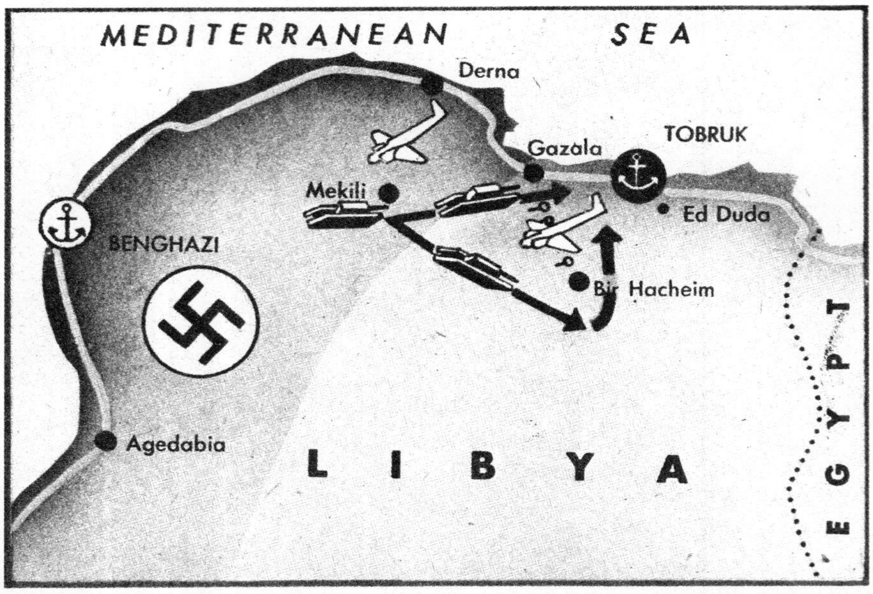

With the bulk of the Nippon fleet active north of the Equator, the tension "down under" was eased somewhat. Jap submarines lobbed shells for an hour into Sydney's waterfront the night of June 8. Fighting continued on New Guinea, but American troops in Australia went on with their preparations for eventual Japanese invasion. They were comforted by the knowledge that time was, for the moment, on their side and that enemy lines were being stretched ever farther, ever thinner, over the Pacific. Some time, they were confident, those lines would stretch to the breaking point.

And on Land . . .

In China the Japs pushed on, but at tremendous cost. Westward from the East China Sea, they inched toward the rail center of Chuhsien, paying with many lives for each foot of ground taken from the Chinese. In three days of fighting outside the old walled city 11,000 of them fell, Chinese sources declared. If the Japanese could capture Chuhsien, they could control the Thailand-Indo-China railroad, assuring an overland supply route to their newly conquered territories south.

An ominous huddle was taking place, meanwhile, in a little room in Chungking, end of the Burma

Road. Chiang Kai-shek was conferring with General Stilwell, his American chief of staff; General Brereton, head of the American air force in India, and General Chennault, leader of the American Volunteer Air Force, which has been driving the Japs nuts in southern China and Burma.

It looked as if Uncle Sam and his Western allies were planning hurry-up help for the hard-pressed Chinese.

Bad News for Adolf

On the other side of the world, bad news flowed in a steady stream into the Wilhelmstrasse. Rommel's Afrika Korps had been stopped again in Libya. The Russians continued to hold in the East. The R.A.F. was sending planes, a thousand at a time, to level whole areas of war industries. And now over the radio the British were warning the French, in effect:

"If you value your lives, get out of the coastal areas, from the Belgian frontier down to the Pyrenees. We can't tell you where, and we can't tell you when, but we're coming."

Black-faced Commandos paid nightly visits to Channel ports, sniping at sentries, damaging docks, destroying airdromes and harrying an already nervous defense force. With them were American staff officers, preparing for the night when an ordinary Commando raid might develop into something a little bigger.

R.A.F. Hammer-Blows

The R.A.F. was building up toward peak activity. As many as 1,200 planes roared across the Channel, seconds apart, to bomb German cities.

"City by city," Churchill had said, when he told how the British and Americans would avenge Coventry. And city by city it began to be. First Cologne—Rhineland city of 800,000, turning out war products day and night. Stirlings, Halifaxes, Wellingtons, Whitleys, Lancasters and Hampdens dumped

New U. S.-built tanks and powerful air support helped British stop Marshal Rommel's Afrika Korps in sixth big campaign of Libyan desert war. Failing in pincer drive toward Toburk, Nazi forces were nearly trapped in bitterest fighting desert has seen.

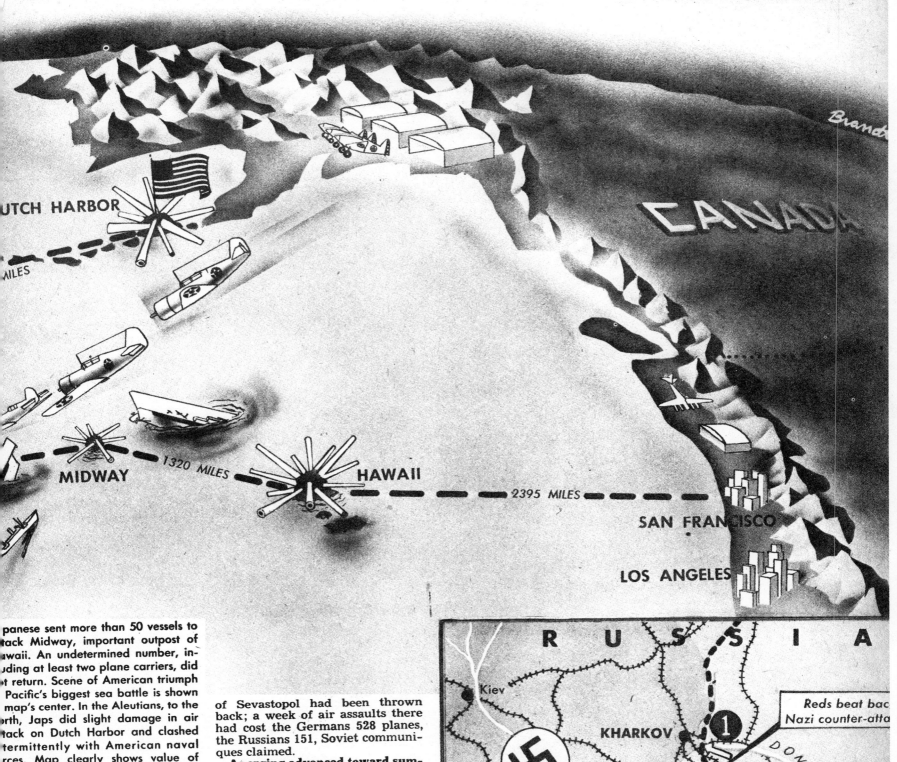

Brandt

UTCH HARBOR

MILES

CANADA

MIDWAY   1320 MILES   HAWAII   2395 MILES

SAN FRANCISCO

LOS ANGELES

panese sent more than 50 vessels to
tack Midway, important outpost of
awaii. An undetermined number, in-
uding at least two plane carriers, did
t return. Scene of American triumph
Pacific's biggest sea battle is shown
map's center. In the Aleutians, to the
rth, Japs did slight damage in air
tack on Dutch Harbor and clashed
termittently with American naval
rces. Map clearly shows value of
eutians to the U. S. as base for at-
cks upon Jap stronghold of Paramu-
iro, or upon Tokyo, and as defense
for Alaska, logical invasion point.

---

eir bundles. Blenheims, Beau-
ghters, Bostons and Havocs ho-
ered by to protect them. When
ey left, Cologne's famous 14th
century cathedral still stood. Little
lse.

The homeless from Cologne
treamed to other cities. Essen
mong them. There again they
eard the drone of planes, and
here again they saw a city erupt
flames. Bremen, with its wharves
nd factories, was next. . . . "City
y city," Churchill had said.

ussia-Trouble

The Nazis had aerial might to
rotect their cities—but they dared
ot take it from the task in the East.
here Russia had beaten them to
he punch on the long-awaited
pring offensive. The Red Army
vas hammering at the gates of
Kharkov and had even gone beyond
t to the south. Repeated Nazi tank
ttacks upon the Black Sea fortress

of Sevastopol had been thrown
back; a week of air assaults there
had cost the Germans 528 planes,
the Russians 151, Soviet communi-
ques claimed.

**As spring advanced toward sum-
mer, the Nazis were hard put to
prevent an offensive, let alone
launch one.**

Rommel Again

In North Africa the Nazis decided they were strong enough to
take the offensive. Marshal Rommel's tanks started eastward across
the Libyan desert—The Caldron, as
the British called it—toward
Egypt's border.

They met a British force more
powerful by far than any that had
crossed and recrossed the desert in
five previous campaigns. It had new
U. S.-built tanks, with range and
fire power equal to if not better
than the German machines.

After two weeks in which at
times 1,000 tanks were locked in
battle, the desert south of Tobruk
was littered with sun-charred
bodies and twisted shells of tanks,
and a battered Nazi corps fought to
hold a nine-mile gap in the front.
Beaten so far, the Nazis were apparently striving to reorganize for
another thrust.

Clouds Over Europe

Inside Europe, unrest grew.
Storm troopers were shot, restaurants bombed, in Paris. The Comitadji, fast growing guerrilla army,
made war still necessary in the conquered Balkans. Each dawn re-

RUSSIA

Kiev

KHARKOV   Reds beat bac
Nazi counter-atta

DONETS R

Stalino

Rostov

DNIEPER R   Taganrog

Odessa

Sea of Azov

KERCH

Sevastopol

Jumping the gun on Nazi spring offensive, Russians put Nazis on defensive at
Kharkov (1), but were themselves fighting hard to hold Sevastopol in Crimea (2).
Light area southwest of Kharkov shows extent of Reds' advance in attempt to
encircle Kharkov.

vealed new corpses of German soldiers floating in Holland's canals.
Two Czech patriots, snapping their
fingers at Gestapo terror, ambushed
and shot to death brutal Reinhard
Heydrich, deputy Gestapo chief

and Hitler's overlord of Czechoslovakia. Throughout the continent,
Nazi agents exacted in reprisal an
ever soaring toll of lives. Food.lines
lengthened. They cast shadows,
long shadows.

THE POETS CORNERED

Nor all your piety and wit
Shall lure it back to cancel half a line.
Omar K., Pfc. 1st Pyramidal Tent Co.

PILL ROLLER

There was a draftee from Podunk
Who said, "I'm a medico punk,
To relieve their congestion
And aid their digestion
I've been rolling these pills till I'm
sunk."

THE YANKS ARE EN ROUTE

Now there's a slim and pretty girl in
France,
Descended from the one of Armen-
tieres;
And only bat-eyed hangmen watch her
dance.
Hold on, and keep your smile, for
we'll be there.
And there's a brave and dark eyed
girl in Greece,
Who lives through hope in days of long
despair,
And has no bread nor wine to make
her laugh.
Hang on, and don't give up, for we'll
be there.
In Holland, where the tulips are all
dead,
There waits a maid with yellow hair,
Praying while her country's veins are
bled.
Stay brave, and keep your faith, for
we'll be there.
From Greece to Spain, from Poland to
the sea,
The girls who lost their smiles can still
compare
A tyrant to a man, and wait to cheer
The flag with Stars and Stripes. And
we'll be there.
Pvt. Arthur Emmons—10th Engrs.

MY ONLY PLEA

"Still laugh," said I, "when I'm away,
And gather all the flowers of May;
Still keep my room, the pictures all,
That I have loved upon the wall;
For I shall want them every one
The moment that the war is won.

Still play the records, dance and sing,
And spread no fears by sorrowing;
Be happy, every time you can,
For victory, work and pray and plan;
For I shall want you looking well
When we have fired the final shell.

Still bake the pies, as it might be,
That I were coming home to tea;
Still plant the garden, roundabout,
Still grub the sturdy thistles out;
And stake the blue delphinium,
As if this war had never come.

For if this struggle shall be long,
At home there must be mirth, and song;
Since these are what we fight to keep,
So hide away, when you must weep;
And be as brave at home, as we
Who fight in sky, on land and sea."

SERGEANT GEORGE L. DAVIDSON
Headquarters Company
116th Infantry

THE BUGLER

The bugler wakes us up each day;
I wish to heck that he would play
Over the hills and far away.

CORPORAL ARDEN L. MELOTT
Headquarters Company
722nd Military Police Battalion (ZI)

A TANKMAN AT THE GATES

A tankman at the Pearly Gates
Was faced by Old St. Pete,
And told to go on down below,
Because he was not neat.
Says he, "I'm dirty all the time,
I live in grease and murk;
I don't sit at an office desk,
I do the dirty work.
I don't march up and down a post
In uniforms so neat,
Nor strap a pack upon my back,
Nor blister up my feet.
I know not what it is to bathe
And shave, most every day,
A bath tub or a sink inside
A tank is in the way.
Now if I were artillery
I'd primp up every night,
And look like Esquire all the time,
But never know a fight.
Or if I were a Q. M. lad,
With uniforms so snappy,
I'd catch most everybody's eye,
And make the girls so happy!
But being just a tankman
I'm used to dirt and stuff;
Now may I enter thru the Gates?
I've lived thru Hell enough.
Yes, being just a tankman
I'm not much used to waitin';
Now may I live in Heaven, Sir,
Or must I call on Satan?"

SERGEANT JOHN V. SULLIVAN
Company A
191st Tank Battalion

Mail Call

Somewhere in Ireland

Dear Yank:
If Yank is going to be another of those corny Army papers with cartoons about rookies peeling potatoes and jokes about supply sergeants and top-kicks, you can cancel my subscription before I even subscribe. Before we left the United States it looked like all we ever saw about the Army was that sort of thing. And I for one do not want to be chased all over northern Ireland by the same damned thing. What do you say about giving us a break?
Sgt. Anthony J. Lavagetto

We promise to do our best to keep the corn out. To us, the potato peeler and the supply sergeant have grown a little thin and none of our readers are rookies. We will step heavily on those antique stories and cartoons. Brother, you are among friends.

Somewhere in Australia

Dear Yank:
There isn't anything down here but lizards. What I mean is that there isn't anything extra to listen to. We have a short wave that's pretty good, but there isn't enough of it. So we figured that you'd be willing to write Crosby and Allen, and maybe Benny, and tell them to talk louder or more often or something.
Very truly yours,
T/Sgt. Mander Lunk
Don't worry. You'll be getting more broadcasts.

LOUDER PLEASE!

Trinidad

Dear Yank:
We were looking over an old Lee-Enfield rifle the other day, and it reminded me of different kinds of rifles, which I've always been interested in. A new magazine like yours might want to feature for-eign rifles sometimes. I mean with pictures and making comparisons with our Garands and Springfields. I thought it would be interesting. Just a suggestion.
Yours truly,
Pvt. Homer Alexander
We'll see what we can do.

WE LIKE TO STICK JAPS WITH ALL RIFLES

Somewhere in Australia

Dear Yank:
A bunch of us were arguing last night about gas, and somebody said the worse a gas smells the less harmful it is. Lewisite smells like geraniums, phosgene smells like hay and tear gas smells like apple blossoms. That kind of stuff. Does it work that way all the time?
Pvt. Marvin Wilson
What about mustard gas—or do you like the smell of garlic anyway? There's ethyldichlorarsine, which has a biting odor and blisters the bejaysus out of you. There's chlorpicrin, or "puking stuff," which smells like flypaper. White phosphorus, which can burn your arm off, smells like burning matches. Gas is gas, no matter how it smells.

YANK

Acting Managing Editor, Pvt. Bill Richardso[n,] Sig.; Acting Assistant Managing Editor, Cor[p.] Harry Brown, Engr.; Acting News Editor, P[vt.] Robert Moora, Inf.; Acting Feature Editor, P[vt.] Douglas Borgstedt, Serv. Unit; Acting Photo E[di]tor, Pvt. Ralph Stein, Med.; Acting Art Edito[r,] Pvt. Arthur Weithas, DEML; Washington Co[r]respondent, Sgt. Donald A. McGuire, FA.
Contributing Editors, T/Sgt. Burgess H. Sco[tt,] Inf.; Sgt. Edward Cunningham, Med.; Sgt. To[m] Long, MP; Sgt. Mack Morriss, Inf.; T/4gr Joh[n] Bushemi, FARTC; Corp. Marion Hargrove, FART[C;] Corp. Peter Paris, Engr.; Corp. Peter Woolle[y,] Serv. Unit; Corp. David Breger, Specl. Serv[.;] Corp. Gordon Frye, Engr.; Corp. Fred Rose[,] CASU; Pvt. 1cl Frank Brandt, Med.; Pvt. [] John Hay, Inf.; Pvt. Al Hine, Engr.; Pvt. Lloy[d] Shearer, Specl. Serv.; Pvt. H. N. Oliphant, Eng[r.]
Circulation, Pvt. Donald Cooke, FA; Pv[t.] G. S. McBride, Inf.; Pvt. William Potter, DEM[L]
Officer in Charge, Lt. Col. Egbert Whit[e;] Business Manager, Major Franklin S. Forsber[g;] Executive Editor, Capt. Hartzell Spence.

YANK

5¢ By the men for the men in the service

JUNE 17, 1942
VOL. I, NO. 1

Here's the YANK, brother.

This is our newspaper, solely and exclusively for us in the ranks and for nobody else.

It's not G.I., except in the sense we are G.I.

It's ours alone.

Because we fight, it is a fighting newspaper.

Because it is ours and because we are fighting men, it is here to reflect pride when we are proud, anger when we are sore.

It is OUR record of what we're doing—in black and white.

It IS us.

When there is poetry, it will reflect our poetry. War always produces poetry.

When there is griping, it is here for that. War always produces griping.

The YANK is each one of us.

As a reflection of ourselves, YANK is freedom, too; something our enemies are afraid to duplicate, and couldn't if they dared.

They don't think like us.

Our enemies will see YANK as us, because it is US.

They will tear it apart. Their psychologists will analyze the words in YANK, our words.

What a hell of a laugh!

They can't figure it out.

Because YANK is ours.

Here's the YANK, brother.

"IF YOU'RE THE SON OF HEAVEN, PAL, NOW'S THE TIME TO USE SOME OF THAT PATERNAL AID—"

HON. JAP. NAVY

U.S. FLEET

A Few Items That Require No Editorial Comment

Albert de Vleeschauwer, a member of the Belgian Government-in-Exile, says his people are "praying" for a Yank-British invasion of the European continent. Vleeschauwer has just reached the U. S. on a secret mission.

Belgian resistance to the Nazis, the spokesman reported, is taking the form of industrial slowdown in factories and sabotage of vital machinery. An underground resistance system is aiding British pilots shot down over Belgian soil and sneaking them back to England, hiding Allied secret agents and similar tasks, Vleeschauwer said. Also 52 underground newspapers are published in Belgium to counteract Nazi propaganda.

Reports from Europe say that Hitler is patching up the Siegfried Line. A group of land mines, a crop of machine guns.

Frederick Oeschner, the United Press correspondent, says that Adolf planned the Siegfried Line in one hell of a hurry. Oeschner, who was in Berlin when we entered the war and was therefore interned, until an exchange of journalists last week, says that Hitler swiped a copy of a private edition of plans for the French Maginot Line, stayed up all one night and a day reading it, then built his own Siegfried Line from those specifications.

Hitler did a good job, too, Oeschner says, considering the fact that the fable insists he just spent some few hours designing it. Of course, he let the generals execute the orders, but he turned around and reciprocated to the generals months later, squaring the matter.

OTTAWA — Canada ordered a 100% increase in draft inductions effective July 1, according to official announcement by the Canadian Defense Department. During June 7,000 men were called; during July the figure is 15,000. In addition there have been 10,000 voluntary enlistments per month.

Canada's enlisted army will be 600,000 strong within a year, the announcement said, not counting undisclosed thousands already in Britain or now in training under enlistments prior to inauguration of the Canadian draft this year.

NORWALK, Conn.—Mrs. Stanley Knowles, sister of the late Brigadier General Billy Mitchell, is "safe and in good health" in a German concentration camp at Liebenau in Wuerttemburg, according to her daughter, Mrs. Albert K. Yohn. Mrs. Knowles was captured in the invasion of Yugoslavia, where she was reported to be a member of the Comitadji, Yugoslav guerrilla organization.

Latest intelligence from Honolulu:

Current joke is that the CO on Midway Island sent the following communique to Admiral Nimitz:

'"Japs lose pants trying to save face."

Four Japs, killed in an abortive submarine raid on Sydney, were cremated with full military honors and their ashes started on the long voyage home via a Swiss war aid organization.

Four Jap families are going to have a lot less hate in their hearts from here on out. Religion or not, they can't ignore that.

Beau geste, Australia.

BERLIN — Official Nazi radio broadcasts admit that the Czech town of Lidice has been wiped off the map because its inhabitants sheltered the patriots who assassinated Nazi gorilla Reinhard Heydrich.

Every man in the village was killed. Every woman was sent to a concentration camp. Every child was put in a Nazi "educational" institution. The Germans say the population of the village was 483. Free Czech spokesmen say that may be all that were left for the final purge, but that before the Nazis took over, the town numbered 1,200 persons.

Anyway, the town is gone. Its name has been extinguished, its buildings destroyed. All because a conquered people couldn't take the brutalities of Heydrich any longer, and gave him what he deserved.

That's life under Hitler.

CAN YOU DRAW, PAINT, OR MAKE CARTOONS?

YANK HAS THE ANSWERS....

. . . to your problems. We'll settle all arguments on military etiquette, love affairs, the National League and how to cook beans. We'll sound off on who's right and who's wrong, and you can beat us up after the war's over. Write to YANK!

Entire Issue Copyright, 1942, by The Yank.
Printed in U.S.A.

The following listing will give you, page by page, sources of all photographs in this issue of YANK.

Cover page—Sgt. John A. Bushemi. 2—Pix Inc. (Bob Leavitt). 3—U. S. Government. 4—Paramount Pictures, United Artists. 5—Sgt. John A. Bushemi. 8—Sgt. Peter Lashe. 9—Arnold Rubin, Corp. Gordon T. Frye. 12—British official photos. 13—British official photos; bottom left, International News Service. 16—International News Service. 18—Acme. 19—NBC photo; bottom, Acme. 20—RKO Radio Pictures. 21—RKO Radio Pictures. 22—International News Service. 23—Corp. Gordon T. Frye.

YANK wants artist contributors! If you can draw cartoons or make action sketches of what goes on where you are, send it to us at YANK, 205 East 42nd St., New York City.

'H. M. S. Pepperpot' Brings Cargo of Tales

Maskrey was short, jolly, and ruddy. Cassidy was moderately tall, dark, and somber. They are both able-bodied seamen in the British Navy, and they were sitting in a U. S. city Union Jack Club drinking warm American beer.

Maskrey and Cassidy are watchmen on the cruiser Penelope, now in an Eastern port for repairs. They do twenty-four hours off and twenty-four hours on, and when they're off duty they usually hang around the Club.

The Penelope comes from Malta. While there she stood up under seven air raids a day until constant firing began to wear out her guns.

"She's a good old girl," Maskrey said. "We called her 'H.M.S. Pepperpot' for awhile, because the Jerries put so many little holes in her decks. We filled up the holes with planks and called her 'H.M.S. Porcupine.' Finally the bombs threw so much debris on her that we called her 'H.M.S. Rockgarden'."

"We ought to call her 'H.M.S. God 'Elp 'Itler' now."

Cassidy laughed. "I can't forget Malta," he said. "We were there, lying at anchor, when the Jerries threw over the worst they had. The ship ran out of water, and we couldn't send to shore for any because the small boats would have been strafed. We had to wait until night to get a drink. We were really parched then, I can tell you. Nothing makes a man thirstier than firing a gun all day."

"Remember Good Friday morning?" Maskrey asked.

"Good Friday morning was the worst," Cassidy said. "Worst of them all. We even used the six-inchers as flak."

"Four-inchers too," Maskrey added.

A Fair Hot Time

"Everything," Cassidy said. "They came over like bloody beetles, the whole damned Luftwaffe, it seemed like. One would go away and two more would come along. It was a fair hot time. They hit us hard that day."

Maskrey grinned. "We're still afloat," he said.

"The bootlicks were shaking," Cassidy said. "Bootlicks are Marines. We call them bootlicks or flunkies. They were shaking that day, all right."

"So was I, mate," Maskrey said. "I never thought I'd see the tykes again."

"There were minutes on Good Friday morning when I never thought I'd get to stand up to the altar," Cassidy said. "But now I'm going to. I'll be going back with a convoy one of these days."

"Lucky bloke," Maskrey said. "I've got to hang around. But I'll hang around until Michaelmas if I can't find a tommy-gun for my tyke."

"I've got some shopping to do, too," Cassidy said. "I've got to buy my girl some silk stockings. You can't get silk stockings in England, either."

Maskrey and Cassidy are puzzled by America. "I don't mind the tall buildings," Cassidy said. "You get used to tall buildings. But the people are impolite. The men don't give up their seats in the busses. At home a conductor would tap a man on the shoulder and make him give up his seat."

"You're right, mate," Maskrey said. Maskrey is from Lancastershire, and he says "coom" for "come." His town is Manchester, and it is a matter of pride with him that his home is only twenty minutes from where Gracie Fields, the comedienne, was born. Cassidy doesn't think much of Gracie Fields. "Ella Logan lived only three streets from me in Glasgow."

And She Says

The pace of American life is odd to them. They like Americans, and neither of them has had a fight with an American sailor, though Cassidy was once struck by a woman on a New York street. "She comes up to me," he said, "and she's a bit under the influence. 'Hello, you dirty Limey,' she says. 'Why aren't you off fighting your war?' and then she belts me one. I pacified her."

Maskrey wants to get home for Christmas, and right now he's looking around this town for a toy tommy-gun to take to his little boy. There are no toy tommy-guns in England. He has Christmas day all planned out. "First I'll go around to the brewery and get a goose," he said. "They give a goose each Christmas to everyone who's worked for them. An Irish goose. There's nothing like a goose or a turkey for Christmas. I like a goose, though. A turkey's too dry, but a goose is oily and smooth. There's nothing like an Irish goose."

"I'll take mutton any day," Cassidy said.

"Mutton is all right when it's hot," Maskrey said. "When it's cold, though, I don't like it."

Mutton-Fed Fighters

"You should have been at Tobruk, mate," Cassidy said. "There were a lot of Aussies there, blokes who'd been raised on mutton. Any one of those blokes would have given his grandmother's teeth for a slice of cold mutton."

Maskrey nodded solemnly. Cassidy is a Naval Reserve man. He was called up when war was declared, and he has been serving in the Mediterranean ever since. He was on his cruiser when, with other units of the British Mediterranean Fleet, she caught up with a big Italian ("Ities," Cassidy calls them) convoy off Sicily. The convoy totaled 15 ships and five destroyers, and the British sent 10 ships and three destroyers to the bottom. "It was a good go," Cassidy said.

Cassidy's cruiser spent six days in Tobruk harbor when German and Italian desert forces were besieging the place. He has great respect for the Australian and Indian troops who held the battered town. "It was no spot to be in," he said. "Everyone in the town had malaria or scurvy or dysentery. The water they drank could get up and walk away. They sent airplanes over the place every day, dive bombers and God knows what else. They used to try and knock us off. Poorest marksmanship I ever saw, though. They never even blistered our paint."

The Germans claimed this was a British ship that Stukas reduced to ruin, but th don't prove it. To the left, two English sailors tell about Stukas and destroyers, l they prove it.

Swagman by the Billabong

Somewhere in Australia—They were guzzling suds at a bar, a handf of Aussies and a half dozen Yanks, and when their throats became t moist for conversation they began to swap songs.

The sandy-haired lad from Metuchen, N. J., put his glass on the ba and grinned. Here, he thought, is where these babies get a taste of re American folk music. And he opened his mouth and bellowed forth th first bars of that old favorite, "Hut Sut Ralson on the Rillarol."

It was a hit all right, and the Aussies were properly impressed. The wanted to know what a "hut sut" was and if the "Rillarol" flowed into th Atlantic or the Pacific. They insisted that the words be written out. Then-

The Hit Parade—Close Order

"We got a pretty good one ourselves," said one. And not one, nor tw but the gang of them opened up on a little ditty called "Waltzing Matilda

That was a night or two after the boys landed. Today there's hardly Yank in Australia who isn't familiar with "Matilda," though the percen age of those who know the words is small. It's the favorite of the Aussie and it'll probably be a favorite on the juke-boxes back in the States whe the boys come home. It'll have to be.

"It's the damnedest song you ever heard," said one of the American "We thought 'Hut Sut' was a tongue twister. Hell, it's a nursery rhym alongside o' this thing. An' slang! It's got our jitterbug lingo stopped!"

Here are the words to "Waltzing Matilda":

Once a jolly swagman camped by a billabong
Under the shade of a coolibah tree,
And he sang as he watched and waited till his billy boiled,
You'll come a-waltzing, Matilda, with me.
Waltzing, Matilda, Waltzing Matilda,
You'll come a-waltzing, Matilda, with me.
   (Repeat third line of preceding verse.)
You'll come a-waltzing, Matilda, with me.
Down came a jumbuck to drink at the billabong.
Up jumped the swagman and grabbed him with glee.
And he sang as he stowed that jumbuck in his tuckerbag:
You'll come a-waltzing, Matilda, with me.
Waltzing Matilda, Waltzing Matilda, etc.
Up rode the squatter mounted on his thoroughbred,
Up rode the troopers, one, two and three.
Where's that jolly jumbuck you've got in your tukerbag?
You'll come a-waltzing, Matilda, with me.
Waltzing Matilda, Waltzing Matilda, etc.
Up jumped the swagman and sprang into the billabong,
You'll never take me alive, said he.
Now his ghost may be heard as you pass by the billabong,
You'll come a-waltzing, Matilda, with me.
Waltzing Matilda, Waltzing Matilda, etc.

It didn't take long to catch on to Aussie slang. Matilda wasn't a fair-haired, full-bosomed lass who had been done wrong by. In fact, to th consternation of the Yanks, Matilda wasn't a gal at all. Matilda was loo and waltzing was carrying it—in a tuckerbag, of course, which is the ba any jolly swagman, or hobo, carries his loot in. A jumbuck was an animal native to Australia, a billabong was a stream and a squatter was a land-owner — which made the song a ballad about a poor hobo who took a powder rather than let the bulls pinch him for poaching.

The song was first sung, incidentally, 'way back in World War days. There are varying versions of the lyrics, and there are varying versions of who sang it first, but most of the Aussies credit it to their cavalry during the Allenby campaign in Palestine. As a marching song, it's right in the groove.

What's your Problem?

WE HEAR THAT

With all this talk in Congress about a pay increase for us, how about some figures on the U. S. Army pay scale in comparison with that of other armies. **PVT. B. SOLSTEIN**

For your $21 or $30 right at the moment, basic minimum monthly pay for soldiers in other armies is:

Australia $45.00; Canada $30.00; Germany $21.60; Mexico $12.40; Britain $12.20; Argentina $4.76; Russia $4.00; Brazil $2.80; Italy $1.51; Turkey $0.40; Japan $0.30; China $0.28.

See story elsewhere in this issue on what you'll be getting soon.

* * *

Once and for all, what's the score on this left-handed salute business in the Army? Is it permissible, and if so, when?
S/SGT. A. MOLINSKI

Don't know any more about than what the AR says: that the hand salute, rendered anywhere, is with the RIGHT hand. Some people may take exceptions, but the book says uh-uh.

* * *

*When I took out Class N Insurance I was under the impression it paid off only in case I should happen to kick off for keeps. Later on I was told the policy contains provisions for collection on injuries, too.
How about it?*
CORP. C. CONDOS

Class N pays off certain amounts for total disability, or disability which renders you unfit for military service. For the details, talk to your CO.

* * *

Would you mind educating a poor dog-face as to the origin of this Horst Wessel Lied referred to in everything coming out of Germany?
CORP. A. V. L.

Horst Wessel was a bully boy in Munich who was shot by a couple of guys for personal-political reasons during the earlier days of Hitler's scramble for power. Wessel had written words to an old Austrian drinking song and, sensing a martyr angle, Mouthpiece Goebbels grabbed it up and made a national party song of same. The martyr idea was that the mortally-wounded Nazi supposedly refused to admit a Jewish physician who was called to treat him and as a result died of pure pig-headedness.

* * *

How many four star generals have there been? How many are alive now? How many are in active service now? This is to settle a bet.
PVT. HERB FICKES

Here's the dope: There have been eleven since the rank was created in 1799. First to hold it was Ulysses S. Grant. After him came William T. Sherman, Philip H. Sheridan, and Tasker H. Bliss. Seven men still alive have held or still hold the rank. They are Generals Pershing, March, Summerall, Hines, Craig, Marshall, and MacArthur. Only the last two, Marshall and MacArthur, hold the rank in active service. Hope you won your bet.

We've been having an argument for the past three weeks on which is better, the Garand M-1 or the old Springfield. Everybody admits the M-1 fires faster, but a lot of the guys say it isn't accurate and also that its machinery inside is too complicated and is liable to crack up under combat conditions? Could you throw any light on the argument?
CORP. HARVEY MILFORD

Was a time, a year or so ago, when this subject would have been too hot a potato for us to handle. People were furiously debating the merits of the Springfield, the M-1, and the Johnson automatic rifle. Each weapon had its fans and a stranger horning in on the argument was lucky to out with a whole skin. Now, under combat conditions in the Philippines, the Garand has proved itself beyond question. After a few clips, the Garand is not quite as accurate as the old Springfield, but its firing-speed and the fire-power built up through that firing-speed more than make up for this. Its inner mechanism is more complicated than the Springfield's, but not so complicated as to go haywire under field conditions. Garands stood up on Bataan, and that was no picnic. We're not trying to talk down the Springfield; it's a swell rifle. But, for all-around combat use and as a basic arm, you can't beat the Garand, and General MacArthur said so, publicly, not long ago.

* * *

I haven't seen any tank warfare yet, but I think I'm going to before the war is over. I wonder if you could tell me whether and how often tanks are likely to be stopped by rifle fire?
PVT. CAHIR PRYGELSKI

Definite dope on this question is almost impossible to assemble. And, if we could get it, it would probably come under the heading of "Military Secrets." Light and medium tanks are vulnerable to rifle fire. It's the old combination of luck and good marksmanship that can disable them. Using armor-piercing ammunition (the bullets with the black tips) and aiming at the firing slits, you may be able to louse up the occupants of any size tank. Even with regular ammunition, a strong fire concentration will force the enemy tank boys to keep their firing and steering slits closed to the minimum, will make them lose visibility and maneuverability, will help to make them easy prey for your own anti-tank outfit.

* * *

What's the low-down on soldiers' marrying? When I left the States, I understood that a private was supposed to get permission from his superior officer in order to marry. Of course, hardly anyone did, but that was the way it was on the books. Now I hear that this has been changed. Has it? And, if it has, how?
PFC. CHARLEY BROWN

Your rumor was correct. As you said, it used to be necessary (for the record) for a soldier to get permission to marry. Now, however, you can marry whom you like, but try to do it during off-duty hours. By the way, how *are* the girls in Iceland?

"I'll have to search her myself, Gibson, if that's all you can find on her."

PHILADELPHIA — Search for the thief with the delicate touch is on. He stole a fire alarm box, disconnecting it without setting off the alarm.

HEMPSTEAD, L. I. — A bonfire spread to a building at 228 Front St., did $10,000 damage and caused injuries to five firemen.

PORTLAND, Ore. — What Iceland needs is not a good cigar—but a good hamburger stand. That's the opinion of Marine Private James I. Smith, stationed on the frigid isle, who says the food is fine, but "an American hamburger" would look awfully good.

BOSTON — The run of weakfish on the Atlantic Coast continues to be composed principally of small 'uns. This doesn't include Nazi submarines, but the Navy admits the fishing for this species is good this season.

WASHINGTON, D. C. — The practice of soldiers and civilian strangers exchanging letters has received a stern frown from the War Department. The reason is obvious. Some of those strangers are not just writing for fun.

ST. LOUIS, Mo. — It looks as if the "good old days" were coming back, at least, in St. Louis. A bill has been introduced prohibiting stables within 100 feet of dwelling places. Numerous complaints have been coming in about persons converting their garages into horse barns.

RED ARMY TANK BASE — A brigade of American medium and light tanks has been assembled and is ready to go into line. They will be joined with Soviet and British tanks at the front. Two or three American tanks are now at the front going through rugged tests, but nothing definite has been heard from them as yet. Several other brigades are in the process of formation.

TOKIO — The tunnel recently completed under the Shimonoseki Strait, between the cities of Shimonoseki and Moji in southern Japan, will be opened soon for freight traffic only.

ASHTABULA, O. — The Ashtabula Court House, built in 1884, has burned, destroying all marriage, birth and other vital statistics records of the entire county for the last 60 years.

CORWELL, Miss. — Ideal weather has given this region its biggest tomato crop since 1923, in a season when prices are highest in years.

GEORGETOWN, N. Y. — Joseph H. Morris, 29, and Fred Sebring, 27, were killed when the truck on which they were riding overturned near here. Both were Georgetown football stars of the 1933 undefeated high school team. Both were due for army induction soon.

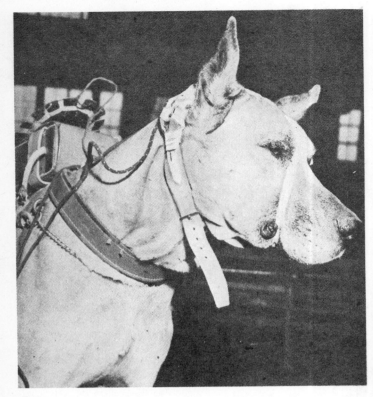

Dogs for Defense

U. S. Training Thousands for War; Russia, Germany Both Using Them

It's a dog's life, you say? Maybe you're right, brother; they're even drafting dogs for it now.

The Army wants 2,000 of them, from Great Danes to poodles. Once trained, they can do plenty to help the guy up front—run messages, do sentry duty, string telephone wires and tote ammunition and medicine.

Dogs for Defense, a non-profit organization, is doing the job. At 20 canine training camps in the U. S., DFD's volunteers—dog fanciers, trainers and handlers—are whipping in shape the nucleus of an eventual corps of 50,000. Already at numerous Army posts, airfields and munitions plants, thoroughbreds from 16 breeds are patrolling with sentries. One sentry with a dog, DFD figures, is worth six without.

The idea is not new. In World War I 75,000 dogs were used, among them the late film star Rin-Tin-Tin. Washington became dog-conscious when the American Kennel Club reported long before Pearl Harbor that the Nazis had shipped to Japan 25,000 dogs trained for military service. Investigation showed that in 10 years Germany had trained 200,000 for army and police work.

Small dogs, such as Scotties, wire-hairs, Manchesters and poodles are particularly good at guard duty where they can remain inconspicuously in one small area. The Navy has asked for Scotties to stand watch when ships are in dock, and munitions plants are using them to guard warehouses. For front-line duty, however, they have not sufficient speed or endurance.

Medium - sized dogs — Afghans, airedales, Dalmatians, greyhounds and, of course, shepherds—are best in combat. They are alert, fast and small enough to be difficult targets. Oddly, hunters are not good war dogs. By instinct they are silent when they scent a quarry, whereas the good war dog must voice a warning promptly.

For its recruits DFD depends on patriotic dog owners. There are plenty. A Pearl Harbor widow brought in a Great Dane on her way to work in a defense plant. An eight-year-old Buffalo boy donated the boxer bitch he got for Christmas. Hundreds of others volunteered their pets.

Basic training for the canine soldier lasts six weeks. If he turns out to be pampered or just plain dumb, he will be found out in that time. Otherwise, at the end of the course, he is ready for the field or his sentry post. He comes to his handler's side immediately when told to "heel." He scouts through indicated woods or fields at the command "out." He returns promptly when told to "come." Of primary importance, he sounds off as soon as he detects strangers. His trainers boast that he has six times the perception of a human guard and can warn of an enemy 100 to 200 yards away.

After the final week, in which he gets acquainted with the soldier assigned to handle him, the new member of the canine corps receives his uniform, a white rubberized harness. And, of course, his dog tags.

Out in Los Angeles, Prince Carl demonstrated a short-wave device which is used for transmitting instructions by remote control to army dogs in the field. Prince Carl, with his radio, is shown upper left. And above, he demonstrates his army tactics in giving "little aid or comfort" to the enemy.

Berlin Overseas Show

He Did It Before and He Is Doing It Again

In the last war the Army put on a musical comedy, *Yip, Yip Yaphank*, that finally hit France, and an Army musical comedy will play to A.E.F. audiences in this war too, if ex-Sgt. Irving Berlin has anything to say about it. *Yip, Yip, Yaphank* was his baby, and his new musical comedy, *This Is The Army*, is now in rehearsal.

It's purely a G.I. show. Until recently Berlin's headquarters were at Camp Upton, L. I., and rehearsals were put on in the guard house. Berlin lived in barracks so that he could be closer to the cast and to S/Sgt. Ezra Stone (Radio's Henry Aldrich), who is his co-director.

Big Names

There are 200 men in the show. Some of the cast are rookies, some veterans. Few are what Broadway calls Big Names; they're just guys who like to hoof a little or sing. They're working their necks off, too.

Customs Are Customs

The troupe will not have to stand guard, but one full platoon, drawn from the cast, stands retreat every night.

"We've got some sweet musicians in the orchestra," Stone says. "Johnny Mince is at clarinet—he used to be with Tommy Dorsey. From Jimmy Dorsey's band we've got Joe Lippman, piano, and Don Matteson, trombone. We've got them from Army bands, from Lopez, Goodman, Lewis, Shaw, the Philadelphia Symphony and the Philharmonic. Our stuff isn't all sweet and it isn't all swing, and the boys are a scream in some rehearsals. The classical boys feel a little sad when they have to beat out honest-to-God swing, and the swing boys feel cheated when they have to play strictly from the book. Between them we've got an orchestra that would open your eyes."

"It's a fast-paced show," Berlin says. "A show that the boys will like, 90% song and dance. Last time, we got *Yip, Yip* right up to the front, and this time we're going to try to do the same thing. The front today is all over the world, and it's going to be hard to do. We may have to split up into small touring companies, but some way, somehow, we're going to get it across."

Out at Camp Upton, Long Island, Irving Berlin is back where he was stationed in 1918. But this time he's producing his own musical show,

G.I. Shakespeare

Macbeth and Macduff hacked away at each other in an Army camp this month. The camp was Fort Meade, and the occasion was the first time that Shakespeare has hit a G.I. audience. The Bard went over big. Bucks from Boston and yardbirds from Ypsilanti cheered the Maurice Evans production; it took seven curtain calls to satisfy them.

Frankly an experiment, the performances of "Macbeth" were free, Evans footing the expenses of the three-night stand himself. During intermissions questionnaires were distributed to the audience. Did Private Rheum like the show? Did Private Stock want more Shakespeare? The answer to both questions was *yes*.

One Man's Meat . . .

The military man's reaction to the play varied with the military man himself. Some soldiers were frankly enthusiastic, others rather bewildered. All, however, were excited by what is probably the most compact and tense of Shakespeare's plays. It was the first legitimate production that some men had ever seen.

Maurice Evans and Judith Anderson, who must have felt that they were on the spot, acted beautifully; their voices carried to the farthest reaches of Fort Meade's Theater No. 4.

Our correspondent, himself a private, went around after the performance to get reactions to the play. He found that almost all the men he questioned wanted to see more Shakespeare, one sergeant saying that he hoped they'd try "Romeo and Juliet" next. Several claimed that they enjoyed "Macbeth" more than the run-of-the-mill musical shows that have been going around to the camps. Prize reaction was obtained from a rookie from Senaca Falls, New York. "I liked them dools," he said simply.

Evans hopes to be able to take "Macbeth" on an extended tour of Army camps in the fall.

At the present time there are three organizations in the States concentrating on short wave broadcasts to the A.E.F.: The Columbia Broadcasting System, the National Broadcasting Company, and the Coordinator of Information. Below you will find the stations affiliated with each outfit. In practically all cases all the stations in one organization carry all its programs.

Short wave being what it is, do not take the directional beams listed too seriously. A station beamed on Northern Europe for example may very well be picked up in Australia.

That's what the Signal Corps told us anyway.

CBS
WCBX—15270 KC—19.6 meters
Beamed on Europe
WCRC—11830 KC—25.3
Beamed on Europe
WCDA—11830 KC—25.3 and 17830 KC—16.9
Beamed on Latin America

NBC
WRCA—15150 KC—19.8 and 31.02
Beamed on Europe and Australia
WNBI—17780 KC—16.8 and 25.23
Beamed on Europe and Latin America
WBOS—15210 KC—19.72 and 25.26
Beamed on Europe and Latin America

COI
WRUL—11790 KC—25.4
Beamed on Far East
WRUW—9700 KC—30.9
Beamed on Far East
WRUS—6040 KC—49.6
Beamed on Far East
WJQ—10010 KC—30.0
Beamed on Australia
WBOS—15210 KC—19.72
Beamed on Europe
WCW—15850 KC—18.9
Beamed on Europe
WCB—15580 KC—19.3
Beamed on South Africa
Beamed on Europe

Add Hardships of War

If your favorite program on the air from the States is cut off suddenly and your radio dummies up all over the band, blame it on the Axis.

When the Japs raided the Dutch Harbor Base off Alaska on June 3rd, all radios along the West Coast from Canada to Mexico were silent for eight hours as a precautionary measure. A second silence was ordered the following night by the Western Defense and Fourth Army Interceptor Fighting Command.

The reason is obvious: transmitters are silenced to prevent enemy planes, if any, from locating themselves and coming in on the beam.

It's Dinah Shore, she with the soft voice, and a bunch of soldiers. The soldiers are not exactly veterans. They have been at an Army Air Force Replacement Center for just three days now. Dinah is short-waved to the A.E.F. by NBC on its "Fashions in Jazz" program.

A. E. F. RADIO SCHEDULE*... *Indicates the program runs daily through the week*

MONDAY, JUNE 15th

*12:00 M	12:30 AM	Here's News From Home WRUL, WRUW, WRUS
3:00 AM	3:30 AM	Here's News From Home KWID
* 6:30 AM	7:00 AM	Here's News From Home WJQ
7:00 AM	8:00 AM	Kate Smith Hour.....(CBS)
* 8:30 AM	9:00 AM	Here's News From Home WJQ
9:00 AM	10:00 AM	The Army Hour......(NBC)
9:30 AM	10:00 AM	Here's News From Home WDO
10:15 AM	10:30 AM	Songs ....(NBC)
10:30 AM	11:00 AM	Fashions in Jazz.....(NBC)
*12:30 PM	1:00 PM	Here's News From Home WRUL, WRUW, WDO
* 1:00 PM	1:15 PM	Esso Reporter .....(NBC)
1:15 PM	1:45 PM	Wheeling Steelmakers (NBC)
* 1:45 PM	2:15 PM	Here's News From Home WBOS
* 2:30 PM	3:00 PM	Here's News From Home WBOS
* 3:00 PM	3:30 PM	Here's News From Home WCB, WCW
*11:00 PM	11:15 PM	American Hour News.(NBC)
*11:15 PM	11:30 PM	Sports ....(NBC)
11:30 PM	12:00 M	Victory Parade ......(NBC)

TUESDAY, JUNE 16th

6:45 AM	7:00 AM	Gene Autry ....(CBS)
7:00 AM	7:45 AM	We the People ......(CBS)
9:00 AM	9:30 AM	Service Serenade ...(NBC)
10:30 AM	11:00 AM	Information Please ..(NBC)
11:00 AM	11:30 AM	Truth or Consequences (NBC)
1:15 PM	1:45 PM	Doctor I.Q. ....(NBC)

WEDNESDAY, JUNE 17th

7:00 AM	7:30 AM	Take It or Leave It...(CBS)
7:30 AM	8:00 AM	The First Line........(CBS)
9:00 AM	9:30 AM	Service Serenade ....(NBC)
1:15 PM	1:45 PM	Horace Heidt ....(NBC)

THURSDAY, JUNE 18th

7:00 AM	8:00 AM	Lux Radio Theatre ...(CBS)

9:00 AM	9:30 AM	Service Serenade ....(NBC)
10:00 AM	10:30 AM	Famous Jury Trials ..(NBC)
10:30 AM	11:00 AM	Kay Kyser ....(NBC)

FRIDAY, JUNE 19th

6:45 AM	7:30 AM	Family Hour ....(CBS)
7:30 AM	8:00 AM	Gay Nineties Revue..(CBS)
9:00 AM	9:30 AM	Service Serenade ...(NBC)
10:00 AM	10:30 AM	Army-Navy-Marine Band (NBC)
10:30 AM	11:00 AM	Fashion in Jazz .....(NBC)

SATURDAY, JUNE 20th

6:45 AM	7:00 AM	Sports Review ......(CBS)
7:00 AM	8:00 AM	Cheers from The Camps (CBS)
9:00 AM	9:15 AM	Service Serenade ...(NBC)
9:15 AM	9:30 AM	Sports Program .....(NBC)
10:00 AM	10:30 AM	Bob Hope ....(NBC)
10:30 AM	11:00 AM	Schaefer Revue .....(NBC)
11:00 AM	11:30 AM	Fanny Brice & Ralph Morgan (NBC)
11:30 AM	12:00 Noon	The Aldrich Family.(NBC)
12:00 Noon	12:30 PM	Ellery Queen Mysteries (NBC)
12:30 PM	1:00 PM	Burns & Allen ....(NBC)
1:15 PM	1:45 PM	Al Pearce & Gang ...(NBC)
1:15 PM	11:30 PM	Dramas by Olmstead.(NBC)
11:30 PM	12:00 M	Basin Street ......(NBC)

SUNDAY, JUNE 21st

4:30 AM	5:00 AM	Command Performance(KGEI)
9:00 AM	9:15 AM	News ....(NBC)
9:15 AM	9:30 AM	Bill Stern ....(NBC)
9:30 AM	10:00 AM	Fitch Bandwagon ...(NBC)
10:00 AM	10:30 AM	Command Performance (NBC)
10:30 AM	11:00 AM	Fibber McGee & Molly (NBC)
11:00 AM	11:30 AM	Command Performance(KGEI)
11:00 AM	11:30 AM	National Barn Dance.(NBC)
11:30 AM	12:00 Noon	Command Perform..(NBC)
12:00 Noon	1:00 PM	Kraft Music Hall ....(NBC)
1:15 PM	1:45 PM	Johnnie Presents .....(NBC)
1:30 PM	2:00 PM	Command Performance(WGEA)
9:15 PM	9:45 PM	Command Performance (NBC)
11:15 PM	11:45 PM	Command Performance (NBC)

All times listed are Eastern War Time. By consulting the time guide and employing a little elementary arithmetic, you can figure out when each broadcast will reach your base.

This is purely an experiment—noble or not. It's a picture of Maurice Evans, with a beard, and it's his experiment, not ours. Evans, a Shakespearean actor, wanted to determine whether American soldiers liked Shakespeare. Here's he shown at Ft. Meade, Md., at a debut performance. With him, Miss Judith Anderson.

Purged of soap-opera corn, singing advertising and amateur music from the hills, radio programs representing a million dollars worth of talent are being beamed by short wave to G.I.'s on foreign service around the world.

The War Department says its "Command Performance," all-star show aired Sunday nights, is heard all over. Letters from Surinam, Guatemala, Greenland, Iceland, the Canal Zone and other spots show the AEF is picking it up on all fronts.

Talent Terrific

With NBC contributing the bulk of the overseas shows at the moment, the concentration of available talent reads like a gold star edition of the Radio Guide annual: Dinah Shore, Jack Benny, Kay Kyser, Fibber McGee and Molly, Fred Allen, Henry Aldrich, Bob Hope, Phil Baker, Al Pearce, Burns and Allen, Bing Crosby, Fanny Brice, Bill Stern, Ted Husing and Grantland Rice, to name a few.

CLIP AND SAVE

TIME IN IMPORTANT AREAS OF THE WAR WORLD

When it is noon (Eastern War Time) in New York City:

Place	Local STANDARD Time
Aleutian Islands ..	5:00 AM
Hawaii	5:30
Alaska 5:00-7:00	
Nome	5:00
Fairbanks	6:00
Juneau	7:00
Mexico	10:00
Guatemala	11:00
Panama	11:00
Jamaica	11:00
Cuba	11:00
Aruba (D.W.I.) ...	11:30
Nova Scotia	12:00 Noon
Puerto Rico	12:00
Bermuda	12:00
Trinidad	12:00
West Indies	12:00
Dutch Guiana ...	12:19:25 PM
Newfoundland ...	12:29
Brazil	1:00 PM
Greenland ......1:00-2:00 PM	
Iceland	3:00
West African Coast	3:00
England	4:00
Northern Ireland .	4:00
Egypt	6:00
Syria	6:00
Iraq	7:00
Lower Red Sea region	7:00
India (except Calcutta)	9:30
Calcutta, India ..	9:53:21 PM
Burma	10:30
Philippines	12:00 Midnight
Australia	12:00 Mid.-2:00 AM next day
Perth & West Australia	12:00 Midnight
Adelaide	1:30 AM next day
Darwin	1:30 AM next day
Sydney & Melbourne ..	2:00 AM next day
New Zealand	3:30 AM next day

JANE RANDOLPH

You'll be seeing her overseas soon. She played bits in the movies until some smart director picked her for leading role in "Highways By Night." The film will reach the troops in the near future. Jane comes from Youngstown, Ohio; was a photog's model in New York before she migrated West. Five-foot-five, 125, likes the outdoors and is single.

MOVIES OVER SEAS

(All pictures reviewed in this column are scheduled for distribution to overseas forces by the Special Services. This is designed as a brief preview of what's in the works.)

THE INVADERS (Columbia)

Eric Portman (a tough Nazi), Raymond Massie (a tougher Canadian private), Laurence Olivier (a French-Canadian trapper), Leslie Howard (a literary guy).

Six Nazi fugitives from a U-boat land in Hudson Bay and try to beat their way to freedom across Canada. It proves, but not heavily, that we don't think and live like Nazis.

KING'S ROW (Warner)

Robert Cummings (hero), Ann Sheridan (a nice Irish dish), Ronald Regan (a small-town playboy), Claude Rains (a wise old doctor), Charles Coburn (a sadistic old doctor), Betty Fields (wacky daughter of the wise old doctor).

This one is about the private lives and conflicts in a small American town in the early 1900's. Don't let that deceive you. Plenty goes on, both wholesome and unwholesome.

BROADWAY (Universal)

George Raft (tough), Pat O'Brien (rough), Janet Blair (m-m-m), with good support by Brod Crawford, Anne Gwynne and Marjorie Rambeau. The treatment novel since it is a biography of Raft. He is seen in the first part of the picture as himself. The story then cuts back to the "roaring '20s" to deal with the stage hit, "Broadway."

YANKEE DOODLE DANDY (Warner Brothers)

James Cagney (Yankee), Joan Leslie (Dandy), Entire cast (good). "Yankee Doodle Dandy" tells the story of the life of George M. Cohan, and his theatrical triumphs on Broadway as a producer, writer, composer and star. It proves, without trying to, that this army needs a marching song.

MRS. MINIVER (M-G-M)

Greer Garson (a beautiful woman), Walter Pidgeon (a London husband in the Blitz). This is one of the war's best movies so far. It's the spirit of ordinary people under fire. Recommended for men who think all the fighting is done by soldiers.

MAISIE GETS HER MAN (M-G-M)

Ann Sothern (and you know what we mean), Red Skelton (funny), Allen Jenkins, Donald Meek, Leo Gorcey, Fritz Feld, Rags Ragland (all as crazy as you'd expect).

This is a typical Maisie yarn. There's an Army camp sequence at the end that's good for a laugh and is strangely accurate for Hollywood. The title tells the story.

THE SPOILERS (Universal)

Marlene Dietrich (herself), Randolph Scott (manly), John Wayne (equally manly).

This is blood-and-thunder stuff about the Yukon gold rush, features one of the nicest knock-down, drag-out fights ever screened. If you like action, if you like Dietrich, you'll cheer this.

TAKE A LETTER, DARLING (Paramount)

Rosalind Russell (lovely), Fred MacMurray (she thinks he's cute, too), Robert Benchley (the business man).

This is about a dame advertising executive who falls flat on her face in love with her male secretary. Light as the crust on mother's pies, but good entertainment.

That Ain't Hay

The highest-paying audience in the history of any theater bought $5,500,000 worth of War Bonds to see the world premiere of "Yankee Doodle Dandy," motion picture story of the life of George M. Cohan, at the Hollywood Theater in New York. Prices ranged from bond purchases of $25 to purchases of $25,000 and the theater was filled to its 1,554 capacity.

This Indiana girl who is making good out Hollywood way is Anne Baxter. She was chosen by Orson Welles for a starring role in his forthcoming "The Magnificent Ambersons." She is only five feet, weighs 110.

Discord

Sweet music will not console the French, Adolf Hitler has learned. Der Fuehrer, a devotee of the Berlin Philharmonic, sent the orchestra to Nantes on the French coast to give a concert. The folks weren't interested. Fearful of humiliating their chief, storm troopers finally rounded up an audience. The orchestra played one piece and packed up its instruments. The audience response had been terrific—all boos.

Whether you're wooing a spirited colleen under an emerald moon in North Ireland, rhapsodizing a dusky queen under a wavy palm in Honolulu, crooning in your best bath-house manner to a lovely lady in Darwin, or merely making a pass at a babe near the Brooklyn Navy Yard, you're going to have the best in music to help you along.

That's the promise of RECORDS FOR OUR FIGHTING MEN, INC., a new non-profit organization composed of the world's top-flight musical artists, which is rushing plans to supply U. S. service men all over the globe with the tops in current recorded melody. It will supply not only the records but the machines on which to play them.

Kay Kyser, Lily Pons, Kate Smith, Benny Goodman, Gene Krupa and Richard Crooks are among those on the RFOFM roster.

A drive is under way by hundreds of volunteer workers to collect 10 per cent of the 200,000,000 used discs believed to be lying mute in American attics. The platters thus obtained will be sold to prominent recording companies whose experts will use the shellac to cut new ones, which will be sent to soldiers, sailors and marines wherever they are stationed, at home or abroad.

Best Sellers

FICTION

The Moon Is Down, by John Steinbeck (Viking)

And Now Tomorrow, by Rachel Field (Macmillan)

Islandia, by Austin Wright (Farrar & Rhinehart)

GENERAL

The Last Time I Saw Paris, by Elliot Paul (Random House)

Washington Is Like That, by W. M. Kiplinger (Harper)

Victory Through Air Power, by Alexander P. Seversky (Simon & Schuster)

BOOK REVIEWS

PRIVATE PURKEY IN LOVE AND WAR

By H. I. Phillips

(Harper Brothers)

"Dear Harriet—Just a couple of lines to let you know I've found out I'm not in Ireland after all . . ."

Private Purkey has been in the Army for over a year, but he leads a life of utter confusion. His letters to his sweetheart, to his other girls, to his relatives are a chronicle of chaos. "All I know is that I am not on no transport because I still feel two good. And Sergeant Mooney is in fine health and as noisy as ever witch he wood not be if he was on the ocean."

Where women are concerned his lines are tangled. Between a movie starlet and a covey of home-town correspondents, he has a strategist's nightmare trying to keep communications open to his true love, Harriet. The offended sincerity of a soldier is echoed in "P.S. If the Army trusts me why can't you?"

There's fast, familiar reading here. Mr. Phillips can write a funny book about the Army without poaching on anybody's corn-field. This is it.

MECHANIZED MIGHT

By Maj. Paul C. Raborg

(Whittlesey House)

This will give you cold dope on the growth of motorized warfare, with special emphasis on the tank.

As a sample, did you know Winston Churchill was one of the fathers of the modern tank? As First Lord of the Admiralty in 1915, he authorized their construction by calling them "land battleships," a neat red-tape dodge. To keep the new weapon secret, the British referred to it in all communications as a "water carrier." This was soon shortened to "tank" and the name stuck.

"Didn't you tell me this hygiene movie was gonna be about bees and flowers?"

SOLDIERS, SAILORS PLAY MAJOR LEAGUE ALL-STARS

CLEVELAND — Lieut. Gordon Cochrane, U.S.N. (you used to call him Mickey, pal, but salute him now), has been chosen to pilot a service men's all-star baseball team in combat with a picked major league team here July 7. Sports writers predict it will rival the seventh game in a World Series as a drawing card.

From 22 or more former big-leaguers in uniform, Lieut. Cochrane believes he can train a crack squad. He has plenty of material—pitchers who can let loose like a 75 mm., batters who have blasted veritable anti-aircraft barrages of baseballs in their day, and men like Hank Greenberg who can out-reach a barrage balloon any day in the Army seven-day week.

The opposition — or the enemy, so to speak — will be chosen from both sides of two major league all-star teams which will play a twilight game in New York the preceding day.

Bob Feller Is One

To start with, Lieutenant Cochrane will have three of the brighter stars of the game: Bob Feller, Cleveland's ace who is now in the Navy; Hank Greenberg, the hard-hitting Detroit first baseman and outfielder; and Cecil Travis, Washington shortstop and runner - up last year for the American League batting championship. The latter two are Army.

For mound duties, Cochrane also has service men Johnny Rigney, the former White Sox hurler; Bill Posedel, formerly of the Braves; Porter Vaughan, of the Athletics; Hugh Mulcahy, of the Phils, and John Grodzicki, ex-Cardinal. Other talent includes:

Catchers—Ken Sylvestri (Yankees), Don Padgett (Cardinals) and Joe Grace (Browns). Grace also played the outfield, and Padgett has doubled in leather in the infield and the outfield as well.

Infielders—Henry (Cookie) Lavagetto, from the 49th state known as Brooklyn; Benny McCoy (Athletics); Johnny Sturm (Yankees); George Archie, Johnny Lucadello and Johnny Beradino (Browns), and Al Brancato (Athletics).

Outfielders — Sam Chapman (Athletics); Buddy Lewis (Senators), Pat Mullin (Detroit), Carvel ('Bama) and Rowell (Braves).

Mickey hopes he can get his players off duty for a week's practice before the game, but he will throw his team together a few seconds before game time, if necessary.

Foxx in New Lair

Jimmy Foxx, veteran of 18 American League campaigns, made an inauspicious debut in the National League on June 4, following his sale by the Boston Red Sox to the Chicago Cubs. He lifted an easy pop-fly in a pinch-hitting role.

Foxx will take over first base from Glen Russell, who will be shifted to the Cub outfield.

Another veteran American Leaguer, Catcher Frank Hayes, changed an Athletic uniform for the flannels of the fast-stepping St. Louis Browns. Connie Mack got Catcher Bob Swift and Pitcher Bob Harris in exchange. First string maskman for the A's now is Hal Wagner, 27-year-old Duke alumnus.

14 Major Leaguers In Uniforms Soon

Fourteen major league baseball players soon may swap their club-owned flannels for G.I. khaki or Navy blue. Most of them have been classified 1A in the military draft.

An equal number are likely to be reclassified and made eligible for military service.

The pennant races this year may well be decided by the draft call. The draft is close to Pee Wee Reese at Brooklyn, and to Enos Slaughter, St. Louis Cardinals' hard-hitting outfielder.

Yanks May Lose Henrich

The first division hopes of the Boston Red Sox revolve around Johnnie Pesky, the star rookie shortstop who may put on a khaki uniform. Even the star-studded New York Yankees would miss Tommy Henrich. The Reds may lose Ray Lammano, rookie catcher.

The Red Sox soon will be deprived of Ted Williams, the American League batting king, who has volunteered for Naval service.

Two Detroit players, Catcher George Tebbetts and Outfielder Barney McCosky are unmarried but currently in 3A because of dependents. Other Detroiters in 3A but possibly subject to re-classification since they are married but have no children, are Pitcher Hal White, Infielder Murray Franklin and Outfielders Bob Patrick and Ned Harris.

Most of the other major leaguers are in 3A, but many of the young married players without children are likely to be re-classified to 1A.

Major leaguers now in 1A:

AMERICAN LEAGUE — Outfielder Tommy Henrich, New York; Shortstop Johnnie Pesky, Boston; Third Baseman Bob Kennedy and Pitcher John Rigney, Chicago, and Pitcher Newman Shirley, Philadelphia.

NATIONAL LEAGUE — Outfielder Willard Marshall and Infielder Babe Young, New York; Outfielder Enos Slaughter, St. Louis; Infielders Sebby Sisti and Lou Gremp and Pitchers Tom Earley, Lou Tost and Art Johnson of Boston.

Horse racing, which has been called a laggard on Army-Navy Relief, took a deep breath last weekend at Belmont and announced that; after returns were in from the all-service Saturday show, racing's contributions to the war chest were crowding the half million mark.

Huck Geary, Minneapolis shortstop is watched by the Giants. He's a hitter and they have him tagged as "another Rizzuto."

Johnny Mize of the Giants slides home as the ball takes its time getting to Catcher Livingston of the Phils. The New York boys defeated Philadelphia by a score of 3 to 2, continuing a winning streak that puts them high on the list for the Service game—if they can catch up.

PITCHING RECORDS

AMERICAN LEAGUE

	G.	IP.	H.	BB.	SO.	W.	L.	PC.
Bonham, N. Y.	8	71	45	7	20	8	0	1.000
Haynes, Chicago	10	26	18	10	7	5	0	1.000
Borowy, N. Y.	6	39	28	17	26	3	0	1.000
Bridges, Detroit	9	73	52	25	33	7	1	.875
Chandler, N. Y.	7	59	57	23	23	6	1	.857

NATIONAL LEAGUE

	G.	IP.	H.	BB.	SO.	W.	L.	PC.
French, Bklyn	11	37	24	11	16	4	0	1.000
Davis, Bklyn	9	70	54	22	18	8	1	.889
Wyatt, Bklyn	9	60	51	20	24	5	1	.833
Starr, Cincin.	11	93	71	34	41	7	2	.778
Tost, Boston	11	53	48	20	14	6	2	.750

LEADING BATTERS

AMERICAN LEAGUE

	G.	A.B.	R.	H.	PC.
Gordon, N. Y.	43	164	24	64	.390
Doerr, Boston	40	161	19	59	.366
Dickey, N. Y.	28	100	10	36	.360
Spence, Wash.	48	201	31	69	.343
Fleming, Cleve.	49	177	29	60	.339

NATIONAL LEAGUE

	G.	A.B.	R.	H.	PC.
Phelps, Pitts.	31	83	10	31	.373
Reiser, Brooklyn	40	158	35	55	.348
Owen, Brooklyn	34	98	17	33	.337
Medwick, Brooklyn	44	161	20	53	.329
LaManno, Cincin.	34	110	13	36	.327

HOME RUNS

AMERICAN LEAGUE

Williams, Boston	15
York, Detroit	13
DiMaggio, New York	10

NATIONAL LEAGUE

F. McCormick, Cincinnati	9
Marshall, New York	8
Camilli, Brooklyn	8

SPORTS HERE AND THERE

Pinch hitters in Cincinnati seem to stick close to the formula of "Casey at the Bat." Of 31 men on the special slugging detail this year, only two have made safe hits. Only six even poked the ball out of the infield.

"Flash" Gordon of the Yanks is in a hitting streak that for early season form rivals the 59-game record of Joe DiMaggio. Gordon has already hit safely in 24 consecutive games.

The whole Yank club is whittling at records. It has boosted the home run total to 34, and its double-play tally for the year to date is a wholesome 69.

On the hole-in-one front at Lancaster, Pa., Bob Eicholtz saw his drive dribble into the cup, but he still had to score a three on his card. His first two drives were out of bounds and the lucky shot was a penalty repeat.

The Office of Defense Transportation has banned special trains to race tracks.

LEAGUE STANDINGS

AMERICAN LEAGUE

	New York	Cleveland	Detroit	Boston	St. Louis	Washington	Chicago	Philadelphia	Won	Lost	Percentage	Games behind
New York	—	2	5	4	2	9	8	6	36	12	.750	—
Detroit	2	—	3	6	3	6	4	30	26	.536	10	
Boston	3	3	—	4	2	4	6	26	23	.531	10½	
Cleveland	2	3	2	—	6	3	4	7	27	24	.529	10½
St. Louis	3	4	2	6	—	4	5	4	28	26	.519	11
Wash'ton	1	4	3	1	4	—	3	5	21	31	.404	17
Chicago	0	5	2	3	5	3	—	3	19	31	.380	18
Phila.	1	5	6	0	3	5	1	—	21	35	.375	19
Games lost	12	26	23	24	24	31	31	35	—	—		

NATIONAL LEAGUE

	Brooklyn	St. Louis	Boston	New York	Chicago	Cincinnati	Pittsburgh	Philadelphia	Won	Lost	Percentage	Games behind
Brooklyn	—	1	4	6	8	4	8	6	37	14	.725	—
St. Louis	5	—	7	4	3	5	2	29	20	.592	7	
Boston	1	6	—	2	6	6	3	3	27	24	.529	10
New York	5	3	4	—	4	2	3	5	26	26	.500	11½
Chicago	3	1	5	—	3	4	10	26	29	.473	13	
Cincin.	2	3	2	3	3	—	3	23	30	.434	15	
Pittsb'gh	2	3	2	2	—	5	7	23	28	.451	14	
Phila.	2	1	3	1	4	3	—	16	36	.308	21½	
Games lost	14	20	24	26	29	28	30	36	—	—		

DUGOUT DIRT

BY HEYWOOD HALE BROUN

FT. BRAGG—There's been considerable debate as to what part American sports should play in the war program. One group thinks organized sport should be abolished until Berlin and Tokyo are parade grounds for American soldiers. Another thinks sports should be expanded for the sake of national morale. In between is a majority which keeps on going to the games and the tracks without thinking much about the principle one way or another.

What the soldier thinks about it is a matter of conjecture, but one thing seems certain. When a soldier gets a chance to go to a ball game he goes, and if he doesn't have a chance to go he reads the score in the papers, and if he can't get the score he wonders about it and hopes that this, at last, is the pennant year for his pet club.

Baseball and boxing have earned praise in the press for their contributions to the Army Relief Fund. Mike Jacobs' fight shows have been quite unlike the old benefits where the beneficiary got "10 per cent off the top," which turned out in most cases to be like the top on beer, mostly foam.

Blue Monday Money

The little promoters have pitched in, too. Many a small fight club has stretched its shoestring to the limit to put on a good attraction for the army.

Major league baseball has been both good and bad. A few clubs have used blue Monday games against cellar opposition for the relief fund—and saved the creamy crucial battles for the Home for Retired Baseball Magnates.

The New York Giants and the Brooklyn Dodgers have made a bigger-than-usual gesture. Their struggles always draw large crowds anyway at the usual $1.10 a head, but Brooklyn, with its flair for the unusual, collected not only from the customers but also from the baseball writers, the players, the umpires and the getcha-redhots boys. Some persons bought tickets and did not attend the game.

War Comes First

However, it will take more than a willingness to contribute funds to keep professional sports on anything like a business-as-usual basis. An omen of the future is the banning of night baseball in coastal cities as part of the antisubmarine effort. Where sports interfere with the war, they're out.

Two important points should be made: First, the commander-in-chief has given baseball the green light. Second, untold numbers of those under him—in other words, we guys in uniform—follow everybody from the big leagues down to the bottom bushes. When these fans—and only these—decide that professional sports should close up shop for the duration, they ought to stop even if the Yankees and Dodgers are in the ninth inning of the seventh game of the World Series.

Racing has taken some heavy raps because it hasn't seemed as yet to have done as much for army and navy relief as some other sports, but it has promised a $2,-000,000 contribution and may soon move into high gear on this promise.

Antidote to War Nerves

Racing is obviously not conditioning anybody for military service, but it relieves the strain of war nerves. This is proved by the attendance and betting records it's setting despite gasoline rationing and the fact that the fans don't have as many spare afternoons as they used to.

Nobody need fear that the military chiefs are going to let sports go to excess. The closing of Santa Anita racetrack, the banning of night baseball and the recent stern message to Belmont Park racetrack to fix up its air raid precautions or else, show that control will be exerted. It might be a good idea to leave that controlling up to the military instead of to those strange crusaders who always pop up when there's a chance to knock off a few amusements in the name of progress.

V-for-Victory Ball Fools Yanks' Foes

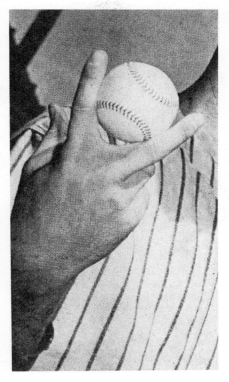

Ask the New York Yankees about "V for Victory" and they'll point out the first and second fingers on the steam-shovel right hand of Ernie Bonham. Those two fingers put the blitz on almost every enemy bat in the American League until the Cleveland Indians broke Bonham's eight-game winning streak June 7.

Bonham used his victory grip when the batter had him on the short end of the count. The slow twisting pitch, used instead of the curve, which Ernie admits was never much good, has fooled Ted Williams, Jimmy Foxx and many other American League sluggers.

LOUIS NEEDS BENEFIT BOUT—FOR SELF

NEW YORK — Cpl. Joe Louis Barrow, who has donated the proceeds of his recent fights to Army and Navy relief funds, would like to have another bout soon — this time for his own benefit. He needs the dough.

The Collector of Internal Revenue has been waiting for Joe to come around with $117,000 in 1941 income taxes. Joe went to see Joseph T. Higgins, the tax collector, but he didn't take the 117 grand.

Things are tough right now, Joe told Mr. Higgins. His farm is running at a loss and he is making only $54 a month from the army, which is a very small drop in a very large bucket. He didn't make a dime out of his last two fights, with Buddy Baer and Abe Simon, because he donated both purses, totaling $85,-000, to Army and Navy relief.

Pay Up or Else

Mr. Higgins was sympathetic. He gave Joe until July 15 to pay up. The corporal is privileged to ask for an exemption on the tax payment until six months after his discharge from the Army, but he'd rather pay it now.

Joe would like to take on Pvt. Billy Conn in what should be the first intra-Army world's heavyweight championship bout in history. However, if the Pittsburgh Irishman's injured hand won't permit it, Louis is willing to risk his title against such civilian challengers as Bob Pastor, Melio Bettina or Lee Savold.

Legal difficulties also bother the champion. A Chicago attorney entered suit for $10,500 fees against Joe, an aftermath of Mrs. Louis' contemplated divorce action last year. Although Joe won the first round last week when a Federal judge ruled out the suit until after the war, he faces the legal action when he leaves the Army.

That Ain't True What They Say

The Axis rumor boys have been staying up nights thinking of clever stories about the Yanks. Here's one that came over the air from "neutral" Lisbon recently.

"Several American aviators, apparently seeking romance and excitement in a city somewhere in western China, entered a Chinese theater where they saw a beautiful dancing girl in a stage play. The so-called 'Flying Tigers' in cowboy fashion kidnaped the girl and went for a moonlight ride in a jeep, only to find that 'she' was a female impersonator."

———

Sam Parks, 1935 U.S. open golf king, was defeated in the Hale American qualifying rounds. Parks lost the play-off he needed to qualify after tying Ted Huge, pro from South Euclid, Ohio.

SPORTS SHORTS

Chief Petty Officer Sam Chapman, who patrolled the outer gardens for Connie Mack's Athletics until he enlisted in the Navy early this year, is taking a voluntary "bust" to seaman, second class, to get a crack at Navy flight training. Sam, who has been a physical instructor at the Norfolk, Va., naval base, will seek a commission in the Naval Reserve Air Corps when he reports later for training at a Washington aviation base.

Ring rumors say that Pvt. Barney Ross, now at the Marine Corps Barracks, San Diego, may get a crack at his old welterweight title now that Boatswain's Mate Red Cochrane, the present 145-pound king, has been transferred from Newport, R. I., to the West Coast. . . . Lew Elverson, Penn's "Destiny Backfield" ace and later grid coach at Swarthmore, is now with Lt. Comdr. Tom Hamilton's Naval Air Fitness group at Annapolis.

Coaching the Camp Edwards, Mass., baseball squad is Pvt. Hugh Mulcahy, the Phillies' mound ace who was the first big league player to trade his diamond flannels for O.D.'s. Mulcahy has an able assistant coach in Jumpin' Joe Dugan, former Yank third baseman, who was assigned to the job in a civilian status.

The Army bowed to the Navy in the recent National PGA golf tourney at Atlantic City when Sam Snead topped Cpl. Jim Turnesa of Fort Dix, two and one, in the final round. Sam has been sworn in but hasn't been called to duty in the Navy yet.

For the first time in history, the 1942 service classic between the Naval Academy and West Point will be broadcast under commercial sponsorship. The $100,000 paid by Standard Oil of N. J. for radio rights of the game in Municipal Stadium, Philadelphia, Nov. 28, will be split between the Army Emergency Fund and the Navy Relief Society.

Purdue's 1942 gridiron slate includes two games with service teams, the Camp Shelby, Miss., eleven and the Great Lakes Naval Training Station team.

Two Sports Carnivals Will Aid War Funds

NEW YORK—War relief funds will benefit in June from two big sports events, one an All-Sports Carnival to be held at the Polo Grounds June 14 and the other the American Athletic Union's 55th national outdoor track and field meet at Triborough Stadium June 19-20.

In the carnival, Cpl. Joe Louis Barrow and his sparring partner, George Nichols, will give a four-round exhibition; an all-star Army baseball team, with Bob Feller pitching, will play the Norfolk Naval Training Base; Craig Wood, national open golf champ, will compete in an accuracy driving test against the Army's three golfing corporals, Vic Ghezzi, Ed Oliver and Joe Turnesa; and on the tennis courts Don Budge and Alice Marble will be matched against Wayne Sabin and Frank Shields.

In the track meet, Greg Rice, Connie Warmerdam, Al Blozis and Johnny Borican will defend their national track titles, and the New York Americans will meet the Brookhattans in soccer.

YANK

THE ARMY NEWSPAPER

5¢ By the men for the men in the service

JUNE 17, 1942 VOL. 1, NO. 1

War-Time Vacation Tip

Harley Archie Olson had a wonderful vacation. The 22-year-old ship's radio operator spent it fishing from an old settee he had rigged up. At the end of 29 days he was fat and tanned. He felt like a million bucks.

It was odd that Olson should look so well, because his "vacation" was spent on a raft. On April 19 his ship was torpedoed, and he spent nearly a month lolling contentedly on the bosoms of a surprisingly friendly sea.

The F.B.I. couldn't understand it. According to all information on the subject, Olson should have been dead, or at least a babbling wreck. The F.B.I. wanted to ask questions.

"Are you sure you weren't sent from a German submarine?"

"Aw, sure."

Olson explained what had happened. He put a lot of wreckage together and made a seaworthy raft. He even found an old settee which he pulled aboard. For 29 days he fishing and napped. His fishing tackle was a net made of bandages from a first-aid kit. "I caught all kinds of fish," he said. "All small ones, of course. Mackerels, herrings, and some peculiar varieties. Only thing is, I had to eat them raw."

"Did you think you'd be picked up?" the F.B.I. wanted to know.

"Aw, sure," said Olson. "I never was nervous. Gentle waves rocked me to sleep every night."

Another Name for Him

You've called the company bugler a lot of things in your time, but from now on in mixed company he's known as a "trumpeter."

That's official, and comes from the War Department Bureau of Public Relations. Puckered lips isn't all that qualifies a good trumpeter. He must also have one hell of a memory because the rules require him to know by heart 41 G.I. calls.

In addition to the one that gets us up in the morning, puckerlips — trumpeter to you—must know a good many fancy cadenzas. One is Overcoats, a notification that the formation to follow will be in overcoats, even if it's in Libya. Another is School Call, which trumpets you into classrooms for heavy brainwork. Another, that you ought to remember as well as the trumpeter, is Pay Day. That's followed by the call in hotlips known as "Roll the Bones" but that last one isn't in the manual.

Dear Sue

Please write. Your letters used to shine my days.
And all I want to hear is how you are,
Just what you do, and where you go, that's all.
And if I find your eyes in every star,
I still can't hear you tell me what they see.
Just let me know about yourself, that's all.

Sgt. Milton P. Coen
609th Engr. Bn.

Peel Away

I'm on KP from dawn till eve,
Just apples and onions to make me grieve.
Peel away, peel away.
I think of the pies that ma could bake,
And I have to grieve for her dear sake.
Peel away, peel away.

Pfc. Ralph Lusby—M. P.

ARE YOU A FRUSTRATED POET?

YANK wants your poetry, even if your best pal won't read it. Long or short, funny or serious, mail it to us from wherever you are and we'll print all we can. Just address YANK, 205 East 42nd St., New York City.

G. I. JOE

by Corp. Dave Breger

YANK

THE ARMY WEEKLY

5¢ **MAR. 19 1943**
VOL. I, NO. 39

By the men .. for the men in the service

CANNONEER

This artilleryman with two bluebirds tattooed on his chest, sketched at Guadalcanal by YANK's staff artist Sgt. Howard Brodie, is Pvt. Steven Kitt of Wilmington, Del., who won the Purple Heart at Pearl Harbor before he went to the Solomons. For more Brodie sketches, see Pages 7, 8, 9 and 10.

Sgt. Howard Brodie
Guadalcanal '43

Does Your Family Need Money in a Hurry?

READ ABOUT THE RED CROSS PERSONAL PROBLEM SERVICE, PAGE 20.

·The first PX opens up in southern Tunisia. The complete supply is on the table and French girl-ambulance drivers hand it out free to the Yanks.

Yanks in Africa

Infantrymen look over a captured German Schmeisser machine pistol.   Under French guard, Nazi prisoners (left) and Italian dig trenches.

American Commandos, who first saw action with the Canadians at Dieppe, run a show of their own and score a clean knockout blow.

By Sgt. RALPH G. MARTIN
YANK Field Correspondent

SOMEWHERE ON THE TUNISIAN FRONT [By Radio]—The moon went down at 3:15 A. M.
A half hour later a well-fortified Axis outpost was a shambles, thick with the dead bodies of some newly imported crack Italian troops. The night-raiding Rangers had completed their first mission on the Tunisian front.

They had piled into fast-moving trucks the previous evening, rode for several hours not knowing where, then double-timed with full equipment over eight miles of rugged country. They bivouacked several miles from their objective with nothing but thin shelter halves for cover.

The next day was devoted to careful reconnaissance and observation of the enemy, and some final detailed planning. During the waiting period the edge was taken off the mass tension when three Arabs came up to the front lines and tried to sell some oranges and eggs. Nobody was taking any chances. After the boys finished laughing they put the Arabs under guard until the attack was over.

The raid was a complete surprise to the enemy. There was no rattling of helmets or creaking of shoes (the Rangers wear shoes with special treads). The Italians were literally caught with their pants down. Most of them were in bed or on the way to bed.

At the first sign of action, Axis officers in the rear hopped on their motorcycles and scrammed, leaving the men to figure out their own angles.

Most of the enemy's fireworks came from 37-mm cannon which were dropping shells all around Lt. Col. William O. Darby's CP. The cannon were near the main objective of Capt. Murray's company. Col. Darby got Murray on the field radio and said, "Captain, when are you going to reach your objective?"

"The objective's been reached, sir," the captain replied.

"Well, when are you going to knock out those blasted 37-mms?" the lieutenant colonel asked.

Just then two of Murray's boys parked a few grenades on the cannon.

"The 37-mms have been reached and destroyed, sir," the captain said.

That's the way the show worked—like clockwork.

The concussion of a grenade that landed about a foot from Pfc. Imbre Biro picked him up and threw him down three feet away. It made the former New York City dead-end kid so mad he got up, shook the shock off, grabbed a tommy gun, and waded in after the guy who threw it.

An embarrassing moment almost proved fatal to Capt. Murray when he jumped into a fox hole and reached for his Comanche knife and found it wasn't there. It was lucky for him that the Italian didn't want to fight, anyway.

As soon as they had rounded up a dozen prisoners, the order came out: "No more prisoners." And there weren't any.

One Italian, who had been shooting up a lot of Rangers from a good vantage point, decided to take the easy way out and yelled, "Kamerad!"

"Kamerad, hell!" one of the Rangers said, and kept on shooting.

Lt. Col. Darby called Capt. Max Schneider, another of his COs. "Captain, have you got any prisoners?"

"I think I have two, sir," replied the captain.

The field connection was bad and the colonel asked him to repeat what he said. Meanwhile the two Italians tried to pull a fast sneak, and Capt.

Ranger Raid
IN TUNISIA

U. S. Army nurses outside the grass hut in which they live in Burri, one of the Fiji Islands. Just shows they can make it look domestic anywhere.

In India, three G.I.s cheer the elephant which has just turned up with their bedding. He goes along on marches but often by his own route.

Schneider, a sharpshooter from Shenandoah, Iowa, fired two shots. He said to the colonel, "Sir, I *had* two prisoners."

The Rangers really messed up that outpost when six mortar crews went into action. Cpl. Richard Bevin of Estherville, Iowa, went up ahead to determine the positions. He radioed

Yanks at Home Abroad

Boy Rangers in U. S. Stand Behind Their 'Big Brothers'

SOMEWHERE IN TUNISIA—The quickest way to make an American Ranger mad is to walk up to him and murmur sweetly, "Hi yo, Silver!" It drives him nuts.

But the Rangers here got a big kick out of a V-letter which they received recently from the president of the Boy Rangers of America. It said:

"I am very anxious to make the acquaintance of our big brother Rangers overseas. Upon receipt of this letter, please write and tell us of your experiences in France and North Africa and we will assign one of your little Ranger brothers to tell you of our doings."

And then the letter was signed, "Yours for Victory—Trusty Tommy."

back the information and added, "And throw in the kitchen sink"—which they did.

Most of the Rangers were having fun but nobody enjoyed it more than T/5 Stanley Bush. Bush got the Purple Heart for action in the Dieppe raid. Cpl. Franklin Koons, the Dieppe hero who was the first Yank to get the British Military Medal in this war, also came along on this Tunisia raid.

This was one show where the big boys didn't sweat it out at headquarters in the rear echelon. Not only was Lt. Col. William O. Darby up there in the thick of it, but with him were his executive officers, Maj. Herman Dammer of New York, and his chief medical officer, Capt. William Jarrett of New York. All of them are as tough and hard as their men.

Capt. Jarrett and his crew of Ranger medics use a pistol or an M1, when they're not tying bandages. They don't wear Red Cross arm bands. They don't want special consideration from the enemy. And they don't give any.

Four medics on the raid treated two officers and 18 wounded enlisted men — guys partially shell-shocked, temporarily blinded from grenade concussion, or with gaping shrapnel wounds in their bodies. All of them insisted on walking back to the rear, nine miles away.

It was the first all-Ranger raid. At Dieppe, a small selected group worked together with the British Commandos. When they wiped out four German coastal guns at Arsew, they served as the spearhead of the Nov. 8 landing attack on North Africa. Now for the first time they were

putting on their own show. They don't chew nails or spit rust but the day after the raid one Ranger said, "Now we know we are tough."

Since their arrival in North Africa, their force has been supplemented by 100 enlisted men and six officers who came directly from the States. This unit represents the sum total of all Rangers anywhere.

The youngest is Pfc. Lemuel Harris of Pocohontas, Va., who has just turned 18. The oldest is 25-year-old J. B. Coomer of Amarillo, Tex. J. B. says he averages $1,000 a month with his card winnings and sends it all home to his wife. For a two-month stretch he didn't gamble. But the next month he sent home $3,000 dollars.

"My wife appreciates a little extra money," he explains.

They've even got a full-blooded Sioux Indian, T/5 Samuel P. Oneskunk of Cherry Creek, S. Dak. Cpl. James Haines of Lexington, Ky., used to be a lion tamer for Frank Buck and two brothers in the outfit, Pvt. Othel Greene and Sgt. Dick Greene of Des Moines, Iowa, are former Golden Glove boxing champs.

They've also got their own photographers—soldiers assigned to them who shoot only with cameras. Sgt. Phil Stern is a former magazine and newspaper photographer, and T/5 Henry Paluch shoots movies.

There are wrestlers, bull-fighters, clerks, poets. Any one of them can break you quietly in two.

The Rangers don't like to be left behind when something exciting is in the air. The night before this latest raid, a broad-shouldered guy, Cpl. Bob Halliday, a former radio crooner from Syracuse, N. Y., had just come off guard duty. He was all pooped out, having slept only two hours out of the past 24. But as soon as he heard of the im-

pending raid, he went up to the CO, grabbed him by the arm and pleaded, "Let me go along, sir; please let me go along."

Everybody got quiet and looked at the lieutenant and the lieutenant looked at Halliday for a moment and frowned. Then he said, "OK. You can come."

That's the kind of a guy a Ranger is.

Moscow Gals Are Pretty and Smart But Nid Means No the Same Old Way

(As mechanic with the plane that flew Gen. Patrick J. Hurley to Russia, S/Sgt. George W. Bowne of Turtlecreek, Pa. has hit military zones in which the average G.I. is scarcer than lemonade in the Sahara. He's been on this slick detail since Oct. 16, 1942. When Sgt. Bowne was tapped to tend the motors of the Hutley DC-2, he didn't know that he was to take an American officer to Russia. As a matter of fact, when it came to front-line flying in the U.S.S.R., he and his fellow G.I.s were switched for a Russian crew. But he has seen a hell of a lot more Soviet territory than most G.I.s. Here's what he says about the place according to Sgt. Al Hine, YANK staff correspondent:)

SOMEWHERE IN THE MIDDLE EAST—It was a pretty amazing experience. Some of it was tough flying, like over the desert when heat pockets would pull you down from 2,000 to 200 without a hell of a lot of warning.

In Russia we had to fly at low altitudes. That's all right even if it does bring the mountains up a little too close for comfort. But one time we had an embassy official with us who was up front having the controls explained to him. He pushed the stick experimentally and zowie! we were suddenly flirting with some very high-class peaks. The general described a gentle arc and fortunately landed in one piece as the pilot brought us out of it.

Russia itself wasn't bad. There was caviar

YANK, The Army Weekly, publication issued weekly by Headquarters Detachment, Special Service, War Department, 205 East 42nd Street, New York City, N. Y. Copyright, 1943, in the U. S. A. Entered as second class matter July 6, 1942 at the Post Office at New York, New York under the Act of March 3, 1879. Subscription price $3.00 yearly. Printed in U. S. A.

frequently but I never got to like it too much. There was vodka but it was expensive.

The movies we saw were good but for an American soldier, at least, a little too heavy on the propaganda angle. The news reels were the best things we saw. Sitting in the theater you'd be able to be right along with a Russian sniper and watch him knock off a Nazi. It was more like seeing action, real war, than we'd seen in any news reels anywhere.

There was good entertainment in Moscow. I went to the ballet one night and I still don't know whether I liked it or not. It was swell music. The ballet I saw was "Swan Lake." And the dancing was good; you could tell it by the way the crowd applauded. I thought some of the men looked pretty silly jumping around in tights. The girls—that's a different matter. I didn't need anyone to tell me they were good.

The Russian girls generally were pretty. The majority of them dressed in clothes that were sensible, not smart. They wore gray felt-lined boots that hit their knees, and longish coats. You can tell a rich woman or a woman who is married to a foreigner by her silk stockings. The girls all seem to know how to say "nid." And that means "no."

There's practically no prostitution in Russia. There's probably a normal amount of playing around but the "oldest profession" is pretty well beat up.

One thing that gave me a kick was a Russian jazz concert. It was the only jazz band I've ever seen that had 14 violins. But they swung in spite of that. The music was solid. The featured dancer with the band was a tap dancer and a good one, but when he tried to dress like an American, he wore the bell-bottomed trousers and wild suits of the torrid '20s. The songs were mostly about six years old. Still, when you hear "Sweet Sue" played in Moscow, it sounds mighty, mighty good.

One other thing I learned was that a Russian can really drink. Don't ever fool yourself that you can outdrink him. He'll put you under the table before you know what hit you.

There was one nice, quiet Russian officer who

met us once when we had a couple of quarts of Scotch on us. We knew him and offered him a drink. He poured out a full tumbler and we gasped. He was apologetic and asked, "Did I take too much?"

We said no because we didn't know what else to say. He downed the whisky with a "bottoms up" and had a second one. He was walking straight as a die when he left us.

In one way he was typical of the sort of thing Russians admire. The one guy they respect is the man who can do something big—bigger than taking a drink, of course—and laugh it off with "nichevo"—which means "there's nothing to it."

Three of a kind. The Aldinger triplets—William F., Robert J. and Henry L.—of Long Island, N. Y., draw their G.I. equipment after enlisting in the Army. They are 18 years old and going strong.

All the Way on the Cuff From Peacock Alley to Tripoli

TRIPOLI—When American news correspondents moved into this city's swank, bepalmed Grand Hotel after the British occupation, they were warmly greeted by its manager, William Gaudenzi.

Gaudenzi said he was a former assistant manager of the Waldorf-Astoria in New York and produced a card to prove it. He said he had been in New York for 10 years, leaving in the early '30s to come to Tripoli.
—**YANK Field Correspondent**

WORDS ACROSS THE SEA

Jordan   Coursen   Graber

Pvt. **Darrell Jordan** sends this message to 3/C Petty Officer Tommy George: "I'm working in an Air Force electrical shop in England, but craving to get my mitts on that lug Hitler. Maybe we can do it soon together." . . . **Sgt. Melvin M. Coursen**, England, optimistically regards Cpl. Eugen Renwick, stationed at Hammer Field, Calif., as his future brother-in-law. He says: "Why don't you write your sis, Thelma. If you do, be sure and say I love her." . . . **Cpl. Ben Graber** has lost touch with his pal Pvt. Walter Weinberger and wants to remind him that his address is still the same base in the South Pacific at which he has been stationed for the last year.

Tonne   Padgett   McKenna

Pfc. **Jerome Tonne** sends "Hi" to his brother, Bob, a Navy cadet, and "Hi, sir" to his other brother, Bill, who rates a salute now as a shavetail. . . . **Sgt. Merle Padgett** wants to get in touch with him: "My address is Hq. 7th Bomb. Gr., APO 886, N. Y. How about a letter soon?" . . . **Les McKenna** is a mess corporal with a New Zealand unit in a South Pacific base. He liked Mess Sgt. James E. Wovels, whom he met when they served chow together in the Fiji Islands. To Wovels: "I found your methods of putting out chow very successful. Best of luck to you and stay away from this bloody island. Drop me a line at Hqs. Kiwi Div., APO 502, San Francisco, Calif."

Davidson, Blalock   Julks   Schmitt

Two ex-hams, **Glenn Davidson** and **Clif Blalock**, Hqusaf, APO 860, N. Y., collaborate on a code message to two guys they knew on the air in the old days, Lt. Art Carlson and Joe Parker "WE STL HAVNT FERGT SWL QSO'S WE HAD ON 40 ES 80 AND R LKING FWRD TO C-ING U AGN BACK ON AIR. FR NW 73's." . . . Pfc. **William Julks** is in England and has this to say to his cousin, Cpl. Levy Julks of Baton Rouge, La.: "The folks asked about you in their last letter. Why don't you write more often?" . . . From England, Pvt. **Maurice Schmitt** tells his pal Leonard Connors in a U. S. training camp: "When you go to Carroll (Iowa) drop in and see my friend at the Heires Electrical Co."

Westlake   Kiersh   Kamp

Sgt. **Bert Westlake**, of the RAF, stationed in Ottawa, Canada, says his girl friend in the WAAFs, whose name is Moralee, has just been promoted from the airmen's mess to officers' mess. "Has your cooking improved?" he asks her. . . . From England, Pfc. **Reubin Kiersh** sends this message to Sgt. Herbert Leibowitz of Brooklyn, N. Y., now overseas: "Your folks haven't heard from you for three months. For all they know you might be a colonel by now." . . . S/Sgt. **Melvin Kamp**, an aerial engineer, has this to say to his cousin, Howard Goldstein: "I hear you joined the Navy. How about writing me, you gob? The address is APO 873, N. Y. The war should be over soon now that we're both in the service."

MESSAGE CENTER

Pvt. **T. W. Oliver** would like to exchange insignia, regimental crests and divisional sleeve patches—both foreign and domestic. His address: Med. Det., 187 FA, Fort Ethan Allen, Vt. . . . Pvt. **M. Joe Turner**, Co. B, 701 Bn., Fort Custer, Mich., wants the address of **Ray Boyes** formerly with the race track, and S/Sgt. **Jan Jankowske** once at Fort Jay, N. Y. . . . Cpl. **C. H. Nonnenmacher**, Hq. Det., 305 Med. Bn., Camp Forrest, Tenn., is paging Pfc. **George Catullo** of Revere, Mass. . . . Jack F. **McNamara,** Med. Det., 180th Inf., APO 45, c/o PM, Pine Camp, N. Y., wants mail from Henry F. **Spinney**. . . . Pvt. **Don Shauger**, St. Hospital, Harding Field, La., wants news from Pfc. **Gordon Rechcygl**, a Marine last heard from in Hawaii. . . . **Dan Egan**, New Caledonia, Jimmy Jones, Africa, get in touch with Sgt. **Joseph Langhans**, 24th Sec., Am. Tr. Sep., CA Bn., c/o Btry. C, APO 862, c/o PM, N. Y. . . . Anyone knowing S/Sgt. **William T. Biddinson's** location write Pvt. **Richard Bond**, Prov. Casual Det., NOSA, New Orleans, La. . . . Pvts. **Harold Burch** and **Ernest Near** get in touch with Cpl. **John Huber**, 14th Photo Recon. Sqdn., USAAB, Colorado Springs, Colo. . . . Pvt. **Gene A. Trace**, Base Hq. APO 813, N. Y. C., wants to hear from S/Sgt. **Louis Priest**, Sgts. **Donald Allumbaugh, Johnny Davey, Leo Roller**, Cpls. **Harold Reynolds, Bill Carlisle,** Pfc. **M. Kackenmeister** and Pvts. **Jimmie Pecarro, William Downey, Mike Sobol, Joe Pendergast**. . . . **James S. Fergerson**, S1c, please write Pvt. **Harry J. Rice**, Btry. C, 161 CA Bn. (AA) Camp Haan, Calif. . . . Will S/Sgt. **Richard Hoptner** and other friends write Sgt. **Mrozek**, 18th Anti-Sub Sqdn., Langley Field, Va. . . . Pvt. **Jack Clingerman**, 24 (CA) Btry. C, APO 864 c/o PM, N. Y. wants to hear from Cpl. **Robert C. Jackson.** Any information welcome. . . . Pfc. **Robert L. Maxham**, 214 CA (AA) Btry. G, APO 502 c/o PM, San Francisco, Calif., wants to let the men in his old outfit know where he is, especially "**Skipper**." . . . Pvt. **Edgar C. Leachman** write to T/Sgt. **William Don Leachman**, 872 Two Eng. Flying Trng. Sqdrn., Blackland Army Flying School, Waco, Tex. No letter since Dec. 7, 1942. . . . A/C **Harry M. Hill**, Sqdn. 84, SAAAB, Santa Ana, Calif., wants mail from S/Sgt. **Pilot Loyd Hoffman**, once stationed at Decatur, Ala. . . . **W. A. Humes**, composer, wishes a libretto to set to music. His address: 1008th Sch. Sqdrn., AAFAFS, La Junta, Colo.

Allies Fight to Clear Mediterranean Sea

As long as the narrow Straits of Sicily are guarded by Axis forces on both sides, the Mediterranean is closed to Allied convoys and invasion of Europe is impossible from the south.

The maps, above, show how the closing of the Mediterranean affects U. S. shipping lines, with Italy and Germany dominating the vital Straits of Sicily.

F IT's hard to figure out why a little place called Tunisia is holding up Allied invasion plans of Europe, a look at the map should put you straight. That 300-mile battlefront is one of the most vital fronts of the whole war. With the Germans in Tunisia, the Mediterranean is of small use to the Allies; with the Mediterranean closed to the Allied convoys, invasion of Europe from the south is impossible.

German-held Tunisia cuts the Mediterranean right in two. Germany commands the North African side of the narrow Straits of Sicily; Italy commands the opposite side from strongly fortified Sicily. The distance is only 90 miles from the mainland to the island base.

The Allies fight in North Africa to clear this bottleneck; and that is why Tunisia is the key to the invasion of Europe. Allied shipping lines get into the Mediterranean on either end, but they can't get through.

The direct routes to North Africa are bad enough. From New York to Gibraltar, U. S. ships have to travel 3,685 miles. From Gibraltar, it is still 297 miles to Oran by coastal road, 494 miles to Algiers. From Algiers, it is more than 400 miles over the most difficult terrain to Gen. Eisenhower's troops. Distance from New York to Algiers, by sea, is 3,820 miles.

It is more than 3,600 miles from New York to Dakar, from where supplies must be shipped across Africa by plane, truck and railroad.

But supplies to our Allies on the eastern side of the Mediterranean bottleneck, and to our soldiers stationed in Iran and Iraq must travel a much more circuitous route. It is 12,000 miles by way of the Cape of Good Hope to Alexandria; it is approximately the same distance to Basra, at the head of the Persian Gulf. With the Mediterranean open, this distance would be only 5,000 miles and the Allies could save from 10 to 20 valuable days getting supplies and equipment where it is needed.

Turkey's present position would be greatly strengthened by the opening of the Mediterranean. Turkey's President Inonu said, "We will do everything possible not to become involved in this war, but we know now that it is not within our power to remain out."

With the Mediterranean open, the way would be clear to clean out the Axis troops in Crete and the Aegean Islands, thus supporting Turkey on her European front and opening the possibilities of a Balkan front into Europe.

Meanwhile, Rommel's retreat in central Tunisia turned into a near rout, and Gen. von Arnim made thrusts in the north against the British positions at Medjez-el-Bab, Beja and the Djebel Abiod Pass. His obvious attempt was to pin the British First Army down so that it could not move south against Rommel's badly beaten troops.

The Germans suffered heavy casualties, and made very slight gains. But they were accomplishing their purpose, which is to delay the Allied invasion of Europe until Hitler can dig himself in more securely.

Kasserine was retaken by the Allies, and it was expected that the enemy would be forced to give up Feriana and Sbeitla.

Highly significant was the fact that light patrols of Gen. Montgomery's Eighth Army swept around the Mareth Line to points where they were only 40 miles from Kasserine. The Eighth Army proper is still separated from central Tunisia, however, by the great salt marshes and the Mareth Line.

Wilhelmshaven, the vital submarine base in Germany, was pounded furiously from the air by Allied planes, and Cologne was quivering under its 113th devastating raid. Lorient and St. Nazaire, U-boat bases on the coast of France, were reported to be out of commission.

"Road to Kokumbona"

The Last Days at Guadalcanal

Here are nine sketches of scenes and men drawn at the front lines by Sgt. Howard Brodie during the Army's final battle against the groggy Japanese defenders.

YANK's staff combat artist, Sgt. Howard Brodie, completed the sketches on this and the following three pages at Guadalcanal on Feb. 9, the day the last Jap resistance on the island ended. By that time, Brodie was as tired as the jungle fighter in his portrait at the left. He had been working for weeks at the front under difficulties that would have forced most artists to throw away their pencils and pads in despair.

Brodie sketched most of his pictures in fox holes, CPs, dressing stations and artillery positions. He was never able to complete a drawing without being interrupted by air raids, mortar bursts and Jap snipers who seemed to delight in taking pot shots at him just when he was beginning to concentrate on his model. "I don't know which was worse—the snipers or the bugs," he says. "I think I was bitten by every insect on the island."

After he did his original sketch on the front lines, Brodie would take it back to the tent he shared with Sgt. Mack Morriss, the YANK staff correspondent who works with him in the South Pacific area. There he would darken and finish the drawing. Brodie did all his sketches in pencil on thin paper and, by the time the fighting ended, most of his pencils were short, one-inch stubs.

Soldiers from California are probably familiar with Brodie's drawings. He was a staff artist on the San Francisco *Chronicle* for seven years before enlisting in the Army last August. He was training to be message-center clerk with the Signal Corps at Camp Crowder when he was transferred to YANK.

Two days after the fighting on Guadalcanal stopped, Morriss and Brodie left the island to try to gain back some of their recently lost weight before proceeding to their next assignment.

"I wouldn't have missed Guadalcanal for anything," Brodie said. "But I was damned glad to leave the place."

Sgt. Brodie at work on Guadalcanal

This marine officer, Lt. Col. M. L. Curry, was sketched as he came up to confer with Army infantry officers.

This infantryman came in from a patrol and dropped down to show me how he had just fired his Reising gun at Jap snipers.

"Along the Kokumbona Road" Inf. pull a 50 cal machine gun cart.

Infantrymen lugging Jap prisoner back on shelter-half who wouldn't walk and wanted to die — On the "Horse's Neck" front. sketched between daytime air-raid alarms.

I sketched this battalion commander, Lt. Col. Earl J. Rijnstra of Nashville, Tenn., in his fox hole at the front.

Pvt. Merlin Murray sits on a ridge, guarding native supply bearers from Jap snipers. Notice the matches stuck in his helmet.

Burial on the spot—

VOL. 1, NO. 39
MAR. 19, 1943
By the men .. for the men in the service

THE LIQUOR BAN

A COUPLE of weeks ago, YANK carried an item in the Strictly G.I. column about a new War Department order prohibiting the sale in military areas of liquor stronger than 3.2 beer. We think this order important enough to discuss a little further.

As everybody knows it was directed chiefly against the sale of liquor in commissioned officers clubs located on Army posts.

The picture of well-stocked bars in officers' clubs in posts where enlisted men were restricted to weak G.I. beer at PXs rubbed a lot of guys the wrong way.

For one thing, it didn't fit into their conception of an army based on democratic tradition. It suggested an autocratic privilege that, simply doesn't belong in an army which is fighting, among other things, to destroy certain autocratic privileges elsewhere.

We hope task force commanders outside the U. S. will take similar action. If special privileges in our Army don't belong inside the U. S. they certainly have no place on the fighting fronts.

Navigator-Bombardier Training

THE soldiers who drop the bombs are going to be trained to shoot the stars, too, and vice versa. WD announces that aviation cadets heretofore, trained as either navigators or bombardiers will now get training for both—30 weeks in all, plus five weeks of aerial gunnery school. The purpose of the change is not to economize in crewmen, but to let men switch jobs during a flight to cut down fatigue (or to take the place of a casualty). Cadets will be appointed flight officers or commissioned second lieutenants after the first phase of their training, and the flight officers will get their gold bars at the end of the training.

Delay on AAF Technician Badges

Ever since we announced authorization of an AAF Technicians Badge last November, we have been swamped with questions about it. To wear it, you must have been in the AAF more than six months and graduate from a technical training school. To make the badge prettier, you can add a bar for each specialty you qualify in—radio operator, parachute rigger, and so forth. But the QM won't say exactly *when* you'll be able to pin these badges on. Whenever we ask them about it, they always answer, "These devices may be supplied on regular QM issue to those organizations entitled thereto," which could mean almost any time between now and six months after the duration.

Venereal Statistics

The present venereal disease rate in the U. S. armed forces is 40 per 1,000 per year, according to the National Research Council. This figure, the lowest military rate in our history, compares with a venereal disease rate of 84 per 1,000 in the first World War. The present civilian rate in the U. S. is 4 per 1,000 for syphilis; 6 per 1,000 for gonorrhea.

The Old Man Talks

The familiar ritual of "Pvt. Smith has permission of the first sergeant to speak to the company commander" is out at Fort Knox, Ky. A recent order by Maj. Gen. Charles S. Scott, CO of Fort Knox, specifies that at certain times "every company commander in this center will make himself available to any man in his company, and no bumptious company clerk or first sergeant is going to stop him."

The Iowa

Some interesting facts about the Navy's newest battlewagon, the 45,000-ton *Iowa*: Carries more ak-aks and heavy guns, including 16-inchers, than any other ship. She is 880 feet long and her beam is 108 feet—just a few inches narrower than any lock in the Panama Canal. The *Iowa's* surface area covers nine and a half acres. She has 800 miles of welding, 250 miles of electric cable, and her generators produce enough power to run a city of 20,000 population.

The *Iowa* is the fourth Navy ship to bear that name. The Navy says she is the most powerful ship afloat.

Army Post Named After Private

A special order of the WD has named Camp Mackall, Hoffman, N.C., in honor of Pvt. John T. Mackall, 2d Battalion, 503d Infantry. Pvt. Mackall died Nov. 12, 1942, of wounds received in action.

North African Fire Water

Everybody is telling the story about the two G.I.s in Casablanca who managed to get a quart of bootleg brandy and prepared to sample it in a hotel room, which they had hired for the purpose. The first soldier lifted the bottle and took a couple of snorts. But he reached over and pushed the bottle away when the second soldier put it to his lips.

"Don't drink that stuff," he yelled.

"Aw, gwan," muttered the second soldier. "Leave me alone."

"I'm telling you—don't drink it," screamed the first soldier. "I just looked out the window and saw President Roosevelt riding down the street in a jeep."

Song of the Volga Boatmen

Items That Require No Editorial Comment

Nazi Joke Book

Dr. Alfred Rosenberg, the Nazi super-race mythologist, gets all burned up when he hears people in Germany joke about the war. "If you hear anyone tell such jokes," he advises in an article in *Der Angriff*, "knock him down." Latest joke to annoy Wotan Rosenberg is the one about the Berlin worker who asked a bank clerk how to invest his life savings of 1,000 marks. "Buy state bonds," suggested the clerk. "Suppose the state collapses?" asked the worker. "Isn't it worth the investment?" replied the clerk.

They Did It With Mirrors

Italian version of recent military developments in the South Pacific as broadcast over the Rome radio. "After wiping out American forces at Buna, New Guinea, and Guadalcanal, Japanese troops withdrew to better positions in spite of heavy enemy attacks."

Those Stubborn Aussies

The difficulty of taking over Australia is explained by the Tokyo newspaper *Asahi*: "As this race enjoys complete freedom, great obstacles must be overcome to make it cooperate with Japan as a member of the Greater East Asia Co-Prosperity Sphere, and to make it grasp peacefully the significance of our new order."

No Help Wanted

Unemployment problems which may worry the Allies aren't giving the Nazis any trouble. Because, explained an article in Hitler's *Voelkischer Beobachter*, "we solved our economic problems under a system that guarantees full employment for all Germans. That is another proof of the genius that guides the New Order. The democracies as usual are confused; but we have our own Nazi ways of solving unemployment."

Like at Stalingrad?

YANK is published weekly by the Enlisted Men of the U. S. Army, and is for sale only to those in the Armed Services.

YANK EDITORIAL STAFF

Managing Editor, Sgt. Joe McCarthy, FA; Art Director, Sgt. Arthur Weithas, DEML; Assistant Managing Editor, Cpl. Justus Schlotzhauer, Inf.; Assistant Art Director, Sgt. Ralph Stein, Med.; Pictures, Sgt. Leo Hofeller, Armd.; Features, Sgt. Douglas Borgstedt, DEML; Cable Editor, Cpl. Durbin Horner, QM; Sports, Sgt. Dan Polier, AAF.
Washington: Sgt. Earl Anderson, AAF; Cpl. Richard Paul, DEML.
London: Sgt. Bill Richardson, Sig. Corps; Sgt. Harry Brown, Engr.; Cpl. Ben Frazier, CA; Sgt. Walter Peters, QM; Sgt. Jack Scott, FA; Sgt. Charles Brand, AAF; Cpl. Thomas Fleming, DEML; Col. Stephen Derry, DEML; Cpl. Louis McFadden, Engr.
North Africa: Sgt. James Burchard, Inf., Sgt. Peter Paris, Engr.
Cairo: Sgt. Burgess Scott, Inf.; Sgt. George Aarons, Sig. Corps.

Tehran: Sgt. Al Hine, Engr.
India: Sgt. Ed Cunningham, Inf.; Sgt. Robert Ghio, MP.
China: Sgt. John P. Barnes, AAF.
Australia: Sgt. Don Harrison, AAF.
South Pacific: Sgt. Mack Morriss, Inf.; Sgt. Howard Brodie, Sig. Corps.
New Guinea: Sgt. Dave Richardson, CA.
Hawaii: Sgt. Merle Miller, AAF.; Sgt. John Bushemi, FA.
Alaska: Sgt. Georg N. Meyers, AAF.
Alcan Highway: Pvt. Donald Seely, Engr.
Panama: Sgt. Robert G. Ryan, Inf.
Trinidad: Cpl. Frank H. Rice, Inf.; Sgt. Tom Vahey, AAF.
British Guiana: Pvt. Fred A. Peruzzi, Inf.
Puerto Rico: Cpl. Byron B. Evans, Inf.
Nassau: Cpl. David B. Fold, MP.
Iceland: Cpl Dennis Weigand, AAF.
Marines: 1st Sgt. Riley Aikman.
Navy: Robert L. Schwartz Y3c; Allen Churchill Y3c.
Officer in Charge: Lt. Col. Franklin S. Forsberg; Editor, Maj. Hartzell Spence; Detachment Commander, Capt. Sam Humphfus; Officer in Charge for England: Lt. Col. Egbert White.

Full 24-hour INS and UP leased wire service.

MAIN EDITORIAL OFFICE
205 EAST 42ND ST., NEW YORK CITY, U.S.A.

FIGHTING SCOT. A Highlander and his Sten gun. This tough and cheerful soldier serves with a famous unit in the British Eighth Army.

MOVING UP. One of a column of U. S.-built tanks snapped drove toward Tunisia. The English said: "They're the best we've h

FIGHTERS IN

DESERT SALVAGE. An RAF truck (left), hauling plane wings back to repair shops in the rear, passes by the charred and twisted wreck of an Italian fighter plane. From Egypt to Tunisia the desert shows these signs of Axis defeat. (Pictures on this page are by Sgt. George Aarons.)

YANK's Cameramen Click on the Americans and British Who Battle the Axis Armies in Tunisia.

HASTY CHOW. Yanks in Tunisia eat English kidney stew mixed up with some dates. (Pictures on this page are by Sgt. Pete Paris.)

CAPTIVE GUN. Pvt. Jeremiah A. Heffernan (right) explains German light machine gun to Pfc. William DeFroscia. Heffernan captured it.

SAFETY FIRST. Before taking off for chow these doughboys look out from their Tunisian airfield "barracks" for possible enemy planes.

ALABAMA

Birmingham's vacant lots were alloted for victory gardens. Alabama teachers asked an increase of $10 per month in minimum pay scales; Jefferson County teachers asked a 15-percent boost. Mrs. H. M. Ball, Homewood, was killed in Birmingham when an L. & N. train struck her automobile. C. Pratt Rather and Maclin F. Smith were named co-chairmen of Jefferson County's Red Cross War Fund drive.

CALIFORNIA

San Francisco's $500,000 Langley Porter Clinic for mental diseases was opened near the University of California Medical Center. Norvell, famous Hollywood astrologist, was arrested on fortune-telling charges. Two San Quentin prisoners were charged with printing bogus checks on the prison's press to be mailed to confederates outside. A San Francisco bus driver, angered by back-seat drivers, refused to let passengers off until they said "please"; they called police. Mrs. Ann Inrene Peile, 31, sued a Los Angeles hospital for $110,000 for telling her she'd given birth to a boy, then telling her it was a girl.

COLORADO

Higley Field at Denver was re-opened, designated as operations base for the Colorado Civil Air Patrol. The Army began a $50,000 repair job on South Platte River levees in Adams County. Ben H. King, former state director of markets, was tried at Denver on embezzlement charges. Mrs. Thelma Jereaw, 38, was near death at Denver after she cut off her tongue; she scrawled, "I have blasphemed the Lord." A 25-year-old parrot awakened residents when fire swept through a Denver rooming house; the people escaped but the parrot perished.

CONNECTICUT

Hartford barber shops upped hair-cut prices to 75 cents for adults, 60 cents for children. Gov. Baldwin opposed construction of a new governor's mansion until after the war. Peter Gurski, Terryville machinist, was executed at Wethersfield for killing Miss Ellen Bourke, 66-year-old retired school teacher, near Plymouth. At Bridgeport, six Norwalk office-holders were fined for absentee-ballot law violations. Hartford women organized a forest fire-fighting crew. The Four-Town Fair was called off at Somers. Miss Jennie O'Neill, 80, went to work on the 3-to-11 P. M. shift in a war plant at Middlebury.

DELAWARE

Delaware set a turkey-production goal of 120,000 birds, 18,000 more than in 1942. Eighteen Elsmere women were awarded Red Cross nursing certificates. At Wilmington, 67 persons were injured when a switch engine rammed the Pennsylvania Railroad's train Cavalier. No candidates filed for municipal offices at Blades. The Wilmington Teachers Association asked additional 5-percent pay boosts for Delaware teachers.

GEORGIA

Twenty-one south Georgia counties planned to buy and operate the Georgia Power and Light Co. George L. Rice of Dalton was named president of the Georgia Bankers Association. Mark Pulliam was sentenced at Chatsworth to life for burning his home and killing his wife and five children. Seven percent of Georgia's autos and trucks left the roads last year. Georgia income-tax payments were below normal.

Sam Phelps, Elberton (Calif.) cobbler, was swamped with work after shoe rationing went into effect.

IDAHO

The State Game Department moved 150 young elk from Jackson's Hole to Owyhee County. Mayor Walker of Boise filed for a second term. A 67-year-old great-grandfather was hired as a telegraph messenger at Twin Falls. Lambing began in the western part of Idaho's sheep country. Dr. F. D. Haines resigned as president of Boise Junior College and returned to California.

ILLINOIS

Mayor Kelly won the Democratic renomination in Chicago with more votes than all other Democratic and Republican candidates combined; George B. McKibbin is the Republican nominee. Cairo's 88-year-old Holliday Hotel, once Grant's headquarters, burned. Emily Sekoskey got judgment at Chicago against Michael Z. Pavolich for $178.89 she spent for meals and movies; he'd married another woman. The federal government paid $6,000,000 for Chicago's 3,000-room Stevens Hotel. Fiatt's Christian Church was 100 years old. The wife of U. S. Senator Wayland Brooks sued for divorce. Illinois in 1942 supplied half the nation's war-vital soybean crop. Oil began pouring through the newly completed 531-mile oil pipeline from Longview, Tex., to Norris City. Chicago aliens admitted to citizenship in 1942 totalled 21,801. Of Shawneetown's original 2,000 population, 500 residents have refused to move from the oft-flooded old town to the new, floodproof site.

INDIANA

Evansville's remaining street-car rails will be removed. Fire destroyed the X market on Booneville's square. Mrs. Martha Dunn of Arthur and Donald Morton of Winslow were killed in a bus accident at Petersburg. Nobleville's First Christian Church burned a $15,000 mortgage. Many towns asked removal of highway traffic signs, saying they're no longer needed. Three downtown business buildings at Terre Haute were destroyed by fire with $350,000 loss; a market at Booneville burned, and the Little Ridge school, near Marion, was razed by fire.

IOWA

The State Liquor Commission ordered store managers not to sell more than one-sixth of their stock in any week. The Rev. Frederick C. Volzke, Algona, succeeded the Rev. Donald Duncan as Baptist pastor at Shenandoah. Primghar schools will end their term April 30 to allow pupils to help on farms. Fire damaged St. Joseph's Mercy Hospital at Cresco, destroyed the Maire-Walgreen drug store and the Jewell Building at Newton. Iowa's first meat-bootlegging injunction petition was filed against William Pratt, Runnels farmer.

KENTUCKY

Five western Kentucky coal operators signed 6-day-week contracts with the Union Mine Workers. Fire destroyed $100,000 worth of coffee, sugar and beef at Glasgow, and the $30,000 Kimmel Theater at Henderson. Logan County schools began a 6-day week. Harlan's Belmont Hotel was closed by Judge F. M. Meadows because of unsanitary conditions. A block of 600 cells was added to Eddyville State Prison. TVA began negotiations to buy the Kentucky Utilities properties at Paducah. The Lowes (Graves County) Commercial Club held its 36th annual Mule Day. Boyd Lakes was charged with killing a University of Kentucky senior in a Negro dance hall at Lexington. Thomas Minch was charged with slaying Thomas Cory, Covington liquor store operator, on information from Minch's wife. A. J. Hoffman, Evansville, Ind., bought the old Herald Post Building on Fifth Street in Louisville.

LOUISIANA

Two thousand goats used as grass cutters on the Bonnet Carre spillway were killed for their 160,000 pounds of meat. Ration cards indicated New Orleans has grown to 650,000. Mrs. Fay Atchison, Miss Beatrice Samson and 5-year-old Ethlyn Rose Cook were burned to death in a New Orleans rooming-house fire. The Landry Memorial School band gave its annual benefit concert at Lake Charles. Judge Mark Pickrel at New Orleans recommended commutation to life imprisonment of the death sentence of Finnon Burks, convicted with Toni Jo Henry. James Philip Gordon admitted at Abbeville the murder of J. E. Miller at Beaumont, Tex. Fire destroyed the Raceland Theater at Raceland, and the J. S. Harrison Wood Products Co. plant at Bogalusa. Lafourche Parish began planting its largest acreage of Irish potatoes. In Avoyelles Parish, 172 new members were added to 4-H clubs. Nathan Samuel Smart, 96, last Confederate veteran of Calcasieu Parish, died.

MAINE

Maine farmers will use boys and girls in summer camps for emergency harvesting this summer. The Rev. Francis E. Whiting became pastor of the United Baptist Church in East Corinth, succeeding the Rev. Charles W. Ellis, now pastor at Kennebunk. The legislature considered legalization of harness-horse racing, with pari-mutuel betting. Miss A. Louise Stone, Kennebunk tax collector for 20 years, retired. John J. McConnell was named police captain at Lewiston. Maine temperatures dropped to 39 below, lowest in history. Six fires caused $250,000 damage at Augusta in one day.

MARYLAND

The Morris Poultry Farm at Bishopville was destroyed by fire with a loss of 40,000 chicks and 2,250,000 eggs. William L. Adams and Homer Gilcrease were killed when a high pressure gas line exploded at Boston and Haven Streets in Baltimore. Mayor Jackson of Baltimore filed for a fifth term. Salisbury asked the legislature to double its police force. Mrs. Julia Hewitt was killed by a locomotive on Haven Street in Baltimore. Mrs. Ida Fretwell and Mrs. Howard Wright were injured when several freight cars crashed into their house beside the B. and O. tracks at Marriottsville. The West Baltimore Methodist Church was a century old. Wooden garbage pails replaced metal ones at Baltimore. The Timonium Fair was canceled; the fairgrounds became an army-truck repair area. Maryland's birth rate rose 19 percent in 1942.

MASSACHUSETTS

Clinon J. Ryan, owner of the Everett Truck Co., was awarded $25,000 at Boston in a suit against the late Charles Schweinert's estate resulting from Schweinert's accusation that Ryan stole an auto. Massachusetts shivered through 26-below temperatures, lowest in years. North Andover police blamed "mistaken identity" for Joseph H. Henderson's murder. A $100,000 fire gutted the D. O. Frost Corporation oil-clothing manufacturing plant at Gloucester. Boston's Back Bay homes were divested of iron fences for scrap. Ludlow laid aside $40,000 in War Bonds for a new post-war town hall. Attleboro planned celebration of its 250th anniversary.

MINNESOTA

Twin Cities furniture manufacturers received federal commendation for devising substitutes for war-scarce metal springs. The State Institute of Governmental Research charged many Minnesota counties are losing one-third or more of available tax receipts through improper assessments. Mr. and Mrs. Ralph Waller died after an auto-truck collision near Belle Plaine; Alfred Albrecht died of heart attack after carrying Mrs. Waller to a doctor's office.

Mrs. Bessie Allison is the first "motorwoman" in Washington, D. C. Others are being trained.

MISSOURI

Dinty Colbeck, leader of the Egan mail robbery gang in the '20s, was tommy-gunned to death in North St. Louis, two years after his release from Atlanta; police blamed a gamblers' quarrel. Legislators protested refusal of Jefferson City hotels to serve a Negro representative. Msgr. Daniel J. Lavery, who founded Holy Rosary Church in St. Louis, died at 83. Russell Cross, convicted at Columbia of murder, asked Judge Dinwiddie to sentence him to die; he got life.

NEBRASKA

Omaha learned a small meat-packing plant had been leased to a firm allegedly controlled by former Chicago Capone gangsters, reputedly to supply black markets. Mayor Dan Butler placed the lid on Omaha gambling. The Innocents, University of Nebraska senior honorary society, added 13 members.

NEW HAMPSHIRE

The legislature junked a proposal to allow each person to kill two deer this season instead of one. The State OPA began a drive to correct coffee rationing inequalities. George M. Dooley, veteran Concord police officer, retired. State Supreme and Superior Court judges were slated for pay boosts from $7,000 to $8,000 a year. New Hampshire income-tax receipts were 25 percent below normal.

NEW MEXICO

Albuquerque consumers will save $62,000 a year under new Gas and Electric Co. rates, approved by the Public Service Commission. The Albuquerque Butchers Union admitted women for training as meat cutters and butchers. Classes were scheduled in Albuquerque to train victory gardeners. Mrs. R. B. Doty and two small sons were killed in an Albuquerque fire. Isleta Indian pueblo mothers gave their church a service flag with 71 stars. Mrs. Josephine A. Fisher pleaded not guilty at Santa Fe to charges she embezzled State Bureau of Revenue funds.

NEW YORK

A Buffalo police shake-up followed a grand jury report that "someone in the Fillmore Avenue police station" caused the death of John Kocemba, 18, arrested for drunkenness. An $80,000 fire destroyed 42 speedboats and cabin cruisers, and the Sylvan Beach boat livery building and dry docks on Oneida Lake at Oneida. James Miller was named president of Buffalo's CIO council. Pet canaries who gave an alarm were credited with saving the lives of residents when gas filtered through an entire block in West New York. The entire New York Philharmonic-Symphony Orchestra threatened to quit after Dr. Artur Rodzinski, new director, fired 14 members. Fireman George Lyons was killed in a fire truck-bus wreck in Buffalo. Fire caused $50,000 loss to Dymac Inc. in Buffalo. Mrs. Jean Gay and her 6-year-old daughter were burned to death at Herkimer. Four persons were injured when a tanker rammed a Staten Island ferry in New York harbor.

NORTH CAROLINA

At Lexington, Mrs. Miley Ann Owens was killed accidentally by officers who came to arrest her two sons accused of

GOLF-LOG is the game in which you shoot for lowest score in changing one word to another, a step at a time.

F'rinstance, last time we changed JEEP to TANK in 8 strokes like this: JEEP. 1. JEER. 2. BEER. 3. BEAR. 4. BEAD. 5. BEND. 6. BAND. 7. BANK. 8. *TANK*.

Note that at each stroke only one letter is changed and each time a change is made a *new word* must be formed.

Today's GOLF-LOG problem is to change TANK into BOMB. Par is 7 strokes. Maybe you can find a way to beat par. If so, send it to YANK's Puzzle Editor, and we'll publish it.

TANK	4.
1.	5.
2.	6.
3.	7. BOMB

Solution on page 22.

ertion; she threatened them with a
otgun. Charlotte cops were forming
union. Judge Zeb V. Nettles padlocked
e Amity Club in Asheville. The legis-
ture killed proposals for a sales-tax
t from 3 to 2 percent and for a liquor
ferendum; approved a school term of
ne instead of eight months. State
AR members met at Winston-Salem.
sper Ozendine, 30, Robeson County
dian, killed his wife and himself after
legedly finding her with another man.
almer Meares, 35, was executed at
aleigh for killing his uncle George
llen in Robeson County last May.
amilton C. Jones and Mayor Currie
omed as leading candidates for mayor
Charlotte. George M. Ivey was, re-
lected president of the Charlotte
hamber of Commerce.

OHIO

Ohio schools considered Saturday
ssions, 3-week term curtailments, to
lease students for farm work. Cincin-
ati's alien detention center was closed.
ternees moved to Chicago. Chester
mith, former University of Cincinnati
hlete, died of injuries received demon-
rating gymnastic routines. Cincinnati
ublic Library has its first girl pages.
obert W. Lindberg, Cincinnati, was
lected regional president of Kiwanis.
he Rt. Rev. J. Henry Schengber,
astor of St. Francis De Sales Church
Cincinnati, celebrated 50 years of
riesthood. A $100,000 explosion wrecked
wing of the Williams Manufacturing
o. plant at Portsmouth. Cincinnati's
3,300,000 War Chest drive was success-
ul. Gov. Bricker signed the bill to
urn Ohio's clocks back an hour, but
leveland and other cities remained on
ar time. About 250 employees of the
azarus store in Columbus became food-
oisoned after eating in the stor afe-
eria: all recovered.

OREGON

*Portland stores and public offices
dopted 9 P. M. closing time twice a
week to accommodate war workers.
Residents of the Lower Siletz River
rea requested a bridge near Toledo.
egislators at Salem considered raising
ruck-weight limits to 71,000 pounds to
acilitate war traffic. The Portland
Chamber of Commerce set up a post-
war planning committee. Eugene sports-
nen gave up rubber boots to farmers.
tephen A. Douglas Meek, 85, died at
Hillsboro; he was the son of Joe Meek,
Oregon's first provisional sheriff who
lanned Oregon's entry into the Union.
orty new Knights of Columbus were
nitiated at Portland. Oregon State Col-
ege at Corvallis set up correspondence
ourses for soldiers.*

PENNSYLVANIA

The Federal Communications Commission approved absorption by the Bell
Telephone Co. of the Keystone system
n Philadelphia. Philadelphia's War
Chest drive exceeded its $7,300,000 goal.
The Army took over the top 14 floors
f the Architects Building in Philadel-
hia. State auto license fees were cut
o $10 flat. Four men were killed in
Pittsburgh when fire destroyed one of
he Golden Triangle's oldest rooming
houses. A Philadelphia-bound bus over-
urned near Stroudsburg and caught
ire, injuring 30. A boiler explosion at
he woolen plant of James Lees and
Sons at Bridgeport injured nine workmen and closed down the plant. Twenty-
ive persons were injured in two war-
plant powder explosions at Philadelphia. The Aliquippa *News Gazette* suspended publication. Stanton S. Herts,
vice president of the Copperweld Steel
Co., and his 13-year-old daughter were
burned to death in their Pittsburgh home.

RHODE ISLAND

Henry J. Kaiser took over the Rheem
shipyard at Providence and promised
to fulfill ship production schedules.
Fourteen-below temperatures, coldest in
39 years, froze the brakes of an auto
at Apponaug, killing Mrs. Grace M. May
of Warwick and fatally injuring her
husband. Louis M. Goldberg was fired
as constable at Misquamicut after Wes-
terly Town Council convicted him of a
"fix" attempt. Gov. McGrath authorized
spring racing at Narragansett Park.
**Washington, Brown and Rhode Island
State Colleges planned limited intercollegiate sports.** The Rev. William J.
Smith, 100, retired Methodist minister,
died at Pawtucket.

SOUTH CAROLINA

The South Carolina Education Association called off its annual convention.
George Mahon, truck driver, was
drowned when the Enoree River bridge,
seven miles from Woodruff, collapsed.
Mary Lattimore, 69-year-old Negro, was
frozen to death at Greer. Lawrence E.
Moore, 35, was burned to death at Conway. Fire destroyed the main building

of Good Hope Plantation three miles
from Ridgeland and the home of Senator Rembert C. Denis near Moncks
Corner. Coker College at Hartsville and
the University of South Carolina began
night classes for war workers.

SOUTH DAKOTA

*Romeo Eugene Koethe, 38, of Salem
was charged at Sioux Falls with killing
Mrs. Francis M. Overdahl in a tourist
cabin. W. C. Vreugdenhill, Union County
farmer, was killed accidentally while
hunting. Six patients died of suffoca-
tion in a fire at the B. K. Gravelle convalescent home in Sioux Falls.*

TENNESSEE

**At Huntingdon, ex-Gov. Gordon
Browning, captain in the first World
War, retired as chancellor to become
an Army captain again.** Mayor Foust
and George Smith, undertaker, filed for
mayor of Jackson. Cary F. Spence, 74,
former brigadier general, postmaster
and vice-mayor of Knoxville, was
drowned while fishing in the Little Tennessee River near Madisonville. A USO
troupe, unable to find hotel accommo-
dations, was provided with rooms in
the Memphis city jail. Daniel M. Baker,
97, McNairy County's oldest resident
and last Confederate veteran, died at
Selmer.

TEXAS

Texas A. and M. experts predicted a
63-percent shortage in vegetable protein
feed for Texas livestock this summer.
The legislature created a commission
to get post-war jobs for discharged
servicemen. Sheriff W. E. Melton was
ordered by the Hopkins County grand
jury to bring in one Adolf Hitler, "notorious paperhanger," indicted for "sundry murders, rapes, robberies, etc." The
War Manpower Commission froze 45,-
000 war workers in the Beaumont-Port
Arthur-Orange district in their jobs.
Dock Dover was acquitted at Beaumont
in the knife murder of Johnny Bean,
labor leader. Leo Lera was executed at
Huntsville for killing Harry Phillips at
Galveston. Thornton Hall, of the San
Antonio *Express-News*, was elected
president of the Texas Newspaper
Publishers Association. Joe Gammon,
Groesbeck grocer, was charged with
arson after a $25,000 explosion and fire
in his store. Ray Spencer of Alvin
bought the Nacogdoches *Daily Sentinel.*

VERMONT

*. Gov. Aiken told the legislature at
Montpelier that Vermont's farm manpower shortage is acute. University of
Vermont instructors doubled up on
work to handle new Army classes. A
special doe season for Windham County
was turned down by the legislature; a
committee approved limiting liquor
sales in Vermont to the hours between
6 A. M. and 10 P. M.*

VIRGINIA

Virginia Electric Power Co. resumed
negotiations with AFL representatives
after Norfolk and Portsmouth transportation employees voted a strike, and
Richmond and Petersburg locals threatened to do likewise. Shield's Lake
near Richmond will be closed again this
summer because chemicals to purify the
water are not available. The Richmond
School Board took over Virginia Mechanics Institute for a vocational school.
Lady Wonder, Richmond's clairvoyant
horse, predicted the war's end next December. The sun-cured tobacco market had its best season: 2,466,200 pounds
at a $22.63 average, $4.74 over last year.

WASHINGTON

A fire in Seattle caused when a
bomber crashed on a packing house
caused a loss of 31 lives. Vancouver
hired 15 new policemen. Gov. Langlie
pardoned 17 long-term convicts previously paroled. The legislature slated appropriation of $2,300,000 to share civilian
defense costs with municipalities. Public utility districts were authorized by
the legislature to make group purchases
of private utilities.

WEST VIRGINIA

The House of Delegates at Charleston
approved a local option beer measure
and prohibited beer sales on Sunday.
Marshall College at Huntington assigned 14 teachers to train Army aviation students. Huntington's $100,000
Community Chest drive fell $27,000
short of its mark. Mr. and Mrs. Melvin
Grimm's 13-month-old son died when
the family car was involved in a wreck
at Martinsburg while the child was being taken to a hospital to have a toy
drum-stick dislodged from his throat.
West Virginia's income-tax law was repealed. Bobby Johnson, 14, charged with
slaying Mrs. J. H. Branham at Charleston, was adjudged insane.

REBUS CITIES

If your home town has over 100,000
population you might find it among the
eight cities pictured below. But don't
expect to recognize it right away because these durn things are Rebus
Puzzles. Can you identify all eight U. S. cities?   *(Solution on page 22.)*

MAIN STREET

Missing Something? The Pullman
Company announced that more than
$100,000 in cash and jewelry had
been left behind by Pullman riders
in 1942.

Cold Weather Hint. Shortage of fuel
made New Yorkers shiver during a
recent cold snap. But Mayor LaGuardia came up with the right answer:
"Take cold baths. It feels so good
when you stop."

A Sit-uation. Edward Sullivan, a
laborer in Los Angeles, thought firemen do too much sitting around. To
remedy the situation, he set fire to
the station house. Now he is sitting
around—in jail.

Always a Bridesmaid. Twenty times
a bridesmaid and never a bride.
That's the record of Carmen Cosio,
Tampa (Fla.) USO head. Miss Cosio
acts as bridesmaid at all USO weddings in Tampa.

Goin' My Way? The share-a-ride
program in Gallipolis, Ohio, has expanded to include perambulators as
well as autos. A shortage in baby
carriages has forced mothers to
double up on babies in conveyances.

What? No Pie Throwing?

Palo Alto, Calif.—Pvt. Bill
Miller and his bride, Harriet,
left on a peaceful honeymoon
after a quiet wedding at which
the maid of honor was rushed
to a hospital for an emergency
operation, a member of the
bridal party backed into a waiter
and upset a tray of champagne,
a bridesmaid fainted, and the
bride's hair caught fire as she
cut the wedding cake.

Resilience. Haled before a justice
of the peace in Marceline, Mo., on
charges of passing worthless checks,
Arthur Fuzzy was fined $17.95. He
handed the judge a check. It
bounced, too.

Served With Onions? Ration-con-
scious readers of the Phoenix (Ariz.)
Republic were told in an advertisement that horse meat is "not only
good—it's delicious!"

Just Call Me Fred. Mr. and Mrs.
Joseph D. Homsi, who are admirers
of Gen. MacArthur, President Roosevelt and Josef Stalin, have named
their new son Douglas Delano Stalin
Homsi.

Checkerboard Strategy

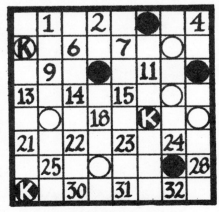

WHITE TO MOVE AND WIN

The score stands: Black, 7 men—White, 5
men. White is two pieces behind. Should he
give up and start a new game?
"Never say die!" say we. Let's examine
the situation.
Yep—it's there all right! The old "wait-
ing-move-and-shot" theme. And—it WINS
FOR WHITE!
Try to figure it out yourself. Here's a hint:
Black is forced into a spot where White
clips off five of his men at once.
The solution is printed on page 22. Number the playing squares of your checkerboard from 1 to 32 as shown so that you can
follow the moves in the solution.

"Yeah, this is room service."

You're in MIAMI Now

A STUDY OF ARMY HOTEL LIFE

By Pvt. R. C. BOLTON, who claims he prefers a tent, and pictures by Sgt. RALPH STEIN, who wants some ice sent up to Room 1004 right away.

M IAMI BEACH, FLA. — So you'd like to spend the winter in Florida? Well, brother, just join the Army. It's as easy as that: But don't say I didn't warn you. You guys who have the weird idea that life here is just one big vacation sprinkled with pay days had better change your brand. Try reefers and get on the beam.

Sure, we are quartered in modern hotels, the beach is at our back doors, the "Moon Over Miami" is as beautiful as the song would have you believe, the climate is delightful, some of us have hotel beds (with double mattresses), each room has a private bath, there are venetian blinds on the windows—and, oh, how we long for the sight of a tent.

Your idea of life in a Miami Beach hotel doesn't include the jeep CQ who comes running through the corridors at 5:20 A.M., blowing his lungs out on a little tin whistle, and, when he has the breath, yelling, "Rise and shine. Up and at 'em, men!" Nor does your notion of life here take into consideration that lowest form of human specie known as hotel sergeant. The toughest top kick in this man's Army is a mere trainee in the hard-boiled class compared to these three-stripers.

Want to know what it's like here? OK, I'll tell you. When the old whistle blows you tumble out of bed and snap on your lights — if you're lucky enough to have lights. They are prohibited in some hotels. But be sure your blinds are tightly closed unless you want the corporal of the guard on your neck in 30 seconds flat. They have what they call a "dimout" here, but it's the nearest thing to a blackout this side of London.

OK, you're up, so now what do you do? Well, there are any number of things you think of doing (getting back into bed being at the top of the list) but you "decide" to fall out for roll call—and I do mean fall out. This is one of the most hazardous jobs in the Army here. Practically all of these hotels have front steps. These are very attractive in the daylight and make excellent places for the boys to sit during their off moments, if any. However, at 5:30 A.M., you can't see these steps even while you are falling down them, which is what usually happens.

You have about 15 minutes now in which to sit and meditate, or you can make your bed. It's a good idea to do the latter, and it's no mean trick. If you think hospital corners are difficult on a G.I. cot, try making them while you juggle an inner-spring mattress that is eight inches thick.

Of course falling out for breakfast is as dangerous as for roll call, and if you think it's fun to stumble in the dark (they call it marching here) to a hotel a block away for chow, you're eligible for discharge as soon as the man in the white coat catches you.

Back in your room (it's now about 6:45) you have a half hour in which

"Have you a reservation?"

to get shaved and clean your room. You learn for the first time why those venetian blinds are on your windows. They're there so you can dust them every morning, and on *both* sides. You probably never stopped to figure that those innocent looking gadgets have about 40 slats and each one must be treated individually. Now you can understand why, with five jeeps in the room, one is assigned to that task alone.

Another job is the sweeping. You're probably one of those unfortunates who has a pretty carpet on his floor of his room. This makes for a homey atmosphere but it also makes for plenty of grief. Be a contortionist and sweep under five beds and you finally wind up with the nap of the carpet in a neat little pile. And don't ever kid yourself into believing that some day you'll have all the nap swept up. You'll be moved to another hotel before that happens, and you can start all over again on a nice new carpet.

Dusting, except for the blinds, is the softest detail. That is grabbed by the "veteran," the fellow who has been longest in the room. You gaze at him longingly each morning and dream of the day when you will have that job. But it never happens. By the time you work your way up to duster, you're transferred to another hotel.

Our days outside the hotel are like those at most any camp. A beautiful golf course is our drill field, and the famous beach is the scene of our calisthenics. But our every waking moment is haunted by thoughts of our rooms and the inspection by the hotel sergeant. Many of our evenings are spent indoors—gigged. When we do get out we rush to a recently opened PX where 16 ounces of beer are handed out for a dime, and the chief topic of conversation is how swell it must be to live in a tent.

But the daily average temperature here is 78. Sun shines all day. Maybe we'd better stay here at that.

"You don't have to carry their bags, sir."

Hollywood — Ann Sheridan has some advice to sweater girls engaged in war industry: "If the sweater's too big for you, look out for the machines. If you're too big for the sweater, look out for the men." . . .

Ann Sheridan

Joe E. Brown, first actor to visit the South Pacific war area, has conferred on himself the title "commander of the beer gardens of the South Pacific." . . . Glenn Ford is Eleanor Powell's best feller. . . . Cesar Romero has joined the Coast Guard and John Payne the Navy . . . Jack Benny is so hateful he steals lollypops from little boys in his new film, "The Meanest Man in the World." . . . Gypsy Rose Lee's shapely little sister June Havoc dances with Jack Oakie in "Hello, Frisco, Hello." . . . Madeleine Carroll, born in England, took her oath as a U. S. citizen on her 37th birthday. Her husband Stirling Hayden is in the Marines. . . . Rationing has hit Hollywood, too. Orson Welles rides to work on horseback. A drive-in sandwich stand has changed to a walk-in, and a shortage of candy at movie houses has sent managers screaming to ration boards. One manager said, "We are facing a grave crisis in chocolate-covered butterfingers." . . . Ingrid Bergman is making a Swedish-language short for the OWI.

Broadway—Olsen and Johnson are finally quitting the Big Town for Hollywood. They'll leave soon to make a movie version of "Sons o' Fun." . . . Abbott and Costello are bemoaning the loss of 17 grand in a gin-rummy game on a train from Chicago. . . . Sgt. Sidney Kingsley has a new play on Broadway. It's called "The Patriots" and is about Hamilton and Jefferson. The sergeant's plays in civilian life included "Dead End" and "Men In White." . . . Margie Hart is quitting burlesque and will have a role in the Chicago cast of "Cry Havoc," the play about nurses on Bataan. . . . "Random Harvest," having shown to 1,600,000 people in 11 weeks at Radio City Music Hall, has broken the longevity record set by "Mrs. Miniver."

TEE-TOTAL

PRIZES are given to the G.I.s who submit the highest Tee-Total scores in each competition. If you haven't taken a whack at this word game, try it now. It's easy—and you may win one of YANK's Puzzle Kits containing a super-dooper collection of tricks, puzzles and games. Names and scores of winners will be published.

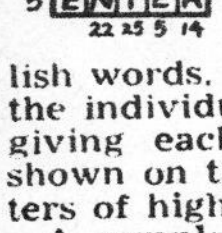

Here's how: Simply fill the diagram with five good English words. No proper nouns. Then total up the individual scores of the 17 letters used, giving each letter a numerical value as shown on the chart. The idea is to use letters of high value.

A sample workout is shown at the left, with a score of 262. Can you beat that par?

LETTER VALUES

A — 6 N — 22
B — 24 O — 8
C — 18 P — 20
D — 17 Q — 1
E — 5 R — 14
F — 21 S — 16
G — 19 T — 25
H — 12 U — 9
I — 7 V — 11
J — 3 W — 23
K — 13 X — 2
L — 26 Y — 10
M — 15 Z — 4

Score: _____ Submitted by _____

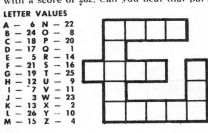

Mail to Puzzle Editor, YANK, 205 East 42nd Street, N.Y.C.

ALTHOUGH her albums of boogie-woogie are played at more than one Army outpost, Hazel Scott thinks the boys across prefer the classics swung in her own style. That's what she gives them short-wave. Her arrangement of "Tea For Two" has domestic priority. In fact, she's sick of it.

Hazel's love is literally with the Army. He is a pilot in the 454th Bombardment Squadron. Consequently this pianist wears more than Air Force wings. Emblazoned on her cream-colored jacket is the squadron insignia, a flying wolf, foaming at the mouth. Like Hazel, it's rather eye-catching.

DOUBLE PUZZLE

First tackle the Picture Puzzle below. Add or subtract the names of the pictured objects, as indicated. The result will be one of the 48 States. Fill this into the Cross-Word Puzzle. 45 Down. Then go to it.

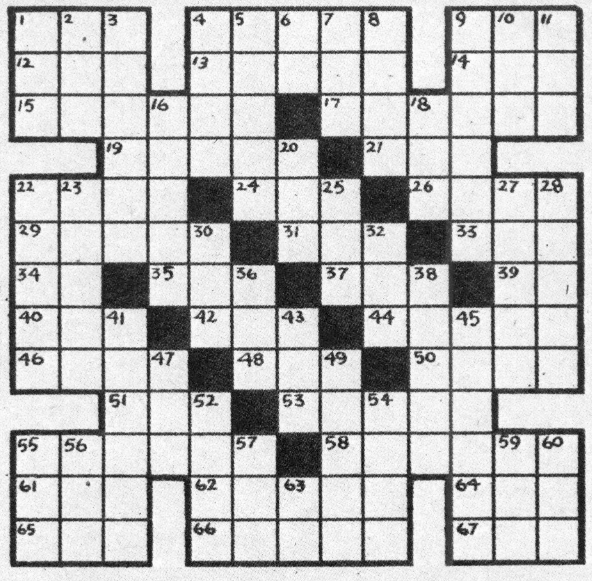

ACROSS
1. Spider's network
4. Blacksmith's hammering block
9. Half a quarter
12. Past
13. Author "The Age of Reason"
14. Beverage
15. Played boisterously
17. Pot
19. Fundamental
21. Rodent
22. Small, light army truck
24. Groove
26. Sport
29. Below
31. Busy insect
33. Age
34. Doctor of Divinity
35. Erase
37. Wholly
39. To the inside
40. Obtain
42. Tibetan gazelle
44. Structure at N. Y. subway entrance
46. British Foreign Secretary
48. Part of a circle
50. Mineral deposits
51. Males
53. French river of first World War fame
55. Plea
58. Trans-Jordan mountain ridge
61. Turn right
62. Snake poison
64. Poem to be set to music
65. Organ of hearing
66. Gapes
67. Likewise not

DOWN
1. We're all in it!
2. Self
3. Dropped explosives upon
4. Imitates
5. Lowest point
6. Six (Roman number)
7. Writing fluid
8. Ogle
9. Military engagement
10. Sick
11. Golf ball rest
16. Document
18. Light blow
20. Young lion
22. Magistrate
23. Finished
25. Beverage
27. Reveille (politely!)
28. The — are coming!
30. Carpet
32. Wapiti
36. South American snake
38. African animal
41. Proneness to anger
43. Supply with weapons
45. (Solve the Picture Puzzle)
47. Born
49. Castrated rooster
52. War vessels, collectively
54. Edges
55. Grow old
56. China berry
57. Meadow
59. Fuss
60. Pronoun
63. Point of compass

(Solution on page 22.)

COMPANY STREET

Here and There. Deflated casanovas at South Plains (Tex.) Army Flying School organized the Jilted G.I. Club; president, thrice-jilted S/Sgt. Enos T. Jones; membership qualifications, two bits and a busted heart; theme song, "Somebody Else Is Taking My Place." . . . The guy who used to trim Greta Garbo's tresses now clips Marine Corps pates at Camp Pendleton, Calif., and, says Pvt. Joseph Zingarelli, "I give the boys the

same careful attention I gave Greta. . . . At Fort Adams, R. I., Pvt. Irving Cohen had his head x-rayed after an injury, was shocked to learn his skull was an exact replica of the skull of prehistoric Neanderthal Man.

KP. Two KPs at Fort MacArthur, Calif., were stopped by a colonel while carrying a steaming kettle out of the mess kitchen. "Get me a spoon," ordered the Old Man. He tasted the contents, spat vigorously, and roared, "D'ya call that soup?" "No sir," was the reply. "We call that dishwater." . . . Camp Edwards (Mass.) candidate for the Army KP marathon: Pvt. R. R. Compt; time: six months. Said he, "I like KP."

Veterans. Cpl. George B. Granger, Camp Williston, Nev.: in service since May 9, 1912. . . . Pvt. Albert Briscoe, Camp Carlson, Colo.: fought on the Mexican Border in 1916, with the Marines in Chateau Thierry in 1917, is now ready for his third campaign. . . . O/C Victor D. Breuille, Fort Benning, Ga.: first enlisted in 1914, was honorably discharged, has re-enlisted six times since, has served in Hawaii, France, Germany and Iceland.

Books. A recently published novel, "Dividends For Louise," arrived at the Barksdale (La.) Field post library and was put on display by Pvt. Norman George Welsh, the book's author. . . . Rookies at Camp Davis, N. C., detailed to move all books out of the post library, left one there because its title was "You Can't Take It With You."

Ratings. Four-months-old Louis Caruso Jr., son of Sgt. Louis Caruso, Camp Hann, Calif., was given the rating of "Technical Prodigy" by post CO Lt. Col. J. P. Jacobs, and became the Army's youngest yardbird. . . . Pvt. Knute Rockne Jr., Camp Perry, Ohio, turned down an officer's commission because "everyone would say I got it on account of my dad."

CHANGE OF ADDRESS

If you're a YANK subscriber, and have changed your address, use this coupon to notify us of the change. Mail it to YANK, The Army Weekly, 205 E. 42nd Street, New York City, and YANK will follow you to any part of the world.

FULL NAME AND RANK _____ SERIAL NO. _____

OLD MILITARY ADDRESS _____

NEW MILITARY ADDRESS _____

THE SAD SACK

"SEX HYGIENE"

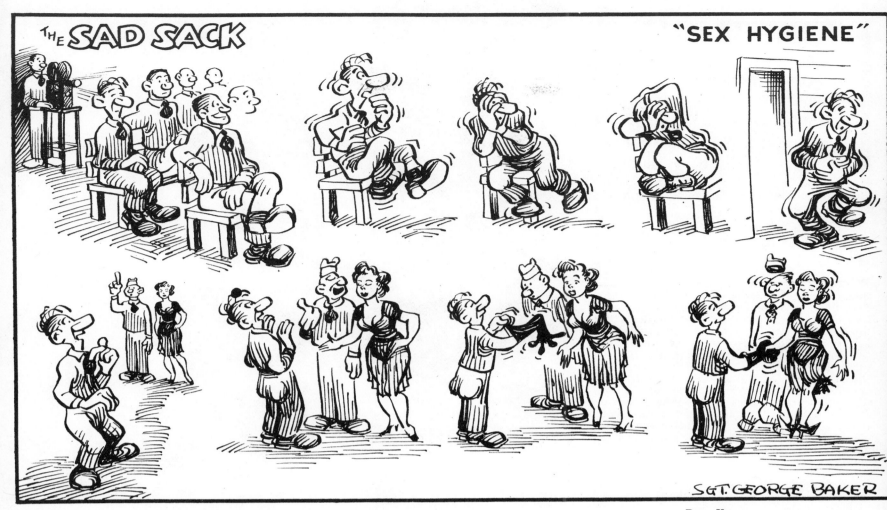

SGT. GEORGE BAKER

Mail Call

Dear YANK:
There's no place where your weekly news is more highly appreciated than by the New Guinea forces. I have spent the past six months in New Guinea so this isn't latrine rumor. I noticed an article sometime ago, "Good News for Chow Hounds," explaining dehydrated food such as potatoes, meat and things. That's really a super idea but there should be a law prohibiting any newspaper from exaggerating the issue. A dehydrated spuds taste more like pine needles than potatoes, and dehydrated sheep tastes like a flock of sheep smells.
—L. CISSON, AEF

Australia

Dear YANK:
Just finished reading the sport page where you wanted the soldiers' opinion on whether baseball should be abolished for the duration or not. Well, I am just like the other boys. The war comes first with me and if ball players are needed, then I say put them in uniform. But I don't think we should give up our best of all sports unless it is really necessary. My idea is that baseball, and what it stands for, is one of the things we are fighting for. So let's keep our good old national pastime, for the present at least.
—Sgt. LOREN R. HENDRYX

Camp Claiborne, La.

Dear YANK:
There's no comparison between Labrador and Greenland. Having been in both of these far-flung "resorts" on G.I. service, I feel qualified to make the following statement: If I had to choose one of the two for further duty, I'd flip a coin. If said coin falls on head or tails, to Labrador I'd go; if the coin stands on edge I'd take Greenland. Get the general idea?
—O/C J. E. MADDOX

Ft. Monmouth, N. J.

Dear YANK:
You're cutting off the best part of your paper when you leave out the cartoon page. The music idea is OK but not good enough to replace the part that is read first and forgotten last.
—Pfc. THURSTON

Camp Ritchie, Md.
■ We'll always try to have a page of cartoons somewhere in the book.

The Barnes Twins

e opposite page brings you a bargain s week, with two girls instead of . They are Lois and Lucille, one of attractions in "Something for the Boys," Broadway musical.

Dear YANK:
Received my second copy of YANK and am not satisfied with it. Take out for two copies and remit the rest of my subscription money.
—Pvt. VERDE C. DOLLARHIDE

Fort Douglas, Utah

Dear YANK:
No doubt the meeting between President Roosevelt and Mr. Churchill deserves every acclaim, but what do you think of this? Today in my ward, there took place a meeting between Jesus Christ, George Washington, Roosevelt, and General Hayes. There were no weighty problems discussed and it was a pleasant meeting throughout. I was an innocent bystander.
—BERYL HARRIS, ANC

Station Hospital, New Orleans, La.

Dear YANK:
Your publication of the poem "Does Victory Depend on Me" by a limited-service MP was read, enjoyed, and clipped by this YANK reader—a "LS-MP." YANK is good—hits the spot with all the fellows in my outfit.
—Pvt. HARVEY R. JOHNSON

Ft. Leonard Wood, Mo.

Dear YANK:
The undersigned, a couple of self-respecting military policemen, have borne with ill-disguised disgust the fact that you are so short-sighted and limited in vision that you are unable to find any material for your appeals to 9-year-old IQs except ridicule and calumny for that noble, self-respecting, God-fearing, brave, clean, efficient, and patient epitomy of what the ideal soldier should be—the Zone of the Interior Military Police. Contrary to popular opinion, we *fight*. And when Joe Dope conducts himself in a manner that would cause a sober engineer to rip him limb from limb, we put a comforting arm around the poor sinner, sober him up at the expense of our own valuable uniform and return him to his unit.
—T/Sgt. DWIGHT H. NETZLY,
S/Sgt. JAMES H. GEORGE JR.

Camp Gordon, Ga.

Dear YANK:
I am on an island somewhere in the Pacific. The place is gorgeous and the natives are very friendly. I haven't seen a white woman in 11 months and by the time you get this letter it will be much more. We get movies once a week and then in different sections of the island. There are hula dances once in a while and also singing. Some of the boys have taught the native girls the American style dancing. Some of the nights the native men play guitars and sing while we dance with the natives. Reading YANK we find out how soldiers are getting along on other islands. I'm surprised nobody from here has written yet.
—Sgt. ROBERT GOETZ

Pacific

Dear YANK:
Maybe YANK can set the guys straight that have the idea the Quartermaster Corps is the WPA of the Army. For almost three years I been givin' my all for Uncle Sam and what do I get? Stuff like, "Yah, goldbrick. A day's work would kill ya." Who do them Infantry guys think they are? Anybody can walk around with a gun on his shoulder and do a right and left face. All the time I am worrying about the shoes they're wearin' out. Some of them guys think I'm the chaplain too. Five minutes after one of 'em has called me a lot of names which ain't nice and explained in detail just how much work I don't do, he is crying on my shoulder. "Good Buddy," he says, "I gotta have shoes as my supply of cardboard is runnin' low. All my socks are worn out and I tore my only good pants. The CO will sure gig me at inspection. Be a pal, will ya?" So as I wipe away my tears I tell 'im, "Okay, send down your supply sergeant and I'll issue to 'im." Always I'm bein' kind to these guys. I figger I saved 'im from gettin' gigged and am just about to mention this fact when he says, "Hello, goldbrick. Haven't they caught up with you yet?"
—S/Sgt. FRANK G. STOKES

APO 983

Dear YANK:
I am writing this because of your article last November on "Convoy Guardian." Not that I have a thing against the Navy but how about letting your readers know about the Army gun crews on transports? We have been stationed on a transport for over nine months in the Southwest Pacific and that article did not make my men feel any too good.
—T/Sgt. PRESTON THOMAS

Overseas

Dear YANK:
You have a very fine paper and we all read it, but if you continue to drift as you are you might as well change the name to "Gripe." Every page is covered with poor Johnnie's story that he has not seen a woman for four months, the beer is warm, the drinks are not so good, or the local women are not like his home-town gal. Every soldier has his troubles but it is damn certain that no one else wants to read about them. Publish your stories and pictures, and let the chronic griper see his chaplain.
—T/Sgt. DON C. JENSEN

Alaska

Dear YANK:
I noticed where one marine was wanting more glory for the Marines and where six soldiers wanted some glory for the Army and Navy. And I also noticed a lot of the boys were wanting to see girls and get furloughs. If you would forget that glory stuff, and the USO girls, and remember that the Army, Navy and Marine Corps are just one big army doing a very big job, you would find fighting and working a lot easier.
—Cpl. W. H. FLETCHER

Alaska

Dear YANK:
I am enclosing a picture of me before I got my "rating." Here you see me as latrine orderly with my helpmate. That building in the background is "it." Inside, you know, is where all the rumors generate. Well, I must stop now because they are yelling for me. One hillbilly sergeant is shouting, "Deen—ah! Deen—ah! P'ivate Fuss Class Deen—ah! Come yeah out of that thar hut 'fo ah beats yo' end off!"
—Pfc. HUGH DEENEY

Camp Blanding, Fla.

The Red Cross does other things besides hospital and recreation work—it's the place to go when you're overseas and hear about sickness or financial worry in the family back home.

By Sgt. JOE McCARTHY
YANK Staff Writer

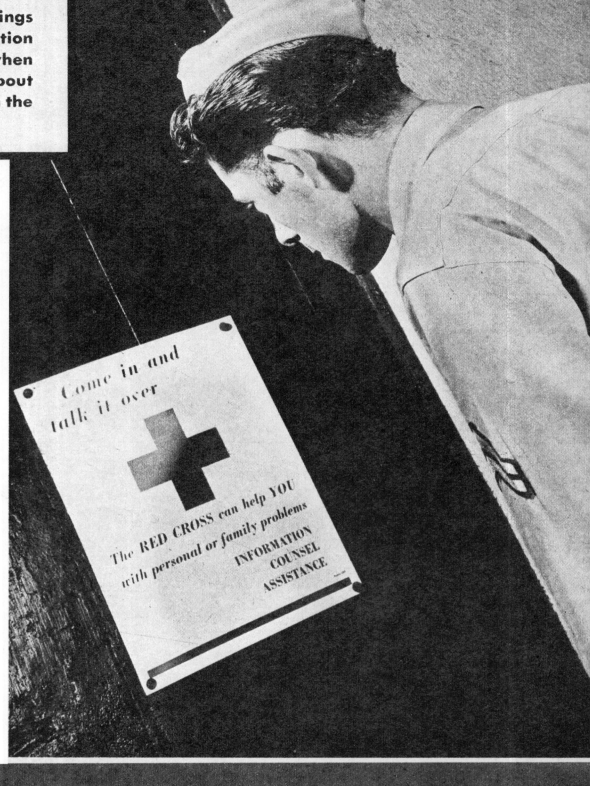

S AN JUAN, PUERTO RICO—Ever since that time back in 1941 when Bubble Butt Nelson and Dinny O'Brien got disgusted with the way things were going in our Field Artillery outfit at Fort Bragg and went over the hill for a week, I have been inclined to be rather skeptical about the American Red Cross and the social service it performs for the enlisted men in our armed forces.

When Nelson and O'Brien returned to the barracks, they told the rest of us how local Red Cross workers had visited them in their homes, describing AWOL as a sucker's racket and urging them to report back to the orderly room as soon as possible. Naturally we were all firmly convinced that the Red Cross had been sending our battery commander hourly reports on the movements of Nelson and O'Brien during their unofficial furlough.

"Why them low bums," declared one private from Scranton, Pa. "Somebody ought to lock them in a garage with the motor running and sophisticate them."

And so when I decided to spend a few days here in Puerto Rico finding out what the Red Cross does to help the soldier or sailor overseas who has personal problems at home, I didn't exactly approach the job in a spirit of friendliness. I was waiting for the Red Cross to show me.

After I was introduced to Moe Frankel of East Orange, N. J., field director of the Red Cross service for the armed forces in this overseas area, I happened to mention the impression that the Nelson-O'Brien episode had left on my mind.

"I don't blame you guys for feeling that way," Frankel said. "But you got the wrong idea. When a fellow goes over the hill, the Army sends the Red Cross a report on him. Then the Red Cross sends a worker to his house who tries to talk him into returning before he gets in too deep. We do that for his own good.

"But the Red Cross never sends any kind of a report back to the Army on the dealings it has with any individual soldier. We never let the military authorities see any records we have of conversations with you men. And that's not just

Trouble at Home?

in AWOL cases, either. It applies to anything we do for you."

That was news to me. So were a lot of the other things I saw the Red Cross doing for soldiers, sailors and marines here in the last few days.

For instance, I didn't know the Red Cross could locate your brother in a combat zone in another part of the world.

A sailor in the Naval Air Station at Puerto Rico heard that his brother in the Army had been shipped overseas. He didn't know when, where or how, and he was getting worried about it.

So he told Frankel the story and gave him the name of his brother's infantry outfit. Frankel sent the information to the Red Cross headquarters in Washington which happened to know where that division was located in North Africa. The Washington headquarters contacted its field man in North Africa who, in turn, located the town

where the sailor's brother was walking guard.

Within a week, the sailor in Puerto Rico received the following radiogram from Oran:

"SAFE AND SOUND FEELING FINE SIGNED TOM."

Getting Rid of a Cheating Wife

I didn't know, either, that the Red Cross could help a soldier overseas get a divorce from his wife back in the U. S. The day I was visiting Frankel's office, a Coast Artillery sergeant came in and showed him a letter from his wife saying that she was six months pregnant.

"Couldn't have been me, sir," the sergeant said. "I been down here in the Caribbean for a year and a half."

I had heard a lot of latrine jokes about this particular type of wartime social problem but, seeing it here before me in real life, it didn't seem so funny.

"What do you want to do about it?" Frankel asked.

"I want to get rid of her," the sergeant said. "I don't want to have no more to do with her."

"Well, if you say the word, maybe we can get you a divorce," Frankel suggested. The sergeant agreed immediately. Frankel collected a few more details about the case and arranged to get the necessary legal aid from the Red Cross chapter in the wife's home town.

After the sergeant went away, I asked Frankel how the Red Cross could arrange such a divorce. I thought it was always necessary for the plaintiff to appear in court and testify in person.

"Oh, no. Several states allow divorces in absentia under these circumstances," Frankel said. "Besides, we've found that the judges nowadays lean over backwards to give every break to a serviceman—especially if he's serving overseas."

Frankel is a typical Red Cross overseas man. He's a Dartmouth graduate, class of 1934, who was just getting established in life with a wife and a new daughter and a good job as head of the social studies department and football coach at Clifford J. Scott High School in East Orange when the war broke out. He gave up all that and a comfortable 3-A classification to volunteer for Red Cross service and, after a short apprenticeship in the States, they shipped him down here to the Caribbean Defense Command.

Now he occupies a small office in the post of San Juan hospital building, an old Spanish barracks, assisted by Richard J. Burtnett, who used to be a safety engineer with a large transportation company in Baltimore, and William Manard, a Notre Dame graduate from Buffalo, N. Y., who takes care of cases at nearby Fort Buchanan. The Red Cross men overseas have been assimilated by the Army and given a rank corresponding to captain so they will be treated as officers in case they are captured by the enemy. But Frankel, Burtnett and Manard are not anxious to wear captain's bars on their uniforms.

"The enlisted men wouldn't feel as free to discuss their personal affairs with us if we were officers," Frankel says. "And, on the other hand, we

couldn't talk as freely to a colonel or a general if we wanted to complain about something. I'm not saying they would pull rank on us—but still it would be possible. We won't put bars on our collars unless they force it on us."

Frankel, Burtnett and Manard have nothing to do with hospital or recreation work. They concentrate entirely on the personal problems of able-bodied men on active service. Burtnett told me they had 136 cases in the past two weeks.

"That is rather slow," he added. "We'll probably have a lot more in the next two weeks."

Frankel showed me a handful of radiograms that he was sending back to the States that afternoon. Here are a few samples, with the names and addresses changed, of course:

Moe Frankel hears a soldier's problem.

"VERIFY SERIOUS ILLNESS MRS MARY RAYMOND 1425 BLANK STREET RICHMOND VA MOTHER OF CORPORAL JOHN RAYMOND"

"CONTACT MRS FRANK COMMINSKY 675 BLANK-VILLE MICHIGAN MOTHER OF LT. MARY COMMINSKY ARMY NURSE VERIFICATION BAPTISM OF NURSE NEEDED FOR MARRIAGE BEING PERFORMED HERE FEB 2, 1943"

"COULD WE HAVE PERIODIC REPORTS FLOOD CONDITIONS IRONTON OHIO FOR PERSONNEL HERE"

"CHECK HOME CONDITION MRS JULIA SMITH 57 NONESUCH STREET JERSEY CITY NEW JERSEY"

Most of the personal problems handled by the Red Cross overseas, and at home, too, are financial ones. Frankel is getting an extra heavy load of financial cases here in Puerto Rico because, for some reason, the allotments for wives and parents made in this area have been slow in paying off. Things are tough in the homes where those allotments are badly needed.

A soldier came to the Red Cross office here a few weeks ago with a typical allotment-trouble story. His wife, living with his father on the farm back in Arkansas, was in her eighth month of pregnancy. She was expecting a hard time with a breech delivery and, because the allotment hadn't gone through, she was absolutely broke. The soldier was broke, too, because he had been redlined and hadn't been paid in a month.

Frankel loaned the soldier $25 on the spot and mailed the money to the wife. He also wrote to the Red Cross secretary in that county of Arkansas, directing her to visit the home and see what help the Red Cross could give. He asked the secretary to see what reductions she could make in the hospital and doctor bills and to arrange for credit until the soldier's allotment arrived.

Report Reveals All is Well

A full report on the case reached Frankel the day I was visiting his office. Things weren't quite as bad as the soldier had suspected. The Red Cross secretary said that breech delivery stuff was a lot of nonsense. The girl was going to give a normal birth and the doctor said she wouldn't have any trouble. The doctor was also perfectly willing to wait until the allotment came before presenting his bill and the Red Cross made a deal with the local hospital to extend credit, too, until that time. The soldier's father said he was able to give the wife plenty of nourishing food and care before and after the confinement and the wife told the Red Cross she was feeling fine. Frankel drove around to the soldier's barracks the next morning and told him the good news, and the soldier relaxed.

Not many soldiers know just what the Red Cross can do to help solve financial problems.

The Red Cross itself can give loans only for pressing emergencies. You can borrow money from the Red Cross for emergency transportation or emergency medical aid for your family back in Ohio. You can also get quick loans for almost any other absolutely necessary expense that must be paid at once. For example, if you broke your glasses and really needed a new pair right away to do your work and couldn't wait six weeks for the Army to get them through channels, the Red Cross would advance you enough money to buy the spectacles.

For other financial headaches, the Red Cross can't give you loans from its own pocket. But it can make arrangements to borrow the dough from the Army Emergency Relief fund or the local relief agencies in your home town. Here's a case that shows how the Red Cross works along that line:

A soldier, broke and waiting for his allotment to be approved, has a penniless wife at home and a mother-in-law who is dependent on him. The mother-in-law has a heart condition, needs $5 a week for a vegetable-and-milk diet and $3 a week

for medicine. They owe the doctor $37 because, in addition to the mother-in-law's heart trouble, the wife of the soldier is pregnant. (The wives of the soldiers who come to the Red Cross for financial or legal help are almost always pregnant, as you've probably noticed by now.) They also owe the grocer $15, the landlord $30, the milkman $12 and the druggist $17. How does the Red Cross handle that one?

Well, the mother-in-law's case is turned over to a local hospital which takes care of her more or less free at its clinic. The Red Cross lends the soldier money to pay the doctor, druggist and milk man because those bills are considered emergency medical expenses. The landlord and the grocer fall into a slightly different category. The Red Cross gets the Army Emergency Relief to pay their bills, with the understanding that the soldier will return the money when his allotment comes around.

Handling Army's Headaches

When Frankel isn't wrapped up with these financial problems, he is launching investigations at the request of the military authorities on behalf of soldiers and sailors who feel that they are entitled to receive dependency or medical discharges. The Red Cross, through its agencies back home in the States, also makes all the arrangements with relatives of servicemen who die or get killed in action overseas. When a soldier's name comes out on the casualty list, the Red Cross sends a representative to his home to help his family fill out the papers for burial and sees that they collect the insurance.

When I got up to leave Frankel's office, I felt somewhat like a heel for denouncing the Red Cross people as a pack of stool pigeons that time in 1941 when Nelson and O'Brien went over the hill. It seemed as though they handled the Army's personal headaches overseas with much more efficiency than the average lawyer or psychiatrist at home.

"You've got a depressing job," I said. "How do you stay so cheerful?"

Frankel smiled and said that, although his daily routine was quite similar to that of Mr. Anthony on the Good Will Court, he usually found something funny in the batch of mail and radiograms on his desk every morning. The other day, for instance, a soldier reported that his father had packed up and left home. The soldier was afraid his father was losing his mind so Frankel had the local Red Cross secretary check on the case.

"Instead of checking on the father, we should have checked on the Red Cross secretary," Frankel said, handing me her report.

"There is nothing wrong with this man's sanity," it said. "He is a spiritualist and he is required to leave home frequently because the spirits are always calling him to other parts of the country."

POST XCHANGE

This Post Exchange, like YANK itself, is wide open to you. Send your cartoons and stories to: The Post Exchange, YANK, The Army Weekly, U.S.A.

If your contribution misses the mark for any reason, you will receive YANK's special de luxe rejection slip that will inspire a more creative mood.

"I am glad you made pfc. Now we can drink better stuff."

THE WIVES

Bless the wives,
They fill the hives
With little bees and honey.
They ease life's shocks,
They mend our socks—
But don't they spend the money!

When we are sick,
They heal us quick—
That is, if they should love us.
If not, we die;
And yet they cry,
And raise tombstones above us!

—Pvt. HAYDEN E. WILLIAMS
Army War College, Washington, D. C.

LETTER

*There's nothing better
Than a letter
Unless it's some remittance
To help along the monthly pittance.*

—Cpl. JACK B. HUGHES
Fort Houston, Tex.

How to Get a Week-End Pass

WALK boldly up to the office of the first sergeant. Catch him off guard, especially when he is busy figuring out pay rolls, rations, KP, and guard duty rosters.

"Hey, bud," you drawl, "how about a week-end pass?"

This method comes as such a shock to the sergeant that he will stammer, "Week-end pass? Sure. How about a three-day? Or a five-day?"

Your pass is recommended and you must now approach the company commander.

Walk boldly to his office, repeating to yourself, "He is only human, shucks, he is only human."

You knock on the door. It is a weak, ineffectual knock. Consequently you get no answer. The lieutenant thought it was his secretary cracking her gum. Knock a little harder. A muffled voice reaches you. You don't understand what it says, so you hesitate. Then you think maybe you had better call the whole thing off. Then suddenly the door opens, and standing in front of you is the lieutenant.

There is a lump in your throat. Your right knee begins to quiver, and your scalp begins to prickle. You fling a salute that almost tears your nose off.

"Sir, the lieutenant has the permission of—"

[Drawing by Walt Owen, from Camp Grant (Ill.) Sentinel.]

No, you fool, that wasn't right. Quick, quick, the lieutenant is waiting. He's scowling.

Only he isn't scowling at you. His thoughts are far away.

Finally you blurt, "Sir, the sergeant says to see you, if I can get a week-end pass, sir."

Your heart stops for a minute. Your blood pressure drops to zero minus. You wait.

At last the lieutenant looks at you. "A week-end pass? Sure. Come on in and I'll fix it up."

See, that wasn't hard, was it?

—Sgt. F. A. PETERSON
Oklahoma City Air Depot, Okla.

A Dogface Answers a Collection Agency

Pvt. Oris Turner, 39168771,
APO 000, c/o Postmaster,
San Francisco, Calif.
Dear sir:

Re: [Creditor's name]—$14.80

YOU have had an opportunity to settle this claim without trouble or expense, but it seems you will not settle until forced to do so. You failed even to reply to our recent letter.

Therefore, unless immediate arrangements are made for settlement, we will have no alternative but to instruct our attorneys to file a complaint against you and have you summoned to appear at the time of trial. An officer of the court will also be empowered to seize your goods, attach your earnings, automobile, bank account, or any other funds or property that may belong to you or be due you.

You would be wise to make settlement, etc., etc.

Yours,
[NAME OF COLLECTION AGENCY.]

New Guinea,
Jan. 26, 1943
Dear sirs:

YOUR letter of 11/19/'42 was duly rec'd today and after reading the contents therein I am pleased to note that I will be summoned to appear in court to make payment due you of $14.30 plus interest and costs.

Gentlemen, the opportunities your letter presents are beyond my wildest dreams.

I believe by law the court is required to send a process server to deliver the summons in person. In that case I will inform you of certain essentials he will require for jungle travel.

The first item advisable is a self-inflating life raft, as ships even in convoys are sometimes sunk. The raft will also be useful later in crossing rivers and swamps in New Guinea. He should also bring the following items: Mosquito bars, head net, pith helmet, quinine, salt tablets, vitamin pills, mosquito and sunburn lotions, medical supplies for tropical infections, poisonous snakes, spiders, steel helmet, gas mask, waterproof tent, heavy calibre rifle for shooting Japs, crocodiles and other game, machete, chlorine capsules, flashlight, and soap.

In choosing this process server make sure that he is not an alcoholic, as there isn't a drink to be found on the whole island. Furthermore, he must not be allergic to mosquitoes, heat rash, malaria, dengue fever, snakes, spiders, lizards, flies, crocodiles, and tall grass with a few head hunters in it. These are trivial matters and he may never come in contact with any of them, especially if his convoy is attacked by the enemy's battle fleet.

I am telling you all this as I am much concerned over his safe arrival. If he reaches this location our meeting will be much more impressive than Stanley and Livingstone's. I will see that the best possible care is taken of him on arrival. As soon as he has recovered from his jungle trip we will be on our way back to civilization and the law court. I trust he is already on his way, and I am packing my barracks bags to avoid any waste of time.

Here's hoping that this letter finds you in the best of health.

Respectfully yours,
—Pvt. ORIS TURNER

"Chaplain's idea, I guess—"

PUZZLE SOLUTIONS

DOUBLE-PUZZLE
A plus CORVETTE plus WAGON minus WAVE minus CAT minus T equals *OREGON*

GOLF-LOG
TANK. 1. BANK. 2. BANE. 3. BONE. 4. CONE. 5. COME. 6. COMB. 7. *BOMB.*

REBUS CITIES
1. INDIANAPOLIS. 2. WASHINGTON. 3. COLUMBUS. 4. BALTIMORE. 5. HOUSTON. 6. HARTFORD. 7. MILWAUKEE. 8. NEWARK.

Tee-Total Winners
Eleven G.I.s came through with the winning solution to the Tee-Total puzzle in YANK of Feb. 10. Their total was 408 and all got it the same way, as shown at left. The winners: Pfc. John P. Grosso, Fort Sam Houston, Tex.; Pfc. S. Watchel, Camp Shelley, Miss.; Cpl. C. P. McLaughlin, Fort Niagara, N. Y.; Pvt. Jack Fisher, Camp Blanding, Pa.; Sgt. Earl A. Bills, Camp Grant, Ill.; Cpl. D. C. Curtin, Fort Hancock, N. J.; Cpl. Clem S. Brandad, Fort Monroe, Va.; Pvt. Paul Cone, Philadelphia (Pa.) Recruiting Office; Cpl. P. Kenner, 113th Infantry, Eatontown, N. J.; Pvt. George R. Pester, Peterson Field, Colo.; Cpl. W. S. Sprouse, Army Air Base, New Orleans, La.

Each of these men receives a YANK Puzzle Kit. Watch for future Tee-Total winners. Send your solutions to Puzzle Editor, YANK, 205 East 42nd Street, New York City.

CHECKERBOARD STRATEGY
White moves 26 to 23. Black king must jump 19 to 26.
White king moves 5 to 9. Black must jump 12 to 19.
White king moves 9 to 6. Black must jump 3 to 12.
Now the White king hops on a merry-go-round for a free ride. He jumps from 6 to 15 to 24 to 31 to 22 to 13, removing 5 Black men in one shot!
Black's position is now hopeless. Two more moves are left him, and then he is completely cornered. WHITE WINS!

North Africa
"She won't talk to him until he thinks up a secret."

SPORTS:

BARNEY ROSS RETURNS FROM GUADALCANAL STILL ON HIS FEET. THAT'S THE WAY HE LEFT THE RING, TOO

By Sgt. DAN POLIER

CPL. BARNEY ROSS came home from the wars the other day. He hobbled down the gangplank of a hospital ship at San Diego leaning heavily on a cane. It was a native-made affair studded with sure enough Japanese buck teeth. The cane was a grim reminder of the harrowing night at Guadalcanal when he flattened 22 Japs. As everybody knows it was one of the few times that Barney was evenly matched.

As he walked down the gangplank, Ross smiled and waved his hand, but his eyes were searching for the ground. When he reached the end of the gangplank he stopped in his tracks, kneeled as if to pray, and kissed the ground. It was good to be home.

"This I vowed to do if ever I saw American soil again—sometimes out there we're not so sure we shall."

Bracing himself with his cane, Barney watched as his buddies were carried from the big hospital ship. They, too, were a grim reminder of the night he stood guard over his wounded comrades in the bloody jungles of the 'Canal.

"The night I spent in that shell hole with five wounded marines and two soldiers was by all odds the toughest round I've ever slugged through," Ross said. "I thought the bell would never sound."

In his time, Barney has slugged through a lot of rounds and slugged a lot of fighters. He won three different boxing titles. But that round he won on the 'Canal is something you just can't measure in titles or service medals. It's different when you are slugging for your life.

Barney continued his story:

"We'd been expecting Army units momentarily when we were cut off by the Japs. We dived for a pair of shell holes about 10 feet apart. I was the only one unhurt.

"It was about 4 P. M., and in the shell hole with me was an Indian named Pvt. Monak. My best buddy, Pvt. R. C. Atkins of Rome, Ga., was in the other hole with two other marines. That night two soldiers wriggled into my shell hole."

The Japs poured mortar and machine-gun fire into the two shell holes until 7 the next morning. Three of the wounded marines were hit again during the terrible night. It was left to Ross to hold the Japs at bay. He crawled around gathering grenades and ammunition. The others were too badly injured to even help load the rifles.

"In all, I threw 21 hand grenades, fired 100 rounds of M1 rifle ammunition and at least 80 rounds from my Springfield," Ross said.

"They never did get a telling punch in on our little group.

"Sometime during the night I got a leg and arm full of shrapnel," Barney related. "But, by golly, I can't tell you when it was—I was just too busy to notice. I had malaria at the time, too.

"The next morning Freeman Atkins suggested that we crawl from our shell hole," Ross continued. "I lifted him up on my shoulder when, looking up, I beheld what looked like angels from heaven coming toward us. It was Capt. LeBlanc, Lt. Murdock and enough of the others to make us realize the round was over."

The round was over all right and Barney had won. The captain counted 22 dead Japs and 30 bullet creases in Barney's helmet.

Barney has been recommended for the Navy Cross or the Army Distinguished Service Cross. He has already been named as boxing's "man of the year." We would like to think of him as just a damn good marine.

Barney walks the gangplank home.

Ross never kissed the canvas as a fighter. This was different. It was good to be home.

Orientation

SGT. JACKIE WILSON (left) took a terrific shellacking from Ray Robinson in the fourth round of their Madison Square Garden fight in New York. Referee Frank Fullam, fearing that the sergeant might not be able to continue, went to his corner after the fourth round and asked:

"Do you know where you are, sergeant?"

"Yes," answered Wilson, "I'm in Madison Square Garden and I'm getting a helluva licking."

Basketball Leaders Sized Up for Tourney

NEW YORK—Any way you look at it, the Metropolitan Basketball Committee is going to make a lot of people mad. Between now and next week they must select eight teams from an imposing list of 38 sectional leaders to compete in the National Intercollegiate Invitation Tournament in Madison Square Garden.

A list of teams considered by the committee:

New York District—St. John's, Fordham, N. Y. U., Manhattan and L. I. U.

New England — Dartmouth and Rhode Island State.

Eastern—Niagara, St. Joseph's, Villanova, Pennsylvania, Seton Hall, Princeton, Washington and Jefferson and West Virginia.

South—Duke, George Washington, Kentucky, Western Kentucky, Georgetown, Murray State and Appalachian.

Mid-West—Notre Dame, Indiana, Illinois, Toledo, De Paul and Hamline.

Missouri Valley—Creighton and Kansas.

Southwest — Arizona, Texas and Texas Christian.

Rocky Mountain—Wyoming.

Pacific Coast—Southern California, Washington, Washington State and Pepperdine.

"I HOPE YOU'RE NOT COMING INSIDE WITH A MUG FULL OF CHAWIN' TOBACCO LIKE YESTERDAY."

YANK

"PVT. WILENSKY, BRING THAT PONTON BACK HERE AT ONCE."

"FADE ME, JOE. I'M SHOOTING THE WORKS."

YANK

THE ARMY WEEKLY

5¢ **JUNE 25 1943** VOL. 2, NO. 1

By the men .. for the men in the service

8 BONUS PAGES

Extra Cartoons • Pin-Ups
Short Story

K RATION

SGT. GEORGE BAKER

FIRST ANNIVERSARY ISSUE

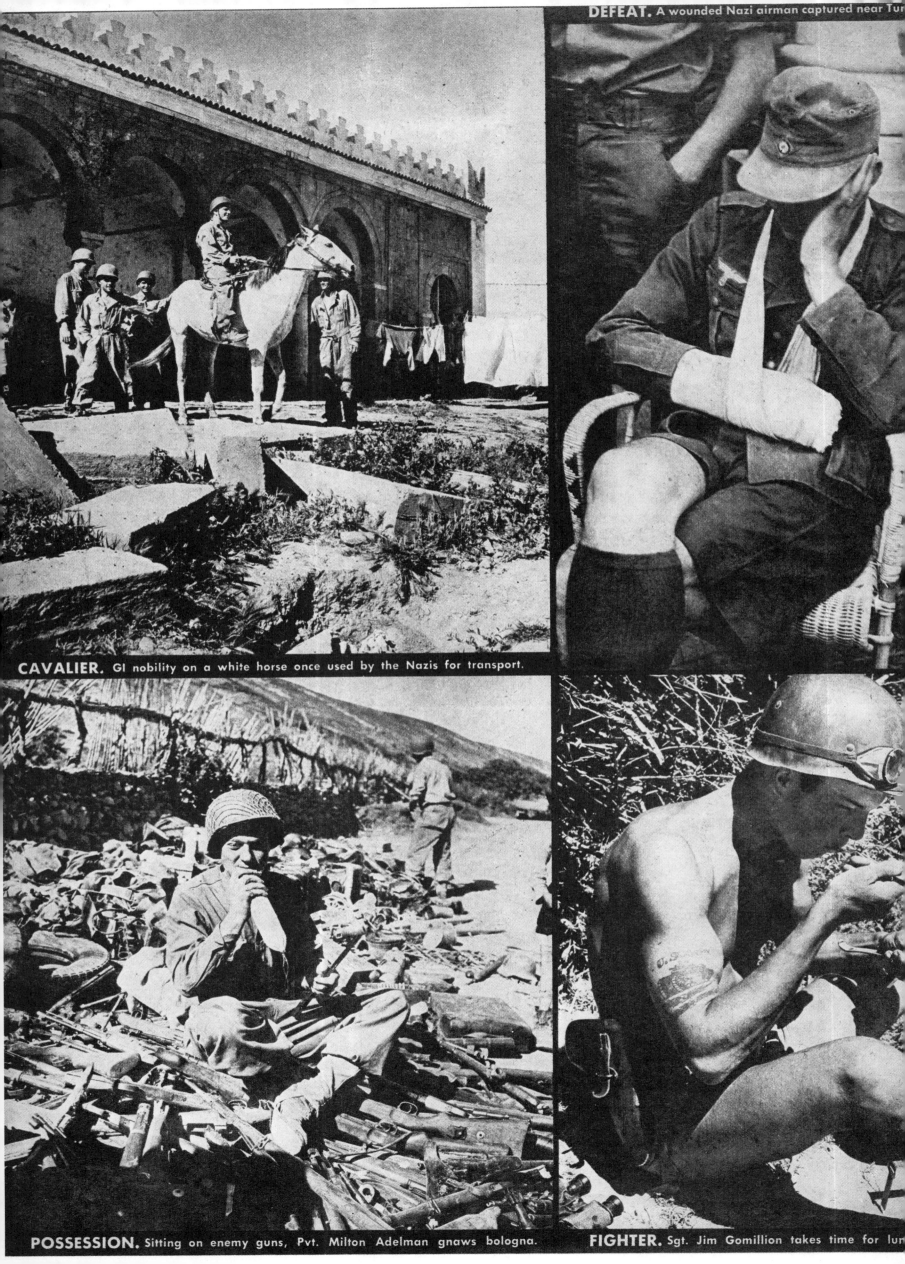

DEFEAT. A wounded Nazi airman captured near Tun

CAVALIER. GI nobility on a white horse once used by the Nazis for transport.

POSSESSION. Sitting on enemy guns, Pvt. Milton Adelman gnaws bologna.

FIGHTER. Sgt. Jim Gomillion takes time for lun

VICTORY. With a Yank in the center carrying the flag of France, British, French and American fighters walk through the streets of Tunis.

Mop-up in Tunisia

YANK'S SGT. GEORGE AARONS,
ONE OF THE FIRST AMERICAN SOLDIERS TO ENTER TUNIS,
MADE THESE PICTURES

TOPPED. Two GIs look over a Mark VI tank, knocked out by Allied shell fire. Sleeve, knocked off cannon's base, rests against muzzle brake.

Command in B-24 over Attu took radio directions from ground during attack, then sent P-38 fighters to raise hell with Jap concentrations.

By Sgt. GEORG N. MEYERS
YANK Staff Correspondent

AMCHITKA, RAT GROUP, ALEUTIAN ISLANDS [Passed by Navy Censor]—Today the feeling among the men was different.

The setting was the same as it had been for a year—a clammy dawn on this sliver of an island that parts the Bering Sea and the North Pacific. The plane was the same—a Liberator, ugly as a blimp but a great worker. The crew was the same—it had flown so often together it was a family.

The men walked out to the ship without any fuss whatever. But this time there was an extra eagerness in their stride. This was the day they had waited for. For a blasted year they had flown in the heavy cold of the Fairbanks country and had dropped supplies to a party testing arctic equipment on Mount McKinley. They had sweated out many hours of ceiling zero along the Aleutian Chain, where the fog gets so tight you'd swear there was no place to come in. Once they had crash-landed on a wild island and had camped all night under the plane's wing before a rescue party found them.

But it was just reconnaissance, so much a routine that they called it "the milk run."

Today it was the milk run no longer. Today this ship and this crew were coordinating air support for ground troops.

They had often talked about this day, longingly as men will when discussing the unattainable. Lately they had begun to hope, for Infantry, En-

gineers and Artillery had been digging in and stretching out in the vast theater of the Arctic islands. But the Ground Forces had been digging in for two years somewhere in Alaska; this might be more of the same.

Of course there had been bombing runs against Kiska and Attu but no ground action. The Air Forces had been at it alone. And Cpl. Alan C. Meador of Nacogdoches, Tex., tail gunner on the *Milk Wagon*, had often complained, "Man, we been doin' all the fightin' up here."

Today, as they took off, Cpl. Meador looked down into the murky haze and fog and said, "It sure is fun to think somebody else is sluggin' it out down there."

To men who had waited so long this was a great day, comparable to the day back home when the circus had actually fulfilled the promise of its big red billboards. And that's why there was an added zip to the *Milk Wagon*. Every man of its crew knew that this morning Ground Forces had been landed on Attu, had cut behind the Japs and were driving toward the beaches.

The joy of Cpl. Meador ran from tail to nose. Up ahead of Meador and YANK's correspondent were Cpl. Charles R. Beckner of Canton, Ohio, photographer; Sgt. Charles E. Balas of Janesville, Wis., left waist gunner; Cpl. Charles Cuneo of Cambridge, Mass., radio technician and right waist gunner; Hugh Goulding of Chicago, engineer; Sgt. Rodgers Oliver of Little Rock, Ark., radio operator; Sgt. James W. Chamberlin of Cleveland, Ohio, top turret gunner and assistant engineer; 1st Lt. James C. Beardsley of Tecum-

This equipment was left behind by the Japs in the Massacre Bay area of Attu, perhaps intended to be used in building a seaplane base.

seh, Mich., navigator; 1st Lt. Robert M. Campion of Dallas, Tex., bombardier; 1st Lt. Martin B. Menger of Gulfport, Miss., co-pilot, and the man at the controls, Capt. John Andrews of Boston, Mass, who, according to his crew, was "the best damned pilot in Alaska or they wouldn't trust him with this job."

And on this trip, inaugurating coordination of Air Force and Ground Force action, there was high rank aboard, Col. John V. Hart, command pilot, chief of staff of the 11th Air Force and CO of the 11th Advance Echelon. Yes, today the *Milk Wagon* had come into its own.

The Liberator lined out for Attu and the waist gunners shifted into heavy clothing and readied their Brownings. Gun-studded Kiska, seat of the main Jap strength in the Aleutians, was directly in their path, and Attu was only 20 minutes away.

Sgt. Balas grinned as he swung his gun out through the open waist panel and went through the motions of machine gunning.

How Planes Support Infantry

Yanks at Home Abroad

Yanks who occupied Attu look over equipment and quarters used by a Jap medical unit. The Japs dug holes and interlacing tunnels through the hill

"I've been waiting a long time for this," he shouted over the thunder of the Liberator's four engines. "Maybe we'll get a chance for some strafing this time."

But he wasn't too hopeful. This was not a bombing mission. Today the *Milk Wagon* was a command plane. And anyway, Sgt. Balas knew the Aleutian weather. If the ceiling proved as low as usual it would conceal the precipitous peaks of Attu and no heavy bomber could risk the narrow valleys under low overcast.

Attu came in sight, and sure enough, the ceiling was too low. A mattress fog blanked out the ridges where the fighting lines were and folded down the cliffs to within 1,000 feet of the beach. Along the shore American tents and supplies were evidences that the Yanks had landed. Outside the shoal water Navy vessels circled in tight patrol, locking out any Jap reinforcements that might try to get in and locking in any Japs who might try to run out. Within the harbors small craft boldly did their work, and Navy PBYs and Kingfishers floated at anchor. The push was on.

The *Milk Wagon's* radio opened up and the crew settled down to enjoy the novel experience of witnessing an invasion. The radio chattered the language of air support for ground troops. All the codes emphasized words containing the letter "l" which the Japs can't pronounce.

Somewhere ashore back in the fog an Air Force liaison officer was moving up with the foot soldiers and artillery, precisely defining for Col. Hart in the *Milk Wagon* the limits of the American positions. He called happily, "Everything south and east of the lines I've given you is open season. There are plenty of the bastards in there, so have a good time."

Col. Hart had a good time. He summoned his heavy and medium bombers. The ceiling held down, though, and they couldn't go in. They patrolled offshore, watching for Jap ships, and Col. Hart sent in the nimble Lightnings. They approached the *Milk Wagon*, swift and graceful, circled for orders, and plunged boldly into the narrow valleys.

And Sgt. Balas, disappointedly fingering his own gun, watched them sweep down the treacherous slopes, buzzing low over the dug-in Japs, tossing light bombs from their wings and throwing quick bursts from their guns.

So close was the terrain that the Lightnings had time only for a quick one before whipping up and banking sharply to avoid crashing into the valley walls. Soon wisps of smoke appeared to Sgt. Balas from the valley, and after a while the tundra grass smoked heavily in a dozen places. Close to shore a rich red fire sent up sooty smoke.

The wave of Lightnings finished its work and raced home. Another wave took over the job. The Liberators and Mitchells meanwhile cruised offshore, cursing the weather. For seven hours they cruised with nothing to do.

And then, at the *Milk Wagon's* signal, they headed for home, their only consolation being the brief moment when they unloaded their bombs on Kiska en route back to their base.

"Anyway," Sgt. Balas concluded, "it's good to see those Ground Forces down there. Maybe we'll have a better break in the weather tomorrow."

New Guinea Alibi

NEW GUINEA—A group of natives were being brought up a river from New Guinea's north shore in small boats to serve as litter and supply bearers. Suddenly a few P-38s roared low overhead. Immediately the natives dived overside and swam ashore.

The American captain in charge of the detail rounded them all up, got hold of the No. 1 boy and explained that the planes were friendly. He ordered the natives not to dive again without his permission.

In a moment, over came more Yank planes. The frightened natives swam ashore a second time, with the No. 1 boy last in line.

Again the captain rounded them up and, seizing No. 1 by his fuzzy-wuzzy head, shouted: "Didn't I tell you not to leave us without orders?"

"Yes," the native replied, "but other boys not know jungle—might get lost. Me follow, show 'em how get back."

—YANK Staff Correspondent

LATEST GI GAGS FROM ALL OVER THE GLOBE

Algiers

Troop-carrier pilots are talking about the commander of a British native company who asked for volunteers. "All who wish to jump from 500 feet report at headquarters in one hour," he said.

The entire company reported, but their spokesman made a request. "We will be glad to jump, sir," he said, "if you make it 300 feet."

The astonished commander looked at him and said, "But, good Lord, man, don't you know a parachute jump from 300 feet would be suicide?"

This time it was the spokesman who was astonished.

"What?" he demanded. "Do you mean to say we are going to get parachutes?"

New Guinea

A unit of Yanks was moving into its first bivouac area on the north side of the Owen Stanley Mountains, a desolate sector near the roving Japanese patrols.

The unit was understandably nervous when it unslung packs and began to dig slit trenches. Suddenly a whistle blew and a noncom shouted, "Front and center, everybody. On the double."

This was it, the Yanks figured, grabbing their rifles and running toward the assembly point. They waited breathlessly for the next order.

"Okay, everybody," the noncom said. "Line up and police the area."

Cairo

The gurkha is a British soldier from India. He operates noiselessly by dark with a curved, razor-sharp knife. German sentries in the African desert didn't like being alone when gurkhas were on the loose.

The best gurkha story, and it's an old one in a new uniform, concerns the gurkha who slipped up behind a careless Jerry, whipped out his knife and snicked.

As the gurkha came around in front of him, the Jerry tightened his grip on his rifle and said, "I've got you now, you schweinhund."

"Oh, have you?" replied the gurkha, politely. "Just wait till you try to turn your head."

Scotland

Pvt. Richard Broome of Brooklyn was enjoying the hospitality of Bob Halliday, genial master of the Red Lion Hotel—not in the hotel from which the Scot had made a tidy sum in his time, but in his stone home north of the village. With nine rooms and two baths, it's the showplace of the section and Halliday was making a ritual of "showing Broome aboot."

They came at last to a robin's-egg-blue tiled bathroom where, attached in gleaming splendor to the tub, was a shower bath. Broome screeched with excitement. Without so much as a by-your-leave he soon had his clothes off and was enjoying his first shower in months.

Halliday roared with laughter and pleasure. "Sa they's wha th' contraption's for," he said. "Aye nae knew before; it just came wi' the tub."

If AAF Guys Fought as They Talk, We'd Lose the War Tomorrow

ENGLAND—Newspapermen trying to get a story out of our airmen who carry daily destruction to Europe are having their troubles. The AAF is composed of fighters, not talkers.

Take for example the following conversation between an inquiring reporter and S/Sgt. Joseph H. Herbert, former grocer's boy from New Rochelle, N. Y.:

Q. *Understand you just returned from a bombing raid over Germany?*
A. Sure as hell did.
Q. *What was it like?*
A. It was fun.
Q. *Didn't it worry you when the flak started coming?*
A. You only see it out of the corner of your eye.
Q. *I'll bet you felt good being assigned to bomb Germany.*
A. I wasn't assigned; I volunteered.
Q. *Well come now, tell me how it felt to be up there over Germany?*
A. I just told you it was fun.
Q. *Did you get anything?*
A. An ME-109.
Q. *Did it give you a good feeling?*
A. A hell of a good feeling.
Q. *How did it happen, exactly?*
A. He came toward me so I let him have it.
Q. *What did it look like?*
A. It looked like a plane being shot down.
Q. *Anybody else get any planes?*
A. Yes. Woody (S/Sgt. Woodrow Smith of Jerome, Idaho) got one and Ed (Sgt. Edward J. Bradford of Washington, D. C.) got one. They did a swell job.
Q. *Are you anxious to get back?*
A. Sure.

—Sgt. WALT PETERS
YANK Staff Correspondent

When out of uniform, this native medicine man sitting on a jeep works on American airfields in Central Africa. Having planes on the brain, he made a headdress in imitation of a B-24.

In Next Week's YANK . . .

NEW FIGHTER-PLANE TRICKS

The Army's Flying Training Command now uses combat-experienced professors from overseas to teach the lessons they have learned the hard way against the enemy. YANK has prepared two articles about those lessons. The first one, next week, explains new fighter technique.

YANK, The Army Weekly, publication issued weekly by Headquarters Branch, Special Service, ASF, War Department, 205 East 42d Street, New York 17, N. Y. Reproduction rights restricted as indicated in the masthead on the editorial page. Entered as second class matter July 6, 1942, at the Post Office at New York, N. Y., under the Act of March 3, 1879. Subscription price $3.00 yearly. Printed in the U. S. A.

Here is our secret bottle weapon which is used to float troops in battle equipment to Germany by the Gulf Stream, if it happens to be going that way.

Secret Weapons

FOR THE INVASION OF GERMANY

By Sgt. RALPH STEIN

More details gladly furnished to any accredited Nazi spy if he encloses a self-addressed stamped envelope

OLD TOWN INVASION BARGE, SUBMERSIBLE, MARK VII, SECTION 8 (WITH PARASOL AND BANJO)

O UR simple-hearted Nazi coast sentry thinks that he sees only romantic couples, spending Sunday afternoon in canoes. But beneath the surface our invading troops are lurking, well supplied with Spam for the fight that looms ahead and studying their comic books as the Zero Hour draws near. *Technical Data:* Notice the young lady, or frail, in the stern of the canoe. She steers the barge with that innocent hand which she trails so languidly in the water and conceals with her distracting legs, or hockeys, the trap door in the floor of the canoe which serves the attacking force as an exit from the barge.

WENCH MORTAR

These weapons create confusion by dropping tasty babes or reasonably exact facsimiles upon installations. Service of the Piece: Tube should be swabbed often with perfume, preferably Chanel No. 5.

NACKWURST AND SAUERKRAUT PROJECTOR, OLFACTORY

[PROJE]CTOR at left carries an engine-driven fan [w]hich forces the odor of knackwurst and [saue]rkraut, cooking on gas range, through the [proje]ctor tube. Drool sergeant at projector [cont]rols can elevate or depress tube through [an a]rc of 70 degrees. Drool meter under Nazi's [nose] registers excitation of salivary gland. If [hi]m doesn't drool enough, put some more [krau]t in the pot. *Method of use:* The enemy [sme]lls the smell of the knackwurst and kraut [and] he is yours. Then you don't let him eat it.

TRACTION REDUCER, BOOT M13, or PRATT-FALL INDUCER

THIS two-man motorized dignity destroyer features a pair of automatic hands which pick bananas very rapidly, dropping the peels in the path of advancing enemy infantry. Rest of the banana goes into GI pudding which is used as a devastating booby trap. Automatic hands can also be used to snap fingers under the noses of enemy officers and make other insulting gestures.

PARACOOK, PTOMAINE

This cruel weapon of invasion is used only under extreme provocation. Cooks and accomplices armed with copies of the Army Cook's Field Manual are dropped behind the enemy's line to cook for him. No special training necessary. Supplies of dried eggs and creamed beef on toast may also be dropped but only as a desperate last resort.

INCENDIARY, PEDAL M1922 or HOT FOOT

THIS is a light, mobile, single-seat infantry cooperation weapon, which can also be used to illuminate GI crap games at night when the invasion is over. *Method of operation:* The bewildered Nazi is chased until exhaustion. Then the embracing ring, or hugger, clamps over his head, pinning his arms to his side while the automatic hand appears with a lighted match, applying a hot foot in the customary manner. When a storm trooper or *oberfeldwebel* is bagged, the weapon applies the blowtorch with satisfactory results. How do the matches get stuck in the boots of the Nazis? They are placed there weeks before the invasion by fifth-columnists disguised as poor but honest shoe-shine boys.

Twelve Months Under Fire

The Army Has Tested New Weapons, Proved Old Tactics, Eaten Plenty of Spam and Found Places Where Scotch Costs $400 a Quart

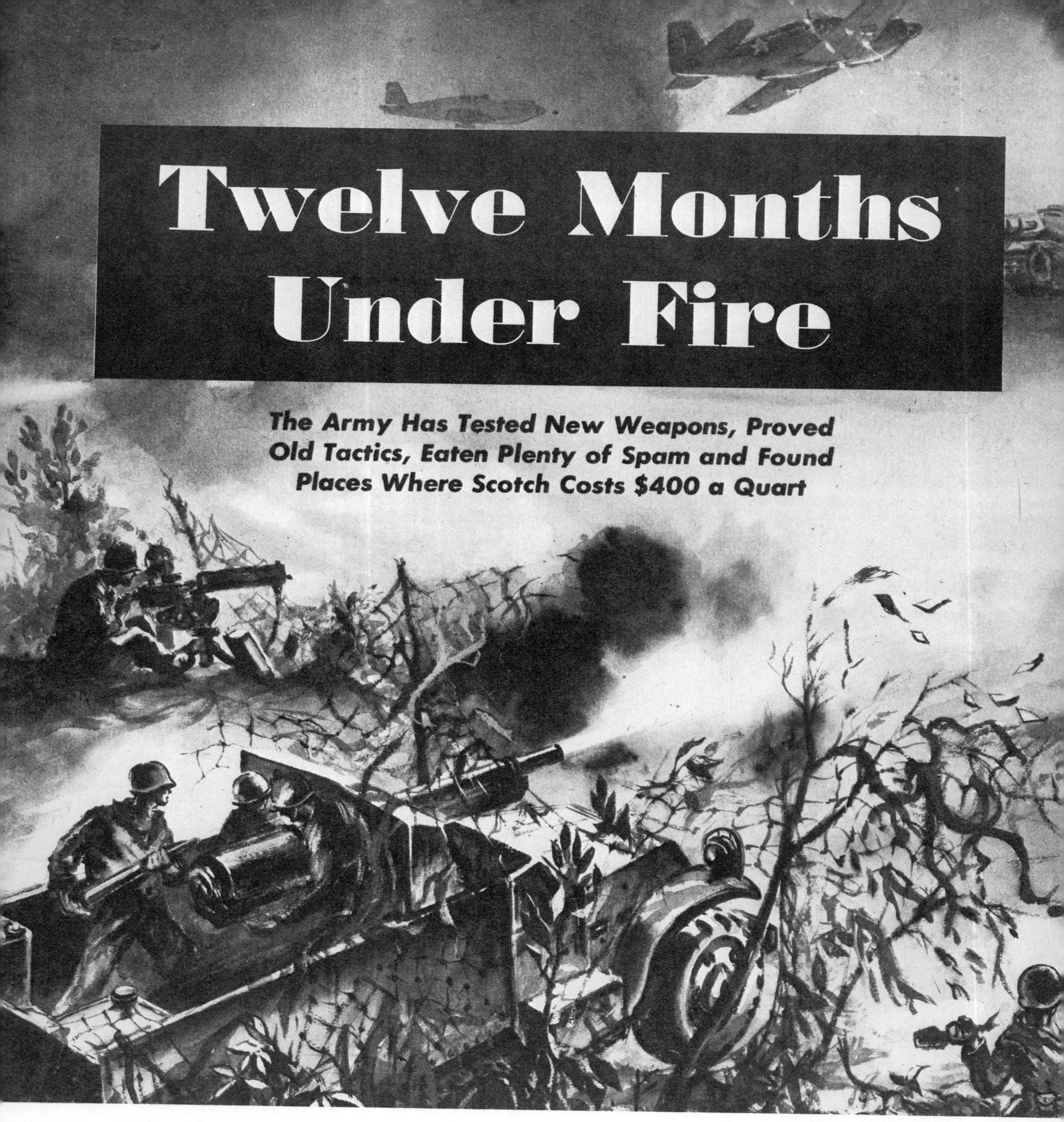

WHEN YANK's first issue was circulated, June 18, 1942, America was doing its fighting exclusively on the sea and in the sky. But in the year that has passed since YANK came into existence, Guadalcanal has been captured, New Guinea cleaned out, Australia freed from the threat of invasion, Africa freed from Axis domination, Pearl Harbor rebuilt and the submarine menace lessened in the Atlantic, and now a drive is under way to push the Japs out of the Aleutians. Soon will come the invasion of Europe.

During that year of war, American soldiers have had a good look at themselves as fighting men. They have had a chance to put the theories they learned during basic training into practice under fire. They have been able to test their weapons against the enemy.

On these pages, YANK has rounded up from reports of its correspondents on every front the general reactions and conclusions of U. S. soldiers concerning their Army's progress in the last 12 months. These pages hold the mirror up to ourselves.

A lot of lessons have been learned and new techniques and equipment developed that we still can't talk about. But here, in brief, is what can be told at this time.

Fighting the Japs

OUR war against Japan was fought chiefly during the last year in the jungles of the Solomon Islands and New Guinea. To our men, jungle warfare was new and strange. They soon discovered that throwing a hand grenade in a dense forest was a hell of a lot different from grenade practice on a parade ground. The men also had to learn the technique of working on their own in small scattered patrols where the natural inclination to bunch up in twos or threes was a fatal error. Each soldier had to do his own thinking, and he had to have enough patience to lie motionless for hours.

Many a soldier in Guadalcanal and New Guinea gladly would have paid $100 for a pair of silent rubber-soled sneakers like those the Japs wore. They even taped their dog tags to prevent them from jingling on patrol missions.

Lessons we learned about jungle fighting:

Our weapons have been away ahead of the opposition in combat except that we had nothing to equal the Jap "knee" mortar, a handy 50-mm portable one- or two-man piece with which the enemy did a lot of damage. Our men like the Tommy gun best for individual shooting and respect the M1.

PVT. JACK COGGINS

The men discovered at Guadalcanal that jungle warfare gave them little opportunity to use the rifle sling. Fast fire in volume was often required. The target usually was obscured, and volume battle fire was most useful. Deluges of rain ruled out compliance with the "soap and water for three days" cleaning rule. Men cleaned bore and chamber of their guns with socks, shirts, undershirts, even tore legs from trousers to get rags.

Cover and Concealment. Through experience our men learned not to neglect the basics of camouflage. They wore green clothes, blacked faces for night work, in the absence of chemicals allowed their beards to grow and learned by hard work to walk quietly, although Jap prisoners said they didn't learn that lesson well enough. They learned that foxholes and slit trenches must be dug well and concealed equally well. They also learned to keep off the trails even when jungle brush was matted, since Jap MG fire covering trails did not traverse.

Infiltration and Diversion. The enemy worked behind defensive positions to create confusion and to draw fire by simple but effective shouting, rock-throwing or feinting away from the main attack. Jap sniper fire proved disconcerting until it was evaluated for what it was—a not-too-effective nuisance.

On the offensive, artillery played the major part in softening up defensive positions, but the Jap usually doesn't quit until an infantryman nails him.

Officers learned not to wear identifying insignia and not to allow their men to call to them by rank or to look at them for orders. The Jap will pass up 20 enlisted men to get an officer. In such a situation, officers had to prove themselves real leaders, and those who were not found themselves in the rear.

Also, our reports from 'Canal say, "you learn, after watching a couple of successful operations, to trust and welcome support from artillery and air and coastwise naval shelling. This is particularly true of artillery, which worked in close cooperation with infantry. You have to have plenty

of faith in the accuracy of somebody else when he's shooting at an enemy 100 yards away—the same faith William Tell's little boy had."

In New Guinea, on the other hand, artillery played a very small part in the Buna and Sanananda campaigns. It was almost impossible to move heavy field pieces in that swampy terrain. The supply problem was terrific and malaria a constant menace. Over the Owen Stanley Mountains the men fought the whole way in stealth and concealment, with little water and much dehydrated food. It was a long, tough haul.

Target designation gave way in New Guinea to concentrated fire power in the general direction of an enemy who did not show himself. Every morning trees were sprayed top to bottom to catch snipers and, in the absence of heavy artillery, 81-mm mortars disrupted enemy supply lines, particularly parachuted supplies.

On the march, such pack essentials as shelter halves, raincoats and mess kits became nonessentials and, along with gas masks, were left in the rear to be brought up by reinforcements. Stripped down to necessities, infantry equipment contained a canteen, sun helmet, fatigue cap, gun, ammunition bandoleers and a little food. Even

blankets were torn in half to lighten the load.

Use of five- and eight-man squads was sometimes moderated owing to density of the jungle, which prevented deployment in force. So the soldier in New Guinea, as at Guadalcanal, had to learn how to do his own thinking and his map- and compass-reading instead of depending upon an officer or noncom.

Chewing gum, pin-up pictures, comic magazines and crunchy candy bars became memories to the men of New Guinea, and while there were sometimes cigarettes, it was hard to find a light. The fighting men had great respect for the QM jeep drivers, the medics and the Fuzzy Wuzzy natives. They also had great respect for the rules for preventing malaria, and the guy who didn't follow those rules was a chump and a very sick one, at that.

Fighting the Nazis

In military tactics as well as in miles it's a long way from the South Pacific to Tunisia. In Tunisia our men demonstrated in highly mechanized warfare that they could take it and could dish it out. War in the Pacific had many of the elements

of Indian fighting before the Revolutionary War. War in the Mediterranean was from the modern assembly line.

Here for the first time we were able to test the glamorized new troops—the armored forces and tank destroyers, heavy hardware, airborne engineers and motorized battalions—against the masters of their use, seasoned German troops.

We learned that these factors are vital but not decisive in themselves. You still must have the solid foundation of artillery and infantry at the pay-off.

The basics of mechanized combat were not changed. The rules don't need rewriting. The men had to learn a lot more about the use of land mines, though; they all admit we should use more of them in the future, sow them more liberally and be more careful about clearing enemy mine fields. As Lt. Gen. McNair says, the way the Germans used mine fields "almost amounted to a new arm."

Artillery concentration followed by infantry advance was proved by the British at El Alamein to be as effective against a mobile mechanized tank army as it was against the trenches on the Somme. The artillery is helped far beyond its former power by aerial bombing, which also is artillery, by aerial reconnaissance, by antitank guns and AA batteries, and by advances in Signal Corps technique which have given artillery a new dimension. But it is still artillery. The infantry now has tanks as blocking backs and planes to heave forward passes, but it is still the infantry that crosses the goal line and kicks the extra point on ground it has occupied and held.

The foxhole and slit trench were the soldier's best friend in Tunisia. Men learned to dig every time they stopped moving, using any damned thing that was handy, even a helmet. Pfc. John Larson, who won the Silver Star and Purple Heart in North Africa, says, "There's something about a flock of machine-gun bullets coming at you from the enemy that says, 'Dig, soldier, dig!'"

Our tank and antitank equipment proved to be so good that the Germans couldn't come near it. But its deployment was not movie-style—in a broad sweep, pennants flying, across windswept space. It was found that tanks are handiest when used as the British use them, as interference for the infantry. Similarly the tank destroyers had to learn they weren't tanks but strictly what their name implied—a defensive weapon best drawn up into strategic position determined by reconnaissance, their high speed used to get them into position, not to chase out into open country. The M10 tank destroyer showed itself, in North Africa, the master of the highly touted German land battleship, the Mark VI.

In spite of so much Spam that everybody got damned sick of it, the ASF did a job in Africa that will find a place in history books. Everything had to be toted from the U. S., including locomotives, not to mention the ordinary mechanized equipment and ammunition. Then when the Second Corps made its epic surprise move from El Guettar to the north, crossing at right angles on its way the supply lines to the British First, the Army Service Forces not only moved it but supplied it without disrupting British traffic or causing delay. They'll be teaching that one at West Point from now on. It was one of the decisive factors of the campaign. The ASF wasn't "too late with too little" in Tunisia.

Alaska

A YEAR and a half of waiting and preparing has paid off in Alaska. There the lessons to be learned were patience and coordination of Army and Navy units. It was a case of waiting for the day, and finally the day arrived when troops and sailors moved into the Aleutians.

The "day" meant many things to many men. To the engineers it proved that the great rush against incredible odds to build the 2,400-mile Alcan Highway was paying off. The Road was open, and how! And the ASF thanked God for its engineers whose guts had put the Road through. The Russians also thanked God for the Road, over which moved supplies to be flown from the terminus of the Road to Russia. Flying that stuff up under the Arctic Circle in fog and ice was a job for the best of Air Force men, who risked their necks every minute of the day.

The lessons in Alaska were in favor of the rule book. Nothing much new to learn, but a lot that had been learned was put to the test of 60-below-zero cold, interminable rain and fog, instantaneous freezing, rugged living. The men got along without women, radios, books, Coca-Cola and sunshine. And they sure want to get the war over so they may get to hell home.

With the movement out along the Aleutian Chain and the victory at Attu, the men began to feel that the war wasn't going to last forever. They understood, then, why they had been stuck in a remote, quiet sector for so long. Alaska was quiet no longer.

Army Air Forces

THE Air Forces made many innovations during the 12 months from June to June. They mastered an air route across the Himalayas from India to China, they met and mastered the *Luftwaffe* in Africa and Europe, shagged Jap airmen from China, and flew through zero ceilings and sub-zero sleet in Alaska. They have for six months been invading Europe almost every day of the week, pounding the Axis arsenal into rubble. They have made the Flying Fortress great because, and only because, great men have flown the Fortress. They have mastered the transition to what Gen. Arnold calls "the last of the small bombers," the B-24 and the B-26. They have taken the curse off the P-38 and the P-40.

Fighter planes have learned not to monkey with individual acrobatics but to stay in formation. Pilots have learned there's a lot of difference between air and ground shooting. Twin-engine pilots have discovered that you can turn in toward a conked-out motor and come out alive. All concede that a bombardier ought also to know navigation and a pilot must be able to give "first aid" repairs to his engines and electrical and hydraulic systems.

Europe. Our Air Forces, with the British, have already invaded Europe. Our Eighth Air Force

and the RAF have had a second front going in the sky for a full year during which time it has constantly grown in intensity and effectiveness to the point where now its commander, Maj. Gen. Ira C. Eaker, says experimental operations over Europe have been concluded.

No section of the U. S. Army has done a tougher or more effective job in the last 12 months than the Eighth Air Force. No target in Germany was too remote for our Fortresses and Liberators. Since last July the Eighth has lost 90 bombers over Europe, in return for which it has collected 356 German planes for sure and many probables.

A trick Gen. Eaker's men have learned is to put fighter planes on the outer rim of formations when the bombers have loads, then when fighter ammunition is about expended to pull the fighters inside the bomber protection for the run home. The men have also had to learn the hard way to be careful in adjusting their electrically heated clothing to prevent frostbite at high altitudes. Gen. Eaker is experimenting, he announced, with bulletproof vests on the order of those worn by Al Capone's boys years ago in Chicago. These are expected to prove helpful against splinters and spent bullets.

Southwest Pacific. The Air Forces successfully carried an invading infantry force into New Guinea, then teamed with ASF to keep it supplied. Aerial troop transports shuttled back and forth delivering reinforcements to areas inaccessible to land and sea. Heavy-caliber artillery was flown over the Owen Stanley Mountains and into such isolated spots as Wau. Lack of heavy naval units at times led to innovations such as skip-bombing.

In the Southwest Pacific, Air Force planes shellacked the Jap Navy in two epic encounters and made the apparently impossible job of aerial warfare over a wide area of islands and sea seem routine. The Air Forces also evacuated hundreds of wounded men from Guadalcanal and other islands to hospitals where their lives were saved.

North Africa. The Air Forces flew in whole crews of engineers to repair airfields under fire, and set up hedge-hopping light planes as reconnaissance units for artillery.

China, Burma, India. The 10th Air Force has learned how to combat dust, heat and monsoon rains. It organized a striking force even though it was at the tail end of the long supply line from the U. S. via Panama, Brazil, Africa, Cairo and India. Its record in that time: 1,000 sorties over Burma with loss of four planes in combat, 500 fighter sorties with loss of two planes. B-24s, B-25s and P-40s kept the Jap constantly off stride and broke up a planned invasion of India. And all the while the 10th so carefully guarded the Air Transport Command's supply lane across the Himalayas that not a single ferry plane was lost through enemy action.

Outstanding development in C-B-I was the 10th Air Force's use of P-40s as dive bombers. They dive at their targets, drop their loads, pull out of the dive and make another run, strafing troops and installations. It has been so successful that the Japs now move over North Burma's railroads only at night. With creation of the 14th Air Force in China, which already has raided the Jap Hainan Islands, things are looking up in the Orient.

The system of Maj. Gen. Chennault for air war against the Japs in China has become as famous in the air as the Notre Dame Shift and the Warner Single Wing Back in football. Since the China Air Task Force took over from the AVG and in turn became the 14th, these flying men, on every occasion badly outnumbered, have scored 182 Jap planes shot down, plus 63 probables at a loss to themselves of 14 pilots. In addition the 14th has been constantly busy with bombing and strafing. One bomb squadron alone has turned in 70 missions with loss of only one plane in combat, and in addition to this bombing it got nine Jap planes confirmed and 13 probables and destroyed 33 Jap planes in the ground. Many of these missions were in conjunction with Chinese ground-force actions. The 14th also made good use of skip-bombing.

Because China is at the end of the supply line, food must be procured locally, and not a man in China but would give a month's flight pay for a good roast-beef dinner with mashed potatoes and gravy. A glass of fresh milk, if auctioned, might bring $30. A bottle of good Scotch costs $400-$600, Chinese money.

Expansion. The big story of the Air Forces in the last 12 months is their expansion. They have doubled in size from a sprinkling of power in England, China, India, Australia and Alaska to

THE ARMY'S NEW M12 IS A 155 MOUNTED ON A MEDIUM TANK CHASSIS

THIS is the M12, the Army's latest model self-propelled 155-mm gun with an effective range of 10 miles, three miles farther than the 105-mm M7 tank-destroyer weapon which proved so successful in the Tunisian campaign firing at distant targets under fire directions relayed from air observers. The M12 is mounted on a medium tank chassis and maneuvers with speed that leaves the average 155-mm field artillery rifle and its prime mover in the dust. Discussing the M12 recently, Maj. Gen. Gladeon M. Barnes, chief of the Army Ordnance Technical Division, disclosed that the weapon can be used not only against ground forces but also as a coast artillery weapon for firing upon prospective landing forces far out at sea. It is particularly valuable in coastal defense because it can be brought into a temporary installation much quicker than other guns of similar size.

14 full-fledged forces in all theaters. New planes like the Lightning have been introduced. Techniques have been perfected. Flying sergeants have become flying officers. Aviation students have become cadets. Gliders are now practical and in use. New gunnery and navigation schools have turned out thousands of experts. And there is no end to AAF resourcefulness. Hell, they are even ferrying fighter planes across oceans, now.

Army Service Forces

THE ASF used to be called the Services of Supply. But whatever they call it, in the last 12 months it has had the biggest supply job in the history of warfare. ASF is the gang you cuss when you get Spam three times a day. But you can thank ASF for mail, medical care, transportation, Ordnance, the QMC, Signal Corps, the Engineers, the WAAC, the MPs, your PXs, movies and recreation, and YANK, among other things.

Just thinking of all the things ASF has to worry about would make anybody dizzy except Lt. Gen. Somervell, the boss.

ASF has moved so fast in the last 12 months it is impossible to report its achievements by theaters. It's all we can do to keep track of them by branches. Here are some of the records:

1. **Bought and delivered world-wide 17 billion dollars worth of supplies.**
2. **Inducted, classified and assigned 4 million draftees.**
3. **Built 6 billion dollars worth of Army installations.**
4. **Moved 14 million tons of supplies and a million men, including you.**
5. **Developed (through the QMC) new clothes to meet new types of war and the dehydrated rations, and took the brass buttons off a lot of uniforms.**
6. **Saved 97 out of every 100 wounded, perfected the use of atabrine, new anaesthetics and pain killers, and through the Medical Department did 100 other jobs that couldn't be done.**

The Engineers built the Alcan Highway, perfected the Airborne Engineers which flew into North Africa to repair bombed-out airports, built Army camps from Hell to Breakfast, and climaxed a brilliant year by keeping the roads clear in Tunisia while the Second Corps moved from Maknassy to the Bizerte sector directly across the Allied line of communications. In North Africa the Engineers built roads at the rate of four miles a day. In Australia and New Guinea the Engineers built 100 airdromes, some actually behind enemy lines.

Construction the Engineers have completed during the year amounts to 20 times the work needed to build the Panama Canal.

Ordnance produced several big developments. The small-arms section developed the bazooka, with a rocket projectile that is strictly from Buck Rogers. For one- or two-man operation, it is our answer to the Japanese "knee" mortar. Ordnance also standardized a corrugated rawhide-handled trench knife. In ammunition, Ordnance substituted the steel cartridge case for brass.

New artillery pieces included a 155-mm 8-wheeler that proved very accurate in Tunisia at up to 20 miles. Antiaircraft has developed a 37-mm and two 50-caliber machine guns on a single mount to fire simultaneously from a half track, a weapon aimed at dive bombers. A new 40-mm AA gun had fine results in Africa. A new 90-mm AA gun drew loud cheers in the two Pacific theaters. Another new piece is the M7 tank destroyer, a 105-mm howitzer called "The Priest" because its 50-caliber machine-gun mount looks like a pulpit, and when it hits you, you need absolution. Tried by the British against Rommel last December, its enthusiasts say it makes tanks obsolete, but don't tell that to a tank man or you'll get a battle. Also first used in Africa was the 155-mm-gun motor carriage. This utilizes a medium tank chassis to tote a 155 rifle that can throw a 95-pound projectile 15 miles and can knock out anything on tracks or wheels. Very new is the gun motor carriage M10 that mounts a 3-inch antitank gun to supplement the M7 howitzer.

There were plenty of other developments during the year, but if we tried to list them all there wouldn't be any space left for the pin-up girls. You will find the regular pin-up as usual on page 24 and eight extras in the middle of the magazine.

LATRINE QUESTIONS A YEAR OF COMBAT DID NOT DECISIVELY ANSWER

1. Whether land-based planes have made carriers obsolete.

2. Whether bombing planes have outmoded the battleship.

3. Whether tanks should fight other tanks or leave that job to tank destroyers and artillery.

4. Whether objective bombing is more effective than area bombing.

5. Whether AA guns should be distributed by units or in mobile masses.

6. When this war will end.

7. Whether Jane Russell or Betty Grable is the better pin-up.

How About Next Year—and the Next 100 Years?

A YEAR ago this week YANK started publication with an editorial announcing that it was strictly an enlisted man's weekly. The enlisted men and nobody else, we said in that first issue, would write YANK's stories, take its pictures, draw its gag cartoons, select its' pin-up girls and determine its editorial policies.

All through our first year, we have kept the magazine that way. YANK belongs to you enlisted men. It reports your fighting and training, prints your literary and artistic inspirations (if you can call them that) and opens its pages to your squawks and gripes. We want you to know that YANK is going to remain an enlisted man's paper for the duration and six months—and even longer if you need it.

Speaking of the future, YANK hopes that you enlisted men will start soon to use the pages of this paper to discuss the peace that will follow the war. Most of us in the Army feel that the men who are doing the fighting should have something to say about the peace, too, and a hell of a lot to say about what kind of a nation America will be after the war. But you enlisted men haven't talked much about the future. Consequently, few people know exactly what you are thinking—if anything. Some people have given out statements quoting soldiers as saying this or that but the statements we've made so far don't add up to much.

Here, in YANK, you enlisted men have a medium for expressing your ideas about the peace and post-war America. We, as editors of your paper, hope that you will make use of YANK in the future for this purpose.

Why don't you?

LET IT SOUND OFF YOUR IDEAS

YANK
THE ARMY WEEKLY

YANK has well earned its acceptance among Army men. It is sprightly and informative. My visits to Army Air Force installations all over the world have demonstrated to me its popularity. To the man overseas, it carries that most welcoming and heartening message—news from home. To the man stationed in the United States, YANK brings vivid and knowing accounts of action at the front.

On this first anniversary of YANK, I extend congratulations to the many enlisted men upon whom falls the responsibility for its actual preparation—the writers, artists and photographers who today are serving alongside their fellow troops on all nine fronts.

—Gen. H. H. ARNOLD
Commanding General
U.S. Army Air Forces

To the staff and contributors of YANK, congratulations on your first year's activities.

Your magazine has been of inestimable morale value to the personnel of this theater. Scattered as we are at isolated outposts on far-flung islands in the Pacific, YANK has been the one magazine hashed and re-hashed. Even our native friends, in their varied (sometimes scanty) attire, look forward to Sad Sack and all his friends.

Keep up the good work—and please don't fail to get each issue out to our people.

—Lt. Gen. M. F. HARMON
Commanding General
South Pacific Area

The most important thing we have learned in the Pacific is the importance of cooperation between the branches of our armed forces. Whenever possible, out there, the Army, Navy, Marines and Coast Guard work together as a fighting unit. No one bothers to think whether the man next to him is a gob, a marine or a soldier. Each one knows that beside him is a fighting man who knows his job—and that's all that matters.

A magazine like YANK helps cement this understanding between the services. It deals with all the services; it's written by all the services.

We look forward to YANK in the Pacific—officers and men both. We think it is doing a first-rate job.

—Capt. JOSEPH FOSS
U. S. Marine Corps

Congratulations on your first birthday. YANK's mission with the Army is one of vital importance. It has been carried out in a commendable manner during the past year.

Speaking for the Army Service Forces, let me assure you that your efforts have been appreciated. We are looking forward to the continued success of the Army's own newspaper.

—Lt. Gen. BREHON SOMERVELL
Commanding General
U.S. Army Service Forces

It is a pleasure to greet the Navy's brothers-in-arms through the Army's voice, YANK.

Soldiers, sailors, Marines and Coast Guardsmen in the Pacific Ocean areas realize the urgent necessity of fighting as a team. The enemy is learning to his sorrow how effective this Army-Navy cooperation can be.

Through YANK I should like to compliment the Army on its fighting spirit, which has already proved itself in battle on many fronts in this war.

—Admiral CHESTER W. NIMITZ
Commander In Chief, Pacific Fleet

Congratulations to YANK on the completion of a very successful year of publication. The Seventh Air Force, Hawaii, has welcomed YANK as a morale builder as well as good entertainment. Keep up the fine work, but we sincerely hope that you won't have occasion to celebrate many more birthdays. Yours for victory—soon and complete.

—Maj. Gen. WILLIS H. HALE
Commanding General
Seventh Air Force, Hawaii

Please accept my heartiest congratulations on YANK's achievements during its first year of publication.

YANK has well earned the popularity it enjoys with men in all branches of the service. We are grateful for the special Marine issues of YANK and for all Marine material included in other editions.

May I, as a regular reader, extend best wishes for your continued success.

—Brig. Gen. ROBERT L. DENIG
Director, Division of Public Relations,
U. S. Marine Corps, Washington, D. C.

I should like to extend my heartiest congratulations to YANK, the Army Weekly, on its first birthday. YANK has faithfully reported the great job our Ground Forces have done in many parts of the world during the past 12 months, and also has published some remarkable pictures of Ground Force operations. During YANK's second year the Ground Forces expect to provide YANK with plenty of important stories. Keep up the good work.

Yours for continued success.

—Lt. Gen. LESLEY J. McNAIR
Commanding General
Army Ground Forces

YANK in the past year has done a noble job as a morale-booster of troops serving in the Caribbean Area.

Soldiers stationed at strategically located defense positions guarding the vital installations of the Panama Canal have brightened long, monotonous hours of watchful waiting by reading their own soldier-edited weekly.

Flavored in a peppy, interesting style, YANK's stories, gags and cartoons fortify the troops on duty here with a desirable type of reading material.

YANK's staff has done splendid work since the inception of the publication last year, and I know the future will bring continued success.

—Lt. Gen. GEORGE H. BRETT
Commanding General
Caribbean Defense Command

As the first year of publication of YANK comes to a close, I congratulate the editors and staff of the newspaper upon the fine work which they have done. As a newspaper published by soldiers and for soldiers, it is the official voice of the American Army and fills a very definite place in the Army life.

In this theater, the newspaper brings up-to-date news of actions and activities in other theaters and tends to create in our men that spirit of pride and comradeship which is most desirable. My thanks to the people responsible for the publication of this newspaper and best wishes for its continued success.

—Lt. Gen. DELOS C. EMMONS
Former Commanding General
of the Hawaiian Department

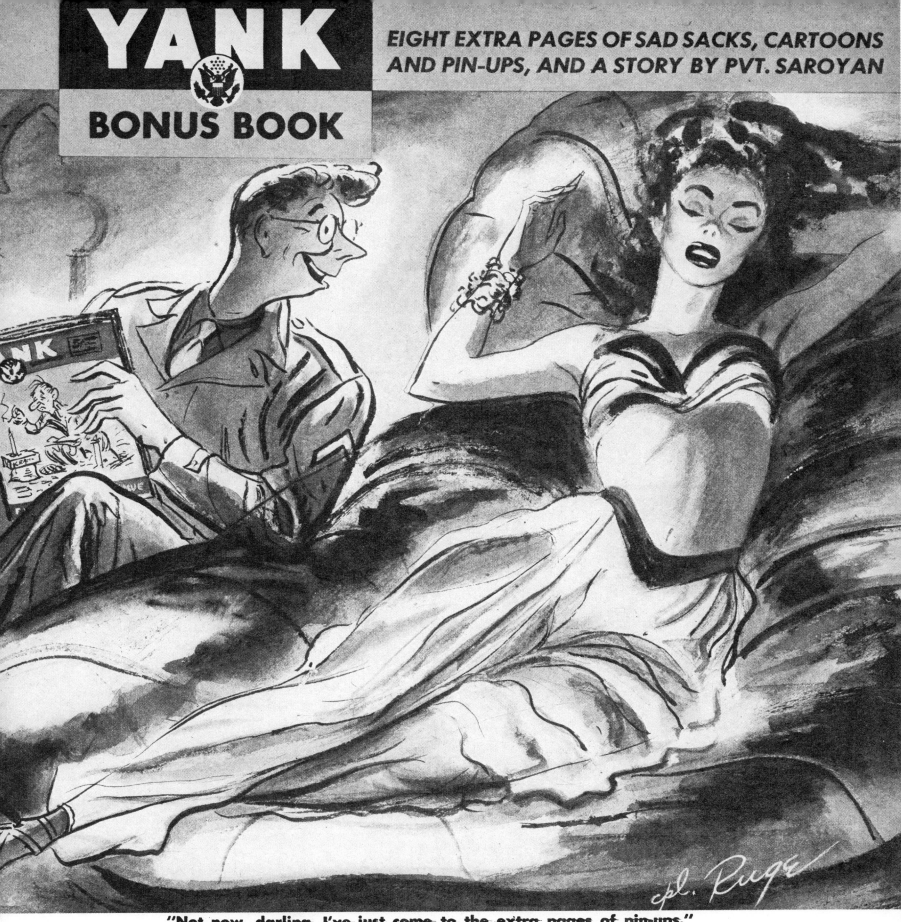

cpl. Ruge

"Not now, darling. I've just come to the extra pages of pin-ups."

"THE UNIFORM

SAD SACK

HIS FIRST YEAR IN THE ARMY

YANK, the Sad Sack is cele-
ating the end of his first year
e Army this week. So we de-
d to turn back his service
rd, bringing out again in this
us Book some of his early ex-
ences in the days when he
to sit on the seat marked
ereals" because he thought
it meant "recruits".

SGT. GEO. BAKER SIGNAL CORPS

"THAT'S HERBERT FOR YOU . . . ALWAYS THE EXHIBITIONIST!"
—Sgt. Irwin Caplan, Fort Knox, Ky.

"AIN'T BEEN IN LONG, HAVE YOU, MATE?"
—Leo Salkin, PhoM3c, USN, San Diego, Cal.

"JUST TO RELIEVE THE MONOTONY, SIR."
—Sgt. Sydney Landi, AAC, Richmond, Va.

"I KEEP HIM HERE FOR SLAMMING DOWN THE TELEPHONE."
—Pfc. Aldo, Jefferson Barracks, Mo.

THE SAD SACK   "REVEILLE"   THE SAD SACK

"I DON'T CARE WHAT HE CALLED TH' DODGERS—SHOOT THAT WAY!"
—Cpl. Bill Newcombe, Fort Knox, Ky.

"THANK YOU FOR A LOVELY EVENING, MISS KINOOK."
—Pfc. Tom Zibelli, Camp Davis, N. C.

"BRING ANY LATE COMICS WITH YOU, MEN?"
—Cpl. E. Maxwell, AAF, Carlsbad, N. M.

"HUT, TWO, THREE, FOUR. HUT, TWO . . ."
—Sgt. Frank Brandt

"SICK CALL"   THE SAD SACK   "DRILL

SGT. GEORGE BAKER

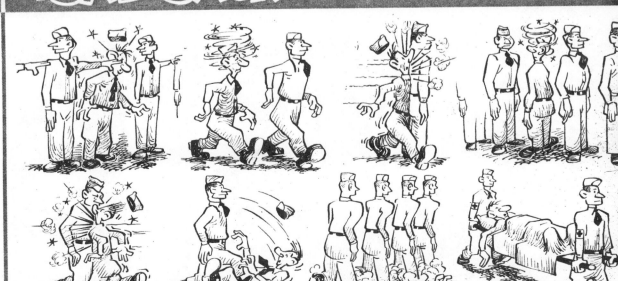

SGT. GEO. BAKER. SIGNAL CORPS P.C.

Brenda Joyce

Jean Parker

Alma Carroll

Betty Grable

Virginia Patton

Doris Merrick

Leslie Brooks

Esther Williams

"TEN-SHUN!"
—Cpl. Bill Newcombe, Fort Knox, Ky.

"ALL I KNOW IS, THEY BEGAN DEVELOPING WHEN I BECAME A SERGEANT."
—Pvt. Bob Abramowitz, Fort Hamilton, N. Y.

"REMEMBER, SIR, OFFICER DATES OFFICER!"
—Cpl. O. L. Dudley, Camp Wallace, Tex.

SAD SACK "GOIN' TO THE P.X.?" THE SAD SACK

SGT. GEORGE BAKER

"TCH-TCH, MULLIGAN! WHEN I THINK OF THE HOURS I SPENT TEACHING YOU JUDO!"
—Cpl. Larry Reynolds, Fort George G. Meade, Md.

"YOUNG MAN, THE IMPORTANCE OF PIGEONS IN THE SIGNAL CORPS HAS BEEN SOMEWHAT OVERESTIMATED."
—Sgt. Ralph Stein

"IT LOOKS LIKE JENKINS IS HAVING A HARD TIME GETTING USED TO THE TROPICS."
—Sgt. Frank Brandt

"PAYDAY"   THE SAD SACK   "IN TOWN"

SGT. GEORGE BAKER

SGT. GEORGE BAKER

The SWEETHEART of Co. D

By Pvt. WILLIAM SAROYAN

THERE is something in the heart of street dogs which draws them close to men, and there is probably no camp or post of the Army which does not have at least one dog, whether the post is in a Far Western desolation or in a suburb of New York, as my post is.

Our Company D has one of these dogs. He is called Shorty by some of the men, Short End by others and Short Arm by still others. Shorty is small, lazy and given to a bitter attitude toward civilians, including children. Somewhere in Shorty's family is a dachshund, as Shorty has the lines of such a dog, but not the hair.

The theory of the men of Company D is that Shorty spends the greater part of his time dreaming of women—or at any rate women dogs. He doesn't come across such creatures very often; he doesn't come across any kind of dog very often. Whenever he does, male or female, Shorty goes to work and gives the matter a stab, so to speak. It is a half-hearted stab, with Shorty more bored than fascinated and not the least bit sure of what he is trying to do, or whether or not he isn't making a fool of himself.

Now and then Shorty will be discovered in the middle of the street, dreaming of love or whatever it is, while two or three trucks stand by discreetly waiting for him to make up his mind. Shorty may have come into the world thoughtlessly, but it is not likely that he will leave any children standing around. He is either too tired, too troubled or too old, even though he is probably not more than 2.

I have observed that Shorty makes himself available to any man in uniform, bar none, and while our post is made up mostly of men of talent, Shorty is not above giving himself over to the affections of a man of practically no talent at all, such as our top sergeant, who was not in civilian life the famous man he is now. Our top sergeant may be a genius, the same as all the rest of us: Two-Teeth Gonzalez, Bicycle Wilkinson, Henry the One Hundred and Fifty-First Million and all the others. He probably deserves a story all to himself, but somebody else will have to write that story, as I want to write sonnets. (That is, if I ever learn to spell.)

MY HERO is Shorty, not our first sergeant. The sergeant is his mother's hero, I suppose, and I wish to God she'd never let him out of the house. If he thinks getting me to do KP is the way we are going to bring the war to a satisfactory conclusion, I believe his education has been neglected. That is not the way to do it. Give me map of the world, a pointer and a good-size audience and I believe I can figure the who thing out in not more than an afternoon. The ide that generals are the only kind of Army person nel capable of figuring out ways and means an all that stuff is unsound. For every general ther ought to be one private on the ground floor. A it is, half the time I don't know what is bein done, what the idea is, or anything else. The re sult is that I must go out into the yard an whistle for Shorty, who instead of leaping to h feet and running to me opens his eyes and wai for me to run to him.

SHORTY knows me all right, but what kind planning can you do with a dog, and a sleep one at that—a day-dreamer, an escapist, a love of peace, an enemy of children in sailor suits? don't know who the chaplain of Company D but for my money he can pack up and go to som other post, because Shorty is doing the sam work and sending in no reports to anybody. He a quiet creature, he is patient, he will listen reason or anything else, and he will get up afte a half hour of heart-to-heart talk and slowl wag his tail. He will wag thoughtfully, with e

THE SAD SACK

fort, and unless you are blind, you will know what advice he is giving you after carefully considering your case.

Now, there was the celebrated case of Warty Walter, the Genius from Jersey, who had a secret weapon all worked out in his head which he believed could finish the war in two weeks. Warty mentioned this weapon to our top sergeant only to hear the man say, "You do what I say, Warty, or you're going to hear otherwise."

Warty went out into the yard to Shorty and unburdened his heart, whereupon Shorty got to his feet, stretched his body until it hurt, wagged his tail three times, kissed Warty on the hand, turned and began wending his way across the street where a girl of 6 in a sailor suit was looking at a movie billboard. That was the end of Warty's secret weapon. The following day he got his orders to go to Louisiana, took Shorty in his arms to say good-bye, and the war is still going on—a good three months after Warty got his idea for the secret weapon. Our top sergeant said, "If it's a secret, what the hell are you coming to me about it for? Keep it a secret."

Not every man at our post is as brilliant or as sincere as Warty, but I can think of no man who is not as devoted to Shorty. No girl of the USO has done Army morale as much good as Shorty. He may not be a dancing dog, but he's got eyes and many a man's seen a lot of understanding in those brooding eyes—many and many a man.

As for the little girl in the sailor suit, she turned and ran, so that Shorty, not knowing what else to do, went up to a second lieutenant and bit him. The following day there was a notice on the bulletin board saying: "Yesterday an enlisted man was bitten by a dog who might or might not have had rabies. Therefore, in the future, any man caught without his dog tags will be given extra duty." This of course was a subtle way of saying that Shorty had rabies, a lie if I ever heard one.

The basic failing of Shorty, if he must be given a failing, is his love of comfort, his passion for food and his devotion to sleep or The Dream. Shorty probably does not know this is 1943. I doubt very much if he knows there is a war going on, and I am convinced he does not know that the men of Company D are soldiers. I believe he has some vague notion we are orphans.

Shorty eats too much and never does calisthenics. He has seen a lot of men come and go. He has loved them all, and they have all loved him. I have seen big men with barracks bags over their shoulders bend down to whisper good-bye to the sweetheart of Company D, get up with misty eyes, swing up into the truck and wave to the little fellow standing there in a stupor. And I have heard them, as the truck has bounced out of the yard on its way to the war, holler out—not to me or to our top sergeant, but to Shorty: "So long, pal! See you after the war!"

I don't think they will see Shorty after the war. I think he will lie down and die of a broken heart once the boys take off their uniforms. Shorty lives to watch them stand reveille and retreat. All that stuff will stop after the war and Shorty will be out in the cold, just another dog of the streets, without honor, without importance —lonely, unfed, despised and unwanted.

That is why I have written this tribute to him.

Artie Greengroin, PFC.

ARTIE, THE WELL-DRESSED MAN

GREAT BRITAIN

"Well, for gaw sake," we said. "What are you doing out of the jug?"

There was Artie Greengroin, big as life and twice as cocky, sauntering along Grosvenor Square, right in the heart of London, where MPs are thicker than cosmoline on a supply sergeant's neck.

"Aw," Artie said, "I beat that rap. It was a pipe. They didn't have nothing on me."

"But what happened to the top?" we asked.

"Three months," said Artie briefly. "Darb of a day, ain't it?"

We grabbed him by the belt. "Wait a minute," we said. "There's something awfully funny here. You mean to say that they never laid a glove on you, but that the top's going to spend the next six fortnights in quod?"

"Thass right," Artie said. "You know, something tells me I'm going to be a corporal one of these days."

"How do you know?" we asked.

"A boid tole me," Artie said, "A little boid."

"Probably a parrot," we said.

"Naw," Artie said, "I think it was a wren. Yeah, thass it. It was a Wren."

"Another dame," we said, "after what the last one did to you with the first sergeant?"

"Never mine that," Artie said. "This one is different. She's a lady. She's got a title. She says she's going to make a gennulman out of me."

"Is she?" we asked.

"Yerse," Artie said.

"What else did she say to you?" we asked.

Artie grinned. "She says I got the smell of the sea in me eyes," he said. "She says I got the heart of a sailor. She's a smart dame, that Wren. I got all them things she says. When I was a kid I used to hang around down by the docks all the time."

"What did you do?"

"I used to fish for flounders," Artie said. "And this doll, she spotted me seafaring background right away. She says she looks on me as a descendant of Drake or somebody. Who is this ole bassar Drake, anyways? I knowed a Willy Drake once. He used to box middle at the Tribulation AC."

"Drake was a great English sailor," we said.

"What did I tell you," Artie said. "That doll really unnerstands me."

"Is she pretty?"

Artie shrugged. "Don't forget they's a war on."

We aren't forgetting for one minute. "How's she fixed for dough?" we asked.

"I tole you she had a title," Artie said, "and if you got a title, you got money. It's nature."

"Oh," we said.

"They don't give you no titles for good looks in the English Isle," Artie said.

"Maybe she'll buy you a yacht," we said.

"Thass a good idea," Artie said. "I'll slip her a spiel on that subjeck next time I see her."

"When's that going to be?" we asked.

Artie dragged out his Ingersoll. "In apperximately six hours and thoiteen minutes," he said.

"You mean to say you're going to see her looking like that?"

Artie surveyed his figure, as crummy as any in the ETO. "Wass the matter with the way I look?" he said. "I'm pressed, shined and poised. I got control over me every gesture."

"Where's your cane?" we wanted to know.

"Me cane?" Artie looked blank.

We said that if we were going out with a title we'd carry a cane.

"Thass a good idea," Artie said. "Thass a very good idea. I'm surprised I never thought of that idea meself. I been needing something to lean on for a long time now. Less see, what else do I need?"

"A hat without a grommet," we suggested.

"You mean I should look dashing, huh?" said Artie. "Maybe you're right. Ain't it a little daring, though?"

"The Air Force does it," we said.

"I'm in the QMC," Artie said glumly.

"The QMC is full of stout hearts and willing hands," we said.

"Thass right," Artie said. "After all, the Air Force drives vehicles in the air and we drive vehicles on the ground. If a air-forceman wants to leave off the grommet from his cap, they's no reason why a QMC can't do the same thing. We got dash, too. Thass what this Army needs. Dash."

"And polished buttons," we said.

"Don't mention them things to me," Artie said. "Them things is a sore subjeck with me. I never polished no gawdam buttons in my life and I ain't going to start for no title. I got honor."

"Hear, hear," we said.

"I think I'll go buy me a cane, though," Artie said.

"Buy a big one," we said.

"And pull out me ole grommet," Artie said.

"Throw it in an MP's face," we said.

"Why," Artie said, "tonight I'll be a new Greengroin, I'll be immaculate. I'll be poised."

"Gently," we said.

"You don't have to worry about me, ole boy," Artie said. "I know how to handle women. I been handling women ever since they stopped handling me when I was 2 years old. I'll go get me a cane and change the whole pitchur of me life."

EER PARTY"

SGT. GEORGE BAKER

Sgts. Mack Morriss and Howard Brodie covered Guadalcanal for YANK.

Sgt. Jack Scott reports the bomber raids on Ge

Our Sgts. Burgess Scott and George Aarons moved with British Eighth Army.

YANK: Its First Year in the Army

YANK, the Army Weekly, has been in the armed forces for a year now but many of the soldiers, sailors, marines and coast guardsmen who read it still don't know exactly what YANK is, how it operates and who publishes it. They don't understand the difference between YANK and such publications as the *Stars and Stripes*, the *Infantry Journal* and the *Army Times*.

That is mostly YANK's own fault because, although we write stories and take pictures of everything else in the Army, we don't talk much about ourselves, the enlisted men who put YANK together every week. A few days ago, however, a sergeant who is one of our staff correspondents in the Pacific wrote to us:

"On every island we've hit, the men have been asking us such questions as 'Does YANK have guys like you everywhere?' and 'Are you GI?' In the first anniversary issue, I think we should give them a straightforward explanation of the whole set-up, told simply and without fluff."

To put it simply and without fluff, YANK is strictly GI. We accept contributions only from enlisted men, and the editors, writers, photographers and artists on the staff are all enlisted men, officially attached to Headquarters Branch, Special Service Division, Army Service Forces. The staff also includes two Navy yeomen and a Marine first sergeant.

This detachment is run just like any other Army installation. It has a first sergeant and an orderly room where he makes out the sick book, duty roster and morning report. YANK's morning report is pretty complicated, though. The orderly room is located in the main editorial office in New York, but most of the men are on de-

tached foreign service as writers and photographers in Tunisia, New Guinea, Australia, the South Pacific, Hawaii, Iran, China, Puerto Rico, Panama, India, the Aleutians, Iceland and Cairo.

Being a regulation Army outfit, YANK also has officers but they have administrative rather than editorial authority over the enlisted men in the detachment. They see to it that YANK gets out every week on time and supervise the endless detail of maintaining a staff of GI correspondents all over the world. But the YANK officers have nothing to say about what goes into the pages, except for such things as making sure that the pin-up girls have enough clothes to keep the magazine from being banned from the mail. The enlisted men make most of the editorial decisions.

This is the difference between YANK and other army publications. The excellent technical magazines like the *Infantry Journal* and *Field Artillery* and *Air Force* are edited by officers. The *Army Times* is a civilian publishing enterprise, edited for soldiers, but not by them.

YANK has no direct connection with the *Stars and Stripes* which is a daily Army newspaper in the European Theater of Operations, but that paper works with our British Edition in circulation. We have a closer relationship with the *Stars and Stripes* in North Africa which is separate from the ETO daily. Sgt. Ralph G. Martin and Sgt. Milton Lehman of that *Stars and Stripes* write for YANK, too, and Sgt. Pete Paris, our correspondent in North Africa, contributes to its columns. However, the Middle East newspaper also called *Stars and Stripes* is published by YANK's Cairo Bureau and the Middle East Command, and it has no connection with the other

Cpl. Steve Derry shoots pictures in Britain.

Sgts. Merle Miller and John Bushemi operate from Hawaii.

Georg Meyers (left, with a pal) was with the Americans who took Attu.

With camera and typewriter Sgt. Pete Paris reported Tunisian campaign.

The enlisted men's weekly which started in New York with a small staff of noncommissioned editors last June now publishes in three different countries and sends its GI correspondents, photographers and artists with U. S. troops to every part of the world.

two papers of the same name. Are we making ourselves clear?

YANK's publishing operation has expanded rapidly during its first year. When it started last June, YANK printed one rotogravure edition in New York for overseas readers only. After six weeks, it was also circulated in camps at home. Now YANK publishes four editions—two in New York (one for the U.S. and the other for general overseas distribution), a British Edition in London and a Caribbean Edition in Puerto Rico. We are also planning to publish YANK in the Middle East Command, Persian Gulf Command, Australia, Trinidad and Panama, and we hope to publish soon in Hawaii and Alaska.

The main reason for these separate editions is to speed up distribution, which has been a problem since the first issue. Shipping YANK by bulk in convoy ships was slow and uncertain, and it didn't take us long to realize that the only way to guarantee regular and prompt delivery overseas was to print on the spot.

Our first overseas printing operation started in London last November with material flown by air mail from New York. GIs in England, amazed to see copies of YANK that weren't six weeks old, bought out the first British Edition immediately and it has been a big success ever since. With Sgt. Bill Richardson as editor, the British Edition now has its own editorial staff in London and combines the regular YANK features with several special ETO pages that don't appear in other editions.

With that start, YANK branched out overseas. Almost every one of the soldiers who put out YANK's first issue last June has been shipped. As you will notice from the pictures on these pages, YANK writers and photographers work together as teams in foreign theaters of operation.

A lot of GIs think that the enlisted men on YANK are all master sergeants. There isn't one master sergeant on the editorial staff. The managing editor, the editor of the British Edition and three overseas correspondents are tech sergeants. Most of the others are privates, T-5s, T-4s, corporals and buck sergeants who earned their ratings in line outfits before coming to YANK.

As a matter of fact, ratings are damned hard to get on YANK. Sometimes a man goes up one grade just before he is shipped overseas but not as a general rule. Marion Hargrove, for instance, came to YANK as a corporal a year ago before his book "See Here, Private Hargrove" made him famous, and he remained a corporal for eight months, even though he was a featured writer. He was always dropping hints about being the ranking corporal in the Army but nobody paid any attention to him. Finally one day Hargrove went to the managing editor's desk in desperation with a newspaper clipping about a very famous editor who had joined the Marines. When the celebrated journalist reported at Quantico, a lieutenant looked over his record and said, "Do you think you can do as much for the Marines as Hargrove has done for the Army?"

"Look at that," Hargrove roared, waving the clipping. "And me just a poor old beaten-down corporal."

But Hargrove remained a beaten-down corporal until he was sent overseas as a correspondent a few months later. Then he finally made T-4.

When Sgt. Robert Ghio clicks his camera we get photo coverage in India.

John Barnes reports the war from China, still wearing his Everett Air Base shirt.

Sgt. Ed Cunningham writes of events in India and Burma.

EVENING MORNING REPORT

HOLLYWOOD. Robert Benchley's next role will be that of a whimsical magazine publisher with an eye for beauty in RKO Radio's "The Sky's The Limit," starring Fred Astaire and Joan Leslie. . . .

Claire Trevor sings for the first time in her film career in "The Gunmaster". . . . The title of "This Land Is Mine" carried a special significance for stars Charles Laughton and Maureen O'Hara and Director Jean Renoir. All three initiated steps to become American citizens while working on the RKO picture. . . . Alfred

Claire Trevor

Hitchcock's habit of appearing briefly in each of the pictures he directs has the cast of "Lifeboat" worried. The entire action takes place in a 26-foot lifeboat and they're wondering where he is going to place his 263 pounds without upsetting the boat—and the picture. . . . Columbia has received a green light from the War Department on "Officers' Candidate School," and Lt. Walter O'Brien, a graduate of OCS at Camp Davis, N. C., has been assigned to act as technical adviser. . . . Monty Woolley, who is making "Holy Matrimony," has been invited to have the imprint of his beard placed in the sidewalk in front of Grauman's Chinese Theater in Hollywood, usually reserved for the footprints of film greats.

BROADWAY. The Twelfth Night Club, a women's theatrical group, is collecting trinkets to be sent to troops in the South Pacific for barter with the natives. . . . Ilona Massey, recently of "Ziegfeld

Follies," is to make a South American goodwill tour. . . . "Arsenic and Old Lace" is the fifth play to exceed the 1,000th-performance mark on Broadway. The others were "Lightnin'," "Abie's Irish Rose," "Tobacco Road" and "Life with Father." Two musicals, "Pins and Needles" and "Hellzapoppin," were also so distinguished. . . .

Ilona Massey

Georgie Jessel goes to Hollywood soon to fill a player-producer contract. He will co-star with his ex-wife, Lois Andrews, in one picture he is signed to make. . . . Ann Corio, the ex-burlesque queen, is considering an offer which would co-star her with Maxie Rosenbloom in a Broadway show. . . . Jimmy Durante had a former lady blacksmith, one Hope Emerson, on his radio program recently. She stands 6 feet 2 and weighs 200 pounds.

BLOCKBUSTER

CAN you make little ones out of big ones? Prizes are awarded to those who do the best job of Blockbusting one big word into many little ones. This week's word is

AEROGRAPHICAL

Here are the rules:
1. Using only letters which can be found in the above word, see how many 4-, 5-, and 6-letter words you can find. Some examples are: CORE, GRAPE, CIPHER.
2. No word may use any letter more often than that letter appears in the word *aerographical*.
3. "Webster's Collegiate Dictionary, Fifth Edition" will be our authority for acceptable words.
4. Write your name, address and total score at the top of your list. Number your words.
5. Mail your entry to Puzzle Editor, YANK, 205 East 42d St., New York 17, N. Y., within two weeks of the date of this issue. Overseas entries, within six weeks. A YANK Puzzle Kit will be mailed to each of the five highest scorers.

CHECKER STRATEGY

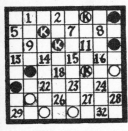

FAIR warning—this one is tough.

So we'll start off by giving you a hint. White makes a few forcing moves, then unleashes the big stroke combination. Black goes down in a blaze of glory.

If that doesn't help, there's the solution on page 30. But first number the playing squares of your board from 1 to 32 as shown.

Jane Russell

he caption writer says this is a picture that doesn't need a caption.

THE POETS CORNERED

*Nor all your piety and wit
Shall lure it back to cancel half a line.*
Pfc. Omar K., 1st Pyramidal Tent Co

KEEP IT CLEAN

Soldiers at Atlantic City (N. J.) Army Air Training Center prohibited from singing eight popular army songs.—News Item.

Oh, let your songs be silent
    And be your voices mute;
A soldier's not an opera star,
    He's just a bloody brute.
A song may lift the sagging heart
    And wing the flagging heel,
But pass the order down the line
    And there'll be no appeal.

Civilian ears are tender
    And soldier songs are crude,
And if some woman heard you sing
    She'd think the Army rude.
So button up your lips, my lads,
    And trudge along unheard;
A soldier's just a bloody brute,
    He's not a blasted bird.

Though singing cuts the miles in half
    And speeds the hike along,
"Mademoiselle from Armentieres"
    Is not a moral song.
Choose something safe and sacred,
    A soldier must not smirch
The Army's honor with a song
    Unfit to sing in church.

Oh, the ghosts of other armies
    That filed into the past
Will listen to your choruses
    And stare at you aghast.
For a dumb and songless army
    You lads will have to be
Unless church hymns and lullabies
    Will set your voices free.
—Sgt. GRANT A. SANDERS

Camp Shelby, Miss.

SOLDIERS WITH A YEN FOR—

Soldiers with a yen for wenches
Usually are found on benches.

Soldiers with a yen for sin
Usually begin with gin.

Soldiers with a yen for vice
Find their week ends very nice.

Soldiers with a yen for trollops
Soon regret the usual follow-ups.
—Pfc. BOB STUART McKNIGHT

Scott Field, Ill.

NOTES ON GUARD DUTY

There's a time 'twixt the day and darkness
That all clock-watching soldiers revile:
When you can't read your watch by the daylight,
Yet you can't read your luminous dial.
—Pvt. JOHN W. SULLIVAN

Beloit College, Wis.

KILL OR BE KILLED

Brass knuckles and knives are your new tools;
Skip the Marquis of Queensbury rules.

Gouge out his eye and kick in his knee,
Knife him from behind when he can't see,
Bludgeon his head and go for his groin,
Honorable ancestor let him join.

Slap the enemy down in the dust,
Using the butt stroke and the short thrust;
Kill with bare hands and let nothing delay
His timely end. Hooray for foul play!

Stamp and crush him with your hobnailed boot;
Bite and kick him. Hell, when do we shoot?
—Sgt. BENJAMIN BORAX

Shreveport, La.

ODE TO MY FOXHOLE

When three quick shots are sounded
And the Nips are overhead,
I wouldn't trade my foxhole
For a pin-up girl in bed.

Ever see Frankie Sinkwich
Streaking downfield for the goal?
Well, he'd look like a turtle
When I'm headed for my hole.

A bomb might have my number
When the Zeros take their toll;
But if they ever get me, Bud,
They must get me in my hole.
—Sgt. MAX SCHERER

New Guinea

WORLD WAR ONE

World War One has started a reign
Of world wars, that is plain;
Or is it just that previous wars
Were given provincial monikers?
—Pvt. LOUIS FISHER

Camp Crowder, Miss.

COMPANY STREET

GI MASCOTS. At **Fort Winfield Scott,** Calif., Punchy, an African lion cub; keeper, Sgt. Joseph Bosi. . . . At **Camp Stoneman,** Calif., Kiki, a brown cat; keeper, Sgt. Leo Gustafson. . . . At **Fort Sill,** Okla., an American eagle *(see photo);* captor and keeper, Pvt. Herman Lanier. . . . At an AAF base in **India:** Taps, a monkey; keepers, an ack-ack crew. Every time Taps hears a Jap plane he chatters like hell to warn the crew, then dives for cover. . . . At

Offutt Field, Nebr., Sgt. Geronimo, a German shepherd paratrooper; keeper, Pvt. Ken Williams. Geronimo has just completed his 13th jump, is now ready for overseas duty.

GUARD DUTY. Pfc. Joe Barbato was on guard duty at **Camp Adair,** Oreg., early one morning when an officer approached. "Halt!" said Barbato. "Who's there?" "Gen. C——," was the answer. "Advance and be recognized," said Barbato. The general advanced, Barbato saw two silver stars and became confused. "Well," barked the general, "should I stand at attention all night?" "No, sir," replied Barbato. "Parade rest!"

QUESTIONS. At **Fort MacArthur,** Calif., Pvt. Steve Crane, who is married to Lana Turner, asked his sergeant for a 24-hour pass. "What dya want a pass for?" asked the zebra. "Are you kidding?" replied Crane. . . . "What would you like to do in the Army?" an interviewer asked Pvt. Quinton Chitwood, **Nashville** (Tenn.) **Air Training Center.** "Latrine orderly," replied Chitwood. "What job do you hold now?" "Latrine orderly." "What else have you done in the Army?" "Latrine orderly." . . . Sgt. Allen Gately, **Fort Devens,** Mass., received a letter from his draft board asking him why he hadn't reported for induction. The letter was dated May 12, 1942.

AWOL. Cpl. Fred A. Loese wired his CO at Westover Field, Mass.: "SIR, WILL BE AWOL SEVEN DAYS TONIGHT SOUNDS ABSURD BUT BEG LEAVE THREE EXTRA DAYS." His CO wired Loese to come back pronto. He did. . . . Pvt. Fred Stein learned camouflage tricks so well at a **Florida** air base that when he went AWOL it took New Jersey state cops 11 weeks to find his hut a couple of feet off the road. . . . At **Miami Beach** (Fla.) **Army Air Base,** Pvt. Ewen J. McNaron got four months for going AWOL and impersonating movie star Jackie Cooper. . . . At **Desert Training Center,** Calif., 39 pigeons went AWOL because they couldn't stand the heat and snakes.

What Happened to My ALLOTMENT?

By Sgt. H. N. OLIPHANT
YANK Staff Writer

A Nebraska farmer whose son is a corporal sent the War Department's Office of Dependency Benefits a letter.

"I am writing," he said, "about a letter I got from your office this morning. Since I didn't open the letter I presume it was my family allowance check. I live on a rural route and on my way back from the mail box I laid the mail down by the pasture gate while I went to rescue a drowning chicken in a nearby tank. When I returned, the check was gone, and I presume one of the cows ate it. I hereby make application for a duplicate check, if this letter you sent contained a check."

That is just one more problem for the Office of Dependency Benefits, which sees that the money you ante up out of your pay each month gets government money added to it, and that the total is delivered to your dependent.

That farmer's carelessness not only means a lot of extra work for the ODB, but it also means he must wait about six months for a duplicate check, because there is just a chance that a cow didn't eat the original. Maybe it blew into the window of a passing car and somebody later cashed it. In that case, the dough is gone, and it's too bad.

The ODB gets about 60,000 letters a day, and a lot of them are similar to the one from the Nebraska farmer. For the ODB pays to soldiers' dependents a total of 175 million bucks a month, which is a lot of dough; in fact, it's more than two billion dollars a year. And it's not just a matter of pushing the button that starts an automatic check-writing machine. Every check must

Eleanor Rajca of Belleville, N. J., files record of family allowance at Office of Dependency Benefits. Most of ODB's 9,000 women workers are relatives of GIs. Eleanor's spouse is in North Africa.

If your allotment check isn't arriving at your home safely, don't be too quick to throw the blame on the clerks at the War Department's Office of Dependency Benefits. They handle the staggering task of delivering 175 million bucks to 3½ million dependents every month and when they don't succeed, it's usually due to carelessness on your family's end of the line.

---

be verified to make sure the money gets in the right hands.

Carelessness is not the only thing that delays delivery of your money to your dependents. Confusion causes trouble, too.

Take a gander at this letter from a private in New Mexico. He was applying for a family allowance for his 19 brothers and sisters, which would seem like a tough enough mathematical problem by itself without the addition of this paragraph: "Of course, I have 12 other brothers and sisters, but they are older and married. However, I would like to get a little money for my brother Edwardo's children. Edwardo has broken both his legs and I'm afraid his 11 children will go hungry. My other 43 nephews and nieces are fairly well provided for by the State of New Mexico, so I don't think they'll need government help at the present time."

You can't throw as tough a one as that at the ODB and expect to get an answer in five minutes. But you'll get an answer reasonably soon, that's certain. The board has not had a single question of dependency that it couldn't solve, even though some of them have been enough to test the com-

bined resourcefulness of Einstein, Mandrake the Magician and Dick Tracy.

Then the ODB gets letters like this one from the wife of a pfc. in Philadelphia: "My husband has been in the service nine months and has never sent me one red cent. Whenever I write to him about money matters, he always answers me back with sweet love words. Now I can't live on sweet love words—I need support."

Despite problems like these, the Office of Dependency Benefits figures out, computes and mails 3½ million checks a month to GI relatives. And the business is growing at the rate of 12,000 new family allowances a day.

There have been some squawks from soldiers that, although their pay has been clipped $22 a month, their families are not getting their checks.

Brig. Gen H. N. Gilbert, director of ODB, says there are cases of that kind—about 30,000 of them—but they constitute only 1 percent of the total. "I can assure YANK," the general said, "that .99 percent of all family-allowance checks and Class E allotments-of-pay mailed from this office are safely and promptly delivered into the hands of the proper payees every month."

What about the 30,000? Most of them can't be delivered because ODB doesn't know where to send them. The customers move without notifying ODB of their change of address.

"Every month," the ODB says, "we can expect about 30,000 checks to be returned undelivered. If your dependent is not getting his or her check, the first thing to do is write to us. Then we know where the dependent lives, and the chances are 30,000 to 1 that there will be no more trouble."

Some confusion arises because it takes about 60 days for the machinery to start working. Suppose you apply (or your dependent applies) for a family allowance during June. The first deduction from your pay is on the July pay roll. The first payment to your dependent goes out the first of August. So don't expect instant action. Wait three months; then if payments are not being made, you can find out why not.

Very few checks are stolen; people who try to cash U. S. government checks illegally have a habit of getting caught. But too many checks are mislaid after the ODB has done its work. The first thing the ODB gets is an excited letter from a dependent, and this starts an investigation.

Cpl. Patsy Cianicullo's wife and baby of Newark, N. J., visit ODB to inquire about family allowance.

Doris Ellison (left) of ODB tells wife of Pvt. Edwin Bartlett her FA application has been approved.

Mrs. Josephine Rowe, with son Bobby, asks about allowance of her husband Pvt. Lewis F. Rowe, Engr.

The thousands of letters the ODB gets indicate that a lot of soldiers and their families don't know the score on the family allowances. To clear up this confusion, Maj. Anson D. Clark of ODB gives us these questions that are most commonly asked and the straight answers to them:

Q. What is a family allowance?

A. It is the government check sent monthly to a soldier's dependent (or maybe dependents) from money deducted from the soldier's pay, plus money added by the government. It is not paid until the soldier or, in some cases, the dependent, applies for it.

Q. Is there more than one kind of family allowance?

A. Yes. There are two kinds. The Class A allowance is for wives and children. The Class B allowance is for dependent parents and minor dependent brothers and sisters, and some others.

Q. How much is taken from your pay for a family allowance?

A. For Class A relatives alone, $22 a month. For Class B dependents alone, $22 a month. For Class A and Class B together, $27 a month.

Q. How much do dependents get?

A. It varies according to the dependents. A wife gets $50 a month. A wife and child, $62. Wife and two children, $72. Father and mother, $47. Wife and parents, $80. But there are about 350 different combinations. The largest family allowance right now goes to the family of a private named Pinkerton, in Chicago, Ill. His wife and 10 children get $152 a month.

Q. Can anybody get an allowance?

A. No. Only enlisted men up to staff sergeants or T/3. Staff sergeants and above, or T/3s and above, are out of luck.

Q. Can your relative apply, or must the soldier do it himself?

A. A Class A allowance can be applied for by the relatives or by the soldier. Class B allowances can be applied for by soldiers or relatives, but the soldier must consent before a deduction is made.

Q. Suppose I don't want a Class A allowance made, even though I have a wife and children.

A. That's too bad. They get it anyway if they apply. They've got to prove the relationship, however.

Q. Suppose I have a divorced wife to whom I was paying alimony. Can she collect?

A. She sure can, but she's got to prove you owe her alimony.

Q. How do you apply for an allowance?

A. There is only one way. You, or your relative, make out form WD AGO 625. Army reception centers have them, also recruiting stations, Red Cross offices, Service Command headquarters, and of course the ODB office.

Q. What proof is needed that the person really is your relative and dependent?

A. Proof must be submitted attached to the application. The ODB will take certified copies of marriage certificates, birth records of your children, and sworn statements from persons who know the other dependents. But you must have proof. Otherwise, no dough.

Q. Suppose several persons are eligible. Is the money sent all in one check to be divided by them?

A. That's up to you or your dependents. If you want separate checks, they'll be sent. But children under 16 or mentally incapacitated adults can't have checks made out to them; someone responsible gets the money for them.

Q. Can aviation cadets get these allowances?

A. No. They aren't low enough in grade.

The rules really are quite simple and work out very well. Occasionally a soldier beefs when his wife corners part of his money without his consent, but not often. And once in a while a squawk arises when a soldier gets nicked by a wife with whom he hasn't been friendly lately.

One disenchanted GI in Australia roared when he heard that his wife was getting an allowance. It was the first he knew of it. Sore as hell, he wrote the ODB that he wouldn't cough up a dime. "That babe," said he, "caused me more trouble than six months of intimate life with mud, snakes and sandfleas. I was separated from her a year before I joined the Army. She never asked for money then. Why should I give it to her now?"

Unfortunately he was stuck. Under the law she's his wife and entitled to the allowance.

The ODB also has a service called Class E allotment-of-pay in addition to the family allowance. This is strictly a service, however, and the government does not add to the kitty. Any soldier, of any rank, officer or EM, can sign form WD AGO 29 and have money deducted from his pay to be sent to his dependents, or to an insur-

ance company to pay premiums, or to a bank for his own account. Officers can have their whole pay sent in this manner if they desire. Enlisted men can send their whole pay except $10. GIs must keep out $10 pocket money. A Class E allotment is strictly voluntary. Right now about a million and a half men are taking advantage of it, 77 percent of whom are EM.

There's nothing to stop you from having a Class E allotment in addition to your family allowance, provided you're eligible for a family allowance. There is nothing, either, to prevent you from discontinuing, increasing or decreasing the Class E allotment at any time. But you can't discontinue the Class A allowance unless you get to be a staff sergeant or T/3 or higher, in which case you become automatically ineligible for it. You can discontinue Class B.

One thing to remember about Class E allotment-of-pay. Suppose you've had $75 a month going to your bank at home. You get promoted to technical sergeant and decide to send $100 home instead. In filling out the allotment form, be sure you authorize the $100 deduction in full. If you just say you want another $25 deducted, you throw a monkey wrench into the machinery.

A GOOD thing to remember about all this allowance and allotment business is this: if you don't know exactly what to do, hunt up somebody who can tell you. Overseas, the Red Cross, the Special Service and the chaplains can answer your questions. In this country, your families can get in touch with Army Emergency Relief, Red Cross or write directly to the Office of Dependency Benefits, Newark, N. J. Or so can you, for that matter.

In its 10 months of operation, ODB has run into some screwy situations. One resourceful gal married six different privates in less than a year, expertly keeping the trick from both the soldiers and the ODB. She was collecting six different family-allowance checks before the law nabbed her for bigamy.

There was also the curious case of the buck sergeant from Indiana who had three wives and no divorces. Each wife applied for a family allowance. As it turned out, wife No. 1 was the only one eligible, because the other two marriages were not legal. Wife No. 2 gladly washed her hands of the whole business. Wife No. 3, however, said she'd forego the allowance if she could keep the sergeant. "He's a fine man," she said. "He has only one bad habit; he smokes."

Occasionally authorities get a letter that makes them feel that everybody is not just out looking for money. Here is a letter, written on plain tablet paper, that was received by the ODB:

"Thanks for offering me the family allowance but I won't take it now as I am able to work and my son overseas sends me money which I can use some of it if I need it. I am saving it for him. I would rather for my part to go to a mother who has little children to feed, and can't get out to work. My son has no brothers and sisters under age."

Having Trouble With Your Family Allowances?

Clip this out and send it to your dependent. One or more of these points may explain why your check is not being delivered.

1. Is your name plainly printed on your letter box? If not, the postman can't deliver a U. S. government check. If you live in an apartment, be sure your name is on the door, even though you live with another family.

2. Stay home on the day you expect the check to come, until after the postman calls. Ask the postman to put the envelope in your own hands. Then it can't get lost.

3. Cash the check at the same place each month. Then you won't have trouble identifying yourself.

4. Do NOT write your own name on the back of the check until the very moment when you cash it. If you write in your name before you leave home and lose the check on the way downtown, you can kiss that money good-bye because anybody can cash it then.

5. Be sure to sign the check exactly as it is made out. If it is made out Mrs. John J. Smith and you, Mrs. John J. Smith, are signing it, don't sign it "Mrs. Anna Smith." Be sure to fill out ALL the information on the back of the check.

6. If you move, report immediately by mail, giving your new address to the Office of Dependency Benefits, Newark, N. J. Don't lose a day in making this report, or you may lose a month's money.

If you've got allowance or allotment problems, shoot your questions to YANK Dependency Benefits Dept., 205 East 42d St., New York 17, N. Y., and we'll give the straight official answers.

ARKANSAS

Arkansas River flood waters cut off Camp Robinson's water supply, compelling the use of emergency wells and sending hundreds of soldiers to Little Rock for baths. Lightning killed L. D. Bolin and Joseph D. Ester while they were at work in a field near De Witt. Ouachita College graduated 97 seniors at Arkadelphia. Maj. James H. Penick, Little Rock banker and veteran of the first World War, re-entered the Army as a fiscal specialist. A state-wide drive was started for 10,000 canning-plant workers. Meeting at Hot Springs, the Arkansas-Missouri Cotton Ginners Association elected John Roberts of Memphis, Tenn., as president.

CALIFORNIA

The Navy announced it would keep Treasure Island as a base after the war. At San Diego, four men were found guilty of the kidnaping and rape of the 19-year-old wife of an Army lieutenant. Lassen County offered $500 reward for the conviction of anyone caught stealing livestock. Al Bolin, Alhambra "Y" secretary, was drafted. Pasadena Junior High students picked 15,000 boxes of oranges. The WMC ordered industry in the seven counties in the San Francisco Bay area to operate 48 hours a week to meet the labor shortage. La Mesa held a reception for Mrs. Arvilla Beckman, 80, California's oldest policewoman. The Southern Pacific Railroad is using 3,000 women on jobs formerly held by men. A six-alarm fire swept a square block of Oakland's warehouse district, threatening the Moore Drydock Co. shipyards.

CONNECTICUT

With the leasing of Hotel Sheridan to the government, Manchester became the only town of its size in the U. S. without a hotel. Hailstones the size of marbles broke windows and damaged gardens in Middletown. Fire destroyed the Marvelous Dye and Printing Co. plant at Derby. Children were blamed for damaging half of Naugatuck's parking meters so badly they could not be used. Danbury became embroiled in a community argument after it was discovered the servicemen's honor roll in Elmwood Park was embellished with the fasces symbol of ancient Rome; under pressure Mayor Hannan ordered the symbol removed, then changed his mind, and Rabbi Malino refused to join in the Memorial Day dedication of the scroll, contending the symbol suggested Italy's Fascist emblem.

FLORIDA

At Tallahassee, the Legislature voted to allow servicemen and women stationed in the state to take advantage of its 90-day divorce law; also passed—a bill forever prohibiting ownership of Florida real estate by persons of Japanese nativity and a labor-regulation bill prohibiting strikes except by majority vote of union members. A four-alarm fire destroyed the Red Cross drug store on Flagler Street, Miami. The Army has Jacksonville's principal airport and the Navy was about to take over its field on the beach road. Willis A. Briggs of Augusta lost a suit for compensation on an appeal to the Florida Supreme Court because, although he had felt a flea bite him while at work, he had not seen it. Died at Palm Beach: Admiral Henry Wiley, 76, commander of the U. S. Fleet from 1927 to 1929.

ILLINOIS

Gov. Green signed bills giving Illinois war veterans State University scholarships and free admission to the State Fair. After an automobile collision involving a Joliet Prison car, the chauffeur unlocked the handcuffs of convict Frank Covelli, who then helped revive his guard, knocked unconscious in the crash. East Moline delayed the dedication of its plaque for servicemen because it was too small to hold all their names. Farmers pooled equipment and labor to plant crops delayed by floods. At Chicago, sailors under 21 from the Great Lakes Naval Training Station were used as decoys in a police drive on saloons accused of selling to minors; Frank Skid and Joe Gironda turned their gasoline station into a livery stable.

INDIANA

The Rev. Andrew J. Patrick, Dover Hill minister, was gored to death by a bull. At Elkhart, Mrs. Eldon Madlem was arrested after plastering the office of Justice of the Peace Myers with rotten eggs. Oil, sucked from power-line transformers by a miniature twister, fell like rain at Kokomo. Carl Burt, athletic director at Manchester College for 18 years, resigned to become superintendent of schools at Warsaw. A $75,000 fire destroyed the Bowden Stone Co. mill at Bedford. Mrs. Solenia Long, believed destitute by her Goshen neighbors, died leaving $900 in cash, 4,000 jars of home-canned fruit and a 1918 Ford. Floods destroyed half of Petersburg's strawberry crop and made 50,000 acres of crop land in the state unsuitable for replanting.

IOWA

Inmates of Wapello County Home were sent to other institutions after its three wells went dry. Ottumwa passed a curfew ordinance and Iowa City planned to invoke an old one. Former Gov. Kraschel's son Dick, 24, was killed at Niagara Falls, N. Y., when his chute failed to open after he jumped from a plane he was testing. Corwith defeated Moneta 9-8 to win the state high-school baseball title. Des Moines East High won the state track meet; Dave Williams of Ottumwa set a discus record of 146 feet 9¾ inches. William Straub, Paullina farmer, was fined $300 and placed on probation for attempted draft bribery in the interest of his son. Died at Decorah: Mrs. Gertrude Hegg, 102.

KANSAS

Gov. Schoeppel asked for immediate farm labor and machinery to prevent millions of acres of productive land in southeast Kansas from going to waste. The only laundry in Dickinson County (pop. 23,000) closed at Abilene. President Butcher retired after heading Emporia State Teachers College for 30 years. Shawnee County farm buildings suffered $100,000 damage from tornadoes. Don F. Geyer, school principal at Hays, was named principal of the Van Buren School in Topeka. A horse owned by the Hills Packing Co., on the loose in Tokepa, foraged many Elmwood Street victory gardens.

KENTUCKY

Reports from 27 counties show Kentucky will be short 2,545 teachers when schools open next fall; in McCracken County half a dozen ministers have offered to teach. Covington police broke up mobs threatening the life of Harry

NEWS from Home

Miller, indicted on charges of attempted rape of two children under 12. Louisville's Mayor Wyatt was back after completing an 8-week assignment for the Board of Economic Warfare in North Africa. Allen County's new $100,000 high school burned. The Owensboro oil field was booming since the opening of a 250-barrel-a-day well on Tom Miller's farm. Mrs. Oma Massie, 30, became Frankfort's first woman bus driver.

MASSACHUSETTS

The Harvard *Crimson*, undergraduate daily, voted to suspend for the duration, but editors said they would publish a semi-weekly for the 8,000 servicemen at the university. Worcester County apple growers expected a bumper crop. At Southbridge, the American Optical Co. announced the use of common household drugs in two new types of sandless glass. Medford's Mayor Carr was commissioned a major in the Army Reserve and George L. Callahan, president of the Board of Aldermen, will fill out Carr's unexpired term. Shades were removed from Brockton's traffic lights as dimout restrictions were eased. At Worcester, Patsy's Main Street barber shop offered a self-shave for 15 cents.

MICHIGAN

Henry Ford, 79, became president of the Ford Motor Co., succeeding his son Edsel, who died of a stomach ailment. At Saginaw, the first Jamaicans recruited to work sugar-beet and bean fields arrived. Ionia residents in a special election approved the establishment of a municipally operated hospital. Lewis G. Hoffman, justice of the peace at Three Oaks, was thrown from his buggy and fatally injured when his horse bolted. Secretary of State Dignan sold his hardware store at Owosso. A $35,000 fire which destroyed a house and garage threatened the entire village of Argyle. Calhoun County has paid $1,200 in fox bounties at $5 a head.

MINNESOTA

With only five fatalities the first quarter of this year, St. Paul was first in its population class in the U. S. in reducing traffic deaths. Thomas and Juan Moreida and Seraido Cruz, teen-age youths, were on trial at Fergus Falls for the alleged kidnaping and assault of Mrs. Minnie Gjelton. David Hillman, Minneapolis infant who weighed 24 ounces at birth, celebrated his first birthday by weighing 21 pounds. The State Executive Council announced a 5-year program to develop 10,000 acres of public hunting grounds in the Whitewater area of Winona County. Motorists whose license plates have become illegible can buy a new pair for 50 cents under a new state law.

MISSISSIPPI

Mrs. Frank Hill, 21, of Biloxi gave birth to triplet girls. The Broad Street Methodist Church in Hattiesburg was dedicated by Bishop Decell of Birmingham, Ala. Paul Cato, a member of the Senate, married Mildred Alexander of Montrose, a member of the House, at Jackson. The famous 155th Infantry, seventh oldest regiment in the U. S., celebrated homecoming day at Camp Shelby with a review. T. B. Murphree, former gridiron star at Mississippi College, was named Hattiesburg High coach. Vera Anderson, 19-year-old welder in the Ingalls Shipyard, defeated Mrs. Hermina Strmiska from Henry Kaiser's Oregon shipyard to win the U. S. woman-welder championship at Pascagoula.

MISSOURI

Near Hannibal, five escaped penitentiary prisoners, captured in Ohio, overcame guards returning them, but one guard successfully talked them out of a second escape. Quick marriages leading to early divorces led Circuit Judge Sartorius of St. Louis to assail the St. Charles "marriage mill." Three GAR veterans, ages 94 to 100, attended the state encampment at St. Louis. The House passed a bill outlawing fortune telling. At St. Louis, Dr. John H. Simon, thrice candidate for mayor, killed himself; Sumner High won the 14th annual Negro public high-school field meet at the Public Schools Stadium.

NEBRASKA

The 1943 national American Legion convention will be held in Omaha Sept. 21-23. The Uni-

A Round-Up of the Week Back in the States

versity of Nebraska graduated 906 seniors. The Rev. Robert P. Hupp, assistant rector of St. Margaret Mary's Catholic Church, Omaha, became a Navy chaplain. Dog lovers and victory gardeners were feuding at Scottsbluff. Two GAR veterans, J. H. Allbee, 98, of Minden and R. E. Coleman, 93, of Lincoln, attended the state encampment at Fremont. South High won Omaha's high-school baseball title. Federal housing projects were approved for Sidney, Bruning, Fairmont, Grand Island and Harvard.

NEW HAMPSHIRE

Figures over a 20-year period show Laconia to be the fastest growing New Hampshire community. Stuart Kingsbury, coach at West Lebanon High for five years, signed a contract to teach and coach at Newport, Vt. The Hollis Congregational Church observed its 200th anniversary. Mrs. Fred Anglehof, wife of the president of the University of New Hampshire, was learning to milk a cow at Durham. State troopers were campaigning against cattle rustlers; new legislation requires licensing of all persons transporting livestock except farmers and common carriers.

NEW MEXICO

Gov. Dempsey asked state departments to build up surplus funds to finance post-war work for returning soldiers. Bernalillo County farmers formed a "co-op" to buy equipment to cultivate potatoes. The annual San Felipe Fiesta was held for two days in Old Town. Stockmen complained that meat rationing threatened to overstock the ranges. Ration-book enrollment showed New Mexico's population as 515,332, a drop of 25,000 since the 1940 census. Mass was said in the 150-year-old San Jose Church of Ranchos de Atrisco for the first time in 18 years.

NEW YORK

Gov. Dewey closed the Whiteface Memorial Highway for the season because of the pleasure-driving ban. Middletown celebrated the 100th anniversary of the arrival of the first Erie Railroad train there; a historical parade depicted "The Evolution of Transportation." Fulton County milk dealers began every-other-day deliveries. Brig. Gen. Gillespie, commandant of Watervliet Arsenal, said the largest cannon factory in the world would open there in July. At Amsterdam, a $200,0000 fire destroyed the McGibbon Building. The *Greater Buffalo*, second luxury steamer converted to an inland-training aircraft carrier, was commissioned at Buffalo. At Corning, over 30,000 gallons of gasoline burned after an Erie Railroad wreck in which 11 tank cars were derailed. Died at Elmira: Edwin Morris, 96, the city's last Civil War veteran.

OHIO

State liquor rationing started with one quart a person each month. Dr. Karl C. Leebrick, president of Kent State University, was not rehired by the board of trustees. A terrific rainstorm flooded the business and residential sections of Elyria. The Legislature voted to allow members of the armed forces to fish, hunt and trap without license and to provide $80 annual tuition in any Ohio college for returning soldiers. Toledo city officials threatened action against downtown building owners whose tenants are in the numbers racket. At Cincinnati, three bandits held up five employees of the Sinton Hotel and escaped with $50,000 worth of jewelry and $10,000 in cash.

OKLAHOMA

After a month-long police controversy at Sand Springs, Wes Carmack resigned as police chief and gave up the keys to the city jail to his successor, Otis Wilson. Harry Wahlgren, chief of Oklahoma City's U. S. Weather Bureau, left to take up a similar post in St. Louis. Oklahoma's A & M College at Stillwater was allocated $16.000 to buy additional dairy farm land. At Miami, cops braved exploding ammunition inside a blazing car to save three of the car's tires. Tulsa beer dealers fought a new law banning dancing in beer taverns. Out-of-state absences caused Oklahoma to have four different occupants of the governor's chair within a week—Gov. Kerr; Robert N. Berry, lieutenant governor; Tom Anglin, president *pro tem.* of the Senate, and Harold Freeman, speaker of the House.

PENNSYLVANIA

Katherine, Rita and Anna Mae Noonan of Drexel Hill married, respectively, a soldier, sailor and marine. Burglars finally gave up an attempt to remove a 1,000-pound safe from the garage of D. Jacoby and Sons at Allentown. Three schools in Duryea were quickly emptied when mine workings beneath the surface settled. The Philadelphia Transportation Co. was training women motormen. At Pittsburgh, Dr. Franz Fielder, German-born chemist, got a 10-year sentence for sedition, charged with attempting to impair the morale of servicemen by letters he wrote them. Cpl. Joseph Selenack of Fort Knox, Ky., was killed when he drove his tank off the road near Philadelphia to avoid collision with a school bus. The Lebanon County Twilight League was reorganized with five teams.

RHODE ISLAND

The Cornell-Dubilier Electric Corp. of Providence sought to reduce absenteeism by raffling two $25 War Bonds a week. Barrington dedicated a servicemen's honor roll. The Catholic clergy and laity of Pawtuxet Valley honored the Rev. Zephyrin Peloquin, pastor of St. Joseph's Church, Natick, on the 50th anniversary of his ordination. Forty-one business and professional men joined the Providence Police Mobile Radio Patrol. Newman Church at Rumford, the oldest Congregational Church in the state, celebrated its 300th anniversary. County Agent Abbey warned Newport County farmers to guard against cattle and poultry rustling.

SOUTH CAROLINA

Judge Mann canceled a court term in Calhoun County to avoid interference with farm work. Claud E. Tate of Columbia was elected president of the South Carolina Junior Chamber of Commerce. A reward was offered for the capture of Fred W. Poole, accused of the fatal shooting of John Kelly at Kelly's home near Columbia. The Rev. Harold W. Seever, pastor of Bainbridge Street Baptist Church, Richmond, Va., was named pastor of the First Baptist Church at Florence. Jake S. Colvin became treasurer of Chester County as successor to Isaac Cross, found dead in his car, apparently the victim of an accidental shooting.

TENNESSEE

At Union City, Bill Deering, 21, and Harry Kennon, 51, each got 99 years in the murder of former Sheriff J. R. McCain, whom Kennon had blamed for burning Kennon's roadhouse. Nashville's Mayor Cummings was re-elected and his supporters won four of seven Council seats in the run-off election. At Memphis, the First and Union Avenue Baptist Church congregations voted against merging. Chattanooga's first lion cub was born in the Warner Park zoo. Bus and streetcar riding in Memphis was double what it was a year ago. At Jackson, 30 law-enforcement officers attended a conference sponsored by the FBI.

TEXAS

A 5-year 125-million-dollar post-war highway program was being considered in Houston for 10 southeast Texas counties. Fingerprints taken when he applied for work in an Orange shipyard resulted in the capture of Wilbert Hard, who escaped prison 27 years ago at Joliet, Ill. Before adjourning, the Legislature refused to increase taxes and lowered appropriations. Mrs. Nora L. St. John, 29, of Houston, whose son is an 18-year-old private in the Army, is believed to be the youngest service mother in the nation.

UTAH

The Legislature reduced residence requirements for divorce from one year to three months. Farmers reported an ample labor supply, but sheep men said that flock masters were having difficulty getting shearers. Construction started on a 341-unit, 2-million-dollar privately financed housing project at Provo. Ira Stormes, sole surviving GAR member in Utah, held his annual one-man encampment and re-elected himself commander. Much of the movie "Buffalo Bill" will be filmed in southern Utah. Granite High, Salt Lake City, won the state high-school track meet at BYU, with Ogden second. Died at Salt Lake City: Sylvester Q. Cannon, 77, president of the Deseret Publishing Co. and member of the LDS Church Council of Twelve Apostles.

VIRGINIA

A murder warrant was issued against T. W. Clatterbuck, Hillsboro businessman, who police said had confessed the murder of A. Morris Love, Love's wife and son and two other persons at the Love farmhouse near Leesburg. The U. S. paid $47,000 for 960 acres in Campbell and Charlotte Counties for a national shrine to Patrick Henry. Richmond's first American Legion unit composed exclusively of veterans of this war was formed by 90 honorably discharged servicemen. Dr. James W. Tipton, Danville physician, was fined $20,000 for income-tax evasion. The state announced plans to complete the Blue Ridge Parkway after the war.

WASHINGTON

Seattle's Mayor Devin ordered Police Chief Kimsey to "resign or be fired" because of alleged vice conditions; Capt. Irene Durham of the women's division was appointed head of the vice squad. Yakima County again headed the apple-producing counties of the U. S. More than 100 pupils and teachers from McLane School near Olympia were victims of food poisoning at a picnic celebrating the end of the school year. A guernsey cow gave birth to quadruplets on Emil Dolter's farm near Burlington. Ronald Paranto, Tacoma shipyard worker, his wife and two young daughters perished when their house burned near Yelm. Agricultural Agent Johnston was seeking city dwellers to work King County farms.

WISCONSIN

F. Robert Buechner, dismissed as Superior's city manager last fall, was rehired by the new City Council. Crawford County's sheriff, Mrs. Helen Day, started cleaning out slot machines around Prairie du Chien. Crop prospects were good but corn will be late. The Polish National Alliance Home in Milwaukee was dedicated. Brookfield taverns were ordered to close at 2 A. M. Mrs. Glenn Frank, widow of the former U W president, gave his library of 5,000 volumes to the State Teachers College at Kirksville, Mo. Died at Oconomowoc: Col. Gustave Pabst, former president of the Pabst Brewing Company, at 76.

New York City's Fifth Avenue looked like that lonesome road after gas cuts drove off busses temporarily.

POST XCHANGE

This Post Exchange, like YANK itself, is wide open to you. Send your cartoons, poems and stories to: The Post Exchange, YANK, The Army Weekly, 205 East 42d Street, New York 17, N. Y.

If your contribution misses the mark, you will receive YANK's special de luxe rejection slip, that will inspire a more creative mood.

The Bathrobe Blues

THE last thing I remember is that Judo class. . . .
The hospital isn't bad. It's just different from what I'd been led to expect after all those Dr. Kildare movies. It isn't the doctors who ride in the wheel chairs at all. In this hospital the patients do it. And all those other things they had in the movies—Laraine Days and sleepless nights, glittering instruments, Technicolor and the romance of the language of medicine ("Don't touch me, nurse, I'm sterile")—none of them is here.

The only vestige of glamor is to be found in the charm of the nurse, a Miss Tangerine Sandbag from Portland, Cement. After a day in bed I was sort of bored. In fact I was so bored *rigor mortis* was setting it; then I saw Miss Sandbag. She had just been sent to our ward from her regular job of retouching X-rays of second lieutenants. Miss Sandbag has big blue eyes, swaying hips and, as they say medically, is quite a dish.

I looked at Miss Sandbag and I could feel my temperature rising. "101," cried the doctor. "102," shouted a ward boy. "103," screamed a warrant officer (junior grade) who happened to be passing. "When it reaches 104," I said, "sell."

"Aha," said the doctor, "a bedpan comedian."

I never imagined I'd spend any time thinking of how nice it would be to kiss a second lieutenant, but here I was, troubled over Miss Sandbag. I got nowhere. She pulled her rank on me

A PAGE FROM A SOLDIER'S SKETCHBOOK

—Sgt. Paul Galdone, Fort Belvoir, Va.

even in my subconscious. Every time my dreams began to get interesting, someone yelled "Tenshun!" and I stood up and saluted. I consoled myself with the old axiom: " 'Tis better to have loved a nurse than never to have loved at all." I'd probably have gotten all scratched up on her bars anyway.

Still, I'm feeling low. I guess I got the bathrobe blues.

Fort Riley, Kans. —Cpl. JULIAN CLAMAN

GIG

I have a date with a pile of dirt
  On Saturday afternoon.
And I was going to see a skirt,
  But I made my plans too soon.

I had just put on my cleanest shirt
  When the sarge walked in—the goon.
I have a date with a pile of dirt,
  And so does half the platoon.

Camp Adair, Oreg. —Pvt. A. L. CROUCH

MY DOG TAG AND ME

As I lay down to sleep last night
  I heard my dog tag say:
"Don't worry, I'm your friend, my lad,
  I'm with you night and day,
And if death should ever part us,
  Don't let it make you blue,
For I'll prove that I am faithful
  By going home for you."

Now it's true my dog tag's faithful,
  And goes where'er I roam;
But I sure will do my damnedest
  To beat my dog tag home.

Camp Sibert, Ala.

"And now I never miss anything."
—A/S Stephen T. Rascoe, Oklahoma City University, Okla.

The Soft Underbelly of Santa Ana

TO the southwest of Santa Ana, Calif., is an Army air base. A Marine camp is on the northeast. Completely outnumbered and hopelessly encircled, the Santa Ana natives have decided to be sensible and take the whole thing good-naturedly.

About 5:30 every evening the marines sweep down from the north. Air Force men simultaneously press upwards along the main north-south highway.

At that hour, the marines and soldiers in town pay no attention to each other. They don't even exchange glances.

If a soldier makes a joke in a soda fountain, the marines never laugh. They pretend not to hear. When marines get loud-mouthed in barrooms, all the soldiers look the other way and smile patiently to themselves.

Lately the MPs have been patrolling the streets of Santa Ana in mixed pairs, one marine MP and one soldier MP. This is an excellent plan—everyone likes to be arrested by his own policeman—yet it may develop certain weaknesses.

But hark! There's a pair of MPs now, walking just ahead of us and twirling their night sticks.

MARINE MP: A pleasant night, but strangely, ominously quiet.

SOLDIER MP: It is indeed. Incidentally, forgive me for mentioning it, Roger, but your tie is slightly disarranged.

MARINE MP: Oh dear. Thanks awfully, old man. Don't look now, but I think there is a soldier coming who is a little out of line. I'll just look the other way while you straighten him out. [*The marine MP pretends to study a drug-store window while his companion straightens out the*

soldier. Then, as they proceed on patrol, the soldier MP straightens out his night stick.]

SOLDIER MP: I notice there are a pair of boisterous marines ahead. I'll drop out while you handle them.

MARINE MP: That's very considerate of you, Phillip. [*He talks to the two erring marines while the soldier MP looks off into space, hums a little tune or studies his fingernails.*]

SOLDIER MP [*as they resume patrol*]: My, I'm afraid there's an argument ahead involving both branches of the service. We'd better handle this together. [*Tactfully they separate the debaters, taking care that no one hits on the break and that no advantage is given either organization. By accident the soldier MP brushes against one of the marines in the general confusion.* "Take ya hands off me, ya soldier ya!" *cries the leatherneck.*]

MARINE MP [*as they continue their beat*]: I'm terribly sorry about that little incident, Phillip. That boy is just back from Guadalcanal, you know, and he's a bit jumpy. And with good cause, I think. Guadalcanal was where the Marines landed first, and then after the tough fighting was finished, the soldiers moved in.

SOLDIER MP: On the contrary, Roger, the Army was called in to mop up, which is the really tough job. Marines are all right in a flash landing, something that's over in a few hours or days. But for really rugged slugging and sustained soldiering they use the Army every time."

MARINE MP [*sharply*]: You are a liar. [*They go at it with night sticks and fists, until a bunch of marines and soldiers finally arrive to separate them.*]

—Sgt. RAY DUNCAN

Santa Ana (Calif.) Army Air Base

PUZZLE SOLUTIONS

CHECKER STRATEGY

White moves 31 to 26. Black king is forced 6 to 9 in order to protect the piece on 17. . . . White squeezes 25 to 22. Black is forced 9 to 13. . . . White moves 30 to 25. Black jumps 21 to 30, crowning. . . . White moves 20 to 16. Black king jumps 30 to 23. . . . White king jumps 19 to 26. Black takes 12 to 19. . . . White moves 3 to 8. Black jumps 4 to 11. . . . White king moves 26 to 30. Black jumps 17 to 26. . . . White king jumps 30 to 23 to 16 to 7 to 14. WHITE WINS.

TEE-TOTAL WINNERS

Winners of Puzzle Kits and their scores in the Tee-Total contest for May 14 are Pfc. D. Lesser, Camp Gordon Johnston, Fla. (442); S/Sgt. Stanley Bartram, N. Kelly Field, Tex. (440); M/Sgt. Harry Chadis, Atlantic Beach, Fla. (439); Pvt. James Wallace, Camp Blanding, Fla. (438). and Sgt. Harold Byer, Clovis (N. Mex.) AAB; Sgt. Donald Farquhar, Tonopah, Nev.; T/Sgt. Harry Stuart, Camp Crowder, Mo.; Pvt. J. G. Yomner, Camp Pinedale, Calif. (all with 437). Lesser's solution is shown at right.

Since you must have a standard in judging these puzzles, YANK has chosen "Webster's Collegiate Dictionary, Fifth Edition." Several solutions were ruled out for the use of *wack, wacky, wicky* and *wych.* Webster's doesn't list them. (Lesser's use of *wahoo* is okay; it's the name of a shrub.) *Welch* was ruled out because it is a proper noun. When in doubt about a word, check with the Collegiate. There should be one in your post library. Otherwise try another word.

SPORTS: ERIC TIPTON, DUKE'S GREAT PUNTER, MAKES THE GRADE WITH CINCINNATI

By Sgt. DAN POLIER

Eric Tipton, who was ear-marked for the majors while still an undergraduate at Duke, slides home to score against the Dodgers. Mickey Owen is the catcher and the umpire is Al Barlick.

VAN LINGLE MUNGO and Babe Barna were sunning themselves just outside the Giant dugout when Eric (The Red) Tipton, Cincinnati's new outfielder, stepped up to the plate to take his practice swings.

"You see this guy Tipton," Mungo said. "He was one of the best football players that ever lived."

"How do you know?" asked Barna.

"Because I saw him. That's how I know," Mungo said indignantly. "I saw him beat Pitt almost single-footed to give Duke the Rose Bowl bid in 1938. There was an inch of snow on the field and this guy Tipton kicked a wet ball from the 50-yard line and it went out of bounds on the one-foot line. The next time he punted, the ball went out 18 inches from the goal. Then he kicked one 75 yards and it stopped dead on the goal line!"

"Yeah, and I understand," Billy Jurges interrupted, "that he can kick a football farther than he can hit a baseball."

The truth of the matter is, Tipton can wallop one as far as he can boot the other. When he was wowing them as an undergraduate at Duke, he didn't get all of his distance on booming 80-yard punts. There was more to his power than that. Those were the days when, with the bases loaded and two out, Eric would bang mighty 400-foot home runs and bat .400 consistently every season for the championship Blue Devil baseball team.

Along with Ace Parker, who played the season before him, Eric was one of Duke's greatest athletes. As a sophomore he started coming fast and when he became a senior he had really arrived and so had the Duke football team. That was 1938, the year the Blue Dukes stormed through an undefeated, untied and unscored-on season. Tipton was the boy that made that team go.

Duke wasn't an offensive club. In fact, it had no offense. There was only one swift running back on the squad, a sophomore named George McAfee, and he was side-lined virtually all season with a foot injury. Wallace Wade was forced to play a defensive game, and it turned out to be a great offense.

Tipton and seven other Duke scholars, affectionately known around Durham as the "Seven Iron Dukes," were that "offense." Tipton could kick, tackle and bust up more passes than a blond in a rumble seat. The Iron Dukes were his 60-minute support. They were always down the field talking with the safety man when Eric's high, lazy punts bounced out on the 18-inch line. It was this combination that won the Rose Bowl bid for Duke. Tipton's magnificent kicking in a driving snowstorm kept Pittsburgh backed up so completely that they were actually calling half their signals from behind their own goal line. It was on just such a play that the Iron Dukes smashed through and blocked a punt for the only score of the game.

If Tipton ever had a bad moment for Duke, it was the time when he let Al Kruger, the Southern California end, slip behind him during the last 45 seconds of the Rose Bowl game and grab that desperate pass from Doyle Nave. It brought the roof down on Duke, 7-3. But we doubt if Wallace Wade ever really held that against Tipton. The redhead had been in the game all the way, kicking the Trojans silly, and in those fading seconds of the fourth quarter he was a weary boy standing there in the cool California twilight. Besides, Wade always did believe that Nave-to-Kruger pass was a screen play and that even Tipton couldn't watch a half dozen receivers.

When Tipton finished at Duke it was no surprise that he signed with the Philadelphia Athletics. A lot of people consider this a post-graduate course in baseball for Duke players because so many of them usually join Connie Mack. There was also strong talk of Tipton plunging into professional football with the Washington Redskins. He might have, too, if he hadn't seen what happened to his predecessor, Ace Parker. The Ace nearly killed himself trying to combine the two. He broke both his legs. Instead, Eric signed as assistant football coach at William & Mary.

The jump from the Duke campus to the Philadelphia outfield was too great for Tipton. He wasn't ready for it. Connie Mack sent him to Toronto and Eric soon found his range and became one of the International League's leading fence-busting sluggers. In fact, one day he really did bust open a fence. He was chasing a foul fly when the outfield fence loomed in his path. He kept right on going, ripped open the fence and barged back unhurt with the ball in his glove.

Cincinnati didn't find Tipton—or vice versa—until last year. Deacon Bill McKechnie, who had already blown over a half million dollars trying to fill his left-field position, was losing Mike McCormick to the Army and he was desperate. McCormick was the only man who could do the job. By this time Tipton had moved to Kansas City and made the American Association all-star team. McKechnie thought Tipton would be a natural for the job.

Eric turned out fine for Cincinnati. He's hitting a cool .300 and fielding his position nicely. McKechnie says he's here to stay. He must be. He has a head full of punctured eardrums and he's color blind—a perfect 4-F.

Maybe it was because his own team lost, but a sailor at the Norfolk Naval Training Station wrote **Arthur Siegel** of the *Boston Traveler* that he wasn't impressed with the major leaguers now playing at his station. The sailor had just watched the North Carolina Pre-Flight School beat the Norfolk station when he wrote this critical review: "Dom DiMaggio is far below par. **Phil Rizzuto** is marvelous and **Benny McCoy** does okay. **Don Padgett** is awfully slow, while **Tom Early** and **Charlie Wagner** do all right. **Pee Wee Reese** of the air station hit into three double plays and I haven't seen him get a hit yet. **Johnny Pesky** of the Pre-Flight School was sleeping. He overran the bag twice and made four errors."

The Army had a look at **Wendell Eads**, the jockey, and said he is not tall and heavy enough to make a soldier. Eads, who once rode Whirlaway, is only 4 feet 10 inches and weighs 106 pounds. . . . Corporal chevrons for lightweight boxer **Ray Robinson** at Mitchel Field, N.Y., and Giant outfielder **Willard Marshall** at the Marine Corps Quartermaster Division in Washington. . . . **Art Pasarella**, the recently inducted American League umpire, divides his time at Camp Grant, Ill., between umpiring ball games and leading the camp band. . . . **Buzz Borries**, Navy's great running back, downed two Jap Zeros during his first five minutes of flying in the South Pacific. The Army is beckoning **Vernon Stephens**, the

SPORTS SERVICE RECORD

After spending a year in the infantry getting his weight down, All-American John Kimbrough (left) begins his basic flight training at Pecos, Tex. Here he is with instructor William Kemerling.

Browns' star shortstop; **Tom Lanning**, Pittsburgh pitcher, and **Dick Wakefield**, Detroit's $52,000 outfielder. Lanning tried to enlist in the Navy a few months ago and was rejected because of hay fever. Wakefield, who is only 22 years old, had been in 3-A because his two brothers were in the Army and he was supporting his mother. . . . There's no chance of **Lew Jenkins** testifying in the Dempsey divorce action. He went over the hill at the Norfolk Coast Guard Station and was assigned to a transport for punishment. . . . **Fred Frankhouse**, who threw a jug-handle curve for the Dodgers, Cards and Braves, has turned up as a shavetail at Fort Hamilton, N.Y.

The Army is standing pat on its policy not to allow its soldier-students to compete in intercollegiate sports. Three former football players now in Congress—Representatives **Mike Monroney**, **La Vern R. Dilweg** and **Samuel Weiss**—had demanded a revocation of the Army ban, pointing out that the Navy permits its trainees to participate if it does not interfere with their training. . . . The scores from that GI basketball tournament in the African desert sound more like baseball returns. One game actually ended 5-4, while the highest score of the tournament was 29 points. The boys blame the freak scores on the ball they were using. Regulation basketballs were not available, so they substituted the smaller, lighter English soccer ball.

"IF WE WENT TO OCS WE COULD GET INSIDE AND PLAY THE SLOT MACHINE."
—Sgt. Irwin Caplan, Fort Knox, Ky.

YANK

"I'M THE NEW TAIL GUNNER, SIR."
—Pfc. Joseph Kramer, Truax Field, Wis.

". . . KEEPING ALWAYS ON THE ALERT AND OBSERVING EVERYTHING THAT TAKES PLACE WITHIN SIGHT OR HEARING."
—Cpl. Ned Hilton, WBGH, El Paso, Tex.

"HEY! ANY YOU GUYS GOT A GOOD RECIPE FOR SPAGHETTI SAUCE?"
—Sgt. Frank Brandt

"WHY CAN'T YOU THINK OF SOMETHING CLEVER TO SAY BACK TO YANK?"
—Pfc. Tom Zibelli, Camp Davis, N.C.

"HE'S BEEN WITH US EVER SINCE WE LEFT ENGLAND."
—Sgt. Sydney Landi, AAC, Richmond, Va.

YANK

THE ARMY WEEKLY

5¢ SEPT. 24 1943
VOL. 2, NO. 14

By the men .. for the men in the service

The Eighth Air Force: Its War Over Europe

PAGE 3

FLYING FORTRESS DRONES OVER THE TARGET, A SYNTHETIC RUBBER PLANT AT HULS, GERMANY

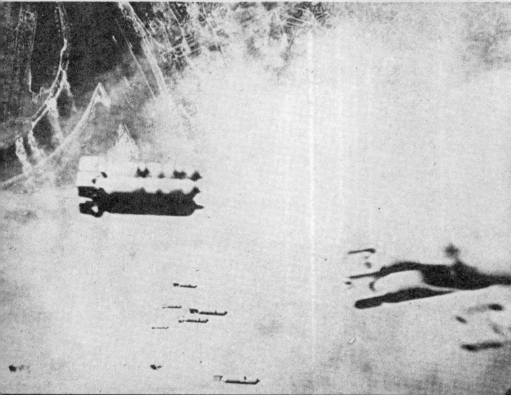

LUSTERS OF INCENDIARY BOMBS SPILL OUT ON THE PORT OF HAMBURG, NOW VIRTUALLY DESTROYED.

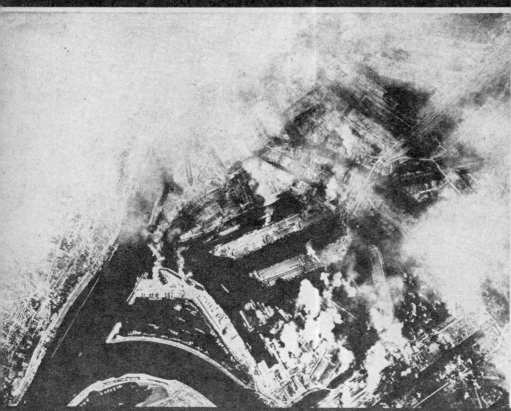

E TARGET, HAMBURG, SMOKES AFTER PLANES OF THE EIGHTH AIR FORCE GIVE IT A POUNDING

Showing the skeptics that Europe can be bombed in daylight with no fighter protection, our flyers in Britain have made a big contribution to the war.

By Sgt. JACK SCOTT
YANK Staff Correspondent

BRITAIN [By Cable]—Along the flat outline of the sky, a wedge of geese appeared, and the Welsh farmer took off his old hat and flapped it toward the sky. The geese were Flying Fortresses. The farmer knew they couldn't see him, for at that altitude the ground was only a crazy quilt far below, yet he always waved at the big American bombers. It was a gallant gesture to a gallant bunch.

The planes passing over his farm were returning to their home base after a raid on Germany that was more than an attack on the enemy; it was a celebration. This was the anniversary of the Eighth Air Force's first year in the European Theater of Operations.

Just 12 months before, Brig. Gen. Ira C. Eaker then chief of the Bomber Command of the Eighth Air Force, led the first All-American heavy

FORMATIONS OF B-17S (FLYING FORTRESSES) WINGING OVER A LAND OF

8th air force

bomber raid against Rouen in occupied France. Today he is a major general and has succeeded Lt. Gen. Carl Spaatz, now in North Africa, as commander of the whole Eighth Air Force.

In the first year of operations, the Americans have convinced the British Air Ministry that our bombers can safely and effectively fly by day, while the British raid by night. This new round-the-clock tempo has been stepped up until now scarcely a day passes without the sullen sound of motors droning over the Channel. The big formations of Flying Fortresses have become as common a "skymark" as the British barrage balloons. That tempo was not reached easily or without cost. Many men who carried the big bombs to Germany and occupied Europe have not returned.

The Eighth Air Force's first big test came on Nov. 9, 1942, when the Fortresses were joined by Liberators in a formation 100 bombers strong, which attacked the enemy locomotive works at Lille in France. That raid provided some of the answers to a couple of important questions:

Could the Fortresses operate as fighter-bombers without any fighter escort? Could they hold their own against the armament of the *Luftwaffe's* speedy fighters? They could and did, but it was a job.

In 82 missions completed in the first year of operations, 419 American bombers have failed to return, well under the 5 percent that is considered a safe margin of loss. On the other side of the ledger are the 1,728 enemy fighters definitely destroyed, 671 probably destroyed and 872 damaged. A total of 15,722 tons of bombs has been dropped on 53 different cities in France, Holland, Belgium, Germany and Norway with proven accuracy.

This arithmetic makes sense. The Eighth Air Force has demonstrated that its formations can penetrate

Sgt. Maynard H. (Snuffy) Smith of Cairo, Ill., Flying Fortress gunner, who was awarded the Congressional Medal of Honor by Secretary of War Stimson for saving his ship and crewmates.

Y'RE ON THEIR WAY TO BOMB WILHELMSHAVEN AND KIEL—AND INCIDENTALLY, TO DOWN ENEMY FIGHTERS

Germany by day, that its combat crews can destroy their objectives by an accurate concentration of bombs from a high altitude and that they can defend themselves against fighter opposition.

When the Forts began to claim enormous bags of enemy fighters on every mission, the British were inclined to doubt the figures, dividing them by three, since their system was to credit a gunner with a definite "kill" only when three men actually saw an enemy plane destroyed or shot down. It didn't seem logical that Fortresses, which were primarily bombers, would be so successful as fighters, too. But today the British confirm the American figures.

In the year of operations there have been many developments in the Flying Fortresses. The original B-17C, a seven-gun model, has been withdrawn from operations over the continent. The Royal Air Force tested the ship over Brest, France, and in the running battle when the German pocket battleships *Scharnhorst* and *Gneisenau* escaped up the English Channel, the B-17C's lack of success was largely the fault of its armament: all seven guns were .30-caliber and there was no tail gun at all. Later the RAF used this model on Norwegian raids and then transferred it to the Coastal Command, where speed and heavy armament are not all-essential.

The lessons learned with the B-17C were used to developed the B-17E and later the B-17F, both wonderful ships with tremendous fire power and absolutely no blind spots. Many changes were included in these models—power turrets have been added, there are 13 guns instead of seven, and the engine and design have been modified.

Among other possible changes is the discarding of all paint on the big bombers. Without paint, the speed of a ship would be increased perhaps 10 to 15 miles an hour, and the bomber's glitter in the sun would make it a difficult target for Jerry fighters.

THE name "Fort" has taken on a special significance, and any great plane with a white star and four motors is immediately called a Flying Fortress—by everyone except the boys who fly them. But our Eighth Air Force is not made up entirely of Fortresses. On almost every raid there have been Liberators (Consolidated B-24s) and Marauders (Martin B-26s).

At first the Eighth Air Force did not know exactly how to use the Marauder, nicknamed the "Flying Prostitute" because, with its short stubby wings, it has no visible means of support. The two-motored, heavily armed bomber was tried out in low-level attacks, but great losses in aircraft and crews proved that this was an error. Now the Flying Prostitute is used at a little higher level and with a new technique. She has lived through her experimental phase

and is going places, four or five times a week.

So are the men of the Eighth. Many of them have set new marks of courage. The story of S/Sgt. Maynard (Snuffy) Smith of Caro, Mich., the little ball turret gunner who was yanked off KP here to receive the Congressional Medal of Honor from Secretary of War Stimson, was one of the most colorful episodes of the war. Snuffy doesn't look like a hero but he behaved like one on his first raid last May.

Snuffy's Fortress was heading out to sea after an attack on the U-boat base of Saint Nazaire, France, when it was engaged by a great number of Focke-Wulfs. There was an explosion inside the plane, and soon the radio control room and the tail section were blazing wildly. Snuffy wrapped his hand in a sweater, seized a fire extinguisher and dove into the flames.

He gave first aid to the wounded tail gunner, helped the left waist gunner to bail out and took time off to man the right and left waist guns against attacks by a swarm of Focke-Wulfs. When all the fire-extinguisher fluid was exhausted, Snuffy urinated on the fire and beat out the flames with his feet.

The crew members of *Old Bill*, the Fortress piloted by Capt. William D. Whitson of Denton, Tex., are among the most decorated bunch of flyers in the Air Forces. They have won eight Silver Stars, two DSCs and seven Purple Hearts. The crew of *Shoot Luke*, a Liberator, has earned four Silver Stars, five DFCs, three DSCs, seven Purple Hearts and a pile of Air Medals.

Sam Junkin of Natchez, Miss., who served with the RAF and later became the first member of the Eighth Air Force to shoot down a Nazi plane, is another who has distinguished himself. But not all have come out as lucky as Snuffy, Sam and the crews of *Old Bill* and *Shoot Luke.*

There were the Mathis brothers of San Angelo, Tex. Jack was killed while he was kneeling over the bombsight in the lead ship of a formation attacking shipyards at Vegesack, Germany. He died before his bombs hit the ground. Mark Mathis, avenging Jack's death, took part in three raids against the enemy as bombardier on the same ship. He was reported missing after an attack on Kiel, his fourth mission.

Members of the ground crews, most of whose work goes unsung, have also won distinction. Pvt. Adam E. Gross of Chicago, Ill., was the first to volunteer to carry away a number of delayed-action bombs, dropped by the *Luftwaffe* on an American airfield in Britain. Pfc. Carmen D' Amanti rushed into a burning bomber on another field and pulled out a number of unconscious men, ignoring the danger of a probable gasoline explosion.

Facing death almost every day, as many of the Eighth Air Force do, they have become quite

religious. Many who hadn't been to church since their early teens now attend regularly. Others have acquired a sense of humor that seems typical of men in dangerous undertakings. They will joke about everything and everybody. Many a Fortress has gone out of its way to help out a sister ship, but when the men return, they kid each other. "We only wanted to save your bunch till pay day. You guys owe us too much money."

Not all the power of the Eighth Air Force comes from bombers. The P-47 Thunderbolts are supplementing the British Spitfires as fighter escorts, meeting the Fortresses somewhere over the Channel and accompanying them across and back. They are not, of course, able to follow the bombers on the deeper raids.

WHEN the first Thunderbolts arrived in this theater, they bore tags on their instrument panels reading, "Please do not fly this ship faster than 427 miles an hour." That was no idle boast; the ships were that fast and faster, though just how fast nobody seems to know, or at any rate nobody is saying.

Many of the P-47 boys in the Eighth Air Force are veterans of the early campaigns in the Pacific, and they would rather fight the Japs, but to a man they call this the hottest aerial theater in the world. "You go out and you get it or you don't" is the motto by which they live. They go out and they do come back. We have lost some P-47s, but the number is minor, and that record is to the credit not only of superior ships but of superior pilots.

Our pilots took the Thunderbolt when it was full of bugs, and they killed those bugs. They killed a few of themselves, too, but they developed the P-47 into one of the finest fighters of them all. In the comparatively short time it has been in action, the Thunderbolt has become a legend, and so have its pilots.

From the British, who have been fighting an air war for four years, has come recognition of the achievements of the Eighth Air Force. Compared with our British allies, we are still recruits in this business of bombing Europe but we are learning and learning the hard way.

The Eighth Air Force was too busy fighting to bother about celebrating its first anniversary with a party. The flyers didn't tell the pretty English girls what wonderful guys they were; they didn't go out and quaff a lot of brew. They took a ride across to Germany and bombed hell out of several important targets. They destroyed more than 40 German fighter planes, and when they came down from upstairs, from the fatiguing 20,000-foot altitude and the 40-below-zero cold, they ate a hearty meal and went to bed. They were tired, and they celebrated by resting up for tomorrow's raid.

The darkness of pre-dawn was lit up by smoke and flame when ships of the U. S. Navy shelled the airfield on the Jap-held base of Munda, New Georgia, later occupied by the Americans.

These pigtailed French Moroccan boys don't particularly care for C rations because they would rather use their bayonets to open Germans and Italians. Tin cans make the blades dull.

By Sgt. RALPH G. MARTIN
YANK Field Correspondent

WITH U. S. FORCES IN NORTHEASTERN SICILY [By Cable] — "Those Goums don't fight fair," an English-speaking German prisoner complained. "They're crazy."

Be that as it may, these French Moroccan native troops took hill after hill here in Sicily, bringing back hundreds of German prisoners and leaving behind many more Jerries quite dead.

All the Goums have an intimate knowledge of French light machine guns, the American tommy gun and the 81-mm mortar. But give them a bayonet and a bunch of grenades, and they'll charge any position anywhere.

They were the first to see action in this northeastern pocket of hills, on the flank of U. S. troops. Their objectives were twin hills, held by two companies of well-entrenched Germans, just outside Mistretta.

The Goums took up their positions in the night, climbed the hill as quietly as mountain goats, heaved several dozen well-aimed grenades and made a "cold steel" attack. When the Moroccans were within 50 yards of the top, the Jerries opened up with machine guns. Instead of falling flat on their faces and hunting for cover, the Goums rushed straight in for hand-to-hand fighting. They drew their 10-inch knives, known as *koumias*, which are used to cut off heads. Once this was a popular weapon with the Goum; now he only uses it when he gets very, very mad. That sometimes happens, as it did on this night, and that is why these big black boys rank so high on the Nazi list of "people we wouldn't want to be with on a desert island."

The Germans definitely don't like the Goums. As for the Italians, they're scared to death of them. In the Mateur and Bizerte sectors, where the Goums were attached to the Ninth Division, three Italian companies surrendered en masse as soon as they heard that the guys in front of them were Goums.

Unlike the Gurkhas, British Indian native troops who look like a bunch of kids but aren't, the Goums look and act as tough as they really are. And they really are tough. Back in 1912, when French troops came to Morocco and overwhelmed the place, the Goums still had very primitive ideas about fighting, torturing and killing. They were just as ready to cut off somebody's head as to tell him "Good morning."

After the French took over and tamed the

NAZIS DON'T LIKE
GOUMS

Goums a little, these native soldiers were absorbed into the French fighting forces but kept as separate units. They were organized into *tabors*, which are the approximate equivalent of our battalions, consisting of four companies with 200 Goums to a company.

Most of these native soldiers have crinkly hair, close-cropped except for a plaited pigtail. The pigtail is worn, the Goums say, so that the Lord

will have something to grab hold of when He yanks them up to paradise.

The Goums, who follow the religion of Mohammed, are of Berber origin. The Berbers, not the Arabs, were the original natives of North Africa. Practically all of the Goums wear beards, because they believe that a man who hasn't seen action and has no beard is no man at all.

That was the explanation offered by 1st Lt.

Bistos Hubert, the Goums' commanding officer. Hubert has been with the Goums for three years. Before that, he served with the Spahis, the French North African native cavalrymen with the red caps and the Technicolor-conscious uniforms.

"These Goums are the best fighters I've seen anywhere," the lieutenant said. "They just don't know when to quit." Besides the commanding officer, each Goum company has one other French officer and 10 French noncoms. In addition, the Goums have their own native sergeants.

They all eat the same food now—C rations— which they don't particularly like. The Goums would prefer a steady diet of bread and green tea, the national dish.

Attached to every *tabor* of Goums is a cavalry unit, in which each man owns his own horse. This unit is employed strictly for reconnaissance, since all Goums fight on foot. Several scores of mules are also attached to each section, to carry ammunition over terrain where even jeeps can't go.

The Goums, though, are crazy about jeeps. It is a terribly funny picture to see one of the Goums, wearing his wool-sack uniform, tearing along in a jeep with his pigtail streaming in the wind.

YANK, The Army Weekly, publication issued weekly by Headquarters Branch, Special Service, ASF, War Department, 205 East 42d Street, New York 17, N. Y. Reproduction rights restricted as indicated in the masthead on the editorial page. Entered as second class matter July 6, 1942, at the Post Office at New York, N. Y., under the Act of March 3, 1879. Subscription price $3.00 yearly. Printed in the U. S. A.

Dressed in camouflaged suits, Marines pay tribute to comrades lost in action at Viru Harbor, New Georgia.

The Sergeant and His Adam's Apple Start a Sensation in China

By Sgt. MARION HARGROVE
YANK Staff Correspondent

SOMEWHERE IN CHINA—Their post is hundreds of miles off any beaten track, and they don't see even an American plane more than once a month or so. There's only a handful of them, with three or four officers. Neither the town nor the hostel offers anything in the way of amusement. There's no radio, no newspapers, not even an occasional GI movie.

"What do you do for entertainment around here, besides wearing out that checkerboard over there?" I asked.

A corporal replied: "We get along. We go shopping in the evenings."

"And we 'make face' with the Chinese," said a sergeant.

This sounding intriguing in a dull sort of way, and since the corporal intended to go to town that night in search of a package of envelopes he had no hope of finding, I decided to tag along.

We passed a couple of Chinese theaters and stopped to see what pictures were showing. There was a double feature at one house—an ancient film starring Jessie Matthews, the British actress, and "The Return of the Cisko Kid." All three of us had seen both of them in better days. The other theater advertised a gripping Chinese drama with some appetizing stills.

"We might see the Jessie Matthews picture and the 'Cisko Kid'," I suggested, but the corporal and sergeant both turned thumbs down. "You wouldn't hear the thing," they explained. "The pictures probably have Chinese subtitles, and when you get a whole house full of the towns-people reading the subtitles aloud to each other, you wouldn't be able to hear even the fire siren."

The only thing left was to go in search of the nonexistent envelopes and attend to the little matter of "face making."

The corporal explained that his command of the Mandarin language was extensive, so he did all the talking. At the first shop we entered there were a number of Chinese envelopes, the kind with the bright red rectangle for the address. After the usual greeting—*"Hao pu hao,"* which literally means "good not good" and passes for "How are you?"—the corporal started his palaver by pointing to the envelopes.

"En lai kan kan," he said. This is very good Mandarin and means "Pick up bring see see." The shopkeeper picked up brought see see. The corporal looked sadly at the envelopes and shook his head. *"Ni yu mei yu mel-kua—?"* he said. This was all right as far as it went; it meant "Haven't you got any American—?" but he got stuck when he came to the word for envelopes.

"That," said the corporal, "is a helluva note." While all this was going on, accompanied by

urgent gestures by the corporal, the sergeant was busy outside "making face" with the Chinese. By this time there were about 50 village children staring and giggling at him.

"Ni kan ni kan," said the sergeant, expressing in beautiful Mandarin the command, "You see, you see." The sergeant pointed to his throat, from which protruded a large but decorous Adam's apple. The children gawked attentively and the sergeant swallowed hard, with a loud and musical gulp. His Adam's apple slid gracefully down his throat and rose majestically again, to await a repeat performance.

The children gasped and burst into roars of wonderment and joy. The performing larynx moved beautifully up and down, making a tuneful gulp with each downward glide, and the children grew tense with excitement. Several of them tried to do the trick themselves but, not having Adam's apples, were unsuccessful.

Now the corporal emerged from the shop, looked with solemn severity over the crowd, and began to wave his finger at child after child as he chanted the mystic phrase: "Meeny, meeny, tipsy teeny." Then, with great dignity, "Apple-jack and Johnny Sweeney. Have a peach, have a plum, have a stick of chewing gum!" The corporal's finger flew at a frightened little Chinese face and the other children shrieked with relief and enjoyment. The corporal swung toward them once more. "O-U-T spells out and out you go, you dirty old dishrag, you!"

The sergeant opened his umbrella and pushed it gently through the crowd, which now numbered at least 150 children and a few scattered adults. We headed down the street and the crowd fell in behind us like a parade. The sergeant began to swing the umbrella the way a drum major twirls his baton, to the immense delight of the children, their parents and a couple of white foreigners who applauded loudly. Away we went.

At the next shop, the sergeant inquired for envelopes, while the corporal "made face" with the townspeople. This time he changed his routine by hotly winking one eye, which is apparently impossible for the Chinese to do, and by wiggling his eyebrows rather furiously.

The crowd had swelled to 225 as we headed for the river. They left us at the bridge, and we entered a tea boat for refreshments. "I've heard a lot about 'making face'," I said over our third cup of tea. "Is that what it is?"

"That's all there is to it," said the corporal. This was a crock of extremely erroneous information.

"You know," said the sergeant, "I've been out here only three months, but they say after you've been here a year or so, you start turning a little whacky." The corporal answered, "That's all imagination. Like as not, China won't have any effect one way or another on either of us."

"No," I said rather weakly, "not a chance." I got the hell out of there the next day.

GI Radioman Pulls a Jap's Leg, Or Maybe the Colonel Is Pulling Ours

SOMEWHERE IN ALASKA—An Army colonel here credits a Yank radio operator with pulling the leg of the Japanese on Kiska, several months before the evacuation of that Aleutian base.

This radio operator, the colonel says, knew the Japanese language, and he practiced for months to imitate the sending peculiarities of a Domei (Tokyo news agency) operator who relayed daily news to the Nip garrison on Kiska.

One evening, as the Domei sender was almost through tapping out the good news from Tokyo, the American radio operator jammed the program so that Kiska did not hear Tokyo sign off. Then, imitating the Tokyo style of sending, the American continued:

"Domei News deeply regrets that Admiral Yamamoto is discredited in imperial circles because he has lost so many valuable ships. The defeat of our naval forces at Coral Sea, Midway and in the Solomons has saddened the imperial household."

The Kiska operator, in precise Morse, acknowledged: "Thank you, Domei, for the excellent news. This is Radio Kiska signing off. Good night."

At least, that's the colonel's story, and he's sticking to it.
                                                    —*Coast Guard Lookout*

FANCY MAIL FROM A SOUTH PACIFIC APO

The postman at Cadieux Road in Detroit wishes he had a few more customers like Mrs. Frank L. Mack. Every letter she gets from her husband wears a brightly colored cartoon on the envelope. He started these mail murals when he was training with the AAF in California and now he's still going strong at a bomber base in the South Pacific.

Those MPs in the Persian Gulf Are Remarkable Guys, Yea Verily

PERSIAN GULF SERVICE COMMAND—It happened in Iran. It actually happened. I seen it.

It was about 8 o'clock in the evening. The streets were crowded with sauntering uniforms, Iranian, British, Russian and American, and street urchins were shouting "Buckshee, Johnny" and "Dailinoose" and "Moscowski Telegramma."

A sergeant, weary and with a three-day beard, shuffled out of a restaurant. He had on a soiled field jacket and a knitted cap. The MP passing by wheeled around and gave him a sharp look.

"Excuse me, sergeant," the MP said, "but we wish you wouldn't wear a field jacket in town in the evening."

The sergeant started to mumble a surly response.

"Now don't apologize," the MP said.

"Ah-ah," thought the sergeant, "here it comes."

"I know just how it is," the MP continued. "Hurried you were and tired. no doubt. Just try to look out for it in the future. won't you? You see, officers notice it and they come to us. Be surprised how much of a bother some of those officers are. Just try to remember the blouse for town after this. will you, sergeant? Good night." And the MP walked off.

The sergeant stood for a minute shaking the cobwebs out of his head. When he got under way again, he was talking to himself in a low amazed voice. The only phrase you could hear was: "Just for that, I think I will wear a blouse next bender!"

—Sgt. AL HINE
YANK Staff Correspondent

In Next Week's YANK . . .

FIJI COMMANDOS

These South Sea native guerrilla troops, who operate under New Zealand officers and noncoms, proved at Guadalcanal that they are probably the best jungle fighters battling the Japanese on the South Pacific front.

Here Is One Place a Private Can Tell a Major Where To Get Off

PEARL HARBOR, HAWAII—Eight Marine Corps privates are teaching combat tactics to members of the U. S. Army's Ranger Battalion, with majors and captains among their pupils at Schofield Barracks.

All graduates of the Marine Corps' own school of combat conditioning at Camp Pendleton, Calif., the marines give classes in the bayonet. combat swimming, the knife, stick fighting and the Reising gun, a weapon new to the Rangers.

The marine instructors are Pvts. June Coghlan of Bogue Chitto, Miss.; Leon Wier of Memphis, Tenn.; Warren Harris of Missoula, Mont.; James Carlos of Mount Clemens, Mich.; Byron Henry of Winamac, Ind.; Michael Geraghty of St. Paul, Minn.; Duke Drakulich of Kimberly. Nev.. and Louis Nagy of Detroit, Mich.

Commissioned officers studying at the Ranger School wear no insignia of rank during the course, so the marine privates can boss them around without fear of consequences.

—Sgt. GENE WARD
Marine Corps Correspondent

The New

Some are scattered with the Allies all over the world but most of them wait with the Princess Irene Brigade in England for the day they'll smash toward home.

By Pvt. ALBERT ORBAAN

A former correspondent for Aneta, the Dutch news agency, and the Netherlands Information Bureau, now training with the Corps of Engineers at Camp Breckinridge, Ky.

TEN miles from home, with a pocketful of nickels and a pay phone right across the street. That's the sweet spot a Dutch Commando named Jans found himself in recently during an across-the-channel raid against the Nazis who have overrun his native land—only they weren't nickels but coins called *dubbeltjen*.

Jans is neither dumb nor timid. He had shot up his share of German installations for the day and he figured that he had a few minutes to spare before catching the raiding party's boat back to England, so he hopped over to the phone and tried to dial his folks' number.

But no go. During Jans' absence from home, the Nazis had confiscated all Dutch coins, substituted German ones of different size and changed all pay-phone slots accordingly. Jans' *dubbeltjen* wouldn't fit and his fondness for Adolf Hitler hit an all-time low.

Which is pretty damn low. There's probably no better bunch of Hitler haters in the world than Jans and the thousands of boys who serve with him in the Princess Irene Brigade, more often known as the Netherlands Brigade or just the Dutch Brigade, which is now in training in its own camp in the Midlands of England. They'll never forget the reckless way in which Hitler sacked their country three years ago last May. With these Dutch soldiers, who have pitched into the fight at the call to arms of their Queen Wilhelmina, it's a grim case of so near and yet

so far. For they are nearer their homes now than a lot of GIs are when they're still at the induction center in the U. S., and yet they haven't a hope of seeing Mom and Pop or the girl friend again until the Nazis are driven back over the boundaries of Germany itself.

The Dutch Brigade is probably an even more cosmopolitan outfit than that famous old catchall of fighting men, the French Foreign Legion. The Dutch have always been a people whose business interests took them abroad in large numbers, but now that their country is in a jam, thousands of them have come back home—or as near home as they can. get at the moment—to join the fight. At least 25 languages are spoken in the brigade's camp, where the men have rigged up a Dutch windmill to remind them of their homeland. Some of the men who before the war lived in Holland had to travel the farthest to report for duty. Unable to escape across the English Channel, they fled to Finland, and went on from there across Russia, the Pacific, the U. S. and the Atlantic to reach England.

Officially named after Princess Irene, a granddaughter of Queen Wilhelmina, the brigade is now the biggest Dutch Army contingent in the world and its men, operating as a distinct Dutch Army within the framework of combined forces, fully expect to form one of the many spearheads which will be necessary for the successful in-

Becoming skilled in the art of camouflage during maneuvers staged by the Dutch Brigade in Britain.

These are "Flying Dutchmen" somewhere over Australia. They've been helping plenty in the war against the Japs.

Dutch Soldier

vasion of the continent. They have yet to see action as a group, but plenty of them, like that fellow Jans, have carried out Commando raids against the *rotmoffen*, or rotten Huns, as they call the Nazis.

The outfit was organized after Germany invaded Holland, when the Dutch began calling up men of military age from all parts of the world. (At present Dutchmen born between the years

Allies: In Australia a Dutch flyer points to his mute mascot, the famous American cartoon figure Popeye.

of 1903 and 1925 are liable for military service in the unit.) The brigade is mechanized and is well equipped with tanks, Bren gun carriers, armored cars, half-tracks, trucks and motorcycles. The equipment is supplied by the British but paid for—as Dutch soldiers are quick to point out—in full and in cash by the Netherlands Government.

The training these Dutch soldiers get is similar to that given to British troops and so are the uniforms they wear. It's not hard to distinguish members of the brigade, though. All orders are, of course, given in Dutch (*op de plaats rust*, for example, means "at ease") and each soldier wears the orange lion of the Netherlands on both shoulders and on his cap. Dutch soldiers who come from South Africa also wear a *springbok* (small deer) emblem and those from Canada a maple leaf. Men from the U. S. wear a maple leaf, too, because the basic-training camp for

them and Canadians alike is in Canada—at Guelph, Ontario. Hollanders in the U. S. may join the American armed forces if they prefer.

The Dutch soldier loves potatoes and at the brigade's camp he gets plenty of them, all the peeling being done by one of those goldbricker's gadgets which spin the spuds around until they look like cakes of soap. The chowhound's favorite dish, however, is a hot pea soup flavored with pigs' knuckles. No one gets extra KP for snafuing — not even the dumbest "turk," which is the Dutch sergeant's pet expression for an eight ball. Restricted to barracks (*patoet*) or weekend sentry duty (*wachie kloppen*) is the usual lot of the transgressor.

The boys get the usual day off every week and a two-day pass every fortnight. There's a town nearby, but most of them seem to prefer to hang around camp, which has plenty of recreation halls, a library and a stage and movie theater. There's a camp choir and an army band, which is well known all over England, and a weekly paper called *De Kampklok*, which means just what it sounds like. There are also two large canteens, one dry and the other selling beer. A Dutch soldier who samples the wares of the latter in moderation becomes *aangeschoten*, or buzzed. If he hangs around all evening he's likely to get *lazarus*, or stinko, and will be lucky if he gets off with mere *wachie kloppen* that week end.

A lot of the men put in for officers' training and those who are accepted from the infantry get the break of going to Sandhurst, which is the British equivalent of West Point. It's a pretty good break, too, as they are the first foreigners ever allowed to enter that famous institution. Officer candidates in other branches of the service are trained elsewhere in England. Dutch officers carry orange lanyards and wear the insignia of their rank on their lapels. Three stars means only a captain, so don't faint. The old man is the *hooge oome*.

In addition to the Dutch Commandos, many other members of the brigade have already seen active duty as gunners in uniform on merchant ships—risky work for which only volunteers are taken. And, of course, no account, however brief, of the Dutch as fighters would be adequate without mention of the "Flying Dutchmen," members of the Netherlands Air Force, who for well over a year now have been hammering with terribly telling results at Japs and Nazis alike.

Op de plaats rust, men.

In Canada, too, the Netherlanders train for the fight against the Axis. These men are charging directly at the camera during vigorous bayonet practice.

After watching the Dutch Army in England hold maneuvers, Ambassador Biddle enjoys refreshments with the troops. They wear British battle dress.

In Australia, 10 members of a Netherlands bomber squadron are decorated.

In England, attentive Netherlanders learn about the sub-machine gun.

Here's a Report on the Fighting Of Each U.S. Division in Sicily

The "Fightin' 1st" veterans from Tunisia distinguished themselves again while others, new to battle, took the campaign in stride.

"WHAT kind of battles did the 45th Division fight? I used to know some of those guys when we were at Pine Camp last summer."

"Before I got into this training cadre, I was with the 16th Infantry. What did they do over there against the Germans?"

These are the questions that the average soldier asks about the Sicilian campaign. We couldn't get the answers from news reports while the fighting was going on because censorship didn't allow the correspondents to name specific units engaged in most of the battles.

Everyone knows now that the American Seventh Army did our fighting in Sicily alongside the British Eighth Army. Commanded by Lt. Gen. George S. Patton Jr., it consisted of six divisions organized into two corps, one under Lt. Gen. Omar N. Bradley and the other under Maj. Gen. Geoffrey Keyes. Here is an account of what each of those six divisions did during the 39-day campaign—gathered by YANK correspondents who covered the action and from other sources. It is as complete a Who's Who of the American forces in the Sicily campaign as we can publish now. A lot of the play-by-play details are still restricted military information, of course, and will probably remain that way until the end of the war.

The map shows clearly the course of battle and the principal routes of invasion followed by each of the American divisions. There were many offshoots from the main invasion routes, as units of the divisions mopped up bypassed areas en route, but only the main invasion routes are indicated. The British and Canadian operations, also shown on the map, were in many respects more important than our own and often even merged with them, but in this summary we are concerned only with the American divisions which YANK readers know.

The first Americans to land on Sicily, after seven days of "saturation" bombing by Allied air fleets and heavy shelling by men-of-war, were the troops of the 82d Airborne Division, pioneer American airborne outfit and without battle experience. The airborne infantry and paratroopers of the 82d, carried to Sicily in giant C-47s and gliders late in the night of July 9, were blown off their course by buffeting winds and landed in scattered groups over an area perhaps 40 to 50 miles wide.

After cutting enemy communications and disorganizing rear installations far inland along a line running roughly from Licata to Vittoria, the paratroopers and airborne infantry re-formed into a solid division. In these operations, separate combat teams mopped up several Sicilian towns, including strategic Vittoria, just north of Scoglitti on the southeast seacoast. One tough 82d detachment was charged by Italian horse cavalry but broke the charge with tommy guns. In a continuous drive along the southern coast, the 82d swept headlong to Campobello and Marsala and seized Trapani on July 25, fanning out from the city to wipe up surrounding areas.

Lt. Gen. George S. Patton Jr.

Maj. Gen. Lucian K. Truscott and Lt. Col. William O. Darb[y]

Maj. Gen. Terry Allen

Maj. Gen. Geoffrey Keyes

Lt. Gen. Omar N. Brad[ley]

A few hours after the 82d descended from the sky, the Rangers, under Lt. Col. William O. Darby, came ashore on the beach at Gela as a shock battalion, paving the way for the main American seaborne invasion force, which landed early on July 10 through waters whipped up dangerously by an unexpected squall.

This main invasion force hit the Sicilian beaches in a three-pronged drive. The 1st Division waded ashore behind the Rangers at Gela. Its right flank was covered by the landing of the 45th Division at Scoglitti. The left flank was protected at first by the 3d Division landing at Licata and later by the 2d Armored Division,

which apparently rolled its tanks and half-tracks out of the boats somewhere between Licata and Gela. Meanwhile, the Rangers were already fighting inland ahead of the 1st Division, veering to the westward out of the line of the 1st's advance. Within 10 days, they took Porto Empedocle and moved swiftly along the southwest shore.

The "Fightin' 1st," under Maj. Gen. Terry Allen, fought one of the bitterest battles of the campaign at the very beginning. Hampered by a lack of tanks, Allen's men were quickly thrown back to the Gela beaches by strong German counterattacks. Aided by airborne troops, but mostly through its own resolute fighting, the 1st Divi-

---

These American Divisions Were in Action at Sicily

 1st Division trained at Fort Devens, Mass. It was the first U. S. division to go into action in 1917, one of the first to land in North Africa and fight in Tunisia.

 45th Division, Oklahoma National Guard outfit, saw action for first time in Sicily. They call it "the Indian Division" because it has some 1,500 Indians from 28 tribes.

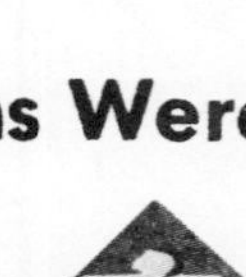

 2d Armored Division got its first real taste of action in Sicily. It used to be Lt. Gen. Patton's old outfit at Fort Benning, Ga., in the days before Pearl Harbor.

 9th Division, activated at Fort Bragg in 1940 by Lt. Gen. Jacob L. Devers, CG of the ETO, was first U. S. unit to enter Bizerte during final drive of Tunisian battle.

 3d Division distinguished itself at the Marne in 1918. It saw limited action in Morocco last fall where it landed after training at Fort Lewis and the Presidio.

 The 82d Airborne Division was Sgt. York's outfit in first World War. It trained at Fort Bragg after it was converted into an airborne division at Claiborne in 1942.

sion clung fiercely to its shaking position until the tanks arrived, then blasted away at the Nazis and rolled the panzers back.

Heading inland, the 1st Division marched directly northward and quickly passed Niscemi, a right flank threat that was met by the 2d Battalion of the 16th Infantry, which fought hard battles early in the march. Within a week the 1st Division was at Barrafranca, where the 26th Infantry had seized the surrounding hills to pave the way for the division's march into town.

In rapid succession the 1st then seized and passed beyond Enna, Petralia, Ganzi and Nicosia. At Enna, an important communications center, the 1st Division and Canadian forces fought together, but the climax of the battle was a dash to the rear of the town by a regiment of American infantry. Between Nicosia and Troina, the 1st Division ran into a long, bitter engagement. Fighting from crest to crest and along sharp turns of the highway at the Falcon Mountain, the division pressed in on Troina.

In the meantime, the 45th, Oklahoma's so-called "Indian Division" commanded by Maj. Gen. Troy H. Middleton, drove hard against the beaches at Scoglitti in a smashing blitz and pushed quickly to Vittoria (already taken by men of the 82d Division), fighting beside the Canadians for a short time. The 45th marched probably the greatest distance in Sicily. It moved from Vittoria to Caltagirone, then swept in a wide arc along a curve covering Mirabella and Aidone, crossing behind the 1st Division and proceeding westward to Caltanissetta. From there it took or bypassed the towns of Mussomeli, Vica-

rello, Montemaggiore, Caccamo and, finally, Termini, just east of Palermo on the northern shore.

At the same time the 1st and 45th were landing at Gela and Scoglitti, the 3d Division, under Maj. Gen. Lucian K. Truscott, and the 2d Armored Division, Maj. Gen. Hugh J. Gaffey's famous "Hell on Wheels," landed at Licata and nearby points. The two divisions quickly took Canicatti and Agrigento and within nine days were near Siculiana. Spearhead of the 3d Division was one of its most famous regiments, the number of which must be withheld. The only battalion not participating in this action was the 3d, which in a daring drive had left the regiment before Siculiana and made a forced march across country from Aaragona to San Stefano, covering 52 miles in 36 hours.

Meanwhile the rest of the 3d Division pushed on to Castelvetrano, then turned northward in a race with 2d Armored Division columns to take Palermo. This town was captured on July 23, the American units then fanning out to break down resistance in nearby areas. The 3d Division is the outfit that on one occasion covered 25 miles in a forced march over mountains without losing a man and then went directly into battle. At Carleone the division walked 32 miles in one stretch and then engaged in an 18-hour close-in battle.

AFTER 15 days about two-thirds of Sicily was under Allied control. The German and Italian lines were withdrawn to the northeast corner of the island, and the American divisions began converging from the south and the west upon the Axis concentrations.

The 9th Division, motorized, commanded by

Maj. Gen. Manton S. Eddy, landed from the sea at Palermo about Aug. 2 under terrific enemy air attacks and rolled quickly along the already-conquered north shore to San Stefano. Then the 9th Division veered sharply to the south as far as Nicosia and joined the 1st Division, engaged in savage battle with the Nazis at Troina. Relieving the 1st, which had already participated in the two greatest American engagements in the campaign, the 9th Division advanced against the Nazis. The 1st Division quickly rejoined the fight, however, and together with the 9th pounded the enemy and captured Troina on Aug. 6.

A week later, the 9th, joined by a British division, was the first American outfit to enter Randazzo, where elements of both U. S. divisions fanned out northward and eastward to cover the southwestern approaches to Messina, important port just across the straits from the mainland of Italy.

The 45th Division, swinging eastward at Termini, and the 3d Division, marching eastward from Palermo, drove along the coastal route toward Messina. The 45th at first led the way along the shore, but later elements of the 3d jumped ahead by means of three "leap frog" maneuvers along the coast. Striking behind the German lines with stabs from the sea, these units landed on Aug. 8, 10 and 16 near Santa Agata, Grojosa Marea and Milazzo respectively. Patrols of the 3d were the first Allied units to enter Messina on Aug. 17. Units of the 45th reached Messina soon afterward.

The campaign was over. Sicily, springboard to the continent of Europe, was in our hands.

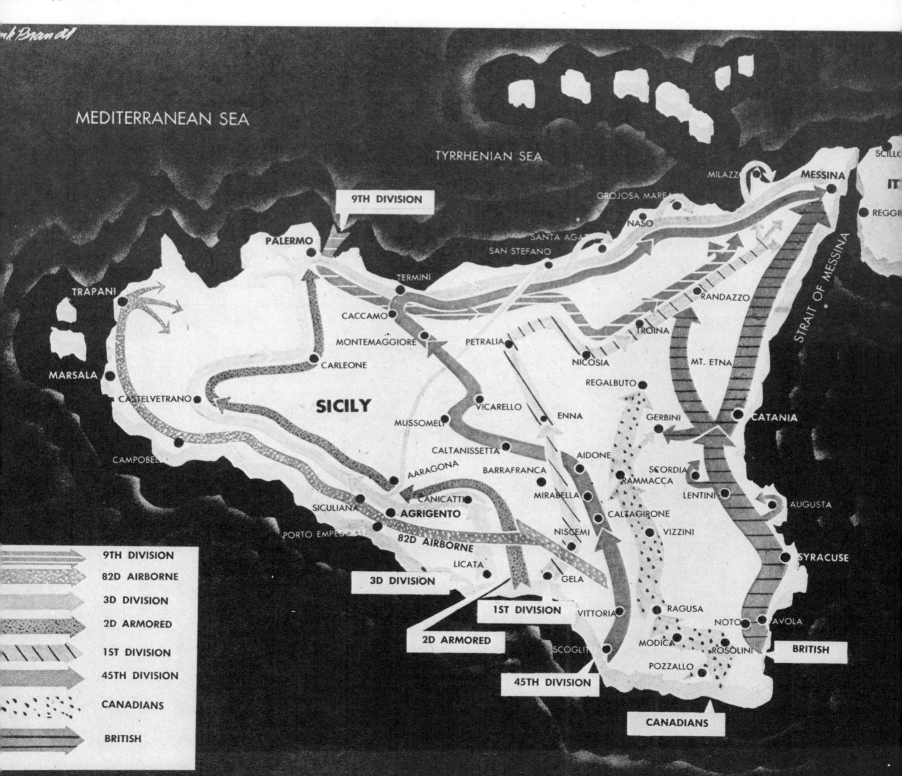

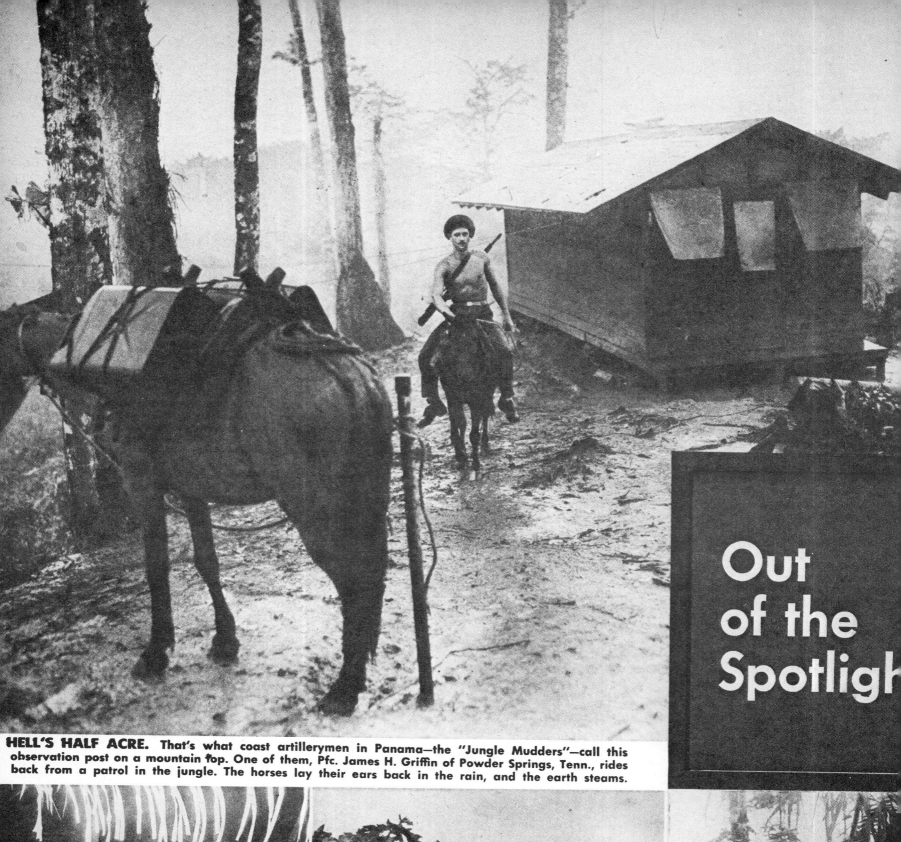

Out
of the
Spotligh

HELL'S HALF ACRE. That's what coast artillerymen in Panama—the "Jungle Mudders"—call this observation post on a mountain top. One of them, Pfc. James H. Griffin of Powder Springs, Tenn., rides back from a patrol in the jungle. The horses lay their ears back in the rain, and the earth steams.

MUD BOUND. Two artillerymen, Pvt. Jim Plante and Pfc. Peter J. Smith, take off their shoes, grown big with mud, before going in.

READY, WAITING. "Jungle Mudders" man a 3-inch coast gun during a practice alert. They built such emplacements themselves, clearing them out of the jungle.

HUNTERS' RETURN. Pfc. Edwin H. Baldwin and Cpl. Bill Kirkpatrick with their trophies—two native birds.

WASH DAY. Army nurses washing clothes at Assam, India, draw a crowd, and some kids get in with the laundry.

HITCHHIKERS. On occasional days off the girls like to take trips to nearby native villages. If it's too muddy to walk they'll take a ride on anything from trucks to bullock carts.

THE coast artillerymen who man the isolated posts in the bush country of Panama and the American nurses stationed at Assam, India, have two things in common: plenty of rain and mud, and the job of carrying on in an obscurity only rarely pierced by newspaper or magazine stories. On these two pages, the camera pays each a visit.

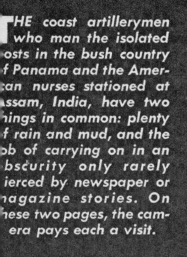

SUNDAY CHOW. That's when the nurses like to put on their cleanest uniforms to walk the chow line. Maybe those nice smiles mean fried chicken.

EXTRA RATIONS. With Ruth Schiffler's sugar and Mary Lozinak's cocoa and nuts, they're making themselves a batch of fudge.

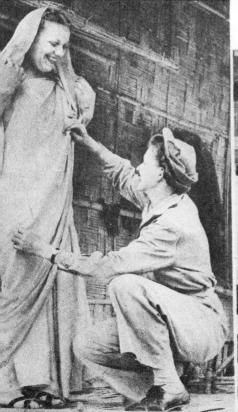

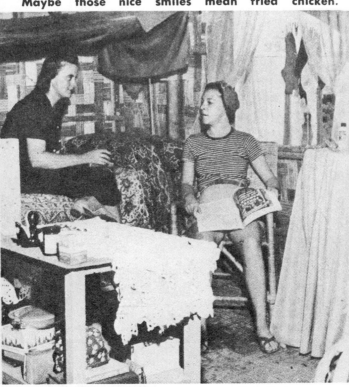

EMERGENCY DRESS. Dorothy Hanson had nothing to wear to a dance and so bought this native Indian dress.

NURSES' QUARTERS. Marie Carroll and Josep...... Sutter have made their bamboo hut as comfortable as possible. Shelter halves keep beds dry when roof leaks.

HELPING TUG. Violet Fisher helps Florence Brunner out of those easy-on, hard-to-get-off rubber boats. They're needed in India's mud.

THE SAD SACK   "DOUBLE OUT"

SGT. GEORGE BAKER
© 1943

Whatever became of the— **Old Fashioned Uppercut?**

By O/C RAY DUNCAN
Camp Davis, N. C.

I HAD the misfortune, a few hours ago, to step on a corporal's shoe in a chow line. It was after our class in judo and hand-to-hand combat. The corporal had just shined his shoes.

He lifted one foot knee high. With a vicious scrape he brought it down against my shin, and at the bottom of the stroke he stamped hard against my instep. As I doubled over in pain he smashed the bridge of my nose with the heel of his hand. Then he went to work on my kidneys with both feet as I lay on my face.

A couple of my buddies rescued me by kneeing the base of the corporal's spine. I'm resting comfortably now—almost through spitting blood—but the incident set me to thinking.

After this war a whole generation of Americans will be trained in judo and hand-to-hand combat. What will that mean to our way of life?

Come with me to the Riff-Raff Room, a cozy little cocktail bar. It is Saturday night and the war has been over for three weeks. Seated at the bar are a former marine sergeant and his former girl.

GIRL: I'm so happy you're back. Isn't it wonderful here?

FORMER MARINE: This place is too noisy. That piano player. I'd like to break his fingers, one by one—like this. [*The girl screams in pain, and a former paratrooper and an artilleryman, just discharged, rush to her aid.*]

FORMER PARATROOPER [*to former marine*]: Take it easy, Mac; yer breakin' the fingers of the girl.

He deftly dislocates the marine's shoulder and

snaps his collar bone in two places. The artilleryman sinks two extended fingers into the marine's abdominal wall. Then they go to work with their feet. Several others join in the melee, and the sound of breaking bones and ripping tis-

sue drowns out everything but the tinkle of the piano. The piano player was banging out "It's Murder, He Says."

The former marine drags himself to the piano and throws an elbow lock on the musician with his one good arm. Then with his teeth he methodically breaks the 10 fingers, counting each one aloud.

L AST time I was on furlough I happened to ask my little brother what he'd been reading.

"What are all the kids reading?" he cried, drawing from his pocket a worn copy of "Kill or Be Killed, a Manual of Dirty Fighting."

If this trend continues, the American home of the future might easily be something like this:

MOTHER: Jimmy! You've been fighting again! [*She anxiously feels the frail little body of her son, who has just come home from kindergarten.*]

SON: Aw gee Mom, I have not! Why?

MOTHER: Your eye—someone's been gouging it again. Your left arm is bent the wrong way. What is it, wrenched socket or fracture? Tell Mommy, honey. Why are you bent to one side? Abdominal wall again?

FATHER [*looking up from the evening paper*]: Stop nagging the child, Miriam. Boys will be boys, you know. Come here, son, and let me set that arm. [*There is a knock at the door and Mr. Robinson, the next-door neighbor, enters. He points at little Jimmy.*]

MR. ROBINSON: That young hoodlum has been fighting my Wilbur again. My boy will be a nervous wreck if your son doesn't stop splitting his kidneys.

FATHER: Either you apologize for calling my son a hoodlum, or I'll crush your spinal base.

MR. ROBINSON: You and who else? [*They circle around each other, crouched low and growling. Mother draws a stiletto from her bosom. Jimmy's eyes are fixed on the visitor's groin. Father lashes out suddenly with a well-placed kick. Mr. Robinson turns white and weakly attempts a right to the jaw.*]

FATHER: Why, you dirty ———. [*He seizes the fist and twists until the wrist snaps. He jabs his fingers into his neighbor's neck, and all struggling ceases. Jimmy kicks to the groin, then rushes to hug his father around the knees.*]

SON: Gee Pop, you're swell! I told that ole Wilbur my pop could kill his pop!

WORDS ACROSS THE SEA

Shandrowsky Terhune Meyers Berger Lea Duncan

From India, **Pvt. Michael Shandrowsky** says hello to all his "dead end" pals of New York City. "Great little wah," says Mike, "but nothing like the old tin-can fights we had in the alley back home." . . . **Pvt. Howard Terhune** of New Albany, Ind., now in Hawaii, wants to get in touch with Pvt. Charley Farnsley, a fellow Hoosier in N. Africa, and Pvt. Carl Wheeler, somewhere in California. Write him c/o YANK's *Words Across the Sea* . . . **Carl Meyers, Cox,** of Alameda, Calif., now in Alaska, has a father in the Seabees and a brother in the Marines and has mislaid them both. His father, E. J. Cedarstaff, and his brother, Pfc. Richard E. Cedarstaff, should write to him c/o YANK's *Words Across the Sea*.

Pfc. Nathan Berger of New York City has been in Panama for more than a year. He tells Sgt. Harold Leinwand, working in the finance department at Newport News, Va.: "Being the chief accountant, those figures must surely make you sweat it out. Down here in Panama it comes out naturally." . . . **Pvt. Harold J. Lea,** Newfoundland, wants to hear from George Hair, Trinidad, and Shay Bankston, N. Africa. They should write him c/o YANK's *Words Across the Sea*. . . . **Marine Gunner Linn G. Duncan** of Rochester, N. Y., USMC, Combat Int. Cen., COMSOPAC, Fleet PO, San Francisco, Calif., sends congratulations to his son Webb on receiving his wings. Says Linn: "Drop your old man a line."

Mail Call

Dear YANK:

In an August issue one of your North African correspondents told how to behave before questioners if captured by the enemy. He advises: "If you are taken before someone who outranks you, salute, even if it makes you squirm." There is nothing in the Geneva Convention which requires the salute to be given enemy officers. And I am sure there is an Army Regulation which specifies the salute is not given enemy officers. I am upset by the apathy with which many of the officers and men regard the enemy. We are not fighting for potato chips. Because a Nazi is captured, it doesn't alter the fact he has been acting for some years as murderer both of people and ideas. The excessive respect and courtesy given captive officers galls me just as if John Dillinger had been feted and handled with kid gloves while he was a prisoner. I'll be damned if I'll salute a Nazi or Jap officer—whether he is my prisoner or I am his.

Newfoundland —**1st Lt. R. W. LIPPMAN**

■ FM 27-10, Rules of Land Warfare, Chapter 4, paragraph 91, states: "Prisoners of war must salute all officers of the detaining power. Officers . . . are required to salute only officers of higher or equal rank." Even if you have to squirm, experience proves it's a good idea to be polite and courteous. The formality of saluting tends to raise a barrier between you and your questioner.

Dear YANK:

The tendency to glamorize the war is nauseating and the film industry is perhaps the worst offender. Hollywood tells us Johnny Doughboy is having a hell of a good time shooting up a few Japs each day and playing tag with hula girls. Then he comes back with medals and wound stripes to marry Susan. Great stuff but it stinks. Tailor-made glamor looks pretty sick compared to a pfc. getting knocked off in New Guinea. It's realized that men must die in war, but why can't the home front accept that fact without making a spectacle of itself covering up with glamor?

AAB, Herington, Kans. —**S/Sgt. MICHAEL J. LAWRENCE**

Dear YANK:

In an August issue I was shocked to discover Artie Greengroin's face had undergone a repulsive transformation. Instead of the old confident but slightly apprehensive Greengroin, we were given a sour sallow individual who stared bitterly down his nose at the title which his countenance belied: "Artie the Optimist." The old Greengroin always bore the marks of last night's festivities, whereas the wizened face of the new Greengroin bespeaks asceticism, repression and malnutrition. The Artie we knew smoked with an air of abandon. The changeling concentrates on a weed like a befuddled addict. How do you explain the switch?

—**S/Sgt. ROBERT VAN BRUGGEN**
Municipal Airport, Memphis, Tenn.

■ We suspect Greengroin of a Jekyll and Hyde existence as well as of asceticism, repression and malnutrition.

Dear YANK:

I feel very much insulted by your article on Tony Galento's come-back in a July issue of YANK. It was an insult to every pro wrestler in the game. Just because Tony hires some punch-drunk tanker like Herbie Katz to take a dive for him, it's no reason for comparing him to pro wrestlers. If you guys think pro wrestling is a fake, just get in and try it.

Australia —**Pvt. FLOYD TEASLEY**

■ Whatcha trying to do? Pull our leg?

Dear YANK:

In *Mail Call* in an August issue Pfc. Roy E. Peck, New Guinea, makes a reckless threat against our "traitorous" labor unions. I must tell him that if ever American labor is faced with the house-cleaning crusade he suggests, it won't have to search far for defenders. Labor shows integrity, courage and democratic faith both in war and peace.

General Hospital, Temple, Tex. —**Pfc. RAYMOND B. COLE**

Dear YANK:

I wonder if the men who read your exotic article about the wonderful treatment of OCS wash-outs at Jefferson Barracks [in a July issue] realized it was pure propaganda. I am an OCS wash-out without halitosis or a mania for homicide, but Col. Pullig didn't greet me or any of the other boys in your Pollyanna style. Instead we were informed by a very bored second lieutenant that we would be here only a few days so not to bother him with "foolishness." That was four months ago and I have now advanced to bayonet drill—at which any one of us could easily massacre our limited-service instructors. We are refused permission to beg or bribe the classification men to ship us out, and our skills are in the advanced stages of decomposition.

Jefferson Barracks, Mo. —**S/Sgt. H. N. NAUMANN**

Dear YANK:

Now that you have printed an editorial about soldiers wearing service ribbons who haven't earned them, why don't you write a piece about our self-appointed Gen. Arnolds? These khaki-clad phonies seem to think that silver wings are something in which one invests a few dollars to make the uniform a bit more resplendent. Last week I was in an Army-Navy store when in stepped a rookie who asked to see some wings. The clerk asked him what kind, but the rookie didn't even know. After being shown three types, he chose the aerial gunner's wings because they were more shiny. When we questioned him he laughed and said, "Everybody is wearing them." My buddies and I expect to earn the right to wear wings in the near future, but we don't think we'll wear them, just to be different.

—**Cpl. LEON WALDMAN**
Douglas Tng. Det., Long Beach, Calif.

Dear YANK:

Your pin-up girls are a work of art. Indeed, better pictures can't be found in *Esquire*. Yes, the pin-up girl is a morale builder all right, and it does my heart good to see "her" bring so much contentment to so many men. . . . But what the hell good is it! Every day we have an inspection and no pictures are allowed to be showing on the walls. I am always reading about soldiers demanding more pin-up girls. But what I want to know is where do we pin 'em?

Camp Howze, Tex. —**Cpl. AL HALPERN**

Dear YANK:

Our battalion commander has issued an order to take all pin-ups off the walls. For months we collected gorgeous women from YANK, but now we have to take them down. We are broken-hearted. Since we have no chaplain here, we would appreciate it if you would punch our TS cards. Thank you.

ASTP, Brookings, S. Dak. —**Cadet DAN WEINBERG***

*Also signed by Cadets Charley Keane, George Reimer and Dale Briggs.

■ You guys are in the same boat with Pvt. Pete La Brie at Camp Barkeley, Tex., whose CO ordered him to have a dress tattooed over the nude female on his left bicep.

Dear YANK:

In a July YANK there was an item about Mae West turning over her jewelry to the WPB to be cut down for use in precision instruments. That's a lot of thinly sliced baloney. 1) Cut diamonds are not used for industrial purposes, 2) there are plenty of diamonds of the proper kind available, and 3) breaking up her jewelry would be analogous to junking a '42 Cadillac to salvage the gaskets.

Fort William Scott, Calif. —**Pfc. LOUIS LICHT**

MESSAGE CENTER

B. Sgt. HYMAN BAND of Brooklyn, N. Y., once at Fort Dix, N. J., see *Message 1.** . . . DAVID JOSEPH BAYER, who lived on Vyse Ave., the Bronx, N. Y., write to Pvt. Jacob Adler; Co. A, 467th QM Trk. Regt., Camp McCoy, Wis. . . . FRANK BAYER, Sicily, write to Pfc. Edward G. Woods, Ward 137, Sta. Hosp., Camp Shenango, Greenville, Pa. . . . Pvt. JOHN BEAL of Brooklyn, N Y., in Panama in 1942, see *Message 2.*** . . . Sgt. JACK BEHR, once at Lowry Field, Colo., write to Pvt. Daniel Friedman, 1879th Ord. Det., Camp Livingston, La. . . . DUDLEY G. BENNETT, once in Bks. 308, Sheppard Field, Tex., see *Message 3.*† . . . AL BERKMAN, last address: Lockbourne AAB, Ohio, see *Message 4.*†† . . . Sgt. JOHN BIRD, once at Fort Bragg, N. C., write Lt. Jesse Tucker, Co. C, 655 TD Bn., Camp Hood, Tex. . . . A/C WALTER BOYCHUCK, last address: Santa Ana, Calif., write to Sgt. G. A. Pifer, Plt. B, 1148th Sch. Sq., Fort Sumner, N. Mex. . . . HARRY BROWN, once at Lockbourne AAB, Ohio, see *Message 4.*†† . . . A/C HAROLD W. BULK, last address: New York City, write to Cpl. Preston Sechrist, 136 First St., Niagara Falls, N. Y.

C. WILLIAM CADMAN, overseas, see *Message 5.*‡ . . . ALBERT B. CALLAHAN of Cleveland Heights, Ohio, write to Pfc. Ralph M. Wefel, Bks. 1211, 804th TSS, Sioux Falls, S. Dak. . . . Sgt. ROBERT CHAUVIN, once in Co. L, 32d Inf., write to M/Sgt. Orville N. Elmore, Sta. Hosp., Fort Snelling, Minn. . . . JERRY (FRENCHIE) CHAWES, once at Lockbourne AAB, Ohio, see *Message 4.*†† . . . Lt. EDWARD C. CHECK, overseas, see *Message 5.*‡ . . . Pvt. GEORGE R. CHENEY, once at Fort Bragg, N. C., write to Sgt. Harry A. Rich Jr., Hq. Co., 67th Sig. Bn., Camp Van Dorn, Miss. . . . Cpl. SHERMAN W. COOKE, last heard from near Tunis, write to S/Sgt. James L. Sobel, Btry. B, 301 FA Bn., Camp Phillips, Kans. . . . ROBERT M. COX, who joined the AAF at Fort Leavenworth, Kans., in 1938, write to Pfc. James B. Ardinger Jr., 397th Tech. Sch., Box 899, Bks. 10, Keesler Field, Miss. . . . JOHN CROFCHECK, last address Jefferson Barracks, Mo., see *Message 6.*‡‡ . . . "PUNCH" CUNNINGHAM of Saint Marys, Pa., now in the S. Pacific, see *Message 6.*‡‡

E. S/Sgt. S. EISENBERG of Brooklyn, N. Y., last address: Grenier Field, N. H., see *Message 1.** . . . Sgt. RAY ERCOLANI, somewhere in Africa, write to Sgt. R. J. Odorisio, Co. K, 390 Inf., Camp Breckinridge, Ky. . . . Pfc. JESSE W. EVANSKI, last address: APO 827, New Orleans, La., write to Pvt. Theo. F. Kubit.

F. DUANE FALCONER, overseas, see *Message 5.*‡ . . . Pfc. ALBERT (BABE) FIO RITA, last address: Patterson Field, Ohio, write to A/C Paul Gardner, Eagle Fields, Dos Palos, Calif. . . . T/Sgt. ROBERT O. E. FISHEL, once at Keesler Field, Miss., write to Lt. Pat Frazier, Hq. 322d Med. Bn., Camp Swift, Tex. . . . Pvt. JOSEPH FOCARINO, last heard from in New York, see *Message 7.*§ . . . JACK FOLEY, once in Barracks 308, Sheppard Field, Tex., see *Message 3.*† . . . CLAYTON FOSTER of Edinburg, Tex., write to Sgt. Charles G. Walker, Sta. Disp., Camp Springs, Washington, D. C. . . . T/Sgt. EDWIN G. FREEHAN, last address: APO 758, New York, write to your wife, Leona M. Freehan, 4622d SU, WAC Det., Fort Sheridan, Ill. . . . Sgt. CHARLES W. FRENCH, once at Schofield Barracks, HD, write to S/Sgt. Melvin Stauffer, Co. C, 6th Bn, Shenango Pers. Repl. Dep., Greenville, Pa. . . . Pfc. VICTOR F. FRIMMEL, write to Cpl. Joseph A. Muzikowski, 20th Photo. Sq. H, Peterson Field, Colo. . . . Pvt. FUNDY, formerly of Btry. A, 6 Bn., Fort Eustis, Va., see *Message 8.*§§

G. Cpl. HAROLD L. GASKINS of Chesterfield, S. C., last address: Fort Benning, Ga., write to Sgt. Eugene Ellison, Rcn. Co. 818, TD Bn., Camp Pickett, Va. . . . 1st Sgt. CHARLES GETGEN, formerly in Co. K, 109th Inf., see *Message 9.**** . . . LOUIS GOLDBERG, last address: Lockbourne AAB, Ohio, see *Message 4.*†† . . . Pvt. GEORGE GUNTFELDER, last heard from in Panama, write to Pvt. D. Johnstone, 403d Fighter Gp. Sq., Selfridge Field, Mich.

H. Pvt. GRADY HARRIS, last post Camp Gordon, Ga., write to Lt. Reuel N. Pomeroy, Weapons Dept., TD Sch., Camp Hood, Tex. . . . 1st Sgt. ALEX HORN, formerly in 37th Ord. Co., Fort Dix, N. J., write Pvt. Bernard B. Amon, Hq. Co., SCNOSA, New Orleans, La. . . . MARVIN HUIRAS, see *Message 5.*‡

M. Cpl. LOUIS MARASCO, last heard from at Indio, Calif., see *Message 7.*§ . . . Pvt. M. MARCUS, USMC, last heard from at Cherry Point, N. C., see *Message 1.** . . . 1st Sgt. S. MILLER, formerly with Co. K, 109th Inf., see *Message 9.**** . . . Pvt. MURPHY, formerly at Fort Eustis, Va., in Btry. A, 6 Bn., see *Message 8.*§§

**Message 1:* Write Pfc. Leo Eisenberg, Hq. Stu. Regt., TD Sch., Camp Hood, Tex.
****Message 2:** Write Pvt. D. Johnstone, 403d Fighter Sq., Selfridge Field, Mich.
†*Message 3:* Write Pvt. Don R. Hook, 1082 Gd. Sq., SAAAF, San Angelo, Tex.
††*Message 4:* Write Pvt. Donald Workman, 729 SAW Co., Camp Gordon Johnston, Fla.
‡*Message 5:* Write Stephen J. Sterbak WO, Dept. of Tactics, AAAS, Camp Davis, N. C.
‡‡*Message 6:* Write James Auman, 6th Bomb. Sq. (H), Gowen Field, Idaho.
§*Message 7:* Write S/Sgt. Alvin Klein, 9th Field Hosp., Camp Rucker, Ala.
§§*Message 8:* Write Cpl. Edward Barkowski, Btry. A, 162 CA Bn. (AA), Fort Brady, Mich.
****Message 9:* Write M/Sgt. H. Wilhelm, Div. Hq. Co., Camp Butner, N. C.

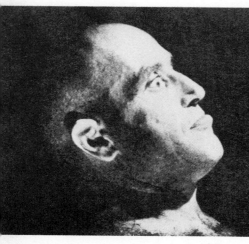

McTURK BATTERS THE BUM

Look at the puss that popped up in the company area to disturb Pvt. Joe McTurk's peaceful fatigue duties. McTurk is played by Pvt. Robert McCracken of Fort George G. Meade, Md. Sgt. Pete Paris took the pictures.

"DAT CHIN looks familyure," mutters McTurk. "Now, where have I saw it before? This must be one of dem new recroots dem quartermasters sent us when we ast for sapolio." Then the light begins to dawn on Joe. "Pardon me for not rekkenizzing yer, chum, but I ain't seen yer in the newsreels so much lately," he explains.

"WHATCHA doin' here?" Joe asks. "I heard yer was goin' outa business but I didn't know it was becuz yer was getting drafted." The guy claims that he would be still going strong only they started rationing balconies back home. "Cantcha salute like that frum der ground?" queries Joe. "Afraid someone might step on yer toes?"

"FUN'S FUN," barks Mac. "But the lootenant is due here any minute an' I got me work to do, so will yez kindly scram and stop handin' me that stuff about de glories of Ancient Rome? Besides d'yez expect me to get all steamed up about yer old glories when yez won't tell me whether dey are blondes, red heads or brunettes?"

BUT THE BUM still holds strong and follows Joe into the barracks. Mac wonders whether he should bother to turn the character into the orderly room. He decides the captain and the first sergeant are busy enough helping the supply sergeant take inventory without cluttering up their morning report with these forgotten men.

"LISTEN, JOIK," Mac yelps. "Fer der last time, I don't care how menny railroads yer made run on time or how yer built the empire. Dat stuff mighta gone over back in 1930 but I gotta clean dis latrine. Now gwan and get outa here before I make a Brenner Pass atcher big lower lip wit me Staten Island fist. So help me."

"YOU AST FOR IT," grumbles Joe as he soberly sweeps the remains out the door. "As if it ain't bad enough keeping dis joint neat and tidy, dey gotta start cluttering up the floor wit ex-dictators. An' jest tink, dis ting here was wunna da reasons why dey stuck me number inna gold fish bowl. Well, it's a small woild."

Our Casualties

HERE are the latest official casualty figures of U. S. military forces from Dec. 7, 1941, to the end of August, 1943:

service	Killed	Wounded	Missing	Prisoners	Total
rmy	9,209	20,159	21,764	19,740	70,872
avy	7,852	2,561	8,914	2,246	21,573
arines	2,005	2,506	663	1,925	7,099
oast Guard	182	22	158	1	363
	19,248	25,248	31,499	23,912	99,907

U. S. Merchant Marine casualties from Sept. 7, 1941 to Aug. 1, 1943: Killed, 627; missing, 124; total, 4,751.

The Army said that 8,748 of its men listed as wounded have either returned to duty or have een discharged from the hospitals.

GIs Gets Tax Extension

The Treasury Department has announced that members of the armed services on active duty ept. 15, 1943, do not have to file income-tax declarations until March 15, 1944. If you make out nd file a final return of income for 1943 and pay he tax shown on it by March 15, 1944, the income filing for 1943 is waived. Even if you had n income this year which was big enough to equire a tax payment you have until March 15, 944 to pay it.

Jove in Australia

The U. S. Army Red Cross field director in Australia has suggested that Aussie girls who ave married American GIs receive instruction n how to fit themselves for home life in the tates. There are now more than 500 such marriages officially recorded, he says, and probably nany more unrecorded. The Red Cross, incidentally, carefully investigates the backgrounds of oth the GI and his girl before they get hitched o make sure each one knows what the score is. arents or guardians of the girl must sign a tatement that they'll care for her in an emerency, and the girl is advised that she can't get o the U. S. until the war's over.

Airborne Insignia?

We have been flooded ith letters from GIs ho want to know if the houlder patch worn by st Sgt. H. M. Longworth n the cover of an August issue of YANK is a ew official insignia for irborne troops. No, it sn't. Sgt. Longworth wears an Air Force insignia ith the word "Airborne" above it (as shown ere) because he is a member of an aviation enineers outfit—part of the Air Forces—attached o an airborne brigade at Alliance, Nebr. But the egular airborne troops are part of the Army round Forces—not the Air Force. Therefore, hey cannot wear this Air Force insignia.

Art and War

The WD has announced that special measures ave been taken to protect art treasures that ome "within the scope of Allied military operaons." Every major unit of the AMG has been ssigned a museums and monuments officer hose duty is to notify commanders of the exstence of art treasures and to direct their presrvation wherever practicable. Combat COs have een furnished with maps showing the locations f widely known art objects, statues and museums so that they can keep them if possible out f firing range.

Permanent Ranks

President Roosevelt has announced the designation of Gen. Dwight D. Eisenhower as a peranent major general in the U. S. Army. Gen. isenhower now holds the temporary rank of eneral and previously held the permanent rank f colonel. Permanent ranks of other Army generals are: Lt. Gen. Mark W. Clark, lieutenant olonel; Lt. Gen. George S. Patton Jr., colonel; st. Gen. Carl Spaatz, colonel; Lt. Gen. George . Kenney, lieutenant colonel; Lt. Gen. Joseph V. Stilwell, brigadier general; Lt. Gen. Milard F. Harmon, colonel; Lt. Gen. Omar Nelon Bradley, lieutenant colonel; Maj. Gen. James arold Doolittle, major; Maj. Gen. Ira Clarence

Eaker, lieutenant colonel; Maj. Gen. Terry De La Mesa Allen, lieutenant colonel. Permanent ranks are those which were held by Army personnel prior to Oct. 1, 1940, and all promotions in rank after that date are temporary. Members of the U. S. Army will revert to their permanent ranks after the duration plus six months. This applies both to officers and enlisted men.

Parachute Bombs

Allied troops in New Guinea have learned that anti-personnel parachute bombs can hang on trees for six months without being affected by heat or rain. These bombs were first used on a large scale in this area, and Allied demolition squads worked for two months destroying all the "duds" they could find. They found several dozen parachute bombs still hanging from trees deep in the jungle and around one bomb crater the bodies of four Aussies. One of them held a shrapnel-torn parachute in his hand.

GI Shop Talk

The WD has announced the posthumous award of the Silver Star to Chaplain Guy H. Turner for gallantry in action in Attu. He was one of 30 chaplains who have died in active duty since Pearl Harbor. . . . WASP, which stands for "Women's Air Force Service Pilots," is the new official title of women pilots of the AAF. Although Wasps wear a distinctive uniform, they serve the AAF in a civilian status and are not members of the armed forces. . . . GIs stationed in areas where rationed goods are plentiful aren't helping their folks by mailing them the stuff back home, says the U. S. Collector of Customs. In every case the correct number of points has to be given up by the person receiving the goods. . . . An AAF P-40 Warhawk group of the Northwest African Air Forces recently celebrated its 100th day of operations by flying on its 100th combat mission in which it brought down five enemy planes and boosted its score of destroyed enemy ships to an even 100 . . . More than 1,000 Wacs will be trained for service in the Army Medical Department in special courses at the Army-Navy Hospital School at Hot Springs, Ark.

LITTLE MAN, YOU'LL HAVE A BUSY DAY.

Fortress Europe

Sgt Adolph Stein

Washington O.P.

GIs are getting the limelight in the Third War Loan Drive now under way. A letter by Cpl. Christopher Hanley, AAF, of Jersey City, N. J., from the Aleutians inspired the kick-off broadcast made by Secretary of the Treasury Henry F. Morgenthau Jr. War veterans will tour the county in transport planes to pep up War Bond rallies. Army posts are supplying talent and equipment for other shows. All together, the Treasury aims to raise 15 billion bucks from civilians and the armed forces. GIs are buying War Bonds on an ever-expanding scale, investing almost 25 million dollars each month.

The first women's service entitled to carry arms are the women guards of the Treasury Department, seven of whom sport revolvers after qualifying on the Treasury pistol range. . . . Gen. Henry H. Arnold, chief of the AAF, picked up the millionth shotgun manufactured for AAF gunnery schools and knocked off a clay pigeon as neatly as you please out at Bolling Field. . . . ASF has changed the name of its weekly radio program to "The Army Services Presents" and hereafter will dramatize the exploits of one individual in each show.

We expect that several more "official" battles will be announced before long by the Awards and Decorations Branch. If you participated in one of them you will be authorized to wear a star on your service ribbon. But don't start putting the stars on yet. So far, only action in the Philippines permits the wearing of a star.

The WD figures that more than 10,000,000 individual Christmas presents will be mailed to GIs overseas during the Sept. 15-Oct. 15 mailing period. That is twice as many as were sent to men overseas during a similar period last year. . . . They tell us the ASTP program is rolling along now, with upward of 100,000 soldiers in training at more than 200 colleges and 16,000 more in STAR units. —**YANK's Washington Bureau**

YANK EDITORIAL STAFF

Managing Editor, Sgt. Joe McCarthy, F.A; **Art Director,** Sgt. Arthur Weithas, DEML; **Assistant Managing Editor,** Cpl. Justus Schlotzhauer, Inf.; **Assistant Art Director,** Sgt. Ralph Stein, Med.: **Pictures,** Sgt. Leo Hofeller, Armd.; **Features,** Sgt. Douglas Borgstedt, DEML; **Sports,** Sgt. Dan Polier, AAF.

Washington: Sgt. Earl Anderson, AAF; Cpl. Richard Paul, DEML.
London: Sgt. Bill Richardson, Sig. Corps; Sgt. Harry Brown, Engr.; Sgt. Ben Frazier, CA; Sgt. Walter Peters, QMC; Sgt. Jack Scott, FA; Sgt. Charles Brand, AAF; Cpl. Thomas Fleming, DEML; Sgt. Steven Derry, DEML; Sgt. Louis McFadden, Engr.; Sgt. Durbin Horner, QMC.
North Africa: Sgt. Peter Paris, Engr. In cooperation with the Stars and Stripes: Sgt. Ralph G. Martin, Inf.; Sgt. Jack Foisie. Inf.; Sgt. Milton Lehman.
Central Africa: Sgt. Kenneth Abbott, AAF.
Cairo: Sgt. Burgess Scott, Inf.; Sgt. George Aarons, Sig. Corps.
Sicily: Sgt. Walter Bernstein, Inf.
Iraq-Iran: Sgt. Al Hine, Engr.; Cpl. James O'Neill, QMC.
India: Sgt. Ed Cunningham, Inf.; Sgt. Robert Ghio, MP.
China: Sgt. Marion Hargrove, F.A.
Australia: Sgt. Don Harrison, AAF; Sgt. Richard Hanley, AAF.
South Pacific: Sgt. Mack Morriss, Inf.
New Guinea: Sgt. David Richardson, CA; Cpl. Thomas St. George, Inf.
Hawaii: Sgt. Merle Miller, AAF; Sgt. John Bushemi, FA; Pfc. Richard J. Nihill, CA; Cpl. James L. McManus, CA.
Alaska: Sgt. Georg N. Meyers, CA.
Bermuda: Cpl. William Pene du Bois.
British Guiana: Pvt. Fred A. Peruzzi, Inf.
South Atlantic: Pfc. Nat Bodian, ATC.

Panama: Sgt. Robert G. Ryan, Inf.
Puerto Rico: Sgt. Lou Stoumen, DEML; Cpl. William F. Haworth. DEML.
Trinidad: Sgt. Clyde Biggerstaff, DEML.
Surinam: Pvt. Bernard Freeman, Inf.
Nassau: Sgt. Dave P. Folds Jr., MP.
Iceland: Sgt. Gene Graff. Inf.
Newfoundland: Sgt. Frank Bode.
Greenland: Sgt. Edward F. O'Meara, AAF.
Marines: 1st Sgt. Riley Aikman.
Navy: Robert L. Schwartz Y2c; Allen Churchill Y3c.

Officer in Charge: Lt. Col. Franklin S. Forsberg; **Detachment Commander,** Capt. Sam Humphfus.

Overseas Bureau Officers: London, Maj. Desmond H. O'Connell; India, Maj. Don Thurman; Australia, Capt. Donald W. Reynolds, 1st Lt. J. N. Bigbee; Cairo, Capt. Hodding Carter; Hawaii, Capt. Charles W. Balthrope; Alaska, Capt. Jack W. Weeks; Panama, Capt. Henry E. Johnson; Iraq-Iran, Capt. Charles Holt; Puerto Rico, 1st Lt. Gerald J. Rock.

YANK is published weekly by the enlisted men of the U. S. Army and is for sale only to those in the armed services. Stories, features, pictures and other material from YANK may be reproduced if they are not restricted by law or military regulations, provided proper credit is given, release dates are observed and specific prior permission has been granted for each item to be reproduced. Entire contents reviewed by U. S. military censors.

Full 24-hour INS and UP leased wire service.

MAIN EDITORIAL OFFICE
205 EAST 42d St., NEW YORK 17, N. Y., U. S. A.

Special Orders

Camp Sibert, Ala.—T/Sgt. Mace E. Taylor is chief order clerk for the Unit Training Center here. He takes his job very seriously, as witness the following announcement which he sent out recently:

HEADQUARTERS
1ST PROVISIONAL TAYLOR HOUSEHOLD
1114 Jupiter Street
Gadsden, Alabama

17 August 1943

SPECIAL ORDERS }
NO. 1 }

1. SHARON SUSAN TAYLOR, seven pounds and a quarter ounces, brunette, and good looking, has reported Holy Name of Jesus Hospital at 0130, 17 August 1943, per paragraph 99, special orders number 297, Headquarters, Camp High in the Clouds, Heaven, and is assigned to Headquarters, 1st Provisional Taylor Household and is designated Chief of Attention Section, vice Technical Sergeant Mace E. Taylor relieved.

By Order of Dr. F. W. McCorkle, M. D.
SUSAN TAYLOR,
Mother (Doing Fine),
H F G.

OFFICIAL:
MACE E. TAYLOR,
Father (Dazed and amazed)

Hide and Seek

Camp Van Dorn, Miss.—Pvt. George Klein of Hq. Battery, 371st FA, on guard duty, saw a dim shape in the darkness some yards away from

CAMP NEWS

PAW SALUTE. Private Buzz, a 5-month-old cocker spaniel seems to be the only dog that can return a GI salute. Trained by Cpl. Joseph F. Notarangelo at Camp Santa Anita, Calif. Buzz can flick up a quick paw but he refuses to salute first

him. He ordered the figure to advance and be recognized.

The trespasser moved closer and halted. Klein, straining his eyes, called out again: "Advance. I still don't recognize you."

The figure moved again and on the third challenge, when Klein announced that he still couldn't recognize him, a voice spoke up: "Hey, buddy, how long is this going on? I'm standing behind you now."

Target Practice

Camp Beale, Calif.—S/Sgt. Jack Butterly of Hq. Co., 83d Armored Medical Bn., entered the dispensary here and told a strange story.

He was walking down a company street and reached toward his pocket for his pipe. He felt something hit his hand hard and looked to see an arrow imbedded in it. Amazement overcame pain. He looked around for the enemy, but no one was in sight.

The doctor examined Butterly, fixed up his hand and came to the conclusion that he wasn't

bait for Section 8. The explanation finally was forthcoming. A group of archery enthusiasts had been practicing and one shaft had missed the target—but not Butterly.

AROUND THE CAMPS

Mobile Headquarters, Third Army, Louisiana—Pvt. R. O. Minnihan, flag orderly with an umpire detail, was crossing the Sabine River during the dark hours. His boat suddenly hit something and stopped. Minnihan, who couldn't swim, thought he'd reached land and stepped out—into 10 feet of water. The boat had hit a snag, but Sgt. Lewis S. Freeman, squad leader, saved Pvt. Minnihan from the results of his error.

Camp Joseph T. Robinson, Ark.—Pvt. Rolly Stroyman reports that GIs attached to Co. C, 68th Replacement Bn., have their doubts about the saying that it's a good cook who eats his

own food. The reason is this notice which appeared on the bulletin board: "Have gone to town for lunch. Will be back at 2 P.M." It was signed by the mess sergeant.

THE BALL FOLLOWS HIM

Sgt. "Duke" Abbruzzi, onetime halfback for Rhode Island State and for three straight years on the All-New England, is still hurling them as assistant athletic director, Hq., Camp Croft, S. C.

BOOKMOBILE READERS. The idea of this portable library was started by the librarian at the Service Club No. 5 in the Harmony Church area, Fort Benning, Ga. Operated for colored troops, this "bookmobile" makes it possible for camp booklovers to get their reading, and to return it, conveniently.

VISITING TROUPERS. Fay McKenzie, singer and leading lady in Gene Autry films, gets her mitts on a machine gun at Wendover Field, Utah, while comedian Billy Gilbert and his wife hope nothing goes off. They visited Wendover to open a new Service Club after coming back from entertaining Yanks overseas

Brooks Field, Tex. — Pfc. Fred Comer, attached to the photo section of the 17th Aviation Sq., was asked by Sgt. Albert E. Musso how he'd feel if he had to bail out at 5,000 feet. Cromer replied: "No, sir, I ain't going to jump from no 5,000 feet. I'm going to wait till that plane gets to about 10 feet from the ground, then I'll jump."

Lincoln Army Air Base, Nebr. — It was to be a gala affair. The newly sworn Wacs were set for a big dinner in celebration of their induction into the Army. Then they remembered that someone would have to stand CQ. The plight of the female warriors found a quick answer from the male GIs here. Cpl. Allen Christensen won a place in the hearts of the Wacs by taking over CQ for the night.

Pine Camp, N. Y. — While T-4 Anthony Cimo of Div. Hq. Co., 5th Armored Div., was catching in a softball game, a batter hit a high foul. Cimo tore off his mask and looked up, but could not locate the ball. He found it a moment later—in his hip pocket where it had fallen.

AAFFTC, Santa Monica, Calif. — S/Sgt. Harry Woods is busy these days giving the Schneider test to air-cadet applicants. One applicant recently told him about a friend of his who had washed out consecutively at Norfolk, Pensacola and Corpus Christi. "What's he doing now?" asked Woods. "Drying off," came the answer.

Camp Atterbury, Ind. — Pfc. Edward Slamovitz of Hq. Section, 1560th Service Unit, is a romantic soul. Each noon, when reading letters from his wife, he smokes a cigar. This ritual is the result of a promise—that he would remember her each day in some special way.

North Camp Polk, La. — Pvt. William Bruner is handling a flame thrower with an armored regiment here and feels right at home. In civilian life he made his living eating fire. Shells of the Axis worry him not, since once he was a human cannonball, and bayonet charges are a cinch, because "I've had my head chopped off a million times. For one season I played the victim in a trick guillotine."

Tampa Air Force Headquarters, Fla. — Sgt. Herman Lowy of Hq. and Hq. Sq. was kidded by barracks mates into believing that he was being restricted because his bed didn't pass inspection. He dashed hurriedly for the orderly-room bulletin board to see just how much of a restriction he was in for. His haste was unwise. He ran into his CO who immediately slapped a three-day restriction on him for not wearing his cap.

Special note to camp PROs and Special Service Officers: YANK wants interesting news items, pictures and features. Pass them on to YANK, Camp Features, 205 East 42d Street, New York 17, N. Y.

HIGH PRESSURE. Or is it advertising? Anyway this was in the *Wright Take-Off*, Wright Field, Ohio, citing improbable advantages of the Army brand.

CANTEEN ENTERTAINER. Sir Toby, the chimp, is doing his part for GIs on leave who visit the "Cage" Door Canteen at the Cincinnati (Ohio) Zoo. At this point in the act he was cutting a very mean rug.

MAN OF PARTS. Sgt. Keith D. Young, with Hq., Third Armored Corps on maneuvers in Louisiana, is an Australian who served in the Aussie Cavalry, was also prospector, pearl diver, aerial surveyor.

ARMY VEGETABLES. Pvt. Frank F. Nemeth shows off some juicy tomatoes grown in a victory garden planted by the 1524th Service Unit, Fort Hayes, Ohio, between barracks on the company street.

TWO ERAS. Cpl. Rosemary K. Babcock, Wac, from Columbus, Ohio, here is chatting with Princess Blue Water of the Sioux Tribe at Fort Warren, Wyo. Both in uniform, the women traded autographs.

BATTLE CONDITIONS. After a heavy rain it began to look almost like New Guinea for men of the 438th CA Bn. who had to negotiate an infiltration course under live bullets at Camp Edwards, Mass.

BOOKS IN WARTIME

'NDER COVER

By John Roy Carlson

For more than four years John Roy Carlson that's not his real name, of course) moved "under over" in America's Nazi underworld. He joined nany seditious groups, met their leaders and ained their confidence. He made friends with nen like Edward Holton James, a New England ristocrat who told him that "the only way to ave America is for Hitler and Japan to smash s," and Joe McWilliams, the Yorkville fuehrer, ho called Adolf Hitler "the greatest philosopher nce the time of Christ." At the end of his four ears Carlson came to the conclusion that the nembers of American Fascist organizations were s dangerous to our democratic way of life as ne Japs and Nazis whom American soldiers are illing on the fighting fronts. "Under Cover" is ill of names, dates and places, and, though ather clumsily written, it is an effective warnig to soldiers who are sure that Fascism can't appen here. Carlson warns us that it not only an happen here, but that there are powerful roups just waiting for the chance to jam it down ur throats. [*E. P. Dutton & Co.*]

ERTICAL WARFARE

By Francis Vivian Drake

This interesting and persuasively written book ies to prove that if the United Nations "had the ill" they could bomb Germany out of the war ithin four months. The book is divided into six spects of aerial warfare, perhaps the most imortant of which is devoted to the "Air Plan." he purport of this plan is that Germany could e bombed into submission if the RAF and the AF combined to destroy 40 percent of Nazi inustrial power. This could be done, says the uthor, in a sustained bombing offensive using 000 bombers at a time in its initial phases and 000 bombers in its final phases. The RAF would equire a bomb tonnage of 180,000 for its "satuation type" bombing, and the AAF 60,000 for its precision type" bombing. The offensive would ist about four months and by that time, the uthor declares, the Nazis would be ready to old up. "Vertical Warfare" contains some strikig air-battle scenes. [*Doubleday, Doran & Co.*]

ICK OUT THE BIGGEST

By Frank Morris

The 10,000-ton cruiser was knifing through the aters north of Guadalcanal on the night of ct. 11, 1942, when word came that Jap ships ere reported to starboard. "How many ships?" sked "Iron Mike" Moran, the *Boise's* skipper. Seem to be five, sir," was the answer. "Pick ut the biggest and commence firing," came the rder. In the next 27 minutes the *Boise* sank two Jap cruisers, each over 10,000 tons; a light cruiser and three destroyers. (There were six Jap ships instead of five.) When the fight was over you wouldn't have given a nickel for the *Boise's* chances of ducking the scrap heap. She had been hit by 11 "straddles" and had a hole in her bow big enough to drive a tank through. She was down by the head and listing heavily to starboard. Most of her guns were blown out of action, and she was blazing furiously in a dozen places. More than 110 of her crew were dead and many others were badly burnt, gassed or wounded. But the *Boise* came through, was finally able to limp into Philadelphia for repairs and is now on the high seas itching for another fight. "Pick Out the Biggest" is a swiftly told, dramatic story of a great ship, an iron-hearted skipper and a bunch of guys who didn't know when they were licked. [*Houghton Mifflin Co.*]

GIVE OUT!

Edited by Eric Posselt

The best you can say about this collection of "songs of, for and by the men in the service" is that it's a good try. Out of 130 songs listed only a dozen were written by enlisted men. Others are by officers and civilians, and a great number are anonymous. Several GI favorites, like "4-F Charlie," "When the War Is Over We'll All Enlist Again" and "I'm Dreaming of a White Mistress," are missing, while old stand-bys like "Anchors Aweigh" and "The Army Air Corps" weren't included because the copyright owners wouldn't okay their use. Many of the songs sound as if they had been written by PROs or Sunday school teachers, and a few, like "Cristofor Colombo" and "The Bastard King of England," are more like the bawdy jingles sung at civilian smokers than by soldiers on the march. Missing also is a five-line ditty without a title which has been sung with great gusto by soldiers while inhaling the dust of southern Virginia. It begins with "Virginia is a helluva state, parlez-vous," and winds up with a certain uncomplimentary reference to Virginia. This song can be sung anywhere in the U. S. by eliminating "Virginia" and substituting the name of the state whose dust you are inhaling. [*Arrowhead Press.*]

CHECKER STRATEGY

Can you take the White side in this position and pilot the pieces through for a win? Although Black has a superiority in numbers, 5 against 4, he *must* lose if White makes the right moves.

Look 'em over and see if you can locate the winning combination.

You can check your analysis with the answer on page 22. Before doing so, number the playing squares of your checkerboard from 1 to 32 as shown.

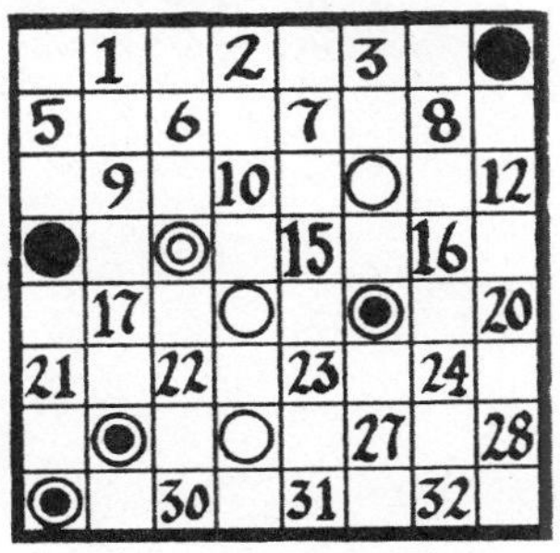

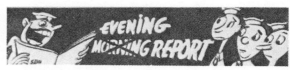

HOLLYWOOD. Laraine Day, who shares honors with Cary Grant in the current "Mr. Lucky," is the 28th cinema-gal to appear opposite him. . . . Objecting to a scene in "Watch on the Rhine" in which a Nazi informer is killed, the Hays Office insisted that there should be punishment for the murder. Lillian Hellman, author of the play from which the film was adapted wrote a note in reply which inquired if the Hays Office was aware that killing Nazis was now a matter of national policy. The scene remained unchanged. . . . Mickey Rooney has been assigned to one of the most dramatic roles of his career, that of Mi in "National Velvet," a story of English steeplechasing. . . . Mona Maris is Hollywood's first refugee from Nazi roles. She recently turned down three spy roles for a bit part in "The Song of Bernadette." "I'm only human," she said. "I'd much rather be kissed than hissed." . . . Joel McCrea will sing in his next picture, "Buffalo Bill." . . . Rita Hayworth, Cary Grant, Janet Blair and Charles Coburn head the roster for Columbia's forthcoming film of old Chautauqua days, "Gone Are the Days." . . . Greer Garson is being tested for the central role of Louis Bromfield's "Mrs. Parkington." . . . Anne Baxter has the role of the wife of the youngest Sullivan in 20th-Fox's "The Sullivans."

Laraine Day

CHANGE OF ADDRESS If you are a YANK subscriber and have changed your address, use this coupon to notify us of the change. Mail it to YANK, The Army Weekly, 205 East 42d Street, New York 17, N. Y., and YANK will follow you to any part of the world.

FULL NAME AND RANK ORDER NO.

OLD MILITARY ADDRESS

NEW MILITARY ADDRESS

Allow 21 days for change of address to become effective

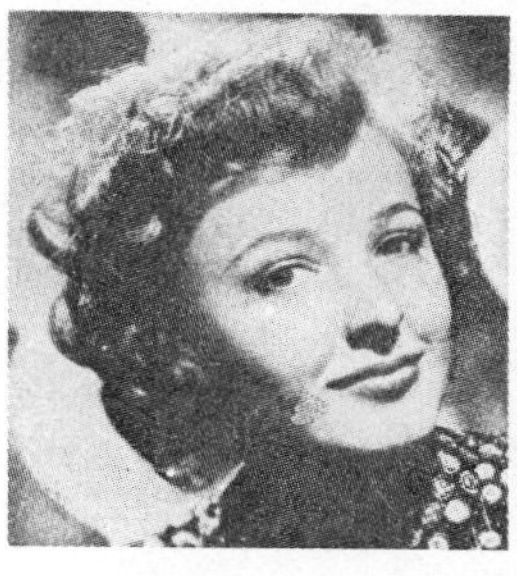

DOUBLE PUZZLE

First tackle the Picture Puzzle below. Add or subtract the pictured objects as indicated. The result will be the name of a country in Asia. Fill this into 1 Down on the crossword puzzle, then solve the rest. (Solution on Page 22)

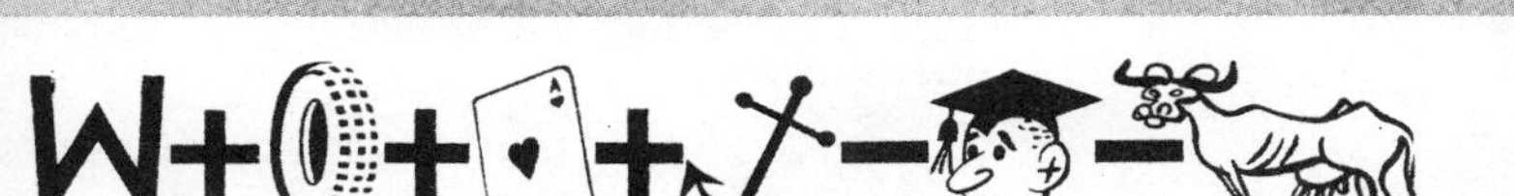

ACROSS

1. Lonesome land
5. Canteen cocktails
10. Conceited
14. Female deer (rare plural)
15. On a *car* it's *shipment*, on *a ship* it's ——
16. Daddy
17. Singing voices
19. The McCoy
20. Press agent
21. Cuddle with a chocolate bar
23. Getting broad
25. Order takers
27. Mixed-up alien
28. Decorating
32. Wriggly fish
33. Symbol for mustard gas
35. Hang-over from a spending spree
36. Civilian bugle
38. No soap ordinance
39. A smart guy
40. Snake's hang-out
41. Character in Othello
42. Wood, layer-cake style
43. Frock for frails
44. Fossilized resin
45. Technical sergeant (abbr.)
46. Beverage
47. Grounds for sentiment if you have a cold
49. Ownership mark on cattle
51. A fuss (two words)
52. Alone on a desert island
55. Dig out
59. Dry
60. Mickey Rooney's British Alma Mater
62. Swiped
63. First name of former heavyweight champ
64. Good luck before a 6, bad luck after
66. Woe is me
67. Prophet
68. At least they beat deuces
69. Loaned

DOWN

1. (Solve the picture puzzle)
2. This takes punishment on the march
3. Answer to "Shall we?"
4. Secret, private
5. State (abbr.)
6. Spare tire in a motorboat
7. Didn't stand pat
8. Anew
9. Army personnel
10. Pertaining to the backbone
11. Society's name for Mary
12. Atop
13. Group
18. Slope
22. ¾ of Ireland
24. Elementary (abbr.)
26. Trap
28. Make suitable
29. Small valleys
30. How to keep out of the guardhouse
31. Transparent sand
33. Famous golfer
34. Nasal horse laugh
37. Article of property
38. Familiar equivalent of Madam
40. Most magnificent
41. Undying
43. Dizzy; and a college supervisor
44. Assistants to superior
46. Swapper
48. Dogface's Operatic Fraternity (abbr.)
49. Ocean to you
50. Discourse
52. Buckles
53. Natural woodwork
54. Classy pigeon
56. Why actors never get hungry
57. Verve
58. Army Alpha
61. Executed Marshal of France

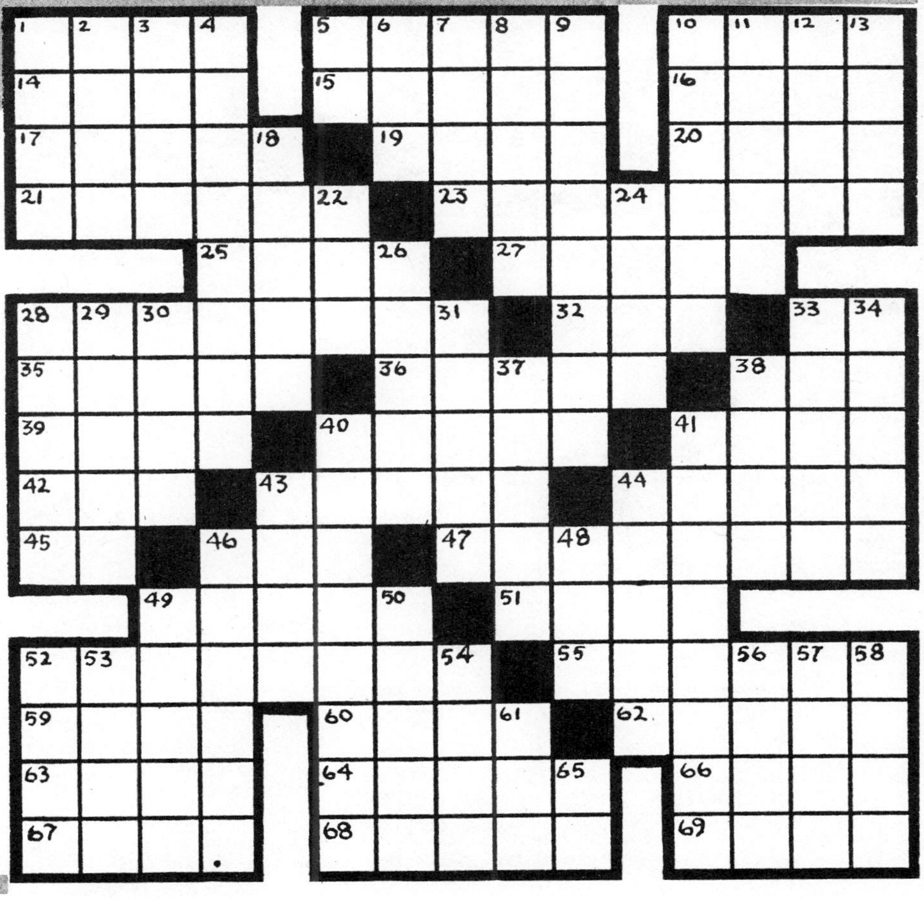

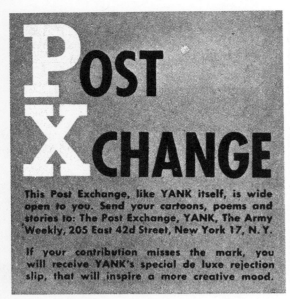

POST XCHANGE

This Post Exchange, like YANK itself, is wide open to you. Send your cartoons, poems and stories to: The Post Exchange, YANK, The Army Weekly, 205 East 42d Street, New York 17, N. Y.

If your contribution misses the mark, you will receive YANK's special de luxe rejection slip, that will inspire a more creative mood.

—Cpl. Don Barber, March Field, Calif.

LATE TO RETREAT
(After reading some poems by A. E. Housman)

These aches and cares that torment me,
How small beside eternity!
The eyes that looked through time with fate
No longer frown, 10 minutes late;
The mind that traveled far-flung space
Can disregard a yard-lost race.
Or so it almost seemed to me,
Immersed in grave philosophy,
Until I woke to sergeant's glare
And now potatoes sadly pare.

Fort Warren, Wyo.   —Pvt. ROLAND A. WHITE

SIZES

One sadly realizes
That the supply-room sarge
Deals only in two sizes:
Too little and too large.

Camp Shelby, Miss.   —S/Sgt. A. L. CROUCH

PREVUE?

Go home and tell your mother
That I hate her very looks.
The only homelier I've seen
Have been in comic books;
But the thing that gripes me most is,
Every time she draws my eye,
I am dismally reminded
What you'll look like by and by.

AAB, Ephrata, Wash.   —Sgt. WILLIAM R. CARTY

The Dog Who Came to Dinner

WHEN the CO called me into his office the other morning, handed me a baggage tag and told me to pick up a crate at the express office, my soldier intuition warned me that trouble was brewing. The crate, explained the CO, contained a dog, and it had been sent by a patron of the squadron who was interested in the welfare of the squadron. The dog was to be the outfit's official mascot.

I hurried to the express office and to my surprise saw a crate big enough to contain a baby grand piano. There was a great deal of movement going on inside the crate, and on the outside a note was tacked which read: "My name is Ralph, what's yours?" I opened the crate and a huge great Dane jumped out, swept up and down the baggage room for a few minutes, knocking over whatever boxes and trunks and workers got in his way. Then he came up to me, put his forepaws on my shoulders and proceeded to lick my face with a tongue like a wet file. After that he gave a few short barks which seemed to say, "Well, what are we waiting for?" and jumped into the jeep.

He insisted on sitting between me and the driver, and all the way back into camp he would blow the horn, shift the gears and even step on the brakes, just to show how smart he was.

It was just my luck to be placed in charge of Ralph. I prepared an enormous box with soft bedding in the basement, but he refused point blank to sleep there. Every night he would run up the barracks stairs, roll me out of my bunk and then sleep there until noon the next day, which resulted in my getting gigged time and again. Then he'd stroll into the mess hall, drool over my shoulder and sniff at my food. Anything that appealed to him was his, and as a result I lost six pounds the first week he was in camp.

He had more unmitigated gall than anyone I've ever met. I arrived at the barracks one evening, dead tired from a 14-mile hike, to find him entertaining two female mutts from a nearby squadron. The pint of gin I had smuggled into camp and carefully hidden in my foot locker was almost empty, and there he sat, with my best pipe in his mouth, belching and having a helluva time.

Unable to control myself any longer, I complained to the CO. The CO listened to my pleas for a few minutes and then cut me short. "I'm afraid," he said coldly, "that you have no appreciation of your responsibilities in this matter. This gentle creature has endeared himself to all who know him. In fact I plan to appoint him the official sweetheart of Squadron D."

After that he not only bawled me out for negligence, but ordered me moved to the basement and gave my bunk and foot locker to the dog.

AAFTTC, Santa Monica, Calif.   —S/Sgt. GORDON CROWE

South of the Border

YOU hear a lot about the Army being a great leveler. Maybe that explains what happened to Pvt. Cornelius Vanderloop.

The minute I land here—in fact I am just dumping my barracks bags on my bunk—when this guy Vanderloop starts being friendly. He is a tall, skinny jerk with horn-rimmed glasses and a studious look. He answers my questions about the camp and tells me I should see Mexico and that he is just the person to show it to me.

Back home I have seen many movies about Mexico with Cesar Romero and these black-haired dolls, and bullfights and dance joints with conga bands. I am very anxious to see all these things, so me and Vanderloop go over the border the next Sunday afternoon.

As soon as we hit the Mexican side there is a dozen cabbies there smiling and saying: "Taxi? See the girls, my fran'?"

I am beginning to think this Mexico may have possibilities.

We go into a restaurant and there is a little pick-up band playing Mexican songs on violins and bass fiddles and a thing like a banjo. There are bright tablecloths and pictures and I am thinking how much it all is like the movies I have seen, when two dolls sit down at the next table. They have black, shiny hair and big brown eyes, and are wearing tight black dresses. The waiter brings them drinks and they talk to each other in Mexican, meanwhile giving us the eye. But Vanderloop don't even look at them. Instead he is talking about the history of Mexico and the Spanish influence, and some guy named Pancho Villa.

My pal orders us a Mexican dinner. I look at the liquor list and I do not believe what I read: "ALL DRINKS 15 CENTS AMERICAN MONEY."

Pvt. Vanderloop is sorry I don't like the dinner, but he says he has something interesting planned for the afternoon. We are going to take a taxi and go somewhere.

We ride out into the country. It is all flat and sandy there and the people live in clay houses. We stop at an old church with walls that have bullet holes in them.

"I want you to see these priceless old bells," Vanderloop says. "They were made in 1569 and the Spaniards brought them all the way here by mule pack. And there's some of the most wonderful mahogany work in the ceiling beams and the altar."

I look at Pvt. Vanderloop and I don't see him. I just see red. I think of the drinks I am missing, the dolls in the shapes and most of all that red-hot dinner. I drag Cornelius back into the hack and tell the driver we want to get back to town.

That was three months ago, and me and Corny have been going over to Mexico regular ever since. He says he hadn't realized the other side of Mexican life could be so interesting.

Fort Bliss, Tex.   —Pvt. FRANC LADNER

PUZZLE SOLUTIONS

DOUBLE PUZZLE. W plus TIRE plus ACE plus ANCHOR minus TEACHER minus COW — IRAN.

CHECKER STRATEGY. White pitches 11 to 8. Black must take 4 to 11. . . . White pitches 26 to 23. Black king must jump 19 to 26. . . . White pitches 18 to 15. Black must jump 11 to 18. . . . White jumps 14 to 23 to 30 to 21. . . . Now Black must throw back the extra checker, by either 13 to 17 or 29 to 25. In either case, White gets the move on the remaining Black checker and wins.

SPORTS: NAVY CARRIES THE BALL IN THE SOUTH WHERE DUKE AND GEORGIA TECH WILL BE POWERS

By Sgt. DAN POLIER

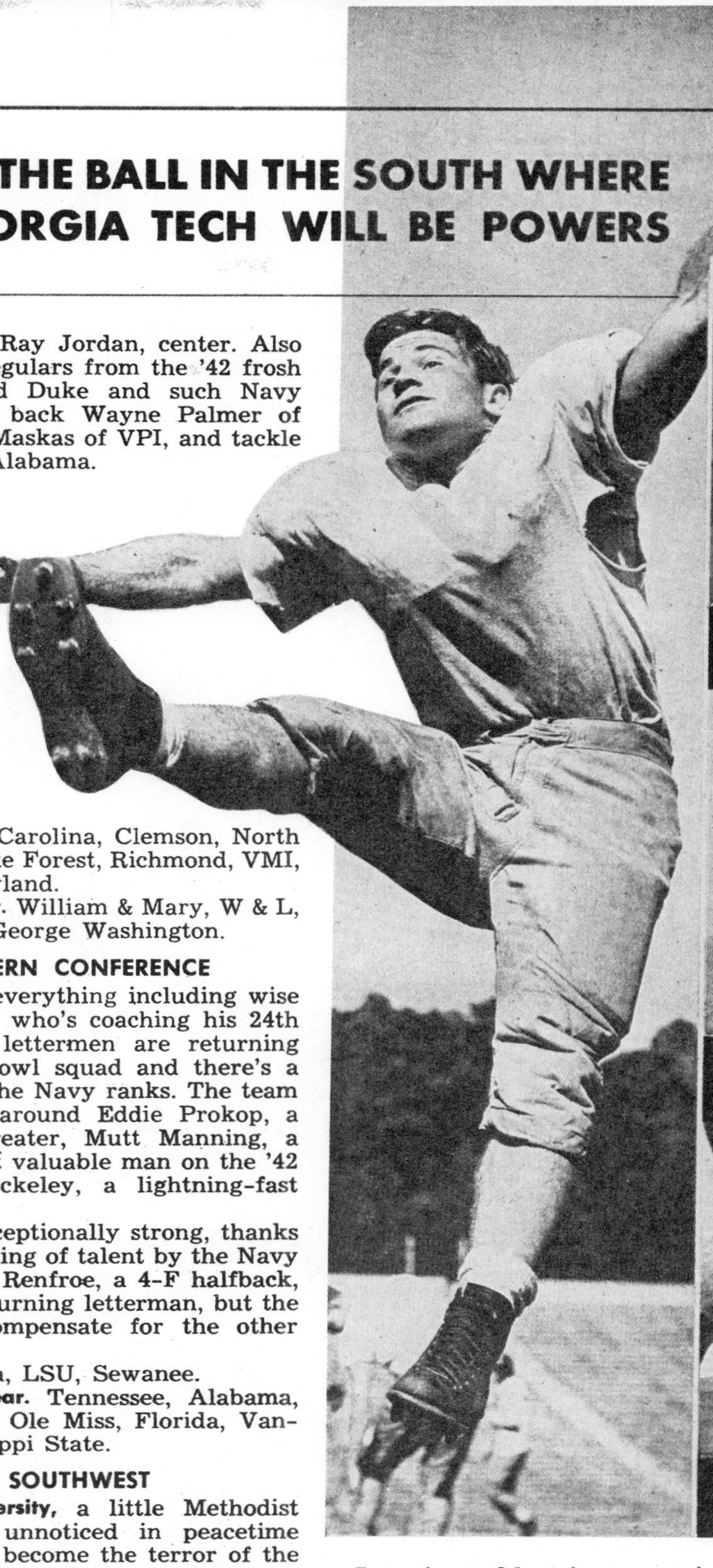

DURING the recent meeting of the Southern Conference a certain representative from the Citadel (all right, we'll name him—Coach Don McAlister) was horror stricken because the league threw all the eligibility rules out the window. He roared that the conference was actually disbanding.

The conference wasn't disbanding. It was just catching up with itself.

As long as the oldest graduates can remember, the Southern Conference has been practicing high-pressure football with little respect for eligibility rules or anything else. The South always gave its football boys room, board, books and tuition as well as furnished them with part-time jobs which gave them spending money. What's more, nothing was ever done to hide the fact.

So why the explosion from the Citadel representative? That's easy.

He knew the action of the conference in discarding eligibility rules gave the green light to its only four members with Navy and Marine students—Duke, North Carolina, Richmond and South Carolina. They would be the big winners, while the 10 other members, stuck with Army trainees barred from athletic competition, would be forced to play 17-year-old neophytes and junior 4-Fs.

At least two schools, Wake Forest College and Davidson College, realized their hopeless condition and asked to be released from Duke's schedule. The others will have to do likewise or follow William & Mary, VPI and Furman to the sidelines for the duration.

Conference by conference, here's how football in the South shapes up:

SOUTHERN CONFERENCE

Duke will be the powerhouse of the conference and one of the strongest teams in the nation. Coach Eddie Cameron has most of last year's mastodonic talent back and his share of Navy and Marine huskies. Some of the Duke veterans—boys like fullback Leo Long, halfback Buddy Luper, guard Bob Nanni and end Bob Gantt—will be playing their fourth year of intercollegiate football as V-12s and can almost double as assistant coaches. Johnny Perry, a great running back who moved from Wake Forest, will be a holy terror running the old reverses Cameron learned from Wallace Wade.

North Carolina may be even better off than Duke. Coach Tom Young had nine lettermen from last year's team dumped back into his lap as V-12s. The veterans are Billy Myers, Shot Cox and Clay Croom, backs; Jack Hussey and Craven Turner, ends; Andy Karres and Ralph Strayhorn, guards; Meredith

Jones, tackle, and Ray Jordan, center. Also available are six regulars from the '42 frosh club that walloped Duke and such Navy prizes as blocking back Wayne Palmer of SMU, tackle John Maskas of VPI, and tackle Don Whitmire of Alabama.

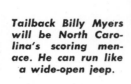

Tailback Billy Myers will be North Carolina's scoring menace. He can run like a wide-open jeep.

Also Rans. South Carolina, Clemson, North Carolina State, Wake Forest, Richmond, VMI, Davidson and Maryland.

No Teams This Year. William & Mary, W & L, VPI, Furman and George Washington.

SOUTHEASTERN CONFERENCE

Georgia Tech has everything including wise old Bill Alexander, who's coaching his 24th Tech team. Eight lettermen are returning from the Cotton Bowl squad and there's a bonus of talent in the Navy ranks. The team will be fashioned around Eddie Prokop, a powerful triple-threater, Mutt Manning, a center and the most valuable man on the '42 team, and Ed Ryckeley, a lightning-fast guard turned end.

Tulane will be exceptionally strong, thanks to the general shuffling of talent by the Navy V-12 program. Joe Renfroe, a 4-F halfback, will be the only returning letterman, but the Navy boys will compensate for the other losses.

Also Rans. Georgia, LSU, Sewanee.

No Teams This Year. Tennessee, Alabama, Kentucky, Auburn, Ole Miss, Florida, Vanderbilt and Mississippi State.

IN THE SOUTHWEST

Southwestern University, a little Methodist school that went unnoticed in peacetime Texas football, has become the terror of the Southwest. The Marines have freighted the finest talent in the Southwest to Coach Medley and he can't miss. Just look at this breath-taking array: From TCU—Hall, Ezell and Bond, backs, and Woodfin, center. From SMU—Maley and McMinn, backs; Martin and Halliday, ends; Dean, tackle, and Wright, guard. From Texas—Collins, Field and Matthews, backs; Watkins, tackle; Fischer and Procter, guards, and Sachse, center.

Howard (Red) Mal[...] Southwestern U

Tom Davis, Duke.

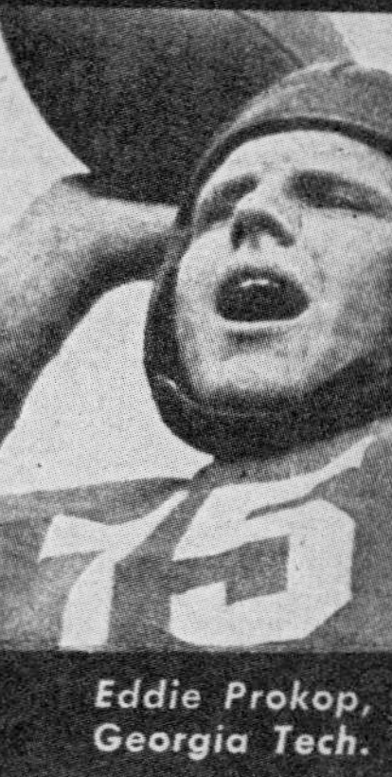

Eddie Prokop, Georgia Tech.

Texas is confident it can retain the conference title and it might at that. Coach Bible is equipped with Navy students, hold-over lettermen and the biggest batch of 17-year-olds in the cow country. Joe Parker, a giant pre-med end, is a sure-fire All-American.

Also Rans. TCU, Texas Tech, SMU, Texas A & M, Rice and Arkansas.

No Team This Year. Baylor.

Next Week: Midwest and West.

As you can see the National Tennis Championship at Forest Hills, N. Y., was virtually a GI affair, with these players (l. to r.): Lt. Elwood Cooke, Lt. Johnny Van Ryn, Cpl. Charles Hare, Pfc. Bitsy Grant, Seaman Jack Kramer and Pvt. Tom Falkenberg.

Sgt. **Max Baer** owes the Army classification office a debt of gratitude. They made him a boxing instructor in the Fourth Air Service Command, which is pretty good for a guy who never learned to box. . . . The MPs collared Sgt. **Joe Louis** the other day in Washington for wearing officer's shoulder loops on his shirt. . . . How's this for irony: **Chalky Wright**, the ex-featherweight champion, was yanked out of the Merchant Marine by his draft board because he enlisted without asking their permission. He was ordered to report for Army induction, then was rejected because he didn't have a bone in his nose. . . . The new heavyweight champion of Iran is a GI, **Jordan Davis**, who weighs only 170 pounds. He recently outpointed the defending champion, who is identified only as **Alexander**.

Ensign Greg Rice has already been dragged out of the water twice while trying to learn to swim at the Merchant Marine Academy. . . . **Lt. Comdr. Jim Crowley** has opened a Navy recreation center in the South Pacific known as Duffy's Tavern. On the same island Crowley has built boxing rings, eight baseball diamonds and a five-hole golf course. . . . Fort Devens, Mass., plans to

have the only hockey team in the service this year. . . . The GIs on New Georgia Island are now carrying baseball bats on night guard duty. . . . Two more major leaguers, Cincinnati's **Bert Haas** and **Gene Hermanski** of the Dodgers, have marched off to war. **Johnny Vander Meer** was supposed to go with Haas, but the Army dropped its option on him because of a chronic intestinal inflammation. Hermanski, who joined the Dodgers unheralded and hit .295 in 17 games, is a Naval aviation cadet at Colgate. . . . **George Cafego** and **Ben Kish** have been given Army CDDs and returned to the football Dodgers.

During the War Bond baseball game in New York, Cpl. **Enos Slaughter** and Lt. **Johnny Beazley** were shooting the breeze with Maj. **Hank Gowdy**.

"You might as well ask Slaughter about his batting average and give him a chance to do some GI lying," Beazley said.

"Lying, sir?" Slaughter screamed. "Everybody in Texas knows I'm hitting .500."

"Approximately?" the lieutenant asked.

"Approximately on the nose. I've made 109 hits in 218 times at bat. Even a guy who's gone through OCS knows that's .500."

YANK

"HAVE YOU EVER SEEN ANYTHING AS
DRAB AND DINGY AS HIS COTTONS?"
—Pvt. Tom Creem

"DAMMIT, THAT'S THE SECOND TIME THIS HAS HAPPENED!"
—Pfc. Tom Zibelli

"AND THEN HE SHINNIES UP THE CABLE."
—S/Sgt. Ted Miller

"THEY'RE AWFUL SMALL, SIR. SHALL I THROW 'EM BACK?"
—Pvt. Robert Bugg

"GOOD MORNING, UNITED STATES ARMY!"
—Sgt. Sidney Landi

YANK

THE ARMY WEEKLY

5¢ **DEC. 10**
VOL. 2, NO. 25
1943

By the men .. for the
men in the service

Pictures of Life Aboard an American Submarine

PAGES 12-13

DARK DAYS. In May 1942 these tired, beaten soldiers were herded to prison camps by their grinning conquerors. Corregidor had fallen. Americans wondered how long they would suffer humiliations of defeat and when they could hit back with enough strength to keep going.

THE Carolina maneuvers had just ended and most of us in the Army that Sunday afternoon of Dec. 7, 1941, thought of only one thing when the news of Pearl Harbor came over the squad-room radio. For three months we had been sweating out 5-, 6-and 17-day problems around Camden, Hoffman, Troy, Belmont and the Pee-Dee River, sleeping in beds only on the rare week ends when we were lucky enough to get a pass to Durham or Charlotte and never changing from those blue fatigue clothes and field jackets with the red or blue ribbons around the left shoulders. All during those months we had been counting the days that were left before we could take off on our Christmas furloughs. When we heard about Pearl Harbor that Sunday afternoon, the first words out of almost everybody's mouth were: "Well, there goes our furlough."

There was plenty of excitement in the Army those next few weeks. A lot of men who were scheduled to be released under the over-28-years-old rule went to the supply room without bothering to ask questions and drew out their equipment again. The guard details were tripled and a lot of new special guards were posted—sabotage guards at the motor pools and aircraft guards in each company area, two or three privates and a noncom pulling 12 hours in a foxhole with a BAR. In fact, during the rest of December and January it seemed as though everybody in the company was either coming off or going on some strange new kind of guard detail.

Then came the day when we heard a latrine rumor about getting Christmas furloughs after all. And the rumor turned out to be true. A week or 10 days instead of the 15 days we had expected before Pearl Harbor, but nobody griped; we were lucky to get anything. About half the company came back from that Christmas furlough married.

December and January were the months of record-breaking enlistments at Army, Navy and Marine recruiting stations. . . . On Jan. 26 the first U.S. troops under Maj. Gen. Russell P. Hartle landed in Northern Ireland; Pvt. Milburn Henke,

MAP CHANGES. A lot of territory in Europe and Africa has changed hands during America's two years of war. White space on the map above shows Hitler's farthest advances. Notice how it has shrunk on map below, showing 1943 Allied advances in Africa, Italy and Russia.

BETTER DAYS. A year and a half after Corregidor, and the United Nations were on the hitting end. Japs and Germans, not Yanks, were falling back or surrendering. Our spirit of offense was winning the war. These German soldiers, being searched by an American sergeant, were captured in Italy.

The Two Years Since Pearl Harbor

Their historic highlights tell an impressive story of America's steady comeback.

...3, of Hutchinson, Wis., was the first enlisted man to walk off the gangplank. . . . The same day President Roosevelt, sending congratulations to Gen. MacArthur on his 62d birthday, praised him for the "magnificent stand you and your men are making" in the Philippines.

In February 1942 the Japs invaded Singapore, and American planes went into action over the Netherlands East Indies for the first time. . . . The Navy sank 16 Jap ships in a raid on the Marshall and Gilbert Islands and formed a court of inquiry to investigate the burning of the *Normandie*. . . . Boston and 18 Connecticut coast towns underwent their first blackout test. . . . U. S. troops arrived at Canton Island, Curacao, Aruba, Bora Bora, Christmas Island and Egypt. . . . An Axis submarine shelled Santa Barbara, Calif., in the first attack of the war on the American mainland. . . . The Army was streamlined into three divisions—the Air Forces, Ground Forces and Service Forces.

The next month Gen. MacArthur eluded the Japs and escaped from Bataan, arriving in Australia to take command of the Allied forces in the Southwest Pacific. . . . Secretary of War Stimson drew the first number from the goldfish bowl to start the new draft of men between 20 and 44. . . . Yanks arrived at Chile, Ascension Island, New Caledonia and Efate Island. . . . Congress approved a bill creating the WAAC.

In April 1942 the Navy for the first time in history opened combat units to Negroes. . . . Three soldiers were shot to death in a fight over use of a telephone at Fort Dix, N. J. . . . Bataan fell on the morning of the 9th, with more than 35,000 soldiers surrendering after three months of heroic resistance. . . . The bloody siege of Corregidor began. . . . On Apr. 18, Tokyo and other Jap cities were bombed in the famous carrier-based raid led by Lt. Col. James H. Doolittle. . . . The first issue of *Stars and Stripes* appeared in London. . . . U. S. troops arrived at Labrador.

In May 1942 Corregidor fell to the Japs after 24 hours of savage hand-to-hand fighting; Lt. Gen. Jonathan M. Wainwright and 11,574 Americans and Filipinos surrendered 150 days after the

war began. . . . American troops arrived in China, India, Espiritu Santo, New Zealand, Liberia, Venezuela, Galapagos and Tongatabu. . . . The House started the ball rolling to raise the private's pay from $30 a month to $50. . . . Gasoline rationing began in 17 Eastern states. . . . The Navy announced that it had 15 battleships in service and 15 more under construction, against a total of 14 Jap battleships built and building. . . . Lt. Gen. Joseph Stilwell, commander of U. S. forces in China, Burma and India and leader of the Fifth and Sixth Chinese Armies, completed his historic trek to India and declared: "I claim we got a hell of a beating. We got run out of Burma and it is as humiliating as hell. I think we ought to find out what caused it, go back and retake it." . . . The Senate Military Affairs Committee approved the bill for dependency allotments. . . . Ted Williams, star Boston Red Sox outfielder, enlisted in the Navy to fly.

In June 1942 the Japs made their nervy but unsuccessful air attack on Dutch Harbor, Alaska. . . . Nine days later, in a thick fog, enemy troops landed on the Aleutians without opposition from Americans, who were not there. . . . The Army began to call 1-Bs—men with slight physical defects—to do limited service. . . . For the first time new Army inductees were granted leaves of 14 days to wind up their personal affairs. . . . The memorable American victory at the Battle of Midway pushed its way into the pages of history. . . . YANK, the new Army magazine, published its first issue for overseas distribution only. . . . Eight Nazi saboteurs, loaded with TNT, $149,748.76 and German orders to wreck vital American installations, were landed by subs on the Long Island and Florida coasts—and were caught by the FBI. . . . The War Department announced that no American soldier in any foreign country or possession could marry without the approval of his commanding officer. . . . It was reported that the Army already had begun negotiations for 1,000,000 service ribbons for an army of occupation in Germany. . . . The War Department

Little Boys Shouldn't Play With Matches.

We drove the Japanese from Guadalcanal.

established the European Theater of Operations under Maj. Gen. Dwight D. Eisenhower. . . . U. S. troops arrived at the Bahamas. . . . American planes bombed Wake Island, flying 2,400 miles to do it. . . . On July 4, American crews, borrowing RAF planes, made the first official U. S. raid on continental Europe.

The Solomons campaigns started in August 1942, when Marines scrambled ashore at Tulagi and Guadalcanal. . . . The airborne division was established by the Army. . . . Clark Gable enlisted in the Army as a private and went at once to the Air Force OCS at Florida, while Rudy Vallee became a chief petty officer in the Coast Guard. . . . Some U. S. Rangers joined the British and Canadians in the murderous Dieppe raid. . . . The 1-B classification was killed, and a man was either fit for Army service or was simply 4-F.

In September and October of 1942 the Japs came within 32 miles of Port Moresby, their closest approach to Australia. . . . Capt. E. V. (Eddie) Rickenbacker, ace of the first World War, crashed in the Pacific and for 23 days clung to a raft before he and six companions were rescued. . . . The Alaska Military Highway officially opened for business. . . . November 1942 marked the great Allied invasion of North Africa under Lt. Gen. Eisenhower. Landings were made at Oran, Casablanca and Algiers. . . . U. S. airborne troops in force penetrated Jap lines near Buna on New Guinea. . . . Mrs. Roosevelt turned up suddenly in Great Britain to talk to GIs. . . . The Army announced it would make barracks out of more than 300 Miami Beach and Surfside hotels. . . . The Navy trounced Jap warships in another great victory when the Nips tried to retake Guadalcanal.

In December 1942 we heard that almost 1,000,-000 in the armed services were overseas at some 65 places throughout the world. . . . The year's production had totaled 49,000 planes, 32,000 tanks and self-propelled artillery, 17,000 antiaircraft guns and 8,200,000 tons of merchant shipping. . . . The new P-47 Thunderbolt reached the record speed of 725 miles an hour in a power dive from 35,000 feet. . . . U. S. soldiers took Buna on New Guinea. . . . The Army Specialized Training Program, designed to enroll 250,000 soldiers in some 300 colleges, was announced by the War Department. . . . The OWI reported that "no American Army in all history has been so orderly," mainly because there was no "excessive drinking" by soldiers.

THE year 1943 began with the activation of the Fifth Army under command of Lt. Gen. Mark W. Clark. . . . The Marines at Guadalcanal were relieved by an Army force, under Maj. Gen. Alexander M. Patch. . . . A unified draft system was

We drove the Axis out of North Africa.

adopted for all four of the armed services. . . . U. S. Flying Fortresses and Liberators, led by Brig. Gen. H. S. Hansell Jr., made the first all-American heavy raid on Germany.

February 1943 marked the first American defeat by Nazis at Faid and Kasserine in Tunisia, but the Yanks, jolted from their positions, hit back within five days and retook their original

ground. . . . Rationing of shoes on the home front went into effect. . . . The Army cleared the last of the Japs out of Guadalcanal on Feb. 9 as official tabulations put the enemy total in the whole campaign at 30,000 to 50,000 men, 1,100 planes and 72 ships. . . . Lt. Gen. Eisenhower was promoted to a full general and put in command over all Allied forces in North Africa. . . . U. S. forces occupied the Russell Islands. . . . Gen. Arnold declared he would keep "an appointment in Berlin" on Feb. 14, 1944. . . . The venereal-disease rate in the Army and Navy was reported to be about 40 per 1,000, the lowest in American military history. . . . Joe DiMaggio, Yankee outfielder, enlisted in the Army.

Early in March 1943 U. S. Air Forces in the Pacific annihilated a 22-ship Jap convoy in the famous Bismarck Sea engagement. . . . The Fourteenth U. S. Air Force was activated in China under Brig. Gen. Claire L. Chennault. . . . The American 1st Division drove 30 miles to take Gafsa in Tunisia.

In May 1943 Lt. Gen. Jacob L. Devers, former Armored Forces commander, was appointed U. S. commander in the ETO. . . . In Africa the American II Corps captured the big naval base at Bizerte in a nine-mile advance, entering the city five minutes before the British First Army seized Tunis in a double thrust that bottled up the retreating Nazis. . . . On May 12 Axis resistance collapsed in North Africa, and in a victory hailed as "one of the most complete and decisive in history" the Allies ended the campaign, which cost the Axis 324,000 casualties in the last few weeks alone and toll of 1,795 planes, against 18,558 U. S. casualties since the African landing and a total of fewer than 70,000 Allied casualties. . . . Army troops landed on Attu in the Aleutians, and in three weeks of savage fighting killed more than 2,000 Japs, taking only 24 prisoners. U. S. losses were more than 1,500.

In June Maj. Gen. Ira C. Eaker, U. S. Eighth Air Force commander, declared U. S. air units in England were growing steadily at a rate of 15 to 30 percent a month and the War Department revealed that more than 2,000,000 U. S. troops were overseas. . . . The movement of troops overseas resulted in the cancelation of Army Air Forces leases on 206 of 434 hotels in the East and South. . . . In a sudden, brilliant move U. S. troops landed at Rendova, five miles from the Jap base at Munda, New Georgia.

July 1943 was an impressive month. . . . The Yanks secured their hold on Rendova, landing the next day at Nassau Bay, New Guinea, 750 miles across the South Pacific, and seizing the tiny islands of Woodlark and Trobriand, in a great three-prong drive aimed at the eventual surrounding of the kingpin Jap base at Rabaul, some 400 miles north. Within seven days U. S. forces landed on Munda, and the long hard push up the New Guinea coast to Lae and Salamaua and up the string of islands in the Solomons—New Georgia, Vangunu, Kolombangara, Vella Lavella, Choiseul, Bougainville—was under way. . . . The scoreboard of operations for the U. S. Eighth Air Force since its first raid on July 4, 1942, revealed that the Yanks had dropped 11,423 tons of bombs in 68 daylight missions over 102 enemy targets, losing 276 bombers against 1,199 enemy planes destroyed, 525 probably destroyed and 501 damaged. . . . The invasion of Sicily, involving more than 3,000 ships, began on the night of July 9, when U. S. glider and parachute troops landed behind the southern coast, and the following morning 160,000 Allied troops, under a formidable air and sea cover, pushed ashore along a 100-mile beachhead. The 39-day campaign, which began the liberation of Europe, cost the Axis more than 135,000 prisoners and 32,000 killed and wounded, and the Allies 21,623 killed, wounded and captured, including 7,500 U. S. casualties. . . . About 500 Allied planes, most of them American, bombed Rome for the first time, selecting only military targets and risking grave danger in their determination to bomb no churches or historic places. . . . Six days later Mussolini quit. . . . The Army revealed that 1,000,000 illiterates had been rejected and every first sergeant found himself quizzically stared at.

On Aug. 1, 1943, more than 175 U. S. Liberators from the Middle East dropped 300 tons of bombs on the Ploesti (Rumania) oil refineries in the biggest low-level mass raid in aviation history, smashing six of the 13 refineries. . . . The Fourteenth Air Force in China reported a 13-month tally of more than 600 Jap planes destroyed or

probably destroyed against only 51 U. S. planes lost. . . . U. S. planes bombed Rome a second time, and American warships shelled the Italian mainland. . . . Yanks seized Lipari and Stromboli, islands in the Tyrrhenian Sea north of Sicily, while on the other end of the world U. S. troops landed on Kiska unopposed, finding that some 10,000 Japs had slipped away in the fog. . . . The Navy reorganized its air arm.

In September 1943 the long-awaited conquest of Europe began when Allied planes and ships covered the successive landings of the British Eighth Army on Italy on Sept. 3 and the Allied Fifth Army at Salerno on Sept. 9. Although Italy surrendered unconditionally and gave up her fleet, the Germans took over and swept southward to meet the invasion, while Yanks and Tommies, after the crucial few days at Salerno, successfully joined forces across Italy's "ankle" on Sept. 17 and 14 days later marched into Naples. . . . In the Pacific U. S. forces attacked Jap-held Marcus Island, Tarawa, Makin, Apamama and Nauru, flying more than 200 sorties and in some of the attacks using both land-based bombers and carrier-task forces. . . . Hundreds of U. S. paratroopers, under Gen. MacArthur's personal command, dropped on Markham Valley, west of Lae in New Guinea, in one of the war's largest parachute jumps and seized the enemy airfield, paving the way for the capture of the two vital Jap bases at Lae and Salamaua. . . . The new B-29 was announced when Gen. Arnold revealed that giant bombers "dwarfing" Flying Fortresses would be used in the near future. . . . Mrs. Roosevelt, visiting the Southwest Pacific front, found many fathers already in the service despite the talk of an "impending" father draft.

In October 1943 the largest air force ever gathered in the Southwest Pacific blasted the Japs at Rabaul, in the first of a series of smashing raids that already have accounted for 11 Jap cruisers and 16 destroyers either lost or damaged. . . . Heavy U. S. bombers effectively shortened the war in one raid on the vital Schweinfurt ball-bearing plants in Germany at a cost of 60 Flying Fortresses. . . . U. S. troops landed on Mono and Stirling Islands, 40 miles south of Bougainville. . . . American paratroops dropped on Choiseul Island. . . . In the 31 days of October the U. S. Eighth Air Force dropped 5,551 tons of bombs over Europe.

U. S. Marines opened November 1943 with an invasion at Empress Augusta Bay on Bougain-

We knocked out the Ploesti oil refineries.

ville, at a spot only 250 miles from the Japs' great base at Rabaul and then fought off a Jap land force north of their position. . . . The new U. S. Fifteenth Air Force was established in the Mediterranean for intensified bombing of Germany and her eastern satellites. . . . Adm. C. W. Nimitz, commander in chief of the Pacific Fleet, warned that "Japan so far has used only about 10 percent of its troops in the island fighting." . . . The *Normandie* was delivered, upright, to the Navy. . . . The dimout was replaced by the brownout.

AS WE look back over those two years, many of the events seem to have happened not two but 20 years ago, for war slows the clock. Now it's almost Christmas again. And our greatest wish—still—is to get home.

Next year's events seem already to be shaping themselves in our minds. The Allies reach the Alps. . . . The Red Army crosses into Germany. . . . The greatest invasion in the history of the world sails for France. . . . Hitler is assassinated and Germany surrenders unconditionally. . . . Combined British and American navies and air fleets turn toward Tokyo. . . . Tojo nobly commits *hara-kiri* and Japan sues for surrender. . . . Each GI can probably take it up from there.

MUDDY AFTERNOON IN ITALY

FIFTH ARMY JEEP SLITHERS THROUGH THE THICK ITALIAN MUD. LONG WEEKS OF RAIN HAVE CHURNED UP THE GROUND AND TURNED JEEP DRIVERS INTO FATALISTS.

By Sgt. WALTER BERNSTEIN
YANK Staff Correspondent

WITH THE FIFTH ARMY IN ITALY—The road through the valley was thick with mud that looked like chocolate-colored whipped cream. The rain dripped steadily from the gray sky, blanketing out the mountains in the distance. Trucks slithered heavily along the road, trying to follow the ruts left by other trucks.

The attack had been successful that morning and two battalions of Infantry now occupied the high ground at the end of the valley. The trucks were bringing up supplies; an ammunition dump had already been established at the base of a hill. and even the tanks were moving up.

The Regimental CP had pulled out as soon as the CO saw that his attack was in. Only two of the drivers from the intelligence platoon were left, waiting for some of their men to come down from observation posts that had been made obsolete by the attack. The drivers stood by the side of the road, taking the misery of the weather in their stride, acutely conscious of the fact that they had driven in worse weather before and would do so again. They stood by their two jeeps and talked of life and second lieutenants.

"Now you take that new lieutenant," one of the drivers said. "That there Ninety-Day Wonder."

"Which Ninety-Day Wonder?" the other driver said. "We got lots of them."

"You know which one I mean, Sam," the first driver said. "The one with the pipe like he's still in college."

"Oh, him." Sam said.

"Why, today I had to show him which way the front was," the first driver said.

"Now, Jesse," said the other.

"I hope to fall right down in a dead faint," Jesse said. "Why, that man couldn't find a hog in a phone booth. He don't even have the cosmoline out of his ears yet."

"Now, Jesse," Sam said. "The lieutenant's all right. He's just young, that's all. You got to excuse them when they're young."

"You got to excuse them," Jesse said. "All I got to do is listen to them."

He started to say something else, but stopped to watch with professional interest as a two-and-a-half almost slid into a ditch.

"Pull her sharp to the left," Jesse called.

The truck driver pulled her sharp to the left and nearly turned over. He stopped cursing the truck long enough to lean out and say a few things to Jesse.

"Mind your manners," Jesse said.

The truck pulled out safely and moved on down the road, and a line of tanks followed it up. The tanks were open at the top, with a man in each turret manning a .50 caliber. They stopped, leaving one tank abreast of Sam and Jesse. The man in this turret was very wet and looked as if he had ulcers.

"Get a horse," Jesse called.

"Why don't you think of something original?" the tankman said disgustedly.

Jesse made a few more tentative comments about what tanks were good for, without appreciable results, and then he suddenly stopped talking. There was the sound of firing up ahead. There was the sudden roar of motors and Sam said, "Jerry planes!"

The tankman didn't look so ulcerish and swung his gun around until it faced the motor sound, now growing louder. Jesse jumped for his jeep, which mounted a .30-caliber machine gun, and started feverishly to prime the piece.

Sam hit the ground, together with everyone else in the vicinity, and the tanks opened up with the 50s. The motor sound grew very loud. and then a plane swept overhead, going very fast and low, the crosses on the wings very big and the flame licking at the sides where the guns were. It was low enough for the men on the ground to see the pilot, who was bareheaded with blond curly hair. Then it was gone, the guns swinging around to follow and the ack-ack increasing down the line. Jesse was still working on his gun.

Then there was another roar and the tanks fired again. Another plane appeared, a little higher this time, its motor drowning out everything else. When it was overhead the plane banked suddenly on one wing and a thing like a football came shooting out, arching over the tanks. Everyone ducked and there was a loud explosion and the plane was gone. The ack-ack followed it along, growing fainter, and finally stopped. Everyone scrambled to his feet. Jesse was still trying to get his gun together.

"You can come away from that now," Sam said gently. "They've gone."

Jesse climbed out of his jeep. "I got to get that thing fixed," he said.

"I wonder did he hit anything," Sam said. "Hey," he said to the tankman. "Did you see where the bomb hit?"

"Didn't hit none of our tanks," the tankman said.

"What did you hit?" Jesse said.

"I didn't hit a damn thing," the tankman said sourly. There was the sound of motors high in the air and then the sound of ack-ack up ahead.

"There they go." Sam said. He pointed up. Very high and just about to enter the clouds were three planes with square wingtips. Tracer bullets followed them up, but they weren't coming anywhere near. The planes entered the clouds and were out of sight.

"I wonder did they get the ammunition dump," Sam said.

THE tanks started their motors again and moved slowly up the road, flattening the mud as they went. A jeep came down from the direction of the front, and Jesse hailed the driver and asked if the ammunition dump had been hit.

The driver shook his head. "Not that I know," he said. "Only thing I know they hit was Jake Hamburg."

"Not Master Sgt. Hamburg out of Service Company?" Sam said.

"The very same," the driver said. "Caught him right in the seat of the pants as he was pulling for an inside straight."

"My," Jesse said.

"Hurt him bad?" Sam asked.

The driver shook his head again. "Just humiliating," he said. He threw the jeep into gear and moved on down the road.

"This war is getting dangerous," Jesse said.

"Naw," Sam said. "It's just what you get for trying to fill an inside straight."

The two of them returned to their jeeps and sat without talking. The rain still fell quietly and steadily. The last of the tanks had passed and the trucks were coming down the road again. It was getting dark.

YANK, The Army Weekly, publication issued weekly by Branch Office, Army Education and Information Division, War Dept., 205 East 42d Street, New York 17, N. Y. Reproduction rights restricted as indicated in the masthead on the editorial page. Entered as second class matter July 6, 1942, at the Post Office at New York, N. Y., under the Act of March 3, 1879. Subscription price $3.00 yearly. Printed in the U. S. A.

SGT. Baskem Bennett, Tank Commander, —— Armored Division: We had started across the field when suddenly 10 German tanks came up on our flank. They opened up on me and hit me three or four times before they came through. Meanwhile we were firing continually.

About that time two 77-mm shells went through the turret and I discovered that my tank was on fire. I called down to the driver and radio man, but they must have been hit, because they didn't answer. The tank was burning badly now so I jumped out with the remainder of my crew. Our tank was burning yet, but it just kept going forward, and we jumped into a ditch and watched it go.

Soon we were surrounded by German tanks. We lay in the ditch for several hours until one of the German tanks started toward us. We thought he was going to run us down so we stood up with our hands over our heads. The German officer in the tank spoke good English. He asked me where our sidearms were and we told him we didn't have any.

He asked where our carrier was and we pointed to our tank which had traveled several hundred yards down the field before burning out completely.

The German officer then pointed towards our lines and told us to go, so we took off quickly.

Sgt. James H. Bowser, Tank Commander, —— Armored Division: The gunnery instruction they gave us in the States was good. There's just one thing you must remember when you're fighting Germans. When you shoot at them they stop and try to kid you into thinking you knocked them out. Then when you turn your back on them,

---

YANK reprints here selections from "Tankers in Tunisia," an excellent book of first-hand combat reports collected in Africa by Brig. Gen. T. J. Camp and now used as a training manual by the Armored Forces. But it is full of valuable advice for the Infantry and Artillery as well as tankers.

---

not get past the machine gun so we were ordered to withdraw.

I would say the enemy's best shots use telescopic sights. Nobody could see that long a distance and be as accurate. One took a piece out of the seat of my pants at what seemed a very long distance. Without a telescope, he could not see to shoot that close. . . .

At one place the enemy had machine guns placed and protected by snipers. We were to take the hill. I was 200 to 250 yards from the enemy and was lying down. I seen a sniper from the top of his nose up. I knew that it would take a good shot and I had my rifle pointed in his direction. I decided to wait and finally he moved up to chest height and I squeezed one off but didn't hit him. Then I seen another, just his helmet. Then he raised and I squeezed another one off. I got him; he raised up on his toes and fell over. I never did get any fire from them. . . .

Sgt. Leland A. Sutherland, —th Armored Infantry: We were attached to the 2d Battalion when the last attack was made and we came under fire. Just the minute we got up there we made a

---

it now anymore, but last Monday we took pretty good beating from their artillery. It w... our second attack and many men were pret... scared, but you readily realize that if you a... in the ground it is pretty ineffective. I try to te... the men to take it easy. . . . No matter how lo... a man has been in the Army, until he hears th... first one go over, he is a rookie.

Lt. Col. L. V. Hightower, Executive Officer, —— A...mored Division: In tank fighting nothing is mo... important than expert reconnaissance of yo... routes of advance and withdrawal. . . . In this cou... try, too, we've learned to move slowly so as not ... reveal our positions. You can't boil up to batt... at high speed without broadcasting your comi... in a big cloud of dust. . . .

The basic training they had in the States mea... a lot to our boys over here. Every time they h... the ground you'll find them digging a helluva b... hole. I have yet to see one man get hit in a pro... erly dug slit trench. One of my lads dug a sha... low one and he came out with a bullet hole cle... through the cheeks of his tail. You don't have ... mention light discipline to them. They'll whoo... and holler at anyone who uses a light at nig... regardless of rank.

We've also learned that it's important f... everyone to know what to do with wounds, e... pecially shock. Although I saw one man die ... shock from a simple hand wound, I've also se... our men save almost 500 casualties by prom... treatment of their wounds with sulfa drugs a... proper treatment for shock. Most of the su... drugs are administered by the men the... selves. . . .

When the Germans go into position they'll hi...

TANKERS IN TUNISIA

These combat stories, told by the men of the Armored Forces in North Africa last April when the going was tough, should be read by every GI in the Army.

FOXHOLE INSURANCE PAID DIVIDENDS.

---

they open up again. We shoot until they stop and then keep shooting until they burn up. . . .

It's a good idea, too, to check your ammunition closely. Once I had to climb out of a tank during an action to ram a bent shell case out of my gun, and then hurry back in before the machine guns got me. . . .

Sgt. William T. Etritge, —th Armored Infantry: Three main things that I think are important: The first is to keep your weapons clean—they won't fire if you don't. Stay under cover—I have had men who were not under cover and they haven't come back. Then get all the fire on the enemy that you can. . . . My men were jumpy but they are better now. We get plenty to eat and get a canteen of water a day.

The enemy has a good machine gun, but if you can get through you have got him. You can get away from his artillery and his mortars.

Three days ago we were going to attack: we were going toward the hill. I put scouts out in front. The enemy let my scouts get within 20 to 25 yards of them and, I guess thinking we were all there, put mortar fire behind us and opened up with machine-gun fire ahead. They got my two scouts. The scouts had got close enough so that they couldn't be hit by mortar or machine gun, but it looked as if they were hand-grenaded. The grenades set the grass on fire under the scouts and when one got up to put out the fire they got him. We seen we could

---

night attack. The scouts drew enemy fire. All the machine guns fired and the men had to learn one thing—that was to stay down. I lost three men. I can harp and preach but the men won't get down. . . . I have learned that artillery couldn't hurt you if you just got down in a foxhole while the firing was going on. The men soon learned to get down while they are firing.

They have guns set up that don't have a grazing fire, but cross-fire. They are set up to get you on the sky line.

I have no experience to relate, but have had the hell scared out of me here for a month or so. I have learned that we have to play for keeps. One thing them Germans and Italians are like, a corporal in my platoon says—like gray squirrels; they can't stay still, and all you have to do is lay down and shoot them as they pop up. . . .

Pvt. Jack Moore —th Infantry: It seems like everything the enemy uses is designed to harass a man. They start firing at night and the guns seem to crack overhead, and it makes it seem as if they were right on top of you. Their tracers seem to have curves on them. But if you wait and take it easy, you can soon tell where they are. They have flares that make it look like convoys coming down the road, and they have flares that are good for nothing but make it seem like an attack is taking place. They have snipers that don't have much of a chance of hitting anything but scare the hell out of you. I am not afraid of

---

their guns and tanks in anything, including Ar... huts. And then they dress their personnel ... Arab garb while going to and from their po... tions. Usually they'll try to suck you inside of ... 1,200-yard range. They frequently use machi... guns to range themselves in, and you can du... their shells by watching their machine-gun fi... When they're moving they'll shoot at anythi... that looks suspicious and they'll generally kno... down every Arab hut in sight. We think that's ... good idea and are beginning to follow suit. Som... times they'll get the range with high burst smo... shells. But when we see three of those in a li... we take off—that's the high sign for the Stuk... When firing, we always shoot low—even t... ricochets will hit them. Most of our misses ha... been high. . . .

Sgt. Becker, —— Armored Regiment: It's a fun... thing, being tank commander. You have got ... run the crew, be stern and show leadership. ... had a new driver for an M3 tank. I told him ... drive up a slope to a certain place and then sto... He got excited and went all the way up the hi... I told him to back up to the right place. He g... excited again and went all the way back dow... the hill. He wouldn't listen to the interpho... communication so I hollered to the 37 gunner ... stop him, as I had my head out. Finally v... stopped him and we drove up to a safe firi... place and I asked him why he didn't pay atte... tion to me.

TANKER WITH A GRANDSTAND SEAT
FOR THE BATTLE OF TUNISIA

INFANTRYMEN OF THE FIRST ARMORED DIVISION TAKE A TOWN IN THE TUNISIAN CAMPAIGN.

Overnight, I explained how I wanted him to drive and how I wanted him to pay attention, and I told him if he didn't I would close his slot up completely and make him drive blind. That fixed him. I think I have a good driver now...

Capt. Gail H. Brown, —th Infantry: . . . Something that I noticed the first night we hit here and made the attack toward the big hill was a massing of troops when they came under fire. They herded together like sheep. I was weapons commander at the time. I found machine guns emplaced close together and where they had no field of fire. The heavy machine guns and light machine guns were placed close together. However, after organizing my own machine guns and mortars and trying to help the infantry to spread out and get a field of fire, they actually learned for themselves, because that night enemy artillery and mortar fell on us. As it was they were spread out and well dispersed. The troops learn fast.

The next thing that I find important is the getting of information down to the troops, for the very simple reason that they don't know what is happening and they don't know what to expect and what to do at the proper time. It has been emphasized before, but the officers don't seem to realize the importance of it. The discipline is very good and the morale high. Replacements seem to help in this because it seems the men have someone new to talk to and tell stories to. At one time we were to get replacements and

were told that they were coming in but they didn't come. The morale went down a lot that night. Last night they came in and we told them to dig foxholes and everything that we had learned by experience. The replacements look like a good bunch of boys. They were a little scared at first because they didn't know what to expect and the people at the rear told them so many different stories. The replacements arrived last night and received baptism of mortar fire this morning. Nobody was hurt because they dug all night and had good foxholes. . . .

S/Sgt. William Hagler, —— Armored Regiment: At Smitty's farm at Medjez-el-Bab on Dec. 10, Germans packed mud on the turrets of their Mark IV tanks to make them look like our M4 tanks. Our own foot reconnaissance picked this up and we were ready for it. Our position was of stationary disguised artillery. We waited until the Mark IVs were within 800 yards, then opened fire. We got five Mark IVs, one of our M3 tanks being used by the Germans and one German motorcyclist in a U. S. Army combat suit. We found only three guns. The German tanks were carrying shock troops.

At El Guettar on Mar. 31 I was protecting the company commander's left flank. His platoon lost one vehicle from 88 fire. He knocked out one 88. By looking through my glasses, I saw it roll over. I knocked one motorcyclist off his cycle with a .45-caliber pistol and broke his hip. I made him

crawl to me and searched him, but found nothing.

Heavy artillery fire was going on with air bursts. I was in a sweat. One crew of my platoon abandoned its tank, which had been hit. Later the company commander, 1st Lt. Boresh, with a driver, went back under fire and recovered the tank. I saw a cyclist getting away and thought he was a messenger, so I shot a super HE ahead of him and he ran into the burst. Pretty expensive shot, but he was out of .30-caliber range.

Afterwards we assembled, gathered the wounded and came out by a roundabout route. I was covering the retreat. I saw a gun crew running to their gun and gave them four supers. They got in the way and we went on. . . .

Spare parts we get now by robbing the battlefields. . . . At present the clothes I have on are all that I have. I wash them in gasoline and they dry in about five minutes. . . . Every man must know his job and the tank commander must know them all. The most important thing I have learned here is the German employment in depth of antitank guns. In tank versus tank, our M4s can handle them two to one.

Sgt. George Cleland, —th Armored Infantry: Men in the States should be trained to dig foxholes. It will save lives. Foxholes are better than slit trenches because they protect a man more and you can fire out of a foxhole and you can't very well out of a slit trench. . . . The first thing I would stress to a new man is leadership. I would make the man have confidence in his leader, and train him in every weapon, camouflage and to dig foxholes; also to cover up tin cans. Tin cans reflect light and give away positions. . . .

GAGS FROM NEW GUINEA

NEW GUINEA—The old gag about bringing a parachute back if it doesn't open was matched on the morning of the amphibious landing near Lae, New Guinea. U. S. amphibian engineers found this notice among their M-1 cartridge clips:

"Return this card to Denver Ordnance Plant when reporting any defects in these cartridges."

Closed for Inventory

Between heavy Jap bombings during the early stages of the Lae battle, a GI asked his supply sergeant for a new helmet. He had lost his old one during a night movement.

"Sorry," said the supply sergeant, pointing to several boxes full of new helmets, "but they can't be given out yet. We have to take inventory."

The Yank was not to be turned down so easily. "Listen, sarge," he came back, "we're in a combat area now. And everything is expendable—especially us."

The sergeant gave him a helmet.

Mess Call

A bunch of amphibian engineers were lined up for chow around noontime one day during the invasion when Jap bombers dropped some eggs. Everybody jumped for a slit trench.

The Jap planes had scarcely had time to unload the bombs and pass on when T-4 C. S. Dodson, a mess sergeant from Mount Pleasant, Tex., bellowed at the Yanks in the ground:

"C'mon, you guys, git out of yore holes and git yore chow while it's hot. This ain't no all-day all-night restaurant."

Aussie Optimism

Americans handling supplies at Busu Village noticed that the Aussies left their big packs and most of their personal gear behind with a few guards when they pushed toward Lae.

Accustomed to lugging around a 40-pound jungle pack, a Yank asked one of the guards why all the gear had been left behind.

"Oh," replied the Aussie, "our blokes reckon it would only slow 'em down when they're chasing the Jap. Besides, they can do without blankets, mosquito bars and other gear for a few days until we take Lae."

Gloomy Send-off

Before the landing craft pulled out for the invasion, I was handed this message assigning me to one of the boats: "Lt. Wentworth—Sgt. Richardson will ride in your LCT. Also two graves registration men."

Signpost to Lae

So swiftly did the Diggers move on toward their objectives in New Guinea that headquarters were usually in jeeps or on foot somewhere along the trail.

When runners were told to take messages to one of these headquarters, they soon learned not to bother going to the place where the headquarters was supposed to be. Instead they walked farther up the trail until they came to Japs who had been killed only a day before.

When they passed these one-day-dead Japs they knew the headquarters was nearby.

—Sgt. DAVE RICHARDSON
YANK Staff Correspondent

This Week's Cover

THE lookout silhouetted on the cover is standing on the bridge of an American submarine, one of our underwater prowlers that have taken such a cheerful toll of Jap shipping. He studies the sky as well as the sea, for the airplane is a deadly enemy of the sub. More submarine pictures are on pages 12 and 13 All are Official U. S. Navy photos.

PHOTO CREDITS: Cover—U. S. Navy. 2—INP. 4—Upper left, Acme; lower left, Sgt. George Aarons; right, INP. 5—Acme. 6 & 7—Sgt. Pete Paris. 8—Sgt. John Bushemi. 9—Sgt. Aarons. 12 & 13—U. S. Navy. 16—Upper left, AAF, Geiger Field, Wash.; upper right, Signal Corps; center left, Sgt. Ben Schnall; lower left, Signal Corps. 17—Upper left, Pvt. David Royter, Camp Shelby, Miss.; upper right, Sgt. Dillon Ferris; center right, Sgt. Schnall. 19—T-5 Harold Weiss. 20—MGM. 21—Columbia Pictures. 23—Upper, PA; lower, Acme.

Editor Backed Lend-Lease Bill; Now He's Down at Lend-Lease Base

TRINIDAD, BRITISH WEST INDIES—"Put up or shut up!" That's what a delegation of irate mothers and fathers told a Corbin (Ky.) editor whose newspaper was crusading for more active American participation in the war. They wanted him to practice what he preached.

So 36-year-old Ernest R. Watkins, editor and owner of the *Tri-County News,* leased his paper, stored his furniture, kissed his wife Mary good-bye and enlisted. Mr. and Mrs. Watkins had established the *News* in 1938.

The paper's editorial columns advocated a more stringent draft bill, passage of the Lend-Lease act and other bills to put the United States on a full-time war basis. "I had intended to join up eventually," Watkins says, "but my callers were in no mood to listen to excuses."

Now Mary is a war worker in Alcoa, Tenn., and Watkins is a corporal and associate editor of *TNT (Trinidad News Tips),* an Army publication sold with YANK. The soldier-editor is through crusading. "It's too hard on the nerves."

Not that Watkins regrets his editorials in the *Tri-County News.* "But when I was hollering loud and long for Lend-Lease," he adds, "I had no idea I would be stationed someday on one of the islands acquired in the deal."

—Sgt. CLYDE BIGGERSTAFF
YANK Staff Correspondent

TS Means Transient Service; It Keeps GI Air Travelers Happy

AN AMERICAN AIR BASE IN BRITAIN—If you're that rare bird, the GI passenger on a military plane, you'll get the surprise of your life at this stop-over base.

Compared with the water convoy, traveling by air is pretty soft, but if you feel like griping there are generally some little things to beef about. Odds are that the mess hall at the base where you land is closed. Your Nissen hut is miles away, and after wrestling your barracks bags through the mud you may find it locked.

It isn't that way here. At this base you are greeted like a visiting general, escorted through the processing, provided with meals and a place to stay, shown where to exchange your currency and guided to the PX and whatever entertainment the place offers. And if you are staying long enough, you'll get a pass to town.

All these minor miracles are the work of the first Transient Service Unit of the Air Transport Command's European Wing. ATC plans to set up similar outfits at all the main air bases.

In a one-month course at the ATC's school in New York, Pan-American Airways officials trained Capt. Warren Freeman of Miami, Fla.; S/Sgt. Johnny A. McCarty of Mountain View, Okla.; Sgt. Lloyd N. Garrison of Blanchester, Ohio, and Pfc. Martin Ampel of New York City.

Most of the Transient Service Unit's enlisted "customers" are on the way to reassignment after completing 50, 70 or 75 combat missions.

—Sgt. BURTT EVANS
YANK Staff Correspondent

Pfc. Bill Crews (above) of Buffalo, Wyo., as well as other American infantrymen in New Georgia, found the solution to rattling dog tags, which might give them away in close jungle combat. Cutting rings of rubber from tubes of gas masks abandoned by Japs, they stretched them to fit around the tags. Noncombatants use them, too, so that the metal, heated by the blistering sun, won't burn their chests.

SGT. Robert Greenhalgh
YANK STAFF ARTIST - RIVER STREET, HONOLULU

AN IMPRESSION OF RIVER STREET IN HONOLULU ON A SATURDAY NIGHT, BY SGT. ROBERT GREENHALGH, YANK STAFF ARTIST IN THE PACIFIC THEATER.

Meet the South Pacific's Ace Rumor-Monger—A Latrine Orderly

AN ADVANCED PACIFIC BASE—When Pfc. Tom M. Gaines isn't helping his ack-ack battery make things hot for the Japs, he works at the most odorous job in the Army. Gaines has been latrine orderly in the same outfit for three years.

Improving on the seven dwarfs who whistle while they work, Gaines yodels while he works —hillbilly songs from back in Henning, Tenn. He considers himself the best-informed soldier in this area; he's collected thousands of hot rumors.

The Tennesseean is proudest of the sturdy brick latrine he built on New Caledonia when the outfit was stationed there. It was rather affectionately known as the "Grand Ole Opry House." Since then he has built, repaired, moved, cleaned and remodeled many a latrine.

When the war is over, Gaines says, "Ah'm gonna go back to mah lil' ole farm in Tennessee and build me the prettiest lil' latrine you ever seen."
—Cpl. HERTZ ROSENBAUM
YANK Field Correspondent

Shipping Overseas, Yank Finds Brother's Name Carved on the Rail

SOMEWHERE ON THE ATLANTIC—Cpl. D. V. Norman of Waco, Tex., stood in the chow line stretching along the ship's rail. Looking at the water and feeling the sway of the ship, he wondered where and when he'd land.

The chow line moved a little, and suddenly there on the rail was his brother's name, carved unmistakably under the initials of a guy from New York: "Pvt. Woodrow Norman, Waco, Tex."

The last time the corporal heard from Woodrow he was in the MPs back in the States. Now, he figures, Woodrow must be in Sicily or Italy; that was where the transport was headed on the trip before this one.
—Sgt. NEWTON FULBRIGHT
YANK Field Correspondent

Second Hand Jeep Corporation Cooks With Gas

BENGAZI, LIBYA—Operating an assembly line that turns out jeeps from begged, borrowed or stolen parts is the spare-time occupation of four men of a U. S. Mobile Ordnance outfit, temporarily located near here.

So far these men have turned out two complete jeeps and they're working on a third. Sgt. Milton E. Rieman, who once operated a garage with 30 mechanics in Spokane, Wash., manages the "Second Hand Jeep Corporation."

As Rieman tells it, he and the other boys went into this spare-time salvage business as a result of a slight annoyance. "Our lieutenant was always bumming the maintenance section's jeep," Rieman says, "and it was never there when we needed it. So there was nothing to do but make him one."

Rieman and his men ranged out over the countryside and rounded up a pile of junk, which they hammered and bolted into a serviceable jeep, complete with top and horn. The happy lieutenant promptly named the vehicle *Spare Parts*, and has bothered them no more.

The corporation's second jeep was turned out after some clever trading on Rieman's part. "Some time before," says Rieman, "I found a boat down at the harbor that somebody had made out of an old airplane ponton. One day I met a man with a jeep body and frame who traded it to me for the boat."

Rieman sent his agents out again and they came in with another load of junk. Into the second jeep's power plant went parts from four discarded engines. Heavily booted salvage-pile tires went on the wheels. A GMC truck speedometer was fitted into the dashboard and a rakish V-shaped windshield from a Dodge truck was welded on. The jeep even has an ashtray.

S/Sgt. John C. Clarke of Chicago, Sgt. Albert Cabot of Filer City, Mich., and Pvt. Hugh Davis of West Plains, Mo., are working with Rieman on a pair of side wings right now. They're making them out of plexiglas from an old P-40. With the side wings, a radiator-cap ornament and a coat of paint, the jeep will almost pass for a new vehicle.

But there's a catch to it. Each jeep, as it rolls off the Second Hand Jeep Corporation's line, has to be numbered, made a part of the outfit's rolling stock and guarded from prying eyes in search of T/BA excesses.

"You see," the outfit's captain wearily explains, "the spare parts, as well as Rieman and his associates, are government property."
—Sgt. BURGESS SCOTT
YANK Staff Correspondent

Sgt. Rieman and the Second Hand Jeep Corporation.

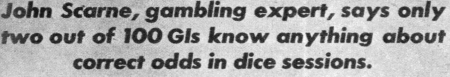
By ALLEN CHURCHILL Y3c
YANK Staff Writer

How many times have you walked down your company street or along the deck of your ship, passing out dollar bills to the guys you meet? Probably never, and probably you never will. But you might as well do this as shoot craps with the odds you get in most camp and ship dice games.

John Scarne, YANK's adviser on gambling, recently made a survey of Army camps and Navy stations. Even Scarne, a hard-boiled citizen, was amazed when he found out how few soldiers, sailors and marines have any idea of fair odds in craps. About two men out of 100, he figures, really know anything about odds.

Shooting dice is like tossing coins. With coins, you take 10 tosses. You may toss 10 heads or 10 tails. Or anything in between. But if you take 100,000 tosses, the heads and tails will inevitably even up. The same holds true for dice.

But say you agreed to take 5 or 10 percent the worst of it on every toss of the coin or roll of the dice. Say you agreed to accept 91 cents every time you won and to pay out $1 every time you lost. If you did this you would be a sucker and go broke in no time. But the odds that most of Uncle Sam's crapshooters are playing are just about as fair as these.

Let's take an example. When a soldier takes the usual even-money bet that he can throw "8", he is cheating himself as much as if he were playing against crooked dice. The proper odds for "8" are 6 to 5, and if he had ever taken time out to think of odds he would know it without being told. But GI suckers seem content to accept the other guy's odds without question.

What's wrong with most of the dice odds used in the armed forces? Plenty—but the reason is simple. They are gambling-house odds. There are three kinds of craps—Bank, Open (Fading) and Army (Private). Army craps is the friendly game of chance that soldiers are supposed to play, while Bank and Open are the big-time games where the house gets a percentage on every bet made. And here is where the dirt comes in. It is hard to believe, but most friendly Army games are played with the same odds that favor the house in Bank and Open.

In short, in most GI games the odds are permanently fixed against the guy who is shooting or betting the dice to win.

The correct dice odds aren't hard to figure. Any GI can figure them out if he takes the time. To save the time, however, John Scarne has done the figuring in the charts presented on these pages. *Charts I and II* are the most important. *Chart I* shows every possible combination on a pair of dice. *Chart II* shows how these combinations can be computed in terms of odds.

The trick is to study these charts and learn how odds are figured out. If you find that few of the odds here tally with those you have been playing it's a sure sign you have been losing money in your dice-playing. By studying the proper combinations, you will become familiar with the proper way of figuring odds. Learn the smaller wagers—the 5- and 10-cent ones—first, and then work up to the big boys.

The first thing to do is determine how many combinations can be thrown with a pair of dice. Use elementary arithmetic for this: There are six numbers on each dice. Multiply 6 by 6 and you get 36 possible combinations. They're in *Chart I*.

Then you figure the number of different combinations or ways each number can be made. By figuring the number of combinations by which the point can be made against the six combinations by which "7" can be made, you can easily arrive at the correct odds on all points and numbers. This is in *Chart II*.

But in case you want more specific examples of how the wrong odds can do you out of your hard-earned GI dough, take a look at the following list of "Do You Knows" that Scarne has assembled. These are only a few examples of the bum dice odds that are being given in the games in the armed forces.

Do you know that if there are only two players in a game, one a steady shooter and the other a steady fader, the shooter will go broke in the long run? The shooter has a disadvantage of about 1.414 percent as soon as he is faded—about 7 cents the worst of it on every $5 bet.

Do you know that when you bet even money you will throw "6," you are taking a beating of 9 1/11 percent, or about 45 cents on every $5 bet you make? The same holds true for "8." These two bets are the surest sucker bets in dice. They show up more often than any other points: in other words, 5 times out of 12, a "6" or an "8" will be the point. The disadvantage of 9 1/11 percent for the right bettor will eventually break him, and that is one of the reasons gamblers say all right bettors must die broke.

Do you know that when you accept 7-to-1 you will make "4" *the hard way* (2 & 2); you are taking 11 1/9 percent the worst of it, or about 56 cents on your $5 bet? Same holds true for "10" *the hard way* (5 & 5).

Do you know that when you accept 7-to-1 on making the "6" *the hard way* (3 & 3) you take a disadvantage of 27 3/11 percent or about $1.36 the worst of it on your $5 bet? Same holds true for "8" *the hard way* (4 & 4).

Do you know that when you accept 4-to-1 you will throw "7" in one roll (*come-out*), you take a disadvantage of 16 2/3 percent or about 83 cents on your $5 bet?

Do you know that when you accept 15-to-1 you will throw "11" in one roll (*come-out*), you are taking 11 1/9 percent the worst of it, or about 56 cents on your $5 bet?

Do you know that when you accept 30-to-1 you will throw "6-6" or any other double numbers in one roll (*come-out*), you're taking 13 8/9 percent the worst of it—about 69 cents on your $5 bet?

Do you know that when you accept 9-to-1 that you will throw "4" in one roll (*come-out*), you have a disadvantage of 16 2/3 percent or about 83 cents the worst of it on every $5 bet you make? Same holds true for "10".

Do you know that when you take 7-to-1 that you will throw "5" in one roll (*come-out*), you are cheating yourself by 11 1/9 percent, or about 56 cents on every $5 bet you make? Same holds true for "9".

Do you know that when you accept 7-to-1 that you will throw craps—"2-3-12"—in one roll (*come-out*), you are beating yourself by 11 1/9 percent, or about 56 cents on your $5 wager?

Do you know that when you accept 5-to-1 you will throw a "6" in one roll (*come-out*), you are 16 2/3 percent a loser before the dice start rolling —about 83 cents on your $5 wager? Same holds true for "8".

Do you know that when you bet the dice to lose the gambling house bars 6-6 on the first roll? This gives the house an edge of 1.363 percent, or about 7 cents on $5.

CHART I: Possible Combinations

"2" can be made in one way	1 & 1
"3" can be made in two ways	2 & 1—1 & 2
"4" can be made in three ways	2 & 2—3 & 1—1 & 3
"5" can be made in four ways	2 & 3—3 & 2—4 & 1—1 & 4
"6" can be made in five ways	5 & 1—1 & 5—3 & 3—4 & 2—2 & 4
"7" can be made in six ways	3 & 4—4 & 3—2 & 5—5 & 2—6 & 1—1 & 6
"8" can be made in five ways	2 & 6—6 & 2—4 & 4—3 & 5—5 & 3
"9" can be made in four ways	6 & 3—3 & 6—4 & 5—5 & 4
"10" can be made in three ways	4 & 6—6 & 4—5 & 5
"11" can be made in two ways	6 & 5—5 & 6
"12" can be made in one way	6 & 6
Total number of combinations	36

Do you know that gambling houses purposely paint their lay-outs to read 8-*for*-1, 10-*for*-1, 30-*for*-1, 15-*for*-1, to mislead players to believe odds are 8-to-1, 10-to-1, 30-to-1, 15-to-1?

Do you know that when you play the field on all the numbers on the lay-out, "2," "3," "4," "9," "10," "11," "12," they total only 16 combinations? The house has 20 combinations against you —an advantage of 11 1/9 percent, or about 56 cents on a $5 wager.

You may think that the above percentages are big, but let's take an example of how percentages work. You are to bet only on the point "6" to win at even money. On the first "6" you bet a dollar and win. On the second "6" you bet the 2 and win; the third "6" you bet the 4 and win; on the fourth "6" you bet the 8 and win, pulling down $16. You are happy, but you are exactly $7.42 short. If you had received the correct odds—that is, 6-to-5—you would have had $23.42. That's how percentages work. John Scarne says there are plenty of dice hustlers in and around Army camps who earn from $500 to $1,000 a month just by hustling "6s" and "8s." They wait for "6" and "8" and bet you even money. You don't.

Craps is an easy game to play, but don't let that fool you, soldier. To play it right requires a little preliminary brain work. Stop being a sucker and study the Scarne charts carefully. Memorize them. Then never accept a bet unless you are offered the correct odds.

CHART II: Odds Against Passing

	CORRECT ODDS	ODDS IN TERMS OF BETS	
"4" can be made in three ways; "7" in six ways	2-to-1	$.10-to-.05	$2.00-to-$1.00
"5" can be made in four ways; "7" in six ways	3-to-2	.30-to-.20	1.50-to- 1.00
"6" can be made in five ways; "7" in six ways	6-to-5	.60-to-.50	1.20-to- 1.00
"8" can be made in five ways; "7" in six ways	6-to-5	.60-to-.50	1.20-to- 1.00
"9" can be made in four ways; "7" in six ways	3-to-2	.30-to-.20	1.50-to- 1.00
"10" can be made in three ways; "7" in six ways	2-to-1	.10-to-.05	2.00-to- 1.00
"6" (3 & 3) or "8" (4 & 4) can be made in one way	10-to-1	.50-to-.05	10.00-to- 1.00
"4" (2 & 2) or "10" (5 & 5) can be made in one way	8-to-1	.40-to-.05	8.00-to- 1.00

CHART III: Odds on the Come-Out (First Roll)

35-to-1 or $1.75-to-.05 against	a Specific Double Number
17-to-1 or .85-to-.05 against	"11"
11-to-1 or .55-to-.05 against	"4"
8-to-1 or .40-to-.05 against	"5"
8-to-1 or .40-to-.05 against	Craps—"2," "3" or "12"
5-to-1 or .25-to-.05 against	"7"
6 1/5-to-1 or .31-to-.05 against	"6"
11-to-1 or .55-to-.05 against	"10"
8-to-1 or .40-to-.05 against	"9"
6 1/5-to-1 or .31-to-.05 against	"8"

Sergeant in Sicily Says Sad Sack Is Shrewd, Sly Spy

ALGIERS—The simple soldier Sad Sack is a Nazi spy!

After months of investigation in the musty files of ancient Sicilian archives during which time 16 investigators almost met a sudden end, the truth about the dirty rotten rat, the Sad Sack, can now be brought to the ears of a waiting world. Sad Sack is neither American soldier nor imaginary cartoon: he is Sad Sach of Nuremberg, Germany, and his black-guard family traces back to one Hans Sad-Sack born to spy in 1494.

The Sack (also spelled Sach) family still has members running around loose all over the world. Although the youngest of the clan, Sad, is now having his fate decided by higher-ups, a tight ring of censorship has been drawn about the case, no doubt caused by Sgt. George Baker, whose deft pen works in cahoots with shrewd Sad. YANK, which claimed to be The Army Weekly and god-fathered the entire scheme by first publicizing the character who always is left holding the sack, is in hot water. If Sad meets his deserved fate, YANK can just about pull in its wings and retire to stud.

These are the events which led to his capture and arrest:

Many months ago, a sergeant whose name cannot now be disclosed because of possible repercussions, first suspected that Sack wasn't as dumb as he was drawn. In one cartoon, Sad Sack wore a cloak about his slim figure. When the clothes dropped off in a later issue, there was Sack with the beginnings of a master sergeant's belly! Nobody can be that dumb and still eat so well. Not in the Army.

When the sergeant went to bed that night, a little bell jangled over his head and rang out the bait for the trap: genealogy! He took

Here is the evidence, a history of the Sack's German family tree, showing that he is a descendent of Hans Sad-Sack, the Teuton poet who died in 1576.

the first plane to Sicily where records are kept concerning villains, spies, pirates and general tramps with enough black sheep in the family to poison future generations for centuries.

There he whisked away to the *Archivia Araldico Cimino, per copia conforme, casellario,* which in plain double talk means "For a buck and a drag on your cigarette, I'll tell you if your old man's grandfather was royalty or just a plain chiseler. For another 20 *lire,* I'll guarantee that he was a baron." The sergeant only paid one dollar.

The sergeant almost dropped dead when the archive director presented him with a genealogical report on the Sad Sack family, complete with coat-of-arms and crest. In the center of the coat-of-arms was a dead rooster plopped up against a golden star. The chicken had the same expression on his mug as Sad.

And this is what the family skeleton contained (guaranteed authentic, one buck):

"Family of Nuremberg and known as Sad Sach, Sad Sack or Sadsack. Its origins are traced back to 1494 to a Hans Sad-Sack, shoemaker, who was a celebrated *meistersinger* and German poet of many works, who died in 1576. Michael Sadsack born in 1808 at Groos Glongan, was an authority on the Orient and died in Berlin in 1864. Melchior Ernest, born in 1843 was a German musical composer at Ratisbon, died in 1900. Parney, born in Baltimore in 1858, was a professor of neuropathology in New York."

This, friends, is not fiction. The sergeant is willing to take the stand. He keeps the Sad Sack secret file open to anyone with guts enough to dispute that Shrewd Sad is a spy

—Sgt. WALTER BERNSTEIN
YANK Staff Correspondent

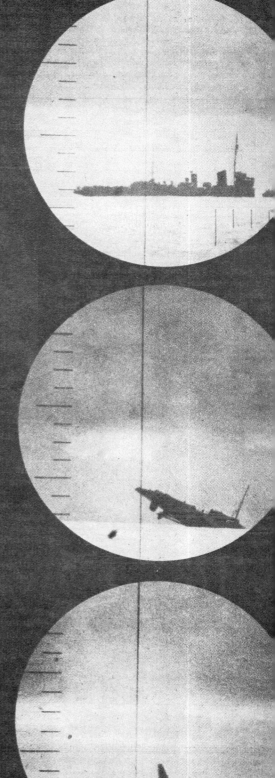

IN THE TORPEDO ROOM A CREW MEMBER GETS A QUIET SNOOZE ABOVE A COUPLE OF DEADLY TIN FISH.

WHEN THEIR SHIP LIES AT ANCHOR SOME OF THE SUBMARINERS JUMP OVERBOARD FOR A WELCOME SWIM.

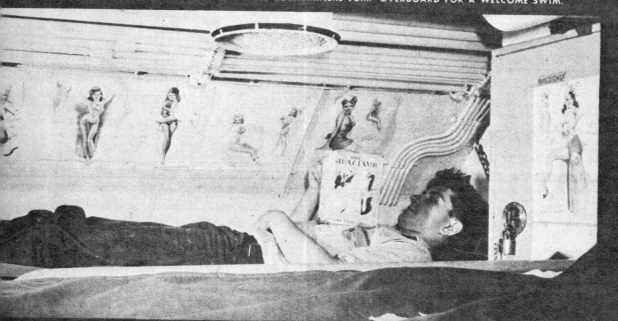

HERE'S A SAILOR WHO USES WHAT SPACE HE HAS TO THE BEST ADVANTAGE. IT'S CLOSE TO REAL COMFORT

THROUGH THE PERISCOPE: A JAP SHIP GOES DOWN

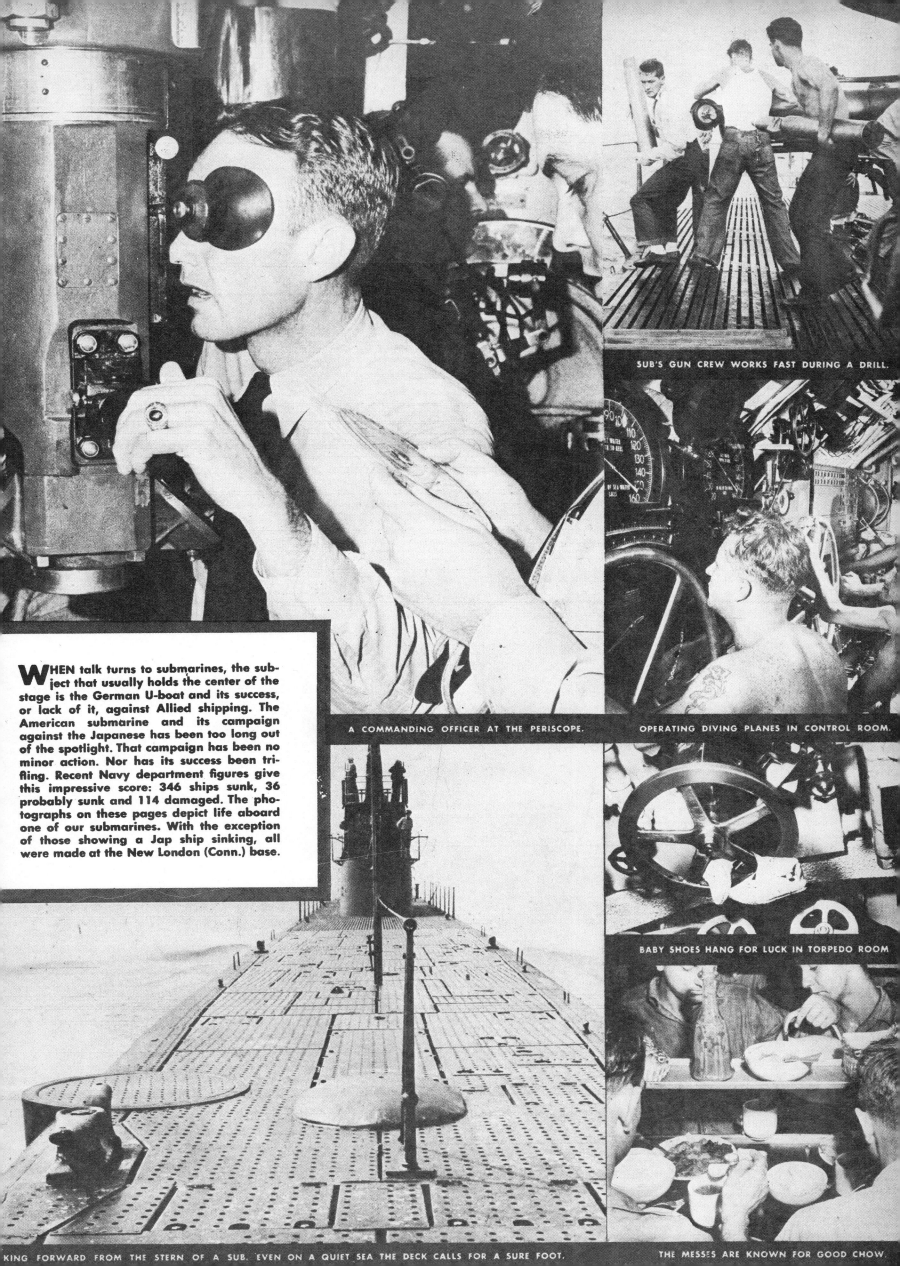

WHEN talk turns to submarines, the subject that usually holds the center of the stage is the German U-boat and its success, or lack of it, against Allied shipping. The American submarine and its campaign against the Japanese has been too long out of the spotlight. That campaign has been no minor action. Nor has its success been trifling. Recent Navy department figures give this impressive score: 346 ships sunk, 36 probably sunk and 114 damaged. The photographs on these pages depict life aboard one of our submarines. With the exception of those showing a Jap ship sinking, all were made at the New London (Conn.) base.

SUB'S GUN CREW WORKS FAST DURING A DRILL.

A COMMANDING OFFICER AT THE PERISCOPE.

OPERATING DIVING PLANES IN CONTROL ROOM.

BABY SHOES HANG FOR LUCK IN TORPEDO ROOM

KING FORWARD FROM THE STERN OF A SUB. EVEN ON A QUIET SEA THE DECK CALLS FOR A SURE FOOT.

THE MESSES ARE KNOWN FOR GOOD CHOW.

ᵀᴴᴱ SAD SACK

"LOST"

SGT. GEORGE BAKER

The Beautiful Bed Check

By Sgt. RAY DUNCAN

A GI musical in two acts, suitable for production by military units as a morale booster. Recommended by leading warrant officers as a gripping statement of a simple soldier's faith in his first sergeant. Production notes are included.

ACT I

[*As the curtain rises on a pitch-dark stage we hear the frank, unaffected snoring of American fighting men. It is that eerie time in the barracks between lights out and bed check. At left, footsteps move slowly and cautiously towards center stage in the darkness.*]

VOICE: Where's m'gahdam bunk?

2D VOICE: Hey, gitcher hands off me, ya lousy drunk! [*There is a creaking of bunks as sleeping men stir.*]

1ST VOICE: Hasa top kick been through yet?

3D VOICE: No, but he's due any minute! Hurry to bed, Butch Norris, the eight-ball of the 8th Platoon! The self-respecting men of the 8th have had about enough of your drunken bungling. You know what the first sergeant said —if you aren't in bed for bed check tonight, we'll all be confined for the week end!

BUTCH: Sounds like Pvt. Buddy Goodwin, best soldier in the 8th Platoon. Blow it out yer barracks bag, Buddy!

[*Chorus sings "Blow It Out Your Barracks Bag, Buddy!" Words and music for this song will be furnished on request, but frankly it's pretty silly. You could have the men sing "I've Been Workin' on the Railroad" instead. Or you could*

simply go ahead with the play, which isn't moving any too fast as it is.]

BUDDY: Hush! Someone's knocking at the door!

ALL: It's the first sergeant! Get in bed quick, Butch!

BUTCH: But what am I goin' t'do with Marge?

ALL: Marge! Who's Marge?

MARGE: Wottinell's it to you who I am, you lousy GI meat-heads? I was in this burg before you guys was shipped in, an' I'll be here after yer gone. For my money this burg was a helluvalot better when the Navy was here!

ALL: Oh! He's brought in a woman again!

BUDDY: Marge, you indecent woman, whoever you are, begone from these barracks. These are American soldiers! Besides, the first sergeant will be here any minute!

MARGE: Stripes don't mean nothin' to me. I'm good enough for top kicks when they're in town, an' I'm good enough fer'm here.

[*She sings "I'm Only His Furlough Girl-O." Incidentally, here's a little suggestion. Why not have some well-known guest star, say Betty Grable or Deanna Durbin, play* MARGE *for you? Any actress will be glad to do it for the publicity. Just drop her a post card, enclosing a self-addressed stamped envelope.*]

FIRST SERGEANT [*knocking again at door*]: Hello in there!

[*Hustle and bustle and squeals of excitement as the curtain falls on Act I. Between the acts you could have a bunch of soldiers dress like girls and do a dance. I think this has been done before, but it will simply knock the audience out with laughter, so what the hell?*]

ACT II

[*Scene, same as Act. I. At rise of curtain we hear the first sergeant knocking on the barracks door. All is quiet within.*]

FIRST SERGEANT: It is I, your first sergeant. Are you covered, fellows? May I come in?

ALL: Do!

[*The sergeant enters and moves slowly across stage, flashlight in hand, checking the beds. The sleeping men gently chant "How Softly Our Sergeant Makes Bed Check." This number is very effective if you care for that sort of thing.*]

FIRST SERGEANT: What was that noise?

[*Marge has jumped out of Butch's bed as the flashlight approaches, and she jumps into bunk with the next man. She continues this, down the line of bunks, always just one jump ahead of the flashlight. But finally she is trapped in the end bunk with Pvt. Buddy Goodwin.*]

FIRST SERGEANT [*shining his flashlight on the two white faces in one bunk*]: Well really! What does this mean?

BUDDY [*staring at his bunkmate*]: Why, Aunt Marjorie!

AUNT MARJORIE: Yes, it is I. I'd no idea you were here.

BUDDY: Whatever brought you to this low condition?

AUNT MARJORIE: Well, I had to put you through the Army somehow. You kept writing for money and after your parents died I was your sole support.

FIRST SERGEANT: Pardon me for interrupting, but this is very irregular. Women are not allowed in barracks.

BUTCH: Wot kind of a outfit is this, fa crysakes, can't a guy's own aunt visit 'm around here?

FIRST SERGEANT: Well—yes. But [*glancing at his watch*] it's past visiting hours! However, I'll take it up with the Old Man in the morning. Meanwhile, madam, you can find lodging at the civilian guest house here on the post. You are a very attractive woman, and if you would consider linking your life forever with that of an humble first sergeant—

AUNT MARJORIE: Buddy, did you hear that? Perhaps if I marry him it will help your Army career!

FIRST SERGEANT: Well, I wouldn't say that. But there does happen to be a new pfc. rating opening up the first of the year.

[*Chorus sings "A Pfc. Rating Is Open!" All join hands and dance as they sing, and curtain slowly comes down.*]

FAMILY REUNION IN TOKYO

Guinea Pigs in Guinea

FIFTY soldiers, plain GI, have been awarded the Legion of Merit for doing nothing.

That is, doing nothing but hard labor in the jungles of New Guinea while *anopheles* mosquitoes chewed on them and their resistance seeped out in the form of sweat through the pores of their skin.

They volunteered for the job and exposed themselves to malarial infection for six weeks, so that the medics could conduct an experiment with two other groups of soldiers to test the comparative effectiveness of atabrine and another suppressive drug that is still new and unproven.

If you think it was easy to let those mosquitoes bite, you've never seen a case of cerebral malaria, or you haven't been in the tropics long enough to see guys' teeth start chattering every time they exert themselves beyond the very lowest level of endurance. A good case of the shivers and shakes sometimes can last a lifetime, or, in some of its forms, it can cut a lifetime down to the few hours men take to pass out in convulsions.

These soldiers were all privates. In the light of combat action's more obvious dangers, their deed might be considered trivial, because the bite of a mosquito is hardly in the same league as the bite of a .31-caliber machine gun.

The volunteers in this case, however, were doing something "beyond the call of duty"—if

not at the risk of their lives, at the risk of their health. If you asked any one of them whether he had the future welfare of the Army in mind, he'd probably laugh at you. If you asked why he volunteered he'd probably tell you it sounded like a good idea at the time, and let it go at that.

That all 50 of them got the Legion of Merit is perhaps as worthy of comment as the experiment's scientific or heroic significance.

The fact is that 50 guys—outside of combat—took a flyer at something out of which none could be absolutely sure of emerging in good condition. And the Army showed them its appreciation.

At least, it would appear, not every noncombatant task in this war is completely thankless.

GI Manpower

A NEW WD order [Cir. 293-43] rescinds previous WD orders on assigning soldiers to jobs on the basis of their physical capacities. Here are some of the more important provisions:

Each EM whose present job is beyond his physical capacity will be reassigned to a job within his capacity, even if he does not meet the current minimum physical standards for induction. The discharge of such men for physical reasons is forbidden as long as they are able to render useful military service in *any* assignment that can reasonably be made available. Assignments will be made "to the most active type of duty" in keeping with physical qualifications and with regard for civilian experience. Only men who are physically unable to handle any assignment that can reasonably be made available will be discharged. If overseas they will be returned to the U. S. for discharge.

Although the use of the term "limited service" is discontinued, this does not mean that men heretofore classified as "limited service" are to be discharged or that the Army will not continue to induct and use men who do not meet the full standards for general service. No man will be discharged for physical disability if he meets the standards for induction for limited service currently prescribed in MR 1-9.

GIs will *not* be shipped overseas if they have the following defects: 1) Pronounced psychiatric disorders (Section 8 cases), 2) hernia, 3) Class I dental defects, with certain exceptions, 4) "enunucleation of an eye with or without prosthesis" (you'd better see your medical officer on that one), 5) tropical diseases which are liable to serious aggravation upon reinfection, 6) defects which are below the minimum physical standards for induction. Exception: Men having defects of type 6 who "have been trained in and have performed adequately in their current assignments" will be kept in their outfits when they go overseas.

The existence of a remedial defect or disease, including uncomplicated cases of malaria, which would disqualify a man for overseas service, will not be sufficient reason to return him to the States from overseas.

EM disqualified for overseas service will be reassigned to duties in the U. S. until their defects are remedied.

Men with venereal diseases, with certain exceptions, are eligible for overseas shipment when otherwise qualified.

For full details read the complete Circular 293

Desalted Sea Water

The Navy Department has announced a new method of desalting sea water in 20 minutes through the use of a compact chemical desalting kit. Devised to meet the desperate need of flyers forced down at sea, the complete equipment weighs less than four pounds and is capable of converting 14 pints of sea water into drinking water—enough to sustain life for two weeks. It consists of a plastic bag with drinking tube and neck cord, and 14 desalting briquets.

New Fourth Air Force Patch

Here is the new shoulder patch authorized for personnel of the Fourth Air Force, HQ, San Francisco, Calif. The patch is 2¾ inches deep and 2⅜ inches wide. It has an ultramarine blue background with a ⅛-inch orange border. A ¾-inch white star is charged with a red disc within a white winged annulet upheld by four golden rays.

Negro GIs

There were 582,861 Negro soldiers in the U. S. Army on Aug. 31, 1943, according to a recent WD release. Of this number 153,900 were overseas. For reasons of security, the release explained, a complete breakdown into components and branches would not be feasible. The following figures, however, were given: Negro GIs in Infantry, 57,323; Coast and Field Artillery, 58,328; Cavalry, 9,750; Engineers, 92,171; other arms and services, 360,903. The figures include Negro Wacs, warrant officers, nurses and 4,386 commissioned officers.

A recent Navy Department announcement reveals that there are 74,013 Negroes in the Navy, of which 7,100 are members of the Seabees.

GI Shop Talk

One of the latest Army guns in action is the 4.2-inch CWS mortar. It fires either smoke, white-phosphorus or 25-pound high-explosive shells. A unit of 4.2 mortars in Italy recently knocked out a battery of Nazi 88s even though the 88s have four times the range and are 30 times heavier. . . . A free memorial flag will be issued by the Navy to the next of kin of anyone who dies in service with the Navy, Marines or Coast Guard. . . . Signal Corps units which went ashore in the first Salerno landing installed 700 miles of communications wire in the first 10 days of the invasion. . . . New British service ribbons, announced in the Canadian Army paper, *Khaki*: For service in North Africa between June 10, 1940, and May 12, 1943, pale buff with central vertical stripe and two narrower ones, one dark blue and one light blue. For service with an operational unit between Sept. 3, 1939, and Dec. 31, 1943, three vertical stripes of dark blue, red and light blue. . . . Representatives of the Protestant, Catholic and Jewish faiths recently joined in dedicating the first American military cemetery in Palestine.

YANK EDITORIAL STAFF

Managing Editor, Sgt. Joe McCarthy, FA; **Art Director,** Sgt. Arthur Weithas, DEML; **Assistant Managing Editor,** Sgt. Justus Schlotzhauer, Inf.; **Assistant Art Director,** Sgt. Ralph Stein, Med.; **Pictures,** Sgt. Leo Hofeller, Armd.; **Features,** Cpl. Harry Sions, AAF; **Sports,** Sgt. Dan Polier, AAF; **Overseas News,** Cpl. Allan Ecker, AAF.

Washington: Sgt. Earl Anderson, AAF; Cpl. Richard Paul, DEML. **London:** Sgt. Bill Richardson, Sig. Corps; Sgt. Harry Brown, Engr.; Sgt. Ben Frazier, CA; Sgt. Walter Peters, QMC; Sgt. John Scott, AAF; Sgt. Durbin Horner, QMC; Sgt. Bill Davidson, Inf.; Pvt. Sanderson Vanderbilt, CA; Sgt. Peter Paris, Engr.; Pvt. Jack Coggins, CA. **North Africa:** Sgt. George Aarons, Sig. Corps; Sgt. Burgess Scott, Inf.; Sgt. Burtt Evans, Inf.; Sgt. John Frano, Sig. Corps; Pvt. Tom Shehan, FA. **Italy:** Sgt. Walter Bernstein, Inf. **Central Africa:** Sgt. Kenneth Abbott, AAF. **Cairo:** Cpl. Richard Gaige, DEML. **Iraq-Iran:** Sgt. Al Hine, Engr.; Cpl. James O'Neill, QMC. **India:** Sgt. Ed Cunningham, Inf.; Sgt. Marion Hargrove, FA. **Australia:** Sgt. Don Harrison, AAF; Sgt. Dick Hanley, AAF; Sgt. Douglas Borgstedt, DEML. **New Guinea:** Cpl. Ozzie St. George, Inf. **Hawaii:** Sgt. Merle Miller, AAF; Pfc. Richard J. Nihill, CA; Cpl. James L. McManus, CA; Sgt. Robert Greenhalgh, Inf.; Sgt. John A. Bushemi, FA. **Alaska:** Sgt. Georg N. Meyers, AAF; Pfc. Robert McBrinn, Sig. Corps. **Bermuda:** Cpl. William Pene du Bois.

Ascension Island: Pfc. Nat G. Bodian, ATC. **Panama:** Sgt. Robert G. Ryan, Inf.; Pvt. Richard Harrity, DEML. **Puerto Rico:** Sgt. Lou Stoumen, DEML; Cpl. Bill Haworth, DEML. Pvt. Jud Cook, DEML. **Trinidad:** Sgt. Clyde Biggerstaff, DEML; Pvt. Bernard Freeman, AAF. **Nassau:** Sgt. Dave P. Folds Jr., MP. **Iceland:** Sgt. Gene Graff, Inf. **Newfoundland:** Sgt. Frank Bode. **Greenland:** Sgt. Edward F. O'Meara, AAF. **Navy:** Robert L. Schwartz Y2c; Allen Churchill Y3c. **Officer in Charge:** Lt. Col. Franklin S. Forsberg. **Business Manager:** Capt. Harold B. Hawley. **Overseas Bureau Officers:** London, Maj. Desmond H. O'Connell; India, 1st Lt. Gerald J. Rock; Australia, 1st Lt. J. N. Bigbee; Cairo, Capt. Robert Strothers; Hawaii, Capt. Charles W. Balthrope; Alaska, Capt. Jack W. Weeks; Panama, Capt. Henry J. Johnson; Iraq-Iran, Capt. Charles Holt.

YANK is published weekly by the enlisted men of the U. S. Army and is for sale only to those in the armed services. Stories, features, pictures and other material from YANK may be reproduced if they are not restricted by law or military regulations, provided proper credit is given, release dates are observed and specific prior permission has been granted for each item to be reproduced. Entire contents reviewed by U. S. military censors.

Full 24-hour INS and UP leased wire service.

MAIN EDITORIAL OFFICE
205 EAST 42d ST., NEW YORK 17, N. Y., U. S. A

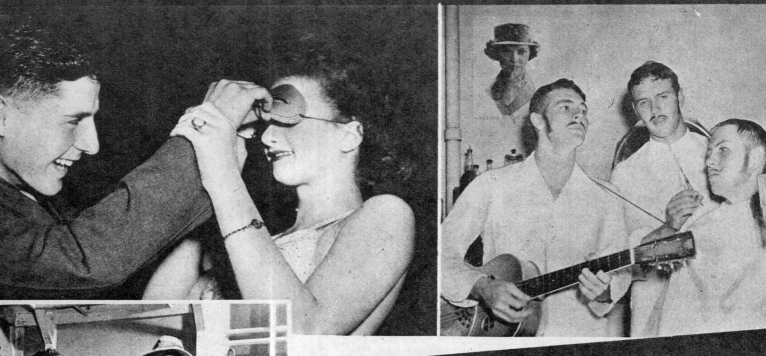

WHO'S THERE? I've gotta see! Pvt. Leonard Cavicchioli tries to complete the picture by taking off his dancing partner's mask. It turned out that her name was Loretta Harvat. She was a guest at a Geiger Field (Wash.) Service Club dance.

BARBER-SHOP ARTISTS. These decorous but carefree gents stepped into [cos]tume to win the costume prize in a quartet contest at Camp Davis, N. C. L. to [r.] Pvt. Francis May, Pvt. Donald Vollner, Pvt. Calvin Mumma and Pvt. Robert Du[...]

CAMP NEWS

BARRACKS CONCERT. A serious musician with some serious listeners. The violinist is Sgt. David Johnson of Co. E, 1210 SCSU at Fort Ontario, N. Y. He studied music at the Juilliard School, New York City.

FAMILY RECRUITS. Pvt. James Davenport visits his mother, Pfc. Marian Davenport, at Camp Joseph T. Robinson, Ark. They were sworn in on the same day at Richmond, Va., but Ma got first promotion.

Strategic Retreat

Camp Gruber, Okla.—Pvt. A. L. Drabin of the 132d Signal Co., pacing his beat on guard duty, probed the chilly darkness ahead when a figure crossed his path.

"Halt, who's there?" he asked.

"Who's there?" the figure echoed. "Advance to be recognized."

"*You* advance to be recognized," said Drabin. "Show me your dog tags."

"Show me *your* dog tags," came the reply out of the darkness.

As he explained it later, Drabin was the first to give in. "What could I do?" he asked. "He was some guy from the Infantry. He had a rifle. All I had was a club."

MISSING COMRADE

Nashville Army Air Center, Tenn.—Pvt. Harry I. Donnelly, 520th Base Hq. & AB Sq., spotted the following classified ad in the Nashville (Tenn.) Banner:

Lost—One half-track M-2 No. C 1-4, name *Comrade*. USA W4011622 — Engine Number 160-AX-1212. Anyone knowing whereabouts of this vehicle notify Provost Marshal, Lebanon, Tenn., or Commanding Officer Co. C, 54th Armored Inf. Regiment, APO 260, care Postmaster, Nashville, Tenn.

Utter Confusion Department

Fort Sam Houston, Tex.—The first sergeant of the 5th Auxiliary Surgical Group found a furlough request on his desk that read as follows:

I would like a furlough to go home to see my folks. My wife is planning to come here and I want to get there before she comes here, because I don't want her to be here when I am there, but I want to be here when she is here.

The GI did not get his furlough. The wife came here.

Romance Marches On

Lincoln Army Air Base, Nebr.—The path of GI romance was aptly illustrated by the selections of reading material seen in the hands of S/Sgt. Walter Biernat.

One night barracksmates found him curled up with a pamphlet titled "What To Do on a Date." The next night he went out on pass. The night after that he was poring intently into a number called "Relationships With the Fairer Sex."

Several nights later still further progress was noted. The sergeant was reading "How To Conduct a Whirlwind Courtship."

AROUND THE CAMPS

Bates Field, Ala.—Cpl. Leonard Richardson s[ays] his favorite President was Harding, and h[e] are his reasons: the corporal was born in Har[d]ing's home town, Marion, Ohio; he went to Har[d]ing High School there; the first man he met [at] the induction center was named Harding; at [the] reception center, his field noncom was nam[ed] Harding; he got his basic training at Hard[ing] Field, La., and while there he went around w[ith] a gal whose name was Harding.

Fort Riley, Kans.—Troopers in the CRTC h[ere] have organized classes in Chinese. Heading [the] "faculty" is Pvt. Ruby Tape of the WAC, assis[ted] by Sgt. Mark Lim and Pvt. Hom Woh. Clas[ses] meet every Tuesday night and so far the [...]

"That's the one, dear!"

—Pvt. Ponce de Leon, BTC 10, Greensboro, N. C., BTC 10-S[...]

have been studying the phonetics of Chinese. [For] their next lesson (they say) they'll take up [the] characters, or words, which run up into som[e]thing like 3,000,000 in all.

Camp Adair, Oreg.—S/Sgt. Corbin Shirley [of] Co. H, 275th Regiment, was overwhelmed rece[nt]ly by fellow GIs who pooled their resources [and] gave him a "baby shower." Included in the ite[ms] for the expected baby were a crib and a virtua[lly] complete outfit of baby clothes.

Camp Pickett, Va. — 1st Sgt. Logan B. Wal[ker] went through the DEML barracks recently loo[k]ing for a detail to assist in fighting a range f[ire]. He reached one stubborn sleeper who failed [to] respond to several calls and taps on the should[er]. "Come on," said Walker finally, roughly shak[ing]

NEAR REALITY. In simulated warfare at Camp Shelby, Miss., soldiers crouch or crawl forward between the lanes on the close-combat range, ready to shoot at any target that comes up. They are in Btry. A, 881st FA, of the 69th Div.

CLOSE HARMONY. This is the kind of autograph, made with lipstick, that a soldier likes best. The lucky man is T-5 John O. Gunn, shown with 20th Century-Fox starlets June Haver (left) and Jeanne Crain, visitors to Camp Perry, Ohio.

HOSPITAL GOLF. S. Sgt. Francis De Angelis (left) and Cpl. Ralph L. Hollis meet a hazard on the miniature course at Grenier Field (N. H.) base hospital.

DONE WITH BLACK GLASSES

Mather Field, Calif.—Sgt. Dick Partridge of the 341st Navigation Training Sq. was walking along the street in San Francisco recently when he was approached by a shabby man wearing dark glasses and carrying a tin cup.

"Sergeant, I'm blind," said the mendicant. "Please give me four bits."

Partridge obliged and continued on down the street. Later it came to him. "How'd he know I was a sergeant?" he asked himself.

he man, "you don't sleep that sound." With that, he GI sat up and replied belligerently: "Who don't?"

Fort Custer, Mich.—Pvt. Harry Cook of the 500th MPEG faced the food on the table before him and went to work silently but efficiently. First he took two solid cuts of beef, then a nice mound of potatoes. These he garnished with a generous coating of gravy. Then as he reached for the pitcher of coffee, he glanced down for the first time. His plate was upside down.

Camp Claiborne, La.—S/Sgt. Edward Peters, 61, of the Provisional Pipeline Hq. Group, EUTC, has some claim to distinction. Forty-three years ago, fighting with the Dutch troops in the Boer War, he was a member of the party that captured a young British journalist named Winston Churchill, now the prime minister of Great Britain.

Camp Carson, Colo.—"Strictly GI" rang up a total of $325,000 in War Bonds here recently and played to an SRO audience. An all-GI show, the revue was the work of Pfc. Peter Preses and S/Sgt. Cyril Morey, who collaborated on the book. Pfc. Carl Kulkman and Pvt. Edward Johnson wrote the music.

Camp Hood, Tex.—Sgt. Francis Hamilton and Cpl. Alton Howell painted the following on a turtle they found roaming around here: "Return to Sgt. Robert Harris, Tank Destroyer School. Reward, $5." Now Harris is getting so many calls that he has about decided to pay the reward to anyone who will give the turtle a home and curb its meanderings.

Fort Knox, Ky.—T-5 Homer Hann packed hurriedly to ship out to cook on a troop train. Getting ready for the return trip from Camp Chaffee, Ark., Hann doffed his cook's garb and started to put on his ODs. He found that he had no OD

trousers. He foresaw a pantsless ride in a civilian coach until an obliging officer of the 19th Inf. at Chaffee supplied trousers for him, just at train time.

Coast Guard Station, N. Y.—Located here is Spar Helen Gragory, 24, founder and organizer of the famed Polish women sharpshooters' civilian regiments which fought the Nazis during the invasion of that country. Helen, who was born in the United States, was taken to Poland by her engineer-father at the age of 2.

Lowry Field, Colo.—Pfc. Bill Walker became incensed recently when an MP told him he couldn't take his gal to the matinee at the post theater. Indignation melted when the MP coldly informed him that "sex morality" was on the bill.

Camp Wheeler, Ga.—Pvt. David Anderson has his own ideas of how to carry on through a KP stint. Recently he appeared at KP roll call in the Co. A (13th ITB) mess hall all set for duty—with his own potato peeler.

Garden City Army Air Field, Kans.—It was an exciting ball game. S/Sgt. Earl J. Finnerty of the PT Dept. had his ear glued to the radio to catch every moment of this World Series drama. The phone rang and Finnerty picked up the receiver automatically. He shouted: "St. Louis Cardinals speaking."

Fort MacArthur, Calif.—The nobility has reported for duty at the reception center here in the person of Baron Gilbert Rothschild, scion of the famous European banking family. Rothschild, who speaks three languages and hopes to get into Intelligence, was in officers' training in Paris before he fled the Nazi occupation in 1940.

Stuttgart Army Air Field, Ark.—Six dogfaces assigned to KP were down in the dumps because their duty would prevent them from attending a shindig to which they had been invited. Then, at the last minute, volunteer replacements appeared, among them a first sergeant, four staffs and a buck.

Keep those contributions coming, whether pictures, news items or features. Share them with other GIs by sending them to the Continental Liaison Branch, Bureau of Public Relations, War Department, Pentagon, Washington, D. C., with a request that they be forwarded to YANK, The Army Weekly.

WORDS ACROSS THE SEA

Cope   Elissomdoberry   Biancalana   Earles

IN THE ALEUTIANS. Pvt. Harold Cope of Salem, Mo., wants to hear from Lee Simmons S1c, with the Navy in the Atlantic. . . . Pvt. John Elissomdoberry of Stockton, Calif., tells Pvt. Elmer Triefembach, elsewhere in Alaska: "The boys all miss you and are sorry you couldn't make the trip." . . . Pvt. Eugen

Biancalana of Chicago, Ill., wants Buddy Ziegler, in the Mediterranean, to "remember our meeting at Wells and Ohio." . . . Pvt. Edward Earles of Los Angeles, Calif., sends a message to his brother, Sgt. Fred Earles, also in Alaska: "I'm all out of cough medicine—anything you can do about it?"

Mail Call

Honorable Discharge Button

Dear YANK:
When will the veterans' lapel buttons be issued? I've already had a fight because someone called me a draft dodger. I've been overseas and seen action and think I deserve to wear this badge.

Chicago, Ill.   —HARRY J. SIMONETTI

Dear YANK:
I certainly don't like the idea of civilian stores selling veterans' lapel buttons. Some time ago the Army promised to give these away free but so far none has been issued. In the meantime stores are selling them for 50 cents apiece. No one should be permitted to sell an award. The veterans' lapel button should be made by the Government and distributed free.

ASOA, Harvard University   —Pfc. MICHAEL LUCKUF

Tribal Blood Dance

Dear YANK:
Your article under the heading "Yank Soldier in Puerto Rico First To View Tribal Blood Dance," which appeared in a November issue of YANK, is so far distant from the truth that I consider it my duty to tell you so, for it might give your readers a distorted idea of what Puerto Rico is and how its inhabitants live. There are neither tribal blood dances nor Madras Hindus in Puerto Rico. Your correspondent must have seen the primitive rites or ceremonies he describes in Panama, where you will find many Hindus.

Camp Davis, N. C.   —OC HORACE QUINONES

■ The story referred to the "'blood dance' of the Madras tribe of Hindus in the West Indies" and did not say the dance took place in Puerto Rico. The writer was referring to the Madras tribe in Trinidad, the British West Indies. Unfortunately there was a Puerto Rican date line on the story, because that is the headquarters of the Antilles Air Task Force, from which the story originated. The heading was incorrectly written. YANK regrets the error. No reflection was intended on the people of Puerto Rico.

Holiday KPs

Dear YANK:
I want to thank Cpl. Rubin Shulman for organizing his Jewish buddies to take over KP and guard duty on Christmas day so the Christian soldiers could have the day off. His letter appeared in a November issue. This is to let him know we pulled KP for his buddies on their holiday.

1st Parachute Troops, Fort Benning, Ga.   —Pvt. J. JONES

Navel Censor

Dear YANK:
If the censor is a good guy, he'll put his stamp in

the right place. The gal on the envelope is a bubble dancer and doesn't want to be embarrassed.
South Pacific   —Cpl. R. E. HUMBERT

Brush-Off Club

Dear YANK:
How do I become a member of the Brush-Off Club? I just received a letter from my girl Jane in Milwaukee who has just become engaged "to the most wonderful man in the world." She said, "I know you will like him when you meet him" and promised to write if I wanted her to. Does this make me a charter member of the Brush-Off Club? T/Sgt. Robert R. Blackney and S/Sgt. Le Roy K. Nelson made up this little wreath in memory of our love.

Guadalcanal   —S/Sgt. POLEWSKI

Dear YANK:
How do I become a member of the Brush-Off Club? My soldier has been wooed away by some Texas girl because she was there with him and I was a thousand miles away. There are many similar cases going on right here: the girls are minus men and just seize someone else's. You need not have any sympathy for me, for it's my own fault that I don't do the same since I come in contact with many servicemen at our Chicago Servicemen's Center where I serve as a junior hostess.

Chicago, Ill.   —(Miss) BINGY PETSCH

■ The parent chapter of the Brush-Off Club in India has no objection to extending its charter to other Army outfits, so go ahead, sarge, and organize. Admission requirement is a broken heart. Qualifications for membership: 1) She has married somebody else. 2) She casually mentions dates with other guys now and doesn't start out "Dearest Darling" any more. 3) Your folks have reported seeing her with other joes. As for Bingy, she seems to be doing all right at the Chicago Servicemen's Center and may not have time to organize a ladies' auxiliary.

11 General Reminders

Dear YANK:
Here are 11 general reminders for Hollywood scenario writers, radio script writers, advertising men, slick magazine writers and all persons who come in contact with the American public through their artistic endeavor: 1) Soldiers are acquainted with girls other than entertainers, debutantes and heiresses. 2) Not all soldiers in the Army are lieutenants in the Air Force. 3) Not all soldiers in the Army are in the Air Force. 4) Occasionally, a soldier's girl friend does not work in a war plant where is manufactured the weapon the soldier is armed with or the airplane he flies. 5) KP includes activities other than potato peeling. 6) Soldiers do not wear their fatigue clothing only when they are on KP or in the guard house. 7) Soldiers aren't fighting the war for Betty Grable. 8) The Stage Door Canteen isn't the first place they hit in New York. 9) Army nurses do not spend most of their time in love affairs with officers. 10) Soldiers cuss once in a while. 11) Not all sergeants growl; nor do they all possess enlarged abdomens.

Fort Jackson, S. C.   —Pvt. SIDNEY SCHLEPP

MESSAGE CENTER

Men asking for letters in this column are all overseas. Write them c/o Message Center, YANK, 205 E. 42d St., New York 17, N. Y. We'll forward your letters. The censor won't let us print the complete addresses.

B. Pfc. GLENDON BAILY, once at Kearns Field, Utah: write Sgt. Joseph Averill. . . . Pvt. EDWARD BOCKEL, once at Fort Eustis. Va.: write Pvt Pasquale J. Colian.

C. Pfc. NORMAN CARNEY, once at Camp Pickett, Va.: see *Message 5.‡* . . . RICHARD M. CARTER once at Camp Breckinridge, Ky.: write Robert D Carter AMM2c. . . . FRANK CAULFIELD, USMC, once at Parris Island. S. C.: see *Message 7.§* . . . ERCOLA J COLIANNO. once at Fort Lewis, Wash.: write Cpl. A C. Leal. . . . Sgt. ALDEN CRONK, USMC, of New Haven Conn.: write Cpl. Joe Darcy.

D. Sgt. ANTHONY DAVID: see *Message 3.†* . . . S/Sgt. CLINTON O. DEWITT, once in Hawaii write Pvt. Gene Manley. . . . Pvt. GORDON DOWLING once at Schofield Barracks, T. H.: see *Message 2.* . . . Capt. A. M. DUXLER, India: write Cpl. Henry S Lond.

F. Pfc. WILLIAM PADEN FINK of Larchmont Acres N. Y., once at Jefferson Barracks, Mo.: see *Message 1.* . . . LEO FORMAN F1c: write W. T. Weston EM3c. . . . Cpl. WALTER B. FULLER of Roxbury, N. C.: write Lt. T. J. Hallman.

H. Pfc. PATRICK HANNON of Yonkers, N. Y., once at Truax Field, Wis.: see *Message 1.* . . . WILLIAM HEMPLE, once in Florida: write Pfc. Robert L Menn. . . . 2d Lt. WILLIAM HILL of Chepachet, R. I. once in Kansas: write Sgt. William E. Fillo. . . . GENE and RAYMOND HISER: write Pfc. Raymond A Del Vecchio. . . . HERBERT HOOPER S1c, once at Pear Harbor: write Cpl. Charles M. Smith. . . . Pvt THOMAS HUDSON of Stamford, Conn., once at Oahu T. H.: write Pvt. Bernard Hoffman.

L. Pvt. VITO P. LAGIOIA, USMC, of Chicago, Ill. write Cpl. Karofsky. . . . Sgt. LARRY LEACH MAN: see *Message 6.‡‡* . . . Pvt. WALTER LENNON o Sparkill, N. Y.: write Pfc. Michael F. Maltese. . . . Pvt. VICTOR A. LINDGREN of South St. Paul, Minn. once at Fort Benning, Ga.: write Cpl. Cliff Boche.

M. Pvt. ROBERT PATRICK McCONAHY of Hunting ton, W. Va.: write Pvt. Lester Edwards. . . . Lt. JAMES (LEFTY) McLAUGHLIN, once at Camp Croft S. C.: write Lt. Meredith Havens. . . . Pvt. JAMES P McMALLEY, Aleutians: see *Message 4.††* . . . Pfc. PET MASUT, once in Australia: write Cpl. John A. Viano . . . S/Sgt. LOUIS S. MEHL, once in Australia: write T-James L. Doody. . . . BUD MILLER, once at Camp Stew art, Ga.: write 2d Lt. William Keeler. . . . S/Sgt. Rex L. MOORE, once in Texas: write S/Sgt. Robert N Richardson.

R. GLENN RIERSON of Leeds, N. Dak.: write Pvt Ralph C. Johnson. . . . HARRY RIXON, Serv. Co. 160th Inf.: write Pvt. George Childs. . . . LAWNDALL ROBINSON of Chicago, Ill.: write Pvt. Michael J. Ancona.

S. Sgt. PETER SAMSELL, once at Schofield Barracks T. H.: see *Message 2.** . . . Lt. ELIO SCOTTI: see *Message 3.†* . . . Pvt. LE ROY SEIRBERT, once at Shenango PRD, Greenville. Pa.: see *Message 4.††* . . . Pvt. STANLEY SHERMAN, once at Base Hosp., Westover Field, Mass.: write Cpl. John A. Dixon. . . . Pvt EDWARD SKOVRAN, once at Shenango PRD. Greenville Pa.: see *Message 4.††* . . . Cpl. CLEATUS SMITH: see *Message 6.‡‡* . . . Cpl. JOHN A. STERK, once at APC 302, New York: write Pvt. Frank A. Sterk. . . . Pvt MURIEL STIGALL, once at Camp Stewart: see *Message 5.‡* . . . ROWEN S. STUFFER, once at Mitchel Field N. Y.: write Lt. Robert L. Redmond.

T. TONY TARANTINO, once at USNTS. Sampson N. Y.: see *Message 7.§* . . . EDDIE TOMAKOWSKI of Detroit, write: Pvt. Henry J. Osip.

*Message 1: Write Salvatore A. Chiodo.
**Message 2: Write Pvt. Stanley Dereniowski.
†Message 3: Write Lt. Peter J. Mamakos.
††Message 4: Write Pvt. George L. Wiedecker.
‡Message 5: Write S/Sgt. Warren Pritchette.
‡‡Message 6: Write Pvt. William H. Glover.
§Message 7: Write Pvt. George Meyer.

SHOULDER PATCH EXCHANGE

The following men want to trade shoulder patches: Lt. William O. Beasley, Engineer Officer. Cent. Sig. Corps Sch., Camp Crowder, Mo.; A/S John W. Foster, 333d CTD Sq. E, George Peabody College, Nashville 4, Tenn.; Cpl. Dora Ann Cessary, 1263 SCSU. ASF, Mason Gen. Hosp., W. Brentwood, Long Island. N. Y.; Sgt. Murray S. Kerner, QM Det., Bushnell Gen. Hosp., Brigham, Utah; Sgt. Ben Schneider, Hq. Bks., 2d Army Hq., Memphis 15, Tenn.; Cpl. S. J. King. Hq. Det., Prisoner of War Camp, Camp Gordon, Ga.; Cpls. Gloria Tipton and Lee Goble, AAF Wac Det., Truax Field, Madison 7, Wis.; Cpl. Robert A. Schmidt, Hq. Co., 89th Div. Camp Carson, Colo.; Sgt. William C. Pearce, 227th Chem. Dep., Camp Sibert, Ala.; Sgt. Bob Diedrich, 1101st Sq., Douglas AAF, Douglas, Ariz.; T-5 Lowell Young, c/o YANK; T-5 William Warren, Troop F, 101st Cav. Camp Ashby, Virginia Beach, Va.; Sgt. Robert Shelley. Troop D, 85th Cav. Rcn. Sq. Mec., Pine Camp, N. Y.; J. C. Edwards, Co. A. Chi Phi House. SCU 4433. ASTP. University of Alabama, Tuscaloosa.

WHEN THE GONG RINGS, ASTP STUDENTS LEAVE THEIR DORMITORY-BARRACKS AND ASSEMBLE OUTSIDE THE UNIVERSITY BUILDINGS TO MARCH TO CLASSES.

A.S.T.P.

By Pfc. J. R. MOSKIN

1551 SU, AST, Indiana University

Dormitory life among the Army's specialized trainees at Indiana University is not a soft existence. But it certainly isn't GI, by any means.

BLOOMINGTON, IND.—More than 2,000 enlisted men are stationed here at Indiana University, racing through rapid-fire specialized training so the Army can use us some day as engineers, doctors or know-it-alls on life and language in such places as Turkey, Yugoslavia, Russia or Germany itself. We have been pulled out of posts from California to Massachusetts and represent every branch of the service from paratroops to chemical warfare.

Some of the men have served in foreign armies—for Hungary, for Poland. Johnny Beadle was torpedoed and spent nine days on a raft. Lou Safford is ready for his three-year-hitch stripe. Johnny Mirsch is a radar specialist. The bulk of us finished basic, maybe went through technical school or maneuvers, and then were switched here to the Army Specialized Training Program to study 10½ hours a day. Although the average is low, ages range between both extremes, from 18 to 38.

This life amounts to a crazy cross between the Army and college. Indiana University is the Big Ten school that was described by *Life* a year or so ago as not knowing a war was going on. She still has traces of peace days, with campus queens, formal dances and sorority teas. But we can't touch that stuff until Saturday night.

College in civilian days was never like this. No fraternity boy ever got up at 6, waited in line 20 minutes for breakfast on a tray and then marched to class. Classes once met three hours a week; now a course will run two and three hours every day.

But, of course, this isn't real Army, either. As a technical sergeant with two years of service says: "It's still the Army but it just ain't GI." A new lieutenant just back from Alaska confessed: "I have been here 10 days now and haven't gotten over the shock yet."

The switch from camp to IU is pretty brutal, almost as bad as the one from civilian life to Camp Upton. Back there we learned that initiative is bucking and that goldbricking is the way of camp life. Now we have to take it all

back and beat our brains out to stay in the program. Only two things count: get good marks and stay vaguely on the GI ball.

Actual physical training in the ASTP has been cut to about seven hours a week. There is no time for prolonged drill sessions or road marches. But none of us puts on weight. Gym periods every other day and the slam-bang routine do not allow it. After the first call at 6, classes run solidly from 8 to 5 o'clock with one hour out for noon chow; then there is required study from 7:30 until 10 and lights out at 10:30.

So we come to live from week end to week end, even though Saturday night can only be spent in a handful of ways—maybe a show or a dance, the rounds of the four on-limits bars on the town square or, as a last resort, a Greyhound to Indianapolis, which is already overcrowded with GIs. Bloomington's square is jammed on Saturday night, but life is peaceful and MPs are unknown. Our only major gripe is having to pay civilian prices on Army pay.

Sex here divides into three categories according to popularity: the co-eds, the 1,000 Waves studying storekeeping on the campus and the town girls from the RCA plant. The co-eds are a bit young perhaps but plenty alive. Navy restrictions send service girls, Cinderella-like, to lonely beds at midnight on the precious Saturday nights. But the Waves move in and out of IU so fast you don't have to worry about long-standing emotional complications anyway. Our real hope in this wilderness is the seven-day furlough the War Department promises us every three months.

Life day by day centers around the dormitories. The area and language and the pre-med students live in a string of converted fraternity houses, and headquarters, the engineers and the 17-year-old AST Reservists are located in what was a girls' quadrangle before last spring. The Navy got here first by almost a year and grabbed up the men's dormitories. So the Army had to

be satisfied with bathtubs instead of showers.

For most part the trainees run themselves by a smooth-functioning cadet system. Cadet officers march the men, head the reviews and take charge of supply and mail call. Then there is an elected 25-man Cadet Student Council, which meets with the colonel once a week.

Col. Raymond L. Shoemaker, head of the 1551st Service Unit here and in Indianapolis, figures his men should be trained for responsible tasks in the future by active learning now. The cadet system is the result, plus help by the trainees in military teaching and administrative work under Lt. Col. Charles M. Munnecke, the plans and training officer. Whether they end up with bars or stripes, the trainees are supposed to know something useful about the Army when they have finished with ASTP.

THE main gripe of the town's civilians is that Washington keeps the Army too busy to play intercollegiate football. Instead, after supper, the men play inter-company games with old college equipment. These draw crowds as large as the Saturday sessions of the varsity.

Some of the men in the unit write and edit a weekly page called "The Service Student" in the college newspaper. Others have organized military and swing bands, a chorus and variety shows. The trainees attend dances, join the Men's Union and get along pretty well with the civilian students. This is to be expected, for many of us, though by no means all, have had at least a year of college. Some have a string of degrees. Others never saw a campus before.

For all of us here, the ASTP is proving the experience and the chance of a lifetime. For the Army it promises to be a source of carefully trained soldier-specialists as the storming of the enemy fortress gains momentum. Meanwhile, we may chant, "Tear down your service flag, mother, your son's in the ASTP," but we find the book grind severe enough to counterbalance the pleasures of life in a college town.

YANK *The Army Weekly* • **DECEMBER 10**

Loretta Young

HOLLYWOOD. Alan Ladd returns to the screen in "And Now Tomorrow," in which he will share starring honors with Loretta Young [*above*]. . . . Eleanor Powell has been signed for the lead in "Sensations of 1944." Other castings include W. C. Fields, Woody Herman and Cab Calloway. . . . Phyllis Thaxter, stage actress, has been signed for an important role in "Thirty Seconds Over Tokyo.". . . Jean Heather, young co-ed discovery, has been given her first starring assignment in "National Barn Dance.". . . Marie Wilson will enact a campus siren in "You Can't Ration Love." . . . Ruth Hussey will be Pat O'Brien's leading lady in "Marine Raiders.". . . Wally Brown and Alan Carney will have the comedy leads in "Seven Days Ashore.". . . Jane Frazee, co-starring with Joan Davis in "Beautiful But Broke," has been signed to a three-picture contract. . . . Charlie Ruggles goes into the cast of "Incendiary Blonde" in a gambler's role. . . . Singer Frank Forest returns to the screen after a five-year absence to do "Take It Big" for Paramount. . . . Lucille Watson plays the role of the Mother Superior of the French hospital in "Tomorrow's Harvest," which stars Maureen O'Hara and Ray Milland. . . . Aurora Miranda, sister of Carmen, has been inked by Walt Disney for a featured role in "The Three Caballeros," which combines live action with cartoons.

COAST TO COAST. James Thurber is taking the *New Yorker* magazine as the subject of his next play. . . . Problem facing Frank Sinatra and the managers of the theaters in which he will appear is how to uproot Frankie's youngster fans after each performance. . . . The Hartmans have replaced Sinatra at New York's Waldorf-Astoria Wedgwood Room. . . . "Life With Father," which has been running continuously at the Empire Theater in New York since 1939, has grossed $3,170,-200. . . . June Walker missed the final performance of her road unit's "Life With Father" in Pittsburgh because of ptomaine poisoning. . . . The Army will have given back 100 hotels to their owners in Miami Beach by Jan. 1. . . . New off-duty unit added to the training schedule at Camp Lee, Va., is the Ballroom Dancers Replacement Center; attendance is voluntary. . . . Fire destroyed the Casino Ballroom at Ocean Park, Los Angeles, causing an estimated $60,000 damage. . . . A total of 130 million records were pressed last year by the three major record companies. . . . Ringling Bros.-Barnum & Bailey Circus broke all-time attendance records with a three-day stand in Miami, Fla., and closed its 1943 season with a two-day engagement at Tampa. . . . Arcadia Rink, Detroit, is getting a face-lifting, with the new color scheme strictly patriotic. . . . The Andrew Sisters are due at the Chicago Theater, Chicago, next month.

THE borough of Brooklyn, N.Y., takes pride in many things: the Brooklyn Dodgers, the Brooklyn accent, trolley cars, the Coney Island hot dog. Lately it has taken special pride in the accomplishments of its native daughter, Lena Horne, the girl across the way, who looks and sounds much better than anything mentioned above. Lena's latest movie for MGM is "Broadway Rhythm."

THE POETS CORNERED

Nor all your piety and wit
Shall lure it back to cancel half a line.
Pfc. Omar K., 1st Pyramidal Tent Co

MY HEART

My heart is like a flower seed
In a jar upon a gardener's shelf;
It is so useless a thing alone by itself.
Yet it will keep when autumn and its winter come;
And then perhaps in spring
Some gentle hand will take it down
From its sad corner of the shelf
And plant it in the blessed ground;
And it will drink the sweetness of the rain
And feel the warmth of sun.

India   —Sgt. CARLYLE A. OBERLE

ODE TO A GUARD

The guard patrols his lonely post,
Finding comfort in the boast
That he alone of all his station
Bears the burden of the nation.

Hears a crunch upon the ground,
Quick as lightning turns around;
Then he grins and feels absurd—
His own footsteps he has heard.

Getting sleepy, names the states,
Whistles snatches, reckons dates,
Counts his steps and counts his turnings,
Figures out his yearly earnings.

Cheer up, sentry, after war
You'll be trained for jobs galore:
Summons server, tax collector,
Postman, cop or bank protector.

I can see you walking floor
For a big department store;
Running wife's errands maybe,
Walking round the room with baby.

And if you should get restless for
Certain features of the war,
Button up your collar tight
And walk around the block all night.

Fort Custer, Mich.   —Pvt. MARTIN WELDON

QUERY?

The purity of Army names
Brings forth this pond'rous question:
Will Gen. Patton then be called
"Aged Plasma and Intestine"?

Fort Benning, Ga.   —Pfc. ROBERT NICOLAI

THE CADENCE BLUES

Oh, listen to the gripers sound
In voices piped and tinny;
Their bitching trails the world around
From Iceland to New Guinea.
They gripe about the terrible heat,
Bemoan the lack of beer;
But me, I like it overseas
Where nevermore I hear
   That horrible chant, the sergeant's roar:
   Hut—two—three—four.

Sometimes the tropics drive men mad,
The heat, the toil, the strife,
And though the fever's plenty bad,
Still I enjoy this life,
Where never a cadence count invades
The quiet, peaceful shore.
I ask, I beg, implore
   No more to hear, no, nevermore;
   Hut—two—three—four.

New Guinea   —Sgt. JOHN READEY

UNRELATED CONCLUSIONS

Any given part of Lana Turner
Is what is known as "cooking on the front burner."

A Flying Fort with a broken rudder
Is as useless as Elsie without her udder.

Maxton AAB, S. C.   —Cpl. BOB STUART McKNIGHT

TOO MANY POINTS?

Be-dewed, be-dipped, befuddled and be-beered,
   I sit here thinking, absent love, of thee
In idioms in which I have been reared—
   The ultimate in numb civility.
When in recorded time did that evoke
   The slightest trace of a responsive fire?
What could such rheumy romance do but choke,
   Before its birth, the wellspring of desire!
Ah, devil a heart was ever won this way,
   And devil a heart by verses such as these,
So slowly I bestir my maudlin clay
   And drain my glass down to its very lees,
Then in the dregs I see your face a-glow:
   I say, "You ought to diet, sweet, you know."

Ephrata AAB, Wash.   —Sgt. WILLIAM R. CARTY

TEE-TOTAL

YANK's big Puzzle Kits will be given as prizes to GIs (and that includes all branches of service—Marines, Coast Guard, etc.) who submit the highest scores on this puzzle. If you haven't tried this word game before, start now.

Simply fill in the diagram with three good English words. Names of persons or places cannot be used. Add up the number values of the 17 letters you have used, giving each letter its value as shown on the chart below. The idea is to use words which contain letters of high value.

In adding your score count each of the 17 letters in the diagram only once.

A sample work-out is shown above, with a score of 178. Can you beat that par?

LETTER VALUES

A — 3		N — 5	
B — 17		O — 1	
C — 7		P — 16	
D — 14		Q — 4	
E — 2		R — 12	
F — 11		S — 6	
G — 19		T — 13	
H — 22		U — 15	
I — 20		V — 26	
J — 9		W — 25	
K — 24		X — 21	
L — 8		Y — 10	
M — 18		Z — 23	

Score .... Submitted by:
....
....
....

Mail to Puzzle Editor, YANK, 205 East 42d Street, New York 17, N. Y., within two weeks of the date of this issue if you are in the U. S., within *eight* weeks if you are outside the U. S. Winners in U. S. will be listed on page 22, Jan. 21, 1944, issue

CARD SENSE

GOT card sense? Then see if you can identify each card from the four clues given below. Par is five minutes.

1. To the left of a club there's at least one diamond.
2. To the right of a diamond there's at least one other diamond.
3. To the left of a king there's at least one other king.
4. To the right of a queen there's at least one king.

(Solution on page 22)

CHANGE OF ADDRESS If you are a YANK subscriber and have changed your address, use this coupon to notify us of the change. Mail it to YANK, The Army Weekly, 205 East 42d Street, New York 17, N. Y., and YANK will follow you to any part of the world.

FULL NAME AND RANK   ORDER NO.
....

OLD MILITARY ADDRESS
....

NEW MILITARY ADDRESS
....

Allow 21 days for change of address to become effective

THE BALLAD OF NUMBER NINE

A bunch of the boys were whooping it up at
  Number Nine PX,
Swigging down their three-point-two and bounc-
  ing rubber checks.
The stock was gone, the shelves were bare, the
  only drink was brew;
The bottles went from hand to mouth and soon
  the beer was through.
Now idle hands are Satan's joy and Satan likes
  his games,
And soon the boys were crowding round and
  bidding for the dames.
"What do I hear for the green-eyed skirt who
  peddles shoe-shine sets?"
"What am I bid for the blond in blue who handles
  cigarettes?"
The party got rougher as time went by and soon
  became obscene,
When a GI angel with khaki wings appeared
  upon the scene.
"Think," he cried, "of your girls at home; rob
  not your GI brother!
"Remember the girl you're bidding for might
  be somebody's mother."
He lifted his voice to dismiss the crowd, but lo!
  the crowd had fled
With vows to leave that beer alone and stick to
  pop instead.
With victory clear the angel smiled a smile both
  glad and wise.
But Satan, smirking, pointed out: "The gals left
  with the guys!"

Camp Swift, Tex.   —T-5 JOHN W. GREENLEAF

POST
P X
CHANGE

This Post Exchange, like YANK itself, is wide
open to you. Send your cartoons, poems and
stories to: The Post Exchange, YANK, The Army
Weekly, 205 East 42d Street, New York 17, N. Y.

If your contribution misses the mark, you
will receive YANK's special de luxe rejection
slip, that will inspire a more creative mood.

VOICE

If the officers' quarters are near
  And a voice there pleads and beseeches,
It's only the chaplain you hear,
  Practicing what he preaches.

Camp Shelby, Miss.   —S/Sgt. A. L. CROUCH

NOTE

I've learned to expect it
And no need to blow up:
Girls who date soldiers
Often don't show up.

Rome Army Air Depot, N. Y.   —Pfc. ARTHUR PECK

"I understand he's a latrine orderly, whatever that is."
—Sgts. Bob Bowie and H. Weisman, South Pacific

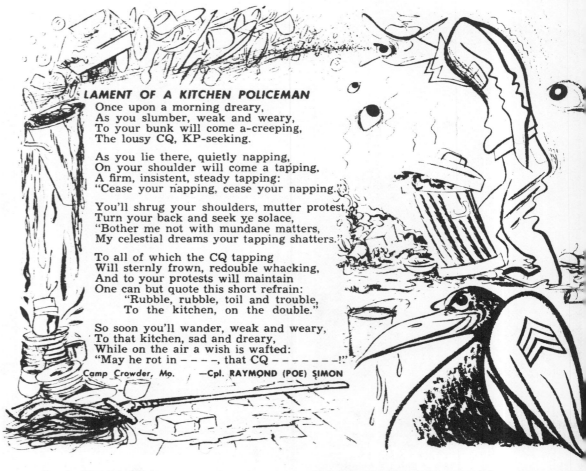

LAMENT OF A KITCHEN POLICEMAN

Once upon a morning dreary,
As you slumber, weak and weary,
To your bunk will come a-creeping,
The lousy CQ, KP-seeking.

As you lie there, quietly napping,
On your shoulder will come a tapping.
A firm, insistent, steady tapping:
"Cease your napping, cease your napping."

You'll shrug your shoulders, mutter protest,
Turn your back and seek ye solace,
"Bother me not with mundane matters,
My celestial dreams your tapping shatters."

To all of which the CQ tapping
Will sternly frown, redouble whacking,
And to your protests will maintain
One can but quote this short refrain:
  "Rubble, rubble, toil and trouble,
    To the kitchen, on the double."

So soon you'll wander, weak and weary,
To that kitchen, sad and dreary,
While on the air a wish is wafted:
"May he rot in – – – –, that CQ – – – – – – –!"

Camp Crowder, Mo.   —Cpl. RAYMOND (POE) SIMON

A Case In Point

PRIOR to my visit to their unpretentious $95-
a-month bungalow, my interest in the Jethro
Willingbys was of a detached nature, but since
the visit I have pondered their case quite seriously. Frankly, I am a little fearful the Willingbys have given me a gander into the future,
a sort of preview of things to come.

Six months ago Jethro was battery clerk in
my outfit at Camp Swale, La. As soon as he
made corporal he and Aux. Mergatroyd Potts
of the WAAC detachment were spliced at the
post chapel. They honeymooned for three days
at the guest house. Some of the boys thought
that was a dumb honeymoon, but Jethro assured me at chow one day that it was really some
pumpkins. Cozy and all that.

Well, it wasn't long before Willingby came up
for medical discharge. Pes planus and scoliosis,
the sawbones said. About the same time, Mergatroyd accepted an honorable discharge from the
WAAC, and the young couple found themselves
chuffing toward the old home town in mufti,
civilians.

I happen to live in the same town, and it was
while on furlough a couple of weeks ago that I
visited the Willingbys. Our acquaintanceship began in the Army and wasn't what you'd call
close, but you know how furloughs are these
days; your friends aren't around, so you cultivate acquaintances.

Mergatroyd answered the door. She was cordial
as could be when she saw who it was, and called
Jethro, who dropped an armful of comic books
to shake hands with me. After the usual pleasan-
tries we repaired to the living room where I saw
the first sign. Smack dab in the middle of one
of the walls was this admonition, neatly framed:

NOTICE
THIS IS OUR HOME
HELP KEEP IT CLEAN
USE ASH TRAYS

"Mergy and I brought the idea home from
Camp Swale," Willingby explained. "We got
signs all over the place, just like in the Army.
How d'you like the one above the phone?" I
glanced toward the telephone stand. Over the
small walnut table was a picture of a T-bone
in a frying pan, smoking to beat hell, and the
legend was: IDLE GOSSIP ONCE RUINED A STEAK.

Then Jethro took me out in the hallway and
pointed out something I hadn't noticed—a bulletin board. Obviously he and Mergatroyd were
proud of the board. One side was devoted to
current poop, such as:

Laundry goes out at 8:30 A.M. Monday.
*The girls will be here for bridge Tuesday eve-
ning.*
Yard will be raked Sunday A.M.
Jethro, remind me to gig the milkman.

The other side of the board, true to Camp
Swale tradition, was strictly eyewash. It included a picture of the Willingbys' pastor, a list
of OCD regulations, rationing schedule, copy of
the Atlantic Charter, a card listing the Ten Com[
mandments, and a photo of Gabriel Ragdale[
Republican candidate for mayor.

Of course the Willingbys escorted me throug[
the house. There were signs in every room, mos[
of them just plain black and white.

About the buffet in the dining room was th[
bold-faced reminder on food conservation[
TAKE ALL YOU WANT, BUT EAT ALL YOU TAKE.

The kitchen, small but utilitarian and tidy
was marred by a large sign which read: TIN CAN[
WILL SPEED THE VICTORY, illustrated with the like[
ness of a smashed-up tomato can.

LET'S KEEP THIS LATRINE CLEAN, said a sign i[
the bathroom.

In all, I counted 38 signs in the Willingby[
home.

My point is this: If the Willingbys, who wer[
never especially GI, have taken the placar[
plague into civilian life with them, what on earth[
kind of affectations will others, more imbue[
with service ideas, take home with them?

For example, there is a definite possibilit[
that the mess sergeant will make his wife brea[
the garbage down into five or six subdivisions[
that the platoon sergeant will send his kids of[
to school in mass formation, that the supply ser[
geant will demand a memo receipt of his wif[
when he brings home the groceries, that th[
latrine orderly will lock the growler door be[
tween 7:30 and 8 A.M. Saturday mornings. E[
cetera, ad infinitum.

I certainly hope the Willingbys do not repre[
sent a trend. Life used to be so simple, so beau[
tiful.

AAA, Buffalo, N. Y.   —S/Sgt. JOHN J. BURN[

OBSERVATIONS OF A JAUNDICED EYE

Army life
Needs a wife.

Army regulations
Forbid vacations.

Army sergeants
Are hard gents.

Army pay
Is hay.

Army medics
Need orthopedics.

Army mess
Is nothing less.

Army beer
Is often near.

Army life
Needs a wife.

University of Pittsburgh, Pa.   —A/S JAMES DENNIS

PUZZLE SOLUTIONS

CARD SENSE. A—queen of diamonds. B—king of diamonds. C—king of clubs.

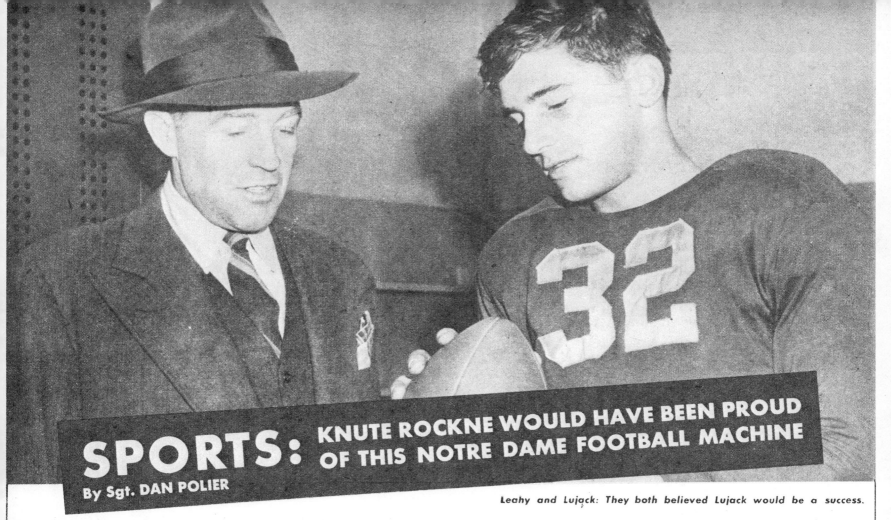

SPORTS: KNUTE ROCKNE WOULD HAVE BEEN PROUD OF THIS NOTRE DAME FOOTBALL MACHINE

By Sgt. DAN POLIER

Leahy and Lujack: They both believed Lujack would be a success.

KNUTE ROCKNE would have liked this Notre Dame football team. It was his kind of ball club: big, swift, poised and powerful enough to knock your brains out.

Rock would have loved that youngster, Johnny Lujack, who came in after the Navy game as Angelo Bertelli's replacement. He's definitely the Rockne type. The old man preferred his quarterbacks cocky, especially when they sincerely believed in themselves. When the game started, Rock used to let Frank Carideo run the show. Lujack fits into the same pattern. He has the same assurance, the same feel of confidence that's typical of all great quarterbacks.

There was a little scene in the Notre Dame dressing room after the Navy game that Rockne would have enjoyed. Bertelli was departing for the Marines and Coach Frank Leahy, fearing that the pressure might be too much for Lujack, called the kid aside to comfort him.

"Johnny, you have a great responsibility in the next four games," Leahy began. "You're going to make mistakes, and I want you to know I expect them. We all make mistakes. But when it happens, forget about it. I have faith in you. I think you'll be an outstanding success."

Lujack looked Leahy straight in the eye and said calmly: "I think so, too."

You know the rest of the story. Lujack,

with exactly 20 minutes of varsity experience behind him, was a tremendous success in the Army game. Sergeants and corporals who had bet their wives' allotments on Army and lost went home muttering, "Who's this guy Bertelli anyhow?" But the Army team wasn't as impressed. They said Lujack had one glaring weakness—that he couldn't pass while lying flat on his back.

Just for the records, we might tell you that without lying on his back Lujack completed eight out of 16 passes against Army, two good for touchdowns. He also exploded through the Army team for another touchdown on a quarterback sneak and prevented an Army score by diving under a blocker to haul down Carl Anderson. Some people have been generous enough to say that was the greatest defensive maneuver of the season.

Rockne would rub his eyes at the sight of Creighton Miller rumbling down the field like a wide-open jeep. Miller has that same clear-cut, compelling quality about his running that Marchie Schwartz and Joe Savoldi had. And there's Jim Mello, Vic Kulbitski, Julius Rykovich and Bob Kelly. . . . Rockne would swear that Leahy has been letting these boys practice with the Chicago Bears.

And what about the Notre Dame line? Wouldn't Rockne say it was something out of

this world? And wouldn't Rockne's body ache all over out of sheer sympathy every time these guys went to work on the enemy?

If Rockne looked long enough he would probably recognize Capt. Pat Filley, the guard. As a kid in South Bend, Pat was always hanging around Rock's practice sessions. Rock would be convinced now that the boy must have been listening to him, because he plays guard as though he invented the position.

Jim White, the tackle, is another boy who would be sure to click with Rockne. The old man would especially have liked Jim's piece of grand larceny in the Army game when he calmly stole the ball away from Glenn Davis to set up ND's second touchdown.

If you could pin Rockne down and ask him to name the player he liked most in the line, he would very likely tell you Jumbo Yonakor, the giant, pass-catching end. Jumbo has that confidence that pleased Rock so much. In the Navy game he played opposite Don Whitmire, who was an All-Southern tackle at Alabama before coming to Annapolis. During the second half Jumbo needled Whitmire constantly by asking him: "Which way do you want us to turn you now, Mr. All-American?"

It was Rock's kind of ball club, all right, but not because it was great. Rather, because it knew it was great.

EVERYBODY was so busy raving about **Sid Luckman** throwing seven scoring passes to break Sammy Baugh's record that nobody noticed that, only the day before, **Glenn Dobbs**, former Tulsa All-American, now playing for Randolph Field, Tex., broke the same record by throwing seven touchdown passes against the Ward Island Marines. . . Here's a story that goes back to the World Series. After the final game in St. Louis, **Bill Dickey** crowded into the same elevator with **Shirley Povich**, the Washington sports writer. An Army corporal pushed his way in beside them. "Hi ya, Bill," said the corporal. "I don't know whether you remember me." Dickey looked him over and said: "Sure I remember you. We used to pitch to you high and inside. When we pitched outside, it was boom, the ball game. Say, what's your name, anyhow?" The corporal's name was **Joe Gantenbein**, and just as Dickey recalled, he could really murder an outside pitch when he played for the Athletics. . . . Uniforms for the Army and Navy football teams playing in Bermuda's second annual Lily Bowl game are being supplied by Fordham University, which abandoned its football team this year.
Inducted: **Ken Sears**, second-string Yankee

SPORTS SERVICE RECORD

Southern California's Dreblow is slowed down, then spilled by Crawford of March Field as the Flyers tramped USC, 35-0. The next day twice-beaten USC was named to meet Washington in the Rose Bowl.

catcher, into Navy; **Mickey Witek**, Giant second baseman, into Coast Guard; **Jimmy Bloodworth**, Detroit second baseman, into Army; **Bobby Cifers**, high-scoring schoolboy football star from Kingsport, Tenn., into AAF; **Hi Bithorn**, Chicago Cub pitcher, into Navy; **Hank Gornicki**, Pittsburgh pitcher, into Army. . . . *Rejected:* **Rip Sewell**, Pittsburgh pitcher and inventor of the ephus pitch; **Jimmy Wasdell**, outfielder-first baseman of Philadelphia Phils; **Bud Metheney**, second-string Yankee outfielder. . . . *Deferred:* **Bill Cox**, owner of Philadelphia Phils. . . . *Ordered for induction:* **Oris Hockett**, Cleveland outfielder; **Spud Chandler**, Yankee pitcher and American League's most valuable; **Jim Bivens**, Negro heavyweight contender; **Tommy Bridges**, Detroit pitcher; **Connie Mack Jr.**, son of the owner-manager of the Athletics; **Ron Northey**, right fielder of Philadelphia Phils. . . . *Discharged:* **Myril Hoag**, former Yankee outfielder, because of severe headaches and dizzy spells. . . . *Commissioned:* **Sid Luckman**, of Chicago Bears, as ensign in the Merchant Marine; **Marty Brill**, coach of Loyola University at Los Angeles, at first lieutenant in the Marines after being released from the Army as staff sergeant; **Patty Berg**, woman golf star, as second lieutenant in the Marines.

"I HATE TO GO HOME ON FURLOUGH. MY WIFE AND I
DO NOTHING BUT FIGHT, FIGHT, FIGHT ALL DAY LONG."
—Sgt. Irwin Caplan

YANK
THE ARMY WEEKLY

"HOW COME THESE SOLDIER GUYS
ARE ALWAYS BUCKIN' FOR STRIPES?"
—Sgt. Bill Newcombe

"HEY MAC, WHERE'S THE REPLACEMENT POOL?"
—Cpl. Hugh F. Kennedy

"COULDN'T USE A CLEVER LITTLE SABOTEUR, COULD YOU?"
—Cpl. Ernest Maxwell

YANK

THE ARMY WEEKLY

5¢

DEC. 31
VOL. 2, NO. 28
1943

By the men .. for the men in the service

ctures of "Fighting 69th" in Invasion of Makin

PAGES 2, 3

WHEN THE NAVY FINISHED SHELLING MAKIN AND THE PLANES STOPPED BOMBING, THE SOLDIERS STEPPED OFF THEIR LANDING BOATS AND WADED ASHORE.

A SOLDIER OF THE SHAMROCK BATTALION WAITS TO PUSH AHEAD.

Lt. Col. Hart's Irish battalion from the famed "Fighting 69th" had a weird night when the Japs staged a series of wild, suicidal attacks on their front-line positions.

By Cpl. LARRY McMANUS
YANK Staff Correspondent

BUTARITARI ISLAND, MAKIN ATOLL [By Cable]—It was a wild mad night, that final period of Jap resistance—a bedlam of infiltration, screams, laughing and suicidal charges against the American perimeter defense. The enemy had been pocketed between two Army forces and was finally crushed between them.

The anvil against which the Japs were crushed was the force on Kuma Island whose machine guns prevented a retreat from Butaritari. The hammer that did the crushing was Lt. Col. Joseph T. Hart's Shamrock Battalion of the 165th Infantry, New York's old "Fighting 69th."

The Jap marines who defended this advance base in the Gilbert Islands were hard to kill. "You can't hurt one of them by hitting him in the head," said Pfc. George Antolak, a machine gunner from St. Clairsville, Ohio. "Three of us were in a machine-gun pit the third night after the landing. The others were trying to sleep and I was on guard. I could hear the Japs a few yards away. They were laughing like crazy men, a weird sort of shrieking laughter. Then about 2300 one of them charged our hole, yelling like hell and slashing around with a saber. My Springfield jammed. The Jap was too close for me to use it anyhow, so I threw it in his face. It smacked him right across the nose. He didn't even slow down.

"Meanwhile I was hollering to the other guys in the foxhole, but it all happened so fast they didn't even get to their feet. I grabbed the barrel of a carbine and let the Jap have it on the side of his head. He kept coming—I tell you, you can't hurt one by hitting him in the head—and swung his saber at me. I grabbed the blade with both hands."

Shamrocks at Makin

STALKING SOME REMAINING JAP SNIPERS, THREE INFANTRYMEN WALK PAST A JAP OIL DUMP, PART OF WHICH IS STILL BURNING AFTER NAVY SHELLING.

Antolak glanced at the bloody bandages on each of his hands.

"That pulled him into the pit and the other guys held him and beat him over the head with helmets while I got the saber and stabbed him in the chest. And still the bastard kept up his awful screaming laugh. We finally got him but he took a lot of killing."

That third night was a frightening nightmare. The Japs, dressed in their best uniforms and wearing their medals, kept attacking in the face of certain death.

The action took place on the eastern end of Butaritari, the principal island of Makin Atoll and the only one heavily fortified by the Japs. Butaritari is shaped like a skinny Italy, with the toe pointing to the northwest and a thin leg stretching to the northeast. It is about eight miles long and averages 500 yards wide. Butaritari covers most of the south side of a triangle of islands enclosing the Makin Lagoon.

Near Butaritari's knee was the atoll's largest village. The Jap defenses were concentrated there to protect four piers extending over the reef into the deep water of the lagoon. At each end of the village the Japs had cleared the coconut trees and underbrush from strips 150 yards wide and extending from the lagoon to the ocean shore. In the center of the clearings were water-filled tank traps, five yards wide.

The original force landed at H-hour, 0830 Saturday, Nov. 20, on "Beach Red" at the sole of the Butaritari boot.

The operation proceeded according to schedule, with one group turning to the right and cleaning out Ukiangong Village, another pivoting to the left to investigate Flink Point, while the main body advanced east toward the Jap fortifications on the island's center three miles from the beach.

Resistance was almost nonexistent—six Jap marines were killed and one Korean laborer captured—as the Beach Red force pushed east up the leg toward the village. But the snipers increased in number as the infantrymen approached the clearing and the tank trap west of the village.

The infantry assault force suffered its first casualties when it came upon Jap pillboxes made of coconut logs and banked with sand. They had to be destroyed by tanks. When he stood up to give orders to the tank commanders, the 165th's CO, Col. James Gardiner Conroy of New York, N. Y., was killed by a sniper's bullet.

At that point the narrow, coral-topped road that ran the length of the island curved north, parallel to the lagoon's shore,

A KOREAN LABORER, TAKEN PRISONER, IS OFFERED A DRINK OF WATER

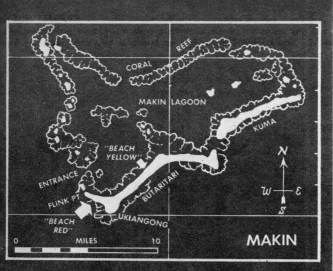

Assault force hit "Beach Red" at 0830 Saturday and pushed up Butaritari to main Jap defenses opposite "Beach Yellow," where second force landed at 1030. The two forces joined Sunday and drove Japs toward Kuma, where third force, which landed Monday, cut off enemy retreat.

where coconut trees grew in profusion and the undergrowth was dense, affording easy cover for many snipers.

Crossing the road to aid a wounded soldier, Capt. Stephen Meany, regimental chaplain of the 165th, was shot and fell into a shell hole. Several hours later, after other attempts to rescue him had failed, Lt. Warren Lindquist of Boonton, N. J., crawled to the hole and dragged the wounded chaplain to safety. A sniper's bullet had struck a religious medal worn on a chain around the padre's neck. The bullet was deflected by the medal, tearing three flesh wounds as it ripped across Father Meany's chest and through his arm.

Two hours after the landing on Beach Red, additional landing boats entered the lagoon and deposited another force on "Beach Yellow," between two of the village piers and directly in front of the principal Jap fortifications.

Despite the tremendous bombardment of the beach before the landing, some of the troops were hit by machine-gun fire as they waded over the 300-yard reef to the shore.

The landing party silenced these machine guns, but they chattered again the next day, manned by Japs who had infiltrated the American lines during the night and taken the old positions.

The Beach Yellow force fanned out to right and left, pushing to make contact with the Beach Red party to the west and advancing against the Japs on the east. The two American forces established contact with each other the morning after the landing.

It was the Shamrock Battalion that was at the front that last wild night. The Shamrocks moved up to the assault position at 0800 Monday and late in the afternoon set up a perimeter defense across the island 3½ miles from the eastern tip. It was there, at night, with the Shamrocks ahead of them and another American detachment waiting on the next island to prevent their retreat from Butaritari, that the Japs made their final eerie series of attacks.

The Shamrocks dug three-man foxholes surrounding the grass shack that had been chosen by Lt. Col. Hart as his CP. Except for a small clearing around the shack, the area was the usual tangle of underbrush and coconut trees, with the island's main road running through the left flank of the American box defense.

The night began quietly enough—for Makin. The sharp tenor crack of sniper's rifles rang out constantly, but the men were accustomed to that by now, and it hardly disturbed their sleep. Two men slept in each foxhole while the third kept guard. The clouds of mosquitoes were more annoying than the snipers.

At 2030 the guards heard a noise—an incongruous sound for a battlefield—and awakened the sleepers, figuring that it was another Jap trick. The sound was repeated—the thin, breathless wail of a baby crying. It came from the Jap lines. Fingers tightened on American triggers as the wail was accompanied by the sound of many feet shuffling down the road toward the Shamrock defenses.

A shaky voice answered the challenge of an American soldier. The voice identified the new-comers as a group of natives—men, women and children—who had fled to the tip of the island

to avoid the American shells and bombs, and now were attempting to return to their village behind the American lines. For their safety, the natives were taken inside the perimeter and ordered to stay until dawn.

A few minutes later, at 2040, a second group was sighted coming down the same path. This time there was no answer to the American challenge. It was a Jap party. Our men opened fire. Four of the enemy were killed and the remainder scattered into the brush.

That was the beginning of the final four hours of Jap resistance. Sgt. Chester Dey of Lambertville, Mo., was in a foxhole between the two machine guns of his section that night. He heard the mad laughter of Japs ahead. "They sounded drunk," he said later. "As if they'd been drinking *sake*." His voice was weak and he spoke slowly in an attempt to reconstruct accurately the events of the night.

"At about 2300 something grabbed my arm and squeezed it so hard it went numb," said Dey. He held out his left arm, covered from palm to elbow by a stained bandage. His pale face very nearly matched the color of the dressing around a head wound.

"This thing—I suppose it was a Jap, I never did see it—held my arm so hard it tore off my wrist watch. I kicked, kneed and pounded with my free hand until I tore myself loose, then I started to crawl to another foxhole to get help from some of my men. Just as I started, something hit me on the head, but I made it to the other hole before passing out. Next morning, when the rest of our forces had advanced, the aid men found me. It was lucky for me they did. I was about out of blood by then."

Another soldier was lying in a foxhole when he heard a clod of dirt roll to the bottom of his pit. He remained still and watched a hand tentatively pat the side of the hole and explore ahead. Finally the hand reached his leg. It drew back a few inches and then went forward again and lightly patted the leg, as though it was making sure that the leg belonged to a dead body. The soldier had been temporarily hypnotized by the whole thing. But now he grabbed the hand, pulled himself erect and, holding his carbine like a pistol, pumped three shots into the Jap on the end of the arm. Then he fired several more rounds at another Jap who was running away from the foxhole.

One group of eight Japs worked their way to within 15 yards of Lt. Col. Hart's CP before they were discovered and killed. The lieutenant colonel's jeep was pierced by several bullets before the skirmish ended.

It was suicide that night to leave a foxhole for any reason. Anything that moved was a legitimate target. The soldiers lay prone before tilting their canteens and lay on their sides to urinate.

Meanwhile, on Kuma Island, separated from Butaritari's northeastern tip by 1,000 yards of waist-deep water, lay a detachment of infantry commanded by Maj. Edward T. Bradt of Schenectady, N. Y. They had landed on Kuma Mon-

day morning. To guard against a possible retreat from Butaritari, they were manning chine guns placed so as to command the joining the islands.

Shortly before 2200 this detachment he woman's voice scream, "Jap boy, Jap boy." guards saw about a dozen persons moving to them from the other island. "We could see clearly, silhouetted against the surf breaki the reef," Maj. Bradt said. "We opened fire must have got all of them or we would have them retreat or heard them splashing i water."

THE next day a party of soldiers and a guide combed the reef for bodies but only two. The rest must have been swept sea by the heavy current that washes bet the islands. One of the dead was a young girl. She was dressed in a grass skirt, dyed and she had been hit twice in the chest.

Beside her lay the body of a Jap sergear the sight of him, the native shook his fis burst into a torrent of excited speech. An preter explained that the sergeant was the hated man on the island. He had been in cl of native labor, and at one time or another, of the island's residents had felt the weig the club he carried.

The girl, the natives said, had a good re tion and was not sympathetic with the Japs. dently they had made her put on the black and forced her to lead the party across the Her cry of warning to the Americans must come as a complete surprise to the Japs.

The natives were not angry or resentful a girl's death. They accepted it philosophical part of the price they had to pay for gettin of the Japs. They had proved their friendshi the Americans from the time they first stagg dazed by aerial and naval bombardment, the dugouts where they had taken shelter the American attack began.

The natives had been ordered to stay in village and not to show lights, but they anxious to help in mopping up the remnan the Jap garrison. When dawn came the Ar cans discovered that the local chief had a his young men with spears that had not used for generations and had stationed the a defense line extending across the island be the American perimeter. Unknown to the A icans, they had guarded their posts all night

Four miles away Lt. Col. Hart's men resu their advance over the bodies of 100 Japs k in the night's attacks. Among the weapons f were five light machine guns and three mortars. A few feet from the CP was a m shell. The excited Jap who fired the mortar failed to pull the pin, and the shell lay u ploded in the center of the area occupied by headquarters group.

At 1010 the Shamrocks reached the en Butaritari, mopped up the area and withdre the narrow neck of land a quarter mile to west to establish a defense line. Makin was

S/Sgt. Mike Thompson, a platoon leader, charged a machine-gun nest 50 yards off and took over.

Lt. Col. James Roosevelt and Col. Clarke L. Ru look over results on the southern part of Butari

The Great Cigarette Mystery

The Quartermaster tells why all those Chelseas went to England and the Pacific and announces good news — only the leading brands will be issued and rationed from now on overseas.

By Sgt. EARL ANDERSON
YANK Washington Bureau

FROM now on, the Army will get the six leading brands of cigarettes in its rations and overseas cigarette issues. The Quartermaster hereafter is buying only Lucky Strikes, Camels, Chesterfields, Philip Morrisses, Raleighs and Old Golds and discontinuing the purchase of less popular brands for these purposes.

For resale overseas, mostly through the PXs, the QM depot will endeavor to supply exactly what brands are requisitioned by the PX officer.

This is the good word for YANK readers from Col. L. C. Webster, officer in charge of the Non-Perishable Section of the Subsistence Branch, Office of the Quartermaster General.

The tremendous job of supplying and packing the cigarettes for millions of rations weekly will throw a heavy load on the six leading brands, already hard hit by the wartime shortage of labor and the wartime increase in smoking. However, the QM expects them to do it in order to give GIs the brands they want.

Since Col. Webster's section buys all the Army's cigarettes for shipment overseas, we popped several other questions at him that have been bothering GIs.

What was the story, for instance, behind the great cigarette mystery of last summer when most of the leading brands disappeared from the PX shelves in England and you couldn't buy anything but Chelseas?

How about the Planters-peanut cans of cigarettes in the Pacific? Why were they always filled with Chelseas instead of Camels, Luckies, Chesterfields, Philip Morrisses or Old Golds?

We told Col. Webster most soldiers overseas were firmly convinced that the War Department owned stock in Chelsea cigarettes. So Col. Webster gave us the War Department's side of the story.

The disappearance of the leading brands from England last year was part of a campaign by the Quartermaster to save GIs there from 5 to 7 cents on each carton—a total saving of about $6,000,000 a year, according to Col. Webster's estimate. Here's how it happened:

The Quartermaster buys cigarettes both for issue and for resale overseas. In purchasing cigarettes for resale, mostly through the PX system, the Quartermaster picked the amount of each brand in proportion to the sales of that brand in this country. Exact cigarette sales here are a closely guarded trade secret. However, *Printer's Ink*, an advertising trade magazine, publishes a yearly analysis of sales that is generally considered to be accurate. From that analysis, the popularity of the leading brands among civilians and soldiers appears to be about like this:

Lucky Strike	25.3%
Camel	23.1%
Chesterfield	17.2%
Philip Morris	9.5%
Raleigh	5.7%
Old Gold	4.7%
All others	14.5%

Actually, however, the Quartermaster normally bought 95 percent of the six leading brands and only 5 percent of Chelseas, Marvels and Twenty Grands. But last year it deliberately bent that yardstick, and the bending caused the temporary flow of Chelseas into England.

Until last July, the Quartermaster had been buying cigarettes from the companies at the regular jobber's price. It felt that the soldiers were not getting an even break under this arrangement because they were paying for merchandising and advertising expenses that the companies incurred in serving commercial jobbers. It therefore asked the companies to sell the tremendous carload shipments that go to the Army at a figure below the jobber's price.

Chelsea and Twenty Grand reduced their prices immediately, but Lucky Strike, Camel, Chesterfield and other major brands refused to go below the jobber's price.

In an effort to make the leading brands fall in line, Quartermaster increased its purchases of Chelseas and Twenty Grands by a few percentage points during July and August. Finally, in September, Chesterfield suggested a reduction of 10 percent in its Army price and the Lucky Strike and Camel people followed suit. Then the Quartermaster went back to the yardstick it had established. But, while the leading brands were making up their minds, a lot of those extra Chelseas bought by the Quartermaster in July and August were going to England. Brig. Gen.

C. A. Hardigg, chief of the Subsistence Branch, and Col. Webster were sorry about the steady diet of Chelseas, but they feel the sacrifice was worth it because of the saving it brought to the GIs.

Those Chelseas in Planter-peanut cans all over the Pacific were the result of a packaging problem. Cigarettes had to be packed in tin to withstand long storage in the tropical climates of New Guinea and the Solomons. But tin was hard to get last year.

Through a stroke of luck, the Quartermaster was able to lay its hands on 8,000,000 cans originally designed for Planters peanuts. But the size of the can did not quite fit the regular-sized cigarette, making it necessary to shorten each cigarette two millimeters under the standard length. This shortening, though barely perceptible to the eye, involved certain adjustments in the machinery of the cigarette companies.

The Quartermaster explained the problem and the necessity for rushing the cigarettes to the Pacific as soon as possible. Then it asked all companies for bids. Chelsea was the only company that responded to the emergency call. It volunteered to fill 2,000,000 cans, and these were delivered ahead of schedule and immediately shipped to the Pacific. When bids were requested a second time, both Raleigh and Chelsea responded, but Raleigh became involved with some WPB priorities on cans. So another shipment of Chelseas went to the Pacific.

In fact, the Chelsea people have gone out of their way on many occasions to cooperate with the Army on special assignments like this. The three cigarettes in C rations, for instance, have to be trimmed to a shorter-than-standard size in order to fit across the top of the can. They also have to be packed by hand. The leading cigarette companies, up to their ears in other orders, found it practically impossible at one time to do the special trimming and special packaging. Hitherto only Chelsea, Fleetwood and Twenty Grand have attempted to do the C-ration job. Hereafter the six leading brands will be used.

Some cases of unbalanced stocks overseas are impossible to explain. A pfc. on one of the Fiji Islands recently wrote to YANK complaining that his PX carried only cans of Wings, Avalons and Twenty Grands. "A few days ago I bought a can of them," he said, "and they were as white on top as the paper around them. It has been this way for the past two months."

YANK turned this news over to the Army Exchange Service, which cabled the Fijis and discovered that the pfc. was absolutely correct. But the Quartermaster doesn't know where the cigarettes came from; it says it never sent canned smokes of those brands to the Pacific.

YANK, The Army Weekly, publication issued weekly by Branch Office, Army Education and Information Division, War Dept., 205 East 42d Street, New York 17, N. Y. Reproduction rights restricted as indicated in the masthead on the editorial page. Entered as second class matter July 6, 1942, at the Post Office at New York, N. Y., under the Act of March 3, 1879. Subscription price $3.00 yearly. Printed in the U. S. A.

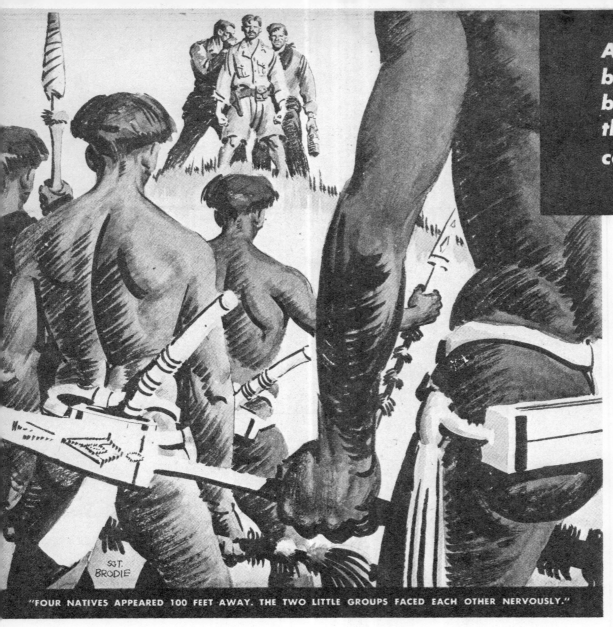

"FOUR NATIVES APPEARED 100 FEET AWAY. THE TWO LITTLE GROUPS FACED EACH OTHER NERVOUSLY."

utes later a C-47 was taking off from the base.

Davies, Wilder and Capt. Lee landed on a hillside hundreds of yards apart but within sight of each other. It was low bush, once cultivated by the natives but now waist-high in grass and shrub. They headed for a path lower down on the hillside, joining forces in about 10 minutes.

Barely a moment later, four natives appeared 100 feet away, each holding a spear. The two little groups faced each other nervously. Then the natives plunked their spears into the ground and picked up branches, a sign of peace. The Americans made friendly gestures and walked forward to meet them.

The natives pointed to a stream in the middle of the valley below and motioned to the Americans to accompany them there. In sign language they told Davies that three other parachutists had dropped from the skies, and soon afterward two of them, Col. Kuo and Sgt. Gigure, came into sight with some other natives.

At the river bank the natives paused, evidently waiting for someone. About 30 more natives emerged from the underbrush, and then a wrinkled little man about 80 years old, apparently the native chieftain, appeared on the scene. A kind of musette bag, containing silver Indian rupees, was slung over his shoulder, and by his side he wore a British sword. He gave a coin to each of the survivors in token of friendship.

Then the chief and his warriors led them on an hour-long, exhausting climb up to his village,

LOST IN HEAD-HUNTER COUNTRY

By Sgt. BOB GHIO
YANK Staff Correspondent

SOMEWHERE IN INDIA—Like stunt flyers in the finale of the Cleveland Air Show, 21 men bailed out from a twin-engined Army transport plane, their parachutes billowing in the bright clear sky. But this wasn't Cleveland; it was the Burma-India border, and the only human beings within hundreds of miles were head-hunting natives and Japanese troops.

Two of the parachutists were government officials, whose capture would be worth thousands of dollars to the Japs. Another one was a foreign correspondent, and the remaining 18 were American and Chinese Army officers and men. Only one had ever jumped from a plane before.

When I met them in the jungle almost a month later, 20 of the men were still alive. Their story involved an encounter with the head hunters, preparation against a Japanese attack, the arrival of medical aid and supplies by air, rescue by a ground force and then a long march back to civilization. They also told of the quick thinking of an enlisted man whose radio signals when the plane was falling saved their lives.

The assorted planeload of 21 had taken off on the morning of Aug. 2 from an airfield in India, bound for China. The trip's normal flying time for the C-46 Curtiss Commando was 2½ hours, and the transport had covered an hour's part of the journey when one motor went out at 0900.

Flight Officer Harry K. Nevue of Cudahy, Wis., pilot of the ship, circled desperately in a struggle to climb over the mountains that were looming ahead. According to his calculations, the transport was over Burma. Even if they survived a crash, they'd probably be captured by the Japs. And Nevue knew that one of his passengers was the political adviser to Lt. Gen.

Joseph Stilwell, John Davies Jr. of the State Department, who could not afford to be captured.

Nevue realized he could never clear the mountains in front of him. He turned the transport toward the valleys and plains lying southwest.

Fifteen minutes later Nevue ordered the passengers to throw out all the baggage. When even that failed to provide more altitude, he gave the order to bail out. They were approaching the Burma-India border, formed at this point by a ridge between two valleys. As the transport was still making considerable speed, the men were scattered over a 10-mile area.

Davies, who had been the first to jump, landed on the Burma side of the ridge with Lt. Col. Kuo Li of the Chinese Army; Capt. Duncan C. Lee of Chatham, Va.; S/Sgt. Joseph J. Gigure of Auburn, Maine; Sgt. E. Wilder of Levelland, Tex.; and Cpl. Basil M. Lemon of Tulsa, Okla.

The others, who hit the India side of the ridge, were William T. Stanton of the Board of Economic Warfare; Eric Sevareid, CBS correspondent; Col. Wang Pao Chao of the Chinese Army; Lt. Roland K. Lee of Hicksville, N. Y.; S/Sgt. Joseph E. Clay of Monticello, Iowa; Sgt. Glen A. Kittleson of Ballantine, Mont.; Sgt. Francis W. Signor of Yonkers, N. Y.; Cpl. Edward Holland of East Cleveland, Ohio; Cpl. J. Sherrill of Burlington, Iowa; Cpl. S. M. Waterbury of Blue Hill, Nebr.; Pvt. William Schrandt of Philadelphia, Pa.; S/Sgt. Ned C. Miller of Ottumwa, Iowa, the transport's crew chief; Sgt. Walter R. Oswalt of Ansonia, Ohio, radio operator; 2d Lt. Charles W. Felix of Compton, Calif., co-pilot, and Nevue.

As the first of the parachutes opened under the faltering transport, Sgt. Oswalt calmly notified the nearest base that the plane would crash in a few minutes. He left the radio circuit open, instructing the base to take a bearing on his position and to send out a rescue mission. Min-

built on a hilltop as a defense against attack. They rested and tried to quench their thirst with zu, a native beer made from rice. Then the chief gave Sgt. Wilder a knife and motioned to him to behead a goat. The head was passed around so that the chief and his guests could drink the blood from the jugular vein, a great delicacy.

Late in the afternoon, a native runner reported to the chief that a plane had crashed in the valley on the other side of the ridge. Davies and Capt. Lee sent a message by another runner to the valley, signed with only their first names, suggesting that survivors return with the guide.

The runner came back 2½ hours later with a note from Eric Sevareid, urging the Davies party to join him instead. Sevareid wrote that one of his companions was injured and added that a friendly plane had sighted them.

Davies and the others set out that same night with native guides to cross the mountain ridge separating them from the native village where Sevareid was apparently situated. It was raining, and the men groped their way along the trail with torches. They were wet and miserable when they reached the village around 2300.

They found Sevareid and 13 others in a native communal hut, some sleeping and some sitting around a fire. The newcomers were told how the transport had crashed and exploded in a geyser of orange flames after Nevue, last of the 21 to jump, left the pilot's seat. Several of them were still in the air when the explosion came, and Sevareid narrowly avoided being blown into the blaze. Sgt. Oswalt, the 210-pound radio operator, broke his ankle when he landed.

Two hours later the C-47, summoned by Sgt. Oswalt's final radio message, flew overhead and sighted the parachutes the survivors had spread out on the ground. A radio receiver, a Gibson girl transmitter, two Springfield rifles and a sig-

After the long march back: Rear row, left to right: P. F. Adams, Sgt. E. Wilder, Col. Wang Pao Chao, John Davies Jr. (in front of Col. Wang), Eric Sevareid, William T. Stanton, S/Sgt. Joseph E. Clay, Cpl. Basil M. Lemon, Sgt. Glen A. Kittleson, Sgt. Francis W. Signor and Cpl. J. Sherrill. Second row: Lt. Roland K. Lee, Lt. Col. Kuo Li, S/Sgt. Ned C. Miller, Flight Officer Harry K. Nevue, S/Sgt. Joseph J. Gigure, Pvt. William Schrandt, Cpl. Edward Holland, Cpl. S. M. Waterbury and Capt. Duncan C. Lee. First row: Sgt. Richard Passey, Lt. Col. Donald D. Flickinger, Cpl. William G. McKenzie and Sgt. Walter R. Oswalt. One of the party died in chute jump.

nal panel set were dropped from the C-47, but the transmitter broke when it landed.

As soon as they set up the radio receiver, the pilot of the C-47 warned the group that there were unfriendly natives nearby and that it would take 12 days for a rescue mission to reach them from the nearest British base. There was no place to land a plane here safely, he said, but it would be easy to drop them any supplies they needed.

Assembling the white cloth signal panels into a message-pattern, Sevareid asked for medical assistance for Sgt. Oswalt. Around 1700 the C-47 returned with medical supplies and three medics, who parachuted down to join the survivors— Lt. Col. Donald D. Flickinger, a Regular Army flight surgeon from Long Beach, Calif., who holds the DFC; Sgt. Richard Passey of Provo, Utah, and Cpl. William G. McKenzie of Detroit, Mich.

Meanwhile the party had found that the natives of the nearby village were not hostile. When Lt. Col. Flickinger arrived and took command, however, he decided to keep the survivors away from the native village as much as possible. It was already overcrowded and he didn't want to take the risk of provoking bad feelings during the time they'd have to wait for a rescue mission.

After some dickering, the natives agreed to build a special hut out of palmetto leaves and bamboo for Lt. Col. Flickinger's men and the survivors, in an uncultivated area some distance from the village, where supplies could be dropped without damaging the native cornfields. From then on two C-47s, piloted by Capt. Hugh E. Wild of Milwaukee, Wis., and Capt. George E. Katzman of Louisville, Ky., flew over the encampment daily to drop medicine, carbines, clothing, food and even Calcutta newspapers.

They read a story in the newspapers about their missing plane, listing Davies among the passengers and saying that news of the mishap had been broadcast by radio. Realizing that Jap agents could read the papers, too, and hear the radio, and that enemy forces would probably be searching the area for the State Department official, Lt. Col. Flickinger assigned his own men to battle stations and they dug a special slit trench

for the injured Sgt. Oswalt to occupy in case the camp was strafed.

As a matter of fact, Jap planes passed near the camp twice. Once an enemy observation plane flew overhead, too high to spot the survivors. Another time a flight of Zeros zoomed just beyond the hill where the village was located.

After organizing battle stations, Lt. Col. Flickinger assigned each man to a special job. Davies, a professional diplomat, was put in charge of relations with the natives. Sgt. Gigure, a mess sergeant, directed the cooking with Cpl. Sherrill as KP-pusher and the two Chinese colonels as "rice cooks."

Stanton was named signal officer and Sgt. Kittleson and Cpl. Holland as his assistants. Capt. Lee served as adjutant and supply officer, Sgt. Clay as supply sergeant and Lt. Lee and Sgt. Signor as quartermasters, bringing in the supplies as they were dropped on the hillside.

Sevareid became camp historian and chaplain. He conducted Sunday religious services and a memorial service for Lt. Felix, the co-pilot, whose body had been found under the tail of the

wrecked plane, where his parachute had evidently caught when he jumped.

The lieutenant colonel and his two medics established a daily sick call, treating natives as well as the Americans and Chinese for sores resulting from leech bites. This free medical attention helped to keep the natives friendly.

To get the men in shape for the coming long march out of the jungle, Lt. Col. Flickinger also conducted a daily calisthenics session. The natives nearly knocked themselves out laughing.

Davies carried on a brisk trade with the natives, exchanging tin cans, cotton cloth and salt —all dropped by the C-47s—for firewood, labor on construction projects, spears, knives and, oddly enough, trinkets. The natives also provided corn, rice, beans, chickens, pigs and cattle.

The salt was reserved as a reward for major services. The natives who constructed the hut and those who found an important packet of papers, which Davies had dropped during his parachute jump, were paid off that way. The biggest payment went to Cpl. Lemon's rescuers.

Lemon had jumped on the Burma side of the

NATIVES CARRY SGT. WALTER OSWALT ON STRETCHER.   DOCTORING LEECH BITES

ridge, but he landed a long distance from the others. For three days and nights he hid out in the mountainous jungles, avoiding the native searchers because he was afraid they would take his head. At night he drank water from a river that ran near his hiding place, but he had nothing to eat except his cigarettes.

On the fourth day after the crash, Lemon was picked up by the natives, his feet badly blistered. He said afterward that he was so weak then that he didn't care who they were. "I was looking for them, head hunters or not," he said.

The day after Lemon was brought to the camp, the chief ordered a friendship ceremony. A *mithon*, a kind of Indian water buffalo, was sacrificed. The ceremonies concluded with the Americans singing "I've Been Working on the Railroad" while the head hunters gaped.

One other ritual helped to pass the time while the men waited for the rescue mission. Schrandt, the only private in the group, was solemnly and formally promoted to acting sergeant so that he could sleep with the rest of the noncoms.

At last, on the sixteenth day after the mass parachute jump, a ground rescue mission reached the village. Headed by P. F. Adams, a young British political officer, the mission included a British Army officer and Capt. J. J. Dwyer of Chicago, Ill.; Lt. Andrew S. LaBonte of Lawrence, Mass.; T/Sgt. Joe L. Merritt of Rosboro, Ark.; T/Sgt. Kenneth E. Coleman of Meridian, Ohio; Cpl. Anthony Gioia of Denver, Colo., and Pfc. Frank Oropeza of Los Angeles, Calif.

Accompanying them were about 50 native porters and 40 of the district's most efficient head hunters. They have no loyalty except to their own villages, and the British maintain order by hiring the fiercest natives as a police force.

This Week's Cover

ON his first night in a foxhole on Makin, Pfc. James McClure heard something moving. He didn't ask questions. He shot. The next morning McClure, of the 165th Infantry, was still there with a dead Jap nearby as mute testimony to his good judgment and aim. See pages 2, 3 and 4 for additional pictures by YANK's Sgt. John Bushemi on Makin.

PHOTO CREDITS: Cover, 2, 3, 4 & 5—Sgt. John Bushemi. 7—Sgt. Bob Ghio. 8—INP. 9—Left, Sgt. Lou Stoumen; right, Acme. 10 & 11—AAF. 12—Upper left, INP; lower left, WW; center, ALCO; right (top to bottom), USMC, Sovfoto, Acme. 13—Upper left & right, INP; center, PA; lower (left to right), Acme, Sgt. Dick Hanley, Acme. 16—Left, AAA School, Camp Davis, N. C.; right, Signal Corps-Fort Blanding, Fla. 17—Upper (left to right), Blythe AAB, Calif., Signal Corps-Fort Sill, Okla., Sgt. Bob Hegge-Lowry Field (Colo.) PRO; center left, U. S. Army; lower left and center, Sgt. Ben Schnall; lower right, Moore Field, Tex. 20—MGM. 23—Right, Acme; left, PA.

Adams told Lt. Col. Flickinger and the others that the natives of both villages visited by the survivors were active head hunters. More than 100 heads had been taken in one village since January. The other village had twice been burned by British expeditions as punishment for excessive head hunting. The memory of these burnings was still fresh when the survivors landed. That's why they weren't molested. The supernatural appearance of their descent, and the prospect of a 500-*rupee* reward (paid in salt) for each parachutist brought in alive to the British authorities, also helped, Adams said.

For two days Adams and his men rested after

their journey. Then, on Aug. 18, he led the party now swollen to a good-sized caravan of Americans, Chinese and natives, on the first lap of a five-day march to his India base. It was tough walking all the way, but they averaged more than 10 miles a day over mountain peaks that sometimes rose to 8,000 feet and along a path sometimes only 10 inches wide.

Adams ordered a halt at one historic ambush point and sent the guerrilla militia ahead to comb the pass. They found no signs of hostile natives and the caravan passed on quietly. A little farther along, all drank beer dropped by plane, the only stimulants they had had since the first night when Capt. Lee handed around a bottle of gin he had hugged tight during his descent.

When the party reached Adams' headquarters a plane dropped containers of hot chicken and gravy, mashed potatoes, ice cream and chocolate cake, and everyone feasted during a one-day stop-over. From this base it is a 2½-day march to the place where the road widens enough to permit the passage of jeeps. I met them one day's march from the head of the jeep trail.

Oswalt was still being carried by eight natives in a bamboo stretcher-chair fashioned by the two Chinese colonels. He told me that at one very bad place in the mountain road a native of half his weight had carried him piggy-back for nearly 50 yards. Oswalt was the only man to gain weight during the 26 days in the jungle.

After reaching the wide trail, the party covered the remaining 40 to 50 miles to the nearest airfield in two hours, making the journey in jeeps, command cars, carry-alls and a couple of trucks. From the airfield, the survivors were flown in two large planes to the station where they had taken off almost a month before.

German Notes on Winter Use Of Infantry Weapons

The following notes, based on directions issued by the German High Command on the use of infantry weapons in winter, are reprinted from the *Intelligence Bulletin* with permission of the Army's Military Intelligence Division.

THE German Army is thoroughly aware that winter cold and snow necessitate special measures concerning the carrying, moving and bringing into position of infantry weapons and ammunition. In this connection German soldiers are reminded of certain fundamental points: that noises travel farther in cold, clear air; that when snow obscures terrain features, there are decidedly fewer landmarks; and that, in winter, distances are generally estimated too short in clear weather and too far in mist. The German High Command adds several other practical suggestions:

It will be especially necessary to practice target designation, distance estimation and ranging.

The rifleman and his weapons must be camouflaged thoroughly. White coats, white covers for headgear, and white overall trousers and jackets will be worn. When necessary, such outer clothing can easily be improvised out of white canvas. The simplest camouflage for weapons will be plain white cloth covers or coats of removable chalk; the former will have the added advantage of affording protection.

At low temperatures, the accompanying weapons of the infantry will fire somewhat short at first. After a few rounds, however, the range to the point of impact will be normal. Before a weapon is loaded, the loading movements should be practiced without ammunition. (In drilling

with pistols, be sure to remove the magazine beforehand.)

Rifles. Rifles are carried on the back, or are hung from the neck and suspended in front. During long marches on skis, rifles are fastened on the side of the haversack.

When the German soldier goes into position, he takes special care not to allow his rifle barrel to become filled with snow. He does not take off the bolt protector and muzzle cap until shortly before he is to use the rifle. The various methods of going into position are practiced in drill.

As far as possible, telescopic sights are not exposed too suddenly to extreme changes in temperature.

Automatic Pistol. The Germans keep the automatic pistol well wrapped and sling it around the neck or over the shoulder. Magazine pouches are closed very tightly.

Light Machine Gun. The light machine gun is slung on the back. In going into position, the Germans use brushwood or a "snow board" for a base. They take care not to disturb, by unnecessary trampling, the snow cover in front of positions. The purpose of this precaution is to avoid recognition by the opposing force.

The simplest kind of mat is taken along so that belts can be kept clear of snow.

The light machine gun is first shot until it is warm and then oiled.

When fire is continued for any length of time, the snow in front of the muzzle turns black; therefore, before the snow becomes blackened, the Germans decide upon prospective changes of position.

If there is to be a considerable interval after the firing of the machine gun, the bolt is changed

and the oil is removed from the sliding parts. (Only an extremely thin oil film is allowed to remain.) This precludes stoppages by the freezing of oil. The new bolt is given a very thin coat of oil before it is inserted.

Replacement ammunition, in pre-filled belts, is carried into action.

Heavy Machine Gun. The heavy machine gun is carried in the usual manner or is loaded on a small sleigh, skis or a *pulk*. A *pulk* is a type of sled used by the Lapps; its front half somewhat resembles that of a rowboat.

When the Germans take the heavy machine gun into position, they use some sort of snow board, the *pulk* or even a stretcher as a base. They take care not to disturb the snow in front of the position.

The Germans try not to expose the sights to temperatures of less than 6° F. During marches these sights are kept in their containers, and before they are used they are gradually warmed in sheltered places or on the human body. The sights are kept mounted on the machine-gun carriage only while the gun is in active use.

Pulk used for transporting machine gun in snow.

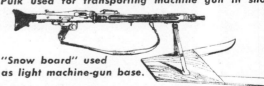

"Snow board" used as light machine-gun base.

Mats are carried so that belts may be kept clear of snow.

For shooting in extreme cold, German range tables provide for the necessary sight adjustments. The heavy machine gun is first shot until it is warm and then is oiled. New positions are decided upon before the snow in front of the muzzle becomes blackened.

The Germans prevent soiling of the machine gun, which leads to stoppages, (a) by keeping the antidust cover closed as much as possible and (b) by not allowing the gun to remain loaded (with bolt backwards) for any length of time.

Speed is considered highly important in readying the gun for firing. While firing is in progress, the bolt remains uncocked in the forward position, the belt is inserted into the belt pawl, and the gunner, remaining in the firing position, withdraws the cocking slide only with a strong jerk and pushes it forward again.

Yanks in Haiti at their Sad Sack Service Club. Left to right, behind bar: Cpl. George Perry Jr.; Edmund Church, local resident; Pvt. Arthur J. Dempsey; S/Sgt. Ernest C. Carlsen. Men in front are club waiters.

Steak, Rum, No KP, No MPs — And Yanks in Haiti Get Paid, Too

PORT AU PRINCE, HAITI—Work details sometimes run to seven 12-hour shifts a week, but apart from that, Yanks stationed in *la republique Haiti* (French is the local language here) have stumbled into a GI paradise.

Voodoo mask

No U. S. quarters or rations are available, so the men live in comfortable barracks belonging to the Haitian Army. They eat succulent Haitian steaks, chops, turkeys and rabbits prepared in a Haitian mess and garnished with mushrooms, spuds, fresh green vegetables and French sauces.

They pull no KP, have their beds made and the floors swept by a houseboy. A reverse Lend-Lease arrangement takes care of guard duty; Haitian soldiers do it. And besides their 20 percent extra for overseas service, the GIs draw a daily $2.75 allowance out of which they pay for quarters and the dream chow. These Haiti Glad Sacks enjoy quick cheap laundry service, too. A uniform can be cleaned and pressed in eight hours for two *gourdes* (40 American cents).

Haitian rum, notably Barbancourt 4 Star, is famed throughout the Caribbean for its smooth, Scotch-like quality. And the GIs here have built their own Sad Sack Service Club, based on the sound principles of good fellowship and U. S. beer. Among the Yanks patronizing the club are Cpl. George Perry Jr. of Oakland, Calif.; Pvt. Arthur J. Dempsey of Jersey City, N. J., and S/Sgt. Ernest C. Carlsen of Kenyon, Minn.

Another advantage of serving in Haiti is the chance to see the misunderstood voodoo rites and to hear the night-long knee-drum jive. At the museum you can take a look at many voodoo relics, including ancient masks from the African Ivory Coast.

All U. S. enlisted men are saluted by Haitian soldiers, but here's the real pay-off to this fairy tale: on the whole island of Haiti there is not one MP.
—Sgt. LOU STOUMEN
YANK Staff Correspondent

In New Caledonia It's the Guys Who Teach the Gals How to Dance

NOUMEA, NEW CALEDONIA—A GI fresh from the States, where USO hostesses are constantly arranging classes to teach the boys to dance, is startled to find the situation reversed at the Noumea Red Cross Servicemen's Club. A sign reads:

"WANTED! EXPERT DANCERS — TANGO, RUMBA, CONGO — TO TEACH THE GIRLS WHOM WE INVITE."

Janice Jarrett of Boston, Mass., formerly the prima ballerina in Catherine Littlefield's group in Chicago, and now stationed here as a Red Cross staff assistant, explained the situation.

Most of the few white girls in Noumea are of French extraction, and they've never been exposed before to American jitterbugging or to Latin-American dance rhythms.

"They have a very different idea of dancing," said Miss Jarrett (quite a jitterbug herself). "When we came the French girls were doing only a fox trot. In fact, it wasn't even a very smooth fox trot. It was rather jumpy."

Now the girls are able to jitterbug with the best of them. But their rumba and conga have to go some before they're quite up to par.

The outstanding GI teachers are Sgt. Donald Hooton of Somerville, Mass., and Pvt. Louis Chabboro of San Francisco, Calif. Hooton was a professional actor and appeared with the St. Louis Opera Company. Chabboro and his wife were a professional dance team. Both Hooton and Chabboro have been rewarded with permanent Monday night passes.

A permanent pass to teach Latin-American dancing once a week may not seem much of a privilege but it is about the only way a soldier can get to a dance here more than once a year or so. Tickets to the regular weekly dance on Thursday are so rare that they are offered as the grand prize at the weekly bingos and quiz programs. The 200 servicemen at each of the dances are chosen for the most part through a Red Cross system of offering block invitations each week to a different organization, usually one that has just returned from the jungle fighting to the north. Soldiers, sailors and marines get the invitation on successive weeks.

The 200 lucky ticket holders find 20 girls at the dance as a rule. Each girl is cut in on 20 times in each set of three dances. The girls call the event their "athletic Thursday."

The Red Cross has its troubles finding even 20 dance partners, because local French ideas about such affairs are very strict. Every girl is accompanied by one or more personal chaperons. The Red Cross sends an automobile to pick up the girl and her relatives and to drive them home.

"The mother may come or both parents," Miss Jarrett remarked. "Sometimes it's the girl's aunts or even her brothers and sisters. When we go to call on a girl, we don't know whether they'll be just two or the whole family."

Sometimes an outfit will try to run a dance on its own, but this generally results in even more critical girl problems. One QM truck regiment ran a dance and only four girls showed up, Miss Jarrett and three of her co-workers from the Red Cross. They had already put in a 12-hour day but danced for six hours more, almost without a break. There were 40 men to each girl. "It was," said Miss Jarrett, "a work-out."
—Cpl. BARRETT McGURN
YANK Staff Correspondent

GI Appendix Removed Despite Close Quarters and Rough Seas

SOMEWHERE IN NORTH AFRICA—While the Liberty ship tossed in seas so rough that a chair was hurled across the little dispensary, Pvt. Herbert Dewey of Adrian, Mich., had his appendix removed in an emergency operation that was among the first of its kind on record.

Other GIs have been sliced up on big transports equipped with an operating room and a reasonable amount of equipment, but Dewey went under the knife in a two-by-four cubbyhole that passed for a hospital on the cargo ship.

Lt. Frank Conole of Binghamton, N. Y., on his third crossing as a medical officer and in charge of the medical detail of the 33d Ship Hospital Platoon, performed the surgery. The lieutenant was called to the dispensary to examine Dewey on the vessel's sixth day out of an East Coast U. S. port. He decided on an appendectomy.

Lt. Conole recruited as his assistants Capt. Walter H. Kwiecten of Bloomfield, N. J., a dental officer, and Maj. Rowland Rushmore of Clinton, Iowa, a veterinarian.

The patient was given pre-operative injections of morphine and atrophine, followed by a spinal anesthesia. Then Lt. Conole made the incision deftly in spite of the motion of the Liberty ship, and sprinkled sulfanilamide powder over each layer of the abdominal wound. A package of sterile towels and drapes, which had been slipped in with the regular dispensary supplies by the Port Surgeon's Office, proved a godsend.

Twelve days after the operation, the stitches were taken out. As a precautionary measure, Dewey donned a snug-fitting "corset" made of sail canvas, hand-stitched by one of the merchant seamen. This provided support for Dewey's abdomen after he was allowed out of bed. When the boat docked, the GI walked down the gangplank under his own power.
—Pvt. TOM SHEHAN
YANK Staff Correspondent

TWO DOWN, TWO TO GO

SOMEWHERE IN THE SOUTH PACIFIC—According to a will left by his grandfather, Sgt. Roman J. Rehegan, USMC, of St. Louis, Mo., must serve a hitch in each of the four branches of the U. S. armed services before he inherits $1,000.

Rehegan, now stationed here, enlisted in the Marines in June 1940 after completing a hitch in the Army. He still has to serve in the Navy and the Coast Guard.
—Sgt. HY HURWITZ
Marine Corps Correspondent

HAPPY LANDING. Or the nicest way for a Wac to leave an Army truck. The scene is Italy; Pvt. Sheldon Howe is catching Pvt. Betty Hoefler, Pvt. Laura Howieson stands at right and yet to jump is Pvt. Rena Hicks.

The Big Three sit for their picture at the Russian Embassy in Teheran while a corps of photographers, including GIs of a Signal Photo Bn., move in for close-up

A GI View of the Teheran Conference

Soldiers in Iran who saw Stalin meet Roosevelt and Churchill no longer look upon their command as the dullest place this side of Cooks and Bakers School.

By Sgt. AL HINE and Cpl. JAMES P. O'NEILL
YANK Staff Correspondents

TEHERAN, IRAN [By Radio]—GIs in Persia, long accustomed to considering their command the most humdrum place this side of a Cooks and Bakers School, were slightly dumbfounded when President Roosevelt, Premier Stalin and Prime Minister Churchill blew into town recently for the most historic conference of the war.

The railroad men, longshoremen and truck drivers who make up the bulk of this important supply depot's Army population couldn't believe their eyes when they saw the crowd of celebrities who followed the three United Nations leaders here for the big international surprise party—Gen. George C. Marshall, Adm. William Leahy, Anthony Eden, V. M. Molotov, W. Averell Harriman, Adm. Ernest King, Gen. H. H. Arnold, Lt. Gen. Brehon B. Somervell, Marshal Klementi Voroshilov, Ambassador John G. Winant and Harry Hopkins, to name only a few.

One GI who had a ringside seat at the conference from start to finish was Cpl. Matt Volenski, a railroad man from Pittsburgh, Pa., who was in charge of the billets for the entire American party.

"There was never a dull moment," Matt says. "A couple of other noncoms and I got our first hint that someone big was coming when they told us to move all our colonels from their regular billets into the wing of the hospital. But

they didn't tell us then what it was all about."

Needless to say, it was a rare pleasure for these corporals and T-5s to be able to tell the silver eagles to pack up and get out.

"We were hearing plenty of rumors about the reasons for the moving," Matt added, "and, of course, the Cairo Conference gave us something to base our rumors on. Sure enough, they told us one morning that the President was coming, so we finished moving the colonels, but fast, and brought in cots, soap, towels, sheets, food, envelopes, toilet paper and everything else we could think of.

"We had a hell of a time getting around, too, because we had no special passes and the whole town was being guarded as tight as a drum. We had to buck Russian guards, argue with our own MPs and run our old beat-up trucks like they were never run before. When the conference got into full swing it was even giddier. I had our minister to Iran, Louis G. Dreyfus Jr., guiding me on one trip from the Russian Embassy where the President stayed for two nights. He hopped on the truck and directed me through the jumble of guards and shrubbery. At one point, I ran up against a Russki secret-service man who gave me a puzzled look from head to foot and then, still puzzled, saluted me. I saluted him back and kept on going."

Since Matt was on duty all the time bringing in food and supplies, he had a good backstage view of the conference. What he didn't see himself, he picked up from the cooks who prepared the meals for the President's party.

They reported that FDR especially liked the gazelle that had been shot here by GI hunters for one of his dinners. His other favorite dishes were odd snacks and fish. The cooks said he made a crack about fish being brain food. The President eats plenty of spinach and likes a little garlic flavoring in his meals.

"That Soviet marshal, Voroshilov, was the

biggest man I've ever seen in this command, Matt said. "And Gen. Marshall certainly looke like a general ought to look. He made a grea hit with the Polish waitresses when he gav them mementos of the visit—wrist bands that h bought here in the GI PX. One waitress said t me: 'Oh, Gen. Marshall is such a clean-cut an good-looking man. He's got such good eyes yo can see that he's foresighted.' She said she wa so nervous she almost went to pieces every tim she waited on him."

They Shot the Works

THE official pictures of the conference were take by six GIs in the 846th Signal Photo Br —T/Sgt. Arthur Daniels, S/Sgt. Robert Davi: Sgt. Robert Murray, Pfc. Munroe Oettinger, Pf William Coggswell and Pfc. Grant Nelrad, a former cameraman at top Hollywood studios.

Their photo section works with a 35-mn Mitchell movie-camera machine propelled by gasoline engine that makes a hell of a racke When they were suddenly called to the Russia legation to shoot conference pictures, they drape camera hoods over the machines to try to cu down on the noise. "The damn thing sounde like a B-24," Sgt. Daniels said afterward.

While these boys, who had taken pictures a El Alamein, Tripoli, Algiers and Malta, wer "shooting" Stalin, Roosevelt and Churchill or the legation porch, a secret-service man cam up and told them one of the hoods was on fire

"To hell with the hood," Pfc. Oettinger tol him. "We're busy. Put it out yourself."

Later the pfc. apologized. "I guess I sort o lost my head," he says. "Just think when thi is all over and the cameramen back on the lo in Hollywood start bragging about the big star they've shot, I'll step in with a story about thi job and top them all."

The six GI photographers never expect t

ocus on anything more important for the rest of their lives. "Even the occupation of Tokyo will be an anticlimax after this assignment," says Sgt. Davis.

Long Way From Home

THE 19th Station Hospital is located on the road that leads to the field where the President reviewed the U. S. Army troops from Camp Amirabaq. All the convalescent patients were allowed to go outside to watch the President pass by. Pvt. William Wiley of Tacoma, Wash., confined to the hospital with a fractured leg, wangled the only wheel chair in his ward and maneuvered it to the side of the road.

When the President came along and saw the patients, he stopped his jeep in front of Wiley's wheel chair. "We're both a long way from home, aren't we, son?" he said.

"Yes, Mr. President, we sure are," Wiley replied. He has been overseas for a year with the 186th Quartermasters.

The Generals Eat Spam

T/SGT. George McClusik, an ex-coal miner from Clarence, Pa., walked into his barracks after a hard day on a bulldozer and bumped into his first sergeant. The first sergeant was carrying McClusik's ODs in his hands. "Here," he said, handing over the clothes. "You're going on guard."

George tried to give the top kick an argument, but before he knew it he was posted outside the door of a small room off the officers' mess where the generals ate their meals. A louey told George not to let anyone through the door unless he gave an okay.

"What will I do if you are not around, sir?" asked George.

"Don't let anybody in except generals," said the shavetail.

George obeyed the rule, with two exceptions—Adm. King and Adm. Leahy. "The louey didn't tell me anything about admirals," he said, "but I figured they rated."

When the generals sat down for their first dinner in Iran the mess officer told Gen. Marshall that he was going to serve them the first fresh meat ever received by the command. It had arrived the night before by boat at a Persian Gulf port and the officials had flown the precious stuff to Teheran for the conference.

But Gen. Marshall refused the meat, graciously but very firmly. "If this is the first meat to arrive here," he said, "I think the men who have been stationed here should have the privilege of eating it. We'll take Spam and bread." And they got Spam and bread.

"This isn't hooey, either," says George. "I heard Gen. Marshall say it. And for my dough, he's a regular guy."

The Intrepid Irishman

CPL. John Kennedy was the guard stationed outside the conference room. He had to check another door to the room. The only way to reach it was to walk right through the conference where the American, British and Russian officials were discussing confidential matters of world-wide significance.

Kennedy, an intrepid Irishman from Philadelphia, Pa., swallowed a couple of times nervously. Then he threw back his shoulders and marched straight into the room past the table where the astonished dignitaries were turning to stare at him. He tried the unchecked door. Then he about-faced and marched smartly out again.

"I sort of had a lump in my throat," Kennedy said. "But I guess those big shots understood that duty is duty. But I could see that they were wondering at first just what the hell I was doing in that room."

When You Gotta Go, You Can't

THE assignment of guarding the President and his party was given to Co. H, 727 Military Police Bn., and this was a great honor for these MPs who, in a noncombatant zone like Iran, usually have nothing to do except boring town-cop duty.

The entire company was placed in strategic spots all over the grounds of the American Legation. They guarded the President so well that first day and night that they were also selected to watch over all three of the conference leaders throughout the historic two-day meeting that followed at the Russian Embassy.

The noncoms and men took their jobs calmly and refused to get excited about the importance of their assignment. They wouldn't let anyone go anywhere without proper authorization. One high-ranking British official, who attempted unsuccessfully to get past them and into the embassy without a pass, shook his head and muttered: "This is the most bloody guarded place I've ever seen."

Pvt. W. G. Atkinson of Scranton, Pa., was the guard on the back door of the embassy when a colonel came up and asked if he could go in to use the latrine. Atkinson refused to allow him near the door.

"Don't you know who I am?" demanded the colonel. He merely happened to be the commanding officer of Atkinson's own MP outfit.

"Sir," replied Atkinson coldly, "until this thing is over, I don't recognize nothing or nobody unless he's got a pass."

The colonel went out into the garden where there were plenty of trees.

Presidential Reviews

REVIEWING the troops here before boarding his plane for home, President Roosevelt drove through the camp to the baseball diamond where he talked to the soldiers from his jeep.

The President took a microphone in his hand. It didn't work. Then he tried another that did not work at first, either. He smiled and said: "And these are supposed to be the most powerful weapons of the war."

His speech was short, lasting only about four minutes. He wore his familiar brown felt hat, a dark coat, a gray flannel suit, a white shirt and black tie. He looked rather tired after the long days of the conference.

He told the gathered troops how he had looked out the window the first morning he woke in Iran and thought at first that he was somewhere in Arizona. The terrain here does resemble that part of America. And he went on to tell them about his meeting with Churchill and Stalin.

"We discussed not only plans for getting the war over," he said, "but also more important plans for peace."

He told the soldiers that the people back home were aware of the fine job they were doing here. He said he wished those people could see the job with their own eyes.

"I am going home now," he concluded. "And I wish I could take all of you with me."

There were no cheers after he finished speaking. Instead there was a hushed silence that seemed to last for a full minute until the troops were called to order arms. The metallic clatter of the pieces rang out over the baseball field. Then the men shouldered arms and began to march away. Many of their faces were bright and many of them had strange marks around their eyes. For most of them, it was the first time they had ever seen a President of the United States.

Declaration Issued by Roosevelt, Churchill and Stalin After the Three-Power Conference at Teheran

WE, the President of the United States of America, the Prime Minister of Great Britain, and the Premier of the Soviet Union, have met in these four days past in this the capital of our ally, Teheran, and have shaped and confirmed our common policy.

We express our determination that our nations shall work together in the war and in the peace that will follow.

As to the war, our military staffs have joined in our round-table discussions and we have concerted our plans for the destruction of the German forces. We have reached complete agreement as to the scope and timing of operations which will be undertaken from the east, west and south. The common understanding which we have here reached guarantees that victory will be ours.

And as to the peace, we are sure that our concord will make it an enduring peace. We recognize fully the supreme responsibility resting upon us and all the nations to make a peace which will command good will from the overwhelming masses of the peoples of the world and banish the scourge and terror of war for many generations.

With our diplomatic advisers we have surveyed the problems of the future. We shall seek the cooperation and active participation of all nations, large and small, whose peoples in heart and in mind are dedicated, as are our own peoples, to the elimination of tyranny and slavery, oppression and intolerance. We will welcome them as they may choose to come into the world family of democratic nations.

No power on earth can prevent our destroying the German armies by land, their U-boats by sea, and their war plants from the air. Our attacks will be relentless and increasing.

Emerging from these friendly conferences we look with confidence to the day when all the peoples of the world may live free lives untouched by tyranny and according to their varying desires and their own consciences.

We came here with hope and determination. We leave here friends in fact, in spirit, and in purpose.

Signed at Teheran, Dec. 1, 1943.   ROOSEVELT, STALIN, CHURCHILL.

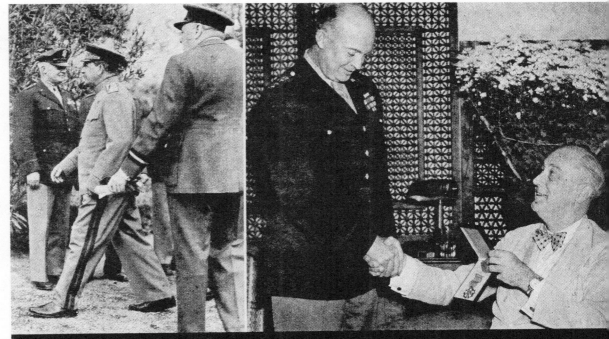

Marshal Stalin, strides past Gen. H. H. Arnold, commanding general of the USAAF and Prime Minister Churchill. During his trip to conferences at Cairo and Teheran, President Roosevelt took time out to award the Legion of Merit to Gen. Eisenhower, commander of Allied Forces in the Mediterranean.

Varie...
PRODUCED BY TH

DEVIL DOG. Caesar, a German shepherd attached to the U. S. rines, was carried back wounded to a dressing station during the of Bougainville. Caesar and other trained dogs have helped ferre Japs in the dense South Pacific jungles and warned many Yanks of

MUDDY WATER. A platoon does its best to avoid a big puddle filling an Italian road. The rainy season has changed any previous ideas about "sunny Italy" for U. S. soldiers.

STAR GUNNER. Senior Sgt. Polienko of the Red is commander of an antiaircraft gun crew which has down 16 German aircraft over Russia. The record is the all to admire in the form of 16 stars on his gun's b

RESULT NOTED. An assembly crew for 105-mm guns at the American Locomotive Co. plant in Dunkirk, N. Y., looking over a story in YANK on a 105 which they helped to make.

UNSCHEDULED. Margaret Adams, MGM actress, got in the way of a wind machine and look what happened. Just look what happened.

FULL SPEED AHEAD. These British infantrymen of the Fifth Army under Lt. Gen. Mark V Clark are in no mood to linger. They have a position to take. Crouching forward they advance ov a blasted railway bridge to take an Italian town on the other side. Then come mountains—and Rom

AT-TOP FOOTBALL. A plane-handling crew s advantage of a quiet moment on the Atlantic to play a brisk game of football on the flight of the *USS Card,* a converted escort carrier.

REQUEST GRANTED. Jolie Bishop, Hollywood actress, wears a grass skirt sent to her from the South Pacific by Pfc. Philip Davis. He wrote that he wanted to see it properly filled.

DECORATED. At a base in England, T Sgt. Harold Rogers, bomber tail gunner, enjoys a party and extra big stripes he earned for completing 25 missions.

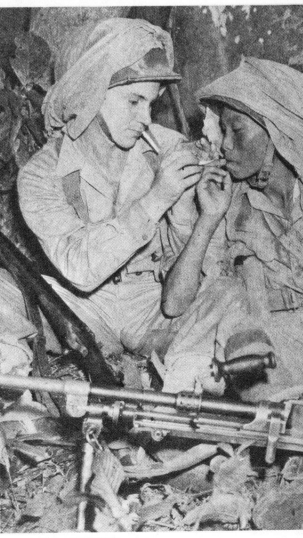

OMECOMING. An Italian woman came back m hiding in the hills when the Nazis were thrown but found her home nothing but a heap of rubble.

PRIDE. Pfc. Harry Kaplan, in Southwest Pacific, is so proud of Purple Heart and ribbon he wears them on fatigues.

TWO ALLIES. Cpl. Rolf Krog, Yank, and a Chinese soldier light up during a U. S.-Chinese operation against Japs in northwestern Burma.

THE SAD SACK

"THE GOOD DEED"

©1943 SGT. GEORGE BAKER

Ratings After the War

Dear YANK:

I hold the temporary rank of master sergeant, although my permanent rank is technical sergeant. I received this promotion after July 1, 1941, the date all advancements in grade went on a temporary basis. Now my question is this: As I have put in almost 30 years of service, will I receive retirement pay based on my temporary master sergeant's rating or will I receive technical sergeant's retirement pay after the war? I've been told that I can only get the technical sergeant's pension. But this doesn't sound right, for I know that in peacetime I would have been promoted to the permanent rank of master sergeant by the time I was due for retirement. I can't see why I should be content with a technical sergeant's pension simply because no permanent warrants can be issued to any soldier in time of war.

Fort Benning, Ga. —M/Sgt. HUGH R. MERRON

■ If you retire now you will get only a technical sergeant's pension, since that is your permanent warrant. All retirement pay is based upon permanent grade only. You do not, of course, have to retire at the end of 30 years' service if you are still physically fit. If you want the master sergeant's pension, you'll have to stay in service after the war is over and earn your permanent warrant. The retired master sergeant receives $138 a month and the retired technical sergeant gets $116.67 a month. It's up to you to decide whether that $21.33 a month is worth waiting for.

Washed-Out Cadet

Dear YANK:

I was an aviation cadet some time ago but washed out due to flying inefficiency. It is Army policy to send some washed-out cadets to schools for bombardier or navigator training, but my score was too low for training in these categories, so I became an enlisted man again. Recently, I applied for reinstatement as a cadet but was informed that my old classification score still disqualified me. But I had been told earlier that I could apply for cadet training again after a year

What's Your Problem?

had elapsed from the date I had washed out. I am anxious to get the latest regulation on this point.

Victory Field, Tex. —Sgt. DAN J. BINDER

■ Aviation cadets who have washed out are not again acceptable for pilot training. Pilot cadets who wash out may, however, enroll for navigator or bombardier training if their classification scores are sufficiently high. If pilot wash-outs fail the bombardier or navigator classification test they may take successive tests every 30 days for as long as the aviation board thinks they might make the grade.

Who's Eligible for Benefits?

Dear YANK:

I am a first three-grader, and I would like to know if I can make out a family allowance for my son, who is under 21 years of age and a private in the Army.

ASTP, University of Alabama —S/Sgt. M. W. SNYDER

■ The legal department of the Office of Dependency Benefits says no go. Former dependents now serving in the Armed Forces are ineligible for benefits.

Dear YANK:

Here is my problem. My wife by a former marriage had three children. Their ages now are 12, 8 and 5. Can I apply for a family allowance for them? We have the birth certificates.

Fort Leonard Wood, Mo. —Sgt. EUGENE E. GLAZA

■ Your stepchildren, if members of your household, are eligible for family allowances. You or your wife should send duly certified copies of the birth certificates, attached to an application for benefits, to the Office of Dependency Benefits, Allowances Branch, 213 Washington Street, Newark, N. J.

Can't Stop Wife's Allowance

Dear YANK:

I am married and have a 2-year-old boy. He is my wife's own child, but mine by adoption. Because the baby's father, my wife's first husband, was dishonorably discharged from the Army for desertion, I arranged to have the child's last name changed to mine. Since I have been away I find

out that she has been going around with other men to such an extent that it can't be called a friendly pastime. One man gave her $100. I can prove that. He also gave her a watch. I can prove that, too. In spite of the fact that my wife is working and making enough to live on, she blows in all of her salary, her family-allowance money and even has cashed and spent all our jointly owned War Stamps and Bonds. Now the pay-off comes in the form of a letter from my mother, who says my wife is threatening to have a civil-court judge write to my CO demanding that I send 20 bucks more a month, in addition to my allowance, "for the care of the little boy." What I want to know is this: Is there any way, short of an M1, that I can stop my wife's allowance? What's equally important, how can I get a divorce? I don't mind if you print this, but don't use my name.

Fort Benning, Ga. —Pfc. E. A.

■ Regrettably, so long as you are married to her, there is nothing you can do to stop your wife's allowance. As the law now stands, even if you obtain a divorce, she can still collect provided she doesn't remarry and is eligible for alimony. Many officials realize that the law in this respect often operates unjustly, but despite their determined efforts to do something about it, no changes are as yet in sight. However, under the terms of the Soldiers' and Sailors' Civil Relief Act, you are entitled to certain specific protections in the courts, and your first move should be to get in touch with your outfit's Special Service officer, who will be able to direct you to the nearest legal-assistance office. (WD Circular 74, March 16, 1943, sets up legal-assistance offices throughout the Army; YANK, Vol. II, No. 15). Meanwhile, if your wife carries through on her threat to go to a local court, you should write to that court setting forth your side of the case. If action is brought and you are unable to retain legal counsel, the court will appoint an attorney to represent you. By law, the attorney so appointed cannot waive any of your rights or bind you by his acts. Finally, even though you are powerless to stop your wife's allowance, you can initiate action that will prevent her from spending your child's legal share of that allowance. In your case, the best thing to do is to write to your mother, asking her to get in touch with the representative in her community of the Veterans Administration or of the Army Emergency Relief, who will investigate the situation and report the facts to the proper authorities.

Ve did it before... UND ve could do it again

Sgt Ralph Stein

When Are We Going Home?

EVERY soldier overseas is looking for an answer to that big important question, "When are we going home?" We all know the war won't be over for a long time. But those of us who have sweated out a year or more in combat zones or the dull noncombat zones like Panama, Iran or Iceland still feel that our outfit is entitled to return to the States for a short time, at least, while somebody else takes over. And we don't see any reason why we should have to wait until the end of the war for such a change in scenery.

There have been all kinds of answers to this question about going home floating around the foreign latrines but all of them have been strictly confidential and highly unofficial answers. In fact, the whole overseas Army is fed up to the ears with unofficial inside dope about new policies and new rules about shipping troops home, none of which, as far as we know, has ever turned out to be correct.

So YANK last week decided to try something different. Instead of concocting an editorial of its own on the problem of when we are going home, it sent a corporal to Washington to ask the War Department for an official reply to the question.

The War Department's answer isn't half as cheerful as the one YANK would have liked to create and it does not jibe with stuff we have been hearing in the chow lines and latrines these last few months. But at least it is straight and official and maybe it will kill a few of the rumors that have been building us up to an awful let-down. Here it is:

"The WD has been studying the problem of rotating personnel outside the continental limits of the United States ever since the beginning of hostilities. However, in every general plan designed to provide a definite time limit for overseas or a definite percentage of personnel to be returned, there is one insurmountable obstacle—insufficient shipping space for the necessary replacements."

In GI language, here's what that means. You can't start to make substitutions in a football game until you first put your full team of 11 men on the field. The War Department says that it needs all its available shipping now to move overseas all the troops that are required there. It can't afford to use ships for the job of making substitutions—sending out replacement units—until it first completes the job of bringing our overseas Army up to its full quota.

When we have all the men we need overseas, the War Department will be able to send out units to take the place of those outfits that have done their share of foreign service. But until then it is just TS and there is nothing we can do about it. Except hope that when replacement shipping becomes available, our outfit will be at the front of the line.

GI Bull Sessions

SOLDIER discussion forums both in the U. S. and overseas have spread so rapidly, says the WD, that the Army now plans to provide special informational pamphlets on subjects in which GIs have shown the most interest. The first series of these pamphlets, which are being prepared by the American Historical Association, will be released early in 1944. GI discussion forums are voluntary and informal and can vary from bull sessions in a rest camp behind the lines to elaborate programs of the kind run twice a week at Camp Lee, Va.

The majority of GI forums, according to the WD release, use the town-hall technique. A soldier with an appropriate background is made moderator, the topic is chosen and men who have a particular knowledge of the subject sit in as "experts." The meeting is opened by stating the arguments, after which the men in the audience give opinions, ask questions and in general pull the subject apart.

Discharged Veterans

A recent report of the OWI states that at least 800,000 veterans of this war have been given discharges by the Army, Navy and Marine Corps.

The Army released 585,000 from Pearl Harbor through Sept. 30, 1943; the Navy 133,155 from Pearl Harbor through Oct. 31, 1943, and the Marines 34,759 during the same period. Of those discharged by the Army, 370,000 were given CDDs; by the Navy and Marines, 46,961. The rest were discharged for various reasons, the majority because they were over age. Of the total number discharged, says the report, 26,000 have applied to the Veterans Administration for continued hospitalization. The majority of discharged GIs, reports the OWI, are getting jobs in war plants.

GI Shop Talk

The 3d Infantry Regiment, one of the first to ship out for foreign service, is back in the States, having been moved from Newfoundland to Camp Butner, N. C. . . . An all-purpose, all-weather gasoline has been developed to meet year-round combat requirements of AGF vehicles. . . . The Northwestern Service Command in Yukon Territory reports the completion of the final link in the first overland telephone line connecting the U. S. and Alaska. . . . GIs in a fighter group in New Guinea built an "airborne" chapel; its materials, excepting timbers and pews, weigh only 900 pounds and can be packed for transportation by air in 53 cubic feet of space. Noncombat Army vehicles manufactured in 1940 or before are being made available for essential civilian use. These do not include jeeps, which were not standardized for Army use until 1941. . . . The Photographic Manufacturers and Dis-

tributors Association claims the first industry-wide plan to absorb returning GIs possessed of technical experience in suitable civilian or war-work jobs. . . . Princeton University sent each of its students in the armed forces a Christmas packet of three pocket-sized books.

Washington O.P.

GI reports of moldy cigarettes, like the one in the cigarette story on page 5 of this issue, burn up Col. Webster of the QM here. He is a bear on the subject of packaging cigarettes; in fact several cigarette manufacturers think his specifications are too strict. In addition to the regular cellophane wrapping on each pack and the regular chipboard carton, he insists that each carton either be double-wrapped in waxed sulphite paper or wrapped once in double-weight paper and then heat-sealed. For each 50-carton shipping case the QM specifies a special water-repellant case liner made of three layers of creped paper and asphalt. The liner is then sealed and the whole business goes into a solid weatherproof fiber shipping case of top quality.

The Army Postal Service, investigating alleged delays in V-mail, examined the dates of letters deposited during one day in a mail box somewhere in England and found some dated three months before mailing. Apparently GIs who had neglected their wives, mothers or girls were predating letters, then blaming slow mail. A good gag; we've used it ourselves. . . . Incidentally, the APS tells us soldier V-mail has increased 200 percent or more in the last 60 days and now equals civilian V-mail in volume.

Somebody in the QMC got to studying about all the good left-hand gloves that are discarded because their right-hand mates wear out faster. Now some types of gloves will be made ambidexterous so you can shift them and make three pairs go as far as four of the old type. . . . The QMC has placed a big order with manufacturers for the new type of battle-dress uniforms. Altogether, the Army will buy 32 million individual garments during the first six months of 1944.

—YANK **Washington Bureau**

YANK EDITORIAL STAFF

Managing Editor, Sgt. Joe McCarthy, FA; Art Director, Sgt. Arthur Weithas, DEML; Assistant Managing Editor, Sgt. Justus Schlotzhauer, Inf.; Assistant Art Director, Sgt. Ralph Stein, Med.; Pictures, Sgt. Leo Hofeller, Armd.; Features, Cpl. Harry Sions, AAF; Sports, Sgt. Dan Polier, AAF; Overseas News, Cpl. Allan Ecker, AAF.
Washington: Sgt. Earl Anderson, AAF; Cpl. Richard Paul, DEML.
London: Sgt. Walter Peters, QMC; Sgt. John Scott, AAF; Sgt. Steven Derry, DEML; Sgt. Durbin Horner, QMC; Sgt. Bill Davidson, Inf.; Pvt. Sanderson Vanderbilt, CA; Sgt. Peter Paris, Engr.; Pvt. Jack Coggins, CA.
North Africa: Sgt. Burtt Evans, Inf.; Sgt. John Frano, Sig. Corps; Pvt. Tom Shehan, FA.
Italy: Sgt. Walter Bernstein, Inf.; Sgt. George Aarons, Sig. Corps; Sgt. Burgess Scott, Inf.
Central Africa: Sgt. Kenneth Abbott, AAF.
Cairo: Cpl. Richard Gaige, DEML; Pvt. Irwin Shaw, Sig. Corps.
Iran-Iran: Sgt. Al Hine, Engr.; Cpl. James O'Neill, QMC.
India: Sgt. Ed Cunningham, Inf.; Sgt. Marion Hargrove, FA.
Australia: Sgt. Don Harrison, AAF; Sgt. Dick Hanley, AAF; Sgt. Douglas Borgstedt, DEML.
New Guinea: Cpl. Ozzie St. George, Inf.
South Pacific: Cpl. Barrett McGurn, Med.; Sgt. George Norford, QMC.
Hawaii: Sgt. Merle Miller, AAF; Pfc. Richard J. Nihill, CA; Cpl. James L. McManus, CA; Sgt. Robert Greenhaigh, Inf.; Sgt. John A. Bushemi, FA.
Alaska: Sgt. Georg N. Meyers, AAF; Pfc. Robert McBrinn, Sig. Corps.
Bermuda: Cpl. Wiliam Pene du Bois.
Ascension Island: Pfc. Nat G. Bodian, ATC.
Panama: Sgt. Robert G. Ryan, Inf.; Pvt. Richard Harity, DEML.
Puerto Rico: Sgt. Lou Stoumen, DEML; Cpl. Bill Haworth, DEML; Pvt. Jud Cook, DEML; Sgt. Robert Zellers, Sig. Corps.
Trinidad: Sgt. Clyde Biggerstaff, DEML.
Nassau: Sgt. Dave P. Folds Jr., MP.
Iceland: Sgt. Gene Graff, Inf.
Newfoundland: Sgt. Frank Bode.
Greenland: Sgt. Edward F. O'Meara, AAF.
Navy: Robert L. Schwartz Y2c; Allen Churchill Y3c.
Officer in Charge: Lt. Col. Franklin S. Forsberg.
Business Manager: Capt. Harold B. Hawley.
Overseas Bureau Officers: London, Maj. Donald W. Reynolds; India, 1st Lt. Gerald J. Rock; Australia, 1st Lt. J. N. Bigbee; Cairo, Capt. Robert Strothers; Hawaii, Capt. Charles W. Balthrope; Alaska, Capt. Jack W. Weeks; Panama, Capt. Henry E. Johnson; Iraq-Iran, Capt. Charles Holt.

YANK is published weekly by the enlisted men of the U. S. Army and is for sale only to those in the armed services. Stories, features, pictures and other material from YANK may be reproduced if they are not restricted by law or military regulations, provided proper credit is given, release dates are observed and specific prior permission has been granted for each item to be reproduced. Entire contents reviewed by U. S. military censors.

Full 24-hour INS and UP leased wire service.
MAIN EDITORIAL OFFICE
205 EAST 42d ST., NEW YORK 17, N. Y., U. S. A.

"Die PW Woche"

Camp Carson, Colo.—*Die PW Woche (The PW Weekly)* is probably the first prisoner-of-war newspaper put out by and for enemy soldiers in this country. It was started Aug. 14, 1943, with just four readers but the circulation has increased to such an extent that 70 percent of the German prisoners here now read it.

Die PW Woche, printed in German, is a 20-page mimeographed, magazine-size publication. It carries a round-up of world news, poetry, fiction, humor, local news, a pin-up picture and items of the sports and amusement fields. Distribution is made by the prisoners themselves and the paper sells for 15 cents, paid for by cantonment tickets received by the PWs for work done.

An officer who was formerly a reporter is the paper's journalistic adviser. The editors meet with camp officials and discuss the contents before publication, eliminating the need for strict censorship.

What Every Joe Should Know

Camp Croft, S. C.—Sgt. Allen E. Klassed and Sgt. Donald L. Reynolds have set about making Army matters clearer for rookies in the 31st Inf. Tng. Bn. They recently published a 20-page mimeographed booklet that covers facts new men should know about the Army and the 31st.

Divided under several headings, the booklet contains a roster of company officers, illustrations of Army rank and insignia, an explanation of military courtesy, training notes, laundry and

AROUND THE CAMPS

Blytheville Army Air Field, Ark.—Sgt. Raymond Wolsfield is the saving sort and out of his GI earnings he has put aside enough to buy an oat-eater named Wizard. Each night Wolsfield hurries to the stables in town where he keeps the horse to minister to it. On stormy nights the sergeant sleeps in the stall with the nag because Wizard is afraid of lightning.

Schick General Hospital, Iowa—Patients here, represented by Cpl. V. Dixon, have high praise for a GI warbler named Jimmie Gill. Pvt. Gill has his own 15-minute program over the Clinton (Iowa) radio station and, says Dixon, "puts more feeling and life into a song than anyone else."

Fort Leonard Wood, Mo.—Cpl. James Woo, cook in the 75th Inf. Div., was walking guard one morning. It was so cold that his sense of smell was not functioning very well. He had an encounter with a skunk as a result. A casualty to the extent of a bitten finger, Cpl. Woo made the mistake of returning to his hutment where he found that there was nothing wrong with his buddies' sense of smell.

Second Army Maneuvers, Tenn.—Sgt. Don Keller asked a small boy on a farm near here if he could ride his cow pony. The boy assented and Keller saddled up. When the boy returned later, he found Keller still in the saddle, but the horse hadn't budged. "I forgot to tell you," the kid said,

as guest soloist with the Chicago Symphony Orchestra, and after that he played in New York Carnegie Hall.

Fort Sam Houston, Tex.—Cpl. Florence Feldman was visiting Corpus Christi with a friend. A handsome marine passed and Wac Feldman remarked: "I know that marine from somewhere. His face is very familiar." The friend said: "It should be. That's Tyrone Power."

Fort Bliss, Tex.—Pfc. Lewis Vilk had a week's furlough but didn't enjoy it. First his train was snowbound; then it got in a collision that caused a further delay. Meanwhile, he lost his ticket and had to buy another. When he got home he

MASTER CRAFTSMAN. S/Sgt. Alfred D. Boyd, MP Det., Army Service Forces, Camp Blanding, Fla., with some of the goods he's carved out of leather sent to him from his ranch in Florida. He only has time to fill a few requests

TWINS AGAIN? Not exactly, at least not in name. Left is Sgt. Hosmer Comfort of San Francisco. The other sergeant is Herb Daugherty of Chicago, both in AAA School, Camp Davis, S. C.

dry-cleaning information, company regulations, an exposition of the art of bunk-making, a clothing list, a map of Camp Croft and one of Spartanburg with the salient points marked and a humorously illustrated line-up of the general orders.

Orders Is Orders

Camp Haan, Calif.—"Climb into the seat," barked M/Sgt. Louis Cherapy, in charge of the headquarters battery's motor pool, to T-4 Fred Kirby, a literal-minded driver. "Now, release the brake," Cherapy went on. Kirby complied.

"Turn 'er over," snapped the sergeant. Kirby stepped on the starter, but nothing happened. The sergeant repeated his order and Kirby again stepped on the starter, but still nothing happened. Cherapy lifted the hood and looked at the motor.

"What's the matter with this danged thing?" he yelled.

At this point, Kirby looked up and quietly asked: "Shall I turn on the ignition now, sergeant?"

Send any pictures, news items or features of interest for these pages to the Continental Liaison Branch, Bureau of Public Relations, War Department, Pentagon, Washington, D. C., and ask that they be forwarded to YANK, The Army Weekly.

"he won't move an inch until you give him a piece of sugar."

Maxwell Field, Ala.—Conjecture filled the air when S/Sgt. Lena Coody, mess sergeant for the WAC Co., married S/Sgt. Anthony Yuhas, mess sergeant of a four-engine school squadron. Who would rule their kitchen after the war? Sgt. Coody put all arguments to rest with: "We're going to hire a cook."

Drew Field, Fla.—T/Sgt. Russ Tittle of the 501st Signal AW Regt. approached a soldier in the dark one night. "Hey, Joe," he said, "have you got the time?" Then the flare of a match revealed an officer. Tittle started to stammer an apology. "That's all right, sergeant," the officer said. "You hit it right—my name is Joe."

Pine Camp, N. Y.—T-5 Bob Lowery of Hq. Co. wanted a new pair of shoes. One of his outfit's lieutenants offered to get him a pair and Lowery advanced the money. The shoes arrived and Lowery was happy about the whole thing until he opened the package—and found the shoes were GI.

Fort Ord, Calif.—Pfc. Andrew Sorentino, member of an ordinance unit here, lost his partial denture plate. A week later it showed up with his laundry and this note: "Partial plate rejected."

Palm Springs Army Air Field, Calif. — Piano-thumpers may be a dime a dozen in the Army, but Pfc. Leonard Pennario is at the top of the heap. He got excellent notices when he appeared

wired for an extension, but received no reply and started back to camp. Five hours later a telegram arrived at his home granting the extension.

Fort Belvoir, Va.—Pvt. Marjorie Davis took pity on a GI wrestling with a typewriter in the Service Club. She typed two letters for him, each to a different girl whom he insisted he adored and would see on his furlough. "I'll probably be too busy to see either of them," he told Wac Davis, then added: "Say, how about a date with you this week end?"

"Come . . . Arise . . . The sun is shining, the lark is on the wing!"

—Cpl. Hugh E. Kennedy, San Bernardino ASC (Calif.) Wing Tips

HERO. T/Sgt. Robert Kessler, 21, was [awa]rded four medals at Army Air Base, [...]he, Calif., for his conduct as an aerial [gun]ner on a B-24 bomber in the Middle East.

SPECIAL HANDLING. With 1st Sgt. James A. Taylor standing ominously behind him at 6 feet 6 inches, Pvt. Marvin T. Fowler, 4 feet 11, gets measured for a proper GI fit at Fort Sill, Okla.

POSTER GIRL. A face like that deserves some kind of title and this is the one she got in a WAC recruiting campaign. She is Cpl. Mary Lou Ferguson, from Pittsburgh, Pa., in the Air WAC Det., Lowry Field, Colo.

ACCIDENTAL FIREWORKS. Though the chances of its ever happening were infinitesimally small, [t]he camera caught a stream of tracers colliding in mid-air during a demonstration at Fort Lewis, Wash.

[O]LD HAND. Sgt. Ralph P. Paquette used [to] work on this boat as a civilian engineer [w]hen it was a general's yacht; now he runs [it for the] QM at Plattsburg Barracks, N. Y.

MATTRESS MASTER. "Familiarity breeds contempt" says Pvt. Baker B. Britton, stacking them up at Boise Barracks, Idaho. Why? Well, he used to run a mattress factory in El Paso, Tex.

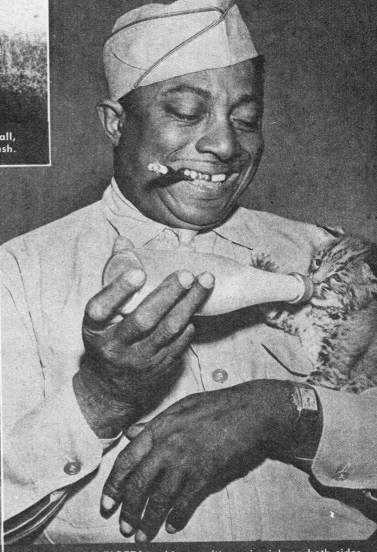

HOLD THAT TIGER! In this case it's a nice job on both sides. Anyway it's a wildcat and a baby. Cpl. Rufus Hawkins found it in a quarry near Moore Field, Tex., and now it's mascot for the 61st Aviation Squadron. Try and hold it when it grows up!

Mail Call

The Face on the Barracks Floor

Dear YANK:
These sketches [above] prove that sometimes a man can do almost the same kind of work in the Army that he did in civilian life. Take me, for instance. When I came into the Army I told the first sergeant I was a painter. He said: "I don't care what you did with a brush; let's see what you can do with a mop." I did—and he was quite surprised with my work.

Camp Fannin, Tex. —Cpl. L. S. GILLAM

B-5th Gr.

Dear YANK:
Stripes painted on the fatigues of ex-noncoms have been bothering my otherwise unoccupied mind. The stripes can't be torn off or washed out. Therefore, I suggest the Army approve a new classification, allowing demoted noncoms to paint a "B" (about the same size as a technicians "T") under their stripes. If this ruling went into effect it would save the Army from having to supply ex-noncoms with new fatigues and would be a fine way to pay respect to their past glory. They could be called sergeant, busted class; corporal, busted class; or whatever their former estate happened to be.

Scott Field, Ill. —Pvt. HALL G. VAN VLACK Jr.

GI Capitalists

Dear YANK:
A few months ago the Office of War Information stated that the pay of the Army private is equivalent to $32.69 a week or $1,696 a year. Upon what is this based? We realize it is a sound accounting practice to consider all expenses involved, but when did it become common practice to include the cost of equipment as part of a man's wages when it is used solely for the purpose of furthering the assignment given him? I suppose the next thing will be a plan for soldiers to pay off the national debt. According to the OWI figures, each soldier will probably owe the Government about $5,000 when he's discharged; so let him sign a promissory note maturing in 10 years and payable in yearly installments. This is not a letter of complaint. It is only to put John Q. Public straight on the rosy life of the "billboard" soldier. We are proud to be members of the Army of the United States. We know we are the best paid, have the finest equipment, clothing, and shelter.

Southwest Pacific —Sgt. PAUL E. ZIMMERMAN

Gen. Patton

Dear YANK:
It was Thanksgiving and all was well until I heard our Gen. Patton was on the carpet in front of Congress. Why the hell don't they mind their own business and leave Patton and Eisenhower alone? The Patton incident reminds me of the story of the men who were gathered at the railing of a ship that they thought would be blown up any minute. They were frantic and all on edge. Then one man started laughing and then everyone did. The ship made shore safely. Now Patton was probably like that man who started to laugh. When a man is frightened there are several ways to bring him around and that could have been Patton's idea. I'm a soldier of nine years' service. Don't put my name on the letter if you print it. I'm in the guardhouse now.

Jackson Barracks, La. —Pvt. A

Veterans' Organizations

Dear YANK:
I noted with much interest the letter from Sgt. David Silver regarding the American Legion in a November issue of YANK. I have been a member of this organization for many years and am at present serving my country in a second war, so it is like a kick in the pants to me to have anyone say I belong to an organization "that leads in the field of attacking civil rights." As for his statements concerning the courtesies extended by the American Legion to Mussolini, it must be remembered that Italy was an ally of the U.S. in the first World War, as was Japan, and up to 1933 there had been no real break between the U.S. and Fascist Italy. I would certainly like to get official proof of his statement that Alvin Owsley, national commander, once described the American Legion as a counterpart of the Fascists in Italy.

NAS, San Diego, Calif. —JOHN H. CONLIN Ptr2c

Dear YANK:
I don't think the veterans of this war will want to be associated with an organization like the American Legion. It's a matter of record that the Legion has been used as a tool for big business and many times operated as a strike-breaking agency. The American Civil Liberties Union has compiled volumes on this.

Camp Lee, Va. —S/Sgt. JOSEPH DAVOLI

Terry Moore's Furlough

Dear YANK:
Listening to the broadcast of the recent World's Series at a jungle outpost we were greatly surprised to hear the announcement that Pvt. Terry Moore, a former professional ball player, who we knew was stationed in the department, was in the stands watching the game. Our curiosity was short-lived as in a November issue of YANK we read: "Pvt. Terry Moore, who is stationed in Panama, saved up all of his furlough time to be with his Cardinal teammates during the series." There are many men in this department who have been at this station for more than three years but who have never received a three-day pass, much less a furlough. Can it be because his name is Terry Moore and ours is just Joe Soldier? The thing that really bothers us is that when they ask us, we have to tell our folks back home that it's impossible to get a furlough. We'd appreciate an explanation.

Panama —Cpl. JULIAN COHN*

*Letter also signed by Pvts. Willie L. Ross, Walter A. Yeargin, Erwin Ensley, M. L. Cannaimo; Pfcs. John Ireland, William L. Russell, John Jackamarch, Gilbert H. Meyer, John J. Scappa, Gerald M. Amidon, John J. Reitz, Clyde S. Kann; Cpls. Elmer J. Sellers, Joseph Salvatore, Gala Gioff, William Hardin, Louis E. Ekhaml, Edward O'Brien, Rolland Biggin, Frank Don Diego, Adrian Pluffpaff, Will T. Harper, John Quaid, Gilbert A. Winders, Reynolds Lyons, David O'Conna; Sgts. Henry J. Borows, Harvey E. Walden, Charles L. Hehnfeld, Norbert Jung, James F. Henegan, Alexander S. Klinghoffer.

■ YANK tried to find out about Terry Moore's furlough but couldn't get a satisfactory answer.

Terry Moore's Ribbons

Dear YANK:
Idle curiosity prompts me to question the three service ribbons sported by Terry Moore in the picture of him at the World Series in an October issue of YANK. I can't understand how the former Card could have possibly earned the tokens, considering that he recently entered the Army in the Caribbean Area where I was stationed, too.

Sedalia AAF, Warrensburg, Mo. —Sgt. HERBERT PIILO

■ Terry Moore is shown wearing two American Theater ribbons and a Veterans of Foreign Wars ribbon. He had two ribbons too many; he should have worn only one American Theater ribbon.

Post-War Policing

Dear YANK:
The following letter to the editor was published by the Sicilian edition of the *Stars & Stripes*. Its unanimous acclaim in this area causes me to submit it to YANK for wider circulation.

Dear Editor:
I suggest that immediately after the day of general armistice all Army personnel who have been overseas during actual wartime, whether or not in combat, be speedily replaced by personnel with only continental service during the war. Post-war occupation duties will not require the experience of seasoned combat troops and transportation will not be the major problem as it is today. Such an arrangement will necessitate additional legislation but I feel that congressmen would do well to take a lead from the many servicemen sharing my opinion on this vital subject.

Sicily —Pvt. EMIL BISCHITZKY

YANK FICTION

1st Sgt. Santa Claus

By Sgt. RAY DUNCAN

OUR first sergeant has the largest stomach in our outfit. That is as it should be, of course. Also it's the reason he was chosen by the captain to play Santa Claus at our unit Christmas party.

Several men in our squadron, for one reason or another, do not like our first sergeant. They allowed their resentment to reach its peak at our Christmas party.

That was very foolish, because in the first place a Christmas party is no place to pay off old grudges. And anyway it is silly to hate the first sergeant for the things he has to do. As he himself told us so often:

"I am only a instrument. I do not do things because I like to be mean. I am a instrument of the captain's wishes and of the Army regulations. As long as I am running this outfit the captain's wishes and the Army regulations is going to be strictly adhered to, or I am going to know the hell why. That's the kind of a potato I am!"

Some of the men disliked that kind of a potato in spite of his explanation, and they looked forward with much interest to the Christmas party. Especially when the grapevine reported that the first sergeant was going to play Santa Claus by order of the captain.

"After all," said T/Sgt. Will Andrews, "he won't be wearing his stripes on his Santa Claus uniform. As far as I can see, anything will go!"

Anything did. We all gathered in the day room about 3:30 on Christmas Eve. There were cigars and cigarettes for everyone, and candy and oranges and apples. There also was beer and, as it later turned out, Coca-Cola.

We were milling around and shooting the breeze when the captain arrived. He climbed up on a table and made a speech, the same one he makes each time our outfit gets together.

"I don't see all you boys together very often. You all have your separate jobs to do all over the camp. However, I think it is a good thing for unit morale when we get together once in a while, and unit morale is a very important thing. Now you men go ahead and enjoy yourselves. I'm afraid I'll have to leave because of other duties."

He climbed down off the table and left. He always did that. He would decide the outfit should have a party, and when we had it he would rush in, dance two dances with his wife, smile twice to give his blessing to the proceedings, and leave.

Nothing else happened for a while, so we all kept on drinking beer and milling around. We were having a very good time. The first sergeant came in with a big bundle and went directly to the day-room latrine.

He came out again in a Santa Claus uniform, the white beard and the black boots and the red coat with a strip of cotton around the edges. Over by the Christmas tree there was a big cardboard box full of presents. He dragged this out in front of the tree.

This also was the captain's idea. Each of us had to bring a present, cost not to exceed two bits, wrapped as a gift but with no name on it. The gifts were all put in the big box to be passed out later.

"All right, gentlemen," called the first sergeant, or Santa Claus.

He had to shout above the din. It was the same familiar reveille-formation voice, although he followed it with a jolly Santa Claus laugh which he apparently had taken some pains to practice for the occasion.

Very few people paid any attention. The noise grew louder.

"C'mon, c'mon men, settle down!" bellowed Santa Claus. "We gotta give out these presents!"

He picked up an empty beer bottle and beat on the floor, but no one seemed to notice. Santa Claus turned very red in the face.

"Listen, wise guys, I know it's Christmas Eve and this is a party, but the least you can do is show a little common courtesy. Now break it up and gather around here in a big circle!"

The noise had subsided while he was talking, but it broke out again immediately. Santa Claus stood there watching for a while, his hands on his hips. Then he took a deep breath and roared:

"Listen, you gahdam meatheads, shut up and get the hell over here!" It sounded very strange to hear Santa Claus swearing.

Bob Wills, a staff sergeant and I believe a ringleader in this thing, had worked his way up to the front of the crowd.

"Look fellows!" he yelled. "Presents!" Everyone became suddenly silent and crowded close as Bob began tossing out presents.

"Get yer hands off them presents, goddammit!" yelled the first sergeant, as he gave Wills a push.

"Who you shoving, graybeard?" said Wills, and he pushed Santa Claus down into a corner. There was a little rough stuff after that. Some of the men began throwing oranges and candy and squirting Coca-Cola at the sergeant. There were some men in the unit who were obligated to the first sergeant to the point of being personal stooges, and they had to try to rescue him. They all got pretty well mussed up.

"Hey, pssst! Aren't you the first sergeant?" hissed T/Sgt. Will Andrews to the badly mauled Santa Claus.

"You know goddam well I am!"

"The trouble is," advised Wills, "you ain't got your stripes on. If you had stripes on these guys would never get away with this!"

The first sergeant was so excited by then that he let Andrews take him over to the barracks and paint six stripes and a diamond on his sleeves with some white poster paint.

WHEN Wills and Santa Claus got back to the day room practically everyone was gone. Only the first sergeant's friends were still there.

Also it turned out that his clothes were gone from the latrine. Since his friends were mostly slender, narrow-chested men, orderly-room clerks, their clothes wouldn't fit him. He had to go home in the Santa Claus outfit with the striped sleeves. Wills rode as far as town with him on the bus, and he said everyone stared at the first sergeant who, to make matters worse, was frowning and muttering to himself.

Some of the boys sneaked back and put the first sergeant's clothes in the bottom drawer of his desk, neatly folded, and they cleaned up the day room. But the day after Christmas we had a special 9 A.M formation.

"Every pass in this outfit is being pulled for a week," announced the first sergeant, "due to misconduct at the unit Christmas party. This was not my idea, it was the captain's wishes. A few troublemakers make it tough for everyone. And if it ever happens again I am going to pull the passes for a month! That's the kind of a potato I am!"

In spite of this unpleasant aftermath nearly everyone said it was just about the best party we ever had in our outfit.

—Pfc. F. Q. Hewitt

"TRANSMISSION HELL! IT'S BARNACLES!"
—Sgt. Irwin Caplan

"WE HAD GIVEN YOU UP FOR LOST."
—Leo Salkin PhoM3c

"SAY WHAT YOU WILL, GIVE ME A GOOD OLD-FASHIONED WALTZ ANY TIME."
—Sgt. Douglas Borgstedt

WHATSA WOID FER—?

ACROSS

1. Hue
6. Flying mammal
9. Pawnbroker's hangout
14. Unaccompanied
15. Get older
16. A bolt for Rosie
17. Musical note
18. Orient
20. Approach
22. First person
23. First woman
25. Rodent
26. You're "it"
27. In U. S. a tramp; in England what he sits on
28. Harvest
30. Right Line (abbr.)
31. Forerunner of oomph
32. Sailors
33. Twilled fabric
35. At no time
37. Captures again
39. More splendid
42. Either
43. Prefix—good
44. City in Sicily
50. Baseball champs' flag
55. Air-raid warning
56. Gaseous element
57. In this place
59. Indefinite article
60. Sun god (Egypt)
61. Trial
64. Perform
65. Consumed
66. Inquire
68. Conflict
69. Lord Lieutenant (abbr.)
70. Top-notch aviators
71. Chirp
73. Exist
74. South American animal
76. Definite article
78. On back of a quarter
80. Overtrained
81. Still
82. Practices

DOWN

1. To supply
2. Italian fruit
3. Behold
4. Unit
5. Part of army stationed behind the rest
6. Engagements
7. Adjutant General (abbr.)
8. Encamping
9. Blow off
10. Atmosphere
11. Fifty-five
12. Madagascar mammal
13. Stalks
19. Three-striper
21. Chow hound
24. Compass point
27. Poet
29. Vegetable
32. Number
34. End of work
36. The Cavalier State (abbr.)
37. Fabulous bird
38. Epoch
40. Even (poetical)
41. Groove
45. English fruit pie
46. Beverage
47. Continent (abbr.)
48. Angry
49. Pardon
50. Military protective wall
51. Rub out
52. Unsatisfactory (slang)
53. Negative adverb
54. Again
57. Best parts of 30-mile hike
58. Brilliancy of effort
62. Fur
63. Woody plants
65. Land measure
67. Retain
70. Be sick
72. Buddy
75. Parent
77. Pronoun
79. The Army way

CUBE CUES

IF you think counting cubes in the AGCT test was hard, try this one. It calls for only one cube—to begin with.

Imagine a cube which is three inches long on each side. Then the camouflage boys get busy and paint it green on all sides. Next a carpenter comes along and cuts the cube up into smaller cubes, each of them an inch long on its sides. Then he piles them all up again to form the original cube.

Now imagine that each one-inch cube is given a quarter turn to the left. Can you visualize how many square inches of *unpainted* surface will be exposed?

(Puzzle solutions on page 22.)

THIS is the kind of girl that makes a soldier appreciate a bathing suit, and even makes a bathing suit thankful there is such a girl. (You'd be surprised what some bathing suits have to put up with.) Petite Diana Lewis comes from a show-biz family, made her theatrical debut at the ripe old age of 2 and at present is appearing in MGM's movie, "Cry Havoc."

POST XCHANGE

This Post Exchange, like YANK itself, is wide open to you. Send your cartoons, poems and stories to: The Post Exchange, YANK, The Army Weekly, 205 East 42d Street, New York 17, N. Y.

If your contribution misses the mark, you will receive YANK's special de luxe rejection slip, that will inspire a more creative mood.

NERVES

The longest war of nerves, I guess,
Is sweating out shipment to OCS.

Sheppard Field, Tex. —Pfc. MARV LORE

Dial 90!

PVT. Manual Ortiz liked the Army very much except for two things: 1) he couldn't understand English well and often got his orders mixed, and 2) he dreaded the obstacle course.

Pvt. Ortiz wanted to be a good soldier, but often when the sergeant bawled out commands in a fast nasal voice, it took him a few seconds to figure out what had been said. By that time the rest of the squad had executed a left flank and Manual would be standing by himself, puzzled and embarrassed at the other soldiers' laughter.

The first day the sergeant asked: "Hey, your ears bad?"

"No, sergeant, but if you would please talk a little slower. Where I come from in southern California we are all Americans, but we do not speak the language much. So if you would so kindly——"

"Dial 90!" the noncom snapped and walked away.

Manual turned to another soldier. "What does that mean?"

The soldier laughed. "That's the chaplain's number. Anytime a guy has a beef, you tell him to dial 90—tell his troubles to the chaplain."

"Where does one find the phone?" Manual asked.

"You kidding? Don't be a dope. It's a gag. Nobody ever calls."

"But there is a padre—a chaplain?"

"Yeah, but I'm telling you it's a gag. Like saying: 'If you don't like it, don't enlist again.' "

Another time the CO read a lengthy notice that all shoes must be handed in for repair on certain days. It was too fast for Manual, and he waited patiently till the officer finished, then asked: "Sir, there is something I would like to know. On what days do we hand in shoes? I have a hole in mine. For some time now."

The officer's face became a dull red as he roared: "Report to the kitchen. That'll stop you from sleeping on your feet!"

"But sir, I——"

"To the kitchen, private!"

As Manual walked away, puzzled, a couple of soldiers grinned and whispered: "Dial 90, buddy."

Each morning the company went over the obstacle course—a daily horror to Manual. When he was a kid he had broken his leg and the memory of it frightened him every time he jumped or scaled a wall. He would lag at the hurdles till a corporal would shout: "Ortiz, either shake a leg or go on sick call!"

"How can I explain it to the doctor?" Manual would ask sadly.

"Aw, dial 90! Jump!"

One morning the sergeant announced that all men who could type should report to the office. "It's a good deal for whoever gets the job—straight office work, no company details, maybe a rating later."

"I can type," Ortiz said.

The sergeant laughed. "You can't even speak English."

"I speak it slowly, but I read and write it very well. In high school I was a good typist—very fast."

The sergeant said "Nuts."

"But it is the truth," Ortiz said. "I type with much speed. It is work I am suited for."

The next morning as the men climbed out of bed for roll call, Pvt. Ortiz remained under the warm covers, a smile on his tan face.

The sergeant came over. "Okay, sleeping beauty. You getting up or do I have to dump your bed?"

Carefully Ortiz took two papers from under his pillow and handed them to the sergeant. "This first one will inform you that I am now the company typist and excused from all company formations and details—roll call for example. The second paper is signed by the doctor and will assure you that I do not have to go over the obstacle course."

The sergeant's long face was full of surprise as he read the letters. "Well I'll be a ——. You really got the job?"

Ortiz nodded. "Yes, I type *mucho*—very fast. The man was most kind and understanding, listened to my troubles and gave me good advice. He also called the office and urged the captain to give me a typing test. He is a very good man."

"Who is?"

"The chaplain," Ortiz said. "I did what you tell me. I dialed 90!"

AAB, Salt Lake City, Utah —Pfc. LEN ZINBERG

PVT. BEN ADAMS

Pvt. Ben Adams (may his rank increase!)
Awoke one night from a deep dream of peace,
And saw within the moonlight in his tent—
Sullen and silent, as on mischief bent—
A sergeant writing in a little book.
Exceeding fear was in Ben Adams' look,
When to the noncom in the tent he said,
"What's that you're writing?" The sarge raised his head
And, with a look made all of sweet accord,
Answered, "The names of those who go on guard."
"And is mine one?" gasped Adams. "Nay, not so,"
Replied the sergeant. Adams spoke more low,
But cheerily now, and said, "I beg you, then,
Go on away and let me sleep again."

The sergeant wrote and vanished. The next night
He came again, with a great wakening light,
And showed the names of those with KP blessed;
And lo! Ben Adams' name led all the rest.

Camp Shelby, Miss. —S/Sgt. A. L. CROUCH

JOTLING

Here's a beer to and a cheer to
The guy who doesn't state
When GI Willy does something silly:
"He's buckin' for Section Eight!"

Camp Davis, N. C. —T-4 T. J. LUNEBURG

"There must be another outfit around here, Hoffman. He doesn't look like one of our own men."
—Sgt. Dick Ericson, Camp Hale, Colo.

A WALK WITH YOU

The lonely stars that stay awake
And keep a vigil all night through
Invite a stroll along the lake
Beside the woodland tipped with dew;
And yet, I do not care to take
A walk with you.

This solitary room can make
A cozy, quiet place for two;
And why, my dear, should I forsake
My haven for a sky of blue?
Ah no, I do not wish to take
A walk with you.

Fort Benning, Ga. —Sgt. LEONARD SUMMERS

GIs YOUNG AND OLD

Oh, the soldier who is younger
Always seems to have a hunger
For places that he never should have been in.
He should really have his whirl in
A place where feet are twirlin'
And not seek low-down dives to drink his gin in.

But the soldier who is older
Seems to be a little bolder
When romance is what he's bent on winnin'.
He eschews the name-band dance halls
And selects the juke-box beer stalls
As the hunting ground to find his sin in.

Now, nobody should quarrel
If this ditty has a moral:
A soldier takes his fun where he can find it.
If he's old and 18 "makes" him,
Or he's young and 40 "takes" him—
It's OK by me as long as he don't mind it.

Somewhere in New England —Sgt. IRVING CARESS

PUZZLE SOLUTIONS

CUBE CUES. 24.

CROSSWORD PUZZLE ▶

SPORTS: MISTER LONG PANTS STARTS NEW CAREER

By Sgt. DAN POLIER

MISTER Long Pants slipped out of baseball just as quietly as he talked or pitched. Except for a matter-of-fact newspaper announcement that Carl Owen Hubbell, after 16 years of loyal service, would become general manager of the New York Giants' farm system, there wasn't much of a fuss made over him.

Nobody suggested that he be honored with a Hubbell Day or a testimonial banquet. He wasn't even presented with a wrist watch or the inevitable leather traveling bag.

In many ways this departure was very much like Hubbell himself. He is the meekest man in sports. He even comes from a town named Meeker, Okla.

Last summer the Giants were playing Brooklyn at Ebbetts Field and before game time Old Hub took his turn shagging flies. Then he walked back to the dugout and watched as the sad Giants got trounced, 7-4. As casually as that, on June 22, Old Hub had celebrated his 40th birthday.

Manager Mel Ott, who used to be Hubbell's roommate, probably knows Mister Long Pants better than anyone else on the Giants. "Carl's shy and he lacks color," Ottie once said. "But he has more important qualities. Like courage, skill, brains, modesty, loyalty and humility. There's character in every game he pitches."

Probably no other pitcher in baseball has been able to put so much of his personality into a ball game as King Carl. His performances reflected his earnestness, his honesty and even his shyness. Hubbell never squabbled with an umpire over a decision or blamed a defeat on his teammates' errors.

"I'm just paid to pitch," he used to say. "I leave the grousing and fighting to those who can handle it. It's not my line."

This attitude was never better displayed than in one of his classic pitching duels with Dizzy Dean in St. Louis eight years ago. Dean was being outpitched and he didn't like it. Finally he became so provoked that he lost his temper and started shelling the Giants with bean balls. Naturally, the Giants didn't take it lying down. They got hotter than a 10-cent pistol and a wild fist fight followed.

Then an unprecedented thing happened. Instead of rallying behind their favorite, Dean, and their own team, the St. Louis fans supported the Giants. It was Hubbell who had won them over. They had watched Mister Long Pants beat Dean with a clean and honest performance and they couldn't help but be impressed. When the fight was over, the St. Louis fans actually booed Dean and cheered Old Hub.

Hubbell, of course, is more famous for his screwball than anything else. And yet it was this trick pitch that caused the Detroit Tigers to send him back to the minors twice. In 1926, when Detroit brought Hubbell up for a second try-out, Manager Ty Cobb said he would never make the grade as long as he used his freak delivery. Cobb warned Hubbell that he would ruin his arm if he continued to throw "that dipsy-do."

Two years later John McGraw bought Hub for an estimated $40,000. It was the best investment the Giants ever made, for Hubbell, in his 16 years with the club, won 253 games and lost 154. He became one of the game's great southpaws, master of the screwball—the pitch that was supposed to ruin his arm—and hurled the Giants to three pennants nd one world championship.

The best description of Hub's screwball was summed up in a remark by Lou Gehrig after the All-Star game in 1934. That was the afternoon when King Carl struck out five of the greatest sluggers in the American League in a row—Ruth, Gehrig, Foxx, Simmons and Cronin.

"I'm still trying to figure out what happened," Gehrig said in the clubhouse. "I took three swings and every time I was positive I was going to hit a home run. The ball was right there, on the bat, and then it wasn't. It disappeared somewhere. No other pitcher throws anything exactly like it."

But Hubbell's success wasn't fashioned around this one pitch. He had a curve and fast ball to go with his freakish drop. The screwball was simply the pitch that identified him. Incidentally, it didn't get its name from the guy who made it famous. He's anything else but.

Carl Hubbell is congratulated by the Giant's brain trust as he steps into the shoes vacated by Bill Terry as head of team's farm system. L. to r.: President Stoneham, Hubbell, Manager Ott, Secretary Brannick.

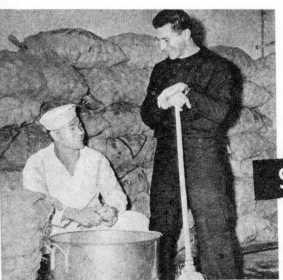

KP KIDS. We don't have to tell you what these two sailors are doing. But we can tell you they're a couple of All-Americans, namely: Bill Daley (left) and Merv Preguiman, both formerly of Michigan. They're in Portsmouth, Va., now, taking boot training.

SPORTS SERVICE RECORD

THIS year's crop of Army football champions: Randolph Field's Cotton Bowlers, with All-American **Glenn Dobbs** pitching, in the Southwest; Camp Davis, N. C., powered by ex-Bear **Norm Standlee**, in the Southeast; March Field, Calif., with at least a dozen "all" guys, in the West; Kearns (Utah) Air Base, with a defensive record of only two touchdowns scored against them, in the Rocky Mountain area; Fort Riley, Kans., in the Mid-West. . . . Incidentally, Fort Riley has the 1940 Olympic walking champion, **Pvt. Bill Mihalo**, as its trainer. . . . **Sgt. Joe DiMaggio** and **S/Sgt. Fred Perry**, the former tennis pro, are working together as physical-training instructors at the Santa Ana (Calif.) Army Air Base. . . . Add the name of **Lt. Derace Moser**, one of the all-time backfield greats at Texas A & M, to the list of All-Americans who have lost their lives in this war. Moser was killed in a Fortress crash near Tampa, Fla. . . . **Lt. Col. Wallace Wade** is still having trouble with his broken leg. He had to be moved from Camp Butner, N. C., where he commands an FA battery, to Oliver General Hospital in Augusta, Ga., for treatment. . . . What's this we hear about GIs in Algiers paying $10 top for ringside seats at soldier boxing shows? *Inducted:* **Luke Appling,** veteran shortstop of the Chicago White Sox and American League batting champion (.328), into the Army; **Bill Veeck,** owner of the Milwaukee Brewers and one of the most colorful figures in sport, into the Marines; **Berkley Bell,** the tennis tourist, into the Army; **Lou Klein,** second baseman of the St. Louis Cardinals, into the Coast Guard; **Elbie Fletcher,** Pirates' first baseman, into the Navy. . . . *Reclassified 1-A:* **Beau Jack,** lightweight champion; **Charlie Keller,** slugging Yankee outfielder; **Bob Carpenter,** newly elected president of the Philadelphia Phillies. . . . *Promoted:* **Birdie Tebbets,** Detroit catcher, to rank of first lieutenant at Waco (Tex.) Army Air Field; **Harry Danning,** the Giants' catcher, to grade of sergeant at Long Beach, Calif. . . . *Commissioned:* **Paul Mitchell,** acting captain of the Minnesota football team and one of the finest tackles in the Big Ten, as an ensign in Navy Ordnance. . . . *Launched:* The **Charles Paddock,** Liberty ship named for the former Olympic sprint champion, who lost his life in a Navy plane crash near Sitka, Alaska. . . . *Decorated:* **Lt. Bob Saggau,** former Notre Dame football star, with the Air Medal for heroism on a dive-bombing mission against enemy shipping in the South Pacific.

YANK
THE ARMY WEEKLY
1944

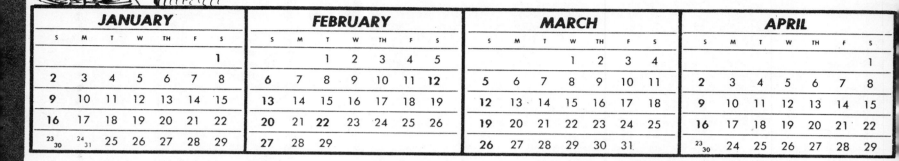

JANUARY
S	M	T	W	TH	F	S
						1
2	3	4	5	6	7	8
9	10	11	12	13	14	15
16	17	18	19	20	21	22
23 30	24 31	25	26	27	28	29

FEBRUARY
S	M	T	W	TH	F	S
		1	2	3	4	5
6	7	8	9	10	11	12
13	14	15	16	17	18	19
20	21	22	23	24	25	26
27	28	29				

MARCH
S	M	T	W	TH	F	S
			1	2	3	4
5	6	7	8	9	10	11
12	13	14	15	16	17	18
19	20	21	22	23	24	25
26	27	28	29	30	31	

APRIL
S	M	T	W	TH	F	S
						1
2	3	4	5	6	7	8
9	10	11	12	13	14	15
16	17	18	19	20	21	22
23 30	24	25	26	27	28	29

MAY
S	M	T	W	TH	F	S
	1	2	3	4	5	6
7	8	9	10	11	12	13
14	15	16	17	18	19	20
21	22	23	24	25	26	27
28	29	30	31			

JUNE
S	M	T	W	TH	F	S
				1	2	3
4	5	6	7	8	9	10
11	12	13	14	15	16	17
18	19	20	21	22	23	24
25	26	27	28	29	30	

JULY
S	M	T	W	TH	F	S
						1
2	3	4	5	6	7	8
9	10	11	12	13	14	15
16	17	18	19	20	21	22
23 30	24 31	25	26	27	28	29

AUGUST
S	M	T	W	TH	F	S
		1	2	3	4	5
6	7	8	9	10	11	12
13	14	15	16	17	18	19
20	21	22	23	24	25	26
27	28	29	30	31		

SEPTEMBER
S	M	T	W	TH	F	S
					1	2
3	4	5	6	7	8	9
10	11	12	13	14	15	16
17	18	19	20	21	22	23
24	25	26	27	28	29	30

OCTOBER
S	M	T	W	TH	F	S
1	2	3	4	5	6	7
8	9	10	11	12	13	14
15	16	17	18	19	20	21
22	23	24	25	26	27	28
29	30	31				

NOVEMBER
S	M	T	W	TH	F	S
			1	2	3	4
5	6	7	8	9	10	11
12	13	14	15	16	17	18
19	20	21	22	23	24	25
26	27	28	29	30		

DECEMBER
S	M	T	W	TH	F	S
					1	2
3	4	5	6	7	8	9
10	11	12	13	14	15	16
17	18	19	20	21	22	23
24 31	25	26	27	28	29	30

YANK
THE ARMY WEEKLY

5¢ **JAN. 28**
VOL. 2, NO. 32
1944

By the men .. for the
men in the service

**GI CLIMBER
IN ITALY**

Why Are We Fighting This World War?

PAGE 8

AS THIS SIXTH ARMY LANDING PARTY MOVED IN, CARRIED BY A FLEET OF LANDING CRAFT, JAP BOMBS KICKED UP GEYSERS OF SPRAY AND BLACK SMOKE AROUND THEM

LANDING FORCE COMMANDER: BRIG. GEN. JULIAN CUNNINGHAM.

ONE OF THE FEW RUBBER BOATS LEFT AFLOAT AFTER FIRST DIVERSIONARY ASSAULT ON ARAWE

A BEACHHEAD ESTABLISHED, THREE YANKS INCH FORWARD AGAINST JAPS.

Sixth Army units seized a foothold on Arawe Peninsula, New Britain, in face of limited opposition. Ten days later Marines landed at Cape Gloucester. Objective of both drives was Rabaul, major Jap base some 260 miles away. Captured airstrips will serve as advance bases for bombers now softening up Rabaul itself.

ATTACK ON ARAWE

By Cpl. RALPH BOYCE
YANK Staff Correspondent

ARAWE, NEW BRITAIN [By Cable]—"Wonder what old Sam Houston would think," said one drawling Texan, "if he could see the flag waving here half way round the world the Alamo?"

American troops of the Sixth Army that seized held this sizable bridgehead on Jap-occupied Britain in the Southwest Pacific were maintional Guard Cavalry from Texas, and they ght with them into battle the flag of the Star State.

o hours before the main landing forces hit beaches, small units of commando-trained s in rubber landing boats made a diversiontab at Umlingolu on the eastern side of the ve peninsula. At 0530 in the bright pre-dawn light, they neared the shore in echelon forn of three boats to a wave.

irty-five yards from shore, as the rubber slid over a reef to the last narrow strip of water, the Japs opened up. Five machine guns, a 37-mm cannon and heavier caliber antiaircraft guns, lowered to fire point-blank, raked the boats in a crossfire.

The Japs were consolidated on a vantage point atop a coral cliff, to which they had hastily withdrawn from Arawe peninsula after the heavy air-naval bombardment the day and night before. Firing down on the assault force, they had the whip hand now.

Men stood up in the rubber boats to rake the shore with tommy-gun fire, and they were cut down. They fought from the boats, and they fought from the water until more than half of them were casualties. Then the Jap guns peppered the survivors as they floundered in the surf, clinging to jagged reefs or to the few boats still afloat or ducking under the boats and holding their breath. Not for three hours could rescue craft get to them, but their position was eased when a U. S. destroyer came out of the haze and with two salvos blew the Jap guns to bits.

As S/Sgt. Bill Hughes of Grand Prairie, Tex.,

said after seeing his platoon leader killed at his side: "Anyone who got out of that—God was on his side."

But the diversion, though costly, was successful. At 0730, two hours after the first troops had set off for "Blue Beach" (Umlingolu), the American Sunday punch struck at the beaches of Cape Merkus and the nearby islands of Arawe and Pilelo. The enemy, elated over his success against the rubber boats, was caught off balance when the main force of the Sixth Army landing party moved in, carried by an armada of the newest type of armored amphibious landing craft.

Unopposed and evidently unnoticed by the Japs, the destroyers and landing craft moved out of the overcast and then their guns opened up. The B-25s of the Fifth Air Force dropped out of the clouds and skimmed over Amalut plantation and Didmap village, strafing as they went.

The main assault was made at House Fireman's beach, west of Cape Merkus, by troops in "alligators" and "buffaloes," queer-looking amphibians propelled in the water by scoops on the trac-

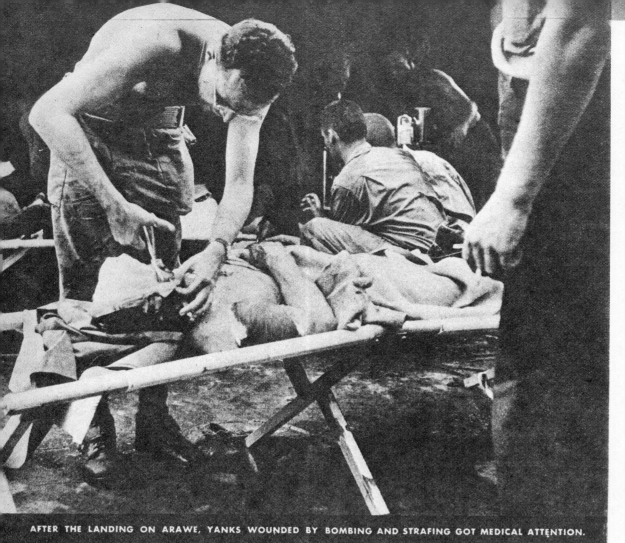

AFTER THE LANDING ON ARAWE, YANKS WOUNDED BY BOMBING AND STRAFING GOT MEDICAL ATTENTION.

tor treads and combining the features of tanks and personnel carriers. Four waves landed 10 minutes apart, meeting no opposition as the carriers rolled up the rough beach and crashed through the coconut grove.

The Yanks had been on the beach little more than half an hour when a formation of Val dive-bombers appeared and attacked the exposed men on the beach and in the plantation. Craters made by American bombers in the softening-up operations preceding the landings, when 856 tons of bombs were dropped, came in handy for GIs seeking cover now from the Jap attack.

Small-arms fire was concentrated on the oncoming enemy planes, and U. S. fighter cover quickly appeared to tangle with the dive-bombers. Two Vals were shot down by light ack-ack from the ground.

Pvt. Lorenzo Duarte, American Indian from Barstow, Calif., manning a .50-caliber atop a buffalo, put his first burst right into the belly of one of the Vals as it swooped low. Duarte jumped to the ground and whooped: "I got the bastard."

A group of five gunners shared honors on the second Jap plane, which they filled fore and aft with ack-ack until it was like a sieve.

The men fanned out quickly toward their objectives. Seven miles east of Arawe is the Arawe Lupin airstrip, built by Australian planters as a pre-war emergency landing ground. Beyond the strip is the Pulie River, lined by several sites suitable for airstrips.

For the week following the landings, the boys of the Sixth Army toiled throughout the day building defenses that would stand up against enemy counterattack, and throughout the night burrowed like prairie dogs while the weight of the Jap air force was thrown against them.

When the week was ended, they could rub tired eyes and flop down beside foxholes, confident that the job was well done. They now held a bit of New Britain that would cost the Japs a small army to retake.

THE success of the week's work was made possible by guts and support—mostly by the guts of the hard-bitten assault troops. They were supported by a close teamwork between fighter cover and ack-ack, which drove off Jap attempts to crush the landing forces from the air.

P-38 Lightnings and P-47 Thunderbolts roared from their base across the Vitiaz Strait to smash almost every daylight bombing attempt before the Japs were over their target area. Amphibian

engineers helped maintain supply lines to the area, while gun crews with land-based ack-ack threw up a protective screen of fire against the few Jap planes that broke through the air cover.

In shell- and bomb-blasted coconut plantations, along coral-reefed beaches and jungled cliffs in the front lines on New Britain itself and on the adjoining island outposts, the American defenses grew as the week progressed.

Sweaty and tiring men strung thousands of feet of barbed wire, dug gun positions, filled sandbags. Several times a day work halted temporarily as alerts sounded and men turned their guns skyward or dropped into the nearest bomb crater.

WHEN those guns did bark at the bombing and strafing Jap planes, there was seldom a full force of raiders. Even those few Jap planes that sneaked through were not safe from fighters of the Fifth Air Force, which often dove into their own ground fire to get a crack at the invaders.

By the end of the week, our pilots were running a 16-to-1 ratio over the Japs. How the men of the ground forces felt about the planes was summed up pretty neatly by Sgt. Oakley Askers of Dallas, Tex. "When I get out of here." he said. "I'm going to kiss the first P-38 I find."

If the days were fairly free from heavy attacks. the nights were not. From the time the moon came up until after midnight, there were Washing Machine Charlies overhead almost constantly. They often came in force, and then the night was lit up with the flash of bombs, the glow of flares and the fire of tracers.

Unwilling to give away gun positions, our troops gritted their teeth and dug deeper into foxholes, feeling for all the world like ducks in a shooting gallery. Before the echo of bombs had died away, aidmen and stretcher bearers were swarming over the area. They found some business but not much. The men were well dug in. and it took almost a direct hit to blast them out.

While the work of building the defenses progressed, the few remaining Japs were mopped up. Along the 200-foot coral cliffs on the east side of the peninsula, some 20 Japs were holed up in numerous caves and crevices. They were trapped, cut off at each end of the cliffs by our patrols and by the ocean down below. In the darkness, several tried to dash over the top but none got through. One soldier in his foxhole wounded a Jap attempting to sneak past, then crawled out of the hole and finished him off with a knife. Two enemy soldiers who tried to charge the CP were

shot by guards. One was killed but the othe who was only wounded, tried to crawl awa unt a lieutenant tossed a hand grenade at him. Pickin up the grenade to throw it back, the Jap had h arm blown off. "That'll teach the sonuvabitch n to touch things that don't belong to him," sai the lieutenant.

Foot by foot our patrols closed in on the snipe in the caves, blasting them out of their hidir places. Assisting the patrols were amphibia engineers in Army vessels patrolling offshor who raked the areas with machine guns.

LT. Edward Coleman of Baltimore, Md., led tw LCVs (landing crafts, vehicle) on a patrol. the boats approached their objective, the lieute ant noticed a camouflaged position on the shor He swung his glasses to the left and made out th stern of a Jap barge. As he ordered T-4 Willia Anthony, the cox'n, to swing the boat aroun Jap guns on the shore and barge blazed out.

Both LCVs returned the fire with their machir guns, and the soldiers in the boats put up smal arms fire. As the leading LCV swung around, bot its gunners were wounded and at the same tim a 20-mm incendiary crashed through the port sid just forward of the wheelhousing. Coleman p out the blaze with a five-gallon can of water.

Meanwhile the second craft, under T-4 Ca Pyles, a cox'n from New Martinsville, W. Va had disappeared from sight around the ben under heavy fire from the Japs. It reappeare some time later, apparently out of control, an ran aground on a reef 300 yards from the enem

While the lead boat laid a protective cone c fire over the stranded vessel, T-5 Clarence Stiffle crawled over the motor hatch, took the wheel an got the boat off the reef. The two boats heade for home with three enemy barges chasing then

As the wounded received first aid, Pfc. Josep Santarsiero of Trenton, N. J., radioed his bas not to fire as the LCVs came in.

That night the precious hours of pre-midnigh sleep were ruined as our artillery barraged th area where the vessels had been ambushed. Nex morning bombs worked over the place, too, an when they were finished, so were 15 Jap barge

On the sixth night after the landing, while o one of these patrols, I had a grandstand seat the heaviest Jap bombing yet received by th American bridgehead. Fifteen planes droppe over 100 bombs in a square mile. The attack laste three hours, and two fires were still burning a dawn of the seventh day as we returned to ou base, expecting to find the worst.

On the bridge, T-5 Lynn Meserole of New Orleans, La., and Pvt. Miguel Lavado of Rye N. Y., the gunners, were talking to T-5 Henry Dolan of Milton, Mass., the cox'n. "I don't give damn how many barges they got," said Meserole "but I don't like to think of the guys we lost.

As we pulled toward shore we passed a burnin barge, and up on the hill we could see a smolder ing fire. In the gunpits along the bomb-pocke beach, crews were tidying up. T-5 Carl Thode of Union City, N. J., met us on the dock. "Oh. he said, "we had a couple of guys wounded her and two or three killed by a direct hit on the hill but nothing worse than that." The Japs had give our positions everything they had, but we wer still holding our beachhead.

ON the afternoon of the seventh day there wa only one fighting Jap left on the entire Araw Peninsula. With a young sergeant I made my wa down to the beach, where someone told me th story of "Yoohoo." This Jap was playing hide and-seek with American patrols in the cliff are all week. His buddies had been knocked off bu he continued his game. Each night he would come within a few yards of our outposts and yell some thing that sounded like "Yoohoo."

Cpl. Levie Hill of Hubbard, Tex., played peek aboo with Yoohoo that way all one night, bu neither Hill nor the Jap dared to fire, for fear o giving away his position. Two of our men were wounded by Yoohoo's sniping in the daytime and on the afternoon before I heard about him Yoohoo had placed a shot within inches of the head of Lt. Frank Fyke of Carrollton, Tex.

With an officer leading the party and accompanied by riflemen, we went along the shore and part of the way up a cliff in the area where the Jap was last seen. The sergeant yelled in Japanese, trying to get Yoohoo to surrender. But ou Jap friend wasn't having any, and we finally gave him up as a bad job.

REPORT FROM GEN. ARNOLD

A few interesting factual highlights from the recent comprehensive 62-page report of the Commanding General of the U.S. Army Air Forces to the Secretary of War.

ET us not gloss over the fact that combat flying is a grim and dangerous business. If our only interest was flying safety in the United States, we would have every man fly a primary trainer on sunny days, and we could cut the accident record to almost zero. If we stopped flying and put the airplanes in hangars we would have no accidents at all. But war is not fought that way. From the outset, the Army Air Forces have taught the men at home the maneuvers that they would execute in combat abroad. In these maneuvers a few are bound to be injured or killed, but the overwhelming proportion of the men are better prepared to defeat the enemy.

There has been an increase in the *numbers* of airplane accidents, but not out of proportion to the tremendous increase in the *numbers of men now flying*. The number of men now in training in the air every day is well over 120,000, approximately equal to the population of Camden, N. J., or Savannah, Ga. It is 25 times as many people as were in the air in this country five years ago. During the fiscal year 1943 the Army Air Forces flew over 3,352,000,000 miles, which is equal to 134,000 trips around the world. This figure is domestic flying only—it excludes overseas or combat flying which has also increased greatly.

Despite the tremendous expansion of Army Air Force flying, the rate of accidents per 1,000 hours flown did not increase as anticipated in the fiscal year ending June 30, 1943, but was, in fact, reduced fractionally from .739 to .716. This rate of accidents was lower than the average rate for the 10 peacetime years of 1931-1940, although more than three times more miles were flown last year than in the whole preceding 20-year period.

Basically, the accident record is good. Ninety-five out of each hundred Army Air Force pilots in training can be expected to fly through the next 12 months without a scratch.

EVACUATION OF CASUALTIES. The first obstacle that had to be surmounted in developing the air evacuation service was the supposed danger of

killing the patient—estimated by some medical authorities to be a real one in the case of head, chest, spine and internal injuries. Yet the safety of transporting wounded by air has been demonstrated beyond doubt. In the Mediterranean theater from the beginning of the Tunisian campaign in November 1942 to the close of the Sicilian campaign in September 1943 more than 25,000 men with all types of illnesses and wounds were transported 8,000,000 miles by air. Only one patient died—one in 25,000.

PACIFIC. Gen. Kenney's surprise and shock tactics have shaken the Japs out of their groove; when their routine is disrupted the Japs are baffled, and baffled Japanese do not fight well.

That is not to say Japan will fold, as the Italian Fascists have, under the mere threat of invasion. There is no doubt but that Japanese industry and shipping will have to be systematically shattered before her armies actually crumble. Our Commander in Chief has said: "There are many roads that lead right to Tokyo, and we're not going to neglect any of them."

Expansion of Aircraft Plants

THE expansion of the aircraft industry is shown in the following table, which was included in Gen. Arnold's report. The table gives the number of aircraft plants in the U. S. engaged in military production only and includes Canadian plants engaged in U. S.-financed activities. Only final assembly plants are listed. Thousands of other plants that produce parts and sub-assemblies are not included.

YEAR	ENGINE PLANTS	PROPELLER PLANTS	AIRFRAME PLANTS
1938	4	2	9
1939	7	4	17
1940	12	4	25
1941	16	9	38
1942	22	13	51
1943	22	19	67

CHINA. Supply is our problem in China. To supply our growing air strength in that country has been perhaps the greatest single challenge to the efficiency of the Air Forces. Every item of equipment necessary for the maintenance and operation of our Fourteenth Air Force must be flown into China from the outside. That is the primary, fundamental fact of our present strategy in Asia.

It may throw some light to consider this fact in terms of gasoline alone. In the round trip over the Hump between Assam and Kunming, the C-87 transport now in use can deliver four tons of 100-octane gasoline. To do so, the airplane must consume 3½ tons of the same precious commodity.

The crews of a heavy bombardment group in China must ferry over their own gasoline, bombs, replacement parts and everything else in their own B-24s (the C-87 is a converted B-24). Before this bombardment group can go on one combat flight, it must make four trips over the Hump. To perform one extremely dangerous mission, those crews must make four separate flights over the most hazardous mountain terrain in the world. Until such time as we conquer the territory and build the road into China, and/or capture a seaport, we must follow this procedure whether it is for 40 aircraft or 4,000.

THE MEDITERRANEAN. The Italians, oddly enough, taught us a fine lesson in Africa as far back as the summer of 1940. They started the Libyan operations of that year with a large, powerful and modern air force. This weapon, which might well have won the campaign for them, was under the direct command of the Italian Ground Forces; local army commanders wasted air power in penny packets to protect their own sectors or to help advance small detachments. The Royal Air Force, consisting of a handful of obsolete aircraft, but employed in concentrated mass as a true air force should be, completely destroyed some 1,100 Italian planes.

Many of our present ideas about the Tactical Air Force were evolved in the heat of these desert campaigns. There is no doubt but that experience and new conditions modify many of our notions, but the present concept of the Tactical Air Force can be regarded as tried and proved in North Africa, Italy and New Guinea.

The Tactical Air Force works in partnership with all the other components of air power. In North Africa it worked with the Strategical Air Force, which concentrated on long-range destruction of targets like munitions establishments and supply ports; it worked also with the Coastal Air Force whose functions consisted of cutting the enemy's sea-borne supply route and of protecting our own. The Tactical Air Force is also intimately concerned with the battlefield itself.

It is misleading to say merely that the Tactical Air Force provides support to the ground troops. The word "support" always makes people think of air power as an ancillary weapon of the Army or the Navy in a land or sea operation—as long-range artillery directed by subordinate ground commanders. This narrow conception appears to be firmly imbedded in the public mind as well as in the thinking of the inexperienced soldier subjected to his first enemy strafing. Fortunately for us, it was a conception shared also by highly experienced Axis strategists.

The Royal Air Force and the Army Air Force functioned as a unit in Africa.

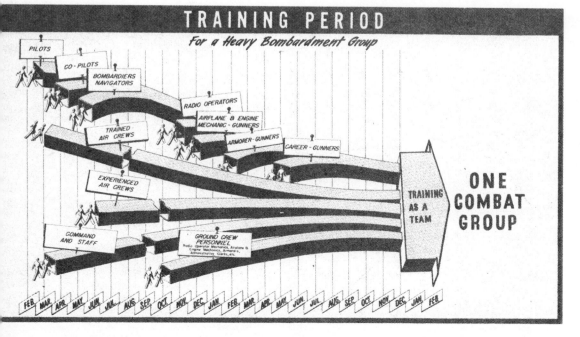

TRAINING PERIOD
For a Heavy Bombardment Group

PILOTS
CO-PILOTS
BOMBARDIERS NAVIGATORS
RADIO OPERATORS
AIRPLANE & ENGINE MECHANIC-GUNNERS
TRAINED AIR CREWS
ARMORER-GUNNERS
CAREER-GUNNERS
EXPERIENCED AIR CREWS
COMMAND AND STAFF
GROUND CREW PERSONNEL

TRAINING AS A TEAM

ONE COMBAT GROUP

FEB. MAR. APR. MAY JUN. JUL. AUG. SEP. OCT. NOV. DEC. JAN. FEB. MAR. APR. MAY JUN. JUL. AUG. SEP. OCT. NOV. DEC. JAN. FEB.

YANK, The Army Weekly, publication issued weekly by Branch Office, Army Education and Information Division, War Dept., 205 East 42d Street, New York 17, N. Y. Reproduction rights restricted as indicated in the masthead on the editorial page. Entered as second class matter July 6, 1942, at the Post Office at New York, N. Y., under the Act of March 3, 1879. Subscription price $3.00 yearly. Printed in the U. S. A.

PANAMA CHOW LINE. Sgt. Stanley V. Sowa, with an aircraft-warning outfit in Panama, saved his fellow GIs from almost starving when he took over mess call for these honey bears. Before the sergeant began feeding them each day at about 1100 and 1600, they were invading the kitchens any time they could for anything they could find. The honey-bear gang is led by a lively monkey named Jocko.

Bloody Basin: An Italian No-Man's-Land Of Black Mist and Enemy Patrols

By Sgt. BURGESS SCOTT
YANK Staff Correspondent

AT THE FRONT IN ITALY—Because so many men from both sides have died here, Yanks of one Fifth Army unit call this sector "Bloody Basin."

The Basin is a shallow depression in a rocky, mountainous setting—a bowl some 200 yards across, with a few battered clumps of mountain scrub and more shellholes than a man can count.

The bottom and sides of the bowl have been pummeled, pounded and powdered by the 105s, 88s, mortars and howitzers until Bloody Basin looks more like a Hollywood battlefield set than like part of the Fifth Army front lines.

At dawn and at dusk, thin layers of mist pour into the Basin and lie in sheets over its scrub and blackened shellholes, making it seem more than ever a no-man's-land.

With nightfall, Yank patrols go out into the Basin to scout out every clump and recon every hole that might contain a Jerry sniper. As they step into the layers of mist, you see only helmets and feet, and then nothing. With darkness enemy patrols venture out, too, and sometimes in the misty blackness the opposing forces come close to each other.

Sometimes they're even within talking distance, and the men tell of weird conversations that follow—snatches of broken German and bits of throaty English exchanged there in the dark.

By day it's almost all foxhole warfare—dug-in Yanks and Jerries cracking at anything that moves opposite them. S/Sgt. James Rutledge of Rising Star, Tex., who has spent many weary days with his rifle in a hole overlooking the Basin, says: "You lie in your hole from sunup to sundown, and the only thing that breaks the monotony is taking potshots at Jerries."

Some unseen artillerymen recently cheated Rutledge out of a German. He had a clear patch of ground across the Basin in his sights, and several times that day Jerries had carelessly wandered across the clearing. Each time he had squeezed his trigger and chalked up another score. "I had the next Jerry lined up in my sights," said Rutledge, "when a 105 made a direct hit on him and destroyed the evidence."

One of the coolest operators in the Basin is S/Sgt. Jack McMillion of Harrisburg, Colo. McMillion was making a report on the field telephone to his lieutenant when he observed three Germans advancing on him up the hill. With one hand he pulled the trigger of the rifle that lay across his knees, while the other hand still held the phone. The lieutenant heard the crack of McMillion's rifle over the phone. That crack dropped one of the Nazis and sent the other two running. Then McMillion completed his report to the officer.

A replacement in the Basin sector, Pvt. Gerald Gralinski of Milwaukee, Wis., got a close shave as an initiation. Gralinski hadn't had time to get into a regular foxhole. He'd scooped the dirt out in a hurry, and his hole was fairly shallow. He'd placed his pack across the front of the hole, laid his rifle across it and was doing a good job when a German machine gunner got him in his sights.

The first burst tore Gralinski's rifle from his hands, crumpling it beyond use. Gralinski yelled to a sergeant in a nearby hole: "Hey, can you get me another rifle?" The sergeant's reply was somewhat profane.

Another replacement fared a little better. Pvt. Martin Krauss of Millville, N. J., a German-born Yank, found that his knowledge of German came in handy on several recon missions. Once Krauss was sent with a couple of other replacements to wipe out a machine-gun nest. They crept within

In Next Week's YANK . . .

POST-WAR PLANS IN OREGON
The Lane County folks have already tackled the problem of making jobs for returning servicemen.

a few yards of the gun, and then, as the othe two covered him with grenades, Krauss com manded the Jerries to surrender, speaking the own language. They came out with their hand up, and the trio of Yanks took them back headquarters.

Sgt. Dan T. Barfoot of Oklahoma did the sam thing, but he did it in English. While on patro Barfoot saw a machine-gun barrel pokin through some brush and saw a Jerry helme behind it. Barfoot pushed his tommy gun in the brush and yelled: "Come outta there." "I coming," answered a voice in good English, an out walked two Germans.

On another mission Barfoot led a patrol of men through the Basin. After they'd walked good distance, he noticed that he had 13 me with him. At the end of the column was a punc drunk German soldier, dizzy from the consta shelling, who had fallen in and was marchin with the Yank patrol. Without saying anythin Barfoot continued the march back to hea quarters.

South Pacific Yanks Witness Dedication of New Zealand Memori

AN ADVANCED PACIFIC BASE—As a bugler soun ed the slow notes of last post, a simple mon ment was unveiled here, honoring the memori of New Zealanders killed in action by a J dive-bombing attack during the occupation this island.

The impressive Sunday-morning memori service was attended by many New Zeala troops and American soldiers and marines. Aft the brief ceremony, the New Zealand and Ame ican national anthems were played by a Na Seabee band.

Built by Kiwi comrades of the honored me the monument consists of a square concrete ba five feet high, topped by a concrete cone. T names of 15 New Zealand artillerymen have be inscribed on a bronze plaque attached to the ba The marker faces the jungle and is situated the edge of the quiet coral beach where the m landed and met the enemy.

The monument dedicated here is believed be the first memorial erected by New Zeala troops in the South Pacific. A similar concre marker will be erected soon on the opposite si of the same beach in memory of the Yanks w fought and died side by side with their N Zealand allies.
—Cpl. HERZL ROSENBAUM
YANK Field Correspond

WISH YOU WERE HERE. When actress J Darrell visited Liberia on a USO trip, she pose T-4 Leon M. Blackley. He's been overseas 18 m but offered to stay 18 years if she would

CEREMONY IN SNOW. In the midst of a driving snowstorm in Iceland, Sgt. Lewis H. Zerbe of Mohnton, Pa., stands before the color guard to accept the award of the Legion of Merit from Maj. Gen. William S. Key. He received it for exceptional conduct as an instructor in small-arms repair at Camp Lee, Va.

A Lover of Nature's Beauties Finds Two of Them in Iran Woods

MOUNTAIN DISTRICT, IRAN—Cpl. Richard Denser is a tall, Ichabod Crane sort of character who likes to wander around the woods.

Denser is librarian for a Special Service detachment that is supposed to supply railroaders up here in this outlying station, 9,000 feet high. But railroad men do not have time to read much, and they prefer comic books or movie magazines to the light tomes like "Decline and Fall of the Roman Empire" that stack Denser's shelves.

So the GI librarian isn't very busy, and he has time to commune with nature if he wants to. There are plenty of wooded mountains around this station, and Denser is usually in them.

At night Denser traipses back to camp and tells his bunkmate, a Cpl. MacLean, about the wonders he has seen in the Iran woods. "Some of the wonders," MacLean says, "are a little unbelievable. Like the time he comes down and tells me he saw a 500-pound bear playing tag with two young gazelles." Another time Denser reported to MacLean, who manages the station PX, that he heard a tribesman taking a few licks of "St. Louis Blues" on his Iranian horn.

The boys in the barracks were beginning to think that Denser had been up in the station too long and maybe they ought to write their CO.

Then one day Denser arrived at the PX on the run and announced that he had seen two girls sun-bathing on a GI blanket in the woods just behind the camp. "One is a blond," the librarian said calmly, "and the other is a redhead, and they called me 'Toots'."

MacLean smiled nervously at his friend and reached for a crowbar that he uses to open PX crates. Then he whispered to the other guys: "Might as well humor him until we tie him up."

"Okay, Denser, old boy," said MacLean. "Let's get a date with those girls."

"Where would we take them?" asked Denser. The boys laughed at this and Denser got very mad. "This is one time," he said, "I can prove I'm not throwing the bull. Follow me!"

The boys followed Denser, MacLean bringing up the rear with the crowbar and some rope. Through the camp, up the hill and into the woods they went, until at last they came to a secluded knoll. There, stretched out on a GI blanket, sat a blond and a redhead playing gin rummy. "H'ya, Toots," the girls said to Denser. The librarian ignored them and turned to his bunkmates. "Who's crazy now?" he asked and wandered off into his woods.

After the guys had stopped MacLean from hanging himself from the nearest tree and had pinched the girls a few times, they asked for an explanation. It seems that the two girls were part of a show called "Liberandos," scheduled to play at the station that night. They had just stepped off their caboose to grab a little sun.

—Cpl. JAMES P. O'NEILL
YANK Staff Correspondent

Big Shots Don't Mean a Thing To This North Africa Car Company

SOMEWHERE IN NORTH AFRICA—Cpl. Floyd Krahnke of Grand Rapids, Minn., assigned to a car company here, can recall driving around San Antonio, Tex., with a lieutenant colonel by the name of Dwight D. Eisenhower in the back seat. The officer was then Third Army chief of staff.

Celebrities like Gen. Eisenhower don't faze Krahnke or other members of his car company. Since the outfit was activated in June 1941, the GIs have driven some of the highest ranking Allied military and political leaders.

The men never know when they report for work at 0700 whether they're going to draw a couple of short driving jobs or set out on a trip that will take them 2,000 miles. Pvt. Joseph E. George of Waterville, Maine, didn't get back for three months from one assignment because the officer he was driving received new orders.

A number of drivers have been under fire. Pvt. Homer Magruder of Brunswick, Mo., was driving Lt. Gen. Lesley J. McNair, chief of the Ground Forces, the day the general received head wounds while visiting the Tunisian front. They had set out in a jeep, but Lt. Gen. McNair dismounted at the base of a ridge and continued on foot. As he reached the top, a German artillery piece cut loose and a shell fragment knocked him down. Magruder rushed up, carried the general back to the jeep and drove him a quarter-mile to a first-aid station. Today the private has an autographed billfold sent him by the general.

Four Wacs have pulled their share of the driving assignments since they joined the company last February. They're all T-5s—Joan M. James of Brighton, Mass.; Cornelia G. Gardner of Passaic, N. J.; Mary H. Lowell of Bono, Ohio, and Ruth C. Perchard of Perth Amboy, N. J.

Forty men are constantly employed in vehicle-maintenance work, and the company operates three gasoline points. Pvt. Arnold Hahn of Swenson, Tex., has a muscle-making job; he hand-pumps an average of 450 gallons of gas into the company's vehicles every day.

—Sgt. GEORGE DORSEY
North Africa Stars & Stripes

This Week's Cover

ON a rocky peak a few miles behind the fighting front in Italy this American soldier is practicing the art of "rappelling" or descending. A rope looped through crotch and over shoulder is carrying him down. He is one of a group of Yanks taking a course in mountain climbing given by both American and Italian experts, the latter being members of the famed Alpini regiments. See pages 12 and 13 for additional photographs of the mountaineers.

WHY ARE WE IN THIS

BETWEEN the Atlantic Charter and the Declaration of Teheran there were some two years and four months, and in that time the fortunes of the Allies turned from possible defeat to certain victory. President Roosevelt and Prime Minister Churchill met at sea early in August of 1941, four months before Pearl Harbor. So the Atlantic Charter, which came out of their conferences, was not a plan of war for the United States; it was a declaration of principles, an international bill of rights. Since then the Allied Nations, at Moscow, Cairo and Teheran, have agreed to make those principles work. They have agreed to crush and to disarm their enemies. But more than that they have agreed to work toward keeping the peace.

THE ATLANTIC CHARTER

"**First**. Their countries [the United States and Great Britain] seek no aggrandizement, territorial or other. **Second**. They desire to see no territorial changes that do not accord with the freely expressed wishes of the people concerned. **Third**. They respect the right of all peoples to choose the form of government under which they will live, and they wish to see sovereign rights and self-government restored to those who have been forcibly deprived of them. **Fourth**. They will endeavor to further the enjoyment by all States, on equal terms, of access to the trade and raw materials of the world. **Fifth**. They desire to bring about closest collaboration between all nations in the economic field, to secure, once and for all, improved labor standards, economic adjustment and social security. **Sixth**. They hope to see established a peace which will afford to all nations the means of dwelling safely within their own boundaries. **Seventh**. Such a peace should enable all men to traverse the high seas without hindrance. **Eighth**. They believe all nations must come to abandonment of the use of force. Since no peace can be maintained if nations threaten, or may threaten, aggression, disarmament of such nations is essential."

THE MOSCOW DECLARATION

"(1) That their united action [the United States, Great Britain, Russia, China] pledged for the prosecution of the war will be continued for the organization and maintenance of peace and security (2) That those of them at war with a common enemy will act together in all matters relating to the surrender and disarmament of that enemy. (3) That they will take all measures deemed necessary to provide against violation of the terms imposed upon the enemy. (4) That they recognize the necessity of establishing a general international organization, based on the principle of the sovereign equality of all peace-loving states. (5) That for the purpose of maintaining international peace and security pending inauguration of a system of general security, they will consult with a view to joint action on behalf of the community of nations. (6) That after the termination of hostilities they will not employ their military forces within the territories of other states except for the purpose envisaged in this declaration and after joint consultation. (7) That they will confer and cooperate with one another and with other members of the United Nations to bring about agreement with respect to the regulation of armaments in the post-war period."

President Roosevelt

Marshal Stalin

Prime Minister Churchill

Generalissimo Chiang Kai-shek

THE CAIRO DECLARATION

"The several military missions [of the United States, Great Britain, China] have agreed upon future military operations against Japan. The three great Allies expressed their resolve to bring unrelenting pressure against their brutal enemies by sea, land and air. The three great Allies are fighting this war to restrain and punish the aggression of Japan. They covet no gain for themselves and have no thought of territorial expansion. It is their purpose that Japan shall be stripped of all the islands in the Pacific which she has seized or occupied since the beginning of the first World War in 1914, and that all the territories Japan has stolen from the Chinese, such as Manchuria, Formosa and the Pescadores, shall be restored to the Republic of China. Japan will also be expelled from all other territories which she has taken by violence and greed. The aforesaid three great powers, mindful of the enslavement of the people of Korea, are determined that in due course Korea shall become free and independent. With these objects in view, the three Allies, in harmony with those of the United Nations at war with Japan, will continue to persevere in the serious and prolonged operations necessary to procure the unconditional surrender of Japan."

THE TEHERAN DECLARATION

"We express our determination that our nations [the United States, Russia, Great Britain] shall work together in the war and in the peace. Our military staff have joined in our discussions and we have concerted our plans for the destruction of the German forces. We have reached complete agreement as to operations from the east, west and south. The common understanding which we have reached guarantees that victory will be ours. We are sure that our concord will make an enduring peace. We recognize fully the supreme responsibility to make a peace which will command good will from the overwhelming masses of the peoples of the world and banish war for many generations. We shall seek the active participation of all nations whose peoples are dedicated to the elimination of tyranny and slavery, oppression and intolerance. We will welcome them as they may choose to come into the world family of democratic nations. No power on earth can prevent our destroying the German armies, their U-boats and their war plants. We look with confidence to the day when all may live free lives untouched by tyranny. We came here with hope and determination. We leave here friends in fact, in spirit and in purpose."

WAR ?

On these pages YANK summarizes the basic objectives for which we are fighting and the basic facts which brought about our entry into the war. These things have been said many times before but they will always bear repeating.

Fascist philosophies must not replace ours

A free country grows with its people; its laws and institutions, art and science change as they do; its beliefs and values accumulate like topsoil on the plains. But the "Holy" Empire of Japan and the Greater German Reich set out to replace the growth of free nations. The Japanese fought to "implant the spirit of the Empire"; the Germans as members of the "Master Race." Why should international agreements or the rights of man mean anything to the future masters of the world? They were ready to destroy what was in their way, and so their creeds allowed no compromise. No nation could be independent if it did not accept the New Orders; and if it accepted, it died.

The law as a racial and national instrument entrusts German parents with the bringing up of their children only on the condition that they bring them up in the manner that the nation and state expect.

—*A German Court*

The purpose of the plebiscite is not to let the people act in the Fuehrer's place or to replace the Fuehrer's decision with the result of the plebiscite. Its purpose is rather to give the whole people an opportunity to demonstrate and proclaim its support of an aim announced by the Fuehrer.

—*Nazi Constitutional Law*

Foreign kings, emperors and presidents are all created by men, but Japan has a Sacred Throne inherited from the Imperial Ancestors. Japanese imperial rule, therefore, is an extension of Heaven. Dynasties created by men may collapse, but the Heaven-created Throne is beyond men's power.

—*Baron Kiichiro Hiranuma*

The law will never make men free; it is men who have got to make the law free. They are the lovers of law and order who observe the law when the Government breaks it.

—*Henry D. Thoreau*

Give me the liberty to know, to utter and to argue freely according to conscience, above all liberties.

—*John Milton*

I have sworn upon the altar of God eternal hostility against every form of tyranny over the mind of man.

—*Thomas Jefferson*

We admit of no government by divine right. The only legitimate right to govern is an express grant of power from the governed.

—*William Henry Harrison*

The Deity has not given any order or family of men authority over others, and if any men have given it they only could give it for themselves.

—*Samuel Adams*

All we national socialists are convinced that we are right, and we cannot bear with anyone else who maintains that he is right. For if he is right, then he must be a national socialist; and if he is not a national socialist, then he is not right.

—*Joseph Goebbels, Nazi Propaganda Minister*

Instead of the army and navy being in the hands of the government, the civil administration is the servant of the fighting men. The power of the army and navy is a kind of dictatorship.

—*"The Japanese Enemy" by Hugh Byas*

The Germanic of the North American continent, who has remained pure and less intermixed, has become the master of that continent. He will remain so until he, too, falls victim to the shame of blood mixing.

—*Adolf Hitler*

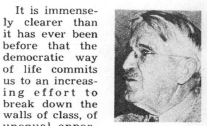

The best test of truth is the power of the thought to get itself accepted in the competition of the market, and that truth is the only ground upon which [men's] wishes safely can be carried out.

—*Oliver Wendell Holmes, U. S. Supreme Court Justice*

In a democracy such as ours military policy is dependent on public opinion.

This is a democratic army working in and for a democratic society. We have to keep our aims and our applications clear in the light of the democratic processes.

—*Gen. George C. Marshall*

It is immensely clearer than it has ever been before that the democratic way of life commits us to an increasing effort to break down the walls of class, of unequal opportunity, of color, race, sect and nationality, which estranges human beings from one another.

—*Dr. John Dewey*

We must put an end to this

In occupied Greece starvation filled this street with dead.

IN EUROPE

Forbidden has been an important word in occupied Europe. For example, it is *Verboten* to cheer prisoners, sing national songs, listen to foreign broadcasts, read un-German books, insult German soldiers, talk to Jews. A "master race" is naturally inclined to forbid. It is also natural that a master should have only contempt for those he conquers. A Nazi leaflet said: "There are no decent Poles just as there are no decent Jews," and that belief brought results. It is estimated that more than 3,000,000 Jews have died in Europe since 1939, and the Inter-Allied Information Committee states that of these, some 1,000,000 or more are Poles who have been "slaughtered, starved or beaten to death."

Part of the doctrine of *Lebensraum* was to "organize great forced migrations of inferior peoples. Posterity will be grateful to us. The colonization of the world by the most perfect race is the wisdom of war." Put into practice that meant round-ups, mass arrests and massacres for occupied Europe. In the winter women and children were jammed into cattle cars to be moved across the continent to places more convenient to the Germans. Thousands of them froze, were trampled underfoot or died of starvation on the way.

It is easy enough to dismiss atrocities as propaganda if you have never seen them, but it is not so easy to deny the facts. German atrocities have been ordered, calculated and ruthless. The Nazis have murdered and burned when they thought it was useful to their plans, having denied "a decent respect to the opinions of mankind." And the record grows as they retreat. In Russia, Rostov reported more than 20,000 civilians "tortured, burned or buried alive," Kiev reported 50,000 machine-gunned and burned, Smolensk reported more than 135,000 persons "were killed by the enemy by execution, starvation, neglect or poisoning." That is only part of the total score which will be added up after the United Nations are victorious.

IN THE PACIFIC

We have learned something of the Jap's cruelty and savage disrespect for life by fighting him. The Chinese learned it before us, on their own soil. Four years before we entered the war Japanese soldiers wer slaughtering thousands of civilians in Nanking and Shanghai. Japan "Greater East Asia Co-Prosperity Sphere" brought 10 million me women and children dead in China since the invasion, plus millior homeless and facing famine and starvation. Japan's economic pillage its flooding of occupied countries with cheap money—is one good caus of hunger, and the conquered peoples of Asia have found that lack rice and mistreatment are more tangible than "Asia for the Asiatics They have found that when the Japs talk about their interest in educa tion they mean: teach your children to speak Japanese or take the cor sequences; and, you can learn nothing from your own country sin Japan is the only teacher. In other words, if Japan takes their foo their resources, their hope, their lives, it is only for the good of th New Order.

But victory alone is not enough

We can stop thinking of the world today as a geographical map—splotches of color that stand only for nations and national possessions. We can begin to think of the human beings who live within those splotches of color as living also within a larger map that marks a single world. We must try to see that all peoples have the means to live and work in that single world so that each can prosper and live with all.
—Wendell L. Willkie

Fascism fights us on both sides of the line. It will fight on from new bases after military victory is complete. Let us not commit the tragic folly of underestimating our enemy. No country has escaped it. The world-wide assault on the power, on the worth and dignity of man is the living issue of our time.
—Vice President Henry A. Wallace

For the purpose of the war we have built up a great store of know edge and of practice which we must be prepared to use for the winnin of the peace. We must turn our machinery of economic warfare in one of economic welfare.
—Sir Stafford Cripp

Our ultimate objective can be simply stated: it is to build for ou selves, meaning all men everywhere, a world in which each individu human being shall have the opportunity to live out his life in peac to work productively, earning at least enough for his actual needs an those of his family; to associate with the friends of his choice; to thin and worship freely; and to die secure in the knowledge that his chi dren, and their children, shall have the same opportunities.
—President Roosevel

The Four Freedoms

From the President's Message to Congress of Jan. 6, 1941

FREEDOM OF SPEECH

FREEDOM FROM WANT

FREEDOM OF WORSHIP

FREEDOM FROM FEAR

By Sgt. JOE McCARTHY
YANK Beautyrest Correspondent

Now that the Post Office authorities have banned *Esquire* and its Varga girls from the second-class mail, I haven't much to do with my spare time except break the arms and collarbones of strange GIs in order to get new specimens for my shoulder-patch collection.

But I had to put this hobby aside last week because I didn't have any way of removing the patches from the latest batch of sleeves that I had wrenched from their sockets and stored away in my barracks bag. The company barber had borrowed my scissors so he could stand a full field inspection. So I decided to while away a few evenings in YANK's *What's Your Problem* department, answering a few of the questions that nobody else would touch with a 10-foot pole.

Most of these questions were a cinch to answer. A couple of them gave me a little trouble, but I figured them out in about 15 minutes with the help of an aiming circle and a few field manuals. For instance:

Q. Why does a major wear gold leaves on his collar?

A. If he wore them on his socks, nobody would see them.

Q. I have a brother 26 years old who has never

This question came from a GI who is supposed to be a dining-room orderly in an Infantry outfit in the South Pacific. That is a tough job because they have no dining room and he has to carry the catsup bottle and the salt and pepper shakers around in the hip pocket of his fatigue clothes. The noncoms in his outfit are fast eaters and when they need salt or catsup they just pick him up and shake him over their mess kits instead of waiting for him to fish the stuff out of his pants. He doesn't mind this so much when the weather is dry, but when it is damp and the salt does not flow freely he gets an awful work-out at each meal.

But, as I was saying before we were interrupted by that long-distance telephone call from Hedy Lamarr, this dining-room orderly had an interesting question. He wanted to know why we have to get up so early in the morning.

Well, there are lots of good reasons why we

boys in the U. S. Army have to get up so early in the morning.

In the first place, if you didn't get up early in the morning, you would miss sick call.

In the second place, people ask too many questions when you don't get up early. A couple of times I tried to stay in bed when everybody else was up, and I couldn't sleep a wink because other GIs kept shaking me and asking me what I was doing in bed so late.

There are lots of other reasons, too. In combat zones you have to get up early because the Germans and Japs get up early. If the Germans and Japs didn't get up so early, it wouldn't make much difference. The first sergeant or the platoon sergeant would wake you anyway so you wouldn't be asleep in case they happened to get up. However, in most combat zones you don't have to worry about whether or not you will get up early in the morning because usually you do not go to bed the night before.

In camps where they have pyramidal tents, you have to get up early because they roll up the flaps on the sides of the tents after breakfast to air the tent out. This lets the sun shine in your eyes. It also exposes you to the KPs when they sneak out of the kitchen to goldbrick around 10 o'clock. They wake you up with foolish remarks.

"If they didn't get up so early, we could stay in bed."

Hey, Joe, why do they wake us up so early in the morning?

"If they didn't get up so early, we could stay in bed."

worked much because he is not interested in anything except being a dramatic critic. He has been deferred from the draft because the Army tried to talk the Navy into taking him and the Navy wasn't interested. He likes to sit around the house a lot. What would you suggest he read?

A. Gas meters.

Q. I understand the Army will let us keep our footwear after the war. Does this mean we can take home our big rubber GI overshoes?

A. Not both of them.

Q. Why does a lieutenant wear gold bars on his collar?

A. If he wore them on his socks, nobody would see them.

Q. My brother has been sent to Fort Bragg where they have put him in a Field Artillery battery. Why did they put him in a battery? He cannot pitch or catch. He always played shortstop or second base.

A. Maybe he knows somebody.

THERE was one question, however, that threw me for a couple of days. I asked the first sergeant about it, but he just glared at me and told me I would be busted if I didn't watch out.

In places where there are barracks with double-decker bunks, you have to get up early so that the GI who sleeps over you won't step on your face while he is making his bed. It is also dangerous to sleep late in barracks because the other men in the room will pile foot lockers and shoes on top of your head while they are mopping the floor.

That brings up another question. Why do men in Army barracks mop the floor every morning?

They mop the floor every morning because they get up so early that they have a lot of time on their hands after they finish breakfast and go to work. They cannot shave because the latrine is being cleaned. They cannot go to the PX because it is not open yet and they cannot go to the orderly room to read the bulletin board because the first sergeant might see them and put them on a detail. There isn't anything new on the bulletin board, anyway. They have to do something. So they mop the floor.

Personally, I think the Army ought to let us sleep later in the morning. For one thing, it would cut down the number of soldiers who get hurt by booby traps. Nobody is going to get hurt by a booby trap if he is in his own bed, sleeping.

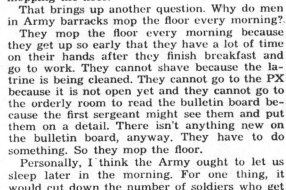

High on a cliff an American soldier student negotiates a hard part of the ascent and another awaits his turn below, while an Alpini instructor guards against a fall.

TRAINING MOUNTAIN FIGHTERS IN ITALY

A middle man in a party climb rests on a pinnacle 1,500 feet above an Italian village.

Instructors of the U. S. mountain-climbing school pose at the end of a day's work. Capt. Edmund Mueller, the CO, is at far left, front row.

Alpini lead man and Yank rest on the peak as third man climbs up.

A FEW miles behind the fighting front in Italy is a class which has a mountain for its schoolroom. It is there that selected personnel from U. S. divisions, officers and enlisted men alike, are taking a course in climbing that will fit them for the extensive mountain fighting that is part and parcel of the war in Italy. Headed by Capt. Edmund Mueller, a Mid-Westerner who has climbed many American ranges, the school is staffed with professional and amateur rock climbers found among the Yanks and a number of officers and men from the famous Italian Alpini regiments. The Italians wear GI uniforms, field jackets, leggings and all, but they still keep their high-crowned Tyrolean felt hats with a feather in the hat band. The staff does not expect its pupils to become experts; it wants them to learn the basic rules of climbing so they can do it sensibly and safely. But it's a tough and intensive course; some of the two- and three-day phases of it would normally take weeks. The men are taught to climb with little more than a rope, to handle extremes of temperature, to accustom themselves to dizzy heights, and to know what types of rock will hold and what will give way. Students who show the greatest climbing aptitude become the lead men in the party climbs when three men ascend together, linked by a 120-foot length of rope. Each man must be prepared to withstand the fall of any other who slips, and he must learn how to "climb with his eyes," using the rope mainly as an assurance and for emergency. These pictures were taken by YANK photographer Sgt. George Aarons.

In a climbing problem for medics a patient is being let down a line.

Two instructors, an Alpini and Pvt. Jack Young of New York City, wind up their climbing ropes.

Medical students in a mountain-climbing class learn how to bring a casualty down the face of a 100-foot cliff on a taut equipment line.

Ascending cliff, Yank reaches stopping point as an Alpini watches.

MAIL CALL

Reserved for Officers

Dear YANK:

In a November issue, T-5 George A. Smith had a complaint about officers having reserved seats in the GI shows [and being first in sick calls or in line for a bus]. If he gets a satisfactory answer, will you please publish it. I'm another one that would like to know.

La Guardia Field, N. Y. —Lt. WARREN J. ECKHARDT

Dear YANK:

I am a Regular Army soldier, and although I will not mention when I came in, I will say I did not come in yesterday. Pfc. Buck and T-5 Smith, I will tell you why I think that the officers should have a reserved section when they go to see a show or anything else. First of all, the officer's uniform represents a great man in this good American Army of ours. So that alone should tell you why you should respect it. Officers have to first be good soldiers in order to become officers. I and every soldier respects a good soldier, but not your kind of soldier, because your kind come a dime a dozen. A good soldier never questions the why or what of an officer. He has already showed his stuff as far as I am concerned by being able to wear the uniform. Your kind of questions helps the Jap and all the rest of the so-and-sos win the war by making remarks that enable them to write propaganda saying that our soldiers and officers don't get along. Think about it, soldier, and respect the uniform if not the man. I myself respect the man because he is able to wear it. That's why I let him have a reserved section at a theater or let him get ahead of me in any kind of line.

Aleutians —1st Sgt. DENNIS TRUJILLO

"Battle for Russia"

Dear YANK:

I have just seen the War Department film "Battle for Russia," showing men, women and children hanged, machine-gunned, gassed, starved to death; kids stripped of clothing to freeze to death. This film is the face of the enemy as the Russian people have seen it. Americans should be urged not to turn aside when they see the hanging bodies in the film, or the frozen babies and mass graves and smoldering ruins. We should be as resolute as the grim-faced Russians who take the oath: "I would rather die fighting than surrender alive to the enemy!" That is the iron in their blood, the granite in their guts. We may recite names, figures and places, but when we know the enemy the way the Russians do, as shown in the Army film, then we shall have taken a long step forward in winning the war.

IV Corps Spec. Serv., Los Angeles —Cpl. DON S. AMTER

Soldier-Voters

Dear YANK:

I am writing this letter because I wonder what other servicemen think about the recent Senate action killing the Green-Lucas bill, thereby practically disfranchising us of the armed forces. From whatever angle one chooses to look at it, this action stands out as a deliberate betrayal of America's 10 Million; more than that, a betrayal of America. The Green-Lucas bill would have created, by Federal action, a bipartisan commission of four to insure every soldier a chance to vote without relying on the chances of state legislatures. This was killed and "recommendations" substituted, throwing the whole thing back into the laps of the states. This is where it was in 1942 when an insignificant 28,000 effective votes were cast.

In practice, it has definitely been proved that state absentee-voting machinery is grossly inadequate to insure the soldiers' vote. These betrayers claim that they are interested in preserving the principles of the Constitution and protecting states' rights. But is that so?

We are selected by the Federal Government. When we are assigned to a unit, it is not the state that assigns us. When we are given KP or latrine duty we cannot refuse on the grounds that it violates states' rights. Everything we do is done in the interests of the nation as a whole. Is it wrong, then, that we receive Federal aid in casting our ballots? It is obvious the states' rights issue has been used to becloud the ugly nakedness of this action to deny the servicemen the chance to cast a ballot.

It has been argued that the soldiers are not interested in voting. Again, that is not the point. Let us have the chance to decide that. I know that's what I'm writing my congressman. What do some of you other GIs have to say about it?

Scott Field, Ill. —Pvt. M. ROSENBERG

Dear YANK:

Congress is now deciding how it can give servicemen a chance to vote, but what, exactly, will we do with the ballots when we get them? You know what happens to the lettuce we get on pay day; the same thing can well happen to the ballots we shall find in mail call. In short, we might gamble most of our votes away. The majority of us don't know more than the two or three top names on the ballot. I've seen a GI in the service club take his fountain pen, close his eyes and make a dot on the ballot. The name the dot came closest to got the vote!

A lot of men in the Army will unquestionably underestimate the tremendous power of their total vote. In examining the civilians who seek government positions in their home towns and in the Federal Government, they will give more weight to what these men have said they will do than to what they have done. Yet that's one thing Army experience should definitely have taught all of us—just because a guy can "sound off" doesn't mean he can do a good job.

All votes should be cast against politicians who consciously or unconsciously are aiding the forces of oppression, intolerance and injustice. That's where the GI vote comes in very strongly. We can fight against those forces in enemy countries with our rifles and other weapons, but to fight them in this country we must use our votes as weapons. Our votes—when we get them—can insure victory on the home front, but only if those votes are cast intelligently.

Camp Edwards, Mass. —Pvt. JEROME E. KLEIN

Soldier Morals

Dear YANK:

A lot of soldiers stationed in this country have broken down the moral barriers at home. The increase in the delinquency of adolescent girls is the fault of soldiers more than any other group in the country, including the girls themselves.

The young girl gone wrong is, because of her youth, only partly to blame. It is the soldiers and sailors who are concerned neither with health nor morals who are much more to blame. Certainly men such as these are as guilty of "prostitution" as the worst woman, for they pick indiscriminately upon girls who have barely reached the age of understanding.

Many people are concerned over the apparent inadequacy of the measures being taken to control youth delinquency. Soldiers and sailors stationed in the U. S. should be equally concerned about improving present deplorable conditions, for which they are mainly responsible.

ASTU, Fordham U., N. Y. —Pvt. STANTON R. GAYLORD

Martha O'Driscoll and GI

Dear YANK:

This is to let my friends from the Bronx and Brooklyn and other localities emit with sighs of envy. The picture of Martha O'Driscoll and myself was taken during her USO tour through Alaska.

Alaska —Pvt. FRANK HOROWITZ

Secret Weapon

Dear YANK:

In the *Current Events Quiz* in a December issue by Sgt. Irving L. Field, it was stated that the P-38 was manufactured by Boeing. Lockheed gets credit for this usually, or have you heard by now?

Scott Field, Ill. —Pfc. RICHARD SIEBEL

Dear YANK:

As every private knows, a sergeant is never wrong. Therefore, we think that it is only your duty to inform Boeing that they are now building P-38s. After all, that Lightning is a hot little baby so why let Lockheed take the credit?

Truax Field, Wis. —Pvt. RAY D. KERSHNER

■ Sgt. Field was wrong, and YANK flunked, too.

Post-War Problems

Dear YANK:

The need for post-war rehabilitation and reorganization seems to be the current topic for debate, but it is imperative that plans be laid now when liberal and clear thinking is predominant. Let us think of the old adage, "In time of peace prepare for war," and so, inversely, in time of war prepare for peace.

Australia —S/Sgt. D. V. THOMAS

Yea 'Bama

Dear YANK:

In the sports page of a December issue you said that in the Alabama vs. Tennessee game of 1935, Paul Bryant [of Alabama] played the full game with a broken leg. Well, who in the hell won the game? "Yea 'Bama!"

Camp McCain, Miss. —Pvt. THOMAS E. BULLEN

■ Alabama 25, Tennessee 0.

Message Center

[Men asking for letters in this column are all overse Write them c/o Message Center, YANK, 205 East 42d Stre New York 17, N. Y. We'll forward your letters. The cen won't let us print the complete addresses.

A. Pfc. JOSEPH ABRIL, USMC, once at Parris land, S. C.: write your cousin S/Sgt. Santos Abril. . . . T-5 HEBRERT ANDERSON of Cincinnati, Oh once at Camp Murphy, Fla.: see *Message 4.*†† . KENNETH and DUANE ATCHISON: write your broth Cpl. Vincent Atchison.

B. Sgt. RODGER BERRY, once in Africa: write S Fred Maier. . . . BOB BRADLEY, formerly at Ke ler and Scott Fields: write Lt. E. R. Cavin. . SAMUEL BRECI, somewhere in the States: write yo brother, S/Sgt. Sebastian Breci. . . . JACK BRO of Dallas, Tex.: write Sgt. Ellis Britain. . . . WALT BUDDEN, formerly at Keesler and Scott Fields: wr Lt. E. R. Cavin.

D. Pfc. JOHN F. DOLDER, once in the AAF in Fl write Pfc. Merle O. Clawson. . . . Sgt. B DURANT, QMC: write your brother, Sgt. L. P. Sh make. . . . Lt. JUSTIN C. DUROCHER, USNR: write B. Bala OS3c.

F. WILLIAM FALVO of Jackson Heights, N. Y.: wr your brother Pvt. Francis Falvo. . . . Cpl. HEIN O. FISCHER, at Will Rogers Field, Okla., in 1942: wr Cpl. Norbert Bykowski. . . . Pfc. JOHN FOSTER of Ci cinnati, Ohio, once at Camp Van Dorn, Miss.: *Message 4.*†† . . . Cpl. GEORGE KENNETH FRY of Ha mond, Ind., and Chicago, Ill., with the Signal Pho Mail Co., ABS: write Pfc. Max Coppage.

G. 2d Lt. GLASS of Newark, N. J., once at F Benning, Ga.: write Lt. Carl B. Hamilton. . FRED J. and CLIFFORD GROTE of Cincinnati, Ohio: *Message 1.** . . . MARTIN GULLEMAN of Cincinna Ohio: see *Message 1.**

J. Lt. JOE JAMAR in an MP Bn., formerly of t Office of Internal Revenue, Houston, Tex.: wr Pvt. Bill Elliott. . . . CHESTER JOHNSON, once in Bt C, 1420 FA, Camp Bowie, Tex.: see *Message 3.*†

K. Pfc. MILTON C. KEES, USMC, in the S. Pacif write Cpl. Elzie L. Kees. . . . JOE and LER KLEMS of Cincinnati, Ohio: see *Message 1.** . . . C WILLARD KLEPPINGER of Northampton, Pa., once Gardner Field, Calif.: write Cpl. Allan L. Stee . . . Pvt. HARRY KLEVAN, once at Camp Shelby, Mis write your brother, Pvt. David Klevan. . . . Ca SID KLIGERMAN, Med. Corps, Australia: write P L. S. Eisenstein.

L. S/Sgt. JOHN LESLIE LANDRUM, once in the 5 Com. Sq., Morris Field, N. C.: write Cpl. Hu Mortimer. . . . ROBERT LAUDATO, formerly with t 501st Prcht. Regt.: see *Message 2.*** . . . 1st Lt. JAM LEGOTT, with the 31st Bomb. Sq.: write your cous Pvt. Legott. . . . RAYMOND LEWIS, once at Camp Mu ray, Wash.: write Pvt. Cecil B. Rosales.

M. ROBERT MARCEAUX JR., USN: write Pvt. Will Simoneaux. . . . Pvt. RALPH MICHAEL of L Angeles, Calif., in the Infantry: write Pvt. Char Levine. . . . Sgt. MERLE MILLER, once with 3d Engr write 1st Sgt. B. H. Thompson.

P. JAMES PALMQUIST, USMC, of Austin, Tex.: wr Cpl. Francis J. Koenig. . . . Pvt. EDWARD PIL once at Fitzsimons Gen. Hosp., Denver, Colo.: wr Pvt. P. C. Curley. . . . DONALD H. PORTER, forme with the 501st and 541st Prcht. Regt.: see *Messa 2.*** . . . Pvt. OSCAR PRINCE, once at Camp Lee, V see *Message 5.*‡

R. CLYDE D. RANKIN, once in Btry. C, 1420 F Camp Bowie, Tex.: see *Message 3.*† . . . C FLOYD REYNOLDS, with the Paratroops in S. Pacif write Sgt. Stephen Van Horn. . . . Cpl. CHALM RIFFLE, once at Fort Belvoir, Va.: write T/S George McClusik. . . . Pvt. LESLIE S. RITZOW, once Calif.: write Pvt. Charles R. Gans.

S. S/Sgt. CHARLES SAYLOR, once at Hampton Ins tute, later at Camp Croft, S. C.: see *Messa 5.*‡ . . . JAY SHARP of Frankford, Philadelphia, P once with the CWS in Maryland: write Sgt. Sam T. Staffieri. . . . VERNON SHAW, once in Btry. C, 14 FA, Camp Bowie, Tex.: see *Message 3.*† . . . JAM L. SUFFLE of Cincinnati, Ohio: see *Message 1.** . Sgt. ANDREW SWASNY, once in Dept. of Air Tr FASM No. 20, Fort Sill, Okla.: write Pfc. Sam Tre marchi.

*Message 1: Write Cpl. George L. Klems.
**Message 2: Write Pfc. Larry Margolis.
†Message 3: Write S/Sgt. Clifford C. Fisher.
††Message 4: Write Sgt. H. A. Fritsch.
‡Message 5: Write Pvt. Willie Saddler.

SHOULDER PATCH EXCHANGE

A mimeographed list of all those wanting to exchan shoulder patches will be sent to soldiers upon request. W haven't enough space to list everyone's name each wee

These men want to trade shoulder patches:

Pvt. James F. Healy, Div. Hq., 18th Corps, Sig. Det., Fort Huachuca, Ariz.

1st Lt. Andrew V. Bakasy, Flt. 9, SO Det. (Pre-Flt.) Maxwell Field, Ala.

Lt. Charles M. Thompson, Co. E, 222d Inf., Camp Gruber, Okla.

Pvt. Oscar Mayers, H Co., 1st Bn., 271st In Camp Shelby, Miss.

Pvt. Ralph Stein, Public tions Dept. Hq., TD Sc Camp Hood, Tex.

Sgt. Nick Worontsoff, C Z, 803 Sig. Tng. Reg Fort Monmouth, R Bank, N. J.

BENNY GOODMAN
Clarinet

LOUIS ARMSTRONG
Trumpet and Male Vocalist

BILLIE HOLIDAY
Female Vocalist

JACK TEAGARDEN
Trombone

OSCAR PETTIFORD
Bass

ART TATUM
Piano

ARTIE SHAW
Favorite in Armed Forces

SIDNEY CATLETT
Drums

RED NORVO
Odd Instruments

LIONEL HAMPTON

COLEMAN HAWKINS
Saxophone

AL CASEY
Guitar

JAM SESSION AT THE "MET"

Hot jazz invaded New York's Metropolitan Opera House on Jan. 18 when first- and second-place winners in the magazine *Esquire's* All-American Jazz Band Poll appeared on the stage of that citadel of the opera. It was the first time the "Met" had opened its doors to the exponents of swing and boogie-woogie. The royalty of Jazzdom, as selected by 16 judges for *Esquire*, put on a jam session that served the additional cause of helping usher in the Fourth War Loan Drive in New York City.

On the roster of judges were two GIs: S/Sgt. George Avakian, a specialist in Chicago style and Dixieland jazz, and Pvt. John Hammond, who had a big part in the launching of such jazz greats as Benny Goodman and Count Basie.

Choices were made from musicians currently active, thus eliminating men in the armed forces and those who, like James Crawford and Gene Krupa, were temporarily out of circulation at the time of voting. Votes were cast for more than 125 performers in 12 classifications.

Benny Goodman led the pack with a total point score of 24 in the clarinet field. Eleven judges picked him for first place while two figured him second. Billie Holiday, who led the field among female vocalists, was second in over-all point scores, with 23 points; she was picked first by nine judges and second by five. Louis Armstrong took first place in two classifications, gathering 16 points in the trumpet department and 11 as top male vocalist. One first-place tie showed up in the odd-instruments field with Red Norvo and Lionel Hampton each getting 15 points.

Other leaders were: Oscar Pettiford, bass; Sidney Catlett, drums; Artie Shaw, favorite in the U. S. armed forces; Jack Teagarden, trombone; Coleman Hawkins, saxophone; Art Tatum, piano, and Al Casey, guitar.

THE SAD SACK

"ROUGH SEA"

©1944   SGT. GEORGE BAKER

What's Your Problem?

Who's Eligible for Benefits

Dear YANK:

My wife has divorced me, and she has married another guy. What I want to know is. can she get a family allowance from me?

FPO, New York, N. Y.   —STANLEY MAZENKAS S1c

■ According to the Office of Dependency Benefits a divorced wife who remarries is not entitled to a family allowance. Write ODB, 213 Washington Street, Newark, N. J., the information that your wife has remarried since she took out her allowance and hence is no longer eligible for benefits.

Dear YANK:

I have a problem about family allowances, and I wish you would help me out. I am not married but as a civilian I did contribute 50 percent of my pay to my mother and father. My mother is not working, but my father has a small place of business and is contributing to the support of my mother and brother, who is 9 years of age. There are many fellows I have come in contact with who have wives who are self-supporting; that is, they are working and are able to get along without help. If this is the case, why can't I apply for an allowance for my mother, who isn't working at all?

800th Ord. Co., Nashville, Tenn.   —Cpl. H. MASLOFF

■ If you contributed to the support of your parents while

you were a civilian, you may take out family allowances for them. Either you or your parents should write to the ODB (address above) stating the degree of their dependence.

Dear YANK:

Please tell me if I can get a family allowance. My son helped me keep my home going while he was a civilian.

George, Tex.   —(Mrs.) ORA MAE SUSEBERRY

■ If he contributed to your support while he was a civilian, you can apply for a family allowance by writing to the ODB. Include in your application affidavits from at least two persons testifying to the extent of your dependence on your son before he went into the Army.

Dear YANK:

I would like to have an answer to the following question: I am one of three sons in the Army. My parents have no income of their own. They are both invalids. Their expenses are approximately $200 per month, including doctor bills, medicine and other living expenses. At present one brother and I each contributes an allotment to their support, but they need more money for a decent living. My other brother was inducted last month. Can he also contribute to their support?

PW Camp, Aliceville, Ala.   —Pvt. JULIUS HESS

■ If your brother can prove that he also contributed to the support of your parents, and if the ODB decides that the combined allowances of your first brother and yourself are not sufficient for your parents, your second brother may also apply for a family allowance. He should write to ODB, Allowances Branch, 213 Washington Street, Newark, N. J., setting forth the details of the help he gave your father and mother before induction.

Religious Preference

Dear YANK:

A friend of mine who belongs to the Greek Orthodox Church wanted to have his religion marked on his dog tags, but he was told that only the denominations of Protestant, Catholic or Hebrew could be stamped on his tags. Is this correct? I think even an atheist should be allowed to express his preference.

Camp Maxey, Tex.   —Pvt. R. S.

■ AR 600-35, Change 25, says: "The religion of the wearer, when stated . . . will be indicated by a capital letter as follows: C for Catholic; H for Hebrew; and P for Protestant." However, it has been the practice in certain units to stamp "O" for "other religion," or sometimes print on the tag the full name of a religion, such as Confucianism. A blank space or an "N" is sometimes used to denote atheism or absence of religious preference.

Ratings in Flight Training

Dear YANK:

I was told that I could become an aviation cadet and keep my present rating through the entire course. Is this correct?

Camp Lee, Va.   —Sgt. CALVIN BAGLE

■ Yes. *AAF Memorandum 35-31* states that an enlisted ma may go through cadet training as an aviation student an hold his rank all the way through. Aviation students receiv the same training as aviation cadets but are permitted to re tain their rank, draw 50-percent increase in base pay fo flying and, if in one of the first three grades and marrie draw an allowance in lieu of quarters for dependents.

Hashmarks for Selectees

Dear YANK:

I would like to know if there is any reason why a selective serviceman can't wear a hash mark when he completes three years' service Many of the first draft men will finish three years soon.

Fort Jackson, S. C.   —S/Sgt. D. P. FLANNAGAN

■ Selectees are entitled to wear a hash mark after three years of honorable service. AR 600-40, Paragraph 46.

Busted in AUS

Dear YANK:

A lot of Regular Army men who have been promoted to temporary grades in the AUS have asked you if they revert back to their permanent ranks in the Regular Army after the war. Now my question is slightly different. I was busted in AUS. Will I revert back to my permanent rating after the war?

Australia   —Pvt A

■ It will depend on how you lost your rating. If you were reduced without prejudice you will revert back to your per manent rating after the war. But if you were broken by sen tence of a court martial you will be broken in the Regula Army even though you received the sentence when you were serving in the AUS.

New Combat Boot

THE QMC has developed a new 10-inch combat boot that is expected to replace the Infantry's shoe-and-legging combination and the special boot now worn by Paratroopers. The lower part of the new boot laces in the conventional manner, and a wide two-buckle cuff at the top permits trousers to be tucked in quickly and easily. The leather in the lower part is turned flesh side outward, leaving the smooth grain side next to the wearer's foot for greater comfort. Sole and heel are of synthetic rubber.

The boot was designed primarily to eliminate the need for leggings and such difficulties as lacings wearing out and coming untied. Tests in combat in North Africa and the Southwest Pacific have proved the new boot to be cooler in warm climates than the shoe-and-legging combination and less easily snagged by underbrush.

Italian Campaign Notes

"Our Infantry soldiers like both the bazooka and the rifle grenade, not only for antitank work, but against personnel," reports Lt. Gen. Courtney H. Hodges, CG of the Third Army, after an observation tour of the Italian front. American arms were so effective, says Gen. Hodges, that the Nazis were often surprised when solid adobe walls, which they believed could withstand anything but artillery fire, were shattered by a weapon in the hands of a GI. Advances in Italy "are necessarily slow" because of the vast quantities of mines and booby traps. "In one division, 91 out of 140 casualties were caused by mines and booby traps." As a result, reports Gen. Hodges, the Infantry and all other arms in addition to the Engineers are being trained in detecting and removing them.

An additional WD report on the Italian campaign states that "German casualties on the Italian front are consistently higher than American, despite the military axiom that an army on the offensive must pay a heavier toll than a defending force."

GI Shop Talk

For every American who had a working knowledge of Japanese when we entered the war, a Navy release says, there were 100,000 Japs with a working knowledge of English. . . . A new group of 105 Wacs recently arrived in North Africa. . . . Each division of the Fifth Army, according to the WD, has its own daily newspaper. News picked up by radio is printed, usually by mimeograph, a few miles behind the lines. . . . The WD announces that 59 percent of the 581 air-crew members originally reported missing on the Schweinfurt raid are prisoners of war, with 217 men still unaccounted for. . . . The first Negro combat battalion to go into action on European soil, the 450th AA Bn., was commended recently by Lt. Gen. Mark W. Clark. . . . Airfields on the Gilbert Islands have been named for Lt. Cmdr. Edward H. (Butch) O'Hare, missing Naval air ace; Rear Adm. Henry M. Mullinnix, missing in action after the sinking of the escort aircraft carrier *Liscome Bay*, and Marine Lt. William Dean Hawkins, killed in action.

"The only thing needed for us to win the European war in 1944 is for every man and woman all the way from the front line to the remotest hamlet of our two countries | the United States and Britain | to do his or her full duty."—Gen. DWIGHT D. EISENHOWER

Short Story Contest

This is a reminder that just one month is left in which you can win the $50 War Bond offered by YANK to the winner of its GI short story contest. Stories must be original and unpublished, and should run from 1,000 to 3,000 words. Contest closes Mar. 1, 1944.

Antiflak Helmets

Two new antiflak helmets have been designed for the AAF—the M3 for pilots, navigators, etc., and the M4 to be worn by turret gunners in cramped quarters. Both helmets are worn over the regulation flying helmets. The M3 is a close-fitting steel cap with ear and eye flaps to fit over earphones and goggles. It has a velvety outer coating

Maj. E. F. Sustrick with M3. Sgt. William Lyon with M4.

that keeps the wearer's hands from sticking to it in subzero weather. The M4 is a smaller helmet made of separate steel plates with a canvas covering, and has no ear flaps over the earphones. Head injuries have been considerably reduced since air crews have been equipped with the new helmets.

Washington O.P.

PVT. Robert Ming, who recently argued a case before the U. S. Supreme Court on Illinois election laws, is believed to be the first EM to argue a case before the nation's highest tribunal. Pvt. Ming, formerly a law professor at Howard University and now stationed at Basic Training Center No. 10, Greensboro, N. C., had to get special permission from his CO to appear in court. He wore civvies, since custom does not permit attorneys to appear before the Supreme Court in uniform. Ming said the *Sad Sack* was his favorite nonlegal reading matter.

Maj. Gen. Frederick L. Anderson Jr., chief of the VIII Bomber Command, told us that Allied bomber attacks on Germany had definitely cut Nazi fighter production 39 percent, and that the bomb tonnage dropped would increase even though weather obscured the targets. In fact, he said, new navigation aids are enabling bombers to hit targets through 25,000 feet of clouds.

The Bureau of the Budget has given the Veterans Administration top priority rating in acquiring new Civil Service personnel. Just as the load was starting to get heavy for the VA, its headquarters here and its more than 100 offices around the country were hard hit by the draft and by loss of employees who took other jobs. The VA has already hired 922 vets of this war and would take on an additional 4,000 if it could get them. . . . Regardless of the priorities that might be set up in local employment stabilization plans, the War Manpower Commission says honorably discharged servicemen will be helped to find jobs of their own choice.

Travel note: Since July 1943 more soldiers have been shipping overseas than have been inducted in the Army. . . . The 555th Service Squadron of the Air Service Command, first American-born Chinese unit in the Army, will be followed by two or three similar units.

—YANK Washington Bureau

YANK THE ARMY WEEKLY

YANK is published weekly by the enlisted men of the U. S. Army and is for sale only to those in the armed services. Stories, features, pictures and other material from YANK may be reproduced if they are not restricted by law or military regulations, provided proper credit is given, release dates are observed and specific prior permission has been granted for each item to be reproduced. Entire contents reviewed by U. S. military censors.

MAIN EDITORIAL OFFICE
205 EAST 42d ST., NEW YORK 17, N. Y., U. S. A.

EDITORIAL STAFF

Managing Editor, Sgt. Joe McCarthy, FA; Art Director, Sgt. Arthur Weithas, DEML; Assistant Managing Editor, Sgt. Justus Schlotzhauer, Inf.; Assistant Art Director, Sgt. Ralph Stein, Med.; Pictures, Sgt. Leo Hofeller, Armd; Features, Sgt. Harry Sions, AAF; Sports, Sgt. Dan Polier, AAF; Overseas News, Cpl. Allan Ecker, AAF.

Washington: Sgt. Earl Anderson, AAF; Cpl. Richard Paul, DEML. London: Sgt. Walter Peters, QMC; Sgt. John Scott, AAF; Sgt. Steven Derry, DEML; Sgt. Durbin Horner, QMC; Sgt. Bill Davidson, Inf.; Pvt. Sanderson Vanderbilt, CA; Sgt. Peter Paris, Engr.; Pvt. Jack Coggins, CA; Cpl. John Preston, AAF. North Africa: Sgt. Burtt Evans, Inf.; Sgt. John Frano, Sig. Corps; Pvt. Tom Shehan, FA.

Italy: Sgt. Walter Bernstein, Inf.; Sgt. George Aarons, Sig. Corps; Sgt. Burgess Scott, Inf. Central Africa: Sgt. Kenneth Abbott, AAF. Cairo: Cpl. Richard Gaige, DEML. Iraq-Iran: Sgt. Al Hine, Engr.; Cpl. James O'Neill, QMC. India: Sgt. Ed Cunningham, Inf. Australia: Sgt. Don Harrison, AAF; Sgt. Dick Hanley, AAF; Sgt. Douglas Borgstedt, DEML. New Guinea: Cpl. Ozzie St. George, Inf.

South Pacific: Cpl. Barrett McGurn, Med.; Sgt. Dillon Ferris, AAF; Sgt. George Norford, QMC. Hawaii: Sgt. Merle Miller, AAF; Pfc. Richard J. Nihill, CA; Cpl. James L. McManus, CA; Sgt. Robert Greenhalgh, Inf.; Sgt. John A. Bushemi, FA. Alaska: Sgt. Georg N. Meyers, AAF; Pfc. Robert McBrinn, Sig. Corps. Bermuda: Cpl. William Pene du Bois. Ascension Island: Pfc. Nat G. Bodian, ATC. Panama: Sgt. Robert G. Ryan, Inf.; Pvt. Richard Harrity, DEML. Puerto Rico: Cpl. Bill Haworth, DEML; Pvt. Jud Cook, DEML; Sgt. Robert Zellers, Sig. Corps. Trinidad: Sgt. Clyde Biggerstaff, DEML. Nassau: Sgt. Dave P. Felds Jr., MP. Iceland: Sgt. Gene Graff, Inf. Newfoundland: Sgt. Frank Bode. Greenland: Sgt. Edward F. O'Meara, AAF. Navy: Robert L. Schwartz, Y2c; Allen Churchill Y3c. Officer in Charge: Lt. Col. Franklin S. Forsberg. Business Manager: Maj. Harold B. Hawley. Overseas Bureau Officers: London, Maj. Donald W. Reynolds; India, Capt. Gerald J. Rock; Australia, 1st Lt. J. N. Bigbee; Cairo, Capt. Robert Strother; Hawaii, Capt. Charles W. Balthrope; Iraq-Iran, Capt. Charles Holt.

PT and Rec Council

Selfridge Field, Mich.—GIs here will have a voice in base sports and entertainment programs through a recently formed Athletics and Recreation Council that serves in an advisory capacity to the physical-training officer and the Special Service officer. The council is composed of two representatives of each base organization, who meet with representatives of the SS and PT offices and four officers.

The group of GIs is headed by Sgt. Garland E. McCleary of the 4th Base Hq. and AB Sq., president; T/Sgt. Henry W. Capron of the 2d Communications Sq. Det., vice president; and Sgt. Mary Jane King of the WAC Det., secretary.

Labor Problem

Camp Roberts, Calif.—When the order came to dig slit trenches at the end of a bivouac march, Pvt. Tom Matthews was tired, so he paid Cpl. Anthony Matymiak $2 to dig one for him. Then he found himself a spot and relaxed. But not for long. An officer spied the private sitting while the others worked and ordered him to the KP tent. There Matthews was assigned to dig the trench for the refrigerator—a 6-by-6-foot job, about three times as big as the trench he had just paid $2 to avoid digging.

Round Table

Camp Sibert, Ala.—Through the establishment of a suggestion box called the "Soldier Round Table," GIs of the 222d Chemical Depot Co. can enter their pet peeves and suggestions, either signed or unsigned. All notes are read by Lt. R. P. Nice, Company CO, and 1st Sgt. L. Modist.

So far, a social and athletic committee has been formed as the result of GI suggestions and a sports program is under way with a team entered in the post bowling league.

GI Galahad

Second Army Maneuvers, Tenn.—Pvt. Dan Brown was seated in the bus awaiting transportation from Nashville to Sparta. A pretty young thing called to him through the open window: "Can I be your wife to Knoxville?"

Surprised at first, Brown remembered that servicemen and their wives had priority on bus seats in this maneuver-crowded area. He nodded. The gal convinced the driver and took her place next to the private.

At Sparta, Brown got off but he fixed things for the young lady in gallant fashion. For the bus driver's benefit he said in a loud voice: "You go on to Knoxville, honey. I got to stop off here and see the colonel."

AROUND THE CAMPS

Camp Santa Anita, Calif.—More than 350 GIs and Wacs recently completed a three-day course of instruction with a faculty composed of Hollywood celebrities. The teaching roster included George Jessel, Eddie Cantor, Perc Westmore, Judith Anderson, Jinx Falkenberg and others. The GIs and Wacs got a taste of every phase of the entertainment field from music to magic to make-up.

Camp Stewart, Ga.—During a recent class in aircraft recognition a private was asked to identify a plane flashed on the screen for the briefest of moments. After a slight hesitation, the GI answered: "It's a two-motored blur, sir."

Camp Gruber, Okla.—Pvt. Russell Sherman of the 242d Inf., a former student at the Kansas City (Mo.) Art Institute, recently held a one-man show of his art work at the Philbrook Museum in Tulsa. Sherman began to display an interest in drawing at the age of 4 and still has some of the sketches he made then.

Camp Carson, Colo.—In the mail came a misdirected letter from a Mid-Western mother. It asked: "Will you please send me a catalogue of the camp and complete information as to what you have to offer a 12-year-old boy and how much does it cost?" One GI joker wanted to answer her with: "Wait until he's 18 and it won't cost you a cent."

Lincoln Army Air Base, Nebr.—Sgt. Walter J. Nakon belongs to that brand of drill sergeants who make basic trainees quake in their GI brogans. One day he bellowed to his flight: "Eyes right!" From the rear rank came an unidentified drawl: "Yo' sure is, suh; you're a sergeant."

CAMP NEWS

DOUBLE EXPOSURE. But it's not the camera's fault that they're twins. Horace and Morris Wofford (center) and Walter and Welton Roberts (right), at Mitchel Field, N. Y., are enough to drive a man dizzy, but Sgt. J. F. Weaver (left) knows them by their voices.

SPECIAL REWARD. Sgt. John W. Atterbury has been general handy artist for so long at Daniel Field, Ga., that they decided to reward him with a job that would be a particular treat to his eyes. So Miss Clara Matthewson of the Finance Dept. agreed to pose.

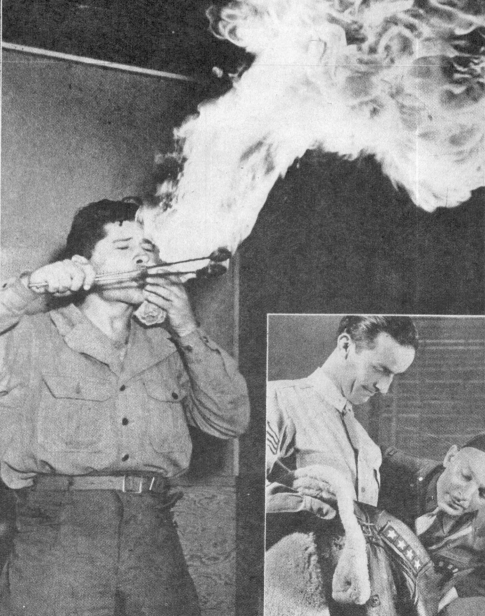

FLAME THROWER. "Step right up, folks, and see the asbestos man!" Pvt. Leroy Scott used to disgorge flame for a fascinated public with Ringling Bros. Circus; now he's at Camp Beale, Calif.

FOUR-STAR SUIT. At Bolling Field, D. C., Supply Sgt. Chris Cosfol checks in a winter flying suit for Gen. H. H. Arnold, AAF commanding general, as Lt. V. A. Evers looks on.

Glendale Army Air Field, Calif.—Cpl. Kirk Trevang of the 435th Fighter Sq. now knows it pays to be honest. On furlough recently he sent the following telegram to his CO: "NO ONE SICK; NO ONE DYING; NO EMERGENCY. HAVING GREAT AMOUNT OF FUN AND ASK FOR FIVE-DAY EXTENSION." He got the extension.

Stewart Field, N. Y.—GIs' hopes soared here when the rumor went around that physical training would be put off until further notice because of the flu epidemic. But Sgt. Bill Fischer of the 820th had the inside dope. "Nothing to it," he said. "They're going to call off the flu epidemic because it conflicts with PT."

Camp Gordon Johnston, Fla.—A whistle used in the last war by 1st Sgt. George Burke of Co. I, 113th Inf., was picked up on the battlefield by a buddy when Burke was killed. Later it was sent to Burke's favorite nephew. Today that whistle is being used by the nephew, 1st Sgt. L. L. McCarty of the Hq. Det. here.

AAF Redistribution Sta. No. 1, N. J.—While shopping for Christmas cards, Sgt. Tom Murphy found one with the word "greetings" in letters an inch high. He sent it to his draft board.

Camp San Luis Obispo, Calif.—Pvt. Robert Callahan of the 322d Inf. did not show the customary eagerness when he opened a large box of home cooking he had received. His hutment buddies could not understand until he smiled: he had just returned from the dental clinic and nary a tooth was left in his head.

Charleston Navy Yard, S. C.—When Dora Mattingly Y3c seemed undecided about a date, another Wave, Jean O. Love, offered to read her palm and advise her. The palm reading predicted

"*. . . and this one's my hat check!*"
—Cpl. Joseph E. Seyk, Hobbs AAF (N. Mex.) *Bomb Blast*

that it would be a great night in Wave Mattingly's life. It was. She hit the jackpot in a bingo game for $245 in War Stamps.

Camp White, Oreg.—When the bulldozer he was driving became overheated, a GI driver went into the Post Sports Arena office and asked Pvt. Ted Woods if he had something in which he could give his "cat" some water. Woods suggested an ashtray. The driver said: "This baby might scratch a little dirt around, buddy, but it ain't that kind of cat."

AAFBTC No. 10, Greensboro, N. C.—T-5 Warren Brushaber was night CQ at the motor pool. With a detail coming up in the morning he asked the telephone operator to give him a call at 6 A. M. When the phone rang, Brushaber answered sleepily: "Thanks a lot, darling." "Okay, sweetheart," came a reply from Lt. Edward Phillips. "Now get over here on the double. You're 10 minutes late."

Truax Field, Wis.—Ten letters arrived before Pfc. D. D. Crawford Jr. was able to figure out why he was getting back the same letters he had received a long time before. The postal dead-letter office confirmed his suspicions; a box of old letters he had mailed home had broken open en route.

Fort Jackson, S. C.—Pvt. Frank J. Conway sent the wrong barracks bag to the laundry. In it were several books and magazines of the kind you wouldn't ordinarily find on your Aunt Bessie's parlor table. When the bag was returned, this note was attached: "We clean your dirty clothes gladly. We can't do a thing with dirty books."

Fort MacArthur, Calif.—T-5 George Gerdes got a sock in the nose recently that paid a handsome profit. He was involved in an accident aboard a Pacific Electric car en route from Los Angeles and got a $100 settlement of his claim.

EX BRAVE. Pvt. Ray Martin of Norwood, Mass., used to be a pitcher for the Boston Braves. Now he's with the 901 QM, Grenier Field, N. H., as a stock clerk where he dishes up supplies instead of balls.

CYCLE CHAMP. Testing, T-3 Robert Hallowell takes his steed over a hurdle at Aberdeen Proving Ground, Md. As a civilian he won a number of motorcycle contests, including 200-mile National in 1939.

WAR LADIES. When Betty Hicks Spc3 of the Spars, golf champion, visited the Wacs at Daytona Beach, Fla., she took a firm hold on the wheel of an Army jeep and saw the sights with Sgt. Gladys Relyea.

MORALE BUILDER. Marguerite Chapman of the movies made the GIs happy by signing autographs at the Salt Lake City (Utah) Army Air Base, but what lifted their morale the most was just seeing her.

THREE JEEPS. S/Sgt. William J. Weber is holding a helmetful of new arrivals at the 275th Infantry, Camp Adair, Oreg. The two boys are slated for pfc. ratings and their sister is going to be a Wac.

MUSIC MAKER. Pfc. Albert De Rose at Fort Ontario, N. Y., doesn't let being a GI keep him from his songs. Composer of "Wherever I May Be," he was arranger for Ina Ray Hutton, Red Norvo and Joe Marsala.

Patricia Dane

YANK

Pin-up Girl

BIVOUAC ON A MOUNTAIN SIDE

I see before me now a traveling army halting,
Below a fertile valley spread, with barns and
   the orchards of summer,
Behind, the terraced sides of a mountain,
   abrupt, in places rising high,
Broken, with rocks, with clinging cedars, with
   tall shapes dingily seen,
The numerous camp-fires scatter'd near and
   far, some away up on the mountain,
The shadowy forms of men and horses,
   looming, large-sized, flickering,
And over all the sky—the sky! far, far out of
   reach, studded, breaking out, the eternal
   stars.
                        —WALT WHITMAN (1819-1892)

*This poem is one of a group called "Drum Taps"
that Walt Whitman wrote about the Civil War.
Other classic war poems will appear in future issues.*

PRAYER, 1944

God, let us have some peace to live,
Carved out from all the time You have in
   store;
Just some centuries that You could give
Without disturbing Your Forevermore.
You've got it pretty soft, God: Your sky
Is silent as the heart of night should be,
With only an occasional meteor going by
To shake the edges of Eternity.
It's a little different, God, down here:
The bitter curse of war is everywhere,
With blood and flame, sorrow mixed with fear,
And Death, instead of Angels, rides the air.

We only ask that You will understand
And drop some quiet mercy from Your hand.
Camp Lee, Va.   —T-4 MYRON W. FISHER

THE NURSE FROM BUTTE, MONTANA

*"The most beautiful girl I've ever seen was a nurse from
Butte, Montana."—From a Curtiss-Wright advertisement.*

I've crossed the rivers of the earth,
The Nile, the Susquehanna;
I've roamed the seven seas, and been
From Guinea to Guiana;
I've been in a thousand towns or more
From Chungking to Savannah,
And had a girl in every town

From Fez to Texarkana;
But the prettiest girl I ever saw
Was a nurse from Butte, Montana.

Some girls have lips with the scent of spring,
And some with the taste of manna;
Some girls converse in a throaty tone,
And some in a clear soprano.
Some girls are flighty, some are calm,
And some like Zola's "Nana";
Some girls may be, like Venus, warm,
And some cold, like Diana;
But the temperature that I like best
I found in Butte, Montana.

I saw some girls in a harem, once;
I've been in a fine zenana;
But my taste runs to the Occident;
I like Americana.
You can have your geisha girls, my friend,
And your brown maids from Havana—
I'll call things square, if I can get
The nurse from Butte, Montana!
Camp Shelby, Miss.   —Sgt. GRANT A. SANDERS

TRIANGLE

Soldier, soldier, to whom do you write?
To my wife back home this very night.
You have new stationery, I see.
That girl in Portland bought it for me.
Camp Shelby, Miss.   —S/Sgt. A. L. CROUCH

A MEMORY'S AN ESOTERIC THING

A memory's an esoteric thing,
You could not make a stranger understand
The value of a melody you sing,
Its tune a spider's web, a thinning strand
Between remembered time and time called
   now.
A huge smooth rock in icy lights of stars
Allows you memory it will allow
No others. Old thought burns and often chars
With bitter black the edges of the mind.
But often more it holds time in its flight,
An anchor to the hurrying feet of life.
Each man remembers something that will bind
The past and present strongly, until spite
And death shall sever them with a quick knife.
Laurinburg-Maxton AAB, N. C.   —Sgt. PHILIP R. BENJAMIN

PEOPLE

People:
You have to like everyone of them
No matter what they are;
You have to like them
When you are one of them;
And you have to believe in them
No matter what they do.
For believing in people
Is like believing in God.
India   —Sgt. CARLYLE A. OBERLE

CHECKER STRATEGY

LOOK what the boys in the barracks have cooked up for us this week. Pvt. William Agan of Pinecastle (Fla.) Air Base submits this little brain teaser. He doesn't claim that the position came up in a game, but we'll bet he wishes it would some day, with him playing the White side. You guessed it. It's White to move and win. 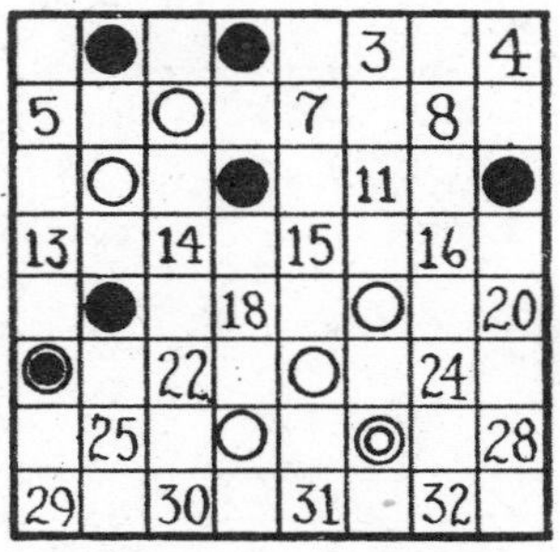
   Number the playing squares of your board from 1 to 32 as shown before checking your analysis with the answer on page 22.

GIRLS who wear bathing suits are often placed in two classifications: those who swim in them and those who look good in them. Patricia Dane (on the opposite page) is the kind of a girl who can and does do both. Her latest MGM movie is "I Dood It." Since making that one she's been appearing with Tommy Dorsey's band. Tommy, you will be sorry to hear, is the guy she married.

COIN SHIFT

THIS toughie was sent in by S/Sgt. Manny Weber of Wendover Field, Utah. It's a coin-shifting problem. You begin by laying out four pennies and three dimes as shown in the diagram, leaving the fifth space blank. If it's too close to pay day, used red and black checkers.

   Now your problem is to rearrange the coins so they lie like this:

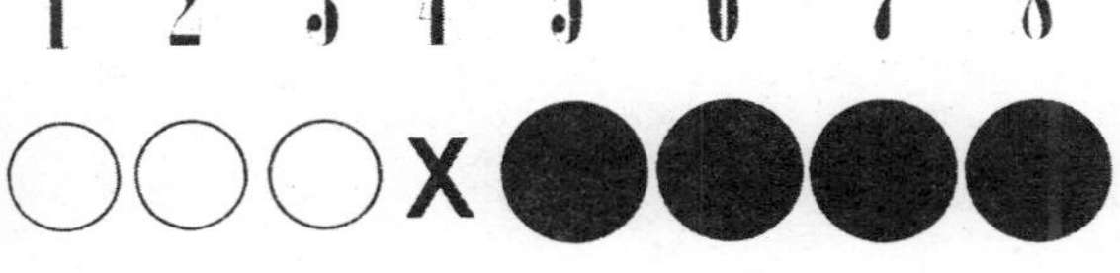

   But these are the conditions: Pennies move only to the right, dimes only to the left. A coin may either move to a vacant space next to it or jump *one* coin next to it into a vacant space.
   This should take you 19 moves if you can dope it out.

(Solution on page 22.)

GOLF LOG

LIKE golf, this word game is won by the player who gets the lowest score. The idea is to change one word to another with a minimum of strokes. At each stroke you change one letter to form a new word with an equal number of letters.
   Example: Change BOY to MAN in three strokes.
BOY: 1. BAY, 2. BAN, 3. MAN. Now try these:

CARD	GIRL	DAWN
1.	1.	1.
2.	2.	2.
3.	3.	3.
4. DICE	4. WIFE	4.
		5. DUSK

(Solution on page 22)

POST X CHANGE

This Post Exchange, like YANK itself, is wide open to you. Send your cartoons, poems and stories to: The Post Exchange, YANK, The Army Weekly, 205 East 42d Street, New York 17, N. Y.

If your contribution misses the mark, you will receive YANK's special de luxe rejection slip, that will inspire a more creative mood.

Genuine Pigskin

THE kid stood on the station platform with his mother and father. They were saying good-bye, and I watched the old man hand the kid a wad of dough. The kid stuck the dough in his pocket and threw back his shoulders and lifted up one of the three valises he had with him. I guess that was the day he became a man.

The kid couldn't carry all three bags. His mother saw me watching them and motioned for me to come over. She told me that her son Arnold had enlisted and he had never been away from home before. She asked me to keep my eye on him and smiled in a nice way and asked me to help him with the bags. I said sure, and the old lady said that it was very sweet for Arnold to have a friend so soon.

The second louey who was taking us up to Upton blew a whistle or something and told us to line up. I grabbed a valise and waited for the kid. He kissed his folks good-bye, even the old man. He wasn't feeling like a soldier yet. The kid's mother was crying and pressing a handkerchief against her mouth. I kind of wished I had some one there to cry good-bye for me, too. That was a hell of a way for me to start my first day in the Army. We started to walk down the ramp to the train.

The kid? I never saw him again. Our names must have been too far apart on the roster. There's the bag, the one I carried for him, over there behind my foot locker.

Sure I kept it, jerk. Genuine pigskin.

AAB, Biggs Field, Tex.   **—Cpl. EUGENE FEIST**

ON SEEING A DRUNKEN DOGFACE WITH A BUCK-TOOTHED GAL

> When GIs get woozy
> They ain't very choosy.

Fort Benning, Ga.   **—Sgt. LEONARD SUMMERS**

—Pvt. J. W. Blake, Camp Wheeler, Ga.

RHYMES FOR THE END OF THE MONTH

THE DANCING IVORIES

Tinkle, tinkle, little dice,
Light-foot foils of avarice;
Joe would like to shoot a pound—
Are there any sports around?
Simper, simper, cubist flirts,
Swirl your scintillating skirts:
Soldiers leap to your commands.
Vying for your wanton hands.
Rumble, rumble, hollow bones!
Join the dirge of hollow groans.
How long till another pay day?
Surely *then* we'll have our heyday.

POKER

There are many rules to the game of poker:
You can play deuces wild or play with a joker.
Five card, seven card, stud or draw—
You can play on a table or play on a floor.
Three small deuces beat two pair:
An inside straight is hard to snare.

But just one thing is firm in my mind:
A full house bows to four of a kind.
I've learned that rule as I learned addition,
By grim, relentless competition,
For whenever my aces are full of kings,
Someone has four of the goddamnest things.

BLACKJACK

If I stand short
And the dealer's got 'em,
My assets' graph
Will reach the bottom.
But if I hit
(As I think I'll do).
Can I hope for less
Than twenty-two?
The deck's against me:
I'm disgusted.
Hit me, brother.
Hell, I'm busted!

Britain   **—Pvt. THOMAS B. LOGUE**

That Must Have Been Fun!

ANNOUNCER: Good evening, friends of the radio audience. Tonight you are to meet Pvt. Padway Gridge. Pvt. Gridge, I understand you hold a most unusual distinction.

SOLDIER: You can say that again, bud.

ANNCR: Is it true that in 3½ years in the Army you've had nothing but basic training?

SLDR: Yeah, I had basic training nine times. My legs is like iron.

ANNCR: I suppose you like Army food, or [*chuckling*] as they call it, chow.

SLDR: Yes, sir.

ANNCR: You don't have to say sir to me, private. We're all one happy family on the air waves. I mean, we're all in this war together.

SLDR: Yes, sir.

ANNCR: Now, tell me Pvt. Gridge, what basic trainings have you had?

SLDR: Well, I started off easy, you might say, with Medical basic.

ANNCR: Oh, that must have been fun. I dare say you met many an interesting nurse.

SLDR: Pretty interesting. Most of 'em came from the same reception center like I.

ANNCR: Oh, I see. Male nurses. Bet that was a good one on you!

SLDR: Uh-huh.

ANNCR: And after that, Pvt. Gridge. What was the next stage in your developing Army career?

SLDR: Then they sent me to Infantry basic. Lots of walking. At night, too.

ANNCR: How healthful!

SLDR: Yeah.

ANNCR: Now, suppose you trace for us the course of the next few basic trainings as you continued to master the exciting arts of soldiery.

SLDR: Well, next I took Artillery basic. Then Tank. Then, let's see, there was Quartermaster. Then I took Infantry again.

ANNCR: How interesting! How did that come about?

SLDR: My old first sergeant asked for me. He owed me a 36-hour pass.

ANNCR: Delightful! Truly a democratic army!

SLDR: Not bad. Then I think there was Engineering basic. Then Tank again. I'm kinda beginning to forget.

ANNCR: Well, Pvt. Gridge, suppose we change the subject for a moment. I'm going to ask you to tear aside the curtain. Tell us just what did you do in civilian life?

SLDR: Oh, nothing much. I was founder and president of a large aircraft firm turning out fast bombers. I employed about 10,000 people and we had 17 million dollars worth of Army contracts when I was inducted. We had to close the place. In my spare time I wrote a three-volume analysis of military strategy that was considered the best work of its kind in a decade.

ANNCR: Anything else you'd like to tell us?

SLDR: Well, my AGCT score was 159. I can type 127 words a minute and take dictation at 136. I hold graduate degrees in medicine, government and Asiatic languages. I am married and have nine dependents. . . . Oh, excuse me I must be going.

ANNCR: Why, Pvt. Gridge, what's your hurry?

SLDR: Well, tomorrow morning I start 17 weeks of basic in the Military Police, and I better get lots of sleep tonight.

ANNCR: Yes, I guess you had better. Will that be your last basic?

SLDR: Maybe. I think after that I'm in line for Cooks and Bakers School.

ANNCR: Grand! Well, thanks so much, Pvt. Gridge, it's been fun. Good-bye and best of luck!

SLDR: Good-bye, sir.

Fort Washington, Md.   **—Pfc. MARTIN WELDON**

PUZZLE SOLUTIONS

CHECKER STRATEGY. White moves 19 to 15. Black jumps 10 to 19. . . . White jumps 23 to 16. Black jumps 1 to 10. . . . White moves 27 to 31. Black jumps 12 to 19. White moves 9 to 6. Black jumps 2 to 9. . . . White moves 26 to 23. Black jumps 19 to 26. . . . White jumps 31 to 22 to 13 to 6 to 15 and the Black king gets trapped in a few moves. White wins.

COIN SHIFT. Move 4 to 5, 6 to 4, 7 to 6, 5 to 7, 3 to 5, 2 to 4 to 2, 6 to 4, 8 to 6, 7 to 8, 5 to 7, 3 to 5, 1 to 3, 2 to 1, 4 to 2, 6 to 4, 5 to 6, 3 to 5, 4 to 3.

GOLF LOG
CARD.	1. CARE.	2. DARE.	3. DIRE.	4. DICE.	
GILL.	1. GILL.	2. WILL.	3. WILE.	4. WIFE.	
GIRL.	1. DARN.	2. DARK.	3. DIRK.	4. DISK.	5. D
DAWN.					

SPORTS: HOW MANY SPORTS CHAMPIONS WILL RETURN AFTER THE WAR?

By Sgt. DAN POLIER

PVT. Luke Appling and Fritzie Zivic both said something the other day that started us to thinking.

Appling was telling a group of GIs in the PX at Camp Lee, Va., that he wouldn't return to baseball after the war because he didn't think his legs could stand the gaff. Zivic echoed the same sentiment in Pittsburgh, wailing loudly that he would hang up his gloves for good when he went into the Navy.

Both Appling and Zivic are fairly ancient for top-line athletes. The luscious Appling is 37 and old rubber legs Fritzie is 30 if he's a day. So there's every reason to believe they won't be coming back after the war. Not even if the war ended tomorrow.

But what about the other athletes now in service? The young champions who are full of vitamins and vinegar? How many of them can return after the duration and six and still do business at the same old stand?

Offhand, you might say Sgt. Joe Louis will have the toughest time when he starts out again in 1945 or '46 as the case may be. Boxers age more quickly than most athletes, because their success depends almost entirely on their legs. Should Louis get back into action as early as 1945, he would be 31 with more than 10 years of wear and tear on him. He wouldn't be as sharp as most of his rivals. Cpl. Billy Conn, for example, would be only 27, and Pvt. Jimmy Bivins just 24. One or both of them might be capable of relieving Louis of his championship.

On top of this, you've got to figure there will be a lot of tough and willing young fellows coming out of the Army who could make Louis's row even harder to hoe. You might paste the name of Cpl. Al Hoosman, a Negro MP from Los Angeles, in your helmet liner as a real contender in '45. He's now in Australia with a MP outfit and just recently slugged the Alabama Kid silly in 10 rounds.

Most of the younger major-league baseball players will be back for the opening of the first post-war season. Lt. Johnny Beazley pitched only one season of big-league ball before entering the Army and he will have a full career ahead of him at 26. CPO Bob Feller will be 27 with 10 more years of good pitching in his right arm. Sgt. Joe DiMaggio at 30 and Ensign Charlie Keller at 31 will be able to pick up their gloves and play at least five more years with the Yankees. A/C Dick Wakefield was only 23 when he joined the

If the war is over in 1945, CPO Bob Feller at 27 will be good for 10 more years of baseball.

Navy last year, and he can start all over again as a rookie. The same holds true for A/C Howie Pollett who was just 22 when he enlisted in the AAF. A/C Ted Williams at 27 will be able to pick up where he left off, too.

Capt. Hank Greenberg and the fellows in his age group, the Tommy Bridges, the Luke Applings and Red Ruffings, will have a harder time winning their jobs back. Greenberg would be 35 if he reported to spring training in 1945 and Ruffing 38. Two summers ago when Greenberg was a buck sergeant at Mac-Dill Field, Fla., he complained after a camp game that he couldn't bring his bat around with anything like the snap he used to have.

"I felt like knocking those fat pitches out of the lot," he said, "but I couldn't connect anymore. My timing was off, and my muscles wouldn't work fast enough. Make no mistake about it, I won't play a lot of ball afterward."

After the last war football really boomed, and there's every reason to believe it will

again. It may boom even more since we now have a professional league. For some reason a fellow never becomes too old to play pro football. Look at Bronko Nagurski, who came back this year to play with the Chicago Bears, and Mel Hein and Tuffy Leemans who are still operating with the New York Giants. So why shouldn't some younger men like Ensign Sid Luckman, Lt. Norm Standlee, CPO George McAfee and Lt. Bill Osmanski come back to take over their old jobs in the Bear backfield for the 1945 or '46 or '47 season?

Golf is another ageless game where a fellow can play until he's 50. Even in their 30s, Lt. Ben Hogan, Lt. Lawson Little and Navy Specialist Sammy Snead won't have any trouble regaining their peak.

It doesn't make much difference whether Ensign Greg Rice or anybody else returns to run the distance races after the war. As long as they keep bringing Haegg over here, the only guy with a chance is Count Fleet.

EX-CHAMP IN AFRICA. Jack Sharkey, former heavyweight champion, who's now touring Mediterranean Army camps, samples some Algerian oranges with T-5 Vera Meyers and Pvt. Ted Rynicki in Algiers.

Cpl. Zeke Bonura, who's doing such a fine job promoting baseball in North Africa, has never worn his stripes and never will. Says he wants to be just one of the boys. . . . **Pvt. Terry Moore,** the ex-Cardinal slugger who flew back to the States to see the World Series, must be the No. 1 pin-up boy in the Panama Canal Department. During the recent boxing championships, thousands of GIs yelled themselves hoarse chanting, "We want Terry Moore." . . . This is **Pvt. Jimmy Bloodworth's** (he's the Detroit second baseman) second hitch in the Army. He served 2½ years with the Engineers before signing up with the Washington Senators. Bloodworth is now with the 37th Engineer Training Battalion at Fort Leonard Wood, Mo. . . . Not to be outdone by all of these "best-of-the-year" awards, the National Semi-Pro Baseball Congress has named **A/C Johnny Pesky** as its Man-of-the-Decade. Pesky played sandlot ball in Silverton, Oreg., before joining the Boston Red Sox. . . . According to **Lt. Cornelius Warmerdam,** who oughta know about such things, 16 feet is the absolute top ceiling for a pole vaulter. Warmerdam, who has cleared 15 feet 42 times, 28 of them outdoors and 14 indoors, works on the theory that no vaulter can go three feet above his gripping point. . . . The biggest news of the East India Lawn Tennis Championships wasn't **Lt. Hal Surface's** singles victory, but those two Indians who played barefooted to defeat Surface and another Special Service officer in the doubles. . . . **Lt. Pug Rentner,** the famous Northwestern halfback, has turned

up in England as an operations officer with the Eighth Air Force. . . . When **Leo Durocher** goes overseas his side kick will be **George Raft** and not **Sammy Kaye.**

Inducted: **Lloyd Mangrum,** pro golfer and veteran of America's Ryder Cup team, into the Army; **Clyde McCullough,** first-string Chicago Cub catcher, into the Navy. . . . *Rejected:* **Bob Swift,** Detroit catcher, because of stomach disorder. . . . *Reclassified 1-A:* **Vern Stephens,** shortstop of the St. Louis Browns, who led the American League batting race for most of the season; **Gene Desautels,** Cleveland catcher; **Steve Sundra,** St. Louis Brown right-hander (15-11 last year). . . . *Discharged:* **Sgt. Steve (Crusher) Casey,** professional wrestler, from the Army; **Ed Levy,** Newark outfielder recalled by the New York Yankees, from the Coast Guard. . . . *Promoted:* **Lt. Jimmy Braddock,** former heavyweight champion, to captain at the Brooklyn (N. Y.) Army Base; **Johnny Rizzo,** Brooklyn outfielder, to chief's rating at Norman (Okla.) Naval Station; **Lew Jenkins S2c,** former lightweight champion, to seaman first class on a Coast Guard transport. . . . *Commissioned:* **Charlie Keller,** Yankee leftfielder, as an ensign in the Merchant Marine. . . . *Transferred:* **Pvt. Luke Appling,** American League batting champion (.328), from Fort Sheridan, Ill., to Camp Lee, Va., for basic training; **Capt. John Whelchel,** Navy football coach, from Annapolis to sea duty; **Capt. Hank Greenberg,** former Detroit outfielder, from Headquarters, AAF Flying Training Command, Fort Worth, Tex., to an undisclosed destination.

SPORTS SERVICE RECORD

"I DON'T MIND THE 24 HOURS EXTRA DUTY SO MUCH, BUT HE TOOK ALL MY FLASH GORDON BOOKS."
—R. P. Canning EM3c

"LIPSKY . . . . STEIN . . . . BRANDT
FRASER . . . . WEITHAS . . . . BECK . . . ."
—Cpl. Hugh E. Kennedy

"HE OWES ME TWO BUCKS FROM A CRAP GAME."
—Pfc. Frank Q. Hewitt

"SOMETHING'S THE MATTER; ALL I CAN
HEAR IS 'PISTOL PACKIN' MAMA.'"
—Sgt. Tom Zibelli

YANK

THE ARMY WEEKLY

5¢

JUNE 16
VOL. 2, NO. 52
1944

By the men . . . for the men in the service

START OF
AN INVASION

First Interview With Marshal Tito in Yugoslavia

1. Infantrymen wait in their assembly area.

2. While on the beach loading is under way.

3. Riflemen with full packs go aboar[d]

6. Before shoving off, services are attended.

7. Hollandia-bound, Navy crewmen man guns.

8. A dry run in gunnery for Leland Bi[rd]

9. Standing offshore, the destroyers range in.

10. And landing craft churn toward a beach.

11. Men search the skies as an LCM mov[es]

Medics with litters move up the ramp

5. Men of the 41st Div. transfer to an LSD

14. Followed by the men who unload supplies

Technique of Invasion

AFTER MORE than two years of war against the Japanese, the United States has polished its Pacific invasion technique to a point approaching perfection in the movement of great armies and vast quantities of material to a given striking point. The operations at Hollandia and Tanahmerah Bay, New Guinea, emphasized this again. On these dual missions, YANK had two photographers. They were Sgt. Dick Hanley and Cpl. Bill Alcine. Their work has been combined to give the remarkably complete coverage of an amphibious operation printed on these and the following two pages.

A weapons platoon hits Tanahmerah beach.

13. And others scramble inland over the sand.

15. Vehicles move along the narrow beach.

16. While the infantry nudges its way ahead.

17. Moving in column of deuces down

9. Across a footbridge toward the objective.

20. Now a machine gun slants in on Hollandia.

21. And the infantry plods through the

24. A well blasted-out Jap barge is scouted.

25. The wounded come back through Hollandia.

26. Five Samurai swords for S/Sgt. Leo C.

YANK, The Army Weekly, publication issued weekly by Branch Office, Army Information, MSD, War Department, 205 East 42d Street, New York 17, N. Y. Reproduction rights restricted as indicated in

Past a supply dump fired by Navy shells.

They relax with souvenirs at a Jap HQ.

23. A fresh-caught Jap, tagged a prisoner of war, is interrogated. A string is holding on his glasses.

Crockery is sorted by Pfc. Claude Hayden.

28. The colonel (A. B. Roosevelt) takes a break.

29. Some Japs had died at Hollandia befo

masthead on the editorial page. Entered as second class matter July 6, 1942, at the Post Office at New York, N. Y., under the Act of March 3, 1879. Subscription price $3.00 yearly. Printed in the U. S. A.

ALASKA HIGHWAY GETS DISCHARGED

By Sgt. GEORG N. MEYERS
YANK Staff Correspondent

FAIRBANKS, ALASKA—The Alaska Highway has been handed its honorable discharge. It's not in the Army any more. But it's still under military control, and you can't drive on it without the War Department's okay.

It's more than two years since Engineer dogfaces were clambering off the train at Dawson Creek, British Columbia, to start clawing out a pioneer trail 1,600 miles north to Fairbanks, Alaska. Now a thin trickle of troops is flowing back over the same path. They're headed for the States and maybe somewhere else overseas. The jobs they're leaving behind are passing to civilians hired by the U. S. Engineering Department.

These are such jobs as barreling trucks through, giving the road its daily shave with graders and massage of gravel, working in the repair shops, filling gas tanks and checking the course of all vehicles at relay stations. Soon the only soldiers

Map locates 1,600-mile route of the Alaska Highway.

you'll see on the Alaska Highway will be doing specialized jobs that Uncle Sam isn't ready yet to turn over to civilian hired hands.

Now that they're turning back, the GIs are taking stock of what became of all their sweat and toil and some blood in the last two years. Some are flabbergasted at the size of their handiwork. The Alaska Highway isn't the Lincoln Highway, but it's not the Old Ox Road, either.

Just saying it's a whale of a project doesn't give you much of a picture, but here are a couple of angles that might. If you took the train from Miami to Tallahassee in Florida, that would be about the same deal as from Edmonton, Alberta, the "gateway to the Alaska Highway," to Dawson Creek, where the road really begins. Then, if you drove from Tallahassee through Birmingham, Ala., Little Rock, Ark., Oklahoma City, Okla., and then swung north and continued to a spot on the Missouri River above Casper, Wyo., you'd have covered about the same ground, with all the twists and turns, as between Dawson Creek and Fairbanks. The only town you'd bump into on that whole trip would be about where you'd hit Oklahoma City. That town would be Whitehorse, Yukon Territory, a village smaller than Carson City, Nev.

Or look at it this way. If you stretched the Alaska Highway in one straight line, including bridges, Winston Churchill could ride in a jeep from the White Cliffs of Dover across the Channel, through Belgium, Germany, Poland and Lithuania, and right up to Joe Stalin's front door in Moscow.

As to scenery, there's no spot on the road as spectacular as, say, Yosemite Valley. The highway starts in the sprawling agricultural acres of British Columbia and winds up in the scattered farm patches around Fairbanks. In between it's mile after mile of skinny white birch, tall sticky spruce, scraggly jackpine, steep gorges, broad glacial bottomlands and rolling hummocky tundra. Curves are gentle and the hills are gradual. The highest point on the route is only 4,214 feet

at Summit Lake, a pass through the Rocky Mountains 400 miles north of Dawson Creek.

All those rugged-looking pictures you used to see of the highway during construction—just a pair of muddy ruts slashing through a narrow aisle in the trees—are ancient history now. For 90 percent of the distance the road is 26 feet between shoulders. In winter the graders keep the surface as hard and smooth as concrete. The speed limit is 35 miles per hour, but you could hit 60 with safety except that it's as slippery as an oyster's abdomen. Last spring the thaw made many sections impassable, and ice wiped out a lot of the temporary bridges. The same trouble is expected this year, but on a lesser scale.

IT'S no secret that nowhere near the amount of freight is moving over the road as there would be if the Japs were still giving us a bad time out in the Aleutians. But that doesn't mean the highway isn't doing a job. Actually it has become the main trunk of a network of facilities that have

Greyhound buses link Dawson Creek with Fairbanks.

brought Alaska closer to the U. S. in two years than in all its previous history.

Running alongside the highway is the longest open wire circuit in the world, connecting Alaska and the U. S. by telephone and teletype for the first time. Signal Corps and Engineer troops helped install the line, sinking about 35 poles every mile for the 2,026 miles between Edmonton and Fairbanks. The line, like the highway itself, cuts through four time zones.

Late in 1943, about the same time the phone line was nearing completion, the longest overland mail route in the world was opened over the highway. This provided daily first-class delivery out of Edmonton. The mail truck makes it from Dawson Creek to Fairbanks in about three days and 19 hours. The service is operated jointly by the U. S. and Canadian Post Offices.

For several hundred miles, the four-inch pipe line of the Canol project follows alongside the highway, and one of the main branches off the highway is the recently opened Norman Wells road. Five QM drivers from Teslin were the first to push through a truck convoy to Norman Wells. They were Cpl. Joseph L. Frey, T-5 Joseph T. Adams and Pfcs. Otis A. Lunyou, Michael Doheny and Joseph T. Smallman.

Another branch of the highway, the Haines Cut-off, gives the panhandle section of southeastern Alaska its first overland connection with the rest of the Territory. This road runs from the Army's old Chilkoot Barracks docks for 154 miles, along the trail trampled out by the herd of cattle Jack Dalton drove north to Dawson City in 1898 and sold as beef for almost their weight in gold. The Haines Cut-off hits the main Alaska highway 100 miles west of Whitehorse.

To top it off, Greyhound buses operated by the Northwest Service Command shuttle over the highway daily between Dawson Creek and Fairbanks. The buses carry GIs going on and returning from furloughs and civilian workers.

In short, except for the sloppy season of thaw, traffic over the Alaska Highway is no longer a catch-as-catch-can affair. Freighting by truck is like the old pony-express system brought up to date. A truck leaving Dawson Creek is loaded, inspected, checked through the dispatch station. The driver jockeys it to the next relay station, about 100 miles away, where another driver takes over. Until the recent shift of administration of the road to the Northwest Division, USED, all drivers were GIs from QM truck companies, and the relay stations were manned by soldier clerks and repair mechanics. GIs also operated the highway patrol that covered the road in 100-mile segments. Each patrol car cruised 50 miles north and south of its station, reporting any bad spots on the road and giving aid to stalled drivers.

SOME of the men are seriously wondering what the post-war prospects are for the Alaska Highway. They'd like to open up tourist camps. S/Sgt. William V. Koeninger of Chillicothe, Tex., already has a spot picked on the shores of Muncho Lake at a site pointed out by Indian Charlie MacDonald, a guide who lives in that section with his 104-year-old father, four sons, six daughters, six horses and six dogs.

Several others have their eye on Lake Therese, a freak hot spring that bubbles up through the snow into a pool of water at a temperature of around 100 degrees. This is a mile off the highway in Tropical Valley, 213 miles north of Fort Nelson.

Most GIs, though, claim they've had their fill of the highway for now and ever afterward. One

This Week's Cover

THROUGH a frame formed by two wire men, YANK's Sgt. Dick Hanley photographed this group of GIs carrying rations aboard one of the LCIs that participated in the invasion of Hollandia, New Guinea. On pages 2, 3, 4 and 5 of this issue, YANK prints a complete picture story of this operation as recorded by cameramen Cpl. Bill Alcine and Sgt. Hanley.

PHOTO CREDITS. Cover—Sgt. Dick Hanley. 2, 3, 4 & 5—Cpl. Bill Alcine & Sgt. Hanley. 6—Sgt. Georg N. Meyers. 8—PA. 11—Sgt. Dave Richardson. 12 & 13—Sgt. John Frano. 18—Upper left, PRO, Fort Monroe, Va.; center & lower right, Signal Corps, Camp Fannin, Tex. 19—Lower left, Signal Corps, Camp Gordon Johnston, Fla; upper right, Acme; center right, USMC; lower right, AAFTC, Columbus, Miss. 20—Warner Bros. 23—Upper, PA; lower, Sgt. Hanley.

of the stock gags is about the yardbird who wanted to get away so badly he was bucking for a Section 8 by biting trees to test their texture.

This skeptical attitude is shared in part by Brig. Gen. James A. O'Connor, who commanded the highway's operations until he was succeeded by Brig. Gen. Ludson D. Worsham of the USED. "The average tourist has two or three weeks' vacation," Gen. O'Conner said. "In most cases it would take at least half that time just to reach Dawson Creek, where the road begins. Its more important peacetime function should be making new mining and settlement areas accessible.

"Primarily the Alaska Highway was built for insurance. We wanted to be sure the line of communication with the north would always be open."

"SOMEWHERE in the CARIBBEAN"

By Cpl. JUD COOK
YANK Staff Correspondent

PARAMARIBO, SURINAM—*Diesie na tro foe na YANK foe de na moro verwondroe prokserie foe mekie wie alla sabie na takkie na wan tala-dei sannie foeden boesi-nengre dei de liebie borokrosie-be foe na kantie na Noord Amerika.* ["This is claimed by YANK to be the strangest ad ever written for publication. The language one used by jungle natives near the shores of North America."]

The second paragraph is a word-for-word translation of the first, which was written in talkie-talkie, a language spoken in only one part of the world—the matted jungles of Dutch Guiana, or Surinam.

Talkie-talkie is a mixture of Dutch, Spanish, French, English, Portuguese and the mumbo-jumbo of the African bush. The lingo is not easy to learn, and there are almost no printed or written records of it. In spite of this, some GIs belonging to jungle-rescue and crash-boat outfits have learned to chew the fat with the natives in the swampy underbrush.

It is in the jungles of the Guianas—British, French and Dutch—that you learn what it means to fight the war in the Caribbean. High above these jungles, Air Transport Command planes fly regular routes day and night. They are doing their job of delivering supplies, but they pay the price exacted by the weather above and the jungle below.

It is not hard to find GIs and officers in the Guianas who have tried their strength against the jungle. There are many who have tasted baboon meat during torturous weeks of pushing through the bush to reach a plane wreck, come nose to nose with a boa constrictor or slept in native huts during their jungle treks.

In the midst of this primitive wilderness, the American GIs have left their trade-mark. From an outpost called Moengo to the eastern boundary of Dutch Guiana, they have slashed "the Million Dollar Highway of the Guianas," so-called because it is surfaced for 30 miles with bauxite, the ore from which aluminum is made. Far back in the bush, where the bauxite mines

are located, American and Puerto Rican soldiers stand guard. Although players are scarce, their baseball diamond is probably one of the most expensive in the world, since it too is richly layered with bauxite. The outfield is fertile tropical grass. Apart from the American national game, there are few diversions at this and other lonely posts except GI movies and some PX beer.

Supplies to Moengo are transported by a Higgins crash boat, skippered by an ex-infantryman who was assigned to the 100-mile, 10-hour river run because he used to own and operate an East Coast fishing boat in the States. In his 15 months on the job, crewmates swear, Pfc. Robert Robinson of Philadelphia, Pa., has come to recognize every tree that slips past his eyes on the long river run to Moengo.

The entire Corps of Engineers at Moengo consists of T-4 Ralph Del Vicario of Providence, R. I., whose job is to keep refrigeration in good shape. In his spare time he has provided the boys in his barracks with a hot shower system, one of the few showers in the Antilles Command where you can turn a faucet and get hot water.

An Americanism that is notably lacking in Dutch Guiana is the slot machine—the coins are square here and don't fit. But at an airfield in British Guiana you can find an honest-to-goodness popcorn machine. Drinking American beer and eating popcorn are one of the best cures for the curse of the Caribbean—utter boredom.

THE average GI down here has been "somewhere in the Caribbean" for at least 18 months and probably as long as two years. He's all ears when you talk about rotation, just as much as the Pacific GI who has seen combat. Probably

he's even a little eager, looking for a match with the enemy he can win instead of one he can take by forfeit.

As for being rotated back to the States instead of to a combat area, one man has been here so long that if he were sent back home, he said, he'd rent a room in a hotel and watch people through his window for a week "just to see how they act." And another was worried that he'd have difficulty with "these new-fangled ration laws."

But the man who's finding it hardest of all down here is T-5 John Price of Newark, N. J., assigned to a maintenance company in Trinidad. It's tough for him to sweat out his time because his daily job is to repair watches.

By Sgt. WALTER BERNSTEIN
YANK Staff Correspondent

Partisan Headquarters, Somewhere in Yugoslavia [By Cable] — Marshal Josip Broz — Tito of Yugoslavia—is a man of high intelligence and sensitivity, dedicated with his people to the job of freeing his country and establishing a federal democratic Yugoslavia.

I can report this after walking from the Adriatic Coast deep into liberated territory to interview Tito. I was the first correspondent to visit him in his Partisan headquarters.

To get here I had to hike day and night for what seemed like months, most of the time over mountains and part of the time through German-occupied territory. It was a tribute to Partisan strength and organization that we finally arrived more or less intact.

The interview took place at night in the house that Tito shares with other members of his staff. The location of the house is naturally secret. It is heavily guarded by tough Partisan soldiers who shoot first and ask you to halt afterward. I was taken there by a young Partisan lieutenant.

The night was very black, and I had no idea where we were going. Once we crossed a stream on a slippery log. Several times we were stopped by guards who appeared silently in the darkness.

In the distance we could hear the roar of a waterfall. The sound grew louder as we approached and finally we could see it, the water churning white and phosphorescent in the night. Tito's house was next to the waterfall, under an overhanging mountain that protected it from air raids.

We walked up to the house. There were more guards at the entrance, young men with tommy guns over their shoulders and captured German pistols in their belts. The lieutenant conferred briefly with them and one of the soldiers went in the house. The rest of us waited outside. It was cold near the waterfall, and the spray fell all around us like thin rain. Finally the soldier came out of the house and led us around to the side.

We stepped up onto the porch and stopped in front of the door. The lieutenant knocked, opened the door and stuck his head inside. Then he pushed open the door and stepped back, and I walked in.

Tito was seated at a desk facing the door, and he stood up when I entered. I didn't know whether to salute, but he held out his hand and I shook it instead. He showed me to a chair next to his desk. A huge dog that looked like a wolf

Interview with TITO of Yugoslavia

was sleeping by the chair. He stirred when I sat down, but Tito said a few words in Croatian and the dog lay still again. Then Tito sat down.

He has one of the most impressive faces I have ever seen. It is Slavic, with high, wide cheekbones. It is a strong face, but not hard. Its most striking quality is one that you do not expect from a leader in such a bloody war, and that is kindness. It is a very kind face, almost gentle. Tito's eyes are set deep and wide apart, and it is difficult to tell their color. The skin underneath is soft and a little pouchy from fatigue. His forehead is high—what people like to call an intellectual forehead—and his hair is abundant and combed straight back. It is brown, with flecks of gray brushed in.

Tito's face is the face of a man who knows himself and the world around him. It could be the face of an artist or of a big businessman who directs a huge industry. And, in a sense, this man is both of these.

He was wearing a gray uniform of heavy wool, simply cut and of excellent material. On each collar he wore three gold quarter-wreaths on a red rectangle, and on the cuff of each sleeve he had a gold half-wreath enclosing a star.

The room was also simple, small and square, with a patterned red rug on the floor. The walls were covered with a kind of wrapping paper, heavily seamed and reinforced with strips of some

white material that looked like parachute silk. One wall was covered with a large map of Yugoslavia. In the corner of the room there was a pot-bellied stove, its pipe running out through the wall. There was little furniture: a small table in a corner, four straight-backed chairs, a large flat desk facing the door and behind the desk a day bed with a dull-green flowered cover. At the head of the bed there were two small tables, each with a radio on it. Even here you could hear the dull roar of the waterfall.

A young girl came in immediately after I had entered and sat down on the other side of the desk. Her name was Olga, and she was an interpreter. Tito speaks fluent German and Russian but no English. The girl spoke English well with a pleasant accent.

Tito would look at her when he talked and then turn to me when he had finished. He talked softly and unhurriedly but without hesitation. As he talked he would finger some of the objects on his desk: a GI flashlight, a copy of "Essential English," a case of British cigarettes. He smoked steadily, putting the cigarettes in a holder shaped like a little pipe. Tito's movements were like his voice—deliberate and sure.

He gave the instant impression of being a leader. I had heard Allied officers refer to Tito as a "big man," and I could see what they meant. He

talked of little things; he was tired and didn't fe like discussing large problems; but even so, th qualities of strength and decision came throug But it seemed a strength with compassion, and decision built out of theory and experience. H seemed that rare kind of man who could achiev a complete fusion of thought and action. Lookin at him and listening to him, I could understan the miracle of organization that the Partisan have created—the formation first of a comple army and now of a state with all its component out of absolutely nothing and against the mo savage terror and treachery.

This was the man who had organized a whol people, bewildered and sold out, into a new an powerful state. Knowing nothing about him, w had called him the "Mystery Man of the Balkans but the only mystery seemed to be why we kne nothing about him, why we had not been informe about this man earlier.

Tito did not talk of his life, but it was eviden in everything he said. He was born in a villag near Zagreb in Croatia. His father was a peasan very poor, and Tito became a metal worker. H was drafted into the Austro-Hungarian army i the first World War and captured by the Russian After the October Revolution in Russia, he aske permission to join the new Red Army and fough

th it for the remainder of the Russian civil
..r. Then he returned to Zagreb, where he be-
..ne a leader of the workers.

But the Yugoslav government imprisoned him,
..d Tito spent four years in jail. He left the
..untry after his release and passed some years
..veling around Europe. He was in Paris when
.. Spanish War broke out. Contrary to pub-
..ned reports, he did not go to Spain himself
..t he organized the large Yugoslav delegation
..t fought there against the Fascists. When the
..rmans attacked Yugoslavia, Tito was already
..Belgrade, preparing to organize resistance.

..ito is married and has two sons. His wife is in
..ovenia, working with the Slovenian Committee
..National Liberation. His 20-year-old son is a
..geant in the Red Army and has been decorated
.. Hero of the Soviet Union. He received the
..ard in the battle of Moscow, where he lost one
.. his hands. He is now in officers' school in Rus-
... The other son, 5 years old, is in Yugoslavia.

..ito holds four positions in the new Yugoslav
..te. He is a member of the executive com-
..ttee, called AVNOJ, which is the Partisans'
..ngress. He is head of the National Committee
..Liberation, which is their cabinet and he is
..nister of war and commander in chief of the
..tional Army of Liberation and Partisan De-
..chments in Yugoslavia. (The National Army of
..peration is Tito's regular army. The Partisan
..tachments are his organized civilian guerrilla
..hters.)

..He is deeply loved by the people of Yugoslavia,
.. only because he has led them well but also
..cause he has fought and suffered with them.
..ere are many stories of Tito's bravery. During
.. first German offensive, he led 12 men in a
..unterattack against an Italian company. He
..s himself wounded in the left arm during the
..rrible fifth German offensive, when it seemed
..at the entire Partisan army would be destroyed.
.. is probably one of the finest strategists of
..s war, mainly because his strategy is based on
..und politics as well as good military tactics.
.. still goes to the front, especially during Ger-
..an offensives.

..ito's cosmopolitan quality becomes more ap-
..rent the longer you are with him. He is no
..nple peasant leader but a man of the world.
..tually Tito is an extremely sophisticated man
.. the highest sense of the word. There are
..o moments when he gives the impression that
.. could have been a fine actor: he carries him-
..lf well and wears his uniform with a flair.

first correspondent from
English-speaking country
..neet the Partisan leader
..s him to be a strong and
..sive man of the world with
..eep admiration for our
American democracy.

..he room was square and simple with a red rug on the floor.

This Story Was a Tough Assignment

Sgt. Bernstein

YANK's Sgt. Walter Bernstein completed one of the toughest assignments ever undertaken by a correspondent in this war when he came out of Yugoslavia with the Marshal Tito interview which appears on these pages. He was the first English-speaking correspondent to talk with the Partisan leader at his headquarters. To get there, Sgt. Bernstein walked for seven days across rugged Yugoslavian mountain country and through German-occupied territory. At one point he and his Partisan guides were forced to cross a road under heavy German machine-gun fire.

"But the walk over the mountains itself was dreadful," Sgt. Bernstein reported later. "We would walk sometimes all night and almost all day, sleeping only a few hours. We would start in the morning and reach the snow line of a mountain about 3 in the afternoon, then come down the other side and start climbing the next one. I lost track of time and would think that the dawn was sunset and vice versa. I was sick when we reached Partisan headquarters, ran a fever for three days and my eyes wouldn't focus." After Sgt. Bernstein's visit, Tito was interviewed by John Talbot of Reuter's and Stoyan Pribichevich of *Time*, representing the combined Allied press. Their stories were published while YANK's interview was being reviewed by the censors.

When he was hiding from the Gestapo in Belgrade or Zagreb, he posed as a wealthy businessman. And he always got away with it.

TITO talked about America. He has a feeling for the U. S. that is characteristic of many Yugoslavs. It stems not only from blood ties with the thousands of Slavs who emigrated to America but also from their innate love of democracy and their conception of the U. S. as a great democratic country. Tito talked about how he had wanted to go to America when he was young but was too poor to make the trip.

He talked of the republican tradition in America and what an inspiration it has been to Yugoslavia. He deplored the idea, prevalent in the U. S., that there is civil war in Yugoslavia and emphasized the unity of the people against the Germans and against the native fascists.

He talked about the Partisan army, proudly and with conviction. He pointed out that they have no discipline problem, that they have succeeded in welding the different racial and religious elements in Yugoslavia into a harmonious whole, and that this unity would continue after the war. He said the major problems of his army are physical: food and tanks and antitank guns and an air force of its own, however small.

Here Tito emphasized that his army had been receiving direct and valuable help from the Allied air forces, but he pointed out that there are many qualified Yugoslav pilots anxious to fly for the Partisans who are just sitting around in Allied territory.

But the food problem is the most pressing. The Partisans can continue to lift arms and ammunition from the Germans but the army cannot function at its highest efficiency on a half-loaf of bread a day. If they could get enough food to feed the army, the civilian population could somehow manage to feed itself, he said. As it is, the civilians have to give to the army and no one gets enough.

He talked briefly about the hardships of the people, speaking without sentimentality and with great pride in what they have done. He spoke particularly about the young girls in the army, marching day and night over mountains and then going straight into battle. He regards this as something not desirable in itself; it is only necessary because other Yugoslavs ran away or refused to fight when the Germans invaded the country.

I asked Tito about the treatment of prisoners. He said it was only recently that the Germans agreed to recognize his forces as an army, Before that they called them bandits and executed all they caught. Now the Germans have been compelled by the size and successes of the Partisans to treat them as they treat other Allied armies. One of the main reasons for this, of course, is that the Partisans have been capturing too many Germans.

Tito leaned forward and emphasized here that there has never been an order issued by his headquarters to kill prisoners, but it is a fact that his army does not take many. By this time the soldiers are a trifle bitter toward the Germans, especially because they have had the habit of killing all the Partisan wounded they could find. Those prisoners that the Partisans do take are usually held for exchange.

This just goes for the Germans. As far as the native fascists—the Ustachi or Croatian fascists—they are considered by the Partisans as beyond any rehabilitation and are usually shot. There are about 100,000, and they occasionally are too bestial even for the Germans, I was told.

Captured Chetniks (Serbian troops of Gen. Draja Mikhailovitch) are first offered the chance to join the Partisans. If they refuse they are sent back to their homes with instructions to stay there and behave themselves. The Partisans regard many of these Chetniks as simply poor, ignorant peasants who were drafted by Mikhailovitch and told they were fighting for the Allies. Most of them, I was told, are glad to escape from service under Mikhailovitch and from collaboration with the Germans, but some do return to their units after being released. One Chetnik was captured 11 different times. I asked why they didn't finally shoot him. "Don't be ridiculous," I was told. "We got 11 rifles from that man."

I asked Tito about the quality of the fascist opposition. He said the Germans were unpredictable, sometimes good, sometimes not so good. It depended largely on how much superiority they thought they had. They don't like to fight at night, and night fighting is right down the Partisan alley. Tito said the Ustachi were good fighters because they know they will be killed if they are caught. The Bulgarians were also good, he said; there is a Bulgarian corps fighting against the Partisans in eastern Yugoslavia, and they are fierce fighters. The Chetniks are not so hot, Tito added—there are only about 15,000 of them at this point, and they are dwindling rapidly. Unless bolstered by a strong supporting force of Germans or Ustachi, he said, they do not have much stomach for fighting.

WE talked about an hour, and then it was time to go. Olga, the girl interpreter, looked tired; everyone I met at headquarters looked tired, which seemed natural under the circumstances. I stood up to go, and Tito rose to shake hands again. He said he hoped the American people would finally learn the truth about Yugoslavia. We stood for a moment without talking, and then he said, half to himself:

"Our people will continue to fight against the invader, no matter who he is, whether German or Chetnik or Ustachi."

We shook hands, and I turned to go. I opened the door, and the young lieutenant moved into the room, holding the door open. It was very dark outside. The noise of the waterfall was suddenly loud, and the cool wet spray drifted lightly into the room. Marshal Tito was still standing behind his desk as I went out. He is not a tall man but he filled the room. Then the door closed.

(Next week's YANK will present Yugoslav Diary, Sgt. Bernstein's description of a week with the staff of an underground Partisan newspaper in a mountain village of Dalmatia, the section of Yugoslavia near the Adriatic coast mostly occupied by Germans.)

Paratroopers are tough guys who tell tough stories about themselves. This is one they tell in Britain. And who are we to doubt it?

By Sgt. ANDREW A. ROONEY
Britain

YEAH, them six holes up there is what the paratroopers left. Tough? They was plenty tough. Here six weeks before they pulled out.

One of 'em's name was Marcetti. Toughest guy I ever see. Damn, he was tough! Marcetti used to be a rigger in a steel mill at Pittsburgh, and when he come into the Army they made an engineer out of him. Sent him to Belvoir and taught him how to make bridges out of them little boats and how to dig. If there was anything Marcetti didn't want to know how to do, it was dig.

They kept him at Belvoir till they found out they'd got the wrong guy to teach digging to. He used to give half his month's pay to a guy named O'Hara to pull his KP for him, and the other half he'd spend on Scotch up to Washington. Hell of a guy he was; sergeants couldn't do nothing but put him in the guardhouse when he popped off. Too good a man for the guardhouse, Marcetti was, and them officers of his knew it.

After they had him about six months they decided they better get someone else to do their

Too Good for the GUARDHOUSE

engineering, so they sent him to Paratroop School where he'd been trying to get since they got him. It wasn't so much they let him go where he wanted but they sure'n hell didn't want him, and the Army just don't send nobody back to a Pittsburgh steel company.

Marcetti got hooked up with this rugged Paratroop outfit—one of the first. Hand-picked, them boys was, back in the days when you hadda be able to lick hell out of three marines before they'd let you in.

They wasn't having no more trouble with him like they was having at Belvoir. He didn't get drunk much, and he begin listening because he figured them babies in the paratroops knew more about stuff than he did. At Belvoir he'd always guessed he could dig as good a hole as the next man without a sergeant telling him how.

Well, hell, first thing you know this Marcetti gets to be the demolition expert of the outfit. Goes to demolition school and learns everything there is to know about blowing things up. Before long the outfit moves over here, and they're the babies that's going to drop right out of the ETO onto Jerry some day when he's still tryin' to figure out what day he's going to get dropped on.

Them six holes is a story. At night Marcetti, Hannock, Taragan and the rest would be sitting around here playing poker for what they had. Marcetti would get restless, and without saying much he'd get up and wander into that little room at the end he had to himself. He'd start taking down all them bottles of stuff he had on the wall.

Damn, he had a pile of the stuff. TNT, nitro, dynamite, everything. Had enough to blow this whole ETO to hell and gone. Under his sack Marcetti kept a hack saw, a bunch of them heavy English beer bottles and three pieces of pipe that run the length of his bed. He'd saw himself off a foot or so of pipe, then he'd come back out here and, talkin' natural all the time, he'd smash himself up about six or eight of them beer bottles in a bucket. He'd go back to his room with the bucket of glass, and pretty soon you'd hear that sound like coal running down a chute when he poured the glass into a hunk of pipe.

Marcetti'd come out of his room with his pipe in one hand and a fuse in the other. He'd sit down with the boys again for a while, talking just like he was knitting a sock as he put the fuse into the moxie he'd packed into that length of pipe.

When he was satisfied with the job he'd lean back in his chair, finish what he was talking about and then wander out. In five minutes he'd be back in his chair again, sitting there talking and smiling.

All of a sudden all hell would break loose. The whole damn hut would shake, and the rivets holding them corrugated-roof pieces together would snap off, a few of 'em. For 30 seconds you couldn't think what was happening for the noise of stones and dirt rattling down on the roof.

You shoulda seen the trees out here at the side. You can still see the scars on 'em. Big hunks of broken bottle stuck into them trees from all angles, and out in the field here they was a hole blown deep enough to bury a horse.

After looking around to see how Marcetti's concoction worked that time, the boys would go back to the hut and start playing cards again. In a few minutes this here meek little shavetail from the provost marshal's office would pull up in a jeep outside. He'd come every time, and I knew he hated to come in that hut worse'n anything in the world. It didn't bother Marcetti and this Paratroop outfit none. Nobody who wasn't a paratrooper bothered them guys none.

This second louey would knock on the door real light and then come into the hut. He'd stand there looking pretty helpless with a .45 on his hip and try to make the boys look up from the game by slamming the door. Hell, everybody that come in there slammed the door.

"Look, you fellows," he'd always say. "I asked you not to pull that stunt any more," he'd say. "Cut it out, will you?" he'd say, pleading. Hell, it was funny. There wasn't anything he could do because no one give a damn. They knew where they were headed for, and what anyone but their CO told them didn't carry no weight.

ONE day they brought some new boys in. Fellows up from an Infantry outfit. They'd been through a pretty rugged course, but they wasn't paratroopers. They'd got most of their training back in the States, and they was pretty cocky. Always showing these paratroopers how they learned it.

Things didn't go too well between 'em, and the CO decided something hadda be done. He gets Marcetti to fix up a bunch of tear-gas bombs under the sacks of a couple of these new joes. They was in here then, and Marcetti and his bunch was over in the bigger hut next door.

That night the Infantry boys come in after a speed march, pretty rugged they was, and a cou-

ple of 'em flops down on these sacks with t[...] tear gas underneath. Boy, you shoulda be[...] around. The bombs go off, and the hut starts fi[...] ing with gas. The boys think they've been [...] direct with HE.

They come hollering and screaming out of t[...] hut like wild Indians. Marcetti is over there [...] the next hut, not even watching—just laying [...] his bunk, looking up at the ceiling and smilin[...]

This new crowd finally catches on. They [...] pretty mad but take it good. Can't get back i[...] their hut, though. All their stuff is in there, a[...] a man can't go near the place for the gas.

This shavetail from the provost marshal's [...] fice comes along to find out what all the excit[...] ment's about. It's getting dark, and he begins [...] worry about the lights in the hut. Doors and wi[...] dows are wide open, and there'd been plenty [...] damn Germans around them nights.

Marcetti hears what's up and comes out of [...] hut. The louey looks at him pained and helpl[...] like. He knows damn well who set them tea[...] gas bombs off.

"Can I do anything for ya, lootenant?" Ma[...] cetti asks, real casual.

"Well," says the lootenant, "I gotta get th[...] lights out some way. If you'd put your gas ma[...] on and put them lights out I'd be much oblig[...] to ya, sergeant."

Marcetti disappears into his hut just like h[...] going in to get his mask like the lootenant sa[...]

Well, the funny thing is that Marcetti d[...] come out with his mask—last thing anyone e[...] pects to see him do. But on his hip he's strapp[...] his .45.

He flips his hat between his legs like [...] taught him at Belvoir and starts fixing the stra[...] on his gas mask. He gets his mask on, puts [...] hat on his head, waves at the louey and star[...] towards the hut. Marcetti is smiling sure as h[...] behind that mask, but you can't see it.

About 20 feet from the door of the hut he stop[...] pulls out his .45 and starts aiming. Everyon[...] expecting something from Marcetti but not th[...] He just plugs away six times at them ligh[...] hangin' there from the ceiling of the hut, knoc[...] 'em clear out and then calmly walks back t[...] wards the louey.

Marcetti pulls off his gas mask. "There y[...] are, sir," he says to the louey and walks ba[...] into his hut and lays down.

That's how them six holes got up there. Ma[...] cetti. Sorta sorry to see them paratroopers g[...] but damn! they was tough.

Merrill's Makeshift Artillery

By Sgt. DAVE RICHARDSON
YANK Staff Correspondent

BEHIND JAPANESE LINES IN NORTHERN BURMA— Jap artillery was pounding Merrill's Marauders again. Three weeks before, the enemy guns had sent shells whistling into Marauder positions facing the Walawbum garrison. Two weeks before, a Jap battery had ranged in on the Marauders during their attack on the enemy supply route at Inkangahtawng. One week before, a couple of rapid-fire guns had hammered the Marauders all night after their capture of a section of the Shaduzup-Kamaing road.

And now Jap artillery was concentrated on a unit of Marauders on Nhpum Ga hill. Another Marauder unit was driving through to relieve the outfit the Japs had surrounded.

As the 70-mm shell blasts reverberated through the jungles. Maj. Edwin J. Briggs of La Grande, Oreg., CO of the attacking unit, sent for a mule skinner and offered him a new job.

S/Sgt. John A. Acker, the mule skinner, was an ex-mineworker from Bessemer, Ala., who had shipped overseas a year before with a pack howitzer outfit. The outfit had gone to New Guinea. After sitting around for months without going into action, Acker and several others grew restless. When a call was made for animal-transportation men to join Merrill's Marauders, they volunteered. That was seven months before.

"Acker," said the major, "I understand you and some of the other mule drivers who used to be in the pack artillery would like to fire some howitzers back at these Japs. Is that right?"

The Alabaman said it was.

"Well, Acker," the major grinned, "this is an emergency. Two 75-mm pack howitzers will be parachuted to us tomorrow. Get two gun crews together and be ready to fire them."

Next day an expectant bunch of mule drivers stood on the airdrop field, watching brilliantly colored parachutes drift lazily down. When the parachutes hit the ground, the mule skinners became artillerymen again. They grabbed the dismantled howitzers and went to work assembling them. The guns were brand new and clean of cosmoline. Within two hours they were assembled, dug in on the airdrop field and firing.

A mile away the Marauder unit that was driving through Jap machine-gun positions along the trail to Nhpum Ga heard the shells whistle overhead. "What the hell is that?" one rifleman asked another. "Jap artillery behind us, too?" Then a radio message explained that it was Marauder artillery. Soon infantry-directed fire was blasting the strong points holding up the rifle platoon.

Two days later Acker and his impromptu artillery crews put their howitzers on mules and climbed the winding trail for three miles. They emplaced their guns on a ridge overlooking the Jap positions between the trapped Marauder unit on Nhpum Ga hill and the attacking unit. While the guns were being set up again T-4 Robert L. Carr of San Luis Obispo, Calif., started for the front as artillery observer with a walkie-talkie.

The point platoon had run smack up against one of the strongest Jap positions yet. This was a perimeter atop a little knoll from which Jap machine gunners commanded a clear field of fire for several hundred feet down the trail. The steep sides of the knoll made flanking difficult. It would have to be taken frontally. The point platoon asked for artillery and mortar support.

Carr, the observer, took his walkie-talkie up to the first squad. "Jap position approximately 700 yards from guns," he radioed, adding the azimuth. "Fire a smoke shell, and I'll zero you in."

The smoke shell whistled over, followed by a few more as Carr adjusted the firing data. Finally he okayed both range and azimuth. Lacking an

These mule skinners gave up their mules for a pack howitzer when Merrill's Marauders needed artillery.

The makeshift gun crew's chief: S/Sgt. Acker.

aiming circle, the only piece of equipment that was not dropped with the guns, Acker and his men were obliged to use an ordinary infantry compass to gauge azimuth.

The order came to fire five rounds. Up ahead all morning there had been constant mortar, machine-gun and small-arms fire. But as soon as the howitzers opened fire, Jap bullets began singing over the artillerymen's heads. All day the Japs reminded Acker's men that they were firing practically point-blank at 700 yards.

Just after the howitzers fired the five rounds, S/Sgt. Henry E. Hoot of Shepherd, Tex., radioman with the guns, shouted to Acker: "Holy smoke! Some Infantry officer is on the radio. He's excited as hell. Says you're right on the target. And—get this—he wants us to fire 'Battery 100 rounds'."

There's no such order in artillery parlance; actually the correct order for a lot of firing is "Fire at will." Acker chuckled at the order. "Okay, boys," he said. "Open those shell cases fast. Gun crews, prepare to fire at will."

In the next 15 minutes, the jungle hills rang as the two pack howitzers threw 134 shells into the Jap perimeter. The crews had been a bit slow two days before because they hadn't seen a howitzer in seven months, but now they performed as artillerymen should.

Up front the point platoon drove through. They found parts of Jap bodies in trees and all over the ground, virtually blown out of their holes. The dense jungle had become a clearing under the terrific blasting. A platoon leader going through the area, a few minutes after the barrage, discovered two shivering Japs deep in a foxhole, unhurt but moaning with fear. He killed them with a carbine. Apparently they were the only ones who had survived and stayed in the area. The platoon moved through unopposed.

For the next few days the artillery worked hand in hand with the point platoon in blasting other Jap positions. On one of these days Pvt. John W. (Red) Seegars of Kershaw, S. C., walked up to the guns with a broad smile. Seegars had been requested by Acker as No. 1 man on one of the howitzers, but because he was a rifleman and was needed in the drive, he had

not been sent back to the guns. Now Seegars was wounded in the left arm.

"As a rifleman I can't crawl with this arm wound," said Seegars, "so they sent me back to the aid station for evacuation. But I'm not going. I can still pull a howitzer lanyard with my right arm." Acker was glad to get him.

MEANWHILE Carr, the artillery observer, found things pretty hot at the front. On an advance with a rifle platoon, he was pinned down on the side of a hill by Jap machine guns and grenades at the top. Two men were wounded near him. He left the radio and dragged each of them back through the fire to an aid man. Returning to his radio, Carr egged the Japs into revealing their positions by throwing grenades, thus drawing fire on himself. Then he radioed the howitzers to shorten their range and swing their azimuth until the shells burst near a Jap heavy machine gun 30 yards away.

All this time, a Jap dual-purpose antiaircraft gun was throwing 70-mm shells into the midst of the trapped Marauder unit on Nhpum Ga hill. Acker got a liaison plane to spot the ack-ack gun's position. Then the howitzers fired on it all day. At dusk the Jap gun tried to fire back at the howitzers, but its trajectory was too flat to hit them. The shells either hit an intervening hill or whistled harmlessly high over the artillerymen's heads.

And that morning the Marauder attacking unit broke through to relieve the unit that had been cut off by the Japs for 10 days. Acker and his men, mule skinners no more, fired a salvo to celebrate.

Edda (she was named after Il Duce Mussolini's daughter) gives her version of the goose step. Ability to do this helps a donkey in stepping over puddles.

She hasn't learned to drive a weapons carrier yet, but give her time. Riding is easy.

BEFORE Sgt. Richard Wallen of Sioux City, Iowa, became a soldier, he was a trainer of performing horses. However, the GIs in his outfit in Italy didn't believe his story. Wallen bought himself a donkey for $10 (he couldn't find a horse) and trained her for almost a year. The skeptics were eventually convinced when they saw what you see on this page.

No tricks here, just a portrait of Edda and her ma[...] At that, getting two ears to stand up so is a [...]

Edda hasn't formed the smoking habit, but she sure likes a chaw of terbaccy. She's taken a cigarette out of Wallen's mouth and doesn't intend to return it.

A donkey with the intelligence of Edda thinks this sort of thing is downright si[...] But as long as they tied a handkerchief on her leg it's up to Edda to open the kn[...]

OAD IN ITALY

This phone system can be used simultaneously by three divers. A diver can talk to the man on deck any time, but Charles Jones MM2c must push switch to talk below.

Before descending some 45 feet under water, a diver puts on 188 pounds of equipment. In addition to being heavy, it's costly. This helmet is worth $650.

A diver's lead-soled shoes. Each weighs 17 pounds. An important item, for a misstep may turn him over.

Diver's knife, his only weapon, is used mostly to cut wire. Local fish aren't dangerous.

IN Africa, in Sicily and now in Italy, Navy divers have been busy with salvage work. They learned their trade in the North River, New York City. Many worked on the Normandie before shipping overseas to dive in more dangerous waters. Pictures were made by YANK's Sgt. John Frano, who also photographed the donkey on the opposite page.

Carrying a wrench, Antony LeBlanc CM1c goes down to fix a damaged LCT. The men who lend a guiding hand are James Schultz CM2c (left) and Tony Scionti CM1c.

This small craft, probably used as a tug, once rested smack on the bottom of an Italian harbor, but Navy salvage crew got it up into the light of day.

MAIL CALL

Army Postal Service

Dear YANK:
Recently you published a letter from Sgt. Al Forristol in your *Mail Call* column. It seems the writer was complaining of not having received mail for almost six months. He properly termed it a "crank letter," and little more need be said on the subject. However, since he is hitting the Army Postal Service decidedly below the belt line, I take it as a personal insult. The cases of people who do not receive mail for long periods are few and far between. In the majority, or about 99 percent, of such cases the man concerned is at fault, as he has failed to cooperate with the Army Postal Service. . . .
The Army Postal Service has a lot of work, and that volume is rapidly increasing. We don't claim to be supermen, and have no time to give personal service to screwballs. If the personnel we serve will just use a bit of common sense and cooperate with the various bulletins that are issued, I am sure that there would be fewer complaints. . . .

Egypt —Sgt. R. C. BUCKRUCKER

Dear YANK:
. . . We can assure Sgt. Forristol that there is no conspiracy to rob him of his precious mail. If his letters to the folks back home were written in the same vitriolic, bad-tempered and insulting tone, then what happened to his mail is no mystery. Who the hell would write to him?

Trinidad —Sgt. THERMAN A. TUCKER*

*Also signed by Sgt. Irving Caress, T-4s T. R. Kleinsasser and F. J. Eggen, Cpls. Clinton L. Clenny, Mead R. Johnson, C. M. Shorr and Nathan Finn and Pfc. K. V. Almirall.

Dear YANK:
After reading Sgt. Al Forristol's letter regarding the Army Postal Service we are inclined to believe that he was thinking only of himself when he mentioned fatheads and things that stink. If you can supply us with his complete address we will see that he gets at least one letter, anyhow, and we guarantee it won't have any lip prints on it, either. . . .

India —Army Postal Personnel

Dear YANK:
. . . We have all read the letter which was written to you from Sgt. Alfred Forristol, and since we find that he is at our station we want to put both him and you straight as to his particular case, also any others who might be complaining. We have tried to locate Sgt. Forristol personally, ever since his letter was published in your magazine, but it seems he has taken cover for some reason, and now we will try and show you why. Sgt. Forristol states that he has not received a letter from home since Sept. 26, 1943, and our records show that he has only been in the ETO for three months, also that this has been his only station since he arrived in the ETO.
We have talked to the unit mail clerks of his squadron, and they recall very distinctly of Sgt. Forristol receiving mail regularly ever since he has arrived at this station; also, at this very moment, we have at this post office 11 letters for this rookie of the ETO. . . .

Britain —T-4 CHARLES A. MILLER*

*Also signed by Cpl. John E. Barnhart and Pfc. Leon Rosen.

The Enemy

Dear YANK:
I have just seen the motion picture "Purple Heart," and I wish to voice some of my feeling about this picture. . . . Aside from certain technical errors, such as a lieutenant being described as a sergeant's "brother officer," the movie demonstrates the stupidity some producers inflict upon us. . . . When I see the Japs once again portrayed as comic-opera characters, thick-skulled and insanely egotistical, I am inclined to walk out. . . . I feel it is very poor psychology for us to be taught that Japs are insignificant little jerks, easily outwitted by any American.
I thought we had passed the stage of underestimating the intelligence of our enemy. As a soldier I would rather learn about the deadliness of the Japs' trickery and their inhuman ferocity. I have friends in the Army recovering from wounds inflicted by members of that "comic opera" race. . . .

Pine Camp, N. Y. —Pvt. ROBERT J. FOGARTY

Dear YANK:
I just finished reading an article [in a recent issue of YANK] and I'm very unhappy. Reason: on page 9 you quote a Russian soldier in this reference to a Nazi: "Babies, he said they were. 'Mama, Mama,' they cried." Are you trying to insult the common sense of the American soldier, or are you ridiculing the feats of the Red Army? This is the theme that has been followed not only by you but by many daily papers, the theme that the Nazis are either cowards or babies.
Is that actually what the American soldiers are up against—a lot of cowards? That's the impression we get, although plenty of us know very well that when we do engage the Germans, we'll not be meeting someone who will throw away his arms and run, crying "Mama, Mama." We'll be meeting soldiers who'll try to kill us. I know that after I have met a German and emerged victorious I certainly want it said that I whipped a damn good soldier and not a baby or a coward.

Camp Maxey, Tex. —S/Sgt. JAMES L. CONDON

Pin-ups

Dear YANK:
We boys do not approve of your very indecent portrayal of the spicy looking female in a recent edition of our much-loved and eagerly read YANK. It seems the intelligent-looking Irene Manning would never pose for such a suggestive-looking picture. We may seem old-fashioned, but sending YANK home to wives and sweethearts with such a seductive-looking picture, we feel compelled to make an apology for this issue.
Is this the much publicized "Pin-Up Girl" that the Yankee soldiers so crave? We have our doubts! Miss Manning is well dressed, but the pose—phew! (Hays office please take note.)
Believe it or not, our average age is 23.

Britain —Sgt. E. W. O'HARA*

*Also signed by Cpl. P. Pistocco Jr. and D. E. Clark.

Dear YANK:
I don't know who started this idea of pin-ups, but they say that it is supposed to help keep up the morale of the servicemen, or something like that. Here is my idea of the help it is. In the first place, I would say that 24 out of 25 of the men in the service are either married or have a girl at home whom they respect and intend to marry as soon as this war is over. . . . How many of you GIs would like to go home and find the room of your wife or girl friend covered with pictures of a guy stepping out of a bath-tub, draped only in a skimpy little towel, or see the walls covered with the pictures of a shorts advertisement or such pictures? None of you would. Then why keep a lot of junk hanging around and kid yourself about keeping up morale? . . .
I would much rather wake up in the morning and see a picture of a P-51 or 39 hanging above my bed or over the picture of my wife, whom I think is the best-looking girl in the world, than of some dame who has been kidded into or highly paid for posing for these pictures.

Myrtle Beach AAF, S. C. —Pfc. JOSEPH H. SALING

Dear YANK:
In two of your recent British editions you put the pin-up girls on the back of the maps. How the hell can you look at the maps and pin up the girls, too?

Britain —Pvt. LAWRENCE A. PETERSON

■ We were beginning to think you didn't care.

Kentucky Derby

Dear YANK:
In an April issue of YANK Sgt. Dan Polier made a little mistake in his Kentucky Derby story which I wish to correct. I'm not stating that Dan doesn't know the difference, but William Woodward's stable and Calumet Farms are two different stables. Woodward's stable is known as Belair Stud and the Calumet Farms are owned by Warren Wright.

Britain —Cpl. ROBERT B. GREGOR

■ Sgt. Polier erred on his stables, all right, but he did a little better on his horses. Back in October 1943 he said: "The Kentucky Derby is still a long way off, but you might paste the name of Ben Jones' colt Pensive in your helmet liner for future reference. He can fly around other horses just like Whirlaway used to do." P.S.—Pensive won the Derby.

Soldier Morals

Dear YANK:
We, the men of this detachment, have just finished reading in a recent issue of YANK the epic of one Pvt. Sir Stanton R. Gaylord, who deplores the state of national morality back home and says that servicemen have done most to cause delinquency among adolescent girls. This is of grave concern to us over here, because most of us have hopes of some day returning to marry some of these girls. Those righteous speeches of Gaylord's sound pretty good to the ear if that's as far as you allow them to go. As yet nothing in our career as soldiers, either in the states or in the 18 months we've been away, has led us to believe that any of those GI "crusaders" are shirking their duty in the seduction of our women. In other words, Gaylord, how much time elapsed between the writing of that classic and the time you arrived at the corner of Broadway and 42d Street in search of a teen-ager to take for a stroll through Central Park?

Iran —M/Sgt. KEN L. WALTERS*

*Also signed by T/Sgts. Ted A. Werling, Jeff J. Phillips and Paul R. Irons and S/Sgts. H. A. Reukapt, Julian Wolfe, Charles H. Rinaldi, Thomas E. Fite and Francis A. Bove and "sergeants, corporals and privates too numerous to mention."

Dear YANK:
. . . I wonder if Pvt. Gaylord ever went into town in an evening? By the tone of his letter I would think that he spends too much time reading books and not enough time getting some practical experience.

Camp Grant, Ill. —Pvt. WALLACE STOCKING

Boche Bomb

Dear YANK:
This is our first gripe in a long period of avid reading of your satisfying and usually authentic rag. However, the instant our eyes fell upon Sgt. Ralph Stein's illustration above the article on aircraft recognition by Sgt. Mack Morriss, we set up a long doleful wailing. As an Ordnance Bomb Disposal Unit, we consider ourselves experts on the missiles of all nations, so bend an ear and be enlightened. The bomb which threatens our hero in the half-track is supposed to be of German origin, judging from the Stuka which is in the upper right-hand corner. Unfortunately, German bombs do not use nose fuses in HE types of that size at all but employ electric fuses in a transverse pocket in the side. Also, German tail assemblies are of the four-vane type without struts of the design shown. The bomb in the cartoon is unmistakably American in shape and markings and is equipped with a British tail unit.

Britain —T/Sgt. ROBERT L. WRIGHT

■ Nice spotting, sergeant, but here's the way we look at it. American and British bombs are being shipped to Germany in quantity lots. Factories there aren't producing as many missiles as they used to. So, a little Nazi TNT, a British tail, an American casing—and *voilà*, a bastard bomb!

Message Center

Pfc. TONY (NINO) GALLETTA, Co. G, 27th Inf.: write Cpl. Marybelle Hauke, WAC Det., Bks. 4006, Aberdeen Prov. Gr., Md. . . . BUDDY or JAMES HERMANN of The Bronx, N. Y.: write Pvt. David J. Bussell, Co. B, 26th Tng. Bn., MPRTC, Fort Custer, Mich. . . . Lt. RUSSELL H. JOHNSON: write 1st Lt. W. W. Moore, 20th AAB Sq., Mountain Home, Idaho. . . . Cpl. H. M. KELLY, formerly of the "Fighting 38th": write Sgt. Helen L. Steffens, Finance Office, Fort Knox, Ky. . . . Sgt. PAUL KERMAN of the Airborne Inf.: write S/Sgt. Garrison Berman, Laboratory Service, Station Hospital, Fort Jay, N. Y. . . . Pvt. CHARLES DON LEGRAND of the USMC in Camp Elliott, Calif.: write Pfc. Frank McCoy, Co. F, 187th Inf., 11th Airborne Div., Camp Polk, La. . . . PAUL CALVIN MONTGOMERY of Pittsburgh, Pa., last heard of at Eglin Fld., Fla.: write Sgt. James B. McGarry, HBC Det., AAF, Ardmore, Okla. . . . Sgt. JAMES H. NEELAN, once at Dalhart, Tex.: write Sgt. A. J. Berwick, Prison Office, Post Stockade, No. Camp Hood, Tex. . . . Pvt. GEORGE NELSON, last heard of in the Hawaiian Islands: write Cpl. Warren Northridge, Co. F, 116th Cav. Rcn. Sq., Carolina Beach, N. C. . . . Pvt. JOHN LESTER OLSEN, once with Co. I, 39th Div.: write T-5 James P. Henchan, Service Co., 114th Inf., APO 44, c/o PM, Shreveport, La. . . . Anyone having any information about 2d Lt. ROBERT F. PURDY's last flight from base in England: write Cpl. Gordon B. Purdy, Hq. Co. 692 TD Bn., Camp Campbell, Ky. . . . S/Sgt. EARL W. RICHMOND, last heard of in Air Corps at Wheeler Fld.: write T/Sgt. D. E. Strawder, Station Hosp., Ward 5, DAAF, Deming, N. Mex. . . . S/Sgt. RAYMOND RITCHIE: write Pvt. Larry Margolis, 1st Hq., 414th Inf., APO 104, Camp Carson, Colo. . . . Lt. HAROLD (DUTCH) ROBINSON, formerly with Btry. B, 52d CA, N. J.: write Cpl. S. Drexler, Btry. B, 286th CA, Fort Custer, Va. . . . T/Sgt. CHARLES TERRACCIO, formerly with the 47th & 44th Ftr. Sq.: write S/Sgt. Cecil Meadows, Sq. A (Prov), AAFRS #1, Atlantic City, N. J. . . . Pfc. MIKE URLETTI, formerly at Camp Breckinridge: write Pfc. Robert J. Orr, Med. Det., WAAF, Waco, Tex. . . . Pvt. LEONARD J. VOS, formerly in Co. L, 168th Inf.: or anyone having information about him: write Pfc. Isburne C. Ash, Hq. & Serv. Co., Fort Knox, Ky. . . . Capt. JAMES P. WALTON, formerly at Camp Roberts, Calif.: write Pvt. Garenette M. Tillitski, Co. 17, 3d Regt., Fort Des Moines, Iowa. . . . Pvt. ROBERT M. YOUNG, once at Camp Luna, N. Mex.: write Sgt. Ernest R. Hansen, c/o Base Tech. Mapertors Office, AAB, Rapid City, S. Dak. . . . M/Sgt. ANTHONY S. ZALENSKI, Hq. Co., 114th Engrs.: write your brother, Cpl. Walter B. Zalenski, 452d SPTS, Hendricks Fld., Fla.

SHOULDER PATCH EXCHANGE. A list of shoulder-patch collectors' names will be sent to you if you write *Shoulder Patch Exchange*, YANK, 205 East 42d Street, New York 17, N. Y. Specify whether you want your name added to the list.

GI Art

TWO soldier-artists attached to the U. S. Army Historical Section in the Middle East, T Sgt. James D. Brooks and T Sgt. Richard H. Jansen, covered plenty of territory in that theater to get material for these paintings. Brooks, the same artist who painted the murals at LaGuardia Field, New York, in civilian life, followed the airfields across the desert to North Africa, while Jansen, a well-known industrial artist whose work used to appear in *Fortune* magazine, traveled by foot, donkey, truck and third-class railway carriages through Iran and the Persian Gulf.

Jansen's "Street Scene in Ahwaz" shows a town in Iran on supply route to Russia.

Jansen's painting "Persian Gulf" depicts a typical scene in an Iranian port where American service forces sweat out the unloading of our Liberty ships.

Brooks calls this North African painting "Dead Birds." The wrecked Nazi planes were shot down by the British during the 1943 drive into Tunisia.

This painting by Brooks shows the crew of a Liberty ship eating dinner, using a hatch cover as a table.

The long-distance perspective in this unusual Brooks painting gives it a strange feeling. A fighter pilot is walking across the desert from his burning plane.

THE SAD SACK

SGT. GEORGE BAKER

TELL IT TO THE CHAPLAIN

By Cpl. GRANT ROBBINS
China

"LOOK," said the first sergeant. "Why don't you just tell it to the chaplain?"

I gave him the look I'd give to a two-headed thing pickled in a bottle, then I turned and walked out. When one has been in the Army for two years, at home and abroad, he becomes a little tired of the so-called GI slang, the oft-repeated phrase picked up in boot camp by a stunned civilian mind and dropped immediately thereafter—unless the mind remains stunned, as in the case of 1st Sgt. Stein.

I had gone into the orderly room because my name was not on a new rating list. My sad story has such a long background of pyramided woes that I shall not go into it more than to say that only a good heart-to-heart talk with someone would straighten me out.

All right, I decided, I *would* see the chaplain.

Of course that interview required considerable preparation, like finding out which chaplain in camp had the highest rank, investigating the CO's religion and memorizing a few chosen texts from my Gideon Bible. It doesn't hurt to talk their language.

The following day I stood before the door of a captain of religion. I was dressed neatly in patched fatigues to give the impression of a poor but honest homespun GI.

"Hello," he said, eying me suspiciously as I closed in on his desk. "Have a cigarette." That wasn't on the schedule, but I sprung a text on him anyway.

"Chaplain," I began, "I was greatly inspired by the sermon you gave on the parable of the loaves and fishes at No. 4 mess hall last Sunday at 2 P. M. Right now I am badly in need of a rod and a staff to comfort me, and I hoped that you might show me how to find a place beside the still waters."

The chaplain winced.

"What have they done to you now?" he asked. "And kindly make it short."

I sat down and let him have it straight. I went back to the very first—the double stretch of infantry training; the misassignment to mechanics school; the lost records and the three solid months of KP; the transfer to an outfit that

didn't need men of any classification but guard; all ratings filled by men ahead of me; no furlough; one small stripe thrown to me like a bone to a starving dog, then held in that rank for eight long hideous months. When the torrent had subsided I sat back and searched the face of the chaplain for a reaction. He gazed at his feet and shook his head slowly.

"I just can't understand the Army," he said. "Now, take me for example. You may think that I am doing pretty well, but I'll tell you appearances are deceiving. After five country churches with an average salary of $10 a week, I finally get settled in a good town with a good congregation. And then, of course, I leave it to become a chaplain. Where do they put me first thing? Out on a sand-blown camp in the desert with a tent to preach in and a bunch of tank men who have no more inclination toward religion than an equal number of Hottentots. Then the wind blows the tent away."

I said that that was too bad.

"That was only the beginning," he continued. "Shortly after I experienced a slight success in bringing some of the boys into the fold, they put another chaplain over me."

He went on and on, from one misfortune to another, and as his story developed one could easily see that he and Fate were at odds, and that it was getting to be too much for him. Tears began to trickle down his cheeks and splash on the bars on his collar.

Since passes were issued now only on Sunday his congregation had suffered a heart-breaking drop in attendance. And he had been ousted from his warm office to make room for the Red Cross. When he protested to the commanding general he was mistaken for a mess officer and installed in a cubbyhole just off the mess kitchen, where from 0600 to 2100 came a heavy odor of frying Spam.

"And to top it all," he said, "I have not received a promotion in 18 months."

I couldn't stand it any longer. I reached across the table, patted him on the shoulder and said, "Keep your chin up, sir. I'm sure things will work out in the long run."

He smiled miserably and thanked me. I tiptoed quietly out the door, leaving him in the throes of his grief.

We Thought You'd Like To Know

You probably read in YANK a few months ago a story about the people in Lane County, Oreg., who have already tackled the problem of making post-war jobs for the servicemen from their towns. We published a detailed report on their plan because it was one of the few post-war job projects we had heard about that was short on sweet talk and long on down-to-earth action.

In a few words, the Lane County Plan provided for public and private work projects designed by a council of 60-odd citizens representing all sections and interests of Oregon's vast Willamette Valley. The people in the county started the plan strictly on their own, aiming to take care of their own boys and girls after the war with their own money and their own enterprise, asking no help from the state or Federal governments. They realized, like most Americans, that their men and women in the armed forces might have a hard time finding jobs when they returned to civilian life but, unlike most Americans, they decided to roll up their sleeves and do something about it immediately.

When YANK described the Lane County Plan and advised its readers to send the story home, a lot of them did just that. A lot of others wrote to us and to people in Lane County wishing the plan the best of luck.

Well, we have just received some additional news about the Lane County Plan from William M. Tugman, managing editor of the Eugene (Oreg.) Register-Guard and one of the plan's original backers. We thought you'd like to know about it. Tugman says:

"Eugene and Lane County have made good on all cash financing for our post-war public projects. County road levies for $500,000 and city levies for $450,000 were adopted recently by a better-than-two-to-one margin with very heavy voting. The cities of Eugene and Springfield will have $4,000,000 to spend on public work projects to make jobs for ex-servicemen and women when the war ends. This leaves the planning council free now to devote all its attention to the creation of private jobs and special projects. We have registered all the Lane County men and women who are in the armed forces, and personal letters have gone out to each one of them concerning their post-war prospects."

This shows what you can do with a tough problem if you have the courage and energy to stand up and face it yourself.

Pass the word back to your home town about the progress Lane

"Poor Heinrich is a nervous wreck. He's just back from a furlough in Berlin."

County has made in its independent drive to make its own jobs for its own servicemen and women. It is about time that other American communities stopped wondering about the post-war world and started to do something on their own to make it a good one.

AAF Score

THE AAF, in operations in all theaters from our entrance in the war through May 15, 1944, destroyed 16,510 enemy planes in aerial combat, probably destroyed 4,650 and damaged 5,546. On the ground the AAF destroyed 3,664 enemy planes, probably destroyed 347 and damaged 432. AAF losses from enemy action totaled 718 combat planes in the air, 236 combat planes on the ground and about 200 noncombat planes. During this period the AAF flew 746,353 sorties and dropped 468,391 tons of bombs.

During the first four months of this year Army Air Forces operating in the Pacific and Asia sank 320,489 tons of Japanese shipping. Tonnage reports by months show a total of 70,160 for January, 159,704 for February, 38,450 for March and 52,175 for April.

Overseas Physicals

Enlisted men with any of the following defects will not be sent overseas, according to WD Cir. No. 164: 1) Pronounced psychiatric disorders, except mild and temporary psychoneuroses; 2) hernia, except small incisional or umbilical; 3) Class I dental defects, unless they can be remedied with false teeth or unless the teeth are not essential; 4) loss of an eye, whether or not the EM has an artificial eye; 5) recurrence or after-effects of tropical diseases which are liable to serious aggravation if reinfected. This last does not include uncomplicated malaria, but EM who have or have had malaria or in whose blood malarial parasites are found will not be sent overseas until six months after recovery or the disappearance of the parasites from the blood.

Combat Jacket

The new field jacket soon to be issued to Yanks in the European Theater of Operations is patterned after the British battle dress and can be used for dress wear as well as for combat. It is made of 18-ounce wool serge in the dark olive-drab shade and lined with Albert twill. The collar is convertible and may be turned up tight about the neck, the shoulder pads are of washable construction and the sleeves have adjustable closures like shirt sleeves. The waist is adjustable by means of side buckles and tabs. The jacket has two outside breast pockets with flaps and two inside breast pockets. It may be worn with regular wool serge trousers or wool field trousers and is especially designed so that it can be worn over a high-necked sweater and under the new M1943 cotton field jacket. The initial procurement of the jacket calls for almost 4,000,000 garments, and the QMC has asked the cooperation of the manufacturers in filling the demand quickly.

Washington O P

SOME common misunderstanding about Army psychoneurotic cases have been cleared up by Maj. Gen. Norman T. Kirk, surgeon general, and Col. William C. Menninger, chief of the Neuropsychiatry Division. Such cases are neither crazy nor goldbricks, according to Col. Menninger. He pointed out that "everyone exhibits mild psychoneurotic reactions in certain situations" and that "every individual has his breaking point." "The greater proportion of psychoneurotic cases in the Army," he said, "is more apparent than real." He revealed that 30 to 40 percent of battle psychoneuroses are salvaged and returned to duty within 48 hours, and that another 40 percent can be salvaged at evacuation hospitals through personal consultation with the hospital psychiatrists. Of those returned to the United States, "many men who a year ago would have been discharged as unfit for duty are being placed in retraining units and trained again to fill specific Army jobs which they are able to perform." Of those who cannot be salvaged for military service, "most . . . will find little difficulty in readjusting themselves to civilian life, for which they are by no means unfitted."

Only half the boys in the last two years of high school are taking physical education, according to the Office of Education. One reason is lack of instructors. At the same time, Maj. Gen. Lewis B. Hershey, director of Selective Service, is urging that the youth of the country be given at least one year of training to fit it for military service. The number of men declared unfit for service in this war is as large as all our armed forces in the last war, he said. —YANK Washington Bureau

---

YANK is published weekly by the enlisted men of the U. S. Army and is for sale only to those in the armed services. Stories, features, pictures and other material from YANK may be reproduced if they are not restricted by law or military regulations, provided proper credit is given, release dates are observed and specific prior permission has been granted for each item to be reproduced. Entire contents copyrighted, 1944, by Col. Franklin S. Forsberg and reviewed by U. S. military censors.

MAIN EDITORIAL OFFICE
205 EAST 42d ST., NEW YORK 17, N. Y., U. S. A.

EDITORIAL STAFF
Managing Editor, Sgt. Joe McCarthy, FA; Art Director, Sgt. Arthur Weithas, DEML; Assistant Managing Editor, Sgt. Justus Schlotzhauer, Inf.; Assistant Art Director, Sgt. Ralph Stein, Med.; Pictures, Sgt. Leo Hofeller, Armd.; Features, Sgt. Harry Sions, AAF; Sports, Sgt. Dan Polier, AAF; Overseas News, Sgt. Allan Ecker, AAF.
Washington: Sgt. Earl Anderson, AAF; Cpl. Richard Paul, DEML. London: Sgt. Durbin Horner, QMC; Sgt. Walter Peters, QMC; Sgt. John Scott, AAF; Sgt. Charles Brand, AAF; Sgt. Bill Davidson, Inf.; Sgt. Sanderson Vanderbilt, CA; Sgt. Peter Paris, Engr.; Cpl. Jack Coggins, CA; Cpl. John Preston, AAF; Sgt. Saul Levitt, AAF; Cpl. Edmund Antrobus, Inf.; Cpl. Joseph Cunningham; Pvt. Ben Frazier. Italy: Sgt. George Aarons, Sig. Corps; Sgt. Burgess Scott, Inf.; Sgt. Burtt Evans, Inf.; Sgt. John Frano, Inf. Cairo: Sgt. J. Denton Scott, FA; Sgt. Steven Derry, DEML; Sgt. Walter Bernstein, Inf.

Iraq-Iran: Sgt. Al Hine, Engr.; Cpl. James O'Neill, QMC; Cpl. Richard Gaige, DEML. China-Burma-India: Sgt. Dave Richardson, CA; Sgt. Lou Stoumen, DEML; Sgt. Seymour Friedman, Sig. Corps. Southwest Pacific: Sgt. Lafayette Locke, AAF; Sgt. Douglas Borgstedt, DEML; Cpl. Ozzie St. George, Inf.; Sgt. Dick Hanley, AAF; Sgt. Charles Pearson, Engr.; Cpl. Ralph Boyce, AAF; Cpl. Bill Alcine, Sig. Corps; Cpl. Charles Rathe, DEML; Cpl. George Bick, Inf.; Pfc. John McLeod, Med.; Sgt. Marvin Fasig, Engr. South Pacific: Sgt. Barrett McGurn, Med.; Sgt. Dillon Ferris, AAF;

Sgt. Robert Greenhalgh, Inf.
Hawaii: Sgt. James L. McManus, CA; Cpl. Richard J. Nihill, CA; Sgt. Bill Reed, Inf.
Alaska: Sgt. Georg N. Meyers, AAF; Cpl. John Haverstick, CA.
Panama: Sgt. Robert G. Ryan, Inf.; Sgt. John Hay, Inf.; Sgt. William T. Potter, DEML.
Puerto Rico: Cpl. Bill Haworth, DEML; Cpl. Jud Cook, DEML.
Trinidad: Pfc. James Iorio, MP.
Bermuda: Cpl. William Pene du Bois.
Ascension Island: Pfc. Nat Bodian, AAF.
British Guiana: Sgt. Bernard Freman, AAF.
Central Africa: Sgt. Kenneth Abbott, AAF.
Iceland: Sgt. Joseph Koren.
Newfoundland: Sgt. Frank Bode, Sig. Corps.
Greenland: Sgt. Robert Kelly, Sig. Corps.
Navy: Robert L. Schwartz Y2c; Allen Churchill Sp(x)3c.

Commanding Officer: Col. Franklin S. Forsberg.
Executive Officer: Maj. Jack W. Weeks.
Business Manager: Maj. Harold B. Hawley.
Overseas Bureau Officers: London, Maj. Donald W. Reynolds; India, Maj. Gerald J. Rock; Australia, Capt. J. N. Bigbee; Italy, Maj. Robert Strother; Hawaii, Maj. Josua Eppinger; Cairo, Maj. Charles Holt; Carribbean, Capt. Walter E. Hussman; Iran, Maj. Henry E. Johnson; South Pacific, Capt. Justus J. Craemer; Alaska, 1st Lt. Harry R. Roberts.

Betty Smith wrote "A Tree Grows in Brooklyn," so husband Pfc. Joe Jones tried his hand with a book, too.

Fort Monroe, Va.—Pfc. Joe Jones, whose wif[e] the former Betty Smith, wrote the year's be[st] seller. "A Tree Grows in Brooklyn," made h[is] own first appearance as a published author whe[n] Harpers released "1-B Soldier," the story [of] Jones' first year in the Army.

Pfc. Jones, now on duty in the PRO here, cam[e] into service on his 36th birthday, going from [a] desk on the Chapel Hill (N. C.) *Weekly* to a C[A] training battery. Like Sgt. Marion Hargrov[e,] Jones told of his experiences in a weekly colum[n] for his old paper, and the book is a compilatio[n]

Jones Joins Smith in P[rint]

of those columns. The background for his exper[i]ences is set at Fort Monroe, the Little Cree[k] Mine Base and Fort Story, Va.

Jones. spent his first year in the service with[out] out getting out of Virginia, but the CA unwi[t]tingly helped him with his story by a quick su[c]cession of transfers back and forth between th[e] three camps and with a variety of duties rangin[g] from the Army's version of stevedoring to se[v]eral types of desk jobs.

A native of Berryville, Va., Jones attended th[e] University of North Carolina and worked on th[e] Chapel Hill *Weekly* for a number of years. A[t] one time he was a waiter, moving with th[e] weather between Lake Placid, N. Y., and Lak[e] Placid, Fla. Since coming here, Jones has bee[n] joined by his wife.

Furlough Bank

Camp Chaffee, Ark.—A company banking ide[a] has earned T-5 Edward Jordan the nicknam[e] of "Thrift Corporal" and has put him in rathe[r] solid with GIs who, because of Jordan's ban[k,] experience no lack of cash when furlough tim[e] rolls around.

Jordan is no money lender, however. What[ever] ever dough is in the kitty for those furloughin[g] GIs is merely the result of their own saving[,] inspired and aided by the facilities which Jorda[n] provides.

Each pay day finds Jordan at a table near th[e] pay-off, so that members of the 561st Ordnanc[e] HM Co. (Tank) can make it the first stop if the[y] want to. They can deposit any amount into th[e] company bank and are given a bank book wit[h] the amount recorded. From there on it's just lik[e] any no-minimum-balance checking account, ex[-] cept that checks may be cashed only by Jorda[n;] they are not negotiable elsewhere. The record[s] show that 80 percent of the men use the bank.

There's nothing in it for Jordan except th[e] work, but he takes pride in the feeling that h[e]

Overseas Vet Hero of Storm Rescue

Camp Fannin, Tex.—Cpl. Clyde H. Banzhof of Lancaster, Pa., who was with the   Inf. on Guadalcanal, was credited recently with quick, heroic action in saving the life of Lt. Charles J. Barrow of Swarthmore, Pa., executive officer of A-82d, 15th Regt., IRTC.

Banzhof, who has already earned a promotion for that feat, was also commended for directing rescue operations when a freak windstorm pinned several platoons of IRTC trainees in a wooded area and left them to the mercy of falling trees.

Two men suffered fatal injuries in the storm, and 11 were hurt, one of them seriously. The storm felled more than 30 trees in the woods near Kernal's Lake, where the soldiers were part of a group returning in a file of twos from a scouting and night-patrol problem.

When the twister struck, the head of the column had just turned around and was moving out of the woods. It was very dark, and the rain was falling in blinding sheets. The column had taken about five steps when Cpl. Banzhof suddenly tackled Lt. Barrow, throwing him heavily to the wet, soggy earth. Just 18 inches away a tree measuring at least 20 inches in girth came hurtling down, pinning nine trainees to the ground. Pvt. James Cox Jr. of Ector, Tex., received fatal injuries in this accident and died at the station hospital the following morning. Pvt. Richard Somers of Raleigh, N. C., sustained a serious spine fracture. The other seven victims were hospitalized with injuries of a lesser degree.

In another part of the woods, similar operations were going on under the direction of Sgt. Otho B. Upchurch of Dahlgren, Ill., and Cpl. Gerauld Collier of Brookfield, Mo. Collier himself had a close call when falling branches from one tree knocked off his helmet and staggered him. The same tree was responsible for fatal injuries to Pvt. Clayton Matlock of Baldwin Park, Calif., who died on the way to the hospital.

Trainees behind Upchurch and Collier were themselves pinned down by a second tree when they went to help the other men. Pvt. Robert R. Samuel of Hood River, Oreg., suffered a mild concussion and a fractured leg. Pvt. Orville E. Lake of Omaha, Nebr., sustained concussion, cuts and bruises and a compound fracture of one finger.

The first ambulance to arrive on the scene crossed the flooded lake area on top of a dirt dam, over which water was beginning to flow. The spillways on the sides were so flooded that trainees, carrying Pvt. Matlock on an improvised stretcher of rifles and a GI blanket, were forced to wade knee deep in water to reach the ambulance.
—S/Sgt. WILLIAM BANCROFT

Lt. Barrow surveys tree which just missed him.

camp new[s]

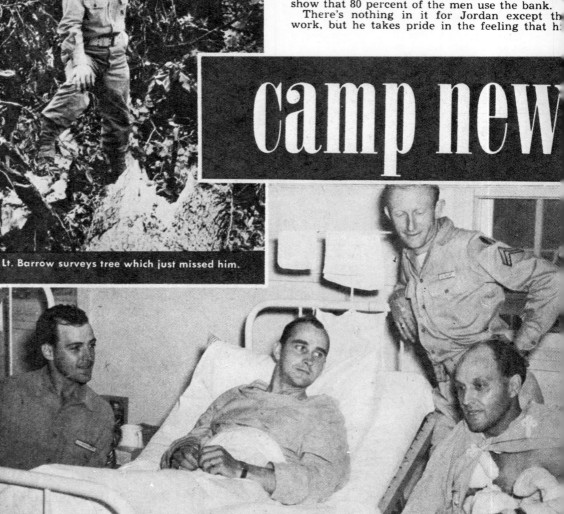

Two 15th Regiment heroes of the freakish windstorm rehash the episode with two of the 19 victims. Left [to] right, they are: Sgt. Otho B. Upchurch, Pvt. Robert Samuel, Cpl. Gerauld Collier and Pvt. Orville E. La[ke.]

idea has encouraged saving and has made it unnecessary for many of his buddies to borrow to defray furlough expenses. In six months of operation, the bank has accepted 487 deposits for a total of nearly $20,000. On 497 checks, withdrawals have amounted to $16,721, of which, Jordan says, more than half has been used to finance furloughs. —T-4 CHARLES CABANA Jr.

Somebody'll Make It

Harding Field, La.—In response to an invitation by the Wacs to attend their anniversary party, 1st Sgt. Russell O. Stevens of Section A, 263d AAF Base Unit, sent the following formal reply to the first sergeant of the WAC detachment:

Section A will be represented in force with the following exceptions: *a*) men in the hospital; *b*) men absent without leave; *c*) men with jealous wives; *d*) men with jealous girl friends; *e*) men working that night; *f*) men on furlough; *g*) men with dates already arranged; *h*) men recovering from Saturday night; *i*) men recovering from Sunday night; *j*) men who don't want to wake up Tuesday morning recovering from Monday night; *k*) men who have no clean pants because 1) same are in laundry, 2) same are not in laundry; *l*) men pulling CG here and there; *m*) men who intend to attend but get lost on the way. —Pfc. MAXINE GARRARD

Dog Dyers, Sound Off

Camp Beale, Calif.—S/Sgt. Thomas H. Sauls of the Service Btry., FA Bn., is confronted with a problem because of Jiggs II, the battalion mascot. Jiggs has passed his overseas physical, has had most of his shots and is all set to go but for one thing—his color.

Jiggs is a white bulldog and, it seems, white dogs are frowned on at the port of embarkation. The only solution, Sgt. Sauls says, is to dye Jiggs a nice neutral OD color.

But, the sergeant wants to know, how do you dye a dog?

No Greater Love

Columbus Army Air Field, Miss.—M/Sgt. Marshal B. Stacey, NCOIC, Inst. Tng. Dept., got a long-distance call from Chicago. The party on the other end was S/Sgt. Walter J. Zapala, who wanted Stacey to do him a favor.

"Not over five bucks, I won't," replied Stacey. "I don't need any dough," said Zapala. "What I want you to do is to assign a couple of guys for latrine orderly Saturday—I forgot to do it before I left."

The call cost $2.50.

A Red Ribbon for Oscar

Camp Haan, Calif.—Pvt. Merle R. Johnson of B Btry., 330th Bn., approached the hostess at Service Club No. 1 and asked for a red ribbon.

"I'll have to look," the hostess said. "What's it for?"

"It's for Oscar," Pvt. Johnson said, reddening.

"Who's Oscar?" asked the hostess.

"Well, if you must know," said Johnson, reaching into his back pocket, "this is Oscar." He pulled out a three-foot gopher snake, very much alive and wriggling.

AROUND THE CAMPS

Camp Polk, La.—When the winner of the manual-of-arms competition among GIs of the 49th Armd. Inf. Bn., 8th Arm. Div., was announced, there were a few red faces scattered throughout the battalion. The winner was Pvt. William L. Arnold who a few weeks before had been transferred to the battalion from an ASTP outfit at the University of Illinois and had had only a three weeks' refresher training here. Arnold credited his squad sergeant for his own proficiency with the M1 rifle.

Kearney Army Air Base, Nebr.—Pvt. Nina P. Morris was featured by the post paper, the *Duster*, as the field's favorite Mother's Day Air-Wac. When her Wac friends went to congratulate her, Pvt. Morris was not to be found until the Wacs went to the mess hall for coffee. There was the favorite mother of the day doing KP.

San Diego Barracks, Calif.—M/Sgt. Raymond C. Morgan, Marine Corps mess sergeant, claims he hasn't received a letter from anyone since November 1933. What he got then was a letter from the Southern California Telephone Company, enclosing a nickel refund for a wrong number.

Stuttgart Army Air Field, Ark.—Pvt. Flavius Long was sent into town to bring back a mule to help him with the victory garden at the station hospital. The mule, named George, had never seen an Army truck before and refused to ride in it. He also refused to let Pvt. Long ride him. There was only one way left, and Pvt. Long took it. He walked George the eight long miles back to the base.

Camp Adair, Oreg.—T-4 George Nikolai has this to say about shaving: "When the weather's cold, I hate to shave in ice water. And when the weather's hot, I'd rather drink the water than shave in it." So Sgt. Nikolai has rigged himself a battery-operated power plant to go with his electric razor. Now he has no trouble keeping himself comfortably clean-shaven without gripes from GIs who claim an electric razor causes interference with radio reception.

Lake Charles Army Air Field, La.—Cpl. J. E. Clark, armorer-gunner of Class 336-22, was credited with a real record. He was the first enlisted man to complete the RTU Ground School with grades of 100 in each of his subjects.

Sioux Falls Army Air Field, S. Dak.—It may not be a record, but Pvt. Mae M. Houston of Burlington, Iowa, a member of the station hospital's staff, has six sons, a daughter and three grandchildren. Four of her sons are in the Navy; one will soon be in the Marines.

Camp Roberts, Calif.—When Pvt. Edgar A. Lawson of Co. B, 85th Inf. Tng. Bn., presented his rifle to the inspecting officer, it was returned without comment. Pvt. John Conley of the second squad, who hadn't tried to do much with his rifle, waited until the officer was at the other end of the line and then exchanged rifles with Lawson. When the officer reached Conley and inspected the rifle, it failed to pass, and Conley was gigged. Later the private learned that the officer had spotted the exchange.

TWIN GABRIELS. Albert and Anthony Mazucca 19, of Tacoma, Wash. give out twin hot licks on their "licorice sticks" in the band at Buckley Field, Colo.

NEAT STACK. Cpl. Darline Long stacks up pretty well herself alongside load of paper gathered in waste-paper salvage drive at Camp Lejeune, N. C.

LEG POWER. Nothing wrong with T-5 Carl Cathey's legs even if he's limited service (punctured eardrum). At Camp Gordon Johnston, Fla., he lifts a jeep.

FATHER TO SON. M/Sgt. John R. Dawdy, 19 years in the Army, pins flying officer's wings on his son, Lt. C. G. Dawdy on graduation day at Columbus AAF, Miss.

Cheryl Walker
YANK
Pin-up Girl

THE DRUMS

[S]ome future year, while man still plays at war,
[A]nd frightened moons float sickly through the
   skies,
[A]ll pale with flame and death—a Man will rise
[U]pon the earth, where once He stood before,
[A]nd raise His voice. And men will stare at crags
[A]nd stumps and shattered city walls and say:
"What have we done? Some dynamiting day
[W]ill fling us, too, among the bloody rags
[O]f sky we've pulled down, fighting to be free!"
[B]ut loud the urgent drums renew the beat
[T]o drown the gentle voice, and man's poor feet,
[A]s if in magic shoes, dance off in glee
[A]nd waltz him to an Armageddon's blast—
[N]ot the first, nor the second, nor the last!

[Ca]mp Butner, N. C.   —Sgt. HAROLD APPLEBAUM

ALEUTIAN LAMENT

We've all got paper dollies;
   They're pinned on every wall,
From a pistol-packin' mama
   To luscious Lucille Ball.

We always find 'em waiting,
   True as any pearl,
But we'd trade our paper dollies
   For a fickle-minded girl.

They've got no animation
   Though posed to hypnotize,
Displaying dainty breastwork,
   Hips and knees and thighs.

We never have a worry
   About 'em doing wrong,
They're only paper dollies,
   Like that one in the song.

We're getting out of practice
   At winking flirty eyes;
We need some real live dollies
   To make us flirty guys.

But we pin 'em up as often
   As we find a shapely lass,
And cuss the Frank Sinatras
   Enjoying all that class.

We'd take our chance on losing
   A dolly that was real:
A blonde, brunette or redhead
   Would have the same appeal.

We are no longer choosy—
   For a short one, fat or long,
We'd trade our paper dollies
   To the guy who wrote the song.

[Th]e Aleutians   —Cpl. JAMES R. GARDNER

The POETS CORNERED

HAPPINESS

Great is the price for happiness:
Yet would I pay the price
A dozen times. I would not once
Consider any cost too great,
For I have tasted happiness
Course through my veins
And stimulate each nerve.
Yet must I flinch before the payment
Of its price; yet I must tremble
Underneath its burden-weight.
I would for freedom's sake
Cheat in its payment where I might;
The evil in my mind would have it so.
But I am seen by eyes
That ever see me as I am. How can I
Cheat and not forever lose the right
To purchase happiness?
There is a light in which I see
The price of happiness is not too great
For me—
Unless I play the coward's part,
And that shall never be!

India   —Sgt. CARLYLE A. OBERLE

OBITUARY

Under a friendly tavern spigot
Lay out my grave and write my ticket.
My life was raw but always cricket
And Bacchus my partner and guide.

This be the verse that you grave for me:
"Here lies a GI where he longs to be
With a flask on his hip and a blonde on his knee
And a quart of shellac in his hide."

Camp Gordon Johnston, Fla.

                                —S/Sgt. FRANKLIN M. WILLMENT

Battle Hymn of the Republic

*Mine eyes have seen the glory of the coming
   of the Lord
He is trampling out the vintage where the
   grapes of wrath are stored;
He hath loosed the fateful lightning of his
   terrible swift sword.
      His truth is marching on.*

*I have seen him in the watch-fires of a
   hundred circling camps;
They have builded him an altar in the
   evening dews and damps;
I can read his righteous sentence by the
   dim and flaring lamps.
      His day is marching on.*

*I have read a fiery gospel, writ in burnished
   rows of steel:
"As ye deal with my contemners, so with
   you my grace shall deal;
Let the Hero, born of woman, crush the
   serpent with his heel,
      Since God is marching on."*

*He has sounded forth the trumpet that shall
   never call retreat;
He is sifting out the hearts of men before
   his judgment seat;
O, be swift, my soul, to answer him! be
   jubilant my feet!
      Our God is marching on.*

*In the beauty of the lilies Christ was born
   across the sea,
With a glory in his bosom that transfigures
   you and me;
As he died to make men holy, let us die
   to make men free,
      While God is marching on.*

This famous Civil War marching song was written by
Julia Ward Howe (1819-1910) in 1861. It is sung to
the tune of "John Brown's Body."

ARMY TIMEPIECE

Dear Mom: Your letter was a welcome lift
   But do not send the watch you plan to buy.
Betimes it would have made a useful gift,
   But that was in civilian days gone by.
Now time has lost its urgency, and so
   I need no watch to mark what hour's fled.
There is a gift that you might send me, though:
   Please send a pocket calendar, instead.

Herbert Smart Airport, Ga.   —Cpl. NATHANIEL ROGOVOY

CRASS-WORD PUZZLE

[O]NE of the definitions Webster gives for *crass* is
"very stupid." With that warning, try this one.
   It works just like a regular cross-word puzzle.

ACROSS
Chew
Insect sting
A snack
   (slang)
Corrode

DOWN
1. Insects
2. Ogles
3. Annoy
4. Comfort

TEE-TOTAL WINNERS

OVERSEAS. Twelfth-time winner: William
Reiter SF2c (score of 397); ninth-time winner: T/Sgt. K. J. Harris (397). Prize puzzle
kits go to these first-time winners: Pfc.
Charles Jefferys, whose solution is shown,
and Cpl. Douglas Booth (tied at 398); S/Sgt.
P. E. Kaltenbach and Sgt. A. R. Brigante
(tied at 397); Pfc. H. Wakefield and Pvt.
[Em]il Wiszowaty (tied at 394) and Sgt. Dodd Fortenberry
[an]d Pvt. V. H. Ruvolo, USMC (tied at 392).

PUZZLE SOLUTIONS

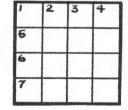

more. Crass, isn't it?
then think over the definitions for 1, 2, 3 and 4 Down or
word: ARE. Fill in the spaces on the diagram according
CRASS-WORD PUZZLE. 1, 5, 6 and 7 Across all are the sa[me]
CARD SHIFT: 4D on 4S; 2D on 2S; 3D on 3S; 5D on 5[S].

[W]HEN Californians boast about their
weather and their women, this is what
[t]hey have in mind. About their women, we
[m]ean. At 17, Cheryl Walker was beautiful
[e]nough to be crowned Queen of the 1939
[P]asadena Tournament of Roses — and she
[h]asn't slipped a bit. Wouldn't be surprised
[i]f she had improved. Her latest movie for
[W]arner Bros. is "Make Your Own Bed."

TEE-TOTAL

[F]EELING bored? Enter this contest and you'll
become exasperated. But you'll get a prize
kit of puzzles if you send in a solution
with a score that is HIGHER than any other
   contestant's score. Here's the way
      to do it:
         Fill in diagram with six dif-
      ferent English words. No names
      of persons or places. Consult Let-
      ler Value table. Add number
      values of the *24 letters* you have
      used, *counting each of the 24 let-*
ters only once. The sample work-out here
totals 252, and you'll have to do a lot better
than that if you want to get a prize.
   Remember: the object of Tee-Total puzzles
is to get the HIGHEST, not the lowest, score.
   In case of word disputes, we'll check with
Webster's Collegiate.

LETTER VALUES

A — 3		N — 14	
B — 16		O — 6	
C — 12		P — 13	
D — 8		Q — 11	
E — 2		R — 10	
F — 23		S — 7	
G — 15		T — 9	
H — 19		U — 1	
I — 4		V — 26	
J — 21		W — 20	
K — 24		X — 17	
L — 11		Y — 5	
M — 22		Z — 25	

Score . . . . Name, ASN and address:

. . . .

. . . .

. . . .

Mail to Puzzle Editor, YANK, 205 East 42d Street,
New York 17, N. Y., within two weeks of the date
of this issue if you are in the U. S., within *eight*
weeks if you are outside the U. S. Winners in U. S.
will be listed on this page in the July 28 issue.

CARD SHIFT

[R]EMOVE these eight cards from a deck and lay them
out as shown.
   PROBLEM: In four moves obtain four groups of
two cards each, each of the groups being made up
of a pair.
   At each move you must pick up a card and jump it
over two adjacent cards, placing it upon the next one
in line.
   With a little preliminary figuring, you ought to be
able to do this on the first try.

It's All a Knack

It's like I say, Eddie, ya gotta know how to handle women. It's all a knack. Take me, for instance.

Last Saturday night I am in Mrs. Snodgrass' Boarding House waiting for my chick and very occupied with a copy of the *Ladies' Home Journal*. On my left is a marine sergeant with a bunch of posies in one hand and a five-pound box of sweets in the other. He is also looking at my copy of the *Ladies' Home Journal*. Looking over my right shoulder is an ensign who is stretching his neck at the girdle advertisements. We are all waiting for chicks.

Right across from us is Mrs. Snodgrass, who looks like her husband was a first sergeant and her face froze while trying to outshout him.

Well, pretty soon a pair of stems comes trucking down the stairs followed by as classy a chassis as I've ever seen. The marine sergeant jumps up from the couch, pulls down his blouse and walks to meet the frill.

"I am the Greek god bearing gifts for the lovely," he says, and he shoves the posies and sweets in front of her.

"Posies!" screams the dame. "Oh, William, you know my hay fever!" and she dumps the flowers in Mrs. Snodgrass' lap.

"And candy!" she wails. "You know I'm on a diet. Oh, William, how could you?"

She reads the riot act to him all the way out, and Mrs. Snodgrass snorts: "Marines, humph!" The ensign and me go back to the girdle advertisements.

The next pair of stems to truck down the stairs is followed by a chest expansion that would make Charles Atlas blush with envy. The ensign jumps up and stalks anxiously towards The Chest. "I have purchased two tickets in the front row for the Follies," he states very proudly. "We will make merry."

The tomato passes her hand wearily over her brow and moans: "Leave us go to the Waldorf Room, Ronald. I need peace and quiet."

The ensign's Adam's apple goes "Gulp!" and I

Contributions for this page should be addressed to the Post Exchange, YANK, The Army Weekly, 205 East 42d Street, New York 17, N. Y.

can almost see $10 cover charges running through his mind. When they start to leave, he carefully knocks the sparks out of the cigarette and inserts it back in the case. He will need it later in the month. Mrs. Snodgrass snorts: "Sailors, humph!"

Now it is my chick's turn, and pretty soon she comes running down the stairs. No click of heels, no mincing walk—just the loveliest long black hair you have ever run your hands through, a black sweater, yellow skirt, yellow socks, and moccasins. You've seen that picture of Muriel in the black sweater that I've got over my bunk, haven't you, Eddie? Every time the captain comes by for inspection it makes him forget all about the dust under my cot. Well, she is wearing that black sweater.

I bounce off the couch and say: "Muriel, you look like something out of a girdle advertisement," and I proceed to plant one right smack on her red ruby lips. "Oh, Muscles," she says as she opens her eyes, "you make my ears jump up and down." To which I gasp: "Leave us go study celestial navigation in the park, honey." Muriel grabs my arm, and I say: "Toodle-oo, Snodgrass. See you in the funny papers." And Mrs. Snodgrass does not snort. "Have a good time, soldier," she says.

It's like I say, Eddie, you got to know how to handle women. It's all a knack.

Gainesville, Fla.   —Pfc. LESTER GROLNICK

Church Service

Sunday morning was a quiet one in Company A's orderly room. It had started to rain about 0300, and by the time the company clerk walked in to relieve the CQ for breakfast the mud was inches deep.

The clerk made out the sick book, took the morning report to regimental headquarters and then had breakfast. It was still quiet when he got back, and he decided to spend a few hours writing letters.

The phone rang. It was the chaplain calling. He wanted 20 more chairs brought to the chapel because it was the kind of morning for a big congregation. The clerk sent out a detail to lug the chairs from the rec hall up the hill to the chapel.

When the phone rang again, it was the guardhouse. Its one prisoner—a boy who had been AWOL and had been returned to camp that week to await trial—wanted to go to church services on his first Sunday back in camp. Someone would have to call for him and take him to church.

The clerk looked over his 20-percent cadre list and called Cpl. Zanowski. The corporal was still sleeping. The men woke him up and told him to get dressed and report to the orderly room on the double.

Zanowski came into the orderly room on the double. He was in fatigues and still smelled of sleep.

"You're on 20 percent," the clerk said, "and the prisoner wants to go to church this morning. You're elected."

"Church!" Janowski shouted. "The prisoner! What the hell does he want to go to church for?"

"He wants to go," said the clerk, "and you're elected."

Zanowski went back to his barracks to dress in ODs.

The phone rang, and it was the guardhouse again. The prisoner hadn't missed a service at home or in camp since he was a kid. He wanted

to make sure he could go to services this morning.

"We're sending a noncom right over," the clerk said. He lit a cigarette and looked out through the window. Up the back road dozens of soldiers were sloshing through the rain toward the chapel.

Zanowski came in, dressed in ODs. "Where the carbine?" he asked. The supply sergeant brought out the carbine and a magazine from the supply room. Zanowski slung the piece on his shoulder, adjusted it and headed for the door.

"On a morning like this," he said, "a guy has to go to church—and I have to take him!"

The clerk called the guardhouse. "Cpl. Janowski is on his way over," he said. "Have the prisoner ready."

He had put the finishing touches on a letter to his wife when the door opened and Zanowski walked in slowly. Zanowski took the carbine off his shoulder, placed it against the wall and laid the magazine on the desk. He sat down in the extra chair.

"Back so soon?" asked the clerk. "The service can't be over yet. It must just be starting now."

"We didn't go to church," said Zanowski. "The prisoner didn't want to go to church."

"But he called up twice," the clerk said. "He didn't want to miss a service. He hadn't missed one since he was a kid."

Zanowski fumbled for a cigarette. "He didn't want to go to church," he repeated. "He didn't want to walk into church with a guy holding a carbine in his back."

Camp Croft, S. C.   —Pvt. SYDNEY BERMAN

"So that's Gordon's idea of a double date!"
—Sgt. Al Kaelin, AAF, Tobyhanna, Pa.

THE SHOW

Uneasily, from time to time I shifted
  Positions in a chair. With throbbing heart
I waited for the time-worn show to start,
  And as the velvet curtain slowly lifted
Revealing lovely scenes, I gently drifted
  Into a world of flesh and fantasy;
And all my friends who saw the show agree
  The star performer of the show was gifted
And now as hazy smoke rings seem to crown
  The whisky bottles in this lowly den
With halos, I still dream and smoke and drown
  Myself in heaven's royal drink, and then
I watch the girl who wears the velvet gown
  I wonder if she'll cross her legs again.

Fort Benning, Ga.   —Sgt. LEONARD SUMMERS

RECIPROCITY

  You've always been considerate
    And I've met none so fair;
  So how can you embrace the thought
    Of giving me the air?

  Remember all the fun we've had
    And friends that we both knew;
  Please love me, dear, just one month more
    Till I get tired of you.

North Camp Hood, Tex.   —Pvt. NAT L. SCHER

THE OPTIMIST

  If the devil takes the hindmost,
    No doubt I'll be behind;
  The gold beyond the rainbow
    Is the gold I'll never find;
  I'm always on the other side
    Of the cloud that's silver lined.

  My life is rugged, really,
    And yet I'm seldom vexed,
  Because I'm stickin' round to see
    Just what the hell can happen next!

Station Hospital, Chico AAF, Calif.   —Pfc. JOHN J. MLOCK

SPORTS: SO YOU KNOW SPORTS? THEN TRY THIS SIMPLE LITTLE QUIZ

By Sgt. DAN POLIER

YANK's third all-purpose sports quiz, ideal for brightening up ten-minute breaks, bull sessions and the lonely war in Alaska.

In scoring yourself for this quiz, allow five points for every question you answer correctly. Eighty or more is excellent, 70 is good, 60 fair, 50 passing, 40 or below failure.

1. Babe Dahlgren has seen service with seven major-league teams and the Pullman Company. Can you name five of the teams he played with?

2. What football player was named on the All-American team for two successive years playing for two different schools?

3. Mel Ott broke in with the Giants at the age of 16 as (a) outfielder, (b) bat boy, (c) catcher, (d) infielder.

4. Name three outstanding professional golfers whose last names begin with the letter "H"?

5. With what sports do you associate each of the following terms: (a) blueline, (b) baseline, (c) balkline?

6. Who was the Cincinnati catcher that committed suicide in a Boston hotel?

7. Ernie Schaaf was killed in a bout with (a) Baer, (b) Carnera, (c) Sharkey, (d) Unknown Winston.

8. What great foreign miler beat Glenn Cunningham in the Princeton meet and later ran away from him in the Berlin Olympics, where he set a new 1,500 meter record?

9. How many of the following pitchers have won 30 or more games in a single season? Carl Hubbell, Jim Bagby Sr., Herb Pennock, Dizzy Dean, Lefty Grove, Lefty Gomez, Bob Feller, Jim Bagby Jr., Babe Ruth.

10. Who is the famous football coach whose name is pronounced the same as that of a great violinist, though the last part is spelled differently?

11. On what college teams did the following professional football players perform: (a) Mel Hein, (b) Dutch Clark, (c) Whizzer White, (d) Beatty Feathers, (e) Ace Parker?

12. What was the last World Series to go the full seven games?

13. Jim Tobin's no-hitter against the Dodgers was the first one in the big leagues since 1941. Who pitched the one in 1941?

14. The only horse ever to defeat Man O' War was (a) Regret, (b) John P. Grier, (c) Upset, (d) Exterminator.

15. When Mel Harder of the Indians won his 201st major-league victory recently, one of the spectators was the only pitcher to win more than 500 games. Who was he?

16. Who was the only boxer to win the heavyweight championship on a foul?

17. What former Duke All-American was responsible for Notre Dame's only defeat of 1943?

18. Identify four well-known golfers known by each of the following nicknames: (a) Silver Fox, (b) Emperor Jones, (c) Joplin Ghost, (d) Wee Bobby.

19. Here are some well-known runners-up. What famous stars used to defeat them, sometimes by a close margin? (a) Helen Jacobs, (b) Blue Swords, (c) Lew Tendler, (d) Gene Venzke.

← 20. Here is a famous sports farewell of 1938 that you should remember. Who is the lone figure and what were the circumstances surrounding his departure?

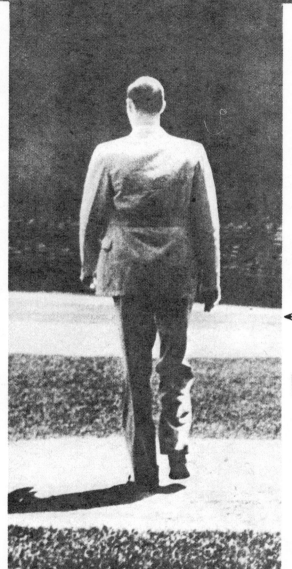

ANSWERS TO SPORTS QUIZ

1. Cubs, Yankees, Red Sox, Braves, Dodgers, Pirates, Phillies. 2. Bill Daley, 1942 Minnesota; 1943 Michigan. 3. Catcher. 4. Ben Hogan, Jimmy Hines, Dutch Harrison, Walter Hagen, Clayton Heafner. 5. (a) hockey, (b) tennis, (c) billiards. 6. Willard Hershberger. 7. Carnera. 8. Jack Lovelock. 9. Jim Bagby Sr., Lefty Grove, Dizzy Dean. 10. Fritz Crisler. 11. (a) Washington State, (b) Colorado College, (c) Colorado, (d) Tennessee, (e) Duke. 12. Reds vs. Tigers in 1940. 13. Lon Warneke, then with the Cardinals, against the Reds. 14. Upset. 15. Denton (Cy) Young. 16. Max Schmeling. 17. Steve Lach of Great Lakes. 18. (a) Tommy Armour, (b) Bobby Jones, (c) Horton Smith, (d) Bobby Cruickshank. 19. (a) Helen Wills, (b) Count Fleet, (c) Benny Leonard, (d) Glenn Cunningham. 20. Schoolboy Rowe leaving Briggs Stadium, Detroit, after a brilliant career with the Tigers. He developed a sore arm and was farmed out to Beaumont.

SPORTS SERVICE RECORD

THIS year's Great Lakes line-up reads like something out of *Baseball's Who's Who*, with such major-league stars as Max West, Billy Herman, Gene Thompson, Schoolboy Rowe, Clyde McCullough, Virgil Trucks, Bill Baker, Merrill May, Johnny McCarthy, Al Glossop and Syl Johnson. And in case Mickey Cochrane ever needs an able pinch-runner he can always call on Apprentice Seaman Glenn Cunningham. . . . Lt. Jim Lansing, the Fordham footballer, who dropped the first bomb on Truk, has signed with the Boston pro Yankees and will join the team after the war. . . . Lt. Ted Williams, the Red Sox slugger, and Lt. Bob Kennedy, former Chicago White Sox third baseman, are Marine flight instructors in the same squadron at the Pensacola (Fla.) Naval Air Station. . . . Add the names of Chief Specialists Pee Wee Reese and Hugh Casey to the long list of major leaguers now serving in Hawaii. . . . Lt. Darold Jenkins, Missouri's All-American center of '41, who was reported missing in action several weeks ago, has turned up as a PW in Germany. . . . Lt. Buddy Hassett, one of Lou Gehrig's successors at first base, has been

appointed recreation officer on an aircraft carrier now nearing completion. . . . Indiana's Archie Harris, who holds the American record for the discus throw, is an aviation cadet at the Tuskegee (Ala.) Army Air Field, where Pvt. John Brooks, the Olympic broad jump star, is a PT instructor.

Decorated: Sgt. Gregory Mangin, one-time Davis Cup winner and national indoor tennis champion, with the Distinguished Flying Cross for shooting down one enemy fighter, forcing a second one to give up the attack on his Fortress, and keeping the other German planes at a safe distance in a raid over Nazi-occupied Italy. . . .

Promoted: Lt. Buddy Lewis, former Washington third baseman, to captain in Burma, where he is piloting a C-47; Lt. Mickey Cochrane, Great Lakes baseball coach, to lieutenant commander. . . . *Discharged:* Al Evans, second-string catcher for the Senators, from the Navy with a CDD. . . . *Ordered for induction:* George Munger, righthander of the Cardinals (4-1 this season) by the Army; Bill Hulse, fastest U. S. outdoor miler (4:06), by the Navy; Al Lakeman, second-string catcher for the Reds, by the Army; Ralph Hodgin, Chicago White Sox outfielder, by the Army; Huck Geary, war-working Phillie shortstop, by the Army. . . . *Rejected:* Ed Sauer, rookie Chicub outfielder, because of high blood pressure; Dain Clay, Reds' outfielder, because of headaches.

EX-GOLF CHAMP, Cpl. Frank Moore, who set a PGA record (136 for 36 holes) when he beat Sammy Snead for the title in 1938, patches up a B-24 Liberator in New Guinea.

"SUPPLIES, SUPPLIES, ALWAYS SUPPLIES! DON'T YOU EVER BRING IN ANY WOMEN?"
—Cpl. Ernest Maxwell

"JEPSON, THE COMMODORE WOULD LIKE MORE GRAVY."
—Pvt. Gerard Otto

YANK
THE ARMY WEEKLY

"QUICK! A TOURNIQUET!"
—Pvt. Thomas Flannery

"I DON'T THINK YOU UNDERSTOOD WHAT THEY MEANT WHEN THEY SAID YOU COULD LIVE OFF THE POST."
—Cpl. Art Gates

YANK

THE ARMY WEEKLY

5¢ **JUNE 30**
VOL. 3, NO. 2
1944

By the men . . . for the
men in the service

**GENERAL IKE AND
HIS INVADERS**

In the face of German machine-gun fire, American infantrymen leave a Coast Guard landing craft and wade chest deep toward the mines and tank traps lining the coast of Normandy. Some, already on land, are crawling forward under the smoke raised by the covering Allied naval barrage.

D DAY, French Coast

FRANCE

Scale of miles
10 5 0 10 20 30 40 50 60 70
International Boundaries
Highways

SALERNO ITALY

LICATA SICI[LY]

a ship that has known the beaches of Sicily and Italy, an American soldier gets a light from an American sailor. Here they are bound for the main show: France.

THE LANDINGS IN FRANCE

By YANK London Bureau

LONDON [By Cable] — The countryside along the Normandy coast in France between the ports of Le Havre and Cherbourg reminds of Connecticut along Long Island Sound or south shore of Massachusetts.

The beaches are sandy, but there are no empty less stretches of sand dunes in back of them. s pleasant green country, divided into pas- s that produce famous Normandy cheeses, etable gardens and orchards, and sprinkled small towns and villages, not unlike West-

port or Stamford in Connecticut, or Cohasset or Duxbury in Massachusetts. The towns are connected by good but rather narrow roads, lined with tall straight poplars. The roads run up and down occasional rises that are not really steep enough to be called hills and through forests that don't look like American forests. The trees are mostly beeches, widely spaced, and there is no thick underbrush. The peasants keep it cleaned out; they need it for their fireplaces.

It was here on June 6, 1944, that the Allies struck the historic first blow in the invasion of western Europe.

First came the airborne troops—four airborne infantry divisions and two paratroop divisions, according to the German count. The paratroops, British and American, jumped two hours before midnight on June 5, landing behind the German shore defenses.

They heard the tow planes coming in slowly behind them, cutting loose the gliders that circled and crashed through the trees. Out of the gliders came the airborne infantry, artillery, 37-mm antitank guns, jeeps and antiaircraft guns.

The paratroopers and the airborne infantry collected their equipment, joined forces and

—and the first wave of U. S. infantrymen wade through the Channel surf toward the beaches of France.

US 207

What the invaders saw: Men in the second waves find half-tracks and a beached duck already on French soil, while up ahead long lines of Yanks are fanning

studied maps. Then they went to work, smashing assigned Nazi coastal gun positions just as they had rehearsed for months back in Britain and setting up defenses around strategic bridges, villages and road junctions.

When dawn began to break, the men near the beaches—who were evading or fighting surprised and still-sleepy German patrols—looked back at the water and saw the minesweepers.

There were 200 of these little British vessels edging their way carefully toward the shore ahead of the main invasion fleet, which numbered more than 4,000 ships, not counting small craft.

And over the horizon thundered the greatest umbrella of airpower ever assembled for invasion protection. More than 7,500 Allied planes went into action over this 50-mile stretch of Normandy coast during the first eight hours of combat. It made the air protection at Tarawa, Kwajalein, Salerno and Sicily seem skimpy.

German shore batteries opened fire on the minesweepers. But the sweepers—an ungainly collection of dirty-looking converted fishing trawlers, tramp coastal steamers and a few modern vessels—treated the bombardment with contempt. They kept on moving straight toward the shore, clearing a path for the landing craft that were already swinging around in wide seasickening circles at the rendezvous points farther back in the Channel.

The minesweepers pulled away, their work done, and the naval vessels began to bombard the beaches. There were plenty of 16-inch shells plowing into that section of the coast. The fleet included such battleships as Britain's huge *HMS Rodney* and the 30-year old *USS Nevada*—back in action after taking a terrific pasting at Pearl Harbor—as well as the 33-year-old *USS Arkansas* and the 32-year-old *USS Texas*. The concussions from their big guns were so great they sprung some of the plates on nearby small landing craft.

Seconds after the bombardment British, U. S. and Canadian infantry poured onto the beaches.

The long-awaited invasion had finally started.

PICKING this particular section of the French coast as the place to start was about the same as trying to bunt in a baseball game with no outs, a runner on first base, the score tied in the

sixth inning and the infield playing in close. It was the obvious thing to do.

Landing conditions on the once-fashionable bathing-resort beaches along the Bay of the Seine were ideal. Farther north, near Calais and Dunkerque, the shore was too shallow, and to the south, nearer Spain in the Bay of Biscay, it was too steep and rocky. Furthermore, this section of Normandy was near the embarkation ports in southwest England and near the important communication lines and highways leading to Paris. And it was near the two best French ports on the Channel, Cherbourg and Le Havre, which the Allies had to get to to supply an extended drive into the Continent.

Perhaps it was because this point was so obviously the place to strike that the Germans were not too well prepared for it.

Resistance was tough enough but no tougher than it would have been in a dozen other sectors of the western European shore. Field Marshal Erwin Rommel was not waiting on the beaches with his panzers to confuse the Allies and to try to knock them back into the sea immediately, as Gen. Sir Bernard Montgomery had expected.

In fact, one of the few enemy forces that was waiting in considerable numbers happened to be on the beach not by plan but by accident.

The three regiments of Germans that were in the right spot at the right time were there only because they had some anti-invasion practice problems on their training schedule the same day the Allied task force arrived.

The practice problems turned out to be more realistic than they had bargained for, but they managed to pull themselves together and put up resistance.

Some of the Americans in the sector, however, ran into luck. The defenses were concrete 88-mm gun emplacements with walls six feet thick. But the two Germans who were supposed to be manning the strongest and most dangerous gun, 200 yards from the beach, were goldbricking back in their living quarters in a tunnel behind the position. Just as the GIs were planning to take the gun, a shell from an American naval vessel landed squarely in the emplacement's muzzle port, knocking the inside of the position to pieces.

The two Germans ran out of the tunnel, scared

to death, and were captured. One was 17, other 18. Like many of the prisoners taken in invasion, they were unenthusiastic soldi scrawny and droopy, glad to be captured evidently impressed by the Americans' bra and equipment.

For the first day of the invasion it seemed if Rommel and the supreme German defe commander, Field Marshal Gerd von Rundste were still unconvinced that this blow at N mandy was Gen. Eisenhower's Sunday pun They hesitated to throw in the full force of th ground troops and the *Luftwaffe* for fear a big Allied amphibious attack might strike at so more improbable part of their Atlantic wall.

There were reports of a huge Allied fleet the Mediterranean off Genoa that might aim

Canadian soldiers stand guard over German pri oners, taken in the first week of the invasio

What the Germans saw: An American second lieutenant and the men of his platoon, carrying full equipment, move forward toward the enemy and into battle.

ward southern France, and in the Low Countries and Norway the Nazi troops also were nervously on the alert.

But throughout D-plus-one and D-plus-two, Gen. Eisenhower continued to pour men and supplies into the Bay of the Seine beachhead and nowhere else. Rommel's intelligence, which reported 12 Allied divisions in Normandy the day after the first landings, said two days afterward there were 20. Correspondents reported the arrival of fresh airborne units in a parade of gliders 50 miles long.

ANY doubts that Rommel and von Rundstedt might have had about this being Eisenhower's main invasion threat, however, must have been dispelled when they learned that their opposition

in Normandy was Gen. Montgomery's British-American-Canadian Twenty-first Army Group. And that Lt. Gen. Omar N. Bradley, favorite of the doughfeet in Tunisia and Sicily and senior U. S. ground-force commander, was on the beach.

The Twenty-first Army Group had been touted all over Britain for the last year as the No. 1 invasion spearhead. When it landed in Normandy, it included two of the best infantry outfits Britain and the U. S. had to offer—the 50th Northumberlands and the American Army's "Fightin' First" Infantry Division.

The slow-speaking North Country men in the British 50th were Gen. Montgomery's favorites in the old Eighth Army during the drive against Rommel in Africa. They were the riflemen who turned the tide at El Alamein, stormed the

Mareth line and fought their hearts out at Catania in Sicily. They had been in France before. They had held off the Germans in 1940 during the evacuation of Dunkerque.

The 1st Division was the first U. S. Infantry division in 1917 to go into action in France, one of the first in 1942 to land in North Africa—where it captured Oran—and one of the first to fight in Tunisia and Sicily. This was the division that fought at Gafsa, El Guettar and Mateur and turned away a desperate German counterattack with its back to the sea at Gela in Sicily. Later it won the bloody battle of Troina.

The division had been the first to have its Springfields replaced by M1s back in the blue-fatigue days of 1941 and the first to get amphibious training before Pearl Harbor. In those days, it was

Down below is France, and when they have fixed their static line, these paratroopers will jump.

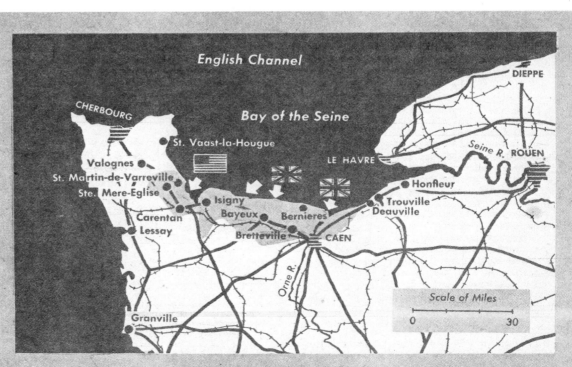

First phase of the invasion: the Bay of the Seine in Normandy. American assault forces struck on the western shore below Cherbourg while British and Canadian troops drove toward Bayeux and Caen.

made up of Regular Army men from Fort Jay, N. Y., a few early draftees and some GIs who volunteered for a year under the Selective Service Act in October 1940. They were mostly from New York, Brooklyn, New Jersey and Pennsylvania. But not many of the original division went to Britain from Africa and Sicily. When the division landed in Normandy, most of the privates and pfcs were replacements.

The 1st Division stepped into some furious hand-to-hand fighting alongside the other American forces on the western shore of the Bay of the Seine, near Caretan and Ste. Mere-Eglise, two towns on the Cherbourg peninsula. Progress was slow there in the beginning because bad weather and rough surf made the landing of reinforcements and supplies difficult.

THE British made out better on the beachhead to the east, which opened with a landing at Bernieras on D Day and then fanned out to cover more than 40 miles of waterfront and about 15 miles of inland depth.

It was here, five miles inland, that the British captured Bayeux, first sizable French town to fall into Allied hands in the invasion. The liberated townspeople gave the British troops a wild reception, breaking out the Tricolor, the Union Jack and the Stars and Stripes from carefully concealed hiding places. They also broke out carefully concealed bottles of wine and toasted the soldiers with "Long live the Allies, death to the Boche" and "Bravo, Tommies!"

Bayeux, like the rest of the Normandy coast, was badly smashed by Allied air and naval bombs. Fearing their heavy bombs would cause so much destruction that the advance of our own troops would be delayed, Allied air chiefs switched to lighter missiles for close-support attacks.

The outstanding military achievement of the first phase of the invasion was the success of the American paratroop and airborne landings in the Ste. Mere-Eglise sector of the Cherbourg Peninsula and the British 6th Airborne Division's attack along the Orne River. This Allied thrust from the sky was far more effective than the famed German airborne assault on Crete three years ago.

Official reports said that only 2 percent of the 1,000 U. S. and RAF planes used in the two attacks were lost. Gliders were landed in far greater numbers than the Germans employed at Crete, and although many of them descended in darkness, casualties were comparatively few. The Americans used Waco CG4A gliders at night and the bigger British Horsas for heavier equipment in the daylight.

One glider landed squarely on the roof of a building on the Valognes-Caretan road. The troops went downstairs and captured the Germans in their beds.

New secret devices enabled the paratroopers to land in carefully designated spots despite layers of clouds. Some of them were driving captured German trucks two hours after they jumped.

After the fall of Bayeux, Rommel hesitated no longer and brought his best armor and ground troops to the front. Canadians attacking the city of Caen on the Orne River found themselves battling the famed 21st Panzer Division, reorganized after its defeat in Africa. The 21st was well equipped and was using some new weapons. One of them, called the "Hornet," was an 88-mm gun mounted on a Mark IV chassis. The Germans were also using the new "Beetle," the tiny tank packed with explosives and controlled with cables from their lines. This contraption had been more or less a flop when it made its debut on the Anzio beachhead.

The British, Canadians and Americans found that Normandy was not a bad place to fight a war, but that the small villages with the tiny picturesque pink-stucco houses were also made to order for the Nazi defenders. These buildings were low two-story structures with thick walls and small windows overlooking the street—but with only a few windows, because of an old law making them taxable. The houses were also joined by thick stucco garden walls, making it easy for the Germans to pass out the back door and into the next building without exposing themselves to fire from the street.

In the countryside GIs found vegetable cellars, or root cellars, dug into the side of slopes along the road. These comfortable caves, with heavy wooden doors, made excellent bomb shelters and dry, protected bivouacs on rainy nights.

There was plenty of rain the second and third

days when the weather turned against the Allies. This was when they needed calm water, and the rough surf made it tough to bring ashore the supplies and fresh replacements Gen. Montgomery wanted in order to capitalize on his first successes.

There are three phases to every invasion operation: 1) the landing and securing of the beachhead; 2) the strengthening and protection of the beachhead and the accumulation there of sufficient supplies and troops to support the drive inland toward military objectives; 3) the battle for those military objectives, which in France are cities like Rouen, St. Nazaire, Le Mans and Paris.

Historians looking back on the first phase of the Allied invasion of western Europe will pronounce it a great success. In fact, Gen. Eisenhower's severest critics, the Germans, have already done so.

Said Adm. Luetzow of the German Navy after D Day: "It is obvious that the light German naval forces were unable by themselves to stop the overpowering enemy forces used in the landing."

Said Wolfgang Rohbeil, a Nazi war correspondent at Caen: "The enemy has succeeded in knocking out our coastal wall defenses on a rather broad front. The German defenders fought like lions, strongpoint garrisons holding out literally to the last man. But the incessant hail of bombs and naval shells, the attacks by endless swarms of low-flying battle planes and the large airborne landings—whole divisions in a matter of hours—were irresistible."

The choice of the obvious landing site in the quaint French countryside that looked like a southern New England summer resort, the selection of the day and the hour, and the expert coordination of air, naval and ground attacks all combined to make the first phase of the invasion live up to our expectations.

The second and third phases were not over yet.

This German machine-gun nest was quickly silenced when Canadians pushed inland after initial assault.

From a B-17 Base

A B-17 BASE IN ENGLAND [By Cable]—D Day for the Eighth Air Force was a day of bombardment across the Channel in France the same kind of bombardment that had been going on for a long time.

At the briefing there was only one new touch —a bombline: a line roughly outlining the area inland from the enemy coast that the Allied penetrations should have covered by the time the mission was scheduled. "You will not," said Capt S. L. Burr, "under any circumstances drop bombs within the bombline."

Out on the hards the newer silver-colored Forts waited beside the older green-painted ones for the start of another raid. In the officers lounge the pilots listened intently to the radio. The broadcaster was talking an awful lot about D Day but saying very little. The pilots were interested; even though they were going to fly in the invasion operation, they had to listen to somebody off in London to get the lowdown.

They made a lot of interesting remarks while they waited for the afternoon raid. "I called Calais," one of them said, "but I was told the telephone line wasn't quite ready yet." Another said: "It's dangerous ditching in the Channel today. There's no room in the water."

They didn't have much to say about the early-morning raid. There had been a ten-tenths' cloud cover. On the way back they had seen landing barges and naval craft in the Channel through a break in the clouds.

Lt. Col. Chester C. Cox of Superior, Wis. strolled around Operations with his hands in his pockets. In the morning, flying in the lead of the earliest formation of American heavies to cross the enemy coast on D Day, he had earned the honor of being the first U. S. heavy-bombardment pilot to drop bombs in direct support of the landings in France. The event had taken place at 0700 hours, but on other mornings Col Cox had seen more flak and more enemy fighters and more merry hell than he had seen on this one. He was taking it easy now.

At 2100 hours the night before they'd been told that the next day was D Day, and there had been a long burst of cheering.

D Day wasn't a good day for flying. There were clouds, and very late in the day there was rain. But the flyers felt a sense of responsibility to the men storming onto the French beaches; short of typhoon weather there would be no halt in the missions.

At 1400 hours there was a briefing. At 1500 the mission was scrubbed. At 1630 it was on again, leaving my chow halfway down my gullet. It might be D Day but it was just like any day at an airfield.

I was assigned to the crew of Lt. James J. Gabler of Pittsburgh, Pa. At the ground-crew tent the flyers stood around and gassed with the

aking a casualty aboard ship bound for England.

echanics. One of the ground-crewmen was 43
ears old, and Lt. Gabler, squinting out at the
ouded sky, said: "I wish I was 43 right now."
hen he moved around trying to imitate some-
ne with St. Vitus dance.

We took off at 1720 hours of a cloudy day
nd climbed up through the overcast to join our
rmation, led by Col. William B. David. Every-
ing was shipshape except that you couldn't see
uch through the overcast and everyone aboard
as much interested in what "our friends" were
ing downstairs. Through an occasional break
the sky we could see the Channel.

When we got over France we solved the mys-
ry of no flak and no enemy fighters. Moving
to our target we could see smoke columns and
es below, although we couldn't tell whether
ey were the result of offshore shelling or of
mb damage. The navigator, 2d Lt. David L.
cGee, handed me a pair of binoculars, and the
es really jumped up through the glasses.

We dumped our load, and the bombardier, Lt.
rry M. Hill, looked satisfied and relaxed. Lt.
abler, the pilot, sounding slightly bored, asked
Sgt. John T. Middleton, the radioman, whether
e could get anything about the invasion.

"I'll see what Jerry has to say," said Middle-
n.

On the way home we followed the most am-
tious traffic pattern ever conceived for aircraft.
ll day long, trains of aircraft had been shuttling
all levels from England to France and home
gain. That meant a careful all-the-way-through
attern, so that the air over England would not
e crowded to the danger point. We swept wide
our return, and that made it a long trip home.

There were broken clouds below us, and
rough them I caught my first real glimpse
the invasion. I could see a mile-long column
ships moving herdlike across the water. Long
reamers of gray gun smoke lay near the water.
Back in England we set down nicely at our
me base at 0010 hours on June 7, or just 10
inutes after D Day had ended. In the rain and
ld wind we asked a ground mechanic: "What's
appening?"

"Churchill spoke," he said. "There's been
ymns and prayers, and the casualties are not as
eavy as expected." Then he went to work on
e Fort.

The interrogation was smooth and over quickly.
nurse grabbed one of the gunners, who had
urt his head in the flight by banging against
mething in the Fort's waist. She ran her fingers
rough his hair, trying to find the wound and
olding him like a big sister.

All the crew went off to bed early because
ere were 15 hours of flying to be done when
ey woke up.

As he headed for his quarters, Lt. Gabler said:
f you really want to do a job, why don't you
me along with us to Berlin sometime?"

—Sgt. SAUL LEVITT
YANK Staff Correspondent

From a Coast Town

A COASTAL TOWN IN BRITAIN—Now that the
invasion is history, we can let you in on
what it was like here before D Day when
troops from all over Britain moved into this sea-
side country to assemble for embarkation.

The assembly areas were really something.
One of them covered 300 square miles—as big as
Fort Bragg, N. C., and more than four times as
big as the District of Columbia. To move the
troops and supplies from the assembly areas to
the water, the Army Service Forces set up complete telephone exchanges and built new roads,
bridges and 150 miles of railroad tracks. In one
area they built three new airfields for the close-
supporting Ninth Air Force.

These assembly areas, or marshaling areas as
they were officially called, were known as A, B,
C and so on. Each area was subdivided into
camps for various units, which were designated
as A-1, A-2, A-3 and on up. The whole set-up
was a masterful achievement in planning.

The GIs arrived for the big event stripped of
all clothing and equipment except the bare combat essentials. They rolled up their shelter halves
and blankets with extra shoes and tent poles,
pins and rope and loaded the rolls onto ducks,
which were to dump them on the sands of France
after the beachheads were established. Back in
their billets, they had packed their blouses, overcoats, go-to-hell caps and everything else connected with garrison formalities into barracks
bags and kissed them good-bye. Maybe the barracks bags would meet the outfit again somewhere in Europe and maybe they wouldn't.

Each man wore OD pants, woolen shirt, field
jacket, leggings, GI shoes with hobnails and steel
heelplates, helmet and gas mask. His combat
pack contained his raincoat, toilet articles, mess
gear and rations. He also carried a shovel or pick
and on his belt his canteen and cup and a first-
aid packet with an envelope of sulfanilamide, a
package of sulfadiazine and a morphine surete.

Every infantryman carried 80 rounds of ammunition and three grenades tucked into an
extra canteen carrier attached to his rifle belt.
Most of the men were armed with M1s. Others
had Springfields with grenade launchers, BARs,
bazookas, flame throwers or TNT pole charges.
Every BARman carried a bag of 240 rounds of
ammunition.

All the money the GIs had was taken away from
them, and each one was given instead 200 *francs*
of French money. Most of the *francs* changed
hands in crap games before the men left Britain.

The GIs spent their last few nights in Britain
sleeping under three blankets on canvas cots in
pyramidal tents. It was cold at night, and some of
the men squawked because they didn't have their
overcoats. But they did not miss their blouses or
neckties. It felt good to be able to walk into
town—after more than a year of strict off-duty
dress regulations—wearing a field jacket and helmet liner with your shirt open at the neck.

The Americans in this town outnumbered the
British civilians 20 to 1 during the week before
D Day. There were soldiers from all branches of
the service and plenty of sailors. A lot of sailors
were dressed in Army OD uniforms with a big
red "N" insignia. They belonged to beach battalions. Other sailors, from landing craft and
combat vessels, stuck to the customary blues.

The soldiers began to disappear from the
streets as D Day drew nearer. Those who had
been briefed on their particular assignments
were restricted to their camp areas and strictly
forbidden to speak to civilians or unbriefed GIs.
Security patrols and Military Intelligence operatives were everywhere.

As a matter of fact, security all over Britain
before the invasion was so strong that Maj. Gen.
Henry J. F. Miller, commander of the Ninth Air
Force Service Command, was reduced in rank to
lieutenant colonel by Gen. Eisenhower and
shipped back to the States because he told somebody at a London cocktail party that D Day
would come before June 15.

Even after they were cut off from outside communication and trained in the pronunciation of
German words for "Halt" and "Put up your
hands" and the French for "Which way is the
boche?", GIs were slightly skeptical about the
whole thing. They wondered if it was just another dry run like the ones that had sent them
through the same routine from A to Z several
times during the spring. On those deals, they had
been awakened during the night and shipped
hurriedly to an assembly area, such as this one,
drawing ammunition and leaving all their personal belongings behind. They had boarded the
landing craft, feeling sure that they were going
to France; then it had turned out to be a practice
landing on the English coast, and a few days
later they were back in their old camps.

But this time, as they found out, it was no
dry run. —YANK London Bureau

From Rome, Where GIs Couldn't Believe the News

By Sgt. JAMES P. O'NEILL
YANK Staff Correspondent

W ITH THE FIFTH ARMY IN ROME [By
Cable]—This befuddled city did not
have time to get over the Fifth Army's
historic and raucous entry into Rome before
the biggest news of the war, the invasion of
France, dropped like a bombshell on the local
hysterical scene.

I went out on the noisy streets after the
astounding news came over the BBC radio and
asked five GIs this question: "What do you
think of the opening of the second front?"

Pvt. Robert J. Kinchen, an artilleryman
with the 85th Division from Vero Beach, Fla.,
where he raised oranges, had been guarding
the street since 0500 hours when I quizzed
him. He was tired but anxious to put in his
two cents' worth. He had heard the news an
hour before the interview.

"I didn't believe it," said Kinchen, "but I
am taking your word for it. I'm damned glad
it finally came. For a long while, especially
when we were at Anzio, we never thought
they'd start it. I hope the boys do not meet
much stuff when they hit the shore. If the
beachhead in France sticks, I guess we will
whip the Germans before the year is out."

Pvt. Jerome B. Kern, an infantryman from
Detroit, Mich., was riding down the Rome
street on a borrowed Italian bicycle when I
got in his way. "You're not kidding me?" he
asked. "I heard it from an Italian, but these
people are so happy today they'll tell you
anything. If it's true, it sure is wonderful
news. I don't mean to be selfish, but I hope it

means we can relax a little. We had our guts
full at Anzio and in the push to Rome. I've
got two pals with the Infantry there; I hope
they get through okay."

Pfc. Bill Ellis, an artilleryman from Mobile,
Ala., was walking down the street in search
of some pals who had whipped off in a weapons carrier and left Ellis stranded in the city.
He was as suspicious as the other two had
been when I told him about the invasion. "It
sure is a hunk of news," he said. "I've been
waiting for that news since North Africa and
was about to give up. Rome and the second
front, both at once, are too much for the Germans. I think we'll be home in six months—
I hope."

S/Sgt. Carl L. Johnson of Minnesota was
parked in a jeep outside a building, waiting
for an officer. He was one of the rare GIs who
had heard the news over the radio; he'd heard
both the German and the BBC reports.

"I got sort of a tickling sensation in my
stomach when the announcer broke the news,"
he said. "I'm happy it came at such a swell
time. I'd sure like to get over there. I can
speak *petite Francais* and could make out
okay with the women. I haven't done so good
here—the language has me whipped."

Pvt. Charles Camp of Dunbar, Pa., a 19-
year-old infantryman who is the only man
left out of a platoon that fought the Germans
for 60 days, said: "It's very good news, but
I am still happiest about getting to Rome; I
didn't think I would make it. My heart is with
those guys in France. I know what they are
going through. But I'm confident they will
push the Germans back just like we did."

Sprawled under poppies lie the German dead, their gaping mouths painted with dust.

Flour and Flats

WITH THE FIFTH ARMY IN ROME [By Cable]—
On the way up to the front, the most common picture you'll see is a line of GI trucks, jammed with soldiers wearing dust goggles over their eyes and handkerchiefs across their noses and mouths. They look like a cross between an old-time highwayman and a two-reeler comedian who has just rolled out of a flour barrel.

Dust grates between your teeth, scrapes down your throat, sifts into your eyes and piles up on your eyelashes until you can feel its weight. It cakes over every inch of your body until you look just as dusty when you step out of your flour-bag clothes as when you're wearing them.

Around almost every bend in the road is a charred German vehicle, bleached and mottled by the dust. Little toy towns, already shelled into white rubble and powder, are whiter still under their covering. The dust colors vast fields of poppies. Sprawled beneath them lie the German dead, dust grotesquely painting their gaping mouths and the fly swarms that once were eyes.

So much dust means that it is impossible to move a vehicle up the road to the front without being spotted by the Germans. It means also that the GI driver balances his life on the rim of his steering wheel every time he goes over 25 miles per hour. Hidden in the shell and mine craters in the road are sharp-edged shell casings, broken *vino* bottles and a thousand and one pieces of jagged metal — the dregs of a beaten army. They are flattening plenty of tires — 10 times as many, motor-pool sergeants tell you, as happened in the once cursed and now blessed mud of a few weeks earlier. Take the case of T-5 Joe Decoster of Jackson, Mich., jeep driver in an armored recon outfit. On the first day of the big push, his jeep came down with 11 flats.

The infantrymen say that the dust works into every inch of their equipment. During each lull in the fighting, doughfeet sprawled in foxholes sweat as they give the tooth-brush treatment to their rifles, machine guns and BARs. Some platoon sergeants have laid down the rule that every shell must be wiped off before it is slipped into a clip to prevent a jam when it counts.

Listen to Cpl. Gene Thompson of Elkhart, Ind., a tank-destroyer gunner. "I never believed," he said, looking inside a C-ration can opened two minutes before, "that they could figure out a way to dehydrate dust."

Message to Garcia

WE were lying in a ditch by the side of the road, looking up at a pretty little town held by the Germans. Like so many pretty little towns in Italy, this one is cocked over one eye of a mountain peak instead of being built in a valley as it would have been in America.

A column of massive tanks clanked up one side of the road, climbing slowly toward the town like a herd of steel elephants. Silent dusty infantrymen 15 yards apart plodded up the other side, their heads down as a protection against the grit that the tanks were billowing up in their faces. The taller doughboys stooped as they walked, to take advantage of a stone wall that ran in and out and under the clots of Jerry vehicles and equipment stretching along the roadside. Each man stepped as closely as he could in the footsteps of the man ahead, following the white tapes laid down by the engineers to mark the path through the enemy mine beds along the road.

Two hundred yards ahead was a sharp twist in the road, with no cover on either side. This was Torpedo Junction, the last exposed stretch before the farmhouse that was our advanced OP. As usual, Jerry's observation was perfect, and he was tossing shells on the bend whenever he spotted anything bigger than a grasshopper moving around it.

Tanks and foot soldiers stopped as the platoon leaders shot up their arms. It looked as if the advance would have to wait until after dark.

Just then a motorcycle came up from the rear like a bat out of hell, dragging a hundred-yard dust tail behind. The driver hunched over the handlebars as he snaked his machine between the shell craters all over the road. Twice we saw the lower half of his body bounding into the air when he didn't quite miss some craters, but he clung to the handlebars and kept going. Then an MP stepped into the middle of the road, and the cycle stopped, motor snorting. The driver's face was a mask of muddy white dust around the goggles.

"Dispatches and maps," he croaked. "Gotta get 'em up to OP." The MP waved him on wearily. "Okay, it's your neck, bud."

A quick twist of one hand and the motorcycle

Shells burst all around the motorcycle. It flew into the air, end over end like a tossed baseball bat.

shot off again. Tankmen leaning out of their turrets and doughboys sprawled in their ditches watched the driver throttle down just before he hit the dangerous bend.

"Damn good thing he knows his stuff," said the MP.

The driver was pulling an old trick. Here in Italy where Jerry is almost always on higher ground, you've got to figure every time you cross an exposed stretch near the line that some Kraut is squinting at you through a pair of binoculars. The idea is to save some speed until you are halfway across, then step on it, hoping that the sudden acceleration will knock the Jerry gunner off their timing.

Sure enough, the motorcycle spurted forward just about where it should have.

But this time the trick didn't work. A cluster of shells burst all around the speeding bike. It flew into the air, whirling end over end like a tossed baseball bat. When the smoke and dust cleared, we saw the driver crumpled in the center of the road.

Inside of 10 minutes, two infantrymen had slung him onto a blanket and carried him back under cover. His shoulder was crumpled queerly, trickles of blood were coming from his left arm and God knows what else was wrong inside him. One of the infantrymen pulled an envelope of sulfa out of his pack and with clumsy fingers tore it in half and sprinkled the white powder

The Dusty Road Through Rome

By Sgt. FRED ROSEN, YANK Staff Correspondent

on the cut. Then he took his own first-aid packet from his belt pouch and slowly and carefully tied up the wound around the oozing pink paste of blood and sulfa powder.

After a while somebody came back with an ambulance from a nearby clearing station. The infantryman who had done the doctoring helped lift up the unconscious man and climbed in beside him.

The motorcycle driver came to while the ambulance was jolting back to the station. He stared for a minute at the brown and gray walls, the grotesque enamel pans and odd-shaped rubber rings and tubes hanging from the ceiling, the worn stretchers with the great brown stains in their middle and the silent infantryman sitting hunched around his rifle. Then he closed his eyes again.

"My leg," he said faintly. "Jesus, my leg."

The clearing station was located under canvas stretched from one side of a trailer to a truck. It was hot and the canvas sagged so that the orderlies had to stoop over as they carried the driver to the operating table. A medic in fatigues and leggings worked swiftly and competently.

"Broken collarbone and shoulder blade," he said briskly.

The orderly, copying down the diagnosis on a tag that goes with each patient, looked up. "Think nothing of it," he said to the motorcyclist. "We'll issue you a new one."

Nobody laughed.

"To hell with all the rest," the driver said through clenched teeth. "Just look at my leg, I tell you."

The orderly shaved around the small cut near the driver's kneecap, and the doctor swabbed on a brown antiseptic. The driver jerked and arched his body. His face contorted.

"After-shaving lotion," said the orderly. "It always stings."

The infantryman squatting against the trailer wheel looked at the orderly. The doctor straightened up.

"He's got a bad shoulder blade," he said, "but there's nothing wrong with that leg. We'll tie up the vein in his arm and they'll stitch it together at the Evac. He'll be all right."

There was a long burst of firing from the distance. We had opened an attack.

The silent infantryman rose and hitched his rifle over his shoulder.

"It takes guts to ride one of them motorcycles," he said as he walked out.

Slang Slants

WHEN the Armored Force boys say something about opening a sardine can, it has nothing at all to do with food. Sardine cans are tanks.

---

tories from the note- book of a reporter who covered the ad- vancing GIs of the Fifth Army during their his- toric capture of the first big capital city in Europe to fall into the hands of the Allies.

And a half-track is rarely called a half-track; it's an ashcan.

For some reason the word Limey, which used to be universal for a British soldier in some outfits, has evolved into "Leroy." You hear "Hiya, Leroy" and even "Here comes a Leroy." The Yanks, naturally, are always Yanks to the Limeys—I mean, Leroys.

One of the most ironic twists of the campaign is the word that meets your eye the minute the Yanks fight their way into a new town. It's "Vincere," meaning "We will conquer"—a hangover from the old Fascist dream of glory. The word is always painted on walls, roofs, signs and fences in the biggest and gaudiest letters possible. Rumor says it is also tatooed on Mussolini's tummy.

Gotta Match?

AMERICAN troops had finally driven the stubborn Nazis out of the town, building by building, cellar by cellar, alley by alley. We were in there, all right, but just managing to hold on by our fingernails and eyelashes, when Jerry began to pulverize the town with a tremendous barrage.

In a cellar right on the main square, a small group of doughboys squeezed their faces against the earth as the plaster rained down steadily with the vibrations of bursting shells. Even in

Each time a shell landed, Vénus danced the shimmy.

the cellar you could hear the 88s, snapping and cracking through the air like giant whips.

Somehow still intact in one corner of the rubble-filled cellar stood a knee-high plaster statue of Venus on a pedestal. Each time a shell landed, Venus quivered as if she were dancing the shimmy.

Every once in a while, Pvt. Tom Robinson of Seattle, Wash., raised himself up and sneaked a quick look to see if our tanks were still in town. They had been sweeping down the street, blasting one shell into each story of a building, then moving on to drop more calling cards at the place next door just in case Jerry snipers were around.

After one of these quick looks, Robinson suddenly froze on one elbow, with his mouth open, and pointed like a madman. "Look," he screamed, "look!" Every grimy face jerked up.

There. right in the open, walking around what used to be a Cupid-fringed fountain, was a ragged old Italian peasant. He was bent over and tapping with a cane. In a couple of seconds his face lit up, and he reached down and picked up something and stuck it behind his ear. It was a cigarette butt.

Supersnake

MANY a replacement, spending his first night in the line, almost busts a gut when he stumbles over a long twisting object that looks exactly like the biggest snake in the world. But it is only part of a snake — a tank tread unrolled from a blasted Jerry tank by direct shell hits. You see these snakes everywhere—coiled around tree trunks, weaving in and out of vineyards, hanging over fences and even rooftops. Add the fact that they have large cleats on their inner surface and usually are covered with blackened blisters and with splotches of flame and rust, and you have something that looks as close to a prehistoric kind of spined supersnake as you can imagine. Some are 30 feet from head to tail.

Valet Service

NO Yank who has fought here will ever forget the Italian refugees. Sometimes, when Jerry rear guards are still withdrawing on one side of town, a long line of refugees appears out of nowhere and trickles back through the other side of town.

Everyone is barefoot, the oldest walking first, the next oldest behind and so on down the line. The women in the procession are always balancing bundles on their heads as big as pianos. It seems as if every woman in this part of Italy has a headpad—a soft cloth on which she can carry anything, from chicken coops to wine barrels to baby carriages. The shape of the load doesn't matter at all. You'll see a woman turn an enormous bundle around and around on her head until she finds just the right point of balance. Then she calmly glides off, never touching another finger to it.

The other day a recon patrol pulled into an abandoned farmhouse to billet down for the night. Right on the dot of midnight the family

that owned the farm filed in. There were 19 in all, ranging from grandpa to the smallest bambino. The Germans had forced them to vacate their home in January. They had spent the winter in a mountain cave, living on dried beans and roots.

Mama was so grateful that she embraced the Yanks and brought out the supply of vino that had been safely hidden in the well. When the boys awoke at daybreak, every man in the outfit found his clothes washed, dried and rolled neatly into his pack.

Esquire, Please Copy

THE Germans go in for a standard camouflage pattern in a big way. You see practically the same blotch-and-blend design of green and brown on all their vehicles, from tanks to the jeep-like volkswagon and also on helmets, machine guns, planes, knee-length frock coats worn by snipers, shelter halves and sometimes even rifles.

The boots worn by the Jerry infantryman look almost exactly like Yank combat boots. They have leather cuffs a few inches above the regular shoe, with two straps around the top. Ours are of better leather and superior workmanship.

Secret Weapons

PFC. HARVEY MALICOAT of Akron, Ohio, temporarily quartered in a cave dugout from which the former German tenants were ousted with bayonets, points with pride to the only piece of decoration his underground bungalow affords. It's a new, self-propelled hand-grenade thrower, which looks like a bazooka but is longer and made of flimsy sheet metal. You hold it under your arm, point it and fire it by pulling a pin. The grenade thrower is another German experiment, and like Jerry's self-propelled baby tanks, it is a complete flop.

Two new Yank weapons were tried out in the same sector on the same day by two pfcs.

Pfc. Aaron Lyberger of Battle Creek, Mich., a signal linesman, was walking through the high grass at night when he stepped into three Jerries, armed to the teeth. Lyberger had only a pair of pliers in his hip holster. He stepped back, whipped out the pliers and looked ferocious. The Jerries shot up their hands and shouted "Kamerad."

On the way back, one of the prisoners offered Lyberger a brand new blanket. He refused to take it. Later the blanket turned out to be a booby trap, wired to explode a hand grenade when it was unrolled.

Pfc. Elton Gorham of Winfield, La., an infantryman, was digging a ditch in the lines when a Jerry suddenly popped up in front of him. Gorham whipped up his shovel like a rifle, and it was all over.

But most of the Yanks hereabouts are sort of old-fashioned. They still rely on their rifles.

Lyberger stepped back, whipped out the pliers and looked ferocious. The Jerries shot up their hands.

YANK'S UNITED STATES

A slap-happy map of 48 certain pieces of terrain in America that will be so nice to come home to.

By Sgt. RALPH STEIN, YANK Staff Artist

MAIL CALL

"Don't Cry, Little Kraut"

Dear YANK:

Referring to the letter of O/C William H. Hall published in a May issue of YANK and appearing below a photo of a captured crying Kraut, which you had captioned "Don't Cry, Little Kraut," O/C Hall seems indignant and deeply moved at your brutal treatment of a little innocent Kraut. He speaks of courage and good taste and accuses you of warming your editorial chair in New York while he battles single-handed the diverse elements of Miami Beach. Emotional Hall is so far removed from the nasty things of war that he apparently doesn't know that many grimacing little and big Krauts, feigning pain or wounds at being captured, evoked the humane sentiments of their captors who, relaxing their alertness at trickery, were shot in the back. I judge from his letter that O/C Hall would be very impressed with the nastiness of things going on around here and think he would do well to stay where he is under the balmy Florida palms because the battlefields are no place for silly humanitarianism, but of stark and brutal reality for life or death with no quarters asked or given.

Italy —Sgt. C. N. LASKARIS

Dear YANK:

I don't know where Mr. Hall gets his ideas. We aren't out for tea and crumpets. It's a little thing like war, in case he's one of the few persons who doesn't know about it. The Germans and Japanese thought we were weak. So now we're showing them. . . . We're through feeling sorry for our enemy. . . .

Aleutians —Pvt. BING HANLEY

Dear YANK:

. . . We wonder whether the Nazis carry their treatment of captured Allied soldiers only to the extent of a photograph and adjoining caption. Were it not for the fact that we have quite a few prisoners ourselves, we doubt whether our men would be receiving the treatment they are supposedly "enjoying." We realize that we're somewhat out of line in our comments, in view of the fact that O/C Hall . . . has probably shown marked intelligence as a leader of men. But we are of the opinion that when and if he is commissioned, and when and if he does see action, his views will change—but radically and right quick, too.

Camp San Luis Obispo, Calif. —T-4 M. BLATTSTEIN*

*Also signed by T-4 C. L. Bartles and Pvt. P. F. Doolin.

Airborne Infantry Bonus

Dear YANK:

After reading that Airborne Infantryman's very, very sad letter many of the paratroopers here shed an abundance of tears. [In a recent YANK, Pvt. R. E. Buckwick complained that glider troops got no extra pay, while paratroopers received $50 a month as jump bonus.—*Ed.*] He was really sympathized with, believe me. He says he rides in gliders. My, that must be thrilling! Hell, we jump from them.

Fort Benning, Ga. —Pvt. S. J. KACZOR*

*Also signed by Pvts. J. Jarvis, A. Guthwirth and W. Harris.

Dear YANK:

I read the letter about "Airborne Infantry Bonus." I feel sorry for those poor glider troops who ride in those dangerous gliders, and especially way back in Camp Mackall, N. C. The glider troops are supposed to be used along with paratroops as a combat team. Maybe they can relate why they have not been used yet. We went into combat eight months ago, but I have yet to see a glider trooper. If they have been used, I assure you I have never seen one that glided in. Some have come in by landing barge. . . .

Anzio Beachhead, Italy —Sgt. GUY CALLEY

Dear YANK:

. . . The American glider troops have played a conspicuous part by their complete absence in this theater of war. About the paratroops' pay, why should Pvt. Buckwick kick when the American doughboy in the front lines, who incidentally draws $50 per month, says we earn every penny? If anyone deserves a pay increase, it's the doughboy on the front lines, not those who have not and probably will not see any action. Who are we? Just a few members of a paratroop outfit overseas, who have made two combat jumps, along with several ground missions, which have kept us busy and made us an active-combat unit eight of our 10 months overseas.

Italy —Paratroop Engineers

Dear YANK:

. . . It was the Paratroops that made the invasion of Sicily and Italy possible. We over here are not trying to take credit for what the boys are doing on the other side. I refer you to the Presidential citation just awarded to the 3d Battalion, 504th Parachute Infantry Regiment, for "outstanding performance of duty in action on the Anzio Beachhead, Italy, during the period 8 to 13 Feb. 1944." The battalion had just been relieved from front-line duty when a vicious German attack (to use the official words) was launched against a nearby British unit and the battalion went right back into action. The citation concludes with: "As a result of the 3d Battalion's tenacious and intrepid action a severe enemy threat to the security of the beachhead was eliminated."

Camp Mackall, N. C. —Pvt. LEO DELCAMBRE

GI Proverbs

Dear YANK:

Don't you think that there are some things which are above the common desire to have fun and get a "kick out of things"? I refer to the article "GI Proverbs From King Solomon" in an April issue of YANK. It is believed that such humor is not necessary but is also carrying a good thing a bit too far. Personally, I do not know too much about the Scriptures, but I do know that making fun of such in the way the above article was presented only shows poor taste. . . . Of course the items were meant for fun and we all like fun, but such as this ceases to be fun, and there are others who share the opinions of the writer.

Africa —Sgt. JAMES M. REDDING

Dear YANK:

How did you ever miss this in your compilation of "GI Proverbs From King Solomon"?

A fool's lips enter into contention,
and his mouth calleth for stripes. [18:6]

Maxwell Field, Ala. —Cpl. AUSTIN C. WEHRWEIN

Dodds' Autograph

Dear YANK:

Shame on you, Sgt. Dan Polier! In your sports article about Gil Dodds in an April issue of YANK you stated that Dodds had been known to autograph 15,000 programs a night. I've spent a lot of time in the direct-mail business, and any time we found a girl who could sign 1,500 letters a day we knew we had a jewel. I'd be willing to wager $25 against your $10 that Dodds couldn't autograph 15,000 copies in a week, let alone add a Biblical verse.

c/o Fleet Post Office, New York —Lt. H. OVERBACK

■ Sgt. Polier was only kidding.

Drafting Women

Dear YANK:

We have just read that there is a movement seeking to pass a bill that will legalize the drafting of women. This movement has been approved by the National Federation of Business and Professional Women's Clubs Inc. It is our opinion, and we believe it is the opinion of the majority of men in the armed forces serving overseas, that this proposed bill is unfair to the soldiers in the armed forces. The only thing that keeps some of us going, when it is tough sledding, is the thought that we are giving our all to protect our loved ones. This will not be true if our wives and sweethearts are drafted into the various branches of the armed services. . . . In closing, we feel that if our country really needs more women in the service, the members of the previously mentioned club should be the first taken.

Iran —Cpl. PATRICK T. McGINNITY*

*Also signed by 23 others.

Prohibition

Dear YANK:

I recently returned from the Asiatic-Pacific theater of war, where I was a gunner on a heavy bomber. I returned to the States after I flew the required number of hours (300) over Jap territory, and 300 hours over enemy territory is no fun. I am now in a con valescent center suffering from operational fatigu I'm an Indian, from Kansas, and because of that cannot purchase beer here in this state . . . [but] I' good enough to wear the uniform and to go on bombing raids over Jap targets.

Fort George Wright, Wash. —S/Sgt. EDDIE RI

General Confusion

Dear YANK:

In a recent issue of a picture magazine Gen. Marshall and Gen. Eisenhower were photographed sitting together. Will you explain the wearing of the generals' stars? Which is correct, Gen. Marshall with four stars on his right collar or Gen. Eisenhower with four stars on his left collar?

Camp Plauche, La. —T/Sgt. NICHOLAS G. SHAHEEN

■ ***AR 600-40, Par. 1b,* states clearly: "All articles of uniform for wear by the General of the Armies, the Chief of Staff, and a former Chief of Staff are such as each may prescribe for himself." Insignia is officially described as part of the uniform, so it is our guess that Gen. Marshall is quite right. Concerning Gen. Eisenhower, we refer you to *Par. 52:* "When the shirt is worn without the service coat, metal insignia will be worn on collar. . . ." General officers of line are supposed to wear the insignia of grade on both sides of the collar. Other general officers, however, are supposed to wear the insignia of grade on the right side of the collar and, on the left side, the insignia indicating arm, service, bureau, etc. Under either of these classifications Gen. Eisenhower *might* be in error. If you think so, you tell him.**

GI Platform

Dear YANK:

Migawdno! regarding Cpl. Lee's suggestion in a April issue that you publish the political platform in the Presidential election. Why take up valuabl space to publish something we know the politicia will forget after election? . . . Now, if you want a *re* platform, listen to mine:

1. Victory (by youse other guys).
2. Rehabilitation of Germany, Japan and Italy. The three, along with U. S., Britain, Russia, China, Franc Canada and Texas, will form the "Big Ten" to contr the world and insure a lasting peace.
3. The Aleutians must be forced on Ireland as penalt for Ireland remaining neutral.
4. Mustering out of servicemen. Each man (and mayb the women) will gladly pay $100 for freedom, thus help ing to reduce the national debt. Each veteran, with n more than two court martials, to receive a pretty ribbo $37.50 in bonds and directions to the nearest USO. In ac dition to above benefits, killers of one German or seve Japs to receive $1.10 in cold cash. Oh yes, all to receiv undying thanks of those unable to enlist or otherwise ke back from the big show.
5. All pin-up pictures to be stored in Fort Knox unt the next war. Smuggling home of these pictures is strict forbidden.
6. More newsprint for YANK (plug).
7. Revision of Mann Act.
8. Less political platforms.

Aleutians —Sgt. ED HARTNE

Message Center

Sgt. WILLIAM T. GARNETT, somewhere in Kingman, Ariz.: write Pfc. Thomas F. Watkins Jr., Co. F, 176th Inf., Fort Benning, Ga. . . . Ens. R. E. GIBSON, King College, class of '40: write Pvt. Walter Caldwell, Finance Office, APO 360, Camp Roberts, Calif. . . . Anyone having any information about 2d Lt. MONROE A. GORDON, navigator, stationed in England and reported missing since Feb. 4, 1944: write Sgt. Alfred Garfield, Co. C, 325 Engr. Bn., APO 447, Fort Bragg, N. C. . . . Cpl. DANIEL HALE GRAY, Phoenix, Ariz.: write Pfc. H. Demke, Co. G, ASTU 3905, Stanford, Calif. . . . M/Sgt. ELVIN O. GREER, once at Bakersfield, Calif.: write S/Sgt. Ernest M. Lee, 744th AFTS, PAAF, Pecos, Tex. . . . Cpl. H. LINDSAY GRESHAM, formerly in Africa, or anyone having information about him: write Lt. Dwight G. Allen, 457 Parachute FA Bn., APO 468, Camp Polk, La. . . . WILBUR HARROLD, once in Camp Roberts, Calif.: write Cpl. Franklin A. Geske, Antitank Co., 140th Inf., Camp Howze, Tex. . . . Cpl. LEON KAMERLING, once at Albuquerque Air Base: write Pvt. Leon Seligson, Co. F, 803d Sig. Tng. Regt., Fort Monmouth, N. J. . . . Cpl. MAXINE LEVY, last heard of at Camp Crowder, Mo.: write Pvt. W. K. Roberts, Co. S, 840th Sig. Tng. Bn., Camp Kohler, Sacramento, Calif. . . . Lt. WILLIAM C. LITTLEWOOD of Chicago, last heard of at Boca Raton Fld., Fla.: write Pvt. Merrill Ormes, 579th Sig. Depot Co., Postal Unit 2, Camp Cooke, Calif. . . . Sgt. LEWIS LOWE, formerly at Scott Fld., Ill.: write Pvt. Anthony A. Szlasa, 20th Academic Sq., Scott Fld., Ill. . . . Sgt. TIM McCARTHY, last heard of in Pine Camp, N. Y.: write A/S C. L. Gerhardt, 21 CTD—C—14, Momer House, Colby College, Waterville, Maine. . . . Anyone knowing whereabouts of Pfc. SACK T. McKEE, last heard of with Fleet Marine Force, Group 23: write Pfc. Charles H. McKee, 383d CCTS, Bks. T-135, Peterson Fld., Colorado Springs, Colo. . . . M/Sgt. GREGORY C. MOIX, last heard of with the AAF, Wheeler Fld., Hawaii: write Pvt. Philip J. Schacca, Med. Det., 424 Inf., APO 443, Camp Atterbury, Ind. . . . Capt. JAMES P. MURI: write 1st Lt. W. W. Moore, 20th AAB Sq., Mountain Home, Idaho. . . . ROBERT RAMIREZ of Jersey City and New York: write T-4 John McGee, 2C Crescent Rd., Greenbelt, Md. . . . EDWARD RHUL, last heard of at Camp Upton: writ Cpl. Guido Cerulli, Advanced Languages Sectio ASTP, 4770th SCU, Grinnell College, Grinnell, Iow . . . BOYD RICHARDS, once an A/C at Stamford, Tex. write Sgt. George J. Murray, 68th BFT Sq., Good fellow Fld., San Angelo, Tex. . . . GEORGE SEVASSEU once of the AAFTD, Univ. of Wisconsin: write Cp Robert Harris, 8th Base Hq. & AB Sq., Scott Fld Ill. . . . S/Sgt. HENRY MANN SILVER II of Newpor R. I.: write T/Sgt. Mike Chamberlain, Rctg. Sta 117 So. Broad St., Philadelphia, Pa. . . . Pvt. ARTHU ULBRAND of The Bronx, believed somewhere in Afri ca: write Sgt. George F. Chace Jr., 81st Fighter Sq CCAB, Cross City, Fla. . . . Pvt. DONALD ULLUM once in the 166th Inf.: write Pvt. W. Knowlton, G T —124th Cav. Regt., Fort D. A. Russell, Tex.

SHOULDER PATCH EXCHANGE. **A list of shoulder-patc collectors' names will be sent to you if you write *Shoulde Patch Exhange,* YANK, 205 East 42d Street, New York 1 N. Y. Specify whether you want your name added to the lis**

FREE LAND IN ALASKA

IN MATANUSKA VALLEY, ALASKA, THE GOVERNMENT MAINTAINS THIS TERRITORIAL EXPERIMENTAL STATION WHERE EXPERTS STUDY FARM PROBLEMS AND GIVE INFORMATION TO THE SETTLERS OF THE FERTILE AREA.

There are 160 acres of good earth waiting for you on America's last frontier. It's yours for the asking. Here is what you have to do.

By Sgt. GEORG N. MEYERS
YANK Staff Correspondent

HEADQUARTERS, ALASKAN DEPARTMENT — Soldier, if the post-war prospect of starting life over back in the States throws a chill into you or maybe looks too tame, there's 160 acres of land waiting for you right here in Alaska —and for free. Under Federal homestead laws, you can stake yourself out a chunk of real estate, and after three years it'll be all yours at the cost merely of the sweat of your brow and some small filing fees.

At one Alaskan District Land Office, more than a half-dozen soldiers have already announced their hankering to apply for homestead entry right now, but unless Congress goes into a huddle on the matter they're legally stymied until after the duration plus.

That's because homestead laws require that you actually live on the land at least seven months a year for three years, and although you're allowed five years during which to fulfill this requirement, it's almost impossible for a soldier on active duty to do this.

The first special servicemen's provisions for homesteading were adopted by Congress in 1872, covering Civil War veterans. In 1901 an act was passed under which veterans of the Spanish-American war and the Philippine Insurrection were given credit toward homesteading for their time in the service.

By an act passed in 1922, Congress decided that any veteran of the first World War who had spent not less than 90 days in the Army or Navy while we were at war and who came off with an honorable discharge was entitled to have a period equal to his term of service (not exceeding two years) deducted from the three years' residence required for homesteading. So far, this provision of law has not been extended to cover service during this war, and credit for your present service does not apply.

It is possible Congress may do something about that, but until it does, you're in the same boat with a 29-year-old staff sergeant from Springfield, Mo., who has his eye on a choice plot near Homer on Kachemak Bay. Next to the Matanuska Valley, the Homer area is the best-known agricultural section in Alaska, but this sergeant is no farmer. He's a welder. He figures that Homer will one day be a helluva lot bigger than its pre-war population of 325 and that they'll need welders around to keep the farm implements in shape.

Like most of the 323 million acres in Alaska subject to disposal under public-land laws, the sergeant's tract is not accessible by road or railroad from his military station. Therefore, he can't even ask for a pass to "live" on a homestead between retreat and first call.

So many soldiers like this Missouri boy have been writing in questions about land settlement in Alaska that Fred W. Johnson, commissioner of the General Land Office in Washington, D. C., issued a bulletin in March, especially prepared for servicemen. If you're interested in homesteading, here are a few things Johnson thinks you ought to know:

The fact that you're a soldier doesn't bar you from making homestead application, but there are some things you'd be required to do that are almost impossible while you're on active service. The first of these is meeting the residence requirement. You must also cultivate at least one-sixteenth of your land by the end of the second year and one-eighth each year thereafter until your residence requirement is satisfied. Before the ground is turned over to you for good, you have to show you've put up a habitable house.

Of those 323 million acres of government land in Alaska, about 200 million have been surveyed and can be located on maps in the District Land Offices at Anchorage, Fairbanks and Nome. If a soldier wants to settle on unsurveyed land, it is not necessary to have it surveyed in advance. For protection against other claims, he should mark his boundaries permanently and file a description of his claim with the U. S. District Commissioner. Then, after final proof, the GI can survey it himself or have it done—by the government or at his own expense.

No one can make application for homestead entry for you or arrange for any piece of land to be held open for you until your discharge. If, however, your family—meaning wife and minor children—is already living in Alaska, they may clinch your rights to a homestead by living on the ground during your absence. In that case, you must execute your homestead application before your CO and forward it to the appropriate District Land Office.

Don't expect the clerk in the District Land Office to be able to give you definite information on the character of a specific piece of ground, but, in general you'll be told that the best prospects for agricultural settlement will be found in the Tanana River Valley, the Cook Inlet-Matanuska Valley area and the Kenai Peninsula. A large bite of the Matanuska Valley already belongs to Alaska Rural Rehabilitation Corporation—the widely publicized Matanuska Colony.

At the moment, no serviceman can expect to get preference over anyone else in the acquisition of public land after the war. Legislation was enacted after the last war that gave ex-servicemen a 90-day jump over the general public in filing entries. This expired in 1940 and has not been renewed or extended by Congress.

THE General Land Office bulletin winds up with a few tips to prospective homesteaders:

"Decide how you expect to make a living. Choose an area for settlement best suited to your liking as to climate, farming, employment, and availability of community services and conveniences. Select good land suited to your needs. Examine the soil for texture and depth. Study climatic conditions, particularly temperature, precipitation and length of growing season. Make inquiry as to crop yields and consider how and where the produce can be sold.

"New land in Alaska, as elsewhere, requires clearing and breaking, planting and harvesting. Hard work lies ahead of the successful settler. To the men in the service seriously interested in full-time farming or in home-site settlement coupled with other employment, there is a real chance for success.

"To others, attracted solely by prospects of free land, there is likely to come disappointment."

THE SAD SACK

"REAR GUARD"

MOVIE STAR IN PERSON
BEST DRESSED SOLDIER TO BE SELECTED AS HONOR GUARD —

SGT. GEORGE BAKER

THE HAND SALUTE

By Sgt. JOSEPH A. KEBLINSKY

A SILENCE fell over the officers' mess as the colonel rose and cleared his throat.

"Gentlemen," he began, "what I am about to say is unpleasant, but it must be faced. We, the officers of this regiment, are the laughing stock of the camp."

He glared about him and 124 officers cringed.

"As you all probably know by this time," said the colonel, and there was sarcasm in his voice, "the first requisite of an officer is to know how to render the hand salute as an officer should. In this very vital military function we are a dismal failure. I repeat, gentlemen—a dismal failure."

He paused to allow the full import of his declaration to sink in. It sank.

"Gentlemen," he said, "you are members of a famous fighting organization, a regiment steeped in tradition. Those of the 8446th who have gone on before—we can not let them down."

The executive officer blew his nose violently, a few majors stealthily wiped their eyes and 33 second lieutenants wept openly and unashamed.

"Now," said the colonel, "is the time for us to forget our past mistakes and look to the future. We shall correct ourselves right here and now. Lt. Lysterbag, front and center!"

A young lieutenant marched forward with fast cadence to hide the trembling in his knees. Three paces from the colonel he clicked to a halt. Smartly his right arm snapped upward, thumb and fingers extended and joined, palm to the left, hand and wrist straight, upper arm horizontal and forearm inclined at an angle of 45 degrees.

"No! No! No!" the colonel screamed, his face livid with anger. "That's just what I've been talking against, and now you come and insult me to my face! You—you young smart-aleck!"

Lt. Lysterbag slowly drew his pistol, shot himself through the heart and fell to the floor, dead.

Willing hands seized his body, dragged it out and dumped it on the garbage rack.

"Now," said the colonel, "here's the way I want you to salute! Watch me closely. I shall explain each movement. Raise your right arm nonchalantly. Cup your right hand with the little finger slightly extended and with the forefinger, middle finger and apex of the thumb almost joining and touching the forehead. Now, drop your hand as though pulling off a wad of chewing gum stuck to your right eyebrow. All right? Now let's all try it together. . . . Again.. . . . Once more. Now, what's so hard about that?"

The officers pressed forward eagerly.

"Looka me, sir," one babbled happily. "Looka me. I can do it good now, sir."

"Very good, Saladoyl. No, not like that, Buckslip. Like this. Now you try it. Only fair, Bedroll. Your forearm is dangerously close to that damn 45-degree angle. Relax, go over in the corner and practice. Cup your hand a little more, Germicide, and roll your eyes upward. That's better."

Each officer received individual instruction; then groups formed and practiced enthusiastically. Col. Rinsewater beamed.

Suddenly, to the sound of screeching brakes and breaking glass, a jeep came to a leisurely halt in front of the mess-hall door. A young captain jumped out, entered the building and pushed his way to the colonel.

Cupping his hand, he saluted.

"Gen. McGoiter's compliments, sir," he said. "Pending written orders which might eventually reach you through channels, sir, you are to observe and comply with the general's VOCO. The order states, sir, that disciplinary action will be taken where subordinate commands infringe upon the customs, privileges and practices of higher headquarters, relating in particular to methods of saluting. The 'chewing-gum-pull' salute is reserved for the exclusive use of the general and his headquarters staff!"

Slowly, slowly, Col. Rinsewater and 123 officers pulled out their pistols. There was a single thundering volley, and Col. Rinsewater and 123 officers dropped to the floor, dead.

The smoke cleared. Reverently the spruce young aide-de-camp paid his final respects. Raising his right arm with ceremonial nonchalance, he cupped his right hand with the little finger slightly extended and with forefinger, middle finger and apex almost joining and touching his forehead. Then he dropped his hand as though pulling off a wad of chewing gum stuck to his right eyebrow. He stepped over the prostrate forms, slipping several times in blood, and silently closed the door behind him.

Thus died the 8446th—bravely and gloriously their traditions upheld to the end.

Sgt. F. Brandt

VOTING REGULATIONS IN FIVE STATES AND TWO TERRITORIES

NAME OF STATE OR TERRITORY	DATE AND KIND OF ELECTION	HOW TO APPLY FOR STATE OR TERRITORY ABSENTEE BALLOT	Earliest Date State or Territory Will Receive Ballot Application	Earliest Date State or Territory Will Send Ballot to Applicant*	Final Date Executed Ballot Must Be Back To Be Eligible To Be Counted	SPECIAL STATE OR TERRITORIAL PROVISIONS
COLORADO	Primary. 12 Sept.	a) In accordance with Colorado law, or b) By sending the WD or USWBC post card to the Secretary of State. Denver, Colo.	21 Aug.	23 Aug.	9 Sept.	
LOUISIANA	2 Primaries: 12 Sept. (first) and 17 Oct. (second)	a) In accordance with Louisiana law, or b) By sending the WD or USWBC post card to the Secretary of State. Baton Rouge, La. One application will suffice for both primaries, unless the applicant has a change of address.	Any time for both primaries.	13 Aug. (first) 1 Oct. (second)	11 Sept. (first) 16 Oct. (second)	Note that Louisiana holds two primaries. One application will suffice for ballots for both elections, but in case of a change of address, a soldier should make separate applications. It is understood that Louisiana is holding a legislative session, which may change some of the facts as given.
MAINE	State Election. 11 Sept.	a) In accordance with Maine law, or b) By sending the WD or USWBC post card to the Secretary of State. Augusta, Maine.	Any time	15 Aug.	11 Sept.	Note that this is not a primary but an election for state and local offices and Representatives of Congress. Voting for the offices of President and Vice President will take place at a general election 7 Nov. 1944.
NEVADA	Primary. 5 Sept.	a) In accordance with Nevada law, or b) By sending the WD or USWBC post card to the Secretary of State. Carson City, Nev.	7 June	15 Aug.	5 Sept.	
SOUTH CAROLINA	2 Primaries: 25 July (first) 22 Aug. (second)	Soldiers may request ballots if enrolled prior to 27 June with a local party club. Application for a ballot should be made to the local club or county secretary by the soldier or a relative or friend acting in his behalf. It can be made with the WD or USWBC post card, on which he has written on both sides the name and address of the appropriate club or county secretary.	27 May (first) 24 June (second)	27 May (first) 24 June (second)	25 July (first) 22 Aug. (second)	Note that South Carolina changed its election laws since YANK announced that soldiers could vote only in person. Note that soldiers must have been enrolled prior to 27 June with a local party club in order to request a ballot, and that those using WD or USWBC post cards should write on both sides of the card the name and address of the appropriate club or county secretary.
ALASKA	Territorial Election. 12 Sept.	a) In accordance with Alaska law, or b) By sending the WD or USWBC post card to the Secretary of the Territory. Juneau, Alaska.	3 Aug.	3 Aug.	9 Sept.	Note that this is the Territorial election. No further election will be held in November.
HAWAII	Territorial Primary Election. 7 Oct.	Hawaii does not provide an absentee ballot for soldiers in the primary.				Soldiers voting in Hawaii can vote only by appearing in person in their home precinct or at a polling place within the Territory, designated by the Governor.

*Application should reach officials on, or as soon as possible after, the date the state or territory starts sending out the ballots.

THIS table explains the voting rules in five states and the territories of Hawaii and Alaska, which are holding primary or general elections in July, August, September and October.

The five states and Alaska permit soldiers to apply for ballots by using either the old WD post card (WD AGO Form 560) or the new United States War Ballot Commission post card (USWBC Form No. 1), although the War Ballot Commission card may not be yet available to you when you make your application. You may also apply by a letter that contains the text of the USWBC post card. If you use such a letter or the old AGO Form 560, be sure it is distinctly marked as ballot material and that it bears the appropriate air-mail marking. Be sure, too, that in addition to signing the application, you print your name and serial number. If you are applying for a primary ballot, remember that you must state your party affiliation.

To be eligible to vote in some states and territories, soldiers have to fulfill other requirements in addition to filing ballot applications. If you're not sure about your eligibility, write at once to the Secretary of State of your home state or to the Secretary of the Territory, if you are from a territory. Your letter should contain this information: date of your birth, date of the election in which you intend to vote; number of years preceding that election that your home residence has been in the state or territory; your town, county, street and number or rural route, and the number of years preceding the election that your residence has been at that place; your voting district to the best of your knowledge.

Since YANK announced that South Carolina soldiers could vote only by appearing in person at the proper local polling places, that state has changed its election laws to permit absentee voting. The new regulations are given here.

The information in this table is taken from WD Circular 221, 3 June 1944.

Washington O P

ASSISTANT Secretary of War John J. McCloy at a press conference described as "arrant nonsense" the reports that Italians in the north of Italy are better off than those in the south. He admitted that AMG made some miscalculations early in the campaign, particularly with regard to food shipments but, he said, "We have accomplished what we have without rounding up hostages, hangings, shootings in the square . . ." Maj. Gen. John H. Hilldring, director of the Civilian Affairs Division, reported that there is less malnutrition in southern Italy now than there was in 1939. Mr. McCloy said that the Italians have been "apathetic" about setting up their local governments. . . . AMG as such will not be used in France, which has been a traditionally friendly country; however, civil-affairs officers will participate in straightening out civilian problems there.

The Civil Service Commission has issued detailed instructions to agencies and departments of the Federal Government concerning the reemployment rights of veterans who leave the Federal service. The CSC circular says that an eligible veteran shall be restored to his old job or a similar one, depending on the case, within 30 days of his application for reemployment. . . . The U. S. Employment Service placed more than 74,000 veterans of the second World War in civilian jobs in February and March. . . . The National Association of Real Estate Boards has set up a committee to help veterans get their money's worth if they buy real estate with their discharge pay or government loans.

Roane Waring, former national commander of the American Legion and vice chairman of the Legion's post-war planning committee, has been asked to accept a post as special consultant to Lt. Gen. Somervell, chief of the ASF. Waring would study WD policies and methods with respect to returning soldiers, especially those concerning hospitalization, reconditioning, rehabilitation, etc.

Mrs. Roosevelt told the ladies at her press conference that many wives of servicemen do not know of the rights they have to free maternity and infant care. To date, 309,000 wives have taken advantage of the Emergency Maternity and Infant Care program operating under the Children's Bureau of the Department of Labor through state health agencies. —YANK Washington Bureau

YANK is published weekly by the enlisted men of the U. S. Army and is for sale only to those in the armed services. Stories, features, pictures and other material from YANK may be reproduced if they are not restricted by law or military regulations, provided proper credit is given, release dates are observed and specific prior permission has been granted for each item to be reproduced. Entire contents copyrighted, 1944, by Col. Franklin S Forsberg and reviewed by U. S. military censors.

MAIN EDITORIAL OFFICE
205 EAST 42d ST., NEW YORK 17, N. Y., U.S.A.

EDITORIAL STAFF

Managing Editor, Sgt. Joe McCarthy, FA; Art Director, Sgt. Arthur Weithas, DEML; Assistant Managing Editor, Sgt. Justus Schlotzhauer, Inf.; Assistant Art Director, Sgt. Ralph Stein, Med.; Pictures, Sgt. Leo Hofeller, Armd.; Features, Sgt. Marion Hargrove, FA; Sports, Sgt. Dan Polier, AAF; Overseas News, Sgt. Allan Ecker, AAF.
Washington: Sgt. Earl Anderson, AAF; Cpl. Richard Paul, DEML. London: Sgt. Durbin Horner, QMC; Sgt. Walter Peters, QMC; Sgt. John Scott, Engr.; Sgt. Charles Brand, AAF; Sgt. Bill Davidson, Inf.; Sgt. Sanderson Vanderbilt, CA; Sgt. Peter Paris, Engr.; Cpl. Jack Coggins, CA; Cpl. John Preston, AAF; Sgt. Saul Levitt, AAF; Cpl. Edmund Antrobus, Inf.; Cpl. Joseph Cunningham, Inf.; Pvt. Ben Frazier, CA; Sgt. Reginald Kenny, AAF.
Italy: Sgt. George Aarons, Sig. Corps; Sgt. Burgess Scott, Inf.; Sgt. James P. O'Neill, QMC; Sgt. John Frano, Inf.
Cairo: Sgt. J. Denton Scott, FA; Sgt. Steven Derry, DEML; Sgt. Walter Bernstein, Inf.

Iraq-Iran: Sgt. Burtt Evans, Inf.; Cpl. Robert McBrinn, Sig. Corps; Cpl. Richard Gaige, DEML.
China-Burma-India: Sgt. Dave Richardson, CA; Sgt. Lou Stoumen, DEML; Sgt. Seymour Friedman, Sig. Corps.
Southwest Pacific: Cpl. Lafayette Locke, AAF; Sgt. Douglas Borgstedt, DEML; Sgt. Ozzie St. George, Inf.; Sgt. Dick Hanley, AAF; Sgt. Charles Pearson, Engr.; Cpl. Ralph Boyce, AAF; Cpl. Bill Alcine, Sig. Corps; Cpl. Charles Rathe, DEML; Cpl. George Bick, Inf.; Pfc. John McLeod, Med.; Sgt. Marvin Fasig, Engr.
South Pacific: Sgt. Barrett McGurn, Med.; Sgt. Dillon Ferris, AAF; Sgt. Robert Greenhalgh, Inf.

Hawaii: Sgt. James L. McManus, CA; Cpl. Richard J. Nihill, CA; Sgt. Bill Reed, Inf.
Alaska: Sgt. Georg N. Meyers, AAF; Cpl. John Haverstick, CA.
Panama: Sgt. Robert G. Ryan, Inf.; Sgt. John Hay, Inf.; Sgt. William T. Potter, DEML.
Puerto Rico: Cpl. Bill Haworth, DEML; Cpl. Jud Cook, DEML; Sgt. Don Cooke. FA.
Trinidad: Pfc. James Iorio, MP.
Bermuda: Cpl. William Pene du Bois, AAF.
Ascension Island: Pfc. Nat Bodian, AAF.
British Guiana: Sgt. Bernard Freeman, AAF.
Central Africa: Sgt. Kenneth Abbott, AAF.
Iceland: Sgt. Joseph Koren.
Newfoundland: Sgt. Frank Bode, Sig. Corps.
Greenland: Sgt. Robert Kelly, Sig. Corps.
Navy: Robert L. Schwartz Y2c; Allen Churchill Sp(x)3c.

Commanding Officer: Col. Franklin S. Forsberg.
Executive Officer: Maj. Jack W. Weeks.
Business Manager: Maj. Harold B. Hawley.
Overseas Bureau Officers: London, Maj. Donald W. Reynolds; India, Capt. Gerald J. Rock; Australia, Capt. J. N. Bigbee; Italy, Maj. Robert Strother; Hawaii, Maj. Josua Eppinger; Cairo, Maj. Charles Holt; Caribbean, Capt. Walter E. Hussman; Iran, Maj. Henry E. Johnson; South Pacific, Capt. Justus J. Craemer; Alaska, Capt. Harry R. Roberts; Panama, Capt. Howard J. Carswell.

YANK
THE ARMY WEEKLY

camp news

Cpl. Howard A. Searfoss

Goes 35,000 Feet 'Up' Without Oxygen

Laredo Army Air Field, Tex.—Cpl. Howard A. Searfoss, a student at the flexible-gunnery school here, made a routine visit to the low pressure chamber and amazed attendants by going to a simulated altitude of 35,000 feet without benefit of oxygen. Searfoss' feat is rare in Army records; AAF medical authorities advocate the use of oxygen at 10,000 feet.

Searfoss, who comes from Wilkes-Barre, Pa., is no husky GI specimen. He is only 5 feet inches tall and weighs 115 pounds. He volunteered to be a subject for study so fellow students might note the reactions of flight at high altitudes without oxygen.

Twenty-two minutes after the heavy door of the pressure chamber had closed, Searfoss was in a pressure equivalent to that at 18,000 feet. There was no apparent effect; he was able to write his name and serial number perfectly and do mental arithmetic problems, and his muscular coordination was good. The "flight" remained at this "altitude" for 12 minutes. At 23,000 feet Searfoss was still apparently normal.

At 27,000 and 28,000 feet Searfoss made two mistakes in spelling. Approaching 30,000 feet, he made several mistakes in simple addition and subtraction but corrected them himself. He even took exercises. He stayed at 30,000 feet for 23 minutes. During that time he could tie his shoe lace with very little trouble and was feeling very happy. He said he'd like to come to the pressure chamber every Saturday night for a cheap drunk.

At 32,000 feet, the "altitude" began to have its first real effect. Cpl. Searfoss' eyes became bleary and his coordination was poor. He told an oxygen-masked observer he was growing weaker and that he felt the need of oxygen.

The flight reached 35,000 feet and remained there for two minutes before a quick "descent" to 32,000. At this point the corporal complained of a pain in his shoulder (bends) and took oxygen for the first time. He was able to put on his mask, but the observer had to turn the oxygen valve for him.

The chamber was "dropped" quickly then, and Searfoss' limbs stiffened and severe tremors developed in both arms and legs. This shaking ceased below 15,000 feet. At "ground level" Searfoss felt weak and very excited. After receiving oxygen on a cot for a half-hour, he was taken to the station hospital for observation. He walked with steady step but appeared dazed. He was given more oxygen for another hour, spent a normal night and left the hospital next morning no worse for his experience. —Pfc. HAL LAUERMAN

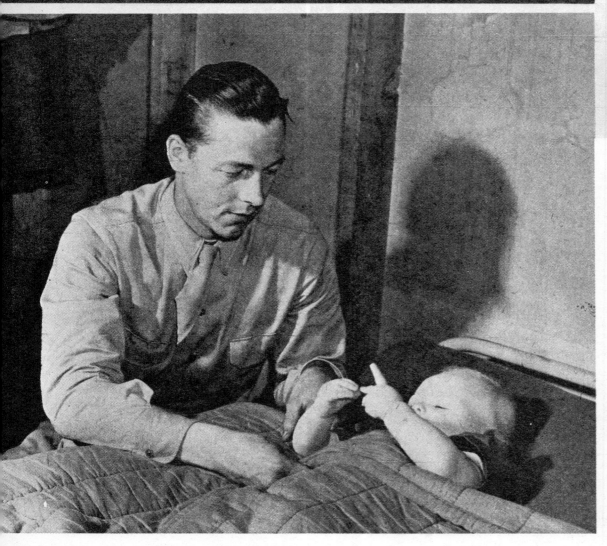

Fireguard Pvt. Chester O. Donaldson looks in on his son, Donald Leroy, acting as assistant CQ.

This Baby Gets an Early Taste of GI Life

Sioux Falls Army Air Field, S. Dak.—While his old man was on all-night fireguard detail, Donald Leroy Donaldson, aged 9 months, took on an Army detail, too. He spent the night in Section A's orderly room, acting as assistant CQ, while the regular CQ, Cpl. John Niziolek, saw that his tour of duty was made as pleasant as possible.

Donnie's presence was occasioned by the predicament his father, Pvt. Chester O. Donaldson, found himself in when Mrs. Donaldson was suddenly taken to the hospital. It was a Saturday night, and Donnie could not be left alone. Not wanting to interfere with someone else's night in town by asking for a substitute to take his all-night detail, Donaldson bundled the baby under one arm, a bottle of milk under the other and brought Donnie to the post.

Tucked into a GI bed, Donnie caused quite a stir among the GIs in Section A and they did their best to amuse and care for him. When the milk ran out, another bottle was procured from the mess hall. Donnie proved to be a true GI. When he hit the sack for good there wasn't a peep out of him the rest of the night.

—Pvt. LARRY C. HIGGINS

Hot Foot, Memphis Style

Memphis Fairgrounds, Tenn.—It was a warm and pleasant day, and Sgt. Lacy L. Hobbs of the 744th FA Bn., stationed at Camp Chaffee, Ark., was tired from his long trip here to pick up a prisoner. He wandered over to Court Square, picked out a tree and stretched out in its cooling shade. He took off his GI brogans to rest his tired feet.

When he awoke his shoes were gone. He walked the long distance back here in his stocking feet, bothered not so much by the curious stares of civilians as by the hot sidewalk. At the Fairgrounds he was issued another pair of shoes, picked up his prisoner and headed back for Chaffee. —Cpl. H. J. GROSS

Alphabetic Squelch

Camp Polk, La.—Pvt. Arthur Epstein of the 8th Armd. Div. has discovered a new way to discourage rank-pulling noncoms. While reading the bulletin board one day, Epstein was elbowed by a sergeant who said curtly: "Haven't you ever heard of RGP?" When Epstein shook his head, the sergeant explained: "Rank Gets Preference."

Epstein then asked the sergeant: "Haven't you ever heard of CDAM?"

"What the hell is that?" asked the sergeant.
"Common Decency Among Mankind," Epstein explained and walked away.

—Pvt. STANLEY WEINSTEIN

Lost—Two Army Wives

Las Vegas Army Air Field, Nev.—On Sunday the wives of A/Cs Harry Hammerlev and Ray Anderson of Squadron 5 arrived in Las Vegas. On Monday their husbands had lost them. On Tuesday they were found. In the meantime two girls and two GIs had spent some frantic moments trying to get together again.

Hammerlev and Anderson took their wives to a motel, but next day they forgot which one it was. Since there are many motels in this part of the country, the GIs were in a spot. They went to the Special Service office for help, and a civilian employee made a telephone canvass of all the motels in the area that had phones only to be given a negative answer by every one. One place remained that had no phone, and when a man was dispatched with a note from the husbands he failed to find the wives there, either.

A motel proprietor, previously polled, called up the second morning and said he had made a mistake. The wives were at his place, patiently waiting and a little worried. —Pfc. LEN S. RUBIN

Saves Chow Truck

Camp Carson, Colo.—When the battery's chow truck caught fire and its interior became filled with fumes and dangerous gases, T-5 Otto V. Holm of Virginia, Minn., grabbed a fire extinguisher and, without thought of personal safety, entered the blazing vehicle. He remained inside for 10 minutes and finally succeeded in extinguishing the flames.

For this act and for the saving of much Government property, Holm, a member of Hq. Btry., 929th FA, 104th Div., was awarded the Soldier's Medal. He's been in the Army since July 1, 1942, and with the 104th since November of that year.

Global Celebration

Camp Lejeune, N. C.—There are 8,000 miles of land and water between Marine Pfc. Martha Blackwell of Oakland, Calif., and her soldier-husband in Australia, but that didn't prevent them from celebrating their wedding anniversary.

Martha invited 15 of her closest friends to the American half of the party; on the other side of the world her husband asked 15 of his buddies to the Australian half. —Cpl. ERNIE HARWELL

Pvt. John W. Mattern

Survives Nazi Terrors, Now in the AAF

ORD, Greensboro, N. C.—One dawn a decade ago, the transport police in Berlin rolled their covered death vans into the yard behind Gestapo headquarters and began removing a pile of corpses for cremation. In the mound they found a man who was still breathing. He was Johannes Wolfgang Mattern, a former captain in the *Luftwaffe* who resigned his commission in 1933 rather than swear allegiance to Hitler.

That man now is at this AAF Overseas Replacement Depot. He is Pvt. John W. Mattern, 36, of the Special Services orientation department. He speaks many times each day before groups here of the "lifetime he lived in a day" under Gestapo questions and of the 51 months he endured in four concentration camps. Even the steady sleepers are wide-eyed at his lectures, and there is a hushed moment when Pvt. Mattern pulls off his shirt and bares his torso that was mutilated by Gestapo and SS torturers.

Accused of being a member of the underground, Mattern was seized early one morning in 1934. There followed 11 hours of beating with clubs and horsewhips. But questioning and violence failed to break him. "So," he says, "they decided finally to kill me. They gave me six dagger stabs in the abdomen, one bullet in the left leg, broke my elbow, knocked out most of my teeth, fractured my skull and threw me on the dead pile."

The next thing he knew he was in the Berlin Moabit Hospital, thanks to the transport police, then not too sympathetic with the Gestapo. There surgeons managed to put him together in six months. But as soon as he was well enough to walk, the Gestapo threw him into the concentration camp at Oranienburg near Berlin. From there he went to Fuhlsbuettel, Dachau and Estervege. "Of these hellholes," he says, "Dachau was the worst. There it was my job with three others to put the corpses in the coffins. We put away so many Nazis who didn't obey orders."

Mattern's father was finally able to get him released and transferred from civilian to military jurisdiction. In 1939 a military tribunal freed him, but he was ordered to report three days a week to the Gestapo in Cologne.

One morning he failed to report. He fled to Austria, then to Liechtenstein, Switzerland, France and finally across the mountains to Spain. He arrived in the United States in 1941. He worked in War Bond and Red Cross Drives and spoke to audiences all over the nation. Under the name of Ernst Winkler he wrote a book, "Four Years of Nazi Torture." "Ernst Winkler," he says, "was one of the first of our group to be murdered by the Nazis. I used his name. Now that I am in the Army Air Forces and hope soon to become an American citizen I speak as John Mattern."

—S/Sgt. MILTON MARMOR

AROUND THE CAMPS

Camp Crowder, Mo.—The Non-Cursist Club of Co. A, 800th Sig. Tng. Regt., amassed a balance of $26 in its treasury from 10-cent fines levied against swearers. "Hell" and "damn" are the only free words allowed members of the club, which is headed by Pfc. Malachy Noone. The money collected goes to pay for a big party every month.

Woodward Army Air Field, Okla.—Pfc. Leo Kaufman, expert swimmer from New York City, became exasperated when an elusive 11-inch bass continually refused to get hooked on his line. Finally he stripped down to his trunks, dove in and caught the bass with his hands.

Truax Field, Wis.—"Toothpick King" is the title GIs here have given Cpl. Jack Denman of Junction, Tex. Before entering the service, Denman once built a working replica of a Ferris wheel,

using 23,000 toothpicks, 14 tubes of cement and 600 hours of labor. As assurance to service-club hostesses inclined to fear for their toothpick supply, Denman says he's given up the hobby for the duration.

Camp McCain, Miss.—Sgt. William Narkowicz sewed some buttons on his shirt and then laid the needle on a 2-by-4 nearby. He forgot about it until the next day when the inspecting officer spotted it. Narkowicz got three hours' extra detail for his oversight.

Alexandria Army Air Field, La.—In the Kerns family of Fairmont, W. Va., there's an obvious fascination for the sound of certain first names. A crew chief here is Sgt. Vester W. Kerns, and his brothers are named Lester, Webster, Nester and Chester.

Camp Roberts, Calif.—Toting a blackboard to field class sessions, an Infantry trainee got a bit twisted on directions to the area his platoon was occupying. "Where do you belong?" barked an impatient platoon leader. "Chicago," replied the bewildered GI.

Newport Army Air Field, Ark.—Every time S/Sgt. Bill Gordon, SSO radio announcer, spoke over the post public-address system his voice came through with an eerie accompaniment. Investigation of the loud speaker revealed a bird's nest full of eggs and tenanted by a mother bluebird that had been adding her maternal muttering to the words of Sgt. Gordon.

Camp Ellis, Ill.—When floodwaters inundated an area near Quincy, Ill., S/Sgt. Roy J. Wilson was one of the GIs from this post who helped in the rescue operations. Sgt. Wilson's big feat was the rescue of a sailor whom he found up a tree and brought to safety in an assault boat.

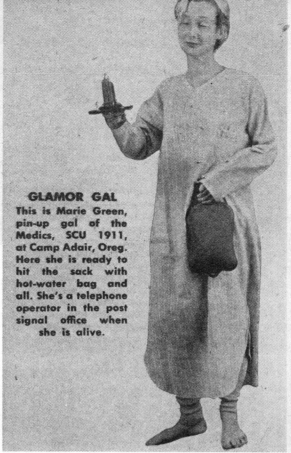

GLAMOR GAL This is Marie Green, pin-up gal of the Medics, SCU 1911, at Camp Adair, Oreg. Here she is ready to hit the sack with hot-water bag and all. She's a telephone operator in the post signal office when she is alive.

HAT STYLIST. Authentic are the skimmers that sit on the head of Cpl. Jerry Eisenberg. Besides directing and producing the "Gay Nineties Review" at AAFTAC, Orlando, Fla., Jerry doubled as prop man.

PERFECT EYE. Sgt. John J. Sutton (left) sights the .57-mm antitank gun with which he fired a perfect 200 at Fort Benning, Ga. Cpl. A. Bushman (center) watches as T/Sgt. T. W. Jackson eyes the target.

REAR WALLOP. The bazooka packs a mean wallop behind as well as in front as demonstrated here by infantry trainees at Camp Roberts, Calif. Target behind bazookamen is blasted by the rocket's backblast.

Jeanne Crain
YANK
Pin-up Girl

NAVY NOTES

HOME STATES. A state-by-state break-down of Navy personnel shows New York first, Texas sixth and Nevada last, the same as in the Army figures published in *Strictly GI* three weeks ago. But California, which was fifth in the Army list, is second with the Navy, making Pennsylvania, Illinois and Ohio third, fourth and fifth, in that order, instead of second, third and fourth, as with the Army. The complete Navy line-up:

New York	272,373	West Virginia	45,871
California	237,292	Connecticut	45,701
Pennsylvania	218,968	Maryland	42,971
Illinois	181,863	Oregon	39,725
Ohio	156,047	Kansas	39,486
Texas	144,284	South Carolina	36,167
Massachusetts	141,955	Arkansas	34,728
Michigan	112,761	Mississippi	33,254
New Jersey	112,566	Colorado	28,418
Missouri	80,506	Nebraska	26,127
Indiana	73,587	Rhode Island	23,746
North Carolina	64,585	District of Columbia	19,612
Minnesota	62,072	Maine	18,315
Virginia	60,198	Utah	15,608
Alabama	58,587	Arizona	12,997
Iowa	57,730	New Hampshire	12,454
Washington	56,954	Montana	12,351
Florida	56,482	Idaho	12,006
Tennessee	56,312	North Dakota	11,183
Georgia	54,810	South Dakota	10,998
Wisconsin	52,575	New Mexico	10,185
Louisiana	51,794	Vermont	6,269
Oklahoma	48,710	Wyoming	6,211
Kentucky	47,906	Delaware	5,702
		Nevada	3,769

LUXURY LINERS. The *USS Wakefield,* formerly the $10,000,000 steamship *Manhattan,* is back on the job after being virtually rebuilt at the Boston Navy Yard. The *Wakefield,* which is manned by Coast Guardsmen, was originally damaged by Jap bombs at Singapore shortly after Pearl Harbor. She later caught fire in the Atlantic while nearing New York.

Work on the *USS Lafayette,* the former French liner *Normandie,* has been halted by a shortage of manpower and critical materials. She will be rebuilt after the war.

PLANE PRODUCTION. Because more and more Navy planes are returning safely from air battles, the Navy Department has ordered a cut in new production. Losses from routine accidents and battle damage are one-third less than the original estimate, and the figures are expected to drop even further as the relative air superiority over the enemy advances.

DREDGINGS. Details on the sinking of the Coast Guard DE *Leopold* in the North Atlantic reveal that she was firing at a sub on the starboard side when another sub put a torpedo in her port side amidships. All of her officers and many of her men were lost, most of them in the icy waters. . . . A new 2,250-ton destroyer will be named the *USS Frank Knox* after the late Secretary of the Navy. . . . Enlisted Navy ratings have jumped from 65 specialties a year ago to almost 100 now. . . . A Navy tug from Bermuda towed a torpedoed tanker 950 miles sternfirst. The trip back to the U. S. took 24 days, but it saved almost all of the tanker's 5,000,000-gallon cargo of aviation gasoline. . . . The Army operates more than 4,000 vessels, most of them small tugs and launches.

Best-selling magazines at Great Lakes NTC are comic books such as "Captain Marvel" and "Superman." Pocket-size detective stories are second. . . . More torpedoes are produced each month than were turned out during the entire first World War. . . . Seabees used empty Jap shell cases to build a 2,000-foot brass drainage system for a Navy hospital at Munda. . . . A Navy pilot at Bougainville, firing his guns to clear them as he climbed on a night interceptor mission, shot down a Jap bomber he didn't know was there.

The Navy has put out a "Functional Components Catalogue," which is the equivalent of a Sears Roebuck handbook for advanced bases. It lists all the items needed for building a new base, and they are ordered from the catalogue. . . . The Pensacola NAS is building a model "survival museum" to teach self-preservation. The exhibit will deal with problems of living on rafts, islands, deserts, ice packs and at high altitudes.

With the advent of the new baby flat-tops the British have discontinued the practice of catapulting fighter planes into the air from the decks of merchant vessels. The "catafighters" were shot into the air for action against subs and enemy planes and then were left to crash when the pilot bailed out after combat. . . . Says the Tokyo radio: "The hardships which confront our seamen in the maintenance of supplies are beyond our imagination." . . . Eighteen men were rescued from the Brazilian jungles in a series of hazardous landings by Navy blimps.

The *Stethoscope,* Navy hospital publication at Bremerton, Wash., held a contest to see who, if any, could identify a photo of Betty Grable's legs. The chaplain won. —ROBERT L. SCHWARTZ Y2c

The POETS CORNERED

ENGINEER BLUES

Where the monsoons sweep and the cobras creep
And darkness falls with a thousand fears,
There the chow is rough and the noncoms tough—
Oh, that's in bounds to the Engineers.

Where the saxes sob and the dancers bob
And the siren from darkened doorway peers,
Where the ivories click and the steaks are thick—
Oh, it's out of bounds to the Engineers.

Where the snipers lurk in the leafy murk,
Where men are bloody and sweaty smears,
Where the Zeros wing and the scorpions sting—
Oh, that's in bounds to the Engineers.

Where the MPs stalk and the hillbillies gawk
And the native soldiers leer,
Where the white wine bubbles to drown your
      troubles—
Oh, it's out of bounds to the Engineers.
India
                              —Pfc. E. V. ANDERSON

ICELANDIC SPRING

This barren land of wind and waste,
This broken rock spewed from the maw
Of a nauseous ocean—ash of the Atlantic,
Beaten down by precipitation,
Numbed by cold gales—
Comes to life sometimes.
Black night turns gray and shrinks
To nothingness.
Wild grass shoots up enigmatically
From volcanic dust
And spreads like moss
On a wet stone.
Iceland
                              —Pfc. THEODORE PROPP

PIN-UP PROBLEM

The pin-up pretties, I am quite sure, were meant
For men in the barracks and men in the tent.
But how can a tent-dweller keep his chin up
When there's no damn place to pin up a pin-up?
New Guinea
                              —T-4 ARTHUR M. ZIPSER

IN YOUR ABSENCE

Innumerable times
Throughout each day
Similies regarding you
Occur in my mind.
Some are corny,
Some are plagiarized,
Some are fair,
And some are of a nature
That at the present state
Must await fermentation
Of that thing called Eros.
When the thought, "She
Is the incarnation of some
Grecian goddess," comes to
Mind for a moment I think
That I've got something,
But the briefest spell
Of time oxidizes it.
Sometimes after some
Rhetorical thought
Has been rejected I
Find myself saying: "She
Simply defies description."
And a short while afterward
The afterthought arrives:
"That would be more pertinent
About five or six years
Ago." And so on and so on
Throughout the day until
Reality does away with it.
Puerto Rico
                              —Pvt. LOUIS FISHER

GO AHEAD, TRY TO INFECT ME

Oh, whisky is a potent brew,
A virile alcoholic dew;
It does amazing things to you,
      A snifter or a shot.

But shots of corn are not as rough
As shots of certain other stuff.
Oh, please, dear Lord, I've had enough.
      My arms have gone to pot.

An ultimate in brutal crime:
My record's lost the seventh time!
The viruses within me climb.
      They've got me on the spot.

With typhus I'm on friendly terms,
I'm intimate with smallpox germs,
My corpuscle in anger squirms—
      It's jealous like as not.

My upper arms are black and blue:
Oh, gentlemen, in pity view
An antipathogenic stew,
      An antiseptic sot.
Robins Field, Ga.
                              —Cpl. SHELDON HARNICK

PUTTING ON THE SQUEEZE

"More and more American women are dispensing with corsets and girdles, under the pressure of wartime rationing. Manufacturers are concerned, fearing a post-war continuation of the trend."—News Item.

In other days, when lace and stays
      Adorned milady's torso,
She yearned to be as willowy
      As Venus—only more so;
She didn't spare her derriere,
      She made her clothes include it—
It may have pained to be restrained,
      But, womanlike, she dood it.

Now, willowy or pillowy,
      A dame is still a dame;
We men don't care what women wear,
      We love them just the same.
If fashion's whim decrees them slim,
      So be it—they are thin;
But thin or stout, we'll take them out
      Whatever shape they're in.

But Sal and Sue are subject to
      Another sort of squeeze—
They'll fret and pout and go without
      Their rubber BVDs;
This war of nerves is tough on curves,
      But easy on the eyes—
When we have peace, will women cease
      To hide their shape and size?
Camp McCain, Miss.
                              —Cpl. ALEX DROGICHEN

TEE-TOTAL WINNERS

OVERSEAS. This time William Reiter SF2c is winning his thirteenth contest with a score of 372. Prize puzzle kits go to these first-time winners: S/Sgt. Paul S. Rhoads, whose solution is shown (score of 377); Cpl. S. Bilsky (373); T-5 Karl Zweiger and Pfc. Ricky G. Kaufmann (372); Pvt. Norbert B. Wittrock (367); and Pfc. Robert C. Richardson (362).

SINCE Jeanne Crain may be your kind of favorite person, you might want to know her kind of favorite fellow. Well, he must be both a "dreamer and a doer." That, undoubtedly, is a unique combination to find in one soldier, but then this rare lass deserves a rare lad. Jeanne's new pictures, both for 20th Century-Fox, are "Home in Indiana" and "Winged Victory."

Nowhere To Go

THE NURSE led her down the long row of beds to where he sat. "You have until 9 o'clock," she said and left them.

They stared at each other for a moment without speaking. Then slowly she bent and kissed him.

She sat on the bed beside him, her eyes never leaving him. They spoke haltingly of unimportant things. Other soldiers moved on their beds and chairs to see them, heads and necks twisted on the pillows, eyes peering over magazines. The nurse moved about them efficiently.

"Let's go outside," he said. He followed her out into the dimly lit corridor and closed the ward door behind him. He turned to her and after a moment passed his arm under hers and around her waist. She quivered.

"What's the matter, darling?"

"It's been 14 months." She held his arm tightly under hers.

A medical officer passed, glancing at them curiously.

"Let's walk," he whispered. He took her hand, and they moved down the narrow corridor. Her hand was warm and moist in his. He turned the smooth yellow wedding ring on her finger slowly around.

Their steps were loud on the wooden floor. They turned the corner, eased against the wall

"Is this the haircut, movie or bus line?"
—Sgt. Tom Zibelli, Camp Davis, N. C.

to let a soldier in a wheelchair pass. They walked again, looking in the open doors of the wards they passed or through the corridor windows to the little roads outside. Everywhere there were soldiers in dark red bathrobes and attendants in whites.

They came to the Red Cross lounge, hesitated and stuck their heads in the door. The men were playing checkers or reading. They walked on. Outside the windows it was getting quite dark.

She stopped at a door and asked: "Is this ward empty?"

"Yes," he said, "but they keep it locked."

He saw her eyes filling as she felt for his hand again. They kept walking down the long corridors—walking, looking, and walking.

—Pfc. MURRAY HARTMAN
104th General Hospital, Camp Pickett, Va.

NOW

Long ago a soldier said to me:
"Enlist in the Women's Army Corps
And be yourself a part of the effort
To hold the head of Democracy
Above the tidal wave of destruction."
And so I did
Because he hinted indirectly
That I was selfish.

I pictured myself near the battlefront
Where bombs rocked the earth about me
And guns chattered from hidden trenches ju[st]
ahead.
All through basic I trained for dangerous work,
Proving my stamina by scrubbing floors,
Marching in Iowa's rain and sleet,
Building fires in the orderly room,
Cleaning latrines.

Then I was assigned to an office desk
on the same post
And all the glamor suddenly left me
high on the rock of discouragement.
I lost my vision in tears of self-pity
Until today when I remembered the words of tha[t]
soldier.
Fort Des Moines, Iowa   —Pvt. JUDITH A. BRIDG[E]

DEFINITION

When majors are seen
Falling in for the muster,
Is that what they mean
By an Oak Leaf Cluster?
Camp Shelby, Miss.   —S/Sgt. A. L. CROUCH

"In lousy weather I always mail mine."
—Cpl. Fred Schwab, Roswell AAF, N. Mex.

The Umpire

THE MAJOR handed Pvt. Ump five tags and said: "Battery A has just been shelled. Go over there and mark some casualties."

"Yes sir," said Pvt. Ump, dismounting from the command car.

An hour later Pvt. Ump reached Battery A. The first men he saw were gathered around a jeep.

"Who's the driver?" asked Pvt. Ump.

"I am," said one of the boys.

"Fine," replied Pvt. Ump as he tied a casualty tag on the driver's blouse. "As of now, you're a casualty."

Continuing his journey, he found a gun crew digging in its weapon. Everyone of the crew looked in the pink of condition except one weary-looking pfc.

Pvt. Ump called to the man: "Come here. I'm going to give you a little rest."

The weary pfc spat on his shovel. "To hell with your rest. Who's gonna dig in the gun—you?"

"Not me," said the Ump, "but you ain't either." And he slipped the tag string around the pfc's jacket button.

"Hell of an Army," the weary pfc swore. "How they expect to win a war when they take a man away from his job?"

Pvt. Ump moved toward the kitchen.

He tied a tag on a KP, and the mess sergeant came flying off the chow truck. "Have a heart," he implored, "I'm short on help. My cooks are sick. I even got to cook myself. I ain't got enough KPs like it is."

"Sorry," said Pvt. Ump, "but business is business."

"Go take the wire section, the detail section. You'll find 'em under the big tree, restin' their fannies."

Pvt. Ump gave a negative jerk of his head.

The mess sergeant put his hands on Ump's shoulders and beseeched: "You can't do that to me, pal. It ain't justice. It ain't the American way of doin' things."

Pvt. Ump's frown said no.

"Look," begged the mess sergeant, "I'll give you C rations, I'll give you K rations. I'll even give you Five in One." He pushed Pvt. Ump down on a box and called to a KP: "A cup of coffee for the gentleman."

When Pvt. Ump had gone halfway through the java the mess sergeant said: "Let's talk this over like sensible people. You get somebody else for a casualty, and I'll fix you up with six cans of C rations!"

Pvt. Ump jumped to his feet and flung the coffee cup at a water can.

"Go away!" he cried, and he strode off indignantly. "C rations!" he mumbled. "That's all I've been eating! Why didn't he offer me a cheese sandwich, the louse?"

At another gun position he fastened a tag on a sleeping sergeant. When the sergeant awoke he found his men standing around him, their faces long and sad.

The sergeant sat up and began to give orders, but no one paid him any attention.

"He wasn't a bad guy," said a melancholy private.

"Blessed be he that enters into the Kingdom of Heaven," another soldier intoned. "Verily."

The first-aid man had told the first sergeant that some umpire was tagging casualties, and the first sergeant told it to his BC, who came storming toward Pvt. Ump, thundering: "Who the hell gave you permission to make casualties? We're not supposed to get any. Nobody told me! Where the hell d'ya get that stuff? You're bustin' up my outfit! Get the hell outa here!"

Pvt. Ump snapped smartly to attention, saluted briskly and militarily announced: "Sir, you are now a casualty."

The BC's face was purple with rage. *"Me!"* he roared.

"You're exhausted," said Pvt. Ump. "You're exhausted and you can't move. Begging your pardon, sir, you must lie down."

The BC sank to the ground, and Pvt. Ump tagged him, saluted, about-faced and started back to the command car, ignoring as he passed the chow truck the frantic cries of the mess sergeant: "Let my KP go! Eight cans of C rations!"

Camp San Luis Obispo, Calif.   —Pvt. R. FRIEDMAN

A FTER all these years we finally have learned why those talent-rich Boston Red Sox never won the American League pennant. The source of our information is none other than James Emory Foxx, who is known in most circles—including one divorce court—as the Beast.

The Beast is no longer connected with the Red Sox and therefore is free to roll out his soap box and speak his piece any time he pleases. When Tom Yawkey began unloading his million-dollar ball club a few years ago, he sold Foxx outright to the Chicago Cubs. After a dismal season with the Cubs in 1942, Foxx retired from baseball, supposedly for keeps, and went into the oil business. But the wartime manpower shortage brought him back, and now he is a part-time third baseman and catcher for the Cubs as well as a full-time authority on the Boston Red Sox.

The Beast didn't come right out and volunteer his information on the Red Sox. Somehow or other the conversation swung around to Connie Mack and Joe Cronin, and we asked why it was that Cronin, after buying up virtually all of Connie Mack's great stars, couldn't win a pennant.

"The difference," the Beast said, "is that one manager knew what he was doing and the other didn't. Cronin didn't. If he had handled our pitchers properly we might have won several pennants. Our hitting was always good, but the pitching didn't hold up. It wasn't the fault of the pitchers, either. They could have won if Cronin had used more judgment in picking their spots. Didn't every one of them turn out to be winners after they got away from Boston?"

Since the Beast turned out to be such a convincing authority on the Red Sox, we wondered if he wouldn't spare us a few words about his present employers, the Chicago Cubs. We asked why Jimmy Wilson was given the opportunity to resign, and if it was true that the Cubs were rehiring all of their old managers until they got Joe McCarthy back.

"Wilson was a good, sound baseball man, and make no mistake about that," the Beast said. "But he was too easy-going for a manager. He would argue with his players instead of telling them off. Now, Charlie Grimm is different. When he took over the team he called us together for a meeting and told us he was boss and that his word would be law.

That was probably the last meeting we'll have, because everybody understood him. That is, everybody but Novikoff. Lou never understands anything the first time anyhow.

"One of the first things Grimm told us was that he expected everybody to be in his room by midnight. He warned us if anybody was caught out after 12 he would be fined $50. Then he turned to Lou and said: 'Novikoff, I'll bet you another 50 you will be the first one I catch.' Sure enough, the very next night Grimm caught Lou out of his room at 1:30 in the morning. He was sitting in the hotel lobby listening to the radio and had forgotten what time it was."

Novikoff is always a good subject, so we kicked him around for a while.

"The trouble with Lou," the Beast explained, "is that he is a bad ball hitter. In the minor leagues he could afford to hit bad balls all day long, because he probably wouldn't look at one good pitcher a week. Up here it's different. He's looking at good pitchers every day. There's only one way to play Novikoff. Just stick him in the outfield and leave him alone. Either he will wake up and learn something or he will be a minor-league player the rest of his life."

The Beast sounded almost like a manager himself. He paused for a moment, then laughed:

"I guess I do at that. Maybe it's because I want to be a manager so badly. Old baseball players usually do."

The Beast is a realist; he admits he's not half the player he was. If it weren't for the war, he wouldn't be playing today. He came back because he wanted to manage some day.

"If I ever do become a manager," he continued, "I hope I can be as successful as Connie Mack. He was the best; he knew his men and he knew how to handle them. There's one incident between Mr. Mack and me that still stands out in my memory. Maybe it will show you what I mean.

"We were playing the Yankees, and it was a tight game. I was leading off in the ninth inning, so I asked Mr. Mack what he wanted me to do. He looked at me coldly and said: 'Jimmy, what have you been drinking?' I was speechless for a minute. I hadn't been drinking and I couldn't understand why Mr. Mack should think so. Finally I said: 'Nothing but water, Mr. Mack.'

"'All right, then,' he answered, 'go up there and use your own judgment.' I worried about this all the way to St. Louis, and the next morning I told Mr. Mack: 'I don't understand that remark you made in Philadelphia. You know I haven't been drinking.'

"'I know it,' Mr. Mack said, 'but there were others listening, and some of them had. I wanted to let them know I would as soon bawl you out for drinking as anybody.'"

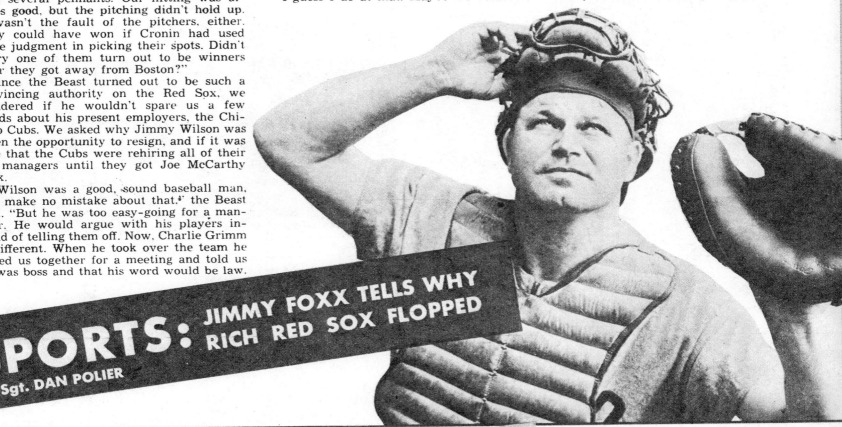

SPORTS: JIMMY FOXX TELLS WHY RICH RED SOX FLOPPED

By Sgt. DAN POLIER

SPORTS SERVICE RECORD

O NE of the first Americans to land in France was Lt. Bob Halperin, an ex-Brooklyn Dodger footballer, who went ashore with the Navy and marked the beaches for the assaulting infantry. . . . When Lt. Col. Wallace Wade, the Duke football coach, was recovering from a broken leg last winter he complained bitterly about being cooped up and wanted to be sent overseas or else given a CDD. Wade got his wish and was shipped to England to command a field-artillery battery for the invasion. . . . Ben Jones' son Jimmy, who helped his father train Lawrin, Whirlaway and Pensive, has been commissioned a lieutenant in the Coast Guard and is stationed in Charleston, S. C. . . . According to Capt. Steve Hamas, who ought to know about such things, the best looking boxing prospect in the ETO is Pfc. Tut (King) Tabor, a sharp-punching middleweight from Oakland, Calif., who wears glasses and looks like Tommy Dorsey. . . . The two top invasion chiefs, Gen. Dwight D. Eisenhower and Lt. Gen. Omar N. Bradley, played on the same football team at West Point in 1915. . . . Lt. Comdr. George Earnshaw, the old Athletic pitcher, was wounded in a naval engagement in the South Pacific. He commands a gun crew on an aircraft carrier. . . . This probably isn't news to anybody in the American League, but Lt. Comdr. Mickey Cochrane says A/S Virgil (Fire) Trucks, former Detroit pitcher, can throw as fast as Bob Feller or Dizzy Dean.

Commissioned: Bill Dickey, veteran Yankee catcher, as a lieutenant in the Navy; Glenn Dobbs, passing star of last year's powerful Randolph Field Flyers, as a second lieutenant in the AAF. . . . Discharged: Pat Filley, Notre Dame football captain, and Wilbur Moore, former Minnesota-Washington Redskin back, from the Marines with CDDs; Sgt. Ray Robinson, uncrowned welterweight champion, from the Army, with a CDD. . . . Ordered for induction: Calvin Coolidge McLish, Dodgers' schoolboy pitcher, by the Navy; Mark Christman, third baseman of Browns, by the Army; George Caster, Browns' pitcher, by the Navy. . . . Rejected: Ron Northey, Phillies' outfielder, because of high blood pressure; infielder Bobby Doerr and outfielder Leon Culberson of the Red Sox, because of knee injuries.

"I'M SURPRISED SOMEONE HASN'T THOUGHT OF IT BEFORE."
—M/Sgt. Jack Lovell

"WHAT MORE SECURITY DO YOU WANT FOR TWO DOLLARS?"
—Sgt. Sidney Landi

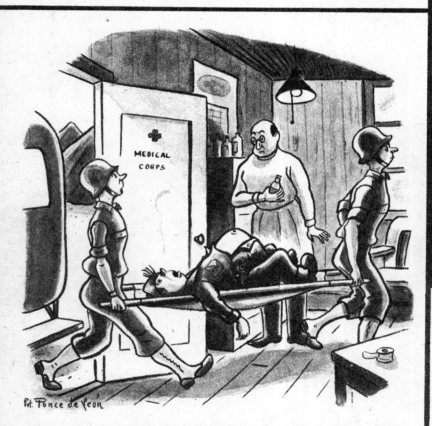

"HE WAS NIBBLING ON SOME DEHYDRATED FOOD IN THE KITCHEN
AND THEN HE DRANK A GLASS OF WATER." —Pvt. Michael Ponce de Leon

YANK
THE ARMY WEEKLY

"THEY CAN TAKE THEIR OLD PSYCHOLOGICAL WARFARE, AND YOU KNOW WHAT THEY CAN DO WITH IT."
—Pvt. Johnny Bryson

YANK

THE ARMY WEEKLY

5¢ JULY 7
VOL. 3, NO. 3
1944

By the men . . . for the men in the service

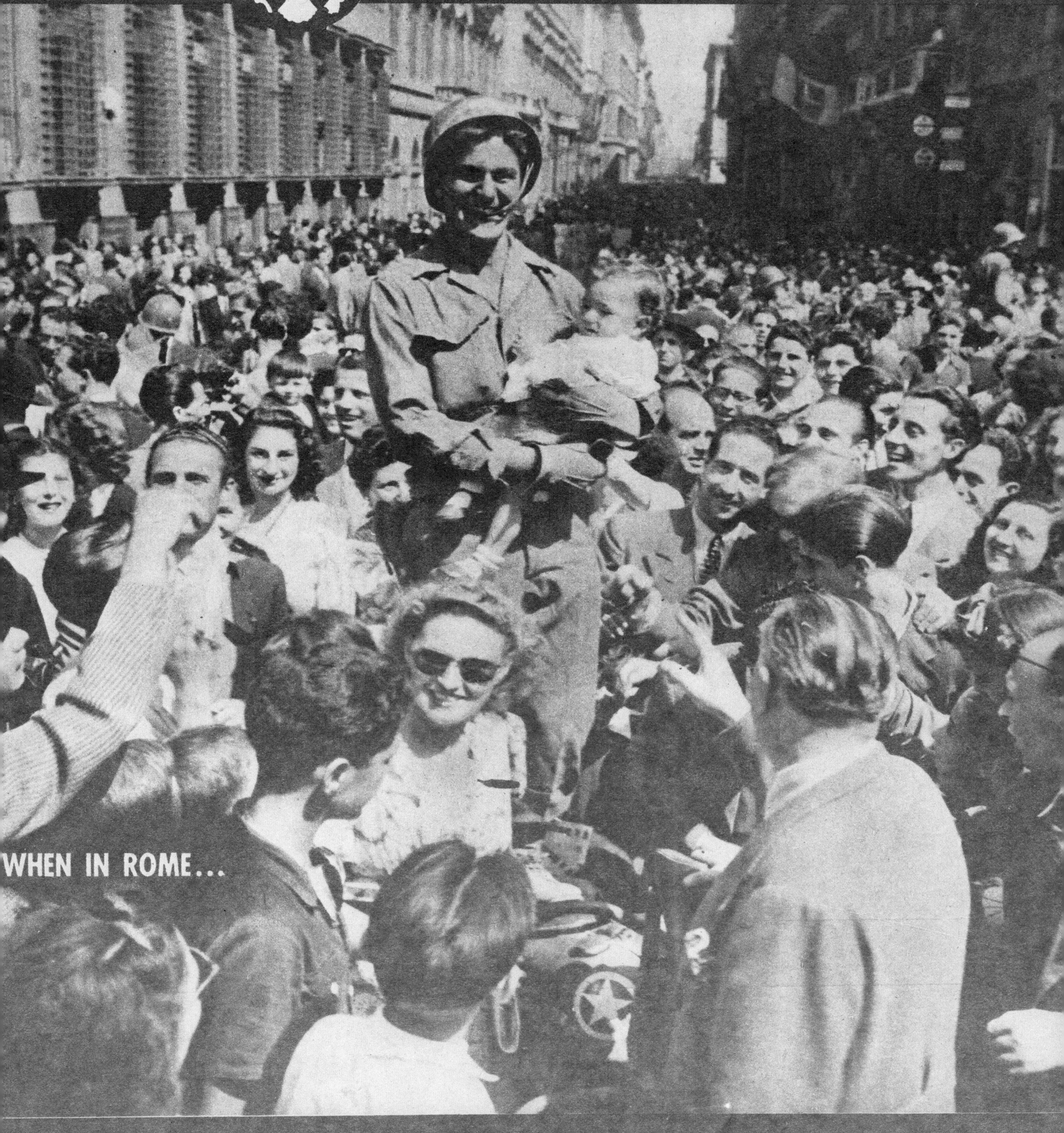

WHEN IN ROME...

Rangers climbed up this rope ladder to surprise and silence a Jerry gun crew at the cliff's top.

1st Division

2d Division

A Who's Who that tells where
each American infantry and air
borne outfit fought against the
Germans on the Cherbourg Peninsula and gives the highlights of
their past combat records.

ONLY a few months ago GIs in the 4th Division were sure they were going to swea[t]
out the rest of the war as garrison so[l]-
diers in the States.

Back in 1918, the 4th or "Ivy" Division land[ed]
in France with only six months' training an[d]
went into action immediately in the Aisn[e]-
Marne offensive. But this time it looked [as]
though things were going to be different. Men [of]
the 4th pointed out bitterly that their divisi[on]
had more shack men than any division in t[he]
Army. A shack man, in case you don't kno[w,]
is a GI so firmly established at a post in t[he]
States that he keeps a house or apartment in t[he]
nearest town and commutes to camp every morn[n]-
ing before reveille.

However, a few months can bring a lot [of]
changes. Wearing the same shoes that had be[en]
soaked so often by the water of Boggy Gut [in]
night problems outside Camp Gordon, Ga., t[he]
shack men of the 4th were among the first Amer[-]
ican soldiers to land on the Cherbourg Peninsu[la]
in France during the invasion of western Europ[e.]

Fighting beside the 4th under the command [of]
Lt. Gen. Omar N. Bradley, U. S. ground for[ce]
chief in Gen. Sir Bernard L. Montgomery's Twen[-]
ty-first Army Group, were three other America[n]
divisions new to combat—the 2d, a Regular Arm[y]
outfit which, like the 4th, was about 80 perce[nt]
selectees; the 29th, a division whose origin[al]
cadre was national guardsmen from Virgini[a,]
Pennsylvania, Maryland and the District [of]
Columbia, and the 101st Airborne, which ha[d]
done most of its training in the old 9th Divisio[n]
area at Fort Bragg, N. C.

And two divisions which had been through th[e]
mill in the Mediterranean—the "Fightin' First["]
and the 82d Airborne. The 1st Division is th[e]
outfit that captured Oran in the North Africa[n]
invasion. Later it fought at Gafsa, El Guettar an[d]
Mateur in Tunisia, and at Gela and Troina i[n]
Sicily. The 82d Airborne saw plenty of action i[n]
the landings at Sicily and Salerno.

On D Day, the 1st and 29th Divisions, with th[e]
2d in close support, fought one of the bloodies[t]
and most heroic battles in U.S. military history[.]
They landed in a sector of the Cherbourg Penin[-]
sula that was elaborately prepared for defens[e]
by the Germans. And a full German division, th[e]
382d, in addition to the regular coastal defens[e]
troops, was lying in wait for them on bluffs over[-]
looking the beaches.

A 40-minute bombardment by Allied aircraf[t]
and naval vessels knocked out some of the sho[re]
guns but failed to dislodge the Germans from th[e]
bluffs. They poured a thick screen of rifle, ma[-]
chine-gun and mortar fire into the men of the[e]
1st and the 29th as they landed. Inland artiller[y]
shelled the invaders with deadly accuracy.

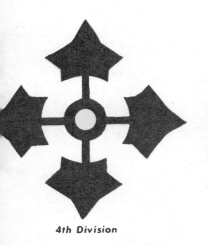
4th Division

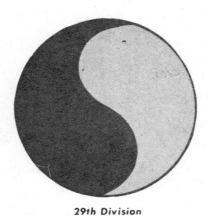
29th Division

82d Airborne Division

101st Airborne Division

U. S. Divisions in France

The only protection on the beach was a gravel ridge along the high-water mark. Those Americans who were able to get through the surf and cross the exposed strip of sand to this ridge, without getting hit, dug in desperately and lay shoulder to shoulder, returning fire from the bluffs above. Some of them were pinned on the ridge for four hours before they could advance. The beach was so hot that landing craft with reinforcements had to stay clear of it. Finally, after another naval bombardment, the 1st and the 29th advanced and captured the bluffs.

Then the 1st pushed inland, capturing the town of Isigny and bridging the Vire River. Meanwhile, on their left flank, farther toward the center of the Allied beachhead, the 2d Division was getting its first taste of combat after three years of training at Fort Sam Houston, Tex., Camp McCoy, Wis., and Northern Ireland—and was doing all right.

As soon as it landed, the 2d Division pushed straight inland to Trevier, toughest enemy strongpoint in that sector. The men reached the outskirts of the town on the third day of their advance and found it loaded with opposition. After several hours of bitter fighting, the 2d drew back and split up into three units. One unit worked its way around the left side of the town while the second bypassed the German positions on the right. After the artillery came up and raked the town, the third unit moved right through the middle, down the main street.

After the terrific beach-bluff stand of the Nazi 382d Division against the 1st and the 29th assault forces, most of the German resistance in the American sector was fluid guerrilla warfare, until the Germans counterattacked toward Montebourg and Carentan during the second week of the battle of Normandy. The 4th and the 101st Airborne met the brunt of these drives against

the two captured key towns of the Cherbourg Peninsula, the first really organized German rally since the Yanks had moved inland.

The 4th met up with the paratroopers and glider troops of the 82d Airborne after it came ashore in the sloppy marshes about 14 miles southeast of Cherbourg. It took the job of protecting the American extreme right flank near Montebourg while the 82d moved into position below the 4th, near Ste. Mere-Eglise. The 101st was on the left of the 82d in the Carentan sector.

When the Germans attacked Montebourg and Carentan, the 4th and the 101st Airborne troops met them in tight hand-to-hand combat. In Montebourg, the 4th mixed it up with the German tanks and infantry in the streets so closely that artillery on both sides had to cease firing.

With the exception of the 101st Airborne, which is strictly a product of modern war, activated only two years ago in Camp Claiborne,

Before they took off for France, the American soldiers learned to say in French: "Which way are the Boches?" Here a French civilian tells a paratroop captain

Drama at the "battle of the beaches." A medic and another British soldier help wounded Tommy up the shore while others crouch for cover or lie where they have fallen in the surf.

German sniper has grandstand seat in a jeep procession in Fran Vehicle mounts two machine guns, one .50-caliber, one .30 lig

La., all of these American divisions have fought in France before.

The 2d Division, as a matter of fact, was organized there in October 1917. In those days, strange as it seems, Marines fought under the command of the Army and the 2d included the 5th and 6th Marine Regiments. It made a brilliant record at Chateau-Thierry, Belleau Wood and in the Marne, St. Mihiel, Champagne and Meuse-Argonne offensives. It captured 12,026 prisoners and 343 artillery pieces during the 66 days it was under fire. After the war, the 2d served in the Army of Occupation in Germany. The boys are hoping they won't have to do the same thing for any great length of time.

The 82d Airborne Division is Sgt. Alvin C. York's old "All-American" Division that saw action in the last war at Toul, Marbache, St. Mihiel and the Meuse-Argonne sectors. Disbanded after the armistice, it was reactivated March 25, 1942, at Camp Claiborne, La., as an infantry division under Lt. Gen. Bradley, who was then a major general.

Morale and efficiency was so high in the 82d that it was converted into one of the Army's first two airborne divisions in August 1942. The 101st was the other. These two outfits trained together later at Fort Bragg, each composed of two-thirds paratroopers and one-third glider infantry and artillery. The 82d went overseas first, arriving in French Morrocco in May 1943.

From there it went to the invasion of Sicily, landing near Gela and later fighting as an infantry division at Trapani. Then its paratroopers jumped again at Salerno when German counter-

attacks were threatening to drive the Fifth Army back to the sea. Some landed behind the German and others came down on the beaches in the height of the battle, helping to turn the tide against the enemy. Units of the 82d Airborne were among the first Allied troops in Naples.

After the Italian campaign, the 82d moved secretly to England and found the 101st waiting for it there. The two divisions trained for the invasion together as they had in Louisiana and North Carolina.

Among these paratroopers who jumped into the swampy section of the Cherbourg Peninsula was a special group of 13 GIs with war paint on their faces and their hair shaved except for a scalp lock. They were 12 Indians and one GI from Brooklyn, N. Y., who had been admitted to the small tribe after cutting his finger and mixing his blood with that of one of the Indians. They smelled strongly. They had taken an oath not to have a bath from Christmas until D Day. In addition to the regulation paratrooper equip-

MAN GETS LADY

LONDON—The problem of what to do with the Allies' first woman war prisoner, the sniper known as Myra, who was captured in civilian clothes in northern France, has been solved. A Home Office spokesman has announced that she probably will be sent to the internment camp for enemy aliens on the Isle of Man.

ment, they carried special knives, machetes, stee knuckles and nylon garrotes.

LIKE the 2d and the 82d Airborne, the 29th o "Blue and Gray" Division served in th Meuse-Argonne campaign in the first Worl War. Reactivated in February 1941 as a squar national guard division, it was streamlined int a triangular division a year later. The 29th ha been in Britain a long time. It arrived there i October 1942, after training at Fort George C Meade, Md., Camp Blanding, Fla., and Cam Kilmer, N. J.

The 4th Division was one of the Army's firs motorized infantry divisions. It was reactivated with half-tracks in June 1940, in the Harmon Church area at Fort Benning, Ga., and move on to Camp Gordon when that infantry train ing center was opened in January 1942. The next summer it lost the half-tracks. That wa when the GIs in the 4th began to doubt that the would ever get out of the States. When the came north to Fort Dix, N. J., in the spring o 1943, rumors began to circulate about oversea duty after all, but they found themselves rakin lawns and painting garbage cans instead o marching onto transports.

Then came amphibious training at Camp Gor don Johnston, Fla., and a stretch at Fort Jack son, S. C. Every time the division moved, it wer nowhere near a POE.

"We're overtrained," the men of the 4th sai "What are we waiting for?"

But in the streets of Montebourg, the 4th foun what it was waiting for.

YANK, The Army Weekly, publication issued weekly by Branch Office, Army Information, MSD, War Department, 205 East 42d Street, New York 17, N. Y. Reproduction rights restricted as indicated in the ma head on the editorial page. Entered as second class matter July 6, 1942, at the Post Office at New York, N. Y., under the Act of March 3, 1879. Subscription price $3.00 yearly. Printed in the U. S. A

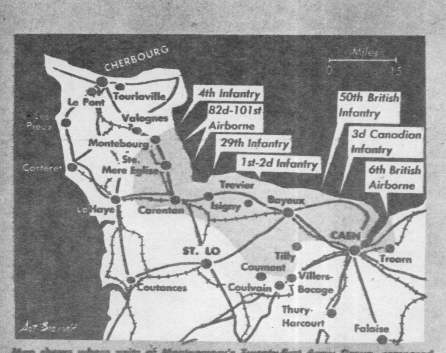

Map shows where units of Montgomery's Twenty-first Army Group, composed of at least six U. S., one Canadian and two British divisions, are fighting.

An American infantryman runs toward a church at Ste. Mere Eglise out a sniper who has been making the going tough. Another Yank covers h

Plan To Combine Armed Forces

Army likes idea of putting both services under one head but Navy disapproves.

By Sgt. MERLE MILLER
YANK Staff Writer

WASHINGTON, D. C.—The Anacostia Naval Air Station and the Army's Bolling Field here in Washington are right next to each other and are connected by a taxi strip.

Each has a control tower and an operations building, and each has an operations officer, weather and communications officers, the EMs who are their assistants and ready crews on duty 24 hours a day.

Each field also has the same kind of fire-fighting equipment, ambulances and hospitals and the personnel to run them.

Robert A. Lovett, Assistant Secretary of War for Air, has called the duplications at Bolling and Anacostia just one example of Army and Navy overlapping. The obvious solution, he says, would be to combine the War and Navy Departments into a single Department of Armed Forces.

Lovett was one of eight WD leaders who made this recommendation in testimony before the newly organized House Select Committee on Post-War Military Policy.

Meanwhile, in the Senate, the proposal for a single department was incorporated in a bill and introduced by Senator Lister Hill [Democrat, Alabama].

The bill, which follows the general outline of the WD chart below, calls for a Secretary of the Armed Forces, who would be a civilian appointed by the President with the Senate's approval; for three other civilians who would be Under Secretaries for the Army, the Navy and the Air, respectively, and for two civilian assistants for each.

For "strategic planning, supply planning and operational direction of all the armed forces," the President would choose from officers of general or flag rank a Chief of Staff to the Commander in Chief, a Chief of Staff of the Army, another of the Navy and a third of the Air Forces. Together they would constitute the U.S. Chiefs of Staff.

Finally, either a Navy admiral or an Army general would be chosen as a Director of Supply to handle the purchase and distribution of supplies for all the armed forces.

Details of the reorganization are not specified in the bill, which is confined to three brief pages; they are left to the experts in both departments. Even if the legislation were to be passed at this session of Congress, the bill provides that the merger should not take effect until six months after the end of the war.

This time lag is in accord with most of the WD suggestions, including that of Secretary of War Stimson, who told the committee that the combination couldn't be undertaken during the war, or at least until the fighting in Europe had ended.

However, there was no WD opposition to eventual merger. Brig. Gen. William F. Tompkins, director of the Special Planning Division, told the House committee: "I can say that of all the officers of the War Department with whom I have discussed the matter, I have yet to find one who did not believe that a single department of the armed forces was the best solution to the problem."

On the other hand, Navy opposition to a merger has been equally unanimous. Secretary James V. Forrestal told the House Committee that such a combination might result in "hamstringing" both the Army and Navy "by the very inertia of size." He said that no such plan should even be considered until admirals like Halsey, Nimitz and King could present their points of view—obviously impossible until the war is over.

A separate Air Force "to the extent that the Army and Navy are separate and distinct"—an idea supported by all the Army witnesses—"is entirely foreign to the Naval concept of its mission and functions," Secretary Forrestal added.

Of the support given by WD leaders, the most detailed came from Lt. Gen. Brehon B. Somervell, commanding general, Army Service Forces. He noted that in March 1942 the WD was reorganized into three major commands—the Air Forces, the Ground Forces and the Service Forces. "The experience over the last two years with this type of organization," he said, "has been sufficiently complete to demonstrate the soundness of its fundamental concept."

As examples of "overlappings and conflict in the present organization," Lt. Gen. Somervell cited duplications in accounting, auditing, procurement, materiel, housing, hospitalization, communications and transport.

He pointed out that the Army and Navy have separate hospitals within a few miles of each other in Washington, San Diego, Memphis and Charleston as well as overseas in Hawaii, New Caledonia and New Zealand. He contended that construction requirements of the Army and Navy could be combined and directed by one agency and make an over-all saving of between 25 and 35 percent. And whereas the Army now has its MPs and the Navy its shore patrol, he said that "if one agency had the responsibility, there would be greater coordination in training and assignment of personnel to town and train patrols."

In general, Somervell concluded, "a suitable combination will result in economy of manpower, saving of money and increased speed of operations."

THERE's no doubt that Congress will spend a lot of time talking over consolidation after it reconvenes next fall, and probably a good many questions, now unanswered, will be debated on the floors of both houses. Some of them may be:

What, under a merger, will happen to the Marine Corps? Will it be incorporated into the Army? Or will it continue as a separate unit under the direction of the Under Secretary for the Navy?

Will the Chief of Staff to the Commander in Chief be an Army general or a Navy admiral? (Adm. William D. Leahy is now personal Chief of Staff to President Roosevelt, but under the terms of the Hill bill the C of S would certainly have greater functions.)

If there is to be one uniform for everybody in the armed forces, should it be GI Army or Navy, a combination of both or something entirely new?

How will the consolidation affect the increasing number of land-based Navy planes? Will all land-based aircraft be the responsibility of the Under Secretary for Air? Will the operation of carrier-based planes be directed by the Under Secretary for the Navy?

And what, finally, will the average GI in all branches of service think about a merger?

These questions and a good many others will be booted around both by soldiers and sailors until Congress acts. And their feelings will play an important part in the decision made.

The GI, after all, has as much at stake in whether or not there is to be a Department of the Armed Forces as any general or admiral.

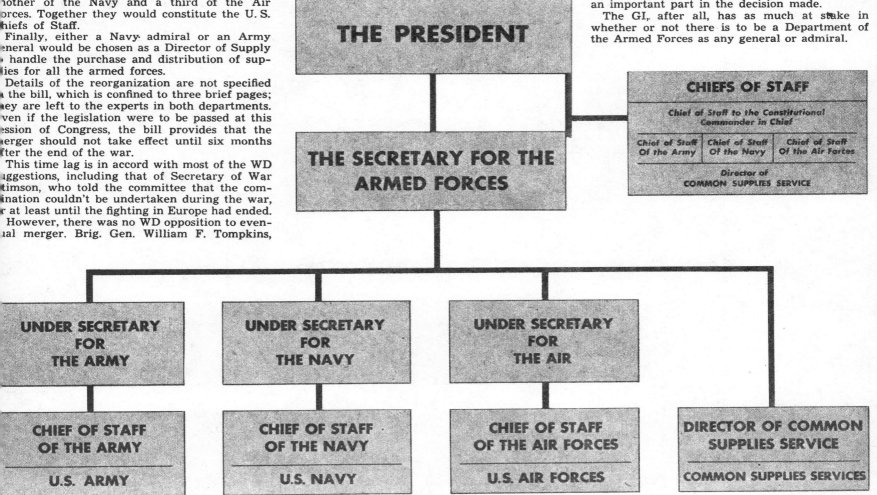

THE PRESIDENT

THE SECRETARY FOR THE ARMED FORCES

CHIEFS OF STAFF		
Chief of Staff to the Constitutional Commander in Chief		
Chief of Staff Of the Army	Chief of Staff Of the Navy	Chief of Staff Of the Air Forces
Director of COMMON SUPPLIES SERVICE		

UNDER SECRETARY FOR THE ARMY	UNDER SECRETARY FOR THE NAVY	UNDER SECRETARY FOR THE AIR	
CHIEF OF STAFF OF THE ARMY	CHIEF OF STAFF OF THE NAVY	CHIEF OF STAFF OF THE AIR FORCES	DIRECTOR OF COMMON SUPPLIES SERVICE
U.S. ARMY	U.S. NAVY	U.S. AIR FORCES	COMMON SUPPLIES SERVICES

An armored half-track personnel carrier rumbles past a line of German infantrymen. In the foreground German officers are taking it on the lam in a Fiat staff car, until lately an Italian civilian's private auto.

Italians display little interest as their unwelcome guests haul away an 88, camouflaged by branches. Use of horses reveals that Allied aerial pasting of enemy rear roads has had an immediate effect in front lines.

These Are Germans Evacuating Rome

Before any Allied troops entered the capital city, an Italian took these pictures of the withdrawing Germans from the upper-story window of a house where he had concealed himself. Later he gave them to YANK's Sgt. George Aarons, who reached Rome with the first Allied patrols.

Significantly headed for the front is an ambulance, once a bus. In opposite direction a prime mover takes personnel and a 10.5-cm gun, past convoy of light c

GIs Take Over Rome

Two reports on the happy day when the Eternal City became the first European capital to get rid of the Nazis and welcome the Allies.

THESE GERMAN PARATROOPERS ARE YOUNG AND HAVE NOT FOUGHT LONG. NOW THEY ARE PRISONERS, CAPTURED AFTER FIERCE ACTION OUTSIDE VELLETRI, BELOW ROME.

By Sgt. JAMES P. O'NEILL
YANK Staff Correspondent

WITH THE 1ST ARMORED DIVISION IN ROME [By Cable]—Eight days ago I was in Teheran, Iran; a few hours ago I was in Naples; now I was in Rome. I entered the city under sniper and machine-gun fire, with the point tanks of the 1st Armored Division, accompanied by riflemen.

Behind a big Sherman, the third tank to enter Rome, our jeep bounced at 1930 hours into this mad town filled with happy, hysterical people, sniper fire, pretty girls, mine explosions and free wine. How I happened to get here is a strange tale.

In Naples we were talking over my plane ride from Iran, the major and I, when a corporal from the censor's office came in and said our troops had entered Rome that afternoon. The major, who is my commanding officer, apologized for interrupting my story. "I'd better get up there and find a press to print YANK on," he said. "I'd better get up there and find a story," I said.

By 1400 hours the major and I, with Cpl. Sal Canizzo as our driver, were speeding toward Rome up Highway 7, the famous Appian Way. The major had decided to take Highway 7 because Sal said that, on the map, it seemed the straightest and easiest road to the Eternal City.

The highway was in excellent condition, and we moved quickly toward the front, slowing down only in towns like Formia, Terracina and Cisterna. There we had to pick our way through

rubble-strewn streets. But if the streets were bad, the towns themselves were terrible. They were towns no longer — just lopsided masonry, dazed peasants, mangled trees and burned tanks. In every town there was the smell of death. You could tell the nearness to war by that smell.

Until we hit Velletri, there was little traffic except an occasional small convoy, and we had

This Week's Cover

WHEN in Rome, hold a Roman baby and be popular with the populace, says Pvt. Ben Pollack who was among the first American soldiers to enter the former Axis capital. YANK's Sgt. George Aarons photographed Pvt. Pollack standing on a motorcycle surrounded by a happy, well-dressed crowd.

PHOTO CREDITS. Cover—Sgt. George Aarons. 2—Acme. 3—Signal Corps. 4—Upper left, INP; others, Acme. 6—YANK Rome Bureau. 7, 8, 9 & 10—Sgt. Aarons. 11—Upper right, MAAF; lower left, Sgt. Dick Hanley; lower right, Sgt. Dillon Ferris. 12—Upper left, Panama Canal Dept.; upper right, Signal Corps; center left, Ted Frutkoff; center right, WW; lower left, Acme; upper right, WW; center right, Acme; lower left, Coast Guard; lower right, Alaskan Dept. 15—Sgt. Steve Derry. 18—Upper, Signal Corps, Camp Polk, La.; lower, AAFTC, Tuskegee, Ala. 19—Upper, Signal Corps, Fort Benning, Ga.; center right, Engr. Gp. Photo. Camp Ellis, Ill.; lower left, AAFEFTC, Greenwood, Miss.; lower right, Base Photo Sec., Fairmont AAF, Nebr. 20—Columbia Pictures. 23—Upper, Acme; lower, M/Sgt. Clyde Henderson, Seventh Air Force.

the highway to ourselves. But when we were about five miles out of Velletri, the road became clogged with traffic—on one lane only, the northbound lane that led to Rome. We zoomed up the outside lane, dodging back into the convoy whenever we spotted an MP.

We passed endless rows of crowded ammo trucks, gas trucks, ambulances, weapons carriers loaded down with equipment and six-by-sixes filled with infantrymen. The road was all dust, dirt and confusion. Whenever we stopped and asked the way to Rome, the MP would shake his head in a puzzled way and point hesitatingly toward the forward end of the dusty column going north on the Appian Way. There was no sign of the enemy; no gunfire of any kind; no planes —ours or theirs—in the sky; no foxholes or tanks. On this sunny afternoon the hustling, bustling column, noisy with yells and friendly curses, reminded me of the impatient crowds bound for dinner after a Saturday football game.

We sped through Albano, where the final push for Rome had started. No sooner had we passed through the quiet town than the whole scene changed. You didn't have to know much about war to sense that you were nearing the front. You could tell by the dust, rising from the road like a giant smoke screen and blotting out the warm caressing sun; you could tell by the absence of vigilant MPs, who up to now had kept shooing our jeep back into the noisy column.

And the column itself had changed. It now consisted of tanks—mostly heavies and mediums

—and trucks mounted with heavy weapons. Straddled out in two single lines, 15 paces apart on both sides of the road, were infantrymen. Their faces were dirty and partly covered by handkerchiefs that helped keep the dust out of their mouths. As they walked up the road, they kept their guns on their hips. Neither the riflemen nor the tank crews talked much; they just moved silently up the road.

The column's pace had slowed down to a crawl when the sounds of shellfire suddenly came from up ahead. The men on the road dove for the safety of the embankment, and the tank crews ducked into their turrets. Sal nudged our jeep over to the embankment, and the three of us got out and lay down with the men at the side of the road. The shelling was over in five minutes, although it seemed like ages; then the column started to move again.

We got into the jeep, and the major looked at his map. For a moment he was silent. Then, taking off his helmet, he scratched his head. "It looks as if that kid from the censor was wrong. We might end up selling these blasted things to the Germans," he said, pointing to the bundle of YANKS we had brought along for promotion work in Rome. "Are you two willing to go on?" Sal, an Italian boy with a terrible yen to get to Rome, yelled "Hell, yes!" I waved my head indecisively. The major took that for an affirmative answer. Our jeep moved on.

Soon the tanks stopped again, and now our jeep was parked protectively behind the third leading tank. There was more fire. It was not the same kind of fire we had heard before; this had a whap instead of a whoosh.

A rifleman came over to our jeep; he was a short squat kid with a dark dirty face, and when he tried to smile you could see he was tired. "Hey, YANK," he said, pointing to the sticker on our jeep, "you're pretty far up to be getting autographs." Then he spotted the bundle of magazines. "Can I have one, sir?" he asked the major. "Sure thing," the major said.

I reached down and handed the rifleman 10 copies. He pulled a knife out of his hip pocket. "Wanna German souvenir, bud?" he asked. He threw the knife into the jeep and started across the road. He gave the rest of the magazines to a bunch of his buddies, and one of them yelled across: "This sure is first-class distribution."

Just then there was another dose of whaps, and one of the infantrymen behind us must have noticed my shaking hands. "Don't worry," he said. "That's just a couple of snipers over in that farmhouse. We're gonna go up and get the bastards in a minute."

The Appian Way had now widened out into a four-lane highway with a trolley line running down the middle. Through the dust you could see the city of Rome. Down the street, ignoring the sniper fire, came citizens of Rome, some of them carrying wine in jugs and bottles. One man came running down the road alone; he wore no coat and was crying. The short dark rifleman talked with him in Italian for a moment, then turned to us and said: "This guy's wife was blown up by a mine. He wants a doctor. You better tell one of the medics."

On the right side of the road three or four dogfaces were talking to the wine-carrying civilians. One of them took a big slug out of a bottle. Suddenly there was a shot, and the GI fell over in the road. The civilians scattered, and the other soldiers bent over their buddy. One of the crew of the lead tank yelled to the crouching rifleman: "Is he hurt bad?" And the little dark kid yelled back: "No, he ain't hurt. He's dead."

A second lieutenant and a squad of riflemen started up the embankment on the left toward the farmhouse from which the shots had come.

The lead tank began to move again. We decided to stay with the tanks, hoping they would finally make town. We felt uneasy on the road and nudged close to the third tank. The three tanks in front of us were the only ones moving; the rest of the column had stopped.

W E made it this time. No sooner had we passed between two long rows of apartment houses, at the point where the Appian Way ends and the city of Rome begins, than the three tanks and our jeep were engulfed by screaming, hysterical Romans. Some were laughing, some were crying and all of them wanted to touch us. One old lady kissed our jeep as if it were her lost son. A dark-haired girl placed a rose in Sal's ear. Somebody threw a bunch of flowers into the jeep and someone else put two bottles of wine alongside the flowers.

The three tanks had met the same fate. Romans swarmed over them like ants. The tanks couldn't move without killing somebody. I jumped out of the jeep and headed for the first tank to get the names of the GIs in it for my story, but it was impossible. Twice I was halfway up when the yelling crowd pushed me off.

Then I spotted an officer in the center of the road, trying to clear a path for the tanks. I went over and talked with him. "How does it feel to be one of the first tanks in Rome?" I asked. He was a tall thin-faced captain. "We're not staying here long," he said. "We're supposed to move up that road toward the Tiber, but these crazy people won't let us. They don't know it, but they're holding up the war."

The officer gave me the names of the men in the lead tank: Lt. Henry Schoberth of Versailles,

"ROMA" sign didn't come with that half-track sco[...]

Ky.; Sgt. John Brown Jr. of Canton, Ohio; T[...] Ernest Barnett of La Grande, Oreg.; Pvt. Tiber[...] Di Julio of Orange, N. J., and Pvt. Antonio Ca[...] of Los Angeles, Calif.

From somewhere came the whoosh of a sel[...] propelled gun. The captain headed for his tan[...] and the tanks began to move to the side of t[...] road for protection. Somehow nobody got hu[...] and this time the Italians cleared a path. The[...] the tanks disappeared down the dark street.

When I reached the jeep, I found that the m[...] jor had picked up an ex-colonel of the Itali[...] Army. "We're going to his house for dinner," t[...] major said. It was a confusing ride. We wou[...] start up one street and meet a bunch of people [...] the corner. They would either swarm all ov[...] our much-abused jeep or scream something abo[...] *Tedeschi*. This, Sal informed us, meant that the[...] were still snipers up the street.

After backtracking over half the city of Rom[...] we finally arrived at the ex-colonel's home. [...] lived in a modern apartment house. We parke[...] the jeep in his garage, locked the door and, aft[...]

The holes in that building aren't shellholes. It's the ancient Colosseum, getting a once-over by Yanks and Italian kids in the armored car and jeeps.

That's Rome up ahead. As infantrymen take 10 and a walkie-talkie relays [...] message, armored cars keep rolling down the highway, past interurban trolle[...]

is knees doubled up in a jeep, the lanky commander of the Fifth Army, Lt. Gen. Mark W. Clark, gets a warm greeting from Italian civilians on his arrival in Rome.

ghting our way through the mob that had ormed in front of the entrance, arrived at our ost's apartment. There we were introduced to is wife, his mother and two of his friends, a middle-aged couple. We had a dinner of ham sliced thinner than a Walgreen special, peas, salad and white wine. We knew food was scarce in Rome and went easy with the ex-colonel's larder.

Through Canizzo's New Jersey-style Italian, we learned that, besides being very happy, these people were interested in two things. The ex-colonel wanted to know how the Allies were going to treat the members of the Italian Army. The other gentleman, a banker, wanted to know what the AMG would do with the *lira*. We could answer neither question.

After thanking them for the dinner, we took off with a volunteer guide for the *Ambasciatori*, one of Rome's swankiest hotels. Our guide found it easily, and we went inside. There were no lights, since the Germans had knocked the powerhouse out of commission. At the desk we found a tall thin man in charge. He spoke good English and did not seem at all ruffled by our presence. "Aren't you surprised to see us?" we asked. "No," he said, "we were expecting you, but not quite so fast." "Are there any Americans here?" we asked. "Not yet," the man said, laughing quietly. "There were German officers in this hotel an hour and a half ago."

A bellboy took us to our rooms. Sal and I shared one with twin beds. He was asleep in five minutes, but I couldn't doze off. There was a lot of sniper fire, and with every whap I could picture some Kraut working his way toward our room. Soon the roar of tanks came up from the streets below. I went out on the balcony and breathed a sigh of relief when I saw they were ours. For a minute or two I watched and then I went back to bed. Soon the comforting roar of the tanks made me drowsy. I remember saying: "This all must be a dream." Then I went to sleep.

EARLY next morning I went down to the bar and met Charlie Castellotti, a famous bartender in the Paris of the hectic 1920s. Three German officers drank at Charlie's bar only a few hours before the arrival of our jeep. "They were sad," Charlie said. "They have felt for a long while that you were going to take Rome."

There was a pretty girl sitting at the other end of the bar with a beautiful dark cocker spaniel at her feet. I went over and petted the spaniel. He didn't seem to like my touch. "His name is Blacky," the girl said. "He was given to me by a German lieutenant last night."

It was a warm lazy day. There were still crowds in the streets. GIs whizzed through town with flowers in their helmets, bottles of wine in their hands and girls hanging on their jeeps.

On one of the main streets a water main had

burst. Four happy dogfaces were pushing each other into the stream. A large crowd gathered and watched the horseplay, cheering whenever a soldier was thrown into the drink.

But not all the Roman scene was hysterical that day. Through one main street, in long serious lines, marched the infantry on its way to the Tiber and the forward positions. On another street tanks, trucks, guns and ammo rolled toward the front.

On still another street a band of civilians, armed with machine guns and wearing red bands on their sleeves, stormed a radio station. They brought out the proprietor and beat him to the ground, using their guns as clubs. Then they carried him off, yelling "*Fascisti*."

The pace was too fast to last. Pvt. Charles Camp of Dunbar, Pa., a rifleman who had fought from the beginning of the push to the very outskirts of the town, put it this way: "Come the MPs and the 'Off Limits' signs, and this town will slow down."

Highway 6

By Sgt. FRED ROSEN
YANK Staff Correspondent

WITH THE FIFTH ARMY IN ROME [By Cable] —Nobody will ever know for certain which were the first Allied troops to enter Rome. During the evening hours of June 4, reconnaissance units, some armor and some infantrymen crept into the city from different directions. In some cases they pulled up to spend the night in houses vacated by Jerry only a half-hour before.

All night long there was sniper fighting throughout Rome as isolated Germans tried to join the rest of their forces fleeing north. German time bombs began booming from different sections of the city during the night. Armed *Partisanos* in civilian clothes, thirsting for revenge, roamed the dark streets, taking pot shots at German vehicles and rushing the buildings where Germans or Fascists were known to be hiding. The last few hours that night Yanks and *Partisanos*, some of them working together, captured a number of Germans trying to escape in civilian clothes.

The city was pitch dark. There was no electricity, no telephones, and water only here and there. The people of Rome sat up all night, peering out of shuttered windows, waiting for the Americans and spitting down curses on the Germans as they caromed through the streets on their way north. At least one of these Jerry vehicles sprayed lead at every window in sight.

At dawn, larger bodies of Allied troops began

entering the city on every road leading up from the south. Most of them somehow came together, forming one great column moving up the Appian Way.

People came pouring out of the houses in a great flood. Hysterical women clasped their hands and rocked back and forth on the curbstones, moaning "*Grazia, grazia*."

WE had reached Rome after a furious jeep trip in pursuit of a picked force of Yanks and Canadians whose mission was to punch through the right flank of the German positions south of Rome and to penetrate the city.

The flying spearhead had met with unexpected success along the broad straight Highway 6, long used by the Germans as their main supply route. Jerry had retreated so fast that he had neglected his usual careful demolition; even the telephone poles were still standing.

Beyond Valmontone, until recently the anchor of the enemy defense line, we came upon the first signs of battle—a half-dozen scorched German tanks and half-tracks, discarded helmets, little heaps of machine-gun shells, a dead German with letters and snapshots on the ground beside him.

The first Yanks we caught up with were tankers, asleep in the turrets or on the ground against the treads. A guard told us they were taking a six-hour break after three days of continuous fighting. Next we came to long lines of infantrymen, tired, dirty but determined. From a farmhouse 20 yards off the road, a couple of riflemen emerged with *vino* bottles in their hands and roses in their "buttonholes."

As we approached Cenecelli, a suburb of Rome, Italians lined the highway, cheering and waving. Old women in black dresses bowed and grinned like mechanical dolls. Men on bicycles leaped off and waved their arms in wild welcome. A kid, sitting on the branch of a tree that stuck out over the road, showered down handfuls of rose petals as we went by.

At the foot of a long upgrade in the road, we came to a cluster of soldiers crouched in a ditch. "Take it easy, there," said a heavy-bearded soldier sprawled in the ditch on one elbow. "This is the end of the line. Jerry is just over the hill." We had caught up with the spearhead.

The Yanks and Canadians had been held up for an hour by a couple of German self-propelled guns and some tanks, dug in over the hill. This effective roadblock had already knocked out two American tanks.

We sat around the ditch. Nobody seemed to know what to do until reinforcements arrived. Two of our tanks went over the hill to try to root the Jerry out, and we could hear the high song of the fast German machine gun that the boys called the diarrhea gun. Two shells burst 20 yards from our ditch. We slammed our faces in-

They tried to clean out a German nest, but shells stopped Pvt. Neal McLean (right, with bazooka) and vino stopped Sgt. Nellis Johnson (left, with BAR).

Here you see what happens to a German 88-mm gun when it meets up with Allied shells. Some Yanks inspect wreckage after the hard fighting for Velletri.

Out for German blood: Armed with rifles, a gang of young Italian *Partisanos* rides through Rome streets in truck, hunting for J___y snipers and stragglers.

to the dirt. Five men crawled down the ditch to join us. They were the crew of one of the tanks, just knocked out by the Germans. "If we could only see where the bastards are," one gasped.

For at least an hour enemy fire kept us pinned down. Whenever a shell burst close to a church near our ditch, it set the bells clanging. We looked at each other and remembered it was Sunday. Suddenly we spotted a wedding procession walking down the road toward the church—eight couples, arm in arm, all dolled up in their Sunday best. The white-gowned bride giggled prettily, as if the roar of shells were her wedding march and the ricocheting bullets were rice.

After another 15 minutes, the lieutenant in charge decided to move up closer to the crest of the hill. We stooped over as we walked up the ditch and carefully avoided stepping on the shoulders of the road—Jerry's favorite place for mines. As the shells whistled and crashed all around us, we turned off the road and sprinted for a half-ruined farmhouse. Some of our tanks roared past, on their way over the hill for another try at Jerry.

Four hours passed while we listened to the battle. Everybody grew restless as the sun got hotter and the flies and the dust increased. Without telling the lieutenant, T-4 Nellis Johnson, an Indian from Pima, Ariz., and Pvt. Neal McLean of Chicago, Ill., crawled through the grass toward the hilltop. McLean had a bazooka, plenty of shells and hand grenades. Johnson had grenades and his favorite weapon, a Johnson automatic rifle, which he calls a "Johnny gun."

Nearly an hour later the two came crawling back. McLean had fired all the bazooka shells into a house where he thought the German guns were located, and had been kept skipping around by machine-gun fire that came back. Johnson was plastered. He had crept around a house to "surround the Jerries" and found a *vino* cellar. The lieutenant burned their ears off for going up without orders. Johnson swayed back and forth, listening meekly and mumbling: "But, sir, we got so tired sitting here!"

Then Jerry began to work on us in earnest. Shells exploded all over the field and the road. "Airbursts," so-called because they exploded before hitting the ground, sent a shower of jagged steel into the backs of the men below. Broken window glass tinkled on our helmets. We had to get shelter—and quick. One of the Canadians shot the lock off a cellar door, but it was no use. The place was full of wine barrels, and we couldn't get in. A shell fragment cut into the Canadian's back; he fell like an empty sack.

An Italian stuck his head out of the farmhouse and told us there were caves in the fields to our left. One by one we rose and walked at a stoop across the fields. The first man didn't run, so neither did the second. Not a man broke into a run. We all crossed safely. The caves were enormous. They were green with fungus, dark and smelly, but they seemed like heaven: there was six feet of rock between us and the shells.

At last the main body of our tanks arrived. In a half hour the job was done; the roadblock was smashed and the advance could continue. We had been held up five hours.

Then a long column of doughboys plodded up the hill. It looked as if the whole damn Army had arrived. The doughboys had marched at least 12 miles in the hot sun, but they just unslung their rifles as they approached the hill crest, bent over a bit and kept going.

THE dome of St. Peter's showed up on the horizon through the mist and smoke. We were nearing the center of Rome, but there still seemed to be German snipers and machine gunners in every other cellar window. It took vicious street fighting before Jerry was driven back.

We stared at the enormous fountains, the huge statues and the gray stone buildings—relics of ancient Rome. There were many priests on the streets. The surprisingly well-dressed crowds were getting wilder every minute. Everyone wanted to shake our hands. Some said "Welcome" and others just yelled "Viva" and waved handkerchiefs and flags around and around their heads. A brown-frocked Franciscan monk stood on the corner and blessed each Allied vehicle as it rolled by. A woman held up her *bambino* so that he would see and remember the great day when the *Americanos* marched in to liberate Mother Rome. Screaming swarms of kids clung to our jeep and tossed bunches of flowers all over her until she looked like a broken-down hag made up to look like Hedy Lamarr. A well-

dressed gentleman jumped on the radiator hung on precariously for a block while he off his chest in broken English the wish America and *Italia* be closa friends forever. girls, eyes flashing, climbed on the fenders, d their hands across their throats and shrie "*Morte Tedeschi!* (Death to the Germans!)"

Around a long bend we sighted the anc Colosseum, and under one of its huge arche crumbling gray stone something that it never seen before in all its years—a jeep v four exhausted Yanks sprawled out sound asl

An average of two or three times every b. somebody would pump our hands up and do wild with excitement, and ask whether we ki his cousin so-and-so who lived in Newark Chicago or Brooklyn. Six Yanks in the jeep ah made it a rule always to say yes; then Italians would drop off, ecstatic.

WE were moving more and more slowly u we came to the great square known as *Piazza Venizza* where Mussolini used to m his famous balcony speeches. Here the cr was so thick that the column stopped complet

A group of Yanks and Canadians who fought in the spearhead force worked their v through the crowd and up through the side c of Mussolini's palace, through its great ga corridors with their gilt ceilings, to the of where the great man used to sit.

Mussolini's huge desk was located at one of the long room, so that visitors who had walk all the way across would feel prope humble by the time they came to the big che himself. Sgt. Sam Finn of St. Louis, Mo., in the chair, put his feet up on the desk, clas his hands behind his head and said: "Not b not bad at all." All around us bustled pal guards and police in musical-comedy unifor with yard-wide cocked hats like the kind I poleon used to wear. We stepped out of the of onto the balcony, and a great roar went up fr the crowd in the square below. We were Mussolini's own balcony, undoubtedly the f Yank uniforms ever seen there.

"*Viva Americanos!*" yelled thousands of peo as they waved their handkerchiefs up at us—same sight Mussolini must have seen as looked down. It was then that Sgt. John Vita Port Chester, N. Y., pulled the historic stunt t will be talked about for the duration and six. stuck out his chin, threw out his chest and di terrific take-off of Mussolini, speaking in Itali The crowds loved it. They nearly went mad w joy when Vita made the exact kind of slap w his left palm against his right bicep as he sl his arm up in the Fascist salute.

That sort of thing went on all day. The fie spirit was broken only by occasional shots mobs went after the stores and homes of Fascis Once in a while we saw trucks and bus jammed with armed *Partisanos*, who fired i the air as they combed the side street and alle

It was a great day and one that no Americ soldier who was there will ever forget. By la afternoon the Yanks who had come in first a then scattered over the city were swinging i line and joining the steady columns of doug boys pouring through Rome all day from sou to north. The doughboys were so tired they ma little attempt to straighten up and parade.

These infantrymen were tired as only m can be who haven't slept two nights in fi days. There were beards on their faces, and the eyes were sunken and red as they plodded siler ly forward. They held their rifles any old w over their shoulders, and many had tied piec of burlap and odd rags around their helmets place of lost camouflage nets.

These were the dirty, tough, goddam wonde ful infantrymen who had fought their way the long bloody mountain path from Salern the men who had lived in underground holes Anzio for months, sweating out the deadly Ge man shellings; the men who always seemed have to fight straight uphill into the muzzl of German guns; the men who had won Rom

They had won Rome, but they did not ha time to stop in it now. Their job was killing Ge mans, and since the Germans were running nor that was where they were heading.

In one long brown column a couple of dough boys were chanting a jingle that expresses, be ter than anything else, the spirit of the Fif Army. It goes this way:

From Sicily to Rome,
Then Berlin and home. . . .

Yanks at home abroad—

Crime and Punishment

SOMEWHERE IN ITALY—There's a tiny village of about 20 houses here, where every person in town thinks he's the luckiest man alive.

Some drunken German soldiers had wandered into the village, broken into the houses, filled themselves with *vino* and used the wine barrels for target practice, laughing loudly when the old wine gushed onto the ground.

Finally the American artillery started shelling nearby, and the Nazi drunks began to stagger out of the place—all except one, who decided to see how his tommy gun worked.

He lined up all the Italians he could find and was all set to start shooting when some shells hit the top of the building across the street and the falling rubble killed several people, including him.

The townspeople buried their own dead but they left the German where he fell. For a week the body lay there, stinking in the sun, and nobody would bury it. Instead, every time the Italians passed the body, they spit.

When the American soldiers entered the town, they buried the German. The Italians still haven't forgiven them for doing that.

—YANK Field Correspondent

Song of the Islands

GUADALCANAL — When Guadalcanal's "Radio City" conducted a band-popularity contest recently, the GIs who operate the new station got the surprise of their lives. Harry James and Benny Goodman trailed Roy Acuff's Tennessee hillbilly band, which received 400 of the 1,000 votes cast by soldiers, sailors and marines of the Canal, on smaller South Sea islands and on patrol ships offshore.

But James is still going to get top billing from the Jacksons who run the broadcasting plant in a three-room shed in a muddy coconut grove. These GI operators, who hail from big cities Chicago, Salt Lake City, Duluth and Cincinnati), claim the vote was a fluke.

They blame T-5 Hyman Averback of Los Angeles, who conducts the station's "Section 8 Program," a session of recorded music and Averback chatter. Far from being a friend of hillbilly chants, Averback is such an ardent hot-music man that he lets his prejudices creep into his running commentary on the platters. "I've got some hillbilly records here," he'll remark, "but who likes hillbilly? Let's have a Harry James."

"That got them riled up," the other operators of the station say, "and resulted in concerted pressure when we took the poll." Just in case this is the wrong explanation, though, the station is going to give more air time to that good old mountain music.

—Sgt. BARRETT McGURN
YANK Staff Correspondent

Temptation

SOMEWHERE IN THE CARIBBEAN—Life on an island down here— a mere shovelful of dirt in the Antilles—is just one long temptation after another.

Across a small body of water you can see a gay, glittering city whose lights beckon to the wayward GI, inviting him to travel the road connecting the island and the mainland.

But passes are scarce, and the trip takes many hours coming and going. So dogfaces on the island naturally cast about for other sources of amusement. There is very little here except rusty huts, shabby fishermen's families and dead fish —and another temptation requiring even more rigid self-control.

The island boasts a distillery, which is one of the largest producers of rum in the Caribbean.

—Pvt. JUD COOK
YANK Staff Correspondent

Don't Wake Me; Let Me Dream

ENGLAND—When Pvt. Charles Schmelze of Pittsburgh, Pa., had finished servicing a troop-carrying glider of the Ninth Air Force for the big invasion hop, he was pretty well pooped. So he climbed aboard the glider, picked himself a comfortable corner and hit the hay.

The glider, towed by a plane piloted by F/O E. G. Borgmeyer of St. Louis, Mo., was last seen landing in a zone of heavy fighting. Pvt. Schmelze had slept his way into history's greatest military operation.

—YANK London Bureau

Fighting Cock

PERSIAN GULF COMMAND — Army pets range from the auk to the zebra, but a trucking station in northern Iran proudly claims a simple barnyard fowl as its mascot. The rooster, a medium-sized Mediterranean Red, doesn't even have a name as yet, but if you believe its owner, T-5 Wallace Grube of New York, N. Y., it is potentially the best fighting cock in the history of the sport.

The Red, a well-fed fowl with an irridescent feathered neck that sparkles like the rainbow, has one of the finest harems in the Moslem Middle East. He struts about the yard daily, the idol of six curvesome hens and the envy of his GI masters. Brought to the post as a present from some visiting British soldiers, he acts as if he were at least executive officer.

The rooster was spotted as a fighter from his first appearance on the scene. Young as he was (and still is), his spurs were well developed and he showed a pleasant tendency to dig them into wrists that were not bearing tribute in the form of chow left-overs. Cpl. Grube, who as chief cook was in a good position to win the confidence of his pet, lost no time finding him a match.

One of the coolies working on the post brought a challenger cock from a nearby native village. The aristocratic Red finished off the contender in 12 seconds flat and had scarcely a blood speck on his comb to show for it. After the fight he went back to his corner strutting, and his hen-wives almost smothered him with congratulations.

"Hen or soldier," says Grube, "he's probably the best combat man in the Persian Gulf Command. Only thing that worries me is, I'm afraid he'll go stale in a nonfighting outfit. I'm checking with the CO to see if I can't get him a transfer to a more active theater.

"Golly, would he go great in the Southwest Pacific."

—Sgt. AL HINE
YANK Staff Correspondent

BEEF. Fed up with eating bully beef at his Fifth Air Force squadron mess in a New Guinea forward area, Sgt. Angelo Luciano of Wilmington, Del., organizes

SCOREBOARD. Pvt. James O'Banner of Memph Tenn., first Negro infantryman to kill a Jap, notc his carbine. He scored the kill on a patrol at B

GOOD GOODS. In Panama City, Sgts. Gerald Hubbush, Louisville, Ky., and Dan Marcus, Norwich, Conn., shop for the home folks. One native isn't interested.

PIONEERS. First Red Cross girls in Burma: Maxine Robertson, Portland, Oreg.; Mary Rogan, Glendale, Ohio; Judy Fitch, Hudson, Ohio; Star Giddy, New York City.

AIMING HIGH. Enemy altitude flyers beware. This U. S. Army 120-mm (gun fires 20,000 feet higher than any other antiaircraft weapon in the

POOL. Don't let the GI's mugging distract yo the pool player. He's Maj. Gen. Arthur Wilson,

ON A LIMB. A Yank paratrooper Down Under has troubles. First he tangled in a tree. Next he opened his emergency chute. Then—aw, what's the use?

TURBAN. When the little woman writes that she needs a new beach hat, tell her what Ruth Roman, screen starlet, did with only a lowly towel. On Ruth it looks good.

HUNGRY HUN. This German prisoner at isn't exactly a young man. But his appetite is He puts away C rations as though they were

NUITY. He hates to walk, so in New Guinea Sgt. Maurice Tombaugh, Minden, tells T-5 John Openshaw how he made a car mainly from plane's belly tank.

MUTUAL ADMIRATION. Hollywood's Donna Reed holds figure of herself in gown for "Dorian Gray." She also has the gown on. That's where it looks best.

ROCKETS AWEIGH. Beaufighters of RAF Coastal Command now carry rocket projectiles. Here two streak out, while their gas starts to blanket plane's tail.

RIPLEY. Believe it or not, Earl N. Phillips, seaman from Rad-Va., fell off a ship in mid-Atlantic. About half an hour later a Guard DE happened along. Result: an invigorating dip for Earl.

CONTRAST. Pvt. Buck Goodwin pauses for his partner, Mrs. Kettleson, to get an eyeful of jit-terbugging. They're at a sourdough dance in a log-cabin recreation building made from local material on an island off Alaska. It took nine long months to build the place, but it's worth it.

MAIL CALL

Saluting German Prisoners

Dear YANK:

I saw the article in a March issue of YANK in regard to the saluting of German officers who are prisoners of war. [YANK in *What's Your Problem* quoted the Provost Marshal General's Office as saying GIs had to salute Nazi prisoners of war.—*Ed.*] I'll have to add my moans to those of the many GIs who wrote to *Mail Call* in the May issue. We have a very good reason to bitch, and I know if some of my old buddies in Africa could see or hear of the above they sure would add a lot more to *Mail Call*. After going through dust, mud and malaria, not to mention a lot of other things, then to have to salute Nazi officers——! . . . The Huns and the Japs are the cause of most of the world's troubles today, then to have to give them the honor of a salute—well, not today or any other day that I am in my right mind. Too many rotten, yellow deals have been pulled by them for me ever to have the sense of mind to salute them. . . . Strange things are caused by war, but this is the strangest yet heard of in a world or country that is supposed to be modern and civilized.

Barksdale Field, La. —Cpl. BYRON O. BARKER

Dear YANK:

. . . Why not have the Germans over for a spot of tea?

Douglas AAF, Ariz. —Pvt. F. A. VALERONI

Dear YANK:

. . . I do not see that our men should salute them. It is not re-education to permit them to retain Nazi psychosis by being saluted by their captors. . . .

India —Cpl. WARD McCABE

Dear YANK:

Deal me in on that deck of sentiments against the saluting of German prisoners. I'm a four-engine first pilot, and the only highball I'd ever "award" the enemy would be if I were knocked down and hauled before the Reich High Command. Then I'd probably thumb my nose at 'em.

Westover Field, Mass. —Lt. SAM C. MECLE Jr.

Dear YANK:

I've noted with amusement the debate over saluting enemy officers. . . . What the hell difference does it make whether you salute an Allied or Axis officer —they're *officers*, aren't they? You're not saluting the man, remember? (If you were, there's some of our own you wouldn't like to salute.) A soldier worthy of being called a soldier salutes rank; but then, lots of us guys are just civilians in uniform.

Any jerk can refuse to salute an enemy, but it takes a man and a sportsman to show an opponent that he's big enough and clean enough not to kick a loser when he's down, no matter how unfortunate the loser is. Salute proudly, soldier; it takes guts to do it sometimes, but you get *respect* when you do it. Would our officers appreciate this gesture in a foreign camp?

Lowry Field, Colo. —Pvt. STEVE CLENSOS

■ In *Mail Call* of an April issue of YANK Cpl. Ernest T. Dutton wrote from Kennedy General Hospital, Tenn., that he was a prisoner of the Nazis in Italy for eight months and that he "never saw any Nazi guard or enlisted soldier salute our officers, British or American."

Sinatra

Dear YANK:

On the behalf of the members of my company I wish to inform you of a new punishment that we were forced to undergo over here in the South Pacific. For 14 months our morale has been strong and our spirits high. We have dodged Japs and falling coconuts, suffered ringworm, fungus, malaria, insects' bites, heat rash and jungle rot, but when they pass out Frank Sinatra in "Higher and Higher" we quit. The war had better end soon if the country is so short of men that the women pick that fugitive from a scarecrow factory for an idol. I might add that the show was crowded when the picture started (we gave him the benefit of the doubt!), but only 10 PWs remained to the end (they were well guarded). When the lights went on, the company doctor passed out Section Eights to the unconscious guards.

Guadalcanal —Pvt. BARNEY KIRK

Dear YANK:

We've just seen the show "Higher and Higher" and have decided that a picture of Frank Sinatra in a bathing suit would help the morale of the women on the home front and in the defense plants. A pin-up picture of Frankie would speed up production at least 20 percent, which would be of great value toward an early victory.

New Caledonia —S/Sgt. W. C. PROWS*

*Also signed by 1st Sgt. Frank A. Traum, S/Sgt. O. D. Winstead, Sgts. Bob Hughes and Fred Brown, Cpls. T. J. Sullivan, W. M. Geiken, Cecil R. Boston, Anthony Donahue and Robert J. Buechel and Pvts. Wm. P. Cashman, Daniel T. Walsh, Garrett Bushman and George Gaastra.

War

Dear YANK:

While riding in a truck the other day I overheard a discussion between two officers which seemed to me to constitute the gripe to end all gripes. As pilots they were bemoaning their luck because ground personnel officers could use command cars to date the lovely ladies of our medical detachment, while they had to be satisfied with the lowly jeep. Man, ain't it a grim war?

India —Cpl. HARRY G. SHIPMAN

Gripe on Gripers

Dear YANK:

We have been reading YANK for many many months, in North Africa, Iran and now here in India. We think it is the best damn weekly publication ever to receive ink from a printing press. However, we think a certain section is being highly abused and slightly degraded. The section is *Mail Call*. There are some darn good questions submitted from time to time and very good answers given in return. But we think that some of our fellow soldiers are just bitching in this column to see their names in print. . . .

India —Pfc. H. CHAMBERLIN*

*Also signed by 56 others.

Dear YANK:

In Joe Valasky's "Gripe on Gripers" he says it's aspirins he needs, since the onslaught of gripers to YANK is giving him a terrible headache. Well, it seems to me that if you didn't have a place where guys could sort of get together and hold a little confab about things that are troubling them, it would be downright unconstitutional. It's free speech and public opinion which mold the course of the world, you know. But those words are high-sounding phrases. What really counts for the griper is that he has the chance to get things off his chest. Then he feels relieved about it.

Central Pacific —Pvt. RALPH EBERT

Unlucky Name

Dear YANK:

In *Mail Call* in one of your recent editions an item titled "Mercy for Japs" was sent in by Pvt. Ralph Luckey. [Pvt. Luckey protested the shooting of Japs on Makin Island when they might have been taken alive as prisoners.—*Ed.*] Unfortunately many of my friends have mistaken the article as my viewpoint since he and I both have the same name. As far as I'm concerned, the only "good" Jap is a dead Jap, and here's wishing more power to all the Yanks who are eliminating them.

Italy —2d Lt. RALPH J. LUCKEY

Honor

Dear YANK:

My mother is very proud of the Purple Heart she received when my brother was killed over France. She wouldn't, I'm sure, be nearly so proud if she knew it ranked just one above the Good Conduct Medal. What a disgrace to all those men who had to die to get it.

India —Cpl. LESTER E. DOLAN

Obvious Boner

Dear YANK:

That cartoon of Pvt. Thomas Flannery's in a recent edition showing the MP dressing up the line in front of the Army Relief Show had one boner that just couldn't possibly be overlooked. An MP always wears his brassard on the left arm.

Britain —Lt. A. J. RUTSHAW

■ What do you mean, "just couldn't possibly be overlooked?" We did, didn't we?

States' Sons in Service

Dear YANK:

. . . Your statement in *Strictly GI* in a June issu [YANK said that the "War Department's new state-b state break-down of personnel statistics gives the to the claim that half the Army comes from Texas." *Ed.*] is not appreciated in view of the fact that th claim that half the Army is made up of Texans wa never made unless in jest. We do know better tha that, even if the Yankees don't think so. We hav claimed the greatest number of troops *per populatio* of the states, the claim based on quotations in new papers. . . . You should print the percentage per sta in the armed forces.

Strother Field, Kans. —Sgt. JOHN C. MA

■ YANK's statistician went right to work to sett this question once and for all. Nevada, with th smallest population of all the states and, there fore, with the smallest number of men in bot the Army and Navy, ranks first on the basis percentage. Texas is topped by 18 other state Here is the full list. The controversy is closed— we hope.

State	Percentage	State	Percenta
Alabama	6.7	Montana	7.3
Arizona	7.8	Nebraska	6.8
Arkansas	6.5	Nevada	11.5
California	9.3	New Hampshire	7.8
Colorado	7.3	New Jersey	9.2
Connecticut	9.2	New Mexico	8.1
Delaware	8.1	New York	8.4
District of Columbia	10.6	North Carolina	6.3
Florida	8.2	North Dakota	6.5
Georgia	6.4	Ohio	8.2
Idaho	7.0	Oklahoma	6.9
Illinois	8.1	Oregon	8.8
Indiana	7.6	Pennsylvania	8.2
Iowa	6.9	Rhode Island	9.2
Kansas	7.4	South Carolina	6.4
Kentucky	6.7	South Dakota	6.2
Louisiana	7.4	Tennessee	7.1
Maine	7.5	Texas	8.0
Maryland	8.2	Utah	8.6
Massachusetts	8.7	Vermont	6.7
Michigan	7.8	Virginia	7.4
Minnesota	7.3	Washington	8.2
Mississippi	6.5	West Virginia	7.9
Missouri	7.4	Wisconsin	6.6
Wycming	8.0		

Message Center

Capt. TOM BIVINS, formerly of the 6th Armd. Div., Camp Cooke, Calif.: write Pvt. Erve Schultz, Military Police, Det. 1, Douglas, Wyo. . . . Sgt. CLARENCE W. BLANFORD, last heard of in the 140th Inf. at Camp Robinson, Ark.: write Joseph R. J. Lesch, Box 559, Seamen's House, 550 W. 20th St., N. Y. C. . . . Pfc. NICK CEROVAC and A/S BOB CHRISTENSON, once at Camp Blanding, Fla.: write Pfc. Andrew R. Kurta, 215th Combat Crew Sec., PO Box 4646, AAB, Pueblo, Colo. . . . Anyone knowing the whereabouts of Sgt. JAMES O. ELLIS, last heard of in Camp Lee, Va.: write Pfc. T. F. Watkins Jr., Co. F, 176th Inf., Fort Benning, Ga. . . . JOHN GOAD, formerly of Co. A, 25th Bn., 7th Regt., Fort McClellan, Ala.: write S/Sgt. Paul G. Faircloth, 426 Base Hq. & AB Sq., SAAF, Stuttgart, Ark. . . . Sgt. VERLIN E. HIGGINBATHAM, once at Station Hospital, San Francisco, Calif.: write Cpl. A. J. Ward, 24th ADG Repair Sq., Kelly Field, Tex. . . . Pvt. PARIS W. HILL, once at Camp Davis, N. C.: write Cpl. James McGee, Hq. Btry., 99th AAA Gun. Bn., Camp Stewart, Ga. . . . S/Sgt. SAUL KLAU, who was attached to Regt. Hq., Camp Shelby, Miss., 1942, now an officer: write Pvt. Samuel Klau, Btry. C, 718 FA Bn., 63d Div., APO 410, Camp Van Dorn, Miss. . . . Sgt. ROBERT S. KNOX: write Pvt. Ernest G. Patton, Co. D, 3d Prov. Regt., ASFTC, Camp Claiborne, La. . . . M/Sgt. CARTER T. LEACH, last heard of at Fort Wayne, Ind.: write Lt. D. F. McCarron, Gen. Del., Baer Field, Fort Wayne, Ind. . . . SHORTY LENZER, once in the 110th Med. Bn., Camp San Luis Obispo, Calif.: write Cpl. Franklin Geske, Antitank Co., 140th Inf., Camp Howze, Tex. . . . 2d Lt. STANLEY LEO LEWANDOWSKI, once at Jefferson Bks., Mo.: write A/C Russell F. Mueller, Sq. 2, Bks. T-801 (CAAF), Columbus, Miss. . . . Pvt. CHARLES F. LOHR, overseas: write Pvt. John W. Gorman, 97th Sig. Co., APO 445, Fort Leonard Wood, Mo. . . . EDWARD P. MULBERRY of Long Island, at Camp Upton in 1942: write Cpl. Robert J. Bolger, Sub Unit E, 113 AAFBU, Charleston, S. C. . . . Pfc. EARL L. ORNETT: write Pvt. Lewis E. Best, 3501 AAFBU, Sec. O, BMC #1, Boca Raton, Fla. . . . BARRIE D. RICHARDSON S2c: write Pfc. R. J. Buckley, Co. B, 519th MP Bn., Camp Chaffee, Ark. . . . O/C FRED RUTHFAUFF, last heard of at Aberdeen Proving Grounds, Md.: write Pvt. Merrill Ormes, 579th Sig. Dep. Co., PO Unit #2, Camp Cooke, Calif. . . . Marin Pvt. FRANKIE SAMMARTANO, once at Naval Base i Jacksonville, Fla.: write Pfc. Daniel S. Karlin, H Co., 3d Bn., 264th Inf., 66th Div., APO 454, Camp Rob inson, Ark. . . . 1st Sgt. JOHN SAVICH or other buddie of the 368th TSS, Scott Field, Ill.: write S/Sgt. Fran cis J. Weaver, 484th BHQ & AB Sq., Willow Run Air port, Ypsilanti, Mich. . . . DOROTHY SHORES, last hear of with the WAVES at Terminal Island, or anyon knowing her whereabouts: write Nibs G. Balbe Btry. B, 199th FA, 410 Gp., Camp Butner, Durham N. C. . . . ROBERT TRAUM & EUGENE TREIBER of Brook lyn: write Pfc. Seymour Posner, Co. H, 202 Inf., AP 411, Camp Gruber, Okla. . . . Lt. BETTY WARDLOU, for merly in Co. 19, 3d Regt., Fort Des Moines, Iowa write Cpl. Claudine Stribling, Co. 8, 22d WAC Regt. Fort Oglethorpe, Ga.

SHOULDER PATCH EXCHANGE. A list of shoulder-patc collectors' names will be sent to you if you write *Shoulde Patch Exchange*, YANK, 205 East 42d Street, New York 17 N. Y. Specify whether you want your name added to the list

EDNA HINDIE, Armenian: They think too much of themselves and brag too much. But I like them, else I wouldn't go out with them as I do.

BARBARA CHARALAMBOUS, Greek: I don't know. I'm afraid to go out with them. They like too much to be naughty.

YANK's photographer Sgt. Steve Derry met these six girls in Cairo, and here's the question he popped to them while he was taking their pictures:

What do you think of American soldiers?

ANNE FANNING, Irish: They are not afraid to do or say what they think. If they want something they go out after it. I should know!

QUEENIE O'HANIAN, Armenian: They're always well dressed; that's all I can say, except my mother don't like for me to go out much.

MARGARET YAZBEK, Syrian: They walk and talk like free people. Not many do that any more. They are serious at work; very good at play.

AZIZA SHOUKRY, Egyptian: They are very natural and probably would be fun to go out with, but I am Moslem and it's against our custom.

THE SAD SACK

"ALL WET"

SGT. GEORGE BAKER

Lost Teeth

Dear YANK:

Does a GI have to sign a statement of charges if he loses the set of false teeth issued to him by the Army? Some guys say you do, and I'm worried. While we were crossing on the ship I was put on a detail as a sort of "bucket brigade" member who passes cardboard cases down to the galley below. One wise guy threw a box at my chest and the jolt bounced my false teeth into the Pacific. It wasn't my fault, and I'll be one damned sore dogface if I am expected to pay for them.

Australia —Pvt. DOMINICK ATRELLIA

■ False teeth are not considered "property" in the usual sense of the word, and the Judge Advocate General has ruled that a GI who accidentally loses his dentures does not have to pay for them on a statement of charges.

Search and Seizure

Dear YANK:

Last week we were suddenly ordered out of our barracks and onto the field and made to submit our wallets for an inspection to see if we had any illegal passes to leave the post. The inspecting officer did not make us give him our wallets, but he did leaf through them and he asked us for any passes we might have on our person. We got real hot, however, when we learned that a commissioned officer came into the barracks while we were away and went through our uniforms, barracks bags and foot lockers looking for passes. The point is this: Do they have the authority to go through a man's private belongings when he is not present?

Hawaii —Cpl. IRA REICHMAN

P.S. They got 20 passes.

■ On an Army post any soldier is subject to search of both his military and personal property when authorities believe a military law has been or is about to be violated.

Sgt. Brandt

What's Your Problem?

Army Nurse Subsistence

Dear YANK:

I'm a private, married to an Army nurse who is a second lieutenant. Now, even though officers are supposed to get extra money for subsistence and rental allowances if they are married, my wife has been told that she can't get this additional money for me. It seems to me that if I can give $22 a month from my pay as a private to provide for a $50 ODB allowance to my wife, a second lieutenant, then she should be able to give *me* what is coming to me. Can I make the Army give my wife (and me) that money?

Britain —Pvt. FRANK JOHNSON

■ You can't get the money. AR 35-2020, Par. 6, states that Army nurses are not entitled to subsistence or rental allowances for their husbands.

Conscientious Objectors

Dear YANK:

When the war began I had strong convictions against fighting. I thought the only way to stop wars was not to fight them. I've changed my mind. The only way to stop wars is to kill the swine who start them. But now I find I can't do much about my change of sentiment because no GI is permitted to volunteer for combat duty. What's worse, my record reads that I am to be assigned to noncombatant service only. What can I do to get that altered so maybe I'll get combat duty?

Puerto Rico —Pvt. F. S. M.

■ It's very easy. WD Cir. 29 (1943), Sec. V, Par. 2, states that conscientious objectors can be transferred from non-combatant to combatant service upon "voluntary request in writing." In short, see your CO. Good luck.

American Theater Ribbon

Dear YANK:

I am stationed on an island 14 miles off the East Coast of the U. S., some of my friends are serving on islands just off the West Coast, and other GIs I know were serving on the beaches of Florida when the German saboteurs landed there. They all tell me that we are entitled to wear the American Theater Ribbon because we served in a combat zone. Is this true?

Cape Lookout, Va. —Cpl. JOHN

■ No. The only personnel entitled to wear the American Theater Ribbon are those serving outside the continental limits of the U. S., and your island and your friends' islands and the beaches of Florida are within these limits. The only exceptions are those GIs who go outside the limits on regular duty such as antisubmarine patrol.

1st Sgt. vs. M. Sgt.

Dear YANK:

Yuk, yuk, yuk. Oh boy, YANK, this is good. We're way down here six miles below hell. One day we were all lounging around, what with the heat, etc., when the first sergeant walked up and started eating us out. Well, there was a master sergeant snoozing in the shade, and the noise woke him. So he got tough, and first thing you know the master sergeant and the first sergeant were having words, as the English say. And, of course, the argument soon boiled down to a question of rank, with each sergeant claiming he was boss since he had the highest rank and precedence among NCOs. Now the whole outfit is divided into two camps, and we're all involved. What's right, YANK?

New Guinea —T/Sgt. VINCENT DOLI

■ Master sergeants and first sergeants are of equal rank, both being in the first grade of enlisted men. Precedence, however, is established as follows: 1) According to the date of rank as stated in the warrants. 2) When the dates are the same, then by length of service in the Army. 3) When both the dates and length of service are the same, then length of service in the Marine Corps or Navy. 4) Finally, if all those tests are not sufficient, the names go into a hat and precedence is determined by lot, believe it or not.

West Point

ENLISTED men over 19 who will not have reached their 22d birthday on July 2, 1945, may apply for admission to West Point under the authority of *WD Cir. 207, 1944*. They must be citizens, they must be unmarried, they must have an AGCT score of 135 or higher, they must have completed a high-school education or its equivalent, they must have completed a full year of active service before July 2, 1945, and they must show a capacity for leadership. Successful candidates must agree to serve for a period of eight years. Applications will be accepted from overseas as well as domestic personnel.

Enlisted men who now hold letters of appointment to one of the other service academies (Navy, Coast Guard) will not be sent overseas, and those who are overseas now will be returned to the States to attend the service academies to which they are accredited.

$10 War Bond

A new $10 GI War Bond, to sell for $7.50, will be available in August for sale to military personnel only. For men who sign up for purchase of the bonds before August under the Class B allotment plan, the WD will date the bonds back to the month of purchase. The new bond, designed for GIs who have a small surplus of cash, is expected to reduce and possibly eliminate installment buying of bonds by military personnel. GIs so far have bought nearly $500,000,000 worth of War Bonds by the allotment plan and are continuing to buy $38,000,000 worth per month.

Pre-Shipping Furloughs

About 97 percent of all Ground Forces personnel transported as overseas replacements in April had furloughs either just before departure or during the preceding six months. AGF's policy is to give, whenever possible, a full 10 days at home to all men headed overseas. A change in the ARs dealing with furloughs says that an EM slated to be sent overseas is eligible for furlough, regardless of length of service, if he has had no furlough since he entered the service.

Combat Wounded

Combat wounded personnel who, as a result of their wounds, are permanently below the minimum standards for induction and are eligible for discharge may now remain in the service at their own request, provided their physical condition permits some useful employment in the service.

War Trophies

GIs returning from overseas are now permitted to bring back war trophies. Such material may also be mailed back to the States if no firearms are included. The trophies must be accompanied by a certificate of permission from the GI's superior officer.

NEW GLIDER BADGE, which fully trained members of glider or airborne units are eligible to wear when they have participated in two glider flights under tactical or simulated tactical conditions. A man entitled to both this and the Parachute Badge may wear whichever he chooses, but only one at a time.

"Sir, we have the first sergeant's permission to capture the commanding officer."

The Women

Wacs with experience in nursing, dietetics or physical therapy may be released from the WAC for appointment in the Nurse Corps or the Medical Department as dieticians or physical-therapy aids. . . . All enlisted Wacs, regardless of age, are now eligible for appointment as officer candidates provided they meet all other requirements. . . . The brown and white pin-striped seersucker uniform worn by nurses overseas is now available to nurses on duty in the U. S.

Washington OP

A BILL is under consideration in the Senate to give a pay increase of $10 a month to wearers of the Combat Infantry Badge and an increase of $5 a month to wearers of the Expert Infantryman Badge. The Secretary of War, in a letter recommending the bill to the Military Affairs Committee, said that in North Africa and Italy the Infantry has made up 19.8 percent of the total strength and has suffered 70 percent of the casualties, while in all theaters the Infantry has averaged about one-fourth of the strength and about half of the casualties.

Veterans of the second World War are not rushing to get their old jobs back. Only 25 percent of the men discharged through hospitals since May 1, 1940, have returned to their pre-induction jobs. The majority of those being discharged now are taking war-production jobs. They usually pay more money, but any rights to the old job evaporate if application isn't made within 40 days. The War Manpower Commission, through the U. S. Employment Service, lines up the new jobs. Test centers set up in Los Angeles, Houston, St. Louis, Minneapolis, Philadelphia, New Haven and Denver to handle placement problems have proved successful and similar centers are blooming in local USES offices.

The U. S. is now producing four planes to every one completed by the Germans, while Japanese production of combat planes is estimated at 13 percent of the U. S. output. U. S. workers, 2,100,000 of them, averaged a plane every five minutes, not counting Sundays, during the first four months of 1944. Our total output for the year will hit 100,000.

Five major headaches of the Army and Navy Postal Service, according to the OWI, are letters to casuals, hospital mail, letters to globe-hopping Air Force personnel, misaddressed letters and matters of security. The Postal Service admits that casuals, hospital patients and Air Force men must expect delays in mail delivery and that in extraordinary cases letters mailed in June and July of 1943 had still not been delivered in the spring of 1944. Some 15 percent of mail is misaddressed, often with the digits transposed in APO and FPO numbers; casuals and Air Force men are often a jump ahead of their latest change-of-address card; secret military operations hold up the mail of their units often until the operation is several weeks old. Mail gets back to the States more quickly than it gets overseas since there is more cargo space on the way back and people at home don't move around so much. Still and all, the Postal Service claims that 90 percent of the men who complain officially are getting their mail before the investigation is finished. . . . GI use of V-Mail caught up with civilian use last December and it's been about 50-50 ever since.

In response to many inquiries since the repatriation of sick and wounded American prisoners began, the Red Cross says that there is no arrangement at present between nations for the exchange of able-bodied prisoners of war.

2d Lt. Ernest Childers and T/Sgt. Charles E. (Commando) Kelly, both Medal of Honor winners, are expected to be assigned to the Infantry School at Fort Benning, Ga., as instructors.

There's a man in this town who spends every Sunday making himself useful to camera-toting couples. He holds the camera so both the guy and the gal can get in the picture at the same time. And on weekdays he writes fairy tales for children. —YANK Washington Bureau

YANK is published weekly by the enlisted men of the U. S. Army and is for sale only to those in the armed services. Stories, features, pictures and other material from YANK may be reproduced if they are not restricted by law or military regulations, provided proper credit is given, release dates are observed and specific prior permission has been granted for each item to be reproduced. Entire contents copyrighted, 1944, by Col. Franklin S. Forsberg and reviewed by U. S. military censors.

MAIN EDITORIAL OFFICE
205 EAST 42d ST., NEW YORK 17, N. Y., U. S. A.

EDITORIAL STAFF

Managing Editor, Sgt. Joe McCarthy, FA; Art Director, Sgt. Arthur Weithas, DEML; Assistant Managing Editor, Sgt. Justus Schlotzhauer, Inf.; Assistant Art Director, Sgt. Ralph Stein, Med.; Features, Sgt. Leo Hofeller, Md.; Features, Sgt. Marion Hargrove, FA; Sports, Sgt. Dan Polier, AAF.

Overseas News, Sgt. Allan Ecker, AAF.
Washington: Sgt. Earl Anderson, AAF; Cpl. Richard Paul, DEML.
London: Sgt. Durbin Horner, QMC; Sgt. Walter Peters, QMC; Sgt. John Scott, Engr.; Sgt. Charles Brand, AAF; Sgt. Bill Davidson, Inf.; Sgt. Sanderson Vanderbilt, CA; Sgt. Peter Paris, Engr.; Cpl. Jack Coggins, CA; John Preston, AAF; Sgt. Saul Levitt, AAF; Cpl. Edmund Antrobus, Inf.; Cpl. Joseph Cunningham; Pvt. Ben Frazier, CA; Sgt. Reginald Arnstein, Inf.
Italy: Sgt. George Aarons, Sig. Corps; Sgt. Burgess Scott, Inf.; Sgt. James P. O'Neill, QMC; Sgt. John Frano, Inf.; Sgt. Harry Sions, AAF.
Cairo: Sgt. J. Denton Scott, FA; Sgt. Steven Derry, DEML; Sgt. Walter Bernstein, Inf.

Iraq-Iran: Sgt. Burtt Evans, Inf.; Cpl. Robert McBrinn, Sig. Corps; Cpl. Richard Gaige, DEML.
China-Burma-India: Sgt. Dave Richardson, CA; Sgt. Lou Stoumen, DEML; Sgt. Seymour Friedman, Sig. Corps.
Southwest Pacific: Cpl. Lafayette Locke, AAF; Sgt. Douglas Borgstedt, DEML; Cpl. Ozzie St. George, Inf.; Sgt. Dick Hanley, AAF; Sgt. Charles Person, Engr.; Cpl. Ralph Boyce, AAF; Cpl. Bill Alcine, Sig. Corps; Cpl. Charles Rathe, DEML; Cpl. George Bick, Inf.; Pfc. John McLeod, Med.; Sgt. Marvin Fasig, Engr.
South Pacific: Sgt. Barrett McGurn, Med.; Sgt. Dillon Ferris, AAF; Sgt. Robert Greenhalgh, Inf.

Hawaii: Sgt. James L. McManus, CA; Cpl. Richard J. Nihill, CA; Sgt. Bill Reed, Inf.
Alaska: Sgt. Georg N. Meyers, AAF; Cpl. John Haverstick, CA; Sgt. Ray Duncan, AAF.
Panama: Sgt. Robert G. Ryan, Inf.; Sgt. John Hay, Inf.; Sgt. William T. Potter, DEML.
Puerto Rico: Cpl. Bill Haworth, DEML; Cpl. Jud Cook, DEML; Sgt. Don Cooke, FA.
Trinidad: Pfc. James Iorio, MP.
Bermuda: Sgt. William Pene du Bois.
Ascension Island: Pfc. Nat Bodian, AAF.
British Guiana: Sgt. Bernard Freeman, AAF.
Central Africa: Sgt. Kenneth Abbott, AAF.
Iceland: Sgt. Joseph Korein.
Newfoundland: Sgt. Frank Bode, Sig. Corps.
Greenland: Sgt. Robert Kelly, Sig. Corps.
Navy: Robert L. Schwartz Y2c; Allen Churchill Sp(x)3c.

Commanding Officer: Col. Franklin S. Forsberg.
Executive Officer: Maj. Jack W. Weeks.
Overseas Bureau Officers: London, Maj. Donald W. Reynolds; India, Capt. Gerald J. Rock; Australia, Maj. Harold B. Hawley; Italy, Maj. Robert Strother; Hawaii, Maj. Josua Eppinger; Cairo, Maj. Charles Holt; Iran, Maj. Henry E. Johnson; South Pacific, Capt. Justus J. Craemer; Alaska, Capt. Harry R. Roberts; Panama, Capt. Howard J. Carswell.

YANK THE ARMY WEEKLY

1st Sgt. Frank J. Wiese reaches out to help Pfc. Ruben Meyer as the 9th Armd. Div. artilleryman lunges across the finish line to chalk up the new record.

All fagged out after setting the record for the 25-mile hike, Pfc. Meyer get support from Pfc. Young Stuhley (right), coach of the 9th's boxing team

Artilleryman Latest To Claim 25-Mile Title

North Camp Polk, La.—Pfc. Ruben Meyer, 31, of Chicago, Ill., an artilleryman with the 9th Armd. Div., became the new 25-mile hike champion of the U. S. Army last month. Covering the distance in four hours, 34 minutes and 24 seconds, Meyer broke the record of four hours and 47 minutes set recently by Pfc. Clarence Blackcloud of the 20th Armd. Div. at Camp Campbell, Ky.

Meyer is in the 3d Armd. FA Bn. and was trying for the record for the first time. With a retinue of coaches, supporters and official observers, he set out at 0400 with full field pack, carbine and steel helmet. He covered the first seven miles in one hour, running and walking.

He was paced at intervals by 1st Sgt. Frank J. Wiese, M/Sgt. William D. Mahoney, S/Sgt. Joseph W. Sylvestre and Sgt. Frederick H. Rudi.

His route took him along the road between the camp and Leesville, while headlights of several vehicles lighted the way as he moved along the shoulder of the road, a rutty and precarious course. At one point he stumbled and fell but was on his feet quickly and off again.

After one hour and 20 minutes of running, Meyer began to tire and brought his pace down to a fast walk. His summer khakis were soaked with sweat by this time, and he had opened his shirt to help cool himself. At 0605 he had reached the halfway mark where he turned

around and started back. His time so far was two hours and 5 minutes.

He stopped several times for water, to douse his legs with liniment and to take salt tablets. He alternated between a dogtrot and a walk and reached the MP gates, about two miles from the finish line, at 0818. He had 28 minutes in which to cover the remaining distance in order to break the record.

Nearing the finish line he broke into a dead run and finished with time to spare. He collapsed at the tape and was taken to the dispensary for a check-up. He'd lost seven pounds, but aside from weariness had suffered no ill effects.

Because Meyer is an artilleryman, the infantrymen of the 9th Armd. are trying to do something about breaking his record. They feel that the 25-mile hike mark is something that belongs in their province.

Voting Orientation

Camp Crowder, Mo.—Pfc. Bernard Schwartzberg is chairman of the Forum Voting Committee, which is going all-out to make sure that GIs at Crowder vote in the coming elections. Outlining the committee's voting-orientation plan, Schwartzberg states it will take the subject of soldier voting "from the realm of words into the field of practical orientation."

The committee set up by the Camp Crowder Forum, a voluntary orientation group, will operate on the following program:

1. Find out election procedures in the 48 states. This material is available through WD circulars.

2. Find out detailed individual voting-eligibility requirements of all states. This is not covered by the WD nor is it included in the CO's responsibilities. Break this information up into readily understood form.

3. Make this information available to all COs and EM by: *a)* Establishing a speakers' bureau which would send out qualified men to deliver voting-orientation talks to all companies; *b)* putting up information booths in all Service Clubs; *c)* distributing voting posters to all day rooms and recreation halls.

Schwartzberg is anxious to pass on his committee's plans and is equally eager to hear from other camps in which voting programs may have been instituted. He claims that voting talks at his post have been followed by almost a third of the personnel applying for war ballots.

"On a nation-wide scale," he says, "it will make the difference between a few soldiers voting and the Army voting. The actual soldier vote can jump from insignificance to a monument to democracy."

Double Steal

Camp Reynolds, Pa.—For seven years Pvt. Bill Purdy of Ithaca, N. Y., had gone steady with a girl from Buffalo. While Bill was taking his basic at Camp Croft, S. C., the girl wrote him often and almost as often sent him packages of cookies.

Then another Bill Purdy came into the outfit. This one began to receive the other's letters and cookies. Finally he wrote the girl to explain the error. Their correspondence blossomed into friendship.

Recently Pvt. Purdy visited his home town

and learned that his girl had married the other Bill Purdy. "I don't mind so much that he stole my girl," he commented, "but what about the cookies?"

Now They Believe It

Fort Sill, Okla.—Pvt. Oscar Simms of Austin, Tex., a member of the 686th FA Bn., recently scored 199 out of a possible 200 with the carbine. When the remarkable score was about to be entered in his service record, doubt arose in the minds of his officers.

So Pvt. Simms returned to the range to prove that such a feat was possible with the light weapon. This time he racked up a perfect mark of 200, firing at 100- and 200- yard distances from prone, standing and kneeling positions. During his basic training, Simms once shot 135 out of a possible 150 with the M1.

Not in the Mood

Malden Army Air Field, Mo.—An air cadet dictated a telegram to Pvt. Scott W. Burge, teletypist in the signal office here. The message concluded with the familiar "All my love."

Burge suggested that if the cadet would eliminate one word, the telegram would be less costly. The cadet thought for a moment and then said:

"Change the last part to read just 'Love.' I don't feel up to giving her all my love tonight anyway."

Geography Lesson

Washington, D. C.—T-5 Harry Miner, on DEML here, noticed a young GI in a local bar wearing a service ribbon that had three vertical stripes of green, yellow and green. "You're pretty young to be wearing that ribbon," Miner told the soldier.

"I got a right," said the GI.

"Okay, maybe you have," said Miner, "but you're a lot younger than I am, I'm sure, and I was only 4 when that ribbon was authorized. That's the Mexican Border Ribbon."

"So what!" snapped the soldier. "I was at Sheppard Field in Texas for three months, and Texas is on the Mexican border, isn't it?"

What's That Name Again?

Stockton Field, Calif.—Cpl. Buddy Miller came into the day room one Sunday afternoon and asked if there had been any phone calls for him. The answer was "No," so Miller sat down to wait. In a few minutes the phone rang and Miller answered.

"Just a minute," he was heard to say, "I'll see if he's around."

Miller took a few steps away from the phone and then halted abruptly. "Say," he said, "that phone call is for Buddy Miller. That's me!"

PARENTAL POINTERS. Cpl. Oscar C. Fish armament man at Tuskegee AAF, Ala., shows Pvt. Oscar H. how to handle a submachine

Three Get Soldier's Medals

Fort Benning, Ga.—Three sergeants were awarded Soldier's Medals and three others received Certificates of Award for heroic action during a training accident here a few months ago. Those honored at a ceremony held at Gordon Field were: S/Sgt. Howard N. Webster of Crewe, Va.; Sgt. William C. Yalenty of Pittsburgh, Pa., and Sgt. John H. Magill of Richmond, Va., who received the Soldier's Medals; T/Sgt. Alvin W. Walker, T/Sgt. Arthur J. Lester and S/Sgt. Edgar T. Simpers, who received the Certificates of Award.

The action for which the awards were granted took place last March during a training demonstration. An assault boat containing members of the 176th sank during the simulated attack of a river line. The six sergeants effected the rescue of many of the men threatened with drowning in the swift waters of the Chattahoochee River.

← *Here is the honored sextet. Left to right: T/Sgt. Alvin Walker, Sgt. William Yalenty, T/Sgt. Arthur Lester, S/Sgt. Howard Webster, S/Sgt. Edgar Simpers and Sgt. John Magill, all of the 176th Infantry.*

AROUND THE CAMPS

Camp Livingston, La.—S/Sgt. Theodore Mooseles of the 86th Division read in his home-town paper that he had become the father of a boy, and the mail that day brought several cards of congratulation. Only one person was more surprised at the news than the sergeant—his wife who lives with him in nearby Alexandria, La.; she didn't know they were having a baby, either.

Boca Raton Field, Fla.—Pvt. William A. Brittain washed out his only good pair of shorts and hung them on the line behind the barracks. While they were drying, two wrens built a nest in the crotch. Brittain removed the nest to a nearby tree, and everybody was satisfied. One crotch was as good as another for the wrens.

Peterson Field, Colo.—S/Sgt. Raymond L. Bretz was elected chairman of the Soldiers and Sailors council at the 106 USO Club recently. Sgt. Bretz succeeds Cpl. Mary Collard of the WAC Detachment, who left this post to undergo training—for overseas duty.

Camp Peary, Va.—Ben Harris S2c, War Bond salesman at Induction, was stumped recently when he faced a prospective customer who could speak only French. Harris went outside and found a recruit in the crowd able to speak French. He sold the bond.

Camp Roberts, Calif.—M/Sgt. Fillmore M. Broom, camp sergeant major, gave an order to the girl driver of the headquarters car to check with him before she took anyone on a trip. Her compliance exceeded even the sergeant's require-ments. When the camp's executive officer, a lieutenant colonel, stepped into the car and told the driver to rush him to another section of the camp, she asked: "Have you Sgt. Broom's permission to use this car?"

Camp Carson, Colo.—GIs were speechless with amazement as they watched Pvt. Tommy Tucker of Co. F, 90th Inf. Regt., put his ice cream between two slices of bread and eat it that way. Tucker's explanation: it kept his fingers from getting sticky.

Camp Kohler, Calif.—Henry S. Troxel, 67, of Kokomo, Ind., traveled 2,300 miles to visit his son, Pvt. Herbert A. Troxell, only to find he was on KP. Mr. Troxel volunteered to share KP with his son and was accepted. Mr. Troxel liked the potato-peeling detail immensely; Pvt. Troxel did not.

Greenwood Army Air Field, Miss.—When it came time for the potato race in the aviation cadets' field day here, a slight hitch developed. Not a potato could be found on the post. Golf balls were substituted.

Camp Adair, Oreg.—T/Sgt. Frank Gilloon of the 70th Div. Hq. Det. got a flat tire driving into camp for reveille one morning. He had no spare, and it looked as if he'd never make it. A car drove up behind him, and the driver said: "Use my spare." The good samaritan was Pvt. Clarence Everett, an MP.

Alexandria Army Air Field, La.—Sgt. Andrew Grisaffi, mail clerk, believes in getting mail to the GIs in his section. When gripes become too frequent and he gets tired of saying, "No mail for you today," Grisaffi writes the men a friendly, cheerful card himself.

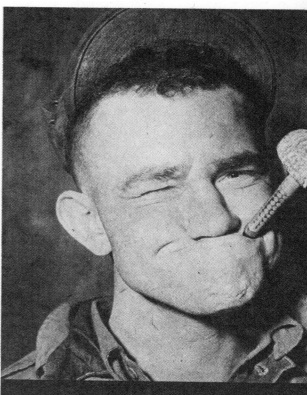

GI POPEYE. "Get your uppers knocked out," says Cpl. Jack Strain, "and you can look like this." He's the roller-rink caretaker at Camp Ellis, Ill.

WHAT'S IN A NAME? There must be something. Here are five unrelated Smiths who won the Green-wood Army Air Field (Miss.) basketball championship. The guy at the left is their coach, S/Sgt. Bill. From there on (l. to r.) it's all "Smith," with A/Cs Bill, Gordon, Otis, Bob and Capt. Jim Smith.

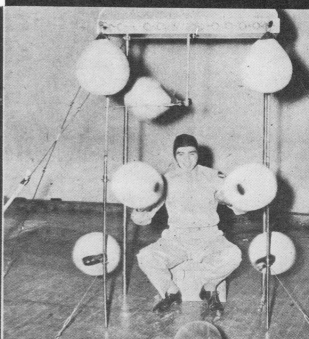

SLIGHTLY PUNCHY. The bags, we mean, not Sgt. Leonard Ross. Here he keeps seven going at

THE HEROES

Upon reading "The Mourner's Bench" in a June issue of YANK.

·soldier said: There is a mourner's bench
here our mothers sit and share their sorrow
or our dead with German mothers—
wailing wall, with Death a bond—
nd little does it matter on which side one fell.

's true, there was a time for mourning.
ne sky was red. They burned the books,
ne temples fell. Old men in prayer shawls
ere dragged and hung with signs: *"I am a Jew!"*
ıt no one cried. They taught their sons
spit into a gagged man's face
ecause he knew such words as "Freedom"
r "Christ" or "Labor Unity" or "Liberty."

ut yet no tears. The guns that held Cassino
ere zeroed at Madrid. "Sieg Heil," "Heil Hitler"
Read "Theft" and "Rape" and "Murder")
rowned out the cries in Holland, Poland,
zechoslovakia, France. The Zeros
nat stunned Pearl Harbor took their test flights
t Kholchingol. The grinning death
nat jumped ashore on Luzon was rehearsed
'ith putrid splendor at Shanghai and Nanking.
nd still no tears. The loving *Hausfrau*
eceived a bundle: there small shoes, a coat,
lood-spattered, fur-lined, warm.
ear wife: Here are some things for Fritzchen.
ut pigs don't cry. They grunt and swallow
children.

ow Hans is dead. And Franz and Fritz.
nd wreaths are hung, and now the cries and
tears
nd wailing. But the tears are cold;
ney will not make the grass grow, and the pain
hollow and a wasted seed.
re dead men heroes just because they died?
re rats like warriors if they bare their teeth?

et them die quickly and be buried quickly,
nwilling graves in a sickened earth. But we
nall waste no breath, no pity on them. We shall
finish
'hat they begot and save our love,
ur heart for all who help us drain
ur world-land from this stench and filth.
et those who learn to follow them be welcome.

amp Reynolds, Pa. —Pvt. RUDY BASS

THIS IS ALASKA

This is Alaska: the towering peaks,
The frozen tundras wide,
The wolf pack's call, the eagle's flight,
The rushing of the tide.

This is Alaska: the sourdough's dream
Of the end of a rainbow's gold;
The flashing of the Borealis' lights;
The snow, the ice and the cold.

This is Alaska: the fog-bound isles,
Volcanoes' fiery breath;
The Last Frontier of America,
Of life and of sudden death.

This is Alaska: lonely caches,
Canyons, glaciers blue;
Land of dream and enchantment
Where sourdough's dreams come true.

Alaska —Pfc. J. FRANKLIN YOUNG

BAR, MOSQUITO

Some Quartermaster master mind
Put in for one more star
Because he is the father of
The famed mosquito bar.
But to the end I'll still contend
The bar is overrated:
You see, my canvas cot and it
Are very much mismated.

For I have yet a night to see
When, sound asleep I seem to be
And my mosquito bar is tucked in,
A damned mosquito hasn't ducked in.

It seems that as I soundly nap
Away the blacked-out night,
Somebody's feet jerk out the sheet
And make my bar untight.
No matter how I fix the thing
It never fails to happen:
When I arise, yawn, rub my eyes,
I see the edges flapping.

My atabrine I'll gladly take
By twos or by the jar
And toss aside the QM's pride—
The brown mosquito bar.

Australia —Sgt. F. H. BOSLETT

THE OVERMEN

Where are the supermen
Whose veins were ducts
For blood more red
Than common kind?

Where are the supermen,
The blond giants,
The bodies beautiful,
Tremendous, powerful?

Where are the superminds,
The men of Kultur,
The intellects more refined
Than common kind?

Prophets of power, of terror,
Overknights of an overrace:
They've made beautiful bodies,
Uncommon bodies,
In a common earth.

IRTC, Camp Wolters, Tex. —Pvt. HERBERT H. BRIN

IN THE SUN

If you feel the warm day coming on,
You step up to the sun and touch it.
You touch it slowly, let it drip.
You like to know that it is warm
And that the sun is on your face.
Sometimes it is closer than that:
It is rolling down your back:
It is a hoop, and a hand
Out of the blue section of the sky
Is pushing it on and on.

She will come to you
In the warm sun and the hot earth
And the hungry days.
She will be touching you
And you will feel naked and humble
Beside her,
And her eyes will be blue,
Her skin will be fair,
Her fingers will not tremble,
But you will hold them
And feel them, soft and firm and warm.

This is a perfect day for a dream
Or something like that.
You are that, soldier:
A person away from the city.
You are thinking of the plum pudding,
Or the corner street light,
Or the bottle of soda, or the schoolroom.

Come, take the sadness from me.
I am waiting here, I am touching you
And, as I kiss you, I hear you say
That the warm sun is in my face,
And your eyes blink,
Because I am in every ray.

SU, Philadelphia, Pa. —Cpl. SARGE D. STERLING

GOLF LOG

ow score wins. See in how few strokes you can change CAMP to SHIP. Maybe you can beat our par of seven strokes.

At each stroke you form a new word by changing ne letter in the previous word. Example: Change RL to WIFE in four strokes—GIRL 1. GILL 2. WILL WILE 4. WIFE.

CAMP

4. ______
5. ______
6. ______
7. SHIP

PUZZLE SOLUTIONS

CHECKER STRATEGY. White moves 23 to 19. Black kin
jumps 15 to 24. . . . White moves 30 to 25. Black jumps an
crowns, 21 to 30. . . . White moves 8 to 11. Black jumps
to 23. . . . White king jumps 11 to 20 to 27 to 18 to 9 to
And White is the winner.

LETTER DIVISION.

0	1	2	3	4	5	6	7	8	9
R	N	I	Y	H	A	T	K	F	E

GOLF LOG. CAMP 1. CARP 2. WARP 3. WART 4. WAIT 5. WH
6. WHIP 7. SHIP.

TOTEM PUZZLE. He built a box seven feet square an
laid the pole on the diagonal.

IF WE must have red tape in the Army, here is the way to have it—wrapped around Rita Hayworth. When she isn't getting into extraordinary poses like this, Rita, who was born Margarita Carmen Cansino, is one of our best screen dancers. Her latest picture for Columbia is "Tonight and Every Night," and we won't stand for wisecracks.

CHECKER STRATEGY

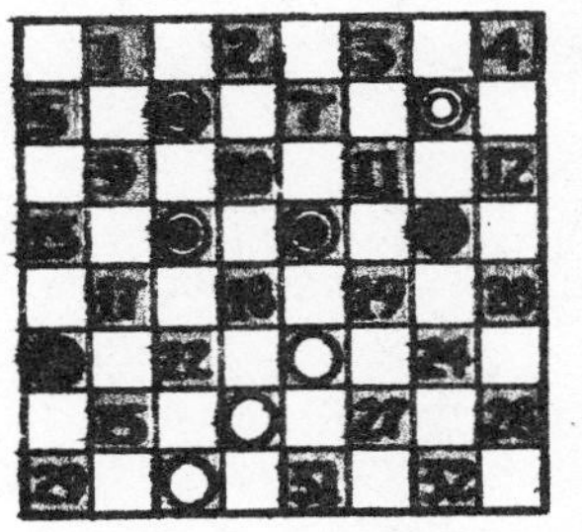

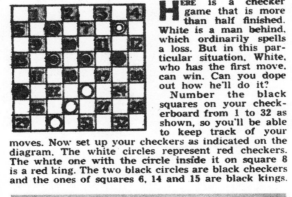

HERE is a checker game that is more than half finished. White is a man behind, which ordinarily spells a loss. But in this particular situation, White, who has the first move, can win. Can you dope out how he'll do it?

Number the black squares on your checkerboard from 1 to 32 as shown, so you'll be able to keep track of your moves. Now set up your checkers as indicated on the diagram. The white circles represent red checkers. The white one with the circle inside it on square 8 is a red king. The two black circles are black checkers and the ones of squares 6, 14 and 15 are black kings.

LETTER DIVISION

THIS is what you get when you substitute letters for numbers in a simple long-division problem. Each number from 0 through 9 is represented by a different letter.

You figure out the numbers. There are plenty of clues. Here's one: N must equal 1 because N times HIKE equals HIKE.

```
          A N R T
        ---------------
H I K E ) I N F A N T R Y
          I N Y E A
          ---------
            H A T T
            H I K E
            -------
              I F K R Y
              I A T K H
              ---------
                Y R I E
```

When you discover the number value of a letter, write down the number in the blank space beneath the letter, wherever it occurs in the diagram. This will help keep you straight.

TOTEM PUZZLE

"A TOTEM pole!" cried the sergeant. "Just what the folks need for the living room!" So he paid $12 for the thing, tied a tag on it and took it down to the express-man.

The pole was 8½ feet long and a foot wide. The expressman took a look at it and shook his head. "No go, bud," he said. "You can't ship that unless you crate it, and be sure your box doesn't measure more than 85 inches long. That's our limit."

Sounds impossible. But without cutting or damaging the totem pole in any way, the sergeant crated and shipped it.

How did he do it?

CHANGE OF ADDRESS If you are a YANK subscriber and have changed your address, use this coupon together with the mailing address on your latest YANK to notify us of the change. Mail it to YANK, The Army Weekly, 205 East 42d Street, New York 17, N. Y., and YANK will follow you to any part of the world.

Full Name and Rank ______ Order No ______

OLD MILITARY ADDRESS

______

NEW MILITARY ADDRESS

______

Allow 21 days for change of address to become effective

The Individualist

"No," said McGillicuddy when he joined the Army. "No matter how hard they try, they shall never mold me."

McGillicuddy thrived on being an individualist. In college he had been a sensation because of his persistent refusal to wear saddle shoes and plaid shirts. In business life he had turned his individualism into temperament and awed his boss at the advertising agency into giving him a raise every six months. For McGillicuddy individualism was not only fun; it paid the rent as well.

When McGillicuddy came into the Army he brought his individualism with him. He kept both pairs of GI shoes in his foot locker, he was frequently seen wearing an OD shirt with fatigue pants, and he had even been known to wear a garrison belt to the service club dances. They may have registered, drafted, immunized and even trained McGillicuddy, but they sure didn't mold him.

For the time being McGillicuddy decided to ride with the tide. He had heard a few things about life in the Engineers, so he decided to become a clerk instead. He was willing to make a few small concessions for this. He stuck to his typewriter and learned about fourth endorsements, message forms and that greatest mystery of them all, the decimal filing system. But still nobody was molding him.

McGillicuddy had a girl. Naturally he loved her like frenzy itself; naturally he wrote long and passionate letters to her every evening. But there came a time when things went slightly more mad than usual in headquarters. A change was being made in the organizational set-up, and McGillicuddy was caught for two weeks in a flood of correspondence.

Eventually McGillicuddy found himself with a few moments in which to repair the damage done to his romance by the long silence.

He rolled a sheet of paper into his typewriter and began to write. A few seconds later he stopped, horrified, to read his first lines. "Dear June:" they went. "Attention is invited to the fourth paragraph of your basic communication."

McGillicuddy ripped the sheet from the machine, rolled in a fresh one and began anew. Before his incredulous eyes his fingers did it again. "My Darling: You can't imagine what I've been through so I am forwarding this as a matter pertaining to a former member of your command."

Great beads of sweat appeared on McGillicuddy's brow. He fumbled weakly for another sheet of paper. "Sweetest 201-Torrance, June (Enl) It seems as though I'll never be trfd in gr to atchd unasg because I want so much to be reprting upon arr to CO because TC will fur nec T when S/R allied papers and baggage will accompany EM."

Something seemed to snap inside him. He struggled on blindly to the last paragraph of "basic communication complied with" through "For the Commanding Officer:" Then he signed his name JOHN N. MCGILLICUDDY, PVT., AUS, and arose from his chair. Without a backward glance he put on his blouse, checked every pocket to see that it was buttoned, placed his overseas cap exactly two inches over his right eye, rolled down the cuffs on his trousers and walked quietly from the room.

"GI McGillicuddy" is what the adjutant affectionately calls him nowadays, and he's a wonder to behold. He never wears his sun-tan shirt with the shoulder tabs, he often volunteers for Sunday CQ, he wears his dog tags on a cotton tape around his neck, and he carefully signs every overnight pass on the back as soon as he gets it.

Fort Sheridan, Ill.   —T-5 JIM HARTER

INFILTRATION

The second day, and now the test—
The short space of time when Death
Will hover close and smile on us.
The heavy pack is absent now;
Steel helmet, rifle, cartridge belt are all we ca
Gather in the clearing, listen to the orders,
Take a final smoke, stand beside your budd
"First wave ready, sir." "File into the tren
Lefty on my right, still laughing, still jokin
A momentary pause—now all is ready.
Lead above our heads is the signal to begin
A first short burst and up we climb,
Out of the trench and close to the ground,
Inch by inch and foot by foot we go.
The midmorn sun is hot—damn hot.
Human sweat and Texas dust mix freely.
The guns are firing faster now.
A foot above our heads the bullets whine.
The first barbed wire! "Over on your backs!
Pry it up with rifle, squirm under like a w
Your clothes are caught, but keep your hea
Tear the cloth and keep on going.
The mines are reached. Turn your head a
A mine goes off—a dull, thick sound.
Flying dirt and gravel clatter from your hel
Keep yelling, swearing all the time;
It makes the bullets sound less near.
Talk to Lefty, keep him coming.
More open space, more mines, more barbed w
More dust, more sweat, more oaths.
Dig your nails in the ground and crawl, cr
    crawl—
Panting harder all the time, straining e
    muscle.
We're almost there, but still keep down.
You risk a look and see guns spitting.
Five more yards, and then the trench.
Roll in and lie—panting, almost sobbing.
A sound behind, and Lefty rolls in.
Suck on your lemon peel, wipe your eyes.
Steady your hand to light a fag.
Your chest recedes to normal breathing.
Lie quiet a while and listen to the others rol
Lefty jokes again, and you laugh with him,
"We did it, boy!" "It wasn't so bad."

Camp Hood, Tex.   —Pvt. WILLIAM N

I Don't Hate You

THE CORPORAL lay stomach down on the grass, his hands to his jaws, his elbows propped on the ground. The lamp shining through the narrow casement window of the gardener's cottage formed a slab of light across his back; it might almost have been pressing him into the ground.

At the end of the long upslope of lawn and darkness stood the house, aureoled in its own light. The top layer of the party sound drifted down to him—the thin, anguished chorusing of the brasses in the orchestra, the cries of restless girls. And from the woods around him came the insistent, wistful shrilling of the crickets.

He ran a hand lightly back and forth across the close-cropped lawn, keeping time with the pompous thumping of the drum.

"Furlough furlough furlough," he said absently. "Feel the grass, like the top of somebody's crew cut."

"Tell me something, John." She was sitting sideways on her thighs, one hand stretched down beside her for support, the other nervously plucking blades of grass from the lawn. "You hate me, don't you?"

He kept rubbing his hand over the grass. "Don't be silly," he said.

"No, I'm serious. Why do you?"

"I don't hate you. You're all excited. The war's got you all excited. The war's got everybody all excited. Would you like to go back to the house and dance?"

"No, I wouldn't." She was pulling up the grass faster now and in larger patches. "I just want you to know that I don't give a damn how you feel. I never have and I never shall. I think you're the most conceited, smug person I know."

For a moment he didn't say anything. Then, as if giving in to the pressure of the slab of light on his back, he put his arms out and laid his face and chest close down in the grass.

"Hear the crickets," he said.

Pratt AAF, Kans.   —Pfc. KNOX BURGER

DID I ever tell you. . . .

. . . *what Lefty Gomez said about Joe Page, the Yankees' new rookie left-hander?*

"There's only one thing wrong with Page. He isn't wild enough for a young left-hander. When I was a Yankee rookie everybody wore masks. They took no chances."

. . . *or what Henry Armstrong said when he was asked to name the greatest fighter he ever fought?*

"Let's say it this way: Ross was the best boxer, Garcia the hardest puncher, Ambers the most cagey and Arizmendi the guy who could take it. He had a 17½ neck, and hitting him on the head was like taking a poke at the Rock of Gibraltar. Garcia couldn't think too fast, but he could belt. Arizmendi worried you because your best punch wouldn't even make him blink; you just had to say to yourself, 'My gosh, what's holding the man up?' and then hit him again. I always called Ambers the 'agony fighter.' Zivic was in a class by himself. He tried to win the best way he knew how, and that was with a glib thumb. And he used to say I was a dirty fighter, too. I guess Ray Robinson was the best all-around fighter I ever met. He could do everything that any of the others could do, and better. He came close to being all those other fighters wrapped into one."

. . . *or what Eddie Arcaro said about Whirlaway?*

"The days I rode Whirly in the Derby and Preakness he was the greatest horse I ever saw, but when I rode him later on I was not impressed anywhere as much. He could really pour it on. It was like stepping on the accelerator of a big Cadillac. He was a hard horse to ride, too. One mistake, and he was beaten. Since he always was coming from behind it was no picnic to be aboard him. But you had to ride him with confidence and wait for the right moment to let him go because once he started to climb you just couldn't slow him down. No sir. Whirlaway was no jockey's horse. The type I like is Devil Diver because he handles easily and invariably can work his way out of trouble."

. . . *or what Herb Pennock said about Leo Durocher?*

"Durocher was the best short-fielder I ever looked at. He was a one-man infield, actually, because he could play second, and third, too. But his greatness came in the pinch. With two out and the tying or winning run coming home, he never made a bad throw. You could depend on that ball getting over to first, straight as a die and in time for the out. He played on his nerve; by that I mean he keyed himself up for a game and never let down while it was going on. How much nervous energy he has expended in a career, I don't know, but he had it. Never believe that a great ball player has to be born. Hundreds have been made; hundreds more have made themselves. Take Pepper Martin and Durocher. I will, any time."

. . . *or what Jimmy Wilson said about Bucky Walters?*

"Everybody says I'm responsible for converting Bucky from an infielder to a pitcher, but I didn't do it. Bucky did it all by himself. He's the most observant man I ever saw. He studies every hitter every moment and never forgets a thing. No one ever worked harder to become a great pitcher than Bucky did. He's tireless, smart and a magnificent competitor. He doesn't enjoy games where he wins by lopsided scores. Give him those 1-0 or 2-1 games, and he loves it. Bucky is the closest I've ever seen to Grover Cleveland Alexander. He has a slider like Alex, a good change of pace and great control. He's quite a guy."

. . . *or what Eddie Brannick, the breezy secretary of the Giants, said about Branch Rickey?*

"The guy is overrated, I tell you. A lot of birds have given him plenty of help, but he's the one who's taken all the bows. A fellow named Charlie Barrett is responsible for the scouting system that Rickey took credit for setting up with the Cardinals. He was the one that had the material pouring in all the time. Who took the bows? Rickey, of course. The tip-off on Rickey is that the only place his name appears in the record books is that more runners stole bases on him than any other catcher. That's his sole claim to fame."

. . . *or what Jimmy Foxx said about Johnny Allen?*

"I just couldn't follow the ball when he pitched. I guess its something about his motion. Buck Newsom used to confuse me, but I finally solved him. But Allen always had my number."

. . . *or what Beau Jack said when he got his draft notice?*

"I'm glad I'm being abducted."

SPORTS: HELP YOURSELF TO A QUOT AS THE GREAT MINDS SPEA
By Sgt. DAN POLIER

Henry Armstrong: ". . . I always called Ambers the 'agony fighter'."

Sports Service Record

IT was bound to happen. **Pvt. Al Blozis**, the shot-put champion, has just set a new Army record for the hand grenade at Fort Bragg, N. C., with a 65-yard heave. A good throw for the average GI is about 50 yards. . . . **S/Sgt. Joe DiMaggio** made his debut at Honolulu Stadium by driving one of his massive clouts far over the leftfield fence for a 453-foot home run. . . . **Col. Bob Neyland**, Tennessee's football coach, is overseas with the Engineers. . . . **Barney Mussill**, the Phillies' rookie pitcher, is one of the few soldiers who have been gassed in this war. He picked up a defective mustard-gas container by mistake at Fort Warren, Wyo., and spent three months in the hospital, almost totally blind. Today he wears thick glasses and can read only one hour out of every 24. . . . **Ens. Greg Rice** is coaching the Merchant Marine Cadet track team at Kings Point, N. Y., and **Glenn Cunningham AS**, is running on the mile relay quartet at Great Lakes. . . . **Lt. Col. Hugh Gallarneau**, former star Stanford and Chicago Bear back, has turned school teacher and is teaching, of all things, public speaking to Marines in the Pacific. . . . **Lt. Booty Payne**, Clemson College's kicking ace, who was missing on a flight over Europe, is now a PW in Germany along with nine members of his crew. . . . What's become of **Bob Pastor**, who went to OCS at Miami Beach last winter?

Commissioned: **Johnny Pesky**, rookie Red Sox shortstop, as an ensign in the Navy. . . . *Ordered for induction:* **Ed Heusser**, Cincinnati right-hander (3 and 3 this season), by the Navy; outfielder **Charlie Metro** and catcher **Al Unser** of Detroit, by the Army. . . . *Rejected:* **Nick Strincevich**, Pittsburgh pitcher, because of gastric ulcers; **Jake Mooty**, right-hander of the Tigers, because of a bone condition resulting from an operation on his pitching arm a year ago.

LATEST BATCH of big-league stars to arrive in Hawaii are, standing (l. to r.): Sgt. Walter Judnich, Browns; Cpl. Mike McCormick, Reds, and S/Sgt. Joe DiMaggio, Yankees. Kneeling: Sgt. Dario Lodigiani, White Sox, and Pfc. Gerald Priddy, Senators.

"SO THAT'S FRANCE, HUH? WELL, I DON'T LIKE IT."
—Pvt. Thomas Flannery

"GOOD MORNING, MADAM. IS THE MAN OF THE HOUSE IN?"
—Sgt. Irwin Caplan

YANKS everywhere . . .

In all parts of the world, Yanks are on the march—not only soldiers, but the soldier's weekly. No matter where you go, you can get YANK by mail. Fill out this coupon NOW.

SEND YANK BY MAIL TO:

PRINT FULL NAME AND RANK

MILITARY ADDRESS

3-3

PLEASE CHECK—New ☐ Renewal ☐
ONE YEAR (52 ISSUES) ☐ $2.00
6 MONTHS (26 ISSUES) ☐ $1.00
Enclose check or money order and mail to:
YANK, The Army Weekly, 205 E. 42d St., New York 17, N. Y.
SUBSCRIPTIONS ARE ACCEPTED ONLY FOR MEMBERS OF THE ARMED FORCES
OR DISCHARGED VETERANS OF THIS WAR

YANK
THE ARMY WEEKLY

"NOW, BEFORE WE GO ANY FURTHER, IS THERE ANYONE WHO DOESN'T UNDERSTAND WHAT WE'RE DOING?"
—Pfc. Joseph Kramer

"MULLIGAN NEVER MISSES A FORMATION."
—Sgt. Charles Pearson

YANK
THE ARMY WEEKLY

5¢ OCT. 6
VOL. 3, NO. 16
1944
By the men . . . for the
men in the service

SOUVENIRS FROM BURMA

YANK Artist's Front-Line Sketches From Guam

PAGES 2-3-4

Getting ready for the Guam show A Liberty ship is loaded with supplies for the assault on the island.

...ennant flying from radio mast, an amphibious tank moves into position. Men look out from open hatches.

Sketches of the Guam Campaign

Marines, relieved from one sector of the front, move on to another combat zone through the town of Agat.

SGT. ROBERT GREENHALGH of YANK made this set of drawings after covering a Marine brigade's operations from its landing on D Day to the capture of Guam air-strip. "Slogging around in the rain and mud," he wrote, "I got my notes soaking wet and now they are almost obliterated. Then the trans-port with my art equipment pulled out. But I found some materials on a flagship, so I was in business again."

A Pack Howitzer Message Center is housed in a Guam mansion. The runner has just arrived from the front.

Wounded ride back from the front on a tank.

Sketches of the Guam Campaign

Marine with automatic in shoulder holster.

Four Marine riflemen search out a Japanese sniper's

Weary Marines rest in the rain and mud of Agat town on the fourth day. The men flop anywhere in the ruins as their lieutenant talks to the MP at the far left

‌ATRIOTS' FUNERAL

By Sgt. HARRY SIONS
YANK Staff Correspondent

‌OUTHERN FRANCE — Paul Dumont and Leon ‌Frallon were young men of Tourves, a small ‌town in the heart of Provence. Dumont was ‌ auxite miner, Frallon a photographer for a ‌ rseilles newspaper. When the Germans over- ‌ France, Dumont and Frallon took to the hills, ‌ thousands of other patriots, to fight the en- ‌ and wait for the Allies to come to their aid. ‌ on after the landings in southern France, a ‌ ment of the 3d Division fought its way close ‌Tourves. Dumont and Frallon volunteered as ‌ es. pointing out German supply dumps, gun ‌ lacements and minefields. The regiment lib- ‌ ed Tourves and swept inland. Dumont and ‌ llon returned to the hills to hunt enemy ‌ ers and stragglers. Townspeople found them ‌ d—shot through the head by the Germans. ‌ wo days later the people of Tourves gathered ‌ pay their final respects to the slain patriots.

1. Funeral services are held at the Town Hall at 10 A. M.

2. Colonials and FFI men guard the caskets.

ruck carrying caskets is escorted to cemetery by cortege of townspeople and patriots.

4. Townsman blows taps as uniformed honor guard stands at attention

 er fighters of the French Forces of the In- ‌ or and colonial troops from Madagascar ‌ med an honor guard for the caskets. Throng: ‌ citizens filled the town square. Among them ‌ d Paul Dumont's kid brother, weeping but ‌ ud, and Leon Frallon's fiancee, her face so set ‌ seemed beyond grief, her hand clutching an ‌ carbine. In the distance boomed the heavy ‌ s shelling Toulon.

 s the Town Hall clock struck 10, friends of ‌ dead placed flowers on the tricolor-draped ‌ kets and the town priest (also the FFI chap- ‌) sprinkled holy water and said a prayer. ‌ small truck, followed by a cortege of the ‌ nspeople, carried the caskets to the church, ‌ ere the priest read the funeral mass.

 rom the church the procession made its way ‌ ough vineyards up a hill to the cemetery. ‌ e, close by a monument to the World War ‌ d of Tourves, the caskets were laid to rest. ‌ e newly elected mayor, leader of the local ‌ istance movement, delivered a funeral oration, ‌ ding: "Adieu, comrades. We will never forget ‌ and the cause for which you died."

 hen the FFI men of Tourves went back into ‌ hills to track down the last of the Germans.

JK, The Army Weekly, publication issued weekly by Branch Of- ‌ Information & Education Division, War Department, 205 East 42d ‌ et, New York 17, N. Y. Reproduction rights restricted as indicated ‌ e masthead on the editorial page. Entered as second class mat- ‌ July 6, 1942, at the Post Office at New York, N. Y., under the Act ‌ March 3, 1879. Subscription price $3 yearly. Printed in the U. S. A.

5. Dead man's fiancee pays last respects.

6. Villagers leaving cemetery console the berea

Yanks at Home Abroad

Building a Russian Base

AN EASTERN COMMAND BASE, RUSSIA—The crew of a Fortress, coming in for a landing here after bombing a German target on a shuttle raid, may not see any Russian women or Cossack cavalrymen down below. But the lusty efforts of the women and Cossacks, combined with the work of the advance party of American GIs, made possible the swift completion of the preliminary skeleton airfields.

One chilly morning an Air Forces sergeant, waiting for a labor detail promised by Russian headquarters to help him plant telephone poles for the new airfield, heard the chant of feminine voices. Looking up, he saw a formation of women, dressed in the Red Army uniform modified by a skirt, make a column right around a brick building. The formation halted near the sergeant and the marching song ceased with the final step.

A woman officer approached the sergeant and said in English: "These are the soldiers who will put up the telephone poles."

A little ill at ease, the sergeant looked over his detail, and his detail looked him over. The women, he noted, carried rifles slung over one shoulder and shovels over the other. Getting hold of himself, the sergeant explained to the woman officer how he wanted the job done. It was done exactly that way.

After that, the women soldiers set up the row of pyramidal tents that were to house the American personnel after their arrival in Russia. They flattened the roads and filled craters so that trucks could bring supplies to the fields. They helped lay the steel matting for the runways. They did, the GIs agreed, everything that men could have done.

It wasn't until later that the Cossacks came into the picture. One night Russian headquarters needed some emergency labor to unload a trainful of American heavy equipment, scheduled to arrive at a railroad station at any minute. The handful of GIs waiting at the platform heard the neigh of a horse in the distance, and then the sound of other horses coming down the road.

It was a detachment of mustachioed Cossacks. Bound back to the rear after front-line service, the cavalrymen had been rerouted to handle the freight. They dismounted, herded their horses together and stacked their arms.

Right about then the train came in, and soon freight was sliding out of dark cars and into Studebaker trucks that rumbled off into the night. By morning the dust had swirled on the road under the hooves of the departing cavalry.

—Pfc. THEODORE METAXAS
YANK Field Correspondent

Rod and Gun in Peru

PERU—GIs at an air base here wish their training had included close combat techniques for use against an opponent who knows more tricks of retreating than Rommel—the deep-sea tuna.

On a free Sunday, these GIs can hire a native fishing boat for less than it takes to buy eight beers at the PX. Some come back with a mess of tuna big enough for an Army truck to carry. Others return with hands cut to the bone, having learned the hard way that they should have asked a native to teach them the ropes.

An inexperienced fisherman is surprised to find the tuna letting itself be pulled in like a dead sheep. But surprise is a mild word for what he feels when the tuna gets close to the boat and then takes off like an express train. Some GIs hang onto the line for dear life and the line scrapes the skin from their hands like a potato peeler. Natives wear down the fish by letting the line out, hand over hand, and a smart soldier who doesn't know the tricks hands the line to a native when the emergency comes.

For soldiers with a yen to be Daniel Boones, there are deer in the mountains 50 miles away. Even when you don't bring home the venison, the hunting is a welcome break from routine. In this part of Peru, the season for deer hunting is never closed.

To get native guides for a Sunday trip, you have to send a "telegram" into the mountains by burro a week or 10 days beforehand.

Sgt. J. C. Gaw of Woodbury, N. J., says: "We usually leave on Saturday afternoon in a borrowed car stocked with supplies for camping out. We travel across miles of hard-packed desert sand and meet the guides, each with a horse or burro, at the foothills. When I went out the last time, we camped in a bowl-like canyon. We ma[de] a fire and had broiled steaks and fried spu[ds]. Then we turned in for the night, under blanke[ts] and mosquito netting."

The mountains are criss-crossed with gar[...] trails. Deer tracks often lead mile after m[ile] down canyon floors, over ridges and up o[ne] mountain side after another. It is much easi[er] to find the trails than it is to find the deer. No[w] and then a GI with a good guide and some e[x-] perience in stalking brings down a buck.

—Sgt. JOHN HA[Y]
YANK Staff Correspondent

The Army's Hide

AN ALEUTIAN BASE—Beefing against the [...] way of life has become such a habit with o[ne] soldier here that he gives the impression of bei[ng] *with* but not *in* the Army. He never misses [a] chance to show his distaste for the whole set-u[p.]

One rainy day this gruff character was u[...] chesting his latest gripes to a jeep driver wh[ile] riding to work. There was a leak in the jee[p] top and rain was trickling through onto the pa[s-] senger's feet.

At the end of the trip the driver got out, b[ut] the other GI sat there, with a disgusted look [on] his face. Pointing at his rain-soaked Army br[o-] gans, he grumbled:

"Look—it's dripping all over *their* shoes."

—Cpl. JOHN HAVERSTIC[K]
YANK Staff Correspond[ent]

This Week's Cover

AT an air base in India, Sgt. Earl Rivard pokes his head out of a bamboo hut and displays souvenirs he picked up behind enemy lines in Burma. He wears a Jap field cap, holds a small antipersonnel bomb in his right hand, a pilot's "honor" dagger in his left. At his elbow is a piece of a Zero.

PHOTO CREDITS. Cover—Sgt. Lou Stoumen. 5—Sgt. George Aarons. 6—Left, Sgt. Aarons; right, Sgt. Stoumen. 8—INP. 9— Upper U. S. Army; lower, Signal Corps. 10—Sgt. Aarons. 11—Acme. 12—Upper, Cpl. Joe Cunningham; lower left, Acme; lower right, Signal Corps. 13—Upper left, Sgt. Eugene Ford; upper right, Acme; center & lower left and lower right, Signal Corps; center right, Cpl. Cunningham. 14—Acme. 18—Signal Corps. 19—Upper right, U. S. Navy; center right, Signal Corps; lower left, Stuttgart AAF, Ark.; lower right, Stockton Field, Calif. 20—RKO Radio. 23—Upper, PA; lower, INP.

LST FLAT-TOP. This Coast Guard-manned LST has been converted into a car-rier. From its deck operate Piper Cubs, baby Army artillery observation planes.

DOUBLE CHARM. Ann Sheridan (right) and Mary Landa meet Maj. G[en.] Chennault of the Fourteenth Air Force during a recent tour of the CBI.

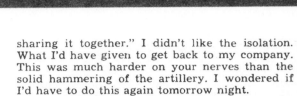

Study in Sound

Relentless barrages of artillery are hard to take but long hours of silence in a forward position are even tougher on the nerves.

By Pvt. JUSTIN GRAY

ITALY—It was a hot day in mid-September. We had expected that Italy would be cooler at that time of year. We had been fighting for 5 days—defensively, merely holding on to a thin peninsula of land that jutted into German territory, holding until the army to the south could reach us. We held the high ground, a mountain ridge. Behind us we could see the invasion armada supplying the main army at Salerno. There were thousands of ships, thousands of men. Ahead of us great naval guns shelled Naples and airplanes bombed the valley below us. But we were isolated: two Ranger battalions facing what seemed to be the entire German Army.

At first the Jerries had attempted to beat us back. Failing this, they subjected us to an almost continuous mortar and artillery barrage. We were vulnerable. They knew exactly where we were. We had to dig in and take it, and we couldn't fight back. Directly below us we could see a constant stream of German trucks on the way to Salerno to meet the main invasion thrust. At first we tried to harass these convoys, but now we no longer dared to go down into the valley. We didn't have the strength. All we could do was cling to the ridge. Our light mortars couldn't reach the German positions.

A few of us had dug a cave. We tried to play cards, but after days of sitting under artillery we were all too tense. When would they send us help? It was long overdue. They told us we'd be in Naples in three days. It didn't look as though we'd ever get there. We were all nervous. Someone remarked: "Gee, I wouldn't mind getting a little wound. Get the hell out of this blasted artillery. If it keeps up much longer I'll be a Section 8 for sure."

We all remembered that young kid Cato a few days before. He burst out crying when he saw an infiltrating German come at him. He yelled: "What'll I do? What'll I do?" Then he was dead. That artillery did things to you. We weren't scared so much, just tired—tired of hugging the ground, of not being able to fight back. We'd been told not to duck when we heard the screaming of the shells; it would be too late. But we ducked anyway. Even the almost silent pop of the mortars was frightening. The sharper sounds of the artillery were always bad. We got to know exactly where a shell would land and played games, calling the shots.

It all seemed so futile. I'd have given anything to get out of it, to do something different, get another job, get moving. A combat patrol, maybe. Anything. Anything at all. Lucky the Germans didn't know how close to cracking we were. I wondered if I could stand another sleepless night. It would be the fourteenth. I knew I couldn't last much longer.

That evening one of us got a break. We were called down to the CP and told we were to guard a mine field that night, about a mile and a half in front of the lines. We were anxious to go. Lt. Davey briefed us. At dusk we were to lay a series of mines completely covering the road leading to the pass. The position had already been picked. We were to cover the mine field with a light machine gun. Our mission was to fire as long as possible at any units that might attempt to infiltrate through the mines. Our firing would alert the Rangers.

The situation was not too clear. To cover the field effectively we had to set up the machine gun in an exposed position. To our left was a steep cliff some 80 feet high. Directly to our right the terrain broke sharply into a 50-foot drop. If we were attacked, we would have no place to go for cover. Even so, it seemed better than sitting on the mountain under artillery.

We collected the necessary equipment and just before dusk we started out warily. We were burdened with a machine gun, ammunition, rifles, mines, grenades and a few blankets we were able to scrounge. That was another break: we'd have blankets on this job. The nights were cold even if the days were hot. We carried no food. Ammunition was of greater importance. Along the way we laid the wire for our field telephone.

In an hour we had arrived, and everything was set up. The mines were laid and the machine gun was in position. The four of us decided to team up in pairs. There were still 12 hours before dawn. That meant six hours a team.

Rona and I took the first six hours. It would be a long vigil, but at least the artillery was going over our heads. We could see the shells landing in the positions we had just left. Rona swore softly: "Those poor bastards up there." He and I sat down back to back, next to the machine gun. The other two rolled up in blankets and went to sleep immediately. I had to smile. They had complete confidence in us.

I had done this many times before. It didn't seem like a very difficult job. It demanded a lot of self-control. Sitting back to back for six hours. Not saying a word. Not smoking. Not even chewing gum. Just searching with your eyes and ears for any movement that might give away the enemy. It was dark now. And way off in the valley I could hear the almost constant hum of German motor transports rushing supplies under cover of night. The sound was irritating.

Then the moon came out suddenly, breaking over the mountain. It made us feel so exposed. I began to worry just a little bit. A child could have dropped a hand grenade on top of us from the cliff to our left. We certainly had chosen a stupid position. Jerry couldn't help but see us.

We were supposed to report back to the colonel's CP every hour. We couldn't talk on the phone. We just tapped on the mouthpiece, and they knew we were all right. That bastard on the phone back in the CP thought we needed a little morale and insisted on spitting out an endless stream of dirty stories. It was disconcerting. We couldn't listen to dirty stories and to the rustle of leaves at the same time. At last we shut him up.

My imagination started to work. Trees began to take human shapes. Scraping leaves on the ground sounded like footsteps. Two birds making love in a tree below us sounded just like an Army. I wanted to throw a grenade, but that was out of the question. We had to be silent at all costs. I began thinking of the time I was out West on a ranch, when I used to guard the camp against bears. I began wondering if the Germans had gotten in behind our position, between us and the main lines. If they had they'd surely find our telephone wire and trace it down to us. What if the Germans counterattacked and pushed the Rangers back to the sea? We would be trapped. We could never get out. I thought of a million things that could happen to us.

My rear end started to go to sleep. I just had to move. But Rona was as silent as ever, so I didn't dare. I could tell whenever he got tense. His back would stiffen up against mine, and I'd hold my breath so as not to interfere with his hearing. I didn't even dare swallow my spit; the sound would have seemed deafening. "Jesus," I said to myself, "I thought it was tense under the artillery fire. At least there we were all sharing it together." I didn't like the isolation. What I'd have given to get back to my company. This was much harder on your nerves than the solid hammering of the artillery. I wondered if I'd have to do this again tomorrow night.

We could hear spasmodic firing back at the lines. I wished I could fire a couple of rounds with the machine gun. The noise would have been satisfying. It was too quiet. I'd be glad when dawn got here.

Our six hours were over. We woke up Stancil and Nichols. They took our place, and I tried to go to sleep. But it was no go. I was too tense. No sounds. No artillery. I couldn't sleep. I just had to sweat out the dawn.

By 0700 we were back at our lines. I began to feel nauseated and seemed to have a temperature. Suddenly I felt very weak and began to vomit, sweating. I could hardly move my legs and arms. I reported to the doc. He gave me a dose of medicine. Then they packed me into a jeep and drove me down to Maori on the water front.

The Rangers had taken over the largest Catholic church in town as their aid station. It was hot. The ward was stuffy. But sick as I was, it looked like something out of a Hollywood movie about the first World War. They carried me to a cot in front of the altar. The altar itself was covered with bandages and medicine. There was one American nurse, a beautiful girl. She was being helped by a number of Italian nuns. I looked around. One soldier was crying in the corner. A nun tried to comfort him. Another was getting blood plasma. The nurse washed my face with alcohol. It cooled me off a bit.

I suddenly realized that it wasn't as quiet as I had thought. The naval guns had opened up. The shells sounded like freight trains right overhead. The whole building shook. But I felt safe. Up on the mountain we had been so far from everything. This clearing station seemed to be a link with home, with the rest of the world. The noise was deafening but comforting. They were our guns, our shells. I fell asleep.

Justin Gray's story is a report on one of his combat experiences. He fought with the 3d Ranger Battalion in Sicily and Italy.

STILWELL: The GIs' Favorite

Our newest four-star general is a tough, plain-speaking soldier who won't allow "Officers Only" signs on cafes in his theater.

By Sgt. ED CUNNINGHAM
YANK Staff Writer

GEN. JOSEPH W. STILWELL, the U. S. Army's newest four-star general, is as regular and down-to-earth as the scuffed GI shoes he wears when tramping through the Burma jungles.

Known among his men as Vinegar Joe or Uncle Joe, he is no glamor-boy general. He's a tough, frank Old Army man who hates Japs with unwavering intensity. One day during the Hukawng Valley campaign a frightened Jap prisoner tried to shake hands with him. Scorning the outstretched hand, Gen. Stilwell snapped: "Not with you, you dirty bastard!"

In the field, where he prefers to be, Stilwell is no collar-ad for what the well-dressed West Point man will wear this season. His usual uniform is a mud-stained field jacket with no rank insignia, ordinary GI pants and leggings, topped off with either a battered felt Infantry campaign hat or a Chinese Army cap.

What goes for Gen. Stilwell goes for his men. They wear clothes best adapted for jungle fighting, without fear of being eaten out by some very GI superior. Uncle Joe justified such departures from military custom with a typical Stilwell explanation: "We're out to win battles, not dress parades."

More than once Gen. Stilwell has been hailed as "Hey, Mac!" by a private who failed to recognize him without his stars. The general recalls with relish the time he was returning from Brig. Gen. Frank D. Merrill's bivouac four miles off the Ledo Road. A pack-mule company of Merrill's Marauders, moving up, forced Gen. Stilwell's jeep to the side of the narrow jungle trail. The general, inelegantly garbed in a Chinese cap without insignia and with a carbine between his knees, was spotted by a GI who turned around and shouted back to his companions: "Hey, look! Duck hunters!"

Another Marauder approached Stilwell's jeep, rested his carbine on the fender and asked: "How far is it to the bivouac area?"

"About four miles," Stilwell replied.

"Holy hell!" the GI hollered. "Couldn't they build the damn thing a little closer to the road? What's the use of having a road if we can't use it?"

Stilwell smiled and, turning to his aide, observed with obvious pride: "These guys are really tough."

DESPITE his 61 years, Gen. Stilwell is the walkingest general in the U. S. Army. Since last Christmas, when he arrived in Burma to direct the Chinese troops there, he has made almost daily trips to forward positions. Most of those trips are on foot because the narrow jungle trails stymie even jeeps. Uncle Joe sets the pace on all hikes. He keeps to a steady 105-steps-a-minute stride with a 10-minute break each hour.

On many of his trips to the front, Gen. Stilwell spends the night with U. S. liaison troops who work with the Chinese. He stretches his jungle hammock between two trees and sleeps there with his clothes on, just as his soldiers must do to ward off the clammy moisture of the Burma night. He often joins in the bull sessions of the corporals and privates as they brew a nightcap of GI coffee over a bamboo-kindled fire. If his men have any complaints, they lay them directly before Uncle Joe.

One night up front, a corporal with blunt GI vigor assailed censorship of mail. "Why is it, general," he asked, "that we can't mention we're in Burma when we write letters home? Guys can say they're in India or China but we can't say we're in Burma."

"We'll see what we can do about it," the general promised.

The next day he radioed the chief censor's office in New Delhi inquiring why letters could not be marked "somewhere in Burma." When no plausible objection was offered, Stilwell ordered that the Burma dateline could be used from then on. However, one mail censor—a scissors-happy second louey—arbitrarily decided that "Burma" must still not be used in letters. The GIs kicked again. Stilwell sent another radio to New Delhi. Two days later the shavetail was relieved of his censoring duties.

Another time Stilwell visited a U. S. base in India where one of the men complained about the ban on pets at the post.

"Let them have pets if they want 'em," ruled Uncle Joe.

Now some U. S. bases in the CBI have virtual menageries of bear cubs, wildcats, dogs, jackals, monkeys, parrots, mongooses and snakes.

Although he is a strict disciplinarian when occasion demands, Stilwell is no stickler for the more rigid military courtesies. At a staff conference shortly after Pearl Harbor, all his officers jumped to attention when he walked in the room.

"Sit down, for God's sake!" he snapped. "We're fighting a war now and we'll dispense with all this jumping-up-and-down business."

Gen. Stilwell side-steps formalities even when presenting decorations. Entering a hospital to award the Silver Star to a wounded American soldier, the general found the GI in bed naked except for bandages and a sheet that covered him to the hips.

Gen. Stilwell introduced himself to the surprised soldier, smiled and said:

"I'm going to have to embarrass you a little."

Then, after his aide had read the citation, the general pulled the sheet over the soldier's chest and pinned the Silver Star on the sheet.

Uncle Joe takes a dim view of decorations for staff men, or even for himself. Returning to headquarters one day after a long trip in the field, he was informed that he had been awarded the DSC.

"Who thought up all this?" he groused. "I'm not so sure about this business of decorating staff men when there are so many men in the front line fighting. I was a lieutenant once and I used to wonder why desk men got so much glory."

STILWELL's understanding treatment of his enlisted men is responsible for his most popular nickname, Uncle Joe. Thanks to his rulings, a GI is not a social outcast in the CBI and "officers only" restrictions are at a minimum. Any enlisted man may visit the best restaurants, night clubs and theaters.

Another popular Stilwell ruling was the one he handed down soon after the first American Wacs arrived in the CBI. The enlisted Wacs were scarcely off their plane when lieutenants, captains and even some of the higher brass were pressing them for dates. The GIs, some of whom had spent two years in the CBI without meeting an American girl whom they could date, figured they were outranked on this deal.

Then came an order from Gen. Stilwell's headquarters forbidding officers to date enlisted Wacs and enlisted men to date WAC officers. The second part of the order was the sheerest of formalities. GIs weren't getting to first base with

THIS STUDY, TYPICAL OF UNCLE JOE, WAS TAKEN DURING ONE OF HIS MANY VISITS TO THE FRONT.

he WAC officers, anyway. Gen. Stilwell's ruling imply rendered unto Caesar the things that ere Caesar's, to GIs the things that were GI.

EAN and wiry, without an ounce of excess weight, Gen. Stilwell has the energy and endurance of a man half his age. His perfect conditioning dates back to West Point, where he as a track star and a 140-pound quarterback on the Army eleven when vest-pocket gridmen were ll but unknown. He wears glasses, smokes cigarettes in a long holder, chews gum frequently nd has his iron-gray hair cropped in GI style.

Uncle Joe can usually be found where the ring is heaviest. He scorns the comfortable rear-chelon headquarters in New Delhi, preferring o stay up with his men. His combat headquarters is usually within artillery range of the nemy's lines.

Recently a Jap artillery shell landed less than 0 yards from Gen. Stilwell during a heavy helling of the position he was visiting. Only the oft, muddy jungle earth, which buried the shell efore it burst, saved the general and his aide rom injury.

Gen. Stilwell was born on Mar. 19, 1883, at alatka, Fla., where his parents were vacationing rom the family home in Yonkers, N. Y. After raduating from Yonkers High School, where he layed football and basketball, he entered West oint in 1900. He graduated with top honors in anguages—he now speaks six fluently, including apanese—and was commissioned June 15, 1904. n the first World War, Gen. Stilwell, then a aptain, served as a liaison officer with the rench and British.

Fortunately for American-Chinese relations, en. Stilwell understands the Chinese soldier as ompletely as he understands the American GIs. n 1920 he went to China as one of the first two J. S. Army officers ever assigned to that country. Ie studied at the North China Language School n Peiping for three years, making frequent trips nto the interior to learn the varied dialects and ustoms of the Chinese people. One summer he vorked as an ordinary day laborer with a coolie ang building roads in Shansi Province.

After six years back in the States, Gen. Stil-

well returned to China in 1929 as executive officer to Gen. George C. Marshall, who was then commanding the 15th Infantry at Tientsin. Later, in 1935, he was appointed U. S. military attache at Peiping.

Despite the administrative nature of his work, Gen. Stilwell was no armchair officer even then. He seldom missed a major military operation in China. Occasionally he was on the Japanese side of the battlefront but he spent most of his time with his old love, the Chinese fighting man. He marched with Chinese troops. He ate Chinese chow with chopsticks. He carried his own bedroll and slept in Chinese bivouacs. He talked with Chinese soldiers in their own language. Gradually he even reached the point where he could think in Chinese.

Gen. Stilwell confers with Gen. Liao Yao-hsiang.

Returning to the States for retirement in 1939, Gen. Stilwell was kept on the active list and ordered to take command of a 2d Division brigade when war threatened. He went to Fort Ord, Calif., in July 1940 as CG of the newly activated 7th Division, which later invaded Attu and the Marshall Islands. The 7th was 85 percent selectees but it ran rings around its "enemies" in the 1941 California maneuvers under Gen. Stilwell's expert leadership.

On one occasion during the maneuvers, the general was absent from his headquarters for two days. His adjutant finally found him sleeping on the floor of a high-school cloakroom in the maneuver area. It was the first sleep he had had in 48 hours.

THE 7th Division's showing in the maneuvers resulted in Gen. Stilwell's appointment as CG of the III Army Corps, a post he held until February 1942, when Generalissimo Chiang Kai-shek asked for a U. S. general to direct American military activities in China. Gen. Stilwell, the U. S. Army's foremost authority on China, was the logical selection. He and his staff arrived at Chungking in late February. Two weeks later he was on the Burma battlefront directing the Chinese forces in his dual capacity as chief of staff to Chiang Kai-shek and CG of Chinese troops in Burma.

Gen. Stilwell took a licking in Burma but he candidly admitted it. Grimly confident, even in 1942's dark days, he said he would go back to retake the ground he had lost. He's making good on that promise now, having recaptured Northern Burma in the only really successful Allied offensive yet staged in the Far East.

Uncle Joe's one ambition is to win the war and get the hell home as quickly as possible. He has no personal post-war political or business aspirations. When peace comes, he plans to retire from the Army and settle down with his family in Carmel, Calif. There on the beach he will be able to don his old corduroy trousers and spend his days slogging through the sands with his favorite dog, a soft-eyed giant Schnauzer named Gareth. The little things in life are what Uncle Joe enjoys most.

UNmilitary Training

Army plans to build up study, recreation and sports and cut down drill in daily routine of GIs stuck in inactive theaters after the defeat of Germany.

By Pfc. IRA H. FREEMAN
YANK Staff Writer

WASHINGTON, D. C.—The Army is planning a big education, recreation and athletic program that will replace most of the military training in the daily routine of GIs who get stuck in the ETO, the Mediterranean and the Middle East after the defeat of Germany.

The powers that be in the War Department feel that there is no sense devoting the whole working day of occupation troops and surplus units awaiting shipment back to the States to close-order drill, gas-mask drill and cleaning of equipment. So they have decided to let GIs spend most of their time in classrooms, in sports competition or participating in musical, dramatic or art activities.

The whole program of education, recreation and athletics will be voluntary. You will be able to take your choice of courses and activities. But each GI will have to take up something in one of the three sections. Or it will be possible to take a major activity from one section and a minor activity from another; for example, you could go to school for three hours a day and then spend two hours every afternoon playing baseball.

The program will not, of course, apply to troops who are scheduled to move on to combat zones in the CBI and the Pacific. They will continue to spend all their time on military training. When the Japanese are finally defeated, this same switch from military to nonmilitary activities in training schedules will probably go into effect in all overseas theaters.

Here are some of the details of the program:

Education

THE Army has fixed its sights on providing at least a fifth-grade elementary-school education for fellows who never had a chance to go to school when they were kids. Vocational training will be available to guys who wish to learn a trade, while the Army will send qualified men to some of the great, world-famous universities in Europe, like Oxford in England and the Sorbonne in Paris. It is possible that soldiers who left school for the service may get credit for study courses taken in the Army when they return to civilian school after demobilization.

Going to one of these temporary Army schools will not affect your chance of getting home. If your shipping orders come through while you are in the midst of a course, you just drop everything and hit the gangplank.

The brass will not attempt to force any GI to go to school. They say that you won't be put on working details, either, if you refuse to study. You will, however, have to choose something from the athletic or recreational list.

The backbone of the Army education program will be the vocational and practical courses given in battalion schools. These schools will offer two-month courses in the following subjects:

Advertising	Carpentry
American Economic	Farm Management
Problems	Foreign Languages
American Government	General Agriculture
Automobile Mechanics	Mechanical Drawing
Beginning Electricity	Personnel Management
Beginning Radio	Psychology
Blueprint Reading	Review Arithmetic
Bookkeeping	Salesmanship
Business Arithmetic	Science
Business English	Shop Mathematics
Business Law	Supervision and
Business Principles and	Foremanship
Management	

There will also be general classes in American history and traditions, as well as guidance courses to help younger soldiers pick a career. In the manual trades, such as carpentry, instruction will include actual on-the-job practice under supervision. Teachers in all these fields will be chosen from experts who happen now to be in the Army, both officers and enlisted men.

Centralized technical schools will be set up in connection with existing civilian schools to teach 150 technical courses, most of them fairly advanced, such as machine-shop practice, radio servicing and repair, refrigeration maintenance, welding and so on.

GIs who have had a high-school education, or its equivalent in technical schools or experience, may take university courses similar to those offered in American colleges. Some of these courses will be given in local civilian institutions in the occupied countries, while others will be available in special Army centers staffed by qualified military instructors. It is expected that American colleges will give students credit for work passed in these foreign universities and Army university centers.

The university courses will include not only general academic subjects, but also professional, preprofessional and graduate study. For example, a lawyer who is a corporal stationed in England, let us say, might get an opportunity of a lifetime: a chance to take a two-month course in international law under a famous professor at Cambridge University.

Recreation

THIS second part of the program of activities for soldiers in inactive overseas areas is subdivided into music, soldier shows and entertainment, and arts and crafts. It is also expected that library facilities will be expanded with the sudden increase in the men's free time, so that each post will have a big book collection like that at camps in the States, with a professional civilian librarian in charge.

As in all the other phases of the program, teachers of music, dramatics and art will be soldiers who used to do such things in civilian life.

In music there will be classes to teach beginners how to play popular instruments, as well as courses in harmony, orchestration and music appreciation. GIs who are already musicians will be able to teach, or take advanced study, or play in bands, small groups or orchestras. Men who merely like to listen to music may get a chance to go to the famous opera houses and concert halls in Europe when those blitzed spots get going again.

Weekly entertainment programs will be put on in each company, with a full-length play or musical comedy produced in the regiment or division at least once, it is hoped, in eight weeks. The better shows will be broadcast and make tours of the theater of operations.

Under arts and crafts, the Army will offer classes in painting and sculpture, photography, wood carving, radio-set making and certain popular handicrafts. Instructors in this section will lead guided tours, from time to time, to the great art museums in Italy, France, Germany, Belgium and the Netherlands.

Sports

PLANS for the Army sports program range from a grand GI Olympic Games with competitors from all theaters of operations down to chess and checker tournaments starting at the platoon level. The equipment is going to cost $20,000,000, which will drain off about 90 percent of all athletic goods made in the U. S. To get this produced, it is possible the sports goods industry will have to be declared essential. Special Services expects 60 percent of GIs in the inactive theaters will take part in the athletic program.

A partial catalogue of sports and games on the program includes:

Acrobatics	Football (regular	Table tennis
Archery	and touch)	Tennis
Badminton	Lacrosse	Track and
Baseball	Soccer	field events
Basketball	Softball	Volleyball
Boxing	Swimming	Wrestling

Special sports, like hunting, fishing, sailing and cycling, are also approved where local conditions and availability of equipment permit. The whole program will be varied, naturally, according to the season and climate.

Competitions, both individual and by teams, will be started at the company level, if feasible, and continue through division, corps, army and finally theater championships. Some international events might be arranged—for example, a tennis tournament among players from the American, British and French forces in Europe.

Coaches and officials for the athletic program will be officers and enlisted men who have had experience that fits them for the jobs. A corps of head coaches is being trained in special courses in the States, and these men will, in turn, instruct other coaches in the inactive theaters.

Sports will include GI Olympic Games similar to this recent inter-Allied track and field meet in Italy.

By Sgt. MACK MORRISS
YANK Staff Correspondent

Pyle Goes Home

PARIS—The medic captain came over to the table smiling and asked: "Aren't you Ernie Pyle?"

"Yes, I am," said Ernie.

"I just want to thank you," said the captain. "You've done some great things for us in your column. I read it whenever I can."

Ernie grinned. "You won't be reading it much longer. I'm going back to the States in a couple of days."

Something like relief passed over the medic's face. "Are you?" he said. "By God, I'm glad. You've seen enough of it. I'm glad you're going."

The conversation went on for a few minutes, the captain standing helmet in hand and the rest of us sitting with dirty clothes and dirty boots at a polished table in a modernistic little bar in the basement of a hotel.

We were drinking champagne cocktails. At this hotel you couldn't get bread. But champagne? *Mais oui, Monsieur.*

"Where are you going when you get back home?" asked the medic.

"To the Pacific, I guess," said Ernie.

"Well, good luck to you, Ernie, and thanks again."

"Thank *you.*" Ernie matched the captain's sincerity, because in this theater there are few men who can stand shoulder to shoulder with the medics when it comes to rating praise. Ernie was a little embarrassed.

But in this theater, too, the legend of Ernie Pyle is a thing of wonder. He is the GIs' war correspondent, the man who loves the soldier of the line. A great deal has been written about Ernie, because he is a phenomenon of this war. He himself, however, sees nothing phenomenal about the work that so far has won him a Pulitzer Prize and the good will of almost everybody in and out of the Army.

"I'm doing the same kind of stuff I've always done in the column," he says, "except that it's on a war basis. Instead of talking to civilians about civilian things, I just swapped over to the military."

Not all that has been written about Ernie has presented him with perfect accuracy. His wife, after reading some of the pieces on Pyle, wrote him: "I am convinced now that nobody can write about you but me." *Time* did an altogether friendly job of profiling him, but Ernie denies the assertion that he has been harboring a "premonition of death," and he would rather people didn't have the impression that he is a gnome-like little character who quivers in his boots, is ashamed of carrying toilet paper in his helmet and was embarrassed by rough-neck soldiery intruding upon him as he "relieved himself," to approximate the *Time* description.

"I've been scared, yes," he says. "Everybody is scared. But I think I've kept myself about as well collected as the next fellow. And I've never been treated with disrespect or in an undignified way in the Army."

Ernie has a great deal of dignity. His uneasiness, which is public property, is the uneasiness of almost any normal person in combat; the difference is that Ernie talks about his anxiety and not everybody else does. Several hundred thousand people, in and out of uniform, share that anxiety with him.

Sitting at that table in Paris, Ernie was a tired man. As every one of his readers knows, he is almost professionally delicate. But as a man, Ernie looks hardly delicate. He has the complexion of a baby, pink and clear, and the contrast with his gray hair, what little there is of it, is striking. He's a wiry little guy who talks with a flat Mid-Western drawl, and he speaks the language of the Army—professionally and with just the amount of four-letter words that a mild man would have occasion to use.

As a working correspondent, Ernie is almost painfully modest. There is just about as much of the Richard Harding Davis or Hollywood war reporter in him as there is in your old grandmother, bless her.

"There are a lot of correspondents who are on the line longer and more often than I am," he assures you. "The way I work is to go up and find a battalion or a company and stay with them a little while and listen to what people tell me, and then come back and write some columns. I usually just take down names and home towns, because a notebook and a fellow with a long pen-

cil scare hell out of a soldier, or anybody else.

"Another reason I don't like notes is that I have to write by mentally carrying myself back to the time and place of the incident I'm writing about. If I had notes I'd just be rewriting them instead of writing about the incident itself, and the column would come out flat.

"Writing comes hard for me until I get started, but once I'm into a column I'm all right. If I write steadily for three or four days, remembering and reliving the things I'm writing about, I'm exhausted. I'm as tired as if I'd been walking three or four days. It takes a lot out of me."

The secret of Ernie's tremendous success and popularity, if there is any secret about it, is his ability to report a war on a personal plane. His capacity for mood and emotion and minor detail has put his columns in a letter-home category. To project this emotion, Ernie has had to feel it himself. The strain of almost constant combat since the African landings is beginning to tell on him. He's had a bellyful.

"I figured if I didn't get out pretty soon I'd be a psycho case or something." Ernie's utterly frank approach to fear and battle pressure has always been characteristic of his writing, and his conversation is just as frank.

"What broke me," he said, "was the bombing that went wrong. I didn't think I could take that. But God knows I don't blame the Air people for it." The bombing that went wrong, which Ernie described in a series of columns, was the one that caught Lt. Gen. Lesley J. McNair and a great many more of our own people. "Those things happen. But that was the worst thing I've ever been through."

In Paris, sweating out a plane for home, Ernie could hardly cover his fatigue.

"I was tired after Italy, and now it's the same thing again," he said. "To tell you the truth, I haven't been on the front here in France as much

as I was in the other places. Damn mortars sound the same here as they did in Italy, and I guess they'll sound the same in the Pacific, I don't know. Frankly, I said three weeks ago that I wasn't going back to the front again, and I meant it. I'm going home now, not because I'm homesick, but because I just about have to."

After almost two years of close association with combat soldiers, about whom he has written with an understanding and sometimes a tenderness that have brought him the admiration of the public and the genuine gratitude of the plain old dogface, Ernie finds himself suffering from one of the most human of all reactions:

"I hate to say it, but I'm sick of the sight of soldiers. I guess in a way I'm a soldier and I'm sort of sick of myself, more'n anything else."

WAR-WEARY or khaki-happy or whatever he is for the moment, Ernie is leaving a hemisphere in which he has produced some real contributions to the American doughfoot. His columns forming the book "Here Is Your War" are being transposed into a movie that will be Hollywood's most ambitious attempt to present the U. S. Infantry in combat. It was in his column, too, that there appeared the first national plea for the Infantry pay raise; but Ernie still doesn't know whether it had anything to do with the bill that was finally passed. "Never did find out for certain about it," he grinned. He also campaigned for something like the present gold service bars for overseas men.

The soldiers who read him in *Stars and Stripes* are his champions. "So you're a war correspondent?" an infantryman will say. "Know Ernie Pyle? There's a guy who knows how it is. He's a good man."

When they talk about Ernie, infantrymen use the same emphasis on the word "good" that Dinah Shore uses in the song about the man she had.

YANKS ROLL PAST A CHURCH STEEPLE, STILL STANDING AMID THE SHATTERED BUILDINGS OF MARIGNY.

Driving Through France

ONE OF FIRST U. S. VEHICLES IN PARIS, AT THE ARC DE TRIOMPHE.

A SHERMAN TANK, KNOCKED OUT BY A GERMAN 88-MM GUN, BURNS BY A ROAD IN SOUTHERN F

NAZI PANTHER STUCK IN A CRATER. THEN AMERICAN ARTILLERY FINISHED IT OFF.

MONT ST. MICHEL, FAMED MEDIEVAL MONUMENT, SUFFERED FEW WAR SCARS.

-STAR GENS. GEORGE S. PATTON (LEFT) AND OMAR L. BRADLEY SHARE A SEAT IN A
GEN. BRADLEY'S TWELFTH ARMY GROUP MADE THE PUSH TO GERMAN BORDER.

TWO U. S. ARMY NURSES, CLOSE BEHIND COMBAT TROOPS, LTS. MARY Mc-
CRACKIN AND RALPHINE MAYNARD, FISH WITH BENT PINS IN A FRENCH STREAM.

A BREAK IN COMBAT AND THESE U. S. ENGINEERS
BLEND HARMONY WITH WINE IN A FRENCH TOWN.

U. S. ENGINEERS, SPLASHED BY GERMAN FIRE, FERRY
A WEAPONS CARRIER ACROSS THE RIVER SEINE.

Merchant Marine

Dear YANK:

In a recent issue of YANK I read the letter by Lt. (jg) Bergen Van Brunt and Harold E. Nelson GM3c, which criticized the Merchant Marine as "civilians who make overly high wages, who cheat on overly high wages, who cheat on overtime" and a score of other stupid charges.

I feel that the letter-writers are guilty of spreading malicious lies about a branch of the service which has undergone many hardships and dangers in order to help defeat our common enemies. I believe I can best answer these charges by quoting the following statement of Lt. (jg) T. A. Potter who knows a great deal about the Merchant Marine:

"This is my third merchant ship . . . in charge of the Navy gun crews. . . . We took part in the invasion of Sicily and saw a good bit of action against Axis planes. Without the fine help of the merchant crew who assisted and augmented our gun crews we never could have maintained the rapid rate of fire necessary to defend the ship. It has been a pleasure to work with these merchant seamen. After watching them perform at Sicily, I can assure you there need be no fear as to the failure of the Allied supply line. They are doing great work."

Need I say more?

Alaska —S/Sgt. A. DIDARIO

Dear YANK:

. . . When I was in the Merchant Marine I was not thinking of money. I was thinking of that brother of mine in a foxhole who needed food and shells. I was thinking of my other brother in the Air Corps who needed gas to take him up in the air. I was thinking of a pal who is in the Navy and who needed oil to run his submarine. . . . My brother in the 29th Division told me to get the hell out of the Merchant Marine before I went down with my ship. He told me to get into the Army, where I would at least have a gun to fight with . . .

Camp Chaffee, Ark. —Pvt. C. J. RICHARDSON

Dear YANK:

. . . When bombs are falling thick and fast a steel deck is a damn hard place on which to dig a foxhole. I know what a part the Merchant Marine plays in this war because they stood by when our transport went down and lent a hand. Out there in a far-away country white markers indicate where some of them are now buried. There are enough of these graves to make a good-sized army. . . .

Percy Jones General Hosp., Mich. —Sgt. W. M. TAEGEL*

*Also signed by Cpls. L. Bazemore and N. B. Carl and Pfc. F. Grizer.

Dear YANK:

. . . I'll salute any man in the U. S. who is doing his part to win this war, whether he is in the Merchant Marine or the Navy. [Lt. Van Brunt said that "It is a pet peeve . . . that GIs salute" the Merchant Marine.] The way I figure it, the only time we enlisted men have to salute an officer is when we are on the beach, and the only time you can think of such minor things as saluting is when you are sitting in a comfortable office. Therefore Lt. Van Brunt must be on the beach. For my money the Merchant Marine is doing a heck of a good job.

FPO, San Francisco, Calif. —PATRICK W. SMITH S1c

Dear YANK:

. . . Our victories would never have been possible without the Merchant Marine. With all respect to the lieutenant's rank I say I am ashamed of his words. I am proud of the Merchant Marine. May God bring them all back home over a peaceful sea some day.

West Coast, Calif. —Pvt. N. F. DOHERTY, USMC

Dear YANK:

We of the Merchant Service have high praise and regard for the Navy and especially the Navy armed guards who cast their lot with the highly vulnerable, poorly armed merchant ships. We ask no glory or praise—only that it be understood that the men who sail the ships do so because it has been their life's work. Just because war converged on them, they did not turn tail and run but accepted their task. Many older men who had retired from the sea returned to do their part and, incidentally, take a thousandfold greater chances and risks than the men on a superbly armed man-of-war.

There are many in the Merchant Marine who have been honorably discharged from the Army, Navy, Marines and Coast Guard who were free to cast off their obligation in this war but who turned to the sea to do their part. Many have said that now, for the first time, they are really doing something quickly and efficiently.

Seattle, Wash. —Ens. K. L. FROST*

*Also signed by Ensigns W. A. Gross (formerly MM1c, USN), C. Corrio (WT2c, USN), C. Alford (EM2c, USN), and D. Cravens (MM2c, USN).

Dear YANK:

. . . Our "haven for those seeking to avoid the armed services" sometimes includes unpleasant details such as trips lasting up to 18 months without liberty except for an occasional evening ashore and trips made in 10-knot ships without convoy and armed with a few popguns manned by boys who would be ashamed to admit that Lt. Van Brunt is in the same Navy with them.

Avalon, Calif. —JAMES G. MORK MM1c, USMS*

*Also signed by John G. Vlahovich SM2c and John E. Thomas StM2c.

Farms for Vets

Dear YANK:

I suggest that the Government put returning soldiers on Government land and furnish them with tools and stock, the soldier to be steward over the property and pay 5 or 10 percent for the use of the

MAIL CALL

land. The rest of the production of the land should be for the use of the soldier and his family. Regardless of the kind of season and what kind of crops were raised, the soldier would pay the Government only 5 or 10 percent of the total income from the land.

France —Pvt. ROY D. CARRICK

Superfortress

Dear YANK:

In several magazines it is stated that the B-29 Superfortress is the largest plane in the world. In YANK itself it is called the heaviest aircraft in the world. These statements are far from true. The biggest airplane in existence is the B-19, which has a wing span of 200 feet. Another plane, the B-15, is about the size of the B-29. In large numbers, however, the Germans have a much bigger plane than the B-29. It is the ME-323, which has a wing span of 171 feet and a much greater carrying capacity than the B-29.

Alaska —Pvt. WAYNE WILSON

■ YANK was referring only to combat planes, not experimental models, transports, etc. The information presently available about the B-29's size is that it is 99 feet long and has a wing span of 141 feet 3 inches. The B-19, although it is 132 feet long and has a wing span of 212 feet, is an experimental ship and only one model was ever built. Its bomb load is 36,000 pounds. The B-15 is 88 feet long, has a wing span of 149 feet and weighs 30 tons, but like the B-19 only one of these models was ever built.

The German ME-323 is 93 feet long, has a wing span of 181 feet and weighs 65,000 pounds. However, it is a transport plane, not a bomber.

The Germans have another plane, the Blohn and Vos BV-222, which is 112 feet long, with a wing span of 150 feet and a weight of 100,000 pounds, but this is a flying boat.

Air Support

Dear YANK:

I have seen a number of items in the newspapers stating that our Air Corps had accidentally strafed some of our own and allied troops. Now that I have seen the Air Corps in action in support of ground troops, I think I know how that may have happened.

A few days ago three of my buddies and myself were on an outpost. We had been there for a short while when we heard some tanks moving up in front of our lines. They were headed our way and were about 150 to 200 yards away. For a few minutes it looked like we were in for a beating. Suddenly, however, a couple of P-47s went into action. It was a wonderful sight.

The first bombs, which looked as if they were going to come awful close to us, found their target. The earth shook, and we felt sure that the next bomb would land right on us. When the P-47s started strafing we were ready to pack up and go. All around us the empty cartridge cases were landing in the hedgerow in which we were hiding, but the real stuff, which set the tanks afire, hit on the targ

It was a really grand job, and my buddies and want to thank those P-47 boys for pulling us out a tough spot. We sure wish we could get to sha their hands and thank them in person.

France —Pfc. A. GRAZIOS

*Also signed by Pfc. E. Clack and Pvts. E. Asborn and J. Sille

Honor Medal Winners

Dear YANK:

I noticed in a recent issue of YANK a picture whose caption stated that Sgt. John Basilone and Pfc. Richard K. Sorenson (*shown above*) are the only living enlisted men of the Marine Corps to win the Congressional Medal of Honor. Haven't you overlooked Pvt. Al Schmid of Philadelphia, who got the Medal of Honor for killing a flock of Japs on Guadalcanal?

Pinellas AAF, Fla. —Pfc. JESSE R. HAGY

■ Marine Pvt. Alfred A. Schmid did not receive the Medal of Honor. He received the Navy Cross for manning a machine gun with two other marines during a Japanese landing operation on Guadalcanal. One member of the squad was killed, Schmid was partially blinded and the squad was credited with killing 200 Japs.

Combat Damage

Dear YANK:

I would appreciate it very much if you wou explain why the American Army pays the civili population in recaptured territory for damage do to their property during battles. In fact, I have ev heard that we pay for the damage done to ea coconut tree in New Guinea.

New Guinea —S/Sgt. NATHAN RICHATO

■ The Army does not pay for damage incident combat action. If a shell knocks down a pa tree during a battle, that's just the owner's tou luck. However, once the Army occupies an ar and there is damage to private property not ar ing from combat, the Army may settle claims f such damage. For that purpose a claims comm sion is provided in *AR 25-90*.

Reserved Seats

Dear YANK:

Our post theater here is divided up into a genera box, an officer's section (with the best seats, seldo crowded), a first-three-graders' section (with all t rest of the good seats) and some punk seats on t sidelines (with poor view and no backs) for the r mainder of the enlisted men. We have an MP patr ling the theater to see that every caste is in its pla

Most outrageous of all is the relegating of the ho pital's ambulatory patients, who have just come from active battlefronts, to a few poor seats down front. If anybody should have good seats set asi for them, I think they should be the ones rather th the noncoms, whose duties are not so exhausting to justify giving them all the good seats.

The effect of the present set-up is that some e listed men don't attend the shows at all for lack good seats, while some of the first-three-grader se are wasted.

I'm not maintaining that good seats should be r served for the lower grades, but merely that th should all be open to whoever gets there first. T would also release the MPs for active duty elsewhe thus increasing the manpower available for direct a plication to the war effort.

Marshall Islands —T/Sgt. BAYARD H. McCONNAUGH

Whipping Boy

Dear YANK:

Just who in hell is the wise guy who answers the bitches in *Mail Call?*

Southwest Pacific —Pvt. DON FAUGL*

*Also signed by Pvt. Tom Hudson.

■ Here he is after a Saturday morning, when the mail is unusually light. He isn't nearly this cheerful most of the week.

Shorter Workday

Dear YANK:

Wouldn't our worries about post-war employme of soldiers come to an end if six months after t war the entire nation went on a six-hour workd instead of the present eight-hour day? Wouldn't th also serve to absorb the workers discharged fro war industries?

India —Cpl. A. FORN

New Zealand

Dear YANK:

I just finished reading your interesting article New Zealand and, having spent eight months Auckland myself, I readily agree on the hospitali and friendliness shown to the Yanks in New Zealar With its numerous pubs, clubs, cinemas, dances a all-around entertainment, it is hard for a GI to unhappy very long. Endless beaches and "Batche on the adjoining small islands make recreation pleasure. The girls are very entertaining and wh you go to their homes you are treated like a lon lost friend. With their time-outs for tea, it see like you are eating all day long.

Camp Alva, Okla. —T/Sgt. H. L. GALBRA

Regulars

Dear YANK:

In a recent issue of YANK I noticed a letter by P Harold R. Newman in which he asked: "Rememb our pre-war Army? It was a pallid stepchild of o Government, and we did not like to show it strangers. The joe who joined it was generally co sidered a lazy, shiftless, moronic lout who lack the brains and ambition to 'make good' in civil life

I would like to say for myself, as well as for oth Regular Army men, that the men who enlisted befo the war were men who had enough ambition to g away from their mothers' apron strings and do thin for themselves. When we came into the Army, the weren't any of the so-called technical schools. W had to learn things the hard way. Had it not be for the men who came into the Army before t war, there would have been no one to train t men that were later drafted into the service.

I think we deserve some credit for our work.

New Guinea —Sgt. JACK MASKE

By Sgt. RAY DUNCAN

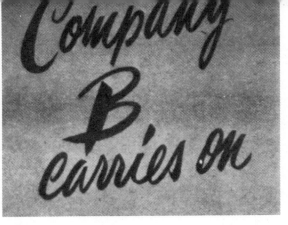

THE ALEUTIANS—Men get a little strange on these island when they're stationed up here too long. Some men do at least. But until last night, when I wandered into B Company, I never had seen a whole outfit acting odd.

"Which way is post headquarters?" I asked the man who was leaning out the sentry box window. His MP brassard had slipped down round his elbow.

"I couldn't say, soldier. This here is B Company."

The crease in his forehead kept getting deeper, and about every five minutes his left eye twitched.

"Tell ya what," he said. "Go up the hill to the orderly room an' ask. Just a few steps up. I'm new aroun' here. Just knock at the door."

I thanked him and his left eye twitched in response.

Halfway up the hill I stopped to rest. Far below, beneath the evening mist rolling up the slope, I heard a bulldozer grunting at work.

I knocked at the orderly-room door. The sound echoed through the building as if it were empty, but I heard somebody walking inside. I knocked again and tried the door. It was locked. Finally a corporal jerked it open.

"Yeah?" he said.

I asked the way to post headquarters and he turned his back on me and growled, "C'mon in." It was a small dusty room, dimly lit through one window. The corporal's desk was in the darkest corner.

"Post headquarters," he said, "is back down the hill. Take the path to your right and turn left by the warehouse."

I leaned forward a little. In the dim light I thought I saw his left eye twitch. The whole musty building, the entire hilltop, was suddenly very quiet. Down below the bulldozer had stopped. For a moment I felt sure that everyone else on the island had just now packed up and shipped out.

"Well, thanks a lot," I said quickly. "I guess I'll shove off."

"Just a minute, soldier."

I stopped in the doorway and turned around. This time, with the help of the light from the door, I saw one eye flicker. "Yeah?" I said, so loud that it made the building ring.

"You got a pass? You can't get out without a pass."

"What?" I'd never heard of passes in these islands, but I was new up here. "The guard at the gate let me in without a pass."

"Yeah, I know, he's always doin' that. You'll hafta see the sergeant about gettin' a pass."

He cranked his field telephone. A little cloud of dust went up from the instrument and faintly, far inside the building, I heard a bell ring.

"Say, sergeant, guy out here wants a pass." While he listened to the reply the corporal's eye twitched again.

"C'mon, soldier." He led me down a dark corridor that connected two huts. "The sergeant'll be here in a minute," he said. "Tell'm what ya want."

THERE was a big desk with in and out baskets on it. Three plywood boards with roster sheets hung behind the desk, and a whistle dangled from a nail in the hut's curved wall. This room, like the other, was dark and smelled of dust.

"Woddya want, fellah?" said the sergeant. He was thin for a top kick, and his blouse was much too big. The bottom rocker reached down to his elbow.

I sat there staring at him. Once again, unmistakably even in the growing darkness, I saw that swift left-eye twitch.

"I want a pass," I cried, "to get out of here."

"Pass! That's all I hear around here—pass, pass, pass! You guys know yer supposed to put in for passes at least 24 hours in advance!"

"Passes in the Aleutians? Sounds like back in the States!"

He shot a swift glance at me. While he pondered my remark his eye twitched twice. "Well," he said very softly, "even if you don't get a pass tonight, you can stay here in our casual area. We can feed you an' put you up."

"No! I gotta get out of here!" I shouldn't have yelled at him like that, for he seemed sincerely anxious for me to stay. But I could see myself eating in a dark mess hall with a bunch of men whose left eyes were always winking.

"Okay, fellah," he sighed, "you'll have to see the Old Man about a pass." He knocked softly on a side door, then tiptoed in. Through the closed door I heard a muffled conversation, then the sergeant came back and said, "Okay, fellah, you can come in here."

He held the door for me. It was a large room, with three doors, and there was a square of brown linoleum on the floor. Behind the desk was a dusty sign which said: THE DIFFICULT WE DO IMMEDIATELY, THE IMPOSSIBLE WILL TAKE A LITTLE TIME.

"Sit here, fellah, the captain'll be here in a minute."

I sat alone for a while, and everything was quiet except for footsteps in the building. Then the captain entered wearing his garrison cap. I jumped up and saluted.

"What's on your mind?" he sighed, wearily returning my salute. His cap visor was pulled too low for me to see his face. The captain's voice was high and strained, and his brass wasn't shined.

"All right," he said, "I'll fix you up. What's your name? Have a chair?" Like all the men in his outfit, he seemed anxious to keep me around for a while.

I sat down as he picked up the field telephone, then I leaped instantly back to my feet. His left eye had twitched. "Sergeant," he was saying,

"fix this man up with a pass." Then he hung up and said: "Sorry I can't offer you transportation out, but we're short of drivers right now. We're on a caretaker basis here, as you can see."

He gazed out the window across the deserted company area to where the wooden doors of ragged tent houses swung in the wind. I thanked him hastily and backed out without saluting.

In a moment the sergeant returned to his office and handed me my pass, but he let me find my own way out of the building. The corporal was gone from his desk by the door. The bulldozer far below had started to roar again.

"Let's button that jacket, soldier," said the MP, who was leaning out his window watching me come down the hill. He studied my pass and winked at it twice. I took off without waiting for him to return it.

THE guys in my hut were drinking our weekly beer ration when I got back, soon after dark. "Look," I said, "what about this B Company up on the hill?"

"Company B," said Davis, "shipped out three weeks ago, the lucky basters." He punched a hole in his beer can with the edge of the hut's red fire-fighting axe.

"No, I was just up there. Queerest outfit I ever saw——"

"Company B," repeated Davis, pointing his beer can at me, "shipped out three weeks ago in a helluva hurry. I know that for a fact. There's only one B man left on this island. Poor guy was in the hospital when they shipped and he got left behind. I work in the hospital, I oughta know."

"Look, Davis, I was just up there——"

"He's kinda funny, got an eye-twitch, but he'll be all right when he gets back to the States in a couple of weeks. Only one B man left, I know that for a fact."

And now that I think about it, Davis might be right. I never saw any of those guys together. But anyhow I'm not going back to find out.

THE SAD SACK

"TOLD OFF"

SGT. GEORGE BAKER

Did I Ever Tell You-?

By Sgt. MARION HARGROVE

"SCHOFIELD BARRACKS was the place, though," said M/Sgt. Clarkin, pouring a slug of walnut wine into his little clay cup and thence down his calloused gullet. "Nineteen years I been in the goddam Army and I never saw a place to beat Schofield. That was the life. That was the goddam life."

I saw that I was in for it again.

He stuck a cigarette into his face and picked up a box of Chinese matches. The first six matches broke. He finally put three together and struck them. It worked.

"Used to have a latrine orderly in my barracks at Schofield named Pop Ballantine. Never will forget the time we had a sex-morality movie and Pop Ballantine showed up dead drunk. He went all the way up to the front row and he must of stumbled and fell eight times before he got there. Funniest damned thing you ever saw.

"We had a dental inspection oncet and old Pop showed up for it with his teeth in his hands. He never wore his teeth; used to leave 'em in his foot locker and the only time he ever took 'em out was for dental inspection. There was one tee-sergeant always used to stick his fingers in Pop Ballantine's mouth and say, 'Bite me, Albert!'

"This Pop Ballantine was the goddamdest rummy you ever saw, though. We'd send him into town to buy toilet brushes for his latrine and he'd get drunk with the money.

"Old Pop used to get his latrine cleaned up in no time at all and then he'd chisel a dime off of somebody—damndest chiseler you ever saw—and he'd sit in the barracks window watching for the beer garden to open up across the street. He'd buy him a 10-cent glass of beer and sit watching like a hawk for somebody to buy a pitcher. Then he'd move in on the guy like he was an old friend. He used to sit in that damned beer garden from the time it opened till the time it closed, except for work call at 1 o'clock.

"There was some staff sergeant, I forget his name now, had jawbone at the commissary. Him and Pop would get Listerine and 7-Up and make highballs out of it. Used to get drunk as hell.

"This guy Pop Ballantine, though, he was conscientious. He was conscientious as hell. Proud of his latrine. You had to watch the old guy or he'd break in on a conversation you were having with ladies and want to show 'em his latrine. He'd explain how he got the stains out of the urinal with sulphuric acid.

"Old Pop had a helluva time when the draftees came, telling 'em about when he was in the Philippines in 1921. He didn't like 'em long, though. The Old Man took his job away from him and gave it to the draftees."

"IT's getting pretty late," I said, "and I've got a motor convoy first thing in the morning. I'd best be turning in——"

"We had another fellow at Schofield," M/Sgt. Clarkin said, "name of Pappy Jackson. Never forget one time he'd been AWOL for a couple of days, shacking up with some woman in town, and they sent the OD in to look for him. The OD found him at his shack and Pappy took off down the street drunk as hell with the OD after him."

He reached again for the walnut wine and I yawned significantly.

"Pappy would almost let the OD catch him and then he'd turn around with his false teeth in his hands and snap 'em at the OD. He'd keep getting playfuller and the OD would keep getting madder. Funniest goddam thing you ever saw.

"Remember one time somebody dropped a match in the seat of Pappy's fatigue trousers to give him the hot seat, you might say. Pappy had his hip pocket full of oily rags and he went up in flames. You ought to seen him running around there beating his hip pocket trying to put the fire out. He seen old Pop Ballantine laughing at him and thought it was Pop did it, so he started a fight. Neither one of 'em could of punched their

way out of a wet paper bag and neither one [of] them got within three foot of the other. Ju[st] bouncing around and feinting and cussing is a[ll] they did. Funniest goddam thing you ever saw[.]

"IF you'll excuse me," I said, "I'd better tak[e] off. I've got a long trip ahead of me."

"I ever tell you about a guy we had at Scho[field named Chaplin? Boys called him Charl[ie] Chaplin; never can remember what his first nam[e] was. Little fellow. Had to get waivers on h[is] height and weight to get in the Army. I remem[-]ber one Armistice Day we put him in a mattre[ss] cover and tied it around his chin and shaved h[is] head. You ought to of seen him hopping aroun[d] in that mattress cover, mad as hell."

"Jeez," I said, "I didn't realize how late it [is] getting."

"This Charlie Chaplin," M/Sgt. Clarkin wen[t] on, "he was scared as hell of the MPs. One nigh[t] we'd been to a *luau*—that's a party—at Wahiw[a.] We were walking back to Schofield, about tw[o] miles, when we saw the MP truck coming up th[e] road. The MPs used an old GMC 1917 with on[e] acetylene light in front, and you could tell it [a] mile away. We were crossing a bridge when w[e] saw it. Old Chaplin had been drinking *okuliha[o]* and it was on his breath. Chaplin thought the ra[il] of the bridge was a fence and he jumped over [it.] Dropped 60 feet into the water, but he wasn[t] hurt any. The MPs hauled him back to the pos[t] and turned him loose and he was mad as he[ll] that he had took the dive for nothing. You shoul[d] of seen him—dripping wet and mad as hell. Fur[-]nest goddam thing you ever saw."

"Excuse me," I said. "I've got to get some ciga[-]rettes." I took off and went to bed and the nex[t] morning I left on my motor convoy.

THE morning I got back, two weeks later, I ha[d] occasion to go into the enlisted men's latrin[e] house and I ran smack into M/Sgt. Clarkin.

"Every time I come into one of these Chines[e] johns," he said, "I think of the beautiful latrine[s] we used to have at Schofield Barracks. We use[d] to have a latrine orderly back at Schofield name[d] Pop Ballantine. One of the funniest old fellow[s] you ever saw."

"A guy with no teeth?" I asked.

"That's right," said M/Sgt. Clarkin. "I remem[-]ber oncet we had a dental inspection——"

'When I think of all the time I spent in basic training creeping and crawling it makes me sick'

The Ninth Army

As we go to press, four American armies are in action against the Germans along the Western front. Latest U. S. army whose presence in France has been officially announced is the Ninth, under the command of Lt. Gen. William H. Simpson, former CG of the 30th Division, the II Army Corps and the Fourth Army. Our other armies in the sector are Lt. Gen. Courtney Hodges' First, Lt. Gen. George S. Patton Jr.'s Third and Lt. Gen. Alexander Patch's Seventh. Security regulations do not permit publication of actual American troop strength in any overseas theater but it has been reliably reported that the U. S. has more troops on the western front than it ever had before on any foreign continent. A total of 2,079,880 American soldiers were shipped to Europe during the first World War, so you can draw your own conclusions.

Battle Honors

Presidential citations have been awarded to seven Infantry units: the 1st Ranger Battalion; Company G, 180th Infantry; Cannon Company, 16th Infantry; 1st Battalion, 16th Infantry (two citations); 2d Battalion, 16th Infantry; Company K, 18th Infantry; Division Headquarters and Headquarters Company, 82d Airborne Division. . . . Troop A of the 8th Cavalry has been cited for action in the Admiralties.

GI Shop Talk

Of the 1,300 general officers on active duty as of Sept. 1, a total of 1,185 were Regular Army officers, 76 were National Guard, 25 were Reserve officers and 14 were commissioned from civil life. The Army has six generals, 34 lieutenant generals, 343 major generals and 917 brigadier generals. . . . The three latest language guides give basic instruction in Danish, Turkish and Swedish. . . . The Swiss legation has informed the WD that the straight-arm salute has been adopted by the German Army and is therefore the proper salute for German prisoners to give in the U. S. . . . As of Sept. 1, there were 243,848 war prisoners being held in the U. S. Of these, 192,846 were German, 50,272 were Italian and 730 were Japanese. . . . For whatever it's worth to the ordinary GI, the WD has announced that the blue dress uniform will not be worn for the duration and six except under specific authorization. . . . Soldiers in a Ledo Road area, working in their spare time, have built and dedicated the first American chapel in Burma, a frame structure covered with tarpaulin.

Divisions on Western Front

Here are a few more U. S. divisions on the western front that the censor will now let us name:

The 5th Division, which has the ace of diamonds for its insignia, fought in the first World War and then served in Luxembourg with the Army of Occupation until July, 1919. It was reactivated Oct. 16, 1939, at Fort McClellan, Ala., and it was stationed at Fort Benjamin Harrison, Ind., and Fort Custer, Mich., before going to the ETO.

5th Division

The 35th Division, a Kansas - Nebraska - Missouri National Guard outfit, is known as the Santa Fe Division and has the Santa Fe cross in its shoulder patch. (The old Santa Fe trail started at a point near the Missouri-Kansas state line.) It was stationed at Camp San Luis Obispo, Calif.; at Camp Rucker, Ala., and at Camp Butner, N. C., before shipping.

The 8th Division did a stretch at Fort Leonard Wood, Mo., before it went to the ETO but it sweated out most of its training in the States at Fort Jackson, S. C. It has also made its home at Camp Forrest, Tenn., and Camp Campbell, Ky.

35th Division

8th Division

Also among those present on the western front are the 4th and 7th Armored Divisions. The 4th Armored is an old Pine Camp (N. Y.) outfit. It was activated there in the spring of 1941. Later it did some time at the Desert Training Center, Camp Young, Calif., and then spent most of the time before it went overseas at Camp Bowie, Tex. The 7th Armored Division was activated Mar. 1, 1942, and assigned to Camp Polk, La., first as a part of the II Armored Corps and later with the III Armored Corps. In 1943 the 7th Armored received desert training at Camp Young, Calif., and then was stationed at Fort Benning, Ga., until it embarked for the ETO.

Washington OP

WASHINGTON has been giving attention lately to the prospect of some sort of compulsory training for American youth after the war. President Roosevelt at a press conference told reporters that he thought the public ought to give some consideration to a government training program for a million or more young men a year between the ages of 17 and 22 or 23. He pointed out that at present there are facilities for training 5,000,000 in this country built by the Army that will last for 25 years and create quite a problem of disposal. He stated that the training need not be completely military in character, and appeared to be suggesting a combination of civilian and military training. As the possible benefits of such a program he listed education in living with a large crowd of people, training in discipline, promoting law and order, education in keeping clean and using muscles, and vocational training.

A few days previously the American Legion made public a letter from Secretary of War Stimson, answering a request from Warren G. Atherton that Stimson outline his views on the subject. "We must not accept the philosophy that this war will end all wars and that there will never again be a need to resort to arms," the secretary wrote. "From all that experience and history can teach us, we will be improvident if we do not adopt a sound peacetime nation-wide form of military service."

In outlining his reasons, the secretary said that our geographic position is no longer a protection, since the development of long-range bombers and amphibious operations. "If in the future we are attacked by a powerful enemy or group of enemies, we may be sure that we will not be given the time to mobilize our industries and to extemporize an Army from the untrained youth of the nation. . . . This means that the youth of the nation must have had the greatest part of its military training before mobilization. The alternative . . . would be a large standing Army. But it is traditional to our democracy to maintain a relatively small regular Army, and in a major emergency to depend, in the main, on the citizens in arms." He added that universal military training for Americans would assure the rest of the world, "that in the future, America will be not only willing but *able* and *ready* to take its part with the peace loving nations in resisting lawless aggression and in assuring peaceful world order."

—YANK Washington Bureau

YANK is published weekly by the enlisted men of the U. S. Army and is for sale only to those in the armed services. Stories, features, pictures and other material from YANK may be reproduced if they are not restricted by law or military regulations, provided proper credit is given, release dates are observed and specific prior permission has been granted for each item to be reproduced. Entire contents copyrighted, 1944, by Col. Franklin S. Forsberg and reviewed by U. S. military censors.

MAIN EDITORIAL OFFICE
205 East 42d Street, NEW YORK 17, N. Y., USA

EDITORIAL STAFF

Managing Editor, Sgt. Joe McCarthy, FA; Art Director, Sgt. Arthur Weithas, DEML; Assistant Managing Editor, Sgt. Justus Schlotzhauer, Inf.; Assistant Art Director, Sgt. Ralph Stein, Med.; Pictures, Sgt. Leo Hofeller, Armd.; Features, Sgt. Marion Hargrove, FA; Sports, Sgt. Dan Polier, AAF; Overseas News, Sgt. Allan Ecker, AAF.
Washington: Sgt. Richard Paul, DEML.
Britain-France: Sgt. Durbin Horner, QMC; Sgt. John Scott, Engr.; Sgt. Charles Brand, AAF; Sgt. Bill Davidson, Inf.; Sgt. Sanderson Vanderbilt, CA; Cpl. Jack Coggins, CA; Cpl. John Preston, AAF; Sgt. Saul Levitt, AAF; Cpl. Edmund Antrobus, Inf.; Sgt. Reginald Kenny, AAF; Pvt. Howard Katzander, CA; Sgt. Mack Morriss, Inf.; Sgt. Earl Anderson, AAF; Sgt. Merle Miller, AAF.
Italy-Southern France: Sgt. George Aarons, Sig. Corps; Sgt. James P. O'Neill, Inf.; Sgt. John Frano, Inf.; Sgt. Harry Sions, AAF; Sgt. August Loeb, AAF; Pfc. Carl Schwind, AAF; Sgt. J. Denton Scott, FA; Sgt. Steve Derry, DEML.

Middle East: Cpl. Robert McBrinn, Sig. Corps.
Iraq-Iran: Sgt. Burtt Evans, Inf.; Cpl. Richard Gaige, DEML.
China-Burma-India: Sgt. Dave Richardson, CA; Sgt. Lou Stoumen, DEML; Sgt. Seymour Friedman, Sig. Corps; Cpl. George J. Corbellini, Sig. Corps; Cpl. Paul Johnston, AAF.
Southwest Pacific: Sgt. LaFayette Locke, AAF; Sgt. Douglas Borgstedt, DEML; Sgt. Ozzie St. George, Inf.; Sgt. Dick Hanley, AAF; Sgt. Charles Pearson, Engr.; Sgt. Ralph Boyce, AAF; Sgt. Bill Alcine, Sig. Corps; Sgt. Charles Rathe, DEML; Cpl. George Bick, Inf.; Cpl. John McLeod, Med.; Sgt. Marvin Fasig, Engr.; Cpl. Roger Wrenn, Sig. Corps.

South Pacific: Cpl. James Goble, Armd.; Cpl. Lon Wilson, Sig. Corps.
Central Pacific: Sgt. James L. McManus, CA; Sgt. Richard Nihill, CA; Sgt. Bill Reed, Inf.; Cpl. Tom O'Brien, Inf.; Sgt. H. N. Oliphant, Engr.; Pfc. George Burns, Sig. Corps; Sgt. Bill Young, Inf.; Ken Harris CPhoM, USCG; Sgt. Barrett McGurn, Med.; Mason E. Pawlak PhoM1c, USNR; Sgt. Robert Greenhalgh, Inf.; Sgt. Dillon Ferris, AAF.
Alaska: Cpl. John Haverstick, CA; Sgt. Ray Duncan, AAF.
Panama: Sgt. John Hay, Inf.; Cpl. Richard Douglass, Med.
Puerto Rico: Sgt. Don Cooke, FA; Pfc. James Iorio, MP.
Bermuda: Cpl. William Pene du Bois.
Brazil: Pfc. Nat Bodian, AAF.
Central Africa: Sgt. Kenneth Abbott, AAF.
Iceland: Cpl. John Moran, Inf.
Newfoundland: Sgt. Frank Bode, Sig. Corps.
Navy: Robert L. Schwartz Y2c; Allen Churchill Sp(x)3c.

Commanding Officer, Col. Franklin S. Forsberg.
Executive Officer, Maj. Jack W. Weeks.
Business Manager, Maj. Charles W. Balthrope.
Overseas Bureau Officers: London, Maj. Donald W. Reynolds; India, Capt. Gerald J. Rock; Australia, Maj. Harold B. Hawley; Italy, Maj. Robert Strother; Hawaii, Maj. Josua Eppinger; Cairo, Maj. Charles Holt; Iran, Maj. Henry E. Johnson; South Pacific, Capt. Justus J. Craemer; Alaska, Capt. Harry R. Roberts; Panama, Capt. Howard J. Carswell; Puerto Rico, Capt. Frank Gladstone.

As One Sgt. Frank Rice to Another

Camp Butner, N. C.—A medal-bedecked soldier. strolled into the Public Relations Office at Camp Butner, the site of the Eastern Personnel Reassignment Center, and remarked: "My name's Frank Rice."

"So's mine," I said. I looked at his sergeant's stripes and then at my own.

"I've just come back from overseas," he continued.

"So have I," I said.

He wore the French Croix de Guerre, the Silver Star, the Purple Heart with cluster, the Defense Ribbon and a few other decorations.

That was something I couldn't top. But I talked with him further and found that his was a story of heroism and devotion to duty that began back in 1936 when he enlisted as a regular and was assigned to the mechanized cavalry. Since then he has soldiered in the Philippines, England, Scotland, Ireland, North Africa, Sicily and Italy.

Wounded several times, Sgt. Rice was among the first troops to storm the coasts of Africa as a member of a Tank Destroyer battalion. His outfit landed a few miles west of Oran and pushed on toward Medjez-El-Bab where they were attached to the British infantry.

"We saw our first action there," Rice said. "but we got the best the Nazis could offer when we reached Tebourba and Tunisia. At that time, around Dec. 2, 1942, we were covering an American infantry position and the shells and planes were doing their best to wipe us out. They tried artillery on us. Then various types of mortars and finally Messerschmitts and Stukas. They threw the book at us."

The first time Sgt. Rice was wounded, which was during the Tebourba-Tunisia engagement. he gave himself first aid and continued fighting.

The second time, he was hit by machine-gun fi and sent to a British hospital. While there he w awarded the Croix de Guerre, but at the time didn't realize what was going on.

"The French kept looking for me and final found me hospitalized," he recalled. "They pinn something on me with much ceremony, but was in French and I couldn't understand it. turned out that I'd been given the highest decortion awarded by the French for heroism battle."

On the way back to duty after recoveri from his wounds, Rice had to abandon the je in which he was riding when it came und enemy machine-gun fire and the driver w killed. After taking cover Rice remembered th valuable military documents were still in t vehicle. For more than 2½ hours he inch toward the abandoned jeep, making only a fe feet at a time, always under heavy machine-g and mortar fire.

"Halfway there," he said, "I was spotted, a they really opened up on me. I had to make dash for it. Bullets flew all around me, but reached the jeep, picked up my dead buddy a drove out of there as fast as I could.

"I brought back information about the enem positions. Since I had been the closest I cou tell our own gunners nearly the exact positic It wasn't long before we got the range and o guns silenced them."

For that little business Rice was decorat again, this time the Silver Star. He went throu the remainder of the African campaign and w into the Italian campaign before he was wound for the third time. That time, however, t wound was so serious that he was returned the States and hospitalized at Butler, Pa., f four months before he was sent here. Before e tering the Army he lived at Cleveland, Ohio.

"No, I don't want a discharge in spite of n wounds," said Sgt. Rice. "I guess I'm out active fighting now. I'm going to miss it, but don't want a discharge."

—Sgt. FRANK H. R

Under machine-gun fire, he inched toward the jeep.

He Felt Like an Officer

Camp Plauche, La.—Sgt. Tom Swan of Headquarters Company, ASFTC, tells this one.

Hurrying to work one morning, Swan was approached by a soldier who asked him gingerly: "Don't you know the first rule of military courtesy, soldier?"

"Say, what is this?" said Swan.

"Don't you salute officers, sergeant?" the other asked.

"Yeah, when there's any around to highball," said Swan. "Why?"

"Well, then——"

And as he spoke the soldier began feeling for brass on his collar, but none was there. A hasty examination of his cap failed to reveal any either. Actually a commissioned officer, he made his apologies. He had forgotten his insignia.

"He turned all colors," said Swan in telling of the incident.

—Cpl. JOHN A. SALDIN

A ROUGH NIGHT

Camp Gordon Johnston, Fla.—It was a hot Florida night. A Pennsylvania boy had just been promoted from T-5 to T-4, and he and his pal had been celebrating. Came closing time and as they left the joint the new T-4 missed the step and fell flat on his face.

"Quit your shoving," he growled.

"I didn't shove you," his pal protested.

Raising himself on his elbow, the promoted one surveyed the situation and said: "Well, then it's damned icy."

Quit Women for Swimmin'

Ardmore AAF, Okla.—One thing the Army can't do is tell a man to dance when he wants to swim, according to Col. H. H. Upham.

The colonel received a complaint from a GI with that old-time civilian gallantry that "the men of this organization ran off to swim and left their dates to dance alone" at an outing sponsored by the outfit.

Answering the complaint in the weekly publication, *Bombs Away*, the colonel stated that section COs cannot dictate to the men what they shall do at a social function. "If swimming is more inviting than dancing," he wrote, "well—."

Camp News

Pro Wrestler Turns Talents to War

Fort Sam Houston, Tex.—Cpl. Frank (Bulldog) Atkinson, onetime professional light-heavyweight wrestler, claims he was one of the first professional athletes to enlist in this war.

On his way to Australia to wrestle, Atkinson was standing near his baggage on Fort Island, a few miles from Pearl Harbor, when the first bombs fell the morning of Dec. 7, 1941. He went to work with the rescue party, removing the dead and injured and making himself generally useful all over the island. Two days later at Schofield Barracks he donned a pair of dog tags.

Bulldog wore an MP brassard for a year in Hawaii and then joined the Infantry as a director of athletics. He saw action at Guadalcanal, Buna and Hollandia, and after he was wounded he was shipped home on rotation and assigned to the Southern Personnel Reassignment Center here. He is a native of Dallas, Tex., and outside the ring he is as meek as a lamb, and a perfect gentleman.

On one occasion in New Guinea, near Buna, his knowledge of wrestling came in handy. He and five other infantrymen were on patrol in the jungle. They proceeded as far as a clearing and pitched camp before they discovered that 25 yards ahead a nine-man Jap patrol lay dug in. At about the same time, it seems, Japs discovered the Yanks.

"We thought the Japs had a regiment or two in back of them," Atkinson says, "and they must have thought the same thing about us, so we set out to wipe each other out quiet-like."

In the free-for-all hand-to-hand tiff that followed, Bulldog broke the arms and legs of at least two opponents with a flying mare, a back body drop and an ogasaki dive, the latter being a Judo touch.

—Pfc. JOE DEITCH

Cpl. Frank (Bulldog) Atkinson used Judo on

tronomical Figures

eenville AAB, S. C.—The following informa-
is presented for whatever it's worth. To
el via a B-25 Mitchell bomber to the M31
ula in the constellation Andromeda, which is
only spiral nebula visible to the naked eye,
following would be required:

,200,000,000 years of flying 24 hours a day at 200
mph.
,563,200,000,000,000 gallons of gas at 100 gallons
er hour.
,564,000,000 Mitchell bombers at 3,000 hours per
omber.
00,000,000 pilots at 30 years of flying per pilot.
,689,600,000,000,000 C ration books.

here the necessary air to support the bomb-
in interplanetary space would come from,
members of the Greenville RTU navigation
did not say.
—S/Sgt. CODY PFANSTIEHL

AROUND THE CAMPS

unicipal Airport, Memphis, Tenn.—S/Sgt. Ralph
alanti of the 26th Squadron here sometimes
ks he pulled the most colossal boner of the
. Making his third trip over the "Hump" from
am Valley in India to Kunming, China, with
rivates and two lieutenants aboard, Galanti
oed when 45 minutes out that he was com-
in with "two Santa Clauses and 14 reindeer
ard." When the transport landed, Maj. Gen.
re L. Chennault, some Chinese generals,
ns of American colonels and all the staff cars
could be assembled were waiting. The code
ase Galanti had erroneously used stood for
generals and members of their staffs.

amp Claiborne, La.—Motion-picture expert of
84th Division is Pvt. Marshall Pitler of Ser-
Battery, 909th Field Artillery. Pvt. Pitler
mates he has seen 3,500 movies in his lifetime
purchased at least 3,000 movie magazines.
personal friends among the stars include
e Kelly and William Wythe. While at Car-
ie Tech studying dramatics he worked with
Pittsburgh Playhouse and since coming into
service has appeared in the USO production
My Sister Eileen," which played hereabouts.

rt Jackson, S. C.—The CO of a combat engi-
s outfit here evidently can't forget the fact
he was a school teacher as a civilian. When
in his company make a mistake on their
dry slips he makes them write "I am sorry
I made a mistake on my laundry slip" 50
s.

amp Crowder, Mo. — When the 529th Signal
rations Company had a field detail sched-
d during a downpour one day, Pvt. Dixon
well reported without a raincoat. Sgt. Wil-
Bader, in charge of the formation, ordered
well to return to the barracks and grab the
raincoat he could find. Stillwell obeyed to
letter and was soon back with the formation.
hours later he returned a muddy and water-
ed raincoat to its astonished and irate owner
t. Bader.

WIRED FOR SOUND

Deshon General Hospital, Pa.—This hospital
specializes in the rehabilitation of the hard-
of-hearing. One of the first steps in the treatment
of such a patient is the selection of a hearing aid
for him.

When questioned on what he was doing at
Deshon, Sgt. Jimmy Shaw of Tampa, Fla., quipped:
"Who, me? I'm being wired for sound."

GHOST STORY

Thayer General Hospital, Tenn.—Lt. Nonnie
Mai Smith telephoned Conditioning Service the
other day and said she was transferring Pvt. Ira
C. Dedman there from Ward 204.
"What was that?" asked the CS telephonee.
She told him.
"I'm sorry, Lt. Smith," said the voice, "this is
Conditioning Service. You want the morgue."

A Wave Chooses To Jump For Her PR1c Rating

Corpus Christi, Tex.—Kathleen Robertson PR1c
is believed to be the first Wave ever to make
the jump as a parachute rigger.

Male Navy parachute riggers earn their rating
by jumping in a parachute of their own packing,
but for Waves the jump is optional. Kathleen
exercised the option. The only girl among the
36 scheduled for the 2,000-foot jump, she calmly
received last-minute instructions, walked to the
open door of the plane when her time came and
took off into space. She landed feet first, fell
backward in the prescribed manner and rolled
back to her feet like a veteran.

"Wonderful," she said. "I can hardly wait to
submit a request for another jump."

Kathleen hails from Norwood, Mass. She enlisted in the Navy in October 1942, received boot
training at Cedar Falls, Iowa, and graduated
from Parachute Riggers School at Lakehurst,
N. J., before she came aboard the Naval Air
Training Center here in 1943.

Kathleen Robertson PR1c is briefed before a jump.

Pfc. Bruce Prouty caught playing at his shell game.

Dull Hours Plus Seashells Equal Paying Hobby

Camp Lee, Va.—One of the deadest places in
the world is an Army dispensary between
the hours of 2400 and 0600, but Pfc. Bruce Prouty
of Madison, Ohio, found a way to make the time
pass profitably and fast.

Last winter, while on a 10-day furlough in
Florida, Prouty noticed the thousands of small
seashells that had been washed ashore by the
tide, and they gave him an idea. When he came
back to the camp he had a suitcase full of them.

In the hours when the rest of the camp is
asleep Prouty spends his time between calls
making costume jewelry of the shells. In one
hour, if he isn't interrupted, he can make a set of
small multicolored earrings or a cross pin. He has
a ready market for them among local Army
nurses and wives of servicemen.

"I get a big kick out of this work," Prouty says,
"and it's a simple way for a pfc to boost his
monthly pay to that of a master sergeant."
—Cpl. GORDON COY Jr.

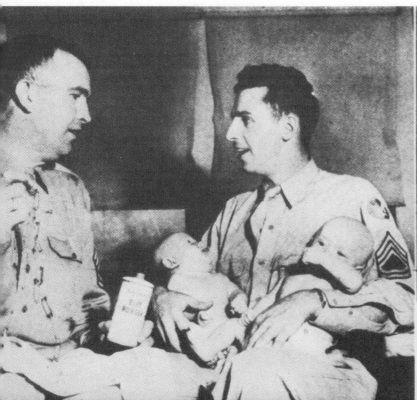
INGING UP FATHER. T/Sgt. Joseph San Fratello (right) of Stuttgart Army
ield, Ark., just got word he was father of twins. T/Sgt. Raymond Pittillo
lends his own twin sons so that the new pappy may get in some practice.

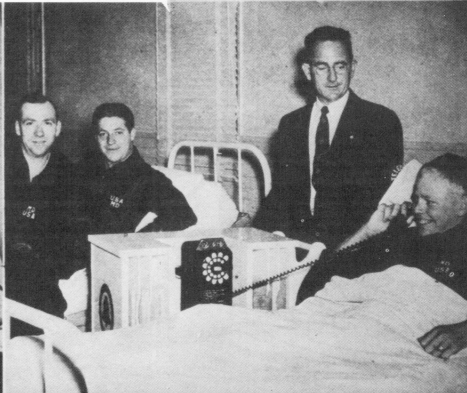
SERVICE DE LUXE. The base hospital at Stockton Field, Calif., has a new
wrinkle in bedside phone service. Here Pvt. E. M. Bryerly puts through a call
to home as E. C. DeVere, local telephone manager, stands by the bed with set.

Elaine Riley

YANK

Pin-up Girl

...e Poets Cornered

FRANCE, 1944

Europe is a quiet land.
There is something dozing
In the soil here
That all the noise and rattle of war
Will never awaken.

It is the sound sleep of the old philosopher
Resting in the shade,
The weary nod of the scholar
With the dusty book and the half-closed eye.

He has been everywhere,
Has seen it all,
And his taste for battle
Has long been satisfied.
Now he will not even turn his head
To watch these new warriors
Crawl through the hedge and
Die on his trampled breast.
He is not moved.

Listen to the earth call to us:
"Come back to your mother's womb
And rest a while."

And the nervous poets look
At the tired dirt
While the jealous claw
That holds them fast to the great root
Of America
Slackens its grip,
As if the journey was over
And this at last
Was perhaps the spirit's final sanctuary.

France —Pfc. JOHN M. BEHM

ELEGY FOR AN AMERICAN

The time to mourn is short that best becomes
The military dead. We lift and fold the flag,
Lay bare the coffin with its written tag
And march away. Behind, four others wait
To lift the box, the heaviest of loads.
The anesthetic afternoon benumbs,
Sickens our senses, forces back our talk.
We know that others on tomorrow's roads
Will fall, ourselves perhaps, the man beside,
Over the world they threatened, all who walk;
And could we mark the grave of him who died
We would write this beneath his name and date:

EPITAPH

Under this wooden cross there lies
A Christian killed in battle. You who read
Remember that this stranger died in pain,
And passing here, if you can lift your eyes
Upon a peace kept by the human creed,
Know that one soldier has not died in vain.

New Guinea —Pfc. KARL J. SHAPIRO

TWENTY-ONE DASH ONE HUNDRED

The old familiar *Basic Field Manual*, officially known as FM 21-100, is no more. A new pamphlet, "Army Life" fills the orientation needs of basic-training recruits, and everything else in the *Basic Field Manual* is either duplicated in other training manuals or is obsolete . . . —YANK, *The Army Weekly*.

Aye, tear its tattered pages out;
Declare it obsolete.
All for the scrap drive's open snout,
Rescind, destroy, delete!

What matter that this midget tome
Was blueprint to our life,
Adviser, counsel, bridge from home
To Army? Whet the knife!

Yes, abrogate, annul, revoke;
Proclaim afar the ban.
Replace the Handbook? Heartless joke!
It fears no mortal man.

It lives, in spite of protocol,
Ingrained in all our brains;
Shot though it was against tne wall,
Its spirit still remains.

Camp San Luis Obispo, Calif. —T-4 JOHN W. GREENLEAF

THE DAY

The day! The day!
Think of the wonder of the day!
Think not about this lonely heart, my mind.
There are fair thoughts for meditation,
And there are fair sights to see.
This moment must be lived! We must not die
Because today is not the same as yesterday;
Each day is fair in its own way.
Laugh now, smile now, now plan, and go about
Your business with a light, free spirit, glad
That when tomorrow opens out the door
Upon tomorrow's garden path
That leads to life and love anew,
There shall be smiles still couching on your lips
And laughter that's not lost its ring;
Sing now that you will not forget the words of
song!

India —Sgt. CARLYLE A. OBERLE

THE REASONS

Resting at sunset, feet in a rut
By the roadside; champing the half-cooked
Hash that unskilled cooks hurl in our kits
In slabs; resting with soft sunset lights
Over the wave of woods dark green
In shadows, emerald under slanting rays,
Peaceful falling shadows (already half asleep);
Ruminating the reasons why men love
A soldier's life. Beauty striking at the heart
At sunset after the long bitter struggle
Over stony trails in pack harness;
The passive acceptance of hardships
(The cool grin at unforeseen orders);
Labor in the muddy gun emplacement;
The ominous port of embarkation
And the sector of trapped jungle,
Fanged Japanese under the dead logs;
Passive acceptance of hardships
(The cool, calculating grin)—how many
Lives for a hundred yards of fever and swamp?
This is why men love a soldier's life:
Sudden beauty by a strange road,
Passive acceptance (sly grin at hardships),
And, high above all, the holy right
To hurl mean flesh at death, to dare
Infinity, the small fears forgotten.
This is why men love a soldier's life.

New Guinea —Cpl. HARGIS WESTERFIELD

THE RECONVERSION

The man you sent off to war may be a problem for a while when he gets home even if he never left the country. That's the opinion of Col. William C. Menninger, chief of the division of neuropsychiatry, Office of the Surgeon General, who believes that many veterans are going to have first-class problems in reconversion on their hands. Some of the worst sufferers, the Army psychiatrist predicted, will be the clerks who became colonels and the messenger boys who became majors.—*Louisville (Ky.) Times*.

When bugles sound their final notes
And bombs explode no more
And we return to what we did
Before we went to war,
The sudden shift of status
On the ladder of success
Will make some worthy gentlemen
Feel like an awful mess.

Just think of some poor captain
Minus all his silver bars
Standing up behind some counter
Selling peanuts and cigars;
And think of all the majors
When their oak leaf's far behind
And the uniform they're wearing
Is the Western Union kind.

Shed a tear for some poor colonel
If he doesn't feel himself;
Jerking sodas isn't easy
When your eagle's on the shelf.
'Tis a bitter pill to swallow.
'Tis a matter for despair;
Being messengers and clerks again's
A mighty cross to bear.

So be kind to working people
That you meet where'er you go,
For the guy who's washing dishes
May have been your old CO.

Fort Knox, Ky. —Pfc. EDWARD BLUMENTHAL

Message Center

FRED ASHLEY of Sioux City, Iowa, last heard of on *USS Mississippi*, 1940: write Sgt. Marvin Lensink, Sec. A, 2516th Base Unit, AAF, Eagle Pass, Tex.... FRANK BOYER, with QM outfit in India: write Pfc. Edward G. Woods, Deshon Gen. Hosp. Annex, New Castle, Pa. . . . Maj. WILLIAM BRADFIELD of Spokane, Wash., in Dutch Harbor in 1941-42: write Cpl. Gil Sodenberg, DA 6-16, CCD, AAB, Dalhart, Tex.... Pvt. DEAN T. CURLEE, inducted at Lubbock, Tex., last January: write Pvt. Patsy R. Stalcup, Sec. D, 701 AAFBU, Wright Field, Dayton, Ohio. . . . FREDERICK HAAS S1c of Los Angeles, Calif., last heard of in 1941 aboard the *USS Tulsa*: write Sgt. Lawrence A. Loquet, Med. Det., 3d Inf., Fort Benning, Ga. . . . Lt. ELIZABETH ISSACS of New Jersey, somewhere in the South Pacific with the ANC: write Cpl. James Dashiell, 640 QM Laundry Co., Camp Gordon Johnston, Fla. . . . S/Sgt. J. JACKSON, once at AAFTTC, Miami, Fla.: write Pvt. Bob Zirk, 13 Tact. Rcn. Sq., AAB, DeRidder, La. . . . Sgt. ALFRED JACOBS with the Air Corps in Trinidad: write Pvt. Julius Kohn, Btry. A, 13th CA, Fort Barrancas, Fla. . . . PAUL KIEL, once at Camp Crowder and Kelly Field: write Cpl. Walter Lloyd, 331st BU, Sq. Y, Barksdale Field, La. . . . T/Sgt. RAY KORMAN, formerly with the 8th Serv. Command, Texas: write T-4 Jake Schoenhof, Hq. & SV Co., 540 Amph. Trac. Bn., Fort Ord. Calif. . . . LARRY LANG, recently inducted: write Pvt. Philip J. Schacca, Med. Det., 424th Inf., APO 443, Camp Atterbury, Ind. . . . T-5 PAT LATESSA, once at Crile Gen. Hosp., Cleveland, Ohio: write Pfc. Nick Fatica, Ward B-1, Sta. Hosp., Camp Crowder, Mo. . . . EDWARD R. MARTIN, last heard of in the 168th FA Bn.: write Cpl. Floyce H. Booker, Hq. Btry., 262d FA Bn., Camp Polk, La. . . . BILL OSTROFF, formerly in the 108th FA: write S/Sgt. Harry Marks, Co. K, 253d Inf., Camp Van Dorn, Miss. . . . Pvt. TONY PERIERA, last heard of in New Guinea: write Sgt. Joe Incas, Ward 14, Oliver Gen. Hosp., Augusta, Ga. . . . DOROTHY MARIE PERRONE, joined WAC in Utica, N. Y., last January: write Pfc. Robert H. Skinner, 2132d AAF Base Unit, Sec. C-3, Maxwell Field, Ala. . . . PVT. STANLEY E. POLLITT, last heard of in Florida: write Cpl. Gene R. Nadig, Co. C, 750th Tank Bn., Fort Jackson, S. C. . . . Pfc. HARRY READY, last heard of in England: write Pfc. Ira Shulman & S/Sgt. Bavio, Co. A, 406th Inf., APO 102, Fort Dix, N. J. . . . S/Sgt. KENNETH RUSHIA, somewhere in Italy: write Pvt. Donald E. Thwaits, 610 AAF Med. Sec. F, Eglin Field, Fla. . . . Pfc. SOL SPIELMAN, formerly with the 135th Engrs., Camp Van Dorn, Miss.: write Pfc. Alfred Myers, 116th AAF Base Unit, AAB, Fort Dix, N. J. . . . Lt. JOAN STERKINBERGE, ANC, once at Sta. Hosp., Lowry Field, Denver, Colo.: write Pfc. William F. Poston, Sec. F3706, AAFBU, Sheppard Field, Tex.... BERT STOUT, formerly from S. Belmar, N. J.: write Sgt. Kittine, A-718 FA Bn., APO 410, Camp Van Dorn, Miss. . . . Cpl. JULIA TAYLOR, WAC, somewhere overseas: write Pvt. Bob Flanagan Jr., Sec. M, Box 374, Keesler Field, Miss. . . . Sgt. JOSEPH A. TOMCZYK, with the 701st Engr. Bn.: write Sgt. Stanley A. Tomczyk, Co. B, 399th Inf., APO 447, Fort Bragg, N. C. . . . Pvt. HARRY TRANSUE, last heard of in ASTU, Providence College, R. I.: write Pvt. Robert C. Beers, 12th Alt. Tng. Unit, CAAB, Columbia, S. C. . . . Lt. ROBERT E. WALTHER, last heard of with 327th Bomb. Sq.: write Pfc. Norman R. Walther, Hq. Btry., 490 Armd. FA Bn., APO 261, Camp Cooke, Calif. . . . JOHN WENE S1c, formerly of Armed Guard Center, San Francisco, Calif.: write A/C George Habeeb, Sec. S, Sq. H, Flt. 3, Class 45-A, AAFPFS, Maxwell Field, Ala. . . . GLENN WIGGINS of Minneapolis, Minn., last stationed in Sicily with an FA Bn.: write Pfc. Don Thorsen, Hq. & Hq. Co. TPS, Fort Benning, Ga. . . . Lt. RICHARD L. WILLIAMS, last heard of in Italy: write Pvt. Herbert K. Williams, Sec. I, AAF, Amarillo, Tex. . . . Lt. JOHN WHITTAKER, stationed at Laurel, Md., before the war: write Pfc. Archie S. Flohr, 213th AAF BU CCTS (H), Sec. A, AAF, Mountain Home, Idaho.

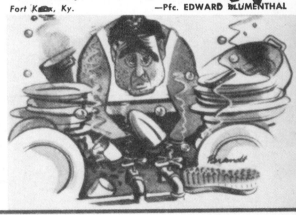

TO PROVE to skeptics that a good-looking girl is not necessarily brainless, Elaine Riley once interrupted her modeling career and became a private secretary. Fortunately for pin-up devotees, she did not continue to hide her lines behind a desk. She pushed back her chair and went to Hollywood. Her new movie for RKO Radio is "The Girl Rush."

CHANGE OF ADDRESS If you are a YANK subscriber and have changed your address, use this coupon together with the mailing address on your latest YANK to notify us of the change. Mail it to YANK, The Army Weekly, 205 East 42d Street, New York 17, N. Y., and YANK will follow you to any part of the world.

Full name and Rank ______ Order No. ______

OLD MILITARY ADDRESS

______

______

______

NEW MILITARY ADDRESS

______

______

______

Allow 21 days for change of address to become effective

Teensy Weensy

Two months ago, while Cpl. Shanks had been on furlough, he had had to watch his Aunt May's pity-me eyes on him and hear her complaints about not even one "teensy weensy" post card from him in the whole year before he'd been home. She said "teensy weensy" in just the same way she'd always spoken to him years before. Like when he first showed resistance to an absurd, pitiful assumption of parental authority.

He sat before the typewriter now, staring at it. The blank sheet of paper inserted in the machine threw a glare from the orderly-room lights. One thing about this outfit, he reflected, corporals pulled CQ, but that was all they pulled. But thinking about that wasn't writing the letter, either.

If you moved the typewriter just a trifle, there'd be no glare on the keys, and that was good when you weren't sure of your typing, anyway.

Aunt May had been a hell of a lot older when he was home this time. It must be lousy to have to beg for a nephew's letter.

Slowly, and in spite of the six or seven GIs kidding around by the first sergeant's desk, he started to type: *Dear Aunt May.*

He remembered the time she begged him not to tell his uncle that she had whipped him. Only she wasn't "teensy weensy" then. She was only scared, he thought as he struggled to grasp the first words for his letter. Or maybe she was scared and glad—glad that she had had the courage to take the place of his mother that much. Until he grew up to run away, and then to stay away, he knew this curious affection that sought to envelop and conquer him.

His uncle wouldn't let her forget: "He's not yours, May. He's not yours." And she grew older and broke her heart standing up to that knowledge.

He sighed and saw his letter get no further. He gave a few unintelligible answers to unimportant questions some of the boys were asking. Who're you writing to, kid? Gotcherself a gal? When's the pin-up coming? So he smiled as he saw his Aunt May, an ageless cadaver in a pink sarong.

Dear Aunt May: How are you? I am fine. Training in our Squadron is coming along fine. This is a wonderful place and quite unlike anything at home. How is Uncle Joe, and did Mrs. Jody have her baby yet? I tried to look up that Master Sergeant who you say is also stationed here and is one of my cousins on Uncle Joe's side, or did you say Uncle Henry's side, or what did you say . . .

The lights in the orderly room got brighter, or Cpl. Shanks got sleepier, but anyway the glare on the keys was back again. He jerked the paper out of the typewriter, got up and walked with it in his hand to the furthermost light and put the light out, walked back to the next light, put it out. Then Cpl. Shanks slowly tore up the letter in his hand into small, deliberate bits as he went back to his desk.

He sat down, rubbed the sleep out of his eyes and shoved the crib of the desk back to let the typewriter roll away out of view.

Then he pulled a picture post card out of his pocket and addressed it in pencil, after which he decided it was about time to check his KP list for the morning.

ACSTC, Fresno, Calif.   —Cpl. VICTOR KLINGER

CODE OF THE LATRINE ORDERLY
When eating oranges, remember our code:
No orange peelin's in the commode!

AAFBU, Inglewood, Calif.   —Sgt. SHELBY FRIEDMAN

RANK REFLECTION
I vow that I
   Would never gripe
Could I but wear
   Just one more stripe.

But then again
   It seems to me
I felt that way
   As pfc.

Camp Atterbury, Ind.   —Cpl. G. G. DOWLING

Dry Wine in the Mess Hall

It all started when the civilian employees on the post began eating at our mess hall. Garbed in rainbow-colored summer outfits, they brought a new glamor to our chow line, even though the rapidly rotating KPs saw the change mainly in terms of more pots and pans to scour.

Some guys were already hurrying back to work when Pfc. Grolnick and I passed them on the morning-glory ramp. "Anything good for chow?" I asked them in passing.

"Spaghetti," answered one of them enthusiastically. Whereupon Pfc. Grolnick did what he did.

"Wouldn't be so bad," he said innocently, "if we had some wine with our meals occasionally."

"Yep," says I, "dry port wine and spaghetti for chow. Really hit the spot."

The damage was done. Some medics must have overheard us, because we traced the story back later on. Wine for chow! Claret, burgundy, muscatel spread over the hospital wards like a California flood.

By the time it reached the medics' orderly room it was cocktails. Yessir, the civilians were dining at mess hall No. 2 and spirits were flowing like water!

Both orderly-room telephones rang continuously. Was it true? How come? What was it? Roma, Cresta Blanca, White Horse Scotch or Vat 69?

The first sergeant sent the assistant first sergeant to investigate. Col. Geoghegan sent Maj. Ecker to check up and bring back the whole story and some samples.

Somebody went running down the street toward headquarters yelling that the war must be over since there was celebrating and drinking. The nearby fire station let go with sirens and whistles. Auxiliary firemen came running and some commandeered cars as per official bulletin No. 24.

The post CO, Brig. Gen. Kynch, called out the MPs and ordered all gates closed. Double guard was thrown around the prisoner stockade. A contingent of Marines from a base nearby, especially trained in handling riots, careened to a stop in front of the gate and ordered the MPs to let them in. Remembering their special orders, the MPs refused, whereupon the Marines opened up with tear gas, climbed the fences and infiltrated toward mess hall No. 2, where all the trouble seemed to have started. Somebody opened the valves on the big water tank and the base unit had its first shower in months.

Things were beginning to get seriously out of hand when Brig. Gen. Kynch radioed a passing Navy blimp that floated in over the base. The quick-witted lieutenant commander aboard the blimp turned on the superdynamic loudspeaker and a terrible voice bellowed out of the heavens, "Hat Ease!"

Everybody stopped, breathless.

The spell was broken. The water tower stopped pouring. KPs and MPs straightened their gig pins and went back to work. And up against the hills a lazy silver blimp drifted into the low fog.

Santa Ana AAF, Calif.   —Pfc. JOSEPH LUFT

LETTER FROM AN ARMY CAMP
I have waited long for the stars tonight,
Waited tense with breath bated; for the stars are clean here
And they cover the sky's water like the foam of waves.
I have waited long for the good darkness to come
And the gentle strength of the night wind; for then
The wind's fingers press the brow and comfort the cheek
And the breeze feels white as it runs through the body.
I have waited long to lie here on the grass again
And look up at the pin-splinters of light in the dark velvet;
For then are you in hand-touch of me
And I can close my tendrils of thought around your image
And know warmth from the thinking of you.

For here in the soft night, the mind refuses distance
And jumps vast beaches of time to nestle close
To your remembrance; for the long, dull, weary
Physical of my life melts in your presence
And memories color the bleak soul and life is a bright picture inside.

It can't be loneliness I feel. A lonely man
Feels clams in the middle of him and spears in his heart;
But here in the open territory of night, beneath the high purple,
I am filled with you and red with the embers
Of your memory, and syllables form on my heart to talk to you.
I have waited long for the night's coming, and the wind-sounds
And you spoke to me as my soul promised.
I can want no more now.

Fort Benning, Ga.   —O/C ELLSWORTH E. ROSEN

CPL. ERNEST MAXWELL GOES FOR A RIDE ON THE TRAIN

Man with no place to go.

Women and children first.

—So long as we have each other.

The fortunes of war.

SPORTS:
By Sgt. DAN POLIER

WHO'LL GO ROSE BOWLING? SOUTHERN CAL? MAYBE UCLA

Bob Waterfield, shown here on 20-yard end sweep, will quarterback UCLA again after spending a year in the Army.

GATHERED around us this week are the five loneliest men in the world. They are the Messrs. L. B. (Stub) Allison, E. C. (Babe) Horrell, Amos Alonzo Stagg, Ralph (Pest) Welch and Jeff Cravat the only active members in Greater Brotherhood of Pacific Coast coaches. So tightly are they bound together that they play each other at least twice during the season and never see an eastern football team anymore, except in the newsreels.

Mr. Allison, don't you find your job at California a lot easier with no Stanford, no Oregon and no Santa Clara to play?

"What's easier about it? Instead of playing a regular schedule we have to double up with UCLA and USC and take two lickings instead of the customary one. I don't think there's any question about the best teams in our league. UCLA and USC are much the best. Just a notch below them I like Washington, College of Pacific, then California. Our backfield is small and lacks a triple-threater. Bob Celeri, quarterback, is only 17 years old and weighs 155 pounds; George Quist and Joe Stuart, halfbacks, are 160-pounders and John Loper at fullback weighs 165 pounds. I don't know what I'm going to do for a triple-threater. I'll probably have to pull center Roger Harding, back to do the kicking. Maybe Mr. Horrell at UCLA could lend me one of his triple-threaters. He's got both Bob Waterfield and George Phillips back this year."

Which is the best, Mr. Horrell? Waterfield, your 1942 star, or Phillips, your 1941 star?

"There's little to choose between them. If the tape and braces hold out Waterfield should be the best passer and punter in the country. Phillips has been shifted from fullback to quarterback to help Waterfield. He's a 6-foot-3, 200-pounder who can really sprint and kick a ball a mile. We should have a strong first team, but I don't think you can compare it with our 1942 Rose Bowl squad. We'll win our share against college competition, but we'll probably take four good lickings from March Field, San Diego Naval, Alameda Coast Guard and St. Mary's Pre-Flight."

Now, gentlemen, let's hear from Mr. Alonzo Stagg, who has already taken a licking from a service team. His College of Pacific Tigers were beaten, 7-6, by the Fleet City Blue Jackets from Camp Shoemaker.

"Last year I had a perfect snap in coaching. All of my boys were fine football players at St. Mary's before they came to me. I didn't have a single jackass on the squad. But this year I expect to earn my salary. I haven't a regular or substitute from last year's team,

and only 10 of my 21 boys have ever played football at all. One end, Milhaupt, used to be a center; both guards, Semon and Cousins, and Pohl at quarterback have never played football before; Jackson at center played only one year of tackle in high school and Muenter was shifted from guard to fullback. Everything depends on how Fred Klemenok, our tailback, holds up. He looks like an excellent broken field runner and passer and both Mrs. Stagg and I like the way he runs the team."

Mr. Welch, for a man who lost 19 lettermen from his Washington Rose Bowl team, you are looking strangely cheerful.

"Well, gentlemen, every cloud has a silver lining. Mine happens to be Andy Walsh, a tranfer halfback from Edinboro State Teachers. He's the best passer we've ever had at Washington and should make a great difference in our team. Besides Andy, we have Jess Simpson, Keith DeCourcey, Bobo Moore, Bob Zech and Bob Gilmore, all veterans. In the line there's Gordon Berlin, a truly great center; Hank Melusky, a fine freshman end, and Jim McCurdy, a guard who used to play center for Stanford. Can any of you gentlemen tell me if those are redwoods or Southern Cal tackles I've been seeing all the way from Seattle."

Come clean, Mr. Cravath. Do you have another Rose Bowl team under your lash at Southern Cal?

"It's almost the same team that played in the Rose Bowl last season, so figure it out for yourself. Six of our first-stringers are lettermen: left end Don Hardy, left tackle John Ferraro, right tackle Marshall Romer, quarterback Jim Hardy, left half George Callanan and right half Gordon Gray. Another letterman, Milt Dreblow, backs up Gray. As I see it, gentlemen, football is war without guns, and who in the hell wants to lose a war?"

SPORTS SERVICE RECORD

HERE'S a new list of big-time athletes now operating in and around Hawaii: **Lt. Frank Leahy**, Notre Dame coach; **Lt. Johnny Beazley**, Cardinal pitching ace; **Lt. Bill Dickey** and **Ken Sears S1c**, former Yankee catchers; **Schoolboy Rowe S2c** and **Virgil Trucks S2c**, Great Lakes pitching stars. . . . **F/O Phil Marchildon**, former Athletics' pitcher, who was reported here as missing after a raid on Kiel, is now a PW in Germany. . . . To give you an idea how good the Great Lakes baseball team was, the poorest hitter of the regulars was **Gene Woodling** with a shameful .342 average. Great Lakes won 48 out of 50 games, a record that's comparable only to the Sampson Naval team, which won 26 of 27 starts.

GIs in Iran are comparing **S/Sgt. Urban Moeller**, right-hander from Scribner, Nebr., with Walter Johnson. They say Moeller has the same easy manner as Johnson, both were relaxed under pressure, both were farmers and you could tell it from the bleachers. . . . When **T-5 Al**

Hostak, former middleweight champ, shoved off for paratroop school he told chums at Camp Bowie: "I'll be taking all my dives feet first from now on." . . . **Moe Berg**, who can catch conversation in seven languages, is attached to the AMG staff in Rome as an interpreter. . . . **S/Sgt. Walt Judnich**, outfielder for the Seventh AAF team in Hawaii, is coming home because he suffers with asthma.

Killed in action: **Cpl. Jim Mooney**, former Georgetown All-American footballer and one of the greatest punters of the past 20 years, in France with the   Infantry Battalion. . *Died:* **CPO Gus Sonnenberg**, exponent of the flying tackle in wrestling, at the Bethesda Naval Hospital following siege of illness diagnosed as leukemia. . . . *Commissioned:* **Al Hust**, captain and end on Tennessee's 1942 Sugar Bowl team, as a second lieutenant in the Engineers. . . . *Transferred:* **Johnny Vander Meer S2c**, Cincinnati's double no-hit ace, from Sampson (N. Y.) Naval Center to the South Pacific; **S/Sgt. Greg Mangin**, ex-Davis Cup star and holder of the DFC and Purple Heart, from Fifteenth AF, Italy, to Redistribution Station, Miami, Fla. . . . *Discharged:* **Sammy Snead S1c**, pro golf star, from the Navy with a CDD because of a back injury.

SOCK TO SCIENCE. Ens. Charlie Keller, Yankee power hitter, does a blood count in the Merchant Marine Laboratory at Sheepshead Bay, N. Y. He's now aboard ship as junior purser-pharmacist's mate.

"SUBSTITUTION! CPL. MITNIK FOR PFC. BITCHWELL!"
—Pfc. Sam Dubin

YANK
THE ARMY WEEKLY

"ERNIE PYLE MISSPELLED HIS NAME."
—Sgt. Al Melinger

"LOOK, FELLAS, I'M A CIVILIAN!"
—Sgt. Tom Zibelli

"SO WHAT DO YOU PROPOSE TO DO—ROTATE ME OR BUST ME?"
—Pfc. Bill Keane

"OH, IT'S SOME NEW IDEA HE'S GOT FOR COMPANY PUNISHMENT."
—Pvt. Walter Mansfield

YANK

THE ARMY WEEKLY

5¢ **MAR. 30**
VOL. 3, NO. 41
1945

By the men . . . for the
men in the service

CALLING THE RANGE

The Battle for Mount Suribachi on Iwo Jima

THE FLAG GOES UP. In what promises to be one of this war's most famous and widely published pictures, men of the 28th Regiment, 5th Marine Division, set up the Stars and Stripes on the summit of Mount Suribachi on Iwo Jima. The volcanic mountain was taken from the Japs four days after the landing.

MOUNT SURIBACHI

e scaling of this peak on Iwo was revenge for the humiliation of Green Beach.

By Sgt. BILL REED
YANK Staff Correspondent

ITH THE 5TH MARINE DIVISION ON IWO JIMA —Anyone who landed there will tell you that naming the stretch of beach just of Mount Suribachi "Green Beach" was urate. "Coffee-Grounds Beach" would de the place better, for the iron-gray volcanic that covers the area resembles nothing so as the dregs in a coffee pot on Monday ng. Members of the 5th Marine Division anded here became extremely intimate with coffee grounds during the first 48 hours of vasion.

sand got into their eyes and caked around eyelashes. It became mixed in their hair gritty dandruff. It invaded small cans of ion ham and eggs as soon as they were d. It crept over the tops of the men's leg and worked to the bottom of their shoes. and was both friend and enemy. It made le digging easy, but it made fast move impossible for men and vehicles.

two days the men who landed on Green were pinned to the ground. Murderous ne-gun, sniper and mortar fire came from of pillboxes 300 yards away in the scrubby bery at the foot of the volcano. No one on each, whether he was a CP phone operator front-line rifleman, was exempt. The sight ead raised above a foxhole was the signal ens of Japs, safely hidden in concrete em nents, to open up. Men lay on their sides nk from canteens or to urinate. An errand en foxholes became a life-and-death mis or the man who attempted it.

two days the Marines stayed pinned to the beach in what seemed to many of them a hu miliating stalemate. Hundreds of green-clad bodies hugged the coffee grounds, spread out helplessly in a scattered pattern, furnishing marksmanship practice for the Japs on the moun tain with their telescopic gunsights.

The Marines had been hopelessly cut up and disorganized when they hit the beach. Their ve hicles bogged down in the sand when they were brought in. Their supplies were ruined. Many of their wounded still lay where they fell, in spite of the heroic efforts of the tireless medical corps men. Bad weather and a choppy ocean prevented the landings of many small boats on the second day and held up the supply of new ammunition and equipment and the evacuation of the wound ed. Though scores of dead marines lay every where, few of our troops had seen a single Jap, dead or alive.

TOWERING over them was Mount Suribachi, a gray, unlovely hulk with enemy pillbox chan cres in its sides. The marines on Green Beach grew to hate the mountain almost as much as they hated the Japs who were on it. Reaching the summit was almost as much of a challenge as destroying the men who defended it.

The supporting air and naval fire did much. Hour after hour of surface and air bombardment couldn't fail to wipe out many emplacements, imprison many Japs in their caves and slowly eat away the mountain fortress itself. But when it came to the specific four-foot-square machine gun emplacements and the still-smaller snipers' pillboxes, there was little the offshore and air bombardment could do except silence them for a few minutes. Everyone knew that in the end the foot troops would have to dig them out.

The foot troops made their drive on the third day. They were aided by a naval and air bom bardment so terrific that the Tokyo radio an nounced that the mountain itself was erupting. They were aided also by our own artillery and rocket guns, landed with superhuman effort the previous day in spite of a choppy ocean and the enemy's guns.

But the foot troops were aided most by the tanks that advanced with them and lobbed shells into the stone and concrete revetments that blocked the way of the foot troops. The Japs were afraid of our tanks. They ducked low in their shelters and silenced their guns when they saw the tanks coming. They had planted hun dreds of tank mines and had dug dozens of tank traps, but that is all they wanted to do. They didn't dare challenge our tanks with their guns.

As soon as the tanks had passed on or had been blown up by mines, the Japs came out of their holes and attacked our men from behind with machine guns and mortars. Between the foot of the volcano and Green Beach the enemy had hundreds of pillboxes and emplacements connected by a network of tunnels. When the Japs were driven from one pillbox, they would disappear until the marines advanced to another, and a moment later they would appear at their old emplacement, lobbing grenades at our men who had just passed.

BY early afternoon of D-plus-2 the Japs at the foot of Suribachi had been silenced. How ever, everyone knew there were still Japs around. There were Japs in the tunnels between the caves and there were Japs in the "spiderwebs"—the one-man sniper pillboxes—who would lift the camouflaged lids of their shelters and take pot

other members of the 5th Division waiting behind them, marines wriggle through the iron-gray sand toward Mount Suribachi, which is hidden by smoke.

Among the first to fall after the landings on Iwo Jima were these two marines who lie dead where they were going forward against the Japs.

After taking him away from the front lines where he was wounded by Jap mortar fi[re] four marines gently lower Cpl. W. H. Porter into a hollow in the volcanic sa[nd]

shots at marines trying to reorganize their outfits.

There were also many Japs who were dead. There were dead Japs in every conceivable contortion of men who meet death violently. Their arms and legs were wrenched about their bodies and their fists were clenched and frozen. Those who had been killed by flame throwers were burned to a black darker than the ashes of Suribachi or scorched to a brilliant yellow. Their clothes had been burned off, and the heat had vulcanized their buttocks together with ugly black strips. It was good to see these sights after having been pinned down to Green Beach for two terrible days.

There were dead marines too. Some platoons had been entirely stripped of their officers and noncoms. Some had lost more than three-fourths of their men since morning.

BUT the worst of the battle for Suribachi was over. Our men had fought their way in under the guns higher up on the mountain. Many of these guns had been knocked out by our tanks and artillery, and our naval and air bombardment. Many others couldn't be depressed far enough to menace our new positions.

There was still much to be done at the foot of the volcano. There were still many emplace-

ments to be cleaned out with flame throwers and tanks, and there were still snipers sneaking through the subterranean tunnels. The third afternoon a detachment of marines fought around one side of the mountain and another detachment fought around the other. Then they dug in for the night. At 0100 hours the Japs counterattacked. They kept coming until daybreak, but the marines held them back. And all day the Americans were busy cleaning out the tunnels, caves and concrete emplacements at the mountain's base.

On the fourth night S/Sgt. Ernest R. Thomas of Tallahassee, Fla., led a platoon whose officer had been killed; it was accompanied by the company's executive officer, 1st Lt. Harold G. Shrier of Richmond, Mo. They dug in for the night at the base of a tortuous path leading to the top of the mountain. It was a bad night. Rain streamed down the mountain in small rivulets that trickled under their clothes and washed the coffee grounds across their bodies. The cold wind made them shiver. They huddled in foxholes, keeping their weapons dry with their ponchos.

At 0800 hours the following morning they began the ascent. The volcanic sand on the steep path offered poor footing. Stubby plants broke off in the men's hands or pulled out by their roots. But the only resistance encountered was

the occasional ping of a sniper's bullet. As t[he] men reached the summit they found a few mo[re] emplacements that were manned by live Ja[ps.] These were cleaned out with flame throwe[rs,] BARs and satchel charges.

AT 1131 hours the Marines were in undisput[ed] control of the top of the volcano. Sgt. Her[bert] O. Hanson of Somerville, Mass., looked arou[nd] for a pole and found a lead pipe on the grou[nd.] At 1137 hours he with Lt. Schrier and other 5[th] Division Marines raised the American flag on t[he] topmost mound of Suribachi.

Far below, Green Beach was rapidly taking [on] the appearance of any other beachhead. The v[ol]canic sand was littered with abandoned equi[p]ment, and the shores were lined with boats d[e]livering more supplies and evacuating t[he] wounded. Far to the north other marines we[re] fighting the battle for Motoyama Airfield No. [1.]

Iwo Jima was far from being secured. But t[he] Marines were on the summit of Mount Suriba[chi,] the fortress that had made them wallow in co[ffee] grounds for two days. Not far from where the f[lag] flew, a communications man shouted, "This [is] easy," into his field phone.

The Marines intended to stay. The humiliati[on] of Green Beach had been avenged.

Knowing that some supposedly dead Japs may be playing possum, ready to pull a grenade, these marines use a sling to remove a body from a dugout.

During the fighting for Mount Suribachi two marines pour on the heat, cleani[ng] out Jap emplacements with flame throwers and blasting a path for the advan[ce]

Yanks at Home Abroad

ck-Book Blues

EW CALEDONIA—It's kind of lonesome these days at a certain Army dispensary here. . Stanley Pryzbyla has quit coming around. his healthy looking 190-pound typist in a Sig- Corps photographic lab has been on sick exactly 103 times in five months. He is proud his record but resents being known about the t as a goldbrick.

It was always legitimate stuff," he says.

irst he got some sort of fungus in his arm- s. That was cured in a few months. Then eone brought a cat into his tent, and Pryzbyla ke out in fleabites. After the fleabites the gus came back. All in all, it was just one nned thing after another.

Tone of this made life any easier for Pryzbyla. lieutenant jumped on him for missing so ch work. And his friends all called him a dbrick.

Things got so bad," Pryzbyla says, "that I ed the doctor to give me some salve to treat self. In the meantime the lieutenant went to Old Man about me missing so much work. ll, you know the regulations—they can't keep nan off the sick book, but they can make it gh for him. So the Old Man put out an order t the sick truck was to quit stopping off at service club. After that, things were pretty ing."

Pryzbyla is a well man now and hasn't seen inside of the dispensary for several weeks. e company clerk is a little sorry. "I was t getting to the point where I could spell his ne," he says.

—T-4 PRESTON CHARLES
YANK Field Correspondent

de and Seek

ITH THE 3D DIVISION IN FRANCE—Pfc. Walter Passon of Duluth, Minn., and Pfc. August dzall of Belleville, Kans., probably owe their es to the snottiness of a German tank driver. he two men had been separated from their fits and were wandering around the front at ht. First a flak wagon chased them, then sson lost his helmet. He saw it lying on the und by a house and started after it. He was tway there when a German soldier turned corner of the building, saw the helmet and ked it up.

Three more Germans followed that one, so the GIs beat it. Finally they came up to what y thought was a Yank tank. They hailed it ectionately, rapped on the side and called etings to the man standing in the turret. This just looked at them for a moment in the k, then turned contemptuously away without ing a word.

hen the Americans saw the Nazi markings the tank. As nonchalantly as they could, y turned around and walked back the way y came. When they were out of sight, they like hell. This time they were lucky. They right into an American CP.

—Pvt. ROBERT E. ABRAMS
YANK Field Correspondent

ki Litter

ITH THE 78TH DIVISION, GERMANY—Sgt. Waldren E. Bliss of Riverhead, N. Y., ent 19 months in the Pacific where there was snow before his transfer to the Western ont, but that didn't stop him from designing ski litter once he got here and saw how the ow made evacuation of the wounded even gher than usual.

Bliss, who is a section leader in the medical tion of the 1st Battalion, 311th (Timberwolf) giment, completed his first model in January d has built others since then.

The litter has cut evacuation time in some ses from 40 minutes to 7. As many as 23 casual- s have been hauled out of tight spots in a gle day. The litter has been pulled over mine ds without setting off charges and, although s used mainly for casualties, it has also hauled pplies to the front.

—Sgt. PETE KELLEY
YANK Field Correspondent

Nomenclature of Road, GI

ITH FIRST CONVOY TO CHINA OVER LEDO- BURMA ROAD—The official Public Relations name for this highway is "Pick's Pike," named for Brig. Gen. Lewis A. Pick, commanding the engineers who built it. But to thousands of GIs it has always been the Ledo Road, and it will probably remain that.

There has been considerable confusion over a fitting name. When our convoy pulled into Yunnanyi, most of us had agreed on "Ledo- Burma Road," but the first thing we saw was a giant sign reading, "WELCOME TO THE FIRST CON- VOY OVER THE STILWELL ROAD." Then a report stated Gen. Stilwell doesn't like that name be- cause it doesn't give credit to the Chinese who did most of the fighting to open it.

Now everyone calls it what he likes, espe- cially the drivers, who call it plenty. The latest report had at least three GIs agreeing on "Tokyo Turnpike."

—Sgt. DAVE RICHARDSON
YANK Staff Correspondent

Rocky

ALAPAGOS ISLANDS—When a guy smacks his lips after a drink of chlorinated water, just like it was Scotch; when he calls every rock he passes by name and greets a goat as he would his girl friend—then he is going "Rocky," which is the local equivalent of heading for a Section 8.

And if you see a GI weaving like a drunk in the distance, he's just wending his way among the rocks in as straight a line as possible. Many men say this method of locomotion will surely carry over into civilian life, distinguishing an ex- "Rock" dweller from one who spent his Army career doubled up in a foxhole or lying in a sack.

—Cpl. RICHARD W. DOUGLASS
YANK Staff Correspondent

Top-Blowing to Generals

UNMING, CHINA—The men stationed here don't tell it to the chaplain when they have something to bitch about. They tell it to the general.

The Red Cross has started a forum called the "Town Club," where GIs get a chance to sound off to invited brass. On two occasions already, Maj. Gen. Gilbert X. Cheves, CG of SOS in the China Theater, has been the guest target.

Topics at these first meetings were mostly limited to war strategy, rather than pet peeves.

INDIAN RELIEF. S/Sgt. Donald Thompson, (right) supervises natives loading .50-caliber ammunition belts for the 7th Bombardment Group, thus reliev- ing Air Force GIs in India and Burma for other work.

The Red Cross says that's because GIs are still a little reticent about blowing their tops before being absolutely sure the blowing won't boom- erang on them. But the project has been success- ful so far, and everyone thinks the discussions will get more and more frank as they go on.

—Cpl. JUD COOK
YANK Staff Correspondent

Backward Typists

RAN—A capable American stenographer, even a sassy one opposed to lap-sitting, could com- mand a high wage in Army offices here. Though many Persian girls have discarded the veil, few of them can speak English. Nor is there any such thing as shorthand in Persian.

Some Iranian girls have proved to be excellent typists, however. Correspondence is written in both English and Persian on double-column sheets. It would impress Ripley to watch an Iranian girl type quickly down one side of the sheet on an American machine, with the carriage moving from left to right, then slip the sheet into a Persian machine and type just as quickly in an entirely different alphabet, with the car- riage moving from right to left.

—Sgt. BURTT EVANS
YANK Staff Correspondent

FRONT LINE JUKE BOX. During the campaign on Luzon a group of Signal Corps men listen to the strains of "Let Me Call You Sweetheart," coming from an old Edison phonograph found in a deserted house.

NK, The Army Weekly, publication issued weekly by Branch Office, Information & Education Division, War Department, 205 East 42d Street, New York 17, N. Y. Reproduction rights restricted as indicated in the thead on the editorial page. Entered as second class matter July 6, 1942, at the Post Office at New York, N. Y., under the Act of March 3, 1879. Subscription price $3.00 yearly. Printed in the U. S. A.

"Easy does it!"

Crew chief and kibitzer prepare dinner.

Blimps

Text and Sketches by Cpl. Ernest Maxwell

THE Navy blimps used to patrol the U. S. coasts can do almost anything. Blimps kept aloft with helium can hang motionless over a target or they can make a mile a minute; they can be brought down to within a few feet of the water or reach an altitude of 8,000 feet. Heavy weather doesn't mean much to a blimp unless it is trying to land in a strong ground gale; in that case it means trouble for the ground crew.

Blimps are particularly effective against submarines because of the all-around vision their crews have, plus the help of mechanical spotting devices. Blimps can put up a fight if attacked but like better to drop TNT on unsuspecting subs.

They're extremely good at rescuing flyers downed at sea; on such jobs they cut off both their engines and get down almost to the surface of the water. Sometimes they also make rescues from isolated ground areas. A Navy pilot once picked up four men, one of whom had died from exposure, from a desolate spot in the California desert. Both propellers of the blimp were bent in the process. The pilot received the Distinguished Flying Cross.

Our blimps have an advantage over the lighter-than-aircraft of other countries in that the U. S. has a monopoly on helium, which is comparatively safe. The only other gas that can be used for airships is hydrogen, which is touchy, highly inflammable stuff.

When a blimp's fuel supply is gone, it becomes a free balloon and can stay up indefinitely. Blimps consume about half as much fuel as heavier-than-aircraft.

Most of the duty time aboardship is spent sweating out subs and other objects in the water subject to patrol. Facilities for relaxation are limited on a blimp.

The machine age gets its start.

"Halt! Who goes there?"

Left: Lots of chow for the cruise.

Above: There are many hours in a day.

Right: A cozy corner in the 'dining hall.'

"Where the hell did that destroyer g

By Pfc. DEBS MYERS
YANK Staff Writer

Arthur H. Vandenberg

WASHINGTON, D. C.—As a onetime reporter, and by his own words a good one, U. S. Sen. Arthur H. Vandenberg believes that one fact is worth five fancy adjectives. On January 1, on the Senate floor, this Michigan Republican stated some views about American foreign policy which may have an important bearing on history. In simple language Vandenberg urged that the United States sign a treaty with her major allies guaranteeing the use of force, if necessary, to keep Germany and Japan disarmed forever.

Most newspapers and magazines hailed Vandenberg's speech as a powerful contribution toward international cooperation; he received 60,000 telegrams, many of them from servicemen. Almost all the telegrams praised the speech. A man in Philadelphia wired: "Finally an understandable speech — made by a man without marbles in his mouth."

Time said: "In bold, constructive terms, the No. 1 Republican spokesman for foreign affairs, long an isolationist, told the U. S. Senate that it was time for the U. S. to stop talking about world collective security and do something to make it real. . . . It might well prove to be the most important speech made by an American in World War II."

Some publications praised the address with reservation. The New York *Herald Tribune,* for instance, said: "At times, Vandenberg seems to recognize this as a struggle for national existence; at others, he seems to see it as one from which we could retire unless all our more idealistic notions were fulfilled."

On the other hand, columnist Walter Lippmann thought it might be one of the few speeches likely to "affect the course of events."

And the London *Daily Telegraph* said: "Sen. Vandenberg, who exercises more influence over Congress than any other Republican, has seized the occasion of the three-power conference to urge with greater vigor than ever that America should now pledge her constant armed cooperation in a collective security scheme with all her major allies."

In his Senate office, after the first tumult over the speech had died down, Vandenberg peered quizzically through rimless spectacles at a stack of telegrams, lighted a denicotinized cigar—the only kind he smokes — and said he wished he were as influential as he had been 40 years ago.

"Forty years ago when I was 20," he said, "in my home town of Grand Rapids, Mich., I was City Hall reporter on the Grand Rapids *Herald.* Made $25 a week and ran the municipal government from the side lines. Never been so influential before or since. There are days when I wonder why a fellow leaves a job on the brick pile to get out front where other people can throw bricks at him. The trouble with authority is that responsibility goes with it."

Not that Vandenberg doesn't like being a United States senator. He likes it good. He has been in the Senate since 1928 and has risen steadily in his party's councils. Both in 1936 and in 1940 he was mentioned as a GOP Presidential possibility, and this talk has been revived by his foreign-affairs speech. The President has named him one of this country's delegates to the United Nations conference to be held in San Francisco April 25—a sure sign of the influence Vandenberg is felt to wield on foreign policy.

Vandenberg stands over 6 feet and weighs more than 200 pounds. He has sparse gray hair, chews gum when he can buy it and takes an occasional highball.

After graduation from Grand Rapids High School in 1900 he got a job as clerk in a cracker factory. When he was fired for going to see Theodore Roosevelt in a parade, he went to work on the Grand Rapids *Herald* as an office boy. Later he became state editor and reporter at $8 a week. In 1906, at the age of 22, Vandenberg became managing editor. He directed the paper's news gathering, wrote editorials, solicited advertising, looked after circulation. Before he was 30, Vandenberg was considered the "editor, oracle and orator" of Grand Rapids.

Vandenberg's first wife, Elizabeth Watson, died in 1916. She was the mother of his three children —two daughters and a son. In 1918 he married Hazel H. Whittaker, a newspaper woman. His son, A. H. Vandenberg Jr., is a captain at MacDill Field in Florida. He came in as a private.

Vandenberg was appointed to the Senate in 1928 to fill the unexpired term of a senator who had died in office. Later that year, he was elected and has served without interruption since.

THE chief cause of this war, in Vandenberg's view, is simple: Failure of the Allies to keep Germany demilitarized.

"Had adequate control been established over German armaments," he said, "GIs would be home now—not fighting in Germany. Obviously, therefore, it is to our American interest—as well as to the interest of Britain, Russia, France, all the European countries—that we don't make the same mistake again and find ourselves with World War III on our hands.

"Therefore, since this is one common interest that we all can agree on, I propose that we shall immediately say so in a hard and fast agreement among the Allies under which the United States will promise to do her full part, with force, if necessary, to keep Germany and Japan demilitarized for keeps.

"When we do that, we will accomplish some other important things. We will eliminate the major reason which our allies give to justify their plans to carve up Europe into zones of special privilege and special interest. Whenever our allies propose to annex some other country, it is always on the plea that they must do it to protect themselves against another world war with Germany. When we take away this reason, we remove the greatest obstacle to a just peace, and only a just peace can be a permanent peace."

That, said Vandenberg, is the sum and substance of his Senate speech. "One reason people liked it," he asserted, "was that they understood it."

Vandenberg emphasized that he didn't want American soldiers serving for a long period as occupation troops. "Immediately following our victory," he said, "there is going to be an unavoidable period when there will have to be military occupation of Germany and Japan pending the time when stable civil governments can be restored. There is no way the Army can avoid this limited postwar service in some degree. But our Army should come home as soon as stable civil government is restored. I don't want to see our men doing a permanent policing job. The organization to handle this supervision of the defeated enemy nations is the new peace league representing the United Nations."

This job of supervision, Vandenberg believes, will largely be one of detection in which trained Allied agents will see to it that Germany and Japan never again have the chance to build up their armament industries.

Vandenberg predicted that this nation's postwar Army and Navy will be composed entirely of volunteers. About compulsory military training, he said: "I want it definitely understood that I'm indefinite about compulsory military training. I want an adequate national defense regardless of treaties. I think compulsory military training should be our last recourse. But I won't run

from it if it becomes necessary. I don't want the country to make a snap judgment about it. I think the men now in the Army and Navy should have their say about it. They know more about it than anyone else. I'm in the show-me class."

About the GI Bill of Rights, of which he was one of the five original authors, Vandenberg said: "We undertook to be as liberal as possible in an over-all program for the benefit of the veterans. I don't want to tamper with it until I see it work. I think weak spots will develop. When they do, they must be promptly corrected."

WHY did Vandenberg abandon isolationism to come out for full American partnership in world affairs? "I never thought of myself as an isolationist," he said. "I was a noninterventionist, or maybe an America First internationalist. In the middle 1930s I was one of the nine Republicans who voted for the World Court.

"What finally happened was this: Up to World War II we thought we enjoyed the isolation of World War I. Since Pearl Harbor the awful mechanisms of war have made such progress that there is no geographical isolation left to us. I recognize this as a physical fact. Contemplate a war of push buttons in which human flesh and blood are at the mercy of mechanized disaster. No nation hereafter can immunize itself by its own exclusive action. Only collective security can stop the next great war before it starts."

Vandenberg wanted it made plain that he writes his own speeches, pecking them out at night on his office typewriter. "I wrote about 20 drafts of my foreign-affairs speech before I finally delivered it," he said. "I had been thinking for about a year that someone should deliver such a speech. Then I got to wondering who should do it. Finally I decided I was the fellow to do the job. And I did it."

DUEREN on the Roer

One of the few things left standing in flattened Dueren was this 25-foot statue of Bismarck, which is now strung with U. S. Army Signal Corps telephone wire

In the battle to cross the last water barrier before the Rhine, two Infantry companies carried the main burden of the assault.

By Sgt. ED CUNNINGHAM
YANK Staff Correspondent

DUEREN, GERMANY—This is the city that lived on borrowed time for three months. Its first brush with doom came last November when American troops drove to the west bank of the Roer, just 40 yards across from the city. Already shattered by Allied air attacks, Dueren—the key city in a road network leading to the Cologne plain—looked like a comparative push-over for the hard-driving First Army forces.

That 40-yard gap was a slim lease on life but it was sufficient for the time being, thanks to the dam system which regulated the flow of water. The dams controlled 160,000,000 cubic feet of water, and the Germans controlled the dams. By blowing two main dams, Schwammenauel and Urfttalsperre, they could inundate the river valley and trap any Allied troops attempting a crossing. Dueren could not be taken until the dams were captured or neutralized. So the First Army units attacked toward the town of Schmidt, the key to the dam defenses. The threat of flood held up our advances and saved Dueren.

Dueren's second reprieve came in mid-December when Von Runstedt's forces crashed through the Ardennes. That automatically

stymied the Allied thrust toward Schmidt. It was not until late in January, when the German counteroffensive had been rolled back beyond the Belgian border, that we could resume our push toward the dam sites.

U. S. First Army troops took Schmidt on February 8 and moved on toward Schwammenauel, the largest of the four dams. But two days later, before we could secure the dam, the Germans opened the flood gates and blew the control gates. The roaring waters rushed west toward Dueren, raising the river level eight feet, flooding the lowlands and doubling the speed of the current. An assault crossing under such conditions was all but impossible, so our First and Ninth Armies had to sit back and wait for the flood to subside.

But Dueren couldn't hold out forever. Its bluff was called on February 23 when the First Army's 8th and 104th Divisions launched a joint assault. Dueren was captured. Here is how it happened:

COMPANY K of the 13th Infantry, 8th Division, had chow at midnight—steak, potatoes, bread, butter, coffee and doughnuts. Some of the men ate it standing around in the mud and rubble of the skeletonized village of Guerzenich. Others carried it back to their billets in the cellars, where they could eat in comparative comfort. There was still an hour before we were to start for the battalion-assembly area on the west bank of the Roer, opposite Dueren.

"That was a pretty good meal," one K company man remarked as he came back for seconds on coffee. "It ought to be," somebody in the mess line said. "If those motors break down tonight,

we'll have to paddle across that damned river and you'll need plenty of energy. The Army's got that angle figured out. What else do you think they are feeding you steak for?"

Some members of the assault teams gave the cooks some last-minute advice when they go their chow. "Don't make the coffee too sweet tomorrow morning," one said. "And let's have some sunny-side-ups for a change," another suggested. "Stop beating hell out of the eggs and serve 'em up the way the hen lays 'em."

"You guys will be lucky if those Krauts give you time enough to eat D rations, let alone ho food," one of the cooks replied.

A couple of rounds of Jerry artillery landed on the other side of the village, rattling the already teetering walls of its shattered houses. "The Jerries must be getting nervous," somebody said

Inside one of the shattered houses the 2d Platoon of K Company was waiting for 0100 T/Sgt. John Demeduk, the platoon sergeant from Ramsey, N. J., and the platoon leader, a second lieutenant, were testing the release valves on their life belts. Pvt. Francis (Doc) Marone, the platoon medic from the Bronx, N. Y., was stretched out on a Jerry mattress on the floor whistling "I'll Walk Alone." Several others were sitting around smoking.

T/Sgt. Edward Kuiken of Fair Lawn, N. J., the mortar-platoon sergeant, came in. "Ready, willing and able?" he asked.

"Able, anyhow," someone answered.

"Say, Ed," the lieutenant said to Kuiken, "I believe we are going to run into trouble at the corner of that *Sportpalast*. The Jerries probably

ave a strongpoint there. So be ready to lay some
if we need help."

"You let me know when you want it, and I'll
laster hell out of them," Kuiken assured him,
en added: "Well, I guess I better shove. It's 10
. Take it easy, you guys, and good luck."

He turned to the lieutenant and put out his
and. "Good luck, Johnny—I mean lieutenant.
ell, I keep forgetting you're an officer now."

"Don't let it bother you," the lieutenant said.
Good luck, Ed. See you over there."

They shook hands firmly, like two men who
njoyed knowing each other. It was a token of
utual respect that knew no rank—respect that
me from fighting together and each one know-
g just what the other could do in a tight spot.
Kuiken and the lieutenant were old K company
en. They joined it together back in 1941, as
rivates at Fort Jackson, S. C. Both were platoon
rgeants when the 8th Division came to France.
ohnny got a battlefield commission for leader-
ip at Brest, when his platoon leader was injured
nd he had to take over. He also got wounds
ere that hospitalized him for four months. He
ad rejoined the company two weeks ago, and
night would be his first action as an officer.

It was 0055. The lieutenant said, "Let's hit it."
he platoon moved out on the moonlit main street
nd fell in with the 1st and 3d Platoons.

"Take it easy with the grenades on those
erry cellars," Doc Marone said. "That's where
ey keep the cognac."

Another voice in the darkness said, "I'd like a
ree-day pass starting immediately."

"Okay, you got it," the lieutenant said. "Only
's made out to Dueren."

"If the Jerries knew what I know," a man in
e front rank said, "they'd be heading back to
erlin right now."

"Yeah," the guy behind him said, "and maybe
you knew what the Jerries know you'd be
eading back to Indiana."

As they moved off in single file on each side
the rubble-heaped street, one optimist said,
Hell, the war might be all over tomorrow."

"Yeah," somebody added. "All over Dueren."

THE artillery began at 0245. Four battalions of
it, two lights and two mediums, delivered
housands of shell-encased notices to the defenders
f Dueren. They fell first on the east bank of the
ver, then on the waterfront buildings, then
astward toward the center of the city, so that
ll of Dueren would know that the mortgage on
is part of Hitler's Reich was being foreclosed.

When the artillery lifted at 0330, the infantry
oved off the west bank to enforce Dueren's
viction notice. Rubber assault boats, powered by
0-horsepower outboard motors, were supposed
o carry the infantry across the treacherous cur-
ent. The motors were to have been warmed up
hile the artillery covered their noise, until the
ery minute before departure. But most of the
otors failed to start. So the infantrymen, who

were supposed to be passengers on this trip,
finished by working their own way, as usual—
this time by paddling instead of walking.

German mortar and artillery fire raked the
bank where the 13th Infantry was making ready
to cross the swirling river. The second lieutenant
of K Company, who was going into action as an
officer for the first time, never even got into his
boat. A mortar burst that landed five feet from
him knocked him out and temporarily deafened
his platoon sergeant, Demeduk. The lieutenant
was returned to the hospital, this time suffering
from concussion and possible internal injuries.
Demeduk was able to stay with the platoon, but
because of his temporary disability, S/Sgt. Harry
B. Laws Jr. of Syracuse, N. Y., took over as
platoon sergeant for the assault.

Meanwhile 1st Lt. Morton S. Mock of Batavia,
N. Y., had landed his Company K assault team on
the enemy-held bank. Less than 50 yards away, a
Jerry machine gun was spraying the other assault
boats coming across. all of which had great
difficulty staying afloat in the rushing current.

Sgt. Bertram West of Meadville, Pa., crawled up
the bank, then into the Jerry trenches and made
his way around behind the MG nest. He threw a
grenade into the hole, routing the three-man
crew. Two tried to make a break for it. West
killed one with his tommy gun, and a BARman,
Pfc. Ray Adamson of King Hill, Idaho, killed the
second. The third Jerry surrendered.

Pfc. Anthony Woody was in another K Company boat. Just as the boat beached, the swirling
waters caught it and carried it away. Seven men
managed to jump clear, but Woody and another
soldier were swept helplessly downstream with
it. A German machine gun sprayed them relent-
lessly, and Woody's companion was killed.

By grabbing the branches of an overhanging
tree, Woody finally got free of the boat and
ashore, only to find that his haven was directly
in front of another enemy machine-gun crew.
He was captured by the gun crew. As the
American troops gradually forced the Germans
to retreat, his captors moved Woody from one
house to another. Late next afternoon they
ordered him to load a wounded German soldier
on a wagon, preparatory to evacuating that part
of town. Just then a platoon of the 104th Division
attacked the area. They shot the horse and the
driver of the wagon and liberated Woody.

Woody, who ran a barber shop in Afton, Okla.,
before the Army made him a rifleman, has only
a skinned ear to show for his experience—where
an MG bullet grazed him while he was in the
boat. His buddies claim it's one for the books when
a barber gets an ear-clipping job himself.

The treacherous current of the swollen Roer
almost proved disastrous to the crossing. Boats
were swept downstream and crashed into the
pilings of a knocked-out bridge that once connected Dueren with the west bank, and many of
the occupants were drowned. Of those who
escaped, some were wounded by enemy fire or

suffered from exhaustion so they couldn't return
to duty immediately despite the critical need of
infantrymen to hold the small bridgehead which
had been established by I and K Companies.

Meanwhile the Germans, profiting from their
well-prepared positions, hung a curtain of mortar,
artillery and MG fire on the river. At daylight,
the intense concentration of fire made it all but
impossible to get more troops across. Two flying
ferries—assault boats tied to trees on our side
and manipulated so that the current carried them
across—were knocked out in less than an hour,
and a footbridge suffered the same fate.

In the city of Dueren, I and K Companies
fought savagely against overwhelming odds.
Forced to carry the load of what was to have
been an entire regiment's attack, these two
companies held out against repeated German
counterattacks and continued to advance slowly
in the city. After 14 hours of fighting practically
on their own, the two units finally got aid at 2200,
when the other companies got across on two
newly established flying ferries. Next morning a
bridge was built on the pilings of Dueren's
original structure and reinforcements poured in
in to help I and K Companies clear the city.

DUEREN, the queen city of the Roer, is nothing
more than a heap of rubble today. Only four
civilian residents of the city's peacetime population of 30,000 are here to see the powdered monument to Germany's dream of conquest.

Oddly enough, one of the few relatively intact
structures in the pulverized city is the 25-foot
monument to Bismarck, Germany's empire
builder of former days. He stands in the middle
of a square whose surrounding buildings have
been reduced to rubble. In his left hand is his
sword, symbol of the power he wielded over Germany's neighbors. In his right is a scroll bearing
the inscription: "Versailles, 18 January, 1871."
That was the date of the restoration of the German Empire at the expense of France.

But the Americans made two modifications in
the statue of Bismarck, neither of which would
have been appreciated by the sculptor or the
people of Dueren who, as the tablet says, "caused
it to be erected in memory of the eminent Reich
Chancellor." Draped over his left shoulder and
resting between the thumb and forefinger with
which he is grasping his sword is a U. S. Army
Signal Corps telephone wire, strung up by an
unawed GI who used the statue as a telephone
pole in the otherwise flattened area.

The other modification is a shell hole, about the
size of a silver dollar, piercing the scroll in his
right hand and cutting off the top of "V", in
Versailles. The American modification of Germany's 19th Century empire builder doesn't stop
there. With true poetic justice, the shell continued
on through the tail of his knee-length military
coat and lodged in the very spot where many of
the subject people of his empire would often
have liked to ram it.

st Lt. Morton S. Mock (left) talks with Pfc. Tony Woody, who was a prisoner for 15 hours after crossing the Roer.

T/Sgt. John Demeduk, platoon sergeant of K Company's 2d Platoon, speaks into his walkie-talkie.

An engineer lies where he was hit and killed by mortar fire as he was crossing the Roer.

Roer Patrol

Before the final break-through that took Dueren, individual patrols did the delicate job of preliminary reconnaissance.

By Sgt. RALPH MARTIN
Stars & Stripes Correspondent

WITH THE NINTH ARMY IN GERMANY—The war was sleeping on both sides of the Roer River, just as it had been sleeping almost every night for weeks and weeks. There were no war sounds, no sounds at all anywhere, except the loud rushing noise of the river itself.

Then suddenly out of the thick mist came the shadows—35 skinny shadows and 10 fat ones. The skinny ones spread out soundlessly along the river bank, flattened themselves on the ground and got their rifles and BARs into position. The fat shadows—face-blackened soldiers wearing Mae Wests—slid into a waiting assault boat and pushed off.

Lt. Roy (Buck) Rogers looked at his watch. It was 1900 hours. So far, so good.

But suddenly the current grabbed the boat, swept it against some debris and tipped it to one side. Just as suddenly the air was filled with flares slicing open the fog. Kraut machine guns started splattering all around the boat, and mortars started plopping in close. The 10 soldiers were no longer fat shadows; they were desperate, fast-moving men, sitting in a spotlight, shifting their positions, trying to get away from the debris and to keep their boat afloat.

On the bank, still stretched out silently, were the 35 skinny shadows. Finally Buck Rogers in the boat grabbed his walkie-talkie. "Fire 15. Fire 17. Fire 25. Repeat. Fire 19. Repeat. Repeat." Seconds after he spoke, the skinny shadows were speaking with their guns.

Even in this blinding mist there was no guess firing. Every Kraut position had been preobserved and located and numbered. 1st Lt. Carl Aamont had spent several days in careful reconnaissance. Everything now was pinpoint precision. Behind the 35 skinny shadows were several heavy-weapons platoons waiting to supply overhead fire, also at numbered targets. Alongside them were some mortar sections.

"Fire 23. Repeat. Repeat."

For a short time the flares stopped. Soon the boat reached the other bank, and three of the fat shadows stayed behind to take care of it—pull it out and hide it. These three were engineers from C Company of the 327th Engineers, temporarily assigned to Buck Rogers' Raiders.

The other seven scooted up the banks and stopped in the wooded slope near the top of the dyke. The dyke top was a long stretch of dirt path, 10 feet wide. "We called it Lovers' Lane," says S/Sgt. Chris Lorenz, one of the seven. "There was a lot of grassy lawn and there were plenty of benches still sitting there. And there were lots and lots of bushes."

Like most of the seven, Lorenz had been here many times before. Crossing the Roer was just a routine job for Rogers' Raiders. And Lovers' Lane was an old friend. It was an old friend because there was this sharp slope that you could hide behind and there were all these thick bushes.

Meanwhile Lt. Rogers was scouring all over everywhere, making his recon-report check-up, finding out what he had been sent over to find out. Buck Rogers insists on going out on almost all the nightly raids. He likes to kill Germans. Two of his kid brothers were killed on this front.

Lorenz likes to kill Germans too. He watched a flare-throwing Kraut having a bull session with a buddy. He waited, frozen still, until the two started walking toward him, then he told his two boys "Now." When their rifles opened up, both Krauts dropped. One of them was still moaning, and Lorenz lobbed over a grenade.

"I always like to make sure," he says.

On the other side of the river, less than 150 yards away, Lt. Aamont was coordinating the mortars and MGs with the rifles and BARs. On the right flank our mortars were dropping three or four rounds a minute, sealing off the raid area.

Meanwhile Lorenz was making a sightseeing tour of the two MG positions. The first was empty because the Krauts were crawling into holes. Pfc. William Drisko spotted one and ordered him to come out with hands up, because the patrol had been told to bring back some PWs. But this Kraut didn't answer; he just kept breathing hard. The breathing turned into moaning when Drisko dropped a grenade into the hole.

"Now, will you come out?" he said in German.

The Kraut complained that he would if he could, but he couldn't because both his legs were broken. He suggested that Drisko come in and get him. Drisko replied by taking another grenade and threatening a repeat performance. The Kraut finally did come out, both legs dangling. He said there weren't any more Germans in the hole, but the skeptical Lorenz yelled, *"Gib auf* (give up)." And, sure enough, another Kraut popped up right in front of him, crying out, *"Polski—nicht schiessen* (Polish—don't shoot)."

"They all claim they are Polish as soon as they are captured," says Lorenz, who knows better. Lorenz was born in Munich in 1922, lived there for eight years before moving to Chicago, Ill., then came back to Europe for a full year in 1936 during the Olympics. He has a Bronze Star with Cluster. "All my relatives are in the German Army," he says. "I wouldn't be surprised if I've killed some of them already."

Buck Rogers now took the other five men ward the second gun position. But before th reached it they bumped into two Germans wa ing fast through the mist, their hands up hi Both quickly explained they were no longer terested in this war. Buck Rogers was going take the wounded PW along with them, but wh the Krauts lifted him he screamed in pain. they left him there.

"I guess the lieutenant was right," says Lore "A wounded guy is a lot more trouble to th Krauts than a dead guy."

Coming back over the Roer, Lorenz baw out, *"Tiefer und haerter* (deeper and harde to the four Krauts doing the paddling. Everybe else was yelling and laughing and cursing.

"We were just feeling good," says Pfc. J McDonald, who studied engineering at Purdue the ASTP. "We were just letting off some ste because we were all still alive, I guess."

THEY were lucky this time. No casualties. last time, 7 out of 12 guys on one patrol Purple Hearts.

But this 43-minute raid was an important, s cessful raid. The patrol did some vital reconna sance, took care of two MG nests, and brou back four PWs.

That's their main job always—to bring some them back alive. That's what the Raiders w first organized for in the first week of Janu The regimental colonel of the 407th was hav lots of trouble with his patrols. Lots of casual and not many PWs. So he called in Buck Rog and Aamont, and told them about an article had read in the *Infantry Journal* about ba patrols composed of small groups of men v did nothing else. Then he told them it was tl baby if they wanted it. They wanted it.

The two loueys called for volunteers and fir ly picked 42 who represented every company this regiment of the 102d Division. Most of th weren't old enough to vote. Most of them w kids who had been yanked out of ASTP coll training when the Army cut it down. Not all college kids, though. S/Sgt. Frank Bartholiv who has a Silver Star and Purple Heart, wa coal miner in Pittsburgh, Pa. He's an old ma the outfit; he's 25. Then there is Pfc. Chief Bea an American Indian from Prescott, Ariz., fought with the ski troops against the Japs Attu.

They volunteered to join Buck Rogers' Raic because they liked the idea of resting during day and going out on patrols at night, or beca they wanted to kill Germans, or because t couldn't get along in their own outfits, or sim because they were young and this sounded lil wonderfully crazy thing to do.

They're the first to admit how young they because they're proud of it.

It was 19-year-old Pvt. Ed Diamond rubbed his beardless chin and said: "The Gill razor-blade people would have a hell of a trying to make any money out of this outfit

Coming up like a mole from underground, where he had been overlooked in mopping-up operations, a German soldier surrenders to Lt. Roy (Buck) Rogers.

Two German snipers raise white handkerchiefs and surrender to U. S. sol on the banks of the Roer. They gave away their position by firing on the Ya

Alaska Sweats It Out

SINCE KISKA, AUGUST 15, 1943, THE BIGGEST BATTLE FOR THE NORTHERN "SNOWFEET" HAS BEEN AGAINST WEATHER LIKE THIS BLIZZARD NEAR FAIRBANKS

Dogfaces on the mainland and in the Aleutian Chain watch the war go by on other fronts, stare out toward the Kuriles and wonder if there's anything cooking.

By Cpl. JOHN M. HAVERSTICK
YANK Staff Correspondent

ALASKA AND THE ALEUTIANS—A corporal said this about the scarcity of combat in Alaska: "We are closeted here in Alaska and the Aleutians like a woman in confinement until the war is over, or else we may become the mother of another offensive. And we all wish we knew which."

The radio stations in Alaska and the Aleutians still sign on and off with slogans like "Broadcasting to you from the northern highway to victory." The foxholes dug during the battle are still on Attu but they are just in the way during practice alerts. The Infantry and Engineers and AAF stumble into the snow-covered holes they forgot were there.

The Aleutians have gone GI to a point where the men stand regular Saturday hut inspections and you no longer turn your back to the wind and use any place on the ground for a latrine. The only reason any soldier on Attu has worn a helmet since July 1943 is a standing rule of the mess halls—"No helmet, no chow."

Just after Kiska, a year and a half ago, most of the war was detoured from this shortest route to Tokyo, and nobody knew then, and nobody knows yet, whether it will ever come through again. So the war in Alaska is mostly against doubt as to whether this theater still matters.

"Look at the maps we use now," says Cpl. Paul C. Legette of San Francisco, Calif. "They aren't even global. There isn't room on them for the Aleutians to be near Japan where they belong, so they are stuck in a box by themselves down in the lower right-hand corner near Seattle."

Not that the men here wouldn't prefer a base near Seattle or that the combat crewmen really want any more combat than they have right now. But what they would all like to know is where they stand in importance.

Actually, of course, Alaska and the Aleutians have been important since Kiska. The ground in the Aleutians is so soft it trembles every time heavy construction equipment passes over it, and the huts on the soft muskeg have trembled ever since Kiska. During all that time the Engineers have been building up bases with airstrips and docks and warehouses for any kind of war that might come.

During the construction period Japan has not been able to return to the islands because of Aleutian-based Army and Navy bombers and Navy task forces that have been crossing 600-odd miles of the North Pacific to raid the Japanese Kuriles. The Kuriles have been hit as regularly as the crews could make it through the fog and wind.

THE Aleutian Chain is the place most soldiers in Alaska want to stay away from. There are very few who like the islands. One of these rare birds is T-4 Dashiell Hammett, 50-year-old author of "The Thin Man" and "The Maltese Falcon." "Why do I like it here?" Hammett sometimes asks. "I don't know—maybe it's the humidity. It slows you up and irritates you, and maybe I like that." When Hammett shows visitors around, he asks how they like *his* mountains.

T-5 Erwin Spitzer, on the other hand, is tired of the mountains. "The scenery here," he says, "is something I've grown very cold about."

Fog covers the Aleutians and the wind has blown down many of the buildings put up by the Engineers. Except for the new Army posts, the islands are barren, and there is nothing queer about a man who has not troubled himself in a year to hitchhike outside his own company area for a look around. All the scenery any man really wants to see is outside Alaska and the Aleutians. They tell about a deckhand on a small power barge who hatched a scheme for escaping from the Chain on his small interisland ship. The place he hoped to reach was Siberia.

On chances for rotation some soldiers quote the king-size ravens that live off the islands. What the ravens say, of course, is "Nevermore."

There are towns near the camps on the Alaska mainland, but on the Chain our men have had to build up islands where there are no towns and no women. A major in the Medics made a survey of his island to find out what happened to these men after a year and a half. The major decided that nothing very serious happened except to the men who would have tripped on the street curbs of their own home towns. He decided that the Aleutians are, strangely enough, a healthier—and safer—place than most overseas theaters.

Rusty Annabel, a war correspondent for United Press and a pre-war resident of Alaska, has never wanted to transfer out of the theater, even though he could be rotated. The reason is that he still thinks he can sweat out Tokyo through the Chain.

Tokyo Rose of Radio Tokyo is still interested in Alaska and the Aleutians, and the theater is humorously important for that reason if for no other. Rose's stories furnish free entertainment to the island-isolated GIs. There is one yarn about the general who flew to the mainland on TD. This general's house caught fire shortly after he left and his plane picked up a radio report describing the fire and telling him he'd better get back. The report, of course, came from Tokyo Rose. According to another of Rose's fables a Jap sub took pictures of one island over a period of days; then the crew came ashore to the island one night and printed their pictures in the airbase photo lab.

THE boys go on listening to Rose for the laughs and wait. The air crews get action now and again, photographing the Kuriles and bombing them. The AAF has hit the Kuriles as far south as Shimushiru, less than 1,000 miles north of Tokyo. And twice in 1944, Matsuwa, 1,100 miles north of the Jap capital, was shelled by a Navy surface force of the Aleutian-based North Pacific fleet.

Except for these air and water excursions, it's still a campaign of boredom in the North, but every soldier knows that in one way or another Alaska does fit into the over-all Pacific picture. Where it fits, though, they don't know. That makes the boredom harder to sweat out—that and the fact that Alaska doesn't have the proper climate to go with sweating.

HUSKIES ABROAD. These team drivers and their dogs are on the Western Front not in the Far North. They picked up wounded soldiers during winter snowsto

PRIVATE STOCK. A Filipino school teacher (center) saved a bottle of whisky for three years to offer Americans when they came back to Luzon. Left and right are Pfc. William Gee and T/Sgt. Floyd Aden.

TUNING. In technical terms, Pvt. Russell Myers of the Signal Corps is che line sag on this pole in France, using the oscillation method for proper wire te

RISKY JOB. A Coast Guardsman clings to a rail as he tries to clear away loose fender from the deck of a tanker in churning South Pacific seas.

DUTCH TREAT. Dressed in their native costumes, these little Hollanders were for a walk by GIs visiting the home in which 145 of them are cared for by

ON ICE. Like everyone else MPs have off-duty hours and these particular ones njoying theirs by spending an afternoon skating in the city of Reykjavik, Iceland.

STOPPING THE SHOW. At a GI night club in Belgium with Belgian entertainers and a soldier dance band, T-5 Walter Goldberg steps before the microphone to sing "Good Night Ladies."

PER LOAD. Bomb-bay doors open and tons of bombs pour out of these B-29s as they fly r enemy positions in Burma. Their target was a Jap supply depot near Rangoon.

C-Y HATS. This is one way of enjoying your off-duty time. In Paris these three visited a famous shop and got a kick out of trying on the latest in spring hats.

TESTING. Barbara Chambliss doesn't need to test. The water is warm, being the Gulf of Mexico, but all the same it's a very nice pose.

THE SAD SACK   "ORGANIZATION"

SGT. GEORGE BAKER

Heavy Dough

Dear YANK:

I have been very lucky with the little white cubes, but I hear tell that I will not be able to bring all my dough back into the States when I finally do get home. The way I get it, I can only bring back $50 in cash. Is that right or is someone kidding me?

Solomon Islands   —Pfc. JAMES WALTERS

■ They're kidding you. There is a Treasury regulation putting a $50 limit on the amount of currency that can be brought into the States from certain foreign countries, but it does not apply to military personnel. So don't worry; the dough is all yours. However, if local theater regulations limit the amount of *cash* you can take back to the States, you can send the rest of the money back via Treasury check or postal money order.

Minority Discharge

Dear YANK:

I was just under 16 when I joined the Navy. Now they have discovered my true age and they are going to discharge me. Is it true that I will get a dishonorable discharge and that I am out of luck on mustering-out pay?

Pacific   —WILLIAM HIGGINS S1c

■ The Navy says that if a man is under 17 when he is discharged, his enlistment is canceled and he gets a discharge "under honorable conditions" but no mustering-out pay. If he is over 17 when discharged, he gets the same "under honorable conditions" discharge and mustering-out pay.

Photos Developed

Dear YANK:

A couple of months ago you had an item in your *What's Your Problem?* column in which

What's Your Problem?

Letters to this department should bear writer's full name, serial number and military address.

you stated that GIs who had undeveloped film which they wanted developed should send it to Rochester, N. Y., for development. Recently I tried to send some film to that address and local censorship refused to let me put it through. Doesn't the answer which you gave apply to men in overseas theaters?

Italy   —Pvt. JAMES J. REYNOLDS

■ The answer YANK gave was intended to apply only to personnel who had returned to the States from an overseas area. GIs in overseas theaters should refer to their theater or base censors for instructions on the handling of amateur film. Overseas theater commanders have issued instructions on the procedure to be followed in disposing of amateur film in their respective theaters. GIs overseas must not communicate unofficially with Rochester about such film.

Insurance Premiums

Dear YANK:

When I entered the Army I took out a $10,000 GI policy but I kept my civilian insurance going because I found it had no "war clause." Now these premium payments on my civilian insurance are beginning to drive me nuts. My policy calls for four payments of $30 each a year. When I was in the States that was OK; I received my notices of premiums due and paid on the nose. However, mail to this part of the world is not what I'd call reliable. I feel sure that my policy will lapse one of these days because of the mail delays as we move from island to island. Is there any way in which I can have the Army take care of my insurance payments by deducting the money from my pay?

Philippines   Cpl. LARRY SMOLLENS

■ You can have the Office of Dependency Benefits do the worrying for you by taking out a Class E allotment to be paid to the insurance company. Although your premiums are due on a quarterly basis, $10 a month will be deducted

from your pay and the payments will be made monthly. A insurance companies have agreed to accept the monthly pay ments from the ODB without regard to the method of paymen specified in the policy.

Clothing Allowance

Dear YANK:

Will you please settle a bet and tell me whethe Navy enlisted men get a clothing allowance afte their first year of service?

Hawaii   —Pvt. RICHARD B. KIN[

■ They do. After each year of service Navy enlisted me receive a clothing allowance which is credited to their pa account each quarter. Chiefs get $18.75 a quarter and a others get $6.25 a quarter.

Clothing Tags

Dear YANK:

After a year and a half in the Army, I find i quite annoying to find some of my equipmen still bearing marking tags. I was convinced tha I had removed the last of these tags but the other day proved I was wrong. Halfway up th sleeve of a field jacket I found one of the familia tags. Why does the Quartermaster permit cloth ing to be bedecked like a Christmas tree?

Camp Barkeley, Tex.   —Pfc. HERBERT N. ROSE[

■ Assembly-line production of Army uniforms makes it neces sary to tag every piece that goes into the making of garment. The tags prevent a size-36 sleeve from going o a size-40 coat and they also keep certain nearly identica materials from getting mixed up in the same uniform. Whe all tags correspond on a completed uniform, the manufacture knows that no mistakes have been made.

kes to a Steak

tt Field, Ill.—When Pfc. Jack Coopersmith of dron C arrived at Scott from overseas, one e first things he did was to take his travel- uniform to the cleaners. But, having missed uple of pay calls, he was financially em- assed when the time came to call for the es. He appealed to the Red Cross and was a loan to cover the cost of the cleaning and toilet articles. He asked for a little more— gh for an occasional coke and a steak—but told that the rules wouldn't permit it. ter paying his cleaning bill, however, he a few cents left and in a wild and woolly e of "dominoes" parlayed his pennies to enough steak. At the PX he was just about to cut a luscious piece of "medium rare" when he the accusing eyes of the man next to him e Red Cross director.

—Sgt. HAROLD L. ASEN

BED CHECK

Camp Hood, Tex.—Returning to the barracks after early chow one morning, a rookie went the task of making up a bunk. He concentrated n the task so intensely that he paid no attention another trainee standing by until the latter said, Thanks, buddy. You really know your stuff."

"Cripes," said the rookie after looking around, 'm in the wrong barracks."

d Men Do Tell Tales

oux Falls AAF, S. Dak.—For the Inquiring Re- er of the post newspaper, the *Polar Tech*, William E. Leeds of St. Louis, Mo., answered question, "What was your closest escape from ible death?" His reply: "I was fooling around a six-cartridge Colt revolver when I was d. I didn't think it was loaded, so I started ing a little game, first clicking the gun at the ror and then at my head. On the fourth shot rgotten bullet exploded and the mirror shat- d into a thousand pieces."

wo days later eagle-eyed Pvt. Lorris R. Miller te in: "Does Pvt. Leeds realize that if his first was at the mirror, his fourth shot would be imself? Brother, he's dead!"

e Navy Lands Again

amp Gordon, Ga.—While 5,000 soldiers were ng in the Sports Arena waiting impatiently the Kay Kyser show to begin, a solitary sailor led in, looking for a seat. At the sight of the y blue, the soldiers broke into cheers and ap- se. The Kyser band picked up the cue and loose with "Anchors Aweigh."

he sailor, R. B. Boyd SK3c, was a native of gusta who had just returned from active duty. ed where he had obtained his ticket, he re- d, "That's a Navy secret." —Cpl. BERNARD BLOOM

ins Gold in Nevada Hills

eno AAB, Nev.—There can't be many bases in this country where you can come back from vo-mile hike with some freshly panned gold, it can be done here, and Cpl. John Miller, an rument specialist, is the man who does it.

tall, gray-haired GI who looks older than his ears, Cpl. Miller makes a hobby of the study collection of minerals. He has any number of cimens from his home state, Maine, and has ed considerably to his collection in his travels n one base to another in the Army. But it n't until he was assigned to this ATC base he took his hobby seriously enough to stake a claim. He hopes, when he gets around to king it after the war, that his claim will yield per, silver and tungsten. In the meantime ning for gold has become his recreation. With pick, shovel, pan and a fluorescent light, goes to a jagged gully halfway up the moun- side about two miles from the base, and pa- tly washes tiny particles of gold from the red vel and black sand of the Nevada soil. A hun- d-odd years ago, $16,000 in gold was taken of this vicinity, practically in one haul, Cpl. ler says. Last summer he and a friend, hoping find the source of the gold they had panned, a tunnel in the gully, but they dug it too h, the corporal believes. Next summer they n to dig a lower tunnel, because the vein easing the gold still has not been found. pl. Miller formerly was engaged in farming, lwork and weaving near Bath, Maine, which still calls home. One of a large religious fami- he carries a Bible with him at all times, ether engaged in his instrument work on C-46 nsport planes or prospecting for gold. He has en brothers in service. —Pvt. KATHERINE S. BELL

AROUND THE CAMPS

AAF Redistribution Station No. 1, Atlantic City, N. J.—Pfc. Louis B. Rorer of White Plains, N. Y., a veterinarian who spent two years in Fairbanks, Alaska, is back in the States because of a timber wolf. "The brute was supposed to be tame," said Rorer, "and I was giving him a rabies shot. He slashed my finger." It was so cold up there the wound wouldn't heal. The bone became infected, so Rorer was ordered home.

Fort Lewis, Wash.—It took Pvt. Jordan Young nearly six months to convince his draft board it should call him. He was in Brazil when we entered the war, so he registered with the American Em- bassy in Rio de Janeiro. When he returned to the States in March 1944, his draft board told him it had no authority to register or draft him because of his registration in Rio.

Brownsville AAB, Tex.—S/Sgt. George Hamod of the AACS received his overseas-shipping orders, effective at once. He wired his new CO requesting an extension of two or three days "to attend to some unfinished business." His CO replied as fol- lows: "Unfinished business over there. Request not granted." —Cpl. P. L. GILMER

Keesler Field, Miss.—Every time the buddies of a certain sergeant slap him on the back and call him by name, the GIs nearby freeze at attention. The reason is that everybody calls the sergeant by his first name instead of the customary "Sarge." He is Sgt. Colonel G. Yates.

Camp Blanding, Fla.—The first two artists who worked on the big mural in Service Club No. 1 received shipping orders while the work was in progress. Pvt. James P. Mealiff, the third to take over, worked in his spare time and finished in five weeks.

Sioux City AAB, Iowa—When a TWX request for 23 Wacs to go overseas arrived at this base, 30 Wacs asked to be sent. Shortly afterward there was another request for 27, and 31 volunteered to go. Both groups are on their way now.

Truax Field, Wis.—Pvt. Winston L. Churchill does not chew big black cigars or settle the world's problems. He is tall, thin, dark and an RM student in Section N.

Camp News

STILWELL INSPECTS. Back from China, Burma and India and now chief of the AGF, Gen. Joseph W. Stil- well (second from right) follows a trainee through a close-combat course at the IRTC, Fort McClellan, Ala.

WAC HOOP CHAMPS. Cpl. Raymond Huckabee (left) coached this winning basketball team of ATC Wacs stationed at Fairfield-Suisun Army Air Base, Calif. They scored seven wins over other WAC teams.

PITTSBURGH, Pa.

The Monongahela and Allegheny Rivers meet the Ohio to form the Golden Triangle of industrial Pittsburgh

The smog that shrouds the city these days is a symbol of war production in plants and mills.

By Sgt. AL HINE
YANK Staff Writer

PITTSBURGH, PA.—The story used to be that the girls in Pittsburgh had such shapely legs because they had to walk up and down so many of the city's hills and the exercise developed their muscles in the right places. Well, the hills are still there and the girls are still there and their legs are just as pretty, but there's far fewer than the usual complement of males to admire them. The hills, we mean.

It takes awhile for you to realize, though, that there has been even that much change in the life of Pittsburgh. It is busier than ever, with the mills along the river flashing a bright backdrop by night to the now-scanty traffic along the Boulevard of the Allies. But the town has been busy before, and to a returning GI the things that are still the same are easier to spot than the changes.

In the winter the snow turns gray just as quickly as ever in most sections and the familiar slush achieves a new tone of black with the help of increased industrial soot. When there isn't snow, this same soot scuts up from the pavements in little black clouds as your shoes strike the ground. You can rest assured that the Smoky City of bad radio jokes is as smoky as ever.

The Pittsburgh that never gets into the jokes is the same, too. South Park and North Park are both lovely in the snow for steak fries by characters who can snare enough ration points, and they're still swell for winter sports. Last spring and summer both parks played host to the usual picnic throngs, which were only a little reduced by the difficulty in getting about on rationed gas. Since Kennywood can be reached by trolley, the amusement park has enjoyed a boom,

with furloughing GIs subtracting a note of color from the crowds.

You don't see as many soldiers in town as you might expect. Camp Reynolds at Greenville, Pa., is the only camp situated near enough to Pittsburgh for GIs stationed there to take advantage of overnight passes to visit the city. There are a few MPs around, of course, and even some SPs. There are some Ordnance guys lucky enough to be stationed in the town itself, checking and doing the paper work on the district's war production, and there are GIs at Pitt and Tech.

But because the ASTP was curtailed last year, there are fewer men in uniform taking courses at the colleges. The GIs are almost the only male students the colleges have. The few civilian collegians are either exceedingly 4-F or painfully young and downy. But the co-ed population has increased during the war. There are girls, girls, girls on all the campuses.

The OD students get worked reasonably hard to balance the luck of being stationed in the United States. For a while Pitt GIs lived cosily in the fraternity houses along Forbes Street, but that was too good to last, and the Army has bundled them off to the Cathedral, where they sleep in disciplined rows in the drafty Gothic skyscraper and have reveille, retreat and so on.

Most of the GIs you see on the streets during the day or in the night spots in the evenings are lucky guys on pre-embarkation or just-back-from-overseas furloughs. There aren't enough of them to give Pittsburgh even the illusion of being a military town, but just as a gesture of something or other the local Provost Marshal has hung his off-limits sign on a couple of bars.

Diamond Street is still the home of the low-price double-header shot, and the Casino is still one of the nation's last stands of old-fashioned burlesque. The Nixon has had good theatrical seasons, getting a lot of road companies playing New York hits. It caters to fewer try-outs, though, since in these times of uncertain transportation most untested shows hesitate to make the long trek from Broadway. The Playhouse

on Craft Avenue still puts on the most polished and popular semipro theatricals in the city, and the little lounge is still jammed a night and on Sundays.

There are still the same one-man clubs designed to outwit the early-closing laws for bars and they still have incredible names like the Benjamin Harrison Literary Association and the St. Cecilia Society. The Continental Bar of the William Penn, the Nixon Cafe, Al Mecur's Music Bar on Graeme Street and the Gay Nineties Room of the Hotel Henry continue to pack in customers of an evening and it is at places like these, after nightfall, that you begin to notice the manpower shortage, nonindustrial. There are tables with three or four girls and only one guy and tables with just three or four girls. And when you see a girl with a date she usually is so self-satisfied that you can't get a good look at her face for the glow on it. The Henry Bar has a sign on the mirror which reads: "UNESCORTED LADIES WILL NOT BE SERVED IN THIS ROOM AFTER 6 P.M."

YOU'LL be able to find practically any landmark you look for. The stone eagles where the boulevard hits Grant Street, across from the *Post-Gazette* building, are dirtier than ever but columnist Charley Danver has given up his crusade to have them cleaned. He figures that the smoke that sullies them is proud evidence of war production and cleaning can wait on peace.

Cold industrial statistics prove Charley's point as convincingly as the smog on the eagles. Late last year Army Ordnance officials revealed that over one-half of all the 8-inch artillery shells produced in the United States came out of the Pittsburgh Ordnance District. And 8-inch shells are only part of the production story.

The steel mills are probably the district's biggest contributors of war materiel, and they have been going full blast since before Pearl Harbor. Though the winter's fuel shortage hampered some of them, they hit their highest production record to date in the week of Feb. 28—an estimated 39,860 tons or 92 percent of capacity.

many of the mills you'll find young girls women doing men's jobs—running donkey nes in the plants, loading cars and such like. y are trying to fill the place of an absent usband or honey. Others have gone into war s simply because they are needed or because like the cash. But most of them seem to have mbition to hang onto their industrial jobs the peace. At Jones and Laughlin's South works the plant manager could think of only girl who wanted to carry on after the war— husband had been killed overseas.

plants like Pittsburgh Equitable Meter and manufacturers of finished products where girls worked even in peacetime, the femi- increase has been tremendous. At the West- ouse Company's East Pittsburgh works, en employees have been known to break she-wolf whistles at the sight of a service- —all in the spirit of good clean fun.

uminum is booming and Pittsburgh, with Kensington up the river, is still the center uminum production in spite of the vast ex- on of the industry elsewhere. Special alloy , machine tools, coal, electrical equipment, and manufactured items of almost every e war. On Neville Island, the Dravo Corpo- turns out PT boats and various other craft he Navy. They go down the Ohio to the ssippi and thence to sea and action. The rivers are crowded with the traffic that Pittsburgh a leading inland port.

TSBURGH has no new wrinkles to add to the od and cigarette shortages found in all cities. ping housewives queue up early in the ings at Donahue's and other food stores to rst grabs at products rumored to be due for ning. Cigar stores along Liberty, at the of the tobacco famine, offered Longfellows se 10-cent dictator-size banquet smokes— eir only available cigarettes. In drug stores can still get Tast-T-Lemmon and Lem-N- l, the fruit juice drinks native to western sylvania.

e migration of Pittsburghers to the suburbs Lebanon, South Hills and the like—con- s. There hasn't been much new building the war, but the North Side and the East re becoming business districts and shopping rs. Squirrel Hill around Forbes and Murray rning into a little East Liberty, and East ty is increasingly like "downtown."

e housing shortage in Pittsburgh—as in other large American city—is acute. The ation has increased, with the influx of in- ial workers from outside more than bal- g the drain of the Army. The Army itself un into the housing problem and has taken the old Municipal Hospital on Bedford t as an MP barracks.

tloose MPs and their freedom-loving pris- used to escape through the back windows e hospital, but this hole has been plugged.

Arlington Heights on the South Side is the only recent substantial housing development.

McKeesport is as overcrowded as Pittsburgh since U. S. Steel moved its Elwood City plant there. Homestead has been half torn down to make room for a new steel plant. The area razed included most of the old red-light district that radiated from Third and Dixon.

Along Fifth Avenue beyond Oakland you'll notice that the old show-place homes are either demolished or dilapidated. Taxes and the love of fresh air have driven most of the wealthy out of town to Sewickly or Fox Chapel. The big, gently sloping lawns and the elaborate gardens are turning into weed patches. Here and there a garage left standing has been rented as a house. The migration to the country would probably have been even faster if the gas shortage hadn't strangled transportation to and from town.

There are more of the new streamlined red streetcars than before, and fewer taxis. There haven't been any new taxis since the war and the old ones are developing creaks. Up on Wylie, in the Hill District, they still have free-lance, non-licensed taxis driven by local boys for music lovers who have stayed up till curfew listening to Honey Boy pound on the drums.

Pittsburgh is full of talk about expansion and improvement schemes for post-war days when construction limitations will be lifted. Last fall City Works Director Frank M. Roessing sub- mitted to the Federal Works Administration a report proposing an expenditure of almost $36,- 000,000 for the first six years of peace.

These projects embrace everything from 50 miles of armored curbing to 36 new public build- ings—mostly police stations and fire houses. Some of the improvements can be begun as soon as Federal authorities give a green light—things like the repaving of Barbeau, Kirkpatrick, Small- man and South 27th Streets and construction of new sewers on Penn, Lemington and North Ave- nues. Other improvements, still in the blueprint stage, are the repaving of the Bloomfield and Manchester bridges and the widening of the south approach to the latter. Still ideas, not yet even on paper, are 36 public buildings and six stations for the City Highway Department.

Roessing's report doesn't include major long- term projects like the proposed $25,000,000 Pitt Parkway, the $15,000,000 restoration plan which will turn Fort Pitt into a park and the $6,000,000 Crosstown Boulevard. Most such big-time oper- ations will be financed jointly by national, county and state governments.

Meanwhile the new streetcars and the old au- tomobiles—and the absence of any cars at all in the dealers' windows—are the changes that you'd most likely spot right off. The sight of sol- diers drilling on the Pitt Campus would proba- bly catch your eye, and you'd be struck by the number of slacks if you drifted into any indus- trial plant. But mostly Pittsburgh is the same. Just a little bigger and busier and dirtier.

The girls' legs are the same as ever.

Kahn's Bar & Grill on Murray Avenue carries on with proprietor Lew Kahn still behind the bar.

Weeds grow over the lawns of the old houses that face on Fifth Avenue. This is Fifth near Shady.

th Avenue, the old Bank of Pittsburgh is parking lot; only its front still stands.

Dorothy Nesbit, from her piano in the Hotel Henry Gay Nineties, entertains a mostly feminine crowd.

People still meet "under the clock" at Kaufmann's department store, downtown on Smithfield Street.

YANK
THE ARMY WEEKLY

YANK is published weekly by the enlisted men of the U. S. Army and is for sale only to those in the armed services. Stories, features, pictures and other material from YANK may be reproduced if they are not restricted by law or military regulations, provided proper credit is given, release dates are observed and specific prior permission has been granted for each item to be reproduced. Entire contents copyrighted, 1945, by Col. Franklin S. Forsberg and reviewed by U. S. military censors.

MAIN EDITORIAL OFFICE
205 EAST 42d STREET, NEW YORK 17, N. Y.

EDITORIAL STAFF

Managing Editor, Sgt. Joe McCarthy, FA; Art Director, Sgt. Arthur Weithas, DEML; Assistant Managing Editor, Sgt. Justus Schlotzhauer, Inf.; Assistant Art Director, Sgt. Ralph Stein, Med.; Pictures, Sgt. Leo Hofeller, Armd.; Features, Sgt. Marion Hargrove, FA; Sports, Cpl. Tom Shehan, FA; Overseas Editor, Sgt. Al Hine, Engr.; U. S. Editor, Sgt. Hilary H. Lyons, CA; Associate Editors, Sgt. John Hay, Inf.; Cpl. Margaret Davis, WAC; Sgt. Ralph Boyce, AAF; Cpl. Max Novack, TC.

WASHINGTON. Sgt. Barrett McGurn, Med.

FRANCE. Sgt. Merle Miller, AAF; Sgt. Charles Brand, AAF; Sgt. Mack Morriss, Inf.; Sgt. Ed Cunningham, Inf.; Sgt. Howard Brodie, Sig. Corps; Sgt. Saul Levitt, AAF; Sgt. Allan Ecker, AAF; Sgt. Reg Kenny, Armd.; Sgt. Robert McBrinn, Sig. Corps; Pfc. Pat Coffey, AAF; Cpl. Howard Katzander, CA; Cpl. Robert Krell, Inf. (Airborne); Pfc. David Whitcomb, AAF; Pvt. David Berger, Engr.

BRITAIN. Sgt. Durbin L. Horner, CA; Sgt. Sanderson Vanderbilt, CA; Sgt. John Scott, Engr.; Sgt. Earl Anderson, AAF; Sgt. Francis Burke, AAF; Cpl. Jack Coggins, CA; Cpl. Edmund Antrobus, Inf.; Pfc. Tom Flannery, AAF.

AUSTRALIA-PHILIPPINES. Sgt. LaFayette Locke, AAF; Sgt. Charles Rathe, DEML; Sgt. Douglas Borgstedt, DEML; Sgt. Dick Hanley, AAF; Sgt. Ozzie St. George, Inf.; Cpl. Roger Wrenn, Sig. Corps; Sgt. Charles D. Pearson, Engr.; Cpl. John McLeod, Med.; Sgt. Marvin Fasig, Engr.; Cpl. Joe Stefanelli, Engr.; Cpl. Frank J. Beck, DEML; Sgt. Roger W. Cowan, DEML; Sgt. Jack F. Crowe, DEML; Sgt. Lionel Wathall, DEML.

CENTRAL PACIFIC. Sgt. Larry McManus, CA; Pfc. George Burns, Sig. Corps; Pfc. John O. Armstrong, Inf.; Sgt. Bill Reed, Inf.; Cpl. James Goble, Armd.; Sgt. H. N. Oliphant, Engr.; Sgt. Bill Young, Inf.; Cpl. Ted Burrows, DEML; Don Morgan Y1c, USCGR; Vernon H. Roberts S1c, USNR; Mason E. Pawlak CPhoM, USNR; Cpl. Len Wilson, Sig. Corps.

MARIANAS. Cpl. Tom O'Brien, DEML; Sgt. Dil Ferris, AAF; Sgt. Jack Ruge, DEML; Pfc. Justin Gray, Rangers.

ITALY. Sgt. Harry Sions, AAF; Sgt. August Loeb, AAF; Sgt. Dan Polier, AAF; Cpl. George Barrett, AAF; Pfc. Ira Freeman, Cav.; Pfc. Carl Schwind, AAF; Pvt. Dave Shaw, Inf.

INDIA-BURMA and CHINA. Sgt. Paul Johnston, AAF; Sgt. George J. Corbellini, Sig. Corps; Sgt. Dave Richardson, CA; Sgt. Lou Stoumen, DEML; Sgt. Walter Peters, QM; Cpl. Jud Cook, DEML.

ALASKA. Sgt. Ray Duncan, AAF; Cpl. John M. Haverstick, CA.

IRAN-IRAQ. Sgt. Burtt Evans, Inf.

PANAMA. Cpl. Richard Douglass, Med.

■

Commanding Officer, Col. Franklin S. Forsberg.

Executive Officer, Maj. Jack W. Weeks.

Business Manager, Maj. North Bigbee.

Supply Officer, Maj. Gerald J. Rock.

OVERSEAS BUREAU OFFICERS. France, Maj. Charles L. Holt; Britain, Capt. Harry R. Roberts; Australia-Philippines, Maj. Harold B. Hawley; Central-South Pacific, Maj. Josua Eppinger; Marianas, Maj. Justus J. Craemer; Italy, Maj. Robert Strother; Burma-India, Capt. Harold A. Burroughs; Alaska, Lt. Grady E. Clay Jr.; Iran, Lt. David Gafill; Panama, Capt. Howard Carswell; Puerto Rico, Capt. Frank Gladstone; Middle East, Capt. Knowlton Ames.

PUERTO RICO. Sgt. Don Cooke, FA; Pfc. James Iorio, MP.

MIDDLE EAST. Sgt. Richard Paul, DEML.

BRAZIL. Pfc. Nat Bodian, AAF.

NAVY. Donald Nugent S1c.

This Week's Cover

AT a forward observation post on Iwo Jima, a marine calls out range instructions to be relayed to artillery and mortar units. He and the two other spotters have located the exact position of an enemy machine gun nest.

PHOTO CREDITS. Cover—USMC. 2—PA. 3—INP. 4—Upper left & right and lower right, PA; lower left, Pfc. A. L. Farnum, MC. 5—Upper, AAF; lower, Cpl. O'Neill. 7—Acme. 8—Sgt. Reg Kenny. 9—Left & center, Sgt. Kenny; right, INP. 10—PA. 11—Ladd Field Photo Section. 12—Upper left, Cpl. Roger Wrenn; lower left, USCG; lower right, PA; others, Signal Corps. 13—Center left, AAF; lower left, Acme; lower right, WW; others, Signal Corps. 15—Upper right, PRO Fort McClellan, Ala.; lower right, ATC Fairfield-Suisun AAB, Calif.; center, PRO Reno AAB, Nev. 16 & 17—Sgt. Ben Schnall. 20—Universal. 23—Upper, Acme; lower, Riverdale Children's Assn.

Mail Call

Correction: No Firearms

Dear YANK:

Please let me take this opportunity to express my appreciation for your wonderful periodical. You may rest assured that it is read from cover to cover by all the officers and enlisted men at this station. It is usually the first medium to disseminate information regarding directives, which usually take some time to filter down through channels. However, I wish to call to your attention your article entitled "Souvenir Savvy."

This article, by the YANK Washington Bureau, is written contrary to directives of Headquarters, ETOUSA, and gives every returning officer and GI the impression that they can take with them to the Z of I enemy firearms of all descriptions, as well as mail back home carbines and other small arms, property of the U. S. Government. You cite in this article *WD Cir. No. 353 1944*, but you will note the article failed to recognize the significance of Par. 3b (3) of Sec. III of the above-mentioned WD circular, which states that the theater commander will determine what can be carried by personnel returning to the Z of I.

For your information I wish to call your attention to *Circular 84, ETOUSA, 1944* series, Sec. iii thereof, which specifically states that firearms, enemy or otherwise, in whole or in part, cannot be retained, carried or mailed by U. S. personnel to the Z of I. It is hoped that you will correct this false impression created in the article at the earliest possible time, as it will create a feeling of resentment by all personnel returning to the Z of I, as under no circumstances will they be allowed to carry with them to the Z of I the equipment mentioned in your article, regardless of any certificate they obtain from their superior officer.

Your cooperation in the matter will greatly facilitate our work at the various replacement centers.

Britain —Col. WILLIAM A. GAYLE

In Defense of MPs

Dear YANK:

The men in my MP outfit are really burned up after reading Pvt. Curt McCoy's rebuke of MPs in a recent *Mail Call*. It strikes us that Pvt. McCoy is just snappin' his cap because he made a mistake in violating speed regulations and got caught doin' it.

I have been an MP for over 3½ years and I have yet to witness any other GI, or group of GIs, dog robbin' for the MPs. If anything, it's the other way round.

Obviously, it has never occurred to Pvt. McCoy that a lot of MPs are (and have been for some time) at the front lines. Who is it that greets the forward echelon of U. S. personnel when they advance to a position that had just been cleared of the enemy? The MPs, naturally. But, then, the rear echelon wouldn't know about that. . . .

Burma —Pfc. PETER E. GARRITY

Dear YANK:

. . . Does Pvt. McCoy know that every beachhead landing has MP personnel who direct movements of troops and materiel right in the line of fire? Does he also know that the MP detachment in India which he so bitterly condemns has received high commendations on its training at home (Infantry training) and the thanks of legions of GIs in India who arrived in a theater strange in custom and weird in living conditions from an American viewpoint?

Pvt. McCoy mentions something about four or five MPs in a jeep parked on a roadside ready to pounce on an unwary GI. This is to advise him that we are one of the few MP units in India and as such we recently oriented about 20 men in MP duties. This was the only conceivable time that four or five MPs could be seen in one jeep. . . .

India —Pvt. HARRY ROSENBERG*

*Also signed by 152 others.

Dear YANK:

In response to Pvt. Curt McCoy's article on "How To End the War," I'd like to add a few remarks. The MPs don't make laws, they enforce them. The orders are set down by the post, camp and station commanders. . . .

Too many soldiers take advantage of an MP who takes it easy on them. A lot of soldiers think the "Out of Bounds" signs are placed in certain areas to curtail their fun. One should walk through the venereal-disease wards to find out just why those signs are placed in those areas. Yes, we have a definite job to do and we're going to do it. . . .

Burma —Sgt. HAROLD DYKSTRA

Dear YANK:

. . . If Pvt. McCoy was still a rookie his gripe could be excused; but he has been in the service long enough to know that orders are orders and they will be carrid out no matter what organization he may be in. . . .

What would his home town be like without a police force?

Iran —Pvt. JOHN E. ANDERSON*

*Also signed by the rest of the men of Company D, 727th MP Battalion.

The War Goes On

Dear YANK:

I have read a lot of bitching in *Mail Call* and now I have one that tops them all. Being in a casual detachment makes me subject to any detail that comes along, but being marched in front of officers for a show is the last damn straw.

Today some jeep came in the barracks for a 10-man detail. Of course I went, and there were about 40 more in the same situation as myself. We went to the theater and some officer (supposed to be) came out and told us that they were giving a show for some visiting brass, but it was pretty dull and we were to walk in front of the stage to give them a laugh. I guess we are here just to give them (officers) something to laugh at. Nothing overseas ever happened like this, and if they would only send me back, then I would be very happy.

Kingman AAF, Ariz. —(Name Withheld)

Officers' Whisky

Dear YANK:

. . . Why is it that only officers are entitled to a whisky ration down here in the Pacific? Is it because an enlisted man can't hold his liquor? If that is the case, then I believe the whisky ration should be done away with altogether because there are some officers who can't hold liquor as well as an EM can.

If whisky were rationed to EM it would do away with a lot of illegal drinking that goes on down this way, which undoubtedly affects a man's health, such as the drinking of butterfly rum, butterfly brandy, cheap wine and other lousy alcohols that a drinking man will drink when there is no good liquor to be had. . . .

We do get a small beer ration out this way. A few bottles a month, but who in hell wants to sit and drink warm beer when someone else is enjoying good mainland whisky?

Pacific —Sgt. E. J. DAMICO*

*Also signed by six others.

Government Salaries

Dear YANK:

Recently I read that there is a mov ment on foot to give members of Co gress a raise in pay. Without enteri into any debate as to whether or n such a raise is now justified, a questi rises in my mind as to whether or not, cases where salary raises for Unit States Government employees are a fected, it would not be more efficient give larger income-tax exemptions i stead of salary raises. The same res would be accomplished with a larger i come-tax exemption or no income tax all; the deserving employee would ha more money in his pockets at the end the year than if he got an increase compensation.

Why do we now give congressmen, se vicemen and others who receive gover ment compensation a sum of money a say to them, "We will require you to gi some of it back at income-tax tim Abolishment of income tax on mon received from Government compen tion would result in a great saving paper work, expense, manpower a headaches. . . .

Italy —Sgt. JAMES S. GOC

One Man's War

Dear YANK:

Not that it would interest anyone particular, but I'd like very much to r cord the following events for posterit

World Affairs	My Contribution
Attu invaded	On KP.
Kiska occupied	Latrine duty.
Tarawa landing	Barracks orderly.
D-Day in France	Signed 104th for havi sleeves up.
Return to the Philippines	Squadron meeting.
Nazis murder 150 Yanks in cold blood	CO spent 2 minutes war news and 20 minu on keeping your sho shined.
Great Russian offensive	Worked on B-24s. (Som one must have slipp up on that day.)

The topper? My wife, an Army nurs is in France and I am in the States.

Tonopah, Nev. —Cpl. ALBERT BARC

An Officer Complains

Dear YANK:

. . . We officers of line companies, cor pany commanders and platoon leade are fighting this war over here, witho the wearing of insignia of rank and wit out title, being called by various nic names, mine being too ribald for tend ears. We take as many hardships a chances as the men. We must always b out in front, for, unless we are, the m are reticent about being aggressive. W are merely another rifleman but with r sponsibility. Yet what is our recognitio Like the aid men, we are taken f granted and when any benefits of a p cuniary nature or postwar opportuni are offered, we are overlooked.

In most cases the junior officers are u married, and most noncoms of marit status make more money than we do. T base pay of a first lieutenant is $166.6 and for foreign service he gets 10 perce of that base pay. He is allowed about $ for quarters—an allowance which h never sees but which we figure we a paying for a foxhole or pillbox sans h

"What makes you think finding your own replacement makes you eligible for rotation?"

ind cold running water. He is allowed $21 a month for meals, and we pay at the rate of 25 cents a meal (about $23.30 a month) and many times the meal consists of C or K ration. We all have the Combat Infantry Badge, but that does not entitle an officer to the $10 each month which goes with this award.

Now the enlisted man. All his worries and cares, outside of the physical hardships and mental dilemmas, are taken care of by officers of the various branches. Besides his base pay he collects 20 percent for foreign service, $10 for the Combat Infantry Award, and he has access to the Soldiers Deposit which gives 4-percent interest. Then the enlisted man gets monetary recognition for certain medals he earns. Warrant officers get 20-percent foreign-service pay and reap many of the advantages given the GI. But the officer is always forgotten. . . .

But here's the pay-off. I refer you to the educational facilities offered to servicemen and women after the war; specifically, to the pamphlet put out by the University of Minnesota, General Extension Division, Correspondence Study Department, Schedule D for U.S. Armed Forces Institute: ". . . The Government will pay one-half the total (not to exceed $20 for any one course) for officers and enlisted personnel in the Navy, Marines, Coast Guard and Waves, and for enlisted personnel in the Army and WAC. . . ."

I cannot understand why the distinction or the ignoring of Army officers. . . . I am the last one in the world to look for favors or money advantages, but we officers are plenty sore and wonder what is the score. Most of us have risen from the ranks. The discrimination certainly does not rest lightly with us.

Netherlands East Indies —Lt. F. P. O'FLAHERTY

ASTP and the Navy

Dear YANK:

We read in *Navy Notes* that the Navy is seeking men between 19 and 29 with language background for enrollment in their Oriental Language Program at Boulder, Colo.

To us this is just another illustration of the lamentable lack of coordination between the Army and the Navy training programs. Why does the Navy have to look high and low to uncover men with language ability? Don't they know that there are hundreds of former ASTP men with 3 to 13 months of language study, now filling jobs in the Army in no way connected with their training? Many of these men have studied the specific languages which the Navy now considers important, viz., Chinese, Japanese, Malay and Russian.

Why can't these Army men (those still in the States) be transferred to the Navy where they can be much better utilized than they are now?

Camp Ritchie, Md. —(Names Withheld)

Discharge Uniform

Dear YANK:

You stated some time ago that the GI would be discharged with only one complete uniform, and all other clothing revoked. What we would like to know is why don't they let the GI keep his clothing issue. We are sure that the majority of this clothing will be destroyed. Many servicemen will have spent from two to six years in the service, and will go back to normal life finding their civilian clothes will not fit, if they have any, and will have no money to buy new clothes. Sure, we get a mustering-out pay, but there will be hundreds of things to do with that. Due to the great demand for civilian clothing at the time of demobilization, you may not be able to buy sufficient clothes. You certainly won't be able to buy clothes the first day you're home, and one uniform won't go far as work and dress clothes.

In our opinion it would be a great asset to the serviceman, and also the Government, if he were permitted to keep his clothing issue. How about that, fellows?

South Pacific —S/Sgt. L. S. OLSZOWY*

*Also signed by three others.

Doesn't Like Beer

Dear YANK:

We have been over here in India 15 months and have been getting our beer rations regularly every month, but there are a number of fellows, myself included, that don't like beer. We wonder why something can't be done about this. Why not a few cases of coke or some other soft drink for us poor unfortunates who don't like beer?

India —T/5 JACK L. YOUNGLOVE*

*Also signed by Pfc. Bruce Worl, T-5 Carl W. Johnson and Pvt. H. Anderson.

"Anyway, the names aren't so hard to pronounce now."

Pallas Athena

Dear YANK:

As a former Greek student at the citadel of classicism, Brooklyn Boys' High School, I really must set you straight on Pallas Athena, whose symbol is worn by the WAC. You stated, quite correctly, that she was the goddess of *a*) War and *b*) Wisdom. However, you failed to mention that she was even more famous as the goddess of *c*) Virginity. (Perhaps virginity, in wartime at least, should be given a higher rating than *c*). Don't forget that when the Athenians built a temple for her, it was called the Parthenon —from the Greek word *parthenos* meaning "virgin."

I leave to you, or to some other modern Aristotle, the philosophical task of showing the relationship of *a*) War and *b*) Wisdom; *a*) War and *c*) Virginity; and *b*) Wisdom and *c*) Virginity. . . .

Arlington, Va. —Maj. FRANKLIN F. RUSSELL

European OPA

Dear YANK:

Much has been said on the subject of American soldiers saving for a rainy day, advising them not to spend their money in occupied countries due to shortages of many popular items and because natives of these countries unscrupulously foster the black market. When Americans are advised, warned or ordered not to do something, that's when they do it.

Statistics recently published indicate that American troops overseas are saving their money to such an extent that even the brass in Washington is now smiling benignly. However, every soldier, regardless of his combat status, has hopes of some day visiting one or more of the liberated capitals of Europe. What does he discover? The natives, at the approach of the Americans, have boosted prices almost beyond his reach.

In the U. S. there is the OPA. Ceiling prices have been established to cope with everybody's pocketbook. Why not establish an agency in these countries until the crisis is over, our troops withdrawn and Europe has regained normalcy? The populace of these countries would profit by curbing prices, and Allied soldiers wouldn't feel that they are suckers to be fighting at all.

France —M/Sgt. J. P. SULLIVAN*

*Also signed by four others.

Compulsory War Bonds

Dear YANK:

. . . By what authority may an order be put out requiring enlisted men to have Class B (War Bonds) allotments taken from their pay before they are eligible to receive three-day passes and furloughs? This prevails on Yuma Army Air Field. . . .

All of us would buy them (and some of us already are) if we were able, but a lot of us have family obligations, and an infrequent, inexpensive three-day pass is our chief source of relaxation.

Yuma, Arizona —(Names Withheld)*

*Signed by 16 EM.

Buzz-Bomb Volunteers

Dear YANK:

So we don't believe in indiscriminate bombing, huh? I think anyone who has sweated out those German fly bombs will heartily agree with me that we had better change that belief, especially those of us who have buddies in hospitals that were hit by the buzz bombs and those of us who have helped carry nurses and other helpless victims of *Der Fuehrer's* death weapon out of these ruins. I think at this time a few hundred thousand of these lovely new fly bombs which we have but don't believe in using would put the fear of God into the German people. Why in the hell should we have scruples with a bunch of bloodthirsty maniacs? The German people themselves have sanctioned the weapon.

I have 50 volunteers, all of whom are plenty mad. If the bombs and ramps are sent to us, we will spend days at regular work and our nights returning bombs we receive each day. We really would enjoy being indiscriminate to those lovely German people who murder our wounded and our heroic little nurses.

France —T/Sgt. JOSEPH ISMAY Jr.

Latrine Guard

Dear YANK:

Only a short time ago I was surprised by the event I saw one night in New Guinea. I found a guard posted at the latrine, guarding the roll of toilet tissue, seeing that no one stole it. I've been in the Army over two years now, but never have I seen anything like this before.

Netherlands East Indies —Cpl. B. L. JOLLEY

Dear YANK:

. . . Here's one for the books. As casuals at a replacement depot, waiting transportation back to our units, we were halted by a guard asking for passes—passes, mind you—to enter an EM latrine. This latrine had no other designation than EM.

New Guinea —Pfc. DONALD SCHMITT*

*Also signed by Pfc. Roy W. Shifflit and Sgt. Floyd Seibert.

Credit for Nurses

Dear YANK:

Being a patient at the 20th General Hospital, it has come to my attention that the American nurses haven't been given as much credit as they deserve. They're doing a swell job of it.

Many of them have been here for two years or more, and I believe most of them will stick it out for the duration. That's what I call the good old American spirit of the American women.

I'm thanking them from the bottom of my heart for their swell services. So what do you say? Let's give them a good cheer.

India —Pvt. EDWARD CORNICELLI

Class Z Movies

Dear YANK:

For the past year we were stationed on a tiny mid-Pacific island where our only entertainment after a hard day's work was the movies. The trouble was that the great majority of these movies weren't just plain bad—they stunk!

Admittedly, movies are fine for the morale provided there's a fair plot and the characters weren't exhumed for the occasion. Believe it or not, it's a fact that a large number of enlisted men in the armed forces are fairly intelligent, and it's an insult to our intelligence to show some of these class Z pictures that so often find their way to our theaters and yet expect the men to enjoy them.

I believe I'm right in assuming that just one of these sub-standard pictures uses enough material to make many thousand rolls of ordinary camera film. Yet it's a rare occasion when my wife is able to buy a roll of film so that I may have pictures of my family, which is something a GI really appreciates.

Pacific —GEORGE L. CARRIER S1c

Strictly GI

Gen. Arnold's Report. Fighter pilots and bomber crews may soon have to dodge bullets while they're in training for combat. A new plastic .30-caliber frangible bullet that breaks up harmlessly upon contact with armor as light as ⅛-inch dural plate was described by Gen. H. H. Arnold, CG AAF, in his second report to the Secretary of War. The bullet is now in the final development stage and its use will be incorporated into all AAF flexible-gunnery training. Gen. Arnold said he believes firing real bullets at real planes will give the boys in training more incentive for accurate shooting.

Gen. Arnold's report contained a reminder that large numbers of robot bombs, reconstructed from the Nazis' V-1 with modifications and improvements, have been ordered for test-firing by the Air Technical Service Command at Wright Field, and that our own models "will soon be available for possible use."

The CG had a good word for AAF mobile weather stations, such as are operating on the Himalaya Mountains, on the plateaus of central China, in Pacific jungles and in many spots in France and Italy. Wherever possible, such stations are transported on trucks or jeeps, but in the Southwest Pacific weather and communications men, working as a team, have had to lug their equipment onto beachheads on their backs. One of the first mobile weather stations was that landed on the Salerno beachhead in September 1943.

Medics' Badge. The War Department has authorized a badge for medics who have served with the medical detachments of Infantry regiments or smaller units since the war started. The award carries no additional pay at present, but there is a bill before Congress to give its winners the same $10-a-month extra paid to combat infantrymen. Medics up to and including captain are eligible. Regimental surgeons, regardless of rank, also can get it.

The badge is elliptical and of silver metal. It shows a litter, a Geneva cross, the striking snakes of the Medical Department caduceus and a wreath of oak leaves. It will be worn on the left breast above decorations and ribbons.

Jet-Propelled Plane. "Fastest fighter in existence" is the description tied onto the new P-80, the AAF's first jet-propelled combat plane, by its manufacturers, Lockheed and the General Electric Company. Unlike the P-59 Airacomet, a Bell-built twin-engined jet fighter-trainer, the P-80 is powered by a single gas-turbine engine. The new ship, called the Shooting Star, has hydraulic aileron boosters for maneuverability at high speeds, and electrically operated flaps. It can carry heavy loads of ammunition, photo equipment, bombs and fuel, and has a pressurized cabin equipped for pilot "G" suits that ease the discomfort and danger of sharp turns and pull-outs. A small maintenance crew can make a complete engine change in 15 minutes.

First announcement of production of the Shooting Star came from Gen. H. H. Arnold. He didn't say when the ship would get into combat.

Jean Trent
YANK
Pin-up Girl

The Poets Cornered

LET THE PEOPLE COME

ɪen this is done, let all the people come
'rom all the lands of earth and walk around
e tattered world. Let them be awed, struck
dumb
3y what they see. Show them the battleground,
e shattered tanks, the buried guns, the stones
)f cities where the bombers passed. Point out
e graves of men or, where they fell, the bones
)f those who died too slow and did without.

ow them the worst of what there is to see;
ɹet them be sickened, horrified, aghast;
t let them look and feel and touch and be
Aware that Future's signpost is the Past,
at these might happen soon again. Let these
3e War's last great advertisement for Peace.

5U, Lake Placid, N. Y. —Sgt. HAROLD APPLEBAUM

THOUGHTS FROM A BOMBER

Which cynical god
In the arrangement of things
Placed this woman
Squatting on a hillside
Near where the ox flings
Moist clods
From an impatient hoof

And gave her
The inscrutable passion
For silent,
Unfeeling stoicism
That moves her to fashion
A tool from
Pieces of blasted roof

'Neath which once
She lived and weaned the child
That today raises
An innocent face
To squint curiously at the wild
Silver bird, once deadly
And now so aloof?

Did this god
Know that from the sky
Men would look
Down at primitive toil
And have time to wonder why
The past lived on
Despite the future's proof?

ipan —Sgt. STAN FLINK

SOAP AND WATER

ou might think this nonsense and so much
palaver
ill you've gone for a month and not even seen
lather.
think someone said that a bath is a bath
'hen a man's in a tub and can both sing and
laugh,
'ith no one to watch him or tell him to hurry
nd soapsuds are flitting about in a flurry.
ve bathed in canteen cups and helmets and cans,
ve gone for three weeks without washing my
hands,
ut I think if I ever get out of this war
ll live in a bathtub for time evermore.

ust give me a tub that is porcelain-lined,
/ith nice tiled floors, and I'll soon be reclined
he full length of that lovely container of water
nd neither my wife nor my son nor my daughter,
hrough threat or enticement, shall lure from
his lair
he father they love. They can pull out their hair,
hey can rave, they can rant, they can scream,
they can roar;
ut I'll smile and remember this bathtubless war,
nd I'll lie midst the wonderful soapsuds, I think,
'ill my skin and my soul are a rose-petal pink.

rance —Cpl. JOHN E. ABEL Jr.

IT seems the Army was partly responsible for putting this trim figure in the movies. Jean Trent was on tour of Army airfields with a Fourth Air Force show and some GIs sent her photograph to Walter Wanger. That brought her an interview and a long-time contract with Universal Pictures. She has a part in Universal's "Salome—Where She Danced."

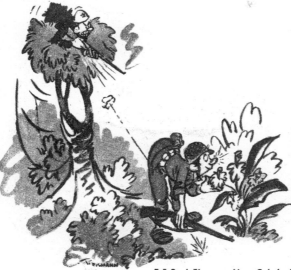

—T-5 Paul Eismann, New Caledonia

SAKI MISSED ME

(Apologies to Leigh Hunt and Jennie)

Saki missed me on patrol,
Peeking from the tree he hid in!
Clerk who checks the morning roll,
Kindly note I ain't been did in!
Mark me AWOL, eat me out,
Say I'm ailing when you list me,
Say I'm late, but never doubt:
Saki missed me!

New Caledonia —S/Sgt. IRA J. WALLACH

IMPRESSION OF THE RAIN

Upon the silent windowpane,
Released from bonds, oblivion bound,
Resound, resound
The milling drops of rain.

Interned and segregated from the clouds,
The heralding murmurs sweep
In crude, transparent shrouds,
Asleep, asleep.

He, instance-bound, adheres
To milling fury and the warning tone,
Alone, alone,
The sheltered and his tears.

New Guinea —T-5 HARRY ECKSTEIN

SONG OF THE EMPTY MAN

I am the empty man who died an empty death.
Not on the seas, clutched by sinuous tentacles of
depth,
Not on high rocks, bruising against the granite,
Nor in forests on a couch of pine.

With mud and dirt cutting my breath,
My dying phrases anticlimaxed oratory,
Frustrated and denied, I turned and bent
Beneath the weight of loathsome slime,
Saw the last dot of blue erased by black
And felt the rasp of gravel in my throat.

Nor did I perish at the battle's height,
In times of glory, famous deeds, heroic circum-
stances.
Much more prosaically, grotesquely too—
Amusing and grotesque I almost laughed
Before my tongue was blocked and I was dead.

It was so long ago, I can hardly remember;
The time was morning and the month November;
The day, strangely enough, was the eleventh.
I am the empty man who died an empty death.

Newfoundland —Pvt. LAURIAT LANE Jr.

QUERY

Breathes there a GI
On the face of the earth
Who possesses the rating
He thinks he is worth?

—Pvt. JULIAN S. WEIL

Cross Word Puzzle

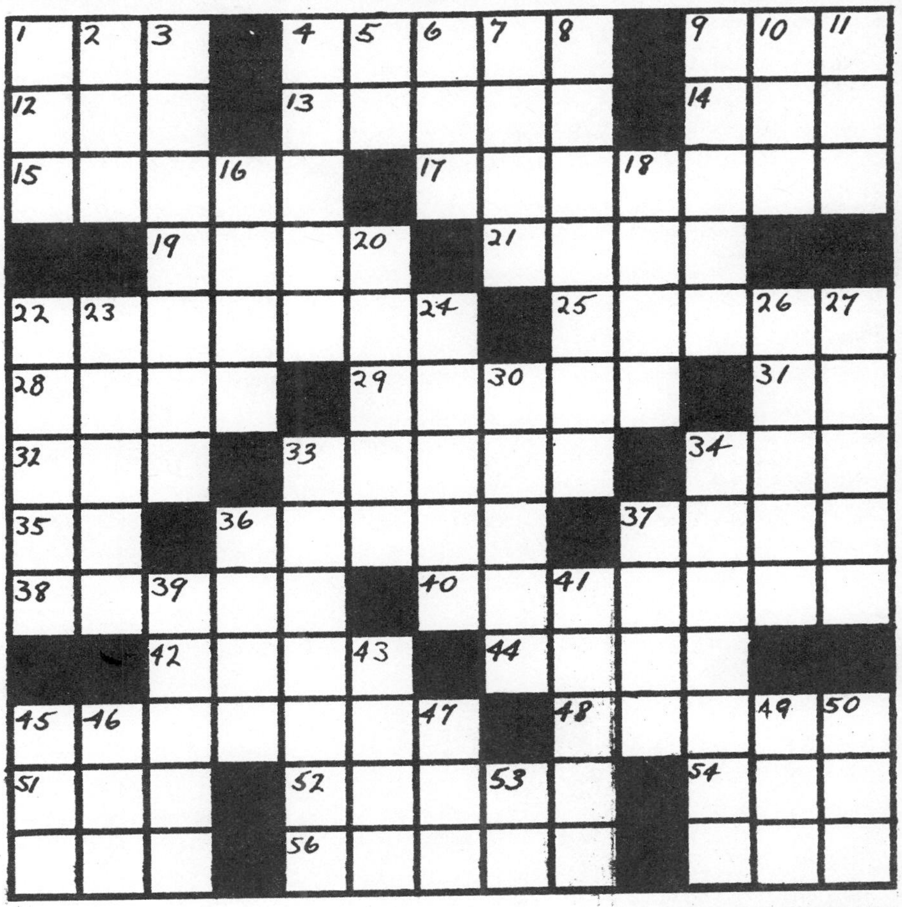

ACROSS

1. Top card
4. Okay in the AAF
9. Park the carcass
12. French street
13. Orphan
14. Hawaiian food
15. Deserve
17. Radioactive element
19. Brain wave
21. Dash
22. Surrendered
25. Girl's name
28. Otherwise
29. Very nervous
31. Either
32. Drunk
33. Baseball player
34. What to call the CO
35. Southern state
36. Old Persian coin
37. Besides
38. Player on the second team
40. GI
42. River in Germany
44. Require
45. Voting tickets
48. Aromatic herb seed
51. ——, sweet as apple cider
52. Military forces
54. Original
55. 24 hours
56. Three stripes or more
59. It goes with a whiz

DOWN

1. Equip for battle
2. Billiard stick
3. Weirdest
4. Fixed the rank of
5. Advance
6. African antelope
7. Ireland
8. One who faces facts
9. Backbone
10. Acknowledgement of debt
11. Man's nickname
16. Not working
18. Not one
20. Protective influence
22. College cheers
23. Pertaining to part of the hip bone
24. Mairzie's follower
26. Din
27. Ball player's slip-up
30. Tear jerker
33. More than half, but less than full, moon
34. Coasting
36. Line of chatter
37. Territory, SW corner of Arabia
39. Pass on
41. To let
43. Sicilian volcano
45. Offer made at an auction
46. —— from Decatur
47. Title of respect
49. Take a look
50. Female sheep
53. Short for telegraph

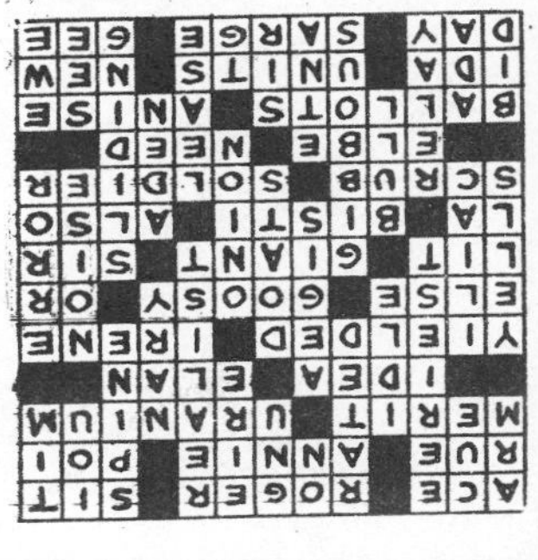

Contributions for this page should be addressed to the Post Exchange, YANK, The Army Weekly, 205 East 42d Street, New York 17, N. Y.

My Soldier Movie

BACK and forth across the country fly the sizzling questions: "Are soldier movies true to soldier life?" and "Is GI Joe really the way the films show him?"

Critics call for greater truth and realism. Hollywood shrugs its shoulders, points to the box-office figures and turns out another blooper about the teen-age crowd at the Stage Door Canteen. The public, caught in the middle and puzzled, looks for someone to whom it can go for the final, authoritative, reassuring word.

Well, here I stand, bursting at the barracks bag with expert opinion, and the only thing anyone ever asks me is "Hey, what's holding up them large plates?" But today somebody else is in the kitchen with Dinah, so attention, please, Hollywood and fans:

The trouble with soldier movies is that they've been glorifying the wrong soldiers. First we get a rash of epics about clean, blond lads in the Air Force saying "Roger!" in clean, blond voices, loving girls with unbearably lovely hair and, at the drop of a propeller, zooming off into the wild blue yonder. Sweet, but is it Life?

No, decides a movie Genius With an Idea, and he rolls back the clock to the last war and comes up with a job about a plain ground soldier, evidently slated for the Infantry. He has this plain soldier spend exactly three-fifths of his basic-training time polishing the insides of garbage cans and another fifth running around with generals (we killed the last fifth New Year's Eve). He finally releases the picture under the hot title of "See Here, Pvt. H--g---e."

There is nothing radically wrong about giving the Air Force and the Infantry an occasional break in the films, but anybody knows that the real heroes of this war are the guys in the station complements and they are the ones who should be glorified. Then we will have a real Army movie, one with the stuff of life in it; a human document—alive, warm, breathing.

I've just about finished the scenario, and I happen to have it with me. Naturally I won't give you all of the plot here, or the dialogue, or even all of the characters. I want to have something in reserve when they get me into one of those story conferences in Hollywood. However, I see no harm in revealing the title and just a few hints about the story.

For a while I played with several titles, each possessing its good points. "Service Unit, I Love You" occurred right away, and for a while I was rather fond of "30 Seconds Over the PX." Then "The Keys of the Typewriter" certainly deserved consideration. I finally decided, though, that you couldn't beat "Well, Well, Pfc. Weldon."

I admit frankly that my decision was caused by a desire to have my name known in every household, instead of merely in most camp latrines. The big advantage of this title is that in making a sequel in a couple of years they won't have to worry about any real-life increase in rating; they can just call the sequel "Well, Well, Well, Pfc. Weldon."

I'm really not the kind of writer who gets into a producer's hair with all kinds of suggestions and demands, but I would like to propose a leading man to play the part of me. What do you think of Gregory Peck? True, this won't be essentially a romantic film—boil it down and it's a case of boy meets Army, boy struggles, Army keeps boy—but I do have my tender side, and Peck, I'd say, has just the right amount of shy charm, coupled with natural, rugged good looks and a thrilling, vibrant voice with wavy hair. And since this will be largely a man's picture, replete with virile action, they needn't go any higher than about Linda Darnell in casting the girl who loves me, or rather adores me.

Now, just a little about the story and I'll get back to my work, as you never saw a garbage truck in the condition this one is.

The action revolves around a captured German service record. A near-sighted, irresistible American soldier (me) discovers the record lying around the headquarters office of a PW camp. The other clerks gave it no heed, figuring the German prisoner was bucking for a discharge and was up before the board. However, our hero (me) knows a few German words—"*frankfurters mitt sauerkraut, mein geliebte*"—and he realizes at once that this is a document of vital importance to the Allied cause, containing as it does the line of duty status of Hipschen von Pippschen, the brains of the Germany army. At this

"I guess I just lost my head, Sarge."

—Sgt. Bob Gallivan, Gowen Field, Idaho

—Sgt. Jerry Chamberlain, Camp Blanding, F

point there is a dissolve. (Whatever that may b Though I made $9,678,137.19 a week as a Holl wood writer, I never did any writing. Just roote in my office making paper airplanes and calli Ingrid Bergman. Called her Ingrid.)

As the next scene opens we see our hero (m keeping the Gestapo at bay (Lower New York while making violent love to the Nazi spy, wh is disguised as a Japanese geisha girl. How t hero thwarts an enemy plot to wreck the mora of the unit by putting rock salt into the pin pong balls, and how he saves the life of the me sergeant, who is being playfully lynched by t KPs, only to have the homely stenograph struggling along on Civil Service pay, throw her dark glasses and reveal a bathing suit hu ging a lovely form, is——

Well, it's something you will certainly nev see in next week's YANK. Order your copy toda

Fort Wadsworth, N. Y.   —Pfc. MARTIN WELD

EVENING AT HOME

As I lay on my cot and I stared at the pages
Of a book where the greatest and best of the sag
Had sprinkled the juiciest thoughts of the ag

Young Roger, my neighbor in pleasure and lab
    My buddy with mop in latrine,
My field-wire reeler, potato peeler
    And expert with TL13,
Came up beside me and forcefully pried me
Apart from the muses, for aces and twoses
    Were vying with ten, jack and queen.

I am not a gambler. I never had played
Rummy or pinochle, bridge or Old Maid,
But friendship is friendship and so I must tra
Two eclogues, an ode, a phillippic tirade—
For a pair of nines and the ace of spade.

Jack sat at my right and Ed dealt the cards,
    Then Jack dealt and I dealt and Roger and Joh
And the minutes flew fast till midnight was pa
    And my dollar and thirty-nine cents were
        gone.
We played and we played for each hand was t
        last—
    Oh, surely—but still it went on.

At a quarter past three,
When the deal came to me,
    I thrust friendship aside and arose;
And my buddies quite weary,
With eyes red and bleary
    Agreed it was time we might close.

Both Caesar and Homer have written of war:
    For Homer 'twas glory,
    For Caesar a story
Of strong men united and pagan defiance.
    For Sherman 'twas gory;
Von Clausewitz described it as theory and scienc

Oh, where in the annals of armies and conque
    Are the words of the erudite seer that writes
Of the battle that barracks-bound soldiers
    Wage over and over on weekday nights?

Port of Embarkation   —Pfc. IRVING RIBN

MY LOVE

My love is tangible to me,
A thing I feel, a thing I see;
A springtime thing I always wear,
Like lilacs, tangled in my hair;
A living thing, forever warm,
Exciting as a summer storm.

Like vapor trails that mark the sky
When early-morning bombers fly,
My love has left a mark on me:
An everlasting melody!

AAFBU, Miami Beach, Fla.   —Pfc. CATHERINE MURRA

"There you go with your rumors again!"

—Pfc. Anthony Delatri, Indiantown Gap. Pa.

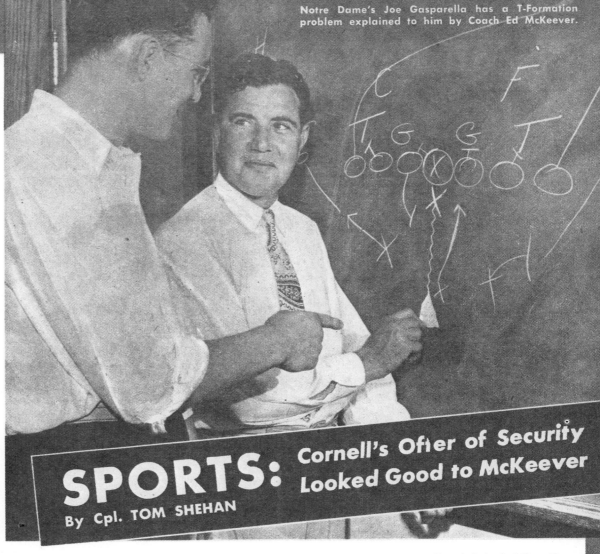

SPORTS: Cornell's Offer of Security Looked Good to McKeever

By Cpl. TOM SHEHAN

Ed McKeever turned down several attractive offers from Fordham, Boston College and a number of professional clubs, and signed a contract to be head coach of football at Cornell because he was looking for security. He wanted to settle down in a nice small town where the 5-year-old McKeever twin girls could start school next fall without worrying about whether they'd have to move again before they got acquainted with the teacher.

"We want to marry our next coach," they told him at Cornell. "We'll promise to honor and obey, in victory and in defeat, and not even the most disgruntled alumnus will make us part."

Ithaca, N. Y., the home of Cornell, looked just right for the twins, who were born in December 1940 while their father and Frank Leahy were taking the Boston College team to New Orleans to beat Tennessee in the Sugar Bowl.

"Get out the marriage license and put that in writing," McKeever said. "I do."

A long-term and well-paid coaching career at a respectable Ivy League school like Cornell must look good to McKeever. He appreciates such a spot because he made his way to the top of the football business the hard way before he became temporary headman at Notre Dame last year, succeeding his best friend, Frank Leahy, who went to the Navy on leave of absence. Just to keep the record straight, in case you haven't seen the newspapers lately, Hugh Devore, the Notre Dame line coach who used to be headman at Providence College, is going to fill in for McKeever at South Bend until Leahy returns.

The new Cornell coach was born in San Antonio, Tex., and played high-school football at St. Edward's University. Prep for Jack Meagher, an ex-Notre Damer who afterward coached at Rice and Auburn. Meagher encouraged McKeever's ambition to play under Knute Rockne, but Ed was only a freshman when the great coach was killed in an airplane crash in Kansas. He lost his enthusiasm then and began to get homesick. So he left South Bend and rode the rods back to Texas.

He first tried to enroll at Rice, but Meagher, his old coach, had to turn him down because the T/O for football scholarships had no vacancies that year. Marchie Schwartz, star of Rockne's last team, had given him a letter of recommendation to Pete Cawthon, the Texas Tech coach, so that was his next stop. Cawthon wasn't sure he wanted McKeever, but he let him sleep in an empty janitor's office on the campus.

Texas Tech then had the reputation of being "the best pro club in the Southwest," but if it was McKeever wasn't one of its highest salaried men. He worked his way through school. Ed and a chum used to catch snakes, skin them and make snakeskin belts which they sold to the freshmen. Summers he worked on the range as a cowhand.

In his first play the day he made his varsity debut as a sophomore in the fourth quarter of the Baylor game, Ed caught a flat pass and raced 35 yards for a touchdown. During the next three years he played right halfback and called the signals while Texas Tech was winning 30 of 35 games. After graduation Cawthon hired him to coach the backs, and between seasons he worked for the gas company in Lubbock, Tex., where Tech is located.

Frank Leahy, then one of Jim Crowley's assistants at Fordham, met McKeever when he went to Lubbock to lecture at a summer school for high-school coaches. "If I ever get a job as head coach," Leahy told Ed, "I'm going to make you my right-hand man." Not long afterward Frank kept his promise. He was hired by Boston College and brought McKeever along to handle his backfield men.

McKeever modestly attributes most of his success to his association with Leahy. "My first big break came when I went to Boston College with Frank," he says. "I've been riding on the Leahy band wagon ever since." While Leahy served as a lieutenant in the Navy, Notre Dame won 8 of 10 games last fall. Ed did an outstanding job in holding the team together after it had been whipped 32-13 by Navy and 59-0 by Army. "It's up to you and the other fellows not to let the youngsters' spirits go down," he told Capt. Pat Filley after the Army game. "Start in on them tonight and don't stop." Notre Dame came back to beat Georgia Tech, a team which had defeated Navy earlier in the year, and Great Lakes.

McKeever's favorite story on the banquet circuit this winter concerned his effort to fire up the team before the Army game with his own version of Rockne's famous Win-This-One-for-George Gipp speech. Ed told the boys that his bedridden father listened faithfully to the Notre Dame games on the radio and that nothing would hasten his recovery faster than a victory over Army.

The Notre Dame boys went on the field all fired up, but the Cadets were too strong for them, to put it mildly. During time out in the last quarter one of the exhausted Notre Dame players looked hopelessly up at the scoreboard. "Fifty-nine to nothing," he sighed. "McKeever's old man must be dead by now."

SPORTS SERVICE RECORD

Lt. Bernie Jefferson, the Northwestern Negro halfback who won Big Ten honors in 1938, is at Atlantic City, N. J., awaiting reassignment after 43 combat missions in Mustang fighters and 65 short-range sorties in P-39s and P-47s in the Mediterranean area. He is entitled to wear the DFC and the Air Medal with six Oak Leaf Clusters. Jefferson got the DFC for a bit of bold flying while on a strafing mission just before the invasion of southern France. The target was two radar towers in Toulon and 180 ack-ack guns. Bernie and 14 other pilots flew the mission and Jefferson hit the towers, pulling up and over a 400-foot cliff and then diving down to knock out the station. . . . Lt. Ray Flaherty, ex-Washington Redskins coach, is now stationed in Brazil. . . . Charlie Berry, the umpire, is telling his friends about the ribbing he received from Pvt. Hank Soar, ex-New York Giants back, during his recent visit to Grenland. Soar suggested a fishing trip, and when they reached the place he explained that the first job was to chop a hole in the ice. Berry started to work and hacked out enough ice to supply a fish market. Then Hank told him the ice was seven feet thick, and it was time to hurry back to camp anyway.

Killed: Maj. William (Memphis Bill) Mallory, captain of the great Yale team of 1923, in a plane crash in Italy; Lt. Comdr. Mack Tharpe, former line coach at Georgia Tech, in action in the Pacific. . . . Rejected: Fritzie Ostermueller, Pittsburgh Pirates pitcher. . . . Inducted: Gordon Maltzberger, 31-year-old ace relief pitcher for the Chicago White Sox. . . . Transferred: Lt. Billy Brown, national hop-skip-and-jump champion, to sea duty from the Bainbridge (Md.) USNTC; Lt. William S. (Billy) Soose, former middleweight boxing champion, from the Solomons (Md.) USNATC to the Armed Guard Center, Brooklyn. . . . Promoted: Maj. Mike Mikulak, former Chicago Cardinals back, to lieutenant colonel in Italy; Lt. Birdie Tebbetts, former Detroit Tigers catcher, to captain at Waco (Tex.) Army Air Field. . . . Cited: Lt. William (Bullet Bill) Osmanski, ex-Chicago Bears fullback now a Navy dental officer of a Marine unit in the Pacific, for rescuing a Navy doctor from quicksand. . . . Discharged: Stan Koslowski, who returned to Holy Cross after having played with the North Carolina Navy Pre-Flight team last fall; Tony Musto, former Chicago heavyweight, from the Navy.

"HAVE WE ANY PLACE FOR A GUY WITH FOUR YEARS AT YALE AND TWO IN THE HARVARD BUSINESS SCHOOL?"
—Sgt. Douglas Borgstedt

"WELL, IF IT AIN'T A MIRAGE I'VE BEEN A DAMN FOOL SINCE EARLY IN 1942."
—Sgt. Ted Miller

"I HEAR THE OLD MAN THREW THE BOOK AT YOU."
—Sgt. Arnold Thurm

YANK
THE ARMY WEEKLY

PLAY IT DOUBLE

"SERGEANT, THIS IS WILFRED APOLLO, WHO WILL PLAY THE ROLE OF YOU IN 'CONGRESSIONAL MEDAL.'"
—Cpl. Art Gates

YANK

THE ARMY WEEKLY

5¢ APR. 6 VOL. 3, NO. 42 1945

By the men . . for the men in the service

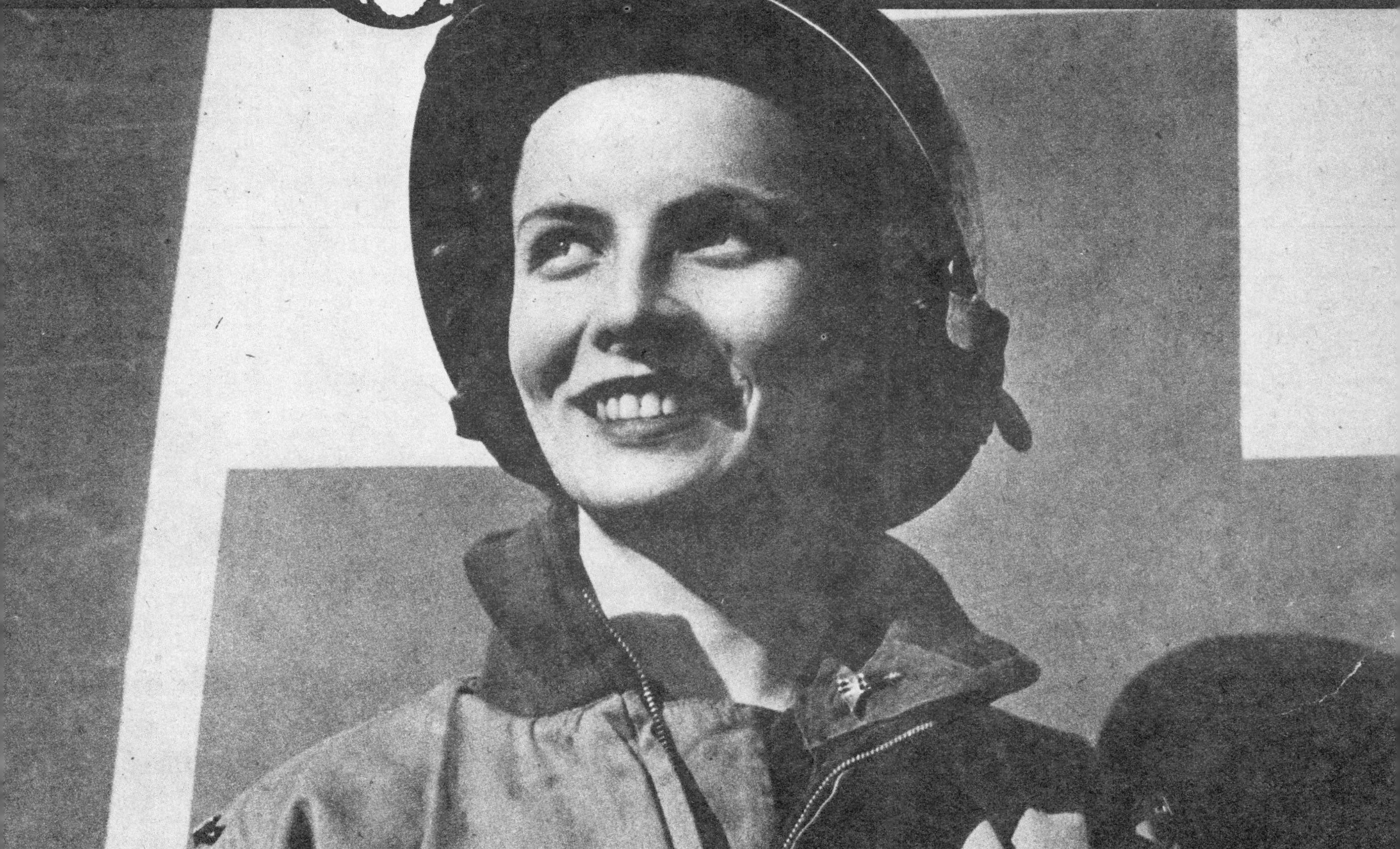

ARMY NURSE

he Ninth Army's Break-Through to the Rhine

PAGES 2, 3 & 4

As Ninth Army soldiers advance, civilians evacuate this front-line German town. The grim housewife at left still wears her apron and is carrying a loaf of bread

The speed of our advance was almost as much of a surprise to us as it was to the befuddled Jerries.

This is part of the steady stream of German prisoners being marched under guard to prisoner-of-war camps while the Yanks were driving from the Roer to the Rhine.

By Sgt. RALPH G. MARTIN
YANK Staff Correspondent

WITH THE NINTH ARMY AT THE RHINE—In a comfortable-looking living room, dirty, bearded doughfeet were puffing on liberated German cigars, discussing interesting characteristics of the different women of the world. Stretched out on a sofa, the platoon sergeant was talking over the telephone.

"Listen, sister," he said, "this is a very damned important call. I have a personal message from the citizens of the Bronx to *Der Fuehrer* himself. Ring him again. I don't care how busy he is."

Everyone in the room temporarily forgot the conversation about women and gathered around the sergeant. The sergeant put the receiver in the center of the group so that all could hear the excited German guttural of the telephone operator.

When they finally stopped laughing, the sergeant said, "I guess they still don't know we took this town."

The Ninth Army sweep from the Roer to the Rhine was so fast that the Nazis didn't know where we were coming from or where we were going or even where we were.

As for us, it was like fever. The speed of it even excited some of the battle-weary boys—cartoonist Bill Mauldin's fugitives from the law of averages.

To the different guys it was the St. Lo breakout, the push up southern France, the race to Rome, the smash across Sicily and the final phase of the Tunisian campaign.

They were all talking like this: "Well, maybe this is it. Maybe we'll meet the Russians in Berlin next week. Maybe we'll all be home in a couple of months. Maybe, maybe, maybe, maybe. . . ."

In the cellar underneath the rubble of Roerich, the general stared at a map, his face shining like a bridegroom's on his wedding night.

"Look where they are now," he said, pointing to a mark on the map. "Hell, they're 12 miles in front of the front."

He was talking about Task Force Church of the 84th Division, made up of beaucoup tanks and truck-loaded troops. At 0700 that morning they took off and just kept going. Whenever they bumped into any SP fire from either flank, they just detrucked some troops, detoured some tanks to mop up and continued to move forward as fast as they could.

Now, only four hours later, they were away in front of everybody. On the map their push looked like a skinny long finger.

Before the day was over, the skinny finger had reached out and captured a rear-echelon German repple depple complete with staff, personnel and more than 100 replacements. Poking around the Nazi rear, the finger also grabbed a whole enemy field-artillery battalion, intact.

The most indignant of all the Nazi artillery officers was the paymaster. "It isn't fair," he protested in German. "You were not supposed to capture me. This wasn't supposed to be a front."

But the front was everywhere. It was sprawling like a fresh ink blot. As soon as the Nazis would try to rush reserves to one sore spot, we would bust out somewhere else. Then the whole front almost completely disintegrated into space.

"I am going nuts here," said an arm-waving MP at the crossroads. "Everybody asks me where this outfit is and where that outfit is. Hell, I don't even know where my own outfit is. One of the boys just passed through this morning and said they were moving, and he didn't know where."

Then he told about a buddy of his who had it even tougher. He was detailed to a guard yard filled with several hundred PWs; then suddenly the detachment got orders to pull out and they forgot all about this guy. Later that afternoon the tired, worried, hungry MP approached Capt. Horace Sutton of New York, N. Y., and the 102d Division, and said: "Look, Captain. I don't know where my outfit is. I don't know if I am getting any relief. And I don't know what to do with all these prisoners. Can you help me?"

Prisoners poured in from everywhere. Long convoys of trucks were packed with them. Hundreds and hundreds of others walked back carrying their own wounded. Occasionally a column of frontward-marching Yanks would pass by a backward-marching column of Jerries. Sometimes there would be a stirring silence. But every once in a while you could hear the doughfeet talk it up:

"Jeez, some of them are babies, just lousy babies."

"Why don't you goose-step now, you sons of bitches."

"And to think that they may send some of those bastards back to the States. Why don't they just keep them here? There's plenty of cities to rebuild."

"Just what is your opinion now of the general world situation, Mr. Kraut?"

ALMOST 3,500 refugees from all over the world crowded together in the huge courtyard in Erkelenz. All of them had been doing slave labor of one kind or another for the Nazis.

"You are now under the supervision of the American Military Government," said Eugene Hugo of St. Louis, Mo. "We will feed you and take care of you until we are able to get you back to your native country."

He made his explanation in English and then translated it into French, German and Russian. The refugees just stood there entranced, as if they were listening to some great wonderful music. Finally one Russian woman broke out hysterically, sobbing, "We have been waiting for this for four years. For four years. . . ."

Erkelenz had been taken only that morning but it was already so rear echelon that the only outfits in town by night were some Quartermaster and service troops. Some QM boys were wandering around in and out of cellars of some of the houses, hunting for liquid refreshment that might have been overlooked, when they stumbled onto a cellar full of Germans. Sitting right next to the Jerries was a pile of unused hand grenades.

The kidneys of the Quartermaster boys almost started functioning again then and there, but the Germans only wanted

Roer to Rhine

Camouflaged Ninth Army tank destroyers move through the broken streets of Muenchen-Gladbach.

to be friends. They explained that they had tried to surrender all day long but nobody wanted to stop long enough to pick them up. So they came down to this cellar, waiting impatiently for somebody to come downstairs so that they could surrender and get something to eat.

They couldn't understand it. Why were the Americans in such a hurry?

It wasn't a breeze everywhere. There were plenty of spots where the Krauts decided to stay put until they were *kaput*. There was this flat, 5,000-yard-long field partially surrounded by a semicircle of thick woods. Planted in the woods were a dozen AT guns, plus some liberally scattered SP guns and machine-gun nests and tanks. The guns were all pointed, waiting and ready for the American armor to try and get through.

G-2 of the 5th Armored knew what the score was, but alternative detours would take too much time, and a slow, slugging battle would be too expensive in the long run, and besides these enemy guns had to be knocked out anyway. So the tank boys just raced across the field at full speed, their guns firing. Not all the tanks made it. Some got hit on the run; others bogged down in the mud and sat like dead ducks until the Nazi AT guns picked them apart and burned them up.

When the show was over, after the last tank had swept past the field, there were no more AT guns in operation, no more SP guns or enemy tanks either. The 5th Armored boys also shot up two American light tanks which the Germans were using minus the USA insignia.

Frenchmen walked down the road, wearing their blue berets and their neat, frayed pants. There had been a strict shortage of MPs, so much so that one MP was often detailed to bring back 300 prisoners all by himself. When these ex-French soldiers volunteered their services, all of them were given K-rations and deputized as prison guards. You could see satisfied expressions on their faces when they prodded the Nazis to walk a little faster.

"It is nice to have a gun pointed the other way," one of them said in French.

There was a lot of cheek-kissing, French style, when the XIII Corps liaison officer, Capt. George Kaminski, spotted one of the incoming French refugees. The two of them had been in the same Infantry company four years before. Now the liaison officer told the refugee about their mutual buddies: this one was wounded and is running a perfume shop in Paris, this other one is down in Colmar, somebody else is dead.

BEFORE the Roer jump-off, our troops had found just as many dead Germans as live ones in these tiny rubbled towns. But Muenchen-Gladbach was different. It was full of live Germans, estimated at 75,000. And practically all of them were trying to butter up to us and sneak inside our sympathies. Especially the women, who felt their favors were worth bartering for food.

"Nazi officers had their own women living here with them," said Capt. Bennett Pollard of Baltimore, Md., at the CP of the 1st Battalion, 175th Regiment of the 29th Division. The CP was a complicated network of hallways and cellars, with triple-decker steel beds for the enlisted men and separate rooms for the officers.

The Nazi CO had a private blonde, who was still there when the troops came into the city during the night. Capt. Pollard held up a flimsy nightgown that he had found on the Nazi's bed. "I guess we really surprised them all right," he said.

The captain told how absolutely still it was when they marched in, how they heard nothing except their marching. There had been no sniping, and the only isolated case of enemy activity

Enemy artillery fire knocked out this U. S. medium tank which burns in a German field.

These two Germans, a man and a boy, were captured with Nazis fighting at the front.

This is the way Duesseldorf looked to GIs reaching the opposite bank of the Rhine.

was the report of two *teller* mines being placed tank treads on the roads during the night. Th had been discovered in time.

Everything was smooth and easy so far. T smooth, he said.

THERE was nothing smooth about the push i Neuss, which sits smack on the Rhine, just posite Duesseldorf.

Outside the town, the Krauts had built a embankment near the railroad tracks, and th studded it with their small, accurate mortars a fast-firing machine guns. After considerable tillery preparation the doggies of Able, Baker a Charley Companies of the 1st Battalion, 32 Regiment of the 83d Division, finally sw through it at 0300 with marching fire. They j walked in and kept shooting.

They kept shooting even when they came do the Neuss main street because the houses w filled with snipers. Within the next few hou some of the Germans ran into the cellars a were burrowed out by hand grenades; some them just continued firing all day long, kill some doughs, and then, when they ran out ammo, came out smiling cheerfully, ready to s render; and some of these *Volksturm* boys i conned the situation, stopped shooting, took *Volksturm* armbands off their civilian clothes a ran outside with bottles of cognac to greet American liberators.

"We caught a couple of those bastards in act," said the battalion CO, Lt. Col. Tim Cook Snyder, Tex. "I had a tough time trying to s my boys from shooting the whole bunch of the

"These people seem to think that if they ta down their Nazi flags and scratch out Hitler's f on the big portrait on the wall of their fr parlor they're automatically anti-Nazis and bosom buddies. I just don't trust any of th bastards."

The first day in Neuss was typical of a wh week's war.

Civilians were strutting around town, not p ing any attention to snipers' bullets, well kno ing that they weren't targets. Shells were dr ping in the town's outskirts, near the river, o a few blocks away, and every once in a while soldiers around the city square would l around for doorways to run into. But most of guys didn't seem to be worried too much. A f of them were tinkering with a nonworking serted civilian auto. Several dozen others w riding around on bicycles. Some were even we ing top hats.

If you wanted to see the Rhine River and Du seldorf, you had to go to the noisy, unhealt part of town and climb to the top of one of big buildings.

Somebody told us where a good spot wa two blocks down, turn right. You can't miss it.

A window in the top-floor toilet was the Battalion OP. From there you could not only Duesseldorf and the big bridge over the Rhi but you could also see war almost as clearly a it were a play and y were sitting in the eig row center.

You could see the Kra dug in for a last-di stand in front of bridge (which was sche uled to be blown soon), and you could our guys ducking a running and falling f And you could see mor fire falling among the During all this, on floor below us, some women were scrubbi floors, occasionally st ing at the visiting Ame can soldiers with expre sionless faces.

Back at the center the town, sitting behi a heavy machine gun, P John Becraft of Broc lyn, N. Y., and C Con pany didn't seem to gi much of a damn abo the Rhine.

"I'd rather see Hudson," he said.

YANK. The Army Weekly, publication issued weekly by Branch Office, Information & Education Division, War Department, 205 East 42d Street, New York 17, N. Y. Reproduction rights restricted as indicated in masthead on the editorial page. Entered as second class matter July 6, 1942, at the Post Office at New York, N. Y., under the Act of March 3, 1879. Subscription price $3.00 yearly. Printed in the U. S.

IWO:D+8

...tour of the beach from the gar-
...son atmosphere of one end to
...e bloody combat of the other.

By Sgt. BILL REED
YANK Staff Correspondent

WITH THE MARINES ON IWO JIMA—On D-Day-plus-8 the southeastern end of Iwo Jima had very nearly gone garrison. This had ...n the invasion beach—the stretch of sand run-...g down from Motoyama Airfield No. 2 to the ... of Mount Suribachi. On D-day the road par-...ling the beach had been covered with mines ... tank traps. Beyond the beach were Jap ma-...e-gun nests and snipers. And the advancing ...ericans headed into one of the worst mortar ... artillery bombardments in Pacific warfare. ...ow MPs ordered marines to police up around ...r foxholes; higher brass was rumored to be ...ing for a visit. Some junior officers already ...pped Rotary Club salutes at their superiors. A ...r-echelon troops were going AWOL to Mount ...ibachi to hunt souvenirs in the caves.

...he beach was busy and confused. Ducks, ...racks, weasels, bulldozers and trucks puffed ...ds of dust as they struggled from one area ... nother. Huge cranes looked like robot giraffes ...hey moved cargo from LSMs, LCMs and LSTs. ... sweated and cursed and wrangled, trying to ...h their freight ahead of someone else's. An ...er's sedan on the road looked as out of place ... dowager in a bawdy house.

...here was a Seabee camp on the beach, and ...w it bulldozers leveled the land and 10 men ... shovels dug graves. A surveying crew took ...surements to fix the exact resting place of ... body. Behind a line of freshly dug earth ...e several rows of filled-in graves. Above each ...ve was a dog tag on a pointed stick. Later the ...ks would be replaced by white crosses. A few ...ines passed between the rows examining the ... tags for the names of their friends.

...allbearers carried bodies shrouded in green ...adcloth to the graves and then returned for ...e. A lieutenant asked Pvt. John W. Conloy of ...Roy, N. Y., in charge of a pallbearer detail, for ...ceipt. Conloy handed him a slip of paper ...tifying the last body buried. "It's too bad, but ... can't even get buried without a receipt," the ...tenant said.

...o the northeast was an artillery post. The ar-...rymen had come in at 0300 on D-plus-1 and ... fired an average of 350 rounds a day since ...ding. Now they were resting while Sgt. Wal-...T. Edwards of Lakeland, Fla., received tele-...ned instructions.

...The first patrol is going into a new village," ...Edwards said.

...hat must be where all those geisha girls are," ...Cpl. George T. Delta of Berkeley Springs, ...Va., one of the crew members. "I hear they ...400 of them."

...here was talk about the geisha girls, and then ...Edwards listened more attentively to his ...phones.

...Okay, let's go," he shouted. The crewmen ...ped to their positions. "Change the deflection ...t, one-three-four—fire!"

...cross from the artillery post was a dump ...d with boxes of D- and C-rations. Cpl. Floyd ...Barton of Sarasota, Fla., sat on a box, mark-...figures on a pad. He had no helmet and his

face puckered in a frown of concentration that was not interrupted by the boom of the gun near-by. His job was distributing rations, and he thought Iwo Jima was a better place to distribute rations than either Saipan or Guam, where he had been before. "It's cooler and there aren't so many insects," he said. The rations were picked up at his dump by trucks that carried them as far to the front as they could go. Then the boxes went the rest of the way on men's backs.

Road traffic dwindled as you moved north. Pfc. Steve A. Trochek of Clairton, Pa., lay on his back on the bank between the road and the first air-strip, repairing a communications line. He had been in the front lines for five days as an artil-lery observer and was working in the rear area as a rest. The line he mended led directly to the front where he expected to return in the morning.

Just two days before, the front lines had strad-dled this first airstrip, and already souvenir hunt-ers had searched through the ruins of Jap fighter planes and bombers strewn across runways and hard stands. A grader worked on one end of the field, and bulldozers, tractors and other graders had been moved up to prepare the base for our own bombers. Pfc. Darrel J. Farmer of Broken Bow, Nebr., ran a grader he had brought in al-most before the Japs moved out. He started his work under mortar and sniper fire, but it was quieter now. "We'll have the field ready in two days," he told bystanders.

Farther up, Pvt. John R. Dober of Milwaukee, Wis., operated a mag-netic mine detector. He was as careful with it as a housewife with a new vacuum cleaner. He had to comb over every foot of the road to make sure it was safe for the bull-dozers that would follow.

A battalion aid station was set up in a clearing above where Dober was working. Corpsmen gave plasma to two marine casualties. Less than an hour had passed since they had been wounded. In another 30 minutes they would be aboard a hospital ship.

A medical officer, just back from the forward CP, told Floyd M. Jen-kins CPhM of Altus, Okla., to prepare to move the station 100 yards closer to the next ridge. "They've been going like hell today," he said, "and they're shoving off again at 1240."

At the top of the ridge the road blended into the sandy plain. Fighting had been vicious here. An American heavy tank lay flopped over on one side, its turret hurled 30 yards away by a land mine. The gunner, carried away by the turret, had been butchered by a jagged piece of iron. Arms, legs and bodies of other members of the crew had been twisted as badly as their tank.

Half a dozen American bodies were piled a few yards above the tank. They were covered with ponchos and shelter halves, and from beneath the covers one clenched fist jutted belligerently. American dead lay everywhere. This battlefield was so new there had been no time to clear it.

Beyond another ridge were the front-line re-

serve troops. They crouched in foxholes and talked quietly. They inspected their weapons and occasionally fired them to make sure they worked. They chewed on fig bars and smoked cigarettes and pawed the dirt restlessly with their feet. Be-yond them were the front lines.

COMPARED with the noise, bickering and confu-sion that surrounded the southern (garrison) end of the beach, the front lines were peaceful. On D-Day-plus-8 we were just in front of Air-field No. 2 and about 700 yards from Sandy Ridge, the last major objective on the island. The battle-field was a flat, desertlike plain with no hills, shrubbery or trees for protection, and it was dominated from the ridge by Jap machine guns, snipers and mortars.

We made headway slowly. Every yard advanced was an individual problem. It was a battle of single-man charges from one foxhole to another. A man would crouch silently in a shelter and look across the sand to a foxhole ahead. He would watch the other men try to reach that foxhole, and he would figure the angle and range of the machine-gun and sniper fire that sputtered to stop them. After watching enough of the others advance successfully, the man would try to make it himself. But when one marine failed, it was a psychological hazard for everyone else.

There were too many failures. There were too many marines sprawled in the dirt with caked blood on their fatigue coats.

The field was a space of great silences. There was no conversation about the war and no curs-ing or bickering. When a man stumbled into a foxhole, the men who were there automatically made room for him. When he decided to leave, there was no melodramatic well-wishing. When enemy bullets dropped a man, he went down like a character in a silent picture—there were no groans or calls for help. It was a hushed panto-mime of war which the sounds from machine guns, sniper fire and mor-tars seemed to accentuate.

Cpl. D. J. Mason, a rifleman from Lincoln Park, Mich., watched from behind a sand dune on the edge of the field. Since early morning he had been moving slowly ahead with the riflemen. He was a reconnaissance man, and it was his job to see that no unnecessary gaps occurred between his regiment and the one on its flank. Since D-Day he had been advancing yard by yard, exactly as he was advancing on D-plus-8. He figured out be-forehand every dash he made between one fox-hole and another. So far he had figured right. Now the vanguard patrols were beyond his range of vision and it was time to dash again.

Souvenir hunters were already at work.

He studied the next foxhole carefully and then he studied the ridge from which a machine gun and two snipers fired consistently at anyone who tried to reach the hole. Dirt had splattered dan-gerously about the feet of two corpsmen as they slid into the foxhole a moment before. A dead marine who had made the wrong calculation lay several feet to the right of the hole.

Mason rolled his tongue in his mouth as his mind worked on the problem. Then he grabbed his rifle and hurled himself toward his objective, his feet pounding out a wake of dust and ashes. As he approached the shelter the machine gun spoke sharply and the sniper's bullet pinged over his head. Then he smashed into the hole. A mo-ment later he crawled carefully up the embank-ment on the other side.

He had figured right again.

Yanks at Home Abroad

Lend-Lease Art

EASTERN COMMAND, USSTAF, SOMEWHERE IN THE SOVIET UNION—Reverse lend-lease in the form of a good-will gesture was made here recently when 1st Sgt. Peter F. Sabakar of the Red Army painted a portrait of President Roosevelt to accompany one of Marshal Stalin. Both portraits now hang on the stage of a theater built jointly by American and Russian GIs.

Sgt. Sabaker, a self-taught artist, did the job in one day from a photograph that appeared in *Stars & Stripes*. He has been in the Soviet Army since the beginning of the war, was awarded the Medal for Courage and was recently retired from active duty because of a bad bullet wound in his hand.

—Sgt. SAMUEL CHAVKIN
YANK Field Correspondent

1st Sgt. Morris Hornstein (center) turns postman for Pfc. Godin (left) and Pfc. Cerrato outside The Tent.

Home Is Where You Make It

NEW HEBRIDES—In the beginning it was just another GI pyramidal tent. Now it's known as The Tent and is the home of Pfc. Gerald Godin of Auburn, Maine, and Pfc. Mike Cerrato of New York City. It has easy chairs, a chicken yard, vegetable and flower gardens and even a mailbox.

Around the front is a white picket fence, with a latticed arch for a gateway. The tent has neatly screened sidewalls. The smooth floor is painted red and white in a checkerboard design. On one side is a kitchen cabinet, equipped with a Coleman stove. On another side is a writing desk with chair to match. About the only things lacking are a piano and the little woman.

The furniture was all made by Godin, a former shipyard worker. Cerrato is responsible for the landscaping details.

Oh, yes. There is also a boarder. He's the first sergeant, who came to dinner one night and has lived there ever since.

—Sgt. JAMES GOBLE
YANK Staff Correspondent

Rough on Rats

MINDORO, PHILIPPINES—Before the war, the owner of the land on which this AAF Squadron built its camp spent $13,000 to clear the area of rats. He was not successful.

The rat situation is so bad on the field that special measures have had to be devised. The I & E Section advertised for a cat because rats were eating their recordings. T/Sgt. Robert C. Wilson and T/Sgt. Lloyd R. Newton built an electronic rat trap, which can electrocute 10 rats at a time. They bait their trap with pork, bacon, corn kernels or cookies. They refuse to use bully beef because they say they don't want to torture the rats, they just want to kill them.

Right now the two men are working on a new model with a mirror arrangement and light beam, to check the height, weight and resistance of each rat. The measuring devices will be hooked onto a voltmeter, which will give small jolts to small rats and large jolts to large rats. The inventors say the saving in juice will be sensational.

T-5 Robert J. Keegan is another who considers the use of bully beef for bait unsportsmanlike. He believes, however, that it is unbeatable in its tin jacket for individual combat with the enemy. In an official combat report, written after an engagement with a rat that was after a sandwich Keegan was eating, he wrote: "The enemy came up from 7 o'clock. I executed an evasive turn, completed it with a snap roll to the left and, as expected, found the enemy in my sights. I used a deflection shot consisting of one two-second burst from my bully-beef can. The enemy took the burst square in the motor and spiraled and when last seen was flaming toward the ground. My camera was not functioning at the time, but Flt. Lt. (T-5 Leon) Shippie, my wing man, will confirm the victory."

The squadron newspaper, *Mud-n-Dust*, spoke for everyone when it said in a flaming editorial: "We will fight them in our tents; we will fight them in the company streets; in the latrine; the mess hall. We will never surrender!"

—Sgt. RAY FORER
YANK Field Correspondent

Amazon Valley Post

SOMEWHERE IN THE AMAZON VALLEY—This emergency-landing strip is 300 miles from nowhere in a land nobody wants, but it is home to the GIs stationed here.

The oldest living resident, S/Sgt. Lonnie Williams of Indianapolis, Ind., has sweated it out for 16 months. The nearest settlement is Amapa, which can be reached by a two-hour boat ride through crocodile- and snake-infested swamps. It consists only of a couple of rows of native grass shacks.

Hunting leads the extra-curricular pastimes. One day some GIs brought back a 17-foot anaconda weighing 187 pounds. Other game includes crocodiles, panthers and leopards.

The climate is also ducky. Rainfall during the December-April season exceeds 160 inches. The entire area becomes a sticky steaming bog, and clothing, bedding, everything mildews. Barracks are built up on pilings like the native huts.

There is a meagerly stocked PX, movies are shown two or three times a week and the chow isn't bad. But that's all, brother. That's all.

—Sgt. DON COOKE
YANK Staff Correspondent

Chocolate Soldier

WITH THE FIFTH ARMY, ITALY—Sgt. Charles Hooper of Woodsfield, Ohio, is not a mess sergeant. He is NCO in charge of a gun section with the 175th Field Artillery, 34th Division. All of which is probably why he has had enough imagination to defy the instructions on his ration wrappers and develop a new dish for winter warfare.

The wrapper on the chocolate bars shipped to the Fifth Army front read "Tropical Chocolate." Sgt. Hooper could read and he knew he wasn't in the tropics. "It just didn't seem to apply here," says Sgt. Hooper. "Since it didn't apply here, I decided to make ice cream out of mine. I chipped the bar up fine, mixed it with some condensed milk and topped it off with some good, clean snow. When I whipped the mixture up, out in the cold, it became ice cream." As easy as that.

—Cpl. NATHAN S. LEVY
YANK Field Correspondent

A Difference in Rank

WITH THE FIRST CONVOY TO CHINA OVER THE LEDO-BURMA ROAD—At one of the many parties thrown for the officers and men of the convoy on its way through China, a member of the Chinese Army was placed as host at each table of GIs.

At one table a GI driver began calling the Chinese Army man "Butch" and getting very chummy, although neither could speak more than a few words of the other's language. Fina[lly] the host asked the GI, "What is your comm[is]sion in the Army, sir?"

The GI grinned and replied, "Corporal. Wh[at's] yours, Butch?"

The Chinese Army man had to get an int[er]preter to find out what the GI said, then answered, "Lieutenant general, sir."

"Geez," said the GI later. "It's good he does[n't] know what a corporal is." —Sgt. DAVE RICHARDSO[N]
YANK Staff Correspond[ent]

Jap Atrocity

WITH THE 41ST DIVISION, THE PHILIPPINE[S]—Men of the 186th Infantry, who captu[red] Puerto Princessa Palattan, the westernmost p[oint] thus far in our Pacific advance, unearthed th[ree] huge pits filled with the charred bodies of J[ap]-massacred American PWs.

The story of what happened to these men w[as] told by nine of their number who escaped. O[ne] was Pvt. Glenn Weddell McDole, who fou[ght] with the 4th Marines on Corregidor. McD[ole] stated that the 40 Americans had congrega[ted] in pits used as air-raid shelters, after the a[ir]-raid warning had sounded.

"Then I looked out of my pit and saw a J[ap] captain come running followed by about 50 [Jap] soldiers armed with light machine guns a[nd] rifles and carrying buckets. I ducked back i[nto] my pit, when all of a sudden an explos[ion] sounded, and I heard men screaming and [the] sound of machine guns. One man looked out [of] the pit and said, 'They are murdering the m[en] in A Company pit.' I looked out and saw one m[an] coming out in a sheet of flame, and he was s[hot] down with a machine gun."

McDole and some others managed to get out [of] their pit through a prepared escape hatch, j[ust] before the Japs threw a bucket of gasoline a[nd] a torch into it. They hid under a pile of rub[bish] on the beach as the Japs went up and down k[ill]-ing all the prisoners they could find.

"About 30 meters down the beach I could [see] six Japs with an American in the center who w[as] being slowly tortured with bayonets while [an]-other Jap joined the group with a bucket a[nd] torch. The American screamed in such a h[igh] voice I could hear him. Then I could see th[em] pour gasoline on one foot and burn it, then [the] other until he collapsed. Then they poured ga[so]-line on his body and set it afire."

The nine prisoners known to have escap[ed] swam the bay and were picked up by guerril[las]. The statements made by all—some sailors, so[me] marines and some soldiers—were identical exc[ept] for minor details.

—Cpl. JOHN F. McLEO[D]
YANK Staff Correspond[ent]

ALTITUDE. GIs of the Seventh Army in France [pay] a visit to Georges Kieffer, "Giant of Alsace." He [is] 8 feet 6½ inches tall, weighs 268 pounds. [He] wears a size 26 shoe. The Nazis didn't draft [him] because they figured his upkeep would cost too mu[ch].

James Dallas was changed from "deferred" to 1-A.

Anthony Gentile, 27, is a 4-F with a punctured eardrum.

Stewart Kent is a discharged combat veteran.

Why Ain't They in Uniform?

Everybody overseas asks that about the young civilians at home. Here are a few of their answers to the big question.

By Cpl. HYMAN GOLDBERG
YANK Staff Writer

PROVIDENCE, R. I.—"How many guys are there still left in civilian clothes back home?" and "Why?" are two questions servicemen overseas ask sooner or later.

I've often wanted to stop some rugged-looking character in civilian clothes and ask those questions myself. Recently I had the chance. With a photographer big enough to take care of any situation that might arise if some character figured I was calling him a draft dodger, I came here to Providence, stood on one of the busiest street corners in town for an hour and talked with the first male civilians of draft age who came along. The corner was at Dorrance and Washington streets, in the downtown section.

The first man who came along was Anthony Gentile, a tall, worried-looking man with glasses. He's 27 years old and a former bartender and lives in Providence. He's a 4-F because he has a punctured eardrum.

"Listen," he said, "you think it's easy for a guy my age not to be in the Army? You think I'm having a good time? Every place I go people spit at me, like. I didn't ask they shouldn't put me in. They said to me, 'Go home, you're no good to us.' That's a fine thing to tell a guy. I didn't even know I got a punctured eardrum. It don't bother me at all, I tell them, but they don't want to listen to me. They say I should go home."

Some time ago bartenders, along with other workers like perfume salesmen and attendants in men's rooms, were declared by the War Manpower Commission to be unessential to the war effort.

"All right, so I'm not essential," said Gentile. "So I go out and get a job in a war plant. I can make a pretty good Martini and draw a neat glass of beer, but about other things I don't know. So I get a job as a floorman. That's what they call it, but it turns out to be pushing a wheelbarrow. Lemme tell you, a guy don't get the feeling he's killing Germans or Japs just pushing a wheelbarrow around. And every place you go, if you ain't wearing a uniform, they spit on you, like. I keep going back to my draft board asking them they should take me in, but they just laugh at me and say I should go home."

A young, healthy-looking fellow wearing a good topcoat and carrying a brief case came down Dorrance Street. He would have looked good in a uniform. He laughed when I asked him how come he wasn't wearing one. He threw open his coat and on the lapel of his blue-serge suit there was a winged discharge button.

"I wore a uniform for 26 months," he said, "and then they wanted it back so I gave it to them, because who am I to quarrel with them?"

He was Stewart Kent, 25 years old, of East Providence. He's a former tech sergeant with the Fifteenth Air Force, which used him as a gunner and radio operator in Italy and North Africa.

"I made 48 missions," he said, "and then I guess my nerves gave out on me or something, and they sent me back home." He came back with the Air Medal and nine Oak Leaf Clusters. He's working as a paint salesman now and doing pretty good.

"It's no wonder you stopped me," he said, "because there are a lot of guys who are out and don't wear their discharge buttons too conspicuously. It gives me a laugh sometimes when I see people looking at me as if they're wondering why I'm not in uniform."

The next man along looked within the draft age. He turned out to be Fred E. Magee, 44 years old but younger looking. He proved Stewart Kent's point about discharge buttons by flipping back his overcoat. There was a gold emblem on his suit too. "I enlisted in the Navy in 1942 and I was a QM2c in the Admiralty Islands, the Solomons and Guadalcanal in the Pacific," he said.

Magee got out on a dependency discharge and now works for the Pullman Company here.

A husky youngster walked up. "Hey, soldier," he said, "d'ya happen to know where the Navy Recruiting Office is?"

He wanted Navy Recruiting, he said, because he was going to enlist. He was Ernest Dube of Providence. "I was 17 years old last June and I got permission from my mother and father to enlist," he said.

"I been a rigger at the Newport Torpedo Station for 18 months. Why? Because I wanted to do what I could to help win the war, that's why. I was going to enlist last June, as soon as I got to be 17, but I broke my leg and I couldn't. My leg is fine now; it's stronger than the other one. Then I was gonna enlist two months ago, but geez, I couldn't get a day off to go to the recruiting office."

James Dallas, who is 27 and lives in West Haven, Conn., came along Dorrance Street. He's married and has a child.

"Right after Pearl Harbor," he said, "I went to the Navy and asked to be put into the Seabees. I'm an electrical expert, and I inspect electrical material for the New Haven Railroad. My brother-in-law went to the Navy with me. They took him, but they turned me down because my teeth weren't good enough."

Dallas has a couple of plates and the Navy told him to go home and wait. If the war continued, they told him, maybe his draft board would call him; anyway, the Navy didn't want him then. When his draft board did call him, the New Haven Railroad got him a deferment. Every six months after that, when the draft board called Dallas again, the railroad got him another deferment.

"I didn't want them to," he said, "but the railroad officials kept telling me that I was doing an important war job and that the railroad needed me and that without railroads the country couldn't fight a war. Well, I guess that's so, all right, but even so, a fellow my age doesn't feel right about staying out. Men older than myself have been called.

"My last deferment has until May yet, but last January my draft board called me and put me in 1-A, and I've just taken my physical and this time it doesn't matter about my teeth. I'm going in in a couple of weeks, and I'm glad about it. I only hope I can get into the Seabees, because I think that's where I can do the most good."

The next civilian to come along was Guido Lorenzo, 29. "Listen Mac," he said, "whaddaya mean why ain't I in uniform?" He flipped open his coat. He had a discharge button on his suit. "Know what that is?"

He had been in the Air Force, with the 326th Fighter Squadron at Santa Rosa, Calif., for almost two years, until July 1944, when they gave him a medical discharge. He's now working in Providence as a maintenance man for the New England Butt Company, which is engaged in the manufacture of war materiel.

Just as the hour was up, a lanky young fellow ambled up to the corner. He said his name was Victor Gold. "Why haven't I got a uniform on?" he repeated in amazement. "Gee whiz," he said, "I'm not old enough. People keep asking me all the time why I'm not in the Army or Navy. I'm only 16 years old."

Victor is in 11-A at Hope High School, where he is studying aeronautics and drafting. "Because in April I'm going to be 17," he said, "and then I'll be old enough to get in the Navy with my parents' permission. All my friends are in, and it's awful lonesome.'"

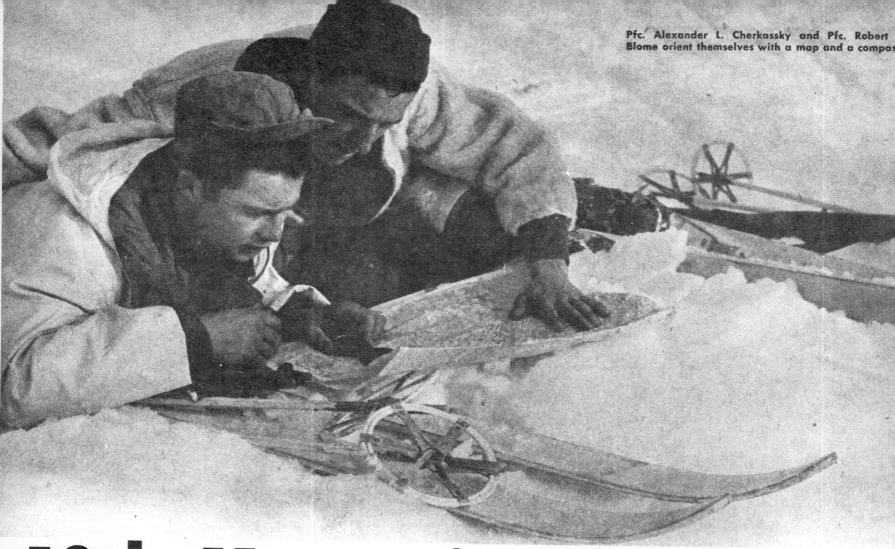

10th Mountain Division

These ski and boot troopers have learned how to get the maximum in mobility and surprise on the snow-covered slopes of Italy.

By Cpl. GEORGE BARRETT
YANK Staff Correspondent

WITH THE FIFTH ARMY IN ITALY—The six-foot-three MP waved the German prisoner into the PW cage with his machine pistol. The Kraut's fingers played nervously with the M1-bullet hole in his right breast pocket. He turned around and said to no one in particular: "They look upon the war as though it were a sport. They are not tired at all. It's all a sport with them." He was talking about his captors.

The PW was one of 388 Germans captured recently in three days by the picked and specially trained "Ski and Boot Troops" of the 10th U. S. Mountain Infantry Division—the same outfit that used to pose for all those snow pictures in the magazines and newsreels when it was training back at Camp Hale in the Colorado Rockies.

In a way the German was right. It sometimes seems as if the 10th regards this slow and punishing war in the Apennines as a part of a college winter-sports carnival. There are regimental orders decreeing undergraduate crew haircuts for every man and encouraging singing. Before the division began its drive on Mount Belvedere in late February—the first successful American offensive action in Italy since the cracking of the Gothic Line five months before—the divisional newspaper published the following:

"In case you're worried about being able to keep that Luger or machine pistol you expect to take from Jerry, forget it. Here's a direct quote from the top: 'I don't want any souvenirs my men may get from a Kraut taken away from them. That Luger or burp gun belongs to that soldier and if he wants to trade it off for cognac or save it for his best girl until after the war—

OK. It's his, to do with as he sees fit. . . . It's open season, and there are plenty of Lugers. Good hunting.'"

The next morning the 10th attacked. Climbing upward over sheer cliffs that the Germans had considered inaccessible and losing men in deep chasms and from dangerously high peaks, they took the strategic mountain which had been lost on two previous occasions. They stripped the burp guns and Lugers, and the periscopes, mortars and knives, from the dead Krauts and rolled the corpses down the mountainside.

"We returned with much booty," said a GI in the 2d Platoon of Company A, 86th Mountain Regiment. "We took a victrola from a German dugout and carted it to our foxhole. Jerry had left a lot of Al Jolson records, and we played them all night long after we took the top of that ridge. Oh, hell, there was nothing dangerous about making all that noise. They knew we were there anyhow. Incidentally, their butter is lousy."

The winter-carnival atmosphere in the 10th is something that might be expected. After all, Walter Prager, the Dartmouth ski coach, is a first sergeant in the 87th Mountain Regiment. Friedl Pfeiffer, U. S. slalom champion and ski instructor at Sun Valley, Idaho, is one of the buck sergeants. Torger Tokle, the national ski-jumping champion, is a tech sergeant. Pvt. Herbert Schneider, scout-observer in the 86th Regiment's I and R Platoon, has spent his whole life at winter-sport resorts; he is the son of Hannes Schneider, the famous Austrian ski instructor. And most of the other men are members of the National Ski Association, which helped the Army organize its first Mountain Infantry battalion in December 1941, at Fort Lewis, Wash.

One of the few soldiers in the 10th who didn't spend all their free time before the war at winter-sports resorts and ski tournaments is the division commander, Maj. Gen. George P. Hays, who flew here from France, where he had been commanding the 2d Infantry Division's artillery, and took over the mountain outfit when it arrived from the States. But Maj. Gen. Hays has

another claim to distinction; he is one of the ra[re] generals who are entitled to wear the Congre[s]sional Medal of Honor ribbon. He won it as [a] second lieutenant in the other World War.

Because the division was drawn largely fro[m] the social class of men who could afford th[e] rather expensive sport of skiing in civilian lif[e] it has more swank than the usual Infantry outf[it.] It is quite normal to hear one of its lieutenan[ts] say, "My platoon sergeant is a Princeton gra[d.]

Pfc. William C. Douglas of Lake Forest, Ill., carefull[y] makes his way across a mountain stream on his sk[is]

uate, *cum laude*," or to get challenged in its area by a sentry with a Harvard accent. Back at Camp Hale, where they bothered about such things, the average AGCT of one of the regiments was 121, which meant that the dumbest buck private was eligible for OCS. If he did decide to take that step, the chances are it wouldn't have gotten him out of the division. Most officer candidates from the 10th, because of their specialized mountain training, go right back into the division after they get their commissions. Nine of the current company commanders used to be enlisted men in the division.

THE men of the 10th have been trained for every kind of mountain fighting, summer and winter—their stub-toed ski boots have heavy rubber cleats for rock climbing—but they are particularly effective in snow operations. As snow troops, according to one platoon leader, patrols of the 10th move "five times as far, four times as fast" as regular Infantry. Winter reconnaissance patrols by the 10th are likely to be more successful than I and R sorties by ordinary Infantry outfits because ski soldiers go higher and deeper into the mountains. If they are suddenly spotted by the Krauts at close range, they have the mobility to get out and away fast.

The 10th faces peculiar difficulties. It is not practical, for example, for skiers to carry their rifles at port in enemy territory; it takes two hands to use ski poles, and skiers must use their poles to climb high ground. Sometimes, under pressure, they have to fire their rifles with these poles still hanging from their wrists. The 12-pound skis and 2-pound poles make it important for the mountain trooper to streamline his movements. He will sometimes carry grenades fastened to his harness so the safety pin will be pulled out automatically when he yanks a grenade off to toss it.

A lot of the special equipment and tactics they cooked up back in the States in training, however, have been discarded at the front. They used to get superstreamlined mountain rations, but they now find that the 10-in-1s are just as good. They don't bother to wear the white ski pants any more; the parka is just as effective for camouflage. Rifles were once painted white, but that is not considered necessary on the line in Italy. Special ski waxes are in the T/E but candles do the trick almost as well.

"We also discovered that the mountains here are a lot steeper and more wind-swept than those in the States," one GI says. "Consequently we learned that we'd probably have to carry our skis a lot oftener than they carried us. On the other hand, the 4,000-foot altitudes in the Apennines are nothing compared with the 10,000 feet of the Rockies, where we trained. It's much easier to breathe over here. Also, during training back in the States we stuck pretty close to the cover of forests, but here we've found we're not taking

many risks if we move in the open, even in daylight, when we are in positions higher than the enemy."

The men find their skis make noise on the hard snow crusts in the Apennines, and they have to take their boards off when approaching a Kraut position. On patrols, the mountain troops often require two scouts, one to break trail and another to do the scouting.

Everybody in the division is trained to move on skis or snowshoes in winter, even the chaplains. The mountain-troopers use the Arlberg technique of skiing. It is slower than the parallel technique but it provides more control on the turns and is a lot surer for soldiers carrying packs and weapons. They can move at 10 miles per hour if they have to make a fast get-away, and a good skier, using $11 GI skis, will cut over the snow at 25 miles per hour on some stretches. What with the back pack and the weapons they carry, this is considered pretty good by the same guys who in pre-war races thought 50 miles per hour was nothing and who made records of 80 miles per hour.

"Snow jeeps"—M29s, or weasels as they are usually called—are the all-purpose vehicles of the 10th. These amphibious tractors—all white, even to the leather seats—haul supplies, tow skiers and do generally on the snow what jeeps do on the dirt. With their tread they can go almost anywhere a mule can go.

The 10th is organized on the combat-team principle. The rugged terrain of the mountains requires that the various units be self-sustaining, because supplies are often impossible to transport. The division's artillery pieces—75-mm pack howitzers—are broken down into sections and carried over the mountains on burros.

Gunners are trained to direct their fire against masses of rock and snow to create avalanches and engulf Kraut positions on the slopes below. These tactics are surprisingly effective. Division artillery officers point out that more than half of the casualties in Alpine fighting during the first World War were caused by avalanches.

Fighting in the mountains as a division presents the 10th with other problems. For example, the length of a battalion going single file up a mountain is four miles, but there may be more than 3,000 feet difference in altitude between the head and the tail of the column, affecting differently the speed and endurance of the men in its various sections.

The 10th probably does more climbing than skiing, and many of their sessions look like something out of a sea story when the GIs practice knots and lashings. They use the Tyrolean Traverse—a two-rope bridge stretched across crevasses and chasms—and improvise cableways to hoist jeeps and supplies up sheer cliffs.

Ropes are standard equipment and are given the same personal care that M1s get. The lore of hemp has been drilled into the men of the

10th. They know that rope will lose 40 percent of its strength in nine months from age alone; that 40 percent of strength is lost when manila is bent sharply around a hook, and that any knot weakens a rope but no knot weakens it so little as the butterfly.

The mountain medics have had to alter ordinary procedure. "Plasma is useless to us," one medic says. "It won't flow in intense cold, and we don't even take it along. In fact, we take very little with us except morphine and bandages. What counts in our work is speedy evacuation. Wounded men relapse into shock cases very fast in the cold at high altitudes, and unless we get them to a warm place soon they're finished.

"The other day we picked up a sergeant in the snow and brought him to the station on a sled; it was fast work but he was in profound shock when we arrived. If we had not been equipped for snow transport the normal delay would have killed him."

The medics are picked partly for their size; they are generally husky guys who have been given intensive training in mountain work. "It takes a strong man to get casualties out of mountain and snow areas," a medical captain points out. "Medics must be experts—in skiing, snowshoe work, ropes and climbing—and they must work in large teams, for it takes six or seven medics to go after, say, one expert mountain-climbing infantryman and bring him back."

The medics' job is made harder by the fact that the ratio of walking-wounded to litter cases is sharply decreased in mountain warfare. Even slightly wounded soldiers cannot stand the heavy strain of struggling on foot down steep slopes and across cliffs. Special precautions must be taken with litter cases. Their helmets are kept on, for example, to protect them from falling rocks. They must be securely but painlessly tied onto the litter across the pelvis so they will not slide off while lurching over the uneven terrain.

"IT's hard to think of any operation of ours that is not different from most outfits' tactics," a captain said. "In general, 10th Division units are told that no matter how small they are they can at any time become independent commands. Mountains separate outfits very suddenly, and on the basis of knowledge that 10th Division troops are extremely alert and intelligent, SOP requires that junior leaders be given the 'big' picture. They are expected to do whatever needs doing to complete the over-all strategy."

Then the captain quoted from the manual: ". . . There are no problems in mountain warfare which an aggressive and indomitable leader cannot solve. The movement of Hannibal's elephants through the Alps, in the dead of winter, without aid of bulldozer, is ancient proof that insurmountable obstacles can be overcome."

"That's from our Army handbook," the captain smiled. "It's the kind of stuff we believe in."

The mountain medics are skilled in getting sleds and litters up steep slopes. The GIs in the foreground are having a rope tossed to them to tie to the sled.

Pvt. Hubert Campbell of Eugene, Oreg., a 10th Division MP, stands guard over a bunch of prisoners just brought in by ski troops. He has an M3 machine pistol.

Burma Hermits

Mail call comes only once a month, there's never any pay day and the jungle is a worse enemy than the Jap.

●

By Sgt. WALTER PETERS
YANK Staff Correspondent

NORTHERN BURMA—One day during the fall of 1942 a clerk at Services of Supply Headquarters in India was studying a requisition form from a Signal Corps Aircraft Warning outfit. After reading the form again he suspected that someone was trying to pull a gag.

The clerk called a sergeant. Then the sergeant called a lieutenant. "Now, what the hell do they want with that kind of stuff?" asked the sergeant. "Colored beads, rock salt, flashy-colored blankets and—well, and all those other crazy items."

Today SOS Headquarters in this theater is no longer surprised at anything that Aircraft Warning may order. Requests for items that aren't strictly GI are complied with quickly and without question.

To accomplish their mission, men of the Aircraft Warning units frequently have to venture into strange and unexplored sections of the jungle. They are often forced to call for the help of natives who have never seen white men before, and these natives usually prefer glittering and flashy objects to money.

During its history, Aircraft Warning has constructed hundreds of miles of jungle and foot trails, and many times, because of the nature of the terrain, its men have had to travel far beyond Jap lines to establish their stations.

The first station was established late in 1942 in the Naga Hills of India, on the Burma border. Later, as the Americans and Chinese fought their way through northern Burma, many other stations were set up in the jungles and hills of that country. Now the network is so vast that a Jap plane can rarely sneak over our lines without being detected.

The station I visited is only a few miles from a road on the Burma-India border. Many other stations, however, are so far back in the jungles that it takes anywhere from 5 to 18 days' walking to get to them. The trails are narrow and snake around steep hills, and often you must ford waist-deep streams.

Our guide was T/Sgt. Fred Fegley of Pine Grove, Pa., a former lineman for the Pennsylvania Light and Power Company. Fegley has spent more than two years at various stations and during that time he figures he has hiked upward of 1,500 miles of jungle trail. "I'm not kicking, mind you," Fegley said as we paused for a rest. "But back in the States nobody in our outfit ever dreamed we would go through anything like this."

Fegley said that the outfit's greatest danger was not from the Japs, but from nature. During monsoon seasons the men don't dare sit on the ground for a rest. "You even pick up leeches when you're walking," Fegley said. "Frequently you have to stop to pick them from your body so they won't suck too much blood out of you.

"And during the monsoons, streams become rivers. There are dozens of streams across the paths to many of our stations. So a station that takes a five-day hike in ordinary times is difficult to get to in twice that time when the monsoons are on."

One thing you can knock off as a myth, ac-

Pvt. George Karastamatis of the Bronx, N. Y., is on duty as ground observer at an AW station in Northern Burma.

These quarters were built by Naga natives. At the table is Cpl. Dale Calderon, cook, and right is Pvt. Karastamatis.

ding to Fegley, is the danger from wild animals ch as tigers and elephants. "Actually our out- has had little trouble from animals," Fegley d. "Most people like to exaggerate the number wild animals they see in the jungle. Of course, u do have to be careful. Once one of our men t up his jungle hammock for the night and his g crept under it to sleep. Next morning there s a pool of blood but no dog."

HE average station is operated by a 10-man team with a staff sergeant in command. The n are required to spend at least six months the jungle before returning to a rear area for rest. But oftener than they like, they have to nain longer. Some teams have served at their sts as long as 11 months without relief.

One of the first acts of an Aircraft Warning m is to call on the village nearest the station. ost natives have been helpful; they've shown e men where to find their water supply and lped build *bashas*—quarters for the men—from mboo and thatching.

The Army's system of going through channels found even among the natives in the jungle. fore hiring anyone the men first contact the adman of the village, who then designates a mber of his people to work at the station. The adman usually sends his own son to act as a rt of straw boss.

"Things have changed from the early days in ese jungles," Fegley lamented. "It used to be e could do a flourishing business with the na- es by trading large tin cans. One can would ing you as much as a chicken. Now there are many tin cans that it's caused inflation. A guy n't even get the shell of an egg for one."

At one station where the men ran out of trin- ts, a GI squeezed all the cream from a Wil- ms shaving tube. Then he very neatly flattened e tube and gave it to one of the natives. The tive wore it as an ornament around his neck— ee advertising for Williams shaving cream.

Medics are highly respected by the natives. t. Eugene Schultz of Buffalo, N. Y., is the edic at the station I visited. All the natives ere call him Doc. "We're too far from a village re," Schultz said, "but at other stations some our medics make weekly calls on the villages. visiting day every woman and child groups ound Doc, and they all pour out their troubles.

native (second from left) plays volleyball with s on a field they constructed on a 4,000-foot hill.

One thing we have been able to accomplish in ese jungles is to teach these people to be eaner. Many of them suffer from malaria and ysentery. Since we've been stressing cleanliness e've found fewer of them with dysentery." During my stay at Schultz's station, a native oman came in with a badly infected foot. chultz tried for days to persuade her to soak in hot water and epsom salts. She finally con- nted after other natives nagged her into it. "Usually you don't have to urge them," Schultz ys. "And, brother, once you get them coming sick call you really get the business. They me whether they're sick or not. When you give

one of them a pill they all demand one. We final- ly got around it by giving salt tablets to those who weren't ill. The salt tablets do no harm and they make the natives happier."

The days at the station are long and boring. Some of the men have taken to writing books and short stories. Occasionally the headman in- vites one of the GIs to a pig roast in the village, but mostly the men spend their time reading or hunting. Every team is given a 12-gauge gun for hunting purposes. Barking deer, pheasants, quail and several species of grouse are the most com- mon game.

Some of the men have taken to teaching the children to read and write, and many natives around the stations have acquired an elementary knowledge of English. Cpl. Russell Higgerson of Albany, N. Y., was teaching two children at the station I visited. "Don't kid yourself about their appearance," Higgerson said. "These kids are as smart as any I've seen back home. I'd love to take one to the States and see what a school edu- cation could do for him."

Mail service is the biggest gripe the men have. Mail, delivered with food and supplies, is dropped by C-47s once a month except during the mon- soon season, when it's even slower. The problem of getting mail for the States out to an APO is more difficult. At some stations the men have worked out a runner system with native messengers. But the men at stations 50 miles or deeper in the jungle have to wait many months before they can send a letter home. To keep their

families informed, the officers at headquarters write for the men.

The men aren't paid until they report back to headquarters for a rest, but since there is no place to spend money, they don't give the pay delay a thought.

SOME men in the outfit have had their share of combat. When Col. Philip Cochran and his 1st Airborne Commandos landed 150 miles behind Jap lines in northern Burma in March 1944, an Aircraft Warning unit went along. Most of their equipment was bombed out after the men had landed, and many of the men suffered from malaria. Nevertheless they went on with their work and established a station.

Last April, when the Japs penetrated into Assam in their threat to invade India, the men in the Kohima district remained at their stations until the enemy almost overran them. 1st Sgt. Daniel H. Schroeder of Casnovia, Mich., a com- munications chief, was one of the last American enlisted men to leave his post when the Japs cut the Manipur Road between Kohima and Dima- pur. And during the Jap drive, Aircraft Warning units were the sole medium of communicating in- telligence to the British. Native scouts reported the Jap movements, and the men at the stations relayed the information to the British.

Fegley was team chief at one of those stations. At 2200 one night, a native reported that the enemy had infiltrated the area near the station. Fegley ordered his men to destroy all equipment. He also ordered that all food cans be broken with axes and creosote poured into them. This was done so that the Japs, who were known to be short on food, could not bene- fit from our supplies.

At 0300 next morning, Fegley and his men took their field equipment, tommy guns and hand grenades and began hiking through the jungles to warn another station. The men walked until 2200 that night, cov- ering a distance of 28 miles. After taking a five-hour break, they re- sumed the trek until they reached the other station, 19 miles farther.

The threat of Jap planes has been eliminated to a great extent in this theater, but the men are still kept busy. These hills are among the most difficult in the world to fly over, and a number of crashes result. When this happens, the stations nearest the crash are called upon to send out searching parties. Dozens of flyers have been saved in this manner.

In August 1943, when John B. Davies, secretary to the American Embassy in Chungking, crashed with a number of American civil- ians and soldiers and Chinese of- ficers, men of Aircraft Warning went to the rescue. The plane crashed in the Ponyo area of the Naga Hills. Some natives in that area are known to be head-hunters and generally unfriendly. There- fore help had to be sent as quickly as possible.

Two Aircraft Warning men—1st Lt. Andrew La Bonte of Lawrence, Mass., and S/Sgt. John L. De Chaine of Oakland, Calif.—together with a British political officer, organized a searching party of natives ac- quainted with that section. The men tramped over narrow paths and through mud and water for five days and covered 125 miles before they found the crash victims.

When the party prepared to leave with 20 survivors of the crash, some natives started a riot over items that were left behind. Sgt. De Chaine, employing a little Yan- kee diplomacy, intervened and quelled the riot.

"In this business you've got to be a diplomat, a businessman, a hermit and an aircraft observer," Fegley said. "Mostly, though, you've got to be ready for surprises. Any- thing can happen here, even if we are a bunch of GI jungle orphans."

Sgt. Eugene Schultz of Buffalo, N. Y., medic for an observation team, treats the foot of a Naga woman.

Cpl. Russell Higgerson of Albany, N. Y., turns school teacher. He is trying to get two Naga kids through the English alphabet.

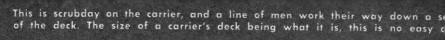

On the way to Tokyo some of the crew members get together for a game of basketball. The court is an elevator that lifts planes from the hangar deck.

This is scrubday on the carrier, and a line of men work their way down a s_ of the deck. The size of a carrier's deck being what it is, this is no easy _

This man, dressed in foul-weather gear, is loading ammunition into the wing gun of an F6F.

The carrier's guns blast at a sleeve towed behind a plane during practice firing en route to Tokyo.

That grin was a promise of things to come. The b_ he handles was last seen blowing up a piece of To_

Air-crewmen gather around as Shelton Garner ACRM marks up on the blackboard the names of the pilots who are to "fly the strike" the following day.

The carrier is somewhere in the waters off Japan, and the day is cold and over_ as the planes on the flight deck warm their motors before taking off for To_

BACK FROM TOKYO, A NAVY FIGHTER, AN F6F, LANDS ON THE WET DECK AS ANOTHER ONE COMES IN BEHIND IT AT RIGHT.

FLAT-TOP

Cpl. Lon Wilson, YANK cameraman in the Pacific, took these pictures aboard a carrier which was part of a fast task force attacking Indo-China and Tokyo.

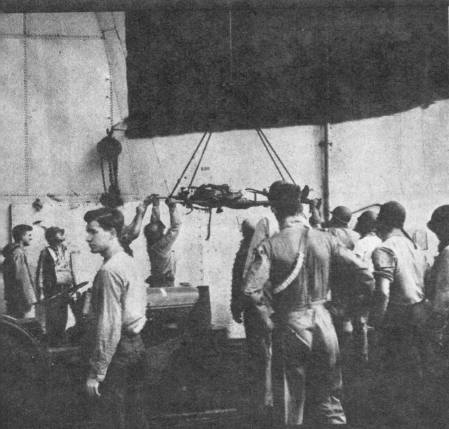

... of those who flew away came back but some of them paid a tough price. Here ...ounded officer is being lowered on a stretcher from the island to the flight deck.

Pilots who have just returned from strikes stop to answer some questions for Air Combat Intelligence officers before leaving the flight deck of the carrier.

THE SAD SACK

"SCREEN CREDIT"

SGT. GEORGE BAKER

By Cpl. TOM SHEHAN

THERE was nothing about T-5 Braidwood Mc-Manus that would suggest he was an athlete. He had flat feet, a perpetual hangover and a bad case of soda-fountain crouch from eating at Liggett's. That's why I was amazed when I read in the *Stars & Stripes* that he had entered the Allied Boxing Championships at the *Foro d'Italia* in Rome.

Naturally I hurried right down to the little bistro on Via Roma where Braidwood held forth, to find out what it was all about. I found him with a cigar stub in his left hand and half a glass of *vino* in the other, talking to a rugged-looking joe with a rather Celtic face.

"What's this story," I asked Braidwood, "about you fighting in the Allied Boxing Championships in Rome?"

"There you go," he said, "jumping to conclusions like you always do. I just wrote Special Services and told them about the Braidwood Mc-Manus entry, figuring I'd get some publicity for my fighter. But I never said that I was going to do any fighting."

"What's the Braidwood McManus entry?" I asked very skeptically.

"Shake hands," said Braidwood, "with Horizontal Hogan. He's going to win the welterweight title at the Allied Boxing Championships."

Before I left the place, Braidwood asked me to ride up to Rome with them the day before the tournament and work in Hogan's corner when he fought.

I'LL say this for Hogan: he talked about as good a fight as I've ever heard. All the way to Rome he kept telling McManus what he was going to do in the tournament, always referring back to what he'd done as a civilian. He had won something like 24 fights as an amateur, if you can call a fighter who sold the watches he won an amateur.

"Remember the time, Mack," he would say, "that I whipped Ripper Ralph Pantelone in the Golden Gloves at the Garden? He was pretty rough until I sunk my hook into his gut. They kept hollering '*A la banza!*' meaning for him to put one in my breadbasket, but he never laid a glove on me. I was a little fat at the time and I couldn't take any chances. Besides, my father had promised me a new green corduroy suit for the Third Avenue Social Club picnic if I won. After I hit Pantelone with that hook and doubled him up, I was able to get in over his guard and I knocked him out in the second round."

I not only had to listen to the guy all the way to Rome; but around the hotel that evening as well. We were stopping at the Moderno, one of those swank joints that used to be popular with the tourists, and Braidwood wouldn't let me out of his sight. Wherever you found Braidwood there was plenty of conversation about Hogan, most of it contributed by Hogan himself.

The next morning we went over to the *Foro d'Italia* for the draw. Braidwood's brow puckered into a permanent wince and his head shrunk back into his shoulders like a worried turtle's when his guy drew Marcel Cerdan for the first round. Cerdan's name didn't mean a thing to me, not even after Braidwood told me that he was the European champion. I'd seen some of those European champions fight at the Garden. But I began to get the idea of how good he was supposed to be when I learned that the French soldiers were offering the GIs odds of four to one that he would knock out Hogan in the first round. Those would be long odds for Joe Louis to knock out my old

man in the first round, but not many GIs we willing to cover the wallpaper money that t *poilus* were waving in their faces.

THERE was a hell of a crowd of French, Britis Italian and American soldiers in the *Foro* walked down to the ring in front of Hogan wi a bucket in each hand, and Braidwood broug up the rear. We climbed into the ring and I cou tell from the noise that went up that the Frenc man was right behind us.

At Cerdan's appearance, those French soldie started clapping their hands in unison and h lering Cerdan's name on the offbeat. "Cerda Clap, clap. "Cerdan!" Clap, clap. They gave h a hell of an ovation. But I didn't see him un Lt. Jack Sullivan, the referee, called us to t center of the ring for pre-fight instructions.

Marcel was a handsome Frenchman with da curly hair. One look at those sloping shoulde and I knew why he had lost only three fights seven years in the ring. But if Hogan was ove awed by his appearance he never showed it. Ba in the corner he shook hands with Braidwoo "Don't worry, Mack," he said. "I'll take care this palooka and be right back."

He made a quick return trip, but not like planned. As soon as the bell rang, Cerdan w out of his corner and across the ring to meet t more sluggish Hogan. He straightened Horizont with a left to the side of the head and the knocked him out with two rights to the chin.

I don't know what Cerdan had in his glov but it took Braidwood and me half an hour bring Hogan to. When the lights came on aga for Hogan, he didn't say much more than enoug to convince us that he was conscious. He st didn't know what had happened.

The sudden ending of the fight spoiled t tournament for us, so we walked back to t Moderno with Hogan. About a block from t hotel it started raining and Hogan, who hadn been very talkative, held out his hand and fe the drops. Then he said to Braidwood, "This probably keep the crowd down, won't it, Mack

Braidwood's answer convinced me that he wa a born fight manager. "Keep the crowd dow hell!" he said. "They called it off!"

Grabinski

camp news

mer Opera Singers Get Tune at Camp Swift

amp Swift, Tex.—Pvt. Edward L. Grabinski, a driver with the 472d Quartermaster Trucking mpany, and Pfc. Richard Holtzclaw, a surgical hnician at the 380th Station Hospital, ex- anged talk of long-haired names and long- red music when they met here recently. Both merly were with the Chicago Opera Company. abinski was on the tenor roster during the sea- s of 1938-41, and Holtzclaw, known profes- nally as Richard Wentworth, sang romantic ritone roles with the company for 3½ years ore he entered the Army last April.

Holtzclaw used to split his operatic seasons be- een the Chicago company and the San Carlo era Company, which annually toured the ited States, Canada, Mexico and Cuba. His ertoire consists of 39 complete operas in Ger- n, Italian and French, including over 1,000 gs. He has sung with such stars as John rles Thomas, Lawrence Tibbett, Martinelli d James Melton, and has been starred opposite h famous divas as Grace Moore, Helen Jepson d Ilona Massey. Besides opera he has appeared Broadway shows, concerts and coast-to-coast lio programs.

Grabinski, whose home is in Moscow, Idaho, s sung as a dramatic tenor with Jan Kiepura, sa Raisa, Dennis King, Alexander Gray, Ruth ting and Vivienne Segal, and has also appeared concert and on the radio. He speaks Russian, lish, Italian, Czech and three Slavic dialects.

"How's your voice these days?" Holtzclaw ked Grabinski.

"I'd say it was pretty good after the third beer," s the reply.

"That's what I was thinking. How about going to Austin some week end and making a record- g after a good sudsing up?" Grabinski agreed.

ld Soldiers Say Good-Bye

Camp Breckinridge, Ky.—Three sergeants of the ld Army stood together at the gate not saying uch of anything. 1st Sgt. Floyd E. (Babe) Knox, ho first enlisted in 1914 and had served a total 26 years, was leaving the Army. M/Sgt. Frank cIlvain, 27 years in the Army, and M/Sgt. S. T. emale, a veteran of 23 years' service, were on nd to wish him good luck on his retirement, t they avoided the subject. All three had rved in France in the first World War and all d participated in the Meuse-Argonne drive.

Sgt. Knox was nicknamed Babe because that's hat he calls almost everybody else. He came to amp Breckinridge with the original cadre July , 1942, and had served as an MP with the 1570th ervice Unit since then. It was at Columbus Bar- cks, Ohio, that he enlisted on July 6, 1914. He ent overseas with the 39th Regiment, 4th Divi- on, and was wounded in combat. Back in the tates, he dropped out of the Army in 1920 for ur years, then joined up again. During his rmy career he was located in San Francisco, alif.; Plattsburg Barracks, Syracuse Fairgrounds nd Camp Mills, all N. Y.; Camp Merritt, N. J.; ort Devens, Mass.; Fort McPherson and Fort glethorpe, Ga.; Fort Thomas, Ky., and in Ha- aii and on the Mexican border. He served with he 39th, 13th, 22d, 35th and 10th Infantry Regi- ents before being assigned to the 1570th SU.

Though born in Phenix City, Ala., he now con- ders Henderson, Ky., his home and lives there ith his wife Mae and his daughter Dorothy enart. Enlisted men and officers at Breckinridge hipped in for a farewell gift when they learned

the old sarge was leaving and Knox managed to choke out that it had been "a damned pleasure" to serve with such men.

Now the two oldest enlisted men of the outfit had come to the gate to bid him good-bye. Sgt. McIlvain spoke up. He said he guessed he and Gemale had better get back to duty. They shook hands with Babe and turned away.

"So long, Babe," they said.

"So long," Sgt. Knox said.

—Sgt. CARL RITTER

SERVING HIS COUNTRY

Camp Gordon Johnston, Fla.—A lieutenant, scouting witnesses for a trial in which he was to be defense counsel, asked a corporal what he was doing the morning of Dec. 28.

"I was doing my duty as a soldier of the United States Army, sir," said the two-striper.

"And what duty were you doing as a soldier of the United States Army?" persisted the louey.

The corporal drew himself up ramrod straight and said, "I was in mess hall No. 2, passing out the bread."

A Book by Any Other Name

Fort Lewis, Wash.—Caroline Paddock and Alma Halverson, librarians of Library No. 3 at North Fort Lewis, tell these anecdotes about the reading tastes of engineers.

One evening a very shy GI came in and asked what books they had by Risqué. "I am in the mood for his works," he said. "How do you spell the name of the author?" asked Miss Halverson. "I'm not sure, but it's a French name," the GI replied, "and his books are generally slightly naughty."

Recently a big strapping three-striper de- manded a copy of "Woman Driver." Miss Paddock had never heard of it, but after the sergeant out- lined the story as he had heard it from a friend, she produced Chevalier's "Drivin' Woman."

AROUND THE CAMPS

Northington General Hospital, Ala.—The weekly gripe sessions here sometimes give the patients a laugh. At a typical session one soldier wanted to know why in hell he had to wait five days for a civilian cleaning plant to return his uniform.

Camp Atterbury, Ind.—Two days before pay day Pvt. Theodore L. Rich borrowed some money from Pvt. John H. Knodt. "That's funny," Rich said. "I'm Rich and he's Knodt, and yet I'm bor- rowing from him." —Pfc. VICTOR W. McGINNIS

1293d SCU, University of Buffalo, N. Y.—When Pvt. Charles DelValle of Company B reported on morning sick call to complain of hemorrhoids, the doctor told him to report for an eye examination. He came back to company headquarters at 1100 with a dislocated knee and at 2100 he was oper- ated on for acute appendicitis.

Camp Blanding, Fla.—Members of the staff of the IRTC visual aids shop here proved that they are the right men for the right jobs by winning the major share of the honors in a camp-wide

WAC STAND-IN. When shots for a movie about Wacs called "Keep Your Powder Dry" were being taken at Fort Oglethorpe, Ga., Pvt. Polly Giloth was chosen as stand-in for actress Laraine Day.

art contest. Cpl. Edward A. Johnson took three first prizes in the oils, prints and drawing cate- gories. Sgt. Alfred Bottare won first in the ren- dering class and Sgt. Theodore Bradford re- ceived honorable mention in the same class. Sgt. Jess Montgomery was second in water colors.

Ben Rocklin

By Pfc. DEBS MYERS
YANK Staff Writer

CHICAGO—When anyone opens the door of Ben Rocklin's knife shop, a burglar alarm jangles, and out from a back room walks Ben Rocklin saying, "What the hell, quiet please."

He sells long-bladed knives that he calls "Jap stickers" to soldiers, and he sells less lethal knives to civilians, provided he likes them. He doesn't sell anything to people he doesn't like. "I am an American citizen, 100 percent," he says, "and I take no guff from any man, unless he is much bigger than I am, and very little guff from women."

In the past three years, Rocklin has sold 6,000 knives to soldiers and marines. Judging from letters he has received, he estimates these knives have been responsible for killing 10,000 Japs. "Old Ben's knives," he says, "have gone across jungles, across deserts and across more than a few gullets. Sometimes, at night when I'm in bed, I say to myself, 'Ben, you old fool, you are such a ball of fire at killing Japs, it is a wonder you're not afraid of yourself.'"

He used to make knives for slicing bread. "I made fine knives," he says, "and housewives praised me in many tongues. Then the bread companies started selling bread already sliced. When this happened Old Ben's heart was broken, but Old Ben is not a man to sit and sulk. I made hunting knives. Old Ben was getting ready. Old Ben knew war was coming. Old Ben knows the Japanese. The Japanese are stinkers."

He bought all the steel filing cases he could get. This was the steel that went into his knives. The knives have blades eight inches long and are sharp on both edges. "Old Ben tooled for war," he says, "from bread knives to Jap stickers. As shy as I am, I sometimes say to myself, 'Ben, you've come a long ways.'"

A Jap, he says, can be trusted no farther than a man can throw an orangutan by the tail. "I fought against the Japs when I was a soldier in the Russian Imperial Army," he recalls, "and even 40 years ago they were stinkers."

Ben Rocklin is 5 feet 4. He weighs 190 pounds. He quit telling about his birthdays when he passed 75. That was a few years ago.

He employs a Chicago telephone directory to illustrate how he used to treat the Japs. The Chicago telephone directory numbers 1,732 pages, is 2¼ inches thick and weighs 4 pounds 11 ounces. Bunching his shoulders, he takes a directory in his thick, stubby hands and twists it into four pieces. "I used to be a strong man," he observes.

Ben has a three-room shop on the second floor of a building at 746 South Halsted Street near Hull House. People in the neighborhood call him the village blacksmith. This he does not like.

"I never shod a horse in my life," he says. "I hate horses. I have ridden many of them and eaten more than a few. I never knew a horse that I liked. Besides, I am a typical small-businessman. When my country was threatened, I became a one-man arsenal of democracy. Also, people were no longer buying bread knives."

Once upon a time—he doesn't remember exactly when—he was a professional wrestler and weight lifter. Many years ago, in Milwaukee, he wrestled the great Frank Gotch, when Gotch was world champion.

"It was a hell of a match," says Ben. "I ga[ve] it to him good."

"Who won?" Ben is asked.

"I was matchless that night, a pillar of flame," says Ben.

"Who won?" Ben is asked again.

"The crowd cheered me wildly," muses Ben. "I was a hero in Milwaukee."

"Who won?"

He grinds a knife, ignoring the question, then looks over his shoulder.

"Gotch," he says, "in 7½ minutes."

On the wall of the shop are Ben's own rules on how to be happy at 75 plus:

"1. Mind your own business and do not u[se] bad remarks about certain people that you mig[ht] be sorry for.

"2. If you have enemies, avoid them. Do not g[o] into places where there is suspicion or whe[re] there is unsafety. Do not hear behind the do[or] people talk or look in keyholes.

"3. Look in all directions when you cross th[e] street; around the corner look out; keep out o[f] arguments about elections.

"4. Eat and drink everything you like an[d] don't deny yourself pleasure.

"5. Watch out for some of your best friend[s] who are your worst enemies."

Ben is writing the story of his life. He think[s] he will probably call it "The Nine Lives an[d] Ninety Thousand Knives of Ben Rocklin."

"It's absorbing," he declares. "I have so muc[h] fun reading it I don't have much time to write it."

One of the great days of history will come, he says, when the Allied armies meet the Russian armies in Germany.

"There'll be Hitler, a pig on a pitchfork," he gloats. "The Russian armies have been under-rated for a long time. All we Russians had wa[s] broomsticks in the old days, and broomstick[s] may be good for riding but they are not good fo[r] shooting. There's only one way to get alon[g] with a German or a Jap. Beat hell out of hi[m] and let him know who is the tough guy. The[n] keep on showing him who is the tough guy. Roosevelt and Churchill and Stalin—they're al[l] tough guys. It's a good thing, too."

BEN cringes a little when he remembers hi[s] own days in the Czarist armies.

"It was very rough," he recalls. "It was no[t] rich living. It was very rough. I had a genera[l] named Gen. Yarovitch. He was big as a stable and smelled like one. He had a great red mustach[e] about six inches wide. When he roared out order[s] his mustache waggled like a flag and he roare[d] most of the time. He was a mean man.

"I was a foot soldier. But one day the cook deserted, and before I could get out of the way and hide, Gen. Yarovitch grabbed me and made me a cook. He carried a long whip called a knout with him all the time, and he shook that whip under my nose and told me I better cook good. Faithfully I promised I would cook good. About that time some Czarist dog shot a rabbit and brought it to the general.

"The general says, 'Ben, cook this rabbit and cook it good or I will skin you and maybe eat you, with garlic, of course.' So I clean the rabbit and fix a stew, but while my back is turned the general's dog steals the rabbit, and when I look around I sit on the ground and put my head in my hands and I sorrow. Old Ben's rabbit is gone. Old Ben's goose is cooked.

"And along comes an old soldier, and he asks me why I sorrow and I tell him. And he says for me not to be a fool but to kill the regiment's cat and cook it for the general. So I do this, with plenty of garlic. And pretty soon along comes Gen. Yarovitch swinging his whip and roaring. And he sits down at his table and I put the plate before him. He takes a mouthful, and he looks at me and says, 'Ben, that is peerless rabbit,' and he tips me a ruble.

"And some years pass and I come to the United States and become a citizen, and I come to Chicago and make knives. And then there is a great World's Fair in Chicago and I go to it. And at the Russian exposition who do I see there but Gen. Yarovitch. His red mustache has turned to gray and he has no whip. But he is still roaring. And he sees me and he hugs me and he says, 'Ben, you rascal. Once you cooked me a peerless rabbit, and I tipped you a ruble.'

"And I'm an American citizen and I'm in a free country and I look back at him and I say, 'Thank you, Gen. Yarovitch, you son of a bitch. But that was no rabbit. That was a cat.'"

By S/Sgt. GORDON CROWE

WHEN the Air Forces reorganized last year, streamlining squadrons and consolidating others into base units, a lot of first sergeants found themselves out of jobs. That's exactly what happened to my old first sergeant, Sam McDougall, as fine a gentleman as any enlisted man could ask for a three-day pass. And McDougall never quite got over it.

McDougall was a veteran of the last war, pushing 50 when he got the urge to enlist right after Pearl Harbor. He went down to the induction center, got a waiver on his age and enlisted as a private.

He wore his ribbons from the last war, including the *Croix de Guerre*, at all formations during basic training, and it wasn't long before the second lieutenant who was acting as drill sergeant pulled Mac out of the ranks and made him an acting drill sergeant. Not long after that, Mac made staff and tech and acting first and finally first sergeant.

He was a kindly, fatherly type. He'd listen to any guy's bitches, never interrupting or making the guy feel like he was wasting his time. He felt very happy and well set in being a first sergeant, since in 33 months' service in the last war all he ever got to be was pfc. He never played favorites, always referred to his charges as "my boys" and said, "We got the best goddam bunch of soldiers in the whole Air Corps."

We were a noncombatant outfit. We gave basic training to pre-aviation cadets and were a small group—160 permanent party in all. We had a squadron fund and every few months we'd pitch a whale of a party in a downtown hotel. Mac would get drunk and interrupt the girls doing a strip tease and make somewhat of an ass of himself, but almost everybody else was pretty high so nothing would ever be said of it after the party was over.

Things were coasting swell. It looked like Mac was set in his job for the duration. Then along came this "reorganization," and Mac found himself a casual along with a lot of the rest of us. He tried to be good-hearted about it for awhile, and when a pfc was assigned to our barracks to see that we kept the place clean and policed the area regularly, Mac just used to laugh and say: "Well, that's the Army for you. Democratic as all hell. Even a first sergeant has got to help police up the place."

But he didn't feel so good when they started posting KP lists and he found his name on them with monotonous regularity. The first time wasn't bad. He pulled it. But after four straight days of KP, he began to get a little irrational and went in to see the new CO. He didn't get anywhere with the new CO. The CO told him he'd have to take his turn on KP, just like the rest of the first-three-graders in the outfit, until he was shipped out or a suitable assignment was found for him.

The CO did give him permission, however, to scout around the post and try to find himself a job. "If you can find a job, then you're out of my hands," the new CO told Mac. "And while you're at it, see what you can do for the nine other first sergeants they've unloaded on me."

Mac went up to the Service Club, where he knew the lady in charge. She was sympathetic and out of pure kindness she gave Mac a job on the cash register, ringing up tabs as you came through with your tray. Mac acted pretty happy over this, and it had its good points. The hours were regular and it kept him off KP. And he could see his friends in his old outfit and he'd always say, "There goes one of my boys—he's a good soldier," or something like that.

But Mac wasn't really happy. You could tell that whenever you'd see him in town. He hung out at the Red Dog saloon nearly every night. He'd get drunk on beer and pick on some civilian and tell him about his "best goddam outfit in the Army." "Yessir," Mac would say nostalgically but making it a point to put in the present tense, "my boys give me a little trouble once in a while, but you know how that is. Boys will be boys."

One night he was pretty stewed when I saw him. (I had a temporary assignment with a crew firing furnaces.) He'd come in with Moraglia, a rather insignificant corporal who used to be a combination runner and file clerk in our orderly room. Moraglia, being aggressive too, had got the same job in one of the base units, and he knew Mac was only a cash-register puncher in the Service Club, so he felt a little lordly at that time, with the help of about 15 beers. They got to arguing about some inane subject, and before anyone

could stop them Moraglia was riding Mac about being a cash-register puncher. I believe it hurt Mac's feelings more than anything else.

"Is that the way to talk to your first sergeant?" Mac demanded.

"Aw g'wan, you ain't no first sergeant any more," Moraglia said. "Why the hell don't you take off them stripes?"

"I'll put you on KP for 15 days," Mac shouted, "and you'll never get another recommendation for promotion out of me!"

Moraglia just stood and laughed sardonically; then Mac took a poke at him, and before we could stop them they were rolling on the floor.

We took them outside and talked to them, but it was pretty hard to calm Mac down. The old man was crying and it was a pitiful sight to see. The owner of the establishment, not wanting to get put off limits, called the MPs, and before we could hustle Mac and Moraglia back to camp, they showed up and hauled them in.

I understand Mac got quite a dressing-down from the provost marshal and that he tried to get a discharge three times on account of his age but was turned down every time. Then he tried to get them to send him overseas, but they vetoed that on account of his age.

I ran into him yesterday for the first time in almost a month. He looked much older than his 52 years, and for the first time I noticed his ribbons were soiled and his pants needed pressing. He forced a smile and said "Hello," but it was false and empty, and the old fire and geniality that were so much a part of McDougall were gone.

"I got a new job," he said, "and it's a pretty good one. I'm in charge of three fellows, and they're going to make the outfit bigger and into a separate squadron. Then I'll get my old first-sergeancy back."

"Gee, that's swell," I said. "What are you doing now, Mac?"

He looked off into the distance and said, "I'm head ticket-taker at the post theater."

Moraglia just stood and laughed sardonically; then Mac took a poke at him.

YANK

THE ARMY WEEKLY

YANK is published weekly by the enlisted men of the U. S. Army and is for sale only to those in the armed services. Stories, features, pictures and other material from YANK may be reproduced if they are not restricted by law or military regulations, provided proper credit is given, release dates are observed and specific prior permission has been granted for each item to be reproduced. Entire contents copyrighted, 1945, by Col. Franklin S. Forsberg and reviewed by U. S. military censors.

MAIN EDITORIAL OFFICE
205 EAST 42d STREET, NEW YORK 17, N. Y.

EDITORIAL STAFF

Managing Editor, Sgt. Joe McCarthy, FA; Art Director, Sgt. Arthur Weithas, DEML; Assistant Managing Editor, Sgt. Justus Schlotzhauer, Inf.; Assistant Art Director, Sgt. Ralph Stein, Med.; Pictures, Sgt. Leo Hofeller, Armd.; Features, Sgt. Marion Hargrove, FA; Sports, Cpl. Tom Shehan, FA; Overseas Editor, Sgt. Al Hine, Engr.; U. S. Editor, Sgt. Hilary H. Lyons, CA; Associate Editors, Sgt. John Hay, Inf.; Cpl. Margaret Davis, WAC; Sgt. Ralph Boyce, AAF; Cpl. Max Novack, TC.

WASHINGTON. Sgt. Barrett McGurn, Med.

FRANCE. Sgt. Merle Miller, AAF; Sgt. Charles Brand, AAF; Sgt. Mack Morriss, Inf.; Sgt. Ed Cunningham, Inf.; Sgt. Howard Brodie, Sig. Corps; Sgt. Saul Levitt, AAF; Sgt. Allan Ecker, AAF; Sgt. Reg Kenny, Armd.; Sgt. Robert McBrinn, Sig. Corps; Sgt. Ralph G. Martin, Med.; Pfc. Pat Coffey, AAF; Cpl. Howard Katzander, CA; Cpl. Robert Krell, Inf. (Airborne); Pfc. David Whitcomb, AAF; Pvt. David Berger, Engr.

BRITAIN. Sgt. Durbin L. Horner, CA; Sgt. Sanderson Vanderbilt, CA; Sgt. John Scott, Engr.; Sgt. Earl Anderson, AAF; Sgt. Francis Burke, AAF; Cpl. Jack Coggins, CA; Cpl. Edmund Antrobus, Inf.; Pfc. Tom Flannery, AAF.

AUSTRALIA-PHILIPPINES. Sgt. Lafayette Locke, AAF; Sgt. Charles Rathe, DEML; Sgt. Douglas Borgstedt, DEML; Sgt. Dick Hanley, AAF; Sgt. Ozzie St. George, Inf.; Cpl. Roger Wrenn, Sig. Corps; Sgt. Charles D. Pearson, Engr.; Cpl. John McLeod, Med.; Sgt. Marvin Fasig, Engr.; Cpl. Joe Stefanelli, Engr.; Cpl. Frank J. Beck, DEML; Sgt. Roger W. Cowan, DEML; Sgt. Jack F. Crowe, DEML; Sgt. Lionel Wathall, DEML.

CENTRAL PACIFIC. Sgt. Larry McManus, CA; Pfc. George Burns, Sig. Corps; Pfc. John O. Armstrong, Inf.; Sgt. Bill Reed, Inf.; Cpl. James Goble, Armd.; Sgt. H. N. Oliphant, Engr.; Sgt. Bill Young, Inf.; Cpl. Ted Burrows, DEML; Don Morgan Y1c, USCGR; Vernon H. Roberts S1c, USNR; Mason E. Pawlak, CPhoM, USNR; Cpl. Lon Wilson, Sig. Corps.

MARIANAS. Cpl. Tom O'Brien, DEML; Sgt. Dil Ferris, AAF; Sgt. Jack Ruge, DEML; Sgt. Paul Showers, AAF; Pfc. Justin Gray, Rangers.

ITALY. Sgt. Harry Sions, AAF; Sgt. August Loeb, AAF; Sgt. Dan Polier, AAF; Cpl. George Barrett, AAF; Pfc. Ira Freeman, Cav.; Pfc. Carl Schwind, AAF; Pvt. Dave Shaw, Inf.

INDIA-BURMA and CHINA. Sgt. Paul Johnston, AAF; Sgt. George J. Corbellini, Sig. Corps; Sgt. Dave Richardson, CA; Sgt. Lou Stoumen, DEML; Sgt. Walter Peters, QM; Cpl. Jud Cook, DEML.

ALASKA. Sgt. Ray Duncan, AAF; Cpl. John M. Haverstick, CA.

IRAN-IRAQ. Sgt. Burtt Evans, Inf.

PANAMA. Cpl. Richard Douglass, Med.

PUERTO RICO. Sgt. Don Cooke, FA; Pfc. James Iorio, MP.

MIDDLE EAST. Sgt. Richard Paul, DEML.

BRAZIL. Pfc. Nat Bodian, AAF.

BERMUDA. Cpl. William Pene du Bois, Inf.

ICELAND. Sgt. John Moran, Inf.

NEWFOUNDLAND. Sgt. Frank Bode, Sig. Corps.

NAVY. Donald Nugent S1c.

Commanding Officer, Col. Franklin S. Forsberg.

Executive Officer, Maj. Jack W. Weeks.

Business Manager, Maj. North Bigbee.

Supply Officer, Maj. Gerald J. Rock.

OVERSEAS BUREAU OFFICERS. France, Maj. Charles L. Holt; Britain, Capt. Harry R. Roberts; Australia-Philippines, Maj. Harold B. Hawley; Central-South Pacific, Maj. Josua Eppinger; Marianas, Maj. Justus J. Craemer; Italy, Maj. Robert Strother; Burma-India, Capt. Harold A. Burroughs; Alaska, Lt. Grady E. Clay Jr.; Iran, Lt. David Gafill; Panama, Capt. Howard Carswell; Puerto Rico, Capt. Frank Gladstone; Middle East, Capt. Knowlton Ames.

This Week's Cover

THIS is 1st Lt. Elizabeth Babarcik of New Cumberland, Ohio, now stationed on the Western Front. In the service for 19 months, she is one of thousands who rate very high with GIs for their work.

PHOTO CREDITS. Cover—Sgt. Reg Kenny. 2—Top, Signal Corps; lower, INP. 3—Acme. 4—Upper, Signal Corps; others, Acme. 6—Left, Cpl. Lon Wilson; right, INP. 7—Pvt. George Aarons. 8—Sgt. Donald Breimhurst. 9—Left, Sgt. Breimhurst; right, Pfc. Werner Wolff. 10 & 11—Sgt. Marvin Kirsten, Signal Corps. 12 & 13—Cpl. Wilson. 15—Upper left, Signal Corps; upper right, Pueblo Ordnance Depot; lower right, WD BPR WAC Group. 16—Chicago Sun. 20—Selznick International. 21—Pvt. Aarons. 23—Acme.

Mail Call

Going Home

Dear YANK:

. . . I have completed 10 years of service this month, holding all ranks from private up to and including captain. I have spent six years and three months overseas (not seeing my wife in over five years). I have fought both Japanese and Germans in China, North Africa, Sicily, Italy, France, Belgium, Holland and Germany, and have served in overseas stations in China, Hawaii, the Philippines, Trinidad, Panama, North Africa, Sicily, Italy, England, France, Belgium, Holland and Germany. I wear the Good Conduct Ribbon alongside the Purple Heart with seven Clusters, the Silver Star with Cluster, the Bronze Star with two Clusters, the Soldier's Medal and, above all, the Combat Infantry Badge.

The loss of hearing in one ear from concussion, the loss of eyesight in one eye from shrapnel, the loss of one lung from a bayonet wound and the partial loss of use of my right leg from German machine-gun slugs put me in the "no longer fit for military service" class.

Now I am being sent home. It may be hard to understand for those who want to go home before the job is finished, but I do not want to go. The prospect of going back to America is not quite so bright with the fight for freedom and security not yet won. I am leaving the field, leaving my men in these stinking fields and villages of Germany, in the sloppy, muddy, snow and ice-lined foxholes and trenches of Germany to fight the battle of life or death for me. I am leaving my men to fight and die (and they do die up there) for the country whose uniform I am so unworthy of wearing. I will be ashamed to look one of those infantrymen in the face and tell him I left him to win the battle when the going was the toughest and went back to the States.

Going back to the United States is not the shining goal it might seem as long as it is still being blurred by the blood of Americans dying for freedom and their loved ones on foreign soil.

ETO —Rifle Company Commander

Wacs' Bonus

Dear YANK:

Where the hell does this guy Pvt. Raymond E. Kaptan get the nerve in saying [in a letter in *Mail Call*] that the Wacs, Waves and Spars shouldn't be granted a bonus the same as men in the service? Maybe this guy would like to leave the beaches of Hawaii and trade places with the Wacs who are with the Fifth Army in Italy.

Pvt. Kaptan made the statement that Wacs, Waves and Spars never had to risk life or limb. May I remind him that there are Wacs in our armed forces today who wear the Purple Heart? Does Pvt. Kaptan have the Purple Heart? As he put it, these Wacs enlisted. Maybe just the guys that were drafted should get such a bonus, huh?

—T/Sgt. ROBERT K. BUCHANAN*
Ardmore AAF, Okla.

*Also signed by 20 other men.

Dear YANK:

In regard to Pvt. Raymond E. Kaptan's letter against granting bonuses to women in service because of voluntary service and absence of danger to life and limb, how about the Wacs in Italy, France and the South Pacific who have endured many bombing raids? Pvt. Kaptan, who is sitting snugly in Hawaii, could take a few lessons from the Wacs in New Guinea and other such places.

As to bonuses, would he have them withheld from women in service because they are women or because they volunteered? What about the *men* who have volunteered? Are bonuses exclusively for those who had to be rounded up and dragged in?

Roswell, N. Mex. —Pfc. MILLICENT PAULTZ*

*Also signed by 14 others.

Dear YANK:

. . . If he [Kaptan] takes his feet off that desk in Hawaii long enough and uses common sense, he would realize that anyone willing to volunteer in the armed forces deserves plenty of credit as well as a bonus.

About risking life or limb, I know of a girl now in England who had her leg amputated as a result of enemy bombing and of several other girls (Wacs) who were on their way overseas when their ship was attacked and they narrowly escaped with their lives. If Pvt. Kaptan is at all interested in this orientation program, I could supply him with a few more instances. . . .

—S/Sgt. ROSAMOND D. ELLIOTT
Kearney AAF, Nebr.

Dear YANK:

. . . Does he forget *why* we voluntarily enlisted when we could have stayed at home and had war jobs with high salaries? We enlisted for him as well as any other soldier, sailor or marine, whether he wants to admit it or not. In the 19 months I have been at my present station I have seen hundreds of men return from foreign and sea duty, and this has been brought about indirectly by the voluntary enlistment of women in the armed forces.

I am also looking forward to my overseas duty (for which I volunteered the first day applications were made available to us) and to making it possible for one more man to come home to the America he has fought for and for which, if it became necessary, I would give up my life. . . .

—C. AYLWARD Y3c
NAAS, Whiting Field, Fla.

Dear YANK:

. . . Does the private suppose that every soldier was drafted? And should those who were not be denied a bonus because they enlisted freely? It seems to me that they rate all the more because they did volunteer. . . .

Drew Field, Fla. —Lt. A. C. LARSON

Dear YANK:

. . . Perhaps if he read a little more of the newspapers, he would also see that one of our Wacs bravely risked her life for a GI overseas by putting out with her own body the flames that were burning him and thereby received the Soldier's Medal. Of course, one couldn't count this as "risking life and limb."

Boston, Mass. —Pfc. BARBARA GAILEY

GI Bill of Rights

Dear YANK:

I have heard so much pro and con
the GI Bill of Rights that I can't compo
myself any longer. I'll grant that it real
gives something to the soldier under
years of age, and it gives a business lo
for those who are just starting in bus
ness—men usually between 25 and
years of age. How about the older m
from 37 to 42 years old—the man w
had just got well started in his busine
but still had an outstanding loan, a
who also owned his home but still had
50-percent mortgage on that? He e
tered the Army to practically let h
business go to pot but that still does
pay the outstanding loan. His wife a
children have a bare existence on t
Army allotment.

This soldier will come back to a de
and have to start his business all ov
again. The mortgage will still be on h
home, which in all probability will ne
a lot of repairs. His age will be again
him as his producing years are sure
numbered. Why not give the old soldi
an amount equal to the cost of the you
soldier's education?

Hawaii —Cpl. JOHN R. NELS

Jobs for Officers

Dear YANK:

Concerning a *Mail Call* letter head
"Commissioned Office Boys" and Ge
Adler's speech entitled "Office Boys Wi
High Rank Worry About Post-War F
ture." It's obvious that there is cause f
such worry and, though I can't promi
these young officers employment wh
the war is finished, I can offer a litt
friendly advice.

There are a lot of older men in th
Army who had their own business e
tablishments or held responsible pos
tions before being inducted. Due to a
limits, these men are not eligible f
OCS or specialized training, so throug
out their whole Army career they r
main Sad Sacks and get pushed aroun
more or less.

But when the shooting is over, the
men will return to their former pos
tions and find themselves on top agai
At that time it's highly probable that a
ex-officer in search of a job will find
necessary to confront an ex-Sad Sac
and, having no other recommendatio
will most likely play up his commissio
in the late war to prove his ability an
accomplishments. Maybe he'll get the jo

"And the pfc stripe I got at Fort Benning, Ga."

—Pfc. Thomas Flannery

TOOTH PASTE IS WINNING THE WAR

Dear YANK:

NOT long ago we heard that a popular weekly magazine in the States had printed an advertisement which was described as having a cartoon with "an indelicate and offensive military angle." However, since I have seen the drawing which was called objectionable I am confused. It shows three soldiers (the home front no longer approves of our calling ourselves GIs) in a lush Pacific jungle, all of them prepared for combat. One gives the order, "We attack at 12:10, take the point at 12:20 and return here for (a popular soft drink) at 12:30."

My chief concern is that this dissatisfaction may result in the total disappearance of poster art with a military angle and rob me of my ties with home and everything that is dear to me.

I submit the following classification of ads which have given me particular pleasure since I have been in uniform:

The first is the "All for Our Boys" ad which may also be called the "you'll get yours later" layout. I first thrilled to this type of display after I had eaten beans, Spam, powdered eggs and C-rations for three weeks and then came upon a picture of myself in one of the popular weeklies. I was in spotless sun-tans, properly tanned, healthy, clean and grinning. I was grinning because I was lugging a bright tray divided into six compartments loaded with a $1.50 steak, fresh vegetables, crisp salad and ice cream. The thing about these ads that pleases me is not the fantasy and imagination employed, but the glamor with which our life is portrayed for those back home. Uniforms are never dirty and unpressed; the portholes of the combat-bound transport always show a travel-talk horizon and a beautiful woman with flowers around her neck, and up beside the now-still howitzer is a full case of that drink I can't do without. I like to see things like that.

My second type is the "Buckies Wuckies Have Gone to War" dirge. Into this classification fall the full pages which reprint letters from former employees to large business concerns telling how they would have been unable to knock out that third tank without that wonderful lubricant which has been specially designed not to freeze, stain, corrode or lubricate (oops!). I suggest that these are highly educational and informative subjects and should not be denied us for their value as combat tips. Why, by the unsolicited testimony of thousands of unprejudiced authorities, battles have been won in 27 countries by spark plugs, shaving cream, condensed milk, chocolate bars and cosmetic tissue. Also by these commercial methods, my wife is happily lulled into thinking that I am issued a spanking new, watertight, oilskin-lined, form-fitting and rust-resisting pouch for used razor blades which was made for me by the former makers of outstanding brassieres.

These same copywriters have comforted much of the home front with pictures of neat, cross-marked graves under which is written "There will be fewer of these if you keep vital information under your (popular brand) hat."

Our third and most exciting type which has given me endless diversion, is the "What Kind of World Are You Returning to?" design, more vulgarly called "After Roosevelt—What?" These combine a "you too can have a private pipe organ" motif with the apology that, due to circumstances not under control of the manufacturer, the item is only being supplied for the armed forces. This last note is stolen from type No. 2. These plastic dreams lead us to believe that no one can live in the postwar world and throw stones. However, some schism in the ranks of copywriters has led to a conflicting and contradictory note. While some of them are suggesting that we expect to return to homes scented with the six delicious flavors, others maintain that we want to come back to find things just the way we left them.

I have not included the "My Reverie" type, for I do not think it represents the high aim of the craft. This version shows a freckled airman (always at least a captain) in an attitude of prayer, hoping that he will come home to find his favorite milk shake still available at the corner druggist's. I have rejected this type because it usually includes the mercenary assurance that he will find it.

Unfortunately most of the magazines available to the forces overseas are printed without advertisements. I have a distinct sense of insecurity when I think that perhaps men may return from the fighting fronts and foolishly demand to get their news and fiction without that necessary embellishment that makes it all readable—the advertisements.

France —T-4 ROSS DONALDSON

---

that way and maybe not, but if he does I don't thing it would be too farfetched to imagine that the employer hired him only for the opportunity to run him ragged and maybe even fasten a broom to his tail and watch him sweep the floor while running.

My advice is: When the time comes to seek employment, sir, don't do any bragging about being an officer veteran. Just forget about it and I think you'll have much greater success in finding that job you're after.

Attu —Pvt. CHARLES KOLBER

Newspapers From Home

Dear YANK:

For several days now I have been listening to the mail clerk bitch, and believe it or not, it is catching. After thinking the matter over, I think he has a darn good right to bitch. He goes after mail daily, rain, shine or snow, with little shine, and what does he bring back? Bags and bags of ancient newspapers, and it is rather disgusting to see the boys get them and then throw them away without even breaking the wrapper. I don't blame the boys, for old newspapers aren't interesting over here.

If there is such a shortage of paper, why doesn't someone get wise and stop the shipment of papers overseas? If GIs themselves could cancel their subscriptions, then we would have more room for first-class mail, to say nothing of the room for supplies. Which do you think is more important?

Not knocking the home-town papers, but they are thousands of miles away from home and from two to three months behind time. As the Italians would say, "They are *nenti bona*."

Italy —1st Sgt. LEONARD L. DURR*

*Also signed by three others.

Dear YANK:

... Why doesn't someone stop the sending of newspapers to China—at least until a landing is made on the coast and newspapers won't fill the valuable transportation space?

China —Sgt. JAMES O. LIDE

Infantry Badge

Dear YANK:

We men of the 103d Infantry Division, qualified wearers of the Combat Infantryman's Badge, would like to register a complaint concerning the present design and construction of the badge. We'd like to offer as a suggestion that the badge be redesigned to include the well-known Infantry emblem—crossed rifles. As for construction, we'd suggest a better alloy. Although the badges we received were stamped "Sterling," we believe they were made of a cheaper metal. After a few weeks of constant wear, the blue enamel chips off, leaving the medal unsightly, and the rifle can no longer be distinguished against the background. We feel that we're not alone in this dislike of the present type of medal. We believe that the medal should be more distinctive because it labels the wearer as an outstanding soldier.

The Army is proud of its Infantry. Let's make the Infantry proud of its badge.

France —Pfc. W. W. VICTOR*

*Also signed by Pfc. Wilson.

Jap Lollapalooza

Dear YANK:

Read your article entitled "The Jap Soldier," and one particular paragraph caught my eye. It stated that the Jap cannot pronounce the letter "L" and gave an illustrative example "lollapalooza." Well, after an exhaustive test, I've found they have no more difficulty with their "L" than any other letter in the alphabet and can say "lollapalooza" just a shade better than a GI from Brooklyn. Who am I to argue with the OWI, but I only know what I hear and "lollapalooza" and "lullaby" are good enough for me.

Marianas —S. H. BLICKMAN PhM3c*

*Also signed by H. Isenberg PhM2c.

Post-War Pilot Training

Dear YANK:

A few weeks ago I read an article in *Mail Call* by some aviation enthusiast and I've given some thought to his suggestion concerning Pilot Training vs. Mustering-Out Bonus. Well, I think he made an excellent suggestion, because there will be, no doubt, quite a few commissioned pilots who would, after the German war is over, be willing to train fellows (who missed out on pilot training for various reasons) to fly light planes while waiting to ship home.

I don't know how much should be taken out of the bonus for such training, but whatever it is, we would have something solid behind us to put to further use in civilian life. . . .

Belgium —Pfc. WM. E. PALLMAN

"Kindly Let All—"

Dear YANK:

Has Sgt. Burtt Evans [in his story, "Kindly Let All Those Who Are Going Out First"—*Ed.*] tried his sentence this way: "Kindly let all those (who are going) out first?" That way, "out," instead of being considered as part of the verb "going," is considered as part of "let." Writing the sentence this way, you'd have: "Kindly let out first all those who are going." Not that it makes much more sense this way.

Perhaps Sgt. Evans can do something with this sentence that used to hang in a Truax Field (Wis.) mess hall some years ago and may still be there: "ALL PERSONS SMOKING IN OR AROUND THIS MESS HALL WILL BE DEALT WITH ACCORDINGLY."

—Pfc. MORRIS FREEDMAN

Randolph Field, Tex.

Can't Write to YANK

Dear YANK:

Well, now this field has issued an order forbidding any of us from writing YANK of any of our gripes or complaints. We are just wondering what is to come next. Is this field run by the Army or not? Please put something in YANK telling all of the GIs just how we stand in this matter.

Eagle Pass AAF, Tex. —(Name Withheld)

10-in-1 Ration

Dear YANK:

I have been eating 10-in-1 rations for quite some time and I haven't been able to find such rations in it as canned peaches, pears, fruit cocktail, vienna sausage, sardines and salmon. I have been trying to figure out for a long time just why they don't put that type of canned food in the 10-in-1 rations, but I haven't been able to do so. If they can put such canned food in them as chopped ham and eggs, corn beef, etc., why can't they put in the type of food I mentioned above?

Before I came overseas there was a lot of talk about food shortages, because they had to ship it to the soldiers overseas on the battle front. I don't think they really meant that, because unless we are stationed at a staging area or some place like Rome, we as front-line soldiers do not get such food. Can you tell me why?

Italy —S/Sgt. LONZIE THOMAS

104th Article of War

Dear YANK:

Let me end this torrent of complaints concerning the abuse of the 104th Article of War by this and that commanding officer by quoting from the 121st Article of War as follows:

"Any officer or soldier who believes himself wronged by his commanding officer, and, upon due application to such commander, is refused redress, may complain to the general commanding in the locality where the officer against whom the complaint is made is stationed. The general shall examine into said complaint and take proper measures for redressing the wrong complained of; and he shall, as soon as possible, transmit to the Department of War a true statement of such complaint, with the proceedings had thereon."

Although I'm sure that you, YANK, are familiar with the MCM, 90 percent of my fellow-GIs aren't.

Camp Lee, Va. —T/Sgt. ALVA L. MEADOR

Strictly GI

M26 Tank. The WD has finally released for publication something that Ordnance and Armored Force people have known for a long time—that we have a 45-ton tank, with a 90-mm gun, which is officially known as the M26 or General Pershing tank. It has more firepower than any other tank produced in the U.S. and is equipped with wide tracks, like German tanks, which are designed to give it better traction in mud.

Service Flags. Honorably discharged veterans may now be represented on service flags hanging in their parlor windows at home. The gold-eagle lapel button for honorable discharge will be used as the flag symbol to replace the blue star that indicates a man in service. Service flags of organizations and industries will display one such symbol with the number of honorably discharged members below it in arabic numerals. To make the symbol stand out from the white background of the flag, the design will be edged in blue.

The WD has also authorized the manufacture of an "official" lapel service button that may be worn by members of the immediate family of any person serving in the U. S. armed forces. The design of this button has not yet been announced.

Generals Nominated. The President has sent to the Senate the nominations of these nine lieutenant generals for promotion to the rank of full general: Joseph T. McNarney, supreme deputy Allied commander in the Mediterranean theater; Omar N. Bradley, CG of the Twelfth Army Group on the Western Front; Carl Spaatz, CG of U. S. Strategic Air Forces in Europe; George C. Kenney, CG of the Far East Air Forces; Mark W. Clark, CG of the Fifteenth Army Group in Italy; Walter Krueger, CG of the Sixth Army in the Philippines; Brehon B. Somervell, CG of the Army Service Forces; Jacob L. Devers, CG of the Sixth Army Group in the European Theater; and Thomas T. Handy, deputy chief of staff of the U. S. Army.

Cindy Garne
YANK
Pin-up G

NAVY NOTES

Navy Leaves. The Bureau of Personnel has issued a summary of its policy on leaves for nlisted personnel and directed all commands to e more strict about entering them on service ecords. Nine classes of leaves are listed and the naximum length in each case is exclusive of ravel time:

1. *Annual Leave.* 30 days in one year, authorized at he discretion of the CO, but should not exceed 15 ays for personnel on shore duty in the U. S. Leave ot taken cannot be carried over to the next year. COs are asked to give special consideration to peronnel returning from overseas whose husbands or vives are also members of the armed forces, and to ive them the full benefit of the 30 days.

2. *Reenlistment Leave.* This 30-day leave, given in eacetime to those who reenlist after their previous nlistment has expired, has been suspended for the luration. Regular Navy men will not forfeit this leave; t will be granted after the suspension has been renoved.

3. *Recruit ("Boot") Leave.* Charged against annual eave and changed according to circumstances. At resent 5 days are prescribed, with travel time in addiion not to exceed 10 days.

4. *Service-School Leave.* Also charged against annual eave and also subject to constant change. It is often uthorized in the form of delayed orders.

5. *Convalescent Leave.* This is supposed not to exceed 0 days but can be almost limitless in individual cases. t is granted only by medical officers and is not charged gainst annual leave.

6. *Emergency Leave.* And they do mean emergency. t is not charged against annual leave, and its length s governed by the emergency.

7. *Rehabilitation Leave.* 30 days, to those who have erved continuously outside the U. S. for one year or nore. In cases where overseas service has been less han a year, 2½ days for each month or fraction of a nonth is allowed. It is deductible from annual leave, but the annual leave is not deducted from rehabilitaion leave subsequently earned.

8. *Survivors' Leave.* 30 days of leave or delayed orders and not charged against annual leave.

9. *Leave on Retirement or Release to Inactive Duty.* 30 days or 2½ days per month of active duty less total eave while on duty, but not if you come under the Mustering-Out-Pay Act.

It will be noted that there is no longer an embarkation leave; all hands are advised to retain sufficient annual leave if they want to visit home before embarking for overseas.

Aid and Comfort to the Enemy. When a detachment of Seabees arrived at Pearl Harbor recently, the censors allowed no mention of the location in letters home. But they gave it away to one Seabee's wife. He started his letter, "Dear Pearl" (that *was* her name), and the "Pearl" was neatly clipped out.

Changes in Regulations. New spectacles or replacement of lenses or frames lost or damaged in performance of duty will now be provided at Government expense. . . . Legal-assistance officers have proved themselves so beneficial to naval personnel that the system is to be extended to include all ships and stations when practicable. . . . Items bought in ship's-service stores which are scarce in the civilian market, such as cigarettes, lighters, alarm clocks, fountain pens, etc., are not to be sent or brought home as gifts to civilians. Strict censorship of mail and gangway inspections are to be used to insure compliance. . . . The AOMB rating (Aviation Bombsight and Fire Control Mechanic) has been changed to AFC (Aviation Fire Controlman). . . . Seamen first class or second class, or their equivalent in any branch, may now submit applications for flight training in the Navy's V-5 program. Previously only petty officers or S1cs with six months' duty in an aviation activity could apply.

End in Sight. Anyone who remembers loading 10 gallons of gas in the jalopy and burning it up of a Sunday afternoon will probably also remember how he could walk into a Western Union telegraph office and, for a quarter, send to anyone in the U. S. a blurb composed by their human-relations department which covered anything from Mother's Day greetings to congratulations on the birth of a baby. They were called fixed-text messages and went out along with the gas for the jalopy. But for servicemen returning to the States for leave, discharge or hospitalization, there are 15 new ones which can be sent from various redistribution centers, hospitals, and receiving stations and they are, we think, properly high-spirited and optimistic. Here they are:

1. Leaving here soon. Home for good. Get my civilian clothes ready. Love.
2. Three cheers. Home for good in 10 days. Can't wait to see you. All my love.
3. Roll out the barrel. The war is over for me. Am on my way home. Love.
4. I'm over here from over there and will be with you soon. Love.
5. Being discharged here. Will be home soon. Round up the gang to celebrate. Love.
6. Back in States. Feeling fine. Furlough soon. Love.
7. Back at last. All well. Here short trip then home. Love.
8. It's good to be back. Hope get furlough soon. Writing. Love.
9. Back in good old U.S.A. All well. Can't wait to see you. Furlough soon. Love.
10. It's a long stretch from no man's land back to you. But I made it well and safe. See you soon. Love.
11. Arrived by plane. Expect to see you soon. Will write at next station. Love.
12. Just arrived. Feeling fine. Hope to see you soon. Love.
13. Arrived here safely. Getting good care and feeling fine. Will write. Love.
14. Passing through here. Will write from next hospital. Feeling fine. Love.
15. Back at last. Feeling OK. Hope to see you soon. Love.

LETTING OFF STEAM. The sluggers in the center of the ring didn't start this bout for fun, but they put on a good show for a crowd of ETO veterans homeward bound on a Coast Guard transport, the *USS General M. C. Meigs.* Two ship's mess cooks started a private argument in the galley. The chaplain stepped in but couldn't make any headway. Finally the boys were persuaded to settle their differences with gloves on one of the ship's cargo hatches. After half an hour's slugfest they staggered away the best of friends.

Believe It or Leave It. Richard R. Torruellas CM2c was an architect in Puerto Rico when he read "I Saw the Fall of the Philippines" by Brig. Gen. Carlos P. Romulo. Impressed by the book, Torruellas joined the Seabees. Gen. Romulo returned to the Philippines with Gen. MacArthur after an absence of 2½ years. Torruellas, now a member of a pontoon-causeway unit, was the first man to greet him.

Coxswain Albert F. Keller of Kennett, Mo., was a gunner on a freighter that was rammed and sunk by a Liberty ship a few miles off the coast of New Jersey last June. The ship went down quickly and Keller lost all his gear. Seven months later he returned to the Armed Guard Center in Brooklyn and picked up a package sent to him from California. In it was the suitcase of gear he'd left aboard the sinking freighter.

Donald E. Murphy of Battle Creek, Mich., and Lester R. Ransbottom of Otsego, Mich. stood side by side as they were sworn into the Navy. They went through boot camp together and then boarded the same transport, bound for Guam. Arriving at Guam, they jumped on the same truck headed inland. The truck crashed and together they were carried to the island hospital. Later they were transferred to a ship returning to the States where they lay side by side until the ship docked at San Francisco. When last reported, Damon and Pythias were in adjoining beds in a West Coast hospital.

A new admiral was recently inducted into the Navy—Arthur Admiral AS of Fort Lewis, Wash. Ens. Chester Ensign is attached to the Naval Air Training Base at Pensacola, Fla. Lt. Shippen Geer was recently detached from Third Naval District PRO. And the *Navy Register* lists the captain who will always be a sailor—Capt. Hobart A. Sailor, USN.

—DONALD NUGENT S1c

BY looking at her picture you might guess that Cindy Garner is the kind of girl who gets where she wants to. She started off as a reporter in her home town of High Point, N. C., and then went clear across the country to get a job as a hat-check girl in a Hollywood night club. Selznick International, with an eye for extra-pretty girls, spotted her there and gave her a contract.

Message Center

S/SGT. RICHARD ARONSTAM, last heard of in England with the Air Corps: write Sgt. Simeon Busenover, 423d AAF BU, Sq. B, Walla Walla, Wash. . . . JOSEPH A. BEERLY of Germantown, Pa., last heard of in Co. H, 18th Inf. at APO 1: write Pfc. Robert L. Lentz, Ward 5, Vaughan Gen. Hosp., Hines, Ill. . . . Anyone having any information concerning PVT. DAVID LIONEL BERMAN, killed in France, formerly with the Med. Det., 12th Inf., 3d Bn.: write Cpl. Stanley H. Pearline, AACS-AAF Det., 200 Mill Road, Upper Darby, Pa. . . . EDWARD L. BIRCHLER, last heard of in Co. 364, USNTC, Great Lakes, Ill.: write Sgt. E. L. Murtha, Hq. Co. IRTC, Bldg. 637, Camp Croft, S. C. . . . LT. TEDDY CARP, last heard of in Hawaii: write Pfc. Isidore Friedman, 878th Med. Sup. Det., Camp Barkeley, Tex. . . . Anyone having information about PVT. JIM COSTIGAN, with Btry. G of 13th CA, Pensacola, Fla., in 1942: write Pvt. Tom Quinlan, Co. B, 91st Sig. Bn., Camp Bowie, Tex. . . . Anyone having information concerning ALICE DELINE S2c, last heard of in USNATC, Norman, Okla., in April 1944: write Lt. H. E. Hargett, Fort Sumner AAF, N. Mex. . . . Anyone having information of F/O WILFRED DESILETS, last heard of with 342 Ftr. Sq., 348 Ftr. Gp.: write A/C Clifford M. Auger, 8023, Sq. I, Box A-5, Gunter Field, Ala. . . . SGT. FRANK FITTIN, last heard of with 364th Ftr. Gp.: write Lt. A. H. Kahrs, 1440 Canal Bldg., New Orleans, La. . . . Anyone having information about SGT. FRANK FAGAN, last heard of in Italy: write Sgt. Charlotte K. Friedly, 600 Buhl Bldg., Detroit 26, Mich. . . . WOJG THOMAS E. FINNERTY, formerly of the 306th CA Bar. Bln. Bn., San Pedro, Calif., and Fort Custer, Mich., now believed to be in the ETO: write S/Sgt. Bernard E. Fischer, 616th MP Escort Guard Co., Camp Stoneman, Calif. . . . PVT. J. C. GORDON JR., last heard of in Det. 53, SFRS, APO 739: write Pvt. J. S. Dudley Jr., Ward 204, Ashford Gen. Hosp., White Sulphur Springs, W. Va. . . . PVT. HARRY KRAM, somewhere in the Pacific: write Pvt. George La Marsh, Hq. Det., 228th Bn., Camp Blanding, Fla. . . . MAJ. CHARLES LADSON, former CO of 793d TSS, Seymour Johnson Field, N. C.: write Pvt. G. W. Jernigan Jr., Gen. Del., Portal, Ariz. . . . Anyone knowing the whereabouts of SGT. PATRICK M. MCCARTHY, formerly of the 26th Rcn. Troop: write S/Sgt. George B. Spring, 3547 Med. Det., Wakeman Gen. Hosp., Camp Atterbury, Ind. . . . A/C LORN G. MAHNEY, last heard of in Class 44-26, Sq. 2 Las Vegas AAF, Nev.: write A/C Raymond G. Cech, Cadet Det., Box 1194, Class 45-1B, Carlsbad AAF, N. Mex. . . . LT. JOHN G. OLDENBROOK, last heard of at Westover Field, Mass., in 1943: write Lt. Melvin W. Norman, Birmingham Gen. Hosp., Van Nuys, Calif. . . . Anyone having any information concerning MAJ. R. B. PARRISH (now believed to be a Lt. Col.): write Pfc. Aaron O. Kelly, USMC, Rifle Range Det., Box 1169, Parris Island, S. C. . . . LT. NORMAN PETERFREUND, last heard of in 1943 at APO 8961: write Ens. Jerome P. Friedman, U. S. Army FS 362, Navy 920, San Francisco, Calif. . . . W. C. PICKNEY, Seabees, last heard of in California: write Cpl. Willie M. Crumbley, WAC Det. No. 3, Regional Hospital, Fort McClellan, Ala. . . . PVT. ROBERT SENELL, last heard of in Mississippi in December 1944: write Pvt. Lillian Roth, WAC, 1010th AAF Base Unit C, Atlantic City, N. J. . . . Anyone knowing the whereabouts of SGT. JAMES THOMAS SUDER, APO 454, who was on a transport reported sunk, now reported missing: write Cpl. Margaret Suder, 759 Walnut Drive, Marietta, Ohio. . . . ARNAT VANDERBURG, last heard of in 1940, then a first lieutenant in the Quartermaster Corps, once stationed at the Army Base in Boston, Mass.: write T-5 Donald F. Brackett, Co. D, 80th Bn., 16th Gp., ASFTC, Camp Claiborne, La. . . . S/SGT. PETER VAN SLYCK, last heard of in England, now believed to be in the States: write A/C William Strang, Cadet Det., Cl. 45-D, Flt. 7, Bks. 672, La Junta AAF, Colo. . . . Anyone having information concerning CPL. E. J. VINCI, last heard of in Co. F, 109th Inf.: write Lt. R. Wanamaker, Luke Field, Ariz. . . . Anyone having information concerning PFC. THOMAS C. WILSON, last heard of in France: write Cpl. James F. Vouts, 7th Hq. & Hq. Det., Sp. Trs. Fourth Army, Camp Bowie, Tex.

Handwriting on the Wall

THERE are some things I don't like about the Army. Oh, I know full well that you will hoot at me and call me a liar and prevaricator and not believe me at all, but I feel I must confess to that failing, improbable as it does seem.

Now that I've got that off my chest (leaving only a fatigue shirt and some woolen underwear between me and the winter wind) I can go ahead and tell you about some of the things I dislike.

I don't care for cartoons about signing statements of charges, I don't like to carry a pack and a rifle, I despise physical training, and I do not rave with joy at the mention of bivouac.

But I have two main pet peeves. First, the Army has taught me to eat too fast. In fact, the word "fast" is as big an understatement as the word "————" in the sentence, "My first sergeant is a ————."

Since entering the armed forces I have learned to devour food with the speed of light, with a quickness and a rapidity which, if transformed to my legs, would enable me to run a 23-second mile. No longer can I dally round the groaning board, spicing the food with light wit and heavy thoughts. No. Now I must make like a steam shovel, excavating the food from tray to gullet with a celerity matched only by the Russian advances.

While this has played havoc with my digestive tract (a play similar in formation to the 6-2-2-1 defense) it has caused me only a fraction of the grief that I get from posters and placards.

I'm sure you are aware of these blatant manifestoes in three and four colors which adorn the walls of day rooms, latrines, orderly rooms and libraries. You know—stuff like a picture of an ape with the caption, "DON'T LET LICE MAKE A MONKEY OUT OF YOU—WASH EVERY DAY."

Well, the point of this blow-up follows immediately. I have seen these displays so often, and the slogans are so catchy, that they have wormed themselves into my speech and form an integral part of my vocabulary. When an officer asks me a question, I find that I answer, "Stoke it—don't choke it" (from the conservation-of-coal series). Sometimes I salute and say, "Don't abuse it—you'll have to use it" (care-and-cleaning-of-the-M1 series) Instead of thinking about my wife, I dream about Margie in the yellow pajamas and the post-war world and War Bonds.

I even think in terms of slogans. I catch myself humming, to that fine old tune, "Dinah," "Nothing could be finer than to have a helmet liner in the mo-o-rning." I turn on the radio and the announcer, to my ears, says, "No shave, no lather, no rubbing. No shave, no sir; it's dubbing."

I went to the medics but they classified me full duty. I talked to the psychiatrist, who was very interested. When he stepped out of the room for a moment, I sneaked a look at his notes and they

"I see a white card with the letters TS on it."
—Pvt. George Halpern, Dyersburg AAF, Tenn.

weren't notes at all. There was a drawing of Wacs, Waves and Spars singing, and the caption bubble showed they were singing "The Army's made a man out of me, a man out of me"!

My friends shun me and I hate myself, but I can't break the habit. I wake up at night and say, "Did anyone ever think of calling OCS the Gold Bar None Ranch?" All my mental pictures are in the form of posters. Like the picture of the typical raw recruit—clothes unpressed, cap askew, straw between the teeth—and the big letters screaming "HALF AN OAF IS BETTER THAN NONE."

"WATER WASTE MEANS WATER SHORTAGE." "NOT THE ENEMY BUT TRENCH FOOT." I tell you, men, it's got me reeling. Right now, while I still retain a toehold on my sanity, I am working on a monstrous, out-sized poster. It will have an OD background and there will be just three objects in the picture. They will be a collar insignia, US, and a collar insignia, EM, and a belt buckle. All will be stained, filthy and as dull as a reading of the *Articles of War*.

The caption? That's simple. Here it is:
"GET OFF YOUR BRASS—AND POLISH IT."

Camp Livingston, La. —S/Sgt. STANLEY MARGULIES

You Never Know

PVT. Harry Chesty was tough. He'd a whole lot rather knock you down than look at you.

The postman had a hard time tagging Harry with greetings from FDR. Harry was traveling with the Unkempt Brothers Shows and the shows existed by traveling fast.

Harry did a strong-man act and most people thought it was pretty good. Young sadists from the audience were permitted to drive railroad spikes into his ears. He bounced manhole covers edgewise off his head. He carried a four-door sedan across the stage. When he didn't have any gas on the stomach, he climaxed the act by eating a rare assortment of goldfish bowls, sanitary plumber's equipment and a crosscut saw.

When Harry entered Camp Bandon Hope, he gave the medics a rough hour or two. For one thing, he got a huge boot out of jerking away so

that four tetanus needles broke off in his arm. He laughed for days.

One night after completing a 30-mile hike through heavy snow, Harry took off for a dance in a town about 20 miles from camp. He missed the last bus back, so he had to leg it. He dog-trotted so he wouldn't be late for reveille.

Harry got into a lot of fights and broke a number of skulls. He was so tough everyone thought he was headed for a clerk's job in headquarters. The funny thing about it is, he was.

Harry had a young brother named Puny Chesty who was emaciated. Puny was hunched over and screwed up from working in an office, and nobody thought he would get into the Army. But he passed his physical somehow. While taking basic training, Puny dropped out on almost every hike and was a regular patron of the sick book.

Pvt. Puny Chesty seemed to be such a poor bet for the Infantry that everyone thought he was headed right for an assignment with the Infantry as a rifleman.

The funny thing about it is, he wasn't. He also was assigned to desk work at headquarters, just like his brother.

So you never know in the Army. That's what we always say. What do you always say?

Camp Breckinridge, Ky. —Sgt. CARL RITTE[R]

MEMORY

There is no beauty like a memory.
There no one dies. The many I have met
Who laughed with me a while, revealed a thought
Or touched with me the joy of sweet content—
Though in the night they quietly slipped away
Into a thousand fields I'll never see,
They are not gone so far that memory
Will not recall them back to me.

Fletcher General Hospital, Ohio —Sgt. JOSEPHINE PAGLIA

"Hey, soldier, don't you know you're not allowed to thumb rides?"
—Sgt. Al Kaelin, Olmsted Field, Pa.

SPORTS

By Cpl. TOM SHEHAN

Mel Ott may not finish the season. He, too, is now 1-A.

THIS is the time of year when all sports columnists are supposed to go into a trance and make with expert opinion about who is going to win the National League pennant. But it so happens that YANK has only one trance on its T/E and it is being used right now by the *What's Your Problem* editor, who went into it two weeks ago trying to find out when the war with Germany was going to end and hasn't been seen since.

So your correspondent decided to turn the task of predicting the National League season over to Mel Ott instead of tackling it himself. We don't need to tell you that Mel is now starting his 20th season as a major-leaguer and his fourth season as manager of the New York Giants. He is 1-A in the draft and wouldn't be at all surprised to find himself soon serving his first season as a private in the Army of the U. S.

Mel thinks that the confused, war-stricken National League situation this year will turn out to be a close, three-cornered battle between the St. Louis Cardinals, the Chicago Cubs and the Pittsburgh Pirates.

He points out that the Cardinals finished 14½ games in front of the Pirates last year, but that they have lost their slugging outfielder, Stan Musial, and that several other Red Birds may have to enter the service some time soon. Best of their new acquisitions is Albert (Red) Schoendienst, who became the International League's batting champion and most valuable player two years ago when he played shortstop for Rochester. Schoendienst was discharged from the Army last summer in time to play 27 games for Rochester. He is now in the process of being converted to a second baseman by Billy Southworth, and will compete with Emil Verban for a regular berth in the St. Louis infield.

"The Cards will be good," Ott says, "but not as good as they were last year.".

A 14-day winning streak of the Pirates last August, which brought 17 victories against one defeat, enabled them to take second place a game and a half in front of the Cincinnati Reds. Frankie Frisch has virtually the same team back in Pittsburgh this spring.

"The Cubs must be good," said Mel, "when they can afford to lose an outfielder like Dallessandro in the draft, release Ival Goodman to manage Portsmouth and let Los Angeles

have Novikoff. Novikoff is no great outfielder, but he hits a long ball, and a lot of clubs could use him if they could get him."

Ott thinks the chances of the rest of the clubs in the National League will depend on the strength of their reserves. "In this kind of wartime baseball you have to prepare for a lot of injuries," he says. "Players are out with injuries oftener than usual because they're older and don't recover as fast. On the other hand, there's such a shortage of men that players on the active list sometimes have to stay in the line-up when they should be resting.

"Last year my whole team took turns being out. Weintraub, Reyes, Medwick and Lombardi were injured during the most important part of the season. I sprained my ankle. A few years ago I would have been back in the line-up in a couple of days, but I was out six weeks. We brought Treadway up from Jersey City to relax some of the pressure, but then he got hurt. If it hadn't been for all those injuries, I honestly think we might have finished fourth." The Giants finished fifth in 1944, eight games behind the fourth-place Cubs and two games in front of the struggling Boston Braves.

Mel thinks that the Giants' prospects are the best since they finished third in 1942, but he has too many TS slips to believe they will be fighting for the pennant. He doesn't know how long Buddy Kerr is going to be around to play shortstop. And he doesn't know how much longer he can stand Danny Gardella, his screwy outfielder, who, despite another year of discipline at Jersey City, has a mouth as loud as ever. Mel has many other personnel problems, but he doesn't want to bore you with them.

The Braves have good pitching and catching but nothing much in the infield. The Phillies are trying out a flock of youngsters, but the tip-off on them is that they have induced Jimmy Foxx to come out of retirement and have given old Gus Mancuso a contract.

THERE was a time when any kind of ball player who donned a uniform could land a spot on an Army camp or regimental team, but not since they started inducting reexamined 4-F athletes at a 50-percent rate. A story now going the rounds concerns a player who entered the service recently and refused to draw a rifle at the induction center. "I'm a ball player," he protested.

"I've seen you play, Bud," the tough supply sergeant told him, "and take it from me, you're gonna need a rifle."

SPORTS SERVICE RECORD

CHICAGO is a wonderful city, according to **Cpl. Erwin Werth.** While he was waiting to buy a ticket for the Chicago Blackhawks-Montreal Canadiens hockey game a man approached him and asked, "Are you alone?" When Werth said he was, the guy handed him a $2 ticket and said, "Here, I'm giving these to servicemen." While Werth was still examining the ticket to see if it was real, another man rushed up, grabbed the ticket, handed him another, went away and returned in a short time with a $2 refund for the first ticket. . . . **Sgt. Gerry Priddy,** former Washington Senators infielder who has been playing ball in the Pacific, is in the Army and Navy Hospital, Hot Springs, Ark., suffering from arthritis. . . . **Tex Hughson,** former Red Sox pitcher, and **Enos Slaughter** and **Howie Pollet,** ex-St. Louis Cards, are on their way to the Pacific to join the Army baseball team there. . . . Rep. Adam Clayton Powell Jr. [Dem., N. Y.] has asked President Roosevelt to make **Sgt. Joe Louis** a commissioned officer. . . . **Lt. Edward W. (Wes)**

Schulmerich, former big-league outfielder who reported to Chapel Hill last fall after service in the Pacific, will coach the North Carolina Pre-Flight nine this year. . . . **Charley Soleau,** quarterback on Andy Kerr's undefeated, untied, unscored-upon and uninvited Colgate eleven of 1932, is a lieutenant in the Navy at Port Lyautey in North Africa.

Rejected: **Mike Garback,** New York Yankees catcher; **Ernie Steele,** Philadelphia Eagles halfback. . . . *Decorated:* **Lt. Bob Herwig,** USMC, former U of California All-American center and husband of Kathleen Winsor, author of "Forever Amber," with the Navy Cross for services in the Pacific. . . . *Inducted:* **Eddie Joost,** Boston Braves second baseman; **Harry Gumbert,** Cincinnati Reds pitcher; and **Dominic Dallessandro,** Chicago Cubs outfielder. . . . *Wounded:* **Lt. Si Titus,** USMC, former Holy Cross and Brooklyn Dodgers lineman, on Iwo Jima. . . . *Discharged:* **Harry Kline,** ex-New York Giants end, by the Navy after being awarded the Purple Heart; **Jimmy Thompson,** long-hitting golf pro, also by the Navy. . . . *Hospitalized:* **Lynwood (Schoolboy) Rowe,** the former speedball pitching star of the Detroit Tigers, in Pearl Harbor with arthritis contracted while serving as a seaman first class in the Pacific.

TWO EX-CHAMPS. Comdr. Jack Dempsey of the U. S. Coast Guard runs into another former heavyweight titleholder, Capt. Jim Braddock of Army Transportation Corps, somewhere in Hawaii.

"IT WAS SIMPLY A MATTER OF MAKING A BETTER MOUSE TRAP."
—Pfc. Walter Mansfield

"PIPE DOWN, MAHONEY. WANNA GIVE AWAY OUR POSITION TO THE ENEMY?"
—S/Sgt. Irwin Caplan

"SEE? I TOLD YOU WE WERE IN FRIENDLY WATERS."
—Cpl. Sol Dember

"I THINK THAT ARGUMENT WITH THE COLONEL MUST HAVE UPSET STANLEY A LITTLE."
—William J. Phelan SA(D)3c

"HOPE WE MAKE NEW YORK TOMORROW. THIS IS THE LAST CLEAN SHIRT I'VE GOT."
—T-5 Steve Milliken

YANK

E ARMY WEEKLY

5¢

MAY 11
VOL. 3, NO. 47
1945

By the men . . . for the
men in the service

e Life of Truman and the Death of Roosevelt

PAGES 2 - 13

HAR

By YANK Washington Bureau

HARRY S. TRUMAN of Independence, Mo., the new President of the United States, was a captain and a major in France in the other war and evidently he wasn't chicken.

Because the men in his outfit—Battery D, 129th Field Artillery of the 35th Division, now fighting in Germany—went out of their way to do something nice for him on the way home after the Armistice. They took a cut from every pot of their crap games on the transport and bought him a loving cup, four feet high.

The cup is still the President's proudest possession and the D Battery men are still his close friends. He has never forgotten the things they talked about on that transport and the hard time he and they had getting back in the swing of Missouri civilian life after they were discharged.

He came home and married his girl, Bess Wallace, in June 1919. He and another veteran raised a little money and opened a small haberdashery store. It failed and they lost everything. Truman had plenty of worries before he started in law and politics a few years later and managed to win election as county judge from his section of Jackson County—not a judicial office as the name implies, for in Missouri the County Court is an administrative agency of government whose members are called judges.

Although it is too early to make predictions about what kind of an all-around job he will be able to do in the White House, it is safe to say that the memory of what he went through 25 years ago as a new civilian makes Truman more aware of veterans' post-war problems than most Presidents we have had.

His first executive order after taking office was one giving veterans of this war job priority in U. S. Civil Service.

His first public speech as President, before Congress, included the words: "Our debt to the heroic men and valiant women in the service of our country can never be repaid. They have earned our undying gratitude."

The next evening he spoke to the armed forces over the radio, reminding them of his own combat service in France with the 35th Division. "I know the strain, the mud, the misery, the utter weariness of the soldier in the field," he said. "I know too his courage, his stamina, his faith in his comrades, his country and himself.

"We are depending on each and every one of you."

Truman's concern for the servicemen has been strong all through his public life. He is an active American Legion man and as a U. S. senator he was an active supporter of the GI Bill of Rights. Only a few days before the death of President Roosevelt brought him into the White House, he devoted his speech at a Grover Cleveland memorial dinner in Buffalo, N. Y., to facts and figures knocking down civilian fear that the returning veterans may flood the labor market and cause widespread unemployment.

As he announced in his address to Congress, Mr. Truman intends to follow the general line of Roosevelt polices. "I will support those ideals with all my strength and all my heart," he said. But Truman's way of supporting the Roosevelt ideals may be as different from Roosevelt's way as the difference between the two men's

The new President knows about a veteran's post-war problems. He had plenty of them when he came home from France in 1919.

These were the President's parents, John and Martha Truman.

Harry Truman (right) as a boy of 4 with his brother, aged 2.

President Truman once operated a haberdashery in Kansas City.

Mr. Truman (back row, left) at a picnic in Kansas City, 1921.

With his mother (now 91) after being elected U. S. senator in 1934.

At a Truman Committee session. It was first set up early in 1941.

As a contender for the Vice Presidency, with his wife and daughter.

He confers with Roosevelt after his nomination for Vice President.

When he took over his duties as Vice President in January 1944.

Y S. TRUMAN

backgrounds and personalities. And that is a difference as wide as the distance between Dutchess County, N. Y., and Jackson County, Mo.

Roosevelt was an Eastern blue-blood who went to Groton School—so exclusive that you can't get in unless your grandfather belonged to the right clubs—and Harvard University. Truman's father couldn't afford to let him go to college. He quit school early and worked in the bank in Lamar, Mo., the town where he was born. Then his family got him to come back and help out on the family farm until he went to war. Roosevelt was a wealthy man. Truman came into the White House with the smallest family fortune of any President of this century.

Roosevelt started mixing into politics as a youngster with a Harvard accent and Brooks Brothers clothes whose neighbors in fashionable Dutchess County had invited him to take part in community affairs. When Truman ran for the judge's job in Jackson County, he needed the money it paid.

When Roosevelt was a bright young Assistant Secretary of the Navy and the up-and-coming Democratic nominee for the Vice Presidency 25 years ago, Truman was just another veteran.

When Roosevelt was nominating Al Smith at the Democratic Convention in 1924, Truman was about to get beaten for re-election as county judge. Roosevelt the next year was a business executive in New York. Truman was back on the farm. He stayed at farming until 1930 when, at the age of 46, he managed to make a come-back and get elected county judge again. Roosevelt by that time was governor of New York and already regarded as a cinch for the Presidency.

Truman didn't get into national politics as a senator until 1934, when Roosevelt was not only President but also was already being referred to as "That Man in the White House." The story is that Truman's debut in national politics was somewhat of an accident. They say he went to see Tom Pendergast, the Kansas City political boss, about a county job. "I'm sorry, Harry," Pendergast is supposed to have said to him. "The only thing I can offer you right now is a U. S. senatorship."

Truman's relations with Pendergast, who was convicted on an income-tax-evasion rap in 1939, have caused some people to raise their eyebrows. The new President makes no bones about the fact that he and the late Kansas City boss were on good speaking terms. He points out calmly that Pendergast never asked him to do anything corrupt and that he got more votes for the Pendergast machine in Missouri than it ever got him. He was re-elected to the Senate in 1940 without Pendergast's help.

The Trumans' family life isn't much like the Roosevelts', either. Back in Independence they lived in a rambling frame house, the kind that has colored glass borders in the parlor windows, built by Mrs. Truman's grandfather 80 years ago. It has a swing on the front porch. The President's 91-year-old mother lives on the old farm at Grandview, not far away. Her boast that Harry could plow the straightest furrow in Jackson County had a big play in the newspapers after her son was sworn in as President.

Mrs. Truman used to sit in front of her husband when they were kids together in the class of 1901 at the three-year Independence High School. (He can name today nearly all of the 4? other boys and girls in the class.) He carried her books home every afternoon and they went to the Baptist Sunday School together, too. When they started keeping company, the whole town approved of the match.

When Mr. Truman came to the Senate in 1934 he brought his wife along as his secretary. "She's my chief adviser," he says. "I never write a speech without going over it with her." Until they moved into the White House, they lived in a small Washington apartment with no maid. Mrs. Truman did her own cooking. Lately, of course, they have been getting invitations to big parties in the Capital. Their easy informality makes a good impression. Mr. Truman at one of the last parties he attended as Vice President played a piano duet of "Chopsticks" with Rosa Ponselle, and it went over big. Mrs. Truman, according to women who know about such things, looks well in evening clothes and doesn't put on social airs. When somebody asked her recently about her previous social life she smiled and said, "Well, there was the Missionary Society, of course, and the Art Club."

The Trumans' 21-year-old daughter Mary Margaret goes along when her parents spend an evening out. She is a pretty girl who would like to study to be a singer, but her father, conscious of his own lack of a college degree, is making her finish George Washington University first. Mary Margaret doesn't have much to say as a rule. At the Chicago Convention, when it began to look as though her father was going to get the Vice Presidential nomination, she jumped to her feet and yelled, "Yea, team!" Then she blushed and looked around to see if anybody had noticed.

Just 2 hours and 34 minutes after the death of President Roosevelt, Harry S. Truman is sworn in at the White House. Left to right: Secretaries Perkins, Stimson and Wallace, WPB Director Krug, Secretaries Forrestal and Wickard, Attorney General Biddle, Secretary Morgenthau, President Truman, Mrs. Truman, Secretary Ickes, Margaret Truman, Chief Justice Harlan F. Stone, Speaker of the House Rayburn, War Mobilization Director Vinson and Rep. Martin, minority leader of the House

Unlike his predecessor, who was very fond of Camels, Mr. Truman doesn't smoke. He takes an occasional drink, usually bourbon. He plays the piano seriously, especially Chopin pieces, and he likes bridge and poker. "I learned poker in France," he says, "and it was a costly education. As yet it hasn't paid any dividends."

PEOPLE in Washington and Missouri who know Mr. Truman intimately say that in supporting the Roosevelt ideals the new President will delegate more authority than FDR, who tried to make most of his own decisions and often became involved in details that might have been pushed off on his assistants. At his first press conference, Mr. Truman said he planned, for instance, to let the State Department handle the San Francisco conference by itself. He explained that he intended to spend most of his Administration in the White House at his desk and pounded it with his fist to emphasize that point.

Roy Roberts, managing editor of the Kansas City *Star*, who knows Mr. Truman from away back, says that this readiness to delegate authority will be the predominating new feature of his Administration. "Each department or bureau head will be expected to go ahead and run his own show," Roberts writes. "If they make good, fine. If they come a cropper—well, Truman is not the sort who will hang onto them long."

Roberts and others who are in the position to make authoritative predictions about Mr. Truman also expect him, as a former senator, to turn more frequently to Congress for advice and recommendations than Mr. Roosevelt did. The first day he was President Mr. Truman broke a precedent by having lunch at the Capitol. Republican leaders in Congress like Sen. Arthur Vandenburg of Michigan and Rep. Joe Martin of Massachusetts are his good friends. He gets along very well with the Southern Democrats in both Houses. Jackson County was largely Confederate in sentiment during the Civil War, and Mr. Truman's father was a Confederate veteran. James F. Byrnes, the former "Assistant President," returned to Washington from Spartanburg, S. C., where he had gone into retirement only a week before, as soon as Mr. Roosevelt died. He was the first person called to the White House for a conference by Mr. Truman. The new President is said to regard Byrnes as one of the ablest figures in American public life.

Mr. Truman now occupies the Presidency, of course, because he won the Democratic Vice-Presidential nomination in Chicago last summer. Two things won him the nomination. The first was the fact that he alone was acceptable to Mr. Roosevelt and to both the conservative element of the Democratic Party and its liberal wing. The second was the excellent performance of the Truman Committee in the investigation of our Government's spending of money for the war effort.

Mr. Truman charged in the Senate in February 1941 that Government agencies were awarding defense contracts to personal favorites, most of them large corporations. He called for the organization of a Senate committee to investigate the situation. A month later, the Senate organized such a committee with him as its chairman. The committee is generally credited with having done a terrific job. It could have been used for sensational, headline-making muckraking. Mr. Truman instead saw to it that the investigations of spending and contract awards were carried on in a spirit of constructive helpfulness. Although he did not hesitate to name names and to let the chips lie where they fell, the people whose work he investigated often thanked him for it afterward.

His committee's first report accused the War Department of "fantastically" poor judgment in the choice of camp sites and in its policy of renting vehicles and equipment for construction programs instead of buying them outright. Gen. Brehon B. Somervell, chief of the Army Service Forces, was quoted later as saying that the Truman inquiry saved the Government $200,000,000.

The Truman Committee also charged that U. S. shipyards were shaking down the Navy for unreasonable profits; that "dollar-a-year men" in key positions in Washington were delaying war production and taking care of their friends with fat contracts; that automobile plants were far behind schedule in converting to war production; that

American fighter planes in 1941 and the early part of 1942 were no good; that housing plans for defense and war workers were snafued; that the big steel firms, trying to squash small competitors, were to blame for the shortage of steel and scrap then prevalent; that the Navy's Bureau of Ships had rejected a design for an effective invasion landing craft and had spent millions of dollars "using models of its own design despite repeated failures thereof"; that I. G. Farbenindustrie and the Standard Oil Company of New Jersey had a cartel agreement which worked to the advantage of the Axis by hindering the development of synthetic rubber in the U. S.

Mr. Truman called on Mr. Roosevelt one day in January 1942 to tell him that his committee was going to recommend that one man should run the whole war-production program. The next day Mr. Roosevelt announced Donald M. Nelson's appointment as war-production head. As a result of the Truman Committee's report, dollar-a-year men bowed out.

Mr. Truman summed up his committee's goal by saying, "The thing to do is to dig up this stuff now and correct it. If we run this war program efficiently there won't be any opportunity for someone to undertake a lot of investigation after the war and cause a wave of revulsion that will start the country on the downhill road to unpreparedness and put us in another war in 20 years."

LIKE Mr. Roosevelt, the new President believes that another war can come just as quickly from a lack of cooperation between nations as it can from the lack of military preparedness. One of the main themes of his campaign speeches last

fall was that the U. S. should never return to isolationism. As a senator who described himself as a "common-sense liberal" he was a strong supporter of the Roosevelt foreign policies. According to his boyhood friend, Charles G. Ross of the St. Louis *Post-Dispatch*, he arranged the luncheon that led to the Ball-Burton-Hatch-Hill Resolution in the Senate calling for a full American share in a world-peace organization.

Once when he was discussing lend-lease, he remarked: "When anybody cries on my shoulder about lend-lease, I always say that for every hundred million dollars we gave them, we saved one hundred thousand lives. If we never get any of it back it will be money well spent."

MR. Truman is the type of President who doesn't stand on pomp and ceremony and likes to call people by their first names. The squads of Secret Service men who follow him around make him feel like a nuisance rather than like an important figure. His friends say he hates to bother or offend people. In that respect, he takes after his parents. His two grandfathers were named Shippe and Solomon. When Mr. Truman was born, his parents didn't want to offend either of them so they gave the boy the middle initial of "S" and let it go at that.

When he was in the Senate, the new President once commented about its ceremony and social procedure. "All this precedence and other hooey accorded to a senator isn't very good for the Republic," he said.

If he felt like that when he was an Army officer, it was no wonder the men in his battery presented him with the loving cup.

President Harry S. Truman meets the press for the first time in the executive room of the White House. The room was jammed with the largest number of newsmen it ever held in the history of Presidential press conferences. There were 348 reporters for newspapers from all over the country, not to mention 50 visitors.

YANK, The Army Weekly, publication issued weekly by Branch Office, Information & Education Division, War Department, 205 East 42d Street, New York 17, N. Y. Reproduction rights restricted as indicated in the masthead on the editorial page. Entered as second class matter July 6, 1942, at the Post Office at New York, N. Y., under the Act of March 3, 1879. Subscription price $3 yearly. Printed in the U. S. A.

After the body was lowered into the gr[...]
Hyde Park, the bugler sounded taps an[...]

The caisson which carried the body of President Roosevelt moved from the Union Station toward the Capitol.

Roosevelt's Funeral

**How the nation took the news of a President's death
and how the word came to GIs overseas.**

men-pallbearers held the flag over the
the Roosevelt family stands in center left.

As the funeral procession arrived outside the White House grounds, the waiting crowd showed its sorrow.

THE funeral march stretched for a thousand miles. The train, with the flag rippling from the engine, had come up from Georgia, past the old battlefields of another war fought 80 years ago. There was a great hush over the land. The people came and stood by the tracks as the long train rolled on, bound for Washington and later a quiet garden high above the Hudson. The President was dead.

The train moved slowly through the night. At Charlotte, N. C., a troop of Boy Scouts started to sing "Onward Christian Soldiers," and massed thousands took it up in a mighty chorus. Along the way people dropped to their knees in prayer. Bells tolled a requiem.

By countless thousands the people came to say good-bye to Franklin Delano Roosevelt. Men in overalls, men with gnarled hands, women with shawls, kids, wet-eyed and solemn, lined the tracks and bowed their heads.

("There is the hope of the future," said the economist who once had been a Brain-Truster. "If Franklin Roosevelt's hopes and dreams are deep enough in the heart of the people, the people will make them come true.")

There had been only one other pilgrimage like this in American history. That had taken place 80 years before, almost to a day, when a wartime President had been borne on a long trek to Illinois and a tomb that became a shrine. His name was Abraham Lincoln.

Across the silent countryside soft with spring, past the sprawling green fields of Virginia, Franklin Roosevelt came back to Washington. There in the Capital, shimmering in the hot sun, where he had four times come in triumph after Presidential campaigns, the President rode again. The last campaign had ended for the man who once described himself as an "old campaigner who loves a good fight." Now he rode in a flag-draped coffin on a black caisson drawn by six white horses.

At the Union Station and along the broad streets leading to the White House, where the President had ridden so often to the crowd's acclaim, the silence was broken only by the muffled roll of drums and the muted dirge.

Five hundred thousand persons saw the coffin on the caisson and sensed that men would speak of this hour 100 years from now.

("Once when I was traveling on a campaign train with Franklin Roosevelt," said the senator, "a little boy came running up the tracks as the train started pulling out of the station. And the little boy yelled, 'Hey, Mr. President, thanks for our new WPA toilet and thanks for everything.' Franklin Roosevelt was the people's hero. The people were his hero. A long time ago he whipped infantile paralysis, and after that he wasn't afraid of anything. No wonder they called him the Champ.")

Mrs. Eleanor Roosevelt had asked that no one send flowers to the funeral, yet in the stately East Room of the White House, where the closed coffin rested, flowers banked three sides of the room, high against the wall. There were flowers sent by kings and flowers sent by obscure people whom the President never saw. A little boy in Chicago sent a bouquet picked from his back yard. "I was sorry," he wrote, "that I couldn't come to the funeral."

The weather was sultry on this funeral day, much as it had been on April 14, 1865, the day Abraham Lincoln was shot in Ford's Theater. And in the East Room, where Lincoln had lain in state, the mourners gathered at the bier of

Franklin Roosevelt. Great men of the world were there. Foreign Secretary Anthony Eden had flown to Washington from London. He looked grave and worried. Prime Minister Winston Churchill had planned also to attend the funeral of this "cherished friend" but canceled his plans because of the urgency of the war situation.

Cabinet members and diplomats were there. Supreme Court justices, congressmen and men famous in literature were there. Mrs. Eleanor Roosevelt was drawn and tired, but her step was firm and her head was high. Harry Hopkins, closest of the Presidential advisers, who had flown to Washington from the Mayo Clinic in Rochester, Minn., where he had been ill, grasped the back of the chair in front of him so tightly that his knuckles gleamed white.

Near the Roosevelt family sat President Truman, his wife and daughter, Mrs. Woodrow Wilson and Crown Princess Martha of Norway. The new President and his family entered the room so quietly that no one had time to rise. He stared straight ahead, his jaw outthrust. In this hour of mourning, he seemed quietly confident, as though at this flag-draped coffin of his fallen leader he was gathering will of spirit for the task ahead.

The coffin was flanked by flags and rested on a catafalque centered near the east wall. From the wall on either side looked down full-length portraits of George and Martha Washington.

At each corner of the coffin was a guard. Two GIs, a corporal and a pfc, and a marine and a sailor all stood rigidly at attention. The stillness was broken only by the gentle whirring of a fan. To one side of the room sat the President's wheel chair, empty.

(And in the park across the street from the White House, where the people had gathered to talk in low tones, the old man said: "The greatest thing that Franklin Roosevelt did was teach the people that this land is theirs; that the earth's abundance belongs to the people; that they need only the will to gain the power.")

In the East Room, rich with history and heavily fragrant with flowers, the Rt. Rev. Angus Dun, bishop of the Episcopal Diocese of Washington, prayed for "steadfast courage in adversity; for sympathy with the hungers and fears of common men; for trials met without surrender, and weakness endured without defeat; for unyielding faith in the possibility of a more just and more ordered world, delivered from the ancient curse of war."

The bishop, at Mrs. Roosevelt's suggestion, quoted the words with which Franklin Roosevelt on a bleak inaugural day more than 12 years before had restored a desperate nation's faith: "The only thing we have to fear is fear itself."

The bishop closed with familiar words that rang through the long room: "Through Jesus Christ, to whom be glory forever and ever. Amen."

The mourners left the White House. Outside, other mourners still stood, crowds of them. They had stood through a sudden downpour of rain, and now their clothes steamed in the sun.

That night, again through hushed, crowded streets, the President's coffin was carried to the train for its journey to Hyde Park, N. Y. Twelve years before, Franklin Roosevelt had come to the White House at a time of crisis, with millions of unemployed roaming the nation's streets, and he had offered sympathy, hope and bold experiment. Now he was no longer untried. Twelve years before he had reassured the people with the solemn word that the "money changers have abdicated . . . the people have not failed." Now the people were telling him quietly and reverently that he had not failed. They watched the hearse roll to the train, and they bowed in honest grief. His place in history secure, the President was leaving the White House forever.

("Some people compare him to Lincoln," said the professor who had once helped draft New Deal legislation, "and it's true that he was attacked and abused like Lincoln. But Franklin Roosevelt patterned himself after Jefferson and Jackson. He proved, as Jefferson did, that a man

can be a great gentleman and at the same t[ime a] great commoner. And he was tough like Jac[kson,] a hell of a fighter.")

ONCE more the body of Franklin Roosevel[t was] borne through the night. And again the [peo]ple in the villages and towns and farms wai[ted in] the darkness while the train rolled past.

Riding with the President on this last jo[urney] were men and women who had come to W[ash]ington 12 years before, eager to wipe out old [laws] and write new ones. This night they were [sad] and troubled. The New Dealers were gettin[g out,] and they had lost their leader. Secretary of [Com]merce Henry Wallace and Secretary of th[e In]terior Harold Ickes had boarded the trai[n to]gether, walking arm in arm. "Roosevelt's m[ourn]eers," said a man in the crowd.

The train moved through the night, an[d the] dim lights of the towns etched the faces [of the] people standing near the tracks. Across on[e sta]tion there was a line of boys and girls—[boys] holding caps in their left hands and girls [with] pigtails. They stood with chests thrust out [at at]tention. A band played "Hail to the Chief." [Some] of the kids were crying.

Northward the train rolled, taking Fra[nklin] Roosevelt home. At the edge of a little to[wn an] old man was spearing waste paper with a po[inted] stick. In his right hand he carried a greasy [old] cap. As the train passed, the old man put o[n his] cap, drew himself jerkily up and saluted. [His] heels were together, his chest was out. Clea[rly he] had saluted before, maybe in some war lon[g ago.]

("I rode with him on all four of his campa[igns,"] said the reporter. "A lot of people praisin[g him] the most now are the ones who fought hi[m the] hardest. That would amuse the old man. [He al]ways knew the pitch on those phonies.")

At lonely crossroads and in great cities [the] common people had come to say their own [good]bye to this crippled man who once had ta[ken a] crippled nation and helped it walk once m[ore.]

Sketches by Sgt. Robert Greenhalgh show men of the honor guard placing the Presid[ent's...]

The next morning was Sunday, April 15, 1945. At 10:15 A.M. Franklin Delano Roosevelt, four times chosen by the people as President of the United States, was committed to the earth of his beloved Hyde Park birthplace.

Against a 15-foot hemlock hedge surrounding the old garden which the President long ago had designated as his burial place, files of soldiers, sailors and marines stood rigidly at attention, their eyes fixed on the flag-draped coffin. A battalion of gray-and-white-clad West Point Cadets was massed at one end of the garden. The cadets' crepe-hung drums rolled mournfully across the chill morning air.

The Rev. Dr. W. George W. Anthony, rector of St. James Church of Hyde Park, quoted from "Requiescat" by John B. Dykes:

"Now the laborer's task is o'er;
Now the battle day is past;
Now upon the farther shore
Lands the voyager at last.
Father, in thy gracious keeping,
Leave we now thy servant sleeping."

Three cadets fired deliberately spaced volleys across the President's grave. A bugler stepped forward and softly blew taps. A sergeant of the honor guard selected to carry the coffin lifted the American flag from the top, folded it carefully and handed it to Mrs. Roosevelt. Mrs. Roosevelt, ashen-gray but dry-eyed, accepted it proudly.

(*"Last time I talked with him,"* said the neighbor, *"the President told me he didn't know how history would record him as a President, but he said he knew for sure that he was one of the best doggoned tree-growers ever to come up the pike."*)

Within a half-hour after the burial all the mourners had left. Franklin Roosevelt was alone in the garden where he had played as a boy and where he had teased a childhood playmate named Eleanor. The only sound was the footbeat of sentries walking their posts.
—Pfc. DEBS MYERS
YANK Staff Writer

The Virginia Depot

LYNCHBURG, VA.—At 2 in the morning it was warm, and the faint scent of flowers mixed with the odors of coal smoke at the station.

The handsome kid who handled the mail sacks cried orders to his driver, who gunned the old Chevy truck noisily. The handsome kid climbed in beside the driver and looked up at the platform above the tracks as the Chevy rolled away—looked up with the magnificent arrogance of a 16-year-old at the legs of the women above.

At track level, two Southern Railway detectives stood in self-conscious importance, knowing that soon they could lift their hands and command all Americans to move aside, move back to a certain line. They were the men in charge, conscious that two hours from now they could report that all had been handled according to instructions. They were hard men, and they had their orders.

"We have our orders," they said. Their credentials were in their left hip pockets. One of them showed his badge to a man who wanted to park his car on the track level.

A few older men stood by the platform railing talking in a soft accent. They were talking about the family. They traded sentences in the sympathetic undertones of old friends of the family; their voices were the voices of those who gather at the home and stand outside on the porch, picking carefully and slowly over the events that follow a death in the family. "One of the boys started home by plane as soon as he heard the news from his mother," a man said solemnly. "I don't guess they all can come."

Two squads of soldiers wearing MP armbands marched in columns of twos down the platform and were posted by a staff sergeant. They took

coffin on its caisson and standing by him in the East Room of the White House.

interval to the left and stood at parade rest. A woman watched the staff sergeant and said, "He don't care how long they stand there, does he?" She marveled at the staff sergeant, marveled that this man could order 24 other men to stand like statues until he said they could do something. "They could stand there until 12 o'clock tomorrow for all he cares." Her voice carried wonderment.

At 3 or a little after a train came in, and the people on the platform watched.

"They're loadin' that one. You know they wouldn't be loadin' express on his train," a man said to his wife. His wife said nothing.

A freight came through and temporarily interrupted the conversation of two Negro men. One had taken off his hat as the earlier train came in, then hastily put it back on when he realized this was not the train. He and his friend were talking about past funerals. They had been talking about whether the President could be buried at Arlington, and now they were talking about soldiers of Virginia who had been buried with honors. "That was the first time I ever saw the Richmond Blues," said one. "I mean all them men was tall, too." The freight rolled off, southbound.

Twenty minutes later two state cops went down and cleared the people from the track level. People moved quietly now, and the talk that had been clear became muted. An older Negro man and his wife stood apart and watched as half a dozen teen-agers invaded the platform from the parking space outside. The teen-age boys wore dark pants and light coats with padded shoulders, and the girls wore slacks and short light coats and had peasant scarves wound in turbans on their heads.

The old Negro couple watched them approach and the old man whispered to his wife, "Now, look at that." His words were scarcely audible. He and his wife moved off, down to the end of the platform where other colored people stood. The old man was scowling. A teen-ager shrilled, "There's Shirley!" and waved.

By 3:40 the people who had waited longest at the platform railing were joined by those who had set their alarm clocks and now began to come, carloads at a time in family groups, to the station. They spoke to one another, these groups, as they found places by the railing. They were compact, clannish groups. One seemed to be composed of civic-club citizens. They spoke biting words aimed at those who had cleared the track level. "It's just

these officials we have here. Why can't we stan[d] down there?" They looked coldly at the cop[s] who were unaware of them.

"Why can't we stand down there?" a black[-] haired young woman said in a sharp accent tha[t] cut deep into the low voices of Virginia aroun[d] her. "His last trip through Lynchburg, too."

A big guy rolled up to the railing and wa[s] greeted by a group. "What brought you dow[n] here?" they asked. "Same thing that brough[t] you," he answered boisterously. "Curiosity g[ot] the best of me." He laughed heartily.

The black-haired young woman looked scor[n]fully across, and her voice was biting. "And [he] had to die——"

The whistle blew far up the tracks, and th[e] sentence was unfinished. The crowd compose[d] itself silently at the railing. From the track lev[el] came the echo-distorted command, "Prese[nt] arms!" The people—400 of a city of 40,000—stoo[d] immobile at 4 in the morning. The noise of drivi[ng] rods cut out from up the track, and then ther[e] was the sound of the bell.

Two engines coasted through, drawing th[e] darkened train, and the people tensed for th[e] sight of something they could remember—ligh[t] in the vestibules and in the lavatories, a man [in] a gray suit with one hand in his pocket ridi[ng] the bottom step of a car.

A light showed in the last car. The car we[nt] by, shades up, and for a moment there showed [a] corner of a flag, red and white, and there was t[he] impression of a red silk bow. Or perhaps the[re] was no bow at all. The train was moving very fas[t.] But there was red and white, and what appeare[d] to be a bow, and that was what the people [on] the upper platform were able to see.

"It was the last thing in the car," a woma[n's] voice said softly.

The people at the railing stood only until t[he] click of the rails was lost in the rising whispe[r] of those who had come to pay their last respect[s.]

—Sgt. MACK MORRISS[ON]
YANK Staff Wri[ter]

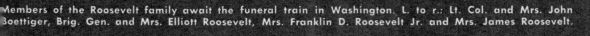

Members of the Roosevelt family await the funeral train in Washington. L. to r.: Lt. Col. and Mrs. John Boettiger, Brig. Gen. and Mrs. Elliott Roosevelt, Mrs. Franklin D. Roosevelt Jr. and Mrs. James Roosevelt.

New York City

NEW YORK, N. Y.—All over New York Ci[ty] people were stunned by the news fro[m] Warm Springs, for this was one of Frankl[in] Delano Roosevelt's greatest strongholds. T[he] news flowed into the subways and busses a[nd] flowed out again over the city.

The people heard it by word of mouth a[nd] radio, and they stood around in little groups [in] the streets waiting for some word that it was a[ll] a mistake and the President was still alive.

When it was learned there was no mistak[e] crepe-draped pictures of the President were p[ut] up in the windows of places as unalike [as] Saks-Fifth Avenue department store and Paddy[s] Clam House. Candy-store owners reached ov[er] and pulled out the plugs from their juke boxe[s.] In the Trans-Lux Newsreel Theater on Broadw[ay] the manager came out and made the announc[e]ment. In 10 minutes more than half the peop[le] in the theater had rushed out, many crying.

Nowhere was grief so open as in the poor[er] districts of the city. In Old St. Patrick's in t[he] heart of the Italian district on the lower East Sid[e] bowed, shabby figures came and went, and by th[e] day after the President died hundreds of candl[es] burned in front of the altar. "Never," a priest sai[d,] "have so many candles burned in this church."

In the poor Jewish district around Delance[y] Street every store was closed on Saturday, no[r]mally the biggest business day of the week. On[e] man started to open his ice-cream parlor [on] Saturday afternoon, but dozens of people gath[e]red in front of the shop, cursing angrily. Th[e] man hastily closed down again.

In the shelter of the Eighth Avenue subwa[y] entrance on Houston Street, a little old woman [in] a black shawl sat on the sidewalk on an empt[y] orange box. She kept swaying back and for[th] and sobbing and saying over and over aga[in,] "He was such a good man, he was such a goo[d] man, he was such a good man."

A cop passed by and he should have made h[er] move, but he made believe he didn't see her.

In all the store windows were *Yahrzeit* glasse[s,] the mourning candles that Jews light on the dea[th] of a member of the immediate family. T[he]

...wling Essex Market, which Mayor LaGuardia ...t to get the push carts off the streets, was ...ed. But inside, the market looked like a sec-... of firmament. There were *Yahrzeit* glasses ...ning on all the hundreds of little stalls.

... man started hawking 1944 Roosevelt cam-...gn buttons in the street, yelling "Get your ...sevelt memorial button — 15 cents." The ...ple drove him off the street. A 6-year-old kid ...t by saying to her mother: "I wished we lived ...Washington. In Washington the kids didn't ...e to go to school." The mother wound up and ...ded one on the kid's backside.

...ust before 4 o'clock when the funeral services ...e about to begin at the White House, Mrs. ...nie Kornberg brought a radio down from her ...e and set it up on the outdoor counter of her ...e store at the corner of Rivington and Essex ...ets. Her store is named Harry's Cut Rate ...dy Corner, Imported and Domestic. Harry is ...ewhere in Germany with the Third Army. ... Kornberg connected the radio, and in 10 ...utes a crowd of about 50 persons gathered ...ng the pickle barrels to listen to the services. ...here were little men in white aprons, old ... with derbies and white beards. There was ...rim woman who looked like a school teacher, ... another who might have been a social worker. ... well-dressed middle-aged man in a gray ...nburg looked strangely like the famous pic-... of the grief-torn Frenchman watching the ...mans roll into Paris in 1940. They all faced ...radio and listened without speaking.

...t 4 o'clock there was a moment of silence, ... on the radio a bell began to toll. It was ...ost a signal. Those who were not already ...ing cried now. The crowd wept with a long, ...longed hum. A woman clasped her 8-year-old ... and said, "Not in my lifetime or in yours, ... we again see such a man."

...bout the same time 35,000 people were gath-...d in City Hall Park to hear formal memorial ...vices conducted by Dr. Nicholas Murray ...ler, president of Columbia University. At 4:05 ... rain suddenly came down in torrents. The ...ple stood bareheaded in the rain and listened. ...ey stood there for nearly half an hour, getting ...nched to the skin. Fewer than 1,000 of the ...000 left to find shelter in the nearby buildings.

—Sgt. BILL DAVIDSON
YANK Staff Writer

The Hudson Valley

...EACON, N. Y.—In 1910 a young man made a ... campaign speech in Bank Square. He wore ...lue flannel coat, white duck pants and white ...es. The speech got a lot of applause, but the ...position felt that notice had to be taken of it. ...It wasn't a great speech," the opposition said. ...e womenfolk were gawking at his fancy ...thes and the men were taken in by that new-...gled auto contraption he brought down here." ...he young man got elected state senator from ...tchess County. He was the first Democrat in ... county who had received that honor in 51 ...rs. His name was Franklin D. Roosevelt.

...After 1910 the young man came back to the ...are seven times to speak to his friends and ...ighbors, Harold Brilliant, the local cop, re-...led. This quiet Sunday morning Harold sat ... the Bank Square curb. There were few people ... the streets, and the square itself was almost ...pty. A warm sun began to nudge over the ...untains and into the Hudson Valley as the ...mes of the Methodist Church on Main Street ...nounced the 6 A.M. memorial service for the ...t President of the United States. The funeral ...in from Washington to Hyde Park was due to ...ss through Beacon about 8.

...Harold took off his faded blue cap, scratched ... head and pointed to the other side of the ...uare. "He'd drive down from Hyde Park ...rough Wappingers Falls and come into the ...uare from North Avenue," Harold said. "Old ...rg Hoyt would be waiting for him. Morg in-...oduced him back in 1910. They always said the ...me things to each other. Mr. Roosevelt would ...y, 'Hello, Morg. You don't look a day older than ...u did back in 1910.' And Morg would answer, ...either do you, Franklin.' Then they both would ...ugh. It was something to see."

...The men of Beacon were full of their mem-

ONE OF MANY

A few days after the death of her husband, Eleanor Roosevelt wrote the following tribute to him in her United Features Syndicate column. When the New York World-Telegram published the column it changed its title from the usual "My Day" to "One of Many."

WHEN you have lived for a long time in close contact with the loss and grief which today pervade the world, any personal sorrow seems to be lost in the general sadness of humanity. For a long time all hearts have been heavy for every serviceman sacrificed in the war. There is only one way in which those of us who live can repay the dead who have given their utmost for the cause of liberty and justice. They died in the hope that, through their sacrifice, an enduring peace would be built and a more just world would emerge for humanity.

While my husband was in Albany and for some years after coming to Washington, his chief interest was in seeing that the average human being was given a fairer chance for "life, liberty and the pursuit of happiness." That was what made him always interested in the problems of minority groups and of any group which was at a disadvantage.

As the war clouds gathered and the inevitable involvement of this country became more evident, his objective was always to deal with the problems of the war, political and military, so that eventually an organization might be built to prevent future wars.

Any man in public life is bound, in the course of years, to create certain enemies. But when he is gone his main objectives stand out clearly, and one may hope that a spirit of unity may arouse the people and their leaders to a complete understanding of his objectives and a determination to achieve those objectives themselves.

Abraham Lincoln was taken from us before he had achieved unity within the nation, and his people failed him. This divided us as a nation for many years.

Woodrow Wilson was also stricken and, in that instance, the peoples of the world failed to carry out his vision.

PERHAPS, in His wisdom, the Almighty is trying to show us that a leader may chart the way, may point out the road to lasting peace, but that many leaders and many peoples must do the building. It cannot be the work of one man, nor can the responsibility be laid upon his shoulders, and so, when the time comes for peoples to assume the burden more fully, he is given rest.

God grant that we may have the wisdom and courage to build a peaceful world with justice and opportunity for all peoples the world over.

These Americans, crowding at the White House gates, were among millions who grieved for the dead President.

ories as they waited for the train. "In the old days," they kept saying, "in the old days. . . ."

Thomas Pendell, owner and publisher of the Beacon *Light*, the town weekly and one of the oldest Democratic papers in Dutchess County, said he had known Franklin D. Roosevelt all his life. In the old days, he said, his father, Robert Pendell, used to talk politics with the young Democrat from Hyde Park.

"We used to have a farm on the corner of Violet Avenue and Dorsey Lane, just about six miles from the Roosevelt farm," Thomas Pendell said. "Young Roosevelt would ride down on his horse, and he and my father would talk politics. Later, after he bought one of the first autos in Dutchess County, he would drive down on a Sunday and take my mother for a ride. They had a standing joke between them. They both would pretend they were courting. It was funny with nine of us kids running around the farm."

Jimmy Dondero, who runs the Dondero candy store on Spring Valley Road with his brother Eddie, remembers things too. His family has owned the store for 50 years, and the young bloods of Dutchess County used to meet there to argue politics. The boys would sit on orange crates, Jimmy said, and gab. The boys were Franklin Roosevelt, Ferd and Morg Hoyt, Jim Meyer, Ed Perkins and young Jimmy Forrestal, who is Secretary of the Navy now.

"Franklin Roosevelt was always asking questions," Jimmy Dondero said. "When the boys would get into an argument he would just listen to both sides, say nothing and then, when it was through, ask more questions. One day he came down here by himself and sat with my brother Ed and I. He began asking those questions and finally I says to him, 'Why are you always asking so many questions?'

"He laughed and said, 'Well, Jimmy, the only way a man can find out what the people want and think is to ask them.' I guess that's what he did down there in Washington. He found out what the people wanted and gave it to them."

Old Sam Middleton said he had never thought much of young Roosevelt's politics. Sam has been a bedrock Republican for the 70-some years of his life.

"I remember him when he was a kid," Old Sam said, "and he used to visit with the gang

that used to hang out in the town cops office at the jail house on Bank Square. I guess he was about 17 then. He would stay there, blowing steam off his belly, until the wee hours. Many's the night there was just old Ted Moith, the night watchman, and young Roosevelt left. I never liked his politics, but I'll say this for him: He was a great gentleman and a good Roosevelt."

Morgan Hoyt, who always introduced Franklin Roosevelt when he came to Beacon to speak, had the most of all to say. Morg is 82 now, and he and young Roosevelt were fast friends, he said, from the time Morg stumped the county for the Hyde Park Democrat back in 1910. They kept up a steady correspondence through the years.

Morg's last letter from his old friend came just after the President returned from Yalta. The letter, addressed "Dear Morg," read:

"Now that I have returned from my trip overseas, I can tell you that I have received a real thrill from your letter of January 25. Those were good days that you recall—that 1910 campaign, the Sheehan fight, and all the other things that went to make life interesting. As you well observe, those tranquil days are a far cry from the present but the comparison helps us to see things in their due proportion.

"I still say, thank God for the old days and for old and tried friends like you."

"There were a lot of things about that first campaign," Morgan Hoyt said, "that showed then the kind of fellow he would turn out to be. A fellow named Harry Yawkey had the first automobile in Dutchess County and we decided it would be a good idea to stump the county in the contraption.

"One day we were up in the Cove—that's up the valley—young Roosevelt, Ed Perkins and myself, and we ran over a farmer's dog. Ed and I decided to get the hell out of there as soon as possible. But young Roosevelt insisted we go up and tell the farmer about the dog. The Cove in those days had some of the orneriest Republicans in the county and we tried to talk him out of it. But he had his way.

"Ed and I expected to get chased off the farm with a shotgun, but when Franklin told him the news the old farmer smiled and said, 'I've had six dogs killed on this farm and you are the first culprit that owned up to it. Young man, I'm going to vote for you.'"

The sun had pushed over the mountains and its light flooded the whole valley. By 8 o'clock everybody in Beacon seemed to be at the railroad station. The crowd was quiet, except for a curly-haired baby who was crying. A low rumbling came from around the bend and the crowd stirred. The curly-haired baby stopped crying.

The train puffed around Beacon Bend. It came slowly through the station, each coach making a melancholy, wind-swishing sound as it passed. In no time at all the train was out of sight, going on to Hyde Park, 19 miles away. Harold Brilliant, the town cop, stayed in the station after the crowd had left. For a long time he said nothing. Then Harold took off his cap and scratched his head.

"He's gone," the town cop said.

—Pvt. JAMES P. O'NEILL
YANK Staff Writer

GIs Overseas

BEFORE the news came over the radio from San Francisco, the GIs in the Eighth Army casual camp in the Philippines were talking mostly about the new adjusted-service-rating cards that two men, fresh from the States, had brought along with their service records and Form 20s. Then an infantryman back from morning chow said that the President had died from a heart attack. Another guy was positive he had been killed in a plane accident on his way to Berlin to sign the peace treaty.

When they got the story straight and realized that it wasn't just another rumor, everybody in the camp was stunned and bewildered.

Pvt. Howard McWatters of Nevada City, Calif., just released from the hospital and waiting to go back to the Americal Division, shook his head slowly. "Roosevelt made a lot of mistakes," he said. "But I think he did the best he could, and when he made mistakes he usually admitted it. Nobody could compare with him as President."

Pfc. David Smith of Council Bluffs, Iowa, railroad man in civilian life and a tank gunn in the Army, said, "Now I suppose the Germa and Japs will think they'll get something weak than unconditional surrender. I suppose the identified Roosevelt with our country so long th they think Roosevelt is America."

There was more talk about the dead Preside and the new one. Somebody remarked that wh you were in a casual camp in the Philippines, y were pretty far away from things. Then grad ally the conversation swung back toward t adjusted-service-rating cards, and an argume started about demobilization points.

In Rome the Allied Command closed its plac of amusement and the Italian officials shut do the civilian movies, the schools, the banks a the opera. "I came out of my tent this mornin said Pfc. Fred Carlson of New York City, a the 1st Replacement Depot, "and I saw the fl at half mast. I asked who was dead. Then th told me. I hope it won't work out like when lost Wilson after the last war."

Pvt. A. J. Smith of Naperville, Ill., an MP Rome, was in the President's motorcycle esc when he visited Oran in 1943. "I stood very cl when he came down the gangplank from t *Iowa*," he said. "He looked tired and aged ther

A Navy lifeguard spread the news among t GIs and sailors on Waikiki Beach in Honolu Most of them walked into the exclusive Outrigg Canoe Club, which is ordinarily reserved members only, and sat silently by the radio their swim suits, listening to the reports of wh had happened in Warm Springs.

At Payne Field, the big ATC base near Cai Cpl. George Patcheck of Chicago was reading t story in the Middle East *Stars and Stripes* whi he waited for customers at the information de in the terminal building. Cpl. O. H. Seals of Mc ristown, N. J., was looking over his shoulder.

"It happens to everybody," Seals said. "The b ones, too."

"But he was an awful smart guy," Patcheck sai

"Sure," Seals said. "But he's not the only sma guy. We've got others. Lots of them."

Sgt. Bob Bouwsma was reading the final ite of the 5 o'clock newscast in the Armed Forc Radio Service station in Panama when Cpl. Re ben Diaz, the station's Spanish announcer, hand him the flash. GIs hearing it at supper in th mess halls didn't believe it at first. Then the st tion's phone started to ring. Sgt. Jim Weathe would pick it up and say, "Yes, it's true." "Ye it's true," he said to each call. "Yes, it's true."

In London, the British civilians lost their tr ditional restraint. They stopped American so diers on the street to tell them how sorry th were, how much the President had done f Britain and for the world. They talked about h trade of the over-age destroyers for their Wes ern Hemisphere bases, about lend-lease, abou the times they had cheered him in the newsree

Sgt. Nelson Endicott of Los Angeles, Calif., Eighth Air Force tail gunner, was walking t ward Piccadilly Circus with some of the men fro his crew. A Canadian soldier stopped them a said, "I see you guys lost your boss." "I thoug for a while it was Ike," said Sgt. Nelson.

Cpl. Helen M. Korsyne of Philadelphia, Pa., Wac attached to Eighth Air Force Headquarte heard it from the landlady at a boarding hou in London. The landlady said she wouldn't ha felt worse if it had been Churchill or the Kin

Cpl. Louis Schier of Chicago, Ill., an armor division artilleryman just back in England fro the German front, said it was like the loss of t major who had command of his task force. "I w just a hundred yards away when they killed hi with a machine pistol," Schier said. "We had tough time after that pulling ourselves togethe It's the same way with all of us now that FD is dead."

In Sydney, Australia, Sgt. Lloyd P. Stallin of San Antonio, Tex., said, "I came down he to have a good time, but now I don't feel cheerful."

Pvt. J. D. Cotter of the Australian Army sai "Wish I knew more about this new bloke."

Outside the Grand Hotel in Paris, Pfc. Leste Rebuck, a medic from the 104th Division, said "It was just like somebody socked me in th stomach when I wasn't looking. I just couldn get it through my head he was really dead. F my money, that guy was one of the greatest guy that ever lived. You can put him next to Lincol or Washington or anybody."

—YANK Staff Corresponder

THE SAD SACK

"DIFFERENCE OF OPINION"

SGT. GEORGE BAKER

Discharged Husbands

Dear YANK:

My husband was wounded in the battle for the Rhine and has been shipped back to the States for hospitalization. I am told that his wounds are such that he will be discharged after a few months of treatment. If that happens he will certainly need me at home to look after him. Can a Wac get a discharge under such circumstances?

Britain —T/Sgt. MILDRED C. McKEE

■ If your husband is discharged for physical reasons as the result of combat wounds you may be able to get a discharge to take care of him. To get such a discharge you will need a doctor's certificate stating that your presence at home is desirable for his health and morale.

Free Schooling

Dear YANK:

Just before I was inducted into the Army I received a four-year scholarship to one of our leading universities. They even promised me they would hold it for me until I get back. I would very much like to study medicine, which is an eight-year course.

Is it possible for me to use this scholarship for my first four years of pre-med and use the educational provisions of the GI Bill of Rights four years later to cover my medical education?

France —Cpl. C. M. HAAYEN

■ You may be able to take advantage of both your scholarship and the educational provisions of the GI Bill of Rights. You need not start taking advantage of the educational benefits of the law until two years after your dis-

What's Your Problem?

Letters to this department should bear writer's full name, serial number and military address.

charge or two years after the end of the war, whichever date is later. In this regard you should remember that the first World War did not officially end until July of 1921. Therefore you may have lots of time to take advantage of the law and there even is a possibility that you will be able to use up the entire four-year scholarship before applying for the GI Bill benefits.

Job Rights

Dear YANK:

My brother was in the office of a general agent of a large insurance company for over 15 years. He entered the Army in 1943 and has been overseas since April 1944. Because he had a large clientele, my mother (age 65) was authorized by the general agent to carry on in my brother's place. Since then a new general agent has taken over and made a lot of changes, firing old employees etc. He told my mother he would keep her on, not because her son was in service, but because she was doing a good job.

Does the law protect my brother in any way? Can my mother carry on his business or can this agent fire her at any time?

Holland —M/Sgt. FRED KAHN

■ The Selective Training and Service Act of 1940, which offers job protection to men in service, does not extend that protection to the person who replaces the soldier. While the insurance company can fire your mother whenever it wants to, that will in no way affect your brother's right to his old job. If he applies for the job within 90 days after he is discharged, he should get it back or a job of like status and seniority.

Surviving Sons

Dear YANK:

My mother tells me that she read in one of [the] papers where it is now possible for a son to [re]quest that he be shipped back to the States if [he] has lost a brother in the war. I tried to che[ck] this with my local command and have been t[old] that it sounds like another civilian rumor. [My] brother was killed in the Philippines. Can I [be] shipped back to the States under that ruling?

India —(Name Withh[eld])

■ You can not. The War Department statement was [that] the *sole* surviving son of a family that had lost *two* [or] more sons in the war could be returned to the Sta[tes.] However, where such a man is engaged in nonhazard[ous] duty overseas he may be kept at his overseas assignme[nt.]

Retirement Pay

Dear YANK:

Some of the men in this outfit insist that N[a]tional Guard time counts toward retirement p[ay.] They say that a guy could sign up in the Natio[nal] Guard, drill one night a week for 30 years a[nd] at the end of that time retire on a Federal p[en]sion. Some others say a guy could count his N[a]tional Guard time toward retirement so that [if] he drilled for 15 years he would only need [a few] more years in the Army to be able to retire [on] a pension. Is either of them right?

Philippines —S/Sgt. E. PAT[T]

■ Neither group is correct. Time served in the Natio[nal] Guard counts toward longevity pay but it does *not* co[unt] toward retirement pay.

Sgt. Elgie (Jump) Jordan

Pvt. Irving Popik

CAMP NEWS

Jump Jordan Dishes Out Jive on Platters

Grenier Field, N. H.—"The Jump Jordan Swing Club" is a jazz program that's jivin'.

When Elgie (Jump) Jordan, a Grenier Field sergeant with a head cocked in the direction of swing music, got the idea of combining his free time with a schoolboy hobby, a good hot jazz program was conceived for station WFEA in Manchester, N. H.

"The Jump Jordan Swing Club" program goes out from WFEA every other Saturday night between 1830 and 1845 and attracts terrific fan mail. It consists of jazz records from Jump's own collection of more than 5,000 dating back to his civilian days in Akron, Ohio. All swing artists of the jazz world are represented, and a War Bond plug is given during each program.

AROUND THE CAMPS

Camp Upton, N. Y.—Pfc. Alfred Palca, a medic in the ASF hospital here, had no shoes to display under his bunk for a Saturday inspection, so he borrowed a friend's pair. He got gigged at the inspection for unshined shoes.

Camp Shelby, Miss.—In its 27 months of operation, the bank on this post, operated by the First National Bank of Hattiesburg, Miss., has passed quite a few million dollars over the counter to GIs yet only two checks have been charged off as dead losses.

Camp Hood, Tex.—There's a grandfather among the trainees of Company B, 152d Infantry Replacement Training Battalion. Pvt. Custer Whisenhunt of Baton Rouge, La., though only 37, has two grandchildren. His son-in-law, the father of his grandchildren, is a staff sergeant in the AAF and a prisoner of war in Germany.

Camp Blanding, Fla.—"To think." moaned one of the two Blanding GIs weeping into their three-point-two over the faithlessness of women, "she took my allotment checks and spent 'em on another guy." "That's nothing," said the other, a pfc, dolefully. "Mine went out with a sergeant until I told her I was getting captain's bars, and now I'm going to have a heck of a time explaining this one stripe."

Laurinburg-Maxton AAB, N. C.—Pvt. Douglas Jones of Sundown, Tex., awaiting overseas or-

JINNIE JEEP. WAC Sgt. Adelaide Lockhart got the title last fall from admirers at Drew Field, Tampa, Fla., where she's stationed.

ders at the I Troop Carrier Command Base here, commented on the enlarged role of women in the world of today. His bride of a year, WAC Pfc. Virginia Jones, has been stationed in New Guinea with the Troop Carrier Command since last November and was in Australia before that. And Jones added: "I guess she's gonna be a 30-year man."
—Cpl. COLIN C. KEMPNER

Fort Worth AAF, Tex.—Home-town newspapers are No. 1 on the preference list of patients at the post hospital of this field, according to Pvt. Lucille Gordon of New York, librarian. More than 20 papers from well-selected geographical areas help satisfy convalescents with a craving for home-town news. Pvt. Gordon also reports that most returned combat men, many of whom have seen many corners of the world, prefer travel books.

Esler Field, La.—The men were all smiles at the end of a recent review of the units of the 1st Tactical Air Division. The reason was an order of the day announced by Brig. Gen. Ford L. Fair, commanding general of the division, which read in part: "In order to promote the comradeship . . . and good will which has always prevailed within this command, it is suggested that at the conclusion of this ceremony all individuals repair to their respective organizational areas where they will find sufficient ice-cold beer . . . to remove all traces of dust and dryness which possibly might have been contracted during the ceremony."
—Cpl. RANDOLPH J. WISE

Combat Engineer Makes Dresses for Wife

Camp Swift, Tex.—Ask Pvt. Irving Popik what he's going to do with his next three-day pass and he'll tell you the same thing he did last time, "Make a new dress for my wife." Stocky, ruddy-faced Popik looks the part of the combat engineer that he is, but give him a sewing machine, some materials and a little time and he can turn out feminine creations that are far from the world of the rugged engineers.

Popik startled the people of the Austin (Tex.) USO the first time he went in and asked to use a sewing machine. But soon their surprise turned to admiration for his work.

"There's really nothing so strange about making clothes for my wife," he says. "I've made them for her ever since I met her."

Popik came to the United States from Poland in 1939. He settled in New York City, and before he entered the Army he operated a design shop there that, he estimates, turned out an average of 500 fashions a year.

He takes the ribbing of his buddies at Camp Swift good-naturedly. "Sewing is fun," he maintains. "But that's where my talents end. I can't cook worth a darn."

Came the Dawn Too Soon

Dibble General Hospital, Menlo Park, Calif.—It was around midnight, and everything was quiet in the WAC barracks. Suddenly a light was turned on, a door opened and a bustle of activity began. The commanding officer was welcoming a new arrival. Then lights began to flash on all over the place. A drowsy private emerged from a room, toothbrush in hand and towel over arm. She started down the hall.

"Where do you think you're going?" the CO demanded.

"Why, to work, ma'am, of course," the private answered.

It didn't take much to convince her she still had seven hours of sleep before duty began.

BATTLE OF BRASS

Mitchel Field, N. Y.—A major in one of the aircraft-warning units on the coast was radioing directions to a fighter pilot who kept replying to his commands with "R-r-roger dodger!" After a few times the major said, "Roger will be sufficient." In spite of his warning the "R-r-roger dodger" continued. Finally the major bellowed: "This is Maj. Lane. I said, 'Roger would be sufficient.'" The voice from the plane replied: "R-r-roger dodger, you old codger. I'm a major too."
—S/Sgt. BERT BRILLER

"Why does an SS man like you surrender?" Bauer asked. The German stopped short. Then he stepped forward and spat out a series of short, ugly Teutonic word

GI Radio Station

IT'S A NEW WEAPON OF WAR

By Sgt. BILL DAVIDSON
YANK Staff Correspondent

LUXEMBOURG [Delayed]—The German medic lieutenant had been captured just a few minutes before, near Ubach in Germany, and he was still sullen and battle-jumpy. He was taken into a garage near the battalion CP. T-4 Fred Bauer of Hollywood, Calif., was waiting for him with a recording machine.

"What is your name, rank and serial number?" asked Bauer in perfect German.

The German told him.

"Why does an *SS* man like you surrender?" Bauer asked quietly.

The German stopped short. Then he stepped forward and spat out a series of short, ugly Teutonic words.

Bauer, a patient young man who had been cut off ahead of the Infantry at Aachen and who had spoken to Nazi Col. "Madman" von Aulock for 12 days through a loudspeaker at St. Malo, let the German medical officer rage on. Then he said softly, "Do you know, *Herr Leutnant*, German doctors like you are even bigger war criminals than the Gestapo in Poland? The Gestapo killed foreigners. You declare the lame, the halt and the blind fit for military service. And in that way you kill your own people."

At the mention of the words "war criminal," the Nazi lieutenant stared. Then he began to break down. "It wasn't I," he said. "I tell you it wasn't I. I knew those men weren't fit to be soldiers. But the Party told me to do it. My God, what can a man do in Germany these days if the Party gives him orders?" He went on like that for about 10 minutes, cursing the Nazi Party for Germany's ills.

When the German was finished, Bauer thanked him for his co-operation and flicked a switch turning off the recording machine that had been on throughout the interview. That night the recording of the Nazi medical officer's outburst against the Nazi Party was broadcast over Radio Luxembourg to every corner of the Greater Reich.

Radio Luxembourg is one of the chief links of the Army's Pychological Warfare Division. Before the war, it was the second most powerful commercial radio station in the world. It blanketed Europe with a broadcast strength of 120,000 watts. Just by way of comparison, the biggest stations in the United States, like WJZ, New York; WGN, Chicago, and KFI, Los Angeles, are all 50,000-watters.

In the German counteroffensive of December, the station transmitter was one of the objectives of the Von Rundstedt push down through northern Luxembourg. On the first Sunday a German tank column got to within four miles of the station. On Monday, strong infantry, ack-ack and antitank detachments around the station were reinforced, and the enemy was driven beyond his starting point. On Tuesday the transmitter went off the air for technical reasons. It came back on Saturday, but in the meantime the Germans did some broadcasting on practically the same wave length from a station in Germany. This led the BBC to announce that Radio Luxembourg had been captured. This was never true. The psychological impact of the recapture of the station was so important to the Germans that they went to all lengths to fake it.

TODAY the station still sends out its signal at 120,000 watts. It is picked up by the small People's radio receiver, distributed by the Nazi Party, which reposes in every good German home, and it can't be jammed because it is practically inside Germany itself. So the U. S. Army is running the station now, allowing a small detachment of Psychological Warfare officers and GIs (many of them born in Germany) to continue to provide inspiring entertainment for the German soldiers and *Hausfrauen* who have been listening to the station for years.

They provided good entertainment for the people of Aachen during the siege of that city. There was excellent music and news. And every half hour announcers Norbert Gruenfeld and T/Sgt. Klaus Brill would get on the air and say, "You now have 12 hours and 30 minutes before your city is blown to pieces," "you now have exactly 11 hours before your city is blown to pieces," and so on. This was after the ultimatum to surrender had been read over the station. It was, of course, impossible for the civilians to surrender, but the constant verbal hammering made a symbol of Aachen.

On another occasion two German soldiers were picked up by a pair of alert GIs near Nancy. The Germans wore civilian clothes. They had been sent into our lines to spy. Radio Luxembourg sent an announcer, K. V. Hagen, and a GI crew down to cover the trial and execution. It was a beautiful play-by-play description. Hagen portrayed the grim prison courtyard. Then he interviewed the two men. Both gave a last message to their families. They said they had had a fair trial with an interpreter and that they had had an American full colonel defending them. They proclaimed that they didn't know the penalty for what they had done was death and that their officers had neglected to tell them. They warned their fellow soldiers against doing likewise. Then Hagen described the men being tied to stakes. There was the click of rifle bolts, the hoarse yell of the American lieutenant giving commands in English, the volley and the echo of rifle fire. It was pretty grim.

All this is tactical. It is a front-line weapon which causes Germans to surrender and saves American lives.

But there is genuine entertainment too. Most of it is listening bait. There is good American music for music-hungry Europe. And there is even a comic character named Tom Jones, who is becoming sort of a Central European Bob Hope. T-5 Tom Jones is supposed to be a typical American GI from Wisconsin. He speaks German with an atrocious American accent (principally because the man who plays the part learned his German at Concordia Institute, near Larchmont, N. Y.). Every night at 2015 he rattles on about his home life in the U. S. and his girl sending him a lemon cake, and about what he found in a captured German mail sack. Every once in a while he drops in a biting gag, such as: "Do you know there are only two ways to get a furlough in the *Volkssturm* [the German Home Guard]? For your baptism and for your golden-wedding anniversary."

The Germans eat this stuff up. The mythical Tom Jones receives dozens of fan letters a week from liberated German-speaking areas. Since there are no mails, all of these letters are delivered by hand. When Strasbourg was taken T-5 Carl Princie of Boston, Mass., was stopped on the streets and asked if he were Tom Jones. Civilians in Luxembourg, Eupen and Aachen go around whistling "As the Caissons Go Rolling Along," Tom's theme song, and the Luxembourg newspaper, the *Luxemburger Wurt,* has been deluged with requests to print the words to the Artillery tune. A German school official in Eupen wrote a literary masterpiece to the station, explaining why he no longer felt himself obliged to subscribe to his oath to Hitler. The letter was addressed to Tom Jones.

DURING the four years of German occupation, Radio Luxembourg was used as part of the Nazis' big propaganda network. It fell into our hands, almost intact, in a strange way. When the American avalanche tore across France and Belgium after the big summer break-through, the Germans began to evacuate the city of Luxembourg. Before they left they called in a Luxembourg engineer whom they had forced to work for them. "How can we destroy the station?" they asked. "Shoot holes in the transmitter tubes," said the Luxembourger, "and the station will be off the air for six months." This the Germans did,

plus extensive demolitions in the studios and master control.

On September 10 the advance echelons of an American task force rolled into town. With the first tanks was a U. S. civilian technical advisor Morrie Pierce, chief radio engineer of the Psychological Warfare Division. He immediately contacted Metty Felton, a Luxembourger, formerly chief engineer of the station, who had been hiding out with the Luxembourg underground. Together they set out for the transmitter, a few miles out of town.

For days the Germans controlled the high ground commanding the station, and once they counterattacked right back to the edge of Luxembourg. But they never fired a round at the transmitter. Up to the last minute they expected to take it back.

In the meantime the Luxembourg engineer who had told the Germans to shoot holes in the tubes came up with a whole new set of tubes he had buried in his garden four years before. John Peyser, formerly of NBC, arrived to take over technical control of the station. Luxembourg's top construction engineers, men like Edmond Ferring, showed up too. They repaired the transmitter and began to rebuild three of the bomb-blasted studios. The GIs arrived, and while everyone worked, Pfc. John Audia of Chicago, Ill., the driver, shuttled back and forth to the town bringing rations and supplies. Finally, at 1845 the evening of September 22, exactly 12 days after the entry into Luxembourg, Peyser got up before a microphone in a tiny, tan-painted, stripped-down studio.

"This is Radio Luxembourg," he said. "This is Radio Luxembourg. . . . Radio Luxembourg returns to the air a free station, with programs of the United Nations." Peyser repeated the announcement in German and French.

Today the men of the Psychological Warfare detachment are spread far and wide to keep the station operating as a tactical weapon. T/Sgt. Stefan Heym went into the Karl-Alexander coal mine near Ubach to interview the German miners now working for us there. He almost got killed by shellfire, but he got a good show that was put to excellent use in the "Don't Sabotage" campaign. The idea of this campaign was to convey this message to the Germans: "Destroy your mines and your factories, and you go without jobs. Destroy your power plants, and you go without light, not us. We carry our own."

There are small recording teams out all the time, with each of the armies. Their big recording trucks often go into jeep-only territory to interview prisoners of war before the shock of capture wears off. A classic broadcast was made on a hill outside of Aachen when a young German theology student, watching shells destroy his home with his parents in it, launched

a terrible tirade against the German Army, political leaders and industrialists. Another time Sgt. Bauer caught three old German ladies just as they were being released from a newly liberated concentration camp. They were singing a pathetic, hate-filled song they had composed about their captivity. In addition to these special hauls the detachments make hundreds of prisoners-of-war recordings which say simply: "Hello, Ma! I'm safe. I'm a prisoner of the Americans." These are used in other programs as bait to attract listeners.

These first-hand interviews with German prisoners are not recorded by trickery. No recordings are made for broadcast purposes without the prisoner's full knowledge and consent. A prisoner's name is never used without his permission and, even then, is not used if it might cause reprisals on his family and friends still under Nazi domination.

BESIDES producing the radio shows, the PWD men in Luxembourg turn out leaflets and three newspapers in German. They understand the German mentality perfectly. They are well-known American newspapermen, like civilian Richard Hanser, or anti-Nazi German and Austrian newspapermen long since thrown out of the Reich and now American citizens, like T-3 Jules Bond, T-5 Otto Brand and T/Sgt. Hans Burger, who got the Bronze Star for bringing in 18 prisoners in Normandy.

T/Sgt. Stefan Heym cut quite a figure in the journalistic and literary world before he enlisted in 1943. As editor of the violently anti-Nazi New York German-language newspaper, *Deutsches Volksecho,* he helped crack the German-American Bund wide open, and his sensational articles helped to convict Fritz Kuhn and several other members of the Bund as embezzlers or Nazi spies. Then he wrote the best-seller, "Hostages," which later become a movie in which Paul Lukas and Luise Rainer appeared. After that he went into the Signal Corps and was transferred to Psychological Warfare.

Capt. Hans Habe, head of the editorial department, is the author of "Kathrine" and "A Thousand Shall Fall," which became "The Cross of Lorraine" on the screen. At the age of 18 he became an editor of Vienna's largest newspaper, *Der Morgen,* and it was he who dug up the photostatic evidence and first broke the story that Hitler's real name is Schickelgruber.

In 1939 Habe enlisted in the French Army as a private. He became a squad sergeant in charge of an infantry scouting detail and was awarded the *Croix de Guerre* for bravery during the battle of France. He was captured by the Germans, posed as a Frenchman, escaped and got into the U. S. on a special visa issued by President Roosevelt to 180 famous European anti-Nazis.

In 1943 Habe enlisted in the U. S. Army. He became a tech sergeant in the new Psychological Warfare Division and went to North Africa for the Battle of Tunisia. There he wrote leaflets in the battalion CPs and was awarded a battlefield commission. He made the initial landings in Sicily with the 45th Division and sweated out the Salerno landings with the 531st Combat Engineers. He came in at H-plus-40-minutes. By 0900 he had interrogated his first German prisoners. By 2100 his first leaflets had been printed, way back in Tunis, and had been dropped on the German troops facing him. At Salerno he lived 48 days in the same foxhole. When this present Psychological Warfare detachment was formed for the invasion of Normandy, Habe was a natural to head it up.

I sat in on one of the daily morning conferences of the editorial staff of the station, in which the material at hand is discussed. Capt. Habe handed out the assignments. Then he said: "Just two more items of interest, gentlemen. On the Third Army front the Germans have been dropping leaflets on their own troops describing Psychological Warfare as the Allied secret weapon and threatening anyone caught listening to our broadcasts with long prison terms. On the First Army front we have captured an order signed by a German divisional commander. The order offers two months furlough at home to any German patrol that can filter through the American lines and blow up the transmitter of Radio Luxembourg."

There was a moment of silence after this. Then someone chuckled. Then Heym said: "Why the silly, stupid, thick-skulled bastards!"

The funny thing was that he said it in German.

From Luxembourg, GIs of the Army's Psychological Warfare Branch broadcast programs that help crack Nazi home-front morale.

Capt. Hans Habe conducts a conference at Radio Luxembourg. Left to right: Capt. Habe, T/3 Peter H. Weidnreich, T/3 Jules J. Bond, Morris Bishop, Richard Hanser, T/Sgt. Stephen Brown-Joussard, T/Sgt. Stefan Heym.

YANK
THE ARMY WEEKLY

YANK is published weekly by the enlisted men of the U. S. Army and is for sale only to those in the armed services. Stories, features, pictures and other material from YANK may be reproduced if they are not restricted by law or military regulations, provided proper credit is given, release dates are observed and specific prior permission has been granted for each item to be reproduced. Entire contents copyrighted, 1945, by Col. Franklin S. Forsberg and reviewed by U. S. military censors.

MAIN EDITORIAL OFFICE
205 EAST 42d STREET, NEW YORK 17, N. Y.

EDITORIAL STAFF

Managing Editor, Sgt. Joe McCarthy, FA; Art Director, Sgt. Arthur Weithas, DEML; Assistant Managing Editor, Sgt. Justus Schlotzhauer, Inf.; Assistant Art Director, Sgt. Ralph Stein, Med.; Pictures, Sgt. Leo Hofeller, Armd.; Features, Sgt. Marion Hargrove, FA; Sports, Cpl. Tom Shehan, FA; Overseas Editor, Sgt. Al Hine, Engr.; U. S. Editor, Sgt. Hilary H. Lyons, CA; Associate Editors, Sgt. John Hay, Inf.; Cpl. Margaret Davis, WAC; Sgt. Ralph Boyce, AAF; Cpl. Max Novack, TC.

WASHINGTON, Sgt. Barrett McGurn, Med.

FRANCE, Sgt. Merle Miller, AAF; Sgt. Charles Brand, AAF; Sgt. Mack Morriss, Inf.; Sgt. Ed Cunningham, Inf.; Sgt. Howard Brodie, Sig. Corps; Sgt. Saul Levitt, AAF; Sgt. Allan Ecker, AAF; Sgt. Reg Kenny, Armd.; Sgt. Robert McBrinn, Sig. Corps; Sgt. Ralph G. Martin, Med.; Pfc. Pat Coffey, AAF; Cpl. Howard Katzander, CA; Pfc. David Whitcomb, AAF; Pvt. David Berger, Engr.

BRITAIN, Sgt. Durbin L. Horner, CA; Sgt. Sanderson Vanderbilt, CA; Sgt. John Scott, Engr.; Sgt. Earl Anderson, AAF; Sgt. Frank Brandt, Med.; Sgt. Francis Burke, AAF; Cpl. Jack Coggins, CA; Cpl. Edmund Antrobus, Inf.; Pfc. Tom Flannery, AAF; Sgt. Rudolph Sanford, AAF.

AUSTRALIA-PHILIPPINES, Sgt. Lafayette Locke, AAF; Sgt. Charles Rathe, DEML; Sgt. Douglas Borgstedt, DEML; Sgt. Dick Hanley, AAF; Sgt. Ozzie St. George, Inf.; Cpl. Roger Wrenn, Sig. Corps; Sgt. Charles D. Pearson, Engr.; Cpl. John McLeod, Med.; Sgt. Marvin Fasig, Engr.; Cpl. Joe Stefanelli, Engr.; Sgt. Robert McMillan, FA; Pfc. Dale Kramer, MP; Cpl. Frank J. Beck, DEML; Sgt. Roger W. Cowan, DEML; Sgt. Jack F. Crowe, DEML; Sgt. Lionel Wathall, DEML.

CENTRAL PACIFIC, Sgt. Larry McManus, CA; Pfc. George Burns, Sig. Corps; Pfc. John O. Armstrong, Inf.; Sgt. Bill Reed, Inf.; Cpl. James Goble, Armd.; Sgt. Bill Young, Inf.; Cpl. Ted Burrows, DEML; Evans Wylie SP1c (PR), USCGR; Don Morgan Y1c, USCGR; Vernon H. Roberts S1c, USNR; Mason E. Pawlak CPhoM, USNR; Cpl. Lon Wilson, Sig. Corps.

MARIANAS, Cpl. Tom O'Brien, DEML; Sgt. Dil Ferris, AAF; Sgt. Jack Ruge, DEML; Sgt. Paul Showers, AAF; Pfc. Justin Gray, Rangers.

ITALY, Sgt. Harry Sions, AAF; Sgt. August Loeb, AAF; Sgt. Dan Polier, AAF; Cpl. George Barrett, AAF; Pfc. Ira Freeman, Cav.; Pfc. Carl Schwind, AAF; Pvt. Dave Shaw, Inf.

INDIA-BURMA and CHINA, Sgt. Paul Johnston, AAF; Sgt. George J. Corbellini, Sig. Corps; Sgt. Dave Richardson, CA; Sgt. Walter Peters, QM; Cpl. Jud Cook, DEML.

ALASKA, Sgt. Ray Duncan, AAF.

IRAN-IRAQ, Sgt. Burtt Evans, Inf.; Cpl. Alfred Kynch, DEML; Pvt. Ray McGovern, Inf.

PANAMA, Cpl. Richard Douglass, Med.

PUERTO RICO, Sgt. Don Cooke, FA.

MIDDLE EAST, Sgt. Richard Paul, DEML.

BERMUDA, Cpl. William Pene du Bois, Inf.

ICELAND, Sgt. John Moran, Inf.

NEWFOUNDLAND, Sgt. Frank Bode, Sig. Corps.

NAVY, Donald Nugent S1c.

■

Commanding Officer, Col. Franklin S. Forsberg.

Executive Officer, Maj. Jack W. Weeks.

Business Manager, Maj. North Bigbee.

Procurement Officer, Maj. Gerald J. Rock.

OVERSEAS BUREAU OFFICERS, France, Lt. Col. Charles L. Holt; Britain, Capt. Harry R. Roberts; Australia-Philippines, Lt. Col. Harold B. Hawley; Central-South Pacific, Maj. Josua Eppinger; Marianas, Maj. Justus J. Craemer; Italy, Maj. Robert Strother; Burma-India, Capt. Harold A. Burroughs; Alaska, Lt. Grady E. Clay Jr.; Iran, Capt. Frank Gladstone; Panama, Capt. Howard Carswell; Middle East, Capt. Knowlton Ames.

This Week's Cover

THE body of our late President and Commander in Chief is borne along Washington's Constitution Avenue toward the White House. His flag-draped coffin is carried on a caisson drawn by six white horses. The picture is by YANK photographer Sgt. John Frano.

PHOTO CREDITS. Cover—Sgt. John Frano. 2—PA. 3—Upper left, INP; right second from bottom, Acme; others, PA. 4 & 5—Acme & INP. 6—Pvt. George Aarons. 7, 10 & 11—Sgt. Frano. 12—Sgt. Art Weithas. 13—Army News Service. 15—Upper left, PRO, Grenier Field, N. H.; upper right, PRO, War Department; center, PRO, Drew Field, Fla. 17—167th Signal Photo Company. 19—Acme. 20 & 21—Sgt. Dil Ferris. 22—Warner Bros. 23—Sgt. Frano.

Mail Call

"Silly Servicemen"

Dear YANK:

I'm wondering if Pvt. Joseph Miller, whose letter on "Silly Servicemen" appeared recently in *Mail Call*, will ever be jolted from beneath his wet-blanket attitude. He implies that the two servicemen who participated in the program "Ladies Be Seated" by sucking milk from nippled bottles acted disrespectfully toward their respective branches of the service. Unless Joe is an old Army man, he realizes that he and most of us are merely civilians in uniform, anyway, and if a man sees fit to do these things as a civilian, why not as a GI? He's still the same man. After all, if sucking milk through a nipple provides a source of enjoyment for people and calls for a 50-buck bonus in addition, then I say let's have more. What's the harm in it? I don't recall an AR which states that a long-faced mask must be worn with GI tans. . . .

Sedalia AAF, Mo. —Sgt. GEORG D. MILLER

Dear YANK:

. . . A great many radio programs give a serviceman preference over the civilians, not because they are trying to make a monkey out of them, but because they know that no enlisted personnel are getting overpaid. I think that we in the service should feel grateful to the radio shows who give us the opportunity to make a little extra cash. . . .

Blackland AAF, Tex. —Sgt. L. A. CHASE

Dear YANK:

. . . As for his reference to the "old bags" who sit in the audience and watch, well, I think my mother and a lot of other soldiers' mothers are entitled to forget their troubles also in this war-weary world. If watching a couple of soldiers supposedly make fools out of themselves will make them forget, then I'll gladly make a fool out of myself to help them. . . .

Besides, for 50 bucks I'd stand on my head and wiggle my bare toes in the air.

Chanute Field, Ill. —Pvt. L. CHAVAK

Dear YANK:

. . . If he does not care to listen to them, it only takes a simple twist of the wrist to turn the dial, and we are sure that no one twisted his arm to get him in the studio and then locked the doors. We had much rather have our sweethearts or, in our case, our wives participating in a program of that kind than we would have them in some roadside hotspot, jitterbugging or even waltzing with one of his kind. . . .

Fort Benning, Ga. —Pvt. EVERETTI S. ORRELL*

*Also signed by T-5 Donald W. June.

Dear YANK:

. . . We think it would be a good idea if Pvt. Miller would take off his tails, put aside his opera glasses, come down to earth, get in the fun and enjoy life like a regular American.

—JOHN TURCOVSKY SM3c*

ATB, Little Creek, Va.

*Also signed by Donald Balvin SM2c.

Yes Sir, Lieutenant

Dear YANK:

For some time now I've been reading gripes from the enlisted men concerning discrimination against enlisted men in favor of officers. Complaints have ranged from "the colonel has an entire roll of toilet paper while I only have nine sheets" to "I'm a college-educated man and that officer who was probably a gas station attendant in civilian life put me on guard duty for failing to salute." Frankly, gentlemen, it's getting very monotonous. Legitimate gripes I favor, as that's the purpose of your column, but I think these trivial gripes are too much.

Four years ago I was farsighted enough to see World War II in the offing and enlisted. (No, I don't have a draft number, and yes, I did have something better to do—a college-sponsored education.) I peeled my share of potatoes for $21 a month but always with an eye to the future. Admittedly rank has its privileges and I determined to share same. If enlisted men resent these privileges, let me remind them that the recruiting offices have been open eight hours a day for the past 50 years at least. Or perhaps the brilliant Phi Beta resents being commanded by a high-school educated lieutenant. I've seen some brilliant bookworms that couldn't have sparked a football team worth a damn. This is a war, not a board of directors having tea. The Army wants fighters, not college professors, theorists and dreamers.

When the Army was clamoring for officer candidates, aviation cadets, glider pilots, etc., everyone had their chance. I took mine and worked hard for my wings and bars. I emphatically do not appreciate derogatory remarks about myself and fellow officers.

France —2d Lt. JOHN L. LOWDEN

Tax Suggestions

Dear YANK:

While reading the latest poop on our staggering national debt and the tax measures that will be necessary to pay it off, it struck me that the guys who fight this war shouldn't have to pay for it too. So how about a lifetime income-tax exemption for combat veterans, something like $1,000 per annum for Infantry and $500 for FA, Medics, Engineers and the rest.

I have seen the unimaginable suffering of the dogface and feel that the nation should make some effort to discharge the invaluable debt it owes him. The magazines at home now admit that the Infantry works hard and Uncle Sam kicks in that dandy $10 bonus, but ask a tanker or a TD man or anyone who operates up front whether he's willing to shoulder a part of the doughface's income tax. You're damn right he is, and so should be the rear-echelon men and the fellows who are dragging down the heavy lettuce back in America. . . .

Belgium —Pfc ROBERT B. ROWON

Dear YANK:

. . . I would give every ex-serviceman who was honorably discharged from service a temporary tax-free period. The extent of the tax-free period would be measured in months. For every month of service with the armed forces, the veteran would be granted one tax-free month. . . .

Italy —Pfc. MURRAY BROWNDORFF

GI Bill of Rights

Dear YANK:

In reply to Pfc. Russel I. Warren's letter, [doubting whether a large percentage of men will ever get "a nickel's worth of benefits" from the GI Bill of Rights] I might say that I am just one of some 80-odd veterans attending this college. The dean told me that it is an increase of more than 50 percent over last term.

I am truly grateful for the benefits I have derived from the GI Bill. . . .

—JERRY THOMAS

Oregon State College, Oreg.

K-Ration Candles

Dear YANK:

. . . Why don't they put about two candles in every K-ration, so that at night, when we are fortunate enough to be in billets or places where we can use a light, we will have one? As you know, the artillery plays havoc with all the power lines and we never have any light except a bottle of gasoline, which is very hard on the lungs. We would appreciate it very much if you would use your influence in getting candles put in the K-type of rations.

Luxembourg —Sgt. DON R. BELCHER

■ According to a recent *Mail Call* letter from Pvt. Johnny Marshall in the Philippines, you can make your own candles with a length of string and the wax scraped off three or four K-ration boxes.

First-Hand Info

Dear YANK:

My outfit is one of the new ones in this area, operating off newly established Superfortress bases in the Marianas, but I'll bet we're way ahead of many other outfits when it comes to close cooperation between air-combat crews and ground personnel.

After our last strike at Japan, our CO called a meeting and told us that after each strike the entire group would receive the briefing given the pilots, the weather encountered, navigational problems, type of bomb raid, fighter and flak opposition, photography results and a detailed account from the men who flew that mission. Well, we've had our first one. The fires in Tokyo are still burning at last reports, and we've been officially congratulated by our commanding general for our participation in the raid.

The idea for making each raid by our group a personal affair for each man was the CO's and one that I hope to hear being duplicated by the other groups in the area.

No more waiting for Tokyo Rose's sugared reports. We've first-hand info now, and coming from the lips of men who thank you for keeping those engines running so smoothly, for keeping those guns working and for bringing them back, it has certainly put more pride and energy on our parts into the performance of our jobs.

Marianas —Cpl. M. B. MUNJACK

Why We Fight

Dear YANK:

I get a kick out of the letters telling why we fight. Actually we're fighting for just one thing: to preserve America as a free sovereign nation. The place these social reformers will have to fight for their reforms is in the States at the voting booths. I would like to remind them that ideals are the cheapest things in the world so long as one doesn't have to fight for them. When it becomes necessary to fight for them then they can be the costliest.

I hope and trust that these ideals for which these people wish to fight mean enough to them that they will be willing to pay any price rather than give them up. I hope they are not like politicians, just jumping on the band wagon because idealism is popular right now. It probably won't be a few years from now, and that's when the real fight will begin.

Italy —Capt. EARL E. ALLEN

Dear YANK:

. . . "Why we fight" may be stated in this way: that we are fighting for the total defeat of our enemies in order that we may return to civilian life as soon as possible. Only as civilians can we begin the fight upon the domestic issues that confront us. Certainly every veteran should acquaint himself fully with these issues, as well as problems in relation to foreign nations, for it will be his responsibility in the post-war world to work out their solutions and insure our having a better America and a better world.

I should like to see a discussion concerning this in your columns. For instance, most veterans will have learned to dislike the policies of labor unions and would be in favor of their elimination, but we must realize there is some protection necessary for the common laborer against unscrupulous employers. Could this need be supplied by a national wage-hour law, increased in size and scope, and national laws insuring decent working conditions and safety precautions?

India —Pvt. WILLIAM K. SIMMS

Don't Starve the Japs

Dear YANK:

. . . Pvt. Elson B. Bruce's letter in *Mail Call* suggesting that we spray the rice-fields of Japan with motor oil in order to destroy their foodstuffs makes me know that Pvt. Bruce has yet to learn the true meaning of the Golden Rule: "Do unto others as you would have others do unto you."

I say punish the Japs, punish them severely, make it impossible for them to commit the act of aggression against our nation or any nation again as long as the world stands and a Jap lives. But let them eat!

The Germans have caused starvation on a large and broad scale in the countries that they have occupied, and much discussion has been allotted to the subject of providing food for those unfortunate countries. Do you agree that this act of brutality on the part of the Germans is the method by which the U. S. should deal with Japan? Shall this, our democratic country, fall victim to such low acts? Would Pvt. Elson V. Bruce want the act of starvation committed against him?

In case anybody is wondering, I am not a Jap sympathizer.

Charleston, S. C. —Pfc. ALLEYNE HENDERSON

More Work

SEND FINANCIAL STATEMENT OF BALTIMORE AND OHIO RR 1940 PENNSYLVANIA RR WIRE COLLECT.

Dalhart, Tex. —Pvt. JOHN B. MILLER

Franklin Delano Roosevelt, 1882–1945

MOST of us in the Army have a hard time remembering any President but Franklin D. Roosevelt. We never saw the inside of a speakeasy because he had prohibition repealed before we were old enough to drink. When we were kids during the depression, and the factories and stores were not taking anybody, plenty of us joined his CCCs, and the hard work in the woods felt good after those months of sleeping late and hanging around the house and the corner drug store, too broke to go anywhere and do anything. Or we got our first jobs on his ERA or WPA projects. That seems like a long time ago.

And since then, under President Roosevelt's leadership, we have struggled through 12 years of troubled peace and war, 12 of the toughest and most important years in our country's history. It got so that all over the world his name meant everything that America stood for. It meant hope in London and Moscow and in occupied Paris and Athens. It was sneered at in Berlin and Tokyo. To us wherever we were, in the combat zones or in forgotten supply and guard posts, it meant the whole works— our kind of life and freedom and the necessity for protecting it. We made cracks about Roosevelt and told Roosevelt jokes and sometimes we bitterly criticized his way of doing things. But he was still Roosevelt, the man we had grown up under and the man whom we had entrusted with the staggering respon-

sibility of running our war. He was the Commander in Chief, not only of the armed forces, but of our generation.

That is why it is hard to realize he is dead, even in these days when death is a common and expected thing. We had grown accustomed to his leadership and we leaned on it heavily, as we would lean on the leadership of a good company commander who had taken us safely through several battles, getting us where we were supposed to go without doing anything foolish or cowardly. And the loss of Roosevelt hit us the same way as the loss of a good company commander. It left us a little panic-stricken, a little afraid of the future.

But the panic and fear didn't last long. We soon found out that the safety of our democracy, like the safety of a rifle company, doesn't depend on the life of any one man. A platoon leader with the same training and the same sense of timing and responsibility takes over, and the men find themselves and the company as a whole operating with the same confidence and efficiency. That's the way it will be with our Government. The new President has pledged himself to carry out its plans for the successful ending of the war and the building of the peace. The program for security and peace will continue.

Franklin D. Roosevelt's death brings grief but should not bring despair. He leaves us great hope.

JAP HUNT on SAIPAN

By Pfc. JUSTIN GRAY
YANK Staff Correspondent

SAIPAN, THE MARIANAS—Official records list this B-29 base in the Western Pacific as having been "freed from organized enemy resistance" on July 9, 1944, after bitter fighting. Since then over 12,000 Jap troops have been killed on the island and 1,100 more have surrendered.

An island is declared "secured" as soon as it can be used as an operational base against the enemy, but to many infantrymen here the word has another meaning. While B-29s have been taking off on their spectacular missions against the Jap mainland, infantrymen have been slowly securing this "secured" island, regularly sending out patrols against enemy troops scattered about in Saipan's wild, hilly terrain. Twisting gullies and steep slopes are covered with tangles of vines, dense fields of tall sugar cane, thickets of banana palms and groves of taller trees.

The main part of the mopping-up has fallen in recent months to the men of the 24th Infantry Regiment—veterans of Guadalcanal, New Georgia and Bougainville with more than 35 months' overseas duty. Although some of the Jap-occupied territory lies not more than a mile from our own installations, the fighting is similar in almost every respect to combat in forward areas.

One night recently OPs on the top of Mount Topotchau, the highest point on the island, located a number of Jap campfires in the hills. Next day three patrols were sent out to investigate these bivouacs, burn the shelters and destroy the food supplies. Leading one 11-man patrol were Lt. Robert E. Sprouce of Wheeling, W. Va., and S/Sgt. Turner L. Ross of Montgomery, Ala.

This squad moved out from Mount Topotchau about 0830, taking along a weapons carrier loaded with 25 gallons of gasoline for burning enemy shelters, plenty of TNT and some wrecking bars. Most of the men carried rifles. Pfcs. Erskine Barnes of West Blocton, Ala., and Samuel Handsel of Fort Worth, Tex., were armed with BARs.

Looking down from the mountain on the enemy-held territory, they could see no sign of Japs on the wild, wooded ridges below. Beyond in the distance, where the flat farmland of the Chamorros stretched along the shore on the far side of the island, they could see the new warehouses the Engineers were building and trucks and jeeps moving along the roadways. Still farther off, across a narrow stretch of ocean,

the low island of Tinian was barely visible in the morning haze.

Moving about in Jap territory in the daytime is a risky operation, with the enemy holding every advantage. There was a real danger of ambush this morning on the narrow trail down which the patrol drove, but a thorough search of the underbrush was possible only in daylight.

THE men rode in the truck until they reached the first Jap bivouac area. It was surprisingly close to our outposts. There was a cluster of wooden buildings which the Japs apparently had been using as a point from which to observe our movements. The buildings had been practically destroyed, probably during the fighting when the island was first "secured," but their frames of hand-hewn timbers had withstood even our flame throwers.

Although it was doubtful that the Japs would remain close to our positions in daylight hours, security had to be maintained every minute on the patrol. Lt. Sprouce sent Ross and a few other men out to search the undergrowth.

At the side of one of the skeleton buildings the Japs had recently built a crude lean-to with a thatch roof, capable of keeping them dry in the worst weather and providing cover for their little fires. Just in front of the lean-to the men found a large cistern. Sgt. Charles Blackwell of Anniston, Ala., the demolition man in the squad, was left with a guard to blow up the cistern. The rest of the patrol moved into the building.

At the entrance Cpl. Frank Wright of Montgomery, Ala., found two dead Jap soldiers wearing GI leggings and shoes. They evidently had not been dead many days, for their skins had not begun to decompose. There were indications that other Japs had been living in the building while the bodies lay at the doorway, and it was possible that the bodies had been booby-trapped. No one touched them.

In the area the men also found a chicken coop made from a 50-gallon GI gas can cut in half, with a strip of chicken wire in front of it. Inside a hen was sitting on 15 eggs.

When the men on security reported no Japs hiding in the vicinity, Lt. Sprouce ordered gasoline poured over the thatch lean-to and lighted. Though it had been raining almost steadily for a week, the thatch caught fire instantly. But the timbered frameworks refused to be destroyed. Pfc. Luther Walker of McKamie, Ark., tried without success to knock down some of the corner posts with a sledge hammer, and the patrol had to move on and leave the job for later.

Since the trail was wide, the men continued in the truck. They passed the site of a building which already had been destroyed and kept going until they reached a small Shinto shrine at the side of the road. Here the lieutenant had the truck halted and everybody climbed out.

The trees and shrubs bordering the trail were so thick at this point that it was impossible to see more than a few hundred yards into the underbrush. But the lieutenant had a map which showed a building of some sort just above on the rise to the right. Pfc. Joe Scale of New York City first made a search of the hillside to the left, and when he had reported all clear the patrol began moving through the trees toward the point indicated on the map. Lt. Sprouce and Ross led the way, with Cpl. Roosevelt Brown of Memphis, Tenn., the radio operator, just behind. For the moment the patrol was cut off from contact with headquarters. Cpl. Brown tried to raise the radio man back at the OP, but the portable radio wasn't powerful enough to reach over the ridge and through the dense woods. The men spaced five yards apart moved quickly, hoping to finish the job in a hurry and get back into an open area where the radio again could make contact. The OP was reporting a lot of movement among bushes which could not be seen by the patrol.

The objective shown on the map turned out to be a frame shack and a thatch lean-to. There weren't many signs that the Japs had been using

Fighting in the Pacific often goes on long after an island has been "secured." Japs still hide out in the hills of Saipan, living off the country, and U. S. Infantry patrols still ferret them out of their holes.

e spot recently, although some breadfruit and tatoes were scattered about. At the rear of the elter there were some empty C-ration and K-tion cases and many strands of wire, indicating at this may have once been an American CP. The lean-to was set afire, and no sooner had it gun to burn than a supply of small-arms mo, which was hidden in the thatch, began to plode. There was a mad scramble to get out the area, and on reaching a clearing Brown anaged to radio back to the OP again.

Security was called in and the patrol moved on ce more. The road led down a hill, and the en proceeded on foot, searching every yard on ch side of the road carefully, with the weapons rrier following at a safe distance. With the plosion of the ammunition, it was impossible r Japs in the area to be unaware of the patrol's esence, and the men were alert for an ambush. The next bivouac area showed signs of having en abandoned this morning, possibly only a w minutes before the patrol arrived. A fire had en recently laid. On a little shelf just behind e fireplace were the shells of about a dozen gs and on the ground nearby was a can of nerican coffee. Behind the buildings another stern was found. Blackwell used two pounds of NT in an attempt to destroy it, but the con- ete didn't even crack.

Just beyond a thatch hut appeared the final ojective, another group of buildings. Since it was parent that the Japs were nearby, the truck mained behind, with Pfc. James Colbert of ewellton, La., as guard. This was not the safest b, for the Japs would attack the truck first. oss, who was leading the patrol, reached the ildings first and immediately noticed in the ft rain-soaked earth the footprints of at least persons. The Japs had made no attempt to sguise the direction in which they had fled. The th led directly to a sharp cliff on the side of a gh ridge.

The patrol formed a skirmish line and started ward the cliff, the scouts moving out ahead.

It was abnormally quiet. No one dared make any noise even though the Japs certainly knew of the patrol's movements. The ridge loomed up menac- ingly. The Japs were in a wonderful defensive position—a couple of grenades from the heights could have wiped out the entire patrol.

Suddenly the air was full of smells. Hiding in the woods for months, the Japs hadn't had a chance to take any baths. At the very base of the cliff the men came to a large bivouac area built around a huge shoulder of rock. Caves had been dug into the rock, and in these the Japs had been doing their cooking. Some of the fires were still hot, though they had been hurriedly covered with dirt and rocks.

The Japs were well stocked. Fresh coffee, rice, water, canned fish and meat and fresh vege- tables were found in quantity. Some of the food was American, but most of the supplies must have come from gardens in the area which the Japs apparently cultivated at night. There were also blankets and articles of clothing.

It was getting late. Before leaving, the men destroyed all the food and equipment. That night the mortars zeroed in on the targets the patrol had marked with fires. The next day the cannon company fired hundreds of shells into the area.

Other men on the patrol were Pfcs. Eddie P. Stile of West Point, Miss., and Charles Jackson of Phoenix, Ariz., who went as aid men, and S/Sgt. George McNeal of Edwards, Miss.

Although the patrol did not make actual con- tact with the enemy, the Japs were undoubtedly hard hit by the mission.

THE 24th Infantry's mopping-up operations are being aided by a propaganda campaign con- ducted by the language section of G-2, using leaflets and broadcasts from portable loudspeak- ers. Between February 14 and March 3 of this year, 58 Japs soldiers and 86 civilians have been induced to come out of hiding and surrender.

The loudspeakers are usually set up on high ground overlooking the caves and underbrush where Japs are known to be lurking. Every half hour, for four or five hours at a time, a spoken appeal in the Japanese language is made over the loudspeaker. Before and after each speech, recordings of Jap folk songs and children's songs are played. This music is chosen to make the lis- teners homesick.

The spoken appeal is made by Cpl. "Ike" Miyamoto of Honolulu, a member of a 10-man language team. Miyamoto never uses the word "surrender." His tone is reassuring, and his spiel runs something like this:

"Hello, hello. This is your friend speaking. Did you hear the music just played? Wasn't it sweet? Weren't they beautiful songs? I am sure the songs brought back memories of home. I have a message for those of you who are still hiding in the mountains. We want to help care for the wounded and sick. We are especially anxious to see that the women and children are brought out to safety. . . . Those who have al- ready come out of the mountains are being treated well. They are well satisfied and very happy to be with their friends in the camp and the stockade. . . . There is plenty of good food, cigarettes and candy. . . ." Then directions are given on how the fugitives may turn them- selves in.

Several individuals who surrendered after listening to such broadcasts have volunteered to return to the hills and bring back their friends. One who was sent back with cigarettes and candy showed up the next morning with 14 civilians in tow, among them two women and three children. Another, a soldier, made two trips into the hills. Each time he came back with a group. In one of these were an infantry lieutenant and five other soldiers.

IT is believed that Jap resistance on Saipan is led by a little fellow who stands about 5 feet 5 and weighs around 130 pounds. He wears a U. S. khaki uniform, leather leggings and a Jap officer's cap and carries a type-94 Jap au- tomatic pistol with a white tassel tied to the holster. Most of his followers are said to fear him as much as they do the Americans, and he ap- parently maintains his control over them by a mixture of threats and promises.

Early this year he promised his followers that on February 11, which was Empire Day (Kigen Setsu), the Jap fleet would sail into Saipan's harbor and drive the Americans away. On that day a U. S. fleet of some 800 ships arrived off Saipan on its way to Iwo Jima. The "boss" lost a lot of prestige on February 11.

Martha Vickers

YANK

Pin-up Girl

By Cpl. TOM SHEHAN
YANK Staff Writer

S_{T.} L_{OUIS}, Mo.—J. G. Taylor Spink, publisher of the *Sporting News*, let out a roar which brought his circulation manager running. Glaring at him over his glasses, Spink threw the letter he had been reading across the desk and bellowed, "Here's a guy on Guam who hasn't seen our paper in a month."

It isn't Spink's fault if a copy of the *Sporting News*—"Baseball's Bible," as the *Saturday Eve-*

Sports-Minded Spink

ning Post called it a few years ago—isn't available in every latrine and day room from the Rhine to Okinawa. Probably no other civilian publication outside of *Time* and *Newsweek* has put so much effort into serving the servicemen.

When the war began the *Sporting News* had a circulation of about 145,000; now it is rapidly approaching the half-million mark, and a large part of it is going to servicemen in this country and overseas.

Besides its regular edition of the *Sporting News*, which averages 24 pages, Spink prints an Overseas Edition and a Service Edition. The Overseas Edition is just what its name implies. The Service Edition goes to camps and hospitals in this country. Originally the St. Louis publisher tried to keep his regular edition standard-sized while publishing the other two as tabloids, but it didn't work out mechanically, and now all three papers are tabloid.

"Going tabloid was the best thing that ever happened to us," Spink says. "We did it to the Service and Overseas Editions to cut down the space in the mail sacks. Now we've found that we get a display on the newsstands that we couldn't get as a standard-sized newspaper. I don't think we'll ever go back to the large size."

Sending his paper overseas to our troops during wartime isn't anything new for Spink. He took over the management of the paper in 1914. By 1918, with most of the country's baseball fans off to war, the circulation dropped to 6,000 copies. He was debating whether he would have to fold the paper for the duration when the late Col. Tillinghast Huston returned from France. Huston, who was then a partner of the late Jake Ruppert in the ownership of the Yankees, told of seeing soldiers at the front pass around a copy of the *Sporting News* until it was in shreds. Ban Johnson, president of the American League, then bought 10,000 subscriptions to be sent overseas.

Spink wasn't caught napping when this war broke out. Right after Pearl Harbor he went to Washington and talked with Lt. Col. Ray L. Trautman, library division of Special Services, and Maj. Paul Postell, his assistant, and arranged to send 14,700 six-month subscriptions to Special Service officers for distribution among the troops. Before those subscriptions had expired the quota was raised to 35,000 and it has been increased steadily ever since.

Liggett & Myers Tobacco Company, the Chevrolet

Division of General Motors, Owens-Illinois Glass and a number of other industrial firms, as well as the major and minor leagues, sponsor subscriptions. And papers purchased by the Joe E. Brown All-Pacific Recreation Fund Inc., which sponsors subscriptions for 15,000 copies per week, were flown to the Marines on Iwo Jima. Sgt. Karl Lipke wrote from that island: "The *Sporting News* was the first Stateside paper here. We distributed over 1,000 copies yesterday."

A typical Overseas Edition carries, in addition to baseball coverage, features on boxing, horse racing, hockey, football and whatever sports are in season; also pin-ups and cartoons. "We make an effort to avoid vulgarity in our pin-ups," says Spink. One of the recent *Sporting News* pin-ups was a picture of Sherry Britton, strip-tease artist at Leon & Eddie's in New York. The caption mentioned that Sherry would be glad to send one of her pictures to anybody who wrote to her at the night club. She received 23,000 requests.

J. G. T_{AYLOR} S_{PINK} inherited his newspaper and his love for sports. His Uncle Al founded the *Sporting News* in 1886, but he soon found publishing a paper, even a sports paper, dull business and sent for his brother Charlie, Taylor's father, to run it for him. Al had written a play about horse racing, a turkey named "The Derby Winner," and immediately on Charlie's arrival from the Dakotas, where he had been homesteading, took it on tour. When Al wasn't touring with his play he was attempting to popularize night horse racing at St. Louis' South Side Race Track.

Charlie dropped the coverage of other sports and concentrated on baseball. He fought for a number of reforms in the game, but it wasn't until the advent of the American League in 1900 that his paper, which backed the Ban Johnson circuit in its fight with the National League, really established itself. When the two leagues made peace they asked Editor Joe Flanner of the *Sporting News* to write the National Agreement. It was set in type at the *Sporting News* office and a proof was shown to Harry Pulliam, then president of the National League. Pulliam was impressed with it, and both leagues adopted it without changing a word of the original copy.

About that time Taylor, who wanted to be a

sportswriter, quit high school to take a job as an office boy in the St. Louis *Post-Dispatch* sports department. Later, when the *Sporting News* office boy quit, Taylor went to work for his father.

Ring Lardner succeeded Joe Flanner as editor of the *Sporting News* before the first World War. The paper went steadily downhill under Ring, who wasn't cut out for an editorial desk job. But it was on the *Sporting News* that Lardner wrote "Pullman Pastimes," the predecessor of his "You Know Me Al" series which made him famous as a short-story writer.

S_{PINK} took over management of the paper from his father not long after Lardner left to write sports for the Boston *Evening American*. Taylor improved it greatly by hiring correspondents in every city which boasted a team in organized baseball. After weathering the first World War, he expanded by starting the *Sporting Goods Dealer*, a trade publication, and publishing baseball guides and record books. In fact, Spink did so well that he was able to have a feud with the late Judge Landis.

"The judge did most of the feuding," Taylor says today. "He was the greatest benefactor the game has had, even if he did act like a ham actor at times."

To make this respectful appraisal of Landis, Spink had to overlook the fact that the judge took away from him the compiling and printing of the official baseball guide, a task Spink and his staff had handled for years, and deprived him of thousands of dollars in income.

Spink gets around. He makes two or three trips a year to New York to take in the shows. He'll go anywhere to attend a sporting event. He's traveled in Europe. The Kentucky Derby is an event he never misses, and he loves to bet on the horses. He arrives at his office early and works late, but when the tracks are open he is in constant touch with one of the St. Louis books.

When friends suggested that he was the man to succeed Landis as commissioner of the national pastime he shouted, "I don't want any part of that job."

"Why?" they asked.

"Why?" he said. "Because I wouldn't be able to bet on the horses—that's why."

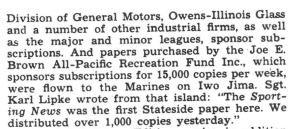

I. G. Taylor Spink uses a Dictaphone to answer all servicemen's letters personally.

"MEET LT. WYMAN, HARVARD—LT. CLARK, PRINCETON—AND CAPT. ESTEY, USAFI."

—Pfc. Willard G. Levitas

"MISS THE FLIGHT DECK AGAIN, HIGGINS?"

—Stan Fine S1c

YANK

THE ARMY WEEKLY

"SOME MORE V-MAIL FOR MULLINS."

—Sgt. Jim Weeks

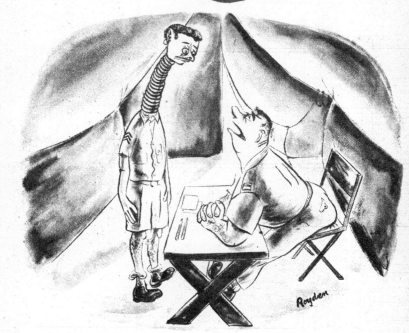

"— ABOUT YOUR RUNNING DOWN TO THE NATIVE VILLAGE ALL THE TIME, MITCHELL —"

—Cpl. Frank R. Robinson

"WELL, WHAT ARE YOU GAPING AT?"

—Pfc. Tom Flannery

VE ISSUE

JUNE 1, 1945
VOL. 3, NO. 50 · 5 CENTS

FADE-OUT

1 For most of us it began on October 29, 1940, when Secretary Stimson pulled out the first number.

2 We repeated the oath before the flag and wondered if we'd be "back in a year, little darling."

3 Trains pulled in at Southern camps, and marched off lugging barracks bags and suitcases

The GI's War in Europe

A Picture Story of the American Soldier's Fight Against Germany and Italy from Induction to Victory

7 And GIs were being sent to Iceland. Traveling on the North Atlantic was often plenty rough

"All present and accounted for." We stood in line, drilled, made packs and stood in line.

5 We hurdled barriers in obstacle courses with those basin helmets sliding around on our heads.

6 Some left the States early. U. S. forces were sent to build bases in Greenland in April 1941.

GI main street in Iceland, lined with Nissen huts. It seemed pretty bleak and far from home.

9 We landed in Northern Ireland in January 1942. Yanks paraded in fresh blouses with gas masks.

10 We were starting to assemble men and supplies in Britain. GIs saw English pubs for the first time.

More and more American planes were flying from English fields as ground crews waved them off.

12 Eighth Air Force Forts first raided Europe in July 1942. These B-17s were bombing in France.

13 B-17 crews were tired after getting back but they usually had plenty of things to talk about.

Krauts were caught napping when the Eighth Air Force first bombed as far as East Prussia.

15 Rangers, back from the Dieppe raid, August 1, 1942, were first to fight German ground troops.

16 The ATC was using Ascension Island (halfway to Africa) as a base but kept it secret until 1943.

CONTINUED

17 The war against fascism brought us to Egypt in 1942, where some of us did a little sightseeing.

18 And the war brought us to Iran, where we kept the lend-lease goods moving toward Russia.

19 On November 7, 1942, bad day for the we landed on beaches of French North A

20 Most GIs who occupied Oran saw a liberated city for the first time and found they liked it.

21 In Tunisia the Germans fought or tried, like this one, to get away. Either way they lost.

22 We fought over the desert and dry hills watched everything the enemy was do

25 When we entered Tunis it was a happy day for Frenchmen, British and Americans alike.

26 When the Tunisian campaign ended, in May 1942, the war was over for a lot of German and Italian prisoners. The Allies had captured 291,000 Axis soldiers, killed 30,000 and wounded 27,000.

28 MPs were about the only GIs who saw the famous Casbah in Algiers. It was out of bounds.

29 Next step was Sicily. In planes, or on landing boats, we wondered how tough it would be.

30 We waded ashore on July 9, 1943, sloshi through the surf and cussing at the mul

23 Infantry and armor took one Tunisian town after another as the Nazi armies retreated.

24 As always, digging a foxhole, like this one by the side of the road, was good insurance.

27 GIs of the Signal Corps worked overtime in North Africa setting up communications.

31 The kids in Sicily were almost as good at observation as we were, being curious—like kids.

32 We fought snipers in the Sicilian towns, with the sun shining through the smoke and dust.

33 The medics did a job in Sicily, as they have done in all other combat areas in this war.

GAFSA 83 KM
MAKNASSY 300 KM
SFAX 130 KM

CONTINUE

34 We invaded Italy in September 1943. The Italians quit, but Nazi bombers still unloaded on us.

35 When we got into Italy we had to cross over one long range of mountains after another.

36 And most GIs who took a hill went o take the next one, but some of them di

40 The Fifteenth Air Force was taking off from Italy. Some ground-crew GIs were fixing up quarters.

41 All Italy and all Allied soldiers who fought there remember Cassino on the road to Rome.

42 We occupied Rome on June 4, 1944. Som a pretty guide to show them the Coloss

46 We were getting set for France in a big way, maneuvering in strength over the English moors.

47 And finally we were jammed up ag the loading docks, ready for sailing o

50 They made it but had to take a bre and were in no mood to smile at the ca

37 The Army nurses were there when we made the Anzio-Nettuno beachhead. We needed them.

38 And we needed artillery. You're a bit more confident with a "Long Tom" backing you up.

39 Another part of war in Italy was the girls who came over to put on a show, rain or shine.

43 Although chasing the enemy, there was time to pause for a little GI side show on the way.

44 As the war went on in Italy you ran across quite a few nice Wacs working in headquarters.

45 Before Rome fell we were still in England, training very hard, getting ready for D-Day.

48 D-Day came, on June 6, 1944. Some lost time in the water before reaching France.

49 It seemed quite a way from the boats to shore. The invaders carried a lot of equipment.

50 We got farther inland and met some of the people. It was easy to get a laugh.

CONTINUED

52 We met up with French civilians who were very nice about quenching a soldier's thirst.

53 The Ninth Air Force needed air fields in France. Engineers were there to lay them out.

54 The break-through at St. Lo began in and then we broke out into the French pl

55 The Krauts retreated, leaving a lot of their baggage twisted and burning on the roads.

56 In Italy we were moving to the shore to board landing craft and invade southern France.

57 We hit southern France on August 15 and some Maquis who were veteran Nazi-figh

58 Ordnancemen had plenty to do keeping guns in repair, even salvaging enemy weapons.

59 We plowed into Brittany and attacked the port of Brest, fighting through the streets.

60 The liberation of Paris came on August and people turned out to cheer and si

62 We went through the old Maginot Line, which didn't look so tough when you got close.

63 For many GIs entering Belgium it was a nice thing to be appreciated by the right people.

64 We got through Huertgen Forest in Novemb but it was a slow, cruel push for the Infant

We couldn't all stay and celebrate in Paris but we put on a good show on the way.

Many GIs found that Army nurses were the only good part of lying wounded in a hospital.

66 Aachen, which was surrendered on October 20, was the first big German city we fought for.

67 A break was a break anyway you looked at it, but having some mail made it even better.

CONTINUED

68 The more casualties the more work for the medics, who were hit themselves often enough.

69 We got through Belgium but we left thousands behind who will never leave Belgian soil.

70 When winter hit the Western Front eve chow didn't keep us warm for very

73 The winter reached its height when we got into Germany. GIs worked in howling blizzards.

74 The Germans under Von Rundstedt started their big counterattack in the Ardennes December 16.

75 GIs will long remember the part the defe of Bastogne played in stopping Von Rund

77 Negro artillerymen helped blast what was left of the Siegfried Line as we went on.

78 The line of prisoners grew as we went from the Roer to the Rhine, and they got less cocky.

79 Some weren't going so fast that they c stop to dance with a few Red Cross

81 Going into Germany we saw refugees all the way, lugging their families and their goods.

82 Cologne was captured on March 7, 1945. And with that the end in Germany was not far off.

83 Also on March 7, First Army GIs fou Remagen bridge intact and crossed the

1 The Infantry filed through the snow-covered Forest of the Ardennes toward the front.

72 The spotlight was on winter in western Europe, but there were snow and cold for GIs in Italy, too.

76 One thing a man can always do to get a welcome relief from war is to look at a YANK pin-up. (Adv.)

0 We took more German cities with empty streets and houses with gaping windows.

4 Then we began to get ponton bridges across the river and the last big offensives were on.

85 The Third Army speeded into Frankfurt. Horst Wessel, Nazi hero, didn't stand for much now.

CONTINUED

The GI's War in Europe

86 Those of us who saw the prison and concentration camps in Germany were no longer suspicious about atrocities. The savagery was there to see.

87 The armies of the Third Reich were folding up, by the thousands hundred thousands. Taking on more prisoners got to be a nuis

90 In Italy we were launching an offensive which ended in Mussolini's execution by the Partisans and a mass surrender by the Germans on May 1.

91 This is where Allied unity became even more real, when GIs of American and Russian armies met near Torgau, in Germany, on Apri

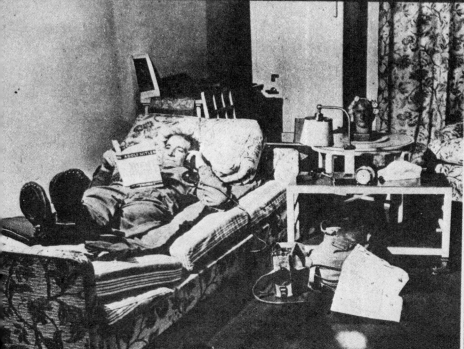

92 We rolled into Munich, birthplace of the Nazi party, on April 29, and took over Hitler's headquarters in the Brown House, with some of his comforts.

93 Von Rundstedt, captured by two GIs on May 1, said we had fought good a war as the Germans had in 1940. He was admitting defe

88 On April 13 our flags flew at half staff in Germany. We didn't want to believe the President was dead; but victory does not wait on mourning.

89 We moved into Nuremberg, appropriately enough, on Hitler's birthday, April 20. In the Nazi stadium GIs were heiling in the *Fuehrer's* face.

ROOSEVELT BLVD.

Adolf-Hitler-Str.

THE two weeks that ended with the Germans' signing an official surrender at 2041 hours, U. S. Eastern War Time, Sunday, May 6, 1945, were crammed with more important happenings than any other equal period of the war. From the fall of Cologne and the massing of Russian assault forces on the east bank of the Oder, the fact of final German defeat had been obvious. The climax came in these last two big weeks and when it came news flash tumbled upon news flash, rumor upon rumor, surrender upon surrender, so quickly that the average GI or civilian could hardly grasp one Allied triumph before he was caught up by the impact of the next.

These two weeks began with the Russian battle for possession of Berlin in full swing. Below Berlin, near Torgau on the Elbe, tankmen of the U. S. First Army were beginning to pick up snatches of Russian combat directions on their mobile radios. Marshal Ivan Konev's forces were moving to meet them. All along the Western Front an Allied nutcracker was breaking up the vaunted "hard core" of German defense. U. S. Lt. Gen. William H. Simpson's Ninth Army was pushing east from Magdeburg, Gen. George S. Patton's tankmen were cowboying toward the Czech border, the First Canadian Army was at Emden, the First French Army was past Stuttgart, Lt. Gen. Alexander Patch's Seventh U. S. Army was south of the Danube near Lauringen, Gen. Jacob L. Devers' Sixth Army Group threatened

Bavaria, British Field Marshal Sir Bernard L. Montgomery's Twenty-first Army Group was bringing complete freedom to the Netherlands and Denmark. From their side the Russians continued the same inexorable squeeze that had forced the Germans back from their high tide of Eastern aggression before Leningrad and Stalingrad. Marshal Gregory Zhukov's First White Russians were in Berlin. Konev was almost to the Elbe River. Gen. Fedeor Tolbukhin's Third Ukrainian Army cut into the Nazi redoubt. Gen. Rodion Malinovsky had pushed through Vienna and was following the Danube deeper into Austria. In Italy the long dull stalemate of Lt. Gen. Mark W. Clark's polyglot armies had been broken. The U. S. 10th Mountain Infantry Division had spearheaded a break-through and the war in Italy had a moving front again—a moving front of Fifth Army veterans, including American Negro troops and Japanese-Americans and Brazilian Allies and free Italian troops, and British and Indian GIs of the famous Eighth which had swept across Africa in 1943—all of them aided by the sabotage and behind-the-lines action of Italian partisans in the North and by the sharp, constant pressure against the German eastern flank from Marshal Tito's Yugoslavs. Hitler's Germany was going down in flames.

Moving forward with the U. S. Ninth Army into the confusion of a dying Reich, YANK staff correspondent Sgt. Allan Ecker observed the symptoms of collapse:

A FERRYBOAT, a big barge propelled by the hand-over-hand cable system, was loaded to the gills with about 60 displaced persons, German nationals and American GIs crossing west over the Elbe from a strictly unofficial American 35th Division bridgehead on the other side of the river. A patrol of K Company of the 137th Infantry under Lt. Howard Pierson of Huntington, Oreg., and S/Sgt. Denzil Lindbom of Peoria, Ill., had made a crossing to the eastern bank for a brief reconnoitering, but they'd run into a peculiar situation.

Everybody and his uncle in the little town of Ferchland insisted on going back with them. So the boys set up a ferryboat. One of the passengers when we went back was a German woman with four kids, the youngest 5 months old, all of them wailing to beat the band. We asked where she was coming from and where she was heading, and her answer seemed to sum up the whole plight of the German nation crushed between two fronts: "We left Brandenburg two days ago," she said, "because the Russian bombs and shells leveled our home there. Where are we going? To a big city where we have relatives."

"Perhaps you've been there? It's called Aachen."

Among the prize catches of the 102d Division was an attractive and much-married female Gestapo agent whose current and fourth husband is an SS major general. Interrogated at her hideaway house in the woods by German-born Edward Hoffer of New York City, the *frau* was much embarrassed by one question. She couldn't remember the first name of her first husband with whom she had lived for 7 years until 1929.

As Russian and American forces converged on the Western Front, a rumor started back among the 8th Armored Division men around Braunschweig that a junction had already been effected. "Just take a look at those two guys if you don't believe it," GIs advised cynics.

"Those two guys" were honest-to-God Red Army first lieutenants, one of them an ex-member of the Crimea General Staff. They were, to be sure, a trifle out of uniform: GI ODs and field jackets, German leather boots and Lugers, Russian shoulder insignia, and GI helmets with big red stars and the words "Soviet Union" painted on them.

Picked out of a horde of Russian slave laborers

and war prisoners wandering along the highways and byways of Germany, the two officers had been given razors, baths and equipment by the 8th Armored's 88th Cavalry Recon Squadron. Thus transformed, they were ready—with the aid of Russian-speaking Pfc. Frank Ilchuk of New York City—to organize some of the thousands of their countrymen into orderly communities in each village. Many starving Russians, newly liberated, have taken to pillaging and cluttering up important roadways. The use of Red Army officers to control them and the requisitioning of rations from local German *burgomeisters* was put into effect to take the load off American combat units until military government authorities arrive in sufficient numbers to take over.

IN the news, as the first of the two last weeks wore on, you heard less about Adolf Hitler and more about Heinrich Himmler, his Gestapo chief. There were increasing rumors of Hitler's disappearance or his death or his madness and with them increasing rumors of a Himmler bid for peace. The peace rumors reached a climax in a false Armistice announcement in the U. S. on April 28. Newspaper headlines screamed "GERMANY QUITS!" and premature celebrations were set off in some communities. They didn't last long in the face of a sharp denial from Supreme Allied Headquarters and the White House.

The fact behind the false armistice—Himmler's attempt to surrender to the U. S. and Great Britain and leave Russia holding the bag—were true. But the chief fact behind the Himmler trial balloon was fear, German fear before an assault the Germans now knew they could not withstand.

Lt. Gen. George S. Patton's Third Army was an arrow aimed at Hitler's Berchtesgaden mountain hide-away. U. S. troops took Italy's chief naval base at La Spezia. Genoa fell. Aged ex-Vichy chief, Marshal Petain, came through Switzerland to give himself up for trial in liberated France. The Germans in Italy were shoved back into the Alps and their lines of possible retreat were all but cut off. Great Britain and the U. S. refused to be parties to any peace overtures which did not include their Russian ally. At Torgau, advance groups of the First Army's 69th Division made contact with the 58th Guards Division of Konev's First Ukrainian Army.

Sgt. Ed Cunningham, YANK staff correspondent, was with the First Army to report the meeting:

A 28-MAN, six-jeep patrol of 69th Division Yanks under the command of 1st Lt. Albert Kotzebue of Houston, Tex., and his platoon sergeant, T/Sgt. Frederick Johnston of Bradford, Pa., and a Russian cavalry patrol made the first link-up between the Eastern and Western Fronts. The meeting took place on a hill outside the village of Zauwitz just before 1330 hours on April 25.

The jeeps roared up the hill smack into the middle of a group of hard-riding Cossacks who were patrolling the area in search of stray pockets of German resistance. Both units recognized each other so there was none of the confusion that attended some later Russki-Yank meetings.

The Cossacks detailed a Russian civilian to guide Lt. Kotzebue and his men to where the CO of the Russian division was waiting to greet them on the other side of the hill. Then they galloped off in search of more Germans.

The American patrol crossed the Elbe in jeeps ferried on a platform raft and fell headlong into a lively Russian celebration.

A Russian major who spoke a few words of English set the tone of the celebration with a toast. "Today," he said, "we have the most happy day of our lives. The years 1941 and 1942 were most difficult time. Germany was at Stalingrad. It was the most difficult time of our lives. At that time we do not think of our lives; we think of our country.

"Just now, our great friends and we have met one another and it is the end of our enemy. Long live your great leader. Long live our great leader. Long live our great countries."

Maj. Fred Craig of Friendship, Tenn., and 2nd Lt. Thomas R. Howard of Mississippi, were in command of the second patrol to meet the Russians. They made contact at 1545 April 25 at Clanzchwitz with a column of Russian cavalry. The Russians galloped across an open field to meet them, throwing their helmets in the air. Maj. Craig was ferried across the river and taken back to the Russian corps headquarters to meet the lieutenant general commanding. The general asked him if he were the highest Ameri-

can officer available to greet him and Maj. Craig explained that his was only a patrol, not the official greeting party.

The major and his men had two meals with the Russians, one at 1900 and one at 0930 the next morning. Once again there were toasts and mutual greetings. The Russians had several cameramen and correspondents on hand to record the meeting and seemed sorry we didn't have any of our own. The general told the major he was sending a message direct to Stalin to inform him of the meeting. The Russians and Yanks fired each other's weapons and criticized them. Red Army men found our M1 too heavy for their taste but liked our carbine and .30-caliber machine guns.

During the night the radio operators at the major's CP on the west bank of the Elbe, relieved each other so they could cross and enjoy the Russian party. A Cossack column stopped by the CP and put on a two-hour serenade of Russian songs with harp, mouth organ and accordion accompaniment.

In the morning a Russian barber shaved the Yanks in bed. It was quite a meeting.

The third U. S. patrol to contact the Russians had a more confusing time of it. It was led by 2nd Lt. William D. Robertson, 1st Battalion, 273d Regiment, 69th Division, who had studied Japanese as an ASTP man, a factor which was as useful as an extra toenail in establishing friendly relations.

Robertson and his three-man patrol reached the town of Torgau on the banks of the Elbe after a 27-mile jeep ride through the no-man's-land

then separating our forces. He spotted Red Army men on the opposite bank and shouted to them: "Amerikanski! Come over, Friends! Tovarisch." But the Russians weren't having any, since a German patrol had tried to get next to them by pretending to be Americans the day before.

Robertson and his three-man GI patrol weren't daunted and proceeded to manufacture an American flag from cloth and red, white and blue paint procured at a Torgau store. They waved their flag at the Russians from the tower of a castle. The Russians fired two colored flares, the agreed link-up signal. But Robertson had no flares to fire back.

The Russians were now thoroughly convinced that something phoney was afoot. They opened up with an antitank gun and small-arms fire on the castle and scored two direct hits.

An American naval lieutenant, a newly-freed PW, came up about that time. He spoke Russian and so did a Russian liberated slave worker who was nearby. Between the two of them, they managed to shout the news across the Elbe that the patrol was really American and wanted to meet the Russians.

THEN and then only did the Russians relent and allow Robertson and his men to cross to their bank. Once across, the meeting followed the pattern already set. There was vodka, and backslapping; there were toasts and mutual congratulations. This third meeting by Lt. Robertson's patrol was the one credited as the first contact in early news dispatches.

The climactic meeting, of course, was when

Maj. Gen. Emil E. Reinhardt of Decatur, Ga., CG of the 69th, made his official visit to Lt. Gen. Rosakov, CG of the 58th Guards Division. The major general and three staff officers crossed the Elbe and returned in a slim German racing boat, so delicately balanced that all the officers had to sit at attention in order not to tip themselves over into the drink. The shell had been designed for sport, not transportation, but it was the only craft available at the section of the Elbe where Gen. Reinhardt crossed and where the Germans had blown the only two bridges.

Sgt. Andrew Marriack of Hudson, N. Y., served as interpreter for a Russian captain who told some of the Americans gathered by the river how his men had taken Torgau. Marriack had learned his Russian as an ASTP student at City College in New York.

"They took this town two days ago," he translated. "It wasn't much of a fight, but the captain got sore because the Germans ambushed one of his patrols. He says a gang of Krauts held up a white flag and when his patrol came over to take them prisoner, they threw down the flag and opened fire, killing two of his men. He says the Germans don't fight like human beings; they're treacherous and they destroy towns and civilian populations without any cause. He says the Russians will stay in Germany until the Germans are capable of respecting the rights of other people. He doesn't. . ."

The roar of an exploding grenade, which landed in the river several yards away from the party, interrupted. Some of the Americans who had just arrived hit the ground. Marriack, who didn't seem disturbed, said, "That's nothing to worry about. Just one of the Russian soldiers showing one of our guys how their grenades work. They always fire their weapons when you ask about them; they figure a demonstration is the best answer they can give."

OUTSIDE of the actual meetings, the unoccupied area which separated the Russian forces on the Elbe from the American forces on the Mulde River was the most interesting and the screwiest part of the link-up picture. Hundreds of German soldiers streamed along the roads leading to the American lines, unguarded and all but forgotten in the excitement of the Russki-Yank junction. They had been disarmed by advance American patrols and ordered to make their own way to our PW cages because we didn't have enough GIs around at the time to escort them. Most of them seemed to be happy to be out of the fighting.

Unlike the reception we got in the dash from the Rhine to the Mulde, where the civilians ac-

The Fall of Germany

ANGELES Times — EXTRA! — MONDAY MORNING, MAY 7, 1945 — 9 A.M. FINAL

THE EVENING SUN — BALTIMORE, MONDAY MAY 7, 1945 — SURRENDER — FLASH

ST. LOUIS POST-DISPATCH EXTRA — The Only Evening Newspaper in St. Louis With the Associated Press News Service — GERMANY SURRENDERS

HAVE NOT YET MADE IT OFFICIAL — AND BIG JOB

MINNEAPOLIS STAR-JOURNAL

Germany's Surrender Announced in Europe — Proclamation

Russian and American soldiers had a celebration after they met near the town of Torgau, Germany, April 25.

The bodies of Benito Mussolini, the "sawdust Caesar" and his Clara Petacci lie in a square in Milan after their execution by partisans.

German officers m_ forces in Netherlan_

cepted our entry in sullen silence, the people between the Mulde and the Elbe welcomed us like returning heroes. They stood on the curbs of no-man's-land towns, waving and laughing.

None of their waves and smiles were returned. The $65 question—the fraternization fine—had nothing to do with the Americans' passive reaction to the sudden German welcome. The Yanks could see through the waving and the smiles. It wasn't that the Germans hated us less; they just feared the Russians more.

FEAR was becoming an all-pervading thing in Germany. No matter which way the Germans turned they found the Allies moving in on them. On April 29, the 12th Armored Division, the 20th Armored Division and the 42d Infantry Division of Lt. Gen. Patch's Seventh Army took Munich, birthplace and shrine of the Nazi party. The Fifth Army took Milan and the British Eighth took Venice and from the north of Italy, from the village of Dongo on Lake Como, came word of the death of Mussolini, tried and executed by Italian partisans. The ex-Duce's mistress, Clara Petacci, was executed with him as were 16 other captured Fascists. The bodies of Mussolini and Clara Petacci were brought to Milan in a furniture mover's van and displayed to the people of the town.

Pierre Laval, the "honest trader" who had sold France out to Hitler, fled from Germany to Spain and was interned. The Seventh Army took Dachau, the most infamous of all Nazi concentration camps and one of the oldest. The Ninth Army made its contact with the Russians just north of the First near Wittenberg. YANK Correspondent Sgt. Ecker was still with the Ninth and observed sidelights of this second junction of Allied armies:

IT doesn't take a second look to know the Russians are planning to stick around for a while in Germany. In our area, American flags are few and far between, mostly on military-government offices, but over on the Russian side almost every window of the occupied town buildings flies a red flag instead of the white surrender flags we leave up. There's another more conclusive proof of permanence of Russian intentions; German signposts, left up in our area, have been torn down by Russians and new ones in their language substituted.

Among the many other things that the Russians can do better than the Germans is the fine art of sloganeering. The Germans in many cities have painted a vast number of inspiration mottoes on the walls of the houses and public buildings but none can quite measure up in concise impact to this Soviet slogan lettered in white on red banners flying in the street here: "Death to the Fascist aggressors." For the benefit of the American allies, a special two-language flag was displayed in Wittenberg, scene of a meeting between the Russian and American corps generals. This is the way it read in English: "Long live the great leaders. President Trumen, Marchall Stalin and Premer Churchill." Lots of wiseacres bet Stalin's

name came first in the Russian version of the same slogan but they were wrong.

THE Allied flood rolled on. It was a great period for capturing Nazi field marshals like Wilhelm Ritter von Leeb and Wilhelm List, both of whom had been kingpins in the Nazi drives that overthrew Poland and France and both of whom had had less luck in the invasion of Russia. Adm. Nicholas Horthy, Nazi-controlled dictator of Hungary was captured. All three were picked up by the Seventh Army. Lt. Gen. Kurt Dittmar, leading German military commentator, surrendered to the Ninth. And then came the biggest story of all. The German radio announced that Hitler had died in action in Berlin. The Russians, who had by this time freed Berlin of all but street fighting, agreed that Hitler was dead, not as a fighting soldier but as a suicide. They said that Josef Paul Goebbels, his warped little propaganda minister, had also died by his own hand. Tired of too many German tricks, most Allied authorities reserved comment; they would believe Hitler dead when they saw his body. But a dead Hitler made for cheerful talk.

In Paris, Sgt. DeWitt Gilpin, YANK field correspondent, took a sample of public opinion on the subject of Hitler's death:

LT. WILLIAM J. CULLERTON of Chicago, a fighter pilot who was left for dead a few weeks ago after a German SS man fired a .35-slug through his stomach, sat in a Paris hotel and talked about the late Adolf Hitler.

"I hope the sonuvabitch was as scared of dying as I was when that SS officer let me have it through the stomach," he said. "I thought I'd had it.

"Now they say Hitler is dead. Maybe he is. If he is, I don't believe he died heroically. Mussolini died at least something like a dictator but somehow I can't figure Hitler dying in action. And I don't think Hitler's death changes anything about Germany. It just might be part of a deal to soften us up so they can stick another knife in the soft spot."

Two Eighth Air Force aerial gunners, who like Cullerton were sweating out a ride back to the States from the same hotel, said that they hadn't believed the news of Hitler's death when they first heard it shortly after the 104th Division liberated them from the Alten Grabow PW Camp.

S/Sgt. Henry J. Smith of Scranton, Pa., said: "I came down near Stutlitz about nine months ago and I just had time to get out of my chute before German civilians started beating me up. One old man of about 60 broke a .22-rifle over me. But when we left Germany all the people were forcing smiles for us. And that old guy would smile too, now. Mussolini is dead, Hitler is dead—but what's the difference? There are lots more."

S/Sgt. William Cupp of Tipton, Iowa, who came down in Belgium and beat his way within 200 yards of the American lines—then near Paris—before the Germans got him, said: "They

want to make Hitler a martyr for the German kids. Most of them are pretty much for him as it is."

At the 48th General Hospital, Sgt. Allan Pettit of Verndale, Minn., and the 78th Division, was well enough to be going out on pass. He had been hit twice before on the Roer River, but this time it was only concussion, and now he had a chance to see Paris.

"Why waste words on Hitler," he said. "And how do you know for sure? Anyway he picked a damned good Nazi to take his place. That crazy Doenitz fought us in the last war."

Over in another ward filled with combat men just in from the front, it was the entertainment hour and as a special favor to Cpl. Peter Stupihin —a Red Army man suffering from prison camp malnutrition—a singer rendered "Kalinka." The GIs thought that was fine, and those who felt strong enough called for tunes like "Stardust" and "I'll Be Seeing You."

A red-headed southerner from the 4th Division was feeling good because the doctor had finished dressing the shrapnel wound in his chest, and he had something to say about Hitler and his Germany between songs.

"I wish I was the guy who killed him," he said. "I'd killed him a little slower. Awful slow."

In the Tout Paree Bar some men from the 101st Airborne and the 29th Divisions worked at having a good time with pilots from the Troop Carrier Command. There were Wacs in the party too, but the attention they were getting came mostly from pilots. Some infantrymen were arguing about what their outfits did and where.

A pianist was pounding out what he considered American swing, and it wasn't the place for a name-and-address interview. An infantry captain who'd had a few drinks didn't waste much time on Hitler.

"Yeah, I guess he's dead," he said, "but so are a lot of good guys. And you just remember that."

Then the infantrymen went back to arguing about what had happened at Bastogne.

AND in a very different setting, in the PW section of a Third Army post in Bavaria, YANK Correspondent Cpl. Howard Katzander, got a very different slant on what might lie behind Hitler's death from a source a little closer to Berchtesgaden:

THE colonel was out of uniform—regrettably so for an officer of his rank in the Third Army area—but he carried it off well. He was average in height, slim and blond-haired. He carried a crooked cane, and was dressed in green cotton trousers, and a pepper-and-salt sport jacket zippered up the front. He wore grey suede gloves and, as he talked he sat cross-legged, occasionally slapping at one trim brown oxford, composed and nonchalant as if he were back on his father's East Prussia estates in the heart of Germany's Junkerland.

The story he was telling was the story of why

on May 3 to surrender rmany and Denmark.

On May 7 Col. Gen. Gustav Jodl, German chief of staff, signs formal surrender terms at SHAEF Headquarters in Reims, France.

After the surrender at Reims, Gen. Dwight Eisenhower holds up the pens with which the documents were signed.

the war did not end last July. It was the story of the attempt to assassinate Hitler and he knew all about it. Because this was Lt. Col. Wilhelm Kuebart, a member of the *Wehrmacht* General Staff, and one of the original plotters.

Kuebart was a *Junker* gentleman of the Prussian militarist class with a long military tradition behind him. His wife was the daughter of a *Junker* general. His uncles were *Reichswehr* officers and before them his grandfather and great-grandfathers as far back as his memory went. Only his father had departed from the tradition to embrace a profession as an architect.

In the fall of 1932 Wilhelm Kuebart entered the *Reichswehr* as an officer-candidate. He was commissioned as a second lieutenant in the fall of 1934.

From then on his rise was rapid and in the best *Junker* tradition. He participated in the Polish campaign in the late summer of 1939 as a first lieutenant and in the summer of 1940 he became a captain and was transferred to the staff of the 18th Panzer Division. In the early spring of 1941 his talents and family background received due recognition and he was sent to the *Kriegsakademie*—the General Staff School—after which he joined Von Leeb's staff in the Central Army Group on the Russian front.

It was there that Kuebart was inoculated with the anti-Hitler virus in its most violent form. Almost the entire staff of this army group was anti-Hitler.

This was not unusual. The *Junker* officer class was probably the most exclusive club in the world. Its members regarded the military as the only career fit for a gentleman and it regarded the *Wehrmacht* as its own private sphere.

Kuebart had taken a pretty dim view of the Nazi regime from the beginning, the way he tells it, and had never joined the National Socialist Democratic Workers Party. Kuebart and his fellow officers felt that their ranks had degenerated under Hitler and they were particularly resentful of Himmler's attempt to spy on the officers and impose *SS* control over them. Hitler's spectacular failures as general and Supreme Commander of the Armies led to open revolt. The disaster at Stalingrad was the last straw.

From that time on the most popular subject of conversation among officers of the old school was the question of how to get rid of Hitler and Himmler. Kuebart had been sponsored for a place on the General Staff by Col. Hansen, Chief of the *Wehrmacht* Intelligence Service, and Hansen was the brains behind the plot against Hitler's life. The *Burgemeister* of Leipzig, Boerdler, was to take political control. Hansen went to Zeitzler, Chief of the General Staff, and persuaded him that immediate action was necessary.

The date for the assassination was set for July 13. The weekly conference between Hitler and his generals was to be held as usual on that day. But, at the last minute, there were two hitches. Himmler was not going to be present and Hitler decided to hold the conference in a flimsy wooden barracks.

The bomb that had been prepared to wipe out Hitler and Himmler was designed for use in Hitler's underground headquarters where heavy concrete walls and the earth itself would confine the force of the blast to the small room.

When the bomb was exploded in the frame building above ground—it had been brought to the conference in a brief case—its force was dissipated. Hitler was injured, but not seriously. The attempt had failed.

It could not be proven definitely that Kuebart had plotted against the Supreme Commander, but it was felt that he had betrayed his trust as an officer of the *Wehrmacht*. Accordingly, a crushing blow was dealt him. He was expelled from the *Wehrmacht* as "*undwirdigkeit*," unworthy of the honor of wearing the uniform. He was forbidden to reenter the army even as a buck private. He was kept under constant *Gestapo* surveillance, apparently in the hope that his movements would betray others who had taken part in the plot.

Kuebart says that 120 high German officers were hanged as a result of the plot, and 700 others are waiting execution.

When American troops overran the area where Kuebart had been living with his wife and two children since his expulsion from the army, he calmly walked into the CP of B Battery, 551st Antiaircraft Artillery Battalion and told his story. He expected to speak his piece and go home to his wife and kiddies. He had papers to show that he had been expelled from the German Army. He assured his interrogators that his group had been prepared to sue for peace immediately if their plot had succeeded.

But he did not go home to the wife and kiddies. Somehow or other, the Third Army did not feel that his expulsion from the army relieved him of responsibility for the part he had played up to that time. He is now in a PW cage and knows no more than anyone else of what actually happened to Hitler this time.

ADM. KARL DOENITZ was named as Hitler's successor—the new Fuehrer. *It was asserted that Hitler himself had nominated the Grand Admiral of the German Fleet to carry on his job. It was possible, Doenitz was a devout Nazi; he was also the man who had helped perfect wolf-pack submarine warfare. Goering, once head of the Luftwaffe, was no longer a factor in anything except guessing games—he was crazy; he was a suicide; he had escaped abroad. Von Ribbentrop was out as German Foreign Minister and cagey Count Lutz Schwerin von Krosigk was in. Berlin fell on May 2. Field Marshal Arnim von Runstedt had already been added to the list of captured field marshals by the Seventh Army. Also on May 2 it was announced that German forces in Italy and Southern Austria had surrendered at Caserta. Free Czechs started their own revolt and battled Germans in Prague. The Fifth and Seventh Armies met at Vipiteno, Italy. On May 4 all the German forces in Holland, Denmark and Northwest Germany surrendered to* Field Marshal Sir Bernard L. Montgomery.

By now the allied advance had gathered unstoppable force. On May 5 the First and Nineteenth Armies, comprising German Army Group G, surrendered to Gen. Jacob L. Devers' U.S. Sixth Army Group in Western Austria and Bavaria; the German First and Nineteenth surrendered to the U.S. Seventh and French First; the German Twenty-fourth Army surrendered to the French First. The Germans were preparing to give up Norway.

On Sunday, May 6, at Reims, France, Col. Gen. Gustav Jodl signed a formal surrender for all German armed forces. YANK's Sgt. Gilpin was at Reims when GIs there got the news:

THE 201st MP Company, whose members handled the guard details when the Germans came to Reims to surrender, is a celebrity-wise outfit. Gen. Eisenhower knows many of the men by their first names and some of them have dined at Churchill's home. They have been the gun-carrying soldiers on hand during a succession of visits to high headquarters by Nazi bigwigs like Franz von Papen, who was described by one of them as looking like "an old goat in golf knickers."

The MPs said Col. Gen. Jodl looked and acted more like the popular idea of a German militarist than any of the other German officers with him at the surrender meeting. He walked and talked with the arrogance that the *Junkers* have developed through a long series of wars. He didn't seem to drink as much as some of the others and before and after each conference the MP outside his bedroom window could see him examining his face in his mirror. After the last conference session Jodl came back to his room, threw open the windows and looked down at Pfc. Jack H. Arnold of Lancaster, Pa. After peering at Arnold, he inhaled deeply and then twisted and pulled at his face before the mirror.

Adm. Hans von Friedeburg, of all the Germans, seems to have impressed the MPs most as what they called a "character." In the words of Pfc. Joseph Fink, who used to build Burroughs adding machines in Detroit, "The Admiral had enough medals hanging on his chest to decorate a Christmas tree."

Fink rode in the car that took the admiral to the German billets. During the ride a British major riding with them brought Friedeburg up to date on current events. He told him the lights were on again in London and Friedeburg, remembering air raids in Germany, replied in English that he hadn't had a good night's sleep in a month. He went on to explain that he had been bombed out of his headquarters three times.

While he stayed in the billets, Friedeburg consumed great quantities of cigars and liquor, but none of this seemed to make any improvement in his testy disposition. When he saw photographs of German atrocities in a copy of the *Stars and Stripes* during a between-conferences discussion of U.S. Army publications he banged his fist on the table in a temper.

Crowds swarmed down Broadway in New York on VE-night, and bright lights were turned on again.

Hitler's henchman Marshal Goering, captured in Austria, posed in his favorite uniform.

Marshal Keitel, German Commander in Chief, signs ratified surrender terms at Russian headquarters in Berlin

Minister Churchill, but, in spite of censorship precautions, it leaked out and set off celebrations in all Allied capitals. YANK reporters in overseas posts from Saipan to Cairo heard the good news as it spread from soldier to soldier, in combat, in camp and on the streets of pass towns:

THE announcement came as an anticlimax to men of the Ninth Army, just as it did to most of the rest of the world. They had been relieved for the last time on the Western Front some days before the signing at Reims and their relief was to them the real end of the war in Europe. Pfc. S. L. Gates, who has a brother in the Marines in the Pacific, figured he'd be heading there soon. Most of the talk was like that—either of home or of possible Pacific duty.

In Paris, where the news had begun as a phoney rumor and then turned true, it was an anticlimax, too. A photographer staged a shot with some French babes kissing some over-happy doughs in front of the Rainbow Corner. "I keep telling everybody that it's over," said an MP at the door of the Red Cross Club who was no longer even checking passes, "but nobody believes me."

Finally, when Paris believed the news, it was just a big-city celebration—crowds and singing and cheers and lots of cognac and girls. People stopped work and airplanes of all the Allied forces buzzed the *Champs Elysees.* Pvt. Ernest Kuhn of Chicago listened to the news come over the radio at the 108th General Hospital. He had just been liberated after 5 months in a Nazi PW camp and he still had some shrapnel in his throat. "I listened to Churchill talk," he said, "and I kept saying to myself, 'I'm still alive. The war is over here and I'm still alive.' I thought of all the guys in the 28th Division Band with me who were dead now. We used to be a pretty good band."

In London there were crowds too, and singing and kissing and cheering. Everybody you spoke to said the news was swell, but they all added a postscript about the Japs. The end of the war in Europe seemed to bring the Pacific war closer than ever to GIs here. Cpl. Robert M. Rhodes of Kittanning, Pa., who works in a base ordnance depot in the U.K., said, "I just can't believe it's over on this side. That is, I can't realize it yet. I figure this VE-day is just one step nearer New York and the Statue of Liberty. I figure it'll take 10 to 12 more months to get rid of the Japs. I'm just going to write home to my wife, 'So far, so good. I'll be seeing you.' "

GI reaction to the surrender was calm in Cairo. There was no singing or dancing in the streets, no great spontaneous demonstration, no fights. T/Sgt. Holis B. Miller of Benedict, Neb., leaning against a staff car parked in front of a downtown hotel, watched the crowds stopping to read the announcement in the extra of the *Stars and Stripes* posted on the hotel wall. "Most of the GIs don't quite know what to make of it," he said. "It doesn't mean much of a change. We won't be getting out of the Army tomorrow or going home." In the Cairo bars, which didn't even enjoy a business boom, men thought mostly of what the celebration might be like in the U. S. "I'll

bet they're having a hot time at home tonight," said Cpl. Paul Furgatch of the Bronx and he ordered another drink.

In the Aleutians there wasn't much formal celebrating either. Mostly there were rumors on "How much better are my chances of getting off this island?" Unit commanders banned "boisterous or disorderly demonstrations" and forbade "discharge of small arms," but many outfits arranged the monthly beer ration to coincide with VE-day. Back of all reaction to the news was the thought that the theater might be due to become important again, that it might live up actively to its slogan, "The Northern Highway to Victory."

In Hawaii there was almost complete lack of interest. The men there were too close to the continuing Pacific war to be unduly jubilant. The ones who got the biggest kicks were those who had close friends or relatives in the European Theater. There wasn't even much talk about VE-day among the GIs. And when they did talk they were usually saying, "Now maybe we can wind *this* war up sooner."

Nobody got very excited on Saipan when the news came over the B-29 squadrons' loudspeakers in the morning. It was like the Hawaiian reaction, only stronger. M/Sgt. Wilbur M. Belshaw, a flight engineer from Vesta, Minn., said what was uppermost in GIs' minds: "The Japs thought they could lick the world. Well, now they've got their chance."

THERE *wasn't much war left in Europe. Germans in Norway moved toward Sweden for internment. The German heavy cruisers Prinz Eugen and Seydlitz were turned over to the British Navy at Copenhagen. A few die-hard groups like the German Seventh Army in Czechoslovakia made a last stab at organized resistance. The official time set for the laying down of all guns in Europe was 2001 hours Eastern War Time, Tuesday, May 8. After that, what fighting remained was unofficial and sporadic. The Russians, justifiably suspicious after earlier Nazi attempts to sign a separate peace with the two other allies, forced Field Marshal Albert von Kesselring to sign a special ratification of surrender in Berlin. Goering turned up, not crazy or dead, but as a prisoner of the celebrity-collecting Seventh Army. Lights went on again in London; the "brownout" was relaxed in New York.*

VE-day had come. People in America had been waiting for it so long they didn't know whether to believe it and, when they did believe it, they didn't quite know what to make of it:

TO GET an over-all view of VE-day in America, YANK asked civilian newspapermen and staff writers in various parts of the country to send in eye-witness reports. From these OPs the reports were much the same. Dallas was quiet, Des Moines was sober, Seattle was calm, Boston was staid.

In some towns crowds gathered and tried to think of something to do to celebrate. Mostly, they didn't seem able to focus their thoughts. Two weeks of spectacular rumors and even more spectacular events had taken the edge off the official victory over Germany. And the press and

The house in which the Germans stayed during the conference looked like a shack on the outside and a palace on the inside. There were paintings on the walls and a grandfather clock, inlaid tile in the bathrooms and comfortable double beds in the bedrooms. There was a bit of a fuss over the first meal because someone had forgotten to get the red wine. Pfc. Frederick A. Stones of Pittsburgh, Pa., commented privately, "If I was running this show I'd throw them a can of C rations."

Stones says that his proposed diet had a practical as well as a vindictive side in that it might have helped shorten the negotiations.

Once Pfc. Joyce Bennet, Wac manageress of the German billets, asked two of the GI orderlies to straighten up the beds of the German officers. The GIs complied but bitched. "We're usually assigned to British Air Marshal Tedder," one of them said, "and he straightens up his own bed and so could these guys."

Speaking of the Germans, a little black-haired Wac from Tarentum, Pa., said, "I felt terribly uneasy serving them coffee. Some officer made a crack about my waiting on Germans while my husband was still shooting them. He didn't stop to think that I'd have preferred to have been spilling the hot coffee down their necks."

On the last day before the Germans signed the piece of paper that officially ended what was to have been Adolf Hitler's New World Order, Col. Gen. Jodl and Adm. Friedeburg were watched by the MPs as they walked in the little garden beside their billet. Friedeburg had relaxed a little, but Jodl was just as stiff necked as ever.

Later, when it was all over except the publicity, the MPs went back to their barracks and had a bull session about the war, the Germans and "Ike." They talked most about "Ike."

Sgt. Henry Wheeler of Youngstown, N. Y., said, "The windup was pretty much what we expected. 'Ike' didn't have anything to do with those phonies until they were ready to quit. Then he went in and told them to sign up.

"And what does he do as he comes out of the meeting? He shakes hands with the first GI he comes to."

And that is the way the war in Europe ended for the 201st MPs.

THE *news of the surrender was to have been held up for a simultaneous announcement by President Truman, Premier Stalin and Premier*

YANK, The Army Weekly, publication issued weekly by Branch Office, Information & Education Division, War Department, 205 East 42d Street, New York 17, N. Y. Reproduction rights restricted as indicated in the masthead on the editorial page. Entered as second class matter July 6, 1942, at the Post Office at New York, N. Y., under the Act of March 3, 1879. Subscription price $3.00 yearly. Printed in the U. S. A.

PAGE 18

dio kept saying: "There's still one war to go."

From Portland, Ore., came a report of a conversation between a Broadway street car conductor and a young woman passenger wearing a service star.

"So this is VE-day," the motorman said. "But we'll have to lick the little yellow men before I go on a toot."

The young woman said: "And my husband will have to come home before I go on a toot."

In Cleveland crowds stood on downtown corners and moved aimlessly along streets where hawkers were selling flags, pompoms, lapel buttons and tin horns. The streets were littered with torn papers and long streamers dangled from office windows and hung from trolley wires—all this the evidence of a brief, wild hubbub following President Truman's 8 A.M. radio announcement on May 8 that victory in Europe really had come.

A man in the Cleveland suburb of Parma painted a fireplug red, white and blue; girls in a candy store threw candy kisses to the crowd; Hitler was burned in effigy at Lakeside and East 9th street; girls danced on the sidewalk; church bells rang; factory whistles blew. But on the whole it was a quiet day, ending with well-attended services in all churches.

Houston's reaction was summed up in one sentence: VE-day came to Houston like Christmas morning to the kid who peeked in the closet the week before and saw his electric train.

New Yorkers milled around the Wall Street district and Times Square, and over a loudspeaker Mayor Fiorello H. LaGuardia told them to behave themselves. In a bar a man said: "I betcha they act like this only in New York and Chicago and San Francisco. "Back in Vermont, where I come from, I betcha they're acting different. I betcha the people are behaving decent, and going to church and praying and not carrying on."

In Chicago a gray-haired man weaved up to the woman behind the cigar counter in the Stevens Hotel lobby. "Aren't you going to celebrate?" the man asked. "Celebrate what?" the woman said. "My two boys are on Okinawa."

San Francisco took it easy. Schools closed an hour early, the Bartenders Union voluntarily shut the saloons. The Junior Chamber of Commerce sponsored an "On to Tokyo" rally in the Civic Auditorium. The United Nations Conference on International Organization went right ahead working in the Opera House and the Veterans' Memorial Building.

In Atlanta the big Bell bomber plant that turns out B-29s operated full blast. Officials said there was no increase in absenteeism.

Des Moines old-timers noted that it was a lot different from the way it had been 27 years before. On Armistice Day, 1918, rioters had filled downtown streets and overturned automobiles, dancing and singing to celebrate the U. S. Army's first victory in Europe. This time, except for a truckload of boys with musical instruments touring the heart of town, there was no revelry.

St. Louis church leaders held services in Memorial Plaza, Emerson Electric Manufacturing, Scullin Steel, Monsanto Chemical and other plants said full crews showed up. Retail stores closed and so did most bars and taverns.

Rain fell in Baltimore during President Truman's speech and streets were as empty as they usually are when it rains at 9 A.M. In the harbor there were impromptu celebrations aboard Norwegian and British vessels.

In Boston office girls sang "Hi, ho, the Merry-O" in Liberty Square, and workmen tearing down the old New England Mutual Building in Post Office Square tolled the bell in the tower. It was the first time the bell had rung in 2 years.

Minneapolis sounded its central air raid warning siren atop the Northwestern National Bank when President Truman officially proclaimed VE-day. For 17 minutes the pigeons in the Loop area wheeled in a capricious wind. Till mid-day the police and fire department kept extra men on hand in case of celebration trouble, but when it was clear that there wasn't going to be any celebration the extras were sent home. Schools and colleges continued classes, and appointments at the Red Cross blood-donor center were kept.

Los Angeles celebrated by launching a 445-foot Victory ship in the California Shipbuilding yards —the 438th ship the yards have turned out. Churches of all denominations held special services, and public offices, retail stores and banks remained open as usual.

Springfield, Mass., stores barricaded their show windows with plywood panels to protect them from VE-day crowds, but there weren't any crowds. The Springfield Armory took down the "Help Wanted" sign which had become almost a landmark at State and Federal Streets. Officials said demands for the Garand rifle had fallen and that lay-offs were expected.

In Thomaston, Conn., an employee of the Seth Thomas clock factory, which has been converted to war production, said: "I don't like to be a fuss-budget, but this doesn't mean much to me. When I stop making fuse parts for shells and start making lock parts again, that will be a wonderful day."

Some German prisoners interned at Fort Oglethorpe, Tenn., near Chattanooga, broke down and cried when they heard it was all over. There was no other display of emotion and no disturbance inside the compound. The post commandant, Col. Howard Clark, made a brief talk at a special retreat ceremony. Thirty minutes later he learned that his son, Lt. William A. Clark, had been killed in action on Luzon on April 18.

Flags were still at half-mast for FDR.

ON OKINAWA, GIs and Marines continued to kill Japs and to be killed by them. It was raining when the VE announcement was broadcast over loudspeakers and the artillery and the noise of planes made it hard to understand. Besides, almost everybody was too busy to pay much attention to it.

SOME of our soldiers may now lay down their arms. For a long time the War Department has planned for this moment when the defeat of our European enemies would permit partial demobilization. It has come nearly 5 years since the first draftees were inducted into the Army in the autumn of 1940—nearly three and a half years since the Japanese attacked us at Pearl Harbor. Part of our mission is now completed. All who can be spared will be released.

The plan for release is based on what the men in the service believed should be the basis of discharge. You yourselves have decided who should be chosen. The needs of war have determined how many shall be chosen and when. You may be assured that the demobilization plan does not interfere with the best strategy we can devise to finish the war with Japan in the shortest possible time and then to get everyone home.

If you are among those selected for discharge, you have my sincere congratulations and good wishes for a deserved return to the country you have served and saved. If you are among those who must continue the fight, you can count upon everything you need to finish the job as soon and with as few casualties as possible. The gratitude of the nation is with you all. May God bless you wherever you are.

HENRY L. STIMSON
Secretary of War

By YANK's Washington Bureau

Now that the war in Europe is over, everybody is talking about what the War Department calls its Plan for the Readjustment of Personnel. This is the plan that will decide who will move from Europe and other inactive theaters to the war against Japan, who will stay behind for occupation and police duty and who will come home, either to stay for awhile in the Army in the U. S. or to get a discharge.

The bare outline of the Plan for the Readjustment of Personnel was announced last September and it hasn't changed much since then. It still calls for enlisted men and women who won't be needed in the war with Japan to be discharged on an individual basis rather than by organizations. It still calls for eligibility for discharge to be decided on a point score system, with the points taking in four factors: length of service in the Army, length of service overseas, the number of decorations or bronze service stars and the number of dependent children you have under 18—but you don't get credit for more than three children.

And it still makes everything in the plan heavily dependent on military necessity. In other words nobody in the Army, no matter how many points he has, will get out unless the Army says that he is not necessary.

As a matter of fact, the only enlisted men in the Army right now who are eligible to get discharged without their commanding officers deciding first whether or not they are essential are men who have been awarded the Congressional Medal of Honor or who are over 42 years old.

The plan still gives no points for age.

Although it has made no fundamental changes in the Plan for the Readjustment of Personnel, the War Department in the past month has thrown a lot more light on some of its details and has revealed some previously secret information on how it is expected to work.

Here are some of the more important facts and figures about the plan that have been revealed:

It has been announced that approximately two million men will be released from the Army during these next 12 months. This two million will include men from the Pacific theaters as well as from Europe. Approximately 1,300,000 of them will be men with high point totals. The rest will be wounded or physically unfit for service or over-age.

Ninety-eight percent of the 1,300,000 men scheduled to be discharged on points during the coming year will have had overseas service.

Seventy-three percent of the 1,300,000 will be men with combat credit—decorations or bronze service stars on their theater ribbons.

Twenty-six percent of 1,300,000 will be fathers.

Redeployment

THE POINT VALUES AND THE CRITICAL SCORE

POINTS. The Army's plan for the readjustment of enlisted personnel calls for an Adjusted Service Rating Card to be issued to each enlisted man and woman. Point totals will be entered on this card covering each of the following four factors:

　　1) Service Credit. One point for each month of Army service between Sept. 16, 1940, and May 12, 1945.

　　2) Overseas Credit. One point for each month served overseas between Sept. 16, 1940, and May 12, 1945.

　　3) Combat Service. Five points for the first and each additional award of the following for service performed between Sept. 16, 1940, and May 12, 1945:

　　　a) Distinguished Service Cross, Legion of Merit, Silver Star, Distinguished Flying Cross, Soldier's Medal, Bronze Star Medal, Air Medal, Purple Heart and Bronze Service Star (battle or campaign participation stars worn on theater ribbon).

　　　b) Credit will also be given to Army enlisted personnel who have been awarded the following decorations by the Navy Department: Navy Cross, Distinguished Service Medal, Legion of Merit, Silver Star, Distinguished Flying Cross, Navy and Marine Corps Medal, Air Medal and Purple Heart Medal.

　　　c) Credit will also be given for those awards and decorations of a foreign country which may be accepted and worn under War Department regulations in effect when readjustment regulations are placed in operation.

　　4) Parenthood Credit. 12 points for each child under 18 years of age born before May 12, 1945, up to a limit of three children.

CRITICAL SCORE. The total of the points earned by the individual enlisted man or woman in the above four categories will be considered a total-point score. The score that the individual must have in order to be eligible for separation from the Army will be known as the Critical Score. The War Department will be unable to announce an official Critical Score until approximately weeks after the readjustment regulations go in operation. There will be one Critical Score for enlisted men in the Army Service Forces and the Army Ground Forces, another for enlisted men in the Army Air Forces and a third one for enlisted women in the WAC.

　　Until it computes and announces these official Critical Scores, the War Department has set for the purpose of aiding immediate demobilization a temporary, "interim" Critical Score of 85 points for enlisted men of the Service, Ground and Air Forces and 44 points for enlisted women of the WAC. These interim Critical Scores will be replaced by the official Critical Scores within the next two months.

In other words 24 percent of the physically fit fathers who are scheduled to be released from the Army during the next year will also be well credited with overseas and combat points. Only 2 percent of the fathers who will be discharged during the coming 12 months will have had no overseas time on their service record. It is a

safe bet that in order to get out they will have to have a very long time in service in the U. S. and the maximum number of three children.

The 1,300,000 will not include many Air Force men. The Air Force will have its own critical score, the term that the War Department is using to describe that very important figure each man's points will have to equal or beat before he can be considered eligible for discharge. The Air Forces critical score will be higher than the critical score for Ground Forces and Service Forces. The WAC critical score will be low because, of course, not many Wacs stand high in overseas or combat points.

The War Department will be unable to compute an official critical score until it does some mathematics during the next two months with individual Adjusted Service Rating Cards and figures out exactly how many men have how many points. Meantime, to start the demobilization of the 1,300,000 able-bodied men, it has set 85 points as an "interim" or temporary critical score not only for the Ground and Service Forces but for the Air Forces as well. The interim critical score for Wacs has been set at 44.

These interim critical scores for the Ground and Service Forces and WAC are expected to be changed to lower figures before they become official.

Another bit of recent news on the Plan for the Readjustment of Personnel, which went over big in Europe, was announced by Gen. Brehon Somervell, Chief of the Army Service Forces. Gen. Somervell said that "the great majority" of the troops in Europe slated for duty in the Far East would go to the Japanese war by way of the States and get furloughs at home en route.

The Army plans to take 3,100,000 men from Europe within the next year, if all goes well, leaving 400,000 behind as occupation forces. Major Gen. Charles P. Gross of the Transportation Corps says that the removal of soldiers from Europe may be done even faster if we can find some enemy passenger ships that are in good condition. The ATC plans to fly home 50,000 men each month.

Gen. Gross estimates that the U. S. Army will leave Europe at the rate of 280,000 men a month for the first quarter of the coming year, 395,000 a month for the second quarter and 269,000 for the third quarter. The rest will be brought home during the last quarter.

Nobody in the War Department has yet made an estimate about the number of men from these 3,100,000 scheduled to leave Europe who will go on to the Japanese war. That depends on a lot of things we don't know the answers to now, such as the progress of our own Pacific campaigns in the next few months, the help we get from Allies and, most important of all, the amount of punishment Japan will take before she quits.

Here are some other details about the Plan for Readjustment of Personnel that you may have missed the last time you read or heard about it:

The War Department says that its point system requirements for eligibility for discharge will remain standard in every theater of operations and in every inactive theater. In other words, a theater cannot set up its own point system.

The War Department says that it will do its best to see that commanding officers do not abuse the military necessity clause, which enables them to keep an enlisted man in the Army no matter how high his critical score happens to be. Theater commanders have been instructed to establish reviewing authorities to pass on individual cases of enlisted men who are being retained in the service despite the fact that their scores are equal to or higher than the critical score.

THIS reviewing deal, of course, like practically everything else in the Army, involves the old business of going through channels. For example, say you're a first sergeant in an outfit in Europe awaiting redeployment. Your CO happens to be the type that leans heavily on others. He has grown to depend on your special knowledge of his company's routine, a knowledge picked up through several years of handling hundreds of details that the CO was either too busy or indifferent to handle. Now, even though you may have no more specialized ability than any other efficient topkick, the CO tags you "essential."

Under the War Department's plan, the CO's word is not final; his request for your retention must go to the next highest in command, your battalion or regimental commander, who can do one of two things. He can approve it, in which case it will be bucked to a higher authority, or he can disapprove it, in which case you will be declared "surplus," and eventually brought back to the States in the prescribed way.

In other words, under WD regulations, your CO's request that you be retained in his outfit can be approved by all of the brass in the Army and still not hold until a reviewing authority puts its stamp on it.

The War Department says that the creation of the reviewing authority was designed to accomplish one thing: to protect a "surplus" man from the whims-and-errors of the brass above him. But there is one catch. There is no time limit attached to the channel-bucking routine. Paper work being what it is, it would probably be a good idea for everyone in this spot to keep his optimism at a reasonably controlled level.

THE Ground Forces men will have an easier time than Service Forces men in getting out of the Army during the coming year. The Service Forces include many highly skilled specialists who cannot be replaced easily, and the supply job in the Far East will be tough.

Under the new regulation Wacs are permitted to apply for discharges if they are married to discharged soldiers.

A lot of outfits in Europe, principally service units of the Service Forces and Air Forces, will have to shove off for the Pacific in a hurry. As a matter of fact, several of them are already on their way. Naturally these outfits will be unable to compute their point scores until after they have been redeployed. That means that men in these outfits with high scores won't know how they stand until they get settled in their new bases. After they get to their new bases, they will have to wait for qualified replacements.

To take care of such cases, the War Department has authorized these outfits to carry a 10 percent overstrength in their T/Os. The overstrength will consist of low-score men who will be trained to replace high-score men on the spot.

The War Department points out, however, that this policy of allowing outfits to carry along replacements as overstrength doesn't necessarily mean that every high-score man in such outfits will be able to get out of the Army fast. There will still be high-score men who may not be replaced until the war with Japan is over.

Here's what is slated to happen to an enlisted man in Europe who has a point total higher than the critical score, who is tagged as not necessary in his own outfit and is therefore declared "surplus." He is transferred to another outfit which is composed of surplus men from other units. This outfit of surplus men will be shipped back to the States directly when and as shipping facilities are available.

In the States, he will be screened to decide whether he will be reassigned to another outfit or discharged. If he is to be discharged, he is sent to a separation center. If he is to be reassigned, he is sent to a Personnel Reception Station near his home. There he draws pay and whatever clothing he needs and gets a furlough. After the furlough he returns to the Personnel Center where he is either sent to a special training combat unit or a station complement outfit.

If a high-score man is declared surplus by his outfit but wants to remain with it just the same, he can do so. But he can't change his mind a few months later and get himself declared surplus again. Once he turns down the chance of becoming surplus, he turns down all chances of getting out of the Army on points until after the Jap war.

Furthermore he has no guarantee that he will be kept in his outfit until the war is over. He stands just as much risk as anybody else of being reassigned somewhere else. For instance, a man may be in an outfit with a soft job he likes and that he would like to keep for a few more years. If he turns down a chance to become a surplus, he may also get reassigned and lose the job within a few months.

Enlisted men in the States will be screened at the base or post to which they are assigned to determine whether or not they are surplus. If they have been overseas and in combat and have high scores, they'll stand as good a chance of getting out as men who are now overseas.

In active theaters like those in Pacific and in China, Burma and India, the plan for returning surplus men won't work in such a wholesale fashion as it will in Europe during the next year. In active theaters there will be no breaking up of whole units. High-score men in the Far East and the Pacific will not be returned until a qualified replacement is available for their job.

The War Department says that officers will have a tougher time than enlisted men in getting released from the service because of their specialized training. They, too, will fill out Adjusted Service Rating Cards and will have point scores. Their point scores will be a secondary consideration, however. The real factor that will decide whether or not they will get out of the Army is military necessity. Officers with long overseas and combat service will get special breaks.

Enlisted men who are declared surplus may have to sweat out long delays before they get back to the States. First of all there will be plenty of slow paper work involved in transferring them to units composed of surplus men. After their transfer, they will have to wait again before the unit is filled with other surplus men.

Then there will be the shipping problem. They will take second place in shipping priority behind men who are going to the Pacific. The equipment in Europe will have to be gathered up and shipped ahead of them and they will have to await the building of special staging areas.

With the cutting down of the Army and the readjustment of its personnel, all physically fit GIs today in the service find themselves in one of four categories:

1) Those who will be retained in their present commands. This includes men on active duty in active theaters, men in troops in inactive theaters slated for occupation duty and men in the States permanently assigned or in training.

2) Those overseas who will be transferred to another theater.

3) Those in the States about to go overseas.

4) Those men overseas and in the States who will be declared surplus and will be screened to decide whether they are essential or eligible to get an honorable discharge.

ADJUSTED SERVICE RATING

LAST NAME—FIRST NAME—INITIAL		SOLDIER'S VERIFICATION
ARMY SERIAL NO.	ARM OR SERVICE	
ORGANIZATION		
MOS TITLE		
SSN	DATE	

TYPE OF CREDIT	NUMBER	MULTIPLY BY	CREDITS
1. SERVICE CREDIT (*Number of months in Army since September 16, 1940*)			
2. OVERSEAS CREDIT (*Number of months served overseas*)			
3. COMBAT CREDIT (*Number of Decorations and Bronze Service Stars*)			
4. PARENTHOOD CREDIT (*Number of children under 18 years old*)			
TOTAL CREDITS			

CERTIFIED BY (*Signature*)

FOR INSTRUCTIONS SEE RR 1-1

WD AGO FORM 1 FEB 1945 **163** This form supersedes WD AGO Form 163, 29 August 1944, which may be used until existing stocks are exhausted.

Here's the official score card.

YANK is published weekly by the enlisted men of the U. S. Army and is for sale only to those in the armed services. Stories, features, pictures and other material from YANK may be reproduced if they are not restricted by law or military regulations, provided proper credit is given, release dates are observed and specific prior permission has been granted for each item to be reproduced. Entire contents copyrighted, 1945, by Col. Franklin S. Forsberg and reviewed by U. S. military censors.

MAIN EDITORIAL OFFICE
205 EAST 42d STREET, NEW YORK 17, N. Y.

EDITORIAL STAFF

Managing Editor, Sgt. Joe McCarthy, FA; A Director, Sgt. Arthur Weithas, DEML; Assistant Managing Editor, Sgt. August Loeb, AAF; Assistant Art Director, Sgt. Ralph Stein, Med.; Pictures, Sgt. Leo Hofeller, Armd.; Features, Sgt. Marion Hargrove, FA; Sports, Cpl. Tom Shehan, FA; Overseas Editor, Sgt. Al Hine, Engr.; U. S. Editor, Sgt. Hilary H. Lyons, CA; Associate Editors, Sgt. John Hay, Inf.; Cpl. Margaret Davis, WAC; Sgt. Ralph Boyce, AAF; Cpl. Max Novak, TC.
WASHINGTON, Cpl. John Haverstick, CA.
FRANCE, Sgt. Merle Miller, AAF; Sgt. Charles Brand, AAF; Sgt. Mack Morriss, Inf.; Sgt. Ed Cunningham, Inf.; Sgt. Howard Brodie, Sig. Corps; Sgt. Saul Levitt, AAF; Sgt. Allan Ecker, AAF; Sgt. Reg Kenny, Armd.; Sgt. Robert McBrinn, Sig. Corps; Sgt. Ralph G. Martin, Med.; Pfc. Pat Coffey, AAF; Cpl. Howard Katzander, CA; Pfc. David Whitcomb, AAF; Pvt. David Berger, Engr.
BRITAIN, Sgt. Durbin L. Horner, CA; Sgt. Sanderson Vanderbilt, CA; Sgt. John Scott, Engr.; Sgt. Earl Anderson, AAF; Sgt. Frank Brandt, Med.; Sgt. Francis Burke, AAF; Cpl. Jack Coggins, CA; Cpl. Edmund Antrobus, Inf.; Pfc. Tom Flannery, AAF; Sgt. Rudolph Sanford, AAF.
AUSTRALIA-PHILIPPINES, Sgt. Lafayette Locke, AAF; Sgt. Charles Rathe, DEML; Sgt. Douglas Borgstedt, DEML; Sgt. Dick Hanley, AAF; Sgt. Ozzie St. George, Inf.; Cpl. Roger Wrenn, Sig. Corps; Sgt. Charles D. Pearson, Engr.; Cpl. John McLeod, Med.; Sgt. Marvin Fasig, Engr.; Cpl. Joe Stefanelli, Engr.; Sgt. Bill Young, Inf.; Sgt. Robert McMillan, FA; Pfc. Dale Kramer, MP; Cpl. Frank J. Beck, DEML; Sgt. Roger W. Cowan, DEML; Sgt. Jack F. Crowe, DEML; Sgt. Lionel Wathall, DEML.
CENTRL PACIFIC, Sgt. Larry McManus, CA; Pfc. George Burns, Sig. Corps; Pfc. John O. Armstrong, Inf.; Sgt. Bill Reed, Inf.; Cpl. James Goble, Armd.; Cpl. Ted Burrows, DEML; Evans Wylie SPlc (PR), USCGR; Don Morgan Ylc, USCGR; Vernon H. Roberts Slc, USNR; Mason E. Pawlak CPhoM, USNR; Cpl. Lon Wilson, Sig. Corps.
MARIANAS, Cpl. Tom O'Brien, DEML; Sgt. Dil Ferris, AAF; Sgt. Jack Ruge, DEML; Sgt. Paul Showers, AAF; Pfc. Justin Gray, Rangers.
ITALY, Sgt. Harry Sions, AAF; Sgt. Dan Polier, AAF; Sgt. Nelson Gruppo, Engr.; Cpl. George Barrett, AAF; Pfc. Ira Freeman, Cav.; Pfc. Dave Shaw, Inf.; Sgt. Don Breimhurst, AAF; Pfc. Werner Wolff, Sig. Corps.
INDIA-BURMA and CHINA, Sgt. Paul Johnston, AAF; Sgt. George J. Corbellini, Sig. Corps; Sgt. Dave Richardson, CA; Sgt. Walter Peters, QM; Cpl. Jud Cook, DEML.
ALASKA, Sgt. Ray Duncan, AAF.
IRAN-IRAQ, Cpl. Alfred Kynch, DEML; Pvt. Ray McGovern, Inf.
PANAMA, Cpl. Richard Douglass, Med.
PUERTO RICO, Sgt. Don Cooke, FA.
AFRICA-MIDDLE EAST, Sgt. Richard Paul, DEML.
ICELAND, Sgt. John Moran, Inf.
NEWFOUNDLAND, Sgt. Frank Bode, Sig. Corps.
NAVY, Donald Nugent Sp(X)3c.

■

Commanding Officer, Col. Franklin S. Forsberg.
Executive Officer, Lt. Col. Jack W. Weeks.
Business Manager, Maj. North Bigbee.
Procurement Officer, Maj. Gerald J. Rock.
OVERSEAS BUREAU OFFICERS. France, Lt. Col. Charles L. Holt; Britain, Capt. Harry R. Roberts; Australia-Philippines, Lt. Col. Harold B. Hawley; Central South Pacific, Maj. Josua Eppinger; Marianas, Maj. Justus J. Craemer; Italy, Maj. Robert Strother; Burma-India, Capt. Harold A. Burroughs; Alaska, Lt. Grady E. Clay Jr.; Iran, Capt. Frank Gladstone; Panama, Capt. Howard Carswell; Middle East, Capt. Knowlton Ames.

FADE-OUT

This Week's Cover

IN the weeks before VE-day Hitler's armies shrank down to nothing. Like his own country, the German soldier on the cover was running toward defeat and fading out of the picture. And Japan, now the subject of our undivided attention, came sharply into focus.

DON'T YOU KNOW THERE'S A WAR OVER?

THE American Army has won another one of its wars. That war smashed one of the greatest military machines in history and saved our country from one of the most dangerous threats its freedom has faced. According to the book the winning of such a big and important war should have brought us a deep feeling of satisfaction and pride and peace. But this war did not end according to the book.

The book does not call for an army to turn away from the successful ending of one war and to find, instead of a farewell pat on the back and mustering-out pay, another war waiting to be finished. The GIs who did the fighting against the Germans were not exactly overwhelmed with satisfaction and pride and peace when they heard the big news of Victory in Europe. They felt a great relief because the danger of getting killed that had been hanging over them since they had landed on the continent was no longer close. Then they started sweating out the Pacific. Nor did most of the GIs fighting the Japs get much satisfaction or pride or peace out of their Army's defeat of Germany. They were too busy to give it a great deal of thought.

Maybe it is good for us to feel that way right now. Maybe this is no time to be throwing out our chests and telling ourselves that we did all right in Europe. Perhaps we should be thinking of what lies ahead in Asia and nothing else.

Maybe, on the other hand, it wouldn't do us any harm to stop for a moment, no matter what part of the world we are in and no matter what part of the present war concerns us most, and look back of what our Army did to the Germans and the Italians during the past three years.

After Pearl Harbor, it was agreed that our best bet was to help the Russians and the British win the European war first. In the summer and early fall of 1942, they stopped the German advance at Stalingrad and El Alamein, the two turning points of the war, and in order to push the enemy back into Berlin they needed everything we could give them. So we sent the bulk of our air and ground forces to the Mediterranean and Western Fronts. The war in Europe became the first big test of the fighting ability of the American soldier and the tactical ability of his commanding officers in modern warfare.

We went up for that test with all the odds against us and very little in our favor. Our new civilian army was facing the most highly trained and efficient soldiers the world had ever known. In preparing for the war, they were years ahead of us.

There were those who also believed that the American Army was surpassed by the German Army in the fundamental things that are more necessary in the winning of a war than training or tactics or weapons. They said that our officers and enlisted men were amateur soldiers at heart. They said that our soft and free democratic way of life would not stand up against the cold regimentation of Fascism when it came to a showdown. They said we did not have the will to fight, the guts to take it and the ruthlessness to hand it out.

That's how it was when we went to Europe in 1942.

But the American Army, so far behind the German Army in experience and knowledge, caught up to it fast and in three years wiped off the best that it had to offer, first in North Africa, in Sicily and then on the Continent.

Our Allied command, supposedly no match for the brains of the renowned German General Staff, baffled them time and again. There was the depth of the invasion bombardment which kept their reinforcements away from the Normandy beaches; the break-through at Saint Lo; the unbelievable shift of the Third Army from the Saar that stopped the Ardennes counteroffensive; the battle of wits along the Rhine that led to the greatest double enveloping movement in military history and the trapping of 317,000 Germans in the Ruhr pocket.

And the American officers and men, despite the softness of their previously unregimented life, managed in some outfits to stand as much as 500 days in the line without displaying any sign of democratic weakness. They crossed the Rapido River in Italy five times without losing their will to fight. They proved at Kasserine, Hill 609, Salerno, Anzio, Omaha Beach, Aachen, Huertgen, Bastogne and many other places that they could take it and dish it out.

Maybe some of us don't know there's a war over. In that war the American Army, combined with the Russian Army, the British Army and the other United Nations forces, played a major role in giving the greatest German Army in history a terrific beating. That makes the American Army today one of the most powerful military machines of all time.

And maybe it isn't considered the proper thing to say from a morale viewpoint right now but we would be glad to put any amount of money on it against Japan.

"All right, men. You've had your 10-minute break. Now start policing up the area."

PFC. Tom Flannery

NEXT TO GO

YANK
THE ARMY WEEKLY

VJ ISSUE
SEPT. 7, 1945
VOL. 4, NO. 12 • 5 CENTS

The answer to the biggest question on any GI's mind is still iffy. YANK assembles here the best dope at the time of going to press on what the WD plans.

By Sgt. H. N. OLIPHANT
YANK Staff Writer

WASHINGTON—The plan the War Department has announced for demobilizing some 5,000,000 men within a year may or may not be your idea of a good deal. But the big question to GIs who remember and were POd by the rotation deal is: Good or bad, will it work?

The WD answers that $64 job this way: The demobilization plan will work okay *if:*

1) We get the breaks on the occupation detail. (Widespread internal disorders in Japan or the threat of a renewal of hostilities would demand the retention of an army considerably larger than that now planned for.)

2) Congressional action doesn't snafu the basic principles of the demobilization pattern as it now stands. (Congress could, for example, abruptly abolish the draft; such action, the WD says, would shut off the monthly supply of thousands of inductees slated to be replacements.)

3) The transportation set-up functions with a minimum of hitches.

All this may sound as if the WD is getting ready to send out TS slips instead of discharge papers. Luckily, that's not quite the case. The WD says it is merely playing it safe by taking into account any snags that may occur in the future. Actually, the sentiment around the Pentagon is that the demobilization machinery ought easily to be able to spring 5,000,000 men out of the Army within 12 months.

The high brass doesn't appear to feel that either Separation Centers or shipping will prove to be bottlenecks. As far as Separation Centers are concerned, the WD points out that the post-VE-Day Readjustment and Redeployment plan gave them a four-month "trial run" and a chance to iron out a lot of wrinkles that emerged.

In addition, the Separation Centers have been expanded and plans are in the works for them to take over certain reception center facilities should the need arise.

A colonel who helped in the evolution of the separation procedure told YANK that further expansion of Separation Centers probably won't be necessary. At the peak, he added, Separation Centers should be able to handle at least 500,000 dischargees a month.

The other possible bottleneck, shipping, should also be a cinch to break. During May, June and July, despite the fact that the overwhelming emphasis was on winning the Far East war, 800,000 men were returned from Europe to the U. S. The Pacific run is twice as long as the Atlantic run. But distance won't matter so much because thousands of tons of shipping formerly used for the redeployment of troops and supplies from Europe to the Far East will now be available for demobilization uses.

The demobilization plan, like the old Readjustment plan put into effect last May, is based on the old point system, and the same point values go for the same four factors: Service credit, overseas credit, combat credit and parenthood credit. But there are at least two important differences between the two plans:

1) R-Day (Redeployment Day), May 12, 1945, the date at which all computations of point scores stopped under the old set-up, will be discarded just as soon as our occupation needs in the Far East are ascertained, and a new date will be substituted, allowing troops credit for service after May 12, 1945.

2) A lower critical score will be established for both EM and Wacs and "further reductions in this score will be made periodically to insure that discharges proceed at the highest rate permitted by transportation." As of the day of Japan's surrender, no definite score had been announced, but most authorities at that time were pretty generally agreed that it would be in the neighborhood of 75 for EM.

Under the demobilization plan, you will compute your score in exactly the same way as you did under the Readjustment plan. When a new critical score is announced, the only difference will be that instead of using May 12, 1945, as your deadline for points, you will include all points you have earned up to the new deadline date.

The demobilization plan does not provide credit for dependents other than three children under 18, and no point credit is given for age. The age limit for the Army, however, has been lowered from 40 to 38, and this limit, according to a Pentagon colonel, will be progressively lowered as demobilization takes full effect.

That worn-out bit of double-talk—the "military necessity" gag—should just about disappear under the demobilization plan. For all practical purposes, the WD insists, the words "essential" and "non-surplus" will be tossed out.

Actually, only men with four types of jobs can be stuck; they really fall in specialized categories: *1)* orthopedic attendants; *2)* acoustic technicians; *3)* electroencephalographic specialists; *4)* transmitter attendants, fixed station.

All this doesn't mean that you can't be retained temporarily even if you don't belong in one of the foregoing groups, but under a regulation being considered by the WD, you can't be held longer than six months after VJ-Day.

THE first job is to get the armies of occupation set. "That job," a Pentagon colonel explained, "takes priority over everything in this plan, just like beating Japan took priority over everything in the Readjustment plan. We've got to make damned sure, in a hurry, that the Japs don't hole up and get a chance to start an underground movement that could cause us plenty of grief later on.

"Therefore, our No. 1 task is to get enough men on the spot as soon as possible and in the right places to insure a real peace. After that has been accomplished and the system of supply for the occupation troops is clicking, the demobilization process can go forward in full swing."

How many men will be needed for occupation duty? The answer to that one depends on several things. First of all, we have no way of knowing as yet what problems we'll encounter in Japan. There is a terrific density of population to consider, and that fact added to the screwy twist in the Japanese mind will in all probability force us to keep plenty of manpower around to police the area constantly and thoroughly. At the same time, our occupation army in Europe—possibly 400,000 men—will continue on the job until Congress decides there's no further use for it.

In addition, we'll have to keep, according to the WD's estimate, around half a million men on duty in the U. S., Alaska, Panama and Hawaii. These will be used to man permanent garrisons and to see that transportation and supply for the occupation armies don't bog down. Finally, all or most of the islands we have captured in the Pacific will have to be garrisoned for an unspecified time. All these needs, the WD figures, will ultimately require a peacetime Army of at least 2½ million men. Presumably, the 2½ million would consist of guys with extremely low point scores, regulars and new inductees.

Many more men than that will be needed at first, principally because of our uncertainty over what the internal situation in Japan will develop into, but most of the big brass here believe that the normal discharge procedure, spreading demobilization over a 12-month period, will insure there being enough troops around to take care of any incidents that may occur in the early phases of the occupation.

Granting priorities to the occupation armies doesn't necessarily mean, however, that the process of getting eligibles out of the Army will be impeded much, if at all. The mechanism for demobilization, says the WD, is tuned so that it can go simultaneously with the machinery that builds and maintains our armies of occupation.

First to be released under the demobilization plan are the 550,000 men who had 85 or more points under the Readjustment plan. According to the colonel, these men are being discharged just as fast as they can be moved to separation centers, or in the case of high-pointers overseas, loaded in ships and planes and returned to the States. While he was reluctant to make any definite prediction as to the exact time it would take to spring *all* high-pointers, the colonel did say, "It is perfectly possible that most of them will be back in civvies within 60 days after VJ-Day."

Of the half-million high-pointers under the original Readjustment plan, those who were in the States when Japan surrendered were necessarily slated to get out first; indeed, the War Department announced that it would try to get all these out by August 31. Accordingly, some guys in the U. S. with a bare 85 points got out sooner than some men overseas with 100 plus.

That may appear unjust, but WD spokesmen justify it on the score of expediency. They describe the demobilization process as a giant funnel. The eligible men already in the States (or en route) would clog the funnel if they were kept sweating it out until overseas troops with higher scores reached the States.

There has been a lot of latrine talk lately about a so-called Army plan to regulate the flow of dischargees back into civilian life, not on the basis of high-point scores but on the basis of whether a guy has a job waiting for him when he gets out. There is no such regulation in the War Department's plan for demobilization and none is being considered, although Congress could conceivably make such a regulation if it decided that it would be in the best interests of the national economy. But not the WD. The WD says its sole job is to get 5½ million men out of the Army just as soon as possible.

Another latrine rumor has it that men eligible for point discharges will be given furloughs in the States before their release so that they can look around for jobs on the Army's time. That's a phony, too. When your number is called you can do only one of two things. You can walk up and get your discharge papers, or you can choose to stay in the Army.

The choice to remain in the Army may sound a little wacky to most of us, but some GIs are thinking seriously about it. High-pointers who elect to remain in the Army have three choices:

1) They can enlist in the regular Army.

2) If they are overseas they can volunteer to remain for the duration-plus-six-months with the occupation army in the theater to which they are presently assigned.

3) Whether they are overseas or in the U. S. they can volunteer for duty in the U. S. for the duration-plus-six.

If you decide to enlist in the regular Army you'll be required to take a three-year hitch. You'll be able to keep the rank you had at time of discharge, but how much freedom you'll have in choosing your arm of service hasn't been decided. The WD is working on plans for an intensive stay-in-the-Army campaign which is expected to include inducements in the way of educational opportunities, easy promotions, retirement privileges, and so on.

The other two deals—volunteering for continued duty for the duration-plus-six—involve several *ifs.* First, if you are overseas you can elect to stay in the theater in which you are presently stationed provided your CO decides there's a legitimate need for your services and if he wants you around. If he accepts you, you're stuck only for the duration-plus-six. You won't be required to join the regulars.

You can volunteer for duty in the U. S., too, without joining the regulars. If there's room for you, you'll probably be accepted. On this deal you also sign for the duration-plus-six.

In case you're still baffled over the "duration-plus-six" business, here are the facts: You were inducted under the law for the duration and six months "after the date of the termination of hostilities." This termination-of-hostilities date has nothing to do with the cease-fire order. It will be a date, defined by law, as "the date proclaimed by the President . . . or the date specified in a concurrent resolution of Congress, whichever is earlier."

THE Marine Corps is using exactly the same plan as the Army used for its Readjustment plan. As of August 14, the day the Japs said they'd quit, it took 85 points to get out of the Marines. The Navy and Coast Guard use a different plan. The Navy gives half a point for each year of age, figured to the nearest birthday; half a point for each full month of active duty since September 1, 1939, and 10 points for a dependent. (It doesn't matter whether you have more than one dependent; you get just 10 points for your total of dependents.) The critical score for Navy EM is 44 points; for enlisted Waves, 29; for male officers, 49; for Wave officers, 35. The Navy, too, will lower its critical scores as "military commitments permit." From 1½ to 2½ million men and women will be released under the Navy's plan within a year to 18 months.

'How soon OUT?"

VICTORY

THREE years, eight months and seven days after Pearl Harbor total victory came to the United States of America and all the Allies. On the 14th of August, 1945, the last Axis enemy went down to that total defeat which the democracies, some of whom had faced up to Rome-Berlin-Tokyo aggression long before the 7th of December, 1941, had solemnly pledged themselves to bring about.

In this nation, and throughout the Allied world, the contrast between those two days was the contrast between shock, dread and near-defeat and relief, thanksgiving and unqualified triumph. There was another difference, too.

To the citizens of the United States—and indeed of all the countries that later became the United Nations—Pearl Harbor had been a blow-without-warning. In its unexpectedness it had brought a mental shock almost as severe as the physical shock of the bombs that fell on Hickam Field and on the ships in harbor. VJ-Day came to a nation waiting for and well schooled in victory.

America's armed forces had had a major share in Allied triumphs all over the globe. The weapons forged in its factories and carried on its ships and planes to every part of the world had proved its industrial supremacy. VJ-Day had come sooner than most Americans had dared hope, but for months none had doubted that it would arrive.

When it did come, after a five-day wait while the Samurai fumed and quibbled over the details of defeat, there was such an outpouring of emotion as Americans had never known. Wherever Americans were gathered together—whether in Louisville, Ky., Berlin or Manila—the pattern of celebration was much the same. There were roars of rejoicing, high hopes for reunions, and prayers. The prayers were offered in gratitude and in remembrance of those who had died for a day they could not mark.

In America the celebration outdid anything within the memory of living men. It made VE-Day seem silent; it far overshadowed Armistice Day, 1918. On the Continent of Europe and on continents and islands where end-of-war had never found U. S. troops before, it was a day without precedent. A chapter, perhaps a whole book, of history had ended, and a word that had figured much in American thoughts for three years, eight months and seven days—a word often spoken, but always in terms of the past or of an unsure future—could be spoken now in terms of the living present. The word was peace.

DALLAS

Peace came to Dallas like a mixture of Hallowe'en and Christmas. The day itself had been quiet, because, as everywhere else, there had been too many false alarms and people had grown cautious. But a White House announcement at 6 P.M. changed all that.

It took just 30 minutes for the celebration to get under way here. From all parts of the city thousands flocked into the downtown area. Bus and streetcar schedules were hopelessly disorganized. The howlingest mob in Dallas's recent history made short work of the anti-noise ordinance, conceived by the city fathers to speed war production.

Sirens came on 30 minutes late, but made up for their tardiness by their volume. Paper cascaded out of downtown office windows, while street sweepers looked on helplessly, then laughed and joined in the fun.

Centering at Commerce and Akard Streets, the celebration fanned out to take in the entire downtown area, with parades of yelling and chanting pedestrians weaving through lines of cars with horns blaring full blast. Elsewhere shirt-tail parades and group singing swelled the volume of sound.

Pillows in the rooms of the Adolphus and Baker Hotels were ripped apart, and their feathery contents floated through the air. Socks came next, with other odds-and-ends following, while Abe Berger, publicity man for the Adolphus, looked worriedly up at the windows and wondered how long they'd stay put.

The long-awaited announcement left many pedestrians silent, however. For one woman the news had come too late. On her shoulder, between

YANK, The Army Weekly, publication issued weekly by Branch Office, Information & Education Division, War Department, 205 East 42nd Street, New York 17, N. Y. Reproduction rights restricted as indicated in the masthead on the editorial page. Entered as second class matter July 6, 1942, at the Post Office at New York, N. Y., under the Act of March 3, 1879. Subscription price $3.00 yearly. Printed in the U. S. A.

the arms of a silver V, was a picture of her son in uniform. He had been killed in action several months ago.

Mrs. Mary Williams, a pretty redhead, said she had been waiting to eat, but her appetite had vanished. "I stepped outside just as the news came," she said. "Then a chill came over me and I had a feeling that was more like sadness than joy." She couldn't help crying, she was so thankful: Her husband, Boyd Williams, is somewhere in the Pacific with the Navy.

A solid mass packed Akard between Commerce and Elm, with cars lined up from signal light to signal light. An Army private walked up to an MP standing at Akard and Commerce. The soldier had made the rounds of the liquor stores just before a telephone conference of owners had resulted in their closing for the night in the midst of a tremendous run. Toting one bottle under an arm and drinking steadily from another, the soldier stared the MP in the face. "Mercy on you, MP," he murmured, "mercy on you," and walked off.

At the USO on Main Street a crowd of servicemen hung over a radio waiting for the President's announcement. When the news came they remained quiet, listening attentively to every word. Then they cut loose with a yell, most of them pouring out into the street to join other celebrators bent on organizing a demonstration.

Some stayed behind. There was Pfc. William E. Boynicki, 39, who sat down at once to write to his wife in Miami, Fla. "All I want to do is go home and tie myself to my wife's apron strings and never leave home again," he murmured. "I've been in this man's army five years. That's enough."

Pfc. Guy Rogers of Dallas, just back from two years and two days overseas, was ready to sit down for a discussion of chemical warfare, a field in which he had worked. The atomic bomb, he figured, had really done the job. Then he paused, struck by an idea. "Now if they would just say that all of us fellows were going to be discharged," he said, "we would really blow our tops."

NEW YORK CITY
At 7:30 A.M. on Friday, August 10, 1945, the thermometer in New York City read 66 degrees, the sun was shining, the humidity wasn't bad, and all in all it was one of the town's better summer mornings. The atomic bomb and Russia were in the war now, and the 7:30 news broadcasts were much concerned with the accomplishments of these new allies.

A moment later it came. Japan, according to the Tokyo radio, wanted out. Word of the momentous broadcast spread quickly, but in New York there was no immediate sense of jubilation. Instead, a mood of trance-like suspense prevailed. Nothing was official, nothing was definite, no one could do anything but hope.

Thin lines of earnest people gathered almost at once in Times Square to await developments as they were flashed on the electric news sign running around the Times Tower Building. They didn't know it then, of course, but they were the advance guard of a host of New Yorkers who would be keeping vigil there for five days and nights to come.

"Whadya say, sarge?" said one GI to another in the ranks of an expectant throng listening to a sidewalk radio in the entrance to a newsreel theater on East 42d Street. "Kinda quiet, ain't it, for a big deal like this? People seem to be walking around in a dream. Yep, that's what the whole thing seems like—a dream."

Among the first in the city to act on the news were the proprietors of establishments in the Times Square area who feared for the safety of their plate-glass windows. By 8 A.M. Toffenetti's Restaurant, on the southeast corner of Broadway and 43d Street, had a crew of carpenters busy putting up barricades as a precaution against crowds, and the Astor Hotel and other vulnerable spots were quick to follow suit.

And so the long morning wore on. Civilians stopped GIs in the streets, offering to buy them drinks, but by and large the GIs didn't seem inclined to accept. Everything was still too uncertain to get party-minded. Down in Wall Street, where ticker tape can be counted on to fly at the first sign of exuberance in the big town, there wasn't so much as a shred of paper in the gutters. A recruiting station for Waves, situated in front of the Sub-Treasury Building at the corner of Wall and Nassau, remained open for business, but there were no customers.

Thousands shouted together when news of Jap surrender came to Times Square in New York.

A sailor and a Wac tore up the sidewalk Broadway with a swinging, strutting victory jiv

Word went out that President Harry S. Truman was calling a Cabinet meeting at 2 P.M.—Somehow or other this was distorted in Manhattan's garment center into a rumor that he had accepted the Jap peace offer, and a celebration, as cockeyed as it was short-lived, began. Seventh and Eighth Avenues from 34th to 40th Streets and the side streets in the area became a crazy quilt of bits and patches of brightly colored cloth thrown from the windows of buildings by excited dressmakers. Vendors popped up from nowhere to peddle VJ-Day buttons at two bits per button. The Department of Sanitation rushed sprinkler trucks around to wet down the mess, but not in time. In the midst of all the excitement, some of the pieces of cloth on Eighth Avenue caught fire from a cigarette butt, and traffic had to be stopped because of the danger to gasoline tanks. "In the garment center, we've always prematured our celebrations," said one disgusted elevator operator.

During the afternoon, 5,000 policemen were stationed in the midtown area to handle anticipated crowds, but at 3:30 P.M. came an announcement that the White House would have no further news until morning and the cops were called in. And so the restless, indecisive day petered out. In the theater district that night there were no more than the usual summer crowds and local radio stations hammered home this message at frequent intervals: "If you have a war job, keep plugging. The war is not yet over."

Nor was the war over during the long weekend that followed. Saturday it was hot—sunny again, and hot. Just after dawn the *Queen Elizabeth* came in with 14,800 GIs from the ETO, a

lot of whom figured that now they wouldn't ha to take another free ocean ride on Uncle Sam, they'd been expecting to. By afternoon the stree were all but deserted and from one end of t city to the other girls sprawled on teneme roofs in skimpy bathing suits, picking up su tans for their legs in place of the silk stockin they couldn't buy. The Japs, the radio said, h been told that Hirohito could stay but that we be the boss, and everyone realized it would no be some time before we'd have an answer to th That evening the West 54th Street police stati reported fewer people in Times Square th there usually are on a summer Saturday nig There was nothing to do but wait.

The skies were clear again Sunday, as inde they were throughout the five days of waiti that seemed like a century, and the thermomet was in the low 80s, making it a fine day to go the beaches. Thousands turned up at Con Island and Orchard Beach, toting portable radi along with them so that they could keep with developments, of which there were non Learned commentators went on the air to expla hat was holding up Japan's surrender, although ey obviously had no more idea than their steners of what the deal was. A mass of thanksving for the peace that had not yet come was ld at St. Patrick's Cathedral on Fifth Avenue. ayor F. H. LaGuardia broadcast this plea: "Do t celebrate unless there is good reason to celebrate."

Then, as it apparently must at the end of any ar, came the phony report of surrender. At 34 P.M. the United Press sent out this flash: ASHINGTON—JAPAN ACCEPTS SURRENDER TERMS F THE ALLIES. Two minutes later came the untermanding order: EDITORS—HOLD UP THAT ASH. But by then it was too late. Radio stations d already broadcast the false news and ousands upon thousands of people had dashed om their living rooms out into the streets.

The U. P. later explained that it hadn't sent t the report and it put up a $5,000 reward for formation leading to the identification and conction of the culprit who in some manner had anaged to slip the hot but screwy dope out er its wires. By that time, however, crowds ere whooping it up in Times Square, a bit synetically, to be sure, since all they had to do as to look up at the electric news sign and read at the war was definitely not over. Most of e hullabaloo was kicked up by kids of bobby-x age just raising the roof for the hell of it. midnight it was way past their bedtimes and, terly pooped out, they straggled home.

Monday was a stinker. The weather was hot d humid and a sweating city was fretfully veating the surrender out. Whereas at first eryone had more or less taken it for granted at Japan would accept our terms, now as the urs passed people began to fear that it wasn't er yet by any means. The day dragged on, a y on which most New Yorkers had thought ey would be celebrating and on which they stead had to return reluctantly to their routine ores. Then, that evening at 6:25, came a radio port that a broadcasting station in Brazzaville, frica, had picked up an announcement from

nitely in the bag. Frenzied babes rushed through the crowds kissing servicemen, and wolves, in uniform and out, prowled about mousing any and every likely-looking number while the cops looked on, grinning indulgently. At 3:17 in the afternoon a sailor and his honey were to be seen lying flat on the pavement necking furiously as the throngs shuffled about them. Traffic was barred from the Times Square area all day so that the mob, which ultimately numbered 2,000,-000, could run loose.

All the way from Staten Island to Van Cortlandt Park, from the Hudson River to the remotest outposts of Queens, the streets were littered with tons of paper torn up and scattered about by New York City's seven and a half million elated citizens. In Chinatown, where the residents have relatives in the land the Japs first tried to overrun, they put on the sacred dragon dance ordinarily staged only on the Chinese New Year. Up in Harlem there was jive and jitterbugging in the streets. Flatbush Avenue and Fulton Streets, two of Brooklyn's main drags, were jammed.

Frantic and madcap as the shindy was by day, however, it was nothing compared to what it became at night after President Truman made his 7 o'clock announcement that the war was over. This, at last, was the official end, and at once the whole city, already a seething turmoil, seemed to explode. To the blasts of automobile horns and the shrilling of whistles the *Queen Elizabeth*, docked in the Hudson, added the deep, throaty boom of her horn. Some of the bars around Times Square closed down, unable to cope with the crush, but it was a cinch to get a drink since scores of people were wandering around carrying quart bottles of the stuff and all were in a generous mood.

On, on, on it went into the night and the next night as the biggest city in the world went its way toward picking up the biggest hangover in its history. It was a hangover few would ever regret.

—Sgt. SANDERSON VANDERBILT

a 40-year-old, rather liquefied, bald-headed gentleman who chose that moment to try to slide, no hands, down the Willard's banister. He made it halfway.

The number of bottles which were passed freely among strangers would have startled anyone who has ever paid $50 for a quart of the stuff in such far-off places as New Georgia. One officer, standing in the middle of Pennsylvania Avenue outside the White House, waved a fifth of rye at arm's length, repeatedly inviting passers-by to "have a drink on the European Theater of Operations."

A T/Sgt. rounded off his night's excitement by shinnying up a light pole in front of the White House and leading the crowd in song, beating time with a small American flag. He concentrated on corny numbers like "Keep the Home Fires Burning" and "Home on the Range," and between songs he led yells of "We Want Harry!" But the President did not repeat his early-evening appearance. There were many officials in Washington that night who were too busy with the new problems of peace to celebrate the end of the war.

Not everyone on the streets was demonstrative, either. "I can't get that jubilant," said a T-5 thoughtfully. "You'd be surprised how many didn't get drunk tonight. I didn't."

And a middle-aged white-haired man with a Scottish burr remarked sadly, "You know, soldier, it's a nice celebration, but I lost two sons—two sons. It might be a joke to some, but . . ."

And the middle-aged man shook his head and walked slowly away.

—Sgt. BARRETT McGURN

CAMP KILMER, N. J.

Dusk had just about settled over the rolling Jersey countryside when the factory whistles of nearby New Brunswick began screaming that the second World War was over.

In War Department Theater No. 1 a captain in a clean, crisp tropical-worsted uniform adorned with an American Defense ribbon was standing on the stage. He was delivering the standard "welcoming lecture" to some GIs who had just got off a ship from Europe and were to be redeployed to the Pacific.

"Now in conclusion, men," he said, "I wish to warn you that any demonstration that results in damage to camp property will result in the postponement of your home furloughs. May your brief stay at Camp Kilmer be pleasant."

Someone hurried onto the stage from the wings and whispered to him: "Captain, President Truman has just announced that the war is over! Tell 'em that before they leave."

"No," replied the captain. "As far as Camp Kilmer is concerned there is to be no announcement of peace until the Colonel hears it from the War Department through channels and announces it officially."

"But President Truman announced it over the radio—it *is* official—"

"Sorry, I'm only following orders."

Over in the barracks area a BAR man was outside in the yard burning the fuzz off his brand-new combat boots in the flame of a can of shoe polish. He heard the factory whistles, looked up and then bent his head to his task again.

Inside barracks T-241 some of the newly-arrived GIs were reading or snoring in their sacks. Others were sitting in little groups, shooting the bull. Still others packed the shower room, luxuriating in the steam.

A little buck sergeant came into the barracks, went over to one group sitting among the double-tiered bunks and said, "The war's over. Just heard about it." They grunted and continued shooting the bull.

A permanent party soldier came in with a handful of overseas caps. "Who wants to buy a hat with blue Infantry braid on it?" he asked. "Only two-fifty. Ya can't buy a cap with braid on it in camp and you can't get outta camp and you gotta take off yer wools tomorrow, so ya better get one."

"Two-fifty!" muttered a big corn-haired guy. "What a racket! Probably cost ya no more'n a buck. You commandos got all the angles, ain't ya! About half an hour ago one of yer pals come in and got rid of two bottles of gin for 15 smackers. Probably cost him about five bucks. Just because we can't get outta camp . . ."

Several of the men bought caps, and the per-

n the White House President Truman, surrounded by members of his cabinet, reads the Jap surrender message. Seated by him are Admiral Leahy, Secretary of State Byrnes and ex-Secretary of State Hull

kyo that Japan would have an important anuncement to make at 8 o'clock the following orning. That made it look as though the situion would remain on ice for the rest of the ght and a large slice of New York City's swelring populace nursed itself to bed early with oling drinks.

That was the last sleep for a lot of people for lot of hours. Tokyo jumped the gun and at 1:49 uesday morning broadcast a statement that pan would accept the Allied surrender terms. hroughout the city late stay-uppers hopped the phone to rouse their friends and tell them e good news. Some made immediately for mes Square, setting off a celebration that was last well over 48 hours. It was still going rong at dawn and carried on right through the y and the next day as more and more yelling, ughing, horn-tooting thousands poured into the ea.

By Tuesday noon there was still nothing official, t from the way the crowds carried on you would ver have suspected that peace wasn't yet defi-

WASHINGTON

This capital city, over which the Japs boasted they would raise their flag within a year after the attack on Pearl Harbor, relaxed its worn nerves and celebrated the winning of the war with a screaming, drinking, paper-tearing, free-kissing demonstration which combined all the features of New Year's Eve and Mardi Gras.

Fraternization among officers and enlisted men was the order of the night in this usually dignified stronghold of brass, where seemingly every second person in uniform is adorned with bars, leaves, eagles or stars. Every girl was fair game, and rank was no obstacle. A buck sergeant and a corporal chased two WAC captains into the doorway of a shop on F Street and kissed their superiors soundly, despite giggled orders to the contrary.

Two Navy officers who warmly invited a victory kiss from a redheaded Wave ensign in the hallway of the Willard Hotel did not make out as well, but their confusion was covered by

This was part of a hilarious two-night celebration in San Francisco. A crowd, a large part of them being sailors, took over some cable cars, stopping traffic.

In Louisville, Ky., soldiers and sailors reacted pretty much as they did other parts of the country. They hoisted their girls into the air and yelle

manent party soldier flashed a sardonic grin at the corn-haired guy.

"By the way," he said, as he headed for the door, "the war's over. Guess you guys won't have to go to the Pacific after all."

"Like hell we won't!" someone shouted from the other end of the room. "We'll get shipped an' you commandos will stay here an' get out."

"Army of occupation in Japan," mused a little Italian from the Bronx. "Geez, why didn't we go over the hill in Austria so's we could of stayed there, fraternizing every night with them gorgeous Heinie babes."

"Oh, Japan ain't so bad," someone chimed in from an upper bunk. "This here book by Roy Chapman Andrews, the explorer, says they got some classy dames in Japan. He says they's one whorehouse there has a huge sign in front of it which says, 'Short time, one yen. All night, including breakfast, three yen.'"

"How much is a yen?"

"You'll find out soon enough, Jack."

"Baloney," said the corn-haired guy. "They ain't gonna ship us to Japan. We at least been overseas 10 months. They'll grab some of these 18-year-olds with peach fuzz on their face."

"That's what you think. Ain't you been in the Army long enough to know it ain't never done a logical thing?"

"Brother," piped a soldier with a Storm Trooper's skull-and-crossbones ring on his finger, "you can say that again!"

"Well, look," said the little Italian from the Bronx, "The war's over. Let's go over to the GI beer hall and toss a few."

Four others went with him. There was a line of more than 200 men in front of the door of the "Gay Nineties," the Area 1 beer hall. They dropped into line. Three-quarters of an hour later they were sitting on the grass outside, drinking beer out of paper cups.

"Nice cool evening, ain't it?" said the corn-haired guy.

"Yeah, quiet, too."

"Shall we sweat out the line for another four cups?"

"Naw, let's hit the sack. We'll be ridin' a train fer purty near two days startin' tomorrow night."

The four ETO veterans got up off the grass and ambled leisurely through the cool, dark night toward barracks T-241. From the direction of New Brunswick came the blaring of horns and the banging of dishpans.

"Well, the war's over."

"Yup."

—Sgt. DAVE RICHARDSON

PASADENA

"A hospital is one hell of a place to be in when a war ends."

That was the majority opinion of the men ranging from private to two-star general who found themselves, on the day of Japan's surrender, patients in the Army hospital ..hich was formerly the swank Vista del Arroyo Hotel. There was bedlam in the hospital, according to Lt. Helen Span, ANC, of Savannah, Ga., when the radio at 4 P. M. brought the official word from the White House.

"They went wild," Lt. Span said of her patients. "They slid down banisters, they chinned themselves on the hospital's chandeliers. The remark most of them made was, 'No Pacific trip now!'"

WAC Sgt. Rayetta Johnson, a former San Diego policewoman, was on MP duty at the hospital's door when the news broke. She held the door open for Maj. Gen. Thompson Lawrence, for the past two years commanding general of the Replacement Training Center, Camp Roberts, Calif., and Mrs. Lawrence. The general, carrying a barracks bag and a suitcase, was entering the hospital as a patient. Leaving off the "sir," Sgt. Johnson said to the general, "It's all over."

The general dropped his bags and grabbed Sgt. Johnson; he and his wife told her that they had two sons in the Pacific.

The hospital rang with shouts, and convalescing patients scurried through the corridors, their maroon robes trailing after them. "All I want," a nurse commented, "is a discharge and some nylons."

"Wotta place to be," moaned a staff sergeant who had been a prisoner in Germany for several months after his B-17 exploded in a raid on Munich. He had come home all in one piece, got his furlough and then banged himself up riding a motorcycle.

Passes were hard to get at the hospital, surrender or no surrender, but the WAC lieutenant who was officer of the day slyly said that as soon as the news came in she had resigned herself to a large number of AWOLs and to much smuggling-in of liquor by visitors. Typical of the passless patients was Pvt. Ted Chuinski of Chicago, back from 14 months in Europe. He sat dejectedly on the front steps, calling out to passing GIs to lend him some clothes. "I couldn't get far in this goddam bathrobe," he said glumly.

—Sgt. LARRY McMANUS

BOSTON

Boston's peace celebration exploded suddenly after the official news of Japanese surrender poured out of countless radios. All morning and afternoon, while many other cities were already wildly celebrating, the Hub, with true New England caution, waited soberly for confirmation.

But this staid attitude was swept away in a surging tide of mass enthusiasm a few minutes after the news came. In a celebration that topped Boston's two-day madness following the collapse of Germany in 1918, over three-quarters of a million people crammed narrow, twisting downtown streets and the famous Common in the wildest riot of noise in the city's long history. It was like 50 New Year's Eves rolled into one.

The most general impulse seemed to be to shout, sing and hug passers-by. For men in uniform the celebration seemed to be more of a kissing fest than anything else. They were seized by girls and women of all ages, and their faces soon burst out in what the movie ads would have called "flaming Technicolor," because of the varied hues of lipstick prints.

Doors of hundreds of churches were opened, and many thousands entered them briefly, if only to pause in silence for a few moments in gratitude

in the midst of an evening in which many ore narily powerful Boston inhibitions were swe aside.

Though nearly 200 persons required treatme for minor hurts, as they were squeezed a pushed around in the throngs, there were serious accidents.

The next day, happily, was a holiday, Boston's celebrators enjoyed a late mornin; sleep. They needed it.

SAN FRANCISCO

Peace broug something akin a state of chaos to the Pacific's largest port embarkation. The good news was almost too mu for San Francisco. Hundreds were injured and number killed in a celebration that lasted tv nights and that at no time had any element of t peaceful about it.

Some of the highlights: Firecrackers, hoard in Chinatown for eight years, rattled like m chine guns. . . . Servicemen and civilians play tug-of-war with fire hose. . . . Market Street, t wide, bar-lined thoroughfare that has long be the center of interest for visiting GIs and sailo was littered with the wreckage of smashed W Bond booths and broken bottles. . . . A plum redhead danced naked on the base of the city Native Sons monument after servicemen h torn her clothes off. A sailor lent the woman coat, and the pair disappeared.

Marine Pfc. James Prim, 34, had as much celebrate as anybody in San Francisco. He h come safely through bitter South Pacific ca paigns. In the early hours of August 15, wh the mass hilarity was at its height, Prim f down a flight of stairs. He died of a fractur skull.

There were thousands of San Franciscans w. marked the day soberly and with prayer, but t end of the second World War seems likely to remembered here as a celebration that got w. out of bounds.

NEW ORLEANS

After celebrating t end of the war pr maturely three times, New Orleans let loose wi everything it had when the official word final came through from the White House.

A snowstorm of paper had pelted down fr office buildings all during the afternoon optimistic citizens hoped for an immediate a nouncement of the war's end. The feel of victo in the air kept office workers downtown pa their normal working hours, and the announc ment caught mobs of shoppers and workers Canal Street.

So wary of unconfirmed rumors were the pe ple of New Orleans that it took a newsboy thr minutes to sell the first copy of the extra pr claiming the real peace. But once they were co vinced, no Mardi Gras was ever as gay or wild as the celebration that followed. Althou all bars closed immediately for 24 hours on o ders from the police, civilians and servicem alike were not slow to bring out bottles.

Mobs jammed the "widest street in the worl from sidewalk to sidewalk. Traffic moved wi the greatest difficulty in spite of the efforts the 150 extra policemen called out to handle the crowds. Sailors swarmed up to street cars as they stopped, kissing willing girls through the open windows. A loaded watermelon truck stalled in traffic on the big street, and sailors took over, handing out the melons to passing celebrants.

As every type of paper, except toilet tissue, which was notably absent, fell to the streets in ankle-deep piles, the Commissioner of Public Works announced that three extra street crews would be put to work cleaning up the mess.

In direct contrast to the shouting in the streets was the quiet of a Jesuit church in the business district crowded with parents, wives, and sweethearts of servicemen, offering prayers of thanksgiving for the end of hostilities and the safety of their loved ones. Men and women clutching newspapers with the banner-line PEACE mingled in front of the church, wiping their eyes unashamedly.

With all the bars closed, the French quarter was deserted as both civilians and servicemen hurried to Canal Street to join the festivities. A scattering of foreign soldiers and sailors were seen among the joyful crowd. A young French aviator, seeking refuge in a recruiting booth, spread a newspaper on the floor in an effort to translate the headlines. A passer-by, seeing his problem, shouted "La guerre est finie!" and the aviator jumped to his feet with a shout and disappeared into the mob.

Shipyards, aircraft plants and other war industries ceased operations shortly after the news was announced.

The *Times-Picayune's* weather forecast read: "Peaceful showers and clouds will be enjoyed by New Orleanians. . . ."

HONOLULU

In Honolulu, where the war began for the U. S., the first news of its ending reached a sleepy-eyed Chinese-American radio technician shortly after 1200 hours when he had just finished making his regular weekly check on KGU's station transmitter and was ready to leave for home.

When technician Harry Chu received the U. P. flash that the Japs had offered to accept the Allied peace terms, he put the transmitter back on the air, telephoned the assistant station manager and marked time until an announcer could arrive by playing records interspersed with the following announcement: "Stand by for important news about the Potsdam ultimatum."

The assistant station manager and two announcers arrived at the studio at about 0245 hours. Ten minutes later the first real broadcast of the news went on the air, and reaction from the late-listening radio audience was immediate.

One of the most spontaneous celebrations was

Victory didn't stop the draft. The day after Jap surrender these men were inducted in Cleveland.

at Hickam Field, where hangars, planes and barracks were strafed by the Japs December 7. Crewmen, technicians and passenger-terminal personnel, working on a 24-hour shift to keep bombers and supplies flowing to the battle lines, heard the first news flash and quickly spread the word. GIs in jeeps and command cars and trucks raced up and down the roads with their horns held down. A soldier woke up six members of the AAF band and their noise soon woke up others. When the first parade started down Fox Avenue there were 40 assorted musicians playing "Hail, Hail, The Gang's All Here."

Flight nurses, Wacs and GIs all streamed from their barracks and joined the howling procession. Forty vehicles, lined up three abreast in back of the paraders, loaded with shouting men, women and children, must have looked pretty puny compared with a Times Square celebration, but nothing ever surpassed them in enthusiasm.

Waikiki Beach, where the Army has its rest camp, Fort DeRussy, and the Navy has the Royal Hawaiian Hotel, at first took the news quietly simply because nearly everyone was asleep. But soldiers and sailors who heard the flash went from door to door pounding and shouting, and within 15 minutes all lights were on and groups had gathered to talk over the historic news.

In the replacement training command depot

where men are assigned to combat units in the forward areas, jubilation was high. Even though men realized that Jap capitulation would not necessarily cancel their trip west, they knew now it would be for occupation duty and not for actual combat.

By 0600 hours thousands of civilian workers, many of them of Japanese descent, began to arrive at the base. They talked excitedly as they went about their jobs, but now it was beginning to look like just another routine day, as busy as ever with nothing slowed down.

Downtown Honolulu didn't seem to be changed much by the news either. Soldiers and sailors filed along Hotel Street doing the same old things they'd always done on pass days—staring at traffic, shopping in curio stores, having their pictures taken with hula girls. But there was a broad grin on the face of Pfc. Nobuichi Masatsugo, a Japanese-American soldier, as he read the headlines.

"I always knew we had them licked, but I never thought the end would come this soon," he said. He wore a Purple Heart won in Italy, where he had fought with the 34th Division.

"I guess my 76 points will be good after all," commented T-4 Cyril D. Robinson of Klamath Falls, Ore., another soldier on pass in town.

Pvt. Mitchell Rosen, a New York City marine who saw action at Iwo Jima, was taking the news soberly.

"You can credit the Marines, the atomic bomb and the Russians for bringing the Japs to their knees," he said, and he emphasized the word "Marines." —Cpl. TOM O'BRIEN

PARIS

The GIs had managed to keep their VJ spirit bottled up through most of the phony rumors, but when the real thing was announced the cork popped with a vengeance. A spontaneous parade, including jeeps and trucks and Wacs and GIs and officers and nurses and enlisted men, snaked from the Red Cross Club at Rainbow Corner down to the *Place de l'Opera* and back.

Jeeps crawled along in the victory celebration so loaded down with cheering GIs that the shape of the vehicles could hardly be discerned. Some GIs showed up with flags to add both color and an official note to the procession. By the time the demonstration hit its full stride trucks and cars were moving five abreast with pedestrian celebrants marching before and behind and between.

The most unusual note of the day was the spontaneous contribution campaign for the Red Cross which started up out of nothing at all except good humor when a GI at the Rainbow Corner pinned a couple of franc notes to a tree, announcing: "This is for the Red Cross."

His idea caught on and soon other GIs were unloading their spare currency. The sport was enlivened considerably by kissing French girls at the tree, whether as a bonus for contributions or just for the hell of it. At any rate, a late afternoon check showed some $14,000 raised for the ARC by what had begun purely as a half-gag gesture of good will.

The whole show was a soldier—especially an American soldier—performance. French civilians were happy and pleased, and they showed it.

SAD SACK — PEACE AT LAST

JAPAN SURRENDERS

SGT. GEORGE BAKER
PHILIPPINES

but they still went about their work as much as usual as was possible. They had been drained of celebration first when their city had been freed and later when the European war had ended.

ATLANTIC OCEAN

GIs aboard troopships at sea, heading back for the States from Europe, heard about the Japanese surrender over the ship's p. a. system barely three minutes after the Washington news flash was received in the radio room, and read details in "extras" of mimeographed and typed ship's newspapers as quickly as the folks back home.

On the *Cape Flattery*, carrying 600 returning officers and low-point EM who'd thought they were headed for the Pacific after a Stateside furlough, each premature announcement was greeted with cheers and then with groans when it turned out to be a false alarm. The *Flattery's* news sheet, the *Bilge*, appeared with a daily news roundup.

One false flash came through at 2 A.M., long after "lights out," so almost nobody heard the news until morning. A pfc was rudely informed by a sergeant who rolled him out of bed at 5:30: "Wake up. The war's over and you're on KP."

But—unlike the boy who cried wolf—the first mate never lost the confidence of his p. a. listeners, and when President Truman made it official, everybody cut loose.

A minute later the chaplain took command of the loudspeaker, leading troops and crew in a prayer for their fallen comrades.

—Sgt. ALLAN B. ECKER

MANILA

The headline, in type so big that the words ran together across the top of the page, said: "NIPS QUIT." The Japanese prisoners of war crowded around the superior private who held the paper. They stood in the sun-baked courtyard of the new

open. About 30 Japs, most of them newly arrived at the prison, lay or sat on blankets spread on the concrete floor. On one side of the room were the day's crop of newcomers. Most of them were just skin and bones, and the GI shorts they wore hung loosely on their flanks as they lay with their thin arms clasped behind their heads, their dead eyes staring at nothing.

On the other side of the room were healthier specimens waiting to be assigned to work companies. It was easy to tell how long they had been prisoners by the amount of meat on their bones.

When the visitors were seated around the superior private's cot (he has a cot because he's a trusty and in charge of this part of the processing center), the interpreter asked him how he felt about the news of Japan's capitulation.

The soldier rubbed his eyes with the palm of his hand and figured out just what he wanted to say.

"I'm not sorry," he told the interpreter. "I'm in a happy mood." He smiled cheerfully to show how happy the mood was. There was a murmur in the room as the word passed from pallet to pallet, and some of those who had been lying down sat up and watched.

He was asked if he wanted to go home now. This was a ticklish one. He wanted to go home, and he didn't want to go home. His relatives and his friends at the aluminum plant where he worked in Tokyo might point at him, he said, and he didn't want to be pointed at. The Japs who had edged into the group all looked at the floor. Nobody said anything for a moment. The superior private looked up and smiled again— his happy mood smile. He was happy that the

After he told the interpreter about his surrender, he spoke rapidly for a moment and the interpreter laughed.

"He wants to go to America," the interpret said.

"Houseboy!" yelled the sergeant in clear English, the first he had spoken.

—Sgt. ROBERT MacMILL

ROME

The people of Rome—Italian civilians and U. S. GIs—took the news the Japanese surrender in their strides. The weren't any parades, bells didn't ring and the were few drunken soldiers. People went abo their business as usual, including the girls on t *Via del Tritone*.

In front of the *Ristorante San Carlo*, a GI re taurant on the *Corso Umberto*, there was t usual line of hungry soldiers waiting to eat. Asi from the fact that most of them were grinni as if they'd just heard a joke, they showed litt reaction to the news. A big, beefy corporal wea ing a Bronze Star ribbon and a blue combat I fantryman's badge, with the Red Bull patch the 34th Division on his shoulder, said, "I do know. Can't believe it. Only two bombs and th give up. Don't sound like all that stuff we hea about the Japs fighting to the end. Seems to there's a catch somewhere. Hey, what the he holding up this line?"

Outside the PX Italian kids were begging cigarettes with "Joe, war *finito*. You give me o cigarette?"

On the night when the papers hit the streets of Manila with headlines of Jap surrender, thousands of Filipinos celebrated.

In London, on Piccadilly Circus, bunch of GIs and a New Zealand sailor (left) hoi an English bobby onto their shoulders when they heard the Japs had offered to

Bilibid Prison south of Manila, where some 8,000 former soldiers of the emperor are confined.

An elderly Japanese civilian interpreter lifted his eyebrows, adjusted his spectacles, and translated.

"*Nippon*," he said. "*Nippon kofuku*."

The superior private glanced sidelong at the older man and laughed at him. The civilian thumped the paper with his forefinger and repeated the translation.

The superior private frowned and stared at the page that said that the war was ending and that his country was offering to surrender. The Japs behind him chattered and stuck their heads over his shoulder to see for themselves. The superior private left the paper with them and walked into the long concrete building where he lived.

I followed with the interpreter

The room, which was part of the processing center for incoming prisoners, was about the size of a Stateside Army barracks. The windows were barred, but the door was unlocked and

war had ended and that the world could know peace again, he said.

The others, watching him, all smiled, too. They put on their happy-mood smiles, and there was the sound of polite hissing.

A muscle-jawed Jap sergeant joined the group. He'd been a prisoner for about a month and was in pretty fair condition. He, too, had been aware of what what was going on.

"I'm much relieved," he told the interpreter. "All my friends [he indicated the Japs along the wall], all my friends have such a mood of mind." The Japs along the wall stared impassively. The sergeant gave his name and said he had no objection to having it published in an American magazine. He was a medical sergeant about 40 years old, and he had an abscess on one leg. He had given up after four months hiding in the hills.

A Nisei staff sergeant from the 442d Regime tal Combat Team came out carrying a paper b full of rations. He grinned and said, "Wonderf news. Almost too good to be true. I'm anxious get home. I hope people there'll realize the wa over. But it's sure fine news—best ever."

In front of the Red Cross a gray-haired te said, "The best news I've ever heard on the rad It's a funny thing. I came out of an Engine outfit that's headed for the Pacific. They pull me out because I got 95 points. I wonder if t boys have left Italy yet. They'll sure have t laugh if they beat me home."

At a sidewalk cafe on the *Via Nazionale* sto a bald-headed GI who was getting a buzz o Laughing and sweating, he showed two Italia pictures of his wife and kids.

". . . and this garage here, you can just s part of it sticking out from the side of the hous I got the sweetest little Buick, what a car. Y *capito* Buick?

Inside the Florida Club, a GI hot spot, thin

looked about the same—a band giving out with some strictly Roman version hot jazz, about 30 couples dancing and several soldiers singing at their tables. A private who said he was attached to the 34th Station Hospital was drinking with an over-bright thin blonde. The private said, "I don't know why, but the thing sort of sneaks up on you. I started out to raise hell tonight but somehow I can't get started. It seems hard to believe. No more worrying about points, stripes or anything. Bud, when I get home now, it's to stay. Maybe when I get home I'll celebrate, really pitch some hell."

"War *finito*," the blonde said. "*Buono*. Americans leave Rome, no?"

It was hard to tell from her voice whether she thought the GIs leaving Italy would be a good or a bad deal.

The private put his arm around her and said, "Yessir, baby, from now on it's home sweet home. Play 'Home Sweet Home,'" he shouted at the orchestra leader.

A GI at the next table said, "That ain't dancing music."

The nine o'clock show at the Barberini Theater was out and the crowd of GIs and Tommies streamed into the streets fresh from seeing Lana Turner in "Slightly Dangerous." An English sergeant said, "Wonderful news. I went to the cinema because I didn't know what to do with myself. Five years of it for me, you know. Nearly four overseas. I was slated for Burma so I'm glad the show's over."

A couple of soldiers were walking down the *Via del Tritone* singing hillbilly songs. Three Brazilian soldiers were sitting in a parked jeep watching the girls as they passed under the street light, laughing and making cracks in Portuguese. On the corner an Italian was selling watermelon slices to a small crowd of civilians who stood around his cart eating and spitting the

These GIs crowded on top of a jeep and drove through the streets of Paris celebrating victory.

seeds out. You could hear them saying, "*Guerra finita . . . bomba atomica . . . molti morti . . .*" while a loud-mouthed buck sergeant from II Corps was happily stuffing himself with melon and explaining how the atomic bomb worked.

In the Borghese Gardens a Fifth Army T-5 was sitting with a slim, pretty Italian girl. "I figured something like this would come. It's been a long war and nobody's sorry it's over. Of course, I married here—this is my wife. Now I wonder how soon I'll go home and if she'll be able to go to the States at the same time. If she gets stuck here, I'm going to ask for a discharge here and sweat out Italy till we can both go to the States. But no more sweating out Japan!"

Near the Galleria Club a Negro sergeant from the 92d Division, wearing a silver star ribbon under his combat Infantryman's badge, said, "I'm glad we didn't have to invade Japan. That would've been a bitch. Got a brother in the Navy in the Pacific and I bet he's shouting now."

Inside the club somebody yelled over the music.

Out in Guam, advance headquarters of the Navy, these servicemen gathered around to cheer the news.

"When you guys get papers from home now you better start reading the want ads columns." The crack brought a wave of laughter.

The Negro GI smiled. "That's a fact. Start thinking about jobs, but after the Army it'll be a pleasure."

An Air Force master sergeant and a Wac corporal were standing in front of the Rome Area Command building, opposite the famous balcony in *Piazza Venezia* where Mussolini used to harangue crowds. The six-striper said, "It's great news all right, although I guess we've been expecting it. Japan can't stand against the world. I'm in an occupation bomb group down at Foggia. You think they'll still keep us here now? I've got 18 months overseas. They ought to send some of these new guys for occupation work."

"They certainly ought to send over men who've never been out of the States," said the Wac. "I think they could even get a volunteer force. I wonder if we or the Chinese will occupy Japan."

"My God, don't even talk about that," said the sergeant, laughing. "Can you imagine Japan with a Chinese occupation force? Damn!"

It was a little after midnight and St. Peter's looked very solemn and impressive against the stars. The church was shut. GIs kept coming up and then standing and looking at the church as if they didn't know what to do. One soldier said, "I thought it would be open tonight."

An elderly Italian said that in Italy all churches close at dark.

"I know, but tonight . . ." the soldier said.

At the entrance to the Swiss Guard barracks a heavy-set guard in the ancient uniform of this small army was standing at the gate. His face was expressionless—his army life not dependent on the war's ending or beginning.

On the day when the greatest and most terrible war in world history came to an end, on the day when fascism was finally broken in the world, Rome—where fascism was born—was quiet and orderly. Rome has seen its share of this war. Maybe there should have been a lot of noise and great rejoicing. Here, where people know war, there wasn't shouting, ticker tape showers or hysterical parades, but the people were merely happy. In Rome most people were merely smiling quietly.

—Cpl. LEN ZINBERG

ALASKA GIs from Fort Richardson tried to take over the nearby town of Anchorage when the final surrender news came through, but the town's six blocks of bars and liquor stores folded under the impact. Anchorage's seemingly inexhaustible supply of liquor just wasn't enough to meet the demand.

The celebration got under way early Tuesday afternoon and continued till 8 P.M. when the bars closed. Civilian neckties keynoted the rejoicing here. GIs bought up all the available ties in Anchorage stores and when the tie supply was exhausted they exchanged OD ties with civilians. MPs removed OD ties from soldiers; the MPs wore civilian ties themselves.

The difficulty for the MPs was telling soldiers from civilians. Officers and EM exchanged insignia and stripes and one sergeant made full colonel during the evening.

Local girls did a strip tease for a couple of hundred GIs. They stripped in a hotel window and tossed their garments to soldiers gathered

below. Telegrams to and from the States quadrupled over the previous day.

The reaction was summed up by Sgt. Bob Kirk of Chicago: "How long is the duration?"

—Sgt. AL WEISMAN

LONDON Two Canadian soldiers walked into a restaurant talking quietly about the Japanese surrender offer. A GI sitting in one of the American-style booths caught their words and let out a whoop. "We're going to tear this place apart!" he announced.

Then he lapsed into silence. Other Americans in the restaurant reacted pretty much the same way. As one soldier remarked, "We're still in Europe, bud."

There was a little more excitement as the evening wore on and there were crowds in Piccadilly Circus and Leicester and Trafalgar Squares. Quite a few people got rid of their waste paper by throwing it out of windows, a sign that the need for saving such things for the war effort was just about over.

Five hundred GIs who arrived that evening on furlough from the continent weren't exactly on fire about the news, either. Duffel bags and toilet kits on their shoulders, they queued up to register for rooms at the Red Cross Club as quietly as they have been queuing up for everything else during their army careers. A lot of the furloughing troops said they didn't believe the war was over and even if it was they'd still have to sweat out transportation home for a long time yet.

Quite a few GIs were more interested in talking about the atomic bomb than about Japan. They were afraid of the new weapon and its potential force for evil. Cpl. Paul Martin of Vauxhall, N. J., an anti-tank gunner with the 9th Division in France, Belgium and Germany and now with the army of occupation in Germany, was a little dazed.

"The news that Japan gave up seems impossible to me," he said. "Especially since the Russians have only been in the thing for one day. This atom bomb is sure a lotta hell; it had a lot to do with the surrender. I have to go back to Germany, but I'm glad for the guys who're sweating it out in the Pacific now. I'll get home eventually and it might be a little quicker than I thought this time last year. How long will we have to stay in Germany? Depends on how long we take to get those *buergermeisters* working right."

"Yeah, I know the atom bomb helped a lot, but it wasn't the only factor in the surrender. Right now I want to go home; I've got 134 points, and I've got a son two years old I never saw and a girl that I only saw once. Who doesn't want to go home, brother?"

Sgt. Bernard Katz of Pittsburgh, Pa., now with the 36th Bombardment Squadron, Eighth Air Force, has been in the Army for five years and had special reactions.

"I'm one guy who ought to be glad, because I saw my first action on Dec. 7, 1941. I was at Wheeler Field on Oahu, the first island the Japs attacked.

"We thought it was an earthquake until we found out that it was war, and war was worse. I jumped under a theater for shelter and found myself lying beside a two-star general. He didn't say anything about saluting, and neither did I.

"Now it's all over. For good, I hope. I think a combination of the Russians and the atom bomb did the trick in about equal proportions. I think the atom bomb is the best weapon to prevent future wars, and I also think it should be given to the whole world so it can be developed to its fullest extent. Even the Japs and Germans should be given it when they're domesticated enough."

—Sgt. FRANCIS BURKE

BERLIN The city that had seen its own brand of fascism and international banditry tumble only a few months before had little energy left for reaction to the fall of Japan. The American Forces network broadcast the first authentic VJ news at 0210, and most of Berlin's polyglot occupation population, as well as most native Berliners, were asleep.

The U. S. Army newspaper *Allgemeine Zeitung* was the only Berlin paper which carried the news the next day. But the four days of false alarms made even the real thing seem unexciting.

Russian GIs interviewed had the same responses as their American counterparts. Said one of them, typically, "Now maybe I can get home to see my wife and children."

Generalissimo Stalin was the only one left of the original Big Three as the Potsdam conference ended.

but equally historic. To San Francisco ca[me] delegates from 46 nations bent on creating world security organization that was to enfo[rce] justice among nations and redeem the sacrif[ice] of the war. The conference itself had b[een] heralded weeks in advance, but the question whether or not it would result in agreement [was] uppermost in millions of minds. Success wo[uld] not necessarily guarantee the peace of the w[orld] for all time, but failure would almost certai[nly] be the first step toward a third World Wa[r,] and for a time it seemed touch and go. Wo[uld] Russia's position on Poland upset the apple ca[rt?] Would the admission of Argentina open the [way] to a renewed lease of life for Fascism? Wo[uld] the small states rebel at a concentration of po[wer] in the hands of the Big Three? Could a so[und] peace rest on a basis of power? All these dou[bts,] and the rumors that accompanied them, c[on-] tributed to the jitters of a nation.

While the earnest delegates successfully str[ug-] gled through political mists thicker than the f[og] that rolled in from San Francisco Bay, w[ord] came from Milan that the first of the dictator[s,] Benito Mussolini, "modern Caesar," founder [of] Fascism, and chest-thumper extraordinary—[had] been shot, along with his mistress, Clara Peta[cci,]

THE LAST 125 DAYS

ALL OVER THE WORLD THINGS SEEMED TO HAPPEN ALL AT ONCE IN THE FINAL FOUR MONTHS OF WA[R]

Men and women everywhere took the death of President Roosevelt, on April 12, as a deep personal loss.

dragged through the gutter and strung up by [the] heels from the girder of a gas station. Pub[lic] figures had been assassinated before, but he[re] was a melodrama of revenge more startling th[an] the blood-and-thunder of the most far-fetch[ed] spy thriller.

THAT was April 28—and for the last time Mu[s-] solini was showing the way to his colleag[ues] in tyranny. Within three days came the startl[ing] announcement from Hamburg that Adolf Hitl[er,] too, had ceased to dishonor the planet with [his] presence, that he had "died at his post" in t[he] ruins of Berlin. It took a while for the news [to] sink in that the man who had plunged the wor[ld] into the greatest misery it had known in ce[n-] turies, who had made fanatic cruelty the la[w] of a nation, who had conquered nearly the enti[re] Continent of Europe and spread his poison to [all] parts of the world—was at last dead and do[ne] for. But here, too, melodrama crept in and ma[de] a big news story doubly intriguing; nobody cou[ld] be quite sure that Hitler really *was* dead, a[nd] the groundwork was laid for the mystery of t[he] century.

Hitler's reported end was the natural prelu[de] to an even bigger story—the collapse of Ge[r-] many, the Nazi state that was to endure for [a] thousand years and make slaves of all the less[er] people of the earth. That story broke — u[n-] officially—on May 7, when morning radio pr[o-] grams in the East (Californians were still aslee[p) were interrupted for a flash report that the Alli[es] had officially announced the unconditional su[r-] render of Germany (which, in fact, they did[n't] get around to doing until the next day). Eve[n] though victory could have been seen approachi[ng] at a gallop for weeks before it arrived, the new[s] was a breathtaker. Celebrations were jubilan[t,] but on all sides they were tempered by wor[ds] of warning: there was still Japan to conque[r,] and that might be a long, costly and bloody busi[-] ness. Six months to a year, said the optimist[s.] A year and a half to two years, countered th[e] cautious. Gradually the excitement died down.

June was, for these feverish times, compara[-] tively calm. There was, of course, the roundin[g] up of the once-proud leaders of the "maste[r] race," the stepping up of the war in the Pacifi[c,] including the great victory at Okinawa, and th[e] successful windup of the San Francisco con[-] ference. But the next really big story, No. [4] on our list, did not break until July 15. On tha[t] day the British were able to announce, in th[e]

By Pfc. ROBERT BENDINER
YANK Staff Writer

NEVER before — to take off on Winston Churchill's famous phrase—has so much history affecting so many people been made in so short a time. In the 125 days starting with April 12 of this year no fewer than 10 world-rocking headlines were splashed across the newspapers of the country, any one of them explosive enough to furnish the average human being with his excitement quota for a year. Raining down in breathless succession, these news bombshells found their target in a public nervous system which should logically be so frayed by this time that it will be fit to take nothing stronger than accounts of tiddly-winks tournaments for at least a year to come.

It is hard to believe that the first of these

four-alarm stories broke on a stunned world only four months ago. On the 12th of April at 3:35 P.M. in the "Little White House" at Warm Springs, Ga., President Franklin Delano Roosevelt died. Papers from one end of the country to the other broke out with the 260- and 300-point woodblock heads reserved for moments of history. Commercials vanished from the air waves, which for 24 hours echoed almost exclusively to solemn tributes and words of mourning. Men and women everywhere took the death of the President as a deep personal loss but beneath this profound emotion ran another—and equally taxing sensation—a strong current of excitement over possible political changes, the feverish speculation that naturally accompanied the first presidential shift in more than 12 years.

Less than two weeks after this emotional outpouring came a story less personal, less dramatic,

ruffled way that characterizes their country;
at they had just experienced the biggest elec-
ral upset in their history.
By a two-to-one count they had voted Winston
urchill, one of the greatest war leaders of
ritish history, out of office in order to install
government that had pledged itself to nation-
ize whole sections of the country's economy
d push toward the goal of socialism. Not since
at remote period before Hitler had embarked
his first aggression, even before Mussolini
d pitted his legions against the Ethiopians, had
itain had a national election. The result was
revelation.

WHATEVER its long-range significance, the election's immediate consequence was the sec-
d substitution in the cast of the Big Three. At
tsdam, on the outskirts of Berlin, the seventh
our heady headlines was in the making. What
osevelt, Churchill and Stalin had started long
o was carried to completion by Marshal
alin, President Truman and Britain's new
ime Minister, Clement Attlee. On August 2,
ter sessions of the strictest secrecy, the fate
Germany and much of Europe was announced
the decision to make Germany a third-rate
dustrial power, incapable of waging war,
ipped of East Prussia and of large areas along
e Oder, and denied a central government for
indefinite future. Equally sensational was the
timatum issued from Potsdam to the Japanese
rms were laid down, and for the first time
e enemy had a concrete picture of what it
uld expect in the event of unconditional sur-
nder. Failure to accept, it was pointed out by
e American, British and Chinese governments,
ould mean the utter destruction of Japan.
That was only a starter for the month of Au-
st, which was to bring the wave of history to a
wering crest. Before August was half over
ree of the biggest news stories of the war—and
e of the biggest in the history of the world—
d broken on a public almost immune to eight-
lumn streamer heads and "flash" interruptions
the morning soap opera.
On August 7, a date that will probably be
emorized by schoolboys for generations, the
orld of the future was ushered in. The power
the atom, the basic energy of the universe,
d at last been harnessed to the uses of man.
s first employment was to blow 60 percent of
e Japanese city of Hiroshima completely out
existence. The tiny atom promised a speedy
d of the war. And, more important in the long
n, it marked out alternative roads for men of
e 20th century to follow: the suicide of our
vilization through atomic warfare, or the sal-
ation of that civilization through peaceful ap-
lication of this monumental scientific advance.
People were still rubbing their eyes and trying
stretch their minds enough to take in the over-
helming significance of the atomic bomb when
tory No. 9 crashed through. Three months from
e date of the German surrender the Soviet
nion entered the war in the Pacific. Long poised
n the borders of Manchuria, the Red Army of
e East plunged across the line from east and
est, and Americans rejoiced that the Japs' crack
wantung Army could be left to the Russians
hile our own forces concentrated on the
nemy's jittery home islands.

IT seemed impossible for the war to go on for
more than a matter of months, but the public
as hardly prepared for the swiftness of the
apanese collapse. Early on the morning of Au-
ust 10 the enemy threw in the sponge. By way
f Domei, the Japanese news agency, came word
hat the Tokyo government was prepared to ac-
ept the Potsdam terms provided the "sovereign-
y" of the Emperor was left intact. Four days
f uncertainty followed, days of feverish con-
ultation in high places and tentative jubilation
n places both high and low. One thing was cer-
ain: the end of the second World War was im-
ninent. The day longed for by an entire world
hrough six tortured years was about to dawn.
In four short months this planet had come a
ong way. Three figures who had dominated the
news of a decade were gone—Roosevelt, Mussolini and Hitler—and a fourth, Winston Churchill,
had passed from leadership of an empire to
leadership of His Majesty's Loyal Opposition.
Nazi Germany had been ground into the dust
and its ruthless leaders either driven to suicide
or brought to the prisoner's dock. The founda-
tions for a durable world security organization

had been laid, and the outlines drawn for a
reconstructed Europe. A Labor government had
swept into power in England, with possible repercussions in all the liberated countries of the
Continent. And the most widespread and devastating war in history was brought to an end
with the capitulation of those Japanese jingos
who had threatened to fight if necessary for a
hundred years. Finally, towering above even
these massive events, a revolution had taken
place in science, which promised in time either
to make the mighty atom work for man or to
destroy man and his world in another war.
After a streak like that it would not be surprising if a revulsion against "big news" should

set in. It may well be that people long to pick
up a paper in which nothing more cosmic is reported than the city's reception of a visiting
channel-swimmer, and nothing more violent than
a tie-up on the Magnolia Avenue trolley line.
On the other hand, "big news" is a potent
drug. On the day between Russia's entry into
the Pacific war and the Japs' bid for peace more
than one American was heard to complain that
things were slow, "nothing new." For such jaded
addicts nothing will do now but an extra with
the eight-column streamer: MOON COLLIDES WITH
EARTH AS MARTIANS CHEER—unless it is that
equally exciting head: ALL GIS DISCHARGED AS
ARMY SCRAPS RED TAPE. But let's not be fantastic.

Whether or not Hitler died in Berlin made a big story
but a bigger one was the German surrender on May 7.

Word came from Milan on April 28 that Mussolini and
his mistress had been shot and strung up in the square.

THE MIGHTY ATOM

This miles-high pillar of smoke represents all that was left of 65 percent of Hiroshima after it was hit by first U.S. atom bomb to be dropped upon Japan.

From it science forged the war' *most fearful weapon, gave Japa* *the final blow and opened a new* *era of vast energy that can, mar* *willing, be harnessed for peace* *These six pages tell the story*

By Cpl. JONATHAN KILBOURN
YANK Staff Writer

THINK of the smallest thing you can conceiv of, then divide it by two billion. That wil give you an approximate idea of the size o the atom, which provides the energy for the mos destructive weapon in the world, the atomi bomb.

The bombs that devastated Hiroshima and Na gasaki contained billions of atoms.

An atom consists of almost inconceivably tin particles of electricity, negatively charged, posi tively charged and "neutral."

Any given amount of any "thing" consists o atoms—billions of them, like the small particle of sand on an ocean beach. Everything you se around you, everything you see or touch is mad of atoms. You are, too.

Each atom is like our solar system in th smallest miniature. In the center is the sun, th nucleus. Around it revolve the planets, called electrons. But they whirl billions of times faste than our world.

Science has broken down into component part the sun of the atom world. This nucleus is com posed of a conglomeration of individual particle of two kinds, protons and neutrons. Protons ar positively charged, neutrons are neutral.

The atom solar system would burst apart i there were not a force to bind it together. Thi force is supplied by the attraction between th one or more protons in the nucleus and the atom' electron planets, which are negatively charged.

HOLDING our little atom system together take terrific energy. This energy, released, mean not only the end of the atom world but, within it sphere, unimaginable pandemonium, like a mi nute Judgment Day. Temperatures of millions o degrees are developed. Pressures produced ar far and away the most violent reactions known Until this reaction was first discovered, humar beings couldn't even conceive of such power.

The reaction depends on no chemical element for combustion; it is entirely self-sustaining. The crashing destruction continues until the entire atomic solar system breaks apart.

What happens to the exploded particles and how can this miniature cataclysm be created? Because the explosion is over so quickly—it takes place in only 1/1,000,000th of a second—the de tails of the reaction are hard to trace.

And bringing about this cataclysm is doubly difficult because atoms are not packed tightly to gether. Trying to smash just any old atom in a molecule or piece of matter would be, as Albert Einstein puts it, like trying to shoot ducks on a dark night in a section where ducks are rare. There would be millions of misses for every hit.

The component parts of the atom world are few and far between, too. Like our solar system, the atom is mostly space. The atom sun occupies only one millionth of a billionth of the atomic solar system's reaches.

If all the electronic planets and empty space were taken from the myriad of atomic solar sys tems that compose a 150-pound man, and only the nuclei remained, there would be left a lump no larger than a ball of buckshot.

Taking the electrons and space from this 150-

d man's miniature solar systems would not, ...ver, leave a neat little lump without pro-...g an explosion beyond imagining. For ...ic disintegration is not the kind of explo-...we are familiar with. Ordinary explosions ...fires are started by the separation from one ...her, and the rearrangement of molecules. ...molecules themselves remain whole, but the ...gy that held them together is released in ...and light and explosive force.

...daily see atomic explosions, but from afar, ...r that we are not familiar with their char-...istics. The sun's heat and light and the many ...it sends forth are produced by such explo-...—explosions that go much farther than the ...separation of molecular groups. Atoms sep-...from one another, and the disintegration ...farther still. The atoms themselves break ...

...n incredibly greater amount of heat and light ...results. Other forces are released, some so ...erful that they have only been guessed at. ...e disintegration of one atom in the labora-...causes havoc in the atom's solar system but ...in the room itself. This is because a chain ...tom worlds—great numbers of them—would ...to go off to equal the detonation of a fire-...ker. Yet a combination of atoms little larger ...a pea could cause terrible destruction be-...e of the billions upon billions of atoms it ...ains.

...create such a combination, and favorable ...mstances for bombarding that combination, ...the primary problems of the atom-smasher ...the makers of the atom bomb. Haphazard ...bardment of the atom is like shooting peas ...n electric fan. The speed of the electrons in ...orbits makes the atom practically impene-...le. Moreover, the electrons successfully resist ...positively charged particles.

...neutron, however, has no electrical charge. ...neither can it move unaided. Because it has ...harge, scientists who wish to break into the ...-defended atom world cannot whirl the neu-...by itself in their giant atom-disrupting cy-...rons or in the atom bombs.

...give the neutron motive power, scientists ...etimes use the heavy hydrogen atom, which ...ains a nucleus in which a proton and a neu-...are combined. The heavy hydrogen atom is ...rled in the magnetic field of the cyclotron. ...en the heavy hydrogen atom hits the target—...uranium atom to be smashed—the hydrogen ...leus breaks apart. Into the uranium atom goes ...neutron.

...he atom target of the neutron can be uranium ...one of the uranium atoms and the atom with ...most powerful electric guards of all. U-235 ...92 positively charged particles in its nucleus ...ch repel any protron stranger that tries to ...h its world. Ninety-two electron planets re-...e around it, and these satellites repel all neg-...e strangers.

...HE reason why scientists use unsociable ura-...nium instead of some more companionable ...terial is that U-235 (the number is its atomic ...ght), one of the atoms in uranium, becomes ...table when its weight is increased by one unit ...shooting a neutron into it. The same is true of ...tonium, the artificial chemical element created ...science to provide a super-atomic energy ...rce, which has an atomic weight of 239, heav-...in existence.

...Whenever the balance of its system is broken ...a neutron, either U-235 or plutonium smashes ...o two nearly equal parts.

...he heavier the atom, the greater the binding ...rgy necessary to hold it together. When the ...nium atom is split in two parts and two ...ster atoms are formed, these two together re-...re less energy to hold together than the atom ...m which they were formed. What's left goes ...in the form of excess energy—it explodes. ...d what's left is 200,000,000 electron volts.

...hat sounds like a lot, but it's just a flicker of ...natch in the atomic universe. Within its sphere ...effect is utterly destructive. But unless the ...mic system's disintegration spreads to other ...ilar systems, it is not observable by the naked ...e of man.

...When the rapidly traveling neutrons hit a ...er, nothing happens in the ordinary nature of ...ngs. At high speeds the 235s are immune. Just ...w the neutron down a bit, however, and the ...m splits. When neutrons float through the air ...ey penetrate the 235s with the greatest of ease.

These are some of the words which everybody uses, sometimes rightly and sometimes wrongly, in talking about the atom bomb:

ATOM—One of the billions of almost inconceivably small "solar systems" of which the 92 separate known *elements* (oxygen, hydrogen, uranium, etc.) of the universe are composed.

NUCLEUS—Center of the atom, containing one or more neutrons and one or more protons.

PROTON—Positively-charged particle found in the nucleus.

NEUTRON—Neutral particle found in the nucleus.

ELECTRON—Negatively-charged particle which speeds in an orbit around the nucleus of an atom.

MOLECULE—One or more atoms joined in chemical combination.

ATOMIC WEIGHT—Number expressing the ratio of the weight of an atom of one element, taking that of oxygen to be 16 (hydrogen's is 1.008).

URANIUM—A luminous white metal which comes from pitchblende and is found principally in Canada and Rhodesia.

URANIUM-235—Uranium atom having an atomic weight of 235.

URANIUM-238—Uranium atom with an atomic weight of 238—heaviest natural atom.

PLUTONIUM—Chemical element created by science as a super-atomic power source. It has an atomic weight of 239.

CYCLOTRON—Giant atom-smashing machine which scientists used for research preceding the development of the atom bomb.

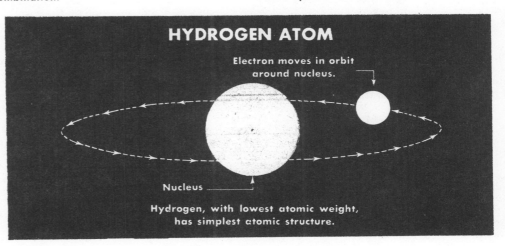

HYDROGEN ATOM

Electron moves in orbit around nucleus.

Nucleus

Hydrogen, with lowest atomic weight, has simplest atomic structure.

URANIUM ATOM

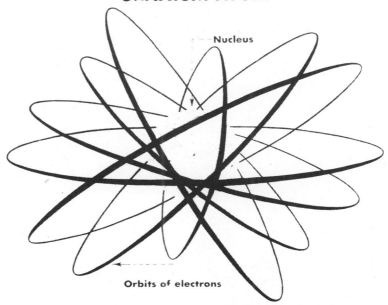

Nucleus

Orbits of electrons

Uranium atom is most complex and rarest of atoms. Its nucleus consists of 92 protons and 143 neutrons, around which whirl 93 electrons in seven orbits.

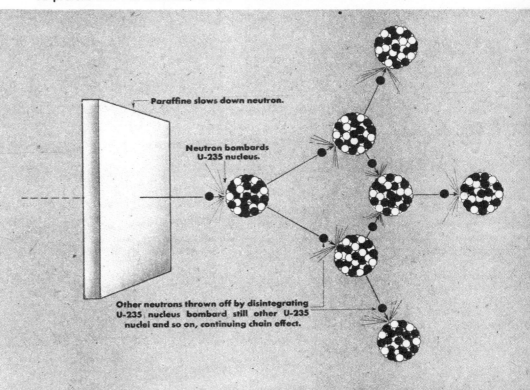

Paraffine slows down neutron.

Neutron bombards U-235 nucleus.

Other neutrons thrown off by disintegrating U-235 nucleus bombard still other U-235 nuclei and so on, continuing chain effect.

Slowed down by frozen paraffine, neutron penetrates atom, splits it, causes chain reaction.

Columbia University and announced the news to an astounded scientific world.

Prof. Fermi then revealed that five years before he had been firing atomic bullets and had been prevented from making the discovery of uranium fission—the splitting of the uranium atom in two—only by a mischance in his technique.

Prof. Fermi, incidentally, is pretty happy today about his failure. When he came so close to making that fateful discovery he was in Mussolini's Italy. Had he succeeded before his exile the Axis might have had atomic bombs with which to begin its war.

The Axis was thwarted again and again by its own tyranny. Among the scientists who helped produce the atom bomb were two Jewish physicists who were forced by the Nazis to emigrate to England and a Danish professor who was smuggled out of German-occupied Copenhagen with atomic secrets which he carried with him to London and Washington. The Nazis raided his laboratory but found nothing.

Another near-miss for the Nazis came when the collapse of France was imminent. Premier Edouard Daladier had sent a secret French mission out of Norway past German spies with heavy water for French physicists, among them Frederick Joliot-Curie, son-in-law of the great Mme. Curie. Heavy water is invaluable in certain methods of atomic fission and is difficult to produce. The water arrived in France just before the capitulation and was carried to England on one of the last ships to leave Bordeaux.

Germany nevertheless continued work on the atom, and Allied leaders were worried. Reports had the Germans working feverishly to forge a weapon from the atom's power. In Britain, alarmed scientists speeded their efforts to solve the secret of atomic fission.

In the U. S., American-born nuclear physicists were so unaccustomed to the idea of using their science for military purposes that they hardly realized what needed to be done. The early efforts to restrict publication on atomic subjects and to obtain Government support for further research were stimulated largely by a small group of foreign physicists living in the U. S. Up to 1940 information on research which was to

lead to America's greatest secret weapon was open to any one.

One of the European physicists-in-exile in the U. S., the great Albert Einstein, had written in 1905 a simple equation which was to be the background for all the research in atomic energy. The equation was part of his relativity theory and indicated that light, which is a form of energy, has mass just as much as a particle of what we usually think of as matter, and that any particle of matter therefore is energy.

The astonishing thing about his equation was that it showed that if only a tiny bit of matter should be destroyed, the result would be enormous energy.

Backed by Einstein and his theory, a little band of scientists—native Americans and exiles from Axis-dominated lands—went to President Roosevelt to interest him in the possibilities of atomic power. The President, convinced that much might come from atom research, appointed a committee to look into the problem. Up to the end of 1941 the total expenditures on atomic research were small, although the amount of work done on the problem by scientists all over the country was great.

Shortly before Pearl Harbor the President wrote Prime Minister Churchill suggesting that any efforts toward the development of an atomic bomb should be coordinated or even jointly conducted by the U. S. and Great Britain.

That December the U. S. National Academy of Sciences issued a report supporting the efforts already made in the atomic field and expressing optimism about the future. Information received from the British was even more optimistic, and the President, the Prime Minister and their advisors decided that the time had come really to push the program. The atom bomb began to take shape.

It was decided to build production plants on a vast scale in the U. S., since Great Britain was already up to her neck in war production and was in range of German bombers and open to sea attack. Britain would therefore furnish her scientists to the U. S. and Canada would furnish indispensable raw materials.

There were many questions for the scientists to decide. First, they had to select a material to give the bomb explosive force. They had several forms of uranium to select from—the uranium "isotopes." There were three of them—uranium 234, 235 and 238, plus plutonium, the artificial element that can be created from uranium. Of these, the scientists knew that only 235 and plutonium could be used.

In a ton of uranium ore there are only 14 pounds of 235, and these are intricately mixed with the other isotopes. It would have taken more than 191 years to obtain a single gram of 235 and more than 75,000 years to obtain a single pound, under methods then in use.

Worst of all—uranium was one of the rarest elements in the world. It was found in pitchblende, which exists only in Canada and Africa in any quantities.

The project and its problems were put under the direction of a group of top-ranking U. S. and foreign scientists working in the newly-formed Office of Scientific Research and Development; its director, Dr. Vannevar Bush, noted electrical engineer, was detailed to report directly to the President. Later, the military value of the experiments became obvious to everybody, and the major part of the work was transferred to the War Department. Practically the same scientific staff continued working, with Maj. Gen. Leslie R. Groves, former Deputy Chief of Construction in the War Department and a veteran Engineer Corps man, in charge.

From here on, work on the atomic bomb became "top secret." In wartime Washington, where practically every project was hush-hush, the atomic work became the best-protected secret of the war.

Information on atom research was so compartmentalized that each person connected with it knew only what he or she had to know to carry out a particular job. A special intelligence organization was set up independent of G-2 to control the security side of the project. Even the FBI was barred from the various installations throughout the country, except where its operatives had special permission to enter.

Congress had to content itself with no more than an assurance from the Army that the $1,-950,000,000 appropriated for atom research was "absolutely essential to national security." Mere

mention of atomic work on the floor of Congre might have been a tip-off to the Nazis and Jap

Once the whole House Appropriations Com mittee became skeptical of the work, sin progress was not so rapid as had been expecte One of the Congressmen called the project "t fantastic" and threatened to tell the House wh he knew and demand more information. Th threat brought Chief of Staff George Marsha before the committee in a hurried secret sessio the committee heeded his plea to keep silent.

The Nazis and the Japs actually did hav agents in the U. S. with specific instructions get information on the bomb, if any, and uranium. The Nazi spies were directed to mak contact with key personnel at any atomic wor plants and to determine the type of protectiv devices used. The FBI learned through a foreig power what the spies were up to and stoppe them.

To make doubly sure that there would be n leak of information, about 20,000 news outlets-newspapers, radio broadcasters, magazines an book publishers—were asked by the Office (Censorship not to publish or broadcast anythin about "new or secret military weapons or ex periments." On the whole, they kept mum. Bu the Army really got in a tizzy when Superma gave a "preview" of the bomb.

One episode showed little Professor Dust challenging Superman to take a 3,000,000-vo charge from a cyclotron. Superman withstood th current, and the professor was so embarrasse by his failure to kill the big guy that he sai "The machine must be out of order."

What followed is still a military secret. At th request of the Office of Censorship, the artist who create the strip promptly discontinued ref erence to atomic power.

Strictest secrecy was maintained throughou the whole project, which was set up as a ne\ district of the Corps of Engineers and official designated the "Manhattan District." More tha 179,000 workers were recruited throughout th country for work in the various laboratories an plants in which the atomic investigations wer carried on. Prospective employees could be tol only that the work for which they were bein selected was "most secret." Many of the men wh were finally chosen were unaware of the purpos of their jobs even after they had been employe for some months.

Although there was still some question as t which of the several theoretically possible meth ods of producing explosive atomic material wa best, the Army decided to go ahead with the con struction of large-scale plants—the biggest Arm construction program of all time—because o the tremendous pressure of time. Two plant were started at the Clinton Engineer Works nea Knoxville, Tenn., and a third at the Hanfor Engineer Works, near Pasco, Wash. Here, too secrecy was essential. Contracts were place with no publicity. Parts were ordered in many cases without the manufacturers knowing wha they were to be used for.

The Clinton site was selected for its large size —59,000 acres—and isolated location, and fo safety against possible unknown hazards. Th Hanford site, too, was isolated, on a 430,000-acr Government reservation.

At the Clinton reservation a Government-owned-and-operated city named Oak Ridge was built. The settlement contains houses and dormi tories, churches, theaters and schools. Today it has a population of 78,000—fifth largest in Ten nessee. At Hanford another city was constructed. Called Richmond, it has a population of 17,000.

Near Santa Fe, N. Mex., a special laboratory most secret of all the secret plants, was built to deal with the hundreds of technical problems involved in putting together an effective bomb. In this largest and most complete physical labo ratory in the world, Dr. J. Robert Oppenheimer brains behind the bomb itself, headed a staff of technicians who worked day and night forging the weapon that gave the final blow to Japan.

All over the country thousands of large and small manufacturing plants and laboratories, uni versities and schools carried on research and worked to develop special equipment, materials and processes for the project. And all of them worked under a blanket of secrecy.

It was due to these hundreds of organizations and thousands of workers that a study which would ordinarily have taken 20 years was com pleted in just three.

The Atomic Age was ushered in on July 16,

Maj. Gen. Groves, O-i-C of the Atomic Bomb Proje (seated), with his assistant, Brig. Gen. Thomas Farrel

5. A tense band of military men and scientists hered in a remote section of the Alamogordo Base on the New Mexico desert 120 miles theast of Albuquerque to witness the results their years of effort—the first fateful test of atomic bomb. It was 5:30 in the morning. darkening sky, rain, lightning and peals of nder heightened the drama.

ension was tremendous. Failure was always sible, and too great success might have meant only an uncontrollable, unusable weapon but death of those who watched. The bomb might st them and their entire efforts into eternity.

he nearest observation post was 10,000 yards th of the steel tower from which the bomb s to be detonated. Here in a timber-and-earth lter the controls for the test were placed. At oint 17,000 yards from the tower which would e the best observation, the key figures in the mic project took their posts.

he time signals—"minus 20 minutes," "minus minutes"—increased the tension. The watchers d their breaths.

'wo minutes before the scheduled firing time st of them lay face down, with their feet nting towards the tower. The moment came. ere was a blinding flash brighter than the ghest daylight. A mountain range three miles ay stood out in bold relief. And then there s a tremendous, sustained roar. A heavy wave pressure bore down upon the observers. Two n who were standing outside the control cen were knocked flat.

A huge, many-colored cloud surged majesti ly upward for more than 40,000 feet. The steel ver was completely vaporized.

he test was over. The bomb was a success.

What is this bomb like? What is its size? How it constructed? Those are still top military crets. Popular science writers say it is likely at the bomb contains plutonium, in great con ntration, as well as some means to split it and ke it release its energy in an explosion.

he detonating mechanism of the bomb must ntain a slow-down device for the neutrons uch are hurled at the uranium or plutonium oms to produce an explosion. Only a neutron, hich is an uncharged particle found in the om's nucleus, has much chance of getting rough an atom's electrical ring of defenses.

Before the war scientists had succeeded, in eir cumbersome cyclotrons, in bombarding anium with neutrons and getting the neutrons rough. It has been estimated that these neu ons had about one chance in 140 of hitting the cleus. When that happened, the uranium atom lit in two, and the result was no longer anium but barium and krypton, a rare gas. at was transmutation, and together with it me the emission of energy, the mass of kryp n and barium being less than that of the orig al uranium atom.

But major mechanical and laboratory advances ve been made. It seems evident that scientists e now able for the first time to separate

uranium in quantity and that a means has been devised to release neutrons to bombard pluton ium and thus detonate the bomb at a desired period after the bomb leaves the aircraft. The War Department has released information sho wing that the weapon is fired before it hits the ground to increase its power to shatter buildings and to disseminate its radioactive products as a cloud. The mechanism that effects such a marvel must obviously be far simpler than a cyclotron, which weighs tons.

How quickly research on the bomb itself has proceeded is shown by the disclosure that the second atomic bomb dropped on Japan at Naga saki, August 9, was a more powerful and a sim pler one, which "made the bomb dropped on Hiroshima obsolete."

But the mechanical details of the bomb did not concern most Americans. When the news came that the greatest weapon in the world had been unleashed upon Japan, the nation's main reaction was one of awe. There was little re joicing.

President Truman voiced the sentiments of the country when he said: "The atomic bomb is too dangerous to be loose in a lawless world. . . . We must constitute ourselves trustees of this new force—to prevent its misuse, and to turn it into channels of service to mankind. It is an awful responsibility that has come to us."

When the awe at the destructiveness of the new weapon began to wear off, the feeling that we were entering a new era—the Age of Atomic Energy—remained. The New York *Times'* three word headline—the like of which had probably never appeared in a newspaper before—summed it up: "New Age Ushered."

Never before had one discovery so caught the imagination of people everywhere. Never before had it been obvious so soon that a scientific dis covery would change the world.

All over the U. S. people started using words they barely understood: "Atom," "electron," "proton," "neutron," "uranium." The nation's press did its best to simplify the scientific prin ciples of atomic energy for its readers. The War Department felt that the subject was too highly complicated for its officers to explain and called in a civilian, the New York *Times'* science ex pert, William L. Laurence, to handle the press releases on the bomb and its background.

There was much disagreement as to when and to what extent atomic energy could be put to peaceful uses. The power, coal and oil industries protested vehemently that it would be years after the lifetime of any one now living before atom energy would take over.

One scientist close to the development of the atomic bomb compares it with the prehistoric discovery of fire and cautions that there was a lapse of centuries and centuries between the discovery of fire and the development of the steam engine. The atomic discovery does not seem as important as the discovery of elec tricity, this scientist says, although it may actu ally prove to be that important in time.

Others were more optimistic. In London, Sir John Anderson, who as Chancellor of the Ex chequer in the Churchill Government super vised the British side of the atomic bomb re

search, said the discovery definitely is greater than that of electricity.

Prof. H. D. Smyth, chairman of the physics department at Princeton University and con sultant on the atomic bomb, has written a de tailed account of the history of the project and of its scientific background with War Department authorization. Smyth says: "There is good prob ability that nuclear power for special purposes could be developed within 10 years and that plentiful supplies of radioactive materials can have a profound effect on the treatment of cer tain diseases in a similar period."

The Rev. Alphonse Schwitalla, S. J., dean of the St. Louis University Medical School, sees in atomic energy a possible key to the mystery of life.

But to make sure that when the secrets of atomic energy become available for peacetime application they will be employed wisely in the interests of security and peace, the U. S., Britain and Canada have taken action to control patents in the field and to obtain control over the uran ium ore which so far appears indispensable to the process. In each country, all scientific and industrial figures involved in the work have been required to assign their entire rights to any inventions to their respective governments, sub ject to financial settlement later.

To consider the long-term direction and con trol of U. S. atomic research, Secretary of War Stimson has appointed a committee to make recommendations. An advisory group of the sci entists and industrialists most closely connected with the development of the bomb is already planning national and international control.

They hope, as the world hopes, that the new Age of Atomic Energy will be an age of peace as well. For if it is an age of war, that war might mean the annihilation of the human race.

—Cpl. JONATHAN KILBOURN

One of the giant production plants of the Clinton Engineering works at Oak Ridge, Tennessee.

ATOMIC BOMB AWAY

By ROBERT SCHWARTZ Y2c
YANK Staff Correspondent

GUAM, THE MARIANAS—It was 0245 when the colonel eased forward on the throttle. The B-29 with *Enola Gay* printed in big block letters on her nose vibrated and began to roll forward. She reached 100 mph in a hurry, then picked up additional speed more slowly. She used up half the runway, and she was still bearing down hard on her spinning tires.

The tail gunner, S/Sgt. George Caron, up near the waist for the take-off, began to sweat it out. Capt. Robert A. Lewis, who usually piloted the *Enola Gay*, would have had her off the ground by this time. But Cap Lewis was only co-pilot on this trip and Caron didn't know the colonel, Col. Paul W. (Old Bull) Tibbets Jr., who had the controls now.

The *Enola Gay* neared the end of the runway and was almost on the gravel when she lifted gently into the dark sky. Caron realized suddenly that the colonel had been fighting to hold the ship on the ground the whole length of the runway just to be absolutely safe. And Caron remembered the bomb.

The men knew about the bomb—that it was something special—but they didn't know it was the atomic bomb. It was important, they knew, too, for in addition to Col. Tibbets' taking over for the trip, there was a Capt. William S. Parsons of the Navy aboard. He was a bomb expert of some kind and had come along as an observer.

Sgt. Joe Steiborik, radar operator, a dark husky Texan who was almost uncannily adept at operating his precision instruments, called the pilot on the intercom and told him he would find a large cloud north of the next island. "Better stay away from it, Colonel," he said. "It's pretty turbulent."

Fifteen minutes later the colonel came to the rear to use the tube. Before the trip was over he was to make a dozen or more such trips. "Coffee," was all he would say. "Drink so damn much of it."

Pfc. Richard H. Nelson, a boyish redhead who looks like every kid in every breakfast cereal advertisement ever printed, settled down to read "Watch Out for Willie Carter," a boxing story. Nelson was teased pretty constantly about his reading, just as he was teased about almost everything. The youngest man on the crew ("I've been 20 for over two months"), he had been nicknamed "Junior" by the four other men of the plane crew. Before the flight was over Junior finished the Willie Carter novel.

The flight engineer, S/Sgt. Wyatt E. Duzenbury of Lansing, Mich., a quiet 32-year-old thin-faced fellow with big ears, sat at his control panel reading innumerable gauges. A pure, undiluted flight engineer, Deuce's only concern during the flight was to wonder how the big explosion would affect his gauges. "He's dial happy," say the others.

Up front sat Col. Tibbets, a young (33) man with an accumulation of war flying experience. He was the pilot of the first B-17 to fly over the English Channel on a bombing mission; he flew Gen. Mark Clark to Gibraltar, he flew Gen. Eisenhower to Gibraltar, and then he flew Gen. Doolittle to Gibraltar; he flew Gen. Clark and Canada's Gen. McNaughton to Algiers, landing on a field he knew would be bombed, and which was actually under attack, before he stopped taxi-ing; he led the first mission to bomb North Africa; returned to the U. S., he flew the first B-29 on test missions; he was made CO of the atomic bomb outfit forming at Wendover, Utah; and now, sitting at the controls of the *Enola Gay*, he was on his way to drop the first atomic bomb in history.

The co-pilot was Cap Lewis, the plane's usual pilot. He had flown four missions against Japan in the *Enola Gay* with this crew. The crewmen all call him Cap, and he is an easy man to know and an easy one to like.

The navigator was Capt. Red (Dutch) Van Kirk, a young Pennsylvanian with a crew haircut that gives him a collegiate look. Van Kirk is a good friend of Maj. Tom W. Ferebee, the bombardier, and they had flown together in

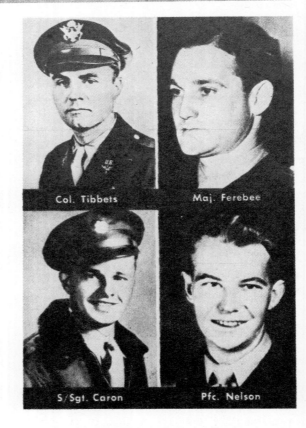

Col. Tibbets   Maj. Ferebee

S/Sgt. Caron   Pfc. Nelson

North Africa and England, usually as navigator and bombardier for Col. Tibbets. They were in on most of the colonel's firsts, and he brought them into his atomic bomb unit as soon as he got it.

The flight was well along now, and Caron, the tail gunner, remembering Cap Lewis' prodigious appetite, crawled forward through the tunnel to get to the food before the co-pilot ate it all. Caron found six apples among the food up forward and threw these the length of the tunnel to Shumard, hoping that they would roll out of the tunnel and fall on a sleeping lieutenant who was flying this mission as special observer. He was Lt. M. U. Jeppson, an electronics officer. Caron wanted to wake him and get him to sit erect, thus taking less space in the waist, but none of the apples went the length of the tunnel, and the lieutenant kept on sprawling.

The flight to the target was routine, and only the thought of what they were going to see kept them active. They read, ate and talked a little and said nothing more historic than "Move over, you bastard, and give me some room," which must have been said on every plane ride since Orville said it to Wilbur at Kitty Hawk.

Occasionally they consulted the various charms and talismans, of which the *Enola Gay* had an inordinate number. These included, in addition to Caron's baseball hat and Shumard's pictures, the following items: Three pairs of silk panties from Omaha, stowed in one corner with a booklet on VD. One picture of Wendover Mary, a group companion during training in Utah. Wendover Mary had on a pair of high heeled shoes. One good conduct ribbon, fastened on the radio set and owned by Junior. Six prophylactic kits, divided equally between Van Kirk and Ferebee and presented by the ground crew in case of forced landing in territory "where the natives are friendly." One ski cap purchased in Salt Lake City and worn by Steiborik. One picture of the lobby of the Hotel Utah at Salt Lake, where Ferebee formed many associations, all of limited length but definite purpose. One lipstick kissprint on the nose, signed "Dottie" and bearing a dateline, "Omaha, onetime," placed there by a civilian girl who worked at an Omaha air base; it had been shellacked over promptly for permanence—source of the crew's common prayer, "Omaha, one more time."

These things were all very important to the *Enola Gay* community and were a binding force. A series of good drunks together in the States had helped weld them into a unit, and they were all very close friends.

They were getting near the target now, and Caron went back to the tail, taking his K-20

along. The plane began to climb, and the pressurized the cabin. The bombardier and th navigator, veterans of 54 and 63 missions, weren worried about their imminent work, though dawned on the navigator, Van Kirk, that "I be the biggest ass in the Air Force if I misse the target." They passed over several secondar targets and found them visible, then continue into Hiroshima. They saw it, lined it up, opene the bomb-bay doors, made the bomb run, and the bomb fall. The plane banked sharply to th right and every one craned to look out.

Back at the right waist window, Sgt. B Shumard, the assistant flight engineer, turne his polaroids to full intensity and prepared take advantage of the fact that he had th best seat for the show. When the bomb we off it looked blue through his polaroids, b he noted that the interior of the plane lighte up as though flash bulbs had been set off insi the cabin. He adjusted his polaroids to mild in tensity and looked down at Hiroshima. A lar white cloud was spreading rapidly over t whole area, obscuring everything and rising ve rapidly. Shumard shouted into the intercom "There it goes, and it's coming right back at us

Looking way down again, he noted that outsi the smoke circle and racing ahead of it we three large concentric circles. These appear to Shumard to be heat rings, since they look like the transparent wavy vapors seen comi off hot objects. He craned to see what happen to them, but the lieutenant who had been asle was now awake and was climbing all over Sh mard's neck. He lost the rings during this i terval and could not find them again.

The engineer noted that his instruments we still functioning normally, and then he look out his little hatch. He said nothing

When Steiborik got no instrument reaction the blast, he looked too.

"Jesus Christ," said Lt. Jeppson, "if peop knew what we were doing we could have so tickets for $100,000."

Van Kirk said nothing, though newspaper r ports later called him "a battle-hardened ve eran who exclaimed 'My God!'" when he sa the blast. The crew still kid him about this.

Ferebee, the bombardier, felt only one rea tion: he was damn glad to be rid of the bom Then he set to work filling out the strike repo form which was to be radioed in.

Back in the tail Caron noted the turbulen and called to the pilot: "Colonel, it's coming t wards us fast." He got no reply, but the pla changed its course and outdistanced the clou

They looked after it as long as they cou see it, a great ringed cumulus-type shaft risi higher and higher through the clouds. Then th flew on and it was gone. The tail gunner call to the pilot: "Colonel, that was worth the 2 ride on the cyclone at Coney Island."

The colonel called back and said. "I'll colle the two bits when we land "

"You'll have to wait till pay day," said t tail gunner

Maj. Ferebee filled out the strike report a gave it to Capt. Parsons who had been in char of the bomb. Parsons took it to Junic

"This report," said the captain, "is going d rectly to the President."

The Navy captain wondered aloud: "How c you destroy so much and sacrifice so little? V didn't even damage a plane."

Some of the men wondered how many it wou take to make Japan surrender; everyone wo dered if the one bomb would end the war. Final they dozed off a little, talked a little and ate little and engaged in brief flurries of speculatio But the *Enola Gay*, the plane that had be named by the crew for the colonel's mother a gesture for the flight, flew on and on. "She sang they say now, with the deep pride that airm feel for a ground crew that can make a pla sing.

Deuce worried about fuel, but Cap kidded hi out of it. Time dragged. Everyone got hungr But then they saw the field, and they were al again.

"I looked at the Old Bull," says Cap Lew "and his eyes were bloodshot and he looked aw ful tired. He looked like the past 10 months, Wendover, and Washington, and New Mexic and overseas, had come up and hit him all once.

"I says to him, 'Bull, after such a beautiful jo you better make a beautiful landing.

"And he did."

Separation

By Cpl. MARTIN S. DAY

FORT MEADE, MD.—Even if you have fewer points than I have, you'll probably be seated across the desk from me one of these days while I try to hand you some separation counseling at the Fort Meade Separation Center here in Maryland. We separation counselors figure that for us it's still a long war.

I know how I'll feel when my chance for discharge comes. "Let's cut the chatter, bud," I'll probably say. "Just give me the white paper and let me take off." Equally impatient right now,

One fellow with 74 points squeezed through to 86, because he had an illegitimate child.

many men try to dash past us without taking full advantage of the separation counselor's advice and assistance. But since they've been away so long from the States and from civilian life, maybe they ought to listen to us.

Almost every man getting out on points has plenty of Spam bars for overseas time and has sweated out more than enough time for a hashmark. No one could deny that the great majority of dischargees on points deserve their release. Many times I've written about a dischargee, "Served as rifleman in North Africa, Sicily, Italy, France and Germany," or "Drove light tank in France, Belgium, Holland, Germany, Austria and Czechoslovakia."

Most of these men came into the Army in 1940 or 1941, and most of them have seen far more than their share of combat. They've earned *WD AGO 53-55* (honorable discharge) the hard way.

Every Army system, however, produces its oddities. I talked to a radio operator-mechanic-gunner on a Liberator who was overseas nine months and collected 60 combat points, while many infantrymen overseas three years got only half that number. A buck sergeant drove a refueling truck on Italian airfields and never even saw an air raid but he collected scads and scads of combat points because his entire squadron received those little bronze stars. On occasion rear-echelon units in AGF and ASF have also picked

up some combat points the easy way. But it does seem a bit screwy for a man who never left England to get the Ardennes star and five more points simply because some planes of his squadron got in the scrap.

One fellow I interviewed had 74 time and combat points and squeezed through to 86 because of an illegitimate child. He had recognized and supported the child for several years, but some of the boys around here were sarcastic. "You do what the medics and the chaplain tell you," they complained, "and you only gyp yourself out of points."

A very few have sweated out the points pleasantly. Recently I had a topkick who was forced to endure the rigors of downtown Honolulu from 1940 until this summer in order to get his release. A fortunate T-4 spent more than three years in Hamilton, Bermuda, before returning to the States in 1944. Early this year he was shipped to India, but the point system tagged him and sent him back for discharge after only three weeks residence in India.

A Regular Army man beat a peacetime desertion rap and is getting a perfectly white discharge that lists more than 900 days bad time. Men with as many as 12 courts-martial are copping the lovely white paper. One youngster is getting a blue discharge because of four AWOLs and a total of 121 days bad time. I've stopped trying to figure this thing out.

If anybody has put this war on a paying basis, I think it's the guy whose feet completely collapsed in basic and sent him back to his wife and three kids after only one month and 12 days in service. In addition to his regular pay he hit Finance for $240 in dependency benefits, $100 in mustering-out pay and 5 cents a mile for the trip back to upstate New York. What are the odds that the joe would have been on flying pay if he'd stuck it out another week or so?

Point system separatees up till now have been about evenly distributed among Regular Army,

His feet collapsed in basic and he went home after one month and twelve days service.

This kid boosted his age to get in the AAF. In two years he got 90 points and is out.

National Guard and Selective Service. Most of them have ranged from 22 to 35 years of age. There's a good percentage of youngsters who lied about their age to get into the Army a few years back. We recently had a kid who boosted his age to join the AAF; in a trifle over two years he amassed more than 90 points and is now back in corduroy pants and polo shirts. He's just a few months past his 19th birthday.

A while back I used to try feebly to kid Regular Army dischargees by saying, "Why don't you RA men stay in and let us civilians out?" I've cut out that sickly gag, largely because most of my RA first-three-graders plan to re-enlist.

One grizzled first sergeant with five hashmarks put it up to me: "They won't let me take my family to Germany. I've got a baby boy I've never seen, and I want to get reacquainted with the missus. Taking a discharge means for me a trip home and $100 a month for a three-month furlough. But after that's over I'll be in for another hitch."

Talking about family reunions, I had one man going to meet his father for about the first time. He was the son of an English girl and an American soldier of the first World War. Born in 1921, he was taken to England by his mother in 1923 when she left her husband in a huff.

After more than one and a half years in the RAF, this man, who was an American citizen because he was born in the States, transferred to the AAF. Coming back to his native land was coming back to an unknown country and to a virtually unknown father. He had been in the States just four days when I talked with him in the interview booth. Very enthusiastic about his brave new world, he remarked in an Oxford accent, "D'you know, old chap, I was always quarreling with those English about how much better the States were."

The GI is more than usually talkative when he gets to us counselors, because he suddenly realizes that for him the Army is on the verge of becoming just a memory, so you ought to come around to this office if you want to hear about Dachau, Bilibid Prison, Anzio or Salamaua.

Older men appear more inclined to want to return to their pre-war jobs than younger men, but 80 to 90 percent of the dischargees I talk with seem to want new and different and, of course, better jobs. The guy who wrote, "How're you gonna keep 'em down on the farm after they've seen Paree?" wasn't just kidding.

From what they tell me, only a very small proportion of farmers plan to return to the farm for good. One pfc blurted out, "I never got much more than 15 miles from home. The Army's taken me through 15 countries from Brazil to Iceland and from Trinidad to Czechoslovakia. After where I've been and what I've seen, I couldn't settle down on any farm."

The number of dischargees expecting luscious jobs paying a la Hollywood·is far smaller than I, at any rate, expected. Most men want steady, lifetime work, and they're willing to study and sweat and take average wages to clinch that permanent job. This generation seems to think pretty much in terms of security.

One ex-farmer said: "The Army's taken me to 15 countries. I couldn't settle down on a farm."

Army counselors can offer extensive referrals and perhaps give you the right steer. Some veterans claim the old run-around is given them by the multitudinous agencies, departments and what-have-you-to-perplex-the-veteran. Tempers and time may be saved, and something vital to you may be gained, if you talk over your job problem with your separation-center interviewer. The T/O lists him as a vocational counselor (262); that means that he should be able to give you advice on job placement.

Surprisingly few of the men I've talked with expect to use the GI Bill of Rights for a full-time education, but many want to take refresher courses at night or other part-time education in the hope of upping their future earning capacity. Many separatees don't realize that all the unemployment or educational benefits they claim will be deducted from any future bonus that may be given to veterans. This really shouldn't be regarded as a disadvantage, however. You have nothing more than a raffle ticket on a future bonus. Do you want the education or the bonus? The education is certain; the bonus at this moment is as unpredictable as a supply sergeant.

Also, it hasn't been universally understood that almost everyone, regardless of age, is entitled to a full year of refresher training. To be eligible

for more than a year's education you must be able to prove that you were under 25 at the time of induction or that your education was interrupted by military service. Your discharge papers are about all you need to produce to be eligible for the one-year refresher course at any school or college of your choice.

Maybe you think I'm fooling you, but I recently had in my booth a staff sergeant who was president of an Alaskan gold mining company. Now 48, he plans a year of advanced metallurgical study before he follows spring up into the Yukon in 1946.

Full publicity has pretty well scotched the hashish dream that everybody could slap the discharge down on the Government counter and say, "Now lend me $2,000, chum." You'll get a loan only from a private lending agency (usually a bank) and only if the lender is willing to risk his own cash on you and your enterprise. Banks are pretty wary these days because most values are now highly inflated. Many loan agencies are backing only gilt-edged, beautifully solvent veterans because they don't want a black eye in the community for foreclosing on an ex-GI.

There are plenty of veterans who are planning to get ahead without borrowing. Take the case of a brawny, Slavic T-5 from Pittsburgh who owns a plot of ground near his postwar place of work.

"First, I'll build a garage with a second floor," he told me. "My wife and I can live in the garage while I build the house in my spare time. I have a little money and I don't want to owe any man a cent." This plan wouldn't work for everybody, and the steel puddler's family won't roll in luxury for a while but, brother, I'm willing to bet the blue chips on that fellow.

The knottiest problem for most men seems to be what to do about their National Service Life Insurance. I've talked with men who have been subject to separation orientation everywhere from Munich or Manila to my desk without getting a clear picture of life insurance conversion. The best advice here is to hold as much of the stuff as you can and thresh out the details with your counselor and with the Veterans' Administration representative nearest your home.

A very poor substitute for Mr. Anthony, I've sometimes found myself dropped into the middle of family squabbles. Not long ago I talked with a poor guy who had been pestering personnel officers all over the ETO. He divorced his wife in 1941 and thought he had done with her, but although she remarried, she didn't forget her first husband. Not this girl. Last summer she produced the license issued for her first marriage and claimed an F allotment from his pay. The GI complained to Regiment, but all he got in the way of satisfaction was, "Oh, yeah? Let's see your divorce papers."

Sent airmail-registered from the States, those papers crawled after the guy across four countries, through two hospitals and around a handful of reinforcement and casual depots. Meanwhile,

One staff sergeant, 48 years old, was president of an Alaskan gold mining company.

He's throwing over a girl in Iceland, a wife and baby in England, for a West Virginia girl.

under protest, he kept paying allotments to another man's wife. I did my legal bit in starting action for him to regain what she had mulcted from him, but I don't know how far he'll push the suit and that's strictly none of my business. "After all," he mused, "she's the mother of my child, isn't she?"

That was a simple case. Sometime ask me to tell you about the medical aidman who has a fiancee in Iceland and a wife and baby in England but wants to throw the three of them over for a gal in West Virginia.

Whatever your problem, we counselors will try to help somehow within the limits of our job. My desk is getting bowlegged from its piles of books and files of addresses and referrals. I'll give you all the time you want, and I've spent as much as 110 minutes with one man.

Usually, the interview here at Fort Meade averages 40 to 50 minutes, and each counselor can handle approximately 10 to 12 men daily. But unless somebody pulls counselors out of a hat, we'll have to speed things up a bit now, because our numbers aren't increasing and the hell-bent-for-civvies boys are really pouring in.

One thing more about your interview with the separation counselor. He'll fill out the Separation Qualification Record which constitutes the Army's job recommendation just as the discharge is the character recommendation. The form has been used extensively by the United States Employment Service and other agencies, and it might be useful to you when you present it to prospective employers.

The interviewer will give you all the breaks in writing up descriptions of your jobs in the Army and in your prewar civilian life. However, just because you've sharpened up a lot while you've been in ODs and suntans, you shouldn't try to sell the counselor a bill of goods unless it's on the level.

I haven't had a downright phony yet, but some of the boys who said they were store clerks when they came into the Army want the Separation Qualification Record to call them department store managers when they go out. Even if you fool the interviewer (and he's talked to hundreds of men and shouldn't be a complete sucker) you probably won't be able to fool a future employer when you're called upon to produce on the job. But I've talked to plenty of GIs and I'm convinced that since they've endured the enemy, foreign parts and the Army, they can be counted on to meet anything the American future may happen to toss at them.

Now I'll admit that I've skimmed over lots of subjects that might be of interest to men on the point of getting out. If you have any questions or just want to kick the subjects around a bit more, just drop in to see me for some separation counseling.

And when I finish shooting the breeze with you and wish you the best of luck in civilian life, please don't break my heart with, "Thanks, same to you. Hope you're out soon."

To cause a successful chain reaction, scientists must arrange things so that the free neutrons are slowed from their dizzying pace.

The neutrons can be caused to collide with frozen paraffine. Hydrogen atoms in the paraffine, about the same weight as the neutrons but active agents, practically stop the neutrons in their tracks—much as one billiard ball can be stopped dead by hitting another.

The neutrons are now shot at the 235s, and the chain reaction ensues. Out of the blast that tears the uranium atom in two come also gamma rays—powerful radiations that sometimes tear electrons off atoms and otherwise shatter them, creating further flying fragments and debris.

The chain reaction is on, carried forward by the swarms of neutrons released from each atom that is split. Rebounding back and forth, the neutrons are sufficiently slowed so that the process is continued, and vast energy is released.

It is this energy that created chaos in Japan. It is this same energy which poses the possibility of a new era, the era of atomic power, in which the vast energies of the atom, harnessed as the atom bomb shows they can be, may give mankind power greater than it has ever had.

This 20-ton cyclotron at Notre Dame is one of many in which scientists smashed atoms prior to invention of the bomb

THE ATOMIC BOMB

"Sixteen hours ago an American airplane dropped one bomb on Hiroshima. . . . That bomb had more power than 20,000 tons of TNT. It is an atomic bomb . . : a harnessing of the basic power of the universe."

THAT simple statement, made by President Truman at 10:30 A.M., August 6, electrified the world. It came as the climax of one of the most dramatic stories in the history of man's long search for the secrets of matter.

The story behind the atomic bomb is a detective story with no Sherlock Holmes for a hero. The number of scientists who took part in the search was without parallel. And when the first of the bombs hit Hiroshima it was a victory for the whole force. No star-performing "special investigator" could claim credit for the breathtaking, earth-shattering climax.

Brilliant deductions had been made, clue after clue tracked down to climactic discoveries. But although the individual findings of many men share the credit for the final, almost incredible success, that success was made possible primarily by the kind of leg work and laboratory work in which a metropolitan police force would take part—leg work and lab work entailing years of drudgery as well as drama, ill-omened activity as well as inspiration, false scents as well as cosmic clues.

The dramatic story opens with Dr. Lise Meitner, a woman scientist and director of the Kaiser Wilhelm Institute in Berlin. In 1938 Dr. Meitner is bombarding uranium atoms with neutrons and then submitting the uranium to chemical analysis.

To her amazement, she and her associates, Drs. Otto Hahn and F. Strassmann, find the element barium in the smashed remains of the uranium. They remember they had put in barium as a chemical "carrier" to precipitate a powerful new radioactive substance present in the debris, but when they try to separate the substance from the barium, it cannot be done.

There is one possible answer, and only one. The mysterious substance is itself barium—a radioactive barium that had been there before the other barium was put in.

But where did the radioactive barium come from? It was a scientific mystery of the first order. It was like finding champagne flowing from your faucet. It just couldn't be.

And then Hitler's racist theories came into the story. Dr. Meitner was a Jewess. Hitler had overruled his own Nuernberg anti-Semitic laws in order to try to compel her to stay in Germany, but Dr. Meitner, outraged by the "new order," escaped over the Dutch border and fled to

Sweden, stopping in Denmark on the way.

With Dr. Meitner in Copenhagen, her former colleagues refused to face the facts of their revolutionary discovery. They reported in a German scientific publication that they could not bring themselves to believe that the radioactive barium came from the uranium.

Lise Meitner was more imaginative. Since the barium was not there to begin with, she reasoned, it must have come from the uranium. That meant it was the result of the uranium atom being split into two nearly equal parts.

She lost no time in getting in touch with her nephew, Dr. Otto Robert Frisch, who worked in the Copenhagen laboratory of the famous Danish physicist, Dr. Niels Bohr. Testing together for the radioactive barium, they saw for the first time the possibility of a geyser of atomic energy.

In the first weeks of 1939 Dr. Frisch succeeded at his task. He split the uranium atom.

Dr. Frisch cabled the news to Dr. Bohr, who was in the U. S. With Dr. John Dunning, Dr. Bohr and Prof. Enrico Fermi, both Nobel prize winners in physics, repeated the experiment at

Little was left of Hiroshima when a reconnaissance plane flew over the devastated city to take this photo day after the first atom bombing. Many buildings and whole city blocks were vaporized.

VJ-DAY

THE announcement everybody had been waiting for—through day after day of rumor and counter rumor—was a long time coming, and relief was as audible as celebration when final word came through. It was what we had been fighting for, the reason we had been in uniform for a year or two or five. Now the war was over.

It is a little hard to analyze the immediate meaning of anything you've been thinking about for so long so intensely. The first feeling is bound to be a bit of a let-down. After you say "It's over" for the first few times and get used to the idea, after you celebrate, after the shouting dies down, there is bound to be a certain hollowness.

The war is over and you suddenly realize that you have been living with war for a good slice of your life. You certainly aren't going to miss the war, but it's hard for a moment for most of us to think of how things will be—are—without it. It's like an itch that you've got used to scratching and all of a sudden along comes a drug that cures it; you still feel a slight inclination to go on scratching and you have to remind yourself that there is nothing to scratch. You have to make an effort to apply yourself to all the things you dreamed of doing if you ever got time off enough from scratching to do them.

The end of the war means for most of us that we will be getting out of the Army—not tomorrow, certainly, and probably not next week or next month, but more or less soon. There is no doubt that this is the biggest immediate meaning of peace to the average man or woman in the service.

One reaction is impatience. All of us are going to be very damn impatient about the speed with which we will be discharged. No matter what system of discharges is put into action there will be kicks, and no matter how good the system is there will be confusion. Recognizing this may make it easier to bear some of the inevitable snafus that will raise their heads in the months to come. We will save a lot of steam if we resist the temptation to bellyache about some of the minor injustices that are in the cards for us, and gripe only when our beefs are legitimate enough and large enough to warrant some attention and action.

Getting out of the Army also means a return to a way of life—a civilian way of life—that has become strange to some of us. It isn't easy to keep from overglamorizing civilian life when you're in uniform and so some of us are going to be disappointed when we get the chance to put on that blue serge or blue denim. Nothing could be so wonderful as the ideal you dream of when you are stuck on some Pacific island or abandoned in some obscure supply command or when you have been engaged in a succession of D-days, each one worse than the one before. It will save a lot of disappointment and bitterness if we can remember that civilian life is not perfect, that there are snafus there, too, and that the mere changing of a uniform for a department store ready-made is not going to solve problems automatically.

Some of the more excitable of civilian editorialists have been doing a heap of worrying about our reabsorption into normal civilian life. YANK thinks a lot of this worry is groundless and it also thinks that one of the biggest jobs we will have as veterans is to prove how groundless it is.

We are not coming back to the States as a bunch of problem children. We have certain rights as veterans and we have certain responsibilities as citizens. We cannot accept the rights without taking the responsibilities, too.

The responsibilities include more than pulling a blind down on our war past and living as useful citizens. We have been in a war and most of us know what war means in terms of death and hardship and hunger and dislocation. One responsibility should be to keep an eye always open for forces that might throw us into another war. We don't want one.

There are eventually going to be over ten million of us. We will have a hell of a lot of potential power. We are going to have to keep continually alert as to how we use that power. There are going to be people who will try to use us for their own ends. There are going to be other people who are going to try to confuse us so thoroughly that our power will be dispersed and useless. Let's not be suckers.

Let's remember that, among other things, this war taught us how costly war can be. And let's, as civilians, pay enough attention not only to our own government but to the affairs of the rest of the world so that another war may be averted.

It may seem silly to worry about far-away places when we will all be so glad to be home again. It may seem silly, but a lot of us spent a lot of time in far-away places and a lot of us died in them to end this war. Unless we pay attention to what goes on in the world today, we may be scattered all over its face, fighting again, tomorrow.

These are the things to remember now that we have the time to think about them. But the most immediate reaction is still the strongest one. The war is over.

YANK THE ARMY WEEKLY

YANK is published weekly by the enlisted men of the U. S. Army and is for sale only to those in the armed services. Stories, features, pictures and other material from YANK may be reproduced if they are not restricted by law or military regulations, provided proper cerdit is given, release dates are observed and specific prior permission has been granted for each item to be reproduced. Entire contents Vol. 4. No. 12, copyrighted, 1945, by Col. Franklin S. Forsberg and reviewed by U. S. military censors.

MAIN EDITORIAL OFFICE
205 EAST 42d STREET, NEW YORK 17, N. Y.

EDITORIAL STAFF

Managing Editor, Sgt. Joe McCarthy, FA; Art Director, Sgt. Art Weithas, DEML; Assistant Managing Editor, Sgt. August Loeb, AAF; Assistant Art Director, Sgt. Ralph Stein, Med.; Pictures, Sgt. Leo Hofeller, Armd.; Features, Sgt. Burtt Evans, Inf.; Sports, Sgt. Bill Estoff, Engr.; Overseas Editor, Sgt. Al Hine, Engr.; U. S. Editor, Sgt. Hilary H. Lyons, CA; Navy Editor, Donald Nugent Sp(X)3c; Associate Editors, Sgt. John Hay, Inf.; Cpl. Jonathan Kilbourn, Sig. Corps; Sgt. Merle Miller, AAF; Sgt. Max Novack, TC.
WASHINGTON, Sgt. Barrett McGurn, Med.; Sgt. H. N. Oliphant, Engr.; Cpl. John Haverstick, CA.
PHILIPPINES, Sgt. Chuck Rathe, DEML; Sgt. George Baker, Sig. Corps; Sgt. Frank Beck, AAF; Sgt. Douglas Borgstedt, DEML; Sgt. Roger Cowan, CA; Sgt. Jack Crowe, Med.; Sgt. Marvin Fasig, Engr.; Sgt. Marion Hargrove, FA; Sgt. Dale Kramer, MP; Sgt. Robert MacMillan, FA; Sgt. John McLeod, Med.; Sgt. Lionel Wathall, Engr.; Sgt. Roger Wrenn, Sig. Corps; Sgt. Bill Young, Inf.; Cpl. Hyman Goldberg, Inf.; Cpl. Tom Kane, Sig. Corps; Cpl. James Keeney, Sig. Corps; Cpl. Joe Stefanelli, Engr.; Pfc. Ralph Izard.
CENTRAL PACIFIC. Cpl. Tom O'Brien, DEML; Sgt. Larry McManus, CA; Sgt. Bill Reed, Inf.; Cpl. George Burns, Sig. Corps; Cpl. Ted Burrows, DEML.
MARIANAS, Sgt. James Goble, Armd.; Sgt. Dil Ferris, AAF; Sgt. Jack Ruge, DEML; Sgt. Paul Showers, AAF; Cpl. Justin Gray, Rangers; Robert Schwartz Y2c, USNR.; Mason Pawlak CPhoM, USNR; Vernon H. Roberts PhoM3c, USNR; Evan Wylie CSp(PR), USCGR.
FRANCE, Sgt. Georg Meyers, AAF; Sgt. Howard Brodie, Sig. Corps; Sgt. Ed Cunningham, Inf.; Sgt. Allan Ecker, AAF; Sgt. William Frazer, AAF; Sgt. Ralph Martin, Med.; Cpl. Pat Coffey, AAF; Cpl. Howard Katzander, CA; Cpl. Debs Myers, FA; Pfc. David Whitcomb, AAF; Pvt. David Berger, Engr.
BRITAIN, Sgt. Durbin L. Horner, CA; Sgt. Earl Anderson, AAF; Sgt. Edmund Antrobus, Inf.; Sgt. Frank Brandt, Med.; Sgt. Francis Burke, AAF; Sgt. Jack Coggins, CA; Sgt. Rudolph Sanford, AAF; Cpl. Tom Flannery, AAF.
ITALY, Sgt. Harry Sions, AAF; Sgt. George Barrett, AAF; Sgt. Donald Breimhurst, AAF; Sgt. Nelson Gruppo, Engr.; Sgt. Dan Polier, AAF; Cpl. Ira Freeman, Cav.; Cpl. Dave Shaw, Inf.; Pfc. Werner Wolff, Sig. Corps.
INDIA-BURMA and CHINA. Sgt. Paul Johnston, AAF; Sgt. Jud Cook, DEML; Sgt. George J. Corbellini, Sig. Corps; Sgt. Walter Peters, QM.
ALASKA, Sgt. Tom Shehan, FA.
PANAMA, Sgt. Richard Douglass, Med.
PUERTO-RICO, Sgt. Donald Cooke, FA.
AFRICA-MIDDLE EAST-PERSIAN GULF, Sgt. Richard Paul, DEML; Cpl. Ray McGovern, Inf.
ICELAND, Sgt. Gordon Farrel, CA.
NEWFOUNDLAND, Sgt. Frank Bode, Sig. Corps.

■

Commanding Officer, Col. Franklin S. Forsberg.
Executive Officer, Lt. Col. Jack W. Weeks.
Business Manager, Maj. Gerald J. Rock.
OVERSEAS BUREAU OFFICERS, France, Lt. Col. Charles L. Holt, Capt. H. Stahley Thompson, assistant; Britain, Maj. Harry R. Roberts; Philippines, Lt. Col. Harold B. Hawley; Central South Pacific, Capt. Merle P. Milham; Marianas, Maj. Justus J. Craemer; Italy, Capt. Howard Carswell, Lt. Jack Silverstein, assistant; Burma-India, Capt. Harold A. Burroughs; Alaska, Capt. Grady E. Clay, Jr.; Panama, Lt. Charles H. E. Stubblefield; Africa-Middle East-Persian Gulf, Capt. Frank Gladstone; Puerto Rico, Capt. Francis E. Sammons, Jr.

This Week's Cover

IT may be necessary to tell some of you who haven't seen one in a long time that this is a suit, American style, of man's civilian clothes. The picture was made by YANK's Sgt. Ben Schnall, a veteran cameraman who would much rather wear the suit than photograph it.

PHOTO CREDITS. Cover—Sgt. Ben Schnall. 3—Sgt. Dil Ferris. 5—PA. 6—Upper, INP; center, PA. 7 & 8—PA. 9—Acme. 10—Left, INP; right, PA. 11—Acme. 12—Upper, PA; lower, Sgt. John Frano. 13—Sgt. Eugene Kammerman. 14—Acme. 16—Upper, Acme; lower, INP. 18—Manhattan Engineer District. 19—Left, INP; right, PA. 22—Sgt. Reg Kenny.

"MEN! Now that the long-awaited word of peace which we have so long awaited has finally and incontrovertibly arrived at this vital outpost in the exterior zone of defense of our glorious nation, I feel it incumbent upon me as your commander to say a few words to the troops who have served with me so long and so faithfully in combatting the menace that menaced the civilization for which we stood and all that we hold dear. Let us not hold this peace we have won lightly, but rather redouble our efforts as personnel of the United States Army better to serve our native land in peace as in war. Through our rich association as officer and men we have come to know each other better, to respect our capabilities and make allowances for our human frailties. Let us remember that the way we act now in the fresh days of peace will be as important as our actions in the sterner tasks of war. The eyes of the world are still upon each and every man of you and there should be no letting up, no relaxation of effort on the part of all of us to bear ourselves fitly as soldiers of our nation. Let us then bend our wills to the manifold and many jobs ahead of us, constant in duty and devotion to all that we hold dear. Let us then remember the cause for which we still soldier and our loved ones at home. Let each man of you remember his obligations as an American soldier and the importance of the part he will play in peace in creating an admirable and accurate impression of the United States of America abroad. The uniform is the mark of the soldier and the clean, well-pressed uniform is the mark of the good soldier so let us concentrate on keeping ever before us as a shining ideal neatness of dress and proper bearing. It is by us that our beloved homeland and the dear ones at home we all hold dear will be judged in these foreign lands. We're all in this thing together men and I'm sure I don't have to emphasize to you the importance of military courtesy—the spirit of the regulations as well as the letter—in the happy years ahead. We'll all be able to pull together as a better team, as the winning team we have proved ourselves, if we keep the snap in our salutes. You can count on me, for one, to return all salutes promptly and with the respect that marks a salute which after all is just a real dandy way of saying a cheery hello between military men. I know that there is no thought among any of you of leaving the service while any part of our great job remains to be done. To you, my troops, I am not ashamed to confess that my eyes are more than a little moist at this hour. One great job lies behind us finished, another great job lies ahead of us unfinished and several other jobs are behind that sand bar in a condition I should not like to describe. Company, Dismissed!"

—Sgt. Ralph Stein and Sgt. Al Hine

"DELIRIOUS AMERICA BLOWS ITS TOP AS WAR ENDS . . . WILD, HYSTERICAL REVELERS OVERFLOW BARS . . . BLARING TRUMPETS . . . NAKED GIRLS . . ."

—Sgt. Ozzie St. George

YANK
THE ARMY   WEEKLY

5c

OCT. 5, 1945
VOL. 4, NO. 16

By and for men in the service

Surrender & Occupation of Japan
PICTURES & STORIES PAGES 2 THROUGH 9

Gen. MacArthur signs as Supreme Allied Commander. Lt. Gen. Jonath[an] Wainwright and Lt. Gen. A. E. Percival, British commander, stand behi[nd]

GIs of the Fifth Airborne hoist the Stars and Stripes over Atsugi Airfield.

By Sgt. DALE KRAMER
YANK Staff Correspondent

ABOARD THE U.S.S. *MISSOURI*, TOKYO BAY—For a while it looked [as] though the proceedings would go off with almost unreasonab[le] smoothness. Cameramen assigned to the formal surrender cer[e]monies aboard the battleship *Missouri* arrived on time and, althou[gh] every inch of the turrets and housings and life rafts above the veran[da] deck where the signing was to take place was crowded, no one fell and broke a collarbone.

The ceremonies themselves even started and were carried on accor[d]ing to schedule. It took a Canadian colonel to bring things back [to] normal by signing the surrender document on the wrong line.

No one had the heart to blame the colonel, though. A mere colon[el] was bound to get nervous around so much higher brass.

The other minor flaw in the ceremonial circus was that it was som[e]thing of an anticlimax. Great historic events probably are always som[e]what that way and this one, to those of us who had taken off thre[e] weeks before with the 11th Airborne Division from the Philippines, w[as] even more so. We had started out thinking in terms of a sensation[al] dash to the Emperor's palace in Tokyo, only to sweat it out on Okinaw[a] and later off Yokohama.

When it did come, the signing aboard the *Missouri* was a show whi[ch] lacked nothing in its staging. A cluster of microphones and a long tab[le] covered with a green cloth had been placed in the center of the dec[k.] On the table lay the big ledger-size white documents of surrender bou[nd] in brown folders.

The assembly of brass and braid was a thing to see—a lake of go[ld] and silver sparkling with rainbows of decorations and ribbons. Briti[sh] and Australian Army officers had scarlet stripes on their garrison ca[ps] and on their collars. The French were more conservative except for t[he] acres of vivid decorations on their breasts. The stocky leader of the Ru[s]sian delegation wore gold shoulder-boards and red-striped trousers. T[he] Dutch had gold-looped shoulder emblems. The British admirals wo[re] snow-white summer uniforms with shorts and knee-length white stoc[kings]

SURRENDER

Gen. MacArthur and Lt. Gen. Sutherland watch Gen. Yoshira Umezu sign for Japanese Imperial General Headquarters on board the *Missouri*.

ings. The olive-drab of the Chinese was plain except for ribbons. The least decked-out of all were the Americans. Their hats, except for Adm. Halsey's go-to-hell cap, were gold-braided, but their uniforms were plain sun-tan. Navy regulations do not permit wearing ribbons or decorations on a shirt.

Lack of time prevented piping anyone over the side, and when Gen. MacArthur, Supreme Commander for the Allied powers, came aboard he strode quickly across the veranda deck and disappeared inside the ship. Like the other American officers, he wore plain sun-tans. A few minutes later, a gig flying the American flag and operated by white-clad American sailors putted around the bow of the ship. In the gig, wearing formal diplomatic morning attire, consisting of black cutaway coat, striped pants and stovepipe hat, sat Foreign Minister Namoru Shigemitsu, leader of the Japanese delegation.

Coming up the gangway, Shigemitsu climbed very slowly because of a stiff left leg, and he limped onto the veranda deck with the aid of a heavy light-colored cane. Behind him came 10 other Japs. One wore a white suit; two more wore formal morning attire; the rest were dressed in pieced-out uniforms of the Jap Army and Navy. They gathered into three rows on the forward side of the green-covered table. The representatives of the Allied powers formed on the other side. When they were arranged, Gen. MacArthur entered and stepped to the microphone.

His words rolled sonorously: "We are gathered here, representatives of the major warring powers, to conclude a solemn agreement whereby peace may be restored." He emphasized the necessity that both victors and vanquished rise to a greater dignity in order that the world may emerge forever from blood and carnage. He declared his firm intention as Supreme Commander to "discharge my responsibility with justice and tolerance while taking all necessary dispositions to insure that the terms of surrender are fully, promptly and faithfully complied with."

The Japanese stood at attention during the short address, their faces grave but otherwise showing little emotion. When the representatives of the Emperor were invited to sign, Foreign Minister Shigemitsu hobbled forward, laid aside his silk hat and cane, and lowered himself slowly

Signed at TOKYO BAY, JAPAN at _____
on the _____ SECOND _____ day of ____ SEPTEMBER ____ ,1945

重光葵

By Command and in behalf of the Emperor of Japan and the Japanese Government

梅津美治郎

By Command and in behalf of the Japanese Imperial General Headquarters

Accepted at TOKYO BAY, JAPAN at ___0908___ T
on the _____ SECOND _____ day of ____ SEPTEMBER ____ ,1945,
for the United States, Republic of China, United Kingdom and the Union of Soviet Socialist Republics, and in the interests of the other United Nations at war with Japan.

Douglas MacArthur
Supreme Commander for the Allied Powers

C.W. Nimitz
United States Representative

Hsu Yung-chang
Republic of China Representative

Bruce Fraser
United Kingdom Representative

Kuzma Derevyanko
Union of Soviet Socialist Republics Representative

T.A. Blamey
Commonwealth of Australia Representative

L. Moore Cosgrave
Dominion of Canada Representative

Jacques Le Clerc
Provisional Government of the French Republic Representative

C.E.L. Helfrich
Kingdom of the Netherlands Representative

Leonard M. Isitt
Dominion of New Zealand Representative

The signature page of the surrender document as signed on the *Missouri*.

Jap soldiers march past American occupation forces on Atsugi Airfield. Advance elements expected trouble but were met by docile Jap officials and soldie

into a chair. The wind whipped his thin, dark hair as he reached into his pocket for a pen, tested it, then affixed three large Japanese characters to the first of the documents. He had to rise and bend over the table for the others.

The audience was conscious of the historic importance of the pen strokes, but it watched for something else, too. Gen. MacArthur had promised to present Gen. Wainwright, who had surrendered the American forces at Corregidor and until only a few days before had been a prisoner of war, with the first pen to sign the surrender. Shigemitsu finished and closed his pen and replaced it in his pocket. There could be no objection. He had needed a brush-pen for the Japanese letters.

When the big surrender folders were turned around on the table, Gen. MacArthur came forward to affix his signature as Supreme Commander. He asked Gen. Wainwright and Gen. Percival, who had surrendered the British forces at Singapore, to accompany him. Gen. MacArthur signed the first document and handed the pen to Gen. Wainwright. He used five pens in all, ending up with one from his own pocket.

Sailors have been as avid souvenir collectors in this war as anyone else, but when Adm. Nimitz sat down to sign for the U. S. he used only two pens. After that the representatives of China, the United Kingdom, Russia, Australia, Canada, France, the Netherlands and New Zealand put down their signatures.

As the big leather document folders were gathered a GI member of a sound unit recorded a few historic remarks of his own. "Brother," he said, "I hope those are my discharge papers."

Reception at Atsugi

By Sgt. KNOX BURGER
YANK Staff Correspondent

Atsugi Airfield, Japan—It was an uneventful reception. C-54s carrying elements of the 11th Airborne Division were coming in low over the coast of Japan in history's gentlest invasion. The narrow beaches, probably the very stretches of sand we would have stormed, were gray and empty. Crowding the beaches were hills and fields, very green and rolling gracefully out from the base of a range of eroded mountains. The fields were thick with rice shoots; from the air they looked like soft flat carpets. Here and there were clumps of trees—willows, evergreens, maples and cherry. Hedges laced the rice paddies. Houses with thatched roofs were built close to the dirt roads. Most of the people walking along the roads carried heavy bundles or pulled carts. They didn't bother to look at the planes.

Atsugi Airfield looked more like the Indiana Country Fair. Two long dirt runways were in the center of some feebly camouflaged hangars and ramshackle barracks. Graveyard-wrecked Jap planes, glinting silver where their green paint jobs had worn off, lay like broken toys at one end of the field, having careened over on their wingtips and noses.

Waiting to meet the ships were members of the 63rd Airdrome Squad and the 21st Air Freight Transport, who had arrived on D-minus-2 to ready the field.

These advance elements had expected to be massacred. Instead, they had been greeted by docile Jap officials, plus a few enthusiastic Russians who had apparently stayed in nearby Tokyo after their government's entry into the war.

Hundreds of square old Jap trucks stood at one end of the runway lined up at close intervals and hundreds of cars were in a big open field at the other end. It looked like the parking lot outside a college football stadium around 1938.

The baggage was piling up in front of the hangars, and troops heavy with packs were climbing into trucks. Jap interpreters, dressed in uniforms or suits or parts of each, stood around in nervous little groups. They had on yellow armbands to denote their calling. Like the Jap truck drivers and work parties, they tried to be impassive. One skinny interpreter wore a faded uniform of black crepe from which dangled bits of dirty gold braid. He looked like a cross between a scarecrow and a kid at a costume party.

On the far side of the field, around the administration buildings, stood armed Jap soldiers. They saluted every American who happened to come within 100 yards of them. Black-uniform cops, carrying small sabers in silver scabbar guarded the roads, looking sinister and se important. A squad of Jap soldiers lay on th straw mats in a car-barn off one corner of t field. Their shirts were off, but they wore leggin; The squad's lieutenant lay on his back, his fe up against his buttocks, making nervous wa movements with his knees.

The barracks and administration buildin were weatherbeaten and somber. They had bleak look that indicated they had been left sag in rain and sun. Here and there a hangar ro had been burned off—or maybe never put on.

The D-minus-2 men were housed in a big ba racks. The Jap Government had supplied the with the services of some waiters from Tokyo Imperial Hotel. The atmosphere was practical lousy with the quiet selflessness that characteriz the breed of good waiters all over the worl "Hail the conquering hero," said one GI as snapped his fingers for more ice-water.

American soldiers stood around and crack about the broken-down automobiles. "I unde stand Henry Ford is coming over to get the ca out of the ditches by Christmas," a corporal r marked drily. The MPs didn't like to let th ancient vehicles cross the field because of the tendency to fall apart in the middle of the ru ways.

In a deserted "shadow factory" dug into th side of the hill next to the field someone found tissue-paper blueprint; it was a design for homemade air-raid shelter. Standing on the roa that criss-crossed the barracks area beside th field, you could feel the ground tremble as truc rumbled past. Underneath was a huge netwo of electric-lighted tunnels where the Japs had s up a complete machine shop.

As MacArthur's entourage pulled out fro the field a car loaded with Jap officials bro down. An officer squatted on the fender ar peered under the hood, his *Samurai* swo dangling grotesquely between his knees. Oth Japs stood by helplessly while a truckload of G wheeled past.

"Why don't you trade that sword in on screwdriver?" called one GI.

GIs of the 188th Parachute Infantry pile into trucks as fast as they can unload from the C-54 transports landing them on Atsugi Airfield outside Yokohama, Japa

A GI eye-witness report on metropolitan landmarks of the air campaign that brought Japan to her knees—Nagasaki, where the second atomic bomb fell, Tokyo, gutted by incendiaries, Hiroshima, where the first atomic bomb leveled 4 square miles.

By Sgt. JOE McCARTHY
YANK Staff Correspondent

IN A B-17 OVER NAGASAKI—Looking down on the vast stretches of level reddish-brown earth that used to be the smoky and crowded industrial section of this big steel city, you can understand why Japan decided to quit the war a few hours after the second American atomic bomb landed here on Aug. 9.

The heart of the city of Nagasaki was squeezed empty by the flash of the bomb, which threw out heat waves estimated by some scientists at 3,600,-000,000,000° F. And even from the windows of this Fortress, as it soars unmolested over the remaining rooftops and dips down to 25 feet above the water along the shipyards and docks, you get the impression that the hearts of the people of Nagasaki are empty, too. A few of them on the streets and at the ferryboat terminal pause to look up at the plane. But most of them just keep on walking, paying no attention. Seemingly they wouldn't give a damn one way or another if 10,000 American planes came over and buzzed their homes.

A popular GI opinion concerning the atomic-bombed cities has been that no American soldier, especially a soldier from the American Army Air Forces, would be able to set foot near Nagasaki or Hiroshima for the next 20 years. They were saying how people here must be filled with bitter longing for vengeance and how they would surely tear to bits any American they could get their hands on. We won't know for sure until we go into Nagasaki on foot, but it doesn't seem that way from our 200- and sometimes 100-foot altitudes. Ours is one of the first unarmed American planes to fly over Japan and at these low altitudes we'd make a nice target for any kind of firearms. But we haven't seen anything below beyond docile indifference.

Eight miles down the bay from Nagasaki there's an Allied PW camp on a small island called Koyagi Shima. Capt. Mark Magnan of Milwaukee, a veteran ETO combat pilot who was flying the *Headliner,* our Fortress, buzzed low over this camp several times while T/Sgt. Jack Goetz of Fayetteville, Pa., engineer, and S/Sgt. George A. Kilzer of Richardton, N. D., tossed 10-in-1 rations out the rear door. The prisoners had rigged up British, American, Chinese and Dutch flags on their buildings and were scattered outside the enclosure, apparently unguarded. If the people of Nagasaki had been filled with bitter hatred of their enemies after the atomic bombing, it seems logical that they

3 BEATEN CITIES

NAGASAKI

This is what was left of the industrial city of Nagasaki after the atomic bomb hit it.

YANK, The Army Weekly, publication issued weekly by Branch Office, Information & Education Division, War Department, 205 East 42d Street, New York 17, N. Y. Reproduction rights restricted as indicated. Entered as second class matter July 6, 1942, at the Post Office at New York, N. Y., under the Act of March 3, 1879. Subscription price $3.00 yearly. Printed in the U. S. A.

would have stormed every nearby PW camp and lynched the inmates.

And every inch of Nagasaki wasn't completely demolished, either. This may have been a result of the geographical layout and the terrain of the city rather than because of any limitation of the atomic bomb. Nagasaki is divided in half by a bay and a river. Part of its residential and downtown section lies in a valley between two hills. The reddish-brown atomic destruction covers almost everything outside the valley but it apparently didn't get inside. About 40 or 50 percent of the town seemed to have been utterly demolished.

The destruction in Nagasaki looks nothing like the debris in Cassino or Leghorn. The strange thing here is the utter absence of rubble. You can see a couple of square miles of reddish-brown desolation with nothing left but the outlines of houses, a bit of wall here and half a chimney there. In this area you will see a road, and the road will be completely clean. It is too soon after the bombing for the Japs to have done any cleaning of the roads and you can't see

a single brick or pile of broken plaster or lumber on any street or sidewalk in the town. Evidently the bomb blast demolishes the wreckage as well as the buildings themselves, just as the scientists say it does.

The bomb blast does strange things. Like that of the V-1s in London last year, it sweeps an area but skips some buildings there altogether. Here and there in the middle of the leveled section of town we could see factories standing alone and looking like hollow boxes, with their roofs, doors and windows gone but with four concrete or stone walls still up. Most of the bridges across the river that divides Nagasaki are still intact. So are the railroad tracks spider-webbing its good-sized freight yard. According to reports, most of the railroad cars came into Nagasaki from other parts of Japan with relief supplies after the atomic bombing, and it is obvious that they wouldn't have been able to make it if the blast had destroyed the tracks they had to travel on.

The atomic blast spread out over plenty of distance where it wasn't halted by hills or wa-

ter. We could see fields far on the town's ou[t]-skirts burned brown.

The Mitsubishi Steel and Arms Works, t[he] same thing to Nagasaki that Jones & Laughl[in] or U. S. Steel are to Pittsburgh, won't be payi[ng] a dividend to its stockholders. Some of its buil[d]-ings are mere twisted piles of girders. Othe[rs] are not around any more.

Flying over Nagasaki, as we did for a fu[ll] half-hour, circling roof tops and diving so lo[w] that you could see clearly the faces of its peopl[e] you get a much more convincing impression [of] the power and the finality of the atomic bom[b] than you can get from any photos that ha[ve] been taken to date. The great empty areas, co[v]-ering so many square miles of city blocks, a[l]-most take your breath away when you first s[ee] them. The thing that hits you is not the terri[fic] bomb damage but the terrific nothingness. It[s] a tough job to describe in writing what Nagasa[ki] looks like today because there's nothing mu[ch] to describe.

More than anything else, Nagasaki looks rig[ht] now exactly like the place the war ended.

In the Ginza district, Tokyo's equivalent of Fifth Avenue, only a few big stores were left intact.

TOKYO—Driving from Yokohama to Tokyo is about the same as driving into New York City from Newark, N. J. You pass through flat, marshy country filled with big factories and industrial towns that are like Kearny and Bayonne and Elizabeth and Jersey City.

To complete the comparison there is an electric railway from Yokohama to Tokyo with overhead trolley wires and the same kind of cars that the Pennsylvania Railroad provides for its Jersey commuters. You keep expecting to see a billboard announcing the rates for rooms at the Hotel New Yorker or advising you to get tickets at once for

"Life With Father." But unlike the Jersey flats, these Tokyo suburbs, which were jammed with factory-workers' houses before Maj. Gen. Curtis LeMay and his men started their devastating series of low-level incendiary-bombing raids last March, are now in burned ruins. The ruins do not look like those of the bombed cities of Europe, which were mostly heavy-explosive, demolition jobs that left piles of broken bricks and plaster and twisted beams. On the road to Tokyo some of the big industrial plants still stand, windowless and charred inside, but the houses and other smaller buildings are flat on the ground and their

A Jap cameraman awaits MacArthur's arriva[l]

remains are burned to almost nothing. You see a bit of machinery or a chimney here and there, and every 50 yards or so a cast-iron or steel safe, probably with a roll of bank notes and the book-keeper's ledger still inside it.

As you bounce your way into South Tokyo, the concrete highways in Japan give you the feeling that they haven't been repaired in five years. There are increasingly more signs of bomb destruction. Jap families have gone back into the ruins of their homes and made little shacks out of the pieces of sheet metal and slabs of black-ened wood, and you get the impression that you're driving through a hobo jungle. Whole families peer out as you pass, and a little boy grins and salutes. On the edge of Tokyo a man and a woman who have evidently heard that the war is over are busy with shovels filling a bomb shelter.

DOWNTOWN Tokyo looks badly beaten. Along the *Ginza*, which is the Japanese Fifth Ave-nue, every other building is either burned to the ground or wrecked inside. A lot of the department stores and smart shops have English and French signs over their doors. The Brett Pharmacy looks like a typical American super-drugstore, but only its front is standing. There is nothing inside ex-cept a stream of water bubbling up from a broken pipe where a soda fountain may have been.

The few large stores which are still intact are swanky ones with indirect lighting and subdued color schemes. Their display windows are covered with heavy, brown, corrugated metal screens and they haven't much to sell. The entertainment and night-club district has also been hard hit. A few of the movie houses are still operating and there are long lines of people outside them waiting to buy tickets. There are lines outside the newspaper offices, too. The press runs of the afternoon edi-tions are small, and it's first come, first served.

The section of Tokyo which suffered most from the punishment handed out by the B-29s was Asakusa Ku, a residential section with a popula-tion of 140,000 per square mile. Probably it was the most thickly populated city district in the world. There is hardly anything left of it today.

Our official estimate of the bomb damage in Tokyo is 52 percent of the city. Air Force Intelli-gence officers visiting Tokyo now think the per-centage is really higher than that. A great many buildings which showed up as undamaged on our aerial photographs are destroyed and useless. The bombing here, of course, was all incendiary work and the targets were whole areas of the city rather than individual buildings. The idea was to get small shops and factories—optical, electrical, tool-making and precision-instrument plants that the Japanese war effort depended on heavily but that could not be attacked individually.

Tokyo looks as though the Strategic Air Forces carried out the idea almost to perfection. You can see evidence of the people's fear of the Superforts everywhere. No city in Europe ever dug as many bomb shelters as this one. Every sidewalk is lined with them. They are shallow affairs, with cement walls and two entrances.

There isn't much traffic on the streets except for dilapidated Army trucks, a few busses and overloaded streetcars and, of course, bicycles. The few people who remain look down-at-the-heel and shabby. Their clothes need cleaning, and only a few of them have leather shoes. Practically all the men and women wear clumsy wooden slip-pers that clack on the pavement. Most of them look as though they have not been eating regu-larly. I haven't yet seen a fat person in Tokyo. The women, who wear baggy pants, look well padded but shapeless, as though they were carry-ing more layers of cotton than flesh.

The people of Tokyo are taking the arrival of the first few Americans with impeccable Japanese calm. Sometimes they turn and look at us twice, but they have shown no emotion towards us except a mild curiosity and occasional amusement. They don't seem to be trying to sell us a bill of goods, as the Germans did after VE-Day. They are still proud and a little bit superior. They know they lost the war, but they are not apologizing for it. In general, their attitude seems to be: The war is over and you won, now you go on about your business and we will take care of ourselves. We don't need any help from you.

The higher-ranking Army officers, wearing their long *Samurai* swords and high tan boots, look at the Americans coldly and cross to the other side of the street to avoid walking near them. The

Japanese enlisted men stare at us with their mouths a little bit open, but without fear or anger.

The Japs are great umbrella carriers. It was drizzling the first couple of days we were in Tokyo and, without doing it noticeably, the Jap girls and older women would maneuver their umbrellas so that when they passed us on the street their faces would be hidden from us. Nobody here wants to have much to do with us. It looks as if there will be no fraternization problem in Japan. It also looks as if we will have no trouble from the Japs. They do a wonderful job of hiding their feelings. I have not seen a single Jap anywhere in Tokyo making any kind of an angry or un-friendly gesture or facial expression.

When we come near to what we think is an average Jap, it is hard to tell yet exactly what he feels about the future and about the way the war turned out for him, because the average Jap speaks no English. The English-speaking Japs are not average Japs. They are people who have lived abroad and who are better educated than the rank-and-file.

One of the English-speaking Japs I talked with in Tokyo was a newspaperman who said that he and most of the other intelligent people in Japan knew for more than a year that Japan was going to lose the war. The suddenness of the ending came as a big surprise to him, however; he said that everybody expected it to last another year. I asked him about the reports I had heard in Guam and Okinawa about the people in Tokyo dancing and singing in the streets with joy when the news of the surrender came. He said that the reaction was just the opposite. Instead of singing, most of the people were crying. For an hour or so, he added, they were excited and sorrowful. After that, they gained control of their feelings.

I asked how much the people knew about the war and if it were true that many of them thought the Japs were fighting in California. He said that nobody here ever believed that their troops had invaded the U. S. and that the Jap Government had never spread such an impression. "But," he added, a little proudly, "we shelled your Califor-nia coast from a submarine early in the war, didn't we?" Then he mentioned the Jap diplomats who conferred with Cordell Hull while Pearl Harbor was being attacked. He seemed to think it was a big joke.

"Do you know that you could have invaded Hawaii easily after that attack on Pearl Harbor?" I asked him. "Our defenses there were not strong. Our defenses in California were not strong, either, in 1941. You could have invaded there. Why didn't you do it?"

He shrugged his shoulders: "The lines of sup-ply would have been too long for us to maintain."

"If the lines of supply were too long for you to maintain, why did you go to war against us?" I asked.

He shrugged his shoulders again, and we changed the subject. He told me that he had been to Hiroshima a few days ago to visit rela-tives and found them all dead from the atomic bombing. "There is absolutely nothing left in Hiroshima," he said, and he wanted to know if it was true that the soil there would be barren for the next 70 years because of radioactivity.

HE asked how much press censorship we had in the U. S. during the war. When I told him that anybody could criticize the war effort in the news-papers and that the press quoted opponents of our administration, he was amazed, although he admitted he had heard such was the case. "That's what we hope to be able to do here in Japan now that the war is over," he added. When I told him that a number of American war correspondents in the Pacific were considering nominating the Domei News Agency for a Pulitzer journalism prize be-cause it had scooped the world on the Jap surren-der, he laughed. Then I showed him some pictures in YANK of the terrific construction job that the Army Engineers and Seabees had done in the Marianas during the past year and told him that they were now doing the same thing in Okinawa. He was hardly able to believe it. "Japan doesn't have equipment for such work," he said.

As a matter of fact, most of the GIs who ar-rived here with the early occupation forces can't get over the lack of transportation and engineer-ing equipment in Japan and the poor quality of the little rolling stock that is available. There are quite a few good American cars—Fords, Stude-bakers and Buicks — but the Japs have ruined

them with poor fuel and bad mechanics. I rode from Yokohama to Tokyo in an antique passenger bus, a sort of motorized Toonerville Trolley with creaking, blue-plush seats. Every two miles or so the driver had to climb out to clear the gas-line.

GIs who have been looking forward to a good time in Tokyo are in for a big disappointment. The town hasn't much to offer. It is too thorough-ly burned out to have much excitement or en-tertainment, and the people are in no mood to give any American a warm welcome. There isn't much to drink except beer, and in most places they don't sell even that in the daytime. *Sake* is rationed.

The food is pretty bad. The Japanese serve canned salmon and canned sardines morning, noon and night, generally with cold potato salad and in a very tasteless fashion. The bread isn't good and the eggs are powdered. The day I arrived here I had lunch at the Imperial Hotel, the best hotel in Tokyo. The meal started with a thick soup made out of barley or some other kind of grain. Then there was a piece of salmon fried in a batter of brown gravy which did not exactly make me smack my lips in glee. Then came a dish with a little boiled cabbage and a lot of things that looked like boiled scallions on it. These turned out to be little pieces of soggy dough. Finally there was a glass of hot tea that didn't taste like tea. The whole meal cost only 30 cents in American money, but it wasn't worth 15.

IF you are lucky enough to find a room in Tokyo, you soon discover that the bed is as hard as a rock. The pillow is a thing shaped like a loaf of bread and filled with something that feels like gravel. They don't have screens on most of the windows and Japan, at this time of the year, is full of mosquitoes and various other kinds of bugs. The bathrooms are really something. They do not have toilets as we know them; just porcelain holes in the floor. They don't have showers or the kind of tubs we use in the States. Instead, each bath-room contains four stone tubs. The first tub is filled with warm water; you get into it and lather and wash off. The next has cold water; you get into it and shiver. Then you dip yourself in the third tub, which has more warm water, and finally you finish off in the fourth, which is cold again.

Tokyo, like every place we've been in Japan so far, is dull, drab and depressing. The first after-noon I was here I went to have a look at the Emperor's palace. It is beautifully laid out in the center of a huge park, but you can't actually see the palace itself. A moat and a high stone wall separate the palace compound from the rest of the world and there is another moat inside the first one that separates the palace from the rest of the palace compound. It is forbidden to drive a vehicle even near the first moat; you have to get out a quarter of a mile away and walk to it. When you get there guards won't let you cross it, but they'll let you stand around. All day long Japs keep coming to the entrance to the palace grounds, alone or in pairs or sometimes in family groups. They stand silently for a few moments facing the Emperor's quarters and then they bow down in prayer. After that, they put on their hats and walk away.

The day I was there a Buddhist priest wearing yellow robes was facing the palace, beating on a drum. Two officers in the Jap Army came up and stood rigidly at attention, gazing in the same direction. Then they bent from the waist, prayed, and snapped a salute. Before leaving, one of the officers turned and looked at me. His face showed nothing, but it was easy to see that he hated my guts and thought it a sacrilege for an American to be so close to the Emperor's presence.

An elderly man with a girl in her 'twenties, maybe his daughter, came up nearby. The girl knelt and leaned forward until her face touched the ground. The old man bent over respectfully and prayed for a few moments while the girl still crouched on the ground. Then the man put on his hat and came over to me, smiling. "You are from Baltimore?" he asked. I told him I wasn't and explained where I came from in the States. "I have been in Baltimore and New York and Chicago many years now," he said. "Well, the war, it is over now and we are no longer enemies. Let us hope we can forget it. There is no need of talking about it."

Just then a B-29 on a sightseeing tour roared low over the palace grounds. The old man looked up at it. "We were wrong," he said. "Yes, we were very wrong."

HIROSHIMA

Two Japanese civilians walk on a road cleared through the dead ruins of Hiroshima. For four square miles the city was left in total destruction by the atomic bomb.

HIROSHIMA—In the bombed-out cities of Europe there were always plenty of eye-witnesses who were only too eager to tell you exactly how it was the day their house fell in. It wasn't like that in Hiroshima when I came here with the first group of Americans to enter the city since it was almost completely destroyed by our atomic bomb on Aug. 6. For the first two hours, as we walked through the utterly demolished downtown section, we couldn't find a single Jap on the streets who had been here when the bomb landed. Practically all eyewitnesses seemed to be dead or in the hospital.

"I knew lots of Hiroshima people, but only one of my friends survived safely," said the Japanese naval officer who acted as our interpreter. "He was at work in the second floor of a building. He fell through to the basement. Everybody else in the building was killed or injured, but he wasn't hurt."

The scarcity of healthy survivors gives some idea what our first and most effective atomic bomb did when it struck Japan. There's no doubt when you look at it that Hiroshima is the greatest man-made disaster in the history of the world.

You can stand at its center and for four square miles around there is nothing but total destruction. The only things left standing are a few concrete-reinforced buildings, with their insides charred and ruined, an occasional bare chimney, and trees with every limb and every leaf torn off.

The fire engines that the city needed so badly are still standing in the fire station, their radiators folded inward like accordions and their mechanisms scattered on the floor.

The hospital which people tried to reach is a hollow, blackened shell.

In parts of the outskirts the smell of the dead under the debris is unbearable. In the center of the town there are not enough ruins to hide a corpse. Everything is level ashes.

We found that the few surviving Japs who had been in Hiroshima the day the bomb fell became inarticulate when we asked them to describe what they had seen and done during the blast and during the few hours that followed the explosions. In reply to our questions, they would just stare at the ceiling and stare at the floor. Then they would make a helpless gesture with their hands and say things like, "The town was in the worst condition you can consider," or, "It was terrible beyond imagination." Evidently the people in Hiroshima were too shaken and too stunned to notice much about what they were doing or what was going on around them that morning of Aug. 6.

One of the Japs we talked to was a Government official named Hirokuni Dazai, a little fellow with a bandaged head who described his job as Commissioner of Public Thought Control in the Hiroshima district. Dazai returned to Hiroshima from a trip to Tokyo only 40 minutes before the bomb fell. There had been an air-raid alarm shortly before 8 o'clock that morning, but Dazai

doesn't remember seeing or hearing any planes overhead. The all-clear signal sounded about five minutes past eight and the people came out of the shelters and started home to have their breakfast. Dazai was standing in front of his house between ten minutes and a quarter past eight when he saw a light moving across the sky.

"It looked like some sort of electric flash," he told us. "It was arc-shaped and bright orange." Then he was knocked to the ground by a wave of concussion. His house shook and fell apart, some of the rubble landing on top of him. That's how he got the bandage on his head. He picked himself off the ground and got his wife and two children out of the ruins. His wife had been knocked out but she came to quickly. The children were unhurt.

"Our house did not start to burn immediately," Dazai said, "but I saw great towers of black smoke advancing toward me across the city from the east, south and north."

Dazai took his wife and children to the home of a relative two kilometers away and tried to get downtown to his office, but the heat of the fire there was too overpowering. He wasn't able to go near his office until after 4 o'clock that afternoon.

The whole city burned steadily for the next two days. Dazai and other officials found relief work almost impossible, since the fire-fighting equipment and the hospitals were destroyed and almost every telegraph pole and wire was flat on the ground. Finally, the Government managed to get some help and supplies up the river by boat to Hiroshima but it wasn't enough.

Later, the trains came into the town. We noticed that there, as in Nagasaki, railroad tracks and bridges had been completely undamaged by the atomic blast. Evidently it doesn't affect things close to the ground.

We asked Dazai how many bombs he thought we'd dropped on Hiroshima. He said at first he thought the city was hit by several hundred but shortly after the blast, when he saw the whole area in burning ruins, he thought it was some new variety of "aerial torpedo." One thing that baffled him and other Japs with whom we talked and who had experienced the bombing, was the complete absence of noise in Hiroshima before and after the bomb landed. One Jap said he was deaf for a week afterward from concussion, but heard no explosion. The Japs at the naval base in Kuri about 12 miles away, however, say they heard a terrific roar. Vice-Adm. Masao Kanazawa said the effect in Kuri was like a tornado. There was "a great wind," he said, and trees around the naval base were bent to the ground by it.

The Japs who went to Manila to arrange the peace signing said their dead at Hiroshima numbered 11,000. That was a great understatement. Reading figures to us from his black notebook, Dazai estimated that the Hiroshima dead so far number around 80,000.

Hiroshima was made to order for effective atomic bombing. It is built on a river delta like New Orleans, and it is as flat as a billiard table. There are none of the hills that protected part of Nagasaki from the blast of our second atomic bomb. Hiroshima was a new and modern city, the home of many Japanese who had lived in the States and had brought back with them American ideas about houses and gardens. It had a population of 343,000 in the 1940 census. Now the population is about 120,000. Most of the residents who are injured or sick as a result of the bombing are living in battered and misshapen houses on the edges of the city.

Dazai said that when the Japs took the first count of the Hiroshima casualties on Aug. 20 there were 3,000 known dead and 30,000 missing persons who had been given up for dead. There were 13,960 "seriously wounded" and 43,500 injured. On Sept. 1 the toll of known dead was up to 53,000.

Japanese doctors who have been attending Hiroshima casualties say that a lot of the weird stories about the effects of the atomic bombings on the civilian population are apparently true. They say that people who were only slightly wounded when the bomb fell and some others who didn't enter Hiroshima until a few hours after the bombing have died from loss of white blood corpuscles. The effect of the atomic bomb as far as they have been able to determine is about the same as over-exposure to the rays of a very powerful X-ray machine. Sufferers, say the Japanese doctors, develop a temperature of around 105°; their hair begins to fall out and they feel ill and vomit blood.

The first thing these Japanese doctors asked was if the Americans who had designed the bomb had also figured out a cure for its after-effects on the human body. So far, the Japanese have found no way of restoring the normal count of white corpuscles. They are trying transfusions, but these seem to have no effect on whatever is destroying the white corpuscles. The corpuscles added to the blood stream by a transfusion are quickly eaten up. We told the Japs that a group of American scientists were coming to Hiroshima soon to study the radioactive effects of the bomb on people and the area.

The doctors also say that the severely blistering X-ray-like burns are generally found only on the side of the body which faced the atomic blast. They say two men were fencing in Hiroshima the morning the bomb exploded. One of these was facing the direction of the blast and died almost immediately. The other, burned only on the back of the neck, lived for a week.

The native doctors also say that clothing serves as protection against atomic burns. People wearing thick undershirts didn't get it as badly as those who had on only a kimono or a shirt. There was a strong rumor, both among Jap civilians here and among GIs back in the Philippines, Okinawa and the Marianas, that anybody even walking into the atomic-bombed area a week or more after would be sterilized by the radioactivity in the soil. Jap doctors haven't had time to check that one yet. They think the victims who were exposed to the bombing itself may not be able to reproduce again, but they don't know for sure. Nor do they know yet how long it will be before Hiroshima will be an absolutely healthful place to live in. Some scientific writer back in the States said recently that Hiroshima's soil would be barren and radioactive for the next 70 years. One Jap doctor says this is the malarkey. He made tests of the soil in Hiroshima a few weeks ago and found no radioactivity in it.

Walking into Hiroshima in broad daylight, wearing an American uniform and knowing that you were one of the first Americans the people in the utterly ruined city had laid eyes on since the bombing, was not a comfortable feeling. I couldn't help wondering what would have happened to me if I'd been a Jap entering Brooklyn after Japan had dropped an atomic bomb, or, for that matter, any kind of bomb, on Flatbush. I was accompanied by the crew of a B-17, who were wearing Air Force insignia all over themselves like an Irishman wears green on St. Patrick's Day, and that didn't help matters. But the Hiroshima Japs—men, women and children—gave us exactly the same treatment we got in Yokohama, Tokyo, Kuri and all the other Jap towns we have visited—the same prolonged, unabashed, curious stares unmixed with any expression either of hatred or welcome.

All through Hiroshima we've passed close to men and women pointing at ashes that evidently used to be homes of relatives or friends. We've seen them at the wrecked police station trying to locate missing people and walking toward their shrines to pray. I noticed one woman leaning over a water faucet, the only thing left of her home, filling a pan to wash some clothes. There was no wreckage around her, no broken walls or glassless windows. Just the water pipe, with the faucet on the end of it, sticking up out of the ashes. "I don't feel sorry for these people," said a GI with me. "It's tough on them, sure, but it saved lots of guys' lives."

One of the Jap Navy officers acting as our interpreter was born in Sacramento, Calif. We asked him if the people in this part of Japan accepted the atomic bomb as one of the misfortunes of war and held no particular resentment against us for it. Or, we asked, do they hate us?

The officer studied his boots and then peered quizzically through his tortoise-rimmed glasses. "They hate you," he said.

Hirokuni Dazai, Hiroshima survivor, tells his story.

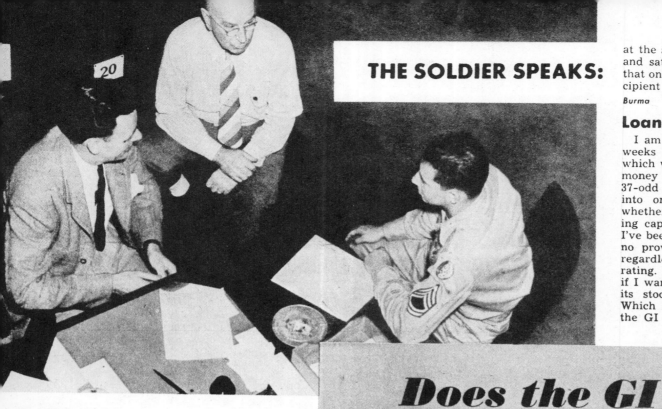

Does the GI Bill of Rights Need Any Changes?

A Mirage

IN my opinion the Bill is like the mirage of a water hole seen by a dying man in the desert. He crawls off to drink and finds it has disappeared. I'm afraid much the same thing happens when we go to drink in the benefits of the Bill. Sure, a serviceman can get credit or a loan, but before he gets it his credit risk will be evaluated in the cold light of sound business, and if it isn't a good risk, no credit. Heck, we can do that without the GI Bill. Sure, a fellow with a wife and family can apply for additional college training. But how is the *average* person going to support his family on the $75 a month he will be given? After being in the Army for three or more years he no longer has the financial reserve to cushion him for another year or more of readjustment.

The GI Bill should give us the means to support us during this schooling or provide for adjusted service compensation to tide us through. Furthermore, the Government should assume the interest on loans it guarantees, lest the burden be too heavy to be of value. (The total cost is negligible when compared with the cost of war, which is a much less valuable contribution to society.)

Ft. Devens, Mass. —T-4 HENRY SCHEIER

Educational Benefits

The requirement in the educational section of the Bill that the soldier start his schooling not later than two years after his discharge or the end of the war, whichever is later, is unwise. This would have the effect of sending those vets who want educational aid off to school all at once and later dumping them on the labor market at the same time. It would be better to spread out the educational benefits over a long period of time. This would help soldiers who want to get jobs after their discharge in order to settle their families. They would feel encouraged to know that they could take advantage of the educational benefits later on.

I believe also that a GI should be entitled to a full education regardless of the age at which he entered the service, and regardless of whether his education was interrupted or interfered with by his induction. Many older men were obliged to go into work which they didn't particularly care for before induction, through the sheer necessity of making a living. Broadening the base of the educational section in this way would be a lifesaver to some of them and might permit them to make a new start.

AAF Base Unit, Hyde Park, N. Y. —S/Sgt. HENRY LEFER

The GI a Good Risk

As the flood of dischargees is finding out, the GI Bill of Rights now provides nothing for the average GI and benefits only those who are well enough off so that they do not need it anyway. There is no need for the stringency of the law, or the present stringency of its administration. Any farm or home loan is automatically secured by the property itself, and with reasonable care,

as is demonstrated by the FHA, the Government takes no loss.

In business loans, the question is simply: Does the Government desire more small business and is it prepared to write off a certain percentage of loss, which is in any case compensated for by the taxes which it collects for as long as the business survives?

As for education, the Government, which is the people, cannot help but benefit, no matter what the expense, by the training and use of talent that would otherwise be lost to it.

New York City —Pfc. L. J. WIEGAND

Elusive Benefits

The great majority of veterans applying for a loan will find out that they can't get one. Either they never had a business reputation before their induction or they were too young to get one, or they have no security to put up for a loan. A man with some social standing previous to his military service is about the only veteran who might be able to obtain a loan, and he is the one vet who doesn't need one.

And how about the educational angle? What family man can live on $75 a month? Even a single man would have a hard enough time. Under the GI Bill, a veteran will have to work his way through school, and I didn't understand that to be its purpose.

As far as I'm concerned I'll take the $300 the Government gives me after my discharge, get myself a job and then let the Government pay for a night-school course to prepare me for the advertising field. I have fought for my country and it should be able to afford that. When I get back I want a decent living for myself, my wife and child, that's all.

Hawaii —Pfc. CHARLES VAN MESSEL

The Kids Could Use It

How about an amendment permitting a soldier to transfer his rights to go to college to one member of his immediate family, his son or daughter? As a great many soldiers, like myself, are too old to continue school and support their families

at the same time, it would be a great advantage and satisfaction to each soldier-parent to know that one of his sons or daughters would be the recipient of a college education.

Burma —Sgt. DOUGLAS E. EAGLE

Loans and Appraisals

I am an honorably discharged veteran. A few weeks after my discharge I went to an agency which was set up to assist veterans in borrowing money for business. This agency is composed of 37-odd banks and trust companies consolidated into one central office. When I asked them whether I could borrow $2,500 to invest as working capital in my father's business, with which I've been associated for ten years, I was told that no provision was made for that type of loan, regardless of character, experience and credit rating. But they said I might be granted a loan if I wanted to buy out an existing business with its stock, fixtures, equipment and good will. Which does me no good. So why not liberalize the GI Bill to include "character" or "working capital" loans for veterans with experience in a particular line of business?

Secondly, the home-buying set-up is a farce. The only advantage offered a veteran is 4 percent interest as against the 5 percent charged by any bank. The red tape and delays which the Veterans Administration requires for an appraiser to make reports would be almost as laughable as some Army regulations if it weren't so unfair to the veterans.

I have been in the real-estate business and I can speak with some knowledge about appraising properties. I have seen appraisals run from 25 percent less than fair-market value to 25 percent higher. In other words, if a fair price for a house is $5,000, one appraiser would say it might be worth $3,750 and another would say $6,250, and either could be right. The VA should do away with the appraisal system. Obviously, the appraiser gets paid for his work, and in many cases the higher the appraisal the higher his fee. I read an article where an appraiser needed two assistants and spent 16 hours on the job on a GI home loan.

That is a crock of good old shellac. I'll appraise any house in a matter of one to three hours. He probably spent 14 hours out of the 16 in making out his report.

Philadelphia —ex-Pvt. GENE LIEBERMAN

Federal Loans Only

I think that any money loaned to a veteran should be loaned by Federal agencies only. Under no condition should the Bill guarantee a loan from banks or any other private lending agencies. These agencies are out to get the GI's losses. The whole thing should be a Government transaction.

I'd like to borrow the money which my grandparents, my parents and I have invested in this great Government. The interest which we are going to have to pay should be an investment as well as a paid debt.

Ft. Benning, Ga. —Pvt. HAROLD L. KELDERMAN

THIS page of GI opinion on issues of the day is a regular feature of YANK. A question for future discussion is "What Reforms Should Be made in the Post-War Army?" If you have any ideas on this subject send them to The Soldier Speaks Department, YANK, The Army Weekly, 205 East 42d Street, New York, 17, N. Y. We will allow you time to get answers here from overseas by mail. The best letters we receive will appear in a future issue.

By Sgt. JAMES P. O'NEILL
YANK Staff Writer

Kansas City, Kansas—In the county court-house here, a tall, middle-aged man with gray hair and horn-rimmed spectacles stood beside a very pretty, very young girl. He held her hand in a casual way and stared abstractedly out of the window as a judge behind a desk intoned the solemn words of a marriage ceremony. The young woman sighed softly and her eyes were starry. When the ceremony was ended the tall, middle-aged man patted the girl affectionately on the back, gave her a fatherly kiss on the forehead and handed the judge a $5 bill.

"Thanks a lot, judge," the bridegroom said.

"What's this one?" the judge asked. "The 38th or 39th?"

"The 39th," the other answered.

The bride, weeping a little, stood hesitantly in the center of the room. The tall man put his arm around her in nonchalant fashion and ushered her out of the courthouse.

"If you'll wait till I call my wife," he said, "I'll take you to lunch."

The bride just nodded her head as if his statement were the most natural one in the world. There wasn't anything wrong with it. Although Thomas H. Finnegan has been married 39 times and has never been a widower or got a divorce, everything was legal.

Under the proxy-marriage law of the state of Kansas, Finnegan takes the vows for overseas soldiers and sailors. And since Kansas is the only state in the Union in which people may be legally married by proxy, there's little doubt among the

PEOPLE ON THE HOME FRONT

Most-Married Man in America

Kansas City courthouse crowd that he is the most-married man in America. Girls have traveled to Kansas to marry him from as far west as Los Angeles and as far east as Corona, Long Island.

Despite his 39 marriages, Finnegan has been happily married to the same woman for 21 years. A successful trial lawyer, he hasn't tried to get rich out of the proxy-marriage business. His fee for a ceremony never amounts to more than $15.

Finnegan got into the marriage-by-proxy game purely by accident. In February 1943, at which time he was head of the Wyandotte County Bar Association, he received a letter from a Miss Brown of the Chicago Legal Aid Bureau. "Miss Brown," Finnegan says, "wrote me that there was a girl out there who had been going steady with a sailor stationed at Great Lakes. They were madly in love and planned to marry but the sailor was abruptly ordered overseas. They still wanted to get married in the very worst way. Some Chicago lawyer mentioned to Miss Brown that he had heard of a marriage-by-proxy law and he thought that Kansas had it. Miss Brown wanted to know if I knew anything about it."

As a matter of record, Finnegan had never heard of such a statute, but he dug out his law books and discovered that the Chicago lawyer was right. Judge Clark E. Tucker of the Wyandotte County Probate Court told Finnegan that while the Kansas law appeared perfectly constitutional, few judges in the state had ever been willing to perform the proxy ceremony.

"Would you do it for a kid in the service who's busy with a few things in the Pacific?" Finnegan asked Judge Clark. Under the circumstances, the judge replied, he guessed he would.

So Finnegan wrote back to Chicago that if the girl wanted to come to Kansas City and be married by proxy, he would not only take care of the license but would act as bridegroom as well. In a few days the girl came to town and she and Finnegan were married, and now she and the sailor, so far as Finnegan knows, are living happily ever after.

A few weeks later Finnegan got another proposal from a Chicago girl, this one engaged to a soldier. Would Finnegan walk down the aisle again? Finnegan would be delighted. In a few months the lawyer was getting married on an average of twice a week.

Shortly before VJ-Day Finnegan had 30 future weddings definitely scheduled and at least 60 in the request stage. Before the war ended he was thinking of hiring an assistant—if he could get one. "Fellows around here are too damned bashful to help me," says Finnegan.

Finnegan, it may please absent bridegrooms to hear, dresses well for the marriage ceremony. His usual garb is a soft gray-flannel suit, a white shirt and a striped tie. He wears a carnation in his lapel and sees to it that the bride has a bouquet. Finnegan knows the marriage ceremony by heart. "If I go through 10 more of these ceremonies, I think I'll be able to recite the whole thing backwards," he says.

Most of the brides are extremely nervous and shy and though the modest lawyer himself won't admit it, his secretary says the girls feel thankful to be able to step up to the altar with such a dapper and understanding man as Finnegan.

"Frankly, the girls expect some old movielike character with a bald head and a big cigar in his mouth," Finnegan's secretary says. "And when they see the boss they're surprised. 'Gee, I didn't know lawyers were so cute,' most of them say."

After the ceremony Finnegan invariably takes the bride out to lunch. "I try to give her a little advice and a few tips I've picked up in 21 years of married life," is the way he explains this part of the ritual.

The luncheon over, the bride usually goes straight back to where she came from. There seems to have been only one occasion on which the bride business disturbed the peace of the Finnegan home. An extremely good-looking girl from Chicago decided to get married in style. She brought along her bridesmaids, well-wishers, wedding dress and even rice, and hired a suite in a local hotel. All through the ceremony she kept calling Finnegan "Joe," her real husband's name. And she insisted that Finnegan come to the reception at the hotel.

"I rarely drink, especially in the daytime," Finnegan says, "but this ceremony made me nervous. It seemed too damned real. I had the guilty feeling I was committing bigamy. And at the reception some of the guests got a little tight and began congratulating me. So I took a snorter to buck myself up."

When Finnegan finally got home, it was past

his dinnertime and he was a little mixed up about things. He had a hard time convincing his wife he hadn't been out on a binge. At last, however, everything seemed to be straightened out, and then he had to go and pull the boner of his life.

"I called my wife 'Elizabeth,'" Finnegan recalls sheepishly. "That isn't her name. That was the name of the girl from Chicago. From there on it was a rough night."

Although the incident marks the only time Finnegan's marriages ever interfered with his married life, his duties as the nation's outstanding proxy husband aren't always finished when he says farewell to the proxy bride. Most of the girls he marries keep up a correspondence with him, letting him know how their married life, if any, is getting on. Finnegan has so far had visits from four husbands for whom he served as stand-in. The visits, he reports, were very pleasant.

One girl who lived near Kansas City was about to have a child when her husband was sent overseas a second time. Finnegan went to the hospital with her and paced the floor in the best expectant-father tradition. "The girl was all alone and in that hospital, and anyhow it's best to have a man around at a time like that to bother the nurses and raise hell with the doctor," Finnegan says.

To date, only one of the Finnegan marriages has turned out badly. A girl he went to the altar with early in his proxy career recently asked Finnegan to handle her divorce. He wrote back that she ought to reconsider and to list all her reasons for wanting a divorce. He also wrote to the husband, suggesting that he tell his side of the case. The correspondence is still in progress.

"I haven't got them together yet," Finnegan says, "but I will. Those kids are wrangling over something very silly and unimportant. My wife and I had the same sort of argument 20 years ago."

Before the war ended, the Kansas City lawyer was planning to use his wife in the business. Seems he had three requests from servicemen in the States who wanted to marry girls stationed overseas.

Mrs. Finnegan, having long ago recovered from the shock of being addressed as Elizabeth, takes her husband's many marriages in entirely good humor. "I don't mind how many girls Tom gets married to," she says, "just so he doesn't go on the honeymoons."

HARTFORD, CONN. Here's how it looked at summer's end in this New England city. The picture was taken from the Hartford Trust Co. at 1 p.m., looking down Main Street. At left is the Phoenix National Bank.

SALT LAKE CITY, UTAH It was a bright morning in Utah's capital city. Pointing down Main Street, with Ensign Peak in the distance, the camera took in the bronze statue of Brigham Young and the famous Mormon Temple of the Latter Day Saints (left background).

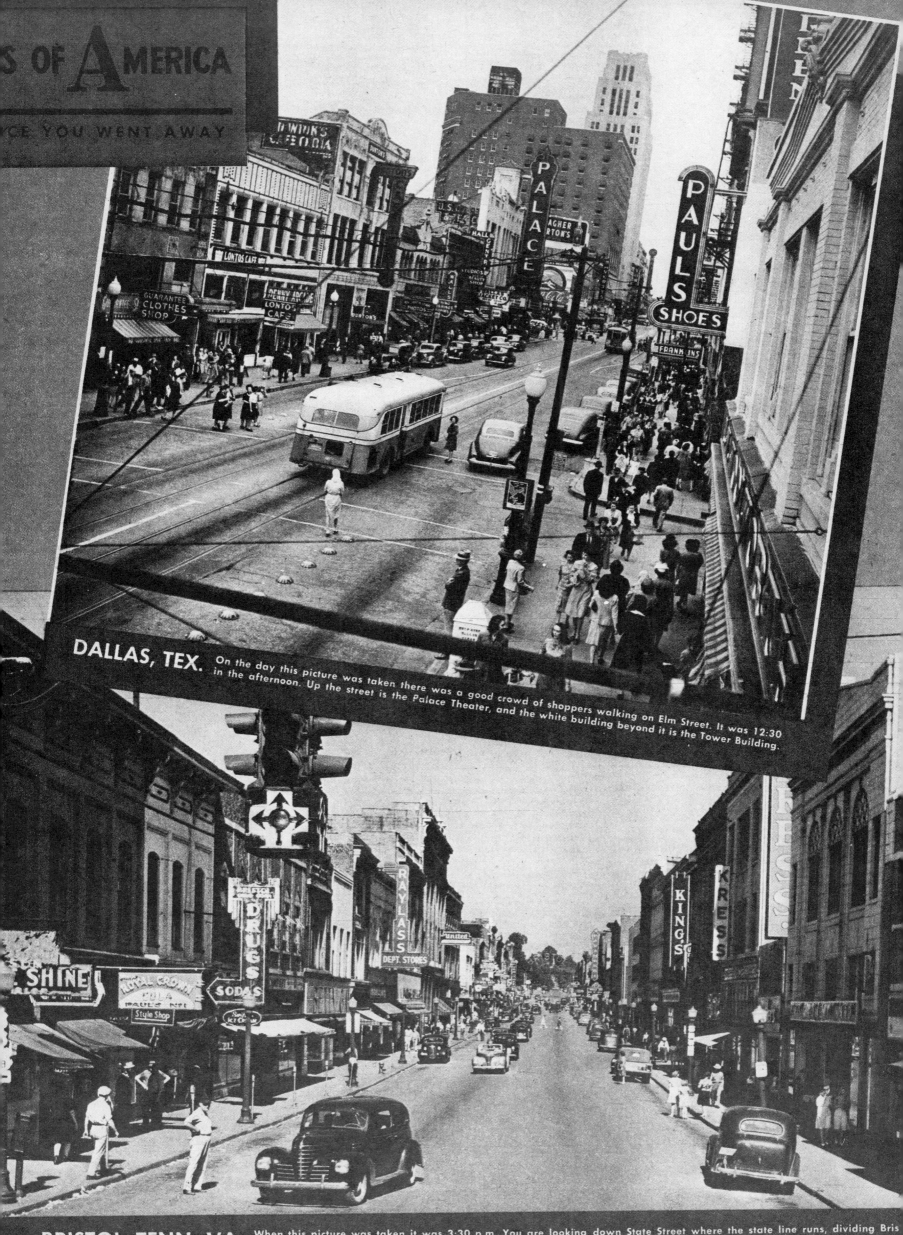

DALLAS, TEX. On the day this picture was taken there was a good crowd of shoppers walking on Elm Street. It was 12:30 in the afternoon. Up the street is the Palace Theater, and the white building beyond it is the Tower Building.

BRISTOL, TENN.-VA. When this picture was taken it was 3:30 p.m. You are looking down State Street where the state line runs, dividing Bris into Virginia on the left and Tennessee on the right. But Bristol, Va., and Bristol, Tenn., spell just one home town for many G

THE SAD SACK

"DITCHED"

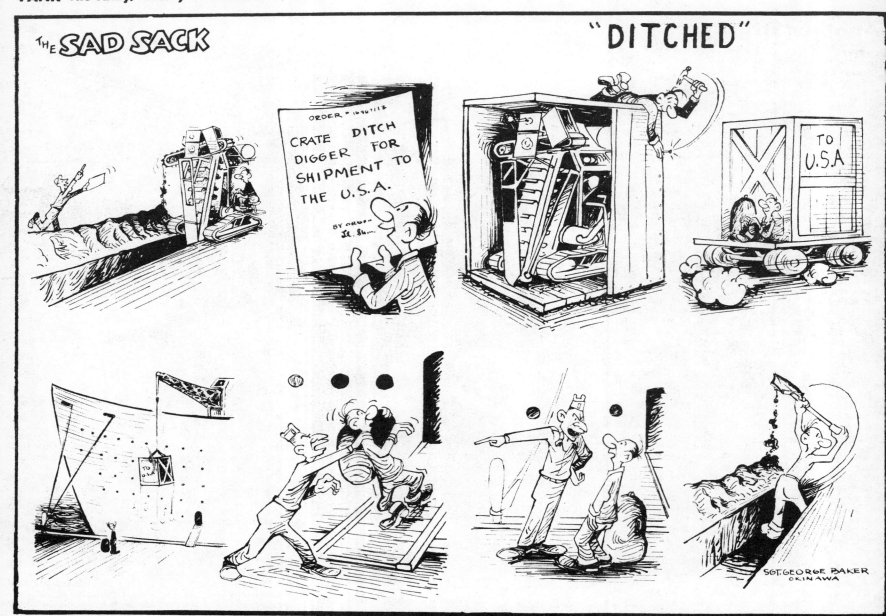

SGT. GEORGE BAKER
OKINAWA

Carnival Marriage

Dear YANK:

After 17 lonely and womanless weeks of training in Texas I was given a furlough. While on furlough I visited a carnival. At the carnival I met a girl and because of my loneliness I asked her to marry me. Although we had just met, she replied in the affirmative, and four days later we were married. Six weeks later I was overseas. I still do not know the girl well nor do I know her family. I do not love her and I am sure I can never be happy with her. I have written her asking for a divorce. She has agreed.

Before coming into the Army I was a male nurse with two years of hospital experience. When I get out of service I want to go to medical school under the GI Bill of Rights. My wife has had only six years of schooling and can barely read and write. She is quite content in her illiteracy. She is anti-social and refuses to go anywhere where there are a number of people. That is definitely a drawback to me. I can never become a doctor with that kind of wife.

I want to know if I, with her consent, of course, can get a divorce while I am still in the ETO?

France   —(Name Withheld)

■ Your right to maintain a divorce action depends on the law of the State having jurisdiction of the case. Many States permit soldier plaintiffs to maintain such actions

WHAT'S YOUR PROBLEM?

Letters to this department should bear writer's full name, serial number and military address.

even though they find it impossible to be physically present during the trial of the case. Whether you have any legal ground upon which to base an action for a divorce is something that only an attorney can advise you about. See your legal assistance officer for further information on that score.

Review of Discharge

Dear YANK:

I was discharged with a blue (without honor) discharge. At the time I didn't think anything of it and figured while I had gotten a raw deal I'd forget about it. Now however I am beginning to see what a difference it makes to receive an honorable instead. I have heard that under the GI Bill of Rights I can apply to the Army Discharge Review Board and get my discharge changed if I can show I shouldn't have received the blue discharge. That's all well and good. I feel sure I can get the necessary proof to convince the board, but what bothers me is that I cannot afford to hire a lawyer. Do I have to get a civilian lawyer in order to present my case to the board?

California   —JAMES L. ALLEN

■ You need not hire a lawyer in order to have your case presented to the Discharge Review Board. The GI Bill of Rights does not require a veteran to hire counsel in order to get a review of his discharge. If a veteran wishes, he may handle his own case before the Review Board.

Points for Stepchild

Dear YANK:

I have a total of 74 points for overseas duty and duty in the States. In April of 1944 I married a divorcee with one child. The father of the child is sending it an allotment through the Office of

Dependency Benefits. I too have applied for an additional allotment on behalf of this child (I have just been told by my orderly room that I am entitled to the allotment). My step-daughter is and has been a member of my household since I was

SIR, HERE IS A PICTURE OF MY NEW DAUGHTER!

married. Now what I would like to know is, am I entitled to 12 points for the child or not? Or, does the child's real father get the 12 points?

Camp Blanding, Fla.   —T-5 WALTER LYNCH

■ You are entitled to the 12 points for the child. In a case of this type the man in whose household the child lives gets credit for the child. The fact that the child's father contributes to the child's support does not change your right to the 12 points.

Back Taxes

Dear YANK:

While I have been in service, taxes on my farm have been piling up (my wife has been living on the farm and running it for me). At present I owe over $600 in back taxes. As you can guess, that is a pretty big load for an ordinary farm to carry. When I get out, will I be able to get a loan under the GI Bill of Rights to pay off these back taxes?

Marianas   —T/Sgt. ROBT. H. STEELE

■ You will. Such a loan will be approved under the GI Bill of Rights. You can get it either as a farm loan or a home loan, and one or the other ought to cover your needs.

Another Stripe

From the day McGregor reported for duty at the statistical office, he felt that tension. He knew there'd be more.

So he began to argue with himself. He would try his best not to become involved in any petty intrigue. He was a big person, and even though he had been in grade longer than Bolton, the other corporal, he knew the Army didn't always give out promotions by virtue of time in grade alone. He'd see to it that he did a better job than Bolton. Then time would tell. At least he would try. There was no harm in trying.

The first week passed amicably enough. They were both feeling each other out—and the lieutenant. He was a tough one. He said very little. He asked few questions. Sometimes, McGregor would ask him a direct question and he wouldn't answer. McGregor would wait tensely, then ask again. Maybe, the second time, the lieutenant would look up and give him some abstract reply. This made McGregor fume inside. So what? What could he expect from his superior officer and his boss? If the lieutenant didn't consider his questions material, then to hell with him. He wouldn't let him know it affected him in the least.

The second week, a Wac pfc was transferred to the office, so they had to rearrange the furniture. The lieutenant had been sitting between Bolton and McGregor, in the middle of the office, but the Wac was to be his personal secretary and she'd have to have a desk within his reach. So Bolton took it upon himself to make the changes.

When McGregor came back from chow one afternoon, he found his desk moved to a far corner of the room, almost out of sight of the lieutenant. Bolton had placed his own desk directly facing the lieutenant's. He'd also brought in a large file cabinet which he put next to his desk so he could reach it without leaving his seat. The width of the cabinet made Bolton's desk protrude into the aisle, making anyone who passed have to take a deep breath in order to get by. He had also placed the small table for the phone between his desk and the lieutenant's. This enabled either of them to reach it without exerting too much effort.

An "in" basket with the name "Bolton" scribbled across it lay on the table. It sat there, ready for any papers that might pass from the lieutenant to him, located conveniently enough to be a stopgap for any other items the lieutenant had no special place for.

This bit of subterfuge lit the candle, even though McGregor was eased somewhat when the lieutenant returned and looked over the new arrangement. His comment was, "The whole set-up looks pretty handy for you, Bolton, but it sure makes it unhandy for everyone else in the office." There was little or no emotion in the lieutenant's voice when he said that. And he didn't intimate that the desks were to be shifted, or the cabinet moved back to the hall. Bolton knew he had scored the first victory.

McGregor tried to keep his mind on his work after that. The first of the month was drawing near and he had it on good authority that there would be ratings. But with the pressure on headquarters for so many promotions, he knew damn well only one of them would make sergeant. At least the lieutenant never complained to him, or turned back any of his work. That was in his favor. But there were little things, things that Bolton managed and he couldn't that stacked the cards so much against him. Like when the phone would ring and Bolton would grab it and say, with a mellifluous purr in his voice, "Lt. Martin's office, Cpl. Bolton speaking." McGregor couldn't do that. He couldn't bring himself to say it, even

"Sure glad you could get home for the holiday, son—we've got a little parade planned."
—Cpl. Frank R. Robinson, Robins Field, Ga.

"It's ours. We made it in our own little workshop."
—Cpl. Bob Schoenke, Ellington Field, Texas

PX

Contributions for this page should be addressed to the Post Exchange YANK The Army Weekly 205 East 42d Street New York 17 N Y

though he tried. Whenever he picked up the receiver, he unconsciously would say, "Post Statistical Office," and once or twice he noticed the lieutenant would look up from his work and give him a half-glare.

He did say, "Lt. Martin's office," once, but it was forced and insincere, and it made him feel uncomfortable because he couldn't buck and he was so afraid it would look as though he were bucking. He'd rather not have a promotion if he had to buck for it, and, damn it, he wouldn't, he assured himself.

And the business of the lieutenant's laundry. That must have taken Bolton a good extra hour of his time when he went to town. It got so the lieutenant would bring in his bundle and put it on Bolton's desk without saying a word. When Bolton would bring back the clean laundry, he'd never mention how much it cost and it might be days before the lieutenant would say, "How much for the laundry, Bolton?" And Bolton would say, "Oh, forget it, sir." And they would banter around until the lieutenant would give him a couple of bills and Bolton would make change. He always managed to have the right change ready.

"Thank you, sir," Bolton would say, with heavy emphasis on the "sir." How many times had McGregor said "sir" to the lieutenant? Damned few. He wasn't discourteous. He always kept his voice in an even tenor when he spoke, but he couldn't tag a "sir" on to the end of every sentence as Bolton did. It just wasn't in him.

"I'm a damn fool," he would say to himself after a conversation with the lieutenant in which he had spoken with an over-amount of coldness and unconcern. "But I'm not bucking. I have that much self-satisfaction."

The day promotions came out, McGregor knew what had happened before Bolton told him, and he had made up his mind to maintain as much disinterest as possible. But Bolton greeted him at the door with a gluttonous smile, waving the order in his face. "I made it, I made it," he said. "Here, have a cigar." And he fumbled in his pocket, pulling out a King Edward that looked as if it had been left over from the time he made corporal.

McGregor flushed and looked Bolton in the eye. "No thanks," he said turning away abruptly. He seemed to choke up as the words came from his lips. He was immediately sorry he'd been such a bad sport, but his attitude didn't even faze Bolton, who just laughed and stuffed the cigar back in his pocket.

The Wac had made corporal, but that didn't bother McGregor. He shook her hand and said, "I'm glad you made it." Bolton stood watching them, still smiling.

Something was sticking in McGregor's throat as he sat down. It was like a big piece of corn in a hen's craw, and he couldn't swallow it. He thought maybe he'd go back to the barracks until he cooled off, but he knew that would be childish. He decided to try to do his work as though nothing had happened.

The lieutenant was late that morning. He came in without speaking, as usual. Bolton gave him a cheery "Good morning," and added, "Thanks for the promotion, sir." The lieutenant mumbled something incoherently as he sat down.

For the rest of the morning nothing could be heard in the office but the monotonous rattle of typewriters, the occasional ring of the phone. Several times, the lieutenant would clear his throat. That was one of his annoying habits.

It was almost noon before the lieutenant said anything. Most of the time he had kept his eyes glued to the mass of papers on his desk, but now he put them aside and looked up.

"I'm sorry I couldn't get you another stripe, too, McGregor," he said. "You know how stingy they are with ratings on this post. Both of you boys have done excellent work. It was too hard for me to decide, so I did the only thing I could. I flipped a coin. Just a case of bad luck on your part."

For the first time, it was the lieutenant who waited for a reply. Interminable seconds went by as the two men looked at each other. Work in the office had come to a standstill. Finally, the lieutenant lowered his head and began to ruffle through his papers absently.

Bolton coughed. "Is your laundry ready to go out, sir?" he asked.

Detroit, Mich. —S/Sgt. GORDON CROWE

TWENTY-FIRST BIRTHDAY

I sit here in my cozy cell;
  My heart is filled with joy,
For I am twenty-one today—
  No longer "just a boy."

My folks and friends remembered me
  With gifts and revenue;
How did the Army celebrate?
  CQ.

Brooklyn Army Base, N. Y. —Pfc. DANIEL WALDRON

"I don't think you've quite gotten the meaning of 'Service Club Commando,' Hubert."
—Pfc. Anthony Delatri, Belgium

By Pfc. ROBERT BENDINER
YANK Staff Writer

In a war which wound up in an atmosphere of scientific marvels, radar ranks high as a stand-out achievement. The Army has taken the wraps off the secret story of what makes radar tick.

BOCA RATON ARMY AIR FIELD, FLA.—In the midst of the vast excitement that followed the unleashing of the atomic bomb, the Army for the first time permitted publication of the basic facts about radar. To a lot of people, the radar disclosure seemed pretty small potatoes compared with the news about the atomic bomb. In the opinion of many well-informed analysts, however, radar's place of honor among the scientific marvels which helped win the war is second to none.

"Radar played a greater part in the whole war than the atom bomb itself," according to Sir Stafford Cripps, formerly Britain's Minister of Aircraft Production. In fact, Sir Stafford adds, "it contributed to the winning of the war more than any other single factor." That is a tall claim, but it is supported by a number of our own Army and Navy authorities. And here are a few of the reasons:

1) It was radar that enabled the RAF to save the day when the *Luftwaffe* threatened to bring England to her knees. No matter how thick the fog or black the night, radar's penetrating eye picked up the German planes as they left the Continent, gave the RAF fighters the maximum time and the most accurate information to counter the attack and sighted the ack-ack guns with deadly accuracy. On Sept. 15, 1940, radar-guided ground and aircraft guns combined to down 185 out of 500 attacking planes. Germany's air arm had met its first serious defeat.

2) It was radar that drove the U-boat from the seas. In 1942 the subs were sinking 16,000 tons of Allied shipping a day. Our Atlantic coast was strewn with wreckage; the loss of life was heavy and the loss of supplies grave enough to threaten our ultimate success in the war.

Carried in aircraft that swept the coasts and the major sea lanes, radar spotted the subs 10 miles off when they surfaced at night to charge their batteries and take in fresh air. High-speed planes were notified and guided direct to the targets. In three months of 1943, 100 U-boats went down.

3) It was radar that played a major part in protecting our convoys so well that we lost only 1/10th of one percent of our convoyed ships; it was radar that directed our bombers in paralyzing German coast defenses on D-Day; radar that guided our paratroopers to landings in Normandy and Holland; radar that put our bombers over Europe in fog, darkness and rain; and radar that made it possible for our ships to steam closer to enemy shores in the Pacific under the cover of night than would have been thinkable to the most daring commander in the days before the "magic eye."

Until a short time ago radar was among the most hush-hush subjects of the war. Thousands of men in the forces had worked with it, but all were sworn to secrecy. Radar operators and observers were known as "radio operators," and students in American radar schools were forbidden to take their notebooks out of the classroom. In Britain, radar development was carried on in a secluded Suffolk manor over whose entrance was a coat of arms with this misleading motto: *Plutôt mourir que changer.* ("Better death than change.") But now the lid has been lifted, though not yet quite all the way.

To understand the underlying principle of radar, you need only know that certain radio waves, or pulses, traveling with the speed of light (186,000 miles a second), bounce when they hit an object in their path. If the object is squarely facing the source from which the waves have been sent, they will bounce back to the source. If the object is partially directed away from the source, only some of the waves will be returned, the others bouncing off at an angle and losing themselves in space.

The principle is simple enough, but the application of it proves very tricky. It was clear from

Radar

This anti-aircraft radar set is manned by four soldiers. The standing GI operates a modulator, and the other three, on high elevated seats, operate the vertical and horizontal position scopes and the range scope. The windmill-like structures are the antennae

the start that if a radio wave of sufficiently high frequency could be directed at a given target and an observation made on the time elapsing between the transmission of the wave and its return, the target's distance could readily be calculated. It was clear, too, that if such waves could be beamed out in all directions, they would, by their return impulse, reveal any targets that happened to be in their path. The problems were to devise a sufficiently powerful short-wave transmitter to do the beaming and a receiver to record the returned waves as they bounced back.

Actually the problems did not at first present themselves in such clear terms. Radar (short for "radio detection and ranging") is, like radio itself, the product of evolutionary development in which each major step opens up new vistas. In its crudest form, the radar principle was first noted in 1922 by two scientists employed by the U. S. Navy, Dr. A. Hoyt Taylor and Leo C. Young. Experimenting with radio communication in the fall of that year, Taylor and Young discovered a distortion in received signals due to the reflection from a small wooden steamer on the Potomac. After further experiments, they reported to the Navy that "destroyers located on a line a number of miles apart could be immediately aware of the passage of an enemy vessel between any two destroyers of the line, irrespective of fog, darkness or smoke screen."

Work in this field progressed independently in the U. S., England, France and Germany throughout the 1920s and 1930s. In this country the Signal Corps, the Navy, private industry and, later, the Air Forces all had a hand in overcoming the technical problems involved in developing radar from its crude beginnings into the highly effective instrument it is today. Means had to be developed for generating pulses of the proper length, a receiver had to be devised which would not be blocked by the transmitter pulses, and a cathode-ray tube had to be designed to display the pulses as they were received.

Step by step, all these technical difficulties were overcome. Radar began to take shape. In 1938 a working shipboard model was installed on the U.S.S. *New York* and in the following year it received a workout in battle maneuvers. In 1938, too, the Coast Artillery gave radar a try-out as an anti-aircraft device.

IN addition to locating planes, the new equipment tracked shells in flight and also guided back to a safe landing an Army bomber that had gone astray during a demonstration and had been blown out to sea. In 1939, the AAF, which had been working closely with the Signal Corps, ordered radar equipment in quantity, and the air arm has since come to be the largest user of radar in the service.

In 1940, an agreement was reached with the British to pool the findings of laboratories on both sides of the ocean, and from that point on progress has been made with such rapidity that an industry which was almost non-existent before 1940 has since sold to our own armed forces alone millions of dollars' worth of equipment. Radar has overnight made electronics an industry comparable in size with the automobile industry before the war.

Basically, all radar equipment has just a few major features. It has, first, a modulator, a device for taking power from whatever generating source is used and applying it to turn a radio high-frequency oscillator on and off. It is this oscillator that emits the necessary waves in short bursts, so timed that returning pulses may be recorded between bursts. For this purpose a highly developed vacuum tube has been evolved; it's capable of operating at a power thousands of times greater than was thought possible a few years ago.

Then there is an antenna which concentrates the radio energy into a well-defined beam. The antenna must be capable of being swung from one point in space to another, so that the direction of the rebounding pulse—and consequently of the target—may be determined. Next, there is the indicator, which presents the information in the form best adapted to the particular radar set. The most striking of these indicators is the PPI, or Plan Position Indicator. This, a round, fluorescent glass disc, the face of a cathode-ray tube, is an ever-changing topographical map. Water, which reflects few of the transmitted pulses, appears as black; land, with a number of smooth surfaces facing in the direction of the plane or

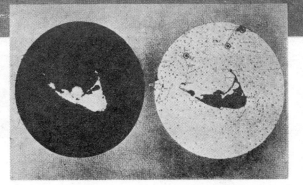

A comparison of an aerial radar photo of the island of Nantucket, Mass., with a chart (right). On the radar screen, land areas appear white and water black. Aircraft or shipping show up as white dots.

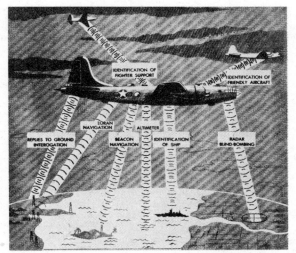

The B-29 is sometimes referred to as a flying radar set. This picture shows the functions of five types of radar equipment which are used by the Superforts.

ship from which the pulses are beamed, shows as gray; while built-up areas, with a great many smooth surfaces directly in the path of the beam, are reflected on the scope as bright patches. Individual objects, such as ships at sea, or airplanes in the vicinity, appear as bright "pips"—"blips," the English call them.

This particular scope is a feature of the amazing BTO set (Bombing Through Overcast). BTO, the peak of electronic development, was kept so secret during the early days of its use that except for the radar operator himself even the crews of planes that carried it were kept in the dark about its details. Crews referred to the BTO mysteriously as "Big Time Operator" and later more widely and more fondly as "Mickey." First used by the British, Mickey was tried out by our Eighth Air Force in the raid on the Wilhelmshaven docks in November 1943. Nine pathfinder planes, each leading a combat wing of 60, were equipped with this marvel, which not only guides a pilot to his target and tells him exactly when to begin his bomb run, but, geared to his bomb sight, also automatically releases the bomb at the strategic moment.

On eight previous raids over Wilhelmshaven our airmen had missed the city's docks entirely. With Mickey, bombing through overcast, they dropped a heavy concentration of bombs on the target area and did considerable damage. Without radar, the Eighth had been compelled to mark time with a force capable of operating 10 to 20 times more often than the target weather would permit. In 1942, our planes were grounded throughout December; in December 1943, using radar, they dropped bombloads that broke the record for any month to that date.

MICKEY did a remarkable job in the air offensive that softened Germany for the kill, but it was only one of the many forms in which radar was used against the enemy. Perhaps the simplest and at the same time one of the most useful applications of the principle was in the Tail Warning Set, most commonly used in night fighters. A fighter pilot, concentrating on maneuvering his ship, might be surprised by a sudden attack from the rear—but not if he had this handy gadget. Let an enemy plane approach within 600 feet and the radar-operated Tail Warner would pick the enemy up, flash a red light on the pilot's instrument panel, and also blow a horn or ring a bell, just to make sure.

Many night fighters were also equipped with AI, or Aerial Interception, a compact radar instrument that was used to track down enemy planes at night or in poor visibility. It required

such close coordination between radar observer and pilot that pairs, once established, were seldom broken up. The observer, watching his scope, would keep up a running flow of chatter which sounded like nothing so much as a broadcaster giving a blow-by-blow account of the heavyweight battle of the century.

An ingenious radar device is IFF (Identification, Friend or Foe). A ground station located, let's say, with an anti-aircraft battery, picks up an approaching plane on its radar set. Unable to tell, through the overcast or darkness, whether it is an enemy plane or one of its own, the station sends out an interrogating pulse. If the plane is friendly, its IFF transmitter is triggered off by the pulse and proceeds, without human operation, to send out a coded signal. The gunners down below hold their fire and, if necessary, the plane is guided on its way.

Then there is the radar altimeter which, by measuring the time required for a pulse to strike the earth and return, reveals absolute altitude, recording even the smallest ridge or elevation below. This is a great advantage over the barometric altimeter, which shows only altitude above sea level. With the radar altimeter a pilot can avoid such hazards as mountain peaks—or even the Empire State Building. An auxiliary attachment to this altimeter provides a three-light warning board to keep a pilot at a predetermined height. If he gets too high, a green light flashes on, if too low he is given a red signal, while amber informs him that all is well. This device is useful in the dropping of parachute troops.

AMONG the newest applications of radar is GCA, or Ground Control Approach. It is aviation's answer to the eternal threat of bad weather and is expected to put civilian air lines on schedules as reliable as the railroads'. This piece of equipment may be set up on any landing field, where it will proceed to pick up planes approaching the field from a distance of five to 30 miles. A ground operator, having located a plane struggling to come down through a heavy fog, communicates with its pilot by radio and, observing every foot of the plane's progress, "talks it in" to a safe landing.

British "Gee" and American "Loran" (Long Range Navigation) are devices that have already revolutionized both nautical and aerial navigation. Based on the transmission of waves broadcast from several fixed ground positions, Loran enables planes or ships to take fixes more readily than by celestial observation and just as accurately. Unlike astronomical bodies, Loran can be consulted in any weather, and it was a major factor not only in putting thousands of bombers over Europe on the blackest nights but in concentrating them at appointed rendezvous.

Radar sounds complex, and the instrument panel of a completely equipped plane does look like a Hollywood scientist's dream, but in fact the operation of most radar machinery may be learned in a matter of hours. Skilled observation, however, comes only with extensive practice.

In the instruction of radar personnel, the services had a monumental task on their hands. Research, development, production and instruction were all carried on at the same time, and equipment, tested in the field by trial and error, gave way to improved versions as fast as men learned to use it.

The entire program, moreover, had to proceed in such secrecy that even mention of radar off the field was grounds for court martial. "Probably no scientific or industrial development in the history of the world," says a report on the subject recently issued by the Office of War Information, "has expanded in all phases simultaneously, and on such a scale."

Starting with small informal classes carried on by the Signal Corps Laboratories in 1937, radar education has grown to such proportions that Navy schools have put more than 125,000 officers and men through advanced courses, while in the Army the Air Forces alone graduated 23,-175 radar men in the first six months of this year, as compared with 818 for the first half of 1942.

The men picked for radar, generally top students at radio schools throughout the service, have tested their gadgets in the clouds over Europe, in the mists of the Atlantic and in the storms of the tropics. They know that the atomic bomb hastened the end of a war whose outcome was no longer in doubt, but they know, too, that radar, the "magic eye," helped tremendously to remove that doubt.

YANK *Mail Call*
THE ARMY WEEKLY

YANK is published weekly by the enlisted men of the U. S. Army and is for sale only to those in the armed services. Stories, features, pictures and other material from YANK may be reproduced if they are not restricted by law or military regulation, providing proper credit is given, release dates are observed and specific prior permission has been granted for each item to be reproduced. Entire contents Vol. 4, No. 16, copyrighted, 1945, by Col. Franklin S. Forsberg and reviewed by U. S. military censors.

MAIN EDITORIAL OFFICE
205 EAST 42d STREET, NEW YORK 17, N. Y.

This Week's Cover

ABOARD the battleship Missouri in Tokyo Bay, the Emperor's delegation surrenders for Japan. As Japanese Foreign Minister Shigemitsu signs the surrender document, Gen. Douglas MacArthur faces him, standing at the right of the desk with his back to the camera. See pages 2 through 9 for other pictures and stories on the surrender and occupation of Japan.

Rank in the Postwar World

Dear YANK:
A story in the Washington *Times-Herald* stated that the War Manpower Commission may favor officers over enlisted men in recommending men for postwar jobs. The following expresses the resentful reaction of the many EM who have read it here.

Enlisted men have borne many indignities and humiliations during the course of their service, and where all else has failed they have maintained a certain philosophic calm in the thought that when the war is over they will return to civilian life, where ability and experience and knowledge will govern their success or failure, all other things being equal. Now we learn that even this small comfort is false—that the officer whose economic status improved considerably after his induction over what he was able to earn as a civilian, and who has become "accustomed to living on an officer's income" will continue to enjoy the benefits that come from having ONCE been at the right place at the right time.

The only conclusion we can reach is that the WMC either is under the thumb of the General Staff, or is headed entirely by ex-officers, or is under the delusion common among civilians that officers are selected by some mysterious system, known only to brass-hats, which infallibly separates the wheat from the chaff. Isn't it high time that the public and its governmental agencies be informed that the process of passing an OCS board combines the worst features of a lottery and a bingo game; that time and place are the most important hazards a contender must pass; that selections are made almost always on an arbitrary basis and frequently on a prejudicial opinion? Shouldn't they be told about T/Os, about "frozen ratings," about "essential enlisted men," about the thousands of EM with AGCT scores much higher than the required 110 who were turned down because of "lack of leadership," "lack of education," lack of skill in apple-polishing, or downright lack of luck? Shouldn't they be told of the thousands of officers who are nothing but highly decorated messengers and name-signers, and who continue to hold their brass only by the sweat, brains, ingenuity and unswerving patriotism of the enlisted men under them?

Mention should also be made of the many EM who ran successful businesses or professional careers in civilian life, building them up painstakingly at the cost of years of effort and thousands of dollars, and who had to sell them at terrific sacrifice or give them away or close them up when the greetings of the President arrived. They had to accustom themselves to living on $50 or less a month, their families had to accustom themselves to living on a ridiculous allotment, and they are now expected by the WMC to continue living on the same scale, in spite of their experience and ability, because in their involuntary shifts from place to place they never arrived at the "right" post or made the "right" connections.

When this war is over and we are out of the Army, let's be OUT of it—let's not let the military caste system take root in and destroy the civilian democracy we have fought to protect. Let ex-officers and ex-EM compete for jobs on terms of proper equality and let the best man win. Otherwise, let's admit that we've beaten the Germans and the Japs—and still have lost the war.

Fort Dix, N. J. —Pvt. MORRIS E. LEVINE*
Also signed by 18 others.

Dear YANK:
In the Dark Ages a man was not expected or permitted to rise any higher than what his forebears had been, but all this was changed—so we thought—on the day this country flung down the challenge to the rest of the world that here all distinctions of class, caste, rank, coterie and clique were to be eliminated for all.

Now we are candidly informed that "in civilian job placements" the august War Manpower Commission has regally decreed, "Officers will be given first chance at administrative and supervisory positions while enlisted men will be channeled into only those jobs requiring special skills or no skills at all."

one of the reasons for this un-American doctrine being that "young officers have married since they were called into service" and "they and their families are accustomed to living on an officer's income."

This is sheer tommyrot and while I doubt very much that any such despicable policy can be foisted upon an informed public, the shameless gall with which the attempt is being made richly deserves the righteous wrath of all good Americans that it will indubitably incur.

Patuxent River NAS, Md. —(Name Withheld)

Dear YANK:
We are all aware of the fact that the Army is based on a caste system not unlike feudalism in the middle ages. Being civilians by nature and soldiers because of necessity, we won't argue the pros and cons of this while we're in uniform. However, when we become civilians again, all such distinctions automatically vanish into thin air. If the Government forces any such distinctions upon us as free Americans it would be the most flagrant violation of the Bill of Rights, our Constitutional rights and privileges. Why does Congress have a Fair Employment Practices Commission to prevent discrimination in the hiring of any American because of race, creed or color, when on the other hand it approves discrimination between all ex-servicemen on the basis of an antiquated undemocratic caste system?

By Army "standards," an officer is *supposed* to be a superior soldier, one outstanding in leadership, initiative, able to bear responsibilities. If this were true, then no officer should have any trouble getting the better jobs on his own abilities and initiative, without help from any employment agency!

All we ask from civilian life is a fair chance to resume our normal way of living in a democratic America based on equal rights and privileges of all free men.

India —T-4 SIEGFRIED ALTSCHER

Dear YANK:
We know the American soldier will never tolerate the existing policies of military caste to be carried over into civilian life. While the average soldier recognizes that some form of military hierarchy is necessary to achieve military goals, he still realizes that certain aspects of enforced disparity between officers and enlisted men are entirely incongruous in an Army of a democracy and he will shed few crocodile tears the day he's no longer compelled to conform to rules of conduct and modes of recognition which he holds as degrading and unjust.

To suggest to the American soldier that officer caste will invade such a monumental field as postwar employment is to invite disunity, bitterness and disillusionment of a kind heretofore unknown. After the last war, when the people felt—and rightly so—that they had been betrayed, there followed a period of social unrest that saw the witch hunts, the bonus marches, race riots and prolonged industrial warfare. Should the proposed plans of the WMC become part of a national policy, the reaction of the people to such a discriminatory trend would cause the above-mentioned disasters to pale into insignificance.

Moreover, we would be announcing to a world which looks to America as the fortress opposing all medieval orders of prejudice and discrimination that we have abandoned our faith, and that in the future the free peoples of all nations must look elsewhere for their leadership.

India —Sgt. GROVER SALES Jr.
Also signed by 155 others.

■ The WMC has since done a certain amount of backtracking.

RHIP

Dear YANK:
In a recent issue of YANK T-5 Neblin stated that the man preceding him in the chocolate-bar ration line received nine almonds in his Hershey bar whereas he himself received only seven. We feel that we can clarify the situation by pointing out that through some gross and unpardonable error the other soldier undoubtedly received an officer's Hershey bar.

—Capt. FRANK L. KIRBY
Baker Gen. Hosp., W. Va.
Also signed by Lt. Andrew J. Lisman and Lt. Gerard M. Nardone.

Battle Stars

Dear YANK:
We are a group of reconverted combat men. We represent that group of Ground Forces men who, because of disabling wounds received at the front were reclassified as Limited Assignment and placed into rear-echelon Air Forces jobs a few months ago.

No one is in a better position to see

"Hey, Sarge, your thirty days are up."
—Cpl. Tom Flannery

ow unfair and unjust these so-called attle participation stars are as a measre of combat points. We know of one an back here who has received credit or three stars without ever having left aples. Once he got one because a forvard group went into a participation one and the whole outfit received redit. Once he was put on TD to an utfit in the area, never joined them at ll, but still got the star. We know of ozens of men who got the latest Italian ampaign stars merely by being on Speial Orders. A number of us were in the etachment of Patients at that time; the ospital staffs got stars, our old outfits ot stars, but not us; we got Purple earts instead.

Although everyone with decent sensiilities and an understanding of the ruth agrees that it is an unfair criterion or determining combat, nobody does nything about it. Are we stuck with his? They repeal bad constitutional mendments, don't they . . . ?

taly —Pfc. HENRY J. BECKER*

*Also signed by five others.

A Home (With Furniture)

Dear YANK:

A short while ago there was a Congressman who was going to introduce a ill in Congress to pay all discharged ervice men and women $5,000. At that ime I thought it was a far-fetched idea and did not approve of it, but I have hanged my mind since then and here s the reason why.

I went home on furlough and looked p some of the old gang and here is what I found. Two of them were still in he Army, three of them had gotten nedical discharges and six of them had never been in the service at all. Of the ine that were out of the Army, eight ad their own homes (with furniture) and these homes were bought since the war started. Besides this, most of them were all paid off. All of them had good ars and a few bucks in the bank.

Now somebody is going to tell me that I have the GI Bill of Rights. OK, so I have—what is that going to get us? Homes, furniture and a few bucks in he bank? The only thing that the GI Bill is good for is fellows that had their education interrupted. The rest isn't worth the paper it is written on. And f these kids do go to school under it and then a bonus is voted later, the cost of their schooling will come out of their onus.

I think that $5,000 is too much money but I do think that there should be some payment made to all fellows with more than one year of service. I will get $300 when I get out. OK, so I buy myself some new clothes at high prices and the $300 is shot. How about it, fellows? Don't you think that we should at least be in the running when it comes to a home (with furniture)?

Ft. Worth, Texas —T/Sgt. E. D. MILLER

Checkmate

Dear YANK:

In the hustle and bustle of war, discharges and reconversion, it is only to be expected, I suppose, that even the most important facts may get lost in the shuffle. My conscience prompts me to do my humble best to remedy a ghastly situation.

Gentlemen, I demand the immediate discharge from the Army of 8,009 expert chess players. Surely you cannot be so blind as not to know what is going on! An entire generation of youngsters is growing to maturity without benefit of any but the most mediocre chess instructions. They scarcely grasp the difference between the English Opening and the Queen's Gambit.

I warn you, gentlemen, unless these abominable conditions are immediately rectified, the country is heading toward mental stagnation, chaos and irrevocable ruin.

China —T-5 EUGENE V. GOLDSTEIN

Pan Mail

Dear YANK:

During all the time YANK has been in existence I believe that its great potential value has been wasted. It has been used mainly as a variety magazine to amuse Army personnel. That is all well and good, but where the Army's Orientation Program has been a miserable failure, YANK could have filled that gap. Most GIs are indifferent to or ignorant of current political, social and economic problems and many are reluctant to avail themselves of such knowledge.

YANK's circulation is probably the largest of any published literature among the American soldiers. For this reason, instead of printing silly poems, non-sensical stories, etc., I believe that YANK should print articles on American history, explain our form of government as compared to the British, Russian and former German types, explain Lend-Lease, problems of Reconversion, taxation, explain Social Security, explain the functions of UNRRA, OPA, WLB, etc.

Maybe these subjects sound dull and uninteresting, but these very thing are pressing our leaders at home every day. It is our duty, yes, duty, as citizens and soldiers to take an interest in all problems which affect us and our neighbors. The day is gone when we isolated our country from the rest of the world and our communities from the rest of the country. We must not continue to isolate our minds from the pressing questions of the day either.

—Cpl. EUGENE SACKS

West Palm Beach, Fla.

Cheerio from Mom

Dear YANK:

. . . It's been two or is it three years now since we first had American boys in this little town. They were not billeted here but just came in from camps to spend their free time.

Now you can guess there was plenty of speculation among the girls and plenty of cautioning from their mothers,

myself included, as I had two daughters just growing up, apart from two still at school.

Well, I thought things over and then I said to my eldest girls, "Now look, there will be a lot of these boys around for some time. They are thousands of miles from home, and what they will need most is a bit of company, or somewhere to sit and talk, so if you must get in company with some of them just bring them home for a cup of coffee and a talk instead of taking them off to the park."

I told them, "It's up to you English girls to keep these boys clean and straight and fit to go back and look the American girls in the face."

Well, I can honestly say my method worked. From the day the first American boy came in to town until now when they are on the eve of going back I can say I've had literally hundreds of these boys visit my home and not one of them has left an unpleasant memory.

True, some of them have imagined they were in love with one of the girls and there has been some amount of heartburning, but it has all come out right and no one any the worse for it.

We've had boys from almost every state in America and what a grand lot they've been and how they have appreciated the little bit of home we have been able to give them—somewhere to spend an evening instead of sitting in a public house, and somewhere to stay overnight on their day off. How they have loved sleeping in a proper bed just for one night in a week. Believe me, if I've been put to any trouble to do this for them it's been well worth it just to hear them say, "Gee, Mom, did I sleep? Boy, oh boy, what a bed."

And if they are grateful to us for what little we could do for them, well so are we grateful to them for their company and talks, giving us a much broader outlook on life and showing us in many ways how we can improve our way of living.

I'd like their mothers to know how much they have helped some of we English mothers. How they have fired us up with ambitions to have much better conditions in our homes. I'd like some of the first GIs to come back now and see the improvements I've made in my little home, and all because they would say to me, "Gee, Mom, you shouldn't have to sweat and work like you do You should have a fireplace that don't need cleaning if you can't have central heating." This being only a small house the central heating was impossible but I did the next best thing and had an old iron fireplace (which took me a half hour every day to clean) taken away and a tiled one put in which takes just five minutes and is a joy to see.

Oh, I could go on forever telling you all sorts of little things they did like sharing their candy ration with the children and their tobacco with Pop, the way they would sometimes tie on an apron and make me sit still while they washed the dishes after a meal.

I'd like to send a letter to every state in America just to let the American mothers know we think they sent over a grand lot of boys and it's been a pleasure to know them. Some day I hope to save enough to visit America. I'd like to meet up with some of my boys, as I call them, although unfortunately I know some of them will never come back to America themselves.

Well, I guess I've written this rather crudely but anyway if any GI reads it, I want to say, "Cheerio, son, it's been grand to have you and come again if ever you can."

England —MOM CANTER

Indefinite Furloughs

Dear YANK:

Millions of service men have endured two, three, four or five years of Army routine and war. Naturally their chief concern is a speedy return to normal civilian life. However, as a victor's reward, they are told they must lay idle in Army camps another six to eighteen months.

The Army contends that they need a large force to occupy the conquered countries, to garrison our outposts and to maintain services of supply. There is a way to prevent mass unemployment, to satisfy the Army's needs and to separate eligible millions of service men in a matter of weeks. Here is the plan:

Indefinite furloughs — After physical examinations at their present bases all eligible men sign a statement waiving disability benefits and are sent home on indefinite furloughs from the armed forces. They will be on reserve and subject to recall in event of an emergency, until discharged. Discharge papers would be handled on a priority basis and would be mailed to the serviceman's local draft board.

Eligibility: All men having served one or more years in the armed forces.

—S/Sgt. CHARLES P. ALLEN

Geiger Field, Wash.

Strictly GI

Demobilization and Redeployment Policy. Following the occupation of Japan, the War Department announced an over-all policy for demobilization and redeployment. While the announcement was partly a summary of rules already adopted, some new regulations were also made public. One such provides that no enlisted man who, as of May 12, 1945, had a point score of 45 or more, or who was 34, 35 or 36 years old (with a minimum of one year of honorable service), should be sent overseas. The reason for this provision, the WD said, is to eliminate transportation to overseas theaters of men who would have less than a year to serve in the theater before becoming eligible for discharge.

Under this ruling, all enlisted personnel with 45 or more points as of last May 12 and all enlisted personnel 34 years old or older were ordered screened out of units and detachments scheduled for redeployment to the Pacific and also out of all units and detachments which might in the future be earmarked for redeployment to that theater. In addition, no EM who falls into these categories will be sent to the Pacific as a replacement or casual. However, men 34, 35 or 36 years old with less than one year of honorable service are still eligible for overseas service. Also, any man may be sent overseas if he volunteers or enlists.

Three exceptions — affecting only a few hundred men—were made to the new screening score of 45 points. These were in the cases of enlisted men in Civil Affairs units which were scheduled for early departure to the Pacific to assist in the vital task of instituting civil government in occupied territories, and enlisted men assigned to the Headquarters of the VII and XVIII Corps, both of which were scheduled for immediate departure at the time the announcement was made. Even in the cases of these exceptions, the WD ruled that no one who had 60 points or more or who was 37 years old or who was 34, 35 or 36 years old with a minimum of one year of honorable military service should be sent overseas.

The WD announced that a revised screening score for overseas service would be made public just as soon as the recomputation of points ordered by the WD as of Sept. 2, 1945, had been completed.

Under the demobilization and redeployment plan for enlisted men in effect as of Sept. 5, 1945, an enlisted man was eligible for discharge if:

1) He had 80 points or more under the Sept. 2 computation of points.
2) He was 38 years of age or older.
3) He was 35, 36 or 37 years of age and had a minimum of two years of honorable military service.

In the case of all overage discharges, commanders have the right to retain applicants for discharge for not more than 90 days after receipt of the discharge application.

The WD announcement pointed out that there are only three highly technical skills which are considered essential to the extent that enlisted men in those classifications must remain in the Army regardless of their point scores. They are: Orthopedic mechanic, transmitter attendant (fixed station), and electro-encephalographic specialist. There are only a small number of these in the entire Army. The list of critical skills, it was noted, was reduced to three from 19 after the acceptance of the Japanese surrender. The WD has ruled that even though an enlisted man has one of the three skills listed as critical, he cannot be held for more than six months after he becomes eligible for release under the point system.

Under demobilization and redeployment policies for enlisted women, a Wac is eligible for discharge if:

1) She has 41 or more points under the Sept. 2 computation of points.
2) She is 38 years of age or over.
3) She is 35, 36 or 37 years of age and has had a minimum of two years of honorable military service.
4) She is the wife of a member of the military forces who has been discharged.

No additional members of the Women's Army Corps are being sent overseas and WAC enlistments were discontinued in August.

The critical scores for discharge (80 and above for enlisted men, and 41 and above for enlisted women) will be lowered progressively and whenever necessary to keep the flow of discharges at the highest possible level, the WD announced.

As previously stated, the Army will continue to use both tactical and transport planes to the maximum extent in order to bring back from Europe and the Pacific those eligible for discharge. As soon as the pool of eligible high-point men starts running low, the critical score will again be reduced so that there will be no slackening of the demobilization movement.

Overseas theater commanders are authorized to return to the U. S. for temporary duty or furlough a limited number of enlisted men who, although not eligible for discharge, can be spared from overseas duty for a brief period. These men will be returned to their overseas assignments upon expiration of their temporary duty or furlough.

WAC Enlistments End. Enlistments in the Women's Army Corps were discontinued as of August 29, Col. Westray Battle Boyce, director of the corps, announced. Wacs are being demobilized on a proportionate basis with men in the Army, Col. Boyce said. Five WAC separation centers have been set up—at Fort Dix, N. J.; Camp Bragg, N. C.; Fort Sheridan, Ill.; Fort Sam Houston, Texas, and Camp Beale, Calif.

Esther Williams

YANK

Pin-up Girl

Navy Notes

Navy and Coast Guard demobilization got under way, following the announcement of a point system. Then the first separatees started grinding through the separator, the first howl went up from the snafued retainees, and the Navy revised its system to allow credit for overseas service.

Under the original system, announced on Aug. 15, no points were allowed for battle stars or more than one dependent and only active duty was counted, regardless of what kind of duty it was. Vice Adm. Randall Jacobs, Chief of Naval Personnel, explained that the Navy had to use a point system more simple than the Army's because its records were not in shape to provide immediate data on overseas service, battle stars and so forth. Adm. Jacobs pointed out that ships move about rapidly, their movements are secret even to BuPers, and transfers occur so often that it would be some time before the Bureau could award proper credit to all its personnel. He also revealed that only seven percent of the Navy has not served overseas.

The reaction among the men on ships in the front line who had hoped to rate something for their combat experience, sea duty and battle stars was a dismal wail.

Then, on Sept. 15, Secretary Forrestal announced that additional points would be given for service outside the U. S. in lieu of any immediate reduction in the critical scores. He said it would be impossible to apply to the Navy any fair formula giving point credits for combat engagements, as is done in the Army.

Forrestal pointed out that Army men generally remained with the units in which they began service and Army combat ribbons and stars provided a basis for computing credits, while, in the Navy, the basic unit is a ship and frequently the most hazardous duties were on ships which technically did not qualify for a combat decoration.

"If we were to give credit to men who were at Midway," the Secretary said, "we ought, by the same token, give credit to every armed-guard crew that made the Murmansk run."

Forrestal also said that the Navy had no intention of making special provision for the release of personnel whose schooling was interrupted by war service. This was in answer to suggestions in Congress that such a policy be adopted.

Here's where the men of the Navy stand as of this writing: ½ point is given for each year of age (nearest birthday); ½ point is given for each month of service on active duty since Sept. 1, 1939 (including service in the other armed branches or in the armed forces of the United Nations); 10 points for one, but no more than one, dependent (determined according to whether a dependency allowance existed prior to 2400 EWT, 15 August 1945); and ¼ point for each month of service outside the U. S. since Sept. 1, 1939.

The total score for discharge is 44 for enlisted men, 49 for officers, 29 for Waves, 35 for Wave officers, 44 for naval aviators, 60 for doctors (MC), 49 for Hospital-Corps officers (HC), and 35 for Navy nurses and women doctors. These scores will be lowered "whenever conditions permit."

There were 3,389,000 men and women in the Navy on Aug. 15 and the Navy proposes to discharge 2,839,000 in one year, leaving it with a force of 550,000. About 750,000 are immediately eligible for discharge, and Secretary Forrestal predicted that within six months, one out of every two men now in the Navy will be home.

Although the service credit carries back to the fall of 1939, relatively few men can get the maximum credit on this score, as the Navy's real expansion came after 1942. There were 125,282 men in the Navy in 1939; 160,997 in 1940; 284,427 in 1941; 640,570 in 1942; 1,741,750 in 1943; and 3,196,158 in 1944. Thus it would appear that a

very real cut in the critical score will have to be made before the Navy can dig very deeply into that proposed 2,839,000 men.

The Coast Guard has already lowered its score to 40 for EM and 43 for officers, and will release 80 percent of its personnel in the next 10 months.

Applications for discharge submitted prior to Aug. 15, discharge by reason of hardship or dependency and directives covering discharge for pregnancy, marriage of Waves, EM on the retired list and for enlisted personnel over 42 years of age remain in effect.

Immediate discharge is also authorized, regardless of points, for Navy personnel who have been awarded the following medals: Medal of Honor, Navy Cross, Distinguished Service Cross (Army), Legion of Merit (if for combat), Silver Star Medal, and Distinguished Flying Cross (if for combat). This provision will release about 20,000 men.

The point system will affect the discharge of all inducted personnel of Class USN(SV), and Naval Reservists whose enlistments have expired, including USNR(SV). Fleet Reservists and other Reservists whose enlistments have not expired will be released to inactive duty. Extended enlistments will be terminated and those not serving in extended enlistment will be discharged for the convenience of the Government.

The following rates are not eligible for discharge until further notice: Classification, Shore Patrol, Punch Card Accounting Machine Operator and Transportation Specialists, Disbursing Storekeepers and Mailmen.

Those in hospitals or undergoing medical or dental treatment will not be eligible until completion of their hospitalization or treatment. Those in disciplinary status will be held until completion of the discipline, including probationary period.

Immediately after the point system was announced, personnel offices began computing the scores of all those in their command and orders for transfer of eligible personnel were sent to the various COs, along with instructions to release a specified percent of their personnel immediately. Among those eligible, preference is to be given to those who have been longest overseas, afloat or ashore. If the CO wishes to retain a man it must be for military necessity as distinguished from military convenience and for not more than 120 days. Meanwhile a replacement must be arranged for.

For those who have the points and yet do not want out, there are two choices: Either to submit an application for enlistment in the Regular Navy, in which case the man will be retained pending final action, or to arrange to be held for the 120 days as a military necessity by the CO, meanwhile writing a letter to the Chief of Naval Personnel requesting retention after this period. The CO is authorized to grant this request without prior reference to the Bureau.

To handle the 750,000 eligibles—and later the millions—the Navy is setting up staging areas at Pearl Harbor, Guam, Saipan, Leyte, Hollandia, Manila and Manus to serve in the first step of that last trip.

The second step will be the receiving station. These will be located at Boston; Portland, Me.; New York; Philadelphia; Norfolk; Charleston, S. C.; Key West; Miami; Galveston; Chicago; San Pedro; Bremerton; Seattle; San Francisco; San Diego; Shoemaker, Calif.; New Orleans; and Farragut, Idaho.

The final line forms at the Separation Centers. These will be located at Bainbridge, Md.; Boston; Camp Wallace, Texas; Charleston, S. C.; Great Lakes; Jacksonville; Lido Beach, L. I.; Los Angeles; Memphis; Minneapolis; New Orleans; Norfolk; Norman, Okla.; St. Louis; Sampson, N. Y.; San Francisco; Seattle, and Toledo.

Seventy-two hours after a sailor enters the Separation Center he comes out a Mister. These hours are said to be filled with friendly advice, good fellowship, movies, laughter, song and—of all things—courteous treatment.

Marine Point System. Since Aug. 15 the Marine Corps has been using the same point system as the Army, with a critical score of 85 necessary for discharge.

Gen. A. A. Vandegrift, Marine Corps Commandant, announced on Sept. 12 the lowering of that critical score to 70 and authorized the release of all Marines 35 years of age and older. These new provisions apply to all Marine Corps personnel,

regardless of whether they are serving within the U. S. or overseas. They do not apply to regulars serving four-year enlistments or extensions. The critical score for members of the Women's Reserve remains at 25 points.

The Marine Corps credit system provides one point for each month of service and an additional point for each month overseas from Sept. 16, 1940, to Sept. 1, 1945; 5 points for each decoration and bronze star; and 12 points for each dependent child.

Scrambled Civvies. With the advent of VJ-Day the Navy announced that personnel within the United States could wear civilian clothes outside of working hours, while on leave or other off-duty status. Two days later Secretary Forrestal ruefully reported that the deal was off.

Seems the Navy thought everybody had old clothes and wouldn't have to buy new ones. Instead, the order produced a buying spree. So it's all off until the clothing industry says that the "supply can stand the shock."

The Secretary was asked if he didn't think the sailors who actually went out and bought new civilian clothes weren't going to be sore about not being able to wear them. The New York *Times* reported that the Secretary winced and did not reply.

Mr. Forrestal quoted Admiral Richard S. Edwards in explanation of the cancellation of the order: "It's far easier to make eggs into an omelet than an omelet into eggs."

He Shall Have Music. Alan C. Wagner AMM3c of Garden City, N. Y., was an amateur pianist—the boogie-woogie kind. He was aboard the aircraft carrier *Bismarck Sea* when she was sunk last February off Iwo Jima and he was severely wounded.

Paralyzed below the waist, Wagner was brought back to St. Albans Naval Hospital, N. Y., where he is undergoing treatment preparatory to a series of operations that must be performed if he is to walk again.

A Garden City neighbor of Wagner's, Mrs. Tinker Connolly, visited him in the hospital and was impressed by the sad fact that, though his greatest desire was to beat out a bit of boogie, the piano didn't exist that he could get next to.

Mrs. Connolly's father, C. Brown Hyatt, is a consulting engineer and something of an inventor. "You can't invent anything that can make it possible for Alan to play," Mrs. Connolly told him challengingly, after explaining the wounded man's predicament.

"The hell I can't," said Mr. Hyatt, and went down into the basement.

The result was brought to Wagner six weeks later as he lay on his stomach getting his regular massage. It was a portable piano-keyboard with the full 88 keys and it could be propped at any angle and in any position on the bed. The keyboard was electrically attached by 88 wires to an upright piano on the floor of the ward. It worked.

Wagner's right hand had been partially useless, but under the stimulation of the music he found that he could use it almost as well as the left.

As the beneficial boogie rolled out of the ward, everybody was happy, most of all C. Brown Hyatt, engineer and occupational therapist.

—DONALD NUGENT Sp(X)3c

ETO-MTO
Track Meet

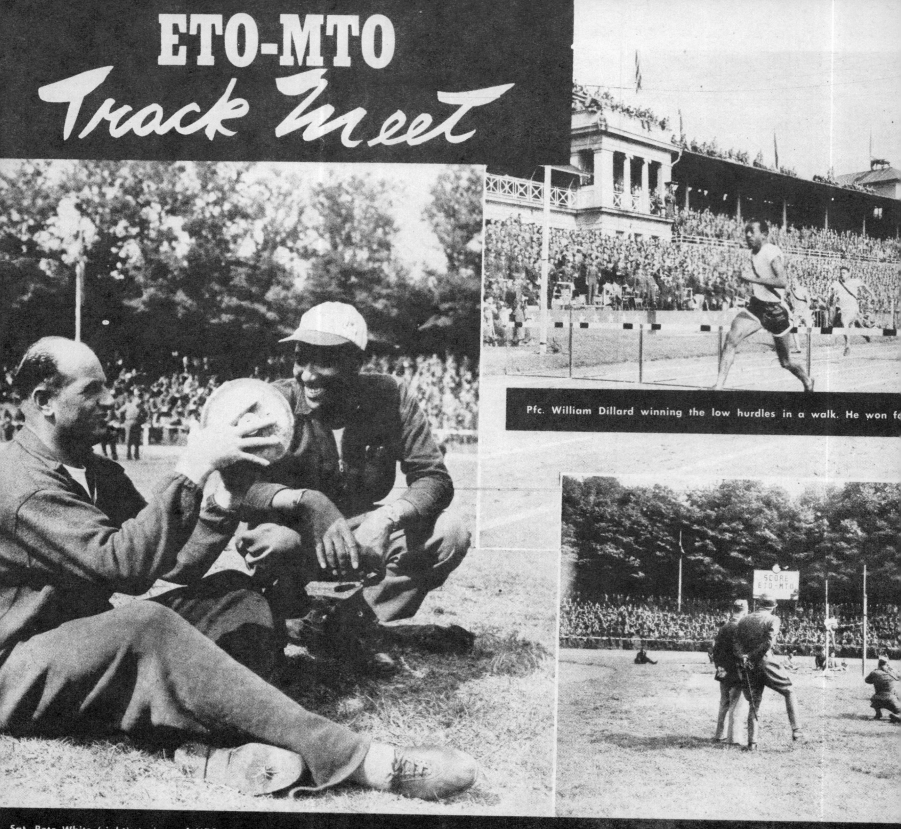

Pfc. William Dillard winning the low hurdles in a walk. He won f[...]

SCORE
ETO-MTO

Sgt. Pete White (right), trainer of MTO track team, talks it over with Joe Tossi, Italian discus thrower.

Gen. Patton, in jodhpurs, helps a high jumper.

By Sgt. LEN ZINBERG
YANK Staff Writer

FRANKFURT-AM-MAIN—A GI trainer has to be an experienced trainer and "operator." Sgt. Pete White of New York City, trainer of the MTO Track Team, is both, and also has seen plenty of combat. Overseas 33 months, he put in five hard months at Anzio, not to mention hitting Salerno a few hours after the 36th Infantry Division made a beachhead.

"Salerno was pitiful," Pete said, standing in the center of the Victory Stadium here, where the MTOUSA-USFET track championships were being held in late August. "But that's all over now. I got 90 points stacked up and expect to be out soon. I was studying physical ed at North Carolina State before Uncle called me. When I get back into tweeds again, I'm going to finish my studying at Cornell, if I can take it under this GI-Bill-of-Rights deal."

It was a hot day and everybody was sweating, especially the ETO team. Pfc. William Dillard had already set a new service record in winning the 110-meter high hurdles, MTO's Lt. Gerald Karver had won the 1,500-meter run with a sensational finish, and the 100-meter dash was about to start. In one corner of the field the high jump was on, and at the other end of the stadium the

boys were tossing the discus around. About 25,000 GIs were having a good time watching the events. Brass was everywhere. One-star generals were almost as plentiful as pfcs.

Pete said. "Dillard is a boy in a class by himself. Only 22. If he gets the right coaching, he'll be better than Jesse Owens. Army life hasn't hurt him much. There is a big difference in conditioning a man in civilian life and in the Army. First off, marching and drilling tighten a guy's legs, and that's bad for a track man. It's hard to get a man excused from details, and all that. Not like in college, where an athlete has everything he wants.

"That's where a GI trainer has to pull what strings he can—operate a bit. Same with transportation; it really takes an operator to get a couple of jeeps. Another bad thing about Army athletics—the competition isn't keen enough to bring out the best in a guy like Dillard. Food is another problem. Once an athlete's stomach is messed up, he's *finito*. Not that Army chow is bad, but there's no such thing as a training table. Of course, we came over here to win a war and not a race. I'm just explaining why the times in an overseas track meet don't compare with a college meet in the States. Just the same, this bunch stacks up with any college team in the States. We had three guys here put the shot over 51 feet.

All ETO boys; we're weak as hell in field events."

In the 100-meter dash, Sgt. Mozel Ellerbee finished third. Pete walked toward him, saying, "Ellerbee is one of the great runners of all time, but he's old now. Track is no place to grow old in, unless you expect to be a coach. I'd like to coach a school team and manage a couple of fighters on the side. That's how I got with 5th Army Special Services. I took a couple of boxers from the 263d QM down to Naples in '43.

"Capt. John Sullivan asked me to go along with the 5th Army team to Algiers, as chief trainer. Easier to train a boxer than a runner. A boxer has one training routine, while you have to train a runner differently for each event. Trained some good boxers in Italy — Ezzard Charles of the 92d and Larry Cisneros, a machine-gunner with the 5th Army. I was with the Joe Louis troupe, too. Ever see Bob Berry of the 19th Engineers? He's in the States now. For my dough he'll be the next heavy champ."

White talked to Ellerbee about the 400-meter relay, while the 400-meter dash was on. ETO took 1st and 2d, cutting MTO's big point lead. Lanky S/Sgt. Peter Watkins of ETO took the high jump with 6 feet, 6 inches. M/Sgt. Lloyd Crable of MTO was third. He was trying to clear the bar at 6 feet, 2 inches, when some jerk yelled, "Get that watermelon, boy!" Crable's brown face

A view of the stands in the big stadium at Frankfurt-am-Main. It was estimated that some 25,000 GIs came to watch the track championships.

ke into a hurt smile, and that was about the
l of his jumping for the afternoon.
TO made a new record in winning the 400-
ter relay, with Dillard running anchor. White
ne back to talk to me after ETO's T-5 Black had
n the 3,000-meter run, beating the famous
nch runner, Bouali.
White said, "Lot of angles to track. ETO pulled
ast one on us—Bouali and Merine can't run
3,000, they consider that a sprint. At 5,000
ters they would have won hands down, but
O wanted it cut to 3,000. But we'll even things
in the discus. Nobody is going to beat Tossi of
Italian Army. Some name for a discus thrower
ossi. He'll be a world's champ, soon as he
rns to put more of his body behind the discus."
Dillard won the 200-meter dash, establishing
other record. ETO took 2d and 3d. White shook
head. "We'll get plenty of firsts, but not
ugh seconds and thirds. That Dillard is a one-
n team. If we had another guy like him—"
MTO won the 800-meter run, S/Sgt. Knowles
king 1st and Sgt. Davies, RAF, coming in 2d to
e MTO three more points. White said, "Things
looking up a little. Good meet. Some stadium.
ankfurt sure was bombed to hell. Wonder how
y missed this place?
"Nothing like track. My old man, Pete White
, was the 200-yard champ back in 1918. He's

chairman of the AAU Track and Field Committee
in New York. He's pounded track into my head
ever since I was a kid. He helped found the
Talem-Crescent A. C. in Harlem. Canada Lee and
Ray Robinson came out of that club."
The 800-meter relay was on. In the final dash,
MTO's James Tucker pulled a muscle. As Edwards of ETO was about to pass him, he turned
his head and said something to Tucker, who then
sprinted like hell, bum leg and all, to win and
set a new service record. Pete ran over to Tucker,
who was tossing on the ground in pain, and
started to rub his swollen leg. Somebody asked
Tucker what Edwards had said.
"Seemed he said, 'Goodbye,'" Tucker said.
"Talking to himself," White grinned.
ETO took the 1,600-meter relay, and then Dillard set another record as he won the 200-meter
low hurdles in 23.6 seconds. White came over
with his arm around Dillard. White said happily,
"Won two-hundred bucks in side bets on you."
Dillard, who is a slender, soft-spoken kid, just
smiled. White went back to help Tucker across
the field. Dillard wasn't even breathing hard,
although he had established four new service
records.
Overseas 11 months, he wears the Combat Infantryman's Badge and took part in the push on
Genoa, when the 370th Infantry marched 105

miles over rough, mountain terrain. Inspired by
Jesse Owens, Dillard began to make a name for
himself in high school and was an English major
at Wallace-Baldwin College when the Army called
him. He went from the Air Corps to study basic
engineering at Hampton Institute, and when the
ASTP program suddenly folded, Dillard found
himself in the Infantry.
"I thought I was done as a runner," he said.
"Infantry sort of takes the edge off an athlete. I
started running again this June, and found I was
in better condition than I expected. I hope to be
in top shape when I return to the States. After
the Army? Well, I want to return to Wallace-
Baldwin. Some day I'd like to be an English
teacher and a track coach. Of course that's all in
the future."
White came over and said, "Come on, let's hit
the showers. You won four medals this afternoon.
You deserve a shower."
Dillard said in his soft voice, "After a while a
fellow gets used to medals. Just something to put
away and look at afterwards."
"Come on," White said, "take that shower. Big
banquet tonight. Chow sure has been good here.
Damn, if we only had more seconds and thirds.
Still, we did okay, everything considered. That
shotput and 3,000-meter run like to have killed
us, though."

"IT'S SOME RARE PHILIPPINE DISEASE. ALL HE CAN DIGEST IS ALCOHOL."
—Sgt. Charles Pearson

"I DON'T KNOW WHAT SCHEDULE YOU'VE BEEN FOLLOWING, BUT HERE'S THE SET-UP FOR THE NEXT 30 DAYS."
—Sgt. Jim Weeks

YANK

"LOOK, YOU GUYS—A PONTIAC!"
—Cpl. Frank R. Robinson

"THESE WILL MAKE A SWELL FLOOR FOR OUR TENT."
—Sgt. Ozzie St. George

YANK

THE ARMY WEEKLY

5¢

DEC. 28, 1945
VOL. 4, NO. 28

By and for men in the service

Army of the United States

Honorable Discharge

This is to certify that

YANK

Army of the United States

is hereby Honorably Discharged from the military service of the United States of America.

This certificate is awarded as a testimonial of Honest and Faithful Service to this country.

Given at   Washington, D.C.

Date   31 December 1945

Dwight D. Eisenhower

CHIEF OF STAFF

Honorable Discharge

"In YANK you have established a publication which cannot be understood by our enemies. It is inconceivable to them that a soldier should be allowed to express his own thoughts, his ideas and his opinions. It is inconceivable to them that any soldiers—or any citizens, for that matter—should have any thoughts other than those dictated by their leaders. . . .

"Upon you, and upon your comrades in arms of all the United Nations, depend the lives and liberties of all the human race. You bear with you the hopes of all the millions who have suffered under the oppression of the war lords of Germany and Japan. You bear with you the highest aspirations of mankind for a life of peace and decency under God."

—Franklin Delano Roosevelt,
from YANK, Volume 1, Number 1.

* * *

AT the time when President Roosevelt wrote this message to GIs for t first issue of YANK, in June 1942, the Japanese were settling down Kiska and Attu and German Gen. Erwin Rommel had just captur Tobruk, Bardia and Bir-el-Gobi. Hulks of American ships were gathering slim under the waters of Pearl Harbor. The Philippines were lost. The Red Army ha evacuated the Kerch Peninsula, and all along a heart-breakingly extended fro its troops fought a delaying action, an armed retreat. Japs swarmed all over t East—New Guinea, the Netherlands East Indies, Malaya, the Solomons.

The American soldier of that June who had seen any action at all, who ha even served overseas, was an exception. There were a few GIs in England a Northern Ireland. Engineers had been stationed in Iceland and Greenland f some months. There were GIs guarding the bauxite mines at Dutch Guiana a British Guiana. There were several shipments of U. S. troops in Australia. The were many too many American soldiers prisoners of the Japs.

The GIs at home were training at a speeded-up rate with the best equipme they could find to train with. Factories were working overtime to break productic records that had to be broken and then broken again. Of course, nobody actual thought we might lose the war, but everybody knew we were in a fight. Lir after line of confused civilian males filed into railway terminals, waving good-by to their families, headed for something strange called camp. There were rumor of worse defeats to come and, ranged alongside rumors, the uncomfortable fa that the enemy had a corner on oil and rubber—and trained manpower. The was a battle going on in the air above Britain while we stumbled about the dri fields of Fort Jackson and Fort Belvoir and Fort Benning and dozens of othe posts, learning to move our feet according to a new rhythm and to sight an M and eat SOS and walk and work and walk and work and sleep like the dead.

YANK was founded to be the publication of the enlisted men of this new Arm of ours. It was to be written and edited by enlisted men for enlisted men a over the world. It was to spread both news and entertainment; not to point officia morals. It was to be a free organ for the legitimate gripes of enlisted men.

It was just as stumbling and hopeful as any other part of the new Army i joined. YANK was sold first only to GIs serving overseas. By its eighth issue i was authorized to sell in U. S. PXs as well. By YANK's eighth issue U. S. marine were fighting on Guadalcanal, and there was something new in the air as w showed our stuff in an offensive action. There was a commando raid on Nazi-hel Dieppe across the English channel that fall, and U. S. Rangers took part in it

YANK had an edition being printed in England by November 1942, and anothe in Puerto Rico. England was an island staging area for nobody yet knew wha invasion. And in the waters off Puerto Rico, German submarines sank Allied ships

In November, too, the secret of the invasion was out. American and Allied forces landed in North Africa under the command of Lt. Gen. Dwight D. Eisen-hower. They had just barely enough men to push through to a successful landing, just barely enough ships to carry them. But the invasion worked. The battle for North Africa was on. And the Germans in Russia were finding out they couldn't take Stalingrad. In a sea battle off the Solomons, 28 Japs ships were sunk.

There were U. S. troops spreading all over the globe. GIs from Arkansas and Oklahoma were standing guard or loading trucks or fighting in places with exotic names like Bandar Shapur, Iran, Karachi, India, Tripoli, North Africa.

The war was still see-sawing. In Burma we hadn't recovered from the "one hell of a beating" Gen. Joseph Stilwell had taken in the early summer. The Germans still had France, even if the British were chasing them out of Egypt, and the Japs still had so much of the Pacific that our gains hardly showed up on the map. But we knew now, surely, and by actual sampling, what we had never doubted —that we could lick the enemy on their own grounds.

In the summer of 1943, six new overseas editions of YANK were started—in Hawaii, in Trinidad, in Egypt, in India, in Australia and in Iran. That fall another was added in Panama.

WE could look at the war with a growing impatience, a heightened sense of progress, instead of with the dogged resolution we had had to live on in those first long months. We had sewed up North Africa and had taken Sicily. We had landed in Italy, kept our toe-hold and moved successfully north, until the Italian Government, in defiance of a fleeing Mussolini, sued for peace. We had taken back Kiska and Attu from the Japs. We were pushing back other Japs the hard way in New Guinea and on Bougainville and in New Britain, and our airmen were pounding Jap supply lines in China.

The year 1944 opened slowly as a war year. There were gains in the Pacific in January on Kwajalein and Majuro. In Italy, GIs landed at Anzio beachhead to lie there week after week, holding a strip of shore under enemy fire. There was another Pacific landing on Eniwetok Atoll in the Marshalls, and Sgt. John Bushemi, YANK photographer, was killed there.

YANK's tenth overseas edition was printed in Italy in March. The war in Italy was still slow. Allied forces to the south finally connected with the orphans of Anzio in May, and the front moved north in June and July. The Pacific war was still a war of strange names and infrequent headlines which didn't mean much except to the men who earned them. In June we landed on Saipan in the Marianas.

And in June the big jump came, the invasion of Europe from across the channel. There were landings in Normandy, and Easy Red Beach and Omaha Beach were added to the war names Americans will always remember. Sgt. Pete Paris, YANK photographer and artist, was killed on D-Day.

That invasion took, too. It pushed from Cherbourg to Caen to Le Mans, and in August another invasion hit France in the south, launched from Italy, landing between Marseille and Cannes. It pushed to Belfort and met the Normandy invaders in the middle. In the Pacific there were landings on Peleliu and Morotai, Angaur and Ulithi Atoll. It was more and more our winning war.

YANK was printing in Paris by September and in Strasbourg by November. The Allies were sweeping through France like the happy ending of a movie. In Italy we had passed and taken Florence.

The Philippines were the hardest, biggest loss of 1942, and in October 1944 we invaded Leyte to begin to win them back. We landed and stayed.

In the China-Burma theater we took Bhamo and lost Kweiling. From the Marianas, raiding B-29s struck Tokyo. The Red Army steam roller, which started its first big push back in June, had never stopped and was now in East Prussia.

At the end of 1944 there was a cornered-rat lunge from the German forces in the Ardennes sector and, caught off-balance, we were knocked groggy. But we hit back. We had regained our losses by the end of January and, in the Pacific, we had wiped up both Leyte and Samar and were striking at Luzon.

We didn't move backwards again for the rest of the war. We crossed the Rhine and pushed on until we met the Red Army at the Elbe and Germany was licked. YANK correspondent Cpl. Bob Krell was killed in the airborne Rhine crossing.

The Philippines were contested all the way, but we took them, and marines on Iwo Jima and marines and GIs on Okinawa carved two more names on our military roll of honor. B-29s pounded hell out of the Jap mainland, and the atomic bomb and the entry of Russia into the Jap war hastened an end already certain.

The Germans surrendered unconditionally on May 7 at Reims. The Japs surrendered on August 14 aboard the U.S.S. *Missouri* in Tokyo Bay.

YANK's last four overseas printings were set up on Saipan in February, in Manila in July, on Okinawa in August and in Tokyo in September—the last one just in time to serve incoming occupation troops.

* * *

THE fighting part is over now and we are winners. If you ever begin to wonder about what we were fighting for, look back to those words of President Roosevelt's at the beginning of this editorial. Read them and try to remember everything that Jap and German domination meant that made us fight it.

We fought it starting from damn near scratch and we beat it. YANK is proud to have been part of the Army that beat it.

Boston is always Boston.

INVENTORY,

By Sgt. ROBERT BENDINER
YANK Staff Writer

FOR close to four years Americans longed for peace, dreamed of peace and tried to imagine what life would be like "when the lights went on again all over the world." Those lights have been on for four months now, and it is possible to piece together a kind of jigsaw picture of a country that has stopped fighting but is only gradually groping its way back to peace.

Millions of men are spending their first Christmas season at home in years, and for them this alone is peace, this is the real thing. But Christmas doesn't last, and the returned GI, looking about him objectively, soon sees that the United States in the fading days of 1945 is not yet the peacetime nation that haunted his dreams on Christmases past as he stared up at the raw boards of a barracks ceiling or sat crouched in a soggy mudhole. Civilians in uniform are still scattered around the globe, still drilling, still pulling details, still sweating out chow lines. No peace treaty has been framed, much less signed. And in the country at large, factories that four months ago stopped grinding out the tools of death have only begun to turn out the comforts of life, those gaudy comforts which the advertising pages of magazines taught us to expect in technicolor, in

abundance and at prices that all could afford.

A quick picture of the U.S.A. in these dawn hours between war and peace is bound to be blurred. Any snapshot of a fast-moving object is likely to be on the hazy side, and the country today is moving as fast as it ever has in all its history. Hundreds of thousands of men and women are streaming out of separation centers, some bent on sliding as quickly as possible into their pre-war grooves, but a surprising number determined to avoid the old grooves and strike out on new courses not yet mapped in their own minds. Trains are jammed, ships are jammed, planes are jammed. The streets of American cities are crowded with men in uniform—on returnee furloughs, enroute to reassignment centers or already in that state of freedom indicated by a gold-eagle patch above the right pocket.

In the civilian population, millions, left jobless when the giant war-production machinery screeched to a stop on VJ-Day, have added the uncertainty of their plans to the national restlessness. Thousands of them are women who are withdrawing from the labor market to return to housekeeping—if they can find a house. Thousands are youngsters who may be induced to return to school, but who may just as well choose to compete for jobs. And hundreds of thousands are men who must stand by and wait for fac-

tories to exchange the belt-lines that turned out guns, bombers and shells for those that will turn out cars, refrigerators and electric trains.

Sgt. Joe Blank, stepping into the civilian world in the closing weeks of 1945, will not see all this. He will not see any over-all pattern, probably, because he will be intensely and naturally concerned with his own immediate affairs and desires—to know his family again, to see his friends, to buy civilian clothes, to take a vacation, to see about getting a job and perhaps to find new quarters and furnishings for a wife and child nearly frantic with the trials of makeshift housing. But it is just these specific desires and problems, multiplied by ten million, which make up that over-all pattern, and it is therefore reasonable to look at the country through his eyes.

After two or three days of saturating himself with the sight, the sound and the feel of home, Joe decides that he had better go downtown and get himself some clothes. Having gone over the subject repeatedly in barracks bull-sessions, he is prepared for an intensive all-day hunt and prices to stagger the imagination. It is a pleasant surprise to discover that he can dispose of the whole business at any respectable department store in a few hours at a cost well within his mustering-out pay. A reasonably good suit, not noticeably different in style from the one he shed at the reception center though inferior in quality, will set him back from $35 to $50. Prices on shirts and shorts are up 50 to 100 percent, but he can figure roughly on an over-all boost of five to 10 percent in clothing prices. And he shouldn't have trouble finding what he wants, provided he doesn't want white shirts or suits of hard-finished worsted. As for styles, he will discover that outside the pages of *Esquire* they have scarcely moved at all beyond a trend in neckwear toward shrieking four-in-hands and long, thin bows, similarly garish.

Having been plunged into the realm of the consumer, Joe checks with his wife, looks at shop windows, and glances at the ads to see how far along the country has come in this "reconversion" that looms so large in the newspaper heads.

Cars, he knows, are far from ready. Government controls have been lifted, but shortages of upholstering fabric, plus strikes, plus the time required to make new dies, have kept the assembly lines down to a painfully slow rate of speed. Nevertheless, the lines are moving, and instead of the 4,000 cars produced throughout the country in August, the December quota is expected to reach 200,000. Like men's suits, motor styles have changed very little. A gadget here and a gadget there are all that distinguish them from the models of 1941, though the air over Detroit is still thick with talk of secret designs for dream cars, and one has been designed without clutches, transmission or even brakes.

Aside from the scarcity of new cars, many other wartime shortages linger on in Joe's new world of peace. He can get metal furniture for that new home he's thinking of, but wooden pieces are either scarce and inferior or prohibitively expensive. And he'll have to wait a while for a new typewriter.

If he can stand up under the battering of a crowd of frenzied women, Joe can probably buy his wife a single pair of nylons, but it will be a long time before he can get her anything in silk. On the other hand, if his wife has long dreamed of an electric refrigerator, a new vacuum cleaner,

a pressure cooker or a laundry machine, he will find that stocks in those commodities are slowly creeping back toward prewar levels, though it's still a case of first come, first served. The same goes for a tricycle for Joe jr.

Toasters, irons, mixers and other small appliances are already amply stocked and can be whisked away for the asking—and the paying. So can the "family planes" now available at a leading New York department store for $2,994. Similarly postwar in spirit are the two-way speaking systems now selling for $33. Designed for use in Army tanks, these gadgets will now link up nursery and mother's bedroom, or outside-gate and butler's pantry.

As for food, the United States finds itself in the winter of 1945-46 embarrassingly glutted while half the world hungers. Beef is coming back so rapidly that the Government has warned feeders that it will soon end its subsidy for fattening cattle. Butter is still spotty in distribution, but eggs are plentiful, and milk and other dairy items are approaching all-time production records. Potatoes, too, are reaching surplus proportions, while fish and vegetables, both raw and canned, are plentiful. Still hard to get, comparatively, are pork and lamb; and the sugar shortage, Joe finds, will be a problem for many months to come, since supplies from the Philippines and the South Pacific cannot be counted on much before 1947.

Dropping into a bar for the first time since his return, Joe discovers that he can get almost anything he wants but a good scotch, and if he's lucky he can get even that. Four Roses and Canadian Club are also a bit on the scarce side, but barring particular brands, he can drink adequately at prices not more than a few cents a shot above the prices he paid before he left.

At the bar the Hot-Stove Leaguers are still mulling over the fantastic Series of two months ago, and the general feeling is that baseball could hardly have survived another wartime season. But things will be different next year. Look who'll be back from the wars: Ted Williams, Enos

Slaughter, Pete Reiser, Henrich and Joe DiMaggio among the sluggers; pitchers Beazley, Higbee, Lanier, Feller and others just as good; fielders Joe Gordon, Rizzuto, Reese and Fletcher.

Boxing, Joe hears, has been even more chaotic than baseball. With the best talent in the services, the fight game was reduced to the status of a cash-register racket, mediocre fighters drew huge gates and there were more mismatches than matches. But now the National Boxing Association has drawn up its first postwar list of ratings, and champions have been notified that they must defend their titles. It will be some time next June before ex-Sgt. Louis slugs it out with ex-Cpl. Conn; and light heavyweight Gus Lesnevich and middleweight Tony Zale will also be given time to rest up from the GI life. But the other champs will have to get on their toes. Aside from Conn, future possible contenders for Louis's crown include Bivins, Mauriello and Bettina, names that still mean little to ex-Sgt. Blank.

On his way home, Joe gives the afternoon paper a thorough going-over, and gathers the impression that a country which achieved remarkable unity during the war has already returned to the squabbles and differences that characterize any democratic country in peacetime. Certain keywords keep popping out at him: strikes, atom secret, unemployment, occupation policy, price controls, peacetime army, Big Three and, far from least, demobilization.

Strikes, he learns, have occurred or threatened to occur, in rapid succession ever since VJ-Day—in autos, oil, steel, lumber, movies, coal, shipping. The case for labor, says one commentator, revolves about the cessation of overtime work. Men who during the war drew time-and-a-half for eight, 10 and even 20 hours beyond the normal schedule find themselves back on a straight 40-hour week, with a consequent loss of income in some cases exceeding 50 percent. At the same time, prices on food commodities have mounted, despite the efforts of the OPA. As a result, labor is demanding a 30 percent boost in hourly wage rates and arguing that industry can well afford

U.S.A.

After the years of war, peacetime takes some getting used to, but the nation is slowly swinging into its postwar stride.

They're still planting in Texas.

to pay the difference out of higher production yields caused by technological improvements, to say nothing of wartime profits. But industry, Joe reads elsewhere, maintains just as stoutly that labor's figures are all wrong, that higher wages will mean higher prices, that nobody knows what prices the Government will allow for their finished product and that a 30-percent raise would be unreasonable and inflationary. Compromise increases, short of the asking price, have already been allowed by some industries, and others are expected to follow suit. Meanwhile the strike wave, paralleling that which followed the last war, runs its course.

Unemployment, Joe notes, is mounting throughout the country, as everyone knew it would, but the rate is not nearly so alarming as the more pessimistic prophets foretold. From the welter of speculation on the subject, he concludes that something of a race is on between full demobilization and reconversion. If industry gets into its production stride before the services are emptied out, unemployment should be brief and not forbiddingly extensive. If it doesn't, the period of joblessness may be longer and more acute. But at worst, it is the consensus of economists that there should be nothing like the crash of 1929 or the prolonged era of apple-peddling. They point out that there is too much in available savings, too much demand for goods of all sorts, too much eagerness for peacetime production profits and too many cushions provided by Government that were not present to absorb the shock in 1929. For all that, several papers, following the lead of *PM*

Quiet as usual in Falmouth, Mass.

in New York, are running free job-wanted ads for veterans, and two movie houses in Detroit flash job-hunters' qualifications on the screen.

Joe's eye falls next on one of those round-up feature stories from Washington, headed "Congress Faces Heavy Session." Skimming through, he is jolted into the realization that, aside from labor relations, unemployment and reconversion, Congress is chiefly concerned with matters that smack more of future wars and international tension than of peace and harmony. There is still the painful question of returning to civilian life millions of Joe's comrades-in-arms. Congressmen are still squirming under a mountain of protest mail and are promising to call on the brass for further explanation. They are also involved in plans for reorganizing the armed forces and perhaps unifying them under a single command. The legislators and President Truman are still fearfully considering ways and means of controlling the Frankenstein monster which appeared on the world scene when the first atom was cracked. Should atomic energy, with its terrific potential for good or for evil, be strictly the province of Government—or should private enterprise be permitted to develop it as it developed electricity and other forms of energy? And should the secrets of manufacturing the atomic bomb be shared with the other nations of the world?

Here the delicate question of our relations with the Soviet Union enters into the picture, and Joe cannot fail to notice the numerous indications that the unity of the United Nations has slipped a cog or two since VJ-Day. Throughout the fall there has been talk of *blocs* again, and mutual suspicions. The peace of the world had a bad jolt in October, when the first Council of Foreign Ministers adjourned in an atmosphere of bickering, without having made any headway toward a framework of treaties on which the peace of the world was to rest. Domination by the Big Three is still a sore point with many nations, and conflicting occupation policies reflect strains even within the Big Three. But also there is determination to overcome all obstacles; they must be overcome, because the threat of the tiny atom is too overwhelming to allow for failure. As one wag put it, "Atomic energy is here to stay. The question is, are we?" By the time Joe reaches home he has read enough of the paper to be convinced that the winning of World War II did not make certain a lasting peace; it only gave us a *chance* to push toward that goal—which is something, at that.

LIKE millions of other Americans, Joe is a bit tired. Life has been grim for a good many months, and for the moment he'd rather leave these headaches to Congress and step out for the evening. A cab, he discovers, is still something to be patiently tracked down, but when landed it turns out to be one of those very few glossy jobs beginning to bob up in contrast with the battered hulks that have carried on through four years of wreck-and-ration.

The Gay White Way of Joe's town is lively and crowded. People have money to spend—more

than they have had at any one time in years, thanks to a long period in which the things they might have bought couldn't be obtained and thanks, too, to the channeling of savings into the U.S. Treasury by way of war bonds. Now they are glad to spend, and theaters, movies and night clubs are enjoying a boom season.

With his wife and a few friends, Joe sits down to a fairly solid meal in a medium-priced restaurant. He thinks the service is bad because they have to wait 15 minutes before the table is cleared of their predecessors' left-overs. But the other members of the party insist that things have improved vastly. Only four months ago diners considered themselves lucky to escape without a bawling-out from an irate waiter.

The talk turns to houses and apartments. On this score the change-over from war to peace has apparently made a strained situation doubly strained. Demand for housing is greater than ever, but new building hasn't been started. Materials are still scarce, and potential landlords are unwilling to embark on new ventures until the OPA lifts rent ceilings. When that happens, Joe's friends fear, rents will go soaring into the blue and tenants soaring into the red. Hotels, too, and rooming houses are still enjoying (if that's the word for it) a wartime boom. Three actresses, stranded in Boston, were so hard put to it for quarters that they pitched a tent on the Common, enjoying the right of eminent domain until ejected by the police.

Joe gets along well enough on the dance floor on what he remembers of the rhumba, the conga and the samba, and he is introduced to the bamba, recently imported from Mexico. He's a little rusty on the songs of the day, but it doesn't take him long to discover that the practice of "adapting" the classics is going strong. Chopin under other names dominates the Hit Parade.

TWO of Joe's old friends are involved in divorce proceedings, so he is not greatly surprised when one of his fellow-diners, just back from Reno, reports that the divorce capital is doing three times the business it enjoyed in 1940. They've had to build an addition to the Washoe County Courthouse to handle the extra traffic, and one Chicago court runs a nursery in the annex. The divorce rate over the entire country is nearly double the pre-Pearl Harbor figure. No wonder marriage figures as the theme in at least two best-sellers—Sinclair Lewis's "Cass Timberlane" and J. P. Marquand's "Repent in Haste."

Parallel with this trend, a new informality and independence are apparent in the public habits of American women. Casual conversation with GIs on trains, cars and buses became an accepted social amenity for American girls during the war, and the habit—simple, friendly and gen-

And Los Angeles is still growing

North Dakota's farms are peaceful and prosperous.

erally harmless—appears to have taken root. Moreover, women who in their husbands' absence paid bills, wielded the checkbook and in general took over the duties of head of the house have inevitably become interested in the world of politics. Selective Service, OPA, taxation and demobilization all struck close to home, and it now seems unlikely that women will once more entirely abandon the political field to men.

This new, free-and-easy air affected by American women is definitely not reflected in their clothes. Here the trend is all in the other direction, toward the frilly and the feminine. The reasons are obvious. Men have been scarce, and the struggle for the pick of the returning conquerors is on. What's more, American girls have been reading a good deal about the charms of their foreign sisters, especially the French, and the competitive urge has taken the form of a greatly heightened emphasis on the sexy, the alluring, the feminine. Tailored suits are ruled out, necks are low and formal evening gowns, almost unseen during the war, are back again.

Fashion authorities report a bit of a struggle between one school, favoring the sheath-like dress and the straight figure, and another, and probably winning, school favoring the return of the hour-glass woman. They even say that in the highest circles of fashion the stomacher has been reintroduced to simulate a tiny waist, and the bustle of grandma's day brought back to add expansiveness to the rear echelon. The top-knot is the prevailing rule in hairdress, and the whole temptress motif is exemplified by the name of the most popular shade in nail polish and lip-tick: "Fatal Apple."

In the field of early postwar books, Joe finds, here are more important trends than the emphasis on the pitfalls of marriage, already cited. Mass production for GIs has given publishers ideas for far wider circulation of books than they ever figured on before the war. At least four concerns are in the field with inexpensive reprints, and the experience of GI libraries and mobile units is being eagerly studied. One result of the war is that hundreds of thousands of men have picked up the reading habit in the endless hours of waiting which all servicemen have had to endure, and publishers are hoping to stimulate that habit before it dies. Books on war subjects are still selling briskly, particularly picture volumes and those that round up and

regroup material treated piecemeal in the hundreds of slim books, on this front and that, which poured out during the conflict. Serious subjects, stimulated by the war, still hold their own on the book-counters alongside the entertainment literature now pouring out for a war-weary nation.

IN Joe's new world of transition, the movies, too, are undergoing a reconversion. All sorts of trends are in the air over Hollywood. Picture makers, for one thing, appear to be convinced that the public is fed up not only with war pictures but with anything serious. Production schedules show musicals due for the heaviest boost, most of them of the super-duper variety long forbidden by wartime budgets. Next in line for volume output are historical and period pieces like "Saratoga Trunk" and "Bandit of Sherwood Forest," and no end of "life stories," particularly of theatrical luminaries. Third in the order of importance are light comedies, typified by the reunion of Bob Hope and Bing Crosby in "Road to Utopia." Escapism is the rule of the day, and themes of social significance appear to be headed for the nearest exit.

Shakeups in Hollywood personnel also are in progress. Tried and true box-office attractions like Robert Montgomery, Jimmy Stewart, Henry Fonda and Clark Gable are back from the war to supplant the collection of aging second-raters who furnished Class-B passion for the duration. Then, too, an increasing number of stars are leaving Hollywood for Broadway. Among those who have already made the shift or are reported about to do so are Spencer Tracy, Katharine Hepburn, Ingrid Bergman, Jean Arthur, Kay Francis and Fredric March.

The loss of other bright-lights is threatened by the appearance in Hollywood of J. Arthur Rank, the fabulous British producer. This pious Sunday-school teacher, who can invest $5,000,000 in a single film and hardly miss it, has been plucking American talent and is regarded on the Coast as the first genuine threat to Hollywood's hitherto unchallenged monopoly in the movie world. Rank, who has already bought into several Hollywood studios, has the British film industry in the palm of his hand. Among his products already released or soon to come are "Blithe Spirit," "Colonel Blimp," Shaw's "Caesar and Cleopatra" with Claude Rains and Vivien Leigh, Shakespeare's "Henry V," and "Mary

Magdalen," a five-million-dollar film starring Ingrid Bergman and Joseph Cotten. Britain's emergence as a film center, thanks to Mr. Rank, is probably the biggest movie news in the fading year, and there is much speculation as to how Hollywood will react to the competition.

Joe has been in places where American radio programs didn't penetrate, and he takes a nostalgic sort of pleasure in learning that, despite FM and other technical advances, the air waves vibrate to many of the same voices he heard before he left home. There is none of the tension, of course, that filled the air in those years in which crisis after crisis mounted in hysterical crescendo from Munich to War-in-the-West, to the invasion of Russia, to Pearl Harbor. News commentators, in fact, have gone into a sharp decline, and round-the-world hookups are neither so numerous nor so fraught with destiny. But otherwise the old familiar voices of radio are still going strong. "Duffy's Tavern" is still serving red-hot boners by Archy, Fred Allen makes his weekly tour of Allen's Alley, Charlie McCarthy carries on his eternal feuds with guest stars, and other veteran standbys—Benny, Durante, Burns and Allen—fill their same comfortable niches in the Crossley ratings. Goodman Ace is doing a series for Danny Kaye, and among the new programs is one by Barry Fitzgerald in the role of small-town barber and justice-of-the-peace. Soap operas supposedly lay bare the hearts of simple folk while commercials lay bare their digestive tracts; and the world's best music still comes to Joe by courtesy of the world's best laxatives.

Joe may well be excused if he looks about him with a certain bewilderment. The dreadful problems of the atom bomb, diplomatic unrest abroad and industrial unrest at home all weigh on the spirit of the country. But on sober second thought Joe knows that no one promised him the millenium, and if peace has not brought with it a world of music and rainbows, neither has it produced those calamities that Joe's more cynical friends predicted—runaway inflation, political war, mass starvation in half the world and general hell-raising all around. Paradise may or may not be just around the corner, and the victories of peace may come as hard as the victories of war, but anyone who has seen what Joe has seen knows that in the last analysis "there is nothing to fear but fear."

By YANK's European Staff

SWEATING IT OUT...

Some occupation deals are good and some are lousy, and the biggest gripe is still chicken.

PARIS—All over Europe the people faced a winter of cold and death, and the GIs left behind to clean up loose ends, to work with Military Government, to route luckier soldiers home, to wait endlessly for their own turn to board a Liberty ship or a transport or a C-47 are an unhappy body of men.

As of now **ENGLAND** is á far cry from the island that was turned into one vast staging area for the invasion of the Continent. About the only unit left organized on a working basis is a longshore outfit engaged in the final work of shipping home some Army equipment and generally policing up the dock area before leaving. Willow Run, which once fed officers on an assembly line schedule in the basement of Grosvenor House, has been long closed, and Grosvenor House itself has returned to being just a hotel. Many of the British girls who married GIs are still awaiting transport home and so are a few soldiers lost in the redeployment shuffle. But a GI who served in England in 1943 or '44 or early '45 wouldn't recognize the place.

Across the channel, **FRANCE** has been returned to the French and almost all the GI offices in Paris have been closed up. A lot of official Army business still passes through the city, but to the average GI stationed on the continent today, Paris is *the* dream place to spend a three-day pass. From every nook and cranny on the continent where Americans are stationed, pulling occupation duty, come the three-day passees, weary and dirty from two- and three-day combination train and truck trips. They are loaded down with pay dirt that has been hard to spend in the small towns of Germany and they are busting to get rid of it.

After a quick shave, shower and shine at one of the many Paris billet hotels, they take off on the town and knock themselves out for a glorious 72 hours.

They soon discover that, although Paris still retains remnants of the city they heard and read wild tales about, it isn't all they thought it was cracked up to be. On the surface, yes. They get out in the middle of the Champs Elysees in front of the Place de la Concorde and gaze down the broad avenue toward the impressive Arc de Triomphe. Paying no heed to the wild-cowboy tactics of French motorists, they take snapshots of each other, legs astride, hands on hips. After half a day of sight seeing at Napoleon's tomb, the Eiffel Tower and the Louvre—where everything from Whistler's "Mother" to Da Vinci's "Mona Lisa" is jam-packed into one gallery—they settle down to the run-of-the-mill GI pastime of drinking bad French cognac at a dollar a snort. Eight out of ten head for the notorious Pigalle section of town. Their Paris-wise buddies back in the outfit had tipped them off that there is where they'd get the "best deal." "Pig-alley," as it's come to be called, is the gaudiest, loosest honkey-tonk section on the Continent—maybe the world. It's rather quiet during the day, but when darkness sets in and the streets light up and the streetwalkers start walking and hawking, it's what's known on Broadway as "out of this world." The ladies of the evening range from 250 *francs* (plus hotel room) upwards to a corporal's pay, and they are not shy about asking.

The men who enjoy "higher class" entertainment, and who have latched onto a "respectable" date, head for Paris' most famous night spot, the Bal Tabarin, where a bottle of sparkling wine sets them back 18 bucks. The Bal is the closest thing to New York's Latin Quarter or Copacabana. Its *frou-frou* revue, with showgirls who wear nothing but a loin cloth and a great big smile, would make a U. S. mayor scream, stomp and call out his vice squad on the double.

The famous sidewalk cafes along the Champs Elysees are closed for the winter, but the side-street bars, cafes and small night clubs off the Champs now handle the GI sidewalk trade. During the past two months an inkling of what Parisian fashions were like in prewar days has hit the Champs promenade. The women are dragging out their Sunday bests—fineries they had stashed away in moth balls during the occupation. They are wearing these cherished garments again because they know that clothes are gradually coming back to Paris and it won't be long before they will be able to replenish their meager wardrobes. Right now, prices are exorbitant and numbers that can be purchased for 15 or 20 dollars in Stateside department stores sell for ten times that much in Paris. But Parisian styling is still tops, and although the materials are inferior to ours, the way the cloth is put together makes the GI window shoppers say, "Goddam, wish I had enough dough to bring one of those home for the wife."

The average Joe limits his Paris gifts to a bottle of perfume, a scarf, a risque pastel print of a half-clad femme sprawled on a divan. The shopwise soldier stays away from the average main-street shops. He sweats out a line at the GI gift store PXs or at the Chanel shop, where he can purchase a decent-size bottle of the famous stuff for six dollars.

The black market in watches, binoculars, typewriters, fountain pens still rages in the Rain-

EUROPE

bow Corner section of town near the Madeleine church. When a GI runs out of ready cash he can always find a buyer for his valuables. Many soldiers wangle passes to Paris for the specific purpose of buying up watches, and bringing them back to Berlin, Vienna and other occupation cities, where they peddle them to the Russians for fabulous sums.

The *Opera Comique*, French ballet and symphony halls are in full swing again, but except for a few long-hairs and the men who are studying at the Sorbonne under the Army's I&E program, the audience is comprised mostly of natives.

There are but a comparatively few American soldiers stationed permanently in Paris, but those few are the ones who really get the "feel" of the city. The three-day pass men say it's okay, but they'll take "Chicago, New York or Los Angeles any day."

The Wacs have left the Hotel California on the Rue de Berri, and Peeping Toms no longer forgather in the offices across the streets to watch the girls get ready for bed. The hotel is now doing a land-office business with American and other foreign businessmen and diplomats, but it isn't as nice as it used to be when the tinkle of girlish GI laughter rang through its halls.

And, at long last, saluting in Paris is no longer required.

The only big installations of GIs left in France are at the staging areas around Reims and at the ports like Le Havre and Marseille, where they step on the boat for home. There are the usual snafus in the returning of men, and some low pointers are getting home before high pointers. The accumulation of justified gripes at the way things are being handled is still a-building. The only thing that erases a gripe is setting foot on a U. S.-bound transport, and there are still plenty of men who haven't had that pleasure.

The ports are working two ways. Every now and then you see a fresh-from-home outfit unloading its complement of new men for the occupation army. There is a universal weariness about most of the incoming GIs, who know that they have come late to a party that may last for a long time. Their presence is, however, one of the few signs of progress that high-pointers waiting for shipment have to cheer them up.

Nice and the rest of the Riviera are still booming as recreation areas for men on pass. They represent a GI approach to paradise, for chicken is taboo and officers are definitely off limits. This side of statutory offenses, a GI can do almost as he pleases in the never-never land of Southern France.

SWITZERLAND is a big-time pass area, too. An RTO sergeant stands on the station platform at Basle on the Swiss border and speaks through a public address system to incoming GIs.

"Fellas," he says, "you are now leaving the land of snafu and entering the country of milk and honey."

Switzerland, for the occupation soldier who is lucky enough to snare one of those $35 seven-day furloughs, almost lives up to the sergeant's pep-talk. The food is good, the hotel beds are soft and the scenery is terrific.

There is no discrimination between officers and EM, and it is first come, first served in hotels and restaurants. There are souvenirs galore and, of course, the inevitable Swiss watch. The watches are reasonable, and you can get a good one without going into hock.

Swiss girls don't seem to rate with GI connoisseurs as highly as the *mademoiselles* and *frauleins*, but they are still plenty nice. One of their added attractions is the fact that most of them speak English—the language is a required subject in all Swiss schools. The girls are anxious to try out their English on qualified GI instructors, and, as an extra-curricular activity, most of them have picked up the art of jitterbugging. The bands in Swiss night clubs play up-to-date American music, both sweet and swing. Night clubs in cities like Berne, Lausanne and Geneva are not inexpensive, but they are well under the stratospheric tariff of the Bal Tabarin.

It is in **GERMANY** with the Army of Occupation that you find the larger part of the GIs who are left in Europe. Most of the high-pointers have been weeded out and at least started home, and the men who are left mostly know that they aren't going to see Missouri or West Virginia or Pennsylvania tomorrow morning.

GIs who live in the beat-up towns of Germany like Nuremberg and Munich envy the men who are quartered in smaller towns untouched by the war. The big beat-up towns are bleak, the people in them are bleak and there isn't much to do except line up for the movies or to dunk doughnuts in coffee at the Red Cross canteens.

Of course, there is always fraternization. But the nights are getting cold and the wind is whipping down through the Bavarian mountains, and some division commanders look down their noses at GIs who go into German houses. So do some German papas who would much prefer that their daughters go around with German boys and that GIs learn to depend solely on their winter longjohns for warmth. Due to the weather, fraternization, particularly in Bavaria, is pretty much an indoor sport nowadays.

The comradeship which existed between officers and men in many outfits during the war—a comradeship born of common danger and common misery—has given way to the more rigid correctness of military courtesy, but most GIs don't find it surprising. They address some officers as sir whom they used to call Bill or Joe, but it's the Army and what the hell. There are separate entrances for officers and men in some ETO headquarters buildings, and this sometimes causes embarrassment. This fall a pfc who used to be with the 1st Division was in a town on pass and encountered a second lieutenant under whom he had served in combat. They had a couple of drinks together and later went to a hotel. There were two doors, one for officers, one for enlisted men. The officer paused before the entrance. "I'll see you inside," he said. "It's a hell of a funny war, I guess."

GIs in Germany are doing most of the chores that any Army garrison does. They drive trucks, fix roads, pull details, stand inspections, do dozens of obscure, dull jobs—many of which have to be done and others of which seem to be simply "made-up" work to keep them busy. There is a tremendous amount of guard duty.

Almost everyone wants to go home, of course, but many men have a vivid enough recollection of combat—either by personal experience or from hearsay—to feel glad still that the shooting is over. And thousands of them are eating off tablecloths and using plates and living in German homes, instead of sitting on the ground and eating out of mess-kits and sleeping in tents.

This doesn't mean that all the GIs in Germany are living in luxury. A lot of them are living miserably, and there is still plenty of high-grade chicken. In a few outfits men who fought in France and Germany are learning once again about nomenclature of the M1 and are doing close-order drill.

One group of GIs living in a little town outside Munich were billeted in an eleven-room German house. They chipped together and hired a maid to clean the rooms every morning. On Saturday morning the GIs were compelled to stand inspection in their quarters while second looeys went around looking at the window panes and feeling door jambs for dust. On these inspection mornings, the maid had to come to work two hours early to make sure the GIs weren't gigged.

Along with the comedy found in some situations there is an ugly undercurrent of German unrest. Some GIs who go out with German girls have been sandbagged by members of the still-existing Nazi underground, and there is everywhere evidence that the war against ideas didn't end with the firing of the last official shot.

The only glamor detail in a publicity sense is that of the soldiers who are guarding the top Nazi war criminals at Nuremberg. In spite of all that has been written about it, it is a rather routine guard job, and top Nazis are about the same amount of bother as bottom Nazis.

In **CZECHOSLOVAKIA**, too, there are GI-policed prison enclosures for *SS* troops, members of the German general staff corps and dangerous Nazis. But most of the American soldiers in the country are stationed in towns. The GIs of the XX Corps don't see why they should be "occupying" a friendly country, especially one whose government has the situation in hand. For their own part, the Czechs wish the Americans (and the Russians, in the eastern zone) would depart and leave the solution of the "German problem" up to them. The Czech girls cannot understand how Americans can fraternize with Germans, and have been known, understandably, to boycott dances to which GIs had also invited *frauleins*.

GIs stationed in **AUSTRIA** admit that the scenery is good, and that the girls are pretty, but they don't like much else. There isn't much else. The shops in Vienna and Salzburg long ago were cleaned out, and recreation is even more limited than it is in Germany. Vienna is one of the saddest, and hungriest, cities in Europe. There is a little more food, and a little more gayety, in the smaller Austrian towns, but not much. The Austrians are living largely on the hope that somehow things will get better, and the GIs in Austria are living largely on the hope that somehow they can get home.

In **ITALY**, as elsewhere in Europe, there are two kinds of GIs left—guys waiting to go home for discharge, and occupation and service troops.

The guys with the points are at the Naples repple depple. Living conditions there are bad, there is a tremendous backlog, and men usually spend several weeks waiting for a boat, living either in overcrowded tents at the race track or in overcrowded barracks. From there some men are sent to Camp Dushane, Casablanca, where they spend another couple of weeks, waiting on a plane ride to the States. Many men at Naples were angry when two big transports were sent to Leghorn and Naples last fall to take the 34th and 92nd Divisions home. The Naples men pointed out with bitterness that most of the men in both divisions didn't have as many points as the repple-depple lads. As late as the end of September, there were still men in the Naples repple depple with as high as 90 points.

There are two main occupation forces. The 88th Division is in the north and is composed mostly of what were looked on as low-point men when the system was first set up. Most of them have 50 points and over two years in the service, however, so they, too, are being weeded out for transport home.

Down near Foggia, there is the 5th Bomb Wing, a heavy-bombardment occupation air force. Living conditions are lousy here. The men live in an area that has dust storms daily, and though the wing is the oldest in Italy the men still live mostly in tents. They only started putting up tuffa buildings last fall.

Chicken has its day in Foggia. For example, 24-hour guard duty is being pulled, something that was never done when the 5th was in actual combat. Going on the theory that the men must be kept occupied, guards are detailed to such ridiculous jobs as doing duty on a baseball field.

In Italy the Italians and the GIs agree on one thing. The Italians want us out of there, as they feel they can never return to normal while GIs boost prices. The GIs want to go home, too.

All over Europe, it's the same. And it's the same in **AFRICA**. Many of the man have forgotten combat, and many of the men are new men who have never seen combat.

One day, outside the little town of Bad Tolz, Bavaria, a corporal and two pfcs were leaning against their truck, eating K-rations. Down the road toward them came a German soldier and a girl wheeling a baby buggy. The German soldier was holding the girl's left hand with his right, and they paid no attention to the GIs.

The German soldier was still wearing his uniform. He had been released from the Army only a few hours before. You could still see the outline, etched in white-dried sweat, of where his pack had rested on his back.

The GIs, members of a victorious Army, looked at the soldier of the defeated enemy.

The corporal flipped a cigarette at the ground.

"There," said the corporal, "goes a lucky son of a bitch."

SWEATING IT OUT.... PACIFIC

From Kilroy to the colonel, everyone wants to go home, and the only question is, "When?"

By Sgt. ROBERT MacMILLAN
YANK Staff Correspondent

TOKYO—The American soldier in the Pacific this winter is either a low-pointer standing at resigned parade rest, guarding something or other, or he is a high-pointer standing beside the redeployment slot-machine, waiting for the right combination to come up and pay off with a trip home.

This goes on from Australia, where summer is coming in, up through the forgotten coastal bases of New Guinea, along the coral stepping-stones to the Philippines; in China, where the marvels of Shanghai await GIs at a price; in Japan, where MPs in lacquered helmets shuffle their feet to keep warm outside the big man's headquarters, and in Korea, where the snow is filling up the jagged crevices of the mountains and the women are adding another layer of underclothes against the coming winter.

In **AUSTRALIA,** where Americans arrived four years ago with old-style flat helmets and plans to defend the countryside along the Brisbane Line, a few officers and GIs are still staying around, paying off the Army's bills, worrying about getting Aussie wives home and letting pretty secretaries go. Soldiers are drinking their last knee-high bottles of Aussie brew and wondering how it will be back where steak does not come mounted with eggs. And a few discouraged MPs are still looking for AWOLs who have settled way out back and who are hoping the Army will forget about them.

In **NEW GUINEA,** practically nothing remains except a murky memory in the skulls of the Fuzzy-Wuzzies. Cities that the Army threw up are fading into nothing. The jungle is obscuring the straight military lines of all the things Americans built to live in, fly from and ride on. At Buna, the Aussies have put up a few signs to mark the place where the Japs were finally stopped and turned back toward Tokyo.

The course of the war up the New Guinea coast and along the little islands nobody ever heard of until Americans started dying on them is marked with the stranded remains of landing craft that brought the Yanks ashore. Crabs scratch around on the rusting metal plates where barnacles are blotting out the olive drab.

GI life on Oahu, **HAWAII,** hasn't changed very much, except for the obvious difference that every soldier is busily figuring out the possibility of discharge in terms of months and weeks and days instead of in years. Most of the old-timers are so PO'd about the clipping a soldier runs into in Honolulu that they seldom even leave their posts when they get free time on Wednesday afternoons and Saturdays. Troops passing through the area on their way home swell the downtown crowds in Honolulu and shell out their jack to the tourist traps.

Transportation home for high-pointers is the biggest and sorest point of discussion. As elsewhere in the Pacific, it is obvious in the islands that not enough GIs who qualify are getting home fast enough. Pacific *Stars & Stripes* in Honolulu investigated the highly-publicized shipment of Army men via aircraft carriers in September and found that only four GIs were shipped Stateside aboard the *Saratoga,* which was crowded with Navy men. The paper ran an editorial cartoon with a caption quoting the original blurb about "Army and Navy men return on Saratoga." The picture showed millions of sailors tramping down the gangplank; buried among them is one lonely GI.

KWAJALEIN, scene of what was probably our most perfect island-invasion operation, is now practically all Navy. The only Army men left are ATC personnel and weather observers and a few other small outfits. The blackboard at ATC is scrawled with remarks about Kilroy not being able to stand it at Kwajalein. Kilroy is the mythical GI character, a Pfc. Paul Bunyan, whose

name is written in every latrine from Hamilton Field and the San Francisco POE to Japan. "Kilroy has been here" is the usual line. And if there is an order posted with an officer's name on the end of it, you find the officer's name scratched out and "Kilroy" scribbled in place of it. The signs at Kwajalein eight months ago used to read: "Welcome, you lucky people." Kilroy and the peace have changed all that.

The island of **SAIPAN** has lost all its work-in-progress look. Main roads are all hard-surfaced, which means that you no longer drive through fog-like clouds of coral dust. The sharp hairpin turn above Tanapag has been rounded into a sensible curve that doesn't require shifting of gears when you're going up hill. As an indication that building is at a standstill, the big coral quarries are almost deserted. Gashes of white still mark their locations on the mountainsides, but there are no longer streams of trucks going back and forth nor busy shovels cutting the coral terraces away 24 hours a day. For the most part, pyramidal tents have disappeared, and in their places are quonsets or prefabs. The whole island is quiet and rear-area.

GUAM is pretty well cleaned out of old men and is getting very chicken. At Harmon Field the MPs make you roll down your sleeves and insist that you wear a sun-tan go-to-hell cap instead of the more comfortable green or khaki peaked, jockey-style hat. You can't wear shorts outside your company area.

In the **PHILIPPINES,** the big ships come in with rations and replacements and go out again, crowded to the anchor-housings with soldiers going home. Repple-depples are jammed with men who have their orders, and more are coming in all the time and people are not happy. Only about one half of the 77,700 scheduled to sail in October made it. Returnees are leaving depots on a first-in, first-out basis rather than according to points. And GIs are unhappy about it.

Sailors and rear-echelon troops swarm along the streets of Manila looking for something to take home to mother and Aunt Sally. The price of native whisky and rum is going down, and eggs don't cost quite as much as pearls any more. Night clubs are going full blast along Rizal Avenue, but the Filipinos still live in corrugated iron shacks among the wreckage of war. About 40 miles south of Manila the Japanese who came soberly down from the mountains when Yamashita surrendered are gathered in vast prison camps waiting for somebody to find ships somewhere to get them home. They know it will be a long wait.

IWO JIMA no longer looks anything like a battlefield. The hills which held Jap gun positions have been leveled, and almost the whole island is covered with flat asphalt runways and good highways. There are radar masts and weather-recording instruments on Mt. Suribachi. And there is a huge cemetery near the volcano with thousands of white crosses laid out to form one mammoth cross.

Iwo is a terrible place to be stationed. The black volcanic dust that covers the island blows incessantly during dry spells and gets into your nose and eyes and throat. There's nothing to do except go to the movies.

When the chicken was setting in on the island this past summer, the officers in an AAF station posted a big sign in their area. "Officers' Country," it read. "—Restricted." The area was between the EM's living area and the place where the EM worked, and the restriction meant that GIs had to make a big circle around it four times a day to get to and from their work—an extra half mile every morning, noon and night. The EM thought things over and came up with a big sign for their own area. It said, "God's Country—No Restrictions." The officers got PO'd and made the GIs take the sign down. But the feeling lingers.

On **OKINAWA,** where the war ended, men and supplies are still coming in to invasion beaches—

when the typhoons will let them. In the dust that was Kadena town, into which troops last Easter picked their way cautiously, an endless stream of vehicles grinds around the great wheel of the traffic circle.

The combat troops are gone today, but service troops still remain with their tents, cutting up the slopes, transforming Jap wagon trails into four-lane coral-topped highways, rebuilding latrines, erecting new quarters as storms blow the old ones down, constructing day rooms and officers' clubs.

The airfields, too—Yontan, Kadena and Naha—are still doing business at the old hardstands. Kadena, where the mightiest air armada ever assembled in the Pacific took off for the final surrender in Tokyo, at the moment lies almost deserted—the sole survivor of six B-29 runways that died a-borning when peace came.

The rubble that was Naha, capital of Okinawa, remains the same. Some of the debris has been bulldozed aside to make room for reefers, warehouses and depots that will some day move out of tents and into quonsets.

Looking down on the ashes of Shuri, where Jap Army headquarters were located, only the forlorn spire of a Christian church remains. The grass is withering between the wooden wheels of the silent guns, and here and there lies a rusting tank or a still-fused shell. Sugar Hill, Chocolate Drop, Three Sisters, Beightler, Bloody Knoll, Suicide Ridge—they too remain open to the sun and wind and rain which, working slower than bulldozers, are nevertheless sure in their job of final obliteration.

As yet no one knows the future of Okinawa—whether it will become a naval base or an Army installation or neither. Thus far it has not been geared to peace. Recreational facilities are almost non-existent. Athletic equipment is scarce, and there is no educational program. So far there exists neither machinery nor equipment for reconversion. As one company commander said, "Well, I guess the men will have to go back to digging ditches." The GIs make no effort to conceal the fact that morale is low and that most of them are good and mad.

In **SHANGHAI** the occupation is a different story. Oriental pitchmen crowd the street with every sundry imaginable, and other salesmen sidle up to the GIs and whisper, "Nice young girl, mister?" Shanghai is a lush utopia to GIs who have spent most of their time overseas in China's interior. You can buy steak for dinner, with French fries and vegetables. There are first-rate night clubs with plenty of beautiful girls anxious to help you spend your money.

Stores are stocked with all sorts of curios at reasonable prices. A dime will still get you a rickshaw ride for a couple of miles—but getting a coolie to understand where you want to go is another matter.

Since all equipment must be flown in, the limited amount the Army was able to bring with it made it necessary at first for the city to furnish rations and quarters. As a result some GIs got housed in the best hotels and drew five to seven bucks per diem.

Keeping warm has become the main problem for occupation troops stationed in **KOREA.** Snow blankets the country from the mountains in the south to Seoul, the American-occupied capital and beyond. Soon the Hangang River, which flows past the capital, will freeze over.

The XIV Corps quartermastered everyone in woolens before the first snowfall, but even then there was a widespread dependence on persimmon whisky and Japanese brandy to keep warm. The national costume of the Koreans has changed little in outward appearance with the weather except for the protective plumpness which the women have assumed. This last, it has been discovered, is due merely to an increase in the number and thickness of undergarments which the women add instead of wearing fur coats.

Dancing is another popular way of keeping

warm. The ballroom of the International Cultural Association, on the fourth floor of Seoul's Mitsubishi department store, offers music—"Dinah," "St. Louis Blues," "My Blue Heaven"—and choice partners, all for two *yen* a dance. The same tunes are to be heard in the host of American-style bars which have sprung up since the curfew was lifted. Each bar is equipped with a corps of hostesses, most of them former *Kee-Sang* girls who entertained in the city's tea houses before the Americans came.

Traffic along Seoul's Bunchung, the Japanese shopping section, is no longer as heavy as it was at first, but the supply of kimonos and lacquerware has not been depleted. Most of the Americans left in Korea now are replacements. Seventh Division veterans of Okinawa, Leyte, Kwajalein and Attu have nearly all gone home.

In **JAPAN** it's getting cold—not as cold as it is in Korea, but cold just the same. Everyone's in ODs. Tokyo still smells of dead fires, dead people and dead fish, and the mysterious little shops along the Ginza are sold out as fast as they get anything in. There's a bull market in kimonos and pearls and silk and lacquer-ware and dolls. Most of Tokyo's *geisha* houses are off limits, but in other places they are still open to GIs. Entertainment is already stripped of Oriental niceties, and joy is reduced to its lowest common denominator.

Probably the saddest outfit in all of the U.S. armed forces is the 97th Infantry Division, now patrolling the area along the Tone River in Honshu, just north of Tokyo, with division headquarters at Kumagaya. The 97th came back from Germany, where it fired one of the last shots of the war, right after VE-Day. The guys got 30-day furloughs and went to Fort Bragg for reorganization and training. They had been at Bragg two

days when they were shipped out to the West Coast (this was after the Japs asked for peace) and hustled on a boat for Japan. Most of them had been in the Army four years and had 50, 60 and 70 points. Four days after they left California, the WD announced that no man with more than 45 points would have to go overseas. They landed in Japan in the middle of September and there they are: standing guard on bridges along the Tone that seems not unlike the Rhine where they were standing guard only a few months ago. Everybody in the division is thoroughly convinced that they'll be in Japan for two years.

The most significant thing about the attitude of occupation troops in Japan—the same as in Germany, no doubt—is that the GIs who are now doing the occupying are mostly low-point men who have never been in combat against the Japs and who haven't had close friends killed. These Johnny-come-latelys naturally don't have the stern attitude toward the Japs that the veterans of the Philippines and Okinawa would have. "Hell, they don't seem so bad," is their attitude. The Japs, naturally, are treating them very nicely.

The chicken is, of course, setting in Japan, and the Army is trying pretty hard to put on a good front. The OD uniforms that are being issued to the troops in Japan are far smarter-looking and better in quality than any ODs issued in the States or in Europe or Australia these last three years (Japan has about the same climate as New York; there is snow in the winter, and it is pretty chilly from October until May). The uniforms include good-looking Eisenhower woolen battle jackets and good OD pants, made from a darker and softer material that looks like more money than anything we had before. The go-to-hell caps are smooth-finished and hard-wool

serge, like officers' caps, and the OD shirts are sharp, with a smooth finish and a low, widespread collar like an expensive civilian sports shirt. They are issuing plenty of sweaters and green combat jackets, with hoods, instead of overcoats. The clothes, in typical Army fashion, are finally getting good now that the war is over and they are no longer as important as they were before.

As a matter of fact, generally speaking, the GIs have made an excellent impression on all Japs. On duty they act correct and off duty they are polite and well behaved. They are nothing at all the way the Jap propagandists said they would be, and the Japs themselves admit that they are nothing like their own soldiers would be if they were occupying America. Getting back to the woman angle again, the GIs have done things like getting up in street cars to give women their seats, which makes a delightful impression on the Jap women and annoys and embarrasses the men. The Jap women have blossomed out in bright kimonos since the Americans have arrived. They had been forced to wear dark, conservative clothes during the war.

In **INDIA** proper where the war was always a waiting war, it's a waiting war still. GIs here used to be waiting for something to happen in Japan, say the end of the war. Now that that's taken care of, the men left in the sub-continent are simply waiting for the same thing everyone else in uniform overseas is waiting for—a quick trip home.

There's a Pacific-wide rumor around that Kilroy has been to Washington and has fixed everything up. He is going to return as Supreme Commander Kilroy of the entire Pacific area. He will convert the major islands of Japan into giant barges and tow all Pacific GIs back to the West Coast. Kilroy's promised New Order will apply only to EM.

YANK
Pin-up Girls

THE OUTER GARMENT

By Sgt. RAY DUNCAN

"**P**UT the flag at half-staff," muttered our CO, "and call a special formation."

There were tears in his steel-gray eyes as he read from WD Circular 288, dated 21 September 1945. "I've seen this coming, men," he said when he had finished. "The Army isn't what it used to be. I'm resigning my commission today. Sergeant, dismiss the troops."

The circular amazed us as much as it did him. "The field jacket," it said, "is authorized to be worn as an outer garment outside the limits of posts, camps and stations."

In those words the Army shattered one of its proudest traditions. I can't imagine how it ever happened in Washington, but it must have gone something like this:

"Gentlemen, I've called you together this morning because we are faced with a crisis. I hardly know how to begin. Certain elements within the War Department have suggested that —it's utterly fantastic—that we authorize the field jacket as an outer garment outside the posts, camps and stations!"

Everyone gasps. "Pardon me, general, but did I hear you correctly? The *field jacket* to be worn in town? By enlisted men?"

"I'm afraid that's right. It's this new, radical element that's come into the Army the past three or four years."

"Smart alecks!" snaps Col. Bioy. "After the long fight we've made to keep EM out of those jackets in town!"

"This strikes a death blow to Army discipline," groans Maj. Riddle, his face buried in his hands. "Don't they realize how good those damn jackets look? What becomes now of the distinction between officers and enlisted men?"

"Well," sighs a colonel, "it won't make much difference now. All the EM are wearing those Eisenhower things anyhow. That was a big mistake."

"Right, colonel. That's what happens when you let combat men start prescribing the uniform. It should be strictly a Washington function."

"When I think," sighs Col. Whistling, "of the long, hard fight I made against the field jacket. I kept my MPs on their toes. Every October I gave them a special pep talk, and they grabbed hundreds of field jackets in town. My guards at the gate were trained to pick up passes ruthlessly whenever they found an EM trying to sneak past in a jacket, and—"

"At my post," interrupts Col. Kidley, "the enlisted men were mighty tricky. They used to smuggle field jackets out in cars, or cram them through the fence."

"Ah, those good old days," says a colonel wistfully. "I always thought AR 600-40 phrased it so beautifully. It was almost poetry: 'The field jacket will *not* be worn outside the limits of posts, camps or stations . . .'"

Everyone sighs deeply. "I made a suggestion, back in 1943, that I still think was rather good," says a colonel. "I proposed at that time that AR 600-40 be amended to forbid the wearing of field jackets *inside* posts, camps and stations as well as outside. EM have been getting too many dates with Government girls working on the posts. Also on the camps and stations. That sort of thing could be prevented. Make them wear the good old EM blouse."

"That brings up a thought," says a colonel craftily. "We can permit the field jacket on EM in town for a while. A lot of them will re-enlist. Then, in a few months, when these radical officers have gone, we can lower the boom! All of a sudden we'll re-invoke old AR 600-40, and—"

"—field jackets will *not* be worn!" chortles a colonel.

"Class-A uniforms only in town!" someone cries.

"Good old EM blouse! Tight across the chest! Narrow shoulders—"

"This time we'll pad the hips. That'll make the shoulders look even smaller—"

"And the little lapels! Those nice, ridiculous little EM lapels."

"We'll change the color—it's too bright now. And the cloth must be coarser, somehow."

"That'll be the day!" cries a general. All the officers rise and shake hands. Then they snap to attention, uncover and chant in chorus: "The field jacket will *not* be worn outside the limits of posts, camps or stations."

Respect the GI

ONE of the most important needed reforms embraces all branches of the armed forces: a merger of the War and Navy Departments.

But, sticking to the Army, I think the Articles of War should be drastically revised. They now provide disciplinary measures against EM for using Government property for personal use, damaging a rifle or staying a few hours over a pass, but they make no provision for penalizing an officer for failing to regard the welfare of the enlisted men or for not respecting his prerogatives, such as they are.

We have taken it upon ourselves to tell other nations how enjoyable life is in a democracy. Let's make the Army consistent with that line. Let enlisted men and officers wear the same clothes; it is really the insignia of rank that distinguishes them from each other. GIs and officers should have the same meals and an equitable distribution of recreational facilities. The privileges granted officers should be in ratio to their responsibility toward the enlisted men under their command.

Germany —Cpl. JOHN J. GATTAS

General Reforms

Here's my list: 1) The Army should consider all soldiers as men of character and intelligence, until they prove themselves otherwise, and should accept them as equals socially and professionally; 2) All soldiers should be dressed alike, from the seventh grade to the fifth star; 3) Greater weight should be given to individual interest in assignment and more flexible standards for promotion should be set up; 4) The Information and Education Division needs to be severed from the Army shackles of "see no evil, hear no evil, speak no evil"; 5) A civilian commission should be provided to hear and evaluate criticism from all grades of Army personnel; it should have authority to give or direct redress in individual cases and to direct the Secretary of War to effect procedural changes when necessary; 6) The Inspector General's office should be removed from the jurisdiction of the War Department.

Grenier Field, N. H. —Pfc. W. J. GREEN

Survival of the Fittest

All commissioned and non-commissioned officers should get annual Civil Service examinations. These examinations would consist of field work and written or oral tests designed to determine developed qualities of leadership, character and integrity. If any man wanted to take an examination for the next higher rank he should be allowed to do so at the time of the annual examination. If his mark were higher than that of the man holding the rank in his outfit, he would replace him and the man replaced would be put in a lower rank or given an opportunity to transfer in grade. Commissions would be awarded only to those who had risen from the ranks after spending a specified period of time as non-commissioned officers.

North Camp Hood, Tex. —Sgt. WILLIAM D. STARNES

A Feudal Society

Our social customs in the Army are based on the relationship of lord and serf. While it is understandable that in feudal times the social customs of the period were carried over into Army life, we should recognize that times have changed. Our modern civilian, accustomed to equality and guaranteed civil rights, is drafted. From the moment he becomes a GI any relationship between what he experiences and democracy is purely accidental.

Our officers are indoctrinated with the need of keeping the enlisted men in their place and maintaining a social position above them. They are impressed with the need for separate, and better, mess, quarters, theater seats and other things.

It is a strange code of ethics which permits fraternization with the ex-enemy, but frowns on informal officer-enlisted men relationships. It would probably never occur to the officers who feted Goering and some other German generals in Germany last May to invite an enlisted man to dine with them.

The enlisted men develop a real appreciation for the benefits of democracy. It is an appreciation which grows in spite of and not because of the social customs of the Army.

THE SOLDIER SPEAKS:

What reforms should be made in the Postwar Army?

The functioning of the business end of the Army must be totalitarian. Discipline must be maintained. The rigid social-class setup, however, needs a bit of streamlining so that it fits in with a democratic form of government. If we fought with weapons as outdated as the customs the Army sponsors, we would be polishing our bows and sharpening our arrows instead of witnessing jet propulsion and the miracle of the atomic bomb.

Africa —Sgt. WILLIAM BROMSEN

Justice in Promotions

One very necessary reform is in the matter of enlisted promotions. Today's army of technical specialization cannot be compared with the army of prewar days. As a result of thinking in outmoded terms, promotional practices, "job grading and appreciation" are brutal.

Too many times men trained in special skills are not considered eligible for promotion because they lack "tactical background," ordinarily known as being a good foot soldier. Too often a GI specialist has little or no contact with his commanding officer and is left to the mercy of the boys who believe mainly in the principle of "brown-nosing."

Different grades could be assigned to each level of responsibility within a job specialty. By this grading policy, together with advancement according to merit and written examinations, much could be done to remedy injustices. Army T/Os specify grades for specialities, but actual results of grading seldom match T/O specifications. I know of one Machine Records unit in which a pfc efficiently did the work of principal clerk in administration because he was the only man who could do it. Yet he was surrounded by men classified as clerks and typists with ratings higher than his.

AAF Base Unit, Santa Ana, Calif. —S/Sgt. JACK A. PEARSON

Trial by Jury

How about having an equal number of officers and enlisted men on a court-martial board? This would permit GIs to have some representation in their trials, and I see no reason why enlisted men shouldn't also sit in when officers are being tried.

If a citizen is qualified to serve as a juror in civilian life and to render a just and honorable decision, there is no reason why he should not be equally qualified in the Army when his fellow soldiers are tried. Jury duty would be required of all men irrespective of rank.

AAF, St. Petersburg, Fla. —Sgt. R. E. NELSON

Eliminate the Chicken

This letter is the result of an informal poll among the GIs in our outfit. Almost to a man their reactions were along the order of "eliminate the chicken."

Of course discipline makes the difference between an army and an armed mob. If orders are to be carried out we need leaders with authority to carry them out. But what the American soldier resents is the petty privileges, the artificial barriers, which make him something apart from and inferior to his officers.

Many officers would like to see changes made in the system. But if they attempt to go along with the GI, to treat him as another man and not just an overgrown 10-year-old, they find themselves on the dirty end of the stick. They find themselves getting all the unpleasant details and being quietly but firmly passed over at promotion time.

Here, in brief, is our own K-ration-inspired reform program: 1) removal of 90 percent of the existing social privileges; 2) a more equitable pay scale; 3) periodic reviews of commissions, resulting in promotion or demotion, conducted by trained and impartial examiners; 4) punishment for officer misconduct and inefficiency on a par with that at present handed out to enlisted men; 5) courts martial where the EM has a voice.

Germany —Pfc. R. E. LEE and T-5 DANIEL W. HOGAN

SEPARATION

When you're on that last lap of Army before getting out, the air is as tense as at induction.

By Ex-Sgt. MERLE MILLER
Former YANK Staff Writer

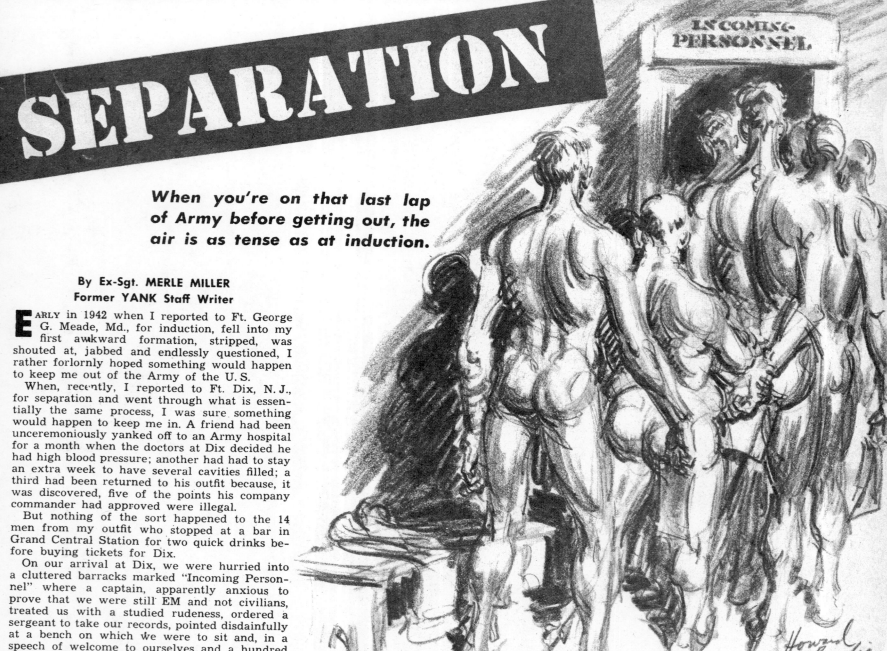

EARLY in 1942 when I reported to Ft. George G. Meade, Md., for induction, fell into my first awkward formation, stripped, was shouted at, jabbed and endlessly questioned, I rather forlornly hoped something would happen to keep me out of the Army of the U. S.

When, recently, I reported to Ft. Dix, N. J., for separation and went through what is essentially the same process, I was sure something would happen to keep me in. A friend had been unceremoniously yanked off to an Army hospital for a month when the doctors at Dix decided he had high blood pressure; another had had to stay an extra week to have several cavities filled; a third had been returned to his outfit because, it was discovered, five of the points his company commander had approved were illegal.

But nothing of the sort happened to the 14 men from my outfit who stopped at a bar in Grand Central Station for two quick drinks before buying tickets for Dix.

On our arrival at Dix, we were hurried into a cluttered barracks marked "Incoming Personnel" where a captain, apparently anxious to prove that we were still EM and not civilians, treated us with a studied rudeness, ordered a sergeant to take our records, pointed disdainfully at a bench on which we were to sit and, in a speech of welcome to ourselves and a hundred other prospective dischargees who soon gathered, several times screamed at us to "pipe down, dammit, or I'll keep you here all day."

Then a corporal who wore a Third Division patch handed each of us a white tag on which, he explained, we were to print our last names, initials and serial numbers before tying the tags to our left breast pockets.

After that, the corporal called out our last names; we shouted our first names and middle initials and stepped up to a counter, where we were given our clothing records and then shown down a long corridor, also lined with counters.

Since my clothing had already been turned in at my previous station, I simply showed a bored private the clean shirt, undershirt, shorts and two pairs of socks in my civilian overnight bag.

"Me," said the private, rather testily, "I'm a lucky bastard. I got 20 goddam points. Twenty." Then, as I turned to leave, he added, "Good luck, chum."

At the end of the corridor, we were met by a pfc who gave us blue cards on which we again printed our names, ranks and serial numbers; then we were herded into a bus and driven to what looked like the company area of any Army post anywhere.

Here we were assigned to a barracks and, once inside, lined up for the usual sheets, pillow cases and GI blankets. As I was making my bunk, slow and easy and being careful to make hospital corners, a weary-looking Fifth Army sergeant said, somewhat sadly, "I'd almost forgotten how, you know, and pretty soon I won't even have to remember."

A sergeant and a corporal were pacing up and down the barracks nervously, chain-smoking but being careful to put each butt in the GI cans conveniently and familiarly placed in front of strategic bunks.

"Anything might happen," said the sergeant. "I had malaria once; they might keep me in for that. Anything might happen."

"A day or so won't matter," the corporal added. "Not after all this time. I mean, even a week or so isn't so much after four years."

They each lighted another cigarette and continued pacing. A few minutes later a permanent-party corporal, who wore a Combat Infantryman's Badge but was obviously on the defensive, came in to tell us there would be a formation at 1645.

"That's 4:45, civilian time," he said.

"How long's it take, corporal?" someone asked him.

"Forty-eight hours," he answered, "after you get on a roster. But it might be a week before you get on one. Might be longer." He said the last somewhat gleefully, as if he hoped it would take longer.

When the corporal left, I dropped off to sleep for what seemed a few minutes, but when I awakened, it was time for the formation. We lined up outside the barracks, almost a hundred of us, and listened to a brash young first lieutenant with a mustache, steel-rimmed glasses and almost no chin.

HE talked in what he obviously hoped was GI jargon, repeating a number of stale jokes and advising us as if we were rather backward children that "pitching woo" (as he called it) in the nearby guest house was frowned on. Then, rather quickly, he told us that the Army was as anxious to get rid of us as we were to get out and that we should be on a roster in the morning.

When he dismissed us, an elderly technical sergeant wearing a patch of the Ninth Division gave him a mock salute and muttered, "Thanks a lot, sonny boy."

By then, it was time for chow, and we fell into a fast-moving line in front of the mess hall.

"I hear the KPs are krauts," said the Ninth Division sergeant. "Dirty krauts." They were krauts, looking surprisingly healthy and well-fed.

"Dirty bastards," the sergeant said, but that was all.

The food was good enough, substantial and unimaginative but plentiful, and after chow we looked at the bulletin boards outside our barracks on which the rosters were posted. We knew our names could not possibly be there until morning, but we looked anyway. It made us feel better.

Then we walked to the PX, bought our cigarette ration and waited at a table in the beer garden until it opened. The beer was warm and not very good, but we drank a lot of it.

"Relaxes you," someone said. "That's the only thing about beer. It relaxes you."

We all agreed that it did, and we spent the evening talking about what we planned to do when we got out, and about officers we'd like to meet again, a few because we suspected that they would really be good guys when they weren't officers any more and a good many more with whom we wanted to settle a score.

When the beer garden closed, we were all a little high, but relaxed, really relaxed. I went to sleep as soon as I hit the sack.

After chow the next morning, we hurried to the bulletin boards, and, sure enough, there were most of our names. Those whose names were missing walked slowly back to the barracks.

"I can't prove I'm not still in Casablanca," said one of them. "I'll probably still be here for the next goddam war."

At 10:15 we lined up outside the barracks, and in a careless, desultory formation walked to a Post Theater. It was the old routine again, like basic training.

Everyone filed into the theater quietly and sat down, nobody talking much.

First, there was the chaplain, a huge, hearty man who boomed at us that we were about to be discharged from the Army, and he supposed we were all pretty unhappy about that. It was a bum gag, but everyone laughed appreciatively. Then he explained about our discharge pay, pointing out that it would be paid in monthly installments, one when we got out, another a month later and, for the great majority of us (those who had been overseas), a third payment a month after that.

He bellowed that we probably wouldn't have too much trouble getting adjusted to civilian life —but that we must be patient with other, more settled civilians. Also that dischargees had a lot of trouble with what he called "pitfalls" in and around Trenton, N. J. He warned us to hang on to our money.

"I hung on to a hell of a lot more money than he's ever seen long before I got in the Army," said a somewhat dispirited man in the row ahead of me.

When the chaplain had finished, a young lieutenant rather diffidently explained that in the afternoon we would meet our counselor, who would tell us about our insurance and the GI Bill of Rights and answer any questions. Then we were handed a card on which to check the questions we wished to ask our counselors.

A few men made checks on theirs, but many of us didn't.

"If they don't know the answer, they may keep you here until they find out," said a corporal. The majority semed to agree with him.

My own counselor was a large, red-faced Irish private who obviously enjoyed beer and drank a good deal of it and explained to me that he had been a newspaper man once himself—and, when he got out of the Army, hoped to be again.

"I guess it's kind of a crowded field, though," he said, rather hopelessly. I agreed that it was.

"You want to know anything?" he asked. I said I didn't.

"Hardly anybody does any more," said the Irishman.

THEN he carefully filled out my Form 100, listing my jobs in the Army and my civilian experience.

"It might come in handy sometime," he said. "I doubt it, but it might."

Then, quite brusquely, he asked: "You don't want to join the Enlisted Reserve, do you?"

"No," I replied

"You know," said the private. "I once had a man who did. He was a pretty smart fellow, too. He thought there was going to be one hell of a depression in this country, and he wanted to keep on eating."

The private paused, then added, "But he was the only one, and I've talked to a lot of guys."

After the counseling, we were through for the day and returned to our barracks. On the way, we passed a formation of men carrying their baggage and with the bright golden discharge emblem on their shirts. They grinned at us.

"Hiya, soldiers," one of them said, then repeated, "soldiers," making it sound like a dirty word.

"A lot of things could still happen," said the sergeant with whom I was walking. "The medics hold up a lot of guys."

"I've got varicose veins," said someone else. "I wonder if that'll make any difference." No one answered. We were thinking of our own minor ailments, wondering if they would matter.

We all drank more beer that evening, but it wasn't as much fun as the night before. Civilian life was too close, and there was still the chance that maybe, somehow, for some obscure Army reason, we wouldn't get out at all.

"We might be civilians tomorrow night at this time," said the technical sergeant from the Ninth Division. "Let's drink to it." We did, but it wasn't much of a toast.

When we marched to the dispensary next morning, nobody talked much, and once inside we took off our clothes and waited. The examination was much like the one that got us into the Army. The doctors looked at us with the same bored expressions.

While we waited for the blood tests, one man paled visibly.

"I've only been back from Paris ten days," he said. "Tell the truth, I'm a little worried."

"You got a bad cavity there," the dentist said to me.

"I know."

"We'd just as soon fix it, free," he continued.

"No," I answered, very politely. "No, thank you very much." The dentist merely shrugged.

After lunch, we turned in our bed clothes and sat down on our empty bunks to wait. The man who could not prove he had left Casablanca was trying to read a book.

"I'll probably have to go back there and then come back here again," he said. "And I'm supposed to meet my girl in New York tonight." He was not even on a roster yet.

When we fell out in front of the barracks with our luggage, the man from Casablanca stood on the porch.

"So long," he said, sadly. "I may not see you again."

We tried to laugh to reassure him, but no one was very successful.

"I heard about a guy that was pulled out at the Finance Office," said the technical sergeant. "It's never too late."

We threw our luggage in a tent that was marked off into compartments, then waited in front of a building marked "Signature Section."

A man had fainted a few minutes before, and the medics had carried him away in a litter.

"They'll probably never let that poor bastard out," said the technical sergeant. He lighted a cigarette, and I was surprised to see that his hand was shaking.

When we got inside the Signature Section, we lined up against a wall and waited until two permanent-party men called off our names. As they reached each name, they placed a folder on a counter, and each man walked over to his own folder.

And then we signed our discharges. I blotted mine in two places. I was still blotting when someone mentioned the Enlisted Reserve again.

At the door we fingerprinted our discharge papers. The corporal in charge of that section was having an argument with a discharge.

"I just asked you to do it the Army way," said the corporal.

The discharge said an unprintable word, then added, "USO Commando."

The corporal did not answer, but when the discharge had gone out the door he said, "I guess it doesn't matter, but I was with the 34th."

Then we walked back and picked up our luggage, waiting outside while a few men ran to another tent to salvage some equipment.

In a few minutes, our guide, a newly inducted private who was an apologetic 18, took us to a squat, unbeautiful building inside of which were rows of men at sewing machines. Each of us had discharge patches sewn over the right pocket of either one or two shirts.

As we put on our shirts again, I felt confident for the first time. But not for long.

"A guy in the barracks got yanked in the Finance Office," repeated the tech sergeant. "Last minute. Been here eight days."

We dropped our luggage in the compartmentalized tent again and walked to the Finance Office. The building was crowded, and our guide told us it would be 45 minutes, at least, before we got in, so we wandered to the PX.

We all ordered cokes, but none of us drank a full bottle.

A corporal, who had loudly sworn off smoking but then borrowed a cigarette, lighted it and said:

"You guys finish your cokes. I think I'll go back."

We all drank a huge gulp of coke, then set down the bottles and hurried back to the Finance Office. We had been gone exactly five minutes, and we still had almost an hour to wait.

Finally we got inside the building and sat on the same kind of hard benches as in "Incoming Personnel." After about 15 minutes more, they began calling our names, and we stepped up to

the cashier's cage, where we were each given $50 in cash, the rest of our pay (minus allotments) in a check, plus the first instalment of our mustering-out pay. Also the small gold discharge button.

As we stepped out into the sunshine again, the tech sergeant smiled for the first time.

"Not a damn thing can happen now," he said. "Not a damn thing. I'm a damn civilian." His eyes were watering, not much, just enough to be noticeable.

When the last man came out of the Finance Office, we lined up quietly and started for the chapel. We knew what was going to happen there; we'd been told at least a dozen times by men who'd already been through it, but we were a little frightened anyway.

AN organ was playing when we marched in, wearing our ties and silent, and we sat down in neat rows, while the organist ran through "The Old Grey Mare," "Glory, Glory Hallelujah" and some hymns I didn't recognize.

A chaplain said something, I don't remember what, and then a very old and very small lieutenant colonel stood up, smiling through what were obviously not his own teeth.

I looked out of the window and saw a handful of new arrivals walking with their barracks bags toward a company area, and I didn't want to pay any attention to what the old colonel was saying. It was corn, pure corn, about the Army appreciating what we had done and about how most of us hadn't gotten the breaks we deserved, but it was a big army and we knew how those things are, and finally about the war we'd won and what a great thing we'd accomplished for our great country.

It was obvious that it was a speech the old man had made many times, but I didn't care. I thought it was a fine speech.

When an enlisted man began calling off the names and men began stepping up to the colonel, saluting him, getting his store-teeth smile and a handshake and their discharge papers, I realized I was making a damned fool of myself. I needed a handkerchief and didn't have one. [ED. NOTE: We feel obliged to point out that ex-Sgt. Miller is the type that also weeps at movies.]

After I had my own discharge paper and was waiting outside, the tech sergeant came up, grinned at me and said, "I think I could kiss you, but I think I won't." Instead, he just patted me on the back, like a football coach congratulating a player after a winning game.

We walked to where we had left our luggage.

"I was planning to knock the block off that bastard captain we saw when we got here—" said the sergeant. Then he paused.

"—but I don't know why the hell I should bother," he concluded.

As we drove out of the gate a few minutes later, a bus load of men who were obviously potential dischargees was just coming in.

"Hiya, soldiers," I said, and waved. "Soldiers," I repeated.

None of them heard what I said, and it really didn't matter. After all, I was a civilian again.

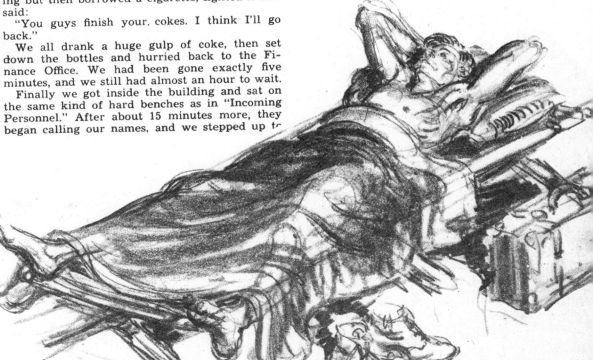

OUT SIX MONTHS

Two veterans separated last spring find that discharge papers aren't passports to every GI dream, but that civilian life still beats the Army every time.

By Sgt. DEBS MYERS
YANK Staff Writer

BACK when he was a pfc in France, Bill Schiffman used to dream about getting out of the Army and having an apartment of his own in New York City, with a fireplace and a black bearskin rug with a blonde cutie nestling on it. In this vision the blonde cutie would fetch steaks and house slippers and cigars and brandy to ex-Pfc. Schiffman, and she would look at him all wriggly-eyed, like he was the greatest and most explosive discovery since gun-powder.

It had to wait, of course, until Pfc. Schiffman got out of the Army, on account when a man got out of the Army there were all kinds of big jobs lying around. All a man had to do was to take a big job and become a wealthy playboy. The newspaper advertisements said so. Pfc. Schiffman couldn't think of anything nicer than being a GI Tommy Manville.

It was nice work, but Pfc. Schiffman didn't get it.

In the first place, he couldn't even get an apartment. He got out of the Army at Fort Dix, N. J., on June 28, 1945, and he is back living where he did before the war, with his parents and two sisters, at 28 Metropolitan Oval, in the Bronx, N. Y.

In case you haven't heard about it, there is a housing shortage in New York City and almost all other cities. There weren't any apartments that he could afford, and there weren't many blondes he could afford either. In both cases there were long waiting lists.

Not, mind you, that Bill is sorry he is out of the Army. He is so glad to be a civilian that sometimes he wakes up in the middle of the night and sits by the window chain-smoking, saying to himself: "I don't have to take any more crap from any sonuvabitch in the world."

For the first three weeks after he got out of the Army, Bill slept a lot, ate a lot and staged a couple of spirited running drunks with his cronies. But he got tired fast of playing the honky-tonk circuit.

"The prices are murder," he said, "and those joints are so full of phonies it makes a guy want to throw up."

After three weeks Bill, who is 25, got a job with the New York *Daily News* as a circulation inspector, which means that he is a trouble-shooter who sees that the papers reach the news-stands on schedule. He makes $40 a week. This is not the kind of money that enables him to go in for black bearskin rugs garnished with blondes, but he is paying his bills and having a good if not gaudy time.

It took about two months for Bill to realize that he actually was out of the Army. He kept being afraid that some officer would find him lolling around enjoying himself and start figuring out ways to make him miserable again.

When he saw an officer coming toward him down the street, Bill always put his hands in his pockets. He wasn't afraid of forgetting himself and saluting the officer, because he always had been an accomplished salute-dodger. Instead, Bill shoved his hands in his pocket as a means of convincing himself that he was his own

Former Pfc. Bill Schiffman turns the radiator up high and the radio low, then sits there feeling good as hell.

boss again—that the days of having to swing his arms by his side were gone forever.

"That's a great thing just in itself," Bill said, "knowing that you can put your hands in your pockets any damn time you want to."

Also, he goes bareheaded a lot. He never liked wearing hats, and he always was sure he looked silly in an Army cap. In five years and two months in the Army he never learned to wear an overseas cap so that it didn't leave about four kilometers of hair sticking out the left side.

WHEN Bill gets up in the afternoon (he works nights), he takes 10 minutes selecting his clothes. This is one of the high points of the day for him.

"That's one of the great things that can happen to a guy," he says, "worrying about whether to wear a blue or a gray suit, and whether to put on a red tie or a green one. For some reason it makes a fellow feel independent as all hell."

He takes at least one and sometimes two or three hot showers a day. He thinks it is criminal letting hot water go to waste without washing in it. He thinks the people talking about another war should have to spend a couple of months washing and shaving out of a half-helmet of cold water.

He talked the Army into letting him wait to have some cavities in his teeth filled until he became a civilian. "It seemed pretty strange," he said, "going to the dentist and having the same dentist work on me from one day to another. This dentist even remembered my name. He called me Mister Schiffman—there was none of that 'sit down, soldier.'"

There were a couple of officers Bill always wanted to sock. He used to tell himself that if the time ever came when he met one of these officers on the street, he would walk up quiet-like and throw his Sunday punch.

The other day he met one of the officers. They

passed each other, nodded and that was all there was to it.

"You know the guy is a bastard," says Bill, "but it isn't important enough any more to do anything about it. You figure the officer probably is having enough trouble, anyway, having to get used to his old job as a soda-jerk or a floor-walker in a 10-cent store."

Bill brought home some pictures he took at the Dachau concentration camp in Germany. Sometimes he shows these pictures to visitors at his home.

"The visitors look kind of hard at these pictures of people who have been starved and tortured," says Bill, "and they usually say something polite about how terrible it is and then they change the subject real fast. They start talking about how the price of lard went up two cents. People don't want to seem to know about bad things. I think it's probably too bad that pictures don't stink. If these people could smell those poor, rotting guys in the pictures, it might do some good."

After Bill went into the Army on April 17, 1940, as a member of the enlisted reserve, he took infantry basic at Fort Warren, Wyo. Then he was shipped to Alaska with a harbor-boat detachment. He went into the Air Cadets, washed out and became a radio operator with an Air Force ground crew. He was in the Sixth Tactical Air Communications Squadron in France, Belgium, Holland and Germany.

He liked only one thing about the Army: the guys he got to know.

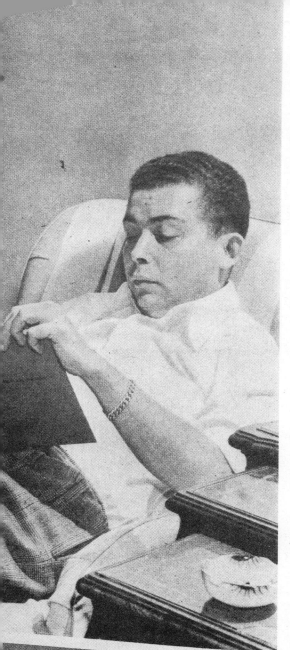

E VEN so, he has lost touch with his old friends, most of whom also are out of the Army and scattered over the country. He has written to several of them, but hasn't received any answers.

Back in France, he used to think that he would spend a lot of time as a civilian bulling around with Army cronies. Instead he came back and started associating with the same friends he had before he went into the Army.

Most of these friends also were in the Army and are out on points or disability. Some of his friends, of course, are still in service. Others won't be coming back at all.

"We almost never talk about the Army," Bill says. "There weren't any of us heroes, and we would feel kind of foolish talking about our experiences. There is one guy who runs around with us who was a 4-F weighing about 110 pounds. Sometimes we kid him a little and call him Atlas, but he is just as much one of the gang as any of us. Not being in the Army doesn't make any difference."

Bill says that a man takes his life into his hands when he goes into a bar these days. There always is a man or two in every bar, he says, who is telling a story about how he was alone on a hill, cut off and surrounded.

"The bullets and the whisky are flying fast as hell," he says. "Some of these guys have been there and know what they're talking about. And there are lots of guys doing a lot of talking who haven't been there. The other day I heard a fellow telling two girls how he strangled one German and bayoneted another one. This guy was wearing only one ribbon, a Good Conduct medal. That guy will be better off if he leaves those girls alone, and puts that Good Conduct medal on his fly."

Now and then, maybe when he has just had a quick drink and a long meal, Bill gets to thinking about the good guys he has known and he thinks maybe the Army wasn't quite as bad as he always knew it was.

When those times come, Bill starts thinking real

Former Pfc. Maurice Elwood found civilian garb cured lots of things.

fast about the rain and the cold, the guff and the chicken, the marches and the mauling, the guys who won't be coming home and those fellows at Dachau with their ribs sticking out of sores on their sides, and Bill knows he is a lucky guy to have made it. He turns the radiator up high and the radio down low. He sits there and feels good as hell.

M AURICE ELWOOD is another discharged soldier who thinks, as Bill Schiffman does, that there isn't much wrong with a soldier that a pin-striped suit and a gray felt hat won't cure. Elwood is a 40-year-old, six-foot Irishman with a brogue that smacks of County Mayo. He was a rifleman with the 141st Infantry, 36th Division. He went into the Army in March 1942 and went to North Africa in April 1943. He fought in Africa, Tunisia and Italy. He was hit in the right leg by shell fragments outside Cassino in October 1944 and finally got a CDD last April. He was a pfc.

Elwood is a maintenance pipe-fitter on the Interborough Rapid Transit lines in New York City. He belongs to the Transport Workers' Union, the Veterans of Foreign Wars and the Catholic War Veterans. He makes $51 a week. He isn't married.

Elwood (he says he doesn't know how he ever got a name like Maurice) thinks it is easier to talk with soldiers, or former soldiers, than it is to talk with people who never have been in the Army.

"Civilians ask such funny damn questions," he says. "They kind of want to handle you with care, like maybe they'll say the wrong thing. Now and then one of 'em will say something pretty silly. Like a friend who asked me the other day if I wouldn't like to take a vacation in the mountains. Mountains, this friend says. Look, after Italy, I'm going to leave mountains strictly to mountain goats and damned fool tourists who think they're mountain goats."

Elwood is a little worried about the talk that soldiers are angry at unions. He prides himself on being a good union man. The union won a 20-cents-an-hour raise for him while he was gone. He thinks the unions did a great job keeping up wage and hour standards while the war was on.

"I don't think the soldiers have heard both sides of the story," he says. "The union side doesn't get printed much. I'm not defending everything that all of the unions have done. But I think, all in all, the unions have done a good job. I think it would be the worst possible thing that could happen to the United States if the veterans and the unions squared off against each other."

Elwood says being home is great, but nothing is as good as a fellow thinks it is going to be, if he thinks about it too much.

"I used to think I was going to eat about five meals a day, once I got home," he says. "Hell, I can't do it. I dunno, maybe a fellow gets out of the habit of eating a lot. I used to dream about eating all kinds of steak and dessert. It's hard on a fellow to realize he can't eat as much as he used to think he could. It's downright humiliatin'."

Elwood believes that Franklin Roosevelt was one of the greatest men who ever lived; that President Truman is doing a good job; that there should be compulsory military training so that the Army discharge rate can be stepped up, and that guys who served together in the Army should keep on being friends after they leave the Army.

But he has just about quit asking what happened to old friends of his in the 36th Division. Too many of them are dead. It was a long road from the desert to the mountains past Rome, and the 36th went all the way.

Elwood doesn't talk about the war. He likes for things to be quiet. He figures that he did enough fighting overseas to last him for a long time. Only once in a while does he get a trifle ruffled.

The other day he went into a candy store. The saleslady looked at him and snapped:

"How is it that a big hulking man like you can stay out of uniform when my little boy had to go overseas last month?"

Elwood rubbed his chin and did a slow burn. He figured it would not be worth it to choke her with her own chocolates.

"I dunno, lady," he said, "some of us Irish are just born lucky."

YANK
THE ARMY WEEKLY

YANK is published weekly by the enlisted men of the U. S. Army and is for sale only to those in the armed services. Stories, features, pictures and other material from YANK may be reproduced if they are not restricted by law or military regulation, provided proper credit is given, release dates are observed and specific prior permission has been granted for each item to be reproduced. Entire contents Vol. 4, No. 28, copyrighted, 1945, by Col. Franklin S. Forsberg.

MAIN EDITORIAL OFFICE
205 EAST 42d STREET, NEW YORK 17, N. Y.

EDITORIAL STAFF

Managing Editor, Sgt. Al Hine, Engr.; Art Director, Sgt. Charles Brand, AAF; Assistant Managing Editor, Sgt. Jonathan Kilbourn, Sig. Corps; Assistant Art Director, Sgt. Frank Brandt, Med.; Pictures, Sgt. Leo Hofeller, Armd.; Features, Sgt. Ray Duncan, AAF; Overseas Editor, Sgt. Debs Myers, Inf.; U. S. Editor, Sgt. Allan B. Ecker, AAF; Navy Editor, Donald Nugent Sp(X)3c; Associate Editors, Sgt. John Hay, Inf.; Sgt. William McNeany, Inf.; Sgt. Max Novack, TC.

WASHINGTON, Sgt. H. N. Oliphant, Engr.; Sgt. John Haverstick, CA.

JAPAN, Sgt. Robert MacMillan, FA; Sgt. Knox Burger, AAF; Sgt. George Burns, Sig. Corps; Sgt. Mike Detzer, Inf.; Sgt. Dale Kramer, MP; Sgt. Bill Lindau, Inf.; Sgt. Jack Ruge, DEML; Cpl. James Keeney, Sig. Corps; Robert Schwartz Y2c, USNR; Evan Wylie CSp (PR), USCGR.

PHILIPPINES, Sgt. Jack Fields, DEML; Sgt. Frank Beck, AAF; Sgt. Joe Stefanelli, Engr.; Sgt. Bill Young, Inf.; Cpl. Jim Gianladis, Inf.; Cpl. Channing Hadlock, AAF; Cpl. Ralph Izard, Engr.; Cpl. Don Michel, AAF.

CENTRAL PACIFIC, Sgt. Harry Tomlinson, DEML.

MARIANAS, Sgt. James Goble, Armd.; Vernon H. Roberts PhoM3c, USNR.

RYUKYUS, Sgt. Norbert Hildebrand, DEML.

FRANCE, Sgt. Georg Meyers, AAF; Sgt. Pat Coffey, AAF; Sgt. William Frazer, AAF; Sgt. David Whitcomb, AAF; Cpl. Howard Katzander, CA.

BRITAIN, Sgt. Edmund Antrobus, Inf.

ITALY, Sgt. Donald Breimhurst, AAF; Sgt. Nelson Gruppo, Engr.; Sgt. Norbert Hofman, DEML; Sgt. Dave Shaw, Inf.; Cpl. Ira Freeman, Cav.

INDIA-BURMA and CHINA, Sgt. John Blay, Inf.; Sgt. Jud Cook, DEML.

ALASKA, Sgt. Tom Shehan, FA.

AFRICA-MIDDLE EAST-PERSIAN GULF, Sgt. Richard Paul, DEML.

ICELAND, Sgt. Gordon Farrel, AAF.

Commanding Officer, Col. Franklin S. Forsberg.

Executive Officer, Lt. Col. Jack W. Weeks.

Business Manager, Maj. Gerald J. Rock.

OVERSEAS BUREAU OFFICERS. France, Maj. Harry R. Roberts; Capt. Jack Silverstein. assistant; Philippines, Capt. Max Gilstrap; Japan, Maj. Lewis Gillenson; Central-South Pacific, Maj. Henry E. Johnson; Marianas, Capt. Knowlton Ames; Ryukyus, Capt. Merle P. Millham; Italy, Capt. Howard Carswell; Burma-India, Capt. Harold A. Burroughs; Panama, Capt. Charles H. E. Stubblefield; Africa-Middle East-Persian Gulf, Maj. Frank Gladstone.

This Week's Cover

is YANK's last cover. It needs no explanation. So long and good luck.

PHOTO CREDITS: 4 & 5—Sgt. George Aarons. 6—Top, Sgt. Ben Schnall; bottom, Sgt. John Frano. 7—Sgt. Aarons. 8—Sgt. DeWitt Gilpin. 10—Sgt. George Burns. 12—Columbia Pictures, 20th Century-Fox, MGM, Michael Levelle, Samuel Goldwyn Pictures, Ewing Krainin, Universal Pictures, Horst, Hurrell, Arthur Macauley, Monogram Pictures. 15—Acme. 18 & 19—Cpl. Brown Roberts.

Mail Call

Lest We Forget

Dear YANK:

Not so many months after they returned from the last war, many of our fathers and older brothers and friends had already forgotten the mud, the trenches and the fatigue, the blood and the fear of battle. They could remember only the camaraderie.

Our fathers forgot the hellish symphony of shells, but the music of "Mademoiselle from Armentieres" stuck in their minds.

In a vague sort of way, the veterans of World War I realized that they had lost something besides time, in the years they'd been in the Army—and that they'd earned more than the mere plaudits of crowds watching them parade. But most of them, those who were comparatively healthy at least, totted it up in terms of wealth. And when they asked to be reimbursed, the vast majority asked for money.

They got their bonus, but in a sense they lost their war. And when, with the advent of World War II, they realized that their own war had been lost, they never realized that they had had a large share in losing it.

The veterans of this war will not, of course, forget the camaraderie any more than did the veterans of the last. The men who fought in World War II will get together, as their fathers did, to shoot the bull about times past, about India, Sicily, Iran, Normandy, Guadalcanal, Okinawa or wherever.

Although they have no common song the equal of "Mademoiselle" to sing, they'll have their ditties and they'll sing them. Some of them will get roaring drunk. And there's nothing wrong with that.

But there is a dreadful danger that these meetings will degenerate into nothing more than this—that the average veteran of this war, like the average veteran of the last, will let others plan his veterans' program—if any—for him. There's a terrible possibility that all of us will forget. Not that we'll forget merely the agony of battle or even the constant, minor humiliations of an EM's garrison life—for these things it's probably best for us at least partially to forget if we are ever to become useful citizens again. The great danger is that we'll forget the reasons why we fought the war.

We must not forget that we fought, if only indirectly and sometimes unconsciously, for the right of peaceful people to live out their lives in pursuit of greater liberty and happiness; against tyranny which would subjugate not only our minds and bodies but those of the whole human race; against fear—the fear of death and the other forms of fear that eat away the mind.

We must not forget that we fought as the free citizens of a democracy, although the Army sometimes failed to allow us to realize it; and that unless we continue that fight for freedom and democracy now and in the future, with the physical battle won, the struggle for which so many of our friends gave their lives will be tragically lost.

Lest we forget all this, I suggest that each man readying himself for the return to civilian life plan a program for himself, a kind of set of resolutions that he can refer to from time to time in the months after he becomes a civilian again. It should be a program that he and his fellow veterans can demand of America in place of, or at least in addition to, any specific individual benefits. It should be a program that will make veterans as a group a potent and meaningful force in America's future.

I don't pretend that my program is complete. But I believe each point in it is important and one that every veteran should be able to—and should—subscribe to. My program would run something like this:

1) The men who fought and died for America were of many races and religions. Negro and Nisei, Catholic, Protestant and Jew all fought valiantly together. You might say, if the Constitution didn't already stress it, that this alone earned them the right to recognition as equals. Let's see that they get it.

2) In the Army we were thrown together with people from all walks of life, farmer and union laborer, small manufacturer and professional man. We learned that most of the men we worked with were not malingerers, and that men who are can come from any group. We learned to respect the other fellow's point of view, to accept what he said, even when we disagreed, as his honest opinion. So even when we disagree with, say, the union man when he goes out on strike, let's realize that he's doing it from honest conviction—and maybe real need. Let's recognize our fellow citizens' right to security and a living wage.

3) We were all fed up with the bull that was thrown at us in the Army, too often, about little things—the importance of saluting, for example—and the big things involved in the war. They only reflected, as we realized, confusion back home—confusion, ineptitude and politics in the Army and, even more, in Congress. More and more of us came to think that much of the bull that is slung in the Army, and on the floor of Congress as well, is the result of corrupt, unthinking political rule—corrupt not in the sense of grafting but in the sense of being in office merely for personal advantage, for what can be gotten out of it. Let's not stand for old-line politics. Let's get into politics ourselves—get in at the bottom, in cities, in the districts of cities. You can't build at the top without rebuilding the rotten underpinnings. Let's demand political straightforwardness.

4) Last of all, let's fight to democratize the Army and follow the fight through logically. Almost all of us will join veterans' organizations. Let's not forget what we learned in the Army about the lack of democracy we all found so galling. Our organizations can fight for a change. But they should do more. Let's not allow our organizations to degenerate into mere drinking and singing societies. Let's have them lead the fight for the democratic spirit throughout the U. S. and the world.

Let's demand these things, when we ask for reimbursement, as veterans, for what we've lost—and for winning what we've won—and make our tentative victory a certain one.

Korea   **Cpl. ACKERMAN J. MICHAELS**

Just Beginning

Dear YANK:

The worst has happened. No longer are the EM one big happy family. We have been divided into two categories—low-pointers and high-pointers. At this repple depple, we low-pointers are looked on as so much dirt. Those with high points remain aloof and don't want anything to do with us.

I know a lot of points have been built up by men having families and battle stars (both the easy way and the line way) and for meritorious-service Bronze

"Oh, Lord, here comes another one!"

—Sgt. Tom Flannery

star medals. But what the hell, whether high or low—we were all put in our respective places to help win the war. Some were fortunate and others got the so-called raw deal.

What I would like to see is more consideration for low-point men. After all, our sweating is just beginning. We are the ones left over here to finish the occupation job. You high-pointers had our sympathy and applause while we were training in the States. What say we turn the tables now? Let's not have a two-way split like the officers; you know—second lieutenants and officers.

Italy —(Name Withheld)

Atomic Secrets

Dear YANK:

I disagree with these learned professors who say we should share the secret of the atomic bomb with other nations.

I remember how not long ago we were selling scrap iron to Japan, only to have it used against our own boys. The atomic bomb is such a terrible weapon of war that it would be a disaster if it got into the wrong hands.

Who holds the atomic bomb holds the destiny of the world, and while I have full confidence in all Allied nations, I think they should in return have sufficient confidence in us to let the U. S. keep the secret of the bomb.

Italy —Pfc. FLAVIUS MORRIS

Dear YANK:

It seems to me that the surest way to bring peace is to give the secret of the atomic bomb to all nations, except, of course, Germany and Japan.

This bomb is so deadly that no country would ever dare to declare war if it knew the other countries were also equipped with atomic bombs. In other words, a nation would be afraid to declare war, knowing the horrible results both sides would suffer.

If we don't share the secret of the bomb, each nation will start a race to develop a super-atomic bomb, with the result that the country that does make such a bomb could rule the world. If all countries had the bomb, no one country would ever be all-powerful.

Italy —Cpl. HARRIS COBURN

Broken Promises

Dear YANK:

Both President Truman and the War Department are advocating the enlistment of enlisted men in the Enlisted Reserve Corps upon discharge from active duty. However, if the campaign to enlist men in the ERC is to succeed, certain discrepancies must be cleared up. Possibly President Truman is unaware of the poor reputation enjoyed by the ERC, but the WD cannot be unaware of the bad feeling that it has stirred up because of its handling of ERC men.

During 1942, a very active bid was made to get enlistments for the ERC. The Army appealed particularly to college students and advertised the ERC as something comparable to the Navy's V-1, V-7 and V-12 programs. ERC men were not to be called to active duty "until exigencies of the service demanded it," were to be given their choice of arm or service and were to be given first opportunity of acceptance for OCS.

As the program was administered, 200,000 men were disappointed and disillusioned with the Army. As soon as enlistments in the ERC were closed, the WD began to announce that ERC men would be called to duty any day. Upon call to active duty, over 90 percent of the men were assigned to IRTC and upon completion of basic were assigned to units alerted for overseas shipment. The WD completely ignored its promises to those men as soon as they had been sworn into the Army. What made the situation worse was that the comparable Navy programs were carried through as they had been represented, and many in the Army felt they had enlisted in the wrong service.

Now the WD is resurrecting the ERC. The promises this time—that men enlisting in the ERC will retain rank held at time of release from active duty, will have opportunity for promotion to higher enlisted grades and in the case of qualified personnel to commissioned grade, etc., etc., etc.—sound good, as did the promises of 1942. Too bad it's impossible to believe them.

—(Name Withheld)

Vaughan Gen. Hosp., Hines, Ill.

Wasted Money

Dear YANK:

Practically every man in this Army has witnessed incidents where the armed forces have squandered public funds to no end. One of the more outstanding examples of such squandering is the magnificent naval officers' club constructed on New Caledonia. This paradise was constructed with Navy labor out of Quonset-type metal buildings which were originally meant for naval warehouses.

The Army also contributed a monument to the taxpayers' money on New Caledonia. They built a junior Pentagon Building for Army Headquarters which will probably be inherited by the French Government. This building was not needed and was uncalled for, because the Headquarters was previously adequately quartered during the period when the South Pacific was a combat theater. This was constructed in the latter part of 1944 after the South Pacific was known as an inactive theater of operations. We were told that the building, which was tremendous and luxurious for an Army headquarters, was constructed from materials found in depot stock which would have otherwise gone to waste.

If this material was going to waste, someone was responsible, and it is hard to believe that such items as mohair rugs, venetian blinds and flush-type toilets could be found in an overseas depot. It is possible that such antics as those above were carried out on other islands in the Pacific, but I feel there is no room for complaints if the islands were to remain U. S. property after the war.

I say, let the public in on some of the deals they faithfully financed with their war bonds.

Philippines —(Name Withheld)

Last Issue

Dear YANK:

I read recently that YANK is scheduled to cease publication in December, and I can only say what a shame. You probably will never fully know how much YANK has meant to millions of soldiers, even less of the great esteem in which you are held by officers, especially ex-GIs, so-called 90-day wonders. We particularly have always turned to YANK (almost surreptitiously at times) for damned fine news reporting and amusing features. Re the latter, the more satirical, the better. And we always felt a sort of secret nostalgic pride in being able to share in the life and living of those from whom we had been arbitrarily isolated by "an act of Congress."

You, YANK, and those of whom you wrote are the real gentlemen of this war. I, for one of many, am truly sorry to see you demobilized, yet equally glad that you can be.

—1st Lt. RICHARD S. BALL

Camp Edwards, Mass.

Labor and Vets

Dear YANK:

For the last 45 months I've listened to Orientation officers and I & E officers tell us how important a job labor did in getting out the war materials and equipment that made us certain of winning the war. And the Army, through its official handouts and statements from the big brass, went out of the way to praise the production on the home front. Well, that made sense to me then and it does now.

But since I've been home from Italy all I read about in the papers is how labor strikes tied up ships that might have been used to bring back the boys from overseas, and in general how much a bunch of dangerous radicals all strikers are. The general effect, if not the purpose, of such articles, seems to be to drive a wedge between labor and the returning veteran, something we've been trying to prevent throughout the war.

Now I'm no authority on labor strikes and I'm not always in a position to know what the issues in a particular strike may be, but I have a suspicion that we're certainly not getting all the facts from many of the newspapers we read. It may be true that the striking longshoremen in New York did hold up GIs returning from Europe, and I agree it's a damn shame. However, it might be a good idea for us GIs to think twice before we go off half cocked on condemning strikers, at least until we make a serious attempt to understand what all these strikes are about. When you get down to it, the problems of labor will be the problems of the great majority of returning servicemen. We're all in the same boat, and the conditions that affect them will affect the GI tomorrow.

So let's be careful that we don't make ourselves a bunch of suckers for a lot of people who would be tickled to death to create an artificial wedge between the returning servicemen and organized labor.

—T/Sgt. SIMEON BRAGUIN

Camp Stewart, Ga.

Lousy Lovers?

Dear YANK:

I am in the mood for passing a few comments on the following clipping from a London paper:

> GIs HAVE LOST THE ART OF LOVE
>
> American soldiers are losing the art of love, says an anonymous letter from an American Army nurse to the U. S. Army newspaper *Stars and Stripes*.
>
> It is because they have had it so easily in Europe with chewing gum and candy bars.
>
> "No wonder we prefer French and British Army personnel who are more subtle," she remarks.
>
> The letter ended with a warning that when the soldiers get back to the States, they were not going to get the first maid with their candy and chewing gum, because that is about all they have left.—Reuter.

I have known many Yanks, the majority all nice boys. Most of them came straight from the States to our country.

I don't believe any of them ever *did* have the art of love-making. I was under the impression that the Americans were great lovers; *they* certainly think they are. But, blimey, they don't know the first thing about love-making.

Incidentally, sincere Yanks and girls here always saw that the kiddies in the street had the candy and gum. Of course, some of our girls were affable when courted with gum, but they are no different than the gold diggers in every country. I suppose the States do have such girls?

So, nurse, I think you are wrong. In fact, the love-making of the Yanks has always left me wondering what American women are like to put up with such poor technique!

Of course, there are always the exceptions, and anyhow, boys, you've been grand company.

Britain —LEE GLITHRO

Military Justice

Dear YANK:

Recent public attacks on the Army courts-martial system have brought into focus a situation which has been in need of corrective action for some time. The appointment of a civilian board of review constitutes a step in the proper direction, but it only catches errors after commission. A possible amendment, much closer to the source and one which would serve to eliminate rather than note discrepancies, has apparently been overlooked, to wit: the discontinuance of the practice of indiscriminately selecting officers to serve as members of the court who lack proper dignity, judicial temperament, training, experience, adaptable backgrounds and an understanding of the fundamentals of military law.

Under the provisions of Article of War 19, courts-martial cases are required to be determined "according to the evidence"—that is, solely on the basis of matters introduced before the court at the trial, and on the basis of the facts of which the court may, under the provisions of the Manual for Courts-Martial, take judicial notice.

Yet, chosen from the organization to which an accused is assigned, through pre-trial discussion, from personal knowledge of the offense and the accused, their belief as to the existence of local regulations, which, in fact, may not be in force, these officers usually, unintentionally but humanly, form a definite opinion as to the accused's innocence or guilt.

Often they come to court without having read the Manual for Courts-Martial in an endeavor to correct their deficiencies and to see that justice is properly administered, thereby rendering themselves incompetent to serve as members of a courts-martial board. It is conceivable that they do not have time to ferret out the principles of military justice; but, whatever the reason, it cannot justify the fact that as a result of their misconceptions and ignorance of the rules they materially injure the rights of an accused by basing decisions on personal knowledge, what may be no more than rumor, or someone else's opinion.

This present method, which so apparently precludes impartiality, could be effectually remedied and the rights of an accused substantially protected, if a system corresponding to the following general outline could be established:

1) The designation of the Judge Advocate General's Department as a separate arm or service.

2) The founding of a School of Military Justice to which qualified candidates could be detailed as has been done with other branches of OCS, said school to be operated under the supervision of the aforementioned arm or service.

3) The inclusion in each T/O of at least one commissioned graduate of the School of Military Justice.

4) The establishment of a Judicial-Administrative School for enlisted men which would teach the fundamentals of military law and the proper procedure for the preparation of legal records.

5) The inclusion in each T/O of a minimum of one graduate of the Judicial-Administrative School whose duty would be to assist the Military Justice Officer.

India —(Name Withheld)

Dear YANK:

Yesterday we received two simultaneous announcements of courts-martial proceedings and their findings. One case involved an officer who was caught red-handed trying to steal Quartermaster rations. When apprehended by the guard, he offered him a bribe (whisky and a wrist watch). The officer was found guilty on several counts and given a $100 fine and reprimanded by the commanding general.

The other case involved a private who misconducted himself while drunk, offering no violence, but simply acting boisterous. This private received a six-month sentence at hard labor, in addition to other penalties.

I, as well as most of us, donned the uniform of our country to fight for various reasons. Is it small wonder then that we've come to hate the very instrument that was supposed to have established the four freedoms all over the earth?

Things of that nature will never be erased from our memories, and they serve to make us lose faith in the great ideals that we have just fought for.

Britain —(Name Withheld)

More Chicken

Dear YANK:

If you think that cutting grass with bayonets is bad, what do you think of moving the great Mohave Desert with shovels and brooms? That is exactly the situation that exists here at Muroc.

Having nothing better for the crews (all back from the Twentieth Air Force for lead-crew training) to do, the administrative officers decided that all enlisted men and one officer from each crew should spend time sweeping and shoveling the ever-shifting sand from the streets and squadron area.

We don't doubt the fact that this work is very effective, but that effect is short-lived, for after about five minutes a strong wind replenishes the layers of sand in the squadron area from the never-ending supply of the Mohave.

Muroc AAF, Calif. —(Four Names Withheld)

Dear YANK:

This morning our company again formed for morning exercises. The exercises were again an example of the additional humiliation that is being heaped upon us before discharge.

We were assigned a partner. Told to put our right hand around his neck. He did likewise. The order was tramp on your opponent's feet or he on yours. A despotic order. Failure to comply with same would bring you additional humiliation in front of the entire company, as I was soon to find out. The second exercise was completed by placing heads against each other's shoulders, pushing forward, punching your opponent in the stomach.

The third routine was accomplished by placing the right hand on the opponent's neck while the left hand was placed against the opponent's right. The order was to wrestle until one man fell. As I didn't (get this chicken) "put enough into it," I was ordered to give a demonstration by our company commander (former West Point lad). The company witnessed same in silence while the officers watched laughing, as they had previously while the other boys pummeled themselves for fear of the consequences.

This is an example of what returning vets are going through before the great day when our points total discharge.

Camp Carson, Colo. —(Name Withheld)

YANK
THE ARMY WEEKLY

CARTOONS

"Oh, fudge."
—Sgt. Douglas Borgstedt

"He's what is known as an enlisted man."
—Sgt. Jim Weeks

"Don't be silly, darling. They'll adore you!"
—Pfc. Joe Kramer

"Frankly, fellows, I need the extra dough."
—Cpl. Hugh Kennedy

"—In short, the paper shortage at this station may be termed critical."
—Cpl. Frank R. Robinson

"Excellent wine, Captain. Put this place off-limits at once."
—Cpl. Irwin Touster

—Pvt. Walter Mansfield

"I've been restricted to quarters aga
—Pvt. Art K

"Who's runnin' this ship, anyhow? . . .
You or me?"
—Sgt. George Mandel

"Is that you, Master Sergeant O'Leary?"
—Sgt. Frank Brandt

—Sgt. Tom Flannery

"They call him Radar. He'll pick up anything."
—Sgt. Tom Zibelli

suppose you know you're out of uni-
rm . . ."
—Sgt. Ozzie St. George

"He's not much good, but he rattles the
other pitcher."
—Sgt. Charles Pearson

—Sgt. Bill Mauldin

"I need fatherly advice, sir."
—Cpl. Ernest Maxwell

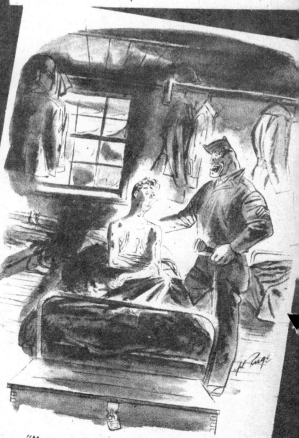

"Merry Christmas. You're on KP."
—Sgt. Jack Ruge

VETERAN'S
20th *Annual*
★ REUNION ★

"... So I said to the general, 'The way I figure it is, they'll try to strike on our left flank, and if I were you, sir'—I still called him sir, understand, because I was as yet a pfc—'if I were you, sir, I'd pull the heavy-weapons company around there.' Well, to make a long story short, that's how we managed to close the gap. Mind you, you won't find it in the history books, but it was no coincidence that I made corporal the next week. There was some talk about a Congressional Medal, but about that time I was shacking with a little number the colonel in charge of the motor pool had his eye on. One night he comes around to her place, early, and I don't take off in time because I don't hear him coming. Well, to make a long story short, that's how I got busted to private. I never told you, did I, about the time Ike inspected our outfit and there I was in the front rank? Well, he comes up just in time, because I had the germ of an idea kicking around in my head and I couldn't get next to our own CO, on account of prejudice against me from some of the junior officers, so I caught Ike's eye as he was passing down the line, and I said, 'General, the way I see it is . . .'"

—Sgt. Tom Flannery and Sgt. Al Hine